USA in Space

Fourth Edition

USA in Space

Fourth Edition

Volume 2

International Ultraviolet Explorer—Space Shuttle: Radar Imaging Laboratories

Edited by

David G. Fisher

SALEM PRESS

A Division of EBSCO Information Services, Inc.

Ipswich, Massachusetts

GREY HOUSE PUBLISHING

Publisher's Cataloging-In-Publication Data
(Prepared by The Donohue Group, Inc.)

Names: Fisher, David G., editor.
Title: USA in space / edited by David G. Fisher.
Description: Fourth edition. | Ipswich, Massachusetts : Salem Press, Inc., [2019] | Includes bibliographical references and index.
Identifiers: ISBN 9781642653137 (set) | ISBN 9781642653663 (v. 1) | ISBN 9781642653670 (v. 2) | ISBN 9781642653687 (v. 3)
Subjects: LCSH: Astronautics--United States.
Classification: LCC TL789.8.U5 U83 2019 | DDC 629.40973--dc23

FIRST PRINTING
PRINTED IN THE UNITED STATES OF AMERICA

Table of Contents

Complete List of Contents

Volume 2

Volume 3

International Ultraviolet Explorer

Date: January 26, 1978, to September 30, 1996
Type of program: Scientific platform

The International Ultraviolet Explorer (IUE) was conceived as a next step in increasingly sophisticated orbiting observatories designed to observe the ultraviolet portion of the spectrum. Launched in 1978, it proved to be the most productive and oldest functioning observatory in the history of the space program until the Hubble Space Telescope.

Key Figures

Yoji Kondo, NASA project scientist
Leon Dondey, NASA Astronomy Explorers manager
Albert Boggess, Jr., IUE project scientist
Robert Wilson, European IUE project director
George Sonneborn, IUE resident astronomer

Summary of the Satellite

The International Ultraviolet Explorer (IUE) was a joint project between the National Aeronautics and Space Administration (NASA), the European Space Agency (ESA), and the British Science and Engineering Research Council (SRC). Each agency contributed financially as well as scientifically to the project. NASA provided the spacecraft and scientific instruments. It launched the IUE and set up a ground station at Goddard Space Flight Center in Greenbelt, Maryland. The ESA provided the solar arrays, which supply the spacecraft with power, and built a second ground station in Villafranca del Castillo, Spain. The SRC took responsibility for the satellite's four television cameras.

IUE carried a 45-centimeter telescope equipped with two spectrographs. A spectrograph records information by passing light or other radiation through a narrow slit and then through a prism, which separates the radiation into its component wavelengths. The result, a spectrogram, was then recorded on film.

The two spectrographs on board IUE were designed to study short and long ultraviolet wavelengths in the electromagnetic spectrum. Light waves are measured in angstroms, which are equal to one one-hundred-thousandth of a centimeter. Ultraviolet wavelengths range from 100 to 4,000 angstroms. Between its two spectrographs, IUE was able to measure ultraviolet radiation from 1,150 to 3,200 angstroms. Along with the spectrographs, two fine error sensors tracked the stars and allowed ground observers to aim the telescope at specific stars.

The satellite, weighing 671 kilograms, measuring 4.3 meters long, octagonal in shape, and with a rocket engine and a telescope tube extending from opposite ends, sported two large arrays of solar cells extending to either side, looking somewhat like a pair of wings. It was launched by a Delta rocket from Kennedy Space Center on January 26, 1978. IUE was placed into an elliptical orbit inclined 34.5° with respect to the equator, having a closest approach distance of 30,252 kilometers and a maximum distance of 41,315 kilometers. The orbit was such that IUE was in communication range with the ESA facility for only ten hours daily. NASA used the satellite sixteen hours a day, and the European agencies operated it for the remaining eight hours.

A sophisticated computer console called the experiment display system was used from the ground for operations coordination and image processing. All spacecraft systems, including those that control orientation, focusing, telescope temperature, and the status of the spectrograph cameras, were monitored from this console. A television monitor displayed spectra from the objects under observation, and a built-in computer allowed a quick preliminary analysis of the images.

The IUE was the first space mission designed to be used by visiting scientists rather than by a select group of researchers. Astronomers from around the world used the satellite if their observing proposals were accepted. In its first year of operation alone, more than two hundred scientists from seventeen countries participated in research using the IUE.

The International Ultraviolet Explorer was run much like a traditional observatory. The visiting astronomers directed the operations in real time. That is, the telescope responded immediately to the operators' instructions, and raw data were displayed directly after exposure, allowing the astronomer unprecedented flexibility. Research plans could be modified as the session proceeded, based on the results as they were obtained. The scientists went to the ground facility, either at Goddard or in Spain, spent several days making observations, and then returned home to analyze their data.

The IUE could be oriented to point anywhere in space, but it had to be at least 43° away from the Sun. If it was closer than that, the Sun's heat would disturb the temperature balance of the mechanism that focused the telescope. Although each day one quarter of the sky could not be observed by IUE, over the course of a year the entire sky could be scanned.

The core of the science hardware of the IUE. The telescope tube and sunshade extend above the pivot point of the support stand, the cameras are just below, and some of the mirrors and diffraction gratings are at the bottom. The box extending from the midpoint of the assembly covers the location of the spacecraft gyros. (NASA)

To make observations, the satellite was skewed to point at the target area, and a television image of that field of view was transmitted to the ground. The exact target was then identified, and the light from the target was directed into one of the spectrographs. The spectrum was then recorded and transmitted to the ground, where it was reconstructed on the screen of the monitor in the control room. Once the spectrum had been recorded, the image was processed by the computer to provide the type of information requested by the observer.

To help visiting researchers, the IUE ground facilities had a full-time staff of experts who supervised scientific operations, conducted image processing, and maintained the calibration of the spacecraft. For the first six months, the original observer had exclusive rights to his or her data. After that, all data passed into the public domain. Observations made using IUE are collected in the IUE Archive at Goddard Space Flight Center. The archive continues to be a tremendous resource. Astronomers can request data about whatever they are studying and perhaps gain information in areas that the original observer did not consider.

The IUE was designed to last for three years, but it exceeded all expectations, providing more than ten years of service. In large part, the ingenuity of its operators accounts for its longevity. In August, 1985, NASA engineers and scientists rescued the spacecraft from certain death after one of its three remaining gyroscopes had failed. Three gyroscopes are necessary to position the spacecraft to point at different targets and to maintain contact with Earth. By using other instruments aboard the satellite in conjunction with the two working gyroscopes, engineers solved the problem and IUE continued to function. After that, NASA developed a plan to control the telescope with only one working gyroscope.

In addition to its longevity, IUE proved to be a source of other pleasant surprises to scientists and engineers working with it. When the satellite was launched, it was expected to be capable of exposure times of fifteen to twenty minutes. By testing its capabilities, researchers were able to make exposures of up to fifteen hours, with a record exposure time of twenty-four hours. Such long exposures allowed study of very faint objects outside the Milky Way, as well as cool stars, which do not radiate strongly in the ultraviolet. In many such instances, IUE proved itself capable of making observations that its designers never intended it to make. In one case, in order to observe Halley's comet close to the Sun, the telescope was manipulated so that it could be pointed toward the Sun, violating the 43° limit.

IUE was shut down on September 30, 1996. It produced more published scientific papers than any previous astronomical satellite. It provided information about physical conditions in the central regions of distant galaxies that may contain black holes. It also provided scientists with more knowledge of the physical conditions in very hot stars, the effect of solar winds on the atmospheres of the planets in our solar system, and the loss of mass from stars when stellar winds and flares occur.

Contributions

The International Ultraviolet Explorer revolutionized almost every area of astronomy. It was instrumental in gathering research on hot and cool stars, energetic galaxies, x-ray sources, solar system objects, and quasars, and was particularly useful to scientists studying binary star systems.

The IUE was especially suited to the study of young, hot stars, because the bulk of their radiation is emitted in the ultraviolet range. With information provided by the IUE, researchers were able to map the regions of star formation in the Milky Way and other galaxies. A major breakthrough in the study of stars revealed that many stars have hot outer atmospheres similar to that of Earth's Sun. Cooler stars were also studied extensively. The Sun is a cool star, and data on cool stars help scientists to learn not only about other stars but also about processes occurring in the Sun itself.

One of the landmarks of ultraviolet astronomy has been the discovery of the nature and character of the dust and gas between the stars, the interstellar medium. It was found to be quite different from what was expected. One of the major findings was the discovery of hot gases as well as cool material between the stars.

IUE research confirmed some standard theories that had been hypothesized for some time. One was the presence of a hot halo of gas around the Milky Way, first proposed by the astrophysicist Lyman Spitzer, Jr., in 1956. IUE has also discovered evidence of a "gravitational lens," in which a double image of an object is created when the gravitational field of a very massive body acts as a lens, splitting the light from the more distant object. The idea of a gravitational lens was intimated by Albert

Einstein's theory of general relativity but until the IUE had never been supported by solid evidence.

Another area where IUE has contributed significantly is in the study of novae, events in which a star suddenly brightens thousands or millions of times. IUE observed more than one dozen novae in its lifetime. It was also instrumental in the study of Supernova 1987A, in which a star in a galaxy located fairly close to the Milky Way exploded. IUE helped researchers determine which star had exploded.

IUE also pointed its ultraviolet telescopes toward comets. It observed Comet Kohoutek finding a spectacular object in the ultraviolet spectrum (the visible display in the night sky had been disappointing). It also observed Comet- IRAS-Iraki-Alcock in 1983 and Comet Halley in 1986. It was found that the compositions of comets are similar, suggesting a common origin.

Besides being an important tool of research on its own, IUE was extremely useful when used in conjunction with other space missions. When several instruments sensitive to different wavelengths are used simultaneously, information on many levels can be obtained. The satellite was also used successfully during the Voyager flybys of the outer planets. The resolution of the instrument and its ability to observe over long periods of time allowed discoveries that would not otherwise have been possible.

In addition to solving many mysteries and casting light on others, IUE created a few mysteries of its own. For example, a number of objects have been detected for which there is no known object in the visible spectrum. It has also been found that other, previously known stars have very odd ultraviolet spectra that do not agree with current theories.

Context

Scientists can discover the nature of celestial objects only by the way those bodies emit, absorb, or alter electromagnetic radiation. The celestial objects that are most familiar emit light in the visible spectrum. Yet visible light is only one portion of the electromagnetic spectrum, which can be considered a range of wavelengths of energy. The longest wavelengths have the lowest energy. These are the radio waves and infrared radiation (heat). Visible light is approximately in the middle of the spectrum. Radiation of progressively shorter wavelengths than that of visible light moves into the ultraviolet and finally into the x-ray and gamma-ray ranges.

The more information one can uncover about a celestial object in each of these ranges, the more completely one will understand its nature. For example, a star may be quite dim in the visible portion of the spectrum but at the same time be a source of intense radio or x-ray emissions. Because the human eye cannot record information from the whole range of electromagnetic radiation, instruments must be designed to be sensitive to and record these wavelengths.

The ultraviolet spectrum is particularly difficult to observe from Earth, because Earth's atmosphere filters out most of the ultraviolet radiation coming from space. Many of the most abundant elements are detected only in the ultraviolet range. It is therefore important to the study of the universe to place instruments outside Earth's atmosphere in order to glean information from this important range of the spectrum.

Because of the necessity of observing from outside Earth's atmosphere, ultraviolet astronomy did not begin until the 1950's, the dawn of the Space Age. At that time, scientists were dependent on rockets and balloons to carry ultraviolet experiments. In the late 1960's, orbiting satellites began to carry ultraviolet telescopes. Most notable of these was the third Orbiting Astronomical Observatory, also known as Copernicus. Starting from virtual ignorance about the ultraviolet, researchers used the early satellites to pave the way for this area of astronomy. Yet none of these instruments had the resolution to detect information from very dim or distant sources. Because of a relatively low orbit, Earth blocked out much of the satellites' range, and they could not remain in continuous communication with receiving stations on Earth.

With the launch of the IUE, ultraviolet astronomy took a giant leap forward. There are few areas of astronomy to which IUE observations have not made significant contributions. The IUE satellite was a telescope in the groundbreaking stages of a new science. Although it had unprecedented resolution for an ultraviolet instrument and had observed objects fainter than those observed previously, its capability allowed only the strongest ultraviolet sources to be observed.

At the time that the IUE was conceived, in the late 1960's, the space program enjoyed a level of government and public support that was destined to diminish in the subsequent decade. The IUE was considered another step along the way to the Hubble Space Telescope, a 2.4-meter orbiting telescope that would be the first permanent optical and ultraviolet space observatory. The Hubble Space Telescope was launched aboard *Discovery* in April, 1990. Until then, IUE remained the sole orbiting observatory surveying the ultraviolet sky. In spite of the tremendous progress made by the IUE, the future of ultraviolet astronomy lies in the future of the space program, when launches of new and more sophisticated instruments can be made.

—*Divonna Ogier*

See also: Far Ultraviolet Spectroscopic Explorer; International Sun-Earth Explorers; Orbiting Solar Observatories; Telescopes: Air and Space.

Further Reading

Ahrens, C. Donald. *Essentials of Meteorology: An Invitation to the Atmosphere.* 4th ed. Pacific Grove, Calif.: Thomson Brooks/Cole, 2005. This is a text suitable for an introductory course in meteorology. Comes complete with a CD-ROM to help explain concepts and demonstrate the atmosphere's dynamic nature.

Cornell, James, and Paul Gorenstein, eds. *Astronomy from Space: Sputnik to Space Telescope.* Cambridge, Mass.: MIT Press, 1985. An overview of twenty-five years of astronomical research from space. Summarizes what has been learned in different areas of astronomy in the form of short articles written by experts in each field. Suitable for those with some science background.

Henbest, Nigel. *Mysteries of the Universe.* New York: Van Nostrand Reinhold, 1981. Explores the limits of what is known about the universe. Ranges from current theories about the origin of the solar system and the universe to exotic astronomy and astronomy at invisible wavelengths. Contains information about ultraviolet astronomy and some results of IUE observations.

Hofmann-Wellenhof, Bernhard, and Helmut Moritz. *Physical Geodesy.* London: Springer- Praxis, 2005. This is an update to a text considered by some to be the introductory book of choice for the field of geodesy. Includes terrestrial methods and discusses contributions made through the Global Positioning System (GPS).

"Infrared Cirrus (Infrared Astronomical Satellite)." *Sky and Telescope* 73 (June, 1987): 601- 602. An article similar to the one in *Astronomy* magazine cited below, but generally more in-depth and slightly more technical. Geared toward the student with some background in astronomy and spaceflight.

Kaula, William M. *Theory of Satellite Geodesy: Applications of Satellites to Geodesy.* New York: Dover Publications, 2000. Discusses how Newtonian gravitational theory and Euclidean geometry are used together with satellite orbital dynamic data to determine geodetic information. Requires familiarity with introductory calculus.

Kivelson, Margaret G., and Christopher T. Russell. *Introduction to Space Physics*. New York: Cambridge University Press, 1995. A thorough exploration of space physics. Some aspects are suitable for the general reader. Suitable for an introductory college course on space physics.

Leverington, David. *New Cosmic Horizons: Space Astronomy from the V2 to the Hubble Space Telescope*. New York: Cambridge University Press, 2001. This is a broad treatise exploring the development of space-based astronomical observations from the end of World War II to the Hubble Space Telescope and other major NASA space-based observatories.

Parks, George K. *Physics of Space Plasmas: An Introduction*. 2d ed. Boulder, Colo.: Westview Press, 2004. Provides a scientific examination of the data returned during what might be called the "golden age" of space physics (1990-2002) when over two dozen satellites were dispatched to investigate space plasma phenomena. Written at the undergraduate level for an introductory course in space plasma, there is also detailed presentation of NASA and ESA spacecraft missions.

Shore, L. A. "I.U.E.: Nine Years of Astronomy." *Astronomy* 15 (April, 1987): 14-22. This article describes the satellite, giving information on its status as well as the results of observations. Details about working with the telescope from ground stations are provided. Directed toward general audiences, although the language is sometimes technical. Illustrated.

Wheeler, J. Craig. *Cosmic Catastrophes: Supernovae, Gamma-Ray Bursts, and Adventures in Hyperspace*. New York: Cambridge University Press, 2000. A complete exposé of high-energy processes at work in the universe. Includes contributions made by the Compton Gamma Ray Observatory and other space-based observatories to that understanding.

Zaehringer, Alfred J., and Steve Whitfield. *Rocket Science: Rocket Science in the Second Millennium*. Burlington, Ont.: Apogee Books, 2004. Written by a soldier who fought in World War II under fire from German V-2 rockets, this book includes a history of the development of rockets as weapons and research tools, and projects where rocket technology may go in the near future.

Interplanetary Monitoring Platform Satellites

Date: November 26, 1963, to October 25, 1973
Type of program: Scientific platforms

The ten Interplanetary Monitoring Platform satellites (IMPs), part of the Explorer program, measured cosmic radiation levels, magnetic field intensities, and solar wind properties in the near-Earth and interplanetary environment.

Summary of the Satellites

The Interplanetary Monitoring Platform (IMP) program included ten missions and formed part of the Explorer program. A primary scientific goal was to collect data from a particular region of interplanetary space for a significant portion of the solar cycle (an interval of approximately eleven years during which sunspot activity reaches a peak, then diminishes); as a secondary goal, the IMPs were intended to help provide some operational support for the crewed Apollo missions by sensing radiation levels in space between Earth and the Moon.

Each of the IMP spacecraft was known by at least two labels: An IMP letter designation was assigned prior to launch, and an Explorer number designation was given afterward. Some of the satellites were also known by an IMP number. IMP A (also known as IMP 1) was built by the Goddard Space Flight Center, part of the National Aeronautics and Space Administration (NASA), which also contributed some scientific experiments on board the spacecraft. Other experimenters included groups from the University of California at Berkeley, the University of Chicago, the Massachusetts Institute of Technology, and the Ames Research Center.

The first seven IMPs had designs similar to Explorers 12, 14, and 15. Each had a main structure with a flat, octagonal shape 71 centimeters across and 20 to 30 centimeters deep, and an average mass of 76 kilograms. An octagonal structure allowed easier access for testing and replacement of components. Each spacecraft used four solar panels as well as rechargeable silver-cadmium batteries to provide power for the experiments and telemetry transmitters. The average data rate for the transmitters was 10 to 100 bits per second. Most IMP spacecraft had two prominent magnetometers mounted on 2-meter (6- to 7-foot) booms extending from the main body. On some IMPs, a third magnetometer was mounted on top of the spacecraft on a telescopic boom. The first generation of IMPs (IMP 1 through IMP 5) was spin-stabilized at 20 to 28 revolutions per minute about an axis perpendicular to the plane of the octagon.

IMP 1 (Explorer 18) was launched from Cape Canaveral on November 26, 1963, using a specially modified Delta launch vehicle (the third stage provided an extra 1,227 newtons of thrust). The spacecraft achieved an elliptical orbit with a perigee (the closest distance to Earth's surface) of 192 kilometers and an apogee (the farthest distance from Earth's surface) of 197,585 kilometers, giving it an orbital period of approximately 2,294 hours. The orbital inclination (the angle between the orbit's geometric plane and Earth's equatorial plane) was 33°. IMP 1 carried seven experiments, including a rubidium-vapor magnetometer (housed in a 33-centimeter-diameter sphere on the telescopic boom);

two flux gate magnetometers (for measuring magnetic field intensity and direction); a low-energy charged particle detector and a grid device for separating electrons and low-energy positive particles, particle telescopes (Geiger-Müller counters), and an ion chamber (all for detecting and measuring the direction, intensities, and compositions of cosmic rays); a curved-plate electrostatic analyzer; and a thermal ion electron experiment.

IMP 2 (Explorer 21) was launched from Cape Kennedy on October 4, 1964, but because of a failure in the Delta-Thor launch vehicle, it achieved an elliptical orbit with an apogee of only 95,575 kilometers instead of the intended 203,539 kilometers. IMP 2 was inclined 37.5° to the equator and had an orbital period of approximately thirty-five hours. The principal consequence of the failure was that the spacecraft could provide data on the magnetic field only from within the magnetosphere (the intense portion of Earth's magnetic field that deflects much of the highly energetic stream of charged particles from the Sun) rather than from the transition region (essentially, the boundary of the magnetosphere). IMPs 2, 3, D, and E carried sets of experiments similar to those on IMP 1.

IMP 3 (Explorer 28) was launched from Cape Kennedy on May 29, 1965, into an elliptical orbit of 195 by 263,604 kilometers (this was higher than the intended apogee of 209,170 kilometers because of an overextended propellant burn in the launch vehicle's third stage). The spacecraft's orbital inclination was 34° and the orbital period was approximately 142 hours.

IMP D (Explorer 33) was launched on July 1, 1966, from Cape Kennedy, using a three-stage, Thrust-Augmented Delta launch vehicle. Because the second and third stages of the Delta provided too much thrust, the retromotor (which was to have slowed the spacecraft for injection into lunar orbit, "anchoring" it there) was able only to inject the spacecraft into an elliptical Earth orbit of 15,897 by 435,331 kilometers, with an inclination of 29° and an orbital period of approximately 309 hours.

IMP E (Explorer 35) was launched from Cape Kennedy on July 19, 1967, and achieved an orbit about the Moon with perilune (the closest distance to the Moon's surface) of 805 kilometers and apolune (the farthest distance from the Moon's surface) of 7,401 kilometers, at an inclination of 147°. Its lunar-orbit period was approximately eleven hours.

IMPs 4 and 5 departed significantly from the preceding satellites in the series by carrying eleven and twelve experiments, respectively. These experiments included a three-axis flux gate magnetometer, a range-versus-energy-loss detector, an energy-versus-energy-loss detector, a low-energy proton and alpha particle detector, an ion chamber, a low-energy solar flare electron detector, a solar proton monitoring experiment, a cosmic-ray angular distortion analyzer, a low-energy telescope, a plasma experiment, and two low-energy proton and electron differential energy analyzers.

IMP 4 (Explorer 34) was launched on May 24, 1967, from Vandenberg Air Force Base in California into an elliptical orbit of 248 by 211,080 kilometers, with an inclination of 67° and an orbital period of approximately 104 hours. IMP 5 (Explorer 41) was launched on June 21, 1969, from Vandenberg Air Force Base into an elliptical orbit of 338 by 213,812 kilometers, with an inclination of 83.8° and an orbital period of approximately 106 hours.

The second generation of IMP spacecraft used a considerably larger structure to support a greater number of experiments. Each vehicle consisted of a sixteen-sided drum, approximately 1.35 meters in diameter and 1.83 meters high. Most of the electronics and experiments were mounted on an aluminum honeycomb shelf in the upper part of the drum. Electrical power was provided by three solar arrays attached to the outside of the drum, with silver cadmium batteries for storage; the average power consumption was 110 watts. Because of their average mass of 278 kilograms, the spacecraft required larger launch vehicles; IMP 6 (Explorer 43) used a Delta M-6 (a Thor liquid first stage with six solid-fueled rocket boosters). Data were sent back to Earth at rates of 1,000 to 1,600 bits per second.

IMP 6 (Explorer 43) was launched on March 13, 1971, from Cape Kennedy into an elliptical orbit of 235 by 196,533 kilometers, with an inclination of 28.8° and an orbital period of approximately 94 hours. IMP 7 (Explorer 47) was launched on September 22, 1972, from Cape Kennedy into an elliptical orbit of 249,395 by 397,423 kilometers, with an inclination of 17.2° and an orbital period of approximately 21 days, 20 hours. IMP 8 (Explorer 50) was launched on October 25, 1973, from the Cape into an elliptical orbit of 226,869 by 465,001 kilometers, with an inclination of 27.8° and an orbital period of approximately 24.1 days. IMPs 7 and 8 were positioned so that during a solar flare one satellite could observe the effects on the dark side of Earth, while the other was making the same observations on the sunlit side.

Contributions

Collectively, the ten IMP spacecraft contributed significantly to knowledge of space physics in the near-Earth, Earth-Moon, and interplanetary environments. Like other long-term-programs, such as the Orbiting Geophysical Observatory satellites, the IMP series provided an extended examination of the interactions of the solar wind with Earth's magnetic field over a substantial portion of one solar cycle. A large part of the data collected pertains to specialized areas in space physics; only those findings of general interest from particular satellites are mentioned here.

IMP 1 discovered a region of high-energy radiation beyond the Van Allen radiation belts (the bands of energetic, charged particles trapped in the geomagnetic field). In addition, the satellite provided data indicating that the solar wind has a spiral character in interplanetary space, resulting from the rotation of the Sun as it emits the streams of particles. Most notable was the discovery of a stationary shock wave in the solar wind. This is a region where the flow properties of the wind change drastically; these changes are caused by interaction of the geomagnetic field and the magnetic field generated by the wind. The shock wave precedes Earth in its motion through the solar wind by 86,250 kilometers.

IMP E in its lunar orbit recorded no such shock wave in the solar wind, indicating no lunar magnetic field. Consequently, the Moon has no radiation belts, ionosphere, or magnetosphere as Earth does. The probe also encountered a wake in the region "behind" the Moon in its motion through the solar wind (a region shielded from the solar wind by the Moon) extending more than 160,000 kilometers from the Moon. One result of this absence of charged-particle flow is a distortion in the interplanetary magnetic field in the wake region.

Context

The IMP missions played a significant role in extending knowledge of the near-Earth, Earth-Moon, and interplanetary magnetic fields and their interactions with the solar wind. This information was used to construct new maps of the field in these regions and to create more accurate models of the dynamic magnetic field-solar wind interactions. In addition, the satellites helped to provide operational support for several of the piloted Apollo missions to the Moon, giving real-time information to Apollo mission controllers on solar flares and the attendant increased radiation levels.

The second group of IMPs, starting with IMP 6, were part of a new generation of satellites in the U.S. space program; they were larger and were capable of supporting greater numbers of even more complex scientific experiments.

—Robert G. Melton

See also: Explorers: Solar; Goddard Space Flight Center; International Sun-Earth Explorers; International Ultraviolet Explorer; Orbiting Geophysical Observatories.

Further Reading

Baker, David, ed. *Jane's Space Directory, 2005-2006*. Alexandria, Va.: Jane's Information Group, 2005. This reference work, devoted to the various international space programs, gives considerable background on the technology used for space exploration. Its section on the IMP satellites is easy to read and informative.

Corliss, William R. *Scientific Satellites*. NASA SP-133. Washington, D.C.: Government Printing Office, 1967. Gives a history of scientific satellite missions from 1958 to 1967. Describes major subsystems common to all satellites, devoting significant coverage to scientific instrumentation for spacecraft use. Includes an appendix of all U.S. scientific missions (with descriptions of the satellites and their experiments) flown through early 1967. For technical audiences.

Davies, John K. *Astronomy from Space: The Design and Operation of Orbiting Observatories*. New York: John Wiley, 1997. This is a comprehensive reference on the satellites that have revolutionized twentieth century astrophysics. It contains in-depth coverage of all space astronomy missions. It includes tables of launch data and orbits for quick reference as well as photographs of many of the lesser-known satellites. The main body of the book is subdivided according to type of astronomy carried out by each satellite (x-ray, gamma-ray, ultraviolet, infrared and millimeter, and radio). It discusses the future of satellite astronomy as well.

Gavaghan, Helen. *Something New Under the Sun: Satellites and the Beginning of the Space Age*. New York: Copernicus Books, 1998. This book focuses on the history and development of artificial satellites. It centers on three major areas of development—navigational satellites, communications satellites, and weather observation and forecasting satellites.

Heppenheimer, T. A. *Countdown: A History of Space Flight*. New York: John Wiley, 1997. A detailed historical narrative of the human conquest of space. Heppenheimer traces the development of piloted flight through the military rocketry programs of the era preceding World War II. Covers both the American and the Soviet attempts to place vehicles, spacecraft, and humans into the hostile environment of space. More than a dozen pages are devoted to bibliographic references.

Johnson, Francis S., ed. *Satellite Environment Handbook*. 2d ed. Stanford, Calif.: Stanford University Press, 1965. This excellent technical overview covers all near-Earth environments, including the magnetosphere. Includes graphs, illustrations, and references.

King, J. H. *IMP I, H, and J: Final Report*. Springfield, Va.: National Technical Information Service, 1973. Gives detailed engineering descriptions of Explorers 43, 47, and 50, including accounts of the construction and testing of these satellites. For technical audiences.

---. *IMP Series Report/Bibliography*. NASA TM-X-68817. Springfield, Va.: National Technical Information Service, 1971. Includes descriptions of the engineering subsystems of Explorers 18, 21, 28, 33, 34, 35, 41, and 43, as well as summary logs of the activities involved in construction and testing of the spacecraft. Contains an extensive bibliography of NASA publications related to these missions. For technical audiences.

Kivelson, Margaret G., and Christopher T. Russell. *Introduction to Space Physics*. New York: Cambridge University Press, 1995. A thorough exploration of space physics. Some aspects are suitable for the general reader. Suitable for an introductory college course on space physics.

Launius, Roger D. *NASA: A History of the U.S. Civil Space Program.* Malabar, Fla.: Krieger Publishing Company, 1994. This is an in-depth look at America's civilian space program and the establishment of the National Aeronautics and Space Administration. It chronicles the agency from its predecessor, the National Advisory Committee for Aeronautics, through the present day.

Leverington, David. *New Cosmic Horizons: Space Astronomy from the V2 to the Hubble Space Telescope.* New York: Cambridge University Press, 2001. This is a broad treatise exploring the development of space-based astronomical observations from the end of World War II to the Hubble Space Telescope and other major NASA space-based observatories.

Yenne, Bill. *The Encyclopedia of U.S. Spacecraft.* New York: Exeter Books, 1985. This well-illustrated volume provides an overview of all craft, including the IMPs, used in the U.S. exploration of space. Includes several appendices and a helpful table of abbreviations and acronyms.

Zimmerman, Robert. *The Chronological Encyclopedia of Discoveries in Space.* Westport, Conn.: Oryx Press, 2000. Provides a complete chronological history of all crewed and robotic spacecraft and explains flight events and scientific results. Suitable for all levels of research.

ITOS and NOAA Meteorological Satellites

Date: January 23, 1970, to May 30, 1979
Type of spacecraft: Meteorological satellites

ITOS is an acronym for Improved TIROS Operational System, a series of meteorological satellites developed by the United States to maintain constant surveillance of weather conditions around the world. The National Oceanic and Atmospheric Administration operated the ITOS satellites during the 1970's.

Summary of the Satellites

Among the first applications devised for artificial satellite technology was the monitoring and analysis of global weather conditions. Scientists quickly recognized the value of satellites for the tracking and reporting of weather systems and for predicting weather patterns.

The surveillance technology aboard these satellites improved quickly over the first twenty years of the space era, resulting in increased efficiency and capabilities. Early experiments with balloons and relay satellites led to the discovery of a variety of atmospheric characteristics previously unknown to scientists who studied the atmosphere. These discoveries included the existence of a band of radiation around Earth (the Van Allen radiation belts) and other phenomena that scientists began to suspect were key elements in Earth's ever-changing weather patterns.

At the time, the only way to study these phenomena was to place satellites containing specialized sensors in orbits that would make possible the identification of relationships between changes in activity such as solar radiation or cosmic-ray bombardment of Earth's surface and weather change. The necessity for such satellites led to development of sophisticated television cameras and infrared sensing instruments that, when placed aboard orbiting satellites, proved to be even more useful as

tools of meteorology than had been expected. As a result, weather-sensing technology was among the first to be applied to artificial satellites placed in orbit by the United States.

The first weather satellite, launched in 1960, was TIROS 1. (TIROS is an acronym for Television Infrared Observations Satellite.) In 1966, the TIROS Operational System (TOS) was established to provide daily observations of global weather without interruption. It included a number of satellites of similar configuration and was operated by the Environmental Science Services Administration (ESSA), which was succeeded by the National Oceanic and Atmospheric Administration (NOAA) in 1970. Thus, TIROS satellites were succeeded by other first-generation satellites known as the ESSA series, which was followed by ITOS/NOAA. Once operational, NOAA weather satellites became part of that agency's National Operational Meteorological Satellite System (NOMSS).

ITOS, an acronym for Improved TIROS Operational System, was the second generation of weather satellites. It included six satellites launched between January 23, 1970, and July 29, 1976. The ITOS satellites were built by RCA, under the direction of engineers at the Goddard Space Flight Center, an arm of the National Aeronautics and Space Administration (NASA). The ITOS series was designed to provide daily real-time coverage of

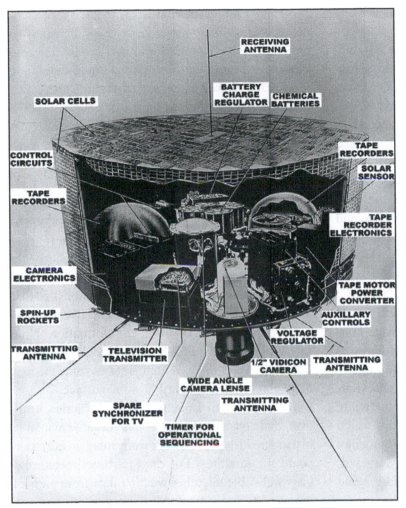

Instruments and equipment of TIROS-1. The main sensors that provided the cloud pictures were television cameras. The TIROS cameras were slow-scan devices that take snapshots of the scene below; one "snapshot" was taken every ten seconds. These were rugged, lightweight devices weighing only about 4.5 pounds (2 kg) including the camera lens. TIROS I was equipped with two cameras. One had a wide angle lens providing views that were approximately 750 miles (1207 km) on a side (with the satellite looking straight down), and a narrow angle camera with a view that was about 80 miles (129 km) on a side. (NOAA)

Earth's cloud cover and other atmospheric conditions, using daytime and nighttime instrumentation.

The first of these satellites, ITOS-1, provided meteorological data that were dramatically improved over the data that had been relayed to Earth by the earlier TIROS and ESSA satellites. It included equipment that could provide direct automatic picture transmission and that could gather and store data for relay at a later time. It was the first satellite to provide around-the-clock radiometric data, and its imagery was significantly better than that of TIROS. The satellite weighed 313 kilograms and was 1.24 meters high and 1.02 by 1.02 meters wide. With shields and antennae deployed, it had a span of 4.3 meters. On board were two advanced 2.54-centimeter vidicon television cameras and two automatic picture transmission devices. Each of the satellite's three wing-like panels contained solar cells. There were four communications antennae, two vertical-temperature profile radiometers, two high-resolution radiometers, and two solar proton monitoring systems. Visible channel resolution was 3.7 kilometers, and infrared resolution was 7.4 kilometers. The second ITOS satellite was NOAA-1 (or ITOS-A), launched on December 11, 1970.

Within ITOS, which represented the second generation of weather satellites, was a second generation of ITOS satellites, ITOS-D. Similar to ITOS-1 and NOAA-1, this series of satellites was more sophisticated. They were also a bit larger; each weighed 340 kilograms and measured 1.016 by 1.016 by 1.219 meters. Rectangular in shape, the main structure of the satellite was a three-axis stabilized despun platform, a major improvement in design that facilitated continuous orientation toward Earth's surface. New onboard equipment included very high resolution radiometers and scanning radiometers, along with vertical temperature profile radiometers for keeping track of atmospheric temperatures. It also contained equipment for monitoring proton and electron flux, phenomena related to solar activity that are thought to affect weather.

Six ITOS-6 satellites had been planned, but only four were launched, because of the unexpected longevity of the individual satellites. The ITOS-D series included NOAA-2 (ITOS-D), launched on October 15, 1972, NOAA-3 (ITOS-F), launched in 1973, NOAA-4 (ITOS-G), launched in 1974, and NOAA-5 (ITOS-H), launched on July 29, 1976.

The ITOS satellites were placed in Sun-synchronous orbits. These orbits were near-polar, the most efficient for the observation of Earth's surface and its near atmosphere. They were placed at an altitude of 1,463 kilometers, and the duration of each orbit was 115 minutes. Sensors aboard the satellite were able to view a track of such width that Earth's entire surface was covered in only 12.5 orbits each day.

Data gathered by the ITOS satellites were continuously fed to automatic receiving stations around the world. These stations were referred to as APT stations, for automatic picture transmission. Additional data stored by the satellite were periodically fed to receiving stations in the United States, which then relayed them to the National Environmental Satellite Service facilities at Suitland, Maryland. There the information was processed before being distributed around the world.

The ITOS program was superseded by the third-generation operational polar-orbiting environmental satellite system, with the launch of TIROS N in 1978. The last of the ITOS satellites, NOAA-5 (ITOS-H), remained in orbit until the summer of 1979.

Contributions

ITOS satellites enabled a significant increase in the amount and quality of meteorological data sent back by artificial satellites. Their increased sophistication meant that more area could be covered in less time with more accuracy than had been the case with the first series, the TIROS and ESSA satellites. Ten TIROS satellites had been launched between

1960 and 1966 in the first effort to use space technology for weather surveillance. Each carried two miniature video cameras, and half carried infrared sensors and radiation sensors that could determine how much radiation entered the atmosphere and how much was reflected by Earth's surface. ITOS series cameras were equipped with vidicons that were larger than those installed in the TIROS cameras and thus could cover more area.

The TIROS satellites did not provide constant, real-time weather information on demand. Imagery they sent back was sporadic, as their mission was to determine the feasibility of using satellites for meteorological purposes rather than to function as a full-fledged monitoring operation. It was not until the TIROS Operational System was established that a satellite was used as a constant, twenty-four-hours-a-day source of weather information. Nine satellites in this, the ESSA series, were launched between 1966 and 1969. With this series came the first daily photography of Earth's entire surface.

It was not until launch of the ITOS series, however, that consistent, reliable data became available instantaneously, as well as from images stored on board the satellites. For the first time, meteorologists were able to gather weather data from parts of the world that contained no reporting stations. These regions included much of the ocean areas in both hemispheres, as well as largely uninhabited deserts and inaccessible or inhospitable regions, such as the North and South Poles.

The range of information collected by the ITOS satellites was enormous. They could detect tropical storms that often turn into hurricanes or typhoons, other less violent storm systems, jet-stream variations, storm fronts, upper-level disturbances, snow cover, even fog. These satellites have enhanced the ability of meteorologists to forecast the weather, often on a long-term basis, and to track dangerous storms on a minute-by-minute basis. The ITOS satellites were also the first to be equipped with instrumentation designed to sense changes in atmospheric conditions caused by solar activity.

Another important function of the ITOS satellites was to provide infrared images that could be used to prepare special Earth surface temperature charts. These charts, which were regularly updated, included surface temperatures of the oceans by regions, which made them useful to the captains of oceangoing vessels, commercial fishermen, and others in the maritime industry. These infrared data were also extremely important to meteorologists, who, through analysis, were able to locate and document conditions that might lead to tropical storms on the world's oceans.

Before the age of satellite imagery, weather conditions had been determined by the amassing of data from observation points around the world. Often, these data were incomplete or outdated because of the difficulty of obtaining accurate readings or updates, particularly in areas that were inaccessible or inhospitable. During the first half of the twentieth century, the United States began to employ aircraft to gather meteorological data. This development was a major step forward, but it proved to be a technique that had significant shortcomings, because it was impossible to get the global weather picture quickly and accurately. When satellites became available, they first served to corroborate or support the information coming in from weather observation posts and aircraft and helped in the analysis of those data. After the satellites took over the task of daily, continuous monitoring of the weather, the roles were reversed, with aircraft used

Inside the B16-10 spacecraft processing hangar at Vandenberg Air Force Base, Calif., workers oversee the lifting and rotating of the National Oceanic and Atmospheric Administration (NOAA-L) satellite to allow for mating of the Apogee Kick Motor (AKM). (NASA / Vandenberg AFB)

to enhance and support satellite-generated meteorological data.

Context

Since the earliest days of the space era, artificial satellites have been invaluable in keeping track of global weather conditions. The impact of ITOS and other meteorological satellites has been felt in agriculture, maritime shipping, air transportation, and weather-disaster warning and control efforts worldwide. They have also been used in conjunction with Earth resources satellites and other land-sensitive satellites to track ice floes in the polar regions, in an effort to determine the effects of such phenomena on global weather. Later generations of weather satellites would be equipped with search-and-rescue instrumentation that would help locate downed or lost aircraft and oceangoing vessels anywhere on Earth's surface.

This technology also has military and defense applications, as demonstrated by the United States Department of Defense weather satellite program that began operation during the mid-1960's. Known as the Defense Meteorological Satellite Program (DMSP), it was a polar-orbiting satellite system, operated by the United States Air Force. Its purpose was to support military operations around the world and to engage in research that would help engineers design more sophisticated and efficient sensing technology for installation in future meteorological satellites.

The United States was not alone in the use of satellites to keep track of Earth's weather. In fact, a working cooperation among several nations existed under the auspices of an international agency, the World Meteorological Organization, which included Japan, the United States, the Soviet Union, and the European Space Agency (ESA) nations. The United States also entered into a cooperative venture with France, which led to the establishment of a program known as EOLE. EOLE was an 84-kilogram satellite launched in August, 1971, to receive and retransmit data from five hundred weather balloons that contained instrumentation designed to monitor the upper atmosphere.

In 1977, a Japanese satellite, Himawari 1, was launched from Cape Canaveral and positioned over the Pacific Ocean. During that same year, Meteosat, a satellite constructed for ESA, was launched from Cape Canaveral and positioned over the eastern Atlantic Ocean, where it worked in concert with Himawari, ITOS, and other international satellites to acquire and transmit global weather data. This cooperation led to increased use of satellite data by

scores of countries, among them several in the Third World.

The Soviet Union was also an early player. Beginning in the early 1960's, it began to experiment with weather-sensitive technology as part of the Kosmos series of satellites. Weather satellites were placed in polar orbits at altitudes of approximately 900 kilometers. For the Soviet Union, polar orbits are required because of its geographical position, which includes territory too far north to be photographed from an equatorial orbit. The Kosmos series eventually led to the Meteor series of meteorological satellites, each of which provided continuous, uninterrupted data in conjunction with others to provide wide-ranging weather coverage. Meteor 1 was launched from Plesetsk on March 29, 1969.

Early Soviet satellites carried video cameras and infrared scanners. The Soviets indicated that they were instrumental in predicting snowmelt from mountain ranges, an important element in the evaluation of prospects for spring flooding, irrigation, and seasonal crop yields. Since the 1970's, the Soviets developed geostationary weather-monitoring satellite technology to support the polar-orbiting satellites.

International space cooperation has been consistent and productive from the earliest days of the space era. The ITOS program, which was developed and operated in conjunction with other programs around the world, remains a monument to such cooperation. The real-time capabilities of its technology resulted in many useful real-world applications that have made satellite meteorological imagery accessible to ordinary people. Today, daily newspapers and radio and television broadcasts include up-to-the-second satellite weather data as part of their weather coverage. Tropical storms, hurricanes, tornadoes, thunderstorms, and snowstorms can be viewed by the public as they are developing as a result of technology advanced through the research and development in the ITOS program. While that technology has advanced significantly since the 1970's, the ITOS satellites were the first to prove that a consistent, reliable, dependable, twenty-four-hours-a-day weather-monitoring system could be established using space hardware. Indeed, it set the standard for technology that would follow.

—Michael S. Ameigh

See also: Environmental Science Services Administration Satellites; Interplanetary Monitoring Platform Satellites; Meteorological Satellites; Meteorological Satellites: Military; Seasat; SMS and GOES Meteorological Satellites; TIROS Meteorological Satellites.

Further Reading

Ahrens, C. Donald. *Essentials of Meteorology: An Invitation to the Atmosphere*. 4th ed. Pacific Grove, Calif.: Thomson Brooks/Cole, 2005. A thorough examination of contemporary understanding of meteorology. Includes the contributions made by satellite technology.

---. *Meteorology Today: An Introduction to Weather, Climate, and the Environment*. 7th ed. Pacific Grove, Calif.: Thomson Brooks/Cole, 2002. A thorough examination of contemporary understanding of meteorology. Includes the contributions made by satellite technology.

Bader, M. J., G. S. Forbes, and J. R. Grant, eds. *Images in Weather Forecasting: A Practical Guide for Interpreting Satellite and Radar Imagery*. New York: Cambridge University Press, 1997. Offers meteorologists and forecasters an overview of the current techniques for interpreting satellite and radar images of weather systems in mid-latitudes. Heavily illustrated.

Gavaghan, Helen. *Something New Under the Sun: Satellites and the Beginning of the Space Age*. New York: Copernicus Books, 1998. This book focuses on the history and development of artificial satellites. It centers on three major areas of development—navigational satellites, communications satellites, and weather observation and forecasting satellites.

Heppenheimer, T. A. *Countdown: A History of Space Flight*. New York: John Wiley, 1997. A detailed historical narrative of the human conquest of space. Heppenheimer traces the development of piloted flight through the military rocketry programs of the era preceding World War II. Covers both the American and the Soviet attempts to place vehicles, spacecraft, and humans into the hostile environment of space. More than a dozen pages are devoted to bibliographic references.

Hoyt, Douglas V., and Kenneth H. Shatten. *The Role of the Sun in Climate Change*. Oxford, England: Oxford University Press, 1997. This book discusses the interaction between the Sun and the Earth's atmosphere and how the latter is shaped by solar activity. It describes many of the different cyclic events that affect our climate and how they can be used or abused. It contains an extensive bibliography.

Ley, Willy. *Events in Space*. New York: Van Rees Press, 1969. Features summaries of all satellite programs, national and international, that were carried out during the 1960's. Particularly useful is a series of tables and glossaries that define space jargon and describe many of the satellite and rocket series of the decade. Also included are lists of satellite launches, complete with launch dates and other information relative to the satellites and the programs with which they were (or are) associated.

National Aeronautics and Space Administration. *NASA, 1958-1983: Remembered Images*. NASA EP-200. Washington, D.C.: Government Printing Office, 1983. This paperback book traces various programs of the space agency from its beginnings. Included is a chapter on space sciences as well as one on Earth-orbit applications, including meteorology. Heavily illustrated with color photographs.

Parkinson, Claire L. *Earth from Above: Using Color-Coded Satellite Images to Examine the Global Environment.* Sausalito, Calif.: University Science Books, 1997. A book for non-specialists on reading and interpreting satellite images. Explains how satellite data provide information about the atmosphere, the Antarctic ozone hole, and atmospheric temperature effects. The book includes maps, photographs, and fifty color satellite images.

Paul, Günter. *The Satellite Spin-Off: The Achievements of Space Flight.* Translated by Alan Lacy and Barbara Lacy. New York: Robert B. Luce, 1975. A survey of the commercial, scientific, and communications applications that developed from the space research of the 1960's and early 1970's. Contains a comprehensive account of the early developments in scientific research that led to the evolution of weather satellites. This book is written from the perspective of the European community. In addition to meteorological applications, space medicine, communications, cartography, agriculture, and oceanography are discussed.

Seinfeld, John H., and Spyros Pandis. *Atmospheric Chemistry and Physics: Air Pollution to Climate.* New York: John Wiley, 1997. This is an extensive reference on atmospheric chemistry, aerosols, and atmospheric models. While the book may be too complex for the average reader, it is extremely useful as a research tool on the science of atmospheric phenomena.

Zimmerman, Robert. *The Chronological Encyclopedia of Discoveries in Space.* Westport, Conn.: Oryx Press, 2000. Provides a complete chronological history of all crewed and robotic spacecraft and explains flight events and scientific results. Suitable for all levels of research.

James Webb Space Telescope

Date: March 30, 2021 (planned)
Type of mission: Space telescope

Projected to launch in the spring of 2021, the James Webb Space Telescope is an infrared-optimized telescope that will serve as the National Aeronautics and Space Administration's (NASA's) successor to the Hubble Space Telescope in that it will surpass Hubble's sensitivity and resolution. However, unlike Hubble, the JWST will be capable of observing in the infrared portion of the electromagnetic spectrum, allowing for discoveries that were not previously possible.

Key Figures

Sir Frederick William Herschel (1738-1822), British astronomer

Charles Piazzi Smyth (1819-1900), English astronomer

Seth Barnes Nicholson (1891-1963), American astronomer

Edison Pettit (1889-1962), American astronomer

James E. Webb (1906-1992) Second NASA Administrator

Bill Ochs (b. 1957), Project Manager

John Mather (b. 1946) Senior project scientist

Gregory L. Robinson, Program manager

Summary of the Technology

The field of infrared astronomy began in the year 1800 when it was discovered that there were other types of light that were unable to be seen. British astronomer, Sir Frederick William Herschel, conducted experiments that unveiled energies that surpassed those of the red portion of the visible spectrum; we now know these to be infrared light. Herschel used different colored filters to view sunlight and noticed that they varied in the amount of heat they let through. Thinking that the colors may be different temperatures themselves, he used a glass prism to filter light into a spectrum and then measured the temperature of each individual color. He discovered that the temperature increased when going from violet to red and, being curious, decided to measure the temperature just past the red end of the spectrum. This ended up having an even higher temperature, indicating an invisible source of energy.

Through the majority of the 1800s and into the early 1900s, infrared radiation was being detected from various types of astronomical sources. In 1856, Charles Piazzi Smyth, Astronomer Royal for Scotland, detected radiation from the Moon. In the 1920s, Seth Barnes Nicholson and Edison Pettit developed technology that could detect infrared radiation from a few hundred stars.

Infrared astronomy did not gain much traction until the 1960s when scientists attached infrared detectors onto balloons and, later, onto high-flying aircraft, in order to make detections. It was eventually noted that, even though putting the detectors higher in the atmosphere yielded better results, they would still need to put instruments outside of the Earth's atmosphere in order to get the most accurate view of the infrared Universe.

Over the next several decades, space-based infrared observations were beginning to be made. In the 1980s, the first infrared telescope, the Infrared Astronomical Satellite (IRAS), a joint project with NASA, The Netherlands, and England, was launched and mapped the entirety of the sky. From there came the Spitzer Space telescope, then the Hubble, and soon the JWST.

The JWST will be launched on an Ariane 5 rocket from the Arianespace's ELA-3 launch complex near Kourou, French Guiana in South America. At 1,491,200 kilometers (932,000 miles) away, its orbit will be more than three times the distance from the Earth to the Moon. The mirrors and sunshield of the telescope will be able to fold up into the rocket, and will not deploy until they are almost at their orbit location.

JWST was named after James Edwin Webb, the second NASA Administrator who served from 1961 to 1968, and was responsible for over 75 launches. His contributions allowed for major advancements in the space program such as the Apollo lunar landing.

The fundamental difference between Hubble and the James Webb Space Telescope is that JWST will observe mostly in the infrared, rather than visible light. In addition, it will have seven times the collecting area of Hubble, with similar resolution. While the Spitzer Space Telescope also observed in infrared, JWST will have 50 times the area of Spitzer's mirror, making for much higher sensitivity.

The telescope will be comprised of three separate sections. The Integrated Science Instrument Model (ISIM) will hold the instruments, the Optical Telescope Element will collect and focus light from deep space in the infrared portion of the spectrum, and the Spacecraft Element will contain the sunshield and the Spacecraft Bus, which in itself contains the communications, electrical power, command and data handling, propulsion, thermal control, and altitude control subsystems.

The Near-Infrared Camera (NIRCam) is being built by the University of Arizona and will follow in the footsteps of Hubble by continuing to produce amazing astrophotography. It will look at near-infrared wavelengths and have a wide field of view as well as high angular resolution. In addition, it will

monitor image quality to determine when and how an adjustment needs to be made.

The Near Infrared Spectrograph, (NIRSpec) is being built by the European Space Agency and will allow scientists to observe over 100 objects within a 9-square-arcminute all at the same time.

The Mid-Infrared Instrument (MIRI) was developed as collaboration between 10 different European institutions as well as NASA's Jet Propulsion Laboratory and arrived at Goddard Space Flight Center in early 2012. This instrument will serve as both a spectrograph and an imager.

The Fine Guidance Sensor/Near-Infrared Imager Slitless Spectrograph (FGS/NIRISS) was developed by the Canadian Space Agency and arrived at Goddard in mid-2012. The Fine Guidance Sensor is responsible for the JWST's accurate pointing which is needed to obtain high-quality photos. The Near-Infrared Imager Slitless Spectrograph is designed for first-light detection (from the Big Bang), detection and characterization of exoplanets, and exoplanet transit spectroscopy.

As previously mentioned, the primary mirror of the JWST will be substantially larger than that of Hubble's. This is being accomplished through building it in relatively small segments, 18 to be exact, each 1.3 meters long and shaped like a hexagon. By doing this, the mirrors will have an effective collecting power of a single mirror that is 6.5 meters long. They will be made out of beryllium, which is lightweight and resists warping and cold temperatures, and coated in a thin layer of gold due to its ability to reflect infrared light.

Because heat and infrared detectors do not get along very well, JWST must be kept at unbelievably low temperatures while avoiding extensive cryogenics. The sunshield will allow for the needed cold by splitting the telescope into two sides, forming a barrier around the heat sources (the Sun, Earth, Moon, and the telescope). The hot side will reach temperatures of 359 kelvins (185 degrees Fahrenheit or 86 degrees Celsius), while the cold side will drop as low as 40 kelvins (-388 degrees Fahrenheit or -233 degrees Celsius).

JWST's sunshield will protect the telescope from heat by incorporating five layers of Kapton, a heat-resistant material coated in silicon. When unfurled, the sunshield will be close in size to a regulation tennis court, measuring 22 meters by 10 meters.

JWST will be stationed at the L2 Lagrangian point. There are five such points in total, where the gravity of the Earth and the Sun effectively cancel each other out and allow an object to remain stationary. Because it is so difficult to accomplish, a special Lissajous orbit, called a halo orbit, will have to be employed. This occurs when the spacecraft remains near the Lagrangian point, and proceeds to do a circular/elliptical loop around it.

Contributions

As the telescope has yet to be launched, it does not currently have any tangible contributions; however, it is expected to provide the scientific community with a plethora of new astronomical data.

JWST will be capable of seeing the very beginnings of the universe including young galaxies and possibly even the first exploding stars. Through these observations, scientists will seek to gain a better understanding of how stars and galaxies were born out of the chaos that was the early universe, suggested by evidence to have begun about 13.7 billion years ago.

As difficult as it is to believe, astronomers today still do not have a solid grasp on the origins of our very own solar system, located in the Milky Way galaxy. JWST will turn to stellar nurseries, areas where many stars form, within our shared galaxy to gather insight into how planets like Earth are formed; this will give them a better understanding as to how our solar system came to be.

With the emerging field of exoplanets, it is crucial that astronomers are capable of gathering data on the planets rather than simply detecting them. JWST will have both the sensitivity and resolution needed to detect water vapor and possibly even

oxygen, carbon dioxide, and methane in the atmospheres of distant planets. With this information, civilization will be brought one step closer to answering one of the most fundamental questions- are we alone in the Universe?

Context

The James Webb Space Telescope is especially important because if successful it will be the largest and most complex observatory that humans have ever put into space. Unlike previous space telescopes, the JWST will have its large sunshield that allows it to separate the warm and cold sides of the telescope. This is an innovative design that will possibly change the future of space telescopes, pending its success.

The collaboration between nations is rather impressive as it includes NASA, the Canadian Space Agency (CSA), and the European Space Agency (ESA). The countries that are providing hardware components to build the telescope are Austria, Belgium, Canada, Denmark, France, Germany, Ireland, Italy, the Netherlands, Spain, Sweden, Switzerland, the United Kingdom, and the United States of America. Finland, Greece, Luxembourg, Norway, Poland, Portugal, the Czech Republic, and Romania are also members of the ESA and will be contributing to the success of the JWST in some way. The telescope is being launched from French Guiana, located in South America. Once JWST is launched and operational, astronomers from all over the world will be able to use the telescope and/or the data that it provides. The collaborations will hopefully make way for more large-scale international collaborations in the future of astronomy.

While the astrophysics community is very excited for this telescope and the results it will yield, there has been a large amount of issues on the backend. The project quickly became harder to build and even more costly. NASA has struggled with Congress to convince them that it remains a high-priority scientific endeavor. Whether or not JWST will be in space before Hubble's mission ends is still unknown, but it is on track now for its currently scheduled launch in 2021.

—*Melissa A. Shea*

See also: Hubble Space Telescope; Infrared Astronomical Satellite

Further Reading

Clements, David L. *Infrared Astronomy – Seeing the Heat: from William Herschel to the Herschel Space Observatory.* CRS Press, 2015. This book talks of the major observational infrared telescopes, how infrared light is detected, what it reveals about astronomical bodies, and the problems that infrared astronomers face.

Ivanova, Nelly. *James Webb Space Telescope: Science Guide.* 1.2 ed., Space Telescope Science Institute, 2012. This short, interactive e-book touches upon the JWST's need for infrared light detection, its instruments, technology, goals, and how it will go about achieving them.

NASA and World Spaceflight News. *Complete Guide to NASA's James Webb Space Telescope (JWST) Project.* Amazon Digital Services LLC, 2017. This comprehensive book includes complete data on the JWST mission, investigations, instruments, subsystems, as well as coverage of the funding controversy between NASA and Congress and testimonies of real Congressional hearings.

Jet Propulsion Laboratory

Date: Beginning December 3, 1958
Type of facility: Space research center

The primary responsibility of the Jet Propulsion Laboratory (JPL) to NASA is exploration of the solar system with unpiloted, robotic spacecraft. At JPL, scientists and engineers work on some of the world's most advanced technology.

Key Figures

Frank J. Malina (1912-1981), first director of JPL

Theodore von Kármán (1881-1963), developer of the California Institute of Technology

William H. Pickering (1901-2004), JPL director, 1958-1976

Bruce C. Murray (b. 1932), principal investigator, planetary missions, JPL director, 1976- 1982

Lew Allen, Jr. (b. 1925), JPL director, 1982-1990

Edward C. Stone, Jr. (b. 1936), JPL director, 1991-2001

Charles Elachi (b. 1947), JPL director 2001-present

Summary of the Facility

The Jet Propulsion Laboratory had its origins in the mid-1930's at the Guggenheim Aeronautical Laboratory of the California Institute of Technology (GALCIT). Under the leadership of Theodore von Kármán, a small staff, and a group of graduate students, a number of rocket engine experiments were conducted in the Arroyo Seco, north of Pasadena, California, close to the site of the present Laboratory.

Funds and encouragement were lacking in the early stages of experimentation until Weld Arnold, a meteorology student at the California Institute of Technology, managed to scrape together one thousand dollars to purchase chemicals and equipment for the project. Later, the National Academy of Sciences provided ten thousand dollars for the development of rockets that could assist U.S. Army Air Corps planes at takeoff. The Laboratory staff expanded to include Apollo M. O. Smith, a GALCIT graduate student; Frank J. Malina, a leading aerodynamicist; Hsue Shen Tsien, a brilliant graduate student from China; John W. Parsons; Edward S. Forman; and Weld Arnold.

The group was studying high-speed flight and the limits of propeller-engine propulsion for aircraft. Robert A. Millikan, then head of the California Institute of Technology, was a member of a committee appointed by the Daniel and Florence Guggenheim Foundation to advise on the support being given by the foundation to Robert H. Goddard for the development of a high-altitude sounding rocket (a rocket used to collect information on the condition of Earth's atmosphere at various altitudes).

GALCIT had been experimenting with two kinds of rocket engines that could be adapted for jet-assisted takeoff (JATO); one used a solid propellant, and the other used liquid propellants. After numerous trials, a solid-propellant rocket engine was developed that produced 125 newtons of thrust and operated for twelve seconds. The Army Air Corps watched with interest when on August 12, 1941, three rockets were attached to each wing of a light monoplane. Army and Navy personnel watched the plane roar down the runway after the pilot had thrown the switch to ignite the JATO units. Calculations showed that the JATO units had shortened the

The Jet Propulsion Laboratory in the upper Arroyo Seco and San Gabriel Mountains foothills, of Pasadena and Altadena, Southern California. (NASA / JPL)

time and distance required for takeoff by 50 percent.

The JATO units' disadvantages prompted more experimentation with ways of controlling the burning rate of solid propellants and greater efforts to develop a liquid-fueled rocket that might serve as a JATO unit. The work was recognized by the aircraft industry. The Consolidated Aircraft Company of San Diego, California, may have been the first American commercial organization to recognize the potential applications of rocket-assisted takeoff. The National Academy of Sciences provided funds for further research.

Early jet propulsion research was applied to the development of "superperformance" aircraft. The researchers looked for ways to shorten the time and distance required for takeoff, to increase the rate of climb temporarily, and to increase level flight speed temporarily. GALCIT was authorized to work on both liquid- and solid-propellant rocket engines.

In early 1944, the Army asked the Laboratory to begin a research and development program on long-range guided missiles. This required basic research

in physics, chemistry, metallurgy, aerodynamics, and electronics. With funds provided by the Army Ordnance Corps and the Laboratory, investigations began on new propellants, metals to withstand heat and corrosion, and remote-control devices. The staff was enlarged, new facilities were added, and the work intensified.

During World War II, a number of firsts were achieved. JPL was the first U.S. government-sponsored group devoted to the study of rockets. JPL developed the first successful jet-assisted takeoff units, the first operational restricted burning solid-propellant rocket motor, and the first liquid-fuel engine to use a special, spontaneously igniting mixture. In 1942 JPL produced the first assisted takeoff of an airplane with a liquid-propellant rocket engine. The first graduate course in jet propulsion was inaugurated in 1944. In 1945 JPL designed and developed a sounding rocket that reached a record altitude of 27.9 kilometers.

JPL was also a pioneer in telemetry, the technique of transmitting instrument recordings via a radio link. Telemetry was necessary to the gathering of flight performance data from rockets and to the eventual development of guided missile systems. Successful development of the Bumper-Wac, which reached a record altitude of 155 kilometers, in 1947; the Loki solid-propellant antiaircraft rocket in 1951; and, in 1953, the Corporal, the United States' first surface-to-surface guided missile, led to the triumphant launch of the United States' first successful Earth satellite, Explorer 1, on January 31, 1958.

Explorer 1's success was heralded as a moral achievement as well as a scientific and technological achievement. Only three months after the Soviet Union had orbited the world's first artificial satellite, Sputnik 1, the Army Ballistic Missile Agency-Jet Propulsion Laboratory (ABMA-JPL) had redeemed the United States' honor. On board the Explorer satellite was an experiment that reported a mysterious saturation of radiation counters at an altitude of 965 kilometers. James A. Van Allen, the scientist who had created the experiment, interpreted this as evidence for the existence of a dense belt of radiation (now called the Van Allen radiation belt) around Earth at that altitude. Another scientific first had been achieved.

In the mid-1950's, U.S. agencies involved in space activities included the National Advisory Committee for Aeronautics, the Atomic Energy Commission, and the Department of Defense. The consensus in Washington was that the United States needed a national space program. The military component would be under the Department of Defense, but a civil component would forge an expanded program of space exploration in concert with the military. The National Aeronautics and Space Administration (NASA) came into being on October 1, 1958, when President Dwight D. Eisenhower signed the National Aeronautics and Space Act of 1958. The act established a broad charter for civilian aeronautical and space research.

On December 3, 1958, JPL was transferred from the Army's jurisdiction to NASA's. The Laboratory would continue to be operated by the California Institute of Technology. JPL's research emphasis changed from missiles to lunar and planetary exploration. New facilities were erected, and additional scientists, engineers, and support personnel were hired.

The Laboratory pledged to support the national interest through spaceflight projects, a deep-space network, a science program emphasizing flight experiments, national security projects, and the application of advanced technology to selective fields such as energy.

Major NASA/JPL spaceflight projects have collected a wealth of information on the physical constitution of Earth's celestial neighbors and the interplanetary medium. In 1958 and 1959, Pioneer 3 and Pioneer 4 were launched. The latter was the first successful U.S. Moon probe. It collected data on particles in lunar space.

From 1964 to 1965, three Ranger spacecraft made contact with the lunar surface. High-resolution photographs of the Moon were sent to Earth by television. From 1966 to 1968, there were five successful soft landings on the Moon by Surveyor probes. The Surveyors observed details of the lunar surface and demonstrated that it was safe for astronauts.

The Mariners were planetary research vehicles. Mariner 2, the first interplanetary spacecraft, collected data from Venus. Mariner 4 traveled past Mars; it returned the first close-up photographs of the Martian surface and discovered craters there. Mariner 5 made the second flyby of Venus; it obtained data on the atmosphere of the planet. The Mariners that followed provided information about Mars. Mariner 10 was the first dual-planet, gravity-assisted mission. In 1974 and 1975, the spacecraft photographed cloud patterns and atmospheric circulation on Venus. Later, it took high-resolution photographs of Mercury's surface and achieved three new encounters with Mercury.

The Viking mission to Mars was another JPL achievement accomplished in concert with Langley Research Center. Two Viking spacecraft were launched toward Mars, the first on August 20, 1975, and the second on September 9, 1975. Viking 1's lander reached the surface of Mars on July 20, 1976, the seventh anniversary of the Apollo crewed landing on the Moon. Viking 2 landed on September 3. During the primary mission, which lasted until mid-November, the Vikings took more than ten thousand photographs from orbit and from the surface; conducted a search for microbial life; performed organic and mineralogical studies of the Martian soil; studied physical and magnetic properties of the soil; made daily weather reports; and listened for seismic activity. The extended mission lasted about three and a half years; one lander, however, remained operational at a low level of activity until November, 1982.

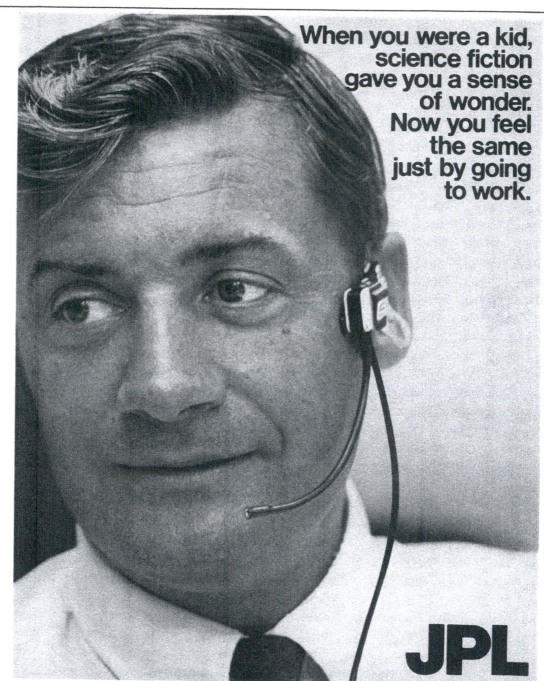

A 1960s advert running in Scientific American *reads: "When you were a kid, science fiction gave you a sense of wonder. Now you feel the same just by going to work."* (via Wikimedia Commons)

Launched from Kennedy Space Center in the late summer of 1977, two Voyager spacecraft are among the most rewarding flight missions managed by JPL. Equipped with television cameras and a variety of other scientific instruments, the Voyagers performed thorough studies of Jupiter, Saturn, and Uranus. In 1988, Voyager 1 was heading out of the solar system, searching for the boundary between the solar system and interstellar space. After having passed the Jovian and Saturnian systems, Voyager 2 achieved a highly successful flyby of Uranus in January, 1986. The spacecraft's encounter with Neptune's north pole and Neptune's satellite Triton occurred in 1989. Studies of the Jupiter and Saturn systems started by the Pioneer 10/11 and Voyager 1/2 flybys were advanced by the Galileo orbiter/probe and Cassini orbiter/probe, respectively.

JPL is also involved in studies of our own planet and its environment. The Solar Mesosphere Explorer has measured concentrations of ozone and other chemicals in Earth's atmosphere, and space shuttles have carried JPL experiments and a JPL scientist into Earth orbit.

The Shuttle Imaging Radar (SIR) and shuttle multispectral infrared radiometer, geologic and resource-mapping instruments that were part of the first shuttle's scientific payload, helped prove the usefulness of the shuttle for science experiments. Another experiment, the Active Cavity Radiometer Irradiance Monitor (ACRIM), flew in Spacelab 1 and measured the Sun's energy output to help determine how variations in solar energy affect Earth's climate.

JPL's Earth-orbiting satellite Seasat demonstrated the feasibility of global monitoring of sea conditions and determined key features of an ocean dynamics monitoring system.

Another of JPL's projects was the Infrared Astronomical Satellite (IRAS), a satellite that carries a cryogenically cooled telescope designed to survey and map the entire sky at infrared wavelengths. IRAS discovered many cold astronomical objects, interstellar clouds of dust, and sites of star formation. Along with three years of Earth-based observation, IRAS's observations revealed the density of Pluto's atmosphere to be greater than previously believed. JPL and University of Arizona planetologists learned that Pluto is different from asteroids and the icy satellites of giant planets. They obtained precise measurements of the diameter of Pluto and of its satellite, Charon.

Ground-based scientists were active in 1986 as the famous Halley's comet passed Earth on its seventy-six-year-period trip through the solar system. Scientists were able for the first time to observe the comet at close range with spacecraft. The European Space Agency, the Soviet Union, and Japan launched flight missions to study Halley's comet. JPL and the University of Erlangen-Nuremberg in West Germany were the centers for eight observing networks.

Spacecraft and the tasks they perform have evolved side by side with computer technology. For decades, JPL has been in the vanguard of advancing microelectronics technology. Developing computers to handle more complicated tasks and solving problems with new computer architecture are among the projects in JPL's Center for Space Microelectronics Technology.

One of the center's most exciting projects, the Hypercube, a concept in computer architecture, was invented at the California Institute of Technology (CalTech) and developed at JPL with strong CalTech participation. The talents of 120 scientists, engineers, and technicians trained in solid-state physics, materials science, chemistry, electrical engineering, and computer science are invested in the project. The CalTech/JPL group has written more than forty applications programs that run on the Hypercube, and several private companies have adopted the technology.

Biomedical research was one of the first nonspace endeavors at JPL; the Laboratory used computer-enhancement techniques borrowed from planetary projects to improve x-ray images of human skulls. JPL continues to do research in areas

Mars Science Laboratory mockup (right) compared with the Mars Exploration Rover (left) and Sojourner rover (center) by the Jet Propulsion Laboratory. (NASA / JPL / Thomas "Dutch" Slager)

such as atherosclerotic disease, laser medical applications, and various forms of cancer.

Context

JPL was chosen to be the nation's first space research facility because of the Laboratory's history of rocket research, which began in 1936 when Theodore von Kármán and several graduate students from the California Institute of Technology did their pioneering rocket experiments in the foothills of the San Gabriel Mountains in Southern California.

That early research led to the development of solid- and liquid-fueled rocket engines. Their first application came in 1940 with jet-assisted takeoff for aircraft. After eighteen years of work for the Army, JPL was transferred to NASA's jurisdiction. Under a NASA-California Institute of Technology contract, JPL received its first assignments to lead the nation's exploration of deep space.

For NASA, JPL has successfully completed robotic missions to the Moon and planets and opened the new frontier of the solar system. Among JPL's achievements are the Ranger and Surveyor lunar projects; the Mariner missions to Mars, Venus, and Mercury; Viking's mission to Mars; a survey of the sky at infrared wavelengths by the Infrared Astronomical Satellite (IRAS); the exploration of Jupiter and Saturn by Voyagers 1 and 2 and Uranus and Neptune by Voyager 2; Magellan, which orbited Venus and mapped its hidden surface with imaging radar; Galileo, designed to orbit Jupiter and send an instrument-laden probe into the planet's atmosphere for the first direct sampling of the planet's clouds; and Ulysses, a joint project between the European Space Agency and NASA to fly past Jupiter and then over the poles of the Sun, scanning the regions of the Sun that have never been seen before and studying interstellar space above the Sun's poles.

JPL's spacecraft are tracked and commanded by way of the Deep Space Network (DSN). In the spring of 1958, the Laboratory had been looking for a site on which to build a space vehicle tracking facility. The ideal location was determined to be at the U.S. Army's Camp Irwin, 72 kilometers north of Barstow, California, in the Mojave Desert. There, JPL engineers built a parabolic receiving dish 26 meters in diameter and 34 meters high. This dish antenna collects and focuses radio signals from space vehicles and is able to track satellites and space probes across the plane of the horizon. The data are collected and relayed to JPL's computing center in Pasadena for analysis.

More recent JPL missions of note include Mars Observer, the Magellan mission to Venus, Galileo to Jupiter and its moons, Ulysses solar-polar investigations, Mars Global Surveyor, Mars Pathfinder, Cassini to Saturn, Deep Space 1, Mars Climate Orbiter, Mars Polar Lander, the 2003 Mars Exploration Rovers Spirit and Opportunity, and Mars Curiosity. NASA's Hubble Space Telescope, freed from the blindfold of Earth's atmosphere, would bring the most distant reaches of the universe many times closer for astronomers. Among the telescope's instruments was a wide-field planetary camera, designed and built by JPL and the California Institute of Technology.

In other fields, too, JPL has turned its scientific and engineering expertise to solving major problems. JPL has been committed to the United States' energy self-sufficiency program since the energy crisis of the 1970's. The Department of Energy named JPL its lead center for solar-photovoltaic development and applications. (Photovoltaic cells are solid-state solar energy devices that convert sunlight directly to electricity.)

The U.S. air carriers, and the people who operate and control them, look to space-age technology to improve conditions for the flying public. JPL has contributed to the Federal Aviation Administration's attempt to improve air safety with a computerized voice-switching and control system.

Research into new technologies is among the most fascinating work pursued at JPL. Many of the new technologies are intended to solve problems that have been with us for decades. JPL's major function, however, continues to be exploration of the solar system.

—Clarice Lolich

See also: Asteroid and Comet Exploration; Explorers 1-7; Infrared Astronomical Satellite; Mariner 1 and 2; Mariner 3 and 4; Mariner 5; Mariner 6 and 7; Mariner 8 and 9; Mariner 10; Mars Curiosity; Mars Exploration Rovers; Pioneer Missions 1-5; Pioneer Missions 6-E; Ranger Program; Seasat; Space Centers, Spaceports, and Launch Sites; Space Shuttle: Radar Imaging Laboratories; Viking Program; Voyager Program.

Further Reading

Bilstein, Roger E. *Orders of Magnitude: A History of the NACA and NASA, 1915-1990*. 2d ed. NASA SP-4406. Washington, D.C.: Government Printing Office, 1989. This brief volume covers the U.S. history of aeronautics and space development, from the first aircraft to the space shuttle.

Burrows, William E. *This New Ocean: The Story of the First Space Age*. New York: Random House, 1998. This is a comprehensive history of the human conquest of space, covering everything from the earliest attempts at spaceflight through the voyages near the end of the twentieth century. Burrows is an experienced journalist, who has reported for *The New York Times*, *The Washington Post*, and *The Wall Street Journal*. There are many photographs and an extensive source list. Interviewees in the book include Isaac Asimov, Alexei Leonov, Sally K. Ride, and James A. Van Allen.

Davies, John K. *Astronomy from Space: The Design and Operation of Orbiting Observatories*. 2d ed. New York: John Wiley, 1997. Coverage of all space astronomy missions, with tables of launch data and orbits as well as photographs of many satellites. Organized by type of astronomy: x-ray, gamma-ray, ultraviolet, infrared and millimeter, and radio.

Hamilton, John. *The Viking Missions to Mars*. Edina, Minn.: ABDO and Daughters Publishing, 1998. Although this is a juvenile book, it does give a good overview of the Viking missions to the Red Planet.

Heppenheimer, T. A. *Countdown: A History of Space Flight*. New York: John Wiley, 1997. A detailed historical narrative of the human conquest of space. Heppenheimer traces the development of piloted flight through the military rocketry programs of the era preceding World War II. Covers both the American and the Soviet attempts to place vehicles, spacecraft, and humans into the hostile environment of space. More than a dozen pages are devoted to bibliographic references.

Klerkx, Greg. *Lost in Space: The Fall of NASA and the Dream of a New Space Age*. New York: Pantheon Books, 2004. The premise of this work is that NASA has been stuck in Earth orbit since the Apollo era, and that space exploration has suffered as a result.

Koppes, Clayton R. *JPL and the American Space Program: A History of the Jet Propulsion Laboratory*. New Haven, Conn.: Yale University Press, 1982. This volume discusses basic space and weapons research during World War II and the decades that followed. It describes the relationships between the California Institute of Technology and JPL and between JPL and NASA. More than half the volume is devoted to JPL's space projects.

Lambright, W. Henry, ed. *Space Policy in the Twenty-First Century*. Baltimore: Johns Hopkins University Press, 2003. This book addresses a number of important questions: What will replace the space shuttle? Can the International Space Station justify its cost? Will Earth be threatened by asteroid impact? When and how will humans explore Mars?

Lee, Wayne. *To Rise from Earth: An Easy to Understand Guide to Spaceflight*. New York: Checkmark Books, 1996. This is a good introduction to the science of spaceflight. Although written by an engineer with the NASA Jet Propulsion Laboratory, it is presented in easy-to-understand language. In addition to the theory of spaceflight, it gives some of the history of the human endeavor to explore space.

National Aeronautics and Space Administration, Jet Propulsion Laboratory. *The Deep Space Network*. Pasadena, Calif.: Author, 1988. This booklet explains the nature of the Deep Space Network, the largest and most sensitive scientific telecommunications and radio navigation network in the world. With illustrations and photographs, it describes the applications of the DSN in JPL's space programs.

---. *Jet Propulsion Laboratory 1987 Annual Report*. Pasadena, Calif.: Author, 1987. Recovering from the tragedy of the *Challenger* gave impetus to a period of research in robotics, automation, machine intelligence, astrophysics, and new computer architecture. JPL researchers expanded observations of Earth's oceans and climate from space. The book contains many black-and-white photographs.

---. *JPL Closeup*. Pasadena, Calif.: Author, 1987. This is an attractive booklet with clear, black-and-white, scientific photographs. It summarizes the findings of the planetary missions launched to date and then presents an overview of immediate and long range plans for JPL's future endeavors. The publication touches on the Deep Space Network and the Hypercube, a concept in computer architecture invented at the California Institute of Technology.

---. *JPL Highlights 1987*. Pasadena, Calif.: Author, 1987. Rather technical, this volume covers deep-space exploration, information systems and space technology development, defense and civil programs, and Earth-orbital applications. Contains photographs and sketches.

Ramana Murthy, Poolla V., and Arnold W. Wolfendale. *Gamma-Ray Astronomy*. 2d ed. New York: Cambridge University Press, 1993. This book, which is a fully updated new edition of the authors' earlier volume published in 1986, is invaluable in providing the background science to this important field. In assessing the current state of the art, the book also indicates the exciting basis from which new discoveries will be made. The concentration on phenomenology makes this book a fine introduction to gamma-ray astronomy. It is of use to all students and professional astronomers who are working in this developing field.

Spilker, Linda J., ed. *Passage to a Ringed World: The Cassini-Huygens Mission to Saturn and Titan*. Washington, D.C.: National Aeronautics and Space Administration, 1997. Edited by the Cassini deputy project scientist, this collection provides a preview of the Cassini- Huygens mission. Chapters include details about the spacecraft, as well as Saturn and its moon Titan. There are numerous photographs and illustrations, a glossary of terms, an acronyms and abbreviations list, and a bibliography.

Stern, S. Alan, and Jacqueline Mitton. *Pluto and Charon: Ice Worlds on the Ragged Edge of the Solar System*. New York: John Wiley, 1997. This book discusses scientists' knowledge of the Pluto-Charon system obtained from ground-based observations and images taken by the Voyager spacecraft and the Hubble Space Telescope. The book covers the advances made possible by dramatic improvements in ground-based astronomical instrumentation and the revolution in scientific perspective wrought by spacecraft visits to the planets. From its discovery in 1930 by Clyde Tombaugh to future exploration by the Pluto- Kuiper Express, this illustration-packed work thoroughly explores these two icy-cold worlds.

Westwick, Peter J. *Into the Black: JPL and the American Space Program 1976-2004*. New Haven, Conn.: Yale University Press, 2006. A scholarly history of a major portion of the history of the Jet Propulsion Laboratory. Includes program management, spacecraft preparations, and mission operations for a wide range of JPL investigations.

Wolf, Marvin J. *Space Pioneers: The Illustrated History of the Jet Propulsion Laboratory and the Race to Space*. Santa Monica, Calif.: General Publishing Group, 1999. This is an in-depth look at the Jet Propulsion Laboratory and the space missions—both piloted and robotic—to explore the depths of space. The book covers JPL from its inception through 1998. There are numerous photographs and tables.

Johnson Space Center

Date: Beginning November 1, 1961
Type of facility: Space research center

Johnson Space Center (JSC) is NASA's lead center for development of piloted spacecraft, training of space crews, and direction of piloted space missions. It is also responsible for research and development in a number of areas, including life sciences and remote sensing of Earth resources.

Key Figures

Robert R. Gilruth (1913-2000), Manned Spacecraft Center (MSC) director, 1961-1972

Christopher C. Kraft, Jr. (b. 1924), MSC/JSC director, 1972-1982

Gerald D. Griffin (b. 1934), JSC director, 1982-1986

Jesse W. Moore, JSC director, 1986

Aaron Cohen (1931-2010), JSC director, 1986-1993

Carolyn Huntoon (b. 1940), JSC director, 1994-1995, and the first woman to hold the position

George W. S. Abbey (b. 1932), JSC director, 1996-2001

Roy S. Estess (1930-2010), JSC director, 2001-2002

General Jefferson D. Howell, Jr. (b. 1940), JSC director, 2002-2005

Michael L. Coats (b. 1946), JSC director, 2005-2012

Dr. Ellen Ochoa (b. 1958), JSC director, 2013-2018

Mark S. Geyer (b. 1960), JSC director 2018-present

Summary of the Facility

Johnson Space Center (JSC) was formed early in the U.S. space program to take charge of all U.S. piloted spaceflights. It evolved from the Space Task Group (STG), a special detail formed by the National Aeronautics and Space Administration (NASA) on November 5, 1958, and charged with starting preliminary work on a crewed spacecraft. STG was located at the Langley Research Center in Hampton, Virginia, and borrowed thirty-three of Langley's engineers. Nine days after its formation, the STG wrote "Specifications for a Manned Space Capsule," sending copies to fifty prospective bidders. On December 17, this "manned space capsule" project was named Mercury. In early 1959, STG became one of six departments in the newly formed Goddard Space Flight Center in Greenbelt, Maryland. Because of its rapid growth, though, the group never moved to Goddard. Instead, it was made an independent entity on March 1, 1961, and a search for a new home began. Encouraged by Rice University's offer of free land and by Vice President Lyndon B. Johnson's support, NASA selected Clear Lake City, a suburb of Houston, as the site of its crewed spaceflight headquarters on September 19, 1961. On November 1, the new facility was named the Manned Spacecraft Center, a name it held until February 17, 1973, when it was renamed in honor of the late President Johnson. Some STG offices moved as early as October, 1961, and were temporarily housed in quarters at nearby Ellington Air Force Base and in Houston. The move was completed after the last Mercury mission, and the center was formally opened in February, 1964.

Designed like a college campus, JSC has more than thirty major buildings, ranging from the office building for headquarters personnel to the

An astronaut training in the Neutral Buoyancy Laboratory at JSC. (NASA)

windowless Mission Control Building. The growth of the shuttle program spurred development of a number of off-site contractor support facilities to handle engineering and support work.

JSC's first director, Robert R. Gilruth, managed the center from its origins in the Space Task Group until January, 1972, when he was appointed to be NASA's director of Key Personnel Development. He was succeeded by Christopher C. Kraft, Jr., a member of the original STG team and a former flight director. Kraft managed JSC until his retirement after seeing the shuttle program into its initial flights. He was replaced by Gerald D. Griffin, who served until after the 1986 *Challenger* accident. Griffin was succeeded by Aaron Cohen, a former manager of the shuttle orbiter project, who left in 1986 to become NASA deputy administrator. George W. S. Abbey became JSC director in January, 1996. He was succeeded briefly by Acting Director Roy Estess (2001-2002), and then by General Jefferson D. Howell, Jr., who had to deal with the *Columbia* accident and the "Return to Flight" efforts that resumed shuttle missions to the International Space Station. Howell retired in 2005, and was replaced by former astronaut Michael L. Coats

who held the JSC director position through the end of 2012. Former mission specialist Dr. Ellen Ochoa became director at the start of 2013 and kept the position through 2018 at which time Mark S. Geyer assumed the leadership of Johnson Space Center.

Reorganization in May, 1963, divided the center into separate operations and development branches. In November of that year, a further change gave the space center's director and his deputy joint responsibility for four assistant directors—of Flight Operations, Administration, Engineering and Development, and Flight Crew Operations—and for the Apollo and Gemini Program offices. Flight Operations included four major divisions: Flight Support, Mission Planning and Analysis, Flight Control, and Landing and Recovery. Flight Crew Operations included the Astronaut Office, headed by a chief astronaut; an Aircraft Operations Office; and a Flight Crew Support division. An assistant director for life science research was added later.

The number of employees at JSC changed with the fluctuating NASA budget over the years. In 1969 the space program had become so retrenched that JSC managers could hire only one employee to replace every fourteen who left. The Apollo-Soyuz Test Project (ASTP), although criticized by some as a scientific dead end, did in fact help to retain a number of skilled flight controllers who might otherwise have left the space program in the long hiatus between Skylab and the space shuttle. Mission Control, the best-known facility at JSC, operated as a backup during the Gemini 2 and 3 missions in 1965. Starting with the Gemini IV mission, however, Houston was the primary control center. It was crewed twenty-four hours per day during crewed space missions, and anyone at the center was on standby to assist with any problems that might arise during a mission. (This tradition would continue: NASA crews at JSC worked around the clock to refine their understanding of the shuttle's strength margins when erratic winds threatened to delay the STS-26 mission in 1988.)

As the Gemini Program progressed and the Apollo Program began, crew members became less dependent on Mission Control for routine operations; nevertheless, they still required guidance updates and schedule revisions, because each mission was subject to minor variations. Mission Control is responsible for a mission from the time the launch vehicle "clears the tower" at the Kennedy Space Center until "wheel stop" at landing or splashdown depending on the nature of the piloted mission.

Mission Control's value was best shown during the Apollo 13 mission in April 1970 when an oxygen tank explosion nearly doomed the crew in flight. The crew, unable to diagnose the problem, relied on the alert ground control team of engineers and flight directors who quickly devised emergency life-support procedures and altered the flight plan to return the crew safely.

Although the public most often sees the "trenches" in the flight control room and hears the voice of the capsule communicator, or CapCom, Mission Control actually comprises a number of support rooms and staff members. There are two complete facilities in the Mission Control Center. The one on the second floor is used for civilian shuttle missions; the one on the third floor is dedicated to military missions. The entire building, like other buildings at JSC, has a special security cardkey system—which did not exist during the comparatively open Apollo era—and the third-floor facilities are enclosed in an electronic screen to prevent eavesdropping on discussions during a flight.

The flight control room encloses three rows of computer terminals where more than twenty flight controllers can be seated. All three rows face a wall-sized map of the world that indicates the spacecraft's position and orbital path and the locations of tracking stations. On either side of the wall map were technical status displays and, on the right side, a television image transmitted from the spacecraft.,

There are ten key positions in Mission Control. The flight director has overall responsibility for the conduct of the mission and final authority for major decisions. The space communicator—or CapCom, from Mercury's capsule communicator—is an astronaut. The CapCom acts as the liaison between ground and flight crews. The flight dynamics officer is responsible for spacecraft maneuvers, the guidance control officer oversees the onboard navigation and guidance software, and the Flight Surgeon is in charge of crew health and life-support monitoring. There are five Systems Engineers: The Data Processing Systems Engineer monitors the onboard computers, the malfunction displays, and the caution and warning system; the Booster Systems Engineer covers the solid-fueled rocket booster, main engine, and External Tank during countdown and ascent; the Propulsion Systems Engineer is in charge of the reaction control and orbital maneuvering systems; the Guidance, Navigation, and Control Systems Engineer monitors those systems, along with abort conditions; and the Electrical, Environmental, and Consumables Systems Engineer is responsible for the power supply and distribution, environmental control, and life-support systems. Personnel in a number of "back rooms"—the multipurpose support room, the Payload Operations Control Center, and several Mission Control support areas— provide expertise for various systems and activities.

Each crewed space program has required the construction of simulators in which the astronauts may train for their missions. Relatively crude simulators for Mercury and Gemini were located at other NASA centers and contractor sites as well as at JSC. More sophisticated simulators were assembled for the Apollo Program. The interiors were virtually identical to the flight vehicles, but the exteriors were covered by a complex array of boxes enclosing sophisticated optical instruments that could project the same views that the crew would see in space. The Lunar Module simulator also had a large model of the lunar surface on which the crew would "land," using the image from a tiny television camera maneuvered by computer.

Most of the Apollo and Skylab simulators were dismantled or turned into museum pieces and replaced with new, computerized simulators for the shuttle era. It is still not possible to build a single simulator that can serve all crews in all ways, so several have been built for specific purposes. The most important are the Shuttle Mission Simulators (SMS's). The moving-base SMS takes the crew through the full range of motions experienced during a shuttle launch and landing, and the fixed-base SMS has upper and lower decks for simulating orbital activities and experiments. Each SMS is attached to a complex array of computers to link it to Mission Control and to simulate virtually every aspect of spaceflight, from instrument displays and outside scenery to the fraction-of-a-second delay in voice signals traveling through the NASA network.

The crews also train on single-system trainers, which mimic the functions of limited sets of instruments and controls on the flight deck; Earth-normal gravity mock-ups, which have the shape and feel of the shuttle cabin for training in ingress and egress, housekeeping, and maintenance, but are otherwise nonfunctional; the manipulator development center, which duplicates the aft flight deck, payload bay, and robot arm for satellite handling tests with helium-filled balloon mock-ups; the shuttle engineering simulator, in which detailed procedures can be worked out before crew tests are conducted on the SMS; and the shuttle avionics integration laboratory, which mimics the functions of virtually every piece of electronic gear in the shuttle and tests flight software.

The simulators have served as more than crew training aids. They have also served as development tools for new experiments and procedures and as trouble-shooting facilities, because engineers cannot examine hardware while a spacecraft is in orbit. The astronauts, whose time is limited, do not take part until a procedure has been refined and needs their comments.

Pilot astronauts maintain their flying proficiency by flying two-seat T-38 Talon jet trainers operated from Ellington Air Force Base, a few miles from JSC. In addition, two special simulators are operated from Ellington: a shuttle trainer aircraft and a KC-135 cargo jet. The shuttle trainer is a Gulfstream 2 corporate jet refitted with controls, computers, and actuators that make it handle as the shuttle orbiter does during final approach and landing. For familiarization with weightlessness, the astronauts ride aboard the KC-135, which flies roller-coaster-like parabolas to provide about thirty seconds of free fall at each peak. Scientists and engineers also use the jet to test new designs for equipment that might be affected by weightlessness.

JSC has a number of other simulation facilities. The Space Environment Simulation Laboratory has

This overall view of the Shuttle (White) Flight Control Room (WFCR) in Johnson Space Center's Mission Control Center (MCC) was photographed during STS-114 simulation activities. (NASA)

two large chambers (36.6 meters high by 19.8 meters wide, and 13.1 meters high by 10.7 meters wide) in which the Apollo spacecraft were subjected to a spacelike vacuum and to temperatures ranging from 100 to 390 kelvins. The Vibration and Acoustic Test Facility subjects hardware to the noise and vibration predicted during launch. The White Sands Test Facility, in New Mexico, tests the space shuttle's thruster modules.

A flight acceleration building once housed a centrifuge on which riders could experience a force twenty times that of gravity, for sustained periods, or thirty times, momentarily. It was dismantled in the late 1970's, and its building was renovated to house the Weightless Environment Training Facility (WETF), a water tank large enough (10 by 23.7 meters in area, 7.6 meters deep) to house a mock-up of the entire space shuttle payload bay. WETF is used to develop crew procedures for various contingencies, such as manually closing the payload bay doors in an emergency, freeing stuck solar arrays on a satellite, and repairing and maintaining orbiting satellites.

JSC also has a number of research offices. The most famous is the Lunar Sample Building, which houses the Lunar Receiving Laboratory, built to protect the Apollo lunar samples from contamination. When the Laboratory was conceived, mission scientists' first and greatest concern was that lunar samples might harbor life-forms hazardous to life on Earth. As a result, the Lunar Receiving Laboratory included a crew quarantine facility in which the early Apollo lunar crews were held for two to three weeks after returning to Earth. Beginning with Apollo 15, crew quarantine was discontinued because tests had firmly established that the Moon had no indigenous life-forms; nevertheless, samples of space materials are still quarantined so that no terrestrial compounds can contaminate them. Analyses normally are carried out in isolation boxes made of stainless steel and glass and with virtually no organic materials present. To support the work at JSC,

the Lunar and Planetary Institute was established at a small ranch adjoining the center.

JSC and Marshall Space Flight Center helped to define the space shuttle program in the late 1960's and early 1970's. Each center jockeyed for the lead role in the program, JSC claiming that the shuttle was a spacecraft and Marshall claiming that it was a launch vehicle. In the end the program was neatly divided between the two: JSC was named the lead center for integration and for development of the orbiter, and Marshall was given responsibility for the propulsion systems.

JSC has always had a strong interest in advanced programs, especially space stations. Between 1962 and 1968, by one accounting, the center conducted some twenty space station studies at a total cost of $6.3 million. In the late 1960's the studies took two major forms: the Apollo Applications Program, which became Skylab and was ultimately managed by Marshall Space Flight Center, and a long-term, reusable space station, which would have been launched as a single unit by the Saturn V rocket. When Congress canceled funding for further Saturn booster production, JSC began emphasizing the shuttle program in the early 1970's. JSC initiated studies on a number of proposed stations that would be carried up as modules by the shuttle. In 1980 these projects converged as the Space Operations Center (SOC) study. SOC was to be a facility providing maintenance and other support to satellites in nearby orbits; it was designed to expand and encompass crewed research. JSC operates the Space Station Control Center (SSCC), handles crew integration and training, and oversees systems operations for U.S. involvement in the International Space Station. JSC adapts to the mission assigned to it by the White House.

As of 2019 JSC was heavily involved in both commercial crew vehicle development to begin sending astronauts back to the ISS having launched from American soil, and also with preparing the new Space Launch System rocket/Orion spacecraft to begin a second phase of human exploration of the

View of the Shuttle Challenger atop the Shuttle Carrier Aircraft (SCA), NASA-905, during its return to Kennedy Space Center (KSC) and flyover of the Johnson Space Center (JSC) at southeast edge of Houston on Saturday, April 9, 1983. (NASA)

Moon. NASA's mandate as of 2019 was to send the first woman and the next man to the Moon by 2024. That is a monumental task with a relatively strict time frame, but JSC has embraced the urgency of that presidential directive.

Context

The center has retained much of the organizational structure set up in the 1960's, with program offices added to handle the Space Transportation System, the shuttle orbiter, and the Space Station programs. Major changes were made in the hierarchy after the 1986 *Challenger* accident—several top-level managers now are attached to NASA Headquarters, even though they work at JSC—and a special safety, reliability, and quality assurance office was created to provide an objective review of areas outside the control of various program offices. Other major offices include Flight Crew Operations, Mission Operations (which includes Mission Control),Mission Support, Space and Life Sciences, and Engineering. Organizational changes also followed in the wake of the 2003 *Columbia* accident.

Following President Ronald W. Reagan's endorsement in January, 1984, four work packages were divided among the various NASA centers. JSC was allocated WP-2, the second-largest package. It included the outfitting of the U.S. Space Station's crew habitation module; the building of various crew-related systems, guidance systems, and computers; the development of the station's primary structure; and the integration and assembly of the station as a whole. In 1988, advanced studies under way at JSC included the Phase II expansion of the International Space Station, and designers were studying the feasibility of large support beams for experiments above and below the modules.

The Astronaut Office supports a number of NASA programs by providing crew members who can offer users opinions about the experiments and systems that ultimately will be deployed in space. Astronauts, new and veteran, often support crew station and other program reviews. Furthermore, the Astronaut Office has been given a greater role in space shuttle planning and operations decisions since the *Challenger* accident. Several astronauts have taken part in analyses of failures or potential failures, and most are active in the Crewed Spaceflight Awareness program, which assists NASA's quality control efforts.

The National Space Transportation System Office has a major branch and a deputy director at JSC. The office oversees all shuttle mission planning and reports to NASA Headquarters in Washington, D.C., rather than to the field center.

JSC was the lead center for a number of space shuttle payloads, including those dealing with Earth observations and life sciences. The center maintains an active Earth Resources office that has supported the Earth Resources Laboratory at the Stennis Space Center. Life science activities cover work ranging from small, occupational health experiments, designed to develop a larger data pool on space sickness, to the dedicated SLS-1 and SLS-2 Space Life Science missions. JSC has a large cadre of flight medicine specialists and conducts experiments using flight crews and civilian control subjects.

The Lunar Receiving Laboratory's role has expanded to include analyses of comet dust samples collected by high-flying aircraft and of meteorites, especially samples from Antarctica that are believed to be Martian rocks cast across space by massive impacts. Samples returned from space by the Genesis and Stardust robotic probes would begin studies here as well. JSC also supports NASA studies of modules and landers for piloted missions to the Moon and Mars.

—Dave Dooling

See also: Ames Research Center; Cape Canaveral and the Kennedy Space Center; Goddard Space Flight Center; Jet Propulsion Laboratory; Langley Research Center; Lewis Field and Glenn Research Center; Marshall Space Flight Center; Space Centers, Spaceports, and Launch Sites; Space Shuttle.

Further Reading

Allday, Jonathan. *Apollo in Perspective: Spaceflight Then and Now*. Philadelphia: Institute of Physics, 2000. Explains the basic physics and technology of spaceflight and conveys the strides made by the Apollo Program in crews, vehicles, and space suits.

Baker, David. *The Rocket: The History and Development of Rocket and Missile Technology*. New York: Crown, 1978. A thorough, well-researched history of the development of rocketry and of specific launch vehicles. Although the focus is on rocket hardware, there are extensive descriptions of launch preparations and of many of the early failures and their causes.

Bilstein, Roger E. *Stages to Saturn: A Technological History of the Apollo/Saturn Launch Vehicles*. Gainesville: University Press of Florida, 2003. Covers the development of the Saturn launch vehicles.

Burrows, William E. *This New Ocean: The Story of the First Space Age*. New York: Random House, 1998. This is a comprehensive history of the human conquest of space, covering everything from the earliest attempts at spaceflight through the voyages near the end of the twentieth century. Burrows is an experienced journalist, who has reported for *The New York Times*, *The Washington Post*, and *The Wall Street Journal*. There are many photographs and an extensive source list. Interviewees in the book include Isaac Asimov, Alexei Leonov, Sally K. Ride, and James A. Van Allen.

Cernan, Eugene A., and Don Davis. *The Last Man on the Moon: Astronaut Eugene Cernan and America's Race in Space*. New York: St. Martin's Press, 1999. The story of the last two men to walk on the Moon is told by Cernan, commander of Apollo 17, and Davis, an experienced journalist. This autobiography tells the story behind the story of Gemini and Apollo. Cernan, whose spaceflight career spanned both programs, fittingly narrates it. He was the first person to spacewalk in orbit around the Earth and the last person to leave footprints on the lunar surface.

Cooper, Henry S. F., Jr. *Before Liftoff: The Making of a Space Shuttle Crew*. Baltimore: Johns Hopkins University Press, 1987. A highly detailed and engrossing account of several weeks in the shuttle crew's training for the October, 1984, *Challenger* mission. The book portrays the ordinary and extraordinary events and frustrations that take place as a crew prepares for and conducts a mission and explains how those events shape mission plans. Written for a general audience.

---. *Thirteen: The Apollo Flight That Failed*. Baltimore: Johns Hopkins University Press, 1995. This book is a re-release of the 1973 edition, published to coincide with the release of the movie *Apollo 13*. The book details the activities surrounding the extraterrestrial melodrama that captivated a world that had found trips to the Moon to be routine. It would be another sixteen years before the United States again became complacent with spaceflight. That complacency ended with *Challenger*. This is a fascinating look at the efforts to rescue three astronauts "lost in space" aboard the Apollo 13 Command Module. Although it reads like a novel, this work is based upon news reports and interviews with the participants and does not exploit the "newsworthiness" of the story.

Dethloff, Henry. *Suddenly Tomorrow Came: A History of Johnson Space Center*. Washington, D.C.: Government Printing Office, 1994. NASA's official history of the Manned Spacecraft Center and, as it was later known, the Johnson Space Center. It gives a great deal of detail about the Center, as well as the personnel who operated it. Along the way, the history of the American space program is told.

Grimwood, James M. *Project Mercury: A Chronology*. NASA SP-4001. Washington, D.C.: Government Printing Office, 1963. A detailed chronology of America's first crewed space missions, from the space program's postwar beginnings through the start of the Gemini Program. Although not written as a narrative, the book provides accounts of launch preparation activities.

Harland, David M. *Exploring the Moon: The Apollo Expeditions*. New York: Springer-Verlag, 1999. This book covers the history from the early, uncrewed probes, the hard and soft landers, through the Apollo Program to the present-day Lunar Prospector. Emphasis is on the Apollo Program. Written in a very readable manner, *Exploring the Moon* is a travelogue that places the reader on the rover with the astronauts. This is a detailed guide to what the astronauts did, where they went, and what they saw. The book, in an easy-to read style, tells not just of the scientific studies but also of the frustration and exhilarations of the crews. The book also contains many maps and excellent photographs. Some photographs have not been previously published. A complete set of appendices lists the rock samples, scientific missions, and the crew. A geologic glossary is included for the nongeologist. Excellent descriptions of the experiments are given for the nonscientist.

---. *The Space Shuttle: Roles, Missions, and Accomplishments*. New York: John Wiley, 1998. The book details the origins, missions, payloads, and passengers of the Space Transportation System (STS), covering the flights from STS-1 through STS-89 in great detail. This large volume is divided into five sections: "Operations," "Weightlessness," "Exploration," "Outpost," and "Conclusions." "Operations" discusses the origins of the shuttle, test flights, and some of its missions and payloads. "Weightlessness" describes many of the experiments performed aboard the orbiter, including materials processing, electrophoresis, phase partitioning, and combustion. "Exploration" includes the Hubble Space Telescope, Spacelab, Galileo, Magellan, and Ulysses, as well as Earth observation projects. "Outpost" covers the shuttle's role in the joint Russian Mir program and the International Space Station. Contains numerous illustrations, an index, and bibliographical references.

Heppenheimer, T. A. *Countdown: A History of Space Flight*. New York: John Wiley, 1997. A detailed historical narrative of the human conquest of space. Heppenheimer traces the development of piloted flight through the military rocketry programs of the era preceding World War II. Covers both the American and the Soviet attempts to place vehicles, spacecraft, and humans into the hostile environment of space. More than a dozen pages are devoted to bibliographic references.

Klerkx, Greg. *Lost in Space: The Fall of NASA and the Dream of a New Space Age*. New York: Pantheon Books, 2004. The premise of this work is that NASA has been stuck in Earth's orbit since the Apollo era, and that space exploration has suffered as a result.

Kranz, Eugene F. *Failure Is Not an Option: Mission Control from Mercury to Apollo 13 and Beyond*. New York: Simon & Schuster, 2000. This is the autobiography of Eugene F. Kranz, flight director during Apollo 13. Kranz joined the NASA Space Task Group at Langley, Virginia, in 1960, and was assigned the position of assistant flight director for Project Mercury. He assumed flight director duties for all Project Gemini missions and was branch chief for Flight Control Operations. He was selected as division chief for Flight Control in 1968 and continued his duties as a flight director for the Apollo 11 lunar landing before taking over the leadership of the Apollo 13 "Tiger Team."

Lambright, W. Henry, ed. *Space Policy in the Twenty-First Century*. Baltimore: Johns Hopkins University Press, 2003. This book addresses a number of important questions: What will replace the space shuttle? Can the International Space Station justify its cost? Will Earth be threatened by asteroid impact? When and how will humans explore Mars?

Launius, Roger D. *NASA: A History of the U.S. Civil Space Program*. Malabar, Fla.: Krieger Publishing Company, 1994. This is an in-depth look at America's civilian space program and the establishment of the National Aeronautics and Space Administration. It chronicles the agency from its predecessor, the National Advisory Committee for Aeronautics, through the present day.

Lay, Beirne. *Earthbound Astronauts: The Builders of Apollo-Saturn*. New York: Prentice-Hall, 1971. Discusses the development of the Saturn V launch vehicle from the viewpoint of several engineers and managers who worked on the Saturn program. Includes many details of mission operations.

Levine, Arnold S. *Managing NASA in the Apollo Era*. NASA SP-4102. Washington, D.C.: Government Printing Office, 1982. A highly detailed history of the difficulties of and lessons learned from managing a large, growing agency as it developed a complex program to place Americans on the Moon.

Lewis, Richard S. *The Voyages of Apollo: The Exploration of the Moon*. New York: Quadrangle, 1974. Covers the development of the Apollo spacecraft and the conduct of the missions. Includes details on Mission Control operations, especially during the crises of the Apollo 13 flight. Suitable for general audiences.

National Aeronautics and Space Administration. *National Space Transportation System Reference*. Washington, D.C.: Author, 1988. A technical manual written to provide the media with as many details as possible about space shuttle hardware, operations, and missions. Includes descriptions of the shuttle facilities at JSC.

Pellegrino, Charles R., and Joshua Stoff. *Chariots for Apollo: The Making of the Lunar Module*. New York: Atheneum, 1985. A well-written, enjoyable history of the development of the Lunar Module. Although the book focuses on the difficulties of building the spacecraft, much attention is given to the work involved in making the module a suitable payload and in launching it into space.

Shepard, Alan B., Jr., and Donald K. "Deke" Slayton, with Jay Barbree and Howard Benedict. *Moon Shot: The Inside Story of America's Race to the Moon*. Atlanta: Turner, 1994. This is, indeed, the inside story of the Apollo Program as told by two men who actively participated in it. Some of their tales appear here for the first time. It is almost as good as being a fly on the wall during the heyday of crewed spaceflight. The book was turned into a four-hour documentary in 1995.

Slayton, Donald K., with Michael Cassutt. *Deke! U.S. Manned Space: From Mercury to the Shuttle*. New York: Forge, 1995. This is the autobiography of the last of the Mercury astronauts to fly in space. After being grounded from flying in Project Mercury for what turned out to be a minor heart murmur, Slayton was appointed head of the Astronaut Office. During his reign he assigned all of the Apollo crew members to their flights. Later, he commanded the Apollo-Soyuz flight in 1975. This is a behind-the-scenes look at America's attempt to land humans on the Moon.

Wells, H. T., et al. *Origins of NASA Names*. NASA SP-4402. Washington, D.C.: National Aeronautics and Space Administration, 1976. A reference that lists the origins of the names of NASA facilities, vehicles, and programs.

Juno Probe

Date: August 5, 2011 - current
Type of mission: Jupiter orbiter

Juno is NASA's second spacecraft to orbit Jupiter, our solar system's largest planet. It was also chosen as the second mission in the New Frontiers program, a series of missions designed to conduct research on the bodies in our solar system. Its purpose is to better understand the origin and evolution of Jupiter through various measurements and detections that are designed to study its composition, gravitational field, magnetic field, and polar magnetosphere.

Key Figures

Scott Bolton (b. 1958), principal investigator
Rick Nybakken, previous project manager
Ed Hirst, project manager as of 2019
Toby Owen (1936-2017), coinvestigator
Andrew Ingersoll (b. 1940), coinvestigator
Frances Bagenal (b. 1954), coinvestigator
Candy Hansen-Koharcheck (b. 1954), coinvestigator
Jack Connerney (b. 1950), Instrument Lead

Summary of the Mission

The Juno spacecraft is named after the wife of the Roman god, Jupiter. She was said to have looked through his clouds of deception that he created around himself when he was being mischievous, just as the Juno probe will peer through the clouds of Jupiter. The name is also considered a backronym, which is an acronym that is created out of an already existing name; it is sometimes referred to as the Jupiter Near-polar Orbiter. New Frontiers 2 is the third name that Juno goes by as it is a follow-up to the first mission in the New Frontiers program.

The first New Frontiers mission, New Horizons, was designated to conduct a flyby of the dwarf planet Pluto and, ultimately, of a Kuiper belt object. The former portion of the mission was completed in 2015 and the latter in 2019 when it passed by Kuiper belt object 2014 MU_{69}, also known as Ultima Thule. In 2005, Juno was chosen as the newest mission in the series.

Launched atop an Atlas V at Cape Canaveral Air Force Station in Florida, Juno arrived at Jupiter on July 5th, 2016 after a five-year journey totaling a distance of 2.8 billion kilometers or 1.74 billion miles. In units representing the distance between the Earth and the Sun, the total distance was 18.7 astronomical units. Two years after launch, the spacecraft performed a gravity assist to gain speed from the Earth. This is accomplished by using the gravity of a larger object to essentially slingshot an object with lesser gravity. This technique uses less propellant than traveling in a straight line and therefore reduces the cost.

When launched, it was planned that the mission would conduct three 53-day-orbits before switching to 14-day polar orbits. However, due to a problem with the main engine, the burn that was supposed to transition between the two orbits was cancelled and Juno would be kept in its 53-day orbit for the remainder of the mission. Because of these complications, the mission has been extended until July 2021 so they can hopefully make up for any lost data.

When the probe is finally done, it will be de-orbited and burned up in Jupiter's atmosphere.

The Juno spacecraft includes nine instruments to aid in investigating its scientific objectives. They are each explained in more detail below:

The Microwave Radiometer (MWR) is made up of antennas that are designed to measure electromagnetic waves, specifically ones with frequencies in the microwave range that are able to pierce through Jupiter's atmosphere. By doing this, it will be able to measure the abundances of both water and ammonia in order to possibly learn the temperatures of the different portions of Jupiter's atmosphere, which will ultimately help figure out the depth of the atmospheric circulation.

The Jovian Infrared Auroral Mapper (JIRAM) is used in surveying the upper layers of the planet's atmosphere as well as taking images of Jupiter's aurora. In addition, it is capable of detecting ammonia, methane, phosphine, and water vapor. Through its measurements of heat radiating off of the planet's surface, JIRAM will be able to conclude how it is possible for clouds with water to be flowing beneath the surface of the planet's atmosphere.

The Magnetometer (MAG) is designed to map Jupiter's magnetic field and determine both the dynamics of its interior and the three-dimensional structure of its polar magnetosphere (a cavity in the solar wind due to Jupiter's magnetic field). MAG consists of two parts, the Flux Gate Magnetometer (FGM), designed to measure the strength and direction of Jupiter's magnetic field lines, and the Advanced Stellar Compass, which will be responsible for monitoring the MAG sensors' orientations.

The Gravity Science (GS) instrument is meant to create a map of Jupiter's uneven mass distribution by using radio waves to infer the planet's gravitational field structure. It is able to do this because of the small gravity variations in the probe's orbit caused by the unevenness in the mass.

The Jovian Auroral Distributions Experiment (JADE) studies Jupiter's aurora in order to measure the angular distribution, energy, and velocity vector of ions and electrons at low energy that are within it. Meanwhile, the Jovian Energetic Particle Detector Instrument (JEDI) studies Jupiter's polar magnetosphere in order to measure the angular distribution and the velocity vector of ions, particularly hydrogen, helium, oxygen, and sulfur, and electrons at high energy that are within it.

The Radio and Plasma Wave Sensor (Waves) measures the radio and plasma spectra in Jupiter's auroral region in an attempt to identify the regions that define the planet's radio emissions and acceleration of its auroral particles.

The Ultraviolet Spectrograph (UVS) uses a 1024 x 256 micro channel plate detector to provide spectral images of its polar magnetosphere's UV auroral admissions by recording the wavelength, position, and arrival time of UV photons when the spectrograph slit views Jupiter each time the spacecraft turns.

The JunoCam (JCM) is a visible light camera as well as a telescope, so it is able to take pictures that are viewable by humans. Although it started out being more focused on public outreach and education, it was eventually repurposed in order to do research on the clouds that exist at Jupiter's poles and their dynamics.

Contributions

Because only around half of the mission has currently elapsed as of 2019, relatively speaking not all that much has been found yet. The main objectives of Juno are to map the magnetic and gravitational fields of Jupiter in order to reveal its deeper structure, measure cloud motions, composition, temperature, and other properties of its atmosphere, learn more about Jupiter's formation through detecting how much water is in its atmosphere, and study the magnetosphere of the planet, more specifically at the poles where the auroras are. This could help astronomers learn how the atmosphere is affected by the planet's large magnetic force field.

Early results from the mission show that both of Jupiter's poles are covered in storms about the size of the Earth, closely packed and interacting with one another. The MWR showed that the belts at the planet's equator extend all the way down the planet, while other belts and zones seem to change into other things instead as they go farther down. There is also an increase in ammonia deeper down one goes into the planet, at least as far down as Juno is capable of measuring. It was also shown that the magnetic field is lumpy, which may indicate that it was generated closer to Jupiter's surface than astronomers had previously believed.

One of the biggest contributions thus far has come from the images being taken and shared of Jupiter. They have been able to show the public the beauty and mystery of our solar system's largest planet. Time-lapse images are capable of illustrating the dynamics of Jupiter's many large storms which would otherwise be incomprehensible as a human.

Context

For years, there had been a desire for a Jupiter orbiter, however several missions were passed up or cancelled before this one had its chance to shine.

The Internal Structure and Internal Dynamical Evolution of Jupiter (INSIDE Jupiter) proposal was passed over by the Discovery Program.

In 2002, the Europa Orbiter was cancelled and, again, in the early 2000s, the Europa Jupiter System Mission was cancelled due to lack of funding. The latter program eventually evolved into the Jupiter Icy Moons Explorer, a spacecraft in development in 2019 by the European Space Agency. It is slated to launch in June 2022 and will study three of Jupiter's Galilean moons: Callisto, Europa, and Ganymede.

In contrast to other missions to Jupiter powered by radioisotope thermal generators using plutonium fuel, Juno is the first to use solar panels and is also the farthest solar-powered trip to happen since humans first began with space exploration. So it is setting some firsts of its own.

—*Melissa A. Shea*

See also: Galileo: Jupiter; New Horizons; Pioneer 10; Pioneer 11; Voyager 1: Jupiter; Voyager 2: Jupiter; Voyager Program.

Further Reading

Bolton, S. J., and J. E. P. Connerney. "The Juno Mission" *Space Science Reviews*, vol. 213, no. 1-4, 2017, pp. 5-37. As an article written for more advanced learners, this one contains more technical language on the Juno mission's goals and scientific objectives, instrumentation, facilitating science operations, and the data management process.

Eager, Ashley. "Juno Reveals More Complex Jupiter." *Science News*, vol. 191, no. 12, June 2017, pp. 14–15. A rather brief article mentioning the spacecraft's observations of Jupiter and discussing the ammonia in its atmosphere as well as the interactions between its magnetic fields and solar winds.

Smith, Lyn. "Jupiter and the Juno Mission: The Latest Developments." *Journal of the British Astronomical Association*, vol. 126, no. 6, Dec. 2016, pp. 333. This is a one-page section of an astronomy magazine discussing the first two close approaches between Juno and Jupiter and the subsequent trouble that ultimately caused the team to reprogram the spacecraft.

Kepler Space Telescope

Date: March 7, 2009 – October 30, 2018
Type of mission: Space telescope

The Kepler Space Telescope was a 9.5 year mission to discover exoplanets (planets orbiting other stars) that were roughly Earth-sized and within their star's habitable zone. Over its lifetime, Kepler observed 530,506 stars and detected 2,662 planets by analyzing the light curves of their host star. The field of exoplanets grew substantially within the astronomical community as a result of Kepler spacecraft data.

Key Figures

Johannes Kepler (1571-1630), German astronomer
    and mathematician
William J. Borucki (b. 1939), Principle Investigator
Maura Fujieh, Project Manager
Jessie Dotson, Project Scientist
Marcie Smith, Operations Manager

Summary of the Mission

The Kepler Space Telescope was named in honor of Johannes Kepler, a German astronomer and mathematician who first described the planets' motions around the Sun in order to accurately predict their positions. The telescope is aptly named as it will be looking at numerous stars in order to detect their possible planets' motions around them.

While the first suspected evidence of an exoplanet dates all the way back to 1917, this astronomical sub-field did not quite take off until the 1990s with the first confirmed detection taking place in 1992. The real first detection of an exoplanet actually happened in 1988, but it was not able to be confirmed until 2012 and therefore did not gain the distinction of first detected exoplanet.

As part of NASA's Discovery Program, Kepler was launched on March 7, 2009 into an orbit around the Sun. It weighed in at a mass of 1,039 kilograms (or 2,291 pounds) and held a primary mirror measuring 1.4 meters (or 55 inches). The telescope took the record for largest mirror on a telescope outside of Earth at the time of its launch, taken over by the Herschel Space Observatory only a few months later. Under contract to Ball Aerospace & Technologies, the Laboratory for Atmospheric and Space Physics (LASP) out of Boulder, Colorado was responsible for operating the spacecraft.

Kepler used the transit method in order to detect its exoplanets. This is when a planet passes in front of its host star and causes a small dip in the amount of brightness being given off. After three transits are successfully recorded, it can be concluded that the planet's existence is confirmed. Kepler was much more likely to detect planetary transits as opposed to the Hubble Space Telescope because, rather than observing a large amount of different things, Kepler was designed to look continuously at one area in the sky.

Originally planned to last only 3.5 years, Kepler experienced noisy data at the beginning of the mission which meant that extra time was needed to make up for the loss. At first, it was expected to be extended until 2016. However, on July 1, 2012, a failure in one of the spacecraft's reaction wheels put the mission in jeopardy. Unless the other three wheels were capable of remaining reliable, the mission would not be able to continue. Unfortunately, on May 11, 2013, a second reaction wheel failed and very well could have ended the entire mission.

However, NASA was able to give up on fixing the reaction wheels and moved forward with a new phase of the mission altogether.

On November 18, 2013, the proposal for the K2 "Second Light" was reported. It would essentially use the Sun as a "virtual" third reaction wheel in order to detect habitable planets orbiting around smaller, dimmer red dwarfs. The approval for the K2 mission was announced by NASA on May 16, 2014 and ended up being successful just like its parent. On October 30, 2018, NASA announced that Kepler Space Telescope was finally going to be retired due to its lack of fuel. In terms of technology, the spacecraft's camera possessed a total resolution of 94.6 megapixels; at the time of its launch, this was the largest camera system to be sent into space. Manufactured by Corning, Kepler's primary mirror measured 1.4 meters or (4.6 feet) in diameter and was required to be covered in silver, a highly reflective material, in order to have enough sensitivity to detect small planets as they passed in front of their host stars. Kepler's singular instrument was a photometer (an instrument that measures electromagnetic radiation from ultraviolet to infrared) with a fixed field of view that was capable of observing the brightness of around 150,000 main sequence stars at a time. The photometer was less focused on taking sharp images and more on having a soft focus to provide good quality photometry.

Contributions

The Kepler Space Telescope has by far made the largest contributions to the evolving field of exoplanets. In addition to an outstanding number of planets detected and confirmed, the mission in general has also answered some very important astronomical questions.

First, it was found that there are more planets than stars in our galaxy; that may not go for every galaxy, but knowing it about our own is revolutionary. Quite recently, astronomers were not even sure if planets were likely around stars, but now they now that it is actually less likely for a star to have zero planets.

When astronomers first started detecting exoplanets, the majority of them were large and massive like Jupiter; they did not know how common a planet like Earth was in other solar systems. Because Kepler was designed to specifically detect small, Earth-like planets, it was found that there are an abundance of them. The Kepler mission concluded that the percentage of stars to have terrestrial, Earth-sized planets within the habitable zone where life could possibly exist is between 20-50%.

While Kepler has shown that there are small, rocky planets in addition to large, gaseous planets, it has also found that there is a wide array of different types of planets that exist in general. The most common type of planet is one between the size of the Earth and Neptune, though that is something that we do not see in our own solar system.

As evidenced by our own solar system, there can be a large variety of different planets all coexisting and orbiting around the same host star. Kepler has reaffirmed this by finding solar systems with all types of planetary configurations, such as one with eight planets all orbiting rather close to their star.

As of 2019, data are still being analyzed from the 9.5 years that the Kepler and K2 missions were active. There were over 4,000 confirmed exoplanets total by 2019 and almost 4,000 more possible candidates still waiting for confirmation, the majority of those coming from one of these missions.

Context

Previously, other exoplanet search projects were only capable of detecting giant planets around the size of Jupiter and larger, but Kepler was purposefully designed to detect much less massive ones around the mass of the Earth. Kepler has been able to put the amount and types of planets in the galaxy and possibly the universe into a much better perspective.

Because of Kepler, there has been a spark in the field leading to a large amount of interest which allows for NASA to continue these types of missions. It has held many records and served as a pioneer for this new brand of astronomy. At the time of its launch, Kepler held the record for highest data rate out of any NASA mission.

In 2018, a new mission, the Transiting Exoplanet Survey Satellite (TESS) was launched in order to continue the exoplanet search. In addition, the James Webb Space Telescope is planned to launch in 2021 to conduct even more such research.

One notable outcome of the Kepler mission was an increase in the amount of citizen science being conducted. Citizen science is when a project has so much data to be processed by those working on it, that the data set is opened up to the general public. Through a program called Planet Hunters, people with varying levels of interest in astronomy could learn how to analyze light curves to detect exoplanets. With this being such a major success for Kepler data, it has continued for TESS as well, with volunteers clearing through the data just as fast as it is coming in.

—*Melissa A. Shea*

See also: Hubble Space Telescope; James Webb Space Telescope; Transiting Exoplanet Survey Satellite.

Further Reading

Ellerbroek, Lucas, and Andy Brown. *Planet Hunters: The Search for Extraterrestrial Life.* Reaktion Books, 2017. This book describes the field of exoplanet research, the history and ideas leading up to it, the first discovery of an exoplanet, and the invention of the Kepler Space Telescope, as well as meeting with leading scientists in the field.

NASA and World Spaceflight News. *Complete Guide to the Kepler Space Telescope Mission and the Search for Habitable Planets and Earth-like Exoplanets.* Progressive Management, 2013. This book is a comprehensive guide to the Kepler mission and its discoveries as well as a discussion on the overall search for exoplanets currently taking place worldwide.

Tasker, Elizabeth. *The Planet Factory: Exoplanets and the Search for a Second Earth.* Bloomsbury Sigma, 2019. The Planet Factory discusses how exoplanets form, their structure and features, the various detection methods used, and what we can learn about the surfaces and atmospheres of these possibly alien worlds.

Landsat 1, 2, and 3

Date: July 23, 1972, to July 16, 1982
Type of spacecraft: Earth observation satellites

Landsat 1, 2, and 3 were satellites that collected data about Earth: its agriculture, forests, flatlands, minerals, waters, and environment. These satellites helped produce the best available maps and provided important agricultural information.

Key Figures

William T. Pecora (1913-1972), originator of Landsat concept at the United States Geological Survey

Archibald B. Park, originator of Landsat concept at the United States Department of Agriculture

William Nordberg (1930-1976), director of Applications at Goddard Space Flight Center

Paul Lowman (1931-2011), a NASA geologist

Summary of the Satellites

In 1970, the National Aeronautics and Space Administration (NASA) developed a series of satellites specifically dedicated to obtaining useful and practical information about the surface of the Earth. William T. Pecora of the U.S. Geological Survey originated the idea for such an Earth observation satellite in the late 1960's. In the Department of Agriculture, Archibald B. Park was interested in large-scale surveys of crops and forests. Earlier in the decade, weather satellites had taken pictures of Earth, as had the Gemini astronauts. These images had shown survey scientists the orbital satellite's potential to provide maps and other data about Earth.

The Earth Resources Observation Satellite (EROS) program took form early in in 1966. Immediately NASA stepped in and demanded control. In time, a cooperative effort between NASA and the Department of the Interior was effected. The satellite, originally called the Earth Resources Technology Satellite (ERTS), quickly had its name changed to Landsat, short for land satellite. This provided a catchy title for promotion to members of Congress, the executive branch of the federal government, and the general public.

On July 23, 1972, Landsat 1 was launched, followed by Landsat 2 in 1975 and Landsat 3 in 1978. They were sent up on Delta rockets. The Landsat 1 spacecraft was manufactured at the General Electric Company's Spacecraft Operations facility at Valley Forge, Pennsylvania. This spacecraft, an outgrowth of the Nimbus series of meteorological satellites, was designed to carry two remote-sensing systems and a system to collect data from sensors located in remote places on Earth. Landsat 3 was launched along with the Lewis Research Center Plasma Interaction Experiment and the Orbiting Satellite Carrying Amateur Radio (OSCAR) communications relay satellite.

Landsat 1, 2, and 3 were all placed in near-polar, Sun-synchronous, near-circular orbits around the poles at an altitude of approximately 920 kilometers. Landsat's orbit is 99°, which means that it is 9° off a North-Pole-to-South-Pole orbit. A Sun-synchronous orbit enables the spacecraft to cross the equator at the same local time every day—in this case, at about 9:30 a.m.—on the daylight side of Earth. Indeed, it crosses the equator at exactly the same local time on every pass. One benefit of a crossing at 9:30 a.m. is the presence of relatively long shadows on the underlying ground, which help

Landsat 3 being prepared for launch. (NASA)

Programmed ground commands were sent from Goddard Space Flight Center, located in Greenbelt, Maryland. The orbit and field of view were such that any given place on Earth's surface is observed every eighteen days by the same satellite at the same local time. With the launch of Landsat 2, the two satellites were synchronized in orbit so that coverage of any spot on the globe could be obtained every nine days. At sites closer to the north and south poles, the coverage was even more frequent.

Landsat satellites acquired electrical power from the Sun. Banks of silicon cells converted sunlight to electricity. With their Sun-synchronous orbits, the Landsat satellites spent half their time in the dark; thus, some means of storing power was required. A series of batteries stored the power collected while the satellite traveled in the sunlight, releasing it when the satellite traveled in the dark.

The first three Landsat spacecraft weighed about 950 kilograms each, were approximately 3.3 meters tall, and were stabilized by gas jets so that if the orbit varied the spacecraft could be repositioned. This was a critical feature, because it guaranteed that the images recorded would be consistent over time.

The three Landsat spacecraft did not carry ordinary still cameras. Instead, each satellite was equipped with a Multispectral Scanner Subsystem (MSS) as its principal sensing instrument, three special television cameras that were known as the return beam vidicon (RBV) system, and other data collection systems that could obtain information from remote, surface-based, automatic platforms around the world. These platforms were able to

show up the topographical features more clearly. By passing over at exactly the same time every day, sensors can photograph scenes under conditions of light and shade that are relatively constant. There are differences caused by varying amounts of cloud cover and the changing seasons of the year, but these variations are something over which scientists have no control. The orbit simply minimizes the variations.

Each satellite circled the globe fourteen times a day and thus took approximately 103 minutes to orbit Earth. The three Landsat passed over each sector of coverage twice a day, once in the daylight and once at night.

monitor local conditions and relay data to central ground stations whenever the Landsat could simultaneously view the platform and a ground station.

On Landsat 1, the RBV system failed shortly after launch; thus, the key recording instrument became the MSS. This instrument had been tested on high-altitude aircraft, but it was first tested in space on Landsat 1. A scanner mirror rocked from side to side some thirteen times per second. By deflecting light from the ground into the detectors, the mirror scanned the scene below in a series of parallel swatches, rather like someone walking along while sweeping with a broom. Sensors were mounted on the bottom of the spacecraft. The area in each image measured approximately 185 square kilometers.

The MSS was the primary information gatherer. The advantage of this type of sensor over a traditional camera is that the information is sent back rapidly by radio waves to ground stations on Earth instead of being recorded on the camera film, which would then have to be physically transported back to Earth in a costly and complicated process. Sensors could image at wavelengths invisible to both the human eye and conventional cameras such as the infrared portion of the electromagnetic spectrum. Other variables that the use of the MSS avoided included the use of different film-developing practices of various laboratories and the subjective eyes of the technicians who interpret the photographic information.

On Landsat 3, video equipment was greatly improved. As a consequence, so was the quality of the image resolution. The video system for Landsat 1 and 2 had consisted of three television-type cameras, each covering a different spatial region. On Landsat 3, the three cameras were replaced by two improved cameras giving side-by-side viewing at twice the spatial resolution.

These MSS data, and later video data, were principally recorded in digital form. Thus information could be rapidly processed with computers, which could analyze the information so that it could be used quickly and precisely.

NASA operated three ground stations to receive data from Landsat 1, 2, and 3 and control their operation. These stations were located in Greenbelt, Maryland, in Goldstone, California, and in Fairbanks, Alaska. Any one of these three stations could detect the Landsat satellites at any time they were over the continental United States. Additional coverage was obtained from ground stations in Italy and Sweden operated by the European Space Agency (ESA) and from stations in Canada, Brazil, Argentina, South Africa, India, Australia, Japan, Thailand, Indonesia, and mainland China. In addition to real-time coverage permitted by these stations, tape recorders on the satellites allowed the recording of data from areas around the world that were outside the range of the ground stations.

In the early days of the Landsat program, all the data were processed at the Goddard Space Flight Center. After 1979, Goddard and the EROS Data Center in Sioux Falls, South Dakota, shared the processing of information. The whole process took about two weeks. Information gathered by the Landsat satellites was placed in the public domain as rapidly as possible and was stored in two national databases, one operated by the U.S. Department of the Interior in Sioux Falls, South Dakota, and the other by the Department of Agriculture in Salt Lake City, Utah.

Landsat 2 was identical in payload to Landsat 1, and despite a design lifetime of one year, it continued to function satisfactorily for five years. After that time, failure of its primary flight control mechanism became evident, and it was difficult to keep the spacecraft steadily pointed at Earthly targets.

When Landsat 3 was launched in March, 1978, Landsat 1 had been out of service for two months, but Landsat 2 was still operating. It was then arranged so that with overlap the repeat time for any section of the globe was again nine, not eighteen, days. This proved of great value in the surveillance of dynamic events. Landsat 3 carried an MSS with four bands identical to those of Landsat 1 and Landsat 2. It also carried a thermal infrared scanner, but this failed shortly after launch. The video cameras of Landsat 3 gave twice the ground resolution by doubling the focal length of the lens system.

Landsat 2 was removed from service on February 25, 1982, and Landsat 3 was removed from service on March 31, 1983. The Landsat 4 and 5 spacecraft were placed into lower orbits than the previous Landsat spacecraft and carried improved instrument suites. Launched on July 16, 1982, Landsat 4 began experiencing numerous spacecraft malfunctions that limited spacecraft functionality. This prompted the early launch of Landsat 5 in March, 1984, to guarantee continued coverage. Management of the spacecraft was transferred from NASA to NOAA with Landsat 4. Although Landsat 5 continued operations well beyond the time period for which it was designed, the Landsat 4 and 5 spacecraft were superseded by Landsat 6 and 7 which had improved instruments. Unfortunately, Landsat 6 failed to achieve orbit when launched on October 5, 1993. Landsat 7 was launched on April 15, 1999, and entered service very shortly thereafter. It suffered a partial malfunction of its principal sensor in 2003 but continued to provide meaningful data.

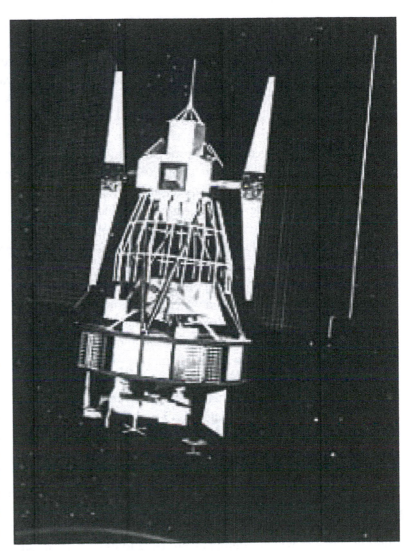

Artist's rendering of Landsat 2. (NASA)

Contributions

The Landsat system was designed to gather information for the better use of Earth resources. Crop information could be gained for better use of land for crop production. Landsat 1, 2, and 3 made it possible to discriminate the patterns of crops, lumber, and vegetation around the world. They could measure crop acreage by species. Precise estimates of the amount and type of lumber resources in the world could be obtained, and the strength and stress on vegetation could be determined. Soil conditions could be monitored, as well as the extent of fire damage.

Moreover, for the first time, an exact determination of the water boundaries and surface water area and volume around the globe was possible. Plans could be formulated to minimize damage from flooding. Scientists were also able to survey snow areas of mountains and glacial features. The depths of the oceans, seas, lakes, and other bodies of water could be calculated and used to plan the better use of water resources. On June 26, 1978, a new experimental satellite, Seasat, was launched; it was designed to test methods most suitable for research about oceans and seas. After only four months of operation, however, the satellite failed, and Landsat continued with this important function.

Mineral and petroleum exploration was also made easier with precise geological data. Maps of rocks and rock types were made for all parts of the globe. More was learned about rocks and soils, volcanoes, changing landforms, and precise land formations. Surface mining could be monitored and land more productively reclaimed. The science of mapping Earth was revolutionized. Urban and rural demarcations were made, and help became available for regional planners. Transportation networks were mapped as well as land and water boundaries. Imprecise maps were updated. Scientists could detect living ocean forms and their patterns and movements. Precious data could be gathered on changing conditions in shorelines, on shoals and shallow areas, and on wave and ice patterns. Scientists were able to gather more precise data on air and water pollution, its sources and effects. They could determine the scope and effects of natural disasters and monitor the environmental effects of defoliation.

Context

Landsat 1 was the first of the ERTS series, the first satellite series in which satellites were used to explore and better understand the planet rather than outer space. A single image from space could encompass large-scale geological features that otherwise would take days or weeks to cover, even with aerial mapping. Better still, such photographs could show features so extensive that they would never have been noticed from the ground or would have been lost in the patchwork of aerial mosaics.

William Nordberg, director of Applications at Goddard Space Flight Center, summarized the results when he said, "Within a few weeks after its [Landsat 1's] launch, we saw that the variety of uses to which Landsat could be used exceeded our expectations." Within a week of the launch of Landsat

1, NASA geologist Paul Lowman was able to make a new geological map of California's coastal ranges near Monterey Bay. In studying this new map, Lowman was able to identify more than thirty previously unknown features, including some geological faults.

This family of satellites has proven an invaluable component of a new approach to locating, monitoring, managing, and understanding many of the natural resources of planet Earth. For those scientists studying Earth, Landsat 1, 2, and 3 have been among the most useful and productive satellites ever launched by NASA. Before Landsat began its systematic sensing of Earth's changing features, cost-effective, broad-scale land monitoring was nearly impossible. Producing comparable maps by conventional methods was costly, and the time required was such that when finally produced, the maps were already out of date.

In the areas of agriculture, oceanography, geology, and environmental studies, scientists were able to gather significant and important data from Landsat 1, 2, and 3—information that could help both in fundamental research and in governmental decision making.

Consider but a few examples of the ways in which the Landsat system benefited humankind. For agriculture, even in the most technologically advanced countries, up-to-date assessments of total acreage of different crops were incomplete before Landsat. After its launch, forests could be managed for both fire control and insect infestation. Wildlife habitats could be monitored and better conserved. More precise, inexpensive maps became available. In terms of land use, vast areas of Africa, Asia, and South America were poorly mapped or even incorrectly mapped before Landsat. Mountain ranges, deserts, vegetable cover, and land use could now be known for all parts of the planet. Landsat information proved so reliable that private industry now makes regular use of it. Landsat can map damage from forest fires more accurately, so that planting can begin again. The same is the case for drought-stricken areas.

Since the mid-1970's, Landsat has marketed several million dollars' worth of products each year to private industry, state governments, and the U.S. Departments of the Interior, Agriculture, and Commerce. With sophisticated computers, the science of knowing Earth, its resources, and its possibilities was greatly advanced.

—Douglas Gomery

See also: Heat Capacity Mapping Mission; Landsat 4 and 5; Nimbus Meteorological Satellites.

Further Reading

Allen, James M., and Shanaka DeSilva. "Landsat: An Integrated History." *QUEST: The History of Spaceflight Quarterly* 12, no. 1 (2005). This article provides historical, scientific, technological, and financial considerations of the Landsat program. Lists numerous references.

Eisenbeis, Kathleen M. *Privatizing Government Information: The Effects of Policy on Access to Landsat Satellite Data.* Lanham, Md.: Scarecrow Press, 1995. The commercialization of the Landsat satellite system in 1984 was a poorly conceived experiment in public policy and a disaster for environmental change researchers. This book analyzes the tragic story of the United States Congress' failure to stop the privatization initiative of the Reagan administration, and describes the subsequent consequences on the ability of U.S. academic geographers to conduct remote-sensing research and to teach using Landsat data. It also discusses the key role that the National Commission on Libraries and Information Science played in preserving the data and establishing the National Satellite Remote Sensing Data Archive. With the repeal of the legislation in 1992, the author revisits the case history and examines the new U.S. remote-sensing data policies.

Harper, Dorothy. *Eye in the Sky.* 2d ed. Montreal: Multiscience Publications, 1983. This clear explanation of the use of satellites includes a survey of the Landsat system. For those with little or no knowledge of space science.

Short, Nicholas M. *The Landsat Tutorial Workbook: Basics of Satellite Remote Sensing.* NASA RP- 1078. Washington, D.C.: Government Printing Office, 1982. A basic guide to the uses of Landsat 1, 2, and 3, this publication is aimed at the user of the data of the Landsat system. Contains numerous charts and diagrams and provides references to numerous publications. Suitable for college-level audiences.

Short, Nicholas M., Paul D. Lowman, Jr., Stanley C. Freden, and William A. Finch. *Mission to Earth: Landsat Views the World.* NASA SP-360. Washington, D.C.: Government Printing Office, 1976. This picture book describes the Landsat program and presents a multitude of maps of Earth made from information gleaned by Landsat 1. It focuses on the wonders of the maps created.

United States Congress. Senate Committee on Aeronautical and Space Sciences. *An Analysis of the Future Landsat Effort.* 94th Congress, 2d session, 1976. Committee Print. This comprehensive report adds much to the knowledge of the Landsat program, its uses and its shortcomings.

Waldrop, M. Mitchell. "Imaging the Earth: The Troubled First Decade of Landsat." *Science* 215 (March 26, 1982): 1600-1603. A comprehensive evaluation of the Landsat program for an important journal. There have been intra-agency political squabbles about the Landsat program, yet that has not stopped it from being a major success.

Williams, Richard S., and William D. Carter, eds. *ERTS-1: A New Window on Our Planet.* U.S. Geological Survey Professional Paper 929. Washington, D.C.: Government Printing Office, 1976. A short, comprehensive guide to the Earth Resources Technology Satellite, which later became known as Landsat 1. This is the pioneering work that laid out the uses of the satellite to map Earth and help plan its management. It is the professional predecessor to *Mission to Earth: Landsat Views the World* (see entry above).

Zimmerman, Robert. *The Chronological Encyclopedia of Discoveries in Space.* Westport, Conn.: Oryx Press, 2000. Provides a complete chronological history of all crewed and robotic spacecraft and explains flight events and scientific results. Suitable for all levels of research.

Landsat 4 and 5

Date: Beginning July 16, 1982
Type of spacecraft: Earth observation satellites

Landsat 4 and 5 were designed to collect data about the Earth: its agriculture, forests, flatlands, minerals, waters, and environment. These satellites continued the mission of the first three Landsat satellites, the first satellites devoted exclusively to Earth resources. Landsat satellites would produce the best maps available and aid farmers around the world to produce more and better crops. All Landsat 4 telemetry data acquisitions were discontinued in August, 1993, due to X-band transmission failure; the K-band transmission had failed in November, 1992.

Key Figures

William T. Pecora (1913-1972), originator of Landsat concept at the United States Geological Survey

Archibald B. Park, originator of Landsat concept at the United States Department of Agriculture

William Nordberg (1930-1976), director of Applications at Goddard Space Flight Center

Paul Lowman (1931-2011), a NASA geologist

Summary of the Satellites

In 1970, the National Aeronautics and Space Administration (NASA) proceeded to design and develop a series of satellites specifically dedicated to obtaining useful information about the surface of Earth, which could then be used on a routine and repetitive basis. William T. Pecora, of the United States Geological Survey, originated the idea in the late 1960's. In the Department of Agriculture, Archibald B. Park believed that large-scale surveys of crops and forests could be conducted with the aid of satellites. As a result, the concept for the Earth Resources Observation Satellite (EROS) took form early in 1966.

This type of satellite, originally designated the Earth Resources Technology Satellite (ERTS), was subsequently renamed Landsat to enhance recognition among members of the United States Congress and influential employees of the executive branch of the government. Landsat 1 was the first in the ERTS series in which satellites were used to explore Earth, rather than outer space. On July 23, 1972, Landsat 1 was launched, followed by Landsat 2 in 1975, and Landsat 3 in 1978; they were all launched on Delta rockets. The Landsat spacecraft, manufactured at General Electric's Space Sciences Facility at Valley Forge, Pennsylvania, was an outgrowth of the Nimbus weather series of meteorological satellites and was designed to carry two remote-sensing systems as well as a system to collect data from sensors located in remote places on Earth.

The Landsat satellites were placed in near-polar, Sun-synchronous circular orbits at an altitude of approximately 920 kilometers. Landsat's orbit is 99°, which means it is 9° off a purely North-Pole-to-South-Pole orbit. A Sun-synchronous orbit means that the spacecraft crosses the equator at the same local time (between 9:30 and 10:00 a.m.) each day, regardless of its locale. At 9:30 a.m., the relatively long shadows on the underlying ground help to enhance the topographical features. Because they passed over at exactly the same time every day, the satellites' sensors were assured of photographing day-to-day scenes under similar conditions of light and shade. In this orbit at this altitude, each Landsat

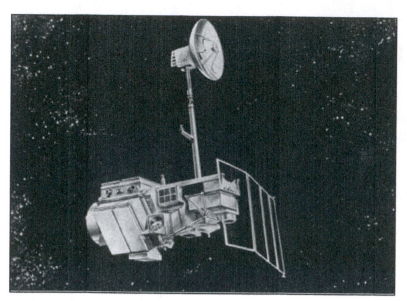

Artist's rendering of Landsat 5. (NASA)

satellite circled the globe fourteen times a day. Programmed ground commands were sent from NASA's Goddard Space Flight Center.

NASA operates three ground stations—in Greenbelt, Maryland, in Goldstone, California, and in Fairbanks, Alaska—to receive data from the Landsat system and to control the satellites' operations. Any one of these three stations could "see" a Landsat at any time it was over the continental United States or in coastal areas. Additional coverage was obtained from ground stations operated by the - European Space Agency (ESA) and stations in Canada, Brazil, Argentina, South Africa, India, Australia, Japan, Thailand, Indonesia, and mainland China, operated by their respective governments.

Information gathered by the Landsat satellites was placed in the public domain as rapidly as possible and in two United States databases operated by the Department of the Interior (EROS Data Center, Sioux Falls, South Dakota) and the Department of Agriculture in Salt Lake City, Utah.

Before launch, the fourth Landsat was referred to as Landsat-D. When it successfully reached orbital altitude, the designation was changed to the appropriate arabic number, in this case Landsat 4. Landsat 4 used a multi-mission spacecraft, an improvement over the original Nimbus series used for Landsat 1, 2, and 3. With an improved launch vehicle, the 3920 Delta, Landsat 4 was increased in size to some 2,200 kilograms and was launched in July, 1982, from the Western Test Range at Vandenberg Air Force Base in California.

Physically, Landsat 4 consisted of two major sections. On board the spacecraft a computer controls power and altitude. This computer also sent commands to the propulsion module that provided the capability to adjust the orbit. The forward end of the spacecraft contained the thematic mapper and multispectral scanner. The antenna mast was 4 meters (13 feet) high.

Landsat 4's orbit differed from those of Landsat 1, 2, and 3. Most significant was the nominal altitude of 705 kilometers, as opposed to the 900 kilometers of the first three Landsats. Additionally, Landsat 4 circled the globe in sixteen instead of eighteen days.

Landsat 4 carried a thematic mapper, which imaged Earth to detect geological features of interest in mineral exploration. Together with the Multispectral Scanner Subsystem (MSS), the thematic mapper also provided information useful for agriculture. The instrument was designed to be most relevant to agriculture experiments that would observe vegetation cover and measure crop acreages. The thematic mapper had better resolution than the MSS and was adapted to estimate crop acreages better in regions with small fields such as China, India, the eastern United States, and Europe. The sensor sent data directly to Earth, in this case to White Sands, New Mexico.

The data collection rate had been improved for Landsat 4. Landsat 1, 2, and 3 programs were primarily for researchers, and a high speed of data transmission was not considered necessary. As familiarity and experience with the use of the first three Landsat increased, they were gradually adapted to digital data. Landsat 4 was designed for digital data transmission from the beginning. The utility of Landsat was, however, somewhat compromised because of a data-relay satellite that malfunctioned at launch. Later engineering problems on board the spacecraft further reduced its performance. Landsat 4 ceased to function in August, 1993.

Landsat 5, which was launched early in 1984 to complete the mission of Landsat 4, was the same size as its predecessor and fulfilled the same functions. Starting in January, 1983, the National Oceanic and Atmospheric Administration (NOAA), rather than NASA, assumed responsibility for operating the Landsat series of satellites. NOAA also assumed responsibility for producing and distributing data and data products, except from the thematic mapper. Landsat 5 synchronized with Landsat 4 to cover the Earth fully in an eight-day orbit. The orbit of Landsat 5 was targeted low intentionally, to ensure that no orbit-lowering maneuvers would be required. Between March 7 and April 4, 1984, a series of eight orbit-raising maneuvers was performed to correct the axis so that Landsat 4 and 5 would be coordinated to cover the entire globe in eight days. Landsat 5, like Landsat 4, achieved a Sun-synchronous orbit and a sixteen-day tracking cycle around the world. The nominal orbits of the two were identical except for their phasing. The eight-day complete coverage of Earth was achieved when Landsat 4 and 5 were on opposite sides of the globe. This phasing also minimized interference between the two satellites. While the satellites were still functional, routine collection of data was terminated in late 1992. Landsat 5's mission officially ended on June 5, 2013 with the spacecraft deactivated and left in a "graveyard" orbit.

Contributions

Landsat 4 and 5 provided more precise data than were gathered by Landsat 1, 2, and 3. The principal uses of the information continually gathered by Landsat 4 and 5 can be grouped into the following broad areas.

With respect to agriculture, forestry, and range land, information could be obtained for better use of land for crop production. Landsat makes it possible to discriminate the patterns of crops, lumber, and vegetation around the world, and it can measure crop acreage by species. The world's lumber resources and their strength and stress on vegetation can be determined, and soil conditions can be monitored, as can the extent of fire damage.

For the first time, an exact determination of the water boundaries and surface water area and volume around the globe was possible. Information could be gathered about floods and flooding, mountains and glacial features, and depths of oceans and other bodies of water. An inventory of lakes was also kept. Mineral and petroleum exploration was made easier with precise geological data and maps of rocks and rock types. Indeed, the knowledge of geology greatly expanded with more information about rocks and soils, volcanoes, changing land forms, and precise land formations. Surface mining was also monitored and land more productively reclaimed as the science of the mapping of Earth was revolutionized. Urban and rural demarcations were corrected, transportation networks were mapped, and help became available to regional planners.

Regarding oceanography and marine resources, floods could now be monitored and measured, and damage delineated and repaired. In desert regions, possible water sources could be more easily identified, and water quality could be monitored. It became possible to detect the pattern and movement of ocean life. Shoreline changes and wave patterns could be mapped, along with shoals, shallow areas, and ice patterns to assist shipping interests.

More precise data on air and water pollution, and its sources and effects, became available, and it became possible to determine the scope and effects of natural disasters. The Landsat also monitored the environmental effects of human activity.

Context

Before Landsat began systematic sensing of Earth's changing features, broad-scale land monitoring was severely limited. Producing comparable maps by conventional methods was costly, and the time required was such that when they were finally produced, they were already outdated.

NASA geologist Paul Lowman used the results from Landsat to make a new geological map of California's coastal ranges near Monterey Bay. Landsat had shown him more than thirty previously unknown linear features, including some geological faults. The Landsat have continued to demonstrate a new approach to locating, monitoring, managing, and understanding many of the natural and non-natural resources on Earth. For those scientists studying Earth, the Landsat series has been among the most useful and productive satellite programs ever launched by NASA.

In the field of agriculture, even in the most technologically advanced countries, up-to-date, complete assessments of total acreage of different crops was incomplete before the arrival of the Landsat system. Forests can now be managed for fire and insect infestation, wildlife habitats can be described, and vegetation and land use can now be known for all parts of the planet. So reliable is the information that private industry has begun to make regular use of it, accounting for one-third of the sales of Landsat images.

The use of sophisticated computers has furthered immeasurably the science of knowing Earth's resources and possibilities. Companies that explore for minerals and petroleum have been quick to realize the efficiency of the Landsat system. Landsat 4 and 5 were instrumental in gathering information about the nuclear accident at Chernobyl in the Soviet Union on April 26, 1986. Although Landsat 5 continued to operate well past the time period for which it was designed, the Landsat 4 and 5 spacecraft were superseded by Landsat 6 and 7, which had improved instruments. Unfortunately, Landsat 6 failed to achieve orbit when launched on October 5, 1993. Landsat 7 was launched on April 15, 1999, and entered service very shortly thereafter. Landsat 7's primary sensor suffered a partial malfunction in 2003, but the spacecraft continued to provide valuable data.

—Douglas Gomery

See also: Dynamics Explorers; Earth Observing System Satellites; Explorers: Air Density; Explorers: Atmosphere; Geodetic Satellites; Global Atmospheric Research Program; Landsat 1, 2, and 3; Landsat 7; Mission to Planet Earth; Private Industry and Space Exploration; Seasat; Tracking and Data-Relay Communications Satellites.

Further Reading

Allen, James M., and Shanaka DeSilva. "Landsat: An Integrated History." *QUEST: The History of Spaceflight Quarterly* 12, no. 1 (2005). This article provides historical, scientific, technological, and financial considerations of the Landsat program. Lists numerous references.

Baker, John. *Landsat-4 Science Investigations Summary*. NASA Conference Publication 2326. Washington, D.C.: Government Printing Office, 1984. This volume provides a summary of the success of Landsat 4 in terms of its ability to map and survey Earth's resources. Some of the material is intended for geologists, but the volume does provide basic information and descriptions for the layperson.

Eisenbeis, Kathleen M. *Privatizing Government Information: The Effects of Policy on Access to Landsat Satellite Data*. Lanham, Md.: Scarecrow Press, 1995. The commercialization of the Landsat satellite system in 1984 was a poorly conceived experiment in public policy and a disaster for environmental change researchers. This book analyzes the tragic story of the United States Congress' failure to stop the privatization initiative of the Reagan administration, and describes the subsequent consequences on the ability of U.S. academic geographers to conduct remote-sensing research and to teach using Landsat data. It also discusses the key role that the National Commission on Libraries and Information Science played in preserving the data and establishing the National Satellite Remote Sensing Data Archive. With the repeal of the legislation in 1992, the author revisits the case history and examines the new U.S. remote-sensing data policies.

Harper, Dorothy, ed. *Eye in the Sky: Introduction to Remote Sensing.* 2d ed. Montreal: Multiscience Publications, 1983. This clear explanation of the use of satellites contains a survey of the Landsat system. It provides its discussion in clear language aimed at the lay reader.

Richter, Rudolf, Frank Lehmann, Rupert Haydn, and Peter Volk. "Analysis of Landsat TM Images of Chernobyl." *International Journal of Remote Sensing* 7 (December, 1986). Landsat 5 provided the images that proved useful in analyzing the results of the Chernobyl nuclear plant disaster. This work is a technical article but contains fascinating information and photographs. This article provides an important example of the success of the Landsat system.

Salomonson, V. V., and R. Kottler. *An Overview of Landsat 4: Status and Results.* Greenbelt, Md.: Goddard Space Flight Center, 1983. This work analyzes how well the thematic mapper is working on Landsat 4. Several helpful diagrams are included, and the details of this measuring and data-gathering device are explained to the reader.

Short, Nicholas M., et al. *Mission to Earth: Landsat Views the World.* NASA SP-360. Washington, D.C.: Government Printing Office, 1976. This picture book does not touch on the Landsat 4 and 5 programs specifically, but it does provide the most useful background to the goals and missions of the Landsat program. It describes the program and presents a multitude of maps of Earth made from Landsat 1.

Zimmerman, Robert. *The Chronological Encyclopedia of Discoveries in Space.* Westport, Conn.: Oryx Press, 2000. Provides a complete chronological history of all crewed and robotic spacecraft and explains flight events and scientific results. Suitable for all levels of research.

Landsat 7

Date: Beginning April 15, 1999
Type of spacecraft: Earth observation satellites

The Landsat 7 mission is a continuation of the Landsat Program, which since 1972 has provided digital images of the Earth's land surface and coastal areas to a diverse group of users. Landsat 7 is the first of these platforms to feature the Enhanced Thematic Mapper Plus instrument.

Summary of the Satellite

Since 1972, the Landsat Program has employed remote-sensing techniques to obtain digital images of the Earth's land and coastal regions. These images have become an invaluable tool for observing conditions and activities on the Earth's surface. Users include environmental researchers, the agricultural and forestry communities, regional planners, commercial interests, and the military. A joint mission of the National Aeronautics and Space Administration (NASA) and the U.S. Geological Survey (USGS), Landsat 7 extended and improved upon the record of images provided by its predecessors.

Landsat 7 was launched on April 15, 1999, from the Western Test Range of Vandenberg Air Force Base in California on a Boeing Delta-II expendable launch vehicle. Three days later, the first image from Landsat 7 (covering southeastern South Dakota and northeastern Nebraska) was acquired. On April 22, 1999, Earth Day, NASA and the USGS officially released this image to the public. For the next two months, Landsat 7 underwent normal post-launch testing and was allowed to acclimate to its new environment. From June 1 through 3, 1999, a Landsat 7 "underflight" of Landsat 5 was conducted. Landsat 7 was maneuvered into a 670- kilometer orbit proximal to Landsat 5, the one other satellite of the Landsat series still transmitting data. The purpose of the underflight was to collect data from both satellites simultaneously, so that the two systems could be cross-calibrated. Once the underfly maneuver was completed, Landsat 7 was repositioned in its operational orbit eight paths to the east of Landsat 5. Routine data acquisition commenced on June 29, 1999.

Landsat 7 cost about $650 million to build and $150 million to launch. The spacecraft, constructed by Lockheed Martin Missiles and Space, is approximately 4.3 meters long and 2.8 meters in diameter, and weighed about 2,200 kilograms at launch. It operates at an altitude of approximately 705 kilometers above the Earth's surface, following a Sun-synchronous, polar orbit (a north-south oriented orbit that carries the satellite over any given point on the planet's surface at the same local time each circuit). The satellite descends across the equator at approximately 10:00 a.m. local time, a time when obscuring cloud cover is at its daily minimum. Landsat 7 provides repetitive coverage—that is, it acquires data from any given place on Earth—every sixteen days (every 233 orbits). Like Landsat 4 and 5, it follows the Worldwide Reference System grid of paths and rows, a sampling scheme that divides Earth's surface into 57,784 images, or "scenes." Landsat 7 passes over roughly 850 land scenes a day. Each scene represents an area 183 kilometers wide by 170 kilometers long. Landsat 7 and 5 overfly the same locations within eight days of each another. Landsat 7 is equipped with a single scientific instrument, the Enhanced Thematic Mapper (ETM+).

Landsat 7 being prepared for launch. (NASA)

(1.55 to 2.35 micrometers), one to near-infrared (0.76 to 0.90 micrometer), and three to visible wavelengths (red, 0.63 to 0.69 micrometer; green, 0.52 to 0.60 micrometer; and blue, 0.45 to 0.52 micrometer). The remaining band is panchromatic, meaning that its sensitivity (wavelengths 0.50-0.90 micrometer) includes most of the visible spectrum. The ETM+ instrument's field of view provides a 185-kilometer swatch of coverage. The ETM+ takes about 25 seconds to collect one scene, which comprises approximately 3.8 gigabits of data. An onboard, solid-state recording device is capable of storing one hundred scenes' worth of data (380 gigabits) until they can be transmitted to ground stations.

The primary ground station for Landsat 7 data is the USGS's Earth Resources Observation System (EROS) Data Center, or EDC, located in Sioux Falls, South Dakota. The EDC includes a receiving station, a data-processing and distribution facility, and archives. Ground control provides the Landsat 7 spacecraft and its instruments with daily commands determining which images to record and when to downlink data to receiving stations. The EDC can receive both real-time and recorded data. U.S. ground stations in Poker Flat, Alaska, and Svalbard, Norway, provide support to and act as a backup for the EDC. There are also International Ground Stations situated on every continent except Antarctica. These stations provide limited regional coverage, receiving only those scenes Landsat 7 acquires in real time and transmits while in range of each station's receiving antenna.

The EDC selects sunlit, substantially cloud-free scenes for acquisition and archiving. The data

Developed by Raytheon Santa Barbara Remote Sensing, the ETM+ is an improved version of the Thematic Mapper (TM) instruments of Landsat 4 and 5. Like the TM instruments, the ETM+ is a passive sensor, one that detects electromagnetic radiation reflected by or emitted from the Earth's surface. It employs an oscillating mirror and arrays of detectors to make east-to-west and west-to-east scans as the satellite passes in its descending (north-to-south) orbit over the sunlit side of the planet. An eight-band multispectral scanning radiometer, the ETM+ collects radiation from different parts of the electromagnetic spectrum. One band is devoted to thermal infrared wavelengths (10.42 to 12.50 micrometers), two to short-wave infrared wavelengths center is able to distribute raw ETM+ data within twenty-four hours of reception and can process and archive up to 250 Landsat scenes every day. Users can determine which scenes they want by viewing lower-resolution images and descriptive information on the Internet. The EDC makes scenes available to users on physical media or via electronic transfer, at the cost of processing, materials, and distribution (about $450 to $600, depending on the level of processing). The EDC releases data only in unprocessed or minimally processed formats; users can perform additional processing themselves or use commercial services.

Contributions

Landsat 7's ETM+ replicates but improves upon the TM instruments flown on Landsat 4 and 5. The ETM+ boasts a panchromatic band, improved sensor performance, superior instrument calibration, and better resolution in the thermal infrared band. Unlike its predecessors, ETM+ components are not susceptible to ice formation that impedes performance.

The Landsat 7 mission also featured improved data capture, transmission, and ground-support capabilities. For onboard data storage, Landsat 5 used a tape-recording device of relatively small capacity, so that the satellite depends heavily upon directly downlinking its data to ground stations around the globe. Landsat 7's onboard recorder could store enough data to enable the newer satellite to generate a complete view of Earth's land surfaces seasonally, or approximately four times per year. Also, the new recording device took less time to transfer its data to receiving stations (150 megabits per second, versus Landsat 5's rate of 75 megabits per second). Landsat 7's upgraded ground data system allowed the receiving station to handle four to five times more data than in previous Landsat missions.

The fact that the Landsat 7 mission is government run and government-subsidized has made its data more readily available to users. As a cost-cutting measure, the commercially run Landsat 5

collected imagery only when a user requested it. Landsat 7, by contrast, gathers data on an ongoing basis, building and periodically refreshing a substantial global archive of images. Commercial Landsat data have proved prohibitively expensive for many users, with value-added pricing. Landsat 7 data, made available to users at cost, are not only comparatively plentiful, but also relatively inexpensive, with per-scene prices running about an eighth of Landsat 5's.

With the Landsat 7 mission's ability to create a seasonal archive, its improved data capture and processing, and its lower data cost, its satellite imagery becomes a more versatile, efficient, and affordable tool for global change studies, land-cover monitoring, and large-area mapping. Among the many users of Landsat 7 imagery are the members of the Landsat Science Team, a multidisciplinary group of researchers who are applying Landsat data to their various areas of expertise.

In Hawaii, where active lava flows pose a public safety hazard, Landsat Science Team members are using Landsat 7 data to monitor volcanic eruptions in real time. These data can also help volcanologists identify areas of increased thermal activity that could be indicative of future eruption. Previous monitoring efforts relied primarily upon lower-resolution remote-sensing data from the Geostationary Operational Environmental Satellites (GOES) used to track weather. Landsat 7's scenes transmitted to a ground station in Hawaii as the satellite passes overhead will provide a means for scientists to produce new maps every eight days that accurately depict volcanic and related wildfire hazards.

In Yosemite National Park, Landsat data have been used to assess the amount and condition of dry biomass that could fuel wildfires. Landsat Science Team members are making predictions regarding wildfire behavior based on these data. The panchromatic band of Landsat 7's ETM+ allows fire managers more easily to distinguish tree density classes, which are directly related to fuel moisture content and wind speeds near the ground. The greater frequency of Landsat 7's observations also facilitates the monitoring of seasonal changes in vegetation.

Other Landsat Team studies concern the rates, causes, and effects of tropical deforestation in the Amazon; changes in the Antarctic ice sheet; the introduction of contaminated spring runoff into the Great Lakes coastal waters; the health of temperate conifer forests; and the growth patterns of urban sprawl. A general scientific goal of the Landsat 7 mission was to gain an understanding of the role vegetation plays in removing carbon dioxide from the atmosphere, and to study the ability of vegetated landscapes such as forests, crops, and rangelands to recover from natural or human-induced disturbances.

Context

The Landsat 7 mission was authorized in 1992 by a directive from President George Bush. That same year saw the passage of the Land Remote Sensing Policy Act, which repealed the Land Remote Sensing Commercialization Act of 1984. Signed into law during President Ronald W. Reagan's administration, the Commercialization Act opened up management of the Landsat program to the private sector. In 1985, the Earth Observation Satellite Company (EOSAT) took over the Landsat Program. By the early 1990's, however, it had become clear that the market for Landsat scenes could not sustain EOSAT's operating costs for the system. When the 1992 act put an end to privatization, oversight of the Landsat program shifted from the commercial sector back to the federal government. The National Oceanic and Atmospheric Administration (NOAA), the agency charged in 1984 with transferring the Landsat program to the private sector, relinquished program management to NASA and the Department of Defense (DoD). The DoD withdrew from the program in 1994, at which time NASA assumed the role of lead agency, with NOAA and the USGS

contributing to program management. NASA incorporated the Landsat 7 mission into its Earth Observing System (EOS), a suite of spacecraft and interdisciplinary investigations devoted to global change research. NASA handled Landsat 7's day-to-day operations until early in the twenty-first century, when the USGS assumed management responsibilities. By 2003, the three ground stations managed by USGS had collected more than 300,000 images for archiving.

Landsat 7 is the sixth successful satellite of the Landsat series (Landsat 6, launched in 1993, failed to achieve orbit). Launched in 1984, Landsat 5 exceeded its original three-year life expectancy by more than a decade, and has exhausted many of its backup systems. Its successor, Landsat 7, had a design life of five to six years. Landsat 5's mission ended on June 5, 2013. The spacecraft was disposed of in a "graveyard" orbit and deactivated. As of 2019 Landsat 7 remained operational.

Begun in 1972, Landsat is the longest-running program for acquiring imagery of the Earth from orbit. With Landsat 7, this program continues well into the twenty-first century, expanding and enhancing the existing data archive. This archive serves as a tool for a wide variety of disciplines and interests, including archaeology, agriculture, forestry, hydrology, geology, geography, mineral exploration, civil engineering, land-use planning, sociology, education, and national security. The broad geographic coverage, detail, and frequency of acquisition characteristic of the Landsat TM and ETM+ dataset make it particularly useful for monitoring environmental change on a regional and global scale; for detecting small-scale processes that instrumentation with lower spatial resolution would miss; and for studying seasonal and year-to-year variations in land cover and other terrestrial and coastal conditions. The global view afforded by Landsat 7 and its predecessors is crucial to humankind's efforts to monitor and assess natural and human-induced changes in the environment—such as deforestation, desertification, sea-level fluctuation, and global climate trends—and to understand them as part of a total integrated Earth system.

—*Karen N. Kähler*

See also: Dynamics Explorers; Earth Observing System Satellites; Explorers: Air Density; Explorers: Atmosphere; Geodetic Satellites; Global Atmospheric Research Program; Landsat 1, 2, and 3; Landsat 4 and 5; Mission to Planet Earth; New Millennium Program; Nimbus Meteorological Satellites; Seasat.

Further Reading

Allen, James M., and Shanaka DeSilva. "Landsat: An Integrated History." *QUEST: The History of Spaceflight Quarterly* 12, no. 1 (2005). This article provides historical, scientific, technological, and financial considerations of the Landsat program. Lists numerous references.

King, Michael D., ed. *EOS Science Plan.* Greenbelt, Md.: National Aeronautics and Space Administration, 1999. This NASA publication, issued before Landsat 7 was launched, discusses the satellite and its ETM+ instrument within the context of the Earth Observing System (EOS) program. See especially Chapter 5, "Land Ecosystems and Hydrology."

King, Michael D., and Reynold Greenstone, eds. *1999 EOS Reference Handbook.* Greenbelt, Md.: National Aeronautics and Space Administration, 1999. This guide to NASA's Earth Observing System (EOS) includes descriptions of the Landsat 7 mission, the ETM+ instrument, and the EROS Data Center.

Mack, Pamela E., ed. "LANDSAT and the Rise of Earth Resources Monitoring." In *From Engineering Science to Big Science.* Washington, D.C.: National Aeronautics and Space Administration History Office, 1998. A brief history of the Landsat program before the launch of Landsat 7, with a focus on the political and bureaucratic forces shaping it. Includes a discussion of the failed privatization effort begun in the 1980's.

Mecham, Michael. "Landsat 7 to Advance Chronicling of Earth." *Aviation Week and Space Technology* 150 (April 12, 1999): 72-73. An informative summary of the mission's instrumentation, platform, capabilities, imaging strategy, and historical background.

Quirk, Bruce, and Ronald E. Beck. "Earth Data for the Future." *Geotimes* 43 (March, 1998): 21-23. The EROS Data Center, Landsat 7's primary receiving station and its archiving and distribution facility, is the focus of this article.

Showstack, Randy. "Landsat 7 Launch Will Extend Long-Term Earth Remote Sensing Mission." *EOS: Transactions of the American Geophysical Union* 80 (April 13, 1999): 167. This brief but thorough article, published shortly before Landsat 7's launch, provides an excellent overview of the Landsat 7 mission and its objectives.

Zimmerman, Robert. *The Chronological Encyclopedia of Discoveries in Space.* Westport, Conn.: Oryx Press, 2000. Provides a complete chronological history of all crewed and robotic spacecraft and explains flight events and scientific results. Suitable for all levels of research.

Langley Research Center

Date: Beginning 1917
Type of facility: Space research center

NASA's Langley Research Center, located near Hampton, Virginia, is the United States' oldest government-run aerodynamic research and testing facility. Built first as a home for civilian airplane development during World War I, Langley conducts and manages a variety of programs on advanced aerodynamics and the future of piloted and robotic space travel.

Key Figures

Samuel P. Langley (1834-1906), aviation pioneer

Leigh M. Griffith, first engineer in charge at Langley

Henry J. E. Reid (1895-1968), Langley center director, 1958-1960

Floyd L. Thompson (1898-1976), Langley center director, 1960-1968

Edgar M. Cortright (1923-2014), Langley center director, 1968-1975

Donald P. Hearth (1928-2013), Langley center director, 1975-1984

Richard H. Peterson, Langley center director, 1984-1991

Paul F. Holloway (1938-2013), Langley center director, 1991-1996

Jeremiah F. Creedon (b. 1940), Langley center director, 1996-2003

Delma C. Freeman, Jr., Langley center acting director, 1996-2003

Roy D. Bridges, Jr. (b. 1943), Langley center director, 2003-present

Richard W. Barnwell, flight director scientist at Langley

Summary of the Facility

Located in the Virginia Tidewater area on the Chesapeake Bay near the city of Hampton, the National Aeronautics and Space Administration's (NASA) Langley Research Center is the nation's oldest and most comprehensive aeronautics research and testing center. Established in 1917 to test civilian aircraft during World War I, Langley quickly became the central experimental and testing facility for state-of-the-art air and spacecraft technology in the United States. Today, Langley Research Center provides vital research and development information on proposed air and spacecraft, equipment, and software systems to civilian government agencies, the military, and private industry. The center also became home to the Scout launch vehicle, as well as numerous space research projects such as the two Viking Mars landing missions, the Echo communications satellites, and the uncrewed Lunar Orbiter from the 1960's. Langley is one of eleven such major facilities operated by NASA out of its headquarters in Washington, D.C.

Langley Research Center was originally created by the National Advisory Committee for Aeronautics (NACA) in 1917. NACA was the first U.S. federal agency dedicated to advancing the principles and practice of powered flight. Langley, NACA's first facility, was named for American aviation pioneer Samuel P. Langley, and run by the first engineer in charge, Leigh M. Griffith. The first testing equipment constructed at Langley, in 1920, was a wind tunnel capable of generating wind speeds of 130 miles per hour. Over the years, Langley's contributions to aeronautic technology grew as the center's resources and responsibilities increased.

Aerial view of NASA Langley in 2011. (NASA)

Virtually all the major advancements in airplane design made since the 1920's in the United States have undergone testing at Langley Research Center prior to production by private industry or the government. When NASA was created in 1958 to oversee the United States' fledgling space program, Langley was one of the first NACA centers incorporated into the new agency. Scientists and engineers who worked at Langley were among the first in the country to look into possible spacecraft design options.

Langley personnel were also part of the team that originally conceived the United States' first program for putting humans into space, the effort later named Project Mercury. The project was managed by the NASA Langley Research Center, which also served as one of the principal training facilities for the first group of seven astronauts selected in 1959. Robert R. Gilruth, a Langley scientist and administrator, headed the team of NACA/NASA experts who created Project Mercury. Because of Langley's wealth of expertise and technical resources, the facility was given managerial control over the project and served as a key training facility for the original seven astronauts.

In 1965, when Project Gemini, the United States' two-person spacecraft program, was put into use,

NASA used Langley personnel to open what would later be called the Johnson Space Center in Houston, Texas, and transferred responsibility for crewed flights from Langley. During and after this period, Langley also managed the Viking Mars orbiter and lander program, the Lunar Orbiter program, NASA's Echo communications satellites, and experiments for various Explorer uncrewed spacecraft, as well as providing research and design support for other NASA piloted and robotic spaceflight projects.

Along with other NASA facilities, such as the Ames Research Center in California and the Goddard Space Flight Center in Maryland, Langley has provided key support in the development and operation of the Space Transportation System(STS), or space shuttle. Langley scientists tested and helped to perfect the shuttle's design and to invent the heat-shielding materials used to protect the shuttle from the intense heat of reentry into Earth's atmosphere. Langley has managed or assisted in the development of several space shuttle payloads: The Langley developed Long Duration Exposure Facility, for example, was a robotic payload delivered into orbit by the space shuttle in 1984 to perform experiments on the long-term effects of exposure to rigors of space on human-made objects. Throughout the space shuttle era, Langley scientists and engineers worked on potential second- and third-generation shuttle designs. In the aftermath of the February 1, 2003, *Columbia* accident (mission STS-107), Langley took on a new function with the establishment of a new NASA Safety Office with agency-wide responsibilities.

In the year 2005, more than 3,800 civil service and private sector contract personnel worked at Langley's nineteen major testing facilities. The center operates twenty-four of the world's most advanced conventional, supersonic, transonic, and hypersonic wind tunnels for testing air and spacecraft design performance characteristics, as well as eight structural laboratories (including a massive aircraft crash test complex), seven engineering and flight simulators, eight facilities for fabricating air and spacecraft designs, seventeen research and support aircraft, a technical reference library of nearly three million titles, and a state-of-the-art supercomputer complex for design and testing support. Langley personnel also publish more than one thousand articles for technical and professional journals, research and project reports, and papers every year.

Organizationally, the NASA Langley Research Center is divided into six research directorates and a congressionally mandated technology

A variety of research aircraft at NASA Langley in 1994. (NASA / LaRC)

utilization program. These directorates (Aeronautics, Electronics, Flight Systems, Space, Structures and Systems Engineering, and Operations) oversee research and testing in such areas as crew emergency rescue systems for the crewed space station, the development of robot arms, wind shear modeling for aircraft, advanced avionics (aircraft electronic systems), high-temperature superconducting materials, and flight simulator designs. The Technology Utilization Program conducts studies to find ways to put NASA-developed technologies into everyday use. Programs in this area at Langley have included stress testing on railroad car wheels, developing improved kidney dialysis machines, and other medical applications.

Context

There are two major ways in which to view the Langley Research Center: first, as an operational research and testing center in the NASA network of space facilities around the nation; second, as a historic milestone in the nation's move into the skies and heavens above the surface of the planet.

The NASA Langley Research Center is one of eleven major research and operational facilities run by the space agency through its Washington, D.C., headquarters. The others are Ames Research Center at Moffett Field, California; Dryden Flight Research Facility at Edwards Air Force Base, California; Goddard Space Flight Center in Greenbelt, Maryland; the Jet Propulsion Laboratory in Pasadena, California; the Lyndon B. Johnson Space Center in Houston, Texas; John F. Kennedy Space Center at Cape Canaveral, Florida; John H. Glenn Research Center at Lewis Field in Cleveland, Ohio; George C. Marshall Space Flight Center in Huntsville, Alabama; John C. Stennis Space Center in southwestern Mississippi; and Wallops Flight Center in Wallops Island, Virginia.

These centers give NASA a multifaceted approach to the science and business of space travel. Langley, like the other NASA facilities, plays a valuable and vital part in fulfilling the space agency's mandate to keep the United States moving forward in the progression into space. Through its advanced research and testing programs, Langley has played an important role in helping the United States to build a viable and competitive aircraft industry. This development, through commercial airlines alone, has revolutionized the world in which we live. The center's design and testing services to the nation's military establishment have reshaped the posture of the United States on the world stage. The center has also contributed significantly to the development of the nation's intercontinental ballistic missile system and other launch vehicles, including the Scout rocket.

Through its aeronautical research, which comprises about 75 percent of the center's activities, Langley also interacts with public and private sector agencies and companies to advance aviation technology. Langley scientists and engineers work to make air travel safer and more efficient through the development of better electronics and aircraft designs, which are then put into production by private companies.

Beyond this role, Langley's creation in 1917 meant that the United States could compete with the United Kingdom, France, Russia, Germany, and other countries in the development of new types of aircraft and new applications of existing aviation technology in the critical first years after the Wright Brothers' first flight in 1903. Langley, in cooperation with the branches of the military, also helped prove the viability of airplanes as weapons and tools in the nation's arsenal, thereby helping prepare the nation for pivotal air confrontations—and dramatic technological advances that resulted—in World Wars I and II, as well as other conflicts.

—Eric Christensen

See also: Ames Research Center; Cape Canaveral and the Kennedy Space Center; Gemini Program; Goddard Space Flight Center; Jet Propulsion Laboratory; Johnson Space Center; Lewis Field and Glenn Research Center; Marshall Space Flight Center; Mercury Project Development; Space Centers, Spaceports, and Launch Sites.

Further Reading

Ezell, Edward Clinton, and Linda Neuman Ezell. *On Mars: Exploration of the Red Planet, 1958- 1978.* NASA SP-4212. Washington, D.C.: Government Printing Office, 1984. This somewhat technical treatise on the nation's efforts to reach Mars is valuable as a definitive look at an important space project. Langley made a significant contribution to this effort.

Hansen, James R. *Engineer in Charge: A History of the Langley Aeronautical Laboratory, 1917-1958.* Washington, D.C.: National Aeronautics and Space Administration, 1987. This is an interesting, well-written examination of the early history of Langley Research Center. Of particular value for its insight into the origins of the Center.

---. *Spaceflight Revolution: NASA Langley Research Center from Sputnik to Apollo.* NASA SP-4308. Washington, D.C.: Government Printing Office, 1995. A part of the NASA History series, this book looks at the contributions Langley researchers have made to the exploration of the atmosphere and space.

Horta, Lucas G. *A Historical Perspective on Dynamics Testing at the Langley Research Center.* Washington, D.C.: National Aeronautics and Space Administration, 2000. This brief report comes from an article in the NASA Technical Memorandum series. It provides insights into the type of aeronautical engineering performed at the Langley Research Center.

Langley Research Center. *Public Information Kit.* Washington, D.C.: National Aeronautics and Space Administration. Numerous brochures, pictures, and other printed materials are available free of charge from NASA on the Langley Research Center and its various activities. Many of these materials are designed for classroom use in all primary and secondary schools.

---. *Research and Technology, [Year]: Annual Report of the Langley Research Center*. Washington, D.C.: National Aeronautics and Space Administration. A series of technical reports published annually which document current and ongoing research projects conducted at the Langley Research Center. In addition to detailed scientific information, many offer a layperson's guide to the importance of the different projects.

Launius, Roger D. *NASA: A History of the U.S. Civil Space Program*. Malabar, Fla.: Krieger Publishing Company, 1994. This is an in-depth look at America's civilian space program and the establishment of the National Aeronautics and Space Administration. It chronicles the agency from its predecessor, the National Advisory Committee for Aeronautics, through the present day.

Ordway, Frederick I., III, and Mitchell Sharpe. *The Rocket Team*. Burlington, Ont.: Apogee Books, 2003. A revised edition of the acclaimed thorough history of rocketry from early amateurs to present-day rocket technology. Includes a disc containing videos and images of rocket programs.

Phillips, W. Hewitt. *Journey in Aeronautical Research: A Career at NASA Langley Research Center*. Washington, D.C.: Government Printing Office, 1998. This is a personal account of a researcher who spent his years at Langley. It is an intriguing behind-the-scenes look at aeronautical research and the way NASA conducts it.

Wallace, Lane E. *Airborne Trailblazer: Two Decades with NASA Langley's 737 Flying Laboratory*. NASASP-4216. Washington, D.C.: Government Printing Office, 1994. This is the story of a unique airplane and the contributions it has made to the air transportation industry. NASA's Boeing 737100 Transport Systems Research Vehicle was the prototype 737, acquired by the Langley Research Center in 1973 to conduct research into advanced transport aircraft technologies. This illustrated work includes source notes, a bibliographic essay, a glossary of acronyms, NASA Boeing 737 Transport Systems Vehicle specifications, and a complete listing of all of its flights.

Launch Vehicles

Date: Beginning 1955
Type of technology: Expendable launch vehicles

The power of launch vehicles and booster rockets is crucial to the establishment and maintenance of a reliable space program. Without powerful rocketry, it would be impossible to leave Earth's atmosphere.

Summary of the Technology

The Vanguard was designed to be the first American satellite-launching vehicle. It was developed, beginning in 1955, by the Naval Research Laboratory in Washington, D.C. The Vanguard rocket was 22 meters long and 114 centimeters at its widest point. It was both cylindrical and finless. Its gross weight at launch was 10,251 kilograms. The Vanguard was designed to place a 9.75-kilogram satellite into orbit.

The first stage of the vehicle was liquid-fueled and generated a liftoff thrust of some 120,000 newtons. The General Electric Company built Vanguard's first-stage engine to lift the vehicle to a point about 58 kilometers above Earth's surface and to attain a velocity of close to 6,000 kilometers per hour.

The second stage, which was also liquid-fueled, contained the guidance system for the entire vehicle. The engine for this stage was built by Aerojet-General Corporation and generated 33,360 newtons of thrust at its operating altitude.

The third stage of the vehicle was propelled by solid fuels and developed about 10,230 newtons of thrust at its operating altitude. The third stage had no guidance system. Stable flight was achieved by rapidly spinning the stage by means of a mechanism that was located in the second stage. After separation of the stages, the third stage was ignited. This firing of the third stage took place at orbital heights of 450 kilometers or greater. The third stage then accelerated the satellite, which was riding on its nose. After orbital velocity was achieved, the satellite was separated from the third stage by a spring mechanism activated by a mechanical timer.

The Juno 1, more commonly known as the Jupiter-Composite or Jupiter-C, was based on the Redstone medium range ballistic missile. The Redstone, which was often called an offspring of the German V-2 rocket, was developed by the U.S. Army in the early 1950's. The missile was 21 meters long and 178 centimeters wide. It was stabilized by four fins at the base of the vehicle. This Chrysler-built, single-stage missile was propelled by a rocket engine using liquid oxygen as the oxidizer and an alcohol-water mixture as the fuel. The engine developed 333,600 newtons of thrust and had a burning time of 121 seconds. The weight of the missile at launch was 27,670 kilograms.

The Jupiter-C consisted of a high-performance version of the Redstone (in addition to enlarged fuel tanks, a change in fuel significantly increased the liftoff thrust) as the first stage and two clusters of solid-propellant rocket motors as the second and third stages. These solid-fueled rockets had been developed by the Jet Propulsion Laboratory in Pasadena, California. Eleven of these rockets were clustered in a ring to form the second stage; three rockets were then clustered together and fitted inside the second-stage ring. The upper stage of the Jupiter-C sat in a bucket-like container atop the Redstone first stage. The bucket was rotated at high

Russian Soyuz TMA-5 lifts off from the Baikonur Cosmodrome in Kazakhstan heading for the International Space Station. (NASA / Bill Ingalls)

2 used the more powerful Jupiter intermediate range ballistic missile as its first stage. The three remaining solid-fueled stages were the same for both the Juno 1 and Juno 2 vehicles. The Juno 2, however, carried a shroud that covered the upper stages to prevent aerodynamic heating during the ascent.

The Thor intermediate range ballistic missile was developed during the 1950's as the Air Force's equivalent of the Army's Jupiter missile. The Thor is a single-stage missile with a liftoff thrust of 765,056 newtons. It is propelled by a single Rocketdyne-built main engine and two small vernier engines for stabilization. The main frame of the Thor, which was built by Douglas Aircraft, was about 17 meters long. The missile weighed 44,900 kilograms fully fueled.

The Thor was used as the first stage for several different missile systems that were used in the U.S. space program, including the Thor-Able, Thor-Agena, Thrust-Augmented Thor, Thor-Delta, and Thrust-Augmented Delta.

The first of these configurations, the Thor-Able, was flown successfully in July of 1958. The Able element of this system consisted of the second and third stages of the Vanguard missile. With these added stages, the Thor became a viable launch vehicle for placing Air Force payloads in space.

Early in 1960, the National Aeronautics and Space Administration (NASA) decided to use the Agena vehicle, which had been developed by the Air Force, as a second stage for the Thor. This combination, the Thor-Agena, stood 23 meters tall (without the spacecraft) and measured about 2

speeds to stabilize the upper stages (much as a rifle bullet is stabilized in flight).

The Jupiter-C was converted into a satellite launching vehicle (Juno 1) simply by adding an instrument package and an additional solid-fueled rocket as a fourth stage. While the Juno 1, or Jupiter-C, used the Redstone as its first stage, the Juno meters at its widest point. Like the Thor, the Agena was a liquid-propelled missile. The two combined provided a total thrust of 827,328 newtons. The Agena was able to be restarted after it had been deactivated in space. This feature permitted great precision in the selection of an orbit. The Agena as modified by NASA was designated Agena B. The Thor-Agena B was capable of sending a 726- kilogram payload into an orbit 480 kilometers high or a 272-kilogram payload into an orbit 1,931 kilometers high.

The Thrust-Augmented Thor (TAT) consisted of the Thor missile with three solid-propellant motors strapped onto its base. With these three motors, the Thor's liftoff thrust was increased to about 1.5 million newtons.

The Thor-Delta was built with the Thor as its first stage, a modified and improved second stage from the Vanguard and Thor-Able designs, and a spin-stabilized, solid-propellant third stage known as Altair. The entire vehicle stood 27 meters high and was capable of launching a 363-kilogram payload into an orbit 483 kilometers high. The gross weight of the vehicle was 50,803 kilograms, and it had a liftoff thrust of 756,160 newtons.

The Thrust-Augmented Delta (TAD) consisted of the Thor-Delta configuration with strapped-on solid boosters. This spacecraft has been continuously upgraded over the years and is today known as the Delta. The liquid-fueled first stage of the 35-meter-tall rocket is augmented by nine solid-propellant motors, six of which ignite at liftoff and three of which ignite after the first six are exhausted, about 58 seconds into the flight. The Delta generates some 3 million newtons of thrust at liftoff. It has a liquid-fueled second stage and a solid-propellant third stage. The Delta's third stage has occasionally been replaced by a Payload Assist Module (PAM). This stage boosts the spacecraft from a low-Earth orbit into a higher one. With the PAM and a modification of the second stage, the Delta can lift 1,270 kilograms into orbit.

The first Delta II vehicle was launched in February, 1989. It consisted of two liquid-fueled stages with a spin-stabilized solid-fueled stage on top. Nine strap-on solid-fueled motors augment the thrust of the first stage and permit the lofting of nearly 1,500 kilograms of payload into a geosynchronous orbit. The Delta II has had only one total failure (and one partial failure, Koreasat-1)—an incredible 98 percent success rate. The Delta II launched the first eight Globalstar satellites, and has lofted fifty-five satellites out of seventy- two in the completed Iridium constellation.

The Delta III was developed by Boeing Aircraft Company as a commercial venture to fulfill customer needs for a launch service to accommodate growing satellite sizes. Its first launch was in August, 1998. The RS-27A main engine powers the Delta III first stage. Boeing increased the diameter of the first-stage fuel tank from that in Delta II to reduce the overall length of the vehicle and improve control margins. To add to Delta III first-stage performance, Boeing uses nine 1.17-meter-diameter solid-fueled rocket motors, which are derived from those on Delta II, but are larger and produce 25 percent more thrust. Three of the new motors are equipped with thrust-vector control to further improve vehicle maneuverability and control. The Delta III second-stage Pratt& Whitney R110B-2 engine is derived from the R110 power plant flown for more than three decades. This second stage carries more propellant than Delta II and burns cryogenic (cold) fuels, which produce more energy, allowing lift of heavier payloads. With a payload delivery capacity to geosynchronous transfer orbit of 3,800 kilograms, Delta III effectively doubles the performance of the Delta II.

The Delta IV launch vehicle uses a new, liquid oxygen/hydrogen "common core" booster powered by a single RS-68 engine. There are several variants of the Delta IV launch vehicle. The Delta IV Medium, which will replace the Delta II, combines the common core booster with the current Delta II second stage and 3-meter fairing. The larger Delta IV Medium Plus (4, 2), which combines the common core and two solid strap-on motors with a modified Delta III liquid oxygen/hydrogen second stage and 4-meter fairing, is capable of placing 5,760 kilograms into a geosynchronous transfer orbit (GTO). The Delta IV Medium Plus (5, 2), which combines the common core and two solid strap-on motors with a large Delta III-type liquid oxygen/hydrogen second stage and a new 5- meter fairing, can place 4,800 kilograms into a GTO orbit. The Delta IV Medium Plus (5, 4), which combines the common core and four solid motors with a large Delta III-type liquid oxygen/hydrogen second stage and a new 5-meter fairing, can place 6,700 kilograms in a GTO orbit. Finally, the Delta IV Heavy combines three common core boosters with a large Delta III-type liquid oxygen/hydrogen second stage and a new 5-meter fairing to place 13,200 kilograms into a GTO orbit. Together, the Delta IV variants are capable of replacing the Delta II and Delta III as well as the heavy Titan IV. In essence, Boeing hopes to use the Delta IV family to address the bulk of the existing and future commercial and government launch market. The first commercial Delta IV order was announced in December of 1999, and the first Delta IV launch was planned for 2001.

The first Delta IV launch occurred on November 20, 2002, and lofted a Eutelsat payload into orbit. The Air Force began using the new booster as early as its second launch, on March 10, 2003. The maiden launch of the Delta IV Heavy occurred on December 21, 2004. Although there were anomalies in the performance of the core boosters, the flight was largely successful, and those anomalies encountered were expected to be easy to correct before the Delta IV Heavy flew again. Its second launch was expected to include a payload destined for operational use, whereas the payloads on the maiden launch were only demonstration satellites.

Over its life span, the Delta family of vehicles has racked up what is perhaps the most successful flight record of any rocket currently in service. At the start of 2005, after some three hundred flights, only about 5 percent had been total failures, thereby establishing a success rate of 95 percent.

In the early 1950's the Air Force began work on its intercontinental ballistic missile programs. The first intercontinental ballistic missile to be developed was the Atlas. The Atlas, built by Convair, was considered to be a stage-and-a-half vehicle. It had two side-mounted liquid-propellant rocket boosters and a liquid-fueled sustainer engine. Two small vernier rockets were located at the base of the Atlas on sides opposite the boosters. When the Atlas was launched, all five of the engines would be running. Atotal of more than 1 million newtons of thrust was produced at liftoff. The vehicle stood 21 meters high, measured about 2 meters in diameter, and weighed 113,400 kilograms at launch.

After it became operational in the late 1950's, the Atlas was used as a first stage for various spacecraft. The Able and Agena configurations, which had been used with the Thor, were now mated to the more powerful Atlas.

In 1966, the Centaur, the United States' first high-energy, liquid-hydrogen, liquid-oxygen launch vehicle stage, became operational. This vehicle was combined with the Atlas. The Atlas-Centaur stood 42 meters tall. Its first stage developed close to 2 million newtons of thrust, and its Centaur stage developed 146,784 newtons of thrust in a vacuum.

The Titan, which was developed by the Martin Company in the late 1950's, was somewhat more sophisticated than the Atlas. Like the Atlas, the Titan was an intercontinental ballistic missile with a designed range of more than 8,000 kilometers. Unlike the Atlas, it was a two-stage vehicle. The first stage produced some 1 million newtons of liftoff thrust, and the second stage produced 266,880 newtons of thrust. Both stages were liquid-fueled. The Titan stood 27 meters tall and was 3 meters in diameter.

Because of military considerations, the Titan was modified and became known as the Titan II. About the only characteristic the Titan II shared with the

Titan was its diameter. The first stage of the Titan II generated close to 2 million newtons of thrust, up from the 1 million newtons of thrust generated by the Titan. Its second stage had a significant increase in thrust. The Titan II stood 31 meters tall and had a weight of 149,688 kilograms at launch.

After various redundant components (multiple devices capable of performing the same function) had been added to ensure the workability of backup systems, the Titan II became human-rated and joined the Gemini crewed spaceflight program in 1965.

The Titan II was eventually modified by the addition of two massive solid-fueled boosters and mated to the Centaur upper stage. This configuration became known as the Titan III-E/Centaur. It was first launched in 1974 and gave the United States an extremely powerful and versatile rocket for launching large spacecraft on planetary missions.

The Titan IV is the largest piloted space booster used by the United States. The vehicle is designed to carry payloads equivalent to the size and weight of those carried on the space shuttle. The Titan IV consists of two solid-propellant motors, a liquid propellant two-stage core, and a 5-meter-diameter payload fairing. The system has three upper-stage configurations that include a cryogenic wide-body Centaur Upper Stage (CUS), but also may be flown with an Inertial Upper Stage (IUS) or No Upper Stage (NUS). Overall length of the system is 62 meters when flown with a 26-meter payload fairing. The Titan IV Centaur is capable of placing 4,500-kilogram payloads into geosynchronous orbit. The Titan IV system is also capable of placing 18,000 kilograms into a low-Earth orbit at 28.6° inclination or 14,000 kilograms into a low-Earth polar orbit. The Solid Rocket Motor Upgrade, used only on Titan IV-Bs, incorporates modern technology to provide increased performance and enhanced reliability. With SRMU, the Titan IV Centaur is capable of placing 5,700-kilogram payloads into geosynchronous orbit or 21,700 kilograms into a low-Earth

orbit. SRMU production started in November, 1993.

Titan launch operations came to a close at Cape Canaveral when a Titan IV booster departed Complex 40 at 00:50 Coordinated Universal Time (UTC) on April 30, 2005. This booster delivered a National Reconnaissance Office classified payload to orbit and put on a spectacular show in the skies along the East Coast of the United States and Canada as it ended more than five decades of heavy-lifting launch services from Cape Canaveral. The launch was the 168th for Titan. In total, there were forty-seven Titan I ICBMs, twenty-three Titan II ICBMs, twelve Titan II Gemini Program support boosters, four Titan III-As, thirty-six Titan III-Cs, seven Titan III-Es, eight Titan 34Ds, four Commercial Titans, and twenty-seven Titan IVs. As of August, 2005, only one final Titan remained to be launched from the Vandenberg site. Then the venerable Titan family would be retired to a rich history that served the national interest in wartime and peacetime, having dispatched both astronauts and highly ambitious robotic probes into space.

The Scout launch vehicle, which became operational in 1960, has undergone several modifications since that time. The Scout is a solid-propellant, four-stage vehicle that stands 23 meters tall. It weighs 21,147 kilograms and has a liftoff thrust of 588,203 newtons. The Scout was originally designed to place small payloads into orbit, but its uprated third stage made it possible to orbit payloads of more than 200 kilograms.

The development of the Saturn series of rockets began in 1958. The first stage of the Saturn I was a cluster of eight liquid-fueled engines of the type used in the Jupiter program. Each engine was capable of generating about 800,000 newtons of thrust. The second stage had six liquid-oxygen, liquid hydrogen engines, each rated at about 65,000 newtons of thrust. The Saturn I stood 38 meters tall and had a base diameter of 6.58 meters. The vehicle was capable of placing a 10,000-kilogram spacecraft into Earth orbit.

The Saturn V was the largest, most powerful rocket ever built. This three-stage vehicle stood 111 meters tall and weighed more than 2 million kilograms when totally fueled. Its first and second stages were each powered by five liquid-fueled engines, and a single engine powered its third stage. The Saturn V was powerful enough to launch 109,000 kilograms into Earth orbit, 41,000 kilograms on a lunar mission, and 32,000 kilograms on a planetary mission.

The space shuttle consists of a delta-winged (a delta wing is a triangular wing with a tapered leading edge and a straight trailing edge) space glider called an orbiter; two solid-fueled rocket boosters (SRBs), which are also reusable; and an expendable external fuel tank containing liquid propellants for the orbiter's three main engines. The assembled space shuttle is 56 meters long and has a wingspan of 24 meters. The shuttle weighs more than 2 million kilograms at liftoff. At ignition, the orbiter's three main engines and the two solid propellant rocket boosters burn simultaneously, generating more than 28 million newtons of thrust.

At an altitude of about 48 kilometers, the used solid rockets are parachuted into the ocean, where they are recovered by waiting ships. The orbiter and the External Tank continue toward Earth orbit. After the orbiter's engines cease to operate, the fuel tank is jettisoned into the ocean. By the use of maneuvering engines, the orbiter is guided into Earth orbit for the duration of the mission. When the mission is completed, the orbiter reenters the atmosphere and returns to Earth, gliding to a landing. The orbiter *Enterprise* was used only for approach and landing tests, and some dynamic testing. Production orbiters that flew in space, listed in order of maiden flights, included *Columbia*, *Challenger*, *Discovery*, *Atlantis*, and *Endeavour*. *Challenger* was lost on mission STS 51-L (1986) and *Columbia* on mission STS-107 (2003).

With the announcement of the Bush Moon- Mars Initiative in the aftermath of the *Columbia* accident, the shuttle fleet was slated for retirement in 2010 after completion of the International Space Station. Project Constellation was tasked with developing a new Crew Exploration Vehicle capable of returning astronauts to human exploration beyond low-Earth orbit, the first time since the end of the Apollo Program in 1972. A new booster would be needed to launch this new piloted spacecraft. Initial consideration was given to using the evolving Atlas-5 or Delta IV Heavy.

Contributions

The Jupiter-C, which was used to orbit the first American satellite, was developed and first used to test nose cones for the Army's Jupiter intermediate range ballistic missile. One of the major problems in the development of ballistic missiles was the aerodynamic heating of the warhead during reentry into Earth's atmosphere. With the development of the Jupiter-C, these problems were solved. This knowledge was later applied to the design of crewed vehicles.

Much knowledge was gained during the early space program on the development of multistage rockets. Because such vehicles were essential for the exploration of space, their early development was critical. Prior to the Vanguard and Jupiter-C rockets, the only real experience American missile designers had had with multistage rockets was a configuration known as the V-2/Wac Corporal. This vehicle was developed in the late 1940's and early 1950's by combining captured German V-2 rockets with the Army's Wac Corporal artillery missile.

In spite of some spectacular successes, early progress was slow, particularly in the Vanguard program. Typical problems encountered with multistage rockets were premature shutdown of stages, the upper stage failing to fire, and stages firing in unintended directions.

Progress was made, however, and by the early 1960's the Redstone and Atlas missiles had been equipped with backup systems and were considered reliable enough to be human-rated. These two missiles then became the boosters for the United States' first piloted spaceflight program, Project Mercury.

Although the Jupiter missile never carried people into space, it did carry two chimpanzees, Able and Baker, on a suborbital flight. Their successful recovery demonstrated that living creatures could survive the heat of reentry.

In 1965, the first multistage rocket in NASA's arsenal became human-rated. The Titan II then joined the Gemini piloted spaceflight program. It is important to note that during the Gemini Program the technique of rendezvous and docking was mastered. Without the ability to rendezvous and dock two spacecraft while in orbit, the lunar missions could never have taken place.

The Saturn project began in 1958 with the long-range goal of producing a vehicle with the capability of orbiting very large payloads. It was decided that the Saturn I should be built from existing, proved hardware. Thus, the first stage of the Saturn I used a grouping, or cluster, of eight liquid-fueled engines of the type used in the Jupiter program. This configuration proved very reliable.

The space shuttle employed a new technology for protection from reentry heat. Previous spacecraft had been coated with layers of material on the underside (the part of the spacecraft that sustains the greatest heat upon reentry). As the layers were heated, the outer layer would ablate, or fly into space, dissipating the heat. The next layers would do the same. Because the space shuttle was designed to be a reusable vehicle, a more efficient method of protecting the spacecraft from the heat of reentry was needed. The solution to this problem was the use of some thirty-four thousand heat-resistant tiles on the underside of the orbiter. These tiles, which conduct almost no heat, were made from fibers of nearly pure silica.

Context

On July 29, 1955, President Dwight D. Eisenhower announced that the United States would launch an Earth satellite during the International Geophysical Year (the eighteen-month period between July 1, 1957, and December 31, 1958). This was the genesis of the Naval Research Laboratory's Project Vanguard. Unfortunately, the Vanguard proved to be unreliable.

The development of the Jupiter-C, or Juno 1 (as it was later designated), marked the U.S. Army's entry in the Space Race. The Army had made a case for the use of its vehicle in the mid-1950's, but the Eisenhower administration had instead favored the Vanguard program. While the Vanguard program was lagging, the Soviets shocked the world with the launching of Sputnik 1 on October 4, 1957. Shortly thereafter, the U.S. secretary of defense gave the Army permission to make launch preparations for its Jupiter-C. Only three months later, Explorer 1 was fired into orbit. The first successful American satellite, Explorer 1 helped to regain some of the prestige lost because of the Sputniks and early Vanguard failures.

Shortly after its formation in October of 1958, NASA announced plans for a piloted Earth satellite program. Because the Redstone had proved to be so reliable in past launches, it was selected as the vehicle that would carry the first Americans into space.

The Army's Jupiter missile did not become part of the piloted spaceflight program but did play an important role in the space effort. In 1958, the upper stages of the Jupiter-C missile were added to the Jupiter to form the Juno 2. On March 3, 1959, a Juno 2 vehicle sent a conical-shaped payload named Pioneer 4 past the Moon and into a solar orbit.

The Air Force's Thor intermediate range ballistic missile became the workhorse of the 1960's and the 1970's, as it was combined with various upper stages. Two of the most notable were the Thor-Agena and Thor-Delta configurations. The Thor-Agena was used successfully in the launching of meteorological, communications, and scientific satellites, including the Orbiting Geophysical Observatories and the Echo 2 communications satellite. It was also used in the launching of various military payloads for the Air Force.

First launched by NASA in May of 1960, the Thor-Delta became a reliable vehicle for a wide range of satellite missions. It launched the first orbiting solar observatory, and satellites in the TIROS, Echo, Telstar, Relay, and Syncom programs.

The intercontinental ballistic missiles Atlas and Titan were used extensively both in the crewed and in the robotic space progams. The Atlas served in Project Mercury, sending John H. Glenn, Jr., and other astronauts into orbit. In addition, the Atlas was united with various upper stages, such as the Agena and Centaur, for uncrewed satellite missions and lunar probes. These included the Applications Technology Satellites and the Ranger and Lunar Orbiter projects. The Atlas was also used as a booster for probes to Venus and Mars as part of the Mariner program.

The Titan was used to launch ten piloted Gemini spacecraft into Earth orbit in 1965 and 1966. It has since been combined with strap-on boosters to form the Titan III-E/Centaur. This vehicle successfully launched two Viking Mars landers, two Voyager spacecraft to the Jovian planets, and two Helios spacecraft toward the Sun.

The Saturn launch vehicle was used in the Apollo piloted lunar-landing program. After the completion of the Apollo Program, the Saturn IB was used to launch three crewed missions to the Skylab space station in 1973. In 1975, it launched the American crew for the Apollo-Soyuz Test Project, the joint United States/Soviet Union orbital docking mission. The massive Saturn V was used to launch the space station Skylab in May of 1973.

The space shuttle, which was first flown in April, 1981, was designed to carry large, heavy payloads into Earth orbit. The shuttle was also designed to serve as a satellite checkout and repair vehicle. (In fact, the most famous success of the space shuttle was the Solar Maximum Mission satellite repair.) In addition, the shuttle has been used for meteorological, oceanographic, and cartographic

study—further establishing the value of research performed beyond Earth's atmosphere.

In the wake of the *Challenger* accident, NASA decided to reinstate expendable launch vehicles. Through the middle of the 1990's, NASA had ten launch vehicles (or variations) in addition to the space shuttle. Pegasus is the first successful space vehicle to be launched from the air. The winged vehicle and its payload are carried to an altitude of about 12 kilometers by a Lockheed L1011 widebody aircraft. It can carry a 300-kilogram payload to low-Earth orbit. A longer version, Pegasus XL, can loft a 450-kilogram satellite to orbit. A ground-launched variation of Pegasus is Taurus, which utilizes a wingless Pegasus atop a large solid-fueled rocket.

The Lockheed Martin Launch Vehicle, LMLV 1, uses two solid-fueled stages, while the LMLV 2 uses three stages and the LMLV3 adds strap-on boosters to the stack. The Titan II was still in operation by the end of the century, launched with and without strap-on solid rocket boosters. The Titan IV variation was the primary launch vehicle for heavy Air Force payloads. The Delta has been upgraded through sixteen variations and has used as many as nine strap-on solid boosters. The final Titan II booster launched from Vandenberg Air Force Base in October, 2003, delivering a military weather satellite to orbit. The final Titan IV-B was scheduled for launch from Vandenberg in late 2005.

NASA's oldest family of launch vehicles, Atlas, has six current models in three basic families: the Atlas-2 (2A and 2AS), the Atlas-3 (3A and 3B), and the Atlas-5 (300, 400, 500, and Heavy Series). The Atlas-2 family is capable of lifting payloads ranging in mass from 2,812 kilograms to 3,719 kilograms to GTO. The Atlas-3 family is capable of lifting payloads up to 4,500 kilograms to GTO. The Atlas-5 family is capable of lifting payloads up to 8,200 kilograms, and over 5,940 kilograms directly to geosynchronous orbit (Atlas-5-Heavy).

The Atlas-3 family builds upon the design of Atlas-2 with the use of a new single-stage Atlas main engine, the Russian RD-180. The Atlas-3A uses a twin RD-180 configuration and has a single-engine Centaur atop it. The changes to Centaur for Atlas- 3B are a stretched tank (1.68 meters) and the addition of a second engine. The first launch of Atlas-3 occurred on May 24, 2000.

The Atlas-5 family uses a single-stage Atlas main engine, the Russian RD-180, and the newly developed Common Core Booster (CCB) with up to five strap-on solid rocket boosters. The CCB is 3.8 meters in diameter by 32.5 meters long and uses 284,453 kilograms of liquid oxygen and RP-1 propellants. The Atlas-5-Heavy configuration will use three CCB stages strapped together to provide capability necessary to lift the heaviest payloads. Both Atlas-5 400 and 500 configurations incorporate a stretched version of the Centaur upper stage (CIII), which can be configured with a single engine or dual engines. The Atlas-5 booster made its inaugural launch on August 21, 2002. The Atlas family of vehicles continues to provide reliable commercial launch services to the world.

—David W. Maguire

See also: Atlas Launch Vehicles; Delta Launch Vehicles; Launch Vehicles: Reusable; Pegasus Launch Vehicles; Saturn Launch Vehicles; Soyuz Launch Vehicle; Space Shuttle; Space Shuttle: Approach and Landing Test Flights; Titan Launch Vehicles.

Further Reading

Baker, David. *The Rocket: The History and Development of Rocket and Missile Technology.* New York: Crown, 1978. A well-illustrated, highly detailed volume recounting the history of rocketry, from the invention of gunpowder to the landing of a human on the Moon. Suitable for general readers.

Berinstein, Paula. *Making Space Happen: Private Space Ventures and the Visionaries Behind Them.* Medford, N.J.: Plexus Publishing, 2002. This work provides insights into the private organizations and entrepreneurs who seek to develop commercial space transportation systems and open up the solar system to economic development.

Braun, Wernher von, and Frederick I. Ordway III. *Space Travel: A History.* Rev. ed. New York: Harper & Row, 1985. A history of rocketry and spaceflight from the ancient Chinese rockets to early Apollo missions. Well illustrated.

Burrows, William E. *This New Ocean: The Story of the First Space Age.* New York: Random House, 1998. This is a comprehensive history of the human conquest of space, covering everything from the earliest attempts at spaceflight through the voyages near the end of the twentieth century. Burrows is an experienced journalist, who has reported for *The New York Times, The Washington Post*, and *The Wall Street Journal*. There are many photographs and an extensive source list. Interviewees in the book include Isaac Asimov, Alexei Leonov, Sally K. Ride, and James A. Van Allen.

Divine, Robert A. *The Sputnik Challenge: Eisenhower's Response to the Soviet Satellite.* New York: Oxford University Press, 1993. This is a dramatic account of the national hysteria surrounding the Soviet Union's launching of the early Sputniks. It details the United States' attempts to put its own satellites into orbit and discusses Eisenhower's role in the early exploration of space.

Emme, Eugene M., ed. *The History of Rocket Technology: Essays on Research, Development, and Utility.* Detroit: Wayne State University Press, 1964. A collection of fourteen papers written by scientists and historians covering the development of rocketry from Robert H. Goddard's first liquid-fueled rocket through Project Mercury. Suitable for general readers.

Fifty Years of Rockets and Spacecraft in the Rocket City: NASA-Marshall Space Flight Center. Atlanta: Turner Publishing Company, 2003. This concise history of rocketry and the development of space travel over the past half-century centers on the contributions made to that effort by the Marshall Space Flight Center. Thoroughly laced with photographs, many of which are not typically included in other such works.

Green, Constance M., and Milton Lomask. *Vanguard: A History*. Washington, D.C.: Government Printing Office, 1970. Part of the NASA History series, this work traces the evolution of the Vanguard program from its genesis to the orbiting of Vanguard 1.

Haley, Andrew G. *Rocketry and Space Exploration*. New York: Van Nostrand Reinhold, 1958. A general history of rocketry from the ancient Chinese to the early years of the Space Race with the Sputniks and the Explorer satellite. Suitable for general readers.

Heppenheimer, T. A. *Countdown: A History of Space Flight*. New York: John Wiley, 1997. A detailed historical narrative of the human conquest of space. Heppenheimer traces the development of piloted flight through the military rocketry programs of the era preceding World War II. Covers both the American and the Soviet attempts to place vehicles, spacecraft, and humans into the hostile environment of space. More than a dozen pages are devoted to bibliographic references.

Holder, William G. *Saturn V: The Moon Rocket*. Edited by Glenn Holder. New York: Julian Messner, 1969. A brief history of the development of the rocket from the ancient Chinese to the American crewed space program. Includes an excellent description of the Saturn V rocket and its launching.

Isakowitz, Steven J., Joseph P. Hopkins, Jr., and Joshua B. Hopkins. *International Reference Guide to Space Launch Systems*. 3d ed. Reston, Va.: American Institute of Aeronautics and Astronautics, 1999. The standard resource for launch vehicles and engines, packed with illustrations, figures, and data for policymakers, planners, engineers, launch buyers, and students.

King, Benjamin, and Timothy Kutta. *Impact: The History of Germany's V-Weapons in World War II*. New York: Sarpedon Press, 1998. The story of the V-1 and V-2 rocket-powered explosive delivery systems is told from their design concepts through their production and use. Their effectiveness as a weapon and the methods the Allies used to destroy them are addressed.

"Launch Vehicles." *Aviation Week and Space Technology*, January 17, 2000, 144-145. This table details the specifications for each of the year 2000 launch vehicles and spacecraft, as well as the current status as of the date of publication.

Levine, Alan J. *The Missile and the Space Race*. Westport, Conn.: Praeger, 1994. This is a well-written look at the early days of missile development and space exploration. The book discusses the Soviet-American race to develop intercontinental ballistic missiles for defense purposes and their subsequent use as satellite launchers.

Ley, Willy. *Rockets, Missiles, and Men in Space*. Rev. ed. New York: Viking Press, 1968. A very detailed work starting with the ideas of early astronomers such as Galileo and Johannes Kepler and building up to crewed spaceflight. The text is suitable for the general reader. The extensive appendices are more technical.

National Aeronautics and Space Administration. *Countdown! NASA Launch Vehicles and Facilities*. Washington, D.C.: Government Printing Office, 1978. A collection of short articles on various NASA launch vehicles, both active and inactive, and a description of NASA facilities.

---. *NASA, 1958-1983: Remembered Images*. NASA EP-200. Washington, D.C.: Government Printing Office, 1983. A well-illustrated booklet describing the first twenty-five years of NASA achievements. Included are tables of launch vehicles and brief summaries of missions.

Ordway, Frederick I., III, and Mitchell Sharpe. *The Rocket Team*. Burlington, Ont.: Apogee Books, 2003. A revised edition of the acclaimed thorough history of rocketry from early amateurs to present-day rocket technology. Includes a disc containing videos and images of rocket programs.

Launch Vehicles: Reusable

Date: Beginning 1991
Type of technology: Reusable launch vehicles

To reduce the cost of delivering satellites to orbit, building and servicing space stations, and launching interplanetary probes, NASA and aerospace companies began developing reusable launch vehicles to replace traditional single-use rockets and the space shuttles.

Summary of the Technology

Reaching Earth orbit is among the riskiest and costliest segments of spaceflight. Until the Space Transportation System (STS) began operation, launchers were used once and allowed to burn up in the atmosphere or fall into the ocean. STS was to lower the cost of each launch—and thereby the per-pound price for lifting cargo into space—by reusing the space shuttle orbiters (flight vehicles in order of maiden voyage were *Columbia*, *Challenger*, *Discovery*, *Atlantis*, and *Endeavour*) in a schedule that anticipated one launch a week. In principle, the program succeeded, but because shuttles were complex and difficult to maintain and prepare for space, only about eight launches per year took place, and the program did not lower expenses nearly as much as had been hoped: A pound of cargo cost about ten thousand dollars to launch into orbit. By the late 1980's National Aeronautics and Space Administration (NASA) managers were looking for ways to save money on launching in order to devote funds to exploration and research. They also knew that the shuttle fleet would eventually have to be replaced.

To solve these problems, NASA Administrator Daniel S. Goldin, acting on orders from President Bill Clinton, established the Space Transportation Program Office in 1994. Its goal was to foster development of a new reusable launcher that would cut the per-pound costs of cargo by 90 percent—to no more than one thousand dollars. Gary Payton, an Air Force officer and astronaut, was named its director. To please a budget-conscious Congress, Payton looked for ways to enlist aerospace companies as partners in designing and building prototype single-stage-to-orbit (SSTO) launch vehicles. Additionally, in 1996 the X Prize Foundation, an aerospace industry-supported organization led by aerospace engineer Peter H. Diamandis, announced that it would present a ten-million-dollar prize to the first company to fly a reusable spacecraft capable of carrying three people into space on a suborbital flight. This "X Prize" succeeded in inspiring fourteen companies to work on designs.

Long before 1994, however, research and development programs for SSTO vehicles were well under way. The experimental vehicles were of two basic kinds: space planes and rockets. Of the first group, the best known was the National Aero Space Plane, a NASA project started in 1983 under the direction of President Ronald W. Reagan. The Space Transportation Program Office canceled this program in favor of designs based on advanced technology.

The Lockheed Martin X-33 is a vertical takeoff, horizontal-landing vehicle whose basic design derives from the lifting bodies, tested in the 1960's. The wedge-shaped body, mounting two stubby rear-mounted wings and two vertical tails for stability, is 21 meters long and 23.5 meters wide. Tanks of liquid hydrogen and liquid oxygen take up about 90

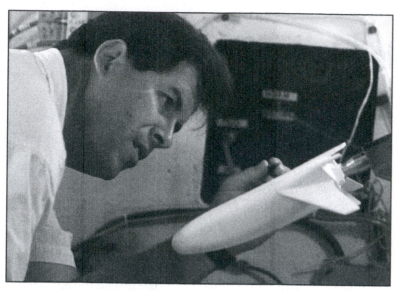

Thomas Horvath of Langley's Aerothermodynamics Branch examines the surface of a model of the X-33 prior to testing in the 20-Inch Mach 6 Air Wind Tunnel at NASA Langley Research Center. The tests, held during the month of September 1997, were conducted to determine aeroheating characteristics of the X-33. (Glenn Research Center)

percent of its volume. Unpiloted, it is designed to reach speeds of up to Mach 13 (Mach 1 equals the speed of sound) in order to test new heat-shielding, ground support management, and engine technology on suborbital flights of about 80 kilometers in altitude (the official threshold to space is arbitrarily designated as 50 miles, which is equivalent to 80 kilometers). The X-33 is a half-size test model of the VentureStar, a commercial, crewed space plane also under development. Capable of flights as long as four days, the VentureStar was designed to ferry passengers to the International Space Station. Its externally mounted payload bay could lift as much as 25,000 kilograms of cargo to low-Earth orbit (LEO). After numerous technological problems, this program was canceled in 2001.

The X-34, developed by Orbital Sciences Corporation, is designed to test reusable rocket engines for carrying small payloads into LEO. Having a delta wing and single vertical tail like the space shuttles, it is 17.7 meters long and has a wingspan of 8.5 meters. It is launched from an airplane like the X-15 and soars up to 80 kilometers at speeds of

up to Mach 8. Fully automatic, the unpiloted space plane lands on a runway. Like the X-33, this program succumbed to the budgetary ax in 2001.

The X-37, developed by Boeing Aircraft Company as part of NASA's Future X program, is a precursor for a piloted military space plane or an unpiloted commercial cargo-hauler. The 8.23- meter-long craft, with wings spanning 4.3 meters, does not take off under its own power. It rides to orbit in a space shuttle cargo bay or atop an expendable booster. Released into space, the X-37 investigates the effects of high speeds, temperatures, and structural stresses during reentry and lands on a runway under power. The X-37 was rolled out in early 2004.

The unpiloted X-43, also known as Hyper X, is intended to test the performance of special jet engines at speeds between Mach 7 and Mach 10. Launched from a B-52 or Pegasus booster, this plane, 3.66 meters long with a wingspan of 1.5 meters, climbs to about 30,488 meters and then is allowed to fall into the ocean. The maiden X-43 test flight failed rather spectacularly on June 2, 2001, but subsequent test flights demonstrated the usefulness of the scramjet. Speed records held by the SR-71 spy plane were broken when the X-43 exceeded Mach 7 on March 27, 2004.

During the late 1990's several companies produced designs for, and even began fabrication of, space planes as private ventures. For example, Pioneer Rocketplane's Pathfinder rocket plane is to have a 1,360- kilogram payload capacity and use existing rocket engine designs. Taking off vertically on a suborbital trajectory, it would release a second stage, which carries the payload into LEO. The Astroliner of Kelly Space and Technology also is intended to take satellites and perhaps passengers into orbit, having a payload capacity of about nearly 32,000 kilograms. The space plane is designed to be towed to 6.1 kilometers by an airliner, where it ignites its rockets for the trip into space. A design by Space Access is to take off vertically and land on a runway under power from special ramjet engines. At altitude it releases two more stages, also winged, that return to the landing site independently.

In addition to space planes, aerospace companies investigated SSTOs that are traditional rockets capable of soft landing. The first major effort was the DC-X (Delta Clipper- Experimental) program, begun in 1991. An unpiloted, one-third-size model for the projected Delta Clipper, it was a suborbital vehicle that took off and landed vertically. McDonnell Douglas built and successfully tested the model (despite one major crash), but NASA canceled the program in 1996 in favor of the X-33.

The F-15B in flight with the X-33 Thermal protection System (TPS) fixture mounted under its fuselage. (NASA / Jim Ross)

Two other designs, privately financed, grew from innovative reentry and recovery concepts. Rotary Rocket Company's Roton is a piloted, fully reusable SSTO vehicle that takes off and lands vertically. Instead of relying on its rockets alone to land, however, it slows its descent with auto-rotating rotors—the marriage of a rocket and a helicopter. The scheme reduces weight from propellant, a major consideration in all designs. The Roton is 19.51 meters long and 6.71 meters in diameter, and is designed to lift a two-person crew and as much as nearly 3,200 kilograms of cargo into LEO. It is fueled by relatively inexpensive, environmentally benign kerosene and liquid oxygen. Successful short-hop test flights took place in 1999.

The unpiloted two-stage K-1 vehicle of Kistler Aerospace also takes off vertically and is fully reusable. The first stage, 18.3 meters long and 6.71 meters in diameter, climbs to 41,159 meters, where it separates from the second stage, restarts its engines for a controlled return trajectory, deploys parachutes at 3,049 meters, and then lands on airbags

that it inflates just before touchdown. The second stage, 18.6 meters long and 4.3 meters in diameter, continues the ascent to orbit, releases its satellite payload, retrofires its rockets to slow for reentry, and then follows the same landing sequence as the first stage.

All the experimental designs underwent some degree of testing by the year 2005. In addition, NASA's Advanced Space Transportation Program was created to study radical new concepts for the agency's "fourth-generation technologies," to be operational around 2040. One is an advanced space plane that would maintain a schedule similar to that of commercial airlines. It would fly to orbit under power from engines capable of breathing air and then converting to rocket power. It would land like an airplane. Another project involves using special lasers to lift an ultralight craft carrying a small satellite payload into space.

The XPrize was won by the SpaceShipOne team on October 4, 2004, after a second piloted flight was conducted within the specified two-week period; actually, the SpaceShipOne team flew two piloted spaceflights within five days with different pilots.

This strengthened the promise of opening up a space tourism business.

Contributions

NASA's experimental space planes allow scientists to examine new technology in realistic flight conditions, although none by itself is designed to be a full-size, ground-to-orbit vehicle. Engines, heating shielding, and handling at hypersonic speeds (greater than Mach 5) are the key subjects of study. However, the organization and management of the support crew that maintains the craft and readies them for space is also a vital concern because the shorter the turnaround time between flights of a reusable launch vehicle, the lower the total per flight costs. The goal for the X-33 program, for example, was to maintain a safe, reliable vehicle with a turnaround of seven days and a total workforce of fifty people. The turnaround time for the VentureStar, it was hoped, would be only two days.

Thrust for the X-33 came from linear aerospike engines, a novel type. The engines, each with multiple combustion chambers, produce thrust by keeping the plume of combusted propellants inside the engine, instead of in an external bell nozzle like traditional rocket engines. This method frees the combustion from the effects of air pressure, allowing the engine to perform efficiently at all altitudes. The X-43 uses scramjet (supersonic hydrogen ramjet) engines, which breathe air like conventional engines but are capable of using air at speeds of more than Mach 6. NASA is also testing an air-breathing rocket engine that during takeoff is a rocket-enhanced jet engine, switches to a jet alone in the atmosphere, and then converts to rocket power in space. All such prototypes are to improve the thrust-to-weight ratio of launch vehicles by decreasing the amount of propellants and oxidizers carried in their fuel tanks.

The X-33 program tested new metals for thermal protection during hypersonic flight. Its heatshield tiles come in seventeen basic shapes and are bolted down, features that would speed maintenance. The skin of the X-34 comprised a carbon composite skin and ceramic matrix composite tiles for the heatshield. Both the X-34 and X-37, which also relies on composite materials, were to test their thermal protection systems during actual atmospheric reentries.

Control of hypersonic aircraft as they ascend is a crucial area of investigation because all spacecraft in the twentieth century entered space attached to rockets. The X-33 and X-43 were designed for the steering and attitude control investigations. The X-34 and X-37 also tested handling conditions under powered reentry. Because the unpiloted vehicles land autonomously, they would provide information for the design of future robotic craft.

Programs such as the Roton and K-1, in addition to trying inventive landing methods for rockets, help private companies learn to manage and finance large space commerce projects. As one aerospace executive put it, financing rocket science is even harder than rocket science.

Context

Interest in reusable launch vehicles intensified during the 1990's because the possible financial rewards rose enormously. As early as 1990 communications corporations announced plans to place hundreds of satellites in orbit in order to create a worldwide high-capacity network for cell phones, Internet linkages, television, and remote sensing. The biggest obstacle to these grand plans was the cost and availability of launchers. Only single-use rockets were in service, and they required from $5 million to $750 million in fees to launch a satellite, depending upon its weight and type of orbit. (Shuttle orbiters no longer launched commercial satellites after the *Challenger* accident in 1986 and after the *Columbia* accident on February 1, 2003, were restricted to orbits compatible with the International Space Station.)

Space commerce planners decided expenses could be reduced by copying the management procedures of commercial airlines. The largest single expense is the labor involved in building rockets and setting them up for launch. Reusable vehicles would drastically curtail building costs, and knowledge gained in the X-33 and X-34 programs was expected to lead to smaller support workforces and faster turnaround times. Unfortunately, both programs were canceled because of technological difficulties and changes in funding priorities.

A vehicle capable of flights every two days would allow NASA to service the International Space Station, launch more deep-space probes, orbit scientific research satellites and telescopes, and perform construction in space—to build a crewed Mars spaceship, for example—for far less money than is required to pay for single-use vehicles. Such a reusable launcher could take satellites into orbit fast enough to be profitable for private companies. Private ventures also expect to start space tourism early in the twenty-first century, first by taking passengers on suborbital flights and later by taking them to space stations built to host daring and wealthy vacationers. Fast package delivery worldwide would also be possible with space planes.

The U.S. military developed its own reusable launch vehicle design in the 1960's. Although its Dyna-Soar project was canceled, the Department of Defense never lost interest. It wants a reliable launcher for reconnaissance satellites. Moreover, in 1999 Secretary of Defense William Cohen announced a new policy for the U.S. Space Command based upon operational military space vehicles that patrol in orbit to protect U.S. space operations and domestic satellites. An X-33 derivative, the X-37, or the X-43 could serve as the prototype for such a space fighter.

—*Roger Smith*

See also: Launch Vehicles; Pegasus Launch Vehicles.

Further Reading

Beardsley, Tim. "The Way to Go in Space." *Scientific American*, February, 1999, 80-97. Beardsley describes the Roton Rotary Rocket, X-43A, space planes, and the K-1 in sidebars in this review article about future spacecraft. Accompanied by dramatic illustrations.

Berinstein, Paula. *Making Space Happen: Private Space Ventures and the Visionaries Behind Them*. Medford, N.J.: Plexus Publishing, 2002. This work provides insights into the private organizations and entrepreneurs who seek to develop commercial space transportation systems and open up the solar system to economic development.

Burrows, William E. *This New Ocean: The Story of the First Space Age*. New York: Random House, 1998. Burrows provides a richly detailed, provocative history of the Space Race, which explains the politics that shaped American programs, including the shuttle, and research to design its replacement. Valuable background reading.

Butrica, Andrew J. *Single Stage to Orbit: Politics, Space Technology, and the Quest for Reusable Rocketry*. Baltimore: Johns Hopkins University Press, 2003. NASA-piloted launch vehicles have traditionally used a multistage approach to reach orbit. This work tells the story of the attempts by research groups and industrial teams to develop a single-stage-to-orbit technology that promises more routine access to space and a lessening of the cost per kilogram for placing payloads into orbit.

Crouch, Tom D. *Aiming for the Star: The Dreamers and Doers of the Space Age*. Washington, D.C.: Smithsonian Institution Press, 1999. A readable general history of spaceflight. The final chapter discusses NASA research efforts and goals, mentioning such reusable launch vehicles as the DC-XA, X-33, X-34, and X-38.

United States Congress. House Committee on Science. *The X-33 Reusable Launch Vehicle: A New Way of Doing Business?* Washington, D.C.: Government Printing Office, 1995. Testimony before Congress from NASA officials and aerospace executives that presents the criteria for a reusable launch vehicle to replace the shuttle, argues for its cost-effectiveness, and explains methods for government-industry partnership in research and development.

United States Congress. Office of Technology Assessment. *Round Trip to Orbit: Human Spaceflight Alternatives.* Washington, D.C.: Government Printing Office, 1989. Intended for Congress, this booklet describes in detail various ways to upgrade the shuttles and designs to replace them. Details the benefits and drawbacks of each option, and summarizes the engineering challenges.

Zubrin, Robert. *Entering Space: Creating a Spacefaring Civilization.* New York: Jeremy P. Tarcher/Putnam, 1999. An extended argument for developing space travel by an aerospace engineer. This book's vision is largely based upon contemporary science and technology. Two chapters discuss the crucial role of reusable launch vehicles and the prototypes under development.

Lewis Field and Glenn Research Center

Date: Beginning October 1, 1958
Type of facility: Space research center

The John H. Glenn Research Center at Lewis Field, Ohio, performs basic and applied research to develop technology in aircraft propulsion, space propulsion, space power, microgravity science, and satellite communications. The center manages projects that validate new technology and produce new flight systems.

Key Figures

George W. Lewis (1882-1948), first director of Research for the National Advisory Committee for Aeronautics (NACA)

Hugh L. Dryden (1898-1965), NACA chair, 1947-1958, who helped transform NACA into NASA

Abe Silverstein (1908-2001), second director of Lewis Research Center

Andrew J. Stofan, fifth director of Lewis Research Center

John M. Klineberg, sixth director of Lewis Research Center

Julian M. Earls, director of Lewis Research Center from 2003

Summary of the Facility

The John H. Glenn Research Center at Lewis Field first was called the Aircraft Engine Research Laboratory of the National Advisory Committee for Aeronautics (NACA). It was renamed the Lewis Flight Propulsion Laboratory in 1948 and the Lewis Research Center in 1958, when NACA became the National Aeronautics and Space Administration (NASA). It was renamed the John H. Glenn Research Center (GRC) at Lewis Field on March 1, 1999, in honor of the Ohio-born astronaut and former U.S. senator.

The first buildings at Lewis were erected on an 80-hectare plot of land next to the Cleveland airport on the extreme west side of the city. Subsequently, another 60 hectares next to the airport were annexed, and 3,200 hectares of land near Sandusky, Ohio, about 80 kilometers west of Cleveland, were acquired to become Lewis's Plum Brook Station.

When it opened in the early 1940's, the research laboratory had the urgent but narrow task of improving the performance of piston aircraft engines. By 1950, however, the focus of its aeronautical work had shifted to gas turbine (jet) engines for aircraft propulsion systems, and the center had begun to expand into rocket propulsion systems for space exploration.

The early work on improving the performance of gas turbine engines concentrated on the basic objective of developing the fundamental operating technology. The next step, in the 1960's, was research geared to developing propulsion systems that would allow aircraft to go higher, farther, and faster and to increase reliability and maintainability. In the 1970's, however, the focus changed again. Work was begun to put propellers back on commercial transport aircraft. New life was breathed into research on a propeller system that would give the performance of a jet engine in terms of speed and altitude with fuel savings of 15 to 30 percent over the most efficient jet engines. The new systems, however, would use modern gas turbine engines instead of piston engines, not to provide thrust but to turn the propellers.

Aerial view of Glenn Research Center at Lewis Field. (NASA)

During the 1970's and 1980's, Lewis managed the Advanced Turboprop (ATP) program, which involved both single rotation and dual counter-rotation propeller systems. Although the technology of each propeller system was distinct, both research efforts were aimed at the "repropellerization" of commercial transport aircraft. The two programs reached their goals in 1987, when a series of flight tests verified the readiness of advanced turboprop technology for use in commercial transport.

One of the oldest areas of aeronautical research at Lewis deals with the causes and prevention of ice formation on aircraft during flight. The icing tunnel at Lewis, built in response to a request from the United States Army Air Corps in 1944, incorporates unique features that have allowed scientists to study icing problems using full-scale aircraft components. The oldest active icing tunnel in the world, it was declared an international historic mechanical engineering landmark in 1987 by the American Society of Mechanical Engineers.

Lewis engineers worked on liquid hydrogen as a fuel during the NACA era and developed confidence in handling it. Nevertheless, the feasibility of a liquid hydrogen-oxygen upper-stage rocket had never been demonstrated. In 1951, Lewis received its first formal appropriation for rocket research,

though the number of people assigned to the rocket section was still small. Lewis's work in high energy chemical rockets led to the development of the Centaur upper-stage vehicle. In 1962, Lewis took on the job of managing the Centaur, which is powered by two liquid hydrogen-oxygen engines with 66,720 newtons of thrust each. Centaur was the nation's first sizable space vehicle able to shut down and restart engines in order to change direction and velocity in space. With both Atlas and Titan rockets as launch vehicles, the Centaur upper stage has been a major factor in the American thrust into space, for it has propelled Surveyor spacecraft to the Moon, scientific satellites to the outer planets, and communications satellites into orbit around Earth. In all, the Lewis-managed Centaur has made more than one hundred successful flights.

The establishment in 1960 of NASA's joint program with the Atomic Energy Commission to develop a nuclear rocket grew out of Lewis's commitment to farsighted research—in this case, investigating nuclear power as a means of aircraft propulsion. Lewis acquired a cyclotron in 1949, and in 1956 the Atomic Energy Commission approved plans for Lewis's nuclear reactor at Plum Brook.

Although nuclear propulsion for aircraft was approached by many with high hopes, problems involving the weight of the necessary shielding and heightened environmental concerns led to the ultimate cancellation of the program in 1961. Nevertheless, the experience gained in nuclear aircraft technology became the foundation for the work on nuclear rockets that continued through the Apollo decade of the 1960's.

Interest in electric rocket propulsion was stimulated originally by an idea dating back to the 1920's: that for space travel, rocket thrust could be produced by the flow of electrically charged particles. The chemical rocket was limited by the enormous amounts of propellant that would be required for flight to distant planets. The advantage of using electric rockets is that although the amount of thrust is small relative to chemical rockets, with a power source in space, electric rockets can produce thrust over longer periods of time. Thus, electric rockets might be useful for long-distance travel between planets. Yet what would their power source be? Their interest stimulated by work described in early papers by European scientists, Lewis engineers began a program to investigate the use of a nuclear reactor to power an electric rocket. Electric propulsion remains a major area of research at Lewis as the United States explores deep space.

Beginning in the early 1970's, work done at Lewis in a joint project with the government of Canada led to the development of the Communications Technology Satellite (CTS). Launched in 1976, CTS was the first communications satellite to incorporate a high-efficiency, high-power transmitting tube invented at Lewis. The tube made it possible for the CTS to operate at power levels ten to twenty times higher than those of previous satellites. It also made possible operation in a new frequency band, the Ku-band. In turn, the improved broadcast capability required much smaller and less expensive ground receiving equipment; it also made possible transmission to remote areas in which terrestrial communications were not highly developed.

Lewis researchers were responsible not only for the development of the high-power transmitter tube for the CTS but also for environmental testing and for the launch vehicle and associated launch services. The spacecraft itself was developed by the Communications Research Center in Canada. The CTS transmitter was turned off in October, 1979, after more than three years of successful experimentation. In 1987, NASA received an Emmy from the National Academy of Television Arts and Sciences for developing technology that had improved television broadcasting throughout the world.

In 1984, Lewis entered the mainstream of the U.S. space program and won the contract to develop the power system for the space station. This power system would serve as a miniature electric utility for a small community of people living and working in space. The total system was expected to generate, store, condition, and distribute electric power to support human life, operate research equipment, and transmit data. Initially, electrical power for the space station was to be provided by solar cell arrays, which would convert the light of the Sun directly into electricity. A solar dynamic system, which would use the heat of the Sun to power a heat engine to turn a generator, was being developed for eventual use in the space station.

Lewis's work in microgravity experiments began in the early 1950's in a small drop tower that could produce reduced gravity conditions for experimental packages during a 30-meter free fall lasting approximately 2.2 seconds. In 1966, a second, larger drop tower, some 150 meters deep, was built. It could produce conditions of one ten-thousandth of Earth gravity for more than five seconds. In 1979, Lewis acquired a Model 25 Learjet, which, when flown in a parabolic trajectory, can provide reduced gravity conditions for 18 to 20 seconds.

The Microgravity Materials Science Laboratory at Lewis opened in 1985. This laboratory is equipped with functional duplicates of the flight hardware used on the space shuttle and the space station. Its purpose is to stimulate the development of experiments in microgravity by offering U.S. scientists and engineers a low-cost, low-risk way to test new ideas for reduced-gravity materials science research. Access to such a facility gives U.S. companies a competitive edge in developing better products through microgravity research. The Micromaterials Science Laboratory has three major sections, for work in metals, alloys, and electronic crystals; glasses and ceramics; and polymers.

In the mid-1970's, Lewis began to conduct research projects on terrestrial energy technology at the request of and with funding from the Department of Energy. As in the case of the advanced turboprop work, this research was driven by a sharp rise in the price of petroleum. There were also environmental considerations. The work included automotive (electric, gas turbine, and Stirling) programs; the development of technology for wind turbine systems (two-bladed windmills) to generate electricity; the development of fuel cell technology for on-site generation; and photovoltaic (solar cell) programs.

Despite the fact that automotive technology was developed to the point that several experimental vehicles were built at Lewis, neither electric nor gas turbine power for automotive applications has become practical. The story of the development of Stirling technology, however, is different. A Stirling engine has pistons that are inside sealed cylinders and are moved by a working gas that expands and contracts with the addition and removal of heat. In automotive applications, the heat comes from the burning of fossil fuels. The experimental vehicles can run on anything from ordinary gasoline to aftershave lotion. Stirling technology also may have application in the power system for the space station. For space uses, the source of the heat could be either solar or nuclear.

In 1987, a wind turbine with a 3.2-megawatt power rating went on line in the utility grid of the Hawaiian Electric Company. That event was the culmination of fifteen years of intensive work by Lewis engineers to harness a renewable energy source, the wind, to generate electric power. The machine has a rotor that spans more than 97 meters tip to tip and can generate more than 13 million kilowatt-hours of electrical energy annually, as much as would be used by 1,300 typical single-family homes.

A fuel cell is a device that generates electricity on site for such commercial and residential applications as apartment buildings, restaurants, retail stores, and nursing homes. In operation, natural gas or some other hydrocarbon is converted into a hydrogen-rich fuel in a fuel processor and fed to one electrode, while oxygen (in this case, from the air)

is fed to another electrode. Electricity is produced by a process similar to that by which it is produced in an automobile storage battery. Because there is no combustion, no pollution-control devices are required. Furthermore, the operation of a fuel cell is virtually noiseless.

Lewis qualified itself for its space station assignment over a period of two decades with basic research in silicon and gallium arsenide solar cell technology. Indium phosphide as a solar cell material also has been investigated. In the 1970's, research moved from the laboratory into the field, in a pilot program that put solar-powered refrigerators in developing countries around the world. The purpose of the program was to demonstrate on-site use of solar cells, in this case to provide the electrical power needed to refrigerate vaccines.

In 1986, Lewis was assigned to play a major role in the development of the propulsion system for the National AeroSpace Plane, a flight vehicle that would take off from a conventional runway, fly to orbit, maneuver in the upper atmosphere, and return to Earth to land at an airport anywhere in the world. The plane also could fly at hypersonic speeds (6,436 to 12,872 kilometers per hour) in the upper atmosphere. Other participants in the program were NASA's Langley Research Center, the Defense Department's Advanced Research Projects Agency, the Air Force, the Navy, and the Strategic Defense Initiative Organization (now called the Ballistic Missile Defense Organization). The National AeroSpace Plane study was terminated in 1994, when it was concluded that the high-temperature materials and air-breathing propulsion technology required for such prolonged high speeds within Earth's atmosphere would take many more years to mature than had originally been estimated.

The STS-50/USML-1 mission in July, 1992, put Lewis in the forefront of microgravity science; it was highlighted by the Surface Tension Driven Convection Experiment, which was built at the center. Restructuring of the International Space Station transferred the Lewis-designed electric power system to Johnson Space Center. In September, 1993, the Advanced Communications Technology Satellite (ACTS) was launched from the shuttle *Discovery*. The satellite was controlled from the ground station at Lewis. Shuttle *Atlantis* delivered the Lewis-managed Mir Cooperative Solar Array (MCSA) to the Russian space station Mir in May, 1996.

The Center contributed three experiments to the Mars Pathfinder mission that landed on July 4, 1997. The successful landing was made possible by testing of the innovative air bags at Lewis Plum Brook Station. Lewis managed the launch services for the Cassini mission to Saturn on October 15, 1997, and provided critical electronic components. Over thirty-six years of history-making achievements came to a close as Lewis transferred its launch vehicle program to the Kennedy Space Center on September 30, 1998.

Lewis provided the ion propulsion system and solar concentrator arrays for NASA's Deep Space 1 mission that launched on October 24, 1998. In December, NASA launched the first U.S. component of the International Space Station, including hardware from NASA Lewis.

Context

For the most part, the political climate in Washington, D.C., in the fall of 1957 was very negative toward space, and any enthusiasm for space research was viewed suspiciously. Against that backdrop of opinion in the capital and throughout the government, Lewis was preparing for its triennial inspection in mid-October by a group of officials and experts that included NACA headquarters personnel, members of Congress, and executives of the aeronautics industry. How should the center's space-related propulsion work be displayed? Causing even more apprehension was the question of how it would be viewed. The Soviets solved both problems.

On October 4, just days before the inspection, the Soviet Union launched Sputnik, changing forever

the nation's and the world's outlook on space exploration. When the visitors arrived, Lewis engineers proudly unveiled their work in spaceflight propellant systems and high-energy rocket propellants. The vision and eagerness of Lewis scientists to venture into the unknown had been more than vindicated.

When NASA was created by Congress in 1958, much more was involved than a mere name change and the substitution of one letter in the acronym for another. The fundamental character of the agency was to undergo a major shift, and the technology it would have to develop would take it down untrodden paths of research. Managing a different type of organization that now would be responsible for missions and operations as well as for its traditional research role would be slightly easier, however, because of the head start in technological development that Lewis had provided.

During the 1950's, Lewis pioneered many important innovations in gas turbine propulsion systems. That work improved the reliability of the gas turbine engine, and by the late 1960's commercial jet passenger service had become a commonplace means of mass transportation over long distances. The piston engine for commercial transport aircraft was gone forever. Propeller technology, however, would return.

Lewis Field and Glenn Research Center 741 Lewis had been involved in advanced propeller research from its very beginning in the 1940's. Early studies indicated the potential for good performance and fuel economy for advanced propeller designs, but with the advent of the jet engine and an abundance of low-cost fuel, propeller work was shelved in the 1950's in response to the public preference for jet-powered aircraft, which could provide fast, comfortable transportation at altitudes well above normal air turbulence.

In the 1970's, however, sharply higher fuel prices and public concern for quality of life and energy use led to research that had environmental and societal goals, and Lewis began to develop technology that would produce aircraft propulsion systems that were cleaner, quieter, and more fuel efficient. The concern for energy conservation, which became a national driving force during the 1970's, led to one of the most unusual research projects ever undertaken at Lewis: work to put propellers back on commercial transport aircraft.

In 1988, the National Aeronautics and Space Administration awarded its prestigious Collier Trophy to Lewis and the NASA/Industry Advanced Turboprop Teams—which included Hamilton- Standard Company, General Electric Company, Lockheed Missiles and Space Company, Boeing Aircraft Company, McDonnell Douglas Astronautics Company, Allison Company, and Pratt and Whitney Aircraft Division—for success in the development of advanced turboprop technology for commercial transport use. Although NACA had received the award several times and NASA has received it for astronautic achievements, this was the first time that NASA had received the award for its work in aeronautics.

—John M. Shaw

See also: Ames Research Center; Cape Canaveral and the Kennedy Space Center; Goddard Space Flight Center; Jet Propulsion Laboratory; Johnson Space Center; Langley Research Center; Marshall Space Flight Center; Space Centers, Spaceports, and Launch Sites; Space Task Group.

Further Reading

Bilstein, Roger E. *Orders of Magnitude: A History of the NACA and NASA, 1915-1989.* 2d ed. NASA SP-4406. Washington, D.C.: Government Printing Office, 1989. A revised and enlarged version of a work prepared originally for the United States' bicentennial celebration. A readable and well-illustrated volume. Covers the period from just before World War I to just before the launch of the first space shuttle in 1981. Recounts NACA's aeronautical achievements and those of Project Mercury, Project Gemini, and the Apollo Program that put Americans on the Moon and established routine access to space as a familiar concept in the American mind.

Glenn, John, with Nick Taylor. *John Glenn: A Memoir.* New York: Bantam Books, 1999. Glenn tells his life story in this well-written and very interesting autobiography. The book covers his career from his days as a Marine pilot, through his Mercury-Atlas 6 orbital mission, and onward to his flight aboard STS-95 in 1998. In between, he was a husband, a father, and a senator from Ohio.

Glover, Daniel R. *History of the Lewis Research Center.* Washington, D.C.: National Aeronautics and Space Administration, 1995. This is the story of the Lewis Research Center and the aeronautical and astronautical research conducted there. It also provides biographical information on George W. Lewis and discusses the National Advisory Committee for Aeronautics.

Graham, Robert W. *Four Giants of the Lewis Research Center.* NASA TM-83642. Cleveland, Ohio: Lewis Research Center, 1984. George W. Lewis, Hugh L. Dryden, Edward R. Sharp, and Abe Silverstein are singled out for their contributions to Lewis and to the development of aerospace technology.

Klerkx, Greg. *Lost in Space: The Fall of NASA and the Dream of a New Space Age.* New York: Pantheon Books, 2004. The premise of this work is that NASA has been stuck in Earth orbit since the Apollo era, and that space exploration has suffered as a result.

Lambright, W. Henry, ed. *Space Policy in the Twenty-First Century.* Baltimore: Johns Hopkins University Press, 2003. This book addresses a number of important questions: What will replace the space shuttle? Can the International Space Station justify its cost? Will Earth be threatened by asteroid impact? When and how will humans explore Mars?

Launius, Roger D. *NASA: A History of the U.S. Civil Space Program*. Malabar, Fla.: Krieger Publishing Company, 1994. This is an in-depth look at America's civilian space program and the establishment of the National Aeronautics and Space Administration. It chronicles the agency from its predecessor, the National Advisory Committee for Aeronautics, through the present day.

Mari, Christopher, ed. *Space Exploration*. New York: H. W. Wilson, 1999. Twenty-five articles, covering the state of the space program at the time of publication, reprinted from magazines, are divided into five sections: John H. Glenn, Jr.'s return to space, the exploration of Mars, the International Space Station, recent mining efforts by commercial industries, and new types of space vehicles and propulsion systems.

National Aeronautics and Space Administration. *NASA: The First Twenty-Five Years, 1958- 1983*. NASA EP-182. Washington, D.C.: Government Printing Office, 1983. Written in a clear, easy-to-read style, this book is meant to be a reference for teachers. It includes a history of NASA and an overview of NASA's work in various fields, including the aeronautics and energy research conducted at Lewis Research Center. Also provides descriptions of the various NASA facilities. Illustrated.

Roland, Alex. *Model Research*. NASA SP-4103. Washington, D.C.: Government Printing Office, 1985. A two-volume historical work that examines NACA as an institution. Attempts to explain how and why NACA functioned and to evaluate it as a research organization.

Sloop, John L. *Liquid Hydrogen as a Propulsion Fuel, 1945-1959*. NASA SP-4404. Washington, D.C.: Government Printing Office, 1978. A misleadingly titled book that gives, in addition to what the reader expects to find, a most lively account of some of the leading figures in the history of Lewis, their contributions, and their personalities. Much of the reading is light and enjoyable.

Lifting Bodies

Date: 1957 to 1975
Type of program: Piloted test flights

The research program on lifting bodies created a fleet of wingless vehicles designed specifically to be able to bring human explorers back to Earth from space and land them on a specified runway, like any airplane. It demonstrated that pilots could maneuver and land lifting bodies safely. The significance of this program is encapsulated in the project's unofficial motto: "Don't be rescued from outer space—fly back in style."

Key Figures

Alfred J. Eggers, Jr. (b. 1922), assistant director for research and development analysis and planning at the Ames Aeronautical Laboratory, who in 1957 conceived the original idea of lifting bodies

R. Dale Reed (1930-2005), NASA engineer who carried the concept of lifting bodies forward and introduced a conceptual design for a lifting body in the form of a truncated cone

H. Julian Allen (1910-1977), an engineer credited with determining that a blunt-nose cone was a desirable shape for a reentry vehicle

Paul Bikle (1916-1991), director of the NASA Flight Research Center, Edwards, California, who approved a program to build and test a prototype based upon the wingless concept in 1962

William "Gus" Briegleb (1912-2002), a sailplane builder who built a plywood shell over a steel frame that was successfully tested in 1963

Milton O. Thompson (1926-1993), the pilot who flew the first lifting body

Summary of the Project

Lifting bodies are wingless aircraft. Instead of wings producing lift, the body itself produces lift. In the 1950's and 1960's, these craft tested the theory that spacecraft could reenter Earth's atmosphere from space and be flown and landed like an airplane. In the atmosphere, they generate lift from the shapes of their bodies without the assistance of propellers and wings.

When an object moves in a fluid such as air, or a fluid moves past an object, the fluid and the object exert forces on each other. Sometimes engineers and scientists focus on the forces exerted by the object on the fluid, as in the case of pumps and compressors. Other times, however, the focus is on the forces exerted by the fluid on the object, as in the case of flying objects such as balloons, balls in flight, airplanes, and space vehicles during reentry into Earth's atmosphere.

The force exerted on a moving object by the surrounding fluid is divided into three perpendicular components. The component that is parallel to the direction of motion is called the drag force. The component perpendicular to the direction of motion but parallel to the direction of gravity is called the lift force. The third component is perpendicular to both the lift force and the drag force. It does not have an agreed-upon common name. If one neglects this third component, then, a simplified theory of flight evolves. It indicates that there are four forces acting upon an airplane in level flight. These are thrust, the force provided by the engine to move the plane forward; weight, the mass as affected by gravity; and lift and drag, which arise from the interaction between the air and the plane.

Lifting body design progression. From left to right: X-24A, M2-F3 and HL-10. (NASA / Dryden Flight Research Center)

While studying flight problems associated with the nose cones of ballistic missiles during reentry, engineers at the National Aeronautics and Space Administration (NASA) found that a blunt nose cone was a desirable shape to survive the aerodynamic heating associated with reentry into Earth's atmosphere. By modifying the shape of a symmetrical nose cone appropriately, engineers could produce the desired aerodynamic lift. These discoveries led to the design of reentry vehicles in the shape of modified half cones. They were flat at the top, rounded at the bottom, with twin tail fins and a rounded nose. These were known by the acronyms M-F, where "M" stood for manned and "F" for flight version. In order to indicate the successive improvements and changes made, numbers were added to each letter to indicate the version of the design: M2-F1, M2-F2, and so on.

A program to build a prototype for a lightweight but unpowered lifting body was approved at Flight Research Center (FRC) by its director, Paul Bikle, in 1962, in order to test the flight characteristics of a wingless craft. The design was affectionately called the "flying bathtub." Its construction was completed in 1963 and was designated the M2-F1. The M2-F1 had elevons, attached to each of the two rudders,

instead of ailerons (which control roll) A large flap on the trailing edge of the body acted as an elevator. The M2-F1 was tested by towing it behind a Pontiac convertible at speeds of 120 miles per hour. Hundreds of such tests were conducted. Following the successful tests, the craft was towed behind a NASA R4D tow plane (Navy version of the C-47) at higher altitudes (3,600 meters). Pilot Milt Thompson glided the M2-F1 back to the base. Since the M2-F1 was a glider, a small rocket motor was added in order to extend the landing envelope.

Dozens of M2-F1 tests were conducted successfully, which led NASA to develop heavyweight lifting bodies. These vehicles used the XLR-11 rocket engine (as had the X-1). The M2-F2 was designed to remedy control problems that were identified during the testing of the M2-F1. A major design problem resulted in airflow separation, which caused aerodynamic instability. The opening footage of the 1970's television show *The Six Million Dollar Man* showed the M2-F2, piloted by Bruce Peterson, crashing and tumbling violently along the runway. Peterson survived to fly again and the craft was rebuilt as the Northrop M2-F3 (1967) with a central rudder to correct the problem.

Horizontal landing models, the so-called HL

series, were designed as well. These heavier designs also used the XLR-11 rocket engine. The Northrop HL-10 (10 is for the tenth lifting body model to be investigated by NASA's Langley Research Center) was built by NASA to evaluate the "inverted airfoil" lifting body and delta plan form. Later, the U.S. Air Force introduced a third design concept known as the X-24 series. These craft were built by Martin Marietta and utilized an upgraded XLR-11 power plant. The first flight of the X-24A took place on April 17, 1969. After its shape was modified and new fins were added, it was renamed the X-24B and flew for the first time on August 1, 1973. The M2-F2, M2-F3, HL-10, X-24A, and X-24B were carried aloft and dropped by the same B-52 used in the X-15 program.

Contributions

Research on lifting bodies contributed greatly to the design of reusable spacecraft that land like an aircraft. The lifting bodies demonstrated the ability of pilots to maneuver and safely land wingless vehicles at a predetermined site. The absence of wings would make the extreme heat of reentry less damaging to the vehicle.

The M2-F1 tested possible lift forces and maneuverability. It demonstrated the feasibility of lifting bodies. The M2-F2 tested heavier aircraft and higher speeds. It helped to refine the design of lifting bodies. The M2-F3 tested the alteration in the shape of the fuselage by adding control surfaces to correct inherent aerodynamic instability.

The HL-10 demonstrated that a space reentry vehicle designed without air-breathing engines could be landed safely. The HL-10 design offered a great amount of internal volume for its size, meaning that an operational version would be able to carry a lot of people or cargo. The X-24A validated the concept that an unpowered space reentry vehicle could be landed safely. The X-24B evaluated "inverted airfoil" lifting (generating negative lift when level) and delta-planform (smaller surface area, lighter weight, greater maneuverability) concepts. It also

showed that an unpowered space reentry vehicle could be landed accurately.

Knowledge and experience gathered from research on lifting bodies led to the development of the space shuttle program. Specifically, it convinced designers that the shuttle's descent from Earth's orbit as an unpowered glider could be controlled and that the shuttle itself could land safely and accurately on a long landing strip, just as an airplane did.

The lifting bodies discussed above also demonstrated the limitations of aircraft without wings. Their primary limitation was their high landing speed, which made controlling them difficult and dangerous. Because of this experience, NASA engineers chose to develop a space shuttle that had wings.

Context

Project Mercury, the Gemini Program (the United States' first piloted space program), and the Apollo Program all used what are termed "ballistic reentry vehicles." During each of these programs, astronauts manually controlled the attitude of the spacecraft during orbital maneuvers, retrofire, and reentry. The Gemini spacecraft and Apollo Command Module gave the pilot some means of flying toward a relatively limited landing area. The method chosen to accomplish this goal was to offset the spacecraft's center of gravity to yield some degree of aerodynamic lift. Using the attitude control system to roll the spacecraft during its flight through the air would control the amount and direction of lift to correct any errors in the predicted landing point.

In order to have a truly reusable piloted spacecraft, it is necessary that it can perform a landing that is both controlled and accurate. This capability required more lift than ballistic reentry spacecraft could offer. By the time this need arose, engineers had accumulated considerable experience with lift. However, their major means for generating lift were either by using wings, as is done with airplanes, or by using spinning propellers, as is done on helicopters. Neither of these conventional ways would be practical during spacecraft reentry, because speeds were very high and aerodynamic heating would require too much weight. Additionally, neither wings nor propellers could survive the tremendous forces exerted on them during reentry.

If neither wings nor propellers could be used, yet lift had to be generated, it became clear that the body of the reentry vehicle itself had to generate the required lift. Unfortunately, the air speed was too great for safe landing by a returning spacecraft. The space shuttle program abandoned the lifting-body concept in favor of a winged orbiter.

After the concept of lifting bodies was abandoned and more or less forgotten, the lifting body reappeared as the HL-20, also known as Assured Crew Return Vehicle (ACRV), the Crew Emergency Return Vehicle (CERV), and the Personnel Launch System (PLS). NASA Langley Research Center designed the piloted space plane as a backup to the space shuttle (in case it was abandoned or grounded) and as a CERV from the Freedom space station. It was designed for two flight crewpersons and eight passengers to make a piloted landing at an airfield on landing gear. Although it was studied by contractors and a full-size mock-up was built, the design was not selected for further development.

Instead, the Russian Soyuz spacecraft was designated as the International Space Station CERV. When doubts about the availability of Soyuz developed in 1995, NASA proceeded with the design of the X-38. A NASA Johnson concept, it was a smaller version of the X-24 lifting body with a parafoil to assist in landing. The one key difference is that the X-38 does not land conventionally on wheels on a runway. Instead, the X-38 deploys a rectangular parachute as it nears the ground and floats to a landing. This method was chosen because NASA learned during its earlier research that lifting bodies have unsafe landing characteristics. The X-38 was designed for indefinite in-orbit storage and uses cold nitrogen gas for attitude control. It was sized for launch on the space shuttle with a wingspan that would fit inside the shuttle cargo bay.

On April 29, 2002, NASA announced the cancellation of the X-38 program due to budget pressures associated with the International Space Station. The X-38 was two years short of completing its flight-test phase.

—Josué Njock Libii and Russell R. Tobias

See also: Launch Vehicles: Reusable; National Aeronautics and Space Administration; National AeroSpace Plane.

Further Reading

Hallion, Richard. *On the Frontier: Flight Research at Dryden, 1946-1981*. NASA SP-4303. Washington, D.C.: Government Printing Office, 1984. A comprehensive look at flight research at Dryden, including the periods before and after the lifting bodies research program.

Reed, R. Dale, and Darlene Lister. *Wingless Flight: The Lifting Body Story*. Lexington: University Press of Kentucky, 2002. A definitive book on the story of the lifting bodies and of R. Dale Reed. Working in their spare time (because they could not initially get official permission), Reed and his team of engineers demonstrated the potential of the design that led to the space shuttle. The book takes readers behind the scenes with just the right blend of technical information and fascinating detail.

Thompson, Milton O., and Curtis Peebles. *Flying Without Wings: NASA Lifting Bodies and the Birth of the Space Shuttle*. Washington, D.C.: Smithsonian Institution Press, 1999. Thompson, a test pilot with the lifting bodies research program, and Peebles, a historian, join forces to give an account of the lifting body test programs.

Lunar Exploration

Date: 1958 to 2019
Type of program: Lunar exploration

The "Space Race" between the United States and the Soviet Union began in 1957, when the Soviets launched two satellites. In response, the United States Department of Defense was authorized to begin lunar exploration. In April, 1961, Russian cosmonaut Yuri A. Gagarin became the first human being in space. In May, 1961—shortly after Alan Shepard's suborbital flight—President John F. Kennedy proposed that the United States send a man to the Moon. Both political desire and a quest for scientific knowledge motivated many lunar missions in the following decades.

Key Figures

Homer E. Newell (1915-1983), NASA associate administrator

Harold Masursky (1923-1990), a scientist at the Jet Propulsion Laboratory

Lee R. Scherer (b. 1919), NASA director of Apollo Lunar Exploration

Clifford H. Nelson (1914-2004), assistant director of Langley Research Center

Robert J. Helberg (1906-1967), manager of the Lunar Orbiter program, Boeing Aircraft Company

Summary of the Missions

The American lunar exploration program began in 1957, before the creation of NASA, as a response to the Cold War political challenge issued by the launching of the first two Earth satellites by the Soviet Union. The U.S. Department of Defense (DoD), through its Advanced Research Projects Agency (ARPA), authorized the Air Force to launch three 45-kilogram Pioneer probes toward the Moon using the Thor-Able booster. The Army was also authorized to prepare two smaller 6- kilogram Pioneer probes for launch by the Juno 2 booster.

The first Air Force Pioneer met with disaster on August 17, 1958, when its Thor booster exploded in flight. A subsequent attempt on October 11, 1958, successfully sent Pioneer 1 into space. However, trajectory inaccuracies caused the probe to fall back to Earth after reaching 115,000 kilometers in altitude. Pioneer 2 also suffered launch failure in November, 1958. The Army rocket team successfully lofted Pioneer 3 into space on December 6, 1958, but again, a faulty aim doomed the probe to fall back to Earth after reaching an altitude of 107,000 kilometers.

Before the next Pioneer could be readied, the Soviet Union succeeded in launching the first craft to break free of Earth's gravity. Russian lunar efforts had previously suffered three secret launch failures in 1958, but on January 2, 1959, Luna 1 left Earth. The 361-kilogram spacecraft, popularly called *Mechta*, or "dream," was intended to hit the Moon, but a guidance error caused the craft to pass 5,955 kilometers from the Moon and enter solar orbit.

An American probe followed the Russian craft on March 3, 1959, when the Army succeeded in launching Pioneer 4 into solar orbit. However, the probe passed 56,350 kilometers from the Moon, too far away to return any lunar data.

Russian lunar efforts achieved two more successes in 1959, when Luna 2 impacted the Moon on September 14, and Luna 3, launched October 4, looped around the Moon and returned crude photographs of its previously unseen far side.

Following Pioneer 4, American lunar efforts were directed by the newly created National Aeronautics and Space Administration (NASA). A heavier series of Pioneer spacecraft, originally designed to study the planet Venus, were diverted toward lunar studies in response to the Russian Luna 3 success. All three launch attempts in 1960 failed when their more powerful Atlas-Able boosters failed in flight. NASA also created two new robotic lunar exploration programs: the Ranger series, which were both to rough-land instruments and to take close-up photographs of the lunar surface before crashing and the Surveyor soft landers, which were to deposit scientific instruments on the Moon.

Initially, the Ranger program had no better luck reaching the Moon than did the Pioneers. Rangers 3, 4, and 5 were to rough-land seismic instruments on the Moon, but after successful launches in 1962, all failed on the way to the Moon. Rangers 6 through 9 were lunar impactors, which were to photograph the surface during terminal descent. After a successful launch on January 30, 1964, Ranger 6 struck the Moon but failed to return any pictures. The long-delayed American lunar success finally came on July 31, 1964, when Ranger 7 returned close-up photographs of Mare Cognitum. Rangers 8 and 9 also returned close-up images in February and March of 1965.

Russian's Luna 9 spacecraft, launched January 31, 1966, achieved a soft landing on the Moon. The craft's 100-kilogram landing spacecraft returned the first images from the lunar surface and recorded radiation levels. Luna 13, launched December 21, 1966, repeated the landing at a different site.

American efforts to soft-land on the Moon achieved success on the first attempt when Surveyor 1 landed on the Moon's Oceanus Procellarum on June 1, 1966. The 995-kilogram lander was considered a test flight and carried only a 7- kilogram television camera. Six additional Surveyor craft were successfully launched toward the Moon in 1966 and 1967. Of these, Surveyors 2 and 4 were lost before landing. The five successful landings returned a total of 87,700 images from the Moon's surface.

The Lunar Orbiter program was conceived from the need for detailed reconnaissance of the lunar surface in order to select suitable Apollo landing sites. The resulting 387-kilogram spacecraft carried a photographic package adapted from a military spy satellite and could map portions of the Moon at 1-meter resolution. All five Lunar Orbiter missions launched in 1966 and 1967 were successful. Of the 2,110 photographic frames available, the Lunar Orbiters returned 1,650 successful images; 78 percent of the photography was scientifically useful.

Between 1969 and 1972, six Apollo piloted landings were carried out. Beginning with the historic first piloted landing on July 20, 1969, Apollos 11 through 17 placed twelve American astronauts on the Moon's surface. Neil A. Armstrong became the first human to set foot on the Moon, while Eugene Cernan was the last human on the Moon in the twentieth century. Apollo 13 did not achieve a landing after an oxygen tank explosion forced the crew to make an emergency return to Earth in April, 1970.

Although the Soviet piloted lunar-landing program was not carried out following the success of the American landings, Russia continued the robotic exploration of the Moon. Luna 16, launched September 12, 1970, soft-landed and robotically returned 101 grams of lunar material to the Earth. This feat was repeated by Luna 20, launched February 14, 1972, and again by Luna 24, launched August 9, 1976. The latter used a specially designed drilling mechanism to retrieve a 1.6-meter core sample. Additional Soviet lunar launches on November 10, 1970, and January 8, 1973, deposited two remote-controlled rovers, Lunokhods 1 and 2, on the Moon. These eight-wheeled robots traversed a combined 47 kilometers of the lunar surface photographing and chemically analyzing the lunar soil.

Since the 1976 Luna 24 landing, no further lunar missions of any kind were carried out by either the

United States or Russia until January 25, 1994, when the U.S. DoD again entered the lunar exploration field. The Clementine spacecraft was placed into orbit around the Moon to gather lunar mineralogical data during a test of military missile detection sensors. On January 6, 1998, NASA also returned to the Moon when it placed the Lunar Prospector spacecraft in lunar orbit to continue lunar mineralogy studies.

The SMART-1 (Small Missions for Advanced Research in Technology 1) is a Lunar Orbiter designed to test spacecraft technologies for future missions. The primary technology being tested is a solar-powered ion drive. It carries an experimental deep-space telecommunications system and an instrument payload to monitor the ion drive and study the Moon. The primary scientific objectives of the mission are to return data on the geology, morphology, topography, mineralogy, geochemistry, and exospheric environment of the Moon. SMART-1 was launched as a secondary payload on September 27, 2003, by the Ariane-5 Cyclad booster.

Lunar Reconnaissance Orbiter (LRO) was sent into orbit about the Moon in 2009 for prolonged lunar research and imaging. LRO had been envisioned to support the planned Vision For Space Exploration which had called for astronauts to return to the Moon as part of the Constellation Program. LRO continued to provide useful information about the Moon long after the Obama Administration cancelled the Constellation Program. In 2019 NASA was challenged to send the first astronauts of the twenty-first century back to the Moon within five years. LRO would continue to provide support to lunar exploration begun over fifty years earlier at the dawn of the Space Age.

Contributions

Although they failed to reach the Moon, Pioneers 1 and 3 made fundamental discoveries by confirming that two zones of high radiation, known as the Van Allen radiation belts, were trapped by Earth's magnetic field and centered at 4,800 kilometers and 11,250 kilometers in altitude. Pioneer 4 demonstrated that above the Van Allen radiation belts out to lunar distances, the normal space radiation environment was low enough to allow humans to safely travel to the Moon.

Prior to the first landing, estimates of the conditions on the lunar surface ranged from hard rock to soft, non-supportive, loose dust, which would swallow a landing craft like quicksand. The successful Luna 9 landing established that the lunar surface would indeed support a spacecraft. Subsequent television pictures from the first Surveyor showed that one of its own footpads had indented the lunar surface only a few centimeters, further demonstrating that the Moon could support a piloted lander. The mechanical and chemical soil analysis performed by the final three Surveyors suggested a general model for lunar composition, which was later confirmed by examination of samples returned by Apollo astronauts.

The most significant result of the space-based photographic reconnaissance of the Moon by both U.S. and Russian probes was the determination that the vast majority of lunar surface features were sculpted by the impacts of meteors, asteroids, and comets, and not by volcanic activity, as previously supposed. Photography also established that chains of craters, even those not radially aligned with nearby large craters, were in fact created by impact ejecta and not volcanism along faults or fractures. It was further established that many volcanic-appearing features associated with individual large craters were the result of impact melting, not true volcanism.

As seen from Earth, the Moon's surface is divided into two geologic types: the light-colored, heavily cratered highlands called terrae, and the dark-colored smoother regions called maria (plural for *mare*, the Latin word for sea). Over its global surface, maria cover 17 percent of the Moon. Orbital tracking of the Lunar Orbiter spacecraft revealed that their initial orbits did not follow that expected for a craft circling a homogeneous body. Instead, areas of increasing gravity centered over the circular lunar maria perturbed the craft. These dark, relatively flat areas were assumed to be volcanic flows across the surface. It was realized that the circular lunar maria were giant impact basins, which had slowly filled with basalt over a period of time. As more basalt flowed into the basins, it slumped and became denser than the surrounding lunar crust. These gravitationally stronger areas are called mascons, for mass concentrations.

Of all the terrestrial planets and their satellites, the Earth and Moon are most like a double-planet system. However, comparing Earth's mean density of 5.5 grams per cubic centimeter and the Moon's mean density of 3.3 grams per cubic centimeter shows marked differences in the overall composition of both worlds. The Moon possesses less volatile substances such as water, sodium, and lead.

The mission of Lunar Prospector ended on July 31, 1999, when it was deliberately targeted to impact in a permanently shadowed area of a crater near the lunar south pole. It was hoped that the impact would liberate water vapor from the suspected ice deposits in the crater and that the plume would be detectable from Earth; however, no plume was observed.

SMART-1 began to monitor the illumination of the lunar poles even before arriving at its final science orbit in March, 2005. The Moon's rotational axis is only 1.5° inclined to the ecliptic plane. This orientation allows areas to exist at the bottom of near-polar craters that do not see direct sunlight and where ice might be trapped. On the other hand, at higher elevations on the rims of polar craters, there are areas that see the Sun for more than half of the time. Following successful lunar orbital insertion, SMART-1's mission was extended a year. It was expected to continue collecting data through August, 2006. The engine would then be used to lower the orbit pericenter to 300-kilometer altitude. It was planned to nominally spend six months in lunar orbit mapping the Moon's surface and evaluating the new technologies onboard.

LRO identified and imaged Apollo program landing sites, and found evidence of water ice at the Moon's south polar region, enough to support a Moon base which was unofficially envisioned as part of the return to the Moon eventually supported by the Trump Administration.

A relatively inexpensive spacecraft identified as LADEE or Lunar Atmosphere and Dust Environment Explorer launched from the Wallops Island facility in southeastern Virginia on September 7, 2013, and performed a seven-month-long investigation of the Moon's tenuous atmosphere and the nature of dust in low-lunar orbit. LADEE found evidence of helium, neon, and argon in the lunar exosphere. After concluding its mission, LADEE was purposed crashed into the far side of the Moon to remove it from orbit.

Context

In the 1950's, spaceflight visionary Wernher von Braun proposed an orderly progression of space exploration events that would ultimately result in humans landing on Mars. An Earth-orbiting space station and piloted flights to the Moon would be stepping stones to the Red Planet. Scientists realized that robotic spacecraft would precede humans to the Moon and determine the general lunar characteristics as the precursors for eventual piloted expeditions. However, this blueprint for piloted space exploration was discarded after the Soviet Union succeeded in launching Sputnik, the first artificial Earth satellite. The political shock of this event was seen by the Western world as a challenge to demonstrate which political system, the free West or the Communist-controlled East, possessed the best industrial and technological base.

The "Space Race" between the United States and the Soviet Union, born from the response to Sputnik, escalated on April 12, 1961, when the Russian cosmonaut Yuri A. Gagarin became the first human being in space. A long string of Soviet technological space "firsts," and American political setbacks on Earth, such as the failed Bay of Pigs invasion of Communist-controlled Cuba, led President John F. Kennedy to seek a national goal in space that offered a reasonable chance of exceeding Soviet efforts. In May, 1961, President Kennedy boldly proposed that the United States send a man to the Moon and safely return him to Earth by the end of the decade. Thus, the U.S. space program was spurred heavily by a political desire to restore American international prestige, and a political timetable was established to conduct the first piloted landing on the lunar surface.

An unfortunate side effect of President Kennedy's mandate was the abandonment of most lunar science. The rush to achieve piloted lunar success before the Soviet Union reduced the Ranger and Surveyor lunar probes to engineering support missions for the piloted landing effort. Any lunar science gained was of secondary importance to the politically driven goal of landing humans on the Moon by the end of the 1960's. However, during the time of active lunar exploration in the 1960's and 1970's, the geology of the Earth was not well understood either. This lent validity to the idea that an understanding of the Moon's geology was essential to understanding the geologic composition of the Earth.

Technical problems in perfecting the complex Ranger spacecraft delayed the results from that program. By the time Ranger succeeded in reaching the Moon in July, 1964, the program was no longer of any direct benefit to the Apollo Program because the design of the piloted lunar lander had already been frozen. Similarly, the Surveyor Program suffered delays when its Centaur booster encountered technical problems and lacked the power needed to loft a full complement of exploratory instruments to the Moon. Conceived a year before Apollo as a science program, Surveyor was thus turned primarily into an engineering test to see whether a soft landing on the Moon was possible.

The early piloted landings of Apollos 11 through 14 were scientifically conservative. Yet, even as the initial piloted lunar landing was conducted by Apollo 11, subsequent missions devoted to lunar science were canceled by Congress. Only Apollos 15 through 17 were upgraded to true lunar scientific efforts.

After four decades of lunar exploration scientists have still not conclusively answered how the Moon was formed almost 4.5 billion years ago. However, post-Apollo studies of the chemical makeup of the Moon now lend strong support to the idea that the Moon was created from the debris flung into space by the impact on Earth of a Mars-sized body. This theory is supported by the similarity between the minerals in the Earth's crust and the composition of the Moon, and the fact that the Moon has no large iron core like that of Earth.

Rock samples returned by the Apollo expeditions show the Moon is lifeless and contains no fossils or organic compounds. The lunar regolith, or surface layer of dust, rubble, and rock fragments created and stirred by billions of years of meteor bombardment, is composed primarily of three basic rock types; volcanic basalts, anorthosites, which are crystalline slow-cooled volcanic rock, and breccias, made up of previously shattered rock fragments welded back together by meteor impact.

The Apollo seismic experiments showed the Moon possesses a crust, mantle, and small core, and were thus differentiated by global melting early in its history. At that time, the Moon was covered with a magma ocean. Today, the lunar highlands are the remains of lower-density rocks that floated to the surface of the early global magma cover. The crust is about three times thicker than Earth's, and the mantle surrounds an iron core that is less than 25 percent of the Moon's radius. Below a 1,000-kilometer depth, the lunar interior is still semi-molten.

The repercussions of the singular national space goal of landing humans on the Moon before 1970 still affect the space programs of both the United

States and Russia. Once the political goal of a piloted lunar landing was achieved, funding for future lunar exploration was severely cut. By the beginning of the twenty-first century, both the United States and Russian space programs had abandoned the technological means for sending humans to the Moon.

—*Robert V. Reeves*

See also: Apollo Program; Apollo Program: Geological Results; Apollo Program: Lunar Lander Training Vehicles; Apollo Program: Lunar Module; Apollo Program: Orbital and Lunar Surface Experiments; Clementine Mission to the Moon; Lunar Orbiters; Lunar Prospector; Ranger Program; Surveyor Program.

Further Reading

Beattie, Donald. *Taking Science to the Moon: Lunar Experiments and the Apollo Program*. Baltimore: Johns Hopkins University Press, 2001. Discusses the struggles to include science payloads as part of the Apollo Program.

Burrows, William E. *This New Ocean: The Story of the First Space Age*. New York: Random House, 1998. An excellent chronology of the Space Age. Good narrative of how the civilian and military space programs grew from their Cold War infancy to the multi-billion dollar programs of today.

Harland, David M. *Exploring the Moon: The Apollo Expeditions*. New York: Springer-Verlag, 1999. A very readable history of lunar exploration. Concentrates heavily on the Apollo piloted landings, but also reviews robotic explorations both before and following the Apollo flights.

Kelly, Thomas J. *Moon Lander: How We Developed the Apollo Lunar Module*. Washington, D.C.: Smithsonian Institution Press, 2001. Grumman Flight Director Engineer Kelly gives a firsthand account of designing, building, testing, and flying the Apollo Lunar Module.

Kozloski, Lillian D. *U.S. Space Gear: Outfitting the Astronaut*. Washington, D.C.: Smithsonian Institution Press, 1994. A museum specialist at the National Air and Space Museum starts with the earliest suits, for high-altitude aviation, and traces the space suit to the current version for the space shuttle.

McDougall, Walter A. *The Heavens and the Earth: A Political History of the Space Age*. 2d ed. Baltimore: Johns Hopkins University Press, 1997. A political history of the Space Age. This well-researched and heavily footnoted historical text describes and analyzes the decisions by the leaders of the United States and the Soviet Union and their effects on the respective space programs. Relates how the American and Soviet space programs became an integral part of Cold War politics.

Nicks, Oran. *Far Travelers: The Exploring Machines*. NASA SP-480. Washington, D.C.: Scientific and Technical Information Branch, 1985. Presents the story of the exploration of the solar system from the perspective of one of the NASA managers who oversaw the development of many robotic lunar and planetary exploratory missions.

Ordway, Frederick I., III, and Mitchell Sharpe. *The Rocket Team*. Burlington, Ont.: Apogee Books, 2003. Discloses much previously classified information about Wernher von Braun's rocketeers, particularly involving the British intelligence effort to learn about Hitler's "vengeance weapons." This revised edition includes a CD-ROM, which includes rare videos and images of the Rocket Team at work.

Reeves, Robert. *The Superpower Space Race: An Explosive Rivalry Across the Solar System*. New York: Plenum Publishing, 1994. A history of the scientific, technical, and political aspects of the robotic exploration of the Moon and planets by the United States and Russia. Presents the history of how America and Russia reached the Moon and planets so quickly early in the Space Age, the Cold War politics that accelerated exploratory programs, and the scientific knowledge gained from these explorations.

Wilhelms, Don E. *To a Rocky Moon: A Geologist's History of Lunar Exploration.* Tucson: University of Arizona Press, 1993. A comprehensive overview of the exploration of the Moon by one of the leading geologic investigators during the Apollo piloted landings. Provides extensive insights into how crewed and robotic lunar exploration was carried out and presents the results of these investigations.

Wilhelms, Don E. *The Geologic History of the Moon.* Scouts Valley, California: Create Space Independent Publishing Platform (Amazon), 2014. Spans the discipline of lunar geology. Considered by some as a seminal work in the field. For technical audiences, but accessible to the interested reader.

Lunar Orbiters

Date: August 10, 1966, to January 31, 1968
Type of program: Lunar exploration

The Lunar Orbiter program was one of three robotic spacecraft programs designed to help scientists select safe landing sites on the Moon for the Apollo Program. In one year, the orbiters provided more new information about the Moon than had been gathered in hundreds of years of observation from Earth.

Key Figures

Homer E. Newell (1915-1983), NASA administrator

Harold Masursky (1923-1990), scientist at the Jet Propulsion Laboratory

Lee R. Scherer (b. 1919), director of Apollo Lunar Exploration, NASA

Clifford H. Nelson (1914-2004), assistant director of Langley Research Center

Robert J. Helberg (1906-1967), manager of the Lunar Orbiter program, Boeing Aircraft Company

Summary of the Technology

The 385-kilogram Lunar Orbiter spacecraft was a spaceborne photographic laboratory. Consistent with the program's primary mission, the major instrumentation aboard the Lunar Orbiters was the photographic subassembly made up of a camera with two lenses—a field lens and a telephoto lens for extreme close-up views—housed in a pressurized and temperature-controlled container. The two lenses operated simultaneously. The camera frame, film supply, and other mechanisms were the same for the two lenses. Exposed film was developed in flight by a damp, monochemical process into a high-quality photographic negative, which was then dried by a miniature heater. A tiny beam of light about as thick as a human hair then scanned the completed negative and converted it into electrical signals for radio transmission back to Earth.

As the target area moved into the sunlit zone, the Lunar Orbiter changed altitude, moving from 200 kilometers to about 46 kilometers (Orbiter 1 went within 39.7 kilometers of the surface), in order to get closer to the Moon's landscape. Each exposure of the dual-lens camera simultaneously exposed one high-resolution and one medium-resolution frame. An overlap of 50 percent or more of the medium-resolution photographs permitted stereo viewing, which discloses surface details not readily apparent from single images. The photographic system allowed versatility in selecting the site to be photographed. Exposed film was developed and stored on a take-up reel for later transmission to ground antennae.

On the ground, a series of antennae picked up the transmitted radio signals and displayed data line-by-line on a kinescope, which looks like a television tube. Cameras on the ground were used to photograph the image on the tube in 35-millimeter film strips from which 23-by-36-centimeter photographs were made. Data recorded on film aboard the Lunar Orbiter also documented the time, spacecraft altitude, location, lighting conditions, and other information needed for analysis by scientists. The first two Lunar Orbiters, for example, covered more than 48,270 square kilometers of landing sites.

Orbiter 3 returned images of those same areas in a confirmation mission.

Without the solar panels and antennae, the Lunar Orbiter spacecraft was about 1.5 meters in diameter and 1.6 meters high. At the time of launch, the solar panels were folded up under the spacecraft base, and the antennae were fixed against the side of the structure. A payload shroud covered the entire spacecraft during the launch phase to protect the structure from atmospheric conditions that might have caused damage.

The spacecraft structure consisted essentially of a main equipment mounting deck and an upper module supported by trusses and an arch. The module supported the control engine and propellant tanks as well as the high-pressure nitrogen tank, which provided pressurization for the engine feed system and attitude control thrusters (a spacecraft's

attitude is its pointing position during flight in reference to some fixed object in space; if the craft began to "fall over," attitude control thrusters automatically spewed nitrogen gas through small jets and forced the craft to return to its original position).

Lunar Orbiter spacecraft launched from Complex 13 at Cape Canaveral, Florida, at approximately three-month intervals throughout the overall project. The launch vehicle for Lunar Orbiter was a combination of two rockets—a 27.4-meter-tall, two-stage Atlas-Agena D rocket. The Atlas rocket sent the payload to about 136 kilometers and then shut down and separated from the group, leaving the Agena to boost the Lunar Orbiter into orbit. The protective payload shroud also was ejected at that time. The Agena booster then ignited and continued pushing its payload forward. Once the Agena established a trajectory to the Moon, it, too, shut down

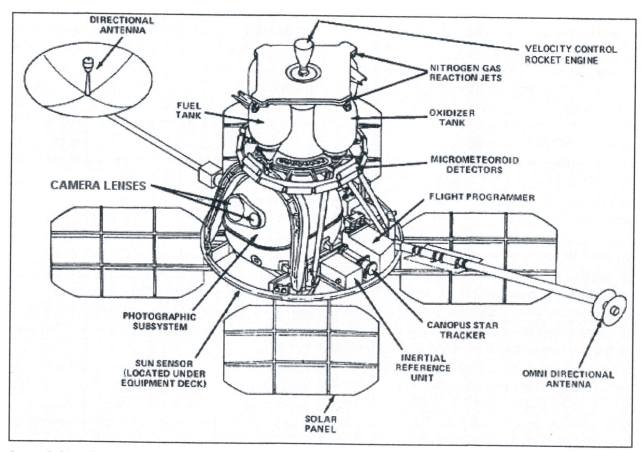

Lunar Orbiter diagram. (NASA)

and separated, leaving only the Lunar Orbiter flying through translunar space. The work of the boosters was finished; the work of the Lunar Orbiter now began.

Early in translunar flight, the Lunar Orbiter solar panels opened out, and the two antennae opened. Control of the mission was then transferred from Cape Kennedy to the Space Flight Operations facility at the Jet Propulsion Laboratory (JPL), in Pasadena, California, which would control and command the Lunar Orbiter for the mission's duration. The spacecraft then turned so that the solar panels faced the Sun and the Sun sensor aboard the craft could identify the Sun as its reference point in space. In addition, Lunar Orbiter had a star-tracker sensor to fix on the star Canopus as another reference point. The journey to the Moon took about three days.

As Lunar Orbiter reached the vicinity of its target, its speed was decreased, allowing the Moon's gravitational field to capture the craft and place it in an elliptical orbit. Orbital adjustments were made by the spacecraft over about three orbits to establish a correct orbital path. A single orbital path of a Lunar Orbiter took approximately three and a half hours.

All five Lunar Orbiters carried instrumentation for additional scientific investigation of the Moon. Information was transmitted about the density of micrometeoroids in the vicinity of the lunar environment, the frequency and severity of solar flares, and the extent of magnetically trapped particles. Specific tracking techniques were designed to refine data about the Moon's gravity and shape.

The basic design of the Lunar Orbiter spacecraft was so reliable and yet versatile that it was never changed during the five flights. At the end of each separate mission, the spacecraft was intentionally crashed into the lunar surface to prevent complications of possible overlapping radio signals from subsequent spacecraft operating near or on the lunar surface. Lunar Orbiters 1, 2, and 3 were downed on the Moon's far side.

Orbiter 1 surveyed sixteen potential Apollo landing sites; Orbiter 2 examined thirteen secondary landing sites and captured the crash site of Ranger 8. Orbiter 3 surveyed forty-one Apollo landing sites and captured Surveyor 1 sitting at its landing site. Orbiter 5 examined five Apollo sites.

Some mechanical anomalies occurred during several flights, most relating to the camera subsystem, but only slight modifications to the original design of the spacecraft were necessary. On Orbiter 1, problems with the camera caused high-resolution film to blur, making 25 percent of its images unusable. The film advance mechanism on Lunar Orbiter 3 broke after achieving only 182 frames, or about 72 percent of its work. Because of the intense heat of the Sun directly on the flat panel protecting the main instruments, several hundred small mirrors, each measuring about 2.5 centimeters square, were added to the decks of Orbiters 4 and 5 to reflect sunbeams and keep the temperature within tolerable limits inside the spacecraft's thermal blanket.

The five orbiters received and executed about twenty-five thousand commands. They performed more than two thousand maneuvers without a failure. In essence, the Lunar Orbiter spacecraft design was an excellent one for the mission. By January 31, 1968, the last orbiter was allowed to impact with the Moon's surface to free up low-altitude lunar space for upcoming piloted Apollo operations.

Contributions

Five Lunar Orbiter missions took place from August, 1966, to January, 1968. During this time, all five spacecraft recorded imagery of the Moon's surface, although nearly all the mission's photographic requirements were satisfied by Lunar Orbiters 1, 2, and 3. As a result, Lunar Orbiters 4 and 5 were assigned chiefly scientific activities, although a few photographic images were recorded on each flight.

Lunar Orbiter missions increased knowledge of the Moon tenfold and represented a quantum leap in understanding the Moon as a body. The urgency of

Lunar Orbiter 3 image of the Moon taken in 1967. (NASA)

As a result of combined Lunar Orbiter and Surveyor photographs, eight landing sites were chosen from an original list of about thirty sites along the Moon's equator. The list of eight sites was then reduced to three or four areas in three lunar sea regions—the Sea of Tranquility, Central Bay, and Ocean of Storms. Orbiter imagery of potential landing sites was sufficiently detailed that surface features as small as 1 meter across could be seen in the telephoto images and 8 meters in the wide-angle photograph. By comparison, the smallest objects on the Moon that can be seen through telescopes on Earth are about 0.08 kilometer across.

For the first time, the Moon's hidden side was almost completely mapped. While circling the Moon on August 8, 1967, Lunar Orbiter 5 recorded the first image of Earth from the Moon, capturing a nearly full Earth view. The missions provided the first definitive information about the Moon's gravitational field, and Lunar Orbiter 1 captured the image of the area where the earlier Surveyor 1 spacecraft had soft-landed. Finally, the mission provided the first views of the Moon's poles, as well as the entire areas of the eastern and western limbs (which are only partially observable from Earth).

the missions to enable scientists to find suitable landing sites for Apollo astronauts was equaled by the need to determine the nature of the environment in order to provide protection for astronauts exposed to the lunar condition.

During the eight hundred days of the five missions, the Lunar Orbiters recorded only eighteen meteoroid hits, in a random distribution pattern, putting to rest fears that moonwalking astronauts would suffer from micrometeoroid bombardment. Radiation levels recorded near the Moon were generally low. Occasional solar flares registered relatively high levels on the radiation-detection instruments.

Maps produced from contributions of the Lunar Orbiter missions are infinitely more detailed and point-accurate than were any previous lunar maps. Stereo views of lunar surface features enabled scientists to calculate near-precise dimensions of craters, crater walls, mountains, valleys and rilles, and scarps, and to speculate on the origins of a number of special features, such as the meandering Prinz Valleys near the Harbinger Mountain. Detailed maps and individual stereo views of various regions significantly increased scientific knowledge about the possible origins of densely cratered areas, mountain ranges, and possible volcanic sites. An oblique view of Crater Copernicus, imaged by Orbiter 2 from an altitude of 45 kilometers, was hailed by scientists as "the picture of the century."

Context

Lunar Orbiter missions were sandwiched among three successful Ranger missions and six Surveyor soft-landing missions to the once-forbidden and hostile world of the Moon. An immense body of information was needed about the physical nature of the Moon before a successful crewed expedition to the stark lunar surface could be mounted. Before then, the unanswered questions about the Moon and about human survival there were nearly endless and included everything from the possible danger of unusually high dosages of radiation (the Moon has no atmosphere to protect it from radiation) that might kill even a thick-suited astronaut, to such mundane puzzles as the distance a person could walk in the deep lunar dust. In 1966, NASA was trying to design a lunar exploration schedule and had to have answers. Lunar Orbiter provided some of those answers.

In the 1960's, it was understood that, if Americans were to reach the Moon before the Russians, if astronauts were to survive the ordeal of the Moon mission, if the United States were to regain international prestige, then it was necessary to define the Moon in understandable terms. The primary task facing NASA was to obtain detailed photographs of selected areas near the Moon's equator to help space scientists choose the safest sites for landings by Apollo astronauts. The Apollo zone of interest lay along the Moon's equator in an area covering east and west longitude 45° and 5° north and south latitude on the Moon's front face. Each of the landing sites was an oval measuring about 4.8 by 8 kilometers, with an approach path 48 kilometers long for the Lunar Module (LM). At the 48-kilometer point,

the LM would be at an altitude of 7,620 meters. Terrain under the approach path had to be familiar to the astronauts. The actual touchdown point for the module would have to be at least 7.6 meters square, free of craters, and sloping not more than 7°.

Although the primary objective of the Lunar Orbiter program was to search for and identify safe landing sites, the overall result of the five missions was something close to miraculous, for what scientists discovered in the process was an entirely new concept of the Moon. Extremely detailed images of lunar topography showed a lunar surface that humans had never seen before and allowed study of lunar terrain features that had not been possible using only Earth-based telescopic instrumentation. In addition to their photographic and measuring functions, the Orbiters served as tracking targets for NASA's Manned Space Flight Network. They provided training for tracking station crews and were used to verify computer programs and orbit determinations for Apollo flights.

Americans were latecomers to the task of photographing the Moon at close range. At the same time that the Ranger-Surveyor-Orbiter triad was at work, the Soviets had already hard-landed Luna 2 near Crater Archimedes in September, 1959. In October of the same year, Luna 3 photographed the Moon's far side and sent the images streaming back to Earth. Then, in January of 1966, six months before the Lunar Orbiter 1 mission, the Soviets were the first to soft-land a photographic spacecraft, Luna 9, onto the Moon in the Ocean of Storms. While television pictures of the surrounding surface were not up to the quality of American photography, the landing proved that lunar soil was shallow enough to support a standing human.

Lunar Orbiter photography provided the definitive source of geographical information about the Moon until the Clementine mission mapped the Moon nearly three decades later with improved technology, providing greater coverage. In fact, enough imagery was generated by the five missions to keep researchers occupied for at least half a century. These images, the photographs taken by the six teams of astronauts who walked on the lunar surface, and those taken by the lone astronaut from within orbiting Command Modules, opened a new era in the scientific study of the Moon. Decades after the conclusion of the Lunar Orbiter program an effort was launched to restore the Lunar Orbiter photographs with modern digital technology even as a new far more sophisticated spacecraft, the Lunar Reconnaissance Orbiter, was busy mapping the Moon and preparing the way for a proposed second wave of human exploration of the Moon.

—*Thomas W. Becker*

See also: Apollo Program; Apollo Program: Orbital and Lunar Surface Experiments; Clementine Mission to the Moon; Explorers 1-7; Launch Vehicles; Lunar Exploration; Lunar Prospector; Ranger Program; Surveyor Program; Viking Program.

Further Reading

Burrows, William E. *This New Ocean: The Story of the First Space Age*. New York: Random House, 1998. This is a comprehensive history of the human conquest of space, covering everything from the earliest attempts at spaceflight through the voyages near the end of the twentieth century. Burrows is an experienced journalist, who has reported for *The New York Times*, *The Washington Post*, and *The Wall Street Journal*. There are many photographs and an extensive source list. Interviewees in the book include Isaac Asimov, Alexei Leonov, Sally K. Ride, and James A. Van Allen.

Cortright, Edgar M., ed. *Apollo Expeditions to the Moon*. NASA SP-350. Washington, D.C.: Government Printing Office, 1975. The best authoritative reference work on the U.S. assault on the Moon, this book includes an excellent but brief review of the Lunar Orbiter program. Included in the review are diagrams and photographs of the spacecraft, mission sequences, and lunar photographing sequences. The volume's most important value is its overall view of the Apollo Program, with the entire American space program as its background.

Gatland, Kenneth. *The Illustrated Encyclopedia of Space Technology: A Comprehensive History of Space Exploration*. New York: Salamander, 1989. The entire history of spaceflight is compiled in this comprehensive encyclopedia, including a brief description of the Lunar Orbiter program. This reliable reference includes illustrations and color photographs.

Heppenheimer, T. A. *Countdown: A History of Space Flight*. New York: John Wiley, 1997. A detailed historical narrative of the human conquest of space. Heppenheimer traces the development of piloted flight through the military rocketry programs of the era preceding World War II. Covers both the American and the Soviet attempts to place vehicles, spacecraft, and humans into the hostile environment of space. More than a dozen pages are devoted to bibliographic references.

Kosofsky, L. J., and Farouk El-Baz. *The Moon as Viewed by Lunar Orbiter*. NASA SP-200. Washington, D.C.: Government Printing Office, 1970. This book contains a compilation of the photographs from the five Lunar Orbiter missions; they were chosen primarily to illustrate the heterogeneous nature of the lunar surface. Included in the introduction are brief descriptions of the Orbiter project, its spacecraft and camera systems, and the lunar surface coverage of the five missions. An appendix includes four stereoscopic views, and a collapsible set of stereo eyeglasses is pasted into the book for the convenience of the reader.

Man, John, ed. *The Encyclopedia of Space Travel and Astronomy*. London: Octopus Books, 1979. This nicely illustrated compendium tends to put the global space community into perspective by discussing the technology of all nations in concurrent situations. The Lunar Orbiter, for example, is explained against the backdrop of the Soviet drive for the Moon.

Mari, Christopher, ed. *Space Exploration*. New York: H. W. Wilson, 1999. Twenty-five articles (reprinted from magazines), covering the state of the space program at the time of publication, are divided into five sections: John H. Glenn, Jr.'s return to space, the exploration of Mars, the International Space Station, recent mining efforts by commercial industries, and new types of space vehicles and propulsion systems.

Nicks, Oran W. *Far Travelers: The Exploring Machines*. NASASP-480. Washington, D.C.: Scientific and Technical Information Branch, 1985. Discusses all major NASA planetary spacecraft during NASA's first quarter-century. Written by a senior NASA official involved with lunar and planetary programs during that era.

Ordway, Frederick I., III, and Mitchell Sharpe. *The Rocket Team*. Burlington, Ont.: Apogee Books, 2003. A revised edition of the acclaimed thorough history of rocketry from early amateurs to present-day rocket technology. Includes a disc containing videos and images of rocket programs.

Shelton, William Roy. *Man's Conquest of Space*. Washington, D.C.: National Geographic Society, 1968. This volume was written and published just before the era of the Apollo Moon landings and contains photographs and some data not readily available. As the definitive work on the human reach into space in 1968, it provides an overview of all the missions and spacecraft.

Swanson, Glen E. *Before This Decade Is Out: Personal Reflections on the Apollo Program*. Gainesville: University Press of Florida, 2002. This oral history of the Apollo Program provides insights into the thoughts of the people who accepted President Kennedy's lunar challenge, sent astronauts to walk upon the Moon, and returned them safely to Earth.

Weaver, Kenneth F. "The Moon: Man's First Goal in Space." *National Geographic* 135 (February, 1969): 207-245. Of all the excellent *National Geographic* magazine articles about the Moon, this one is perhaps the most meaningful because it tells the full story of the people and the processes leading to the unlocking of some of the lunar secrets. Copiously illustrated in color and black-and-white, it is an excellent starting point for anyone seriously interested in knowing more about the Moon and the technology that led to the Apollo astronaut landings.

Vondrak, R.R. and J. W. Keller, editors. *Lunar Reconnaissance Orbiter Mission*. London: Springer, 2010. Provides details of lunar imaging, and contrasts Lunar Reconnaissance Orbiter efforts against a wave of international interest in the Moon involving Japan, China, and India. For the serious reader.

Lunar Prospector

Date: January 6, 1998, to July 31, 1999
Type of program: Lunar exploration

The Lunar Prospector was collecting data while orbiting the Moon in March of 1998, when the spacecraft's instruments detected high levels of hydrogen. Hydrogen seemed to be located in dark craters caused by the impact of comets in years past. NASA scientists, along with engineers and astronomers from the University of Texas, decided to perform a controlled crash with the Prospector to investigate whether the detected hydrogen existed in water ice or some other form.

Key Figure

Alan Binder (b. 1940), Lunar Research Institute founder and director, principal investigator for Lunar Prospector

Summary of the Technology

Since American astronauts last visited the Moon in December, 1972, scientists have become increasingly interested in obtaining more information about the Moon and its characteristics. Most of the information about the Moon came from the Apollo missions. These missions mainly provided data relating to equatorial regions of the Moon's surface. Although these discoveries and the amount of information were startling at that period in time, a more complete set of data was desired in order to better understand the lunar world.

The Lunar Prospector itself was a tiny vehicle relative to previous norms. Measuring 1.3 meters in diameter by 1.4 meters in height with three masts 2.5 meters long for deploying scientific measurement instruments, the vehicle had a mass of only 296 kilograms when fully fueled. Lunar Prospector was built by Lockheed Martin at a cost of $63 million, which included the Athena II rocket launcher. The Lunar Prospector was indicative of the National Aeronautics and Space Administration (NASA) policy that space-discovery missions should be "faster, better, cheaper": more frequent and less costly.

The goal of the Lunar Prospector mission was to provide a more complete understanding of the Moon and its key characteristics. This was to be accomplished by means of data gathering over a one-year period during which Lunar Prospector would orbit the Moon taking measurements with sophisticated instrumentation. The characteristics that scientists selected to study were elemental abundances, gravitational fields, magnetic fields, and radon-outgassing events. Another objective of the mission was to obtain data on the crust and atmosphere, expanding our knowledge regarding certain minerals, water ice, and gases that might be present on the Moon or, more specifically, might be trapped or mixed in the regolith (lunar soil). It was hoped that such knowledge would add significant facts to current theories regarding the beginnings and the evolution of the Moon.

Instruments used and experiments to be conducted were (a) a neutron spectrometer (NS) to detect hydrogen in various forms that would determine if ice deposits existed on the Moon; (b) a gamma-ray spectrometer (GRS) to determine the types and locations of elements on the Moon's surface; (c) the alpha particle spectrometer (APS) to investigate outgassing events; (d) the magnetometer and electron reflectometer (Mag/ER) to study

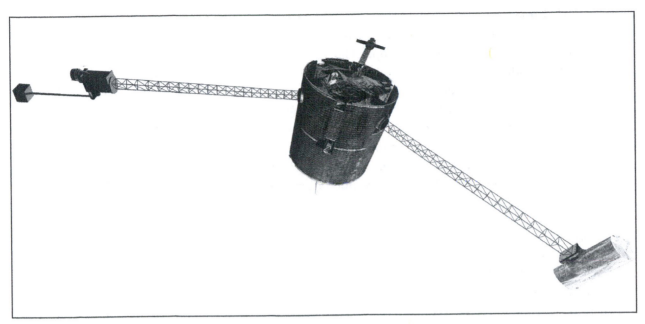

Lunar Prospector. (NASA Ames / Donald Grahame)

the Moon's magnetic fields and its inner core; and (e) the Doppler Gravity Experiment (DGE) to map the gravitational field of the Moon and determine the size of its core.

On January 6, 1998, at 6:28:43 p.m. Pacific standard time, or 04:28 Coordinated Universal Time (UTC), on January 7, a team of scientists led by Dr. Alan Binder launched the small spin-stabilized Lunar Prospector spacecraft. Launch took place from Pad 46 at Cape Canaveral in Florida with the spacecraft on an Athena II rocket. The spacecraft reached its elliptical polar mapping orbit four days (105 hours) later.

In March, 1998, scientists announced that water ice had tentatively been detected at the lunar poles by Lunar Prospector. An initial estimate speculated that as much as 300 million metric tons might be found at these locations. The water was thought to be in the form of ice lying in dark, cold craters of the Moon. This theory dated back to 1961, when scientists determined that permanently shadowed areas were the only locations possible for water ice to exist on the Moon because heat from direct sunlight and the vacuum, due to the relative lack of atmosphere on the lunar surface, would cause rapid

vaporization of water. The craters were remnants of impacts left by comets in the past. Although it was first thought that the water might exist in the form of scattered crystals, later hypotheses were that water ice or hydrated minerals might be buried in the lunar soil, possibly as deep as 18 inches. These later hypotheses were based on the high levels of hydrogen detected by the Neuron Spectrometer (NS) transported by the spacecraft.

In January, 1999, scientists decided to extend the Lunar Prospector mission by six months, bringing Lunar Prospector to very low lunar orbits in order to obtain more and better measurements. Further mapping would now occur at a 30-kilometer orbit, sometimes as low as 10 kilometers.

As the mission and usefulness of Lunar Prospector were coming to an end, engineers and astronomers at the University of Texas/McDonald Observatory worked with NASA to perform a controlled impact of the spacecraft on a crater located in the southern pole of the lunar region. Instead of allowing Lunar Prospector to crash uselessly, this controlled crash was to be a final experiment in which the impact with lunar soil might cause a plume of material in which water vapor or hydroxyl radicals (OH formed by the action of ultraviolet rays from sunlight on water) would rise and perhaps be detected with the Hubble Space Telescope. The controlled crash landing began on July 26, 1999. It was essential to the experiment that the impact should occur in one of the dark craters. For the controlled crash, the Lunar Prospector had to endure an eclipse period that could have damaged certain subsystems on the spacecraft. On July 31, 1999, at 2:51 a.m. Pacific daylight time, the Lunar Prospector successfully crashed on the lunar surface.

Contributions

Lunar Prospector instruments and experiments (NS, GRS, APS, Mag/ER, and DGE) were supported by McDonald Observatory, located at the University of Texas at Austin, Hawaii's Keck Telescope, the Submillimeter Wave Satellite, and the Hubble Space Telescope. The neutron spectrometer detected high concentrations of hydrogen at the lunar poles by analyzing "telltale dips" in the epithermal neutron energy spectra. This led to the speculation that as much as 75 million gallons of water ice might be found at these poles. This was the first interplanetary mission to use NS for the detection of water. NS was also used to map iron and titanium. Two other elements, gadolinium and samarium, were also implicated in the analyses.

The gamma-ray spectrometer determined the distribution of KREEP (rocks rich in K or potassium, REE or rare earth elements, and P or phosphorus) on the lunar surface. This has produced a global map of elemental abundance by analyzing gamma rays. If the Moon was formed from material coming from the Earth's mantle (the giant impact hypothesis), then elemental abundances ought to be similar to those on Earth. However, lunar volcanic and impact events could affect elemental abundances. For example, the detection of thorium in and around the Mare Imbrium supports the theory that the Imbrium Basin was formed by a meteor or comet impact that ejected rocks onto the lunar surface. GRS also allowed the mapping of three major rock types on the Moon: mare basalts, noritic rocks, and anorthositic rocks.

The magnetometer/electron reflectometer results produced a more detailed mapping of the magnetic field variations on the lunar surface. Some larger magnetic fields were found to occur on the far side of the Moon, opposite some large impact basins on the near side, whereas, in other cases, weaker fields than their surroundings were found opposite to impact basins. Studies are being conducted to attempt to understand and explain magnetic field variations detected on the lunar surface. The instrument also provided corroborative evidence that the Moon has a metallic core with a radius of 250 to 430 kilometers.

The DGE improved the calculation of the Moon's polar moment of inertia and established the radius of the iron core at 300-400 kilometers. This small radius supports the idea that the Moon was formed from an impact on Earth. This instrument also uncovered the discovery of thirteen "mascons" that were not known before. Mascons are mass concentrations of high-density materials in or below the lunar crust. They were found on the lunar far side and in the large impact basins. These mascons were thought to exist due to basalt filling in the basins, which were over plugs of dense mantle material. However, no basalt was detected in some of the new mascons, implying that they were caused by the mantle plug.

The APS was used to detect signals of radioactive decay of radon gas and polonium. These findings would help quantify the style and rate of lunar tectonics. If radon, nitrogen, and carbon dioxide are vented, this could lead to the discovery of low-level volcanic activity. APS data were complicated by frequent solar energy particle events, and results are still being analyzed.

Context

Lunar Prospector was not the first robotic program given this name. Early in the 1960's—in addition to the Ranger hard lander, the Surveyor soft lander,

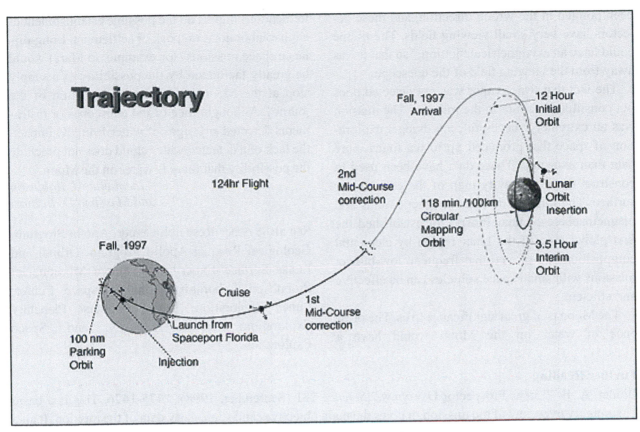

Path of the Lunar Prospector. (NASA)

and the Lunar Orbiter mapping probes—a robotic roving vehicle called Prospector was considered to support anticipated piloted lunar landings. This Prospector mission was canceled early in the design and development phase long before any flight hardware could be built.

The Lunar Prospector mission supplied information invaluable to the scientific community. The mission complemented information previously gained from Apollo, Clementine, and Explorer missions. Along with advancements in technologies and instruments, the Lunar Prospector mission provided a more detailed understanding of the Moon and has strengthened some theories regarding the origin and evolution of the Moon.

In the latter stages of the mission, the main focus was to establish whether water is present on the Moon. Although there was disappointment when a positive result was not obtained from the Lunar Prospector controlled crash landing, there are many possible reasons that no visible water vapor was detected in the ultraviolet regions of the spectral data from the instruments used to observe the experiment. For example, the approach angle was very narrow, making it possible that Lunar Prospector might have missed its target, possibly hitting the rim of the crater instead of the crater itself. Lunar Prospector could have hit a rock or dry lunar soil on impact. Water molecules might not exist in the form of crystals, but instead as hydrated minerals in the rocks. The impact would not have had enough energy to separate the water molecules from these minerals. The hydrogen detected by Lunar Prospector could exist in its pure form, maybe deposited by solar winds. Perhaps the hypotheses and assumptions were false or inadequate, or modeling parameters for plume development predictions may have been inappropriate. Telescopes might have been pointed in the wrong direction, and these detectors have very small viewing fields. The plume could have an asymmetrical "jetting," so that it was away from the viewing field of the telescope.

The fact that water vapor was not detected does not constitute a failure in the mission. The mission was an extremely successful, low-budget exploration of space that produced up to ten times more data than expected. These data have been used to construct the first gravity map of the entire lunar surface. The mission detected magnetic fields and magnetospheres. Lunar Prospector established the first global map of the lunar region by elemental composition and proved that frequent, low-budget missions with small space vehicles can be effective and efficient.

The Moon is of great significance to us. The presence of water on the Moon would have a tremendous impact on the possible establishment of a lunar laboratory, outpost, or settlement. Long-distance space missions (for example, to Mars) would be greatly facilitated by the possibility of a supply stop at the Moon before the continuation of the journey. Although none of the telescopes or instruments detected any signs of water from the impact, the lack of a detected water cloud does not preclude the possibility that there is water on the Moon.

*—Jacqueline J. Robinson
and Massimo D. Bezoari*

See also: Ames Research Center; Apollo Program: Geological Results; Apollo Program: Orbital and Lunar Surface Experiments; Dawn Mission; Jet Propulsion Laboratory; Johnson Space Center; Lunar Exploration; Lunar Orbiters; Planetary Exploration; Private Industry and Space Exploration.

Further Reading

Binder, A. B. "Lunar Prospector Overview." *Science* 281 (September, 1998): 1475-1476. This is a basic summary overview of the mission. It gives the main objectives and some early data of the mission. It also highlights why these findings are important.

Elphic, R. C., D. J. Lawrence, W. C. Feldman, B. L. Barraclough, S. Maurice, A. B. Binder, and P. G. Lucey. "Lunar Fe and Ti Abundance: Comparison of Lunar Prospector and Clementine Data." *Science* 281 (September, 1998): 1493-1496. Compares the analysis of Lunar Prospector data with that of Clementine data. It shows the importance of Fe and Ti, and also explains why the neutron spectrometer is searching for these elements.

Feldman, W. C., S. Maurice, A. B. Binder, B. L. Barraclough, R. C. Elphic, and D. J. Lawrence. "Fluxes of Fast and Epithermal Neutrons from Lunar Prospector: Evidence for Water Ice at the Lunar Poles." *Science* 281 (September, 1998): 1496-1500. This article goes into detail on how hydrogen was detected on the lunar surface. This article also explains the formation of epithermal neutrons and the importance of detecting them.

Goldstein, David B., R. Steven Nerem, Edwin S. Barker, S. Victor Austin, Alan Binder, and William C. Feldman. "Impacting Lunar Prospector in a Cold Tap to Detect Water Ice." *Geophysical Research Letters* 26, no. 12 (June 15, 1999). This article explains how water ice was detected in the shadowed craters. It gives reasons as to why scientists and engineers decided to perform a controlled crash with the Lunar Prospector. It then explains how hydrogen would be detected by a positive reading of water's by-product OH from the plume produced by the crash.

Hartmann, William K. *Moons and Planets.* 5th ed. Belmont, Calif.: Thomson Brooks/Cole Publishing, 2005. Provides detailed information about all objects in the solar system. Suitable on three separate levels: high school student, general reader, and the college undergraduate studying planetary geology.

Lawrence, D. J., W. C. Feldman, B. L. Barraclough, A. B. Binder, R. C. Elphic, S. Maurice, and D. R. Thomsen. "Global Elemental Maps of the Moon: The Lunar Prospector Gamma Ray Spectrometer." *Science* 281 (September, 1998): 1484-1489. This article explains the elements that are detected by the Gamma Ray Spectrometer and shows how they can be used to deduce global maps of elemental abundance.

Lin, R. P., D. L. Mitchell, D. W. Curtis, K. A. Anderson, C. W. Carlson, J. McFadden, M. H. Acuna, L. L. Hood, and A. B. Binder. "Lunar Surface Magnetic Fields and Their Interaction with the Solar Wind: Results from the Lunar Prospector." *Science* 281 (September, 1998): 1480-1484. This article explains the crustal core of the lunar region. This article also explains the localized magnetic fields and how their interactions with solar winds can cause magnetospheres.

Thompson, Dick. "NASA: One Giant Smash-up for Mankind." *Time Notebook*, June 6, 1999. This article tells of the importance of a positive detection of hydrogen/water ice. It also gives a brief summary of the mission, including cost of the mission in comparison with the cost of transporting water to the Moon.

Vondrak, R.R. and J. W. Keller, editors. *Lunar Reconnaissance Orbiter Mission*. London: Springer, 2010. Provides details of lunar imaging, and contrasts Lunar Reconnaissance Orbiter efforts against a wave of international interest in the Moon involving Japan, China, and India. For the serious reader.

Zimmerman, Robert. *The Chronological Encyclopedia of Discoveries in Space*. Westport, Conn.: Oryx Press, 2000. Provides a complete chronological history of all crewed and robotic spacecraft and explains flight events and scientific results. Suitable for all levels of research.

Magellan: Venus

Date: May 4, 1989, to October 12, 1994
Type of program: Planetary exploration

Magellan's primary objective was to map the surface of Venus using powerful radar imaging instruments. This orbiter managed to produce a detailed map of 99 percent of the planet's surface, as well as a gravity map of Venus showing the density distribution of materials beneath the surface. The spacecraft also relayed important information about the Venusian atmosphere.

Key Figures

Anthony Spear, Venus Radar Mapper (VRM) project manager at the Jet Propulsion Laboratory (JPL)

Allan Conrad, JPL manager for VRM, Mission Operations System manager

Douglas G. Griffith, JPL project manager for Magellan

Stephen Saunders, JPL project scientist

Summary of the Mission

The Magellan mission was designed to produce an extremely detailed radar map of surface features on the planet Venus, with a secondary goal of making a gravity map of the planet's subsurface features. The project was named after the Portuguese explorer Ferdinand Magellan (1480-1521), who led the first successful attempt to circumnavigate the world by sea. Although Magellan did not survive the journey, his legacy profoundly changed humankind's understanding of our planet. The spacecraft that bore his name had the same effect on our understanding of the planet Venus.

Radar imaging (using high-frequency radio waves as "light") is required to make images of Venus's surface because the entire planet is perpetually shrouded in a thick cloud blanket laced with sulfuric acid. Unlike visible light waves, radar is capable of penetrating these thick clouds, reflecting off surface features back to a space probe or a ground-based radar station. The first radar images of Venus were produced from Earth-bound radar facilities at Goldstone, California, and Arecibo, Puerto Rico.

The Magellan spacecraft was the culmination of a National Aeronautics and Space Administration (NASA) project begun in 1980 called the Venus Orbiting Imaging Radar Project. This ambitious and costly project was canceled in the fall of 1981, only to be resurrected later as the Venus Radar Mapper Project (VRM) with NASA's Jet Propulsion Laboratory (JPL) in Pasadena, California, given primary mission and systems development responsibilities. Anthony Spear was made overall project manager, and Allan Conrad was assigned the post of Mission Operations Systems manager, the office responsible for designing the actual hardware employed in the final spacecraft. VRM later evolved into Magellan, which was eventually headed by a new project manager, Douglas G. Griffith. Stephen Saunders was made project scientist, the person responsible for organizing and coordinating the gathering and analyzing of scientific data produced by the mission.

Martin Marietta Corporation of Denver, Colorado, was contracted to build the actual spacecraft, while construction of the critical radar sensor was assigned to Hughes Aircraft Company in El Segundo, California. Their task was complicated by budget constraints that demanded that the final craft be as cost-effective as possible. Early complicated

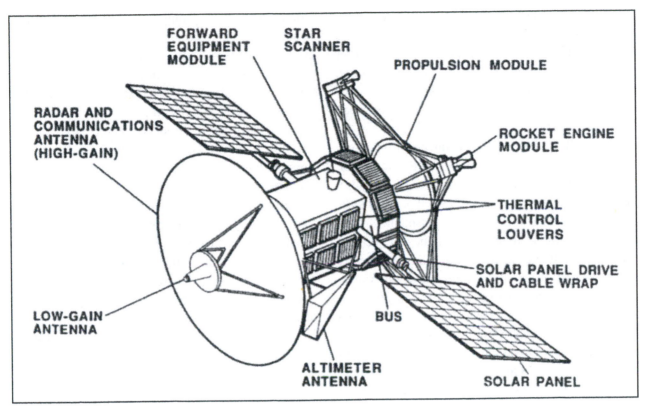

Diagram of the Magellan Venus orbiter. (NASA)

designs produced during the VRM project were rejected as too costly. Spare parts from other missions were used in many critical hardware components, and existing hardware designs were employed where possible instead of creating new configurations. Magellan's large high-gain (highpower) dish antenna, for example, was a spare left over from the Voyager project. Final costs for Magellan amounted to about $450 million.

The final spacecraft was 6.4 meters tall, 3.7 meters across (high-gain antenna diameter), and weighed 3,460 kilograms. The aft section contained a network of support struts and braces supporting the four sets of attitude control rocket engines used to alter the spacecraft's orientation in space. The attitude control system was attached to the main body of the craft consisting aft of a ten-sided instrument package belt, topped off by the boxlike forward equipment module, itself capped by the large (nearly 4 meters in diameter) high-gain dish

antenna. Attached to one side of the large dish antenna was a horn-shaped antenna designed for surface altitude determinations. Projecting from opposing sides of the forward equipment module were two telescoping booms that served to deploy the nearly square solar panels away from the craft after launch and to orient them relative to the Sun for maximum efficiency. The panels were capable of producing the 1,200 watts of electrical power required to operate all onboard equipment. The craft also had a round aperture on the forward equipment module, the star tracker, that was used to orient the spacecraft relative to the star field.

Magellan was originally scheduled for launch in November, 1988, from a space shuttle, using a Centaur rocket booster to achieve initial orbital characteristics. However, after the *Challenger* shuttle accident in 1986, the launch date was moved back to September, 1989. Then the shuttle/Centaur program was canceled, necessitating reevaluation of the booster vehicle needed to send Magellan to Venus. After considering three alternative launch dates and booster configurations, NASA decided on a booster called Inertial Upper Stage (IUS) and a spring, 1989, launch opportunity. The precise window of opportunity for the launch was placed between April 27 and May 17, 1989.

Magellan was eventually launched from Kennedy Space Center aboard space shuttle *Atlantis* on May 4, 1989. After a flawless launch and IUS booster burn, Magellan spent the first part of its fifteen-month journey establishing a spiraling orbit around the Sun. It circled the Sun one and one-half times before finally achieving an elliptical, nearly polar orbit (north-south) around Venus on August 10, 1990. This orbit carried the craft about 200 kilometers from Venus's surface at its closest approach (periapsis), and about 8,500 kilometers from the surface at its farthest point (apoapsis), on the planet's opposite side. One complete orbit took about three and a quarter hours. Radar mapping was done each time the probe dipped down to periapsis, producing high resolution images of the surface of Venus and transmitting them back to Earth. Magellan incorporated a sophisticated synthetic aperture radar (SAR) located in the large Voyager-type dish antenna that revealed objects as small as 120 meters across, one tenth the size previously detectable.

To fulfill its mapping mission Magellan would transmit a radar signal with its SAR on close approach, illuminating a 16-to-28-kilometer-wide, 16,200-kilometer-long swath across the planet's surface. The reflected signal was then stored on tape and periodically played back to Earth through the high-gain antenna located within the large dish mounted on the forward end of the craft. Data from Magellan were beamed back to JPL's Deep Space Network with receiving stations in Spain, Australia, and the Mojave Desert.

However, all did not go according to plan, particularly during initial phases of the radar mapping mission. Twice before mapping began, ground controllers at JPL thought they had lost the craft when the main computer malfunctioned and the high-gain antenna refused to point toward Earth. After thirteen hours of concentrated effort, the JPL team managed to communicate with Magellan through a smaller antenna, and the mission was saved. Three more times over the next several months, however, Magellan went silent (known as loss of signal events) but was revived each time by the resourceful improvisation of the JPL Mission Control scientists. In September, after mapping had begun, one of Magellan's two tape recorders failed. Luckily, the remaining recorder performed flawlessly for the rest of the mission. Loss of signal events were eventually traced to a minor software problem. With this glitch corrected, Magellan never again refused to transmit its valuable data.

For planning purposes, the Magellan mission was divided into mission cycles, one cycle being equal to the very slow rotational period of Venus on its axis, 243 Earth days. At the end of each mission cycle the JPL mission controllers assessed mapping progress by contrast to planned objectives and time tables. Magellan performed far more efficiently than anticipated. For example, at the end of the first mission cycle, cumulative planetary coverage was 84 percent; at the end of the second cycle, coverage had jumped to 98 percent. By the end of the third cycle, 99 percent of the planet had been covered, an area three times as large as Earth's combined continental land masses. Originally, Magellan was expected to cover 70 percent of Venus's surface at most.

On September 15, 1992, Magellan initiated a fourth 243-day mission cycle, this time to perform a global gravity survey. Gravity data help scientists to determine the thickness of subsurface layers on a planet, and to determine relative densities of materials in the planet's interior. For example, low-density areas may suggest hot rising magma—or a deep valley. By the end of mission cycle four, Magellan had generated a gravity map of most of Venus, but the most reliable data were collected when the craft was closest to the planet's surface, within 30° or 40° latitude of the equator. Mission scientists, delighted at having a still functioning spacecraft after four cycles, decided to dedicate a fifth cycle to acquiring high-quality gravity data from the polar regions as well.

To provide better gravity data from Venus's polar regions, JPL mission specialists had to devise a way to alter Magellan's orbit so that it would swoop in closer to the polar regions than its elliptical orbit would allow. This was accomplished in a particularly imaginative fashion, using a technique called aerobraking, which involves using frictional drag with the atmosphere to slow spacecraft momentum so that it assumes a nearly circular orbit. In May, 1993, Magellan became the first spacecraft to use aerobraking to alter its orbital characteristics.

Mission cycle six, Magellan's last, was used to obtain important information about Venus's atmosphere. With its attitude control fuel nearly exhausted, its useful life as a planetary space probe was nearing its end. However, the low circular orbit acquired during cycle five left the craft flying within the planet's atmosphere, allowing measurements of atmospheric density and other parameters. To measure density, Magellan was oriented so that its extended solar panels acted like the blades of a windmill. The force (expended by attitude control rockets) required to keep the craft from rotating provided a measure of the density of atoms and molecules in the atmosphere.

On October 12, 1994, Magellan's radio transmissions to Earth fell silent. Shortly thereafter, the

Magellan being fixed into position inside the payload bay of Atlantis prior to launch. (NASA)

spacecraft, which had orbited Venus for more than four years, was destroyed as it plunged through the atmosphere.

Contributions

The Magellan mission to Venus provided humankind with the most detailed surface map of a planet in the entire solar system. The Venus revealed by Magellan shows a tortured surface, 85 percent of which is covered by volcanic lava flows that form the planet's vast plains. Much of the rest of the surface consists of mountainous highlands criss-crossed by fold belts and rift valleys in complicated patterns. Magellan also revealed for the first time the full extent of impact cratering on the surface. Impact craters are fairly evenly distributed over the entire planet and are much more abundant than on Earth.

Magellan also revealed the planet-wide extent of cratering on Venus from rocky meteoroids originating elsewhere in the solar system. It showed that impact craters less than about 30 kilometers in diameter are rare on Venus, the result of diminished momentum of small bodies encountering the thick carbon dioxide atmosphere. Using crater densities recorded by Magellan (number of craters in a given area) and comparing them to densities on the Earth and Moon, the age of the present crust of Venus was calculated at about 500 million years. Another important Magellan accomplishment was the construction of a high resolution, planet-wide gravity map of Venus. In 1978 the Pioneer orbiter made a gravity map of Venus, but the Magellan map shows superior surface coverage and resolution of fine details. A comparison of the radar-produced topographic map with the gravity map shows an extremely close relationship between topography and gravity; high topographic features (domes, volcanic peaks) show high gravity, whereas low topographic areas (valleys) are associated with low gravity. This close topographic/gravity association is generally not observed on Earth.

Finally, Magellan contributed important information about Venus's atmosphere. Windmill experiments showed expected atmospheric densities at altitudes from 180 to 172 kilometers above the surface where atomic oxygen dominates the atmosphere, but at 160 to 150 kilometers above Venus atmospheric density was about one-half previously estimated values.

Context

Magellan was the twenty-second space probe to be sent to Venus, making Venus the target of more probes than any other planet. The first interplanetary probe, Mariner 2 (Mariner 1 was destroyed on launch), was launched toward Venus in 1962 and made infrared temperature determinations as it flew by the planet. In 1967 the United States launched Mariner 5, and the Soviet Union launched Venera 4, the first spacecraft to drop a probe into the Venusian atmosphere. They confirmed the high temperature readings (minus 30° centigrade at the cloud tops; 477° at the surface) of Mariner 2 and established the atmospheric composition as carbon dioxide-rich and extremely thick (914,000 kilograms per square meter surface pressure; ninety times that of Earth).

Other notable U.S. probes included Mariner 10, which produced the first close-up, high-resolution pictures of the cloud formations on Venus in 1972. Pioneer Venus missions 1 and 2, launched about three months apart in 1978, released four "hard landers" (Pioneer 2; probes designed to fall through the atmosphere and crash on the surface), and made the first gravity map of Venus (Pioneer 1 orbiter). Pioneer also produced rada raltimetry maps that allowed the first delineation of Venus's global topographic provinces. A few months before Magellan reached Venus in 1990, the Galileo spacecraft transmitted detailed images of cloud patterns to Earth as it flew by Venus on its way to a December, 1995, rendezvous with Jupiter.

The Soviet Union launched the most spacecraft toward Venus, fifteen in all. Beginning with Venera 5, these craft included orbiters, atmospheric probes, and soft landers capable of operating on the surface. Notable among the soft landers were Veneras 9, 10, 13, and 14, all of which carried cameras that produced the first images of the surface features. The Venera 15 and 16 orbiters were the first probes to produce radar images of Venus. The last Soviet probes were Vegas 1 and 2, which launched balloons to assess wind patterns in the atmosphere, and landers to assess surface conditions.

The scientific legacy of Magellan is immense. In addition to discovering many new surface features on Venus, Magellan revolutionized scientists' understanding of how the planet has evolved over time. Correlations of topographic features with gravity data show that, unlike Earth, Venus does not have lithospheric plates, thick slabs of rigid crust plus mantle material that slide horizontally over a weak, partially molten layer in the mantle. Sliding motions of these plates on Earth (a process called plate tectonics) accounts for most of the Earth's mountain belts, volcanic chains, ocean basins, and earthquake activity. On Venus high surface temperatures produce ductile (easily deformable) behavior at very shallow depths in the crust, precluding the formation of strong rigid plates.

In terms of technological advances, Magellan demonstrated the feasibility of aerobraking for the first time, a technique that would be used to control the orbit of the Mars Global Surveyor spacecraft launched in 1996. Magellan also demonstrated the feasibility and economy of building a very successful spacecraft out of spare parts from other missions, although this was not without its problems. For example, the Voyager-type antenna dish was not an ideal configuration for radar work and had to be jerry-rigged to adjust itself three thousand times during each mapping pass. Nevertheless, the spacecraft broke records for the amount of data received, exceeding all previous U.S. missions combined. To illustrate the amount of data Magellan collected, a magnetic data tape from just one mapping cycle would stretch halfway around Earth.

—*John L. Berkley*

See also: Hubble Space Telescope; Hubble Space Telescope: Science; Jet Propulsion Laboratory; Lunar Prospector; Mariner 1 and 2; Mariner 5; Mariner 10; National Aeronautics and Space Administration; Pioneer Venus 1; Pioneer Venus 2; Planetary Exploration; Space Shuttle; Space Shuttle Mission STS-26; Space Shuttle Flights, 1994.

Further Reading

Beatty, J. Kelly, Carolyn Collins Petersen, and Andrew Chaikin, eds. *The New Solar System*. 4thed. New York: Sky Publishing, 1999. This is a comprehensive, engaging account of all solar system objects from planets to comets, asteroids, and meteorites. Richly illustrated with color and monochrome photographs, drawings, graphs, and charts, this is the perfect book to start anyone on an exploration of the solar system. Information on Venus is from pre-Magellan probes but is nevertheless very timely. Has an appendix with planetary characteristics, glossary, and suggestions for further reading. Comprehensive planetary maps are also included. Suitable for general audiences.

Cattermole, Peter, and Patrick Moore. *Atlas of Venus*. New York: Cambridge University Press, 1997. This is a complete, up-to-date atlas of the planet shrouded in mysterious clouds. This colorful collection of maps and pictures draws heavily from the Magellan spacecraft's radar imaging, some of it published here for the first time. There are twenty color plates, forty-eight black-and-white photographs, and twenty-two line diagrams.

Cox, Brian and Andrew Cohen. *The Planets*. London: William Collins, 2019. Companion book to an acclaimed BBC science series. Provides understanding of the solar system based on astronomical observations and spacecraft investigations as of 2019.

Grinspoon, David Harry. *Venus Revealed: A New Look Below the Clouds of Our Mysterious Twin Planet*. Cambridge, Mass.: Perseus Publishing, 1998. This is a somewhat romantic look at the lore of Venus and the historical attempts to study it. Grinspoon draws on data from U.S. and Soviet Venusian missions, as well as conventional astronomical observations (and folklore) to present for lay readers the most detailed picture of Venus available.

Hartmann, William K. *Moons and Planets*. 5th ed. Belmont, Calif.: Thomson Brooks/Cole Publishing, 2005. Provides detailed information about all objects in the solar system. Suitable on three separate levels: high school student, general reader, and the college undergraduate studying planetary geology.

McBride, Neil, and Iain Gilmour. *An Introduction to the Solar System*. New York: Cambridge University Press, 2004. This work provides a comprehensive tour of the solar system best suited to a high school or college course on planetary astronomy.

Morrison, David, and Tobias Owen. *The Planetary System*. 3d ed. San Francisco: Addison- Wesley, 2003. Organized by planetary object, this work provides contemporary data on all planetary bodies visited by spacecraft since the early days of the Space Age. Suitable for high school and college students and for the general reader.

National Aeronautics and Space Administration, Jet Propulsion Laboratory. *Magellan: Revealing the Face of Venus*. JPL 400-494 3/93. Washington, D.C.: Government Printing Office, 1993. This is a twenty-five-page booklet produced by NASA to publicize the Magellan mission. It contains full-color diagrams and pictures of the spacecraft itself, colorized radar images including a global view of Venus, altimetry map showing principal topographic regions of Venus, and monochrome images illustrating important geological surface features. The text is packed with interesting facts, including a concise rundown on mission history, spacecraft dimensions and specifications, descriptions of mission objectives and results, facts and figures about the planet Venus, and the procedure for naming newly discovered features on its surface. It also contains a complete list of the principal scientific investigators on the Magellan project.

Saunders, R. Stephen. "The Surface of Venus: Razor-Sharp Images of the Earth's Near Twin Reveal a Mix of Familiar and Perplexing Geologic Features." *Scientific American* 263 (1990). This article by the Magellan project scientist at JPL presents a wide array of excellent radar images of surface features on Venus. Images include impact craters, mountains, faulted plains, and volcanoes, all shown in exquisite detail. Also shows a picture of the Magellan probe and a drawing illustrating how it obtained its images. The text gives a synopsis of the Magellan mission and explanations of the illustrated surface features. This article is easily accessible in the serials section of most libraries. It is intended for general audiences.

Manned Maneuvering Unit

Date: 1965 to 1984
Type of program: Piloted spaceflight

The Manned Maneuvering Unit (MMU) was a device, strapped onto an astronaut's space suit, that allowed independent movement for work in free space. The MMU was modified many times, evolving from a handheld device in the Gemini Program to the space shuttle MMU, allowing an astronaut to maneuver up to 100 meters from the spacecraft.

Key Figures

Edward H. White II (1930-1967), the NASA astronaut and U.S. Air Force captain who used the first-generation MMU, called the Handheld Maneuvering Unit, for the first American spacewalk

Daniel McKee, director of development for the second-generation MMU, called the Astronaut Maneuvering Unit, the first backpack-mounted maneuvering unit

Edward G. Givens, Jr. (1930-1967), NASA astronaut and U.S. Air Force major, also responsible for developing the Astronaut Maneuvering Unit

Bruce M. McCandless II (1937-2017), NASA astronaut who first used the MMU in spaceflight

Summary of the Technology

The Manned Maneuvering Unit (MMU) was an advanced space-maneuvering device that allowed astronauts to engage in extravehicular activity (EVA), or work in free space apart from the space vehicle. Without this kind of device, an astronaut would be virtually helpless in the weightlessness of space.

The MMU was the third generation in a succession of devices designed to help American astronauts perform EVAs. The first was a handheld propulsion device used by Gemini Astronaut Edward H. White II on the first American spacewalk, June 3, 1965. This instrument was called the Handheld Maneuvering Unit (HHMU). It resembled a gun with antennae and was attached to its supply of compressed gas by lines running to the Gemini spacecraft. The astronaut needed to point the HHMU opposite to the direction in which he wanted to move and pull the trigger; a burst of compressed oxygen gas would be released from the gun's antennae (which were actually thrusters), propelling the astronaut through space. The HHMU was used with limited success; its design was too simplistic, and its gas supply was insufficient to provide control for very long.

The National Aeronautics and Space Administration (NASA), with help from the Air Force, had plans for an improved device even as the HHMU flew on Gemini IV. The second-generation device was to consist of the same HHMU, but with modifications. Instead of being attached to the space vehicle by gas lines, the HHMU was to be attached to a supply of Freon 14 contained in a backpack called the Extravehicular Support Package (ESP). The resulting system became known as the Astronaut Maneuvering Unit (AMU). Later versions of the AMU would include twelve thrusters on the ESP backpack itself.

The AMU was designed to be worn by an astronaut during EVA outside the cramped Gemini spacecraft. Designing the AMU was an Air Force project headed by Daniel McKee and Edward G. Givens, Jr. The AMU's first use was planned for

At about 100 meters from the cargo bay of the space shuttle Challenger, Bruce McCandless II was further out than anyone had ever been before. Guided by a Manned Maneuvering Unit (MMU), astronaut McCandless, pictured above, was floating free in space. McCandless and fellow NASA astronaut Robert Stewart were the first to experience such an "untethered space walk" during Space Shuttle mission 41-B in 1984. (NASA)

Gemini VIII, in March, 1966. Unfortunately, that mission was cut short before the planned extravehicular activity could take place, when a thruster malfunctioned—a failure that seriously threatened the safety of astronauts Neil A. Armstrong and David R. Scott.

The AMU was flown again on Gemini IX-A in June, 1966. Astronaut Eugene A. Cernan began his EVA successfully enough, but because of excessive fogging of his faceplate and an inability to don the backpack in the weightless environment, plans for the AMU were aborted late in the EVA.

The ESP backpack was removed from the system for Gemini X (July, 1966), and the HHMU(with nitrogen gas) was used for the flight. The HHMU would be used again on Gemini XI (September, 1966). Finally, the AMU was shelved altogether in late 1966, its technical problems too complex to address during the busy pre-Apollo days.

The AMU eventually reemerged to fly in space again—inside the voluminous Skylab space station on the second Skylab mission (May, 1973). Yet, the redesigned Skylab AMU had undergone significant changes under a Martin Marietta Corporation contract and hardly resembled the original AMU. It was called the M509 experimental unit. M509 was a full generation ahead of the AMU. It closely resembled and would evolve into the Manned Maneuvering Unit, to be used on the space shuttle.

The Martin Marietta Corporation retained the AMU contract during the long hiatus between the last flight of Skylab (November, 1973) and the first space shuttle flight (April, 1981). During intervening years, the AMU was renamed the MMU but retained many of the outward characteristics of the Skylab AMU.

The MMU was a back-mounted maneuvering unit stored in the forward end of the space shuttle orbiter payload bay. It had its own electrical power supply, propulsion gases (compressed gaseous nitrogen), and controls. Like the Skylab AMU, it resembled a chair with armrests supporting control devices.

The MMU was housed in the shuttle's payload bay in its flight support station, which consisted of a mounting bracket and interfaces to the orbiter to supply propellant gases and power. The flight support station also provided restraints necessary for astronauts to don and doff the MMU efficiently in weightlessness. This process took the astronauts about fifteen to twenty minutes to accomplish. In an emergency, however, the astronaut could detach himself from the MMU in less than thirty seconds.

The MMU propulsion system consisted of twenty-four thrusters, commanded by the astronaut through controls located at his fingertips: the rotational hand controller (right hand) and the translational hand controller (left hand). The MMU could be controlled either automatically or manually.

The MMU was capable of producing changes of 0.09 meter per second in translational (moving in a straight line direction) motion and 10.0° per second in rotational (moving as if on an axis) motion, with six degrees of freedom (meaning, it could move six degrees in any direction in free space). It was designed to allow an astronaut to work at distances up to 100 meters from the spacecraft.

The MMU's 16.8-volt batteries, which powered electronic systems and lights, could be replaced in five minutes while in orbit. Gaseous propellants were stored in two 27-liter tanks located within the MMU. Each of the twenty-four thrusters could generate a thrust of 7.5 newtons for a minimum duration of 0.009 second. Drawing from supplies in the orbiter, the gas tanks could be recharged while in orbit in less than twenty minutes. The MMU had thirty-two separate heaters located at specific points within its structure. In addition, special paint and reflective materials helped control the temperature of the unit.

Each MMU had a twelve-year operating storage life. It was designed to fly in space with an active operational life of about four hundred hours. It could be stored in the shuttle's payload bay for fifteen hundred hours. The MMU was designed in such a way that it would not move far from the orbiter if it malfunctioned. Fail-safe mechanisms included those to avoid damaging collisions with the orbiter.

The first use the MMU was made on STS 41-B on February 7, 1984. During that flight, Astronaut Bruce M. McCandless II donned the MMU. For the first time in history an astronaut floated free from a piloted space vehicle, becoming an independent satellite. McCandless and his MMU maneuvered as far away as 98 meters from the orbiter, and both returned safely. The second use of the MMU was the daring retrieval and repair of the Solar Maximum Mission satellite (Solar Max) in April, 1984. STS 41-C astronaut George D. "Pinky" Nelson flew over to the satellite and attempted to attach a grappling device to it. Eventually, the satellite was retrieved and repaired in the payload bay by Nelson and James D. A. "Ox" Van Hoften.

The third and final use of the MMU occurred during STS 51-A (November, 1984) in the spectacular rescue of a disabled Palapa B2 satellite. During this flight, astronaut Joe Allen flew the MMU to the spinning satellite some tens of meters away from the shuttle. He inserted a device called a "stinger" into the satellite's rocket motor. Thus locking himself to the satellite, he used his MMU to counter the spin of the satellite. Stabilizing the entire configuration in space, Allen then used the thrusters on his MMU to tow the satellite to the shuttle's payload bay, where it was secured. Another satellite, Westar 6, was also later recovered on the mission in the same MMU-based manner by astronaut Dale A. Gardner. Both satellites were returned to Earth for repairs and later returned to space.

Contributions

The historic photographs of Edward White outside his Gemini IV spacecraft show the astronaut gripping his HHMU. In retrospect, when placed alongside images of Dale A. Gardner strapped to his MMU and maneuvering toward the disabled Westar, the HHMU seems primitive. Eugene A. Cernan's frustrated attempts to don his AMU stand in sharp contrast to the relative luxury of the MMU's flight support station and illustrate well the successful changes in design.

White's mission demonstrated that the HHMU was extremely sensitive and its propellant supply far too limited. Yet, the HHMU did provide positive control and maneuvering capability necessary to perform fundamental tasks in free space. After White's spacewalk, the HHMU was given larger propellant tanks and attached to the outside of the spacecraft's cabin to allow for more propellant volume, thus ensuring a greater maneuverability.

When the AMU was tested in space, designers realized that merely adding more parts would not solve the problems of the system. The Gemini Program was branching into more fields than there were time and money to support. Because the United States' goal was a flight to the Moon—and since the AMU would not be useful there—the AMU project was put on hold. More thought would have to be put into donning methodology, self-propulsion, in-orbit storage, and the resupply of consumables and power.

These problems were addressed when the AMU was redesigned and flown on Skylab. The Skylab M509 experimental unit solved some basic problems: how to interface a large collection of equipment, power, and plumbing with the human form. Its chair-type design and handheld controls would become lasting contributions to the technology. Ideas on the placement of gas thrusters, propellant storage, and the translational/rotational controls were tested and found to be ideal design characteristics. During Skylab, an effective combination of design modes for storage, doffing, and donning was also verified. Although the M509 never actually saw use in free space, it represented an important link that would lead to the design of the MMU.

When Bruce M. McCandless II strapped himself into his MMU in orbit in February, 1984, he was to test a system that had evolved from several generations of space maneuvering technology. McCandless verified that the whole system was operational and performed as a unit. The ease of donning and doffing, the operability of control systems, the "invisible" heaters and thermal control elements that maintained the system's environment, and the ability to fly slightly beyond the expected distance from the spacecraft convinced technicians that the MMU was a success.

STS 41-B, 41-C, and 51-A would confirm that the United States had a superior, functioning piloted maneuvering capability in space. Useful work was performed to capture satellites, while additional information was being amassed to enable the next generation of MMU—the Simplified Aid for Extravehicular Activity Rescue (SAFER)—to be used to aid astronauts in the construction of the International Space Station.

Context

No one underestimated the importance of the ability of humans to work in space outside the confines of a space vehicle and orbital shelters. From the first EVA on the Soviet mission of Voskhod 2 on March 18, 1965, and Edward White's spacewalk some three months later, the importance of this capability was clear.

With Gemini, the useful work that could be performed in free space was largely experimental. White realized the importance of some kind of maneuvering capability with his very limited HHMU. As the program progressed, leading to the AMU, it became evident that almost nothing useful in space could be performed without a maneuvering capability.

From the start, "work in space" was defined as the ability to move from one point to another and, upon arriving, to stabilize and use tools. This fundamental concept was first tested on the flight of Gemini IX-A. Although the EVA on that mission had its share of problems, it is a milestone in space history: the first time a human, outside the confines of a space shelter, attempted useful work in space.

From Gemini through Apollo, work in free space had consisted of crawling around the external surface of a spacecraft and recovering items. On Skylab, a thermal shield was installed during an EVA, marking the first time that an EVA was accomplished to save a mission. Yet again, it was accomplished without the aid of a maneuvering unit. It was becoming clear, however, that the need to maneuver efficiently and safely in space was basic to the more ambitious space shuttle missions.

The stranded Westar 6 satellite provided the first opportunity to test the full capabilities of the MMU. The MMU performed flawlessly, so perfectly that it appeared nearly invisible in the drama that unfolded around it. The massive satellite dwarfed the astronaut who was approaching it in free space. The MMU provided the stable platform he needed to pinpoint his rendezvous, mate with the satellite, slow its spin, and return it to the shuttle—an astonishing first trial.

The SAFER was designed and developed by the Johnson Space Center in a team project led by the Automation and Robotics Division. It is a small, self-contained, propulsive backpack device that can provide free-flying mobility for a spacewalker in an emergency. It is designed for self-rescue use by a spacewalker in the event a shuttle became unable or unavailable to retrieve a detached, drifting crew member. SAFER is a scaled-down, miniature version of the MMU. It is designed for emergency use only, but without built-in backup systems. SAFER's propulsion is provided by twenty-four fixed position thrusters that expel nitrogen gas. SAFER was not designed as a replacement for the MMU. An improved version of the SAFER was prepared for use on the International Space Station.

SAFER was first tested on STS-64 in September, 1994, ten years after the last MMU mission. Astronauts Mark Lee and Carl J. Meade performed an engineering evaluation, an EVA self-rescue demonstration, and an overall flight quality evaluation, which included a demonstration of precision flying by tracking the Remote Manipulator System arm.

While docked to the Mir Space Station in March, 1996, astronauts Linda M. Godwin and Michael R. "Rich" Clifford attached four experiments, known collectively as the Mir Environmental Effects Payload (MEEP), to the outside of the Mir Docking Module. As a precaution, they each wore a SAFER pack. Astronaut Scott E. Parazynski and Russian cosmonaut Vladimir Georgievich Titov tested the first flight production model of SAFER on STS-86 during the September, 1997, mission. During the third STS-88 spacewalk to assemble the International Space Station, Astronaut Jerry L. Ross achieved only 50 percent of the evaluation objectives for SAFER. Still, the tests were considered successful, and SAFER was worn by astronauts during station construction, repair, and maintenance operations.

—Dennis Chamberland

See also: Extravehicular Activity; Magellan: Venus; Skylab 3; Space Shuttle; Space Shuttle Mission STS-1; Space Shuttle Mission STS-6; Space Shuttle Flights, 1984; Space Shuttle Mission STS 41-B; Space Shuttle Mission STS 51-A; Space Shuttle Flights, July-December, 1985; Space Suit Development.

Further Reading

Allen, Joseph P., and Russell Martin. *Entering Space: An Astronaut's Odyssey*. Rev. ed. New York: Stewart, Tabori and Chang, 1984. A heavily documented essay describing the U.S. space shuttle program. It describes the shuttle's development from processing at the Kennedy Space Center to launch, orbital activities, and landing. The book is aimed toward all readers and is probably the most beautifully photographed and illustrated of all shuttle books.

Baker, David. *The History of Manned Space Flight*. New York: Crown, 1982. This work offers a precise chronology of the history of piloted spaceflight, oriented toward the United States' effort. It is quite a detailed work, tracing the U.S. piloted space program from its beginnings to the dawn of the space shuttle program. Provides detailed analyses of all the Gemini flights. Suitable for all audiences.

Burrows, William E. *This New Ocean: The Story of the First Space Age*. New York: Random House, 1998. This is a comprehensive history of the human conquest of space, covering everything from the earliest attempts at spaceflight through the voyages near the end of the twentieth century. Burrows is an experienced journalist, who has reported for *The New York Times*, *The Washington Post*, and *The Wall Street Journal*. There are many photographs and an extensive source list. Interviewees in the book include Isaac Asimov, Alexei Leonov, Sally K. Ride, and James A. Van Allen.

DeWaard, E. John, and Nancy DeWaard. *History of NASA: America's Voyage to the Stars*. New York: Exeter Books, 1984. A pictorial essay on the history of NASA. It does not go into great detail on the Gemini and space shuttle programs, but it does present a large collection of color photographs from various missions.

Harland, David M. *The Space Shuttle: Roles, Missions, and Accomplishments*. New York: John Wiley, 1998. The book details the origins, missions, payloads, and passengers of the Space Transportation System (STS), covering the flights from STS-1 through STS-89 in great detail. This large volume is divided into five sections: "Operations," "Weightlessness," "Exploration," "Outpost," and "Conclusions." "Operations" discusses the origins of the shuttle, test flights, and some of its missions and payloads. "Weightlessness" describes many of the experiments performed aboard the orbiter, including materials processing, electrophoresis, phase partitioning, and combustion. "Exploration" includes the Hubble Space Telescope, Spacelab, Galileo, Magellan, and Ulysses, as well as Earth observation projects. "Outpost" covers the shuttle's role in the joint Russian Mir program and the International Space Station. Contains numerous illustrations, an index, and bibliographical references.

Hartmann, William K., et al. *Out of the Cradle: Exploring the Frontiers Beyond Earth*. New York: Workman Publishing, 1984. This well-illustrated book concentrates on the future of piloted spaceflight. It presents, with dramatic insight, space exploration in the twenty-first century and the benefits humankind will reap.

Joëls, Kerry Mark, and Gregory P. Kennedy. *The Space Shuttle Operator's Manual*. Designed by David Larkin. Rev. ed. New York: Ballantine Books, 1988. This book contains a wealth of information on space shuttle systems and flight procedures. It is written as a manual for imaginary crew members on a generic mission and will be appreciated by anyone interested in how the astronauts fly the orbiter, deploy satellites, conduct spacewalks, and live in space. Contains many drawings and some photographs of equipment.

Kozloski, Lillian D. *U.S. Space Gear: Outfitting the Astronaut*. Washington, D.C.: Smithsonian Institution Press, 1994. This history of the space suit illustrates the wealth of ingenuity that has gone into dressing for space. Kozloski, a museum specialist at the National Air and Space Museum, begins with the earliest suits, created for high-altitude flight in the 1930's and barely a step up from the Red Baron's leather skullcap, and she ably chronicles the evolution of design and problem solving up to the current gear for the space shuttle.

National Aeronautics and Space Administration. *Simplified Aid for Extravehicular Activity Rescue (SAFER) Operations Manual*. Washington, D.C.: Government Printing Office, 1994. Written as the training manual for SAFER, this is a very good technical reference on the inner workings of the backpack. It is filled with detailed drawings and specifications, as well as operating procedures.

Shayler, David J. *Walking in Space: Development of Space Walking Techniques*. Chichester, England: Springer-Praxis, 2003. Overview of EVA techniques based on original documentation and interviews with astronauts.

Manned Orbiting Laboratory

Date: December 11, 1963, to June 10, 1969
Type of program: Space station, piloted spaceflight

The Manned Orbiting Laboratory (MOL) was the first space station project that evolved beyond the study stage. It also represented the Pentagon's attempt to establish a piloted military presence in space at a time when Cold War tensions between the Soviet Union and the free world were at their greatest.

Key Figures

Lyndon B. Johnson (1908-1973), thirty-sixth president of the United States, 1963-1969

Robert S. McNamara (1916-2005), secretary of defense under the Johnson administration

Cyrus R. Vance (1917-2002), deputy secretary of defense under the Johnson administration

Bernard A. Schriever (b. 1910), commander of the Air Force Systems Command

James E. Webb (1906-1992), flight director administrator of NASA

Joseph S. Bleymaier, Titan III program director

Russell Berg, initial deputy MOL program director

Harry Evans, initial MOL program vice director

Peter Leonard, MOL program science adviser

Melvin R. Laird (1922-2016), secretary of defense under the Nixon administration

Summary of the Technology

In the early 1960's, U.S. Air Force plans for establishing a military piloted presence in space were based on the X-20 Dyna-Soar project. This was a 10-ton "mini-shuttle" space plane that was to be launched by an Air Force Titan III-C booster. As NASA's Gemini two-person spacecraft program evolved in the early 1960's, civilian defense analysts concluded that a modified Gemini might offer a means of performing military piloted space functions better and more cheaply than the X-20.

Secretary of Defense Robert S. McNamara suggested that the Air Force be given an equal management role with NASA in the Gemini Program, thus creating a parallel military "Blue Gemini" program. This drew a heated response from NASA Administrator James E. Webb, who viewed the proposal as a militarization of NASA that would jeopardize its presidentially mandated goal of landing a man on the Moon by the end of the decade. In July, 1963, NASA began to look seriously at the concept of future space stations. It was suggested that an orbiting laboratory based on the Gemini spacecraft would offer the military a separate means to explore its role in piloted spaceflight. This idea marked the birth of what was to become the Air Force's Manned Orbiting Laboratory (MOL) program. The resulting 11,340-kilogram cylindrical space station concept looked like a giant thermos bottle the size of a house trailer.

In October, 1963, McNamara requested that the X-20 be terminated and replaced with Gemini B, a military version of the NASA two-person spacecraft. When McNamara met with the newly installed President Lyndon B. Johnson on December 10, 1963, the X-20 was canceled. The next day, the Gemini B/MOL program was officially announced.

The MOL (pronounced "mole") program inherited some funds from the canceled X-20 and benefited from the ongoing development of the X-20's Titan III-C booster. The original goals of the space station project were modest: to provide a shirtsleeve environment to see how a crew could live and

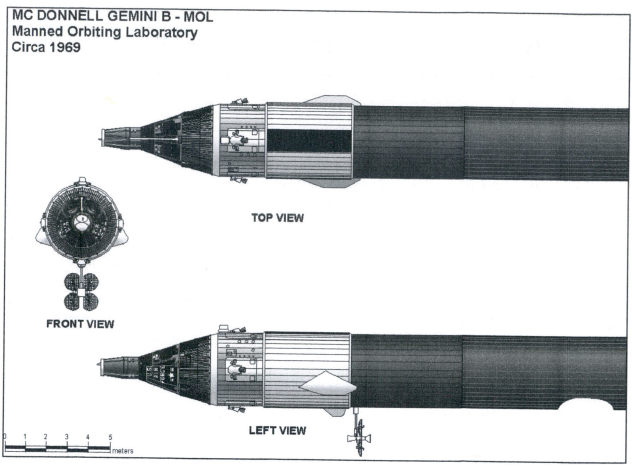

The main features of the MOL. (via Wikimedia Commons)

function in space for extended periods. Plans called for initial mission durations of thirty days.

One of the early surprises in piloted spaceflight was the ability of astronauts to easily spot and track targets on the ground, and to secure amazingly detailed photographs of the Earth with ordinary hand-held cameras. Thus, as the design stage of the program progressed, MOL evolved into a space-based reconnaissance platform to develop surveillance techniques using both advanced sensors and the on-board astronauts. It was assumed that human observers in orbit could selectively choose military and political targets to be photographed and studied. This would eliminate the need for blanket photographic coverage of vast areas of foreign territory and greatly simplify the interpretation of the resulting intelligence. In keeping with this surveillance role, the MOL project is designated in some references as the Keyhole 10 (KH-10), part of a long series of Keyhole military reconnaissance spacecraft. Experiments with communication, meteorology, navigation, and electronic surveillance were also planned.

The project was first envisioned as a $1.5 billion program with the first piloted flight scheduled for 1968. Five orbital laboratories were to be built and launched from Vandenberg Air Force Base, California. MOL was primarily an Air Force project, but plans called for the Navy to have dedicated use of two of the laboratories for perfection of ocean surveillance techniques. The crew was to ride into space aboard the Gemini spacecraft, then transfer into the MOL laboratory once safely in orbit. At the conclusion of the mission, the crew would enter the

Gemini, separate from the MOL, and return to Earth. The laboratory would then be deliberately deorbited into the ocean to prevent its secret reconnaissance equipment from falling into unauthorized hands.

The MOL design evolved into a polar-orbiting cylindrical station 3.3 meters in diameter and 16.8 meters long with the Gemini B spacecraft attached. The laboratory was divided into different sections. The pressurized portion housed two spaces: the experimental laboratory, where the surveillance equipment was to be operated, and a living compartment with consumables to sustain the two-person crew for up to thirty days. The attached unpressurized compartment opposite the Gemini contained housekeeping equipment such as power and oxygen supplies.

Official development approval for MOL was given by President Johnson on August 26, 1965. The timing of the approval is significant because it came while the eight-day mission of NASA's Gemini V, carrying L. Gordon Cooper, Jr., and Charles "Pete" Conrad, Jr., was in progress. The success of the NASA Gemini missions was crucial to the MOL project, as the Gemini spacecraft was a key element in the system.

Douglas Aircraft won the competition to build the laboratory, while the Gemini B spacecraft was to be produced by McDonnell Aircraft, the same company that built the Gemini for NASA's piloted space program. Coincidentally, both prime contractors for the MOL project merged midway through the program's development and became the McDonnell Douglas Aircraft Company.

The MOL was to be launched by the Air Force Titan III-C booster. This was a modified two-stage Titan II ICBM clustered with twin 3.05-meter-diameter solid-fueled rocket boosters. The solid boosters were unique in that they were assembled from separate "segments," which were stacked and bolted together. Their performance could be increased or decreased by adding or subtracting segments. For the Titan III-C, the solid boosters each

contained five segments. The solid-fueled boosters were designated the "Zero stage" and each provided more than 453,600 kilograms of thrust. Both were ignited at liftoff along with the 213,190-kilogram thrust twin liquid-fueled first-stage engines, providing a combined liftoff thrust of 1,133,922 kilograms. This made the Titan III-C the most powerful booster in the free world at the time. The second stage was powered by a single 45,360-kilogram thrust liquid-fueled engine. The launcher was topped with a restartable "transtage," which provided an additional 7,257 kilograms of thrust.

One of the vexing problems facing engineers was how to move the crew from the Gemini B into the pressurized MOL laboratory once in orbit. A number of schemes were investigated, including transfer by extravehicular activity (EVA) or through an inflatable external tunnel connecting the two components of the station. The final solution was to modify NASA's Gemini craft by adding a hatchway through the heatshield between the Gemini and MOL laboratory. This modification was the major difference between NASA's civilian Gemini and the Air Force Gemini B.

The heatshield is a critical item on any piloted spacecraft. If it fails during return to Earth, the crew is doomed to an incendiary death. Many engineers therefore considered the heatshield an inviolable part of the spacecraft. Cutting a hatch through it was regarded by some as a dangerous joke. McDonnell Aircraft engineers in charge of designing the modified shield considered it theoretically workable. Only an robotic space test would validate the design.

By the summer of 1966, the MOL concept had grown more complex, and it accordingly gained weight, swelling to a 13,608-kilogram station. This prompted the switch from the Titan III-C to the Titan III-M. The new rocket used more powerful seven-segment solid-fueled boosters and had a liftoff thrust of 1,363,636 kilograms.

As the program progressed, it became apparent that earlier cost estimates were not realistic. By

Illustration of a Gemini B reentry vehicle separating from the MOL. (U.S. Air Force)

early 1967, the total program cost had grown to $2.2 billion, with the initial piloted launches slipping until 1970. Then the Vietnam War began to take its fiscal toll on the high-technology program. Funds were diverted from MOL to help finance the war effort and the first launch slipped further, to 1971. By 1969, the total program costs had expanded to a projected $3 billion, with the first launch still three years in the future.

Shrinking military budgets and increased Vietnam War costs eventually overtook the MOL project. On June 10, 1969, President Richard M. Nixon's secretary of defense, Melvin Laird, reluctantly canceled the MOL program. After a decade of effort with both the X-20 and the MOL program, the United States' military piloted space program also ended.

Contributions

Had it been completed, MOL would have been the world's first space station. While the goal of long-duration space operation was not achieved, the design and construction of the MOL components by Douglas Aircraft initiated an experience base for

the building of large space structures. At the time of its design and initial fabrication, the MOL laboratory was the largest free-flying single-component piloted space structure yet built.

Although the project was prematurely terminated, MOL progressed through the development and validation of the Titan III-C booster and the initial development of the seven-segment solid booster for the Titan III-M. The seven-segment booster design was also shelved when MOL was canceled, but its development was not wasted. In 1985, the design was resurrected for the even more powerful Titan IV booster, which is the mainstay heavy-lift booster of the current American military space effort.

An robotic MOL development launch designed by the Air Force as OV4 3 was flown on November 3, 1966. The payload consisted of a 3.3-meter diameter, 11.7-meter-long simulated MOL fabricated from a Titan II ICBM oxidizer tank that was topped with a conical Gemini spacecraft adapter. The resulting vehicle was unusually long, 48.2 meters, and one of the design goals of the flight was to gather "long shape" aerodynamic data during the Titan III-C launch.

The Gemini B spacecraft launched atop the dummy MOL was in fact the same spacecraft used by NASA in the Gemini-Titan 2 suborbital flight on January 19, 1965. The NASA flight validated the craft's heatshield for piloted use. In the case of the MOL launch, the same spacecraft was again used to validate the heatshield design, the difference being the second flight used the MOL heatshield, which had a hatch cut into it for the transfer tunnel between the Gemini B and the Laboratory.

The OV4 3 launch was, in all respects, a success. The Titan III-C performed nominally, flying an unusual "roller-coaster" ascent trajectory. Upon reaching an altitude of 210 kilometers, the first burn of the transtage pitched the vehicle downward as it accelerated to 28,255 kilometers per hour. Upon descending to 167 kilometers, the Gemini B spacecraft was released into a reentry trajectory that targeted it into the South Atlantic Ocean near Ascension Island, where it was recovered. The transtage then reignited two more times to place the simulated MOL into a 295-by-296- kilometer orbit. The transtage remained attached to the payload, resulting in the largest military-oriented payload yet placed into orbit.

The OV4 3 mission not only provided operational experience with the flight of the simulated laboratory but also was the first reflight of a spacecraft that had previously flown in space. Many respected engineers were doubtful that the Gemini B heatshield would be structurally sound once the MOL crew hatch had been cut through it. The reentry test showed the modified heatshield did indeed work. Instead of destroying the shield, the heat of reentry "welded" the hatch shut and solidified the heatshield, verifying its design intent.

Although the program was canceled, much of the reconnaissance sensor technology developed for the MOL project was later applied to robotic spy satellites, such as KH-11.

Context

Had the project been concluded, MOL would have been the first piloted space launch to use solid-fueled rocket boosters. Instead, this legacy fell to the space shuttle, which itself owes the use of solid-fueled boosters to the experience gained with the MOL's Titan III booster. The reliability and simplicity of the solid-fueled boosters developed for the Titan III were instrumental in their acceptance into NASA's space shuttle program. Their initial success in the Titan program led to a false sense of security with the solid boosters, which contributed

to the fatal space shuttle *Challenger* accident in 1986.

While the United States did not fly the hardware developed for MOL, the program's existence inspired the Soviet Union to initiate its own piloted space-based reconnaissance system called Almaz ("diamond" in Russian). Almaz was developed in the 1960's by the Soviet design bureau headed by Vladimir Chelomei. It was a twenty-ton cylindrical space station similar to MOL.

The Almaz program suffered delays much as the MOL program did, and it was not ready to fly even when MOL was canceled in 1969. However, in response to the planned 1972 launch of NASA's Skylab space station, the Soviet Almaz was "civilianized" and transferred to the Energia Design Bureau. Launched in 1971 as the Salyut 1 space station, the converted Soviet counterpart of MOL became the prototype of a twenty-five-year-long series of space stations, which has culminated with the Russian Mir Space Station.

The MOL program evolved during a difficult era in American history. Bold space plans outlined by President Kennedy at the beginning of the 1960's clashed with the economic realities of massive government spending on both expanding domestic social programs and the burgeoning war in Southeast Asia. At the same time that President Lyndon B. Johnson's Great Society programs absorbed more of the nation's fiscal resources; the Vietnam War was eating up more of a shrinking military budget. This placed a great strain on development of new technologies such as the MOL. It became the target for continued budget cutting and saw its funding allocation continuously reduced until it could no longer maintain a realistic development schedule.

As MOL faced extended delays, the program had the public appearance of being outdated before it even flew. Based on the Gemini spacecraft that NASA retired in 1966, MOL would seem obsolete by the time piloted launches began in 1972. Other detractors argued that the program was wasteful military duplication of the civilian space station program, which was being advanced as the Skylab program, also slated for its initial launch in 1972.

The reality behind MOL's eventual cancellation in 1969 goes beyond obsolescence or duplication of NASA efforts. The fact was that the operational requirement for a piloted military reconnaissance platform in space had changed. The Air Force had experienced unexpected high success with its robotic space reconnaissance programs. The KH-4 through KH-8 spy satellite series was far more productive than its planners had dreamed. Complex and risky piloted MOL missions were simply not needed for effective space-based reconnaissance.

Thirteen military pilots were selected as astronaut candidates for the MOL program. When the space station was canceled, the seven pilots who fell within NASA's cutoff age of thirty-six were allowed to enter the NASA Astronaut Corps.

Although it would be more than a decade before any of them would fly in space, all seven eventually flew on the space shuttle.

Significant among those who did not transfer to NASA were James A. Abrahamson, Jr., and Robert Herres, both with the Air Force. Too old to become NASA astronauts, they continued their military careers. Abrahamson earned three stars as a general and became first the head of the space shuttle program, then the first director of the Strategic Defense Initiative, or "Star Wars" program. Herres earned four stars and became vice chairperson of the joint chiefs of staff under General Colin Powell.

—Robert V. Reeves

See also: Gemini Spacecraft; Manned Maneuvering Unit; Mercury Project; Rocketry: Modern History; Russia's Mir Space Station; Skylab Program; Skylab Space Station; Space Centers, Spaceports, and Launch Sites; Space Stations: Origins and Development; Spy Satellites; Titan Launch Vehicles.

Further Reading

Braun, Wernher von, and Frederick I. Ordway III. *Space Travel: A History.* Rev. ed. New York: Harper & Row, 1985. Details the development of rockets and the evolution of the Space Age. The historical narrative describes to the layperson how rocketry advanced from Chinese fireworks to the Apollo landings on the Moon.

Bronner, Fritz. *Buzz Aldrin's Race into Space Companion.* Berkeley, Calif.: Osborne McGraw- Hill, 1993. Though billed as a companion volume for Buzz Aldrin's *Race into Space* computer simulation, the first 183 pages of this book provide an excellent nontechnical review of the politics and conduct of the Russian and American civil and military space programs.

Burrows, William E. *This New Ocean: The Story of the First Space Age.* New York: Random House, 1998. This is a comprehensive history of the human conquest of space, covering everything from the earliest attempts at spaceflight through the voyages near the end of the twentieth century. Burrows is an experienced journalist, who has reported for *The New York Times*, *The Washington Post*, and *The Wall Street Journal*. There are many photographs and an extensive source list. Interviewees in the book include Isaac Asimov, Alexei Leonov, Sally K. Ride, and James A. Van Allen.

Gatland, Kenneth. *The Illustrated Encyclopedia of Space Technology: A Comprehensive History of Space Exploration.* New York: Salamander, 1989. This volume is noted for its concise yet detailed descriptions of the world's space programs. It is lavishly illustrated with color photographs and contains many drawings and charts that explain past and current space systems to the layperson in a visually interesting manner.

Hacker, Barton C., and James M. Grimwood. *On the Shoulders of Titans: A History of Project Gemini*. NASA SP-4203. Washington, D.C.: Government Printing Office, 1977. This official NASA history of the Gemini piloted space program is rich in technical detail and personal anecdotes about the development and conduct of the program. It is relevant to the Manned Orbiting Laboratory in that the Gemini spacecraft was to be used by that program.

Heppenheimer, T. A. *Countdown: A History of Space Flight*. New York: JohnWiley, 1997. A detailed historical narrative of the human conquest of space. Heppenheimer traces the development of piloted flight through the military rocketry programs of the era preceding World War II. Covers both the American and the Soviet attempts to place vehicles, spacecraft, and humans into the hostile environment of space. More than a dozen pages are devoted to bibliographic references.

Hobbs, David. *An Illustrated Guide to Space Warfare*. London: Salamander Books, 1986. This profusely and colorfully illustrated book details the development of military space systems from the birth of the Space Age to the modern "StarWars" era. Nontechnical text and excellent diagrams describe various military space programs for the lay reader.

Klass, Philip J. *Secret Sentries in Space*. New York: Random House, 1971. This book was one of the first to detail the Soviet and American military space reconnaissance programs. Although recent declassification has shown that many speculated details about covert programs were in error, the details of publicly discussed military space programs remain historically useful.

Lee, Wayne. *To Rise from Earth: An Easy to Understand Guide to Spaceflight*. New York: Checkmark Books, 1996. This is a good introduction to the science of spaceflight. Although written by an engineer with the NASA Jet Propulsion Laboratory, it is presented in easy-to-understand language. In addition to the theory of spaceflight, it gives some of the history of the human endeavor to explore space.

McDougall, Walter A. *The Heavens and the Earth: A Political History of the Space Age*. 2d ed. Baltimore: Johns Hopkins University Press, 1997. This nontechnical historical narrative deals exclusively with the politics of the Space Age and details how the civil and military space programs of both the United States and the Soviet Union evolved from the Cold War political struggle between the two superpowers.

Mari, Christopher, ed. *Space Exploration*. New York: H. W. Wilson, 1999. Twenty-five articles (reprinted from magazines), covering the state of the space program at the time of publication, are divided into five sections: John H. Glenn, Jr.'s return to space, the exploration of Mars, the International Space Station, recent mining efforts by commercial industries, and new types of space vehicles and propulsion systems.

Peebles, Curtis. *Guardians: Strategic Reconnaissance Satellites*. Novato, Calif.: Presidio Press, 1987. Written for the layperson, yet still detailed and fact filled, this book reviews the military space reconnaissance programs of both the United States and the Soviet Union. Technical details are presented in easy-to-understand context. Well illustrated with charts, diagrams, and photographs.

Shayler, David J. *Gemini: Steps to the Moon*. Chichester, England: Springer-Praxis, 2001. The story of the development of the Gemini Program from the perspective of the engineers, flight controllers, and astronauts.

Strom, Steven R. *The Best Laid Plans: A History of the Manned Orbiting Laboratory*. El Segundo, California: The Aerospace Corporation, 2004. http://www.aero.org/publications/crosslink/ summer2004/02. html. A concise history of the Manned Orbiting Laboratory from the company that designed and built it.

Mariner 1 and 2

Date: July 22, 1962, to January 3, 1963
Type of spacecraft: Planetary exploration

Mariner 1 and 2 were the first interplanetary spacecraft directed to study Venus. Although Mariner 1 suffered a launch failure, Mariner 2's flyby initiated an era of robotic spacecraft returning detailed data about the planetary system. Although it returned no photographs, Mariner 2 revolutionized knowledge of the conditions on Venus.

Key Figures

Jack N. James (1920-2001), Mariner 2 project manager

Dan Schneiderman (1922-2007), Spacecraft Systems manager

Edward J. Smith, principal investigator, magnetometer experiment

Gerry Neugebauer (1932-2014), and

Lewis Kaplan (1917-1999), principal investigators, infrared experiment

J. Copeland, and

D. E. Jones, principal investigators, microwave experiment

Summary of the Missions

The first interplanetary mission began developmental work even before the first Ranger spacecraft was ready for shipment to the Cape Canaveral launch site. (Ranger spacecraft were designed to be launched toward the Moon, taking photographs from a specified altitude until impacting the lunar surface.) The National Aeronautics and Space Administration (NASA) delegated primary responsibility for Mariners A and B to the Jet Propulsion Laboratory (JPL), in Pasadena, California. Mariner A was to be launched to Venus and Mariner B to Mars. Both spacecraft were to be in the 452-to-566-kilogram class. They were to be launched by a new booster consisting of an Atlas rocket with a Centaur upper stage. Centaur was designed to provide higher energy and better performance than previous upper stages. During the 1962-1964 time period, desirable launch windows existed to both Venus and Mars. Program planners expected Centaur to be available to support these launch opportunities.

It became evident by August, 1961, however, that Centaur would not be ready to send Mariner A to Venus for the third quarter 1962 inferior conjunction, when Venus would be in a position between the Sun and Earth. Existing boosters were incapable of sending Mariner A to Venus, as the spacecraft was too heavy. Clearly a problem existed, but the tremendous pressure to encounter Venus during this inferior conjunction prevailed. Under the advice of JPL, NASA developed the compromise Mariner R program, wherein an Atlas-Agena booster would launch a lighter, Ranger-class spacecraft containing modified Mariner A components and experiments.

Mariner R would weigh less than 210 kilograms and carry between 11 and 18 kilograms of experiments. Two spacecraft were to be dispatched from the same launch facility during the fifty-six-day launch window from July to September, 1962. Mission planners, scientists, and engineers had to redesign, build, and test a brand new spacecraft, devise a flight plan, and arrange twin launches in only eleven months. The decision to abandon Mariner A and commit to the new Mariner R spacecraft, redesignated Mariners 1 and 2, came in September, 1961. Test assemblies and design modification in the spacecraft and boosters were hurried along. After only nine months, project equipment was shipped to Cape Canaveral.

The Mariner R spacecraft was slightly more than 3 meters tall and 1.5 meters wide. As soon as the solar panels were deployed and the directional antennae unfurled, these dimensions became 3.5 and 5 meters, respectively. The final design weighed only 202 kilograms, including 18.6 kilograms of scientific equipment for Venus and interplanetary medium studies. The basic structure of the Mariner R spacecraft consisted of a hexagonal frame with superstructure to which a small liquid-fueled rocket motor, attitude control system gas jets, two folding solar panels, an infrared and microwave radiometer, numerous antennae, and other scientific experiments were attached.

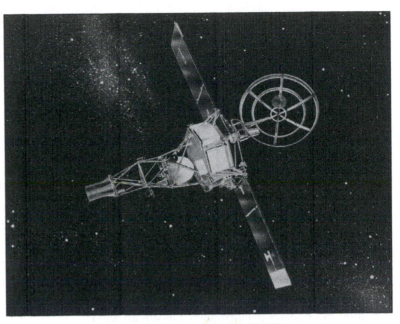

Illustration of of Mariner 2 in space. (NASA / JPL))

Sixty minutes after launch, Mariner R's central computer and sequencer automatically activated the attitude control system to orient the spacecraft's directional antennae toward Earth and the solar panels toward the Sun, using nitrogen gas thrusters to make periodic adjustments to maintain this attitude to within 1 degree. In this attitude, the solar panels provided the spacecraft with 222 watts of power and permitted the telecommunications system to operate on a mere 3 watts of power (even at a distance of 54 million miles from Earth).

The small rocket engine in the hexagonal base contained sufficient fuel for only one midcourse correction firing. Mariner R's speed could be altered by 0.2 to 61 meters per second as a result of burning this engine from 0.2 to 57 seconds.

Three spacecraft (Mariners 1, 2, and a backup) were shipped to Cape Canaveral in late May, 1962. Final flight preparations for Mariner 1 were completed by mid-July. Thus, after only 324 days from program inception, a spacecraft was poised to provide the first close-up examination of another planet. The Atlas-Agena/Mariner 1 vehicle began its final countdown at 11:33 p.m. on July 20 or 03:33 Coordinated Universal Time (UTC) on July 21, but almost immediately, difficulty in the range safety command system forced a hold. (This system had already delayed the initiation of the 176-minute countdown.) The countdown resumed at 12:37 a.m. (04:37 UTC) on July 21, but a blown fuse in the range safety circuit forced cancellation of the launch about two hours later.

The following day, the recycled countdown resumed just before midnight. Difficulties with both ground equipment and the vehicle's radio guidance system plagued the countdown with several unscheduled holds. At 4:16 a.m. (08:16 UTC) on July 22, the countdown resumed after a recycle to T minus 5 minutes. The remainder of the countdown proceeded without incident, and Mariner 1 was lifted from the pad at 4:21:23 a.m. (08:21:23 UTC). Although initial flight telemetry looked promising, the range safety officer noticed an unscheduled vehicle yaw two minutes after liftoff. The vehicle threatened populated areas and the North Atlantic shipping lanes. When corrective commands sent to the vehicle's guidance system proved ineffective, the range safety officer was forced to destroy the vehicle, after only 293 seconds of powered flight. For more than a minute as the Mariner 1 spacecraft fell to the ocean, its transponder transmitted data.

The cause of the Atlas-Agena failure was not immediately clear. Before a commitment to proceed with Mariner 2 could be made, the cause had to be determined and corrective measures taken. After a detailed accident analysis, a simple fault was uncovered in the guidance system programming: A bar (or hyphen) above the element R in the guidance program had been overlooked. This programming error was shared by all previous Atlas launches, but booster performance was not affected by it during these launches because the remainder of the guidance systems functioned properly. On Mariner 1's Atlas, an antenna performed inadequately, causing the guidance signal received by the launch vehicle to be weak and noisy. Eventually, the launch vehicle lost its lock on the ground guidance signal, and when the signal was lost, the ground computer initiated a programmed search for the Atlas radio beacon to restore the proper signal lock. As this was in progress, the Atlas computer suppressed information from this search, according to designed programming, and attempted to restore the signal lock on its own. Unfortunately, the command for that action was bar R. Thus, because the booster's computer was incapable of restoring the lock by itself, a result of the programming error, and was not responding to the ground search efforts, the Atlas was not properly supplied with steering commands and it veered off course.

Thirty-five days after the destruction of Mariner 1, Mariner 2 began its final launch countdown. Like its predecessor, Mariner 2 was plagued by countdown difficulties. The first launch attempt had to be aborted because of a problem with the command-destruct system. The countdown resumed the following evening. During one unscheduled

countdown hold, the primary Atlas booster battery had to be replaced; a planned hold then had to be extended to monitor the battery lifetime. When the countdown reached the scheduled T-minus-5-minute hold, technical difficulties in the radio guidance system forced a further delay. The countdown was able to proceed only to T minus 60 seconds before the radio guidance troubles forced another hold; they also caused a hold at T minus 50 seconds. After a recycle to T minus 5 minutes, the countdown was able to continue without mechanical trouble, but now the Atlas booster battery had only three minutes of pre-liftoff life remaining. To conserve power, flight planners decided not to switch on this battery until T minus 60 seconds. The test director pressed the fire button at T minus zero (1:53:14 a.m., 05:53:14 UTC, August 27, 1962) and the Atlas-Agena/Mariner 2 rose from the pad and followed the desired trajectory. The Agena/Mariner 2 separated from the spent Atlas, and after coasting briefly, the Agena's restartable engine was fired to achieve the desired orbital velocity and a 186-kilometer parking orbit.

Just 16 minutes after orbital insertion, the Agena engine was restarted to increase spacecraft velocity to more than 40,000 kilometers per hour (escape velocity). Mariner 2 separated from the Agena upper stage two minutes after engine shutdown. Forty-four minutes after launch, Mariner 2's central computer and sequencer issued the commands to unfold the solar panels and radiometer dish, thus assuming the in-flight configuration. Sixteen minutes later, the attitude control system began the Sun orientation sequence to align Mariner 2's attitude properly.

Early projections indicated that Mariner 2 was on a flight path that would miss Venus by 373,000 kilometers. In order to obtain meaningful scientific data at closest approach, the spacecraft had to pass within 12,800-64,000 kilometers of the planet's surface. On September 4, a series of commands was transmitted to Mariner 2 to perform a required midcourse correction burn. The spacecraft engine burned for 27.8 seconds. As a result, Mariner 2's velocity decreased by 94.4 kilometers per hour with respect to Earth and increased by 72 kilometers per hour with respect to the Sun, causing the spacecraft to spiral in toward the Sun, passing Earth on mission day 65, and crossing the orbit of Venus on mission day 109.

During its interplanetary cruise, Mariner 2 suffered a series of nagging problems, but none that crippled the spacecraft. As Mariner 2 approached its target, spacecraft temperatures began to rise steadily. In fact, twelve hours before the Venus encounter, it was feared the central computer and sequencer would be unable to command Mariner 2 to initiate its encounter sequence properly because of overheating. As a check, a ground command was radioed to Mariner 2; the spacecraft, then 57.6 million kilometers away, responded by initiating the encounter sequence.

Mariner 2 approached Venus on its night side, making three scans of the planet: one on the night side, one along the terminator, and one on the daylight side. At its closest approach, Mariner 2 was only 34,800 kilometers above the surface of Venus.

Contributions

Mariner R carried six scientific instruments; two were primarily intended for Venus studies and the remaining four for interplanetary medium studies. Mariner's scientific objectives were twofold: measurement of cosmic dust, solar winds, high-energy cosmic rays, charged solar particles, and magnetic fields in the interplanetary medium; and measurement and investigation of the magnetic fields, radiation belts, temperature, surface conditions, and cloud composition of Venus. Data from the scientific instruments were processed for transmission to Earth receiving stations by a data conditioning system.

For the study of the interplanetary medium, the spacecraft contained a cosmic dust detector, a solar plasma experiment, a magnetometer, and a high energy radiation experiment. The cosmic dust detector

measured the flux, direction of origin, and momentum of interplanetary dust and investigated the nature of any hazards this dust could pose to crewed spacecraft. The energy and flux of low-energy positive ions streaming from the Sun were measured by the solar plasma experiment, which consisted of curved electrostatic deflection plates and a collector cup, a sweep amplifier, a programmer element, and an electrometer. The plasma experiment worked in a manner similar to a mass spectrometer, except that the instrument measured the energy of ions (in the range of 240 to 8,400 electron volts, or eV) rather than the mass. Mariner's magnetometer took readings of the magnetic fields in the vicinity of Venus and in interplanetary space with a lower sensitivity limit of 5 gammas. (One gamma is approximately one thirty thousandth the intensity of Earth's magnetic field at the equator.) High-energy charged particles consisting of cosmic-ray protons, alpha particles, electrons, and heavy nuclei were studied by the high-energy radiation experiment. To penetrate the walls of the instrument's ionization chamber, electrons required energies greater than 0.5 million electron volts (one million electron volts is a megaelectron volt), alpha particles more than 40 megaelectron volts, and cosmic-ray protons of more than 10 megaelectron volts. Particle fluxes were measured in a detector consisting of three Geiger-Müller tubes.

For the study of Venus, the spacecraft contained a microwave radiometer and an infrared radiometer. The microwave radiometer scanned the planet at 19-nanometer and 13.5-nanometer wavelengths. Activated ten hours before closest encounter, the instrument had two scan-rate modes, 120° at a rate of 1 degree per second for pre-encounter and 0.1 degree per second at closest approach. Designed to investigate the origin of the high surface temperature emanating from Venus and measure the surface temperature at encounter, the instrument had to be calibrated automatically twenty-three times during flight using a reference antenna system that scanned deep space for an absolute zero reference temperature. The infrared radiometer was attached directly to the microwave radiometer antenna so it would scan the exact area scanned by the microwave experiment at the same scan rate. This instrument scanned Venus at wavelengths in the 8- to 9- and 10- to 10.8-micron ranges of the infrared. A rotating disk alternately passed and blocked planetary emissions to compare the readings of Venus against the background empty-space readings.

Context

Mariner 2 was the first successful interplanetary spacecraft, continuing beyond Venus and reaching solar perihelion (the point in its orbit where it was nearest to the Sun) on December 27, 1962, at a point 104 million kilometers from the Sun. Mariner 2 entered an orbit, that sent it around the Sun coming as close as 40 million kilometers to Earth and as far as 181 million kilometers from the Sun. Spacecraft signals continued to be received until January 3, 1963, when the Johannesburg, South Africa, tracking station shut down the spacecraft following a thirty-minute data transmission. A few days later, the Goldstone station searched for a weak spacecraft signal, but Mariner 2 had gone silent, becoming another relic of humankind's presence in outer space.

Scientists required several months to sift through Mariner 2's data to construct a new picture of the planet Venus. Rich in carbon dioxide and poor in oxygen and water vapor, the Venusian atmosphere consists of a continuous thick cloud layer beginning 72.5 kilometers above the surface and continuing for 24-32 kilometers. This thick cloud layer allowed solar energy to reach the surface but prevented most of the heat from radiating back into space, creating

A long scroll of data from Venus, seen in front of JPL's Mariner 2 mission board. (NASA)

a greenhouse effect. Before Mariner 2, the surface temperature of Venus was estimated to be about 320° Celsius. Mariner data suggested a hotter planet, slightly more than 425° Celsius at the surface. The thick atmosphere conducted heat well and explained why the spacecraft observed no temperature variation between the planet's daylight and dark sides. Mariner 2's magnetometer failed to detect a magnetic field or any belts of trapped charged particle radiation. These observations tended to confirm ground-based data indicating an extremely slow or nonexistent planetary rotation.

Perhaps the most important result of the Mariner 2 mission was the inescapable evidence that interplanetary space was neither empty nor field free, but full of particles having a wide range of energies. It was learned that these particles also contain time-dependent periodic fields with characteristic oscillation periods ranging from 40 seconds to several hours.

With the immense success of Mariner 2, plans for a repeat mission were canceled. Plans began to take shape for a mission to Mars. The earliest "least-energy" opportunity for a Mariner Mars flyby was during 1964-1965. With these seemingly modest efforts, an era of planetary exploration had begun. The Mariner program concluded after ten attempted planetary missions. Two more Mariner spacecraft visited Venus. Mariner 5 flew 3,391 kilometers above Venus (October, 1967), and Mariner 10 flew within 6,000 kilometers of Venus (February 5, 1974) while on its journey toward Mercury. The United States sent Pioneer Venus probes in 1978 to orbit Venus and plunge through its atmosphere. The Soviet Union also investigated Venus, sending Venera probes through the atmosphere, attempting soft landings on the surface. Venera 7 (1970) was the first to transmit data from the surface. Several times the Russians repeated this feat with varying degrees of success; probes, however, cannot survive long in the harsh Venusian environment. Nevertheless, these spacecraft (Pioneer Venus, Mariner 10, and the Veneras) greatly increased scientific understanding of Venus, and the bold step of Mariner 2 paved the way for these more advanced scientific undertakings.

—David G. Fisher

See also: Deep Space Network; Hubble Space Telescope; Jet Propulsion Laboratory; Magellan: Venus; Manned Orbiting Laboratory; Mariner 3 and 4; Mariner 5; Mariner 8 and 9; Mariner 10; Pioneer Venus 1; Planetary Exploration; Solar and Heliospheric Observatory; Viking Program; Voyager 2: Neptune.

Further Reading

Cattermole, Peter, and Patrick Moore. *Atlas of Venus*. New York: Cambridge University Press, 1997. Filled with photography from telescopes and the Mariner, Pioneer Venus, and Magellan spacecrafts, this work provides a complete atlas of Venus and a gazetteer of Venusian place names.

Fimmel, Richard O., James A. Van Allen, and Eric Burgess. *Pioneer Venus*. NASA SP-461. Washington, D.C.: Government Printing Office, 1983. The official NASA history of the Pioneer Venus program. In addition to details about mission events and data, it provides a historical perspective of our scientific understanding of Venus as a result of earlier spacecraft missions (such as Mariner 2).

Fisher, David G. "Mariner: Twenty-Five Years of Interplanetary Space Flight." *Aerospace Educator* 4 (Fall, 1987): 33-37. This work provides details about the spacecraft systems and mission events. Suitable for general audiences.

Greeley, Ronald. *Planetary Landscapes*. 2d ed. New York: Chapman and Hall, 1994. This book presents pictorial geomorphology (study of the form and evolution of planetary surfaces) of all the planets visited by spacecraft prior to 1987 and the moons orbiting those planets. Suitable for advanced high school and introductory college-level audiences. Includes numerous references to more specific scientific papers.

Grinspoon, David Harry. *Venus Revealed: A New Look Below the Clouds of Our Mysterious Twin Planet*. New York: Perseus Book Group, 1998. This work provides both romantic and scientific explanations of the planet closest to Earth, incorporating the latest data from the Magellan spacecraft.

Hartmann, William K. *Moons and Planets*. 5th ed. Belmont, Calif.: Thomson Brooks/Cole Publishing, 2005. Provides detailed information about all objects in the solar system. Suitable on three separate levels: high school student, general reader, and the college undergraduate studying planetary geology.

Heppenheimer, T. A. *Countdown: A History of Space Flight*. New York: JohnWiley, 1997. A detailed historical narrative of the human conquest of space. Heppenheimer traces the development of piloted flight through the military rocketry programs of the era preceding WorldWar II. Covers both the American and the Soviet attempts to place vehicles, spacecraft, and humans into the hostile environment of space. More than a dozen pages are devoted to bibliographic references.

Lee, Wayne. *To Rise from Earth: An Easy to Understand Guide to Spaceflight*. New York: Checkmark Books, 1996. This is a good introduction to the science of spaceflight. Although written by an engineer with the NASA Jet Propulsion Laboratory, it is presented in easy-to-understand language. In addition to the theory of spaceflight, it gives some of the history of the human endeavor to explore space.

Mari, Christopher, ed. *Space Exploration*. New York: H. W. Wilson, 1999. Twenty-five articles (reprinted from magazines), covering the state of the space program at the time of publication, are divided into five sections: John H. Glenn, Jr.'s return to space, the exploration of Mars, the International Space Station, recent mining efforts by commercial industries, and new types of space vehicles and propulsion systems.

Morrison, David, and Tobias Owen. *The Planetary System*. 3d ed. San Francisco: Addison- Wesley, 2003. Organized by planetary object, this work provides contemporary data on all planetary bodies visited by spacecraft since the early days of the Space Age. Suitable for high school and college students and the general reader.

Nicks, Oran W. *Far Travelers: The Exploring Machines*. NASASP-480. Washington, D.C.: Scientific and Technical Information Branch, 1985. This work provides a perspective on planetary and lunar spacecraft programs unique to one who has participated in numerous programs. Illuminates the planning process and evolution of spacecraft programs. Suitable for general audiences.

Mariner 3 and 4

Date: November 5, 1964, to July 24, 1965
Type of spacecraft: Planetary exploration

Mariner 4 was the first U.S. robotic probe to Mars. It provided data that greatly increased our understanding of Earth's neighboring planet. The probe revealed a harsh, cratered wasteland rather than an environment likely to be capable of supporting life, as well as data on Mars's radiation density, cosmic-ray and cosmic-dust bombardment, characteristics of the "ion wind," and properties of the Martian atmosphere.

Key Figures

William H. Pickering (1910-2004), Jet Propulsion Laboratory (JPL) director

Oran W. Nicks (1925-1998), director of Lunar and Planetary Programs, NASA

Dan Schneiderman (1922-2007), Spacecraft Systems manager

John R. Casani (b. 1932), Mariner Spacecraft Systems manager

Robert B. Leighton (1919-1997), television subsystem experimenter, California Institute of Technology

Bruce C. Murray (1932-2013), television subsystem experimenter, California Institute of Technology

Robert P. Sharp (1911-2004), television subsystem experimenter, California Institute of Technology

James A. Van Allen (1914-2006), radiation and charged particles experimenter, University of Iowa

Summary of the Missions

Mariner missions were intended to advance our knowledge of Mars and of the solar system in general by investigating certain physical aspects of the planet and its environs. After the success of Mariner 2, sent to investigate Venus in 1962, the National Aeronautics and Space Administration (NASA) contracted with the Jet Propulsion Laboratory (JPL) of the California Institute of Technology in Pasadena, California, to engage in a series of robotic investigations of Mars over a period of many years. Mariner 3 was to be the first mission in that series.

The Mariner "family" of spacecraft had begun with a highly successful spacecraft, or "bus," on which numerous scientific instruments could be hung. This Mariner system was part of a broader system referred to as the overall "Project," which consisted of all the ground-support, testing, fabricating, launching, telemetry (radio signal data), and data-reception processes required to send the spacecraft to its target, correctly gather data, and return the data to Earth for scientists to interpret. In the case of Mariners 3 and 4, the Project involved a worldwide network of antennae stretching from California to Australia, South Africa, and Spain, as well as many subsystem contractors in the United States.

The Mariner/Mars Project established in 1962 succeeded within a short time in preparing two Mariner craft for launch. At midday on November 5, 1964, Mariner 3 was lofted from Launch Complex 13 at Cape Kennedy by an Atlas rocket. Within a few minutes, it became apparent that the craft was not functioning properly. The "shroud," or protective covering that surrounds the payload during launch (when the possibility of damage is greatest), is normally ejected after the rocket passes through the atmosphere. At that point, the payload can ride safely on the nose of the rocket until it separates from the rocket and is sent on its journey. Mariner 3's shroud, however, would not disconnect and could not be ejected. Unable to shed the weight of the shroud, the rocket was unable to reach sufficient velocity to push its payload far enough out into space. At the appropriate time, Mariner 3 separated from the rocket and tried to extend its solar panels to collect sunlight to convert into energy for powering onboard equipment. Because the shroud still surrounded the Mariner payload, however, this step could not be executed; after a short time the onboard backup batteries failed, leaving the spacecraft dead.

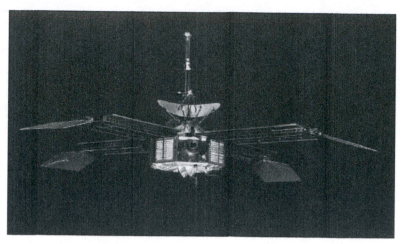

Design of Mariner 3 and 4. (NASA)

After studying the problems with the Mariner 3 craft, the engineering team experimented with a fiberglass payload shroud, redesigning the entire shroud in only three weeks. Toward the end of November, Mariner 4 stood on the launch pad. Itwas launched on November 28, at 9:22 a.m. eastern standard time or 14:22 Coordinated Universal Time (UTC) by an Atlas-Agena rocket. The spent Atlas booster was jettisoned and the Agena continued to push Mariner 4 to an orbital altitude of 185 kilometers and an orbital velocity of 28,157 kilometers per hour. Mariner 4 was on its way. The Agena rocket shut down, and the Mariner craft coasted for 41 minutes in Earth orbit, preparing to swing outward toward Mars. At a predetermined time, the Agena reignited to boost the craft to escape velocity. Then Mariner 4 separated from the rocket, opening its four solar panels. Mariner oriented itself toward the Sun and received energy-giving sunlight, thus activating solar cells in the solar panels, generating 700 watts of electrical power.

The journey to Mars required crossing 523 million kilometers of open space over a period of almost eight months. During this time, the spacecraft used Canopus (one of the brightest stars in this part of the Milky Way galaxy) as its reference point for navigation. A spacecraft in Earth orbit or near Earth can use the planet for fixing its position. At great distances, however, Earth becomes a faint and unreliable reference; thus, Canopus was used.

During the long journey, Mariner continually checked its own performance and status as well as the condition of the space environment. Onboard attitude control thrusters released puffs of nitrogen gas to keep Mariner upright, and the craft was continually balanced and rebalanced against the pressure of the solar wind (the ionized particles that flow out from the Sun) by special vanes attached to the ends of the solar panels. To regulate the temperature of the spacecraft's instruments, special "window shades" fashioned like louvered slats opened or closed to let out or retain heat generated by instruments.

A solar plasma probe was designed to measure the charged particles making up the solar wind. A Geiger-Müller tube measured ionization caused by charged particles. Unfortunately, a massive solar flare on February 5 damaged the instrument and rendered it useless. A cosmic-ray telescope detected protons and alpha particles, while a high-sensitivity helium magnetometer measured magnetic fields. The cosmic-dust detector consisted of a flat plate facing the direction in which the spacecraft was moving, and two surface-penetration detectors were fixed with a microphone to record the impact force and the number of hits from micrometeoroids.

Mariner's camera system was a vidicon television tube mounted behind a telescope; for this mission, it was also fitted with red and green filters that could be used interchangeably. The image falling on the tube was about 0.55 centimeter square. The camera scanned the image in 200 lines of 200 dots for each line, producing a digital signal of 240,000 bits per image, which was recorded on a quarter-inch magnetic tape loop 91 meters long. The recorder stopped automatically between images to save tape. Mariner 4 recorded television images, which were converted to digital form so that the data could be transmitted to Earth for analysis and conversion to print images.

Mariner 4 first encountered Mars on July 14, 1965, after traversing almost 523 million kilometers along the spacecraft's arcing trajectory (215 million straight-line kilometers). In its pass across Mars, Mariner recorded twenty-one images and a small portion of a twenty-second, starting at 18 minutes after midnight UTC on July 25. The imaging sequence took only 26 minutes. The first image was recorded when Mariner was 16,895 kilometers from its target, and the last was recorded at 9,844 kilometers,t At that time, Mars was moving in its orbit around the Sun at a speed 17,700 kilometers per hour faster than Mariner was moving as it crossed in front of the planet.

The digital data recorded on magnetic tape on board the spacecraft were released in a steady stream and rerecorded on magnetic tape by Mariner Mission Control at JPL in Pasadena. The series of Earth antennae, which spread from Goldstone, California, across Australia, South Africa, and Spain, recorded every bit of digital data, and the data then were converted into black-and-white photographs.

Contributions

The Mariner 4 mission completely changed humankind's concept of Mars.. Startling images received from the craft, when compared to even the best photographs taken through Earth-based telescopes, immeasurably increased our knowledge of Mars. The other instruments, each conducting its own separate electronic investigations, also provided amazing information. Mariner 4 was an unqualified success.

Densely packed craters, both large and small, were revealed, as well as an impact basin. In all, more than seventy craters appear in the imagery. The surface of the planet was found to be rough and irregular, not unlike the topography of the Moon. Only in one instance did the Mariner 4 images hint at the presence of water, and that was in the ground haze rimming some of the deeper craters along the northern border of Phaethontis.

Carbon dioxide in considerable amounts was detected in the thin Martian atmosphere, although little nitrogen was discovered. Indeed, a thicker atmosphere might have protected the surface from the meteorite bombardment that produced the

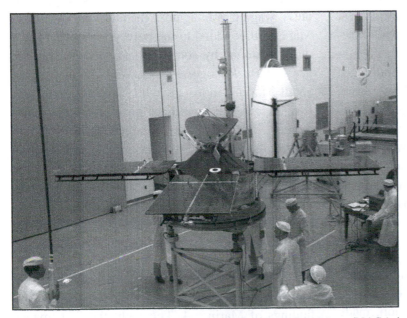

Mariner 4 is prepared for a weight test before launch to Mars. (NASA / JPL)

cratered surface. The absence of radiation belts and magnetic shock layers around Mars indicates that Mars has little or no magnetic field surrounding it. The Mars that greeted Mariner 4 has probably looked the same for millions and millions of years. In a planned spacecraft occultation, the Mariner craft swept behind the planet and sent back to Earth careful readings of the thin atmosphere surrounding Mars. In fact, the ionosphere is virtually undetectable.

During Mariner's 227-day odyssey, about two hundred micrometeoroids struck the craft. The hits apparently increased as the craft approached Mars but then decreased suddenly in the vicinity of the planet; this decrease suggests that Mars sweeps its path clear of cosmic dust as it orbits the Sun. The Mariner mission was undertaken during the period of the "quiet Sun," that time in the eleven-year sunspot cycle when the Sun's activity is at a minimum. At the same time, however, Mariner recorded violent solar eruptions in February, April, May, and June. Some of these flares were seen by telescope from Earth.

The sweep of Mariner 4's observations began at Phlegra, near the region of Cebrenia in the northern hemisphere; moved across the Mesogaea area near Amazonis at the Martian equator and Mare Cimmerium in the southern hemisphere, through Phaethontis and back up across Aonius Sinus; and ended just below and near Xanthe and the Chryse basin. By far the most spectacular image captured by Mariner 4 was image number 11, at 34 south latitude and longitude 199 east. The image showed a large crater in Cimmerium with newer and smaller impact craters overlaying the older large crater. The image also suggests ground haze or possibly frost rimming the large impact crater.

Context

The mission of Mariner 4 took place in that especially delightful era of scientific discovery known as the golden age of planetary exploration, made possible by breathtaking new technologies in space science research. For the first time, human eyes could see—considerably more precisely than Galileo had—the landscape of an alien world. Since 1960, when the world's first weather satellite (TIROS) looked at Earth for the first time, scientists have learned more about the solar system and the universe than had been learned during the preceding five hundred years. Mariner 4 was on the leading edge during that great epoch of lunar and planetary exploration—an exciting time of new discoveries, new theories, new possibilities, and new inventions.

Before Mariner 4, popular conceptions of Mars were determined by theorists who envisioned a planet that was more attractive and infinitely more appealing. Astronomer Percival Lowell had taken up the Martian canal debate and had tried to enlarge the Martian fantasy of earlier astronomers such as Giovanni Schiaparelli, who had claimed to see canali, or channels (which were mistakenly translated as "canals"). This controversy had raised the exciting possibility of intelligent beings who constructed the canals to transport or control the flow of enormous amounts of water.

The comic-strip adventures of Buck Rogers, piously waging war against dictators encamped on Mars, further added to the perception of Mars as a place inhabited by some kind of "people." On the heels of Buck Rogers, H. G. Wells wrote a novel about Martian monsters who came to Earth, destroying cities in their quest for dominion over humanity. The fiction was enlarged upon by Orson Welles, then a radio broadcaster, who added sound effects to the story and used his creation as a huge Halloween prank on the American people. On October 30, 1938, Welles aired his fantasy as *The War of the Worlds*. Thinking that what they heard on radio was really happening, people panicked—some even committed suicide.

Given the prevailing myth of a life-supporting Mars, people the world over were surprised by the findings of Mariner 4. The night the first images came back to Earth, a televised newscast was held at JPL. One by one the images were shown, Disappointment was evident as not the lush landscape of a beautifully adorned planet, but a dry, barren, crater-pocked wasteland was revealed.

Although Mariner 4 brought about an end to a dream, it offered the beginning of another. Every planetary investigation provides new information with which to compare Earth. After the explorations of Venus and Mars by American and Soviet spacecraft, a new Venus-Earth-Mars scenario has slowly emerged, suggesting that the present appearances of these three planets are somehow linked in an evolutionary way. Continued planetary exploration shed light on the nature of that possible evolutionary link, but it is not known if Mars is a failed Earth-like body or a planet geologically dead, or if Venus was once Earth-like but suffered a runaway greenhouse effect, destroying any possibility for the development of life as we understand it. Even more important is comparative planetology: the contrasting of what is found on Venus and Mars with the current geophysical state of Earth. Study in this field will help to deepen our understanding of Earth's past and future dynamic geophysical and biological evolution.

The success of Mariner 4 as a spacecraft led to the use of variations on the Mariner bus—the same type of frame was employed on subsequent missions. Mariner 5 went to Venus and in 1967, Mariners 6 and 7 to Mars in 1969, Mariner 9 to Mars in 1971, and Mariner 10 to Venus in 1974 and 1975. The Mariner design blazed a path for other uncrewed planetary explorers. The remote-sensing system used a flyby technique that was later used on all the Mariner-Mars missions, as well as on Pioneer missions to Jupiter and on Voyager missions to Jupiter, Saturn, Uranus, and Neptune.

The discoveries of Mariner 4 proved enticing. Several more uncrewed expeditions to Mars resulted, including Mariners 6, 7, 9, and 10, Vikings 1 and 2, and the Soviet Phobos probes. Some failures during the Mars science missions of the late 1990's were outshone by the successes of such missions as the Mars Global Surveyor Mars Pathfinder, Mars Odyssey, and the Mars Exploration Rovers Spirit and Opportunity.

—Thomas W. Becker

See also: Deep Space Network; Jet Propulsion Laboratory; Mariner 1 and 2; Mariner 5; Mariner 6 and 7; Mariner 8 and 9; Mars Exploration Rovers; Mars Observer; Mars Odyssey; Mars Reconnaissance Orbiter; Planetary Exploration; Viking Program.

Further Reading

David, Leonard, and Ron Howard. *Mars: Our Future on the Red Planet.* Washington, D.C.: National Geographic, 2016. Provides a detailed description of humanity's evolving understanding of the Red Planet, and projects what may happen in the next 25 years in Mars exploration. For the space enthusiast. Has marvelous images of Mars.

Hartmann, William K. *Moons and Planets.* 5th ed. Belmont, Calif.: Thomson Brooks/Cole Publishing, 2005. Provides detailed information about all objects in the solar system. Suitable on three separate levels: high school student, general reader, and the college undergraduate studying planetary geology.

Hartmann, William K., and Odell Raper. *The New Mars: The Discoveries of Mariner 9.* NASA SP-337. Washington, D.C.: Government Printing Office, 1974. One of the best research works extant for the reader who wants to understand the past, present, and future of Mars and Martian explorations. "Early Mariners and the Profile of the Mariner 9 Mission," as well as the first two chapters of historic data, presents a sweeping view of Mars as the planet of human hopes and fantasies.

Heppenheimer, T. A. *Countdown: A History of Space Flight.* New York: John Wiley, 1997. A detailed historical narrative of the human conquest of space. Heppenheimer traces the development of piloted flight through the military rocketry programs of the era preceding World War II. Covers both the American and the Soviet attempts to place vehicles, spacecraft, and humans into the hostile environment of space. More than a dozen pages are devoted to bibliographic references.

Kaufman, Marc. *Mars Up Close: Inside the Curiosity Mission.* Washington, D.C.: National Geographic, 2014. Although a text primarily about the Curiosity rover on Mars, this work provides historical developments in the space-based exploration of Mars. Includes numerous excellent photographs of the Red Planet and its geology.

Koppes, Clayton R. *JPL and the American Space Program: A History of the Jet Propulsion Laboratory.* New Haven, Conn.: Yale University Press, 1982. A volume that must be considered the definitive work on the subject, this book covers U.S. planetary exploration during its golden age.

Lee, Wayne. *To Rise from Earth: An Easy to Understand Guide to Spaceflight.* New York: Checkmark Books, 1996. This is a good introduction to the science of spaceflight. Although written by an engineer with the NASA Jet Propulsion Laboratory, it is presented in easy-to-understand language. In addition to the theory of spaceflight, it gives some of the history of the human endeavor to explore space.

McBride, Neil, and Iain Gilmour. *An Introduction to the Solar System.* New York: Cambridge University Press, 2004. This work provides a comprehensive tour of the solar system. Suitable for a high school or college course on planetary astronomy.

Mari, Christopher, ed. *Space Exploration.* New York: H. W. Wilson, 1999. Twenty-five articles (reprinted from magazines), covering the state of the space program at the time of publication, are divided into five sections: John H. Glenn, Jr.'s return to space, the exploration of Mars, the International Space Station, recent mining efforts by commercial industries, and new types of space vehicles and propulsion systems.

Morrison, David, and Tobias Owen. *The Planetary System.* 3d ed. San Francisco: Addison- Wesley, 2003. Organized by planetary object, this work provides contemporary data on all planetary bodies visited by spacecraft since the early days of the Space Age. Suitable for high school and college students and the general reader.

National Aeronautics and Space Administration. *Report from Mars: Mariner IV, 1964-1965.* NASA EP-39. Washington, D.C.: Government Printing Office, 1966. This illustrated booklet is a concise, accurate, well-written account of the entire mission, from first contact to imagery and photograph interpretation. An excellent reference source.

National Aeronautics and Space Administration, Jet Propulsion Laboratory. *The Mariner 6 and 7 Pictures of Mars.* NASA SP-263. Washington, D.C.: Government Printing Office, 1971. The official chronicle of the results of Mariners 6 and 7, this volume helps bring the contributions of Mariner 4 into perspective; the first chapter provides a thumbnail sketch of the Mariner 4 mission and other background information.

Nicks, Oran W. *Far Travelers: The Exploring Machines.* NASASP-480. Washington, D.C.: Scientific and Technical Information Branch, 1985. Discusses all major NASA planetary spacecraft during NASA's first quarter-century. Written by a senior NASA official involved with lunar and planetary programs during that era.

Sparrow, Giles. *Mars.* London: Quercus, 2015. Primarily a textbook, but available to the interested reader. Details the state of understanding of the Red Planet as gained by astronomical observation and investigations by spacecraft since Mariner 4. Amazing photographs.

Mariner 5

Date: June 14, 1967, to November 5, 1968
Type of spacecraft: Planetary exploration

The primary scientific objectives of Mariner 5 were to gather data on the atmosphere and the ionosphere of Venus and to study the interaction of the solar plasma with Venus's environment. A secondary engineering objective was to gain experience in converting a spacecraft designed to study Mars into one suitable for studying Venus.

Key Figures

Glenn A. Reiff (b. 1923), Mariner-Venus program manager, 1967

Dan Schneiderman (1922-2007), Mariner-Venus project manager, 1967

Allen E. Wolfe, Mariner-Venus Spacecraft System manager

D. W. Douglas, Mariner-Venus Mission Operations System manager

Nicholas A. Renzetti, Mariner-Venus Trajectory and Data Systems manager

Summary of the Mission

The Mariner program was an early attempt by the National Aeronautics and Space Administration (NASA) to explore the environment of nearby terrestrial planets using robotic flyby space vehicles. The program began in the early 1960's, and the Jet Propulsion Laboratory in Pasadena, California, was charged with the mission. The first two Mariner missions were to return data on Venus. The first Mariner launch, in 1962, was aborted soon after liftoff because of a malfunction. Mariner 2 was launched on August 27, 1962. It encountered Venus on December 14, 1962, and relayed valuable information to Earth. It established the presence and the properties of the solar wind (the plasma from the Sun) but did not provide information regarding its interaction with the environment around Venus, because its orbit did not pass through the zone of interaction.

The Mariner 3 and 4 missions were designed to gather data on Mars. Mariner 3 was disabled because its protective nose shield failed as the probe passed through Earth's atmosphere. Mariner 4, launched on November 28, 1964, performed flawlessly and transmitted data for more than three years.

In December, 1965, NASA authorized two new Mariner programs for the Jet Propulsion Laboratory: one (Mariner 5) to investigate Venus further in 1967 and the other to return to Mars in 1969. A close look at the atmosphere and ionosphere of Venus was intended, and the interaction of solar plasma with the environment of Venus was to be a principal focus of Mariner 5. It was decided that the spare spacecraft designed for the Mariner 4 mission to Mars would be modified for the Venus mission. Seven scientific experiments were planned, and the spacecraft was fitted with appropriate equipment. A solar-plasma probe, a helium magnetometer, and an energetic-particle detector were designed to study the interaction between the planet and the interplanetary medium (the environment of Venus). An ultraviolet photometer was included to measure the properties of the planet's topmost atmospheric layers. S-band radio occultation and dual-frequency radio propagation experiments were to probe Venus's atmosphere at various heights from the surface, and precise measurements of the mass of Venus and the shape of its gravitational field were the aims of a celestial mechanics experiment.

The solar-plasma probe, helium magnetometer, ultraviolet photometer, and trapped-radiation detector experiments were slightly modified from earlier Mariner 4 experiments, and the dual frequency radio experiment was fitted with a newly modified instrument package. The celestial mechanics and the S-band radio experiments involved no new instruments, because they utilized the tracking and communications systems. The instruments were fitted within an octagonal spacecraft bus. Because Mariner 5 would fly closer to the Sun than had Mariner 4 in its mission to Mars, the four solar panels

that powered the probe's instrument package were reduced from 21.5 to 13.3 meters and were isolated and spaced 0.6 meter away from the bus to reduce heat transfer by reflection. The bus was thermally insulated and fitted with a folding, octagonal, aluminized-Mylar sunshade facing the Sun. The bus was also fitted with thermostatically controlled louvers, which opened when the temperature in the bus exceeded a limiting value and closed when the temperature decreased. At the encounter point with Venus, the total heat leakage to the bus was expected to be about 50 watts.

Mariner 5 was equipped with sensors and an attitude control system that oriented the spacecraft to within half a degree with respect to the Sun and the star Canopus. A central computer and sequencer fulfilled timing, sequencing, and other computational functions for the spacecraft equipment. The spacecraft was aimed to encounter Venus on October 19, 1967, at an approximate distance of 8,165 kilometers from the planet's center. It had the capability of two midcourse maneuvers to avoid accidental impact on Venus.

The spacecraft, weighing 245 kilograms, arrived at Cape Kennedy on May 1, 1967. The Atlas-Agena, a multistage rocket with which the probe was to be fitted, was being readied at Launch Complex 12. The Atlas rocket was the main launch vehicle to lift the spacecraft through Earth's atmosphere. It was nearly 20.5 meters tall and 3 meters wide, and contained kerosene-like fuel and liquid oxygen feeding two 733,920-newton-thrust booster engines for liftoff, a 253,536-newton-thrust sustainer engine, and two 2,557.6-newton-thrust vernier control engines to stabilize the rocket. The Atlas rocket was to burn

Launch of an Atlas Agena D with Mariner 5. (NASA)

for about five minutes and then separate. The Agena D upper stage, fitted atop the Atlas, was 6.1 meters long and 1.52 meters wide and was powered by a 71,168-newton-thrust engine. The Agena was to be fired twice—first after the separation from the Atlas booster, to provide sufficient velocity to place the spacecraft in orbit, and again at an appropriate time to power the spacecraft for its journey to Venus. The Agena was fueled by dimethylhydrazine and nitric acid oxidizer.

The launch date was selected in advance to optimize the value of the scientific mission. Mariner 5 was launched at 06:01 Coordinated Universal Time (UTC), on June 14, 1967. Soon after the probe's separation from the Agena, the solar panels and the sunshade were opened and the scientific equipment was powered as Mariner 5 sailed toward Venus. The magnetometer returned measurements of the magnetic field of Earth and the interplanetary field generated by the Sun, and the ultraviolet photometer detected the Lyman-alpha glow caused by atomic hydrogen in the upper layers of Earth's atmosphere. The direction of approach to Venus was controlled by the spacecraft sensors, which aimed constantly toward the Sun and Canopus. A mid-course maneuver was made at 23:08 UTC on June 19.

Data acquisition continued during the four-month flight to Venus. Approximately 850 hours of data (at 33.33 bits per second) were received by the Canberra station of the Deep Space Network during the first forty days. An additional 1,670 hours of data were received before Mariner's encounter with Venus, and 600 hours of data were received after the encounter, at a rate of 8.33 bits per second. Venus blocked Mariner 5 from Earth during the satellite's closest approach. This inhibited communications, and 648,000 bits of scientific data had to be stored in the spacecraft's tape recorder and relayed back to Earth twice during the week following the closest encounter.

During its flight to Venus, an important experiment was conducted with Mariner 5. Ranging experiments had been performed earlier using Earth- and Moon-orbiting satellites, but the first ranging experiment at planetary distance was performed with Mariner 5. By accurately determining the frequency shift (Doppler shift) of a coded radio signal returned by the spacecraft and measuring the total transit time (at approximately 300,000 kilometers per second), it was possible to determine the velocity and the distance of the spacecraft quite precisely. Near its approach to Venus, the accuracy of locating Mariner 5 was about 6 meters in 80 million kilometers.

As Mariner 5 neared Venus, various instruments started monitoring the planet. The encounter sequence with Venus started at 02:49 UTC on October 19, 1967, in response to a command sent by ground controllers. Changes in the readings of the onboard magnetometer and the plasma probe indicated Mariner's passage through the zone of plasma shock. The closest approach to Venus occurred at 17:34 UTC at a distance of 10,151 kilometers from the center (approximately 4,094 kilometers above the surface) of Venus. The planet's strong gravitational pull modified the flight path of Mariner 5 into a tight arc of more than 100° and hurled it toward the Sun at a velocity of 30,650 kilometers per hour. During the three-hour period of the encounter with Venus, the thickness of the plasma shock and the boundary of the planet's influence on solar plasma were determined, ultraviolet photometric observations were completed, an ionosphere was detected, and observations of the atmospheric effect on S-band signals were made. Contact with Mariner 5 was reestablished as the probe emerged from behind Venus.

As Mariner 5 approached the Sun, its telemetry signal grew weaker. The signal was eventually lost on November 21 when Mariner 5 was about 117 million kilometers from Earth and about 98 million kilometers from the Sun. To this point, the spacecraft had performed flawlessly and exceeded all expectations. A large amount of scientific data were collected, and from every perspective the mission was deemed a complete success.

Mariner 5 attained a perihelion (closest distance to the Sun) of about 86 million kilometers on January 4, 1968. The spacecraft was traveling at the remarkable speed of 149,000 kilometers per hour. The strong gravitational attraction of the Sun placed it in an elliptical orbit around the Sun, with an orbital period of 195 days. Mariner 5 would be in the neighborhood of Earth (just outside the orbit of Venus) about every fourteen months.

Because the Mariner 5 mission was such a success, a decision was made to extend the project through January 22, 1969. During this period, interplanetary space would be examined at short wavelengths, the nature of the space around the Sun would be studied during the period of high solar activity. Researchers also wished to gain knowledge of the effects on scientific equipment of the spacecraft's close passage around the Sun.

Attempts to reestablish radio contact with Mariner 5 began on April 26, 1968. After numerous attempts, contact was made on October 14, 1968, but the spacecraft behaved abnormally and did not respond to ground commands. Finally, on November 5, 1968, the project was terminated without achieving its extended objectives.

Contributions

Venus has been termed a twin planet of Earth. It is the planet closest to Earth, it has an atmosphere, and its size (radius about 6,053 kilometers) is comparable to that of Earth (radius 6,371 kilometers). In other ways, however, Venus is very different from Earth.

The atmosphere of Venus was found to be denser and more compressed than Earth's. The ultraviolet photometric experiment indicated the presence of atomic hydrogen, but the upper boundary of atomic hydrogen is only 19,000 kilometers above Venus's surface, or about one-fifth the height for Earth. Consequently, the temperature at this altitude is much lower than at the same altitude above Earth,

suggesting that thermal loss of hydrogen from the Venusian atmosphere is much lower.

Although Mariner 5 was not designed to make direct measurements of the composition, density, and temperature of Venus's atmosphere, estimates were made from various data that it did provide. S-band occultation measurements provided temperature and pressure profiles for Venus's atmosphere in the altitude range of 25 to 90 kilometers. The downward extrapolation indicated the surface temperature and pressure to be in the range of 430° Celsius and 100 bars, respectively. The top of the cloud cover is located at an altitude of 65 to 70 kilometers from the Venusian surface. The dense lower atmosphere acts as a lens to refract light around the surface. Consequently, nights on Venus are expected to be brighter than those on Earth, with sunlight forming smeared rainbows along Venus's horizon.

Mariner's ultraviolet photometer recorded a weak ultraviolet airglow on the nightside of Venus. The origin of this airglow is not known. The instrument failed to record the presence of atomic oxygen in the upper atmosphere, but verified the detection by the Soviet Venus probe, Venera 4, of very small quantities of molecular oxygen and water in the lower atmosphere. The dominant atmospheric constituent is carbon dioxide, which must constitute at least 85 percent, and perhaps much more, of the Venusian atmosphere. Nitrogen concentration is quite low. These observations confirmed the "greenhouse" model of Venus suggested in the early 1960's. Because carbon dioxide is transparent to sunlight but opaque to longer wavelengths (infrared) reradiated from the surface, heat energy builds up in the lower atmosphere. The thick atmosphere prevents cooling of Venus's nightside, and hot winds keep the surface temperature uniformly redistributed over the planet's surface.

Measurements of the magnetic field and ionosphere and their interaction with the solar plasma indicate considerable differences between Venus and Earth. Venus's magnetic field was undetected by Mariner's instruments and so must be at least one thousand times weaker than that of Earth. As a result of Earth's geomagnetic field, the solar plasma is deflected and flows around it, forming a cavity, known as the magnetosphere, into which the plasma cannot enter. The closest approach of the plasma on Earth's sunlit side is 50,000 kilometers from the surface. The deflected plasma causes a bow shock similar to one created by a supersonic plane. An analogous effect has been observed in Venus. In the case of Venus, however, the plasma is deflected not by the magnetic field but by a dense ionosphere on the sunlit side of the planet. The ionosphere prevents the penetration of plasma, piling it up in front and deflecting it on the sides to form a bow shock. The upper boundary of the ionosphere is, however, extremely low, not higher than 500 kilometers above Venus's surface.

The celestial mechanics experiment provided an accurate value for the mass of Venus. Analysis of the range and Doppler radio tracking data indicated, with an accuracy of one part per million, that the mass of Venus is 81.49988 percent that of Earth. The radius of the planet could not be determined through the S-band occultation experiment, as the electromagnetic waves were deflected by the dense lower atmosphere of Venus.

Context

The early 1960's marked the beginning of planetary exploration. The first launch of an uncrewed spacecraft, Venera 1, was in 1961 by the Soviet Union. Both Veneras 1 and 2 (the latter launched in 1965) flew past Venus without relaying any scientific information. Venera 3 landed on Venus in 1966 but failed to operate. Venera 4 was launched on June 12, 1967; it encountered Venus a day before Mariner 5 did. As Venera 4 descended through Venus's atmosphere, it transmitted valuable information on the temperature, density, and composition of the Venusian atmosphere; radio transmission from the

spacecraft stopped, however, at an altitude of 25 kilometers.

Mariner 2 was the first United States probe to fly past Venus. Launched on August 26, 1962, it encountered Venus at a distance of 35,000 kilometers on December 14, 1962. Data from Mariner 2 confirmed the existence of solar plasma, which traveled with a velocity between 350 and 800 kilometers per second; the probe's instruments also measured the density of the plasma. Data showed that the temperature of the Venusian atmosphere was high (around 130° Celsius). The onboard magnetometer failed to detect any magnetic field around Venus.

The interaction of plasma with Earth's Moon has been studied in detail. Because the Moon has no magnetic field, solar plasma strikes its surface and is absorbed, while the magnetic field associated with the plasma passes through the Moon without any interference. Measuring the interaction of the solar plasma with Venus was one of the primary objectives of Mariner 5, the second American probe to Venus. It discovered the bow shock of the plasma and the presence of an ionospheric layer around Venus; it also confirmed the existence of high temperatures, high pressure, and a high concentration of carbon dioxide on Venus.

Subsequent missions to Venus were Veneras 5 and 6, launched in 1969. Like Venera 4, both succumbed to the high atmospheric pressure of Venus and ceased functioning before they landed. Venera 7 operated for only 23 minutes. Venera 8 was more successful; it transmitted valuable information about temperature and wind velocities on Venus.

Mariner 10 represented the second generation of American probes to Venus. It took close-up photographs of the planet's cloud cover and identified weather patterns. Pioneer Venus (1978) and Veneras 15 and 16 (1983) mapped the surface of Venus using radar. The Magellan orbiter dispatched to Venus from space shuttle *Atlantis* on the STS-34 mission provided a high-resolution near-global map of

Venus topography that revolutionized our understanding of the second planet out from the Sun.

Since the days of Mariner 5, much has been learned about the atmosphere of Venus. Ninety-seven percent of Venus's atmosphere is composed of carbon dioxide. Sulfuric acid has been detected, as well as small amounts of hydrochloric and hydrofluoric acids. Most of the molecules of water are locked into the ions of these acids, making the surface of Venus much more arid than deserts on Earth.

The concentration of water vapor is observed to be less than 0.1 percent in Venus's lower atmosphere.

—*D. K. Chowdhury*

See also: Jet Propulsion Laboratory; Magellan: Venus; Mariner 1 and 2; Mariner 3 and 4; Mariner 8 and 9; Mariner 10; Pioneer Venus 1; Pioneer Venus 2; Planetary Exploration; Viking Program.

Further Reading

Carlson-Berne, Emma. *The Secrets of Venus*. Washington, D.C.: National Geographic, 2015. A complete description of spacecraft investigations of Venus. Highly illustrated and comprehensive. Includes Mariner through Magellan spacecraft results.

Cattermole, Peter, and Patrick Moore. *Atlas of Venus*. New York: Cambridge University Press, 1997. Filled with photography from telescopes and the Mariner, Pioneer Venus, and Magellan spacecrafts, this work provides a complete atlas of Venus and a gazetteer of Venusian place names.

Grinspoon, David Harry. *Venus Revealed: A New Look Below the Clouds of Our Mysterious Twin Planet*. New York: Perseus Book Group, 1998. This work provides both romantic and scientific explanations of the planet closest to Earth, incorporating the latest data from the Magellan spacecraft.

Heppenheimer, T. A. *Countdown: A History of Space Flight*. New York: John Wiley, 1997. A detailed historical narrative of the human conquest of space. Heppenheimer traces the development of piloted flight through the military rocketry programs of the era preceding World War II. Covers both the American and the Soviet attempts to place vehicles, spacecraft, and humans into the hostile environment of space. More than a dozen pages are devoted to bibliographic references.

Lee, Wayne. *To Rise from Earth: An Easy to Understand Guide to Spaceflight*. New York: Checkmark Books, 1996. This is a good introduction to the science of spaceflight. Although written by an engineer with the NASA Jet Propulsion Laboratory, it is presented in easy-to-understand language. In addition to the theory of spaceflight, it gives some of the history of the human endeavor to explore space.

Mari, Christopher, ed. *Space Exploration*. New York: H. W. Wilson, 1999. Twenty-five articles (reprinted from magazines), covering the state of the space program at the time of publication, are divided into five sections: John H. Glenn, Jr.'s return to space, the exploration of Mars, the International Space Station, recent mining efforts by commercial industries, and new types of space vehicles and propulsion systems.

Morrison, David, and Tobias Owen. *The Planetary System*. 3d ed. San Francisco: Addison-Wesley, 2003. Organized by planetary object, this work provides contemporary data on all planetary bodies visited by spacecraft since the early days of the Space Age. Suitable for high school and college students and the general reader.

National Aeronautics and Space Administration, Science and Technical Information Office. *Mariner-Venus, 1967: Final Project Report*. NASA SP-190. Washington, D.C.: Government Printing Office, 1971. This report describes the complete project of the Mariner 5 mission. It contains details of the instruments, describes the observations, and analyzes the results. It is appropriate for university-level audiences.

Nicks, Oran W. *Far Travelers: The Exploring Machines*. NASASP-480. Washington, D.C.: Scientific and Technical Information Branch, 1985. Discusses all major NASA planetary spacecraft during NASA's first quarter-century. Written by a senior NASA official involved with lunar and planetary programs during that era.

Snyder, Conway W., et al. "Mariner V Flight Past Venus." *Science* 158 (December 20, 1967): 1665-1690. This collection of scientific articles by the principal investigators summarizes the preliminary findings of the Mariner 5 project. Suitable for university-level readers.

Zimmerman, Robert. *The Chronological Encyclopedia of Discoveries in Space*. Westport, Conn.: Oryx Press, 2000. Provides a complete chronological history of all crewed and robotic spacecraft and explains flight events and scientific results. Suitable for all levels of research.

Mariner 6 and 7

Date: February 24, 1969, to December, 1970
Type of spacecraft: Planetary exploration

Mariner 6 and 7, the second and third robotic missions to Mars, provided valuable photographic information on the surface characteristics of the planet, along with data on temperatures, atmospheric composition, and densities that were vital in planning and executing subsequent missions to Mars.

Key Figures

Harris M. Schurmeier (1924-2013), Jet Propulsion Laboratory (JPL) Mariner 6/7 project manager
John A. Stallkamp, Mariner 6/7 project scientist
Henry W. Norris, Mariner 6/7 Spacecraft Systems manager
Marshall S. Johnson, Mariner 6/7 Mission Operations Systems manager
Robert B. Leighton (1919-1997), principal investigator, Imaging Team

Summary of the Missions

The Mariner 6 and 7 missions were undertaken to acquire information on the Martian surface and atmospheric characteristics in order to provide a firm basis for an effective long-range program of exploration. The selected instrument payload emphasized this purpose.

In late 1965, the National Aeronautics and Space Administration (NASA) had approved the Mariner Mars 1969 project, and the project management responsibility was assigned to the Jet Propulsion Laboratory (JPL), along with the responsibility for providing the spacecraft, mission operations, and Tracking and Data Acquisition (TDA) systems. The Lewis Research Center was assigned the responsibility for providing the launch vehicle system. The spacecraft subsystems were acquired from a number of industrial suppliers and were assembled and tested at JPL prior to being shipped to Cape Kennedy for launch.

The spacecraft system design was derived from the successful Mariner 4 spacecraft, with several significant improvements: The instruments were mounted on a two-degree-of-freedom platform, which made it possible to point the instruments in desired directions during the Mars encounter; dual tape recorders were used to store thirty-five times the amount of data that had been stored on Mariner 4; electronic equipment increased the rate at which data could be transmitted from the spacecraft to Earth to a maximum of 16,200 bits per second (Mariner 4 had transmitted data at a comparative snail's pace, 8.33 bits per second); and a central computer and sequencer, which could be reprogrammed from Earth, allowed information acquired from Mariner 6 to enhance Mariner 7 science data.

The spacecraft was octagonal in structure (as the previous Mariners had been), with electronic equipment mounted on its inner walls; the propulsion subsystem and its hydrazine tank were mounted on one of the faces of this octagon to provide trajectory corrections. The structure also supported the instrument platform, four solar panels that extended like wings to provide electrical power for the spacecraft, and a dish-shaped high-gain antenna that was part of the radio subsystem used for receiving commands from Earth and transmitting data back to Earth. The radio subsystem was also used for navigating the spacecraft. The science payload consisted of two television cameras, two infrared instruments, and an ultraviolet spectrometer.

Two spacecraft could be launched during a "window" between February 24 and April 7, 1969. It was planned to launch Mariner 6 as early as possible during this period to allow for initial midcourse trajectory corrections and, if necessary, any unplanned modifications of the second spacecraft, which had to be launched during the same window. Two Atlas SLV-3C Centaur launch vehicles were prepared for the Mariner 6 and 7 missions.

One and a half weeks prior to the initial scheduled launch, an accidental depressurization of the Atlas booster occurred; the substitution of the launch vehicle designated for the second launch became necessary, and a new Atlas booster was obtained to launch Mariner 7. Rescheduling and extra shifts made it possible for the launch team to launch Mariner 6 at the desired early point in the window, on February 24, 1969. Roughly fifteen minutes into the scheduled one-hour launch window, Mariner 6 separated from its launch platform, at 8:29 p.m. eastern standard time or 13:29 Coordinated Universal Time (UTC). The launch vehicle was required to change its course following the burnout of the Atlas booster to ensure that debris did not fall on the Bahamas or the Leeward Islands. The launch vehicle's performance was excellent, and the spacecraft was safely on its way to Mars. Mariner 7 lifted off at 5:22 p.m. eastern standard time (10:22 PM UTC) on March 27, 1969. A course change following the Atlas booster burnout was not necessary for Mariner 7, and the launch vehicle performance was equal to that for Mariner 6.

Launch trajectories selected for both Mariners were designed to ensure that the unsterilized Centaur stage could not strike Mars. Midcourse maneuvers were required to position the spacecraft roughly 3,200 kilometers above the planet's surface for their

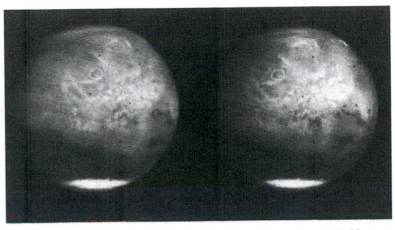

View of the entire planet of Mars from Mariner 7, showing NIX Olympia (later identified as the giant shield volcano Olympus Mons), and polar caps. Photographed from 200,000 miles away. (NASA)

closest observations of the planet. These maneuvers were conducted on March 1 and April 8, 1969, respectively.

Several problems occurred during the missions that required the engineers and scientists to utilize great skill in evaluating problems, with limited data, and then design new operational sequences to overcome and reduce the risks of losing scientific data. The first of these problems occurred when the scan platform (the platform to which all the instruments were attached) was unlocked from the fixed position that prevented it from being damaged during launch. When the platform of Mariner 6 was unlocked, several small particles of dust were dislodged from the spacecraft; they drifted in front of the star tracker, which keeps the roll axis of the spacecraft fixed as it flies through space. As a result, Mariner 6 rolled away from the direction toward the bright star Canopus which was being used at that time as its reference. Standard commands were sent to the spacecraft to lock it back on Canopus.

The flight team recognized that a similar problem could occur during the Mars encounter, when valves would be activated to release the two gases used to cool the detector of the infrared spectrometer. As a result, a change in the encounter sequence was made; the spacecraft would be kept under gyroscopic control during the critical sequence.

Encounter sequences were designed to store primary science data on onboard tape recorders; these data would be played back to Earth at a conservative rate of 270 bits per second. An engineering experiment would allow a faster playback when the large Goldstone, California, antenna was tracking the spacecraft.

On July 29, 1967, the far-encounter sequence—which acquired 33 television pictures of Mars as Mariner 6 raced toward the planet—began. The next day, seventeen images were scheduled as Mariner 6 came even closer. Fifteen minutes before Mariner 6 took the last of these images, alarms rang in the operations center, indicating that radio contact with Mariner 7 had been lost. The emergency occurred when the staff was concentrating on recovering the primary science data on Mariner 6 and most of the tracking facilities were committed to that spacecraft. A small team of engineers was assigned to the Mariner 7 problem. After several hours, Mariner 7 was directed to switch to its omni-directional antenna. After eleven minutes, signals were received on Earth and two-way communications with the spacecraft again were possible.

Obtaining science data during Mariner 6's near-encounter phase on July 31 now became the goal. High-rate data (16,200 bits per second) were received from the spacecraft. All went well, except some difficulties occasioned when the infrared spectrometer's low-temperature detector failed to cool, probably because a particle had lodged in the fine tubing of its refrigerator.

Mariner 7 followed its predecessor five days later, and although considerable data were received on Earth, the navigation team determined that the craft's early failure had changed its flight path by the planet. The team heroically revised all the pointing angles to compensate for this change, sending them up to the spacecraft before its close encounter. The low-temperature refrigerator on the infrared spectrometer also worked on Mariner 7; thus, its information complemented that sent back by Mariner 6.

Following an extensive review of the lost radio signal, analysts finally concluded that the storage battery had failed. One or more of the eighteen sealed battery cases must have ruptured, causing severe power changes, and upsetting electrical circuits on the spacecraft. Liquid discharge from the battery cells also resulted in a small change to the spacecraft trajectory.

In spite of these problems, the flight team was able to reprogram the flight computers. As a result, the mission acquired more scientific data than needed to meet the established mission objectives. This improvement in data acquisition was most notable with the television experiment, in which 16 far-encounter and 48 near-encounter images were required; 2,561 far-encounter and 577 near-encounter images were actually recovered. Six hundred spectral pairs of data, compared with 288 pairs required for the infrared spectrometer, were acquired. Additionally, the infrared radiometer and the ultraviolet spectrometer also modestly increased the amount of information recovered.

Following the encounters with Mars, several engineering experiments and a few scientific measurements were made, but since the payload was entirely planet-oriented, few data were obtained. Toward the end of 1970 altitude control gas on each spacecraft ran low. The missions concluded when transmitters were turned off before the end of December, 1970.

Contributions

Information from the ultraviolet and infrared spectrometers determined that carbon dioxide and its disassociation products were dominant in the Martian atmosphere. A high, thin cloud of atomic oxygen surrounds the outer atmosphere of Mars, just as it does on Earth and Venus. No nitrogen, however, was detected. Nor was any high-altitude ozone. Traces of water vapor and ice were found, and undetected amounts of inert gases such as argon and neon are believed to complete the constituents of the atmosphere.

S-band occultation measurements made at four locations allowed the determination of pressure and temperatures at various altitudes. Thus, the ionospheric layer was detected at an altitude of about 140 kilometers. Surface pressures between 6 and 7 millibars were determined for three of four locations; the fourth had a pressure of 3.8 millibars, and it is believed that the surface at this measurement has an elevation of 5 to 6 kilometers. Clouds of Mars are thin, occur mainly near the polar caps, and are made up principally of dry-ice crystals, water crystals, and dust. Frost and snow forms on Mars.

Martian surface temperatures were measured by the infrared radiometer with two instruments compatible with the narrow-angle television cameras. A high temperature of 289 kelvins was measured in equatorial regions, and low temperatures of 153 kelvins were found near the south pole. The temperatures measured by Mariner 7 as it crossed the southern polar cap are consistent with the frost temperature of carbon dioxide at a vapor pressure of 6.5 millibars; this information confirms that the polar caps are principally frozen carbon dioxide. Dark features on Mars absorb more solar energy during daylight and are warmer than light areas.

The Mariner television cameras acquired approximately two hundred times the imaging data that were obtained from Mariner 4. The near-encounter pictures substantially increased resolution, allowing an improved understanding of the surface features and the geologic history of the planet. Cratered terrain is certainly Moon-like, but weathering has occurred, particularly along the edges of the polar cap. Carbon dioxide snow on the edges of the cap is generally thin; it disappears on the surfaces of craters while remaining on the crater walls, where the Sun does not shine as brightly.

Two new types of terrain were observed on these missions. The Mariner 7 television cameras crossed a southern circular desert area where there are few craters. This featureless terrain must have been significantly eroded, but liquid water cannot exist on Mars because of the planet's low atmospheric pressure. In another area, near the equator, the surface has a series of ridges and depressions that seemingly were created after the craters were produced. This area was identified by the television experiment team as chaotic terrain.

Context

Mariners 6 and 7 were the second and third spacecraft to visit Mars. The Russians had tried several times to visit Mars but were unsuccessful until the 1970's. Mariner 4, the first spacecraft to visit Mars, had discovered the cratered surface of the planet. That spacecraft also was able to determine that Mars has no significant magnetic field; during that mission, the planet's atmospheric density, temperature, and mass were measured. Mariners 6 and 7 were designed only to study the planet and make measurements that would be of value in subsequent long-range explorations of Mars.

Mariners 6 and 7 were able to photograph roughly twenty times the surface area covered by Mariner 4. Three types of terrain were observed: cratered, chaotic, and featureless. Featureless terrain indicates that significant weathering has occurred on Mars, eroding the impact craters that once existed in these areas. Measurement of surface temperatures confirmed those determined by Earth-based observations at the equator and the edges of the polar caps.

Two identical spacecraft were authorized by NASA to ensure that these important data were returned to Earth; this information would be used for future missions to Mars. Only one channel on the infrared radiometer on Mariner 6 worked, but the two working channels on Mariner 7 provided the missing data for the mission. Incorporation of an onboard, reprogrammable computer allowed information obtained from Mariner 6 to enhance that of Mariner 7.

The measurements that were collected by Mariners 6 and 7 do not encourage the belief that life exists on Mars, although the possibility has not been excluded. Nevertheless, if life does exist, it probably is microbial. Absence of atmospheric nitrogen, coupled with ultraviolet rays penetrating the atmosphere, and the scarcity of water, make life-forms such as those found on Earth unlikely. Scientific and engineering data received from these missions, along with the successful demonstration of computer and communications technologies, were of significant value to the planning of the subsequent Mariner 9 orbiting mission of Mars, launched in 1971.

—*Henry W. Norris*

See also: Mariner 3 and 4; Mariner 5; Mariner 8 and 9; Mars Observer; Planetary Exploration; Viking Program.

Further Reading

Chapman, Clark R. *Planets of Rock and Ice: From Mercury to the Moons of Saturn.* Rev. ed. New York: Charles Scribner's Sons, 1982. This readable, well-illustrated book describes what is known of the solid planets and moons. Text includes material acquired by the Mariner 4, 6, 7, and 9 and Viking 1 and 2 missions to Mars.

Collins, Stewart A. *The Mariner 6 and 7 Pictures of Mars.* NASA SP-263. Washington, D.C.: Government Printing Office, 1971. A brief background of previous investigations is included along with technical descriptions of the two cameras used for this investigation. Black-and-white prints of each of the images recorded on the spacecraft are included.

David, Leonard, and Ron Howard. *Mars: Our Future on the Red Planet.* Washington, D.C.: National Geographic, 2016. Provides a detailed description of humanity's evolving understanding of the Red Planet, and projects what may happen in the next 25 years in Mars exploration. For the space enthusiast. Has marvelous images of Mars.

Hartmann, William K. *Moons and Planets.* 5th ed. Belmont, Calif.: Thomson Brooks/Cole Publishing, 2005. Provides detailed information about all objects in the solar system. Suitable on three separate levels: high school student, general reader, and the college undergraduate studying planetary geology.

Heppenheimer, T. A. *Countdown: A History of Space Flight.* New York: John Wiley, 1997. A detailed historical narrative of the human conquest of space. Heppenheimer traces the development of piloted flight through the military rocketry programs of the era preceding World War II. Covers both the American and the Soviet attempts to place vehicles, spacecraft, and humans into the hostile environment of space. More than a dozen pages are devoted to bibliographic references.

Kaufman, Marc. *Mars Up Close: Inside the Curiosity Mission.* Washington, D.C.: National Geographic, 2014. Although a text primarily about the Curiosity rover on Mars, this work provides historical developments in the space-based exploration of Mars. Includes numerous excellent photographs of the Red Planet and its geology.

Lee, Wayne. *To Rise from Earth: An Easy to Understand Guide to Spaceflight.* New York: Checkmark Books, 1996. This is a good introduction to the science of spaceflight. Although written by an engineer with the NASA Jet Propulsion Laboratory, it is presented in easy-to-understand language. In addition to the theory of spaceflight, it gives some of the history of the human endeavor to explore space.

McBride, Neil, and Iain Gilmour. *An Introduction to the Solar System.* New York: Cambridge University Press, 2004. This work provides a comprehensive tour of the solar system. Suitable for a high school or college course on planetary astronomy.

Mari, Christopher, ed. *Space Exploration*. New York: H. W. Wilson, 1999. Twenty-five articles (reprinted from magazines), covering the state of the space program at the time of publication, are divided into five sections: John H. Glenn, Jr.'s return to space, the exploration of Mars, the International Space Station, recent mining efforts by commercial industries, and new types of space vehicles and propulsion systems.

Morrison, David, and Tobias Owen. *The Planetary System*. 3d ed. San Francisco: Addison- Wesley, 2003. Organized by planetary object, this work provides contemporary data on all planetary bodies visited by spacecraft since the early days of the Space Age. Suitable for high school and college students and the general reader.

Nicks, Oran W. *Far Travelers: The Exploring Machines*. NASASP-480. Washington, D.C.: Scientific and Technical Information Branch, 1985. Discusses all major NASA planetary spacecraft during NASA's first quarter-century. Written by a senior NASA official involved with lunar and planetary programs during that era.

Scientific and Technical Information Division, Office of Technology Utilization. *Mariner- Mars 1969: A Preliminary Report*. NASA SP-225. Springfield, Va.: Clearinghouse, Department of Commerce, 1969. The initial report prepared by members of the project team and the scientific investigators, it describes the program objectives and the spacecraft that were built for this dual-spacecraft mission. Brief descriptions of each experiment and the preliminary results of each experiment are included with photographs and charts of the recovered data.

Sparrow, Giles. *Mars*. London: Quercus, 2015. Primarily a textbook, but available to the interested reader. Details the state of understanding of the Red Planet as gained by astronomical observation and investigations by spacecraft since Mariner 4. Amazing photographs.

Wilson, James H. *Two over Mars: Mariner VI and Mariner VII, Feb-Aug, 1969*. NASA EP-90. Washington, D.C.: Government Printing Office, 1971. This report, with good pictures and charts, describes the missions of Mariners 6 and 7 and provides a brief summary of the scientific findings and their potential value to subsequent missions to Mars.

Mariner 8 and 9

Date: May 8, 1971, to October 27, 1972
Type of spacecraft: Planetary exploration

As the first artificial satellite of another planet, Mariner 9 did the work planned for both Mariners 8 and 9. It experienced a huge Martian dust storm, measured the two Martian moons, mapped a complete planet in less than a year, made preliminary determinations of the surface areas upon which landers could be set down, and revolutionized our understanding of the Red Planet.

Key Figures

Dan Schneiderman (1922-2007), Mariner-Mars project manager, 1971, Jet Propulsion Laboratory

Carl W. Glahn, NASA Mariner-Mars program manager, 1971

Robert A. Schmitz, Viking-Mariner-Mars, 1971, participation group manager

Harold Masursky (1922-1990), Mariner 9 Imaging Team leader

Bradford A. Smith (1931-2018), Mariner 9 Imaging Team leader

Summary of the Mission

Conceptually, the Mariner-Mars 1971 mission—the technical designation for the combined launching of Mariners 8 and 9—began under the ambitious but premature first Voyager program, which was fiscally eliminated on October 26, 1967. The initial Mariner projects were approved on July 15, 1960, by T. Keith Glennan, the first administrator for the National Aeronautics and Space Administration (NASA). At first, planners intended to send payloads of between 400 and 700 kilograms to Venus and Mars within the following two years using Atlas-Centaur launch vehicles. However, when the upper-stage Centaur booster continued to be unavailable, the Venus flyby flight (Mariner A) was canceled and that for Mars was successively redefined and rescheduled.

In the interim, the Jet Propulsion Laboratory (JPL) reconsidered several smaller versions of the Atlas-Agena launch vehicle and proposed the pairs Mariner-Venus 1962 (only Mariner 2 completed its Venus flyby) and Mariner-Mars 1964 (only Mariner 4 completed its Mars flyby) and the single remodeled Mariner-Venus 1967 (which, as Mariner 5, completed a Venus flyby). As the Voyager program was phased out, reconsiderations permitted the final flights past Mars with more intensive optical equipment on the pair Mariner-Mars 1969 (which performed successfully as Mariners 6 and 7).

The upper-stage Centaur Satellite Launch Vehicle 3C (SLV-3C) became available in 1966. The Office of Space Science (OSS) proposed in November, 1967, in anticipation of a new Viking project, a pair of orbiters designed to image much of the surface of Mars. The Mariner-Mars 1971 flights were approved August 23, 1968, to send orbiters with landers to Mars (Vikings 1 and 2), ostensibly to search for extraterrestrial life. Photographs from Mariners 4, 6, and 7, while suggesting a lunar-like, cratered surface, had shown a more dynamic planet than terrestrial observation had anticipated.

The Mariner-Mars 1971 mission, with identical spacecraft, was complementary during the ninety days of reconnaissance. Mission A (the prelaunch designation for Mariner 8) was to orbit Mars once every twelve hours, scanning most of the planet's surface, including the polar regions, from an orbit inclined 80° to the Martian equator. The elliptical orbit was to have a periapsis (the closest approach to the gravitational center of the planet) of 1,250 kilometers, thus providing overlap in consecutive images taken directly downward by a wide-angle camera with a resolution of 1,000 meters.

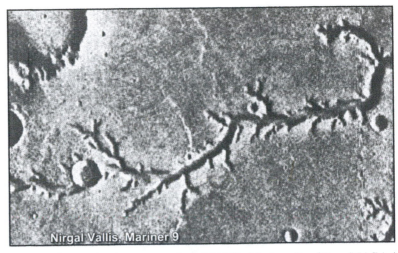

Nirgal Vallis, Mariner 9

The view of channels on Mars from NASA's Mariner 9 orbiter. (NASA / JPL-Caltech)

Mission B (the prelaunch designation for Mariner 9) was to orbit Mars once every 20.5 hours, focusing every five days on details of the variable surface features within its equatorial belt from an orbit inclined 50°. It was to come within 850 kilometers of the surface, from which its high-resolution camera would identify features as small as 100 meters.

Each was to carry three other scientific instruments. The infrared interferometer spectrometer, previously employed on Nimbus weather satellites, was redesigned to measure water vapor in the Martian atmosphere as well as the profile of atmospheric temperature from the surface outward into space. The ultraviolet spectrometer and the infrared radiometer had been employed on Mariners 6 and 7. The ultraviolet spectrometer was to identify the components of the Martian atmosphere and measure atmospheric pressure at the surface of the planet. The infrared radiometer would compare the background coldness of deep space (4 kelvins) and the known temperature of an internal source in the instrument package.

An occultation experiment was to analyze distortion of radio signals passing through the Martian atmosphere. With orbital repetition, the atmosphere could be measured according to latitude, season, or time of Martian day, and the shape of the planet could be determined. A celestial mechanics experiment, using the spacecraft's radio signals, was to determine the size, distance, and position of the planet and detect any large concentrations of mass.

As orbiters, Mariner-Mars 1971 required propulsion subsystems exerting 1,600-meter-per-second velocity changes to inject the craft into orbit. A 1,340-newton engine with restart capability, deriving its propulsion from monomethyl hydrogen and nitrogen tetroxide, was developed from components used on various other spacecraft.

The Mariner craft retained the basic shape and size of Mariners 6 and 7: an octagonal magnesium frame, measuring 138.4 centimeters diagonally and 45.7 centimeters deep. They required larger solar panels, still four in number; these measured 215 by 90 centimeters and spanned 68.9 centimeters. They had a total surface area of 7.7 square meters, and with 14,742 solar cells, they were capable of generating 800 watts on Earth and 500 watts on Mars—maintaining the nickel-cadmium battery at a charge of 20 ampere-hours. Restructuring did not increase the overall size of the spacecraft, but launch weight increased from 412.8 kilograms for Mariners 6 and 7 to 997.9 kilograms for Mariner-Mars 1971.

The launch window of May 6 to June 3, 1971, provided a basic time frame for both U.S. and Soviet efforts to investigate Mars at optimum distance. On August 10, 1971, because of the eccentricity (out-of-roundness) of the Martian orbit, the opposition (closest approach) of Mars and Earth was 56,166,105 kilometers.

Mariner 8 was launched with an Atlas-Centaur booster at Cape Kennedy's Eastern Test Range, Launch Complex 36, Pad A, at 9:11 p.m. eastern daylight time or 13:11 Coordinated Universal Time (UTC) on May 8, 1971. Following a normal countdown and liftoff, a malfunction in the Centaur main engine occurred after ignition, and the Centaur stage tumbled out of control, shutting down the engines. Centaur and spacecraft separated, reentering Earth's atmosphere 400 kilometers north of Puerto Rico.

On May 19, the Soviet Union launched the Mars 2 probe from its Baikonur Cosmodrome near Tyuratam; the probe was placed into Earth parking orbit before being injected into flight trajectory for Mars. The probe weighed 4,650 kilograms. On May 28, the Mars 3 probe was launched.

The loss of Mariner 8 resulted in a revised plans for Mariner 9; it was to accomplish the scientific work of both with minimum loss in data accumulation. A new orbit was assigned with an inclination of 65°, a twelve-hour period, and a 1,200-kilometer periapsis. Mariner 9 was scheduled to arrive by November 14, ahead of both Soviet craft.

At 6:23 p.m. (22:23 UTC) on May 30, Mariner 9 launched from the Eastern Test Range into a direct-ascent trajectory along a 398-million-kilometer path toward Mars. The spacecraft separated from its Centaur booster and deployed its solar panels at 6:40 p.m. (22:40 UTC). At 7:16 p.m. (23:16 UTC), out of Earth's shadow, the craft's Sun sensor was set. At 10:26 p. m., the spacecraft locked its star sensor onto the star Achernar.

On June 4, a midcourse maneuver with a 5.11-second engine burn increased velocity by 6.7 meters per second, adjusting the trajectory and ensuring that the Centaur stage would not impact on Mars and thus potentially negate the results of the anticipated exploratory landings of the later Viking project. The correction aimed the craft so close to

Mars (within 1,600 kilometers) that the anticipated second maneuver was unnecessary. The radio transmitter was switched from low-gain omnidirectional antenna to high-gain, narrow-beam (increased strength) antenna on September 22/23. On November 2, an unexpected anomaly shifted the navigational lock of the star sensor, requiring commands to the craft to search and resume orientation.

Earth-based astronomers were watching the Martian atmosphere. On September 22, a brilliant, whitish cloud appeared, moving rapidly over the Noachis region: The cloud was first photographed by G. Roberts of the Republic Observatory in South Africa. Trackers at the Lowell Observatory in Flagstaff, Arizona, watched the cloud spread from the initial 2,400-kilometer streak; dust-storm clouds obscured nearly the whole planet by the end of the month. Martian dust storms, known since 1892, show an intensity coincident with Martian perihelion (the planet's closest approach to the Sun) and are most visible when perihelion coincides with Earth-Mars opposition. Nevertheless, the intensity, speed, and spread of this storm were the greatest ever observed.

Calibration photographs of Mars were received on November 8, and the significance of the storm became apparent. Mariner 9 began regularly photographing the planet on November 10 through 11 as it approached from 860,000 to 570,000 kilometers. These images were transmitted through the Goldstone Tracking Station to JPL and broadcast live on national television.

On November 13, after a 15-minute, 23-second engine burn, Mariner 9 was inserted into an elliptical orbit with a 64.4° inclination, 12-hour, 34-minute, 1-second period, a 1,398-kilometer periapsis, and a 17,927-kilometer apoapsis (the farthest distance from Mars in its orbit). The initial orbit was intentionally long to allow optimal coincidence between the probe's periapsis pass over the planet and the Goldstone viewing period. By the fourth orbit, synchronization was achieved. An orbit trim maneuver was accomplished on

November 15, yielding a 64.34° inclination, an 11-hour, 57-minute, 12-second period, a 1,394-kilometer periapsis, and a 17,048-kilometer apoapsis. The orbiting spacecraft was affected by an equatorial irregularity of the Martian gravitation, and a second trim maneuver was required on December 30 with a 17-second engine burn giving the craft a 64° inclination, an 11-hour, 59-minute, 28-second period, a 1,650- kilometer periapsis, and a 16,900-kilometer apoapsis.

The dust storm persisted through January, 1972, though by late November some clearing had begun; the rate again slowed in late December. On March 17, cameras were turned off to allow engineers to analyze a malfunction in the onboard computer; photography resumed until March 30, when all science instruments were turned off. The craft had taken 6,876 photographs.

Once each orbit between April 2 and June 4, Mariner 9 passed through the shadow of Mars; during these periods, the craft required battery power. Power shutdown during this interim not only saved the solar cells but also freed the Goldstone Tracking Station to give support to the flight of Apollo 16.

Mariner 9 resumed photography on June 8, giving special attention to the two Martian poles—which were not clearly visible from Earth and previously had been obscured by lingering clouds. From early August, 1972, until October 12, Mars was behind the Sun; Mariner 9 could not be commanded from Earth. The low-resolution camera had mapped most of the surface. The high-resolution camera had covered specially targeted areas over about 2 percent of the surface. The shrinking of the southern polar cap was examined in detail. When operations resumed, map coverage of the northern pole was completed.

Mariner 9 sent its last picture on October 17. By October 27, the spacecraft's mission ended after depletion of its attitude-control gas. Final command 45,960 was given; the telemetry signal ceased during orbit 698. Scientists estimated that the spacecraft would remain in Martian orbit for fifty to one hundred years.

Contributions

Photographic mapping of Mars provided detail superior even to that of the Moon as viewed from Earth; moreover, the mapping covered the entire surface and displayed changes through one-half of a Martian year. The great dust storm provided an opportunity for photographic flexibility—repeated views of areas of interest, attention to Martian satellites, and measurements of the storm itself.

Mariner 9 indicated wind velocities as great as 180 kilometers per hour—an extreme required in low atmospheric pressure to raise dust 50 to 70 kilometers above the surface. Particles ranged from 2 to 15 micrometers in size with a silicon content of about 60 percent.

Mariner 9 measured the shape of Mars. Rather than an oblate spheroid (flattened sphere) like Earth, Mars is a triaxial ellipsoid: 3,396 by 3,394 by 3,376 kilometers. The longer axis passes through the highly elevated Tharsis Ridge, a Martian bulge 6,000 kilometers in surface diameter and 7 kilometers high.

While Mariner 9 did away with the notion of "canals" on Mars, it produced images of giant volcanoes even before the dust cloud settled. The large light spot known since the advent of telescopic observation as Nix Olympica (the snow of Olympus) was reidentified as Olympus Mons, the largest volcanic or mountainous mass known: 500 kilometers wide and rising 29 kilometers above its surroundings. Olympus lies on the western flank of a broad ridge, running diagonally northeast to southwest, which is marked by three great shield North volcanoes-North Spot, Middle Spot, and South Spot—each about 400 kilometers across. These, and other smaller volcanoes, have been active recently enough areologically (areology is the Martian study equivalent of geology) that the plains on Mars appear as volcanic regions covering older cratered areas.

If volcanoes were not impressive enough, as the dust subsided a spectacularly immense canyon within the equatorial belt was identified by Mariner 9. Valles Marineris, named for the spacecraft, stretches from the southeast flank of Tharsis Montes eastward more than 4,000 kilometers; its vertical edges descend up to 9 kilometers deep, and many minor side canyons are 250 kilometers wide, some extending back into surrounding uplands for 150 kilometers.

Numerous channel networks, some broad and sinuous, others narrow and dendritic (branched like trees), occur over widespread areas. Some of the largest, 30 to 60 kilometers wide and up to 1,200 kilometers long, originate in northern plateaus and flow (slope) northward into the Chryse region. Networks of narrower channels come off the sides of craters northwest of the Hellas Planitia. Other varieties demonstrate the exotic character of the planet.

Each polar ice cap has a permanent core containing some frozen water. The enormous expansion in the winters, extending to within 40° of the equator, shows the deposit of frozen carbon dioxide (CO_2) from an atmosphere that, while thin, is about 90 percent that gas. Pitted plains and layered terrains awaited Viking Orbiter photography for further clarification. Carbon dioxide clouds formed and drifted about major topographical features.

While Mariner 9 did not obtain improved photographs of Phobos, the largest of the Martian moons, it did get preorbital pictures, including Phobos silhouetted against Mars. The smaller satellite, Deimos, was photographed while Mariner awaited the settling of the dust storm. Both were measured. Each is a triaxial ellipsoid with axes of 28, 23, and 20 kilometers for Phobos, and 16, 12, and 10 kilometers for Deimos. Both have nearly circular orbits about the Martian equator, keeping the same face (their longest axis) toward the planet. Deimos, at 23,400 kilometers, revolves in 30 hours, 18 minutes; Phobos, at 9,270 kilometers, in 7 hours, 39 minutes. Both are heavily cratered, the largest crater on Phobos some 8 kilometers wide. Their lack of crater erosion permitted some comparative consideration with craters on Mars. Both are among the darkest objects in the solar system.

Context

Space exploration and interplanetary travel were initiated in pre-World War II experimentation and post-World War II (Cold War) competition. Schemes proposed in the 1950's went beyond engineering capacities and budgeting possibilities. Mariner-Mars 1971, reduced to the actual success of Mariner 9, is no exception, as the effort to obtain its real cost illustrates. Figures from $76 to $115 million have been stated, but the reality is lost within a Voyager program that never occurred and a reorganized Viking mission that landed on Mars.

Mariner 9 was the fourth spacecraft of the first ten to reach Mars; six of these had only flyby-status missions. The Soviet Mars 1 spacecraft, launched on November 1, 1962, lost radio contact on March 21, 1963, some 106 million kilometers from Earth. Mariner 3 failed on November 5, 1964, shortly after its launch, when the shroud for the spacecraft did not open; it went into solar orbit. Mariner 4 was successfully launched on November 28, 1964, and took twenty-two photographs. Of them, nineteen were usable and two were beyond the Martian terminator (the darkening line of solar light); they revealed the cratered character of the Martian surface along a single sweep path. The Soviet Zond 2, launched November 30, 1964, failed when its transmission ceased at the beginning of May, 1965.

Mariners 6 and 7 were launched on February 24 and March 27, 1969. Mariner 6 sent 50 far-encounter and 25 near-encounter photographs over July 29-30; Mariner 7 sent 91 far-encounter and 33 near-encounter shots over August 2-4. These hinted at the variety of Martian surface features.

Mariner 8 experienced a launch failure on May 8, 1971. The Soviet pair, Mars 2 and 3, launched May 19 and 28, 1971, successfully reached Mars and went into orbit on November 27 and December 2. Each carried a sterilized scientific lander package.

The Mars 2 lander, ejected before orbit, crashed on the Martian surface. The Mars 3 lander touched down safely and relayed a television signal, which stopped after 20 seconds. Their primary mission was to measure solar wind and cosmic radiation between Earth and Mars. They measured Mars's atmospheric humidity and surface temperature, ending their missions in August, 1972.

One significant result of these efforts was the increased communication between U.S. and Soviet space scientists. The Working Group on Interplanetary Exploration was established under an agreement of January, 1971, by NASA and the Soviet Academy of Sciences. Meeting in Moscow in 1973, the group agreed to exchange on April 15 data from Mars 2 and 3 for pictures and maps made by Mariner 9. During 1973, the Soviets launched four more spacecraft of their Mars series. One of Mars 4's onboard systems malfunctioned, leaving it unable to brake for orbit. It flew by on February 10, 1974, at 2,200 kilometers, taking pictures, and left to continue transmittal of outer space information. Mars 5 entered orbit on February 12, 1974. Mars 7 neared on March 9; its lander separated, but malfunctioning of its onboard system caused it to miss Mars by 1,300 kilometers. Mars 6 approached on March 12, separated its lander at 48,000 kilometers, and continued into heliocentric orbit, passing within 16,000 kilometers. The lander transmitted for 148 seconds.

The U.S. Viking orbiters were launched August 20 and September 9, 1975, and inserted into their respective orbits on June 19 and August 7, 1976. Care was taken to obtain higher-resolution photographs before permitting the landers to descend. Each was successfully landed: Viking 1 on July 20, Viking 2 on September 3. The prodigious output of photographic images (51,539 from the orbiters and more than 4,500 from the landers) was spectacular, while those from the surface had the intrigue of new but limited vision. Biology experiments performed by the landers proved inconclusive, though essentially negative for the immediate regions. Viking Orbiter 2 ceased operating on July 25, 1978. Its lander was shut down on April 12, 1980. Viking Orbiter 1 was silenced on August 7, 1980. Viking Lander 1, with the capacity for direct communication to Earth, continued to supply weekly weather information or the occasional landscape image to indicate any change of surface conditions until contact was lost on January 11, 1983.

—*Clyde Curry Smith*

See also: Mariner 3 and 4; Mariner 6 and 7; Mars Observer; Mars Pathfinder; Mars Reconnaissance Orbiter; Planetary Exploration; Viking Program; Viking 1 and 2.

Further Reading

Cortright, Edgar M., ed. *Exploring Space with a Camera*. NASA SP-168. Washington, D.C.: Government Printing Office, 1968. As spacecraft of various types entered Earth, lunar, or solar orbits, experiments with camera observations, machine or handheld, produced one of the great achievements of the Space Age. Samples, arranged historically and topically and including those from the first lunar lander and the Mariner 4 flyby, receive interpretive commentary.

David, Leonard, and Ron Howard. *Mars: Our Future on the Red Planet*. Washington, D.C.: National Geographic, 2016. Provides a detailed description of humanity's evolving understanding of the Red Planet, and projects what may happen in the next 25 years in Mars exploration. For the space enthusiast. Has marvelous images of Mars.

Ezell, Edward Clinton, and Linda Neuman Ezell. *On Mars: Exploration of the Red Planet, 1958- 1978*. NASA SP-4212. Washington, D.C.: Government Printing Office, 1984. This excellent example of critical scholarship, demanding an attentive and knowledgeable reader, covers the technical details of the various

Mariner and Viking missions and reports the complex web of political, financial, and managerial problems that eventually resulted in a series of firsts on Mars: the first photographing (Mariner 4), the first orbiting (Mariner 9), and the first landing with observational and biological results (Viking). Photographs, drawings, tables, appendices of data, bibliography, notes, and indexes make this the official NASA history.

Hartmann, William K. *Moons and Planets*. 5th ed. Belmont, Calif.: Thomson Brooks/Cole Publishing, 2005. Provides detailed information about all objects in the solar system. Suitable on three separate levels: high school student, general reader, and the college undergraduate studying planetary geology.

Hartmann, William K., and Odell Raper. *The New Mars: The Discoveries of Mariner 9*. NASA SP-337. Washington, D.C.: Government Printing Office, 1974. A generous sample of Mariner 9 photographs, usually of adequate scale, supplemented by historical materials including drawings, telescopic observations, and comparative examples from Mariners 6 and 7, placed within a narrative context that interprets the diverse and novel features from the perspective of new discoveries. A concluding summary itemizes Mariner 9's achievements. For a broad audience.

Heppenheimer, T. A. *Countdown: A History of Space Flight*. New York: JohnWiley, 1997. A detailed historical narrative of the human conquest of space. Heppenheimer traces the development of piloted flight through the military rocketry programs of the era preceding World War II. Covers both the American and the Soviet attempts to place vehicles, spacecraft, and humans into the hostile environment of space. More than a dozen pages are devoted to bibliographic references.

Kaufman, Marc. *Mars Up Close: Inside the Curiosity Mission*. Washington, D.C.: National Geographic, 2014. Although a text primarily about the Curiosity rover on Mars, this work provides historical developments in the space-based exploration of Mars. Includes numerous excellent photographs of the Red Planet and its geology.

Mari, Christopher, ed. *Space Exploration*. New York: H. W. Wilson, 1999. Twenty-five articles (reprinted from magazines), covering the state of the space program at the time of publication, are divided into five sections: John H. Glenn, Jr.'s return to space, the exploration of Mars, the International Space Station, recent mining efforts by commercial industries, and new types of space vehicles and propulsion systems.

Moore, Patrick, and Charles A. Cross. *Mars*. New York: Crown, 1973. A British effort in the wake of Mariner 9's apparent mapping triumph to provide any interested reader with the first real atlas of another planet. Aside from its maps, the volume is splendidly illustrated, carefully written, and indicative of the development of knowledge about Mars.

Morrison, David, and Tobias Owen. *The Planetary System*. 3d ed. San Francisco: Addison- Wesley, 2003. Organized by planetary object, this work provides contemporary data on all planetary bodies visited by spacecraft since the early days of the Space Age. Suitable for high school and college students and the general reader.

National Aeronautics and Space Administration, Scientific and Technical Information Office. *Mars as Viewed by Mariner 9: A Pictorial Presentation by the Mariner 9 Television Team and the Planetology Program Principal Investigators*. Rev. ed. NASA SP-329. Washington, D.C.: Government Printing Office, 1976. The largest and best collection of photographs, with captions expressing an interpretation by one of the members of the Imaging Team. The intelligent commentary reflects the excitement of the initial impact.

Nicks, Oran W. *Far Travelers: The Exploring Machines*. NASASP-480. Washington, D.C.: Scientific and Technical Information Branch, 1985. Discusses all major NASA planetary spacecraft during NASA's first quarter-century. Written by a senior NASA official involved with lunar and planetary programs during that era.

Sparrow, Giles. *Mars*. London: Quercus, 2015. Primarily a textbook, but available to the interested reader. Details the state of understanding of the Red Planet as gained by astronomical observation and investigations by spacecraft since Mariner 4. Amazing photographs.

Spitzer, Cary R., ed. *Viking Orbiter Views of Mars*. NASA SP-441. Washington, D.C.: Government Printing Office, 1980. A carefully selected sample of photographs is presented in a topical arrangement with introductory comments, followed by examples with explanatory captions of sufficient detail to make each photograph more revealing for any audience. Several stereographically matched pairs allow three-dimensional effects when the enclosed viewing device is used. Greater clarity compared to the Mariner 9 equivalents illustrates how much more remains—even now—to be learned from Mars.

Mariner 10

Date: November 3, 1973, to March 24, 1975
Type of spacecraft: Planetary exploration

Mariner 10 collected vital data on the inner solar system, including detailed photographs of Venus and Mercury. The first probe to use the gravitational pull of one planet to help it reach another, Mariner 10 proved the utility of the "gravity-assist" technique for interplanetary travel.

Key Figures

Walker E. "Gene" Giberson, project manager

James A. Dunne, project scientist

Victor C. Clarke, Jr., Mission Analysis and Engineering manager

John R. Casani (b. 1932), Spacecraft Systems manager

Bruce C. Murray (1932-2013), principal investigator, Imaging Team

Norman F. Ness (b. 1933), principal investigator, magnetometer experiment

Summary of the Mission

The Mariner 10 mission performed the first close flyby of the planet Mercury, using the gravity of Venus to divert the spacecraft's trajectory toward Mercury. While multiple-planet swing-bys had been anticipated since the 1920's, it was not until the 1960's, with advanced trajectory-compution techniques, that such methods of interplanetary navigation became feasible. In 1969, the National Aeronautics and Space Administration (NASA) approved a Mariner Venus/ Mercury mission for 1973 (MVM73). In February, 1970, it was discovered that the gravity of Mercury could be used to provide a "free return for a second encounter with Mercury after the probe's initial flyby using a minimum of spacecraft propulsion. The Jet Propulsion Laboratory (JPL) in Pasadena, California, was selected to implement the mission, and the project began in 1970 under the management of Walker E. "Gene"

Giberson. John R. Casani was selected to manage spacecraft development, Victor C. Clarke, Jr., became Mission Analysis and Engineering manager, and James A. Dunne was project scientist. The Boeing Aircraft Company of Seattle, Washington, was selected to build JPL's Mariner spacecraft design.

The spacecraft itself was modeled on the Mariner series: a standard octagonal structure with electronic instrumentation installed in the inner walls, and within, hydrazine fuel tanks to feed propulsion units, which handled trajectory corrections. Supported on this body were twin television cameras; two panels of solar cells extending like wings, which powered the spacecraft; and a dish-shaped high-gain antenna, which was part of the radio system used for relaying data, navigating the spacecraft, and making scientific measurements. Extensive modifications to the design of previous Mariner probes were necessary, such as changing the fuel tanks and attitude control system; others were necessary to protect the probe from the intense heat of the Sun, such as designing the photovoltaic solar panels to rotate and tilt away from the Sun and using new thermal protection techniques. Furthermore, the payload included instruments to take pictures in wavelengths from ultraviolet through infrared and others to measure electromagnetic and charged particle characteristics of the planets and interplanetary space.

The launch window to Venus was open from October 16 to November 21, 1973. Normally, spacecraft are launched as close as possible to the beginning of the period in order to provide a margin for error. NASA, however, approved a launch at the optimal time of 12:45 a.m., eastern standard time or 05:45 Coordinated Universal Time (UTC), November 3, and the launch (achieved by the Atlas SLV-3D/Centaur D1-A launch vehicle) took place within a few thousandths of a second of that desired time.

Instruments for specific experiments were turned on soon after launch and began gathering data on the "solar wind" (the solar plasma that flows out from the Sun) and on the interplanetary magnetic fields. Television cameras were also engaged at that time to calibrate the cameras for Venus by taking pictures of the similarly cloudy Earth and for Mercury by taking pictures of the Moon, whose surface was suspected to be like Mercury's.

MVM73, now called Mariner 10, was—despite its ultimate success—plagued by failures of the spacecraft and of experiments throughout the mission, taxing the ingenuity of engineers and scientists to the utmost. Shortly after launch, a protective shield became stuck and caused much data in the plasma science experiment to be lost. Ten days after launch, during a series of roll maneuvers, the spacecraft's star tracker detected a bright particle (a minute flake of dust or paint from the spacecraft) and followed the particle instead of the intended star, Canopus, thus causing major losses of attitude control gas.

After passing on the darkside of the planet, Mariner 10 photographed the other, somewhat more illuminated hemisphere of Mercury. The north pole is at the top, two-thirds down from which is the equator. (NASA / JPL)

When employing an alternative method of flying the spacecraft, however, the JPL team found that the interaction between the gyroscope control system and the flexible body of the spacecraft produced unforeseen vibrations, again causing the loss of attitude control gas. A further threat to the mission occurred a few months later, when the spacecraft automatically and irreversibly switched from its main power system to a backup system, leaving no room for power failures without jeopardizing the mission. The high-gain antenna and television cameras also experienced recurrent failure, threatening to reduce drastically the amount of data transmitted to Earth.

Fortunately, the JPL team found ways to compensate for these difficulties. Solar panels were tilted so that the pressure of the solar wind could be used to balance the spacecraft and save attitude control gas by a technique called solar sailing. After the Venus encounter, scientists discovered that the trajectory could be corrected by "sunline" maneuvers, which do not require the spacecraft to roll or pitch, thereby avoiding use of the gas-wasting gyroscopes. The high-gain antenna and television camera heaters warmed up and repaired themselves before the Mercury encounter. In addition, the Deep Space Network (DSN), which received the spacecraft transmissions on Earth, made improvements in their large antennae.

On February 5, 1974, Mariner 10 began taking history's first close-up photographs of Venus, beginning with an image of a thin lighted crescent and gradually revealing the entire planet as the spacecraft swung around Venus from its night to its day side. Ultraviolet images showed swirling cloud patterns. At the same time, the high-gain antenna was used to reveal characteristics of both the Venusian atmosphere and the mass and shape of the planet.

On March 16, a sunline maneuver was performed to correct Mariner's trajectory, heading it toward Mercury. The first encounter with the planet occurred on March 29. For eleven days surrounding closest approach, Mariner's cameras transmitted more than two thousand high-resolution pictures back to Earth, displaying a cratered, Moon-like surface. Also, particle and field measurements revealed an unexpected magnetic field.

On May 9 and 10, Mariner was readied to attempt a second, and possibly a third, encounter, using the "free return" gravity-assist trajectory. Two days after the first encounter, however, another power system failure occurred as a result of overheating. In August, 1974, the spacecraft's tape recorder failed, preventing pictures from being obtained when the spacecraft was out of contact with Earth. Part of the computer system also failed, making spacecraft control more difficult. The spacecraft team compensated for these problems, and the mission continued.

On September 21, Mariner 10 passed the day side of Mercury on its second encounter, at a distance of about fifty thousand kilometers. Three antennae of the DSN were arrayed to increase their ability to detect the spacecraft's radio transmissions, resulting in the receipt of about one thousand high-resolution pictures of Mercury from a new southerly viewing angle.

After the second encounter, the spacecraft was placed in a hibernation mode and allowed to roll slowly through space with its cameras deactivated. This move was intended to save attitude control gas and to avoid exercising the unreliable power system. A "back-off" sunline maneuver was required at one point to prevent the spacecraft from actually hitting Mercury on its third encounter. One final malfunction occurred that resulted in the spacecraft rolling into an attitude that blocked radio signals from Earth. By using a combination of DSN antennae, educated guesswork, and analysis of the high-gain antenna transmission power pattern, scientists were able to stop the roll, and the spacecraft was correctly oriented—only thirty-six hours before the third encounter.

On March 16, 1975—nearly one year after its initial encounter with Mercury—Mariner 10 made its final and closest flyby and took its final installment of pictures, with resolutions to 140 meters. Eight days later, its supply of attitude control gas finally exhausted, the spacecraft's radio transmitter was turned off, leaving a silent spacecraft to orbit the Sun. A short time later, the United States Postal Service issued a stamp commemorating the mission.

Contributions

Ultraviolet pictures of Venus revealed a swirling pattern of clouds rotating rapidly (once every four Earth days) around the planet. The clouds move in a direction opposite to the planet's rotation (very slowly, as discovered by Earth-based radar measurements of the surface—once every 243 Earth days). Another experiment determined that the shape of Venus is one hundred times closer to a sphere than is Earth's.

The particle and fields experiments verified that Venus has a weak magnetic field but also confirmed that Venus's ionosphere interacts with the solar wind to form a "bow shock" (a shock wave similar to that produced by a supersonic airplane), which keeps the solar plasma from hitting the planet directly. The ultraviolet experiment found in Venus's upper atmosphere a great quantity of hydrogen, which is thought to control its chemistry, forming clouds laced with sulfuric acid. The infrared experiment determined that the temperature of the cloud tops remained constant (250 kelvins) between the day and night sides of the planet.

As Mariner 10 approached Mercury, the planet, as expected, showed a Moon-like appearance (heavily cratered with large, flat circular basins), suggesting the early bombardment of the inner solar system by meteors. On the second encounter, the back side of Mercury revealed a huge circular feature approximately 1,290 kilometers across, subsequently named the Caloris Basin for its heat. The infrared experiment determined that the surface temperatures—given the long Mercury days and nights and the planet's proximity to the Sun— range from 90 kelvins on the night side to 460 kelvins on the day side.

The radio and ultraviolet experiments confirmed that Mercury, like Earth's Moon, lacks an atmosphere. Unlike the Moon, however, Mercury has large cliffs that are up to 3.2 kilometers high and 480 kilometers long. These are believed to have been caused by the shrinking of the planet during cooling of a hot central core. Mercury is also much denser than the Moon and, like Venus, much more spherical than Earth. Estimates of Mercury's mass were improved one hundred times through the encounter of Mariner 10.

The particle and fields experiments discovered, quite unexpectedly, that Mercury has a significant magnetic field, sufficient to produce a bow shock between the planet and the solar wind. Whereas Venus's bow shock is produced primarily by charged particles in its ionosphere, Mercury, with no atmosphere, must have an intrinsic magnetic field. Mercury's field is Earth-like in its shape, though less intense.

Context

Mariner 10 was the fourth spacecraft to visit Venus and the first to take close-up pictures. The first interplanetary probe, Mariner 2, had made a flyby of Venus in 1962 and used infrared radiometry to determine that Venus had a very high temperature low in the atmosphere as opposed to high up in the atmosphere, as some scientists had proposed. Earth observations of Venus had previously established that the planet showed no surface features, implying an opaque atmosphere. In 1967, the combined measurements from the U.S. Mariner 5 flyby and the Soviet Venera 4, which sent an entry probe into the atmosphere, proved that the Venusian atmosphere was extremely hot and dense and composed primarily of carbon dioxide. None of these missions, however, carried cameras. Mariner 10 identified weather patterns on Venus that have produced data for the prediction of weather patterns on Earth. It confirmed the heat and density of Venus's atmosphere, which are attributed to a "greenhouse" effect resulting from the carbon dioxide atmosphere. This finding shed light on the greenhouse effects that could result on Earth from atmospheric changes caused by industrial pollution.

Later missions to Venus included the U.S. Pioneer Venus (in 1978) and the Soviet Veneras 15 and 16 (in 1983), which used radar to map surface features. Soviet Venera spacecraft were

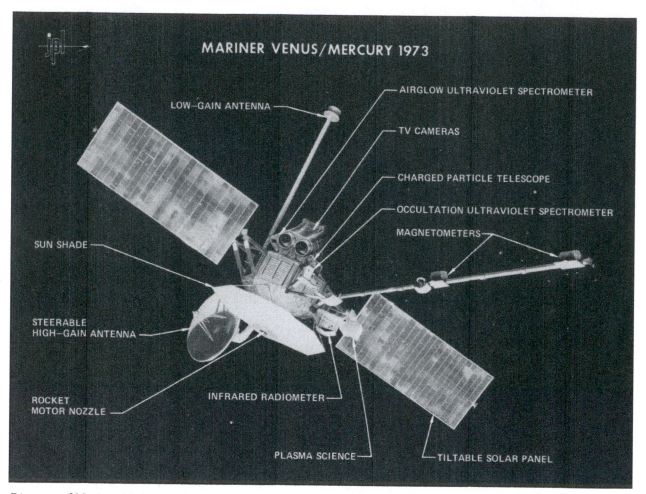

MARINER VENUS/MERCURY 1973

LOW–GAIN ANTENNA

AIRGLOW ULTRAVIOLET SPECTROMETER

TV CAMERAS

CHARGED PARTICLE TELESCOPE

OCCULTATION ULTRAVIOLET SPECTROMETER

MAGNETOMETERS

SUN SHADE

STEERABLE
HIGH–GAIN ANTENNA

ROCKET
MOTOR NOZZLE

INFRARED RADIOMETER

PLASMA SCIENCE

TILTABLE SOLAR PANEL

Diagram of Mariner 10. (NASA / JPL)

landed on Venus in 1975 and 1982, and the Soviet Vega spacecraft (which encountered Halley's comet in 1986) dropped balloons and landers on Venus as it flew by. Between 1989 and 1994, the U.S. Magellan mission produced a detailed map of 99 percent of the Venusian surface.

Mercury observations are important in understanding the overall history of the solar system. Scientists speculate that Mercury and Venus formed originally in a zone around the Sun where there was little water, in contrast to Earth, which formed in a water-rich zone. Comparative studies of Mars, the Moon, and Mercury show that the three bodies were all subjected to a similar meteoric bombardment, including asteroid-sized bodies, between 4 billion

and 3.3 billion years ago. Mercury data suggest that the bombardment could have originated outside the solar system rather than in the asteroid belt, as previously thought.

Earth is in a period of tectonic action—creating volcanoes—and some scientists have speculated that Mars may be entering an active phase of tectonic activity leading to an Earth-like future. Mercury data, however, seem to strengthen a contrary theory, that Martian volcanism took place hundreds of millions of years ago and that the internal heat of Mars is now too low to drive tectonic processes. Such findings, including Mercury's still unexplained magnetic field, have raised new questions and changed scientists' perceptions of the solar system. Many questions remain to be answered.

From the perspective of space technology, Mariner 10 established the viability of the gravity-assist technique, which was subsequently used for the 1977 Voyager 2 encounters with Saturn and Uranus via Jupiter. The gravity-assist technique will undoubtedly play a major role in future interplanetary navigation.

With Mariner 10, for the first time scientists were selected to assist in mission planning early enough to influence the spacecraft design. JPL agreed to implement the mission for the very low budget of $98 million. The mission cost through the first encounter was $1 million less than the $98 million promised by JPL to NASA, including inflation. Costs for the extended mission were less than $3 million, so that the entire mission was achieved for $100 million, which corresponded to about sixty cents for each American.

Three decades would pass before a proposal for another Mercury spacecraft would be funded. MESSENGER (Mercury Surface, Space Environment, Geochemistry, and Ranging), launched on August 3, 2004, and headed toward an orbital insertion around the planet closest to the Sun, thereby providing an opportunity for prolonged measurements and extensive surface mapping. Mariner 10 had imaged only about half of the planet's tantalizing surface. MESSENGER extended that mapping until its mission ended on April 30, 2015 with the spacecraft purposely deorbited to impact on Mercury.

—Donna Pivirotto

See also: Deep Space Network; Hubble Space Telescope; Jet Propulsion Laboratory; Magellan: Venus; Mariner 1 and 2; Mariner 3 and 4; Mariner 5; Mariner 8 and 9; MESSENGER; Planetary Exploration; Voyager 2: Neptune.

Further Reading

Cattermole, Peter, and Patrick Moore. *Atlas of Venus*. New York: Cambridge University Press, 1997. Filled with photography from telescopes and the Mariner, Pioneer Venus, and Magellan spacecrafts, this work provides a complete atlas of Venus and a gazetteer of Venusian place names.

Chapman, Clark R. *Planets of Rock and Ice: From Mercury to the Moons of Saturn*. Rev. ed. New York: Charles Scribner's Sons, 1982. Describes the characteristics of the solid bodies of the solar system, as well as the people and missions that identified those characteristics. Draws comparisons between these planets and moons and draws conclusions about Earth in a planetary context. Includes some photographs of planets. Suitable for general audiences.

Domingue, D. L., and C.T. Russell. *The MESSENGER Mission to Mercury*. New York: Springer-Verlag, 2008. Provides a historical context for the continued exploration of Mercury by the MESSENGER mission. Heavily illustrated. For the more advanced astronomy enthusiast.

Dunne, James A., and Eric Burgess. *The Voyage of Mariner 10: Mission to Venus and Mercury*. NASA SP-424. Washington, D.C.: Government Printing Office, 1978. The official history of the Mariner 10 mission, written by the project scientist. Suitable for high school and college levels, it describes the mission in detail from early Earth observations of Venus and Mercury through the third Mercury encounter of Mariner 10. Contains numerous illustrations and photographs of the spacecraft and the pictures returned from the mission. Among the appendices is a list of the participants in the mission.

Greeley, Ronald. *Planetary Landscapes*. 2d ed. New York: Chapman and Hall, 1994. A pictorial atlas describing the geomorphology (determination of the form and evolutionary history of planetary surfaces) of all the rocky planets and rock/ice moons from Mercury through Saturn. Suitable for advanced high school and college levels, this volume includes many references to books and scientific articles about the planets.

Grinspoon, David Harry. *Venus Revealed: A New Look Below the Clouds of Our Mysterious Twin Planet.* New York: Perseus Book Group, 1998. This work provides both romantic and scientific explanations of the planet closest to Earth, incorporating the latest data from the Magellan spacecraft.

Heppenheimer, T. A. *Countdown: A History of Space Flight.* New York: John Wiley, 1997. A detailed historical narrative of the human conquest of space. Heppenheimer traces the development of piloted flight through the military rocketry programs of the era preceding WorldWar II. Covers both the American and the Soviet attempts to place vehicles, spacecraft, and humans into the hostile environment of space. More than a dozen pages are devoted to bibliographic references.

Hunten, D. M., et al., eds. *Venus.* Tucson: University of Arizona Press, 1983. A collection of scientific essays describing all aspects of Venus. The authors are primarily from the United States and the Soviet Union, and findings from all the Venus missions of both countries are described. Includes a chapter on the history of Venus studies, as well as maps, charts, equations, and calculations describing the geology, atmosphere, and magnetic environment of Venus. College-level material.

Morrison, David, and Tobias Owen. *The Planetary System.* 3d ed. San Francisco: Addison- Wesley, 2003. Organized by planetary object, this work provides contemporary data on all planetary bodies visited by spacecraft since the early days of the Space Age. Suitable for high school and college students and the general reader.

Murray, Bruce C., and Eric Burgess. *Flight to Mercury.* New York: Columbia University Press, 1976. A description of the Mariner 10 mission from the personal viewpoint of the principal investigator of the television experiment team. Written chronologically, it refers to world events of the period, including the Arab oil crisis and the Watergate hearings, to provide historical context for the mission. Suitable for general audiences; includes more than one hundred photographs of Venus and Mercury.

Murray, Bruce C., Michael C. Malin, and Ronald Greeley. *Earthlike Planets: Surfaces of Mercury, Venus, Earth, Moon, Mars.* San Francisco: W. H. Freeman, 1981. This well-illustrated volume includes many black-and-white and some color photographs of the planets. It describes and compares the characteristics of the inner planets—Mercury, Venus, Earth, and Mars—as well as the Moon, and deduces facts about the origin and evolution of the solar system. Suitable for general audiences.

Nicks, Oran W. *Far Travelers: The Exploring Machines.* NASASP-480. Washington, D.C.: Scientific and Technical Information Branch, 1985. Discusses all major NASA planetary spacecraft during NASA's first quarter-century. Written by a senior NASA official involved with lunar and planetary programs during that era.

Pater, Imke de, and Jack J. Lissauer. *Planetary Science.* New York: Cambridge University Press, 2001. This is an advanced text about the physical, chemical, and geological processes at work in the solar system.

Strom, Robert G. *Mercury, the Elusive Planet.* Washington, D.C.: Smithsonian Institution Press, 1987. This readable, well-illustrated book provides a complete description of Mercury, including the history of observations of the planet. Describes the Mariner 10 mission in the context of the subsequent twelve years of interpretation of data from the mission, the geology and magnetic characteristics of the planet, and the theory behind scientific conclusions about Mercury. Includes many photographs, a table of definitions of technical and scientific terms, and a list of the names and locations of surface features.

Strom, Robert G., and Ann L. Sprague. *Exploring Mercury: The Iron Planet.* New York: Springer-Praxis, 2003. A detailed history of our changing understanding of the planet closest to the Sun. Includes Mariner 10 data and describes the goals of the MESSENGER mission.

Mars Climate Orbiter and Mars Polar Lander

Date: December 11, 1998, and January 3, 1999
Type of program: Planetary exploration

As part of the Mars Surveyor Program, NASA's long-term Mars exploration program, Mars Climate Orbiter (MCO) and Mars Polar Lander (MPL) were sent to arrive at the Red Planet in late 1999. They were designed to study Mars's climate and history as well as the nature and extent of its resources. Unfortunately, both missions failed.

Key Figures

Norman Ray Haynes (b. 1936), Jet Propulsion Laboratory (JPL) director of Mars Exploration Directorate

Fuk Li, JPL manager of the New Millennium Program

David Crisp, JPL New Millennium Program scientist

John McNamee, JPL Mars project manager, 1998

Richard Zurek, JPL Mars program scientist, 1998

Glenn E. Cunningham (b. 1943), JPL Mars Surveyor Operations project manager

Sam Thurman, JPL Mars Surveyor Flight Operations manager

Sarah Gavit, Deep Space 2 project manager

Kari Lewis (b. 1973), Deep Space 2 chief mission engineer

Suzanne Smrekar, Deep Space 2 project scientist

Summary of the Missions

Mars Climate Orbiter and Mars Polar Lander were a pair of missions to Mars launched during the favorable launch window of late 1998 and early 1999. They were part of the Mars Surveyor Program, NASA's long-term program to send missions to Mars during each favorable launch window. These windows occur at intervals of a little over two years.

Launched on December 11, 1998, Mars Climate Orbiter was timed to arrive at Mars the following September. The mission plan called for MCO to go into an initial capture orbit with the engines firing for about sixteen minutes. The planned initial orbit was an elliptical orbit. During the first two months after MCO's arrival, the mission plan did not call for any scientific experiments. Rather, the orbiter was to have gradually maneuvered into its final planned orbit. During successive closest approaches to Mars in the elliptical orbit, initially at an altitude of approximately 160 kilometers, atmospheric braking would gradually slow the craft. After roughly two months, MCO would be ready to enter its final nearly circular polar Sun-synchronous orbit.

The first planned mission of Mars Climate Orbiter was to provide support for the Mars Polar Lander during its three-month mission. After completing the support functions, MCO would start its primary mission. Armed with two instruments, it was to have spent one complete Martian year, a little less than two Earth years, studying the climate of Mars through all its seasons. The Mars Color Imager (MARCI) had two cameras to directly photograph the surface and atmospheric conditions. The Pressure Modulator Infrared Radiometer (PMIRR)

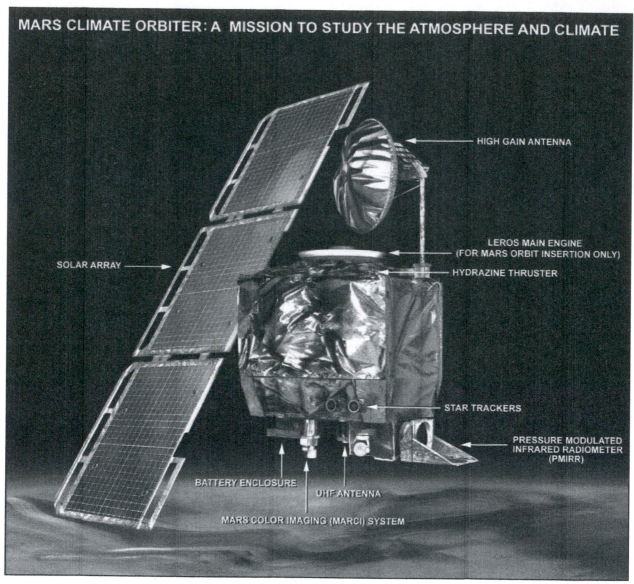

The structure of the Mars Climate Orbiter. (NASA)

was designed to make detailed measurements of various atmospheric conditions. MCO was then to have been free to provide support as needed for future missions to Mars.

Unfortunately, the planned mission was not completed. As Mars Climate Orbiter approached the Red Planet early on the morning of September 23, 1999, contact was lost. The approach altitude to Mars was just under 60 kilometers rather than the originally planned 160 kilometers. The minimum

approach altitude that the spacecraft could survive was between 85 and 100 kilometers. Hence, Mars Climate Orbiter was lost.

Mars Polar Lander was launched on January 3, 1999, by a Delta 7425 rocket. It arrived at Mars the following December, shortly after the Mars Climate Orbiter was to have reached its final orbit. Upon its final approach to Mars the Mars Polar Lander was to separate from the cruise stage of its launch vehicle. This cruise stage provided the needed

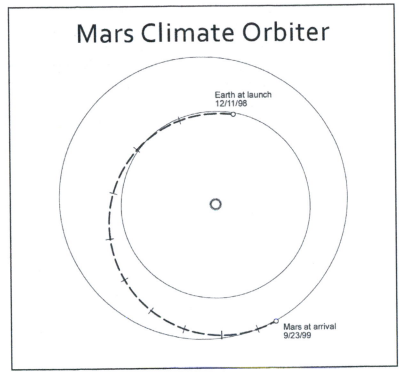

Mars Climate Orbiter

Earth at launch
12/11/98

Mars at arrival
9/23/99

Interplanetary trajectory of Mars Climate Orbiter when en route to Mars. (NASA - JPL)

support, protection, and course corrections during MPL's eleven-month voyage. Just after this separation, two microprobes were to launch from the cruise stage. These New Millennium Program (NMP) probes were designed to fall to Mars without any type of braking. Crash landings at an estimated 200 meters per second would cause them to burrow about 1 meter into the surface at a location roughly 100 kilometers north of MPL's target.

Mars Polar Lander was to have landed near the south pole of Mars. The target site, at roughly 76° south latitude, was at the border of Mars's south polar cap. The landing date was during the southern hemisphere spring on Mars. During its three-month planned mission, MPL was to have studied the transition of the south polar cap as it receded from its southern winter extent to its smaller summer extent.

Mars Polar Lander contained four instruments. The Mars Descent Imager (MARDI) was a camera to photograph Mars's surface during the landing.

After reaching the surface the remaining three instruments were to take over. The Mars Volatiles and Climate Surveyor (MVACS) was a suite of instruments designed to study water and carbon dioxide (volatiles) on the Martian surface. The Light Detection and Ranging Instrument (LIDAR) was supplied by the Russian Space Agency to study ice and dust clouds. The Planetary Society provided the Mars Microphone (MM) to listen for sounds near Mars's surface.

Even though it was very interesting scientifically, the planned polar landing site was riskier than previous landing sites on Mars. The environment is harsher, and the region is not as well studied. Therefore, it is harder to choose a safe, smooth landing site. With the greater risk, contact with MPL was lost as it attempted to land.

Apparently MPL crashed into the surface because a software error caused the landing rockets to shut down ten seconds early. All attempts to reestablish contact with the spacecraft after the descent failed. As was MCO, so too MPL was lost. The two NMP microprobes were also lost.

Contributions

Mars Climate Orbiter and Mars Polar Lander were to have looked for indirect evidence of life on Mars, either past or present, study the climate and climate history of Mars, and study the resources on the Red Planet. The common thread in these three goals was the study of water on Mars, which is needed for life, an important element of climate, and an important resource needed for human exploration.

To accomplish these goals, MCO was to have acted as a weather satellite monitoring the weather on Mars for a full planetary year. The PMIRR would have measured various atmospheric characteristics and their variations with altitude. These characteristics include the pressure, temperature, dust content, water vapor content, and ice content. These observations would have provided information on atmospheric wind patterns, the seasonal Martian dust storms, and the seasonal water and carbon dioxide cycles. Detailed understanding and modeling of Mars's present climate from these observations would have allowed extrapolation backward to deduce Mars's climate history.

Mars Climate Orbiter also contained the MARCI. The resolution of this camera was not as high as that of the cameras on the Mars Global Surveyor, but its images would have been in color. They would have allowed direct visual identification of surface and atmospheric features, including clouds and dust storms.

After Mars Climate Orbiter was lost, the investigation team determined that it went into an initial orbit at an altitude that was too low. The orbit was incorrect because there was a miscommunication between different teams about whether English units or metric units were used to control the spacecraft—an error attributed in large part to "faster, cheaper, better."

Mars Polar Lander was to have worked on its mission goals from a closer vantage point on the surface. This vantage point would have allowed more detailed observations, but for only one stationary point on Mars. The location chosen was near the edge of the south polar ice cap, while it was receding during the southern hemisphere spring.

The primary instrument on MPL was actually a suite of instruments called the Mars Volatiles and Climate Surveyor (MVACS). These instruments would have made detailed studies of water and carbon dioxide, both of which are volatile on Mars, and important factors in the present and past climate. These instruments were not designed to look directly for

life, but they might have revealed whether Mars at one time had a climate more favorable to life.

The MVACS consisted of a robotic arm that could dig a meter deep for soil samples and transfer them to the Thermal and Evolved Gas Analysis (TEGA) experiment. TEGA would have analyzed the samples for water and other gases trapped in the soil. The layers in the meter-deep trenches would have corresponded to a maximum geologic age of one hundred thousand years. Hence, the planned analysis would have provided a detailed climate history of Mars over that recent period.

Mars Polar Lander also contained the Mars Descent Imager to photograph the landing site during descent. Images would have provided a geologic context for the more detailed measurements from the ground, thereby ensuring that the big picture would not get lost in the details.

The LIDAR instrument was to have used a laser beam in a way similar to radar. The laser beam would have reflected off water, ice, and dust clouds to study their content in the Martian atmosphere. A small microphone on board MPL would have listened to wind and other possible sounds on Mars.

The two NMP microprobes, weighing 2.5 kilograms, contained smaller, less elaborate versions of

In the Spacecraft Assembly and Encapsulation Facility-2 (SAEF-2), a KSC technician looks over the Mars Polar Lander before its encapsulation inside the backshell, a protective cover. (NASA)

the TEGA instrument. They were to have penetrated about a meter into the ground to look for layering, water, and ice in the soil. They would also have measured the soil temperatures and would have functioned for only a few days before completing their mission.

Unfortunately, contact was lost with the Mars Polar Lander and the microprobes during the landing attempt on December 3, 1999. An investigation team determined that the most likely cause of the mission failure was a software error that caused braking rockets to stop firing ten seconds early. Hence, MPL crashed into the surface at an estimated speed of approximately 80.5 kilometers (50 miles) per hour. The cause of the microprobe failure remained unknown.

Context

Mars Climate Orbiter and Mars Polar Lander were components of NASA's long-term plans for exploring Mars. These missions were also flown under the cost and time constraints of NASA's "faster, better, cheaper" (FBC) policy, implemented in the early 1990's.

NASA's Mars exploration program began with Mariner flyby missions in the late 1960's. In 1976 the Viking mission landed two robotic spacecraft on the surface of Mars. The Viking mission returned evidence that liquid water had existed on the surface of Mars in the past, even though water can no longer exist as liquid there. These missions found no direct evidence for life on Mars. Consequently, most scientists thought that there was no past or present life on Mars. However, in August, 1996, a

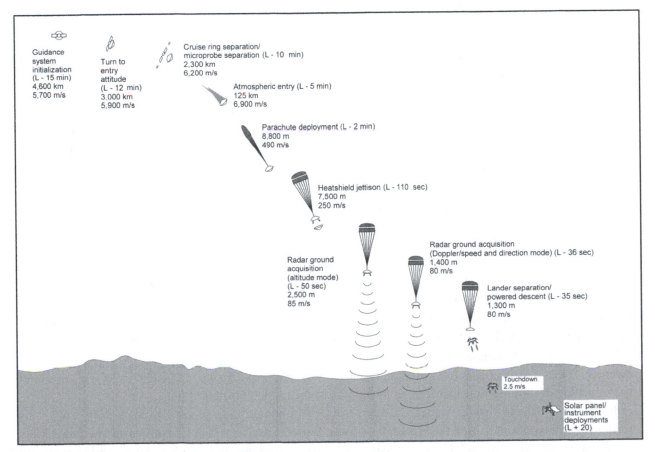

Landing diagram of Mars Polar Lander. (NASA)

team of NASA scientists announced that a Martian meteorite contained evidence of past simple life-forms on Mars. Evidence remains controversial, but it renewed interest in the search for past or present life on Mars. Studies of the climate and volatile histories on Mars that were to have been performed by Mars Climate Orbiter and Mars Polar Lander would not have definitively answered the questions about life on Mars; they would, however, have provided clues in our search to answer these questions.

During the 1990's NASA started the Mars Surveyor Program to send missions to Mars roughly every two years during each favorable launch opportunity. These missions were to be part of NASA's FBC program. Prior to origination of the FBC concept, typical NASA missions had cost nearly a billion dollars, and took years to plan and implement. Price tags and time lines limited the number of possible missions, and increased the consequences of a mission failure. Missions planned under the FBC concept had price tags measured in a few hundreds of millions rather than upwards of a billion dollars. They were also to be planned and implemented in a few years rather than decades. This policy reduced the negative consequences of a mission failure, but at a price as the risk of a mission failure increased.

The first missions to Mars under the FBC concept, the Mars Pathfinder and Mars Global Surveyor, were resounding successes. Therefore, the increased risk of a mission failure seemed worth taking. However, failures of both MCO and MPL forced a reconsideration of the FBC concept. NASA's official *FBC Task Final Report* and the report of the Mars Climate Orbiter Mishap Investigation Board did not recommend that ca the FBC philosophy be scrapped outright noting that failure can be acceptable if a mission is extremely technically challenging and the scientific return is worth the risk. However, failures caused by too much emphasis on the time and cost caps imposed by the FBC policy are not acceptable. The root cause of the Mars Climate Orbiter failure was a lack of communication between different groups working on the project, leading to the failure in unit conversions. The root cause of the Mars Polar Lander failure was apparently a programming error. Management changes were designed to reduce the possibility of making these types of errors and increasing the possibility of repeating them

—*Paul A. Heckert*

See also: Delta Launch Vehicles; Funding Procedures of Space Programs; Jet Propulsion Laboratory; Mariner 10; Mars Observer; Mars Odyssey; Mars Pathfinder; Mars Reconnaissance Orbiter; National Aeronautics and Space Administration; New Millennium Program; Planetary Exploration; Search for Extraterrestrial Life; Viking 1 and 2.

Further Reading

Carroll, Michael. "Divining on Mars." *Astronomy* 27, no. 2 (1999): 42-48. This article, published shortly after the mission launch dates, describes the scientific instruments and planned observations for the mission. There is also some comparison with past and planned Mars missions.

Chaikin, Andrew. "Mars Invasion." *Popular Science* 255, no. 6 (1999): 100-101. Published between the losses of the Mars Climate Orbiter and of the Mars Polar Lander, this article describes the loss and the plan for the Mars Polar Lander mission.

Cowen, R. "Math Error Equals Loss of Mars Orbiter." *Science News* 156, no. 15 (1999): 229. This is a brief news article describing the error leading to the loss of the Mars Climate Orbiter.

Gordon, Bonnie Bilyeu. "Faster, Better, Cheaper, Not Good Enough." *Astronomy* 28, no. 3 (2000): 6-7. This article examines, from behind the scenes, the Faster, Better, Cheaper policy by comparing the failed Mars missions to the still-on-track Cassini mission to Saturn. Hartmann, William K. *Moons and Planets.* 5th ed. Belmont, Calif.: Thomson Brooks/Cole Publishing, 2005. Provides detailed information about all objects in the solar system. Suitable on three separate levels: high school student, general reader, and the college undergraduate studying planetary geology.

Mishkin, Andrew. *Sojourner: An Insider's View of the Mars Pathfinder Mission.* New York: Berkley Books, 2003. A thorough exploration of the Mars Pathfinder mission that also provides a detailed historical perspective on the exploration of the surface of Mars (begun by Viking).

Morrison, David, and Tobias Owen. *The Planetary System.* 3d ed. San Francisco: Addison- Wesley, 2003. Organized by planetary object, this work provides contemporary data on all planetary bodies visited by spacecraft since the early days of the Space Age. Suitable for high school and college students and the general reader.

Oberg, James. "NASA's Not Shining Moments." *Scientific American* 282, no. 2 (2000): 13-14. This brief article reports on the loss of both the Mars Climate Orbiter and the Mars Polar Lander. It concentrates on reasons behind the loss and steps to prevent future losses.

Parsons, Paul. "NASA Scrambling to Surmount Orbiter Loss." *Astronomy* 28, no. 1 (2000): 30-31. Published after, but written prior to, the loss of the Mars Polar Lander, this brief news article describes reactions to the loss of the Mars Climate Orbiter.

Rhea, John. "In the Wake of Mars Failures, Should NASA Still Pursue Faster, Better, Cheaper?" *Military& Aerospace Electronics* 11, no. 1 (2000): 8. This article is an opinion piece in which the author argues in favor of incremental changes to, but not complete elimination of, NASA's Faster, Better, Cheaper program.

Zimmerman, Robert. *The Chronological Encyclopedia of Discoveries in Space.* Westport, Conn.: Oryx Press, 2000. Provides a complete chronological history of all crewed and robotic spacecraft and explains flight events and scientific results. Suitable for all levels of research.

Mars Exploration Rovers

Date: June 10, 2003 to February 13, 2019
Type of program: Planetary exploration

The Mars Exploration Rovers (MERs), twin robotic expeditions exploring the surface of Mars, landed on different locations on opposite sides of Mars to maximize the scientific return. With the ability to trek the length of a football field each day, they can explore a larger portion of the Martian surface than previous missions. Each rover contains a package of scientific instruments designed to analyze Mars's surface geology to help trace the history of liquid water on Mars.

Key Figures

Jim Erickson, project manager
Joy Crisp, project scientist
Albert Haldemann, deputy project scientist
Steve Squyres, science instrument principal
    investigator

Summary of the Mission

The Mars Exploration Rovers (MERs) were launched about a month apart in the summer of 2003, and reached Mars in early 2004. The first rover, Spirit or MER-A, was launched on June 10 on a Delta II 7925 rocket. The second, Opportunity or MER-B, was launched on July 7 atop a Delta 7925H rocket. The "H" indicates Heavy. This configuration was used because the second mission launched when the relative positions of Earth and Mars required more energy to get to Mars. Both were launched from Cape Canaveral, Florida. Both MER missions were timed to take advantage of the closest Mars approach to Earth in approximately sixty thousand years.

The probes took the fastest possible trajectories to Mars, and arrived in January, 2004. After a seven-month journey, Spirit landed at Gusev Crater on January 3, 2004. Opportunity soon followed by landing on Mars at Meridiani Planum on January 25, 2004. Unfortunately two other missions, the Japanese Nozomi probe and the European Beagle 2 mission, which were planned to arrive at Mars nearly the same time did not succeed.

The MER mission used a landing system pioneered by the 1997 Pathfinder mission, which incorporated a combination of rockets, parachutes, and airbags to cushion the blow of striking the Martian surface. Because the MERs were heavier than the Mars Pathfinder, parachutes 40 percent larger were used. After the parachute was opened to provide initial slowing, rockets fired to bring the landers to a stop about 10 to 15 meters above the surface. Finally airbags inflated to cushion the remaining fall. The landers bounced several times before finally coming to rest on the Martian surface and deflating the airbags. The lander's petals were then free to open, allowing the rovers to deploy their solar arrays and begin exploring Mars.

Shortly after landing, the computer on board Spirit experienced some memory difficulties. Mission controllers were able to resolve the problems in a little over a week by purging files and reformatting the flash memory. After this initial difficulty, both rovers performed well for their originally scheduled ninety-day mission and beyond.

Each 170-kilogram rover contained a suite of instruments designed to allow it to explore the geology of Mars. These included cameras and instruments designed for detailed studies of the chemical compositions of selected rocks.

Nine cameras on each rover included six engineering and three scientific cameras. Four Hazard Avoidance Cameras (Hazcams) were mounted on the front and back of the rovers. Their 120° fields of view were pointed downward to see obstacles that might interfere with the rover's motion. Having two in each direction gave three-dimensional images, just as two eyes give human beings three-dimensional depth perception. Two 45° field of view Navigation Cameras (Navcams) provided a three-dimensional forward view higher than the Hazcams and allowed ground controllers to see where the rover was going.

Two Panoramic Cameras (Pancams) had the same resolution as the human eye, so they could mimic what a geologist would see standing on the surface of Mars. Because there were two Pancams, they could also provide three-dimensional imaging. In addition, these cameras had a number of color filters to provide basic spectral information and color pictures. A solar filter allowed the Pancams to locate the Sun's position in the sky. When combined with the time of Mars's day, the Sun's position provided navigational information.

In addition to the large view cameras, the Microscopic Imager (MI) took extreme close-up pictures. This camera was mounted on a robotic arm that could swing into position very close to the rock of interest. The camera was also mounted behind a microscope, so it provided the equivalent of a human geologist's observations of a rock sample through a microscope.

As on most space probes, cameras provide dramatic images, but the information provided by other scientific instruments is at least as important. The Miniature Thermal Emission Spectrometer (Mini-TES) provided infrared spectra of the Martian

An artist's concept portrays a NASA Mars Exploration Rover on the surface of Mars. (NASA / JPL / Cornell University)

rocks, soil, and atmosphere. These spectra revealed much about the chemical composition and mineral structure of the rocks and soil. The Mini-TES was particularly important in searching for minerals that were produced in the presence of water. Atmospheric spectra taken with the Mini-TES told mission scientists about the temperature and the presence of dust and water vapor in the atmosphere.

Two spectrometers studied the chemical composition of the Martian surface. The Mössbauer Spectrometer (MB) was designed specifically to study the iron abundance in the mineral content of Martian rock and soil samples. Because iron is magnetic, the MB also helped scientists study the sample's magnetic properties. Magnet arrays mounted at various positions on the MERs collected magnetic samples for analysis by the MB. Chemical compositions other than iron used the Alpha Proton X-Ray Spectrometer (APXS). Alpha particles emitted during radioactive decay told mission scientists about the presence and abundance of various radioactive isotopes in the mineral structure of rock samples. The x-ray spectra also provided information about the chemical samples' composition.

The Rock Abrasion Tool (RAT), located on the end of the robotic arm, could grind a 4.5-centimeterdiameter hole into a selected rock sample. A half-centimeter hole took about two hours to grind. Mission scientists used the RAT to expose and study the interior structure of rocks.

In late October, 2004, the MER mission passed the 50,000-picture milestone. This number represents more than twice as many pictures as taken by all previous Mars landers. In early November, 2004, the Opportunity solar panels received a mysterious power boost that may have been caused by wind blowing accumulated dust off the solar panels. The MER missions, originally planned for about ninety days, performed so well that on October 1, 2004, the National Aeronautics and Space Administration (NASA) extended the missions for a second time. Some rover components were beginning to show signs of age, but they were still exploring Mars's surface.

On April 6, 2005, with both rovers suffering from only minor problems, and each covering greater and greater distances during translations across the Martian surface, NASA announced that the MER program was being extended for the third time. This latest extension would run for the coming eighteen months. Few program officials and scientists would have been so optimistic before launch to have expected the rovers to last this long in the severity of the Martian environment.

Spirit got stuck in soft sand on May 1, 2009. It took eight months to analyze the situation and devise an extraction procedure. Unfortunately, Spirit could not break free, and on January 26, 2010, NASA revised the rover's mission to be a stationary science platform. Communications with Spirit

ceased on March 22, 2010. The Jet Propulsion Laboratory repeatedly attempted to reestablish a link to Spirit, but on May 24, 2011, Spirit's mission was officially declared complete.

Mars developed a wide-ranging dust storm in 2018. Inside Endeavour crater Opportunity was configured so that it had a decent chance of weathering the dust storm. Alas on June 10, 2018, Opportunity stopped communicating with Earth. Two days later with its power level dangerously low, Opportunity entered hibernation mode. Opportunity never rebooted itself or called Earth after the dust storm abated. Controllers on Earth attempted to reestablish contact with Opportunity without success. Either the spacecraft had succumbed to the cold or had drained its battery since dust covered its solar panels. In any event, after over a thousand signals had been sent to the rover, NASA declared Opportunity's mission completed on February 13, 2019.

Contributions

The primary scientific objective of the MER missions was to find evidence of past water on Mars by looking for signs of past water activity in Martian

The Spirit and Opportunity rovers were named through a student essay competition. The winning entry was by Sofi Collis, a third-grade Russian-American student from Arizona. "I used to live in an orphanage. It was dark and cold and lonely. At night, I looked up at the sparkly sky and felt better. I dreamed I could fly there. In America, I can make all my dreams come true. Thank you for the 'Spirit' and the 'Opportunity.'" (NASA)

rocks and soils. Other important scientific goals included understanding the environmental conditions when liquid water was present on Mars; understanding the composition and distribution of minerals, particularly those containing iron, near the landing site; and understanding the geologic processes that formed the minerals and terrain at the landing sites. Finally, studies on the ground could check the conclusions reached about the local Martian geology from orbiter studies, and thereby provide confidence that conclusions reached from orbital studies elsewhere on Mars were correct.

The Gusev Crater and Meridiani Planum landing sites were chosen for their potential as sites where water once existed. Gusev Crater, the landing site for Spirit, is an impact basin about the size of the state of Connecticut and was once thought to have been a giant lake. However, during the three-month primary mission Spirit failed to find any lake-related deposits at this site. If they ever existed, they have apparently been disrupted by subsequent impacts. Rocks at the Spirit landing site are olivine-bearing basaltic rocks, a type of volcanic rock not previously seen on Mars. The RAT ground off surface layers on rocks at this site, revealing subsurface veins possibly altered by the presence of water. Rock coatings are also consistent with brief periods of moisture in the past, even if not indicative of a large, long-term lake. Spirit also found evidence that subsurface water percolated to the surface at Gusev Crater. After exploring Gusev Crater, Spirit started the trek for the nearby Columbia Hills, named after the crew of the ill-fated STS-107 space shuttle flight (destroyed upon reentry on February 1, 2003), to search for clues to the early history of Gusev Crater. Initial indications are that the hills are layers of volcanic ash.

Meanwhile, Opportunity found evidence of water at Meridiani Planum inside a crater named Eagle. Rocks containing sediments from evaporation appear to have formed in a body of slow-moving salt water, perhaps at the shoreline of a salty sea. Rocks at this site contain high concentrations of hematite which forms in wet conditions. These rocks provide definite direct evidence of liquid water in Mars's past.

Samples collected by the Rovers' magnets indicate that most of the rocks on Mars contain iron. Oxidized iron gives Mars its rusty red color. Studies of patterns on the rocks are also helping mission scientists understand wind erosion on Mars, currently the most significant source of Martian erosion. Some rocks found on Mars resemble meteorites found on Earth that are thought to originate from Mars, bolstering evidence that they truly originated on Mars.

Context

The MER missions are part of NASA's long-term program to explore Mars. The program has four main scientific goals:

(1) to determine if there was ever life on Mars

(2) to understand the Martian climate

(3) to understand the Martian geology

(4) to pave the way for human exploration of Mars

In 1976, the first Viking landers on Mars found no direct evidence for life on Mars but did find evidence suggestive of large amounts of liquid water in the past in the form of dry riverbeds. The MER missions found more direct evidence of geologic processes requiring liquid water on the surface of Mars. The first Viking landers on Mars had no mobility. The 1997 Pathfinder mission was the first rover to land on Mars. The MER rover had greater mobility compared with the Pathfinder, and were able to trek several kilometers from their impact points.

—*Paul A. Heckert*

See also: Jet Propulsion Laboratory; Mariner 3 and 4; Mars Climate Orbiter and Mars Polar Lander; Mars Global Surveyor; Mars Observer; Mars Odyssey; Mars Pathfinder; Mars Reconnaissance Orbiter; Planetary Exploration; Private Industry and Space Exploration; Viking Program; Viking 1 and 2.

Further Reading

Chaisson, Eric J., and Steve McMillan. *Astronomy Today*. 5th ed. Upper Saddle River, N.J.: Pearson Prentice Hall, 2004. The chapter on Mars in this introductory astronomy textbook provides background for understanding the exploration of Mars.

Godwin, Robert, ed. *Mars: The NASA Mission Reports*. Vol. 1. Burlington, Ont.: Apogee Books, 2000. A thorough presentation of NASA documents relating to the Mars programs from Mariner 4 through Mars Global Surveyor. Includes press kits and a CD-ROM filled with special programs and interviews.

---. *Mars: The NASA Mission Reports*. Vol. 2. Burlington, Ont.: Apogee Books, 2004. A thorough presentation of NASA documents relating to the Mars programs from Mars Odyssey through the Mars Exploration Rovers. Includes a DVD of NASA data, bonus interviews, and NASA animation.

Hartmann, William K. *Moons and Planets*. 5th ed. Belmont, Calif.: Thomson Brooks/Cole, 2005. Provides detailed information about all objects in the solar system. Suitable for high school students, general readers, and undergraduates studying planetary geology.

Mishkin, Andrew. *Sojourner: An Insider's View of the Mars Pathfinder Mission*. New York: Berkley Books, 2003. A thorough exploration of the Mars Pathfinder mission that provides detailed historical perspective on the exploration of the surface of Mars begun by Viking and continued by the Mars Exploration Rovers.

Moomaw, B. "Spirit Lands at Gusev." *Astronomy* 32, no. 4 (2004): 32. This article tells the inside story of Spirit's landing on Mars. Page 48 of the same issue also has an article titled "Envisioning Mars" with many good images of Mars.

Naeye, R. "Red-Letter Days." *Sky and Telescope* 107, no. 5 (2004): 44. This article describes the MER mission through April, 2004, giving both mission details and scientific results.

---. "Software Links Pediatric Doctors with New Research." *Obesity, Fitness and Wellness Week*, October 30, 2004, p. 231. This article describes a virtual pediatric intensive care unit that uses modified software similar to that used by the MER mission.

National Aeronautics and Space Administration, Jet Propulsion Laboratory. "Mars Exploration Rovers." http://marsrovers.jpl.nasa.gov. Accessed June, 2005. This official Web site for the Mars Exploration Rovers contains a wealth of information about the mission, including overviews of the program, the science, the people involved, and mission details.

Mars Global Surveyor

Date: November 7, 1996 to November 21, 2006
Type of program: Planetary exploration

Mars Global Surveyor (MGS) was designed to spend more than a full Martian year, 687 Earth days, mapping the surface of the Red Planet with unprecedented accuracy making high-resolution images, observing short-term and seasonal changes on the surface and in the atmosphere, and measuring gravitational and magnetic properties of Mars.

Key Figures

Thomas E. Thorpe, Mars Surveyor Operations project manager at the Jet Propulsion Laboratory (JPL)

Arden L. Albee, Mars Surveyor Operations project scientist at JPL

Summary of the Mission

Mars Global Surveyor (MGS) was launched from Cape Canaveral November 7, 1996, aboard a Delta rocket. The scientific payload consists of five instruments: a camera, a laser altimeter, a thermal emission spectrometer, magnetic field sensors, and a special radio transmitter. MGS also has a relay antenna designed to pick up transmissions from future surface probes and relay data back to Earth. Major components of the spacecraft itself include communication equipment, solar panels, reaction wheels and steering thrusters (for pointing the craft), and a rocket engine. That engine was first used to take MGS to Mars, and then to put it into an orbit around Mars that ranged from 262 kilometers to 54,026 kilometers above the Martian surface.

Because the Delta launch vehicle was not powerful enough to allow MGS to carry enough fuel to put MGS into its mapping orbit, aerobraking was used to lower MGS into the orbit. Using aerobraking, the low point of MGS's orbit is lowered into the upper Martian atmosphere so that air drag slows the spacecraft. One of the two solar panels had been slightly damaged shortly after launch, and when it bent alarmingly under the atmospheric drag forces, aerobraking was halted. After some study, engineers decided to resume aerobraking, but at a much gentler rate so that mapping orbit was only achieved in March, 1999, instead of January, 1998. The mapping orbit has an average altitude of 378 kilometers.

The Mars Orbiter Camera (MOC) used regular arrays of thousands of tiny sensors in charge coupled devices (CCDs) to record images. When the camera lens formed an image on the array, the sensors converted position and intensity information into electrical signals. These signals were then digitized and stored until they were broadcast to receiving stations on Earth. The MOC's telephoto lens was actually a 35-centimeter-diameter telescope. While its field of view was narrow and it made only black-and-white images, it could show details on the Martian surface as small as 1.4 meters. Two wide-angle fish-eye lenses generated spectacular panoramic images. One was filtered to transmit blue light and the other to transmit red light so that a color image could be obtained by combining their data. In early February, 2005, MOC took its thousandth image.

The Mars Orbiter Laser Altimeter (MOLA) sent pulses of infrared laser light down to the Martian surface. Some of this light was reflected back to the

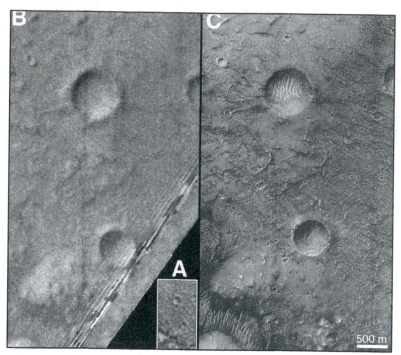

Three images of Airy-0 taken by, from A to C, Mariner 9 (1972), Viking 1 (1978) and Mars Global Surveyor (2001). Airy-0 is the larger crater towards the top center in each frame. (NASA / JPL / MSSS)

spacecraft and focused with a 50-centimeter-diameter parabolic mirror onto a detector. Because the speed of light is well known, measuring the time elapsed between the outgoing pulse and the detection of the reflected pulse allowed the distance to the surface to be determined. MOLA could measure the height of terrain to within 2 meters locally and 30 meters globally. (Global accuracy was diminished because data had to be taken over various orbits and be combined.)

The thermal emission spectrometer (TES) contained three detectors. The Michelson interferometer analyzed infrared light by spreading it into a rainbow, or spectrum, of infrared colors and measuring how much of each color is present. Because different elements and minerals have different infrared spectra, analysis of TES data provided information on which minerals cover the Martian surface and which gases and mineral particles (dust) are present in the Martian atmosphere. The second detector was a broadband infrared sensor that could

determine the temperatures of infrared sources. Various substances exposed to the same amount of sunlight absorb and radiate heat at different rates, so the temperature of a substance was a clue to its identity. The third detector measured the brightness of reflected sunlight in the visible and near infrared ranges.

Two magnetometers (MAGs), mounted on the outer ends of the solar panels, reduced interference from other instruments on the spacecraft. They measured magnetic fields near the spacecraft by comparing voltages in special pairs of coils. The electron reflectometer (ER) used a clever trick to measure the magnetic field closer to the Martian surface. The solar wind consisted mainly of high-energy protons and electrons streaming outward from the Sun. Because the Martian atmosphere is so thin, electrons may penetrate to within several tens of kilometers of the Martian surface. When a magnetic field is present, electrons spiral around that field in helical paths as they approach the surface. Electrons traveling nearly parallel with the magnetic field penetrate deep into the atmosphere and are absorbed, but other electrons traveling at larger angles with respect to the field stop their forward motion and then spiral back out into space. It was possible to determine the magnetic field nearer to the surface by measuring the range of angles over which the reflected electrons strike the ER.

The Radio Science experiments depended on the Ultra-Stable Oscillator (USO), which very precisely controlled the radio's carrier frequency. For a few minutes during each orbit, radio signals from MGS passed through the Martian atmosphere as MGS disappeared behind Mars and then again as it reappeared from behind Mars. Carefully measuring the intensity and frequency (tone) of the radio carrier wave allowed scientists to calculate how the pressure of the atmosphere changed with height over a given location on Mars. The second experiment detected changes in the Martian gravitational field. Small changes in the thickness and density of the Martian crust could be measured because they would cause MGS to change its orbital speed very slightly. These speed changes resulted in slight changes in the radio's carrier frequency by the Doppler effect.

NASA extended the Mars Global Surveyor mission with the possibility that it could be extended even further if a more fuel-conservative orbit was achieved. Indeed, the Mars Global Surveyor continued to play a significant role in support of the Mars Exploration Rovers Spirit and Opportunity in 2004 and 2005. Mars Global Surveyor on January 1, 2003, started a relay mission in support of the Spirit and Opportunity landings. On March 30, 2004 Mars Global Surveyor provided a remarkable image of Spirit and the wheel tracks that it had made in the Martian soil during its first 85 days of surface travel. About a year later MGS was able to for the first time photograph a spacecraft orbiting a planet other than Earth from another orbital vantage point. It was able to record two images of NASA's Mars Odyssey and one of the European Space Agency's Mars Express.

Another mission extension, Mars Global Surveyor's third, started on October 1, 2006. This was intended to last two years. However, on November 2, 2006, while attempting to reorient a solar panel, controllers on Earth lost contact with MGS. Three days later a weak signal was picked up briefly from MGS, but it was not continuous. NASA announced on November 21, 2006, that MGS was most likely lost. Then on April 13, 2007, the space agency released an accident report which indicated that spacecraft communications were probably lost as a result of a software issue involving an error in a parameter update. Therefore MGS had not suffered a hardware failure. Rather, loss of the spacecraft was due to human error. Left in a nearly polar orbit at an altitude of 450 kilometers, MGS was expected to remain circling the Red Planet until 2047.

Contributions

Has it ever rained on Mars? Did Mars ever have any lakes or oceans? There is ample evidence of catastrophic flooding, places where permafrost melted or underground springs broke the ground open to send cubic kilometers of water rampaging across the planet's surface. The Mars Pathfinder spacecraft landed at one such site in 1997. While there are many ancient river channels that were apparently fed from underground, there are very few channels that show the fine network of sources displayed by streams fed by surface runoff on Earth. Two sites where MGS images show evidence of surface runoff are in the Libya Mountains south of the Isidis Basin and in the Loire Valley. Only two sites out of the thousands examined, the Nanedi Valley and the Nirgal Valley, show an inner channel within a broader channel, a sign of continuing water flow over a long time. If rain occurred only early in Martian history, it may be that most of the evidence for it has been eroded away or covered by drifting sand.

The northern lowlands are unusually flat and smooth and are sufficiently reminiscent of an ocean bottom that scientists examined the surrounding terrain looking for shoreline features. The most likely shoreline is called Contact 2. Careful inspection of MGS high-resolution photographs showed these shoreline features to be illusory. However, data from the MOLA show that Contact 2 is a plausible shoreline for a northern ocean. Nearly all of Contact 2 is at the same elevation, and the terrain below this "shoreline" is significantly smoother than the terrain above it. Six large outflow channels empty into the lowlands approximately at the level of Contact 2, and their abrupt termination there strongly suggests that they emptied into a standing body of water.

Consistent with previous measurements, MGS detected no significant planetary magnetic field that could shield Mars from the solar wind. Instead,

MGS discovered that the solar wind interacts directly with the Martian ionosphere and upper atmosphere. However, as MGS dropped below the ionosphere during aerobraking it detected a weak field from magnetized crustal rock. Further measurements showed that only rock in the southern hemisphere was magnetic, so the discovery was somewhat fortuitous. The original aerobraking plan required MGS to dip low into the atmosphere over the northern hemisphere, not the southern. Had the damaged solar panel not necessitated a change in plans, the discovery might have been missed.

The terrain where the magnetized rock occurs is some of the oldest on Mars. In a situation reminiscent of a mid-oceanic ridge on Earth, the rock is magnetized in parallel bands tens of kilometers wide, and the direction of magnetization reverses in adjacent bands. The TES found that the surface materials are primarily volcanic, as had been supposed. The ancient, heavily cratered southern hemisphere is dominated by the volcanic rock basalt, while the younger northern hemisphere is dominated by a different type of volcanic rock called andesite.

A 200-by-500-kilometer-wide area in the Sinus Meridiani is covered with coarse-grained hematite, and there is a smaller deposit covering a crater floor in the Aram Chaos area. It is likely that these are evaporites—deposits left behind when a large body of water evaporates. Most of the Martian meteorites found on Earth contain carbonates, and it was anticipated that MGS would find large carbonate deposits. However, with the exception of the hematite deposits, MGS has not found large deposits of evaporites—such as carbonates, salts, or sulfates—that were anticipated. There is some evidence that MGS's instruments were not as sensitive to carbonates as had been supposed, and it is also possible that carbonate deposits may have eroded away or been buried beneath the sand. Detection of a hematite signature from orbit assisted the Mars Exploration Rover team in selecting landing sites for Spirit and Opportunity. Hematite can be an indication of water, and so the rovers were placed where hematite was likely to be found on the surface.

Context

The emerging picture of Mars is that it was initially volcanically active, and that a molten layer in its interior produced a global magnetic field. The southern highlands formed in various episodes as molten basaltic rock flowed over surface rock that was weakly magnetized as it cooled in the global magnetic field. Combining gravity data from the Radio Science experiments with topographical data from MOLA allowed scientists to calculate that the Martian crust ranges from 70 kilometers thick beneath the southern highlands to 40 kilometers thick beneath the northern lowlands. These data also reveal several vast, buried channels that may once have carried water to a northern sea. Erosion of ancient craters shows that the early atmosphere was much thicker, and there may have been rain. Two large impact craters in the southern hemisphere, Hellas and Argyre, have very smooth bottoms and may have contained seas at one time. MGS data show that Hellas is 4,000 kilometers across and 9 kilometers deep, which makes it the largest known impact basin in the solar system. It is nearly twice the diameter of the Lunar South Pole- Aitken Basin, the previous record holder.

Northern lowlands are made of andesite, a volcanic rock richer in silica than the highland basalt. Formation of andesite on Earth occurs when ocean water is drawn deep into the crust below oceanic trenches and mixed with magma, so finding large amounts of andesite on Mars was a surprise since there is little evidence of plate tectonics on Mars. The process may occur in a different fashion on Mars, but large amounts of andesite are another sign that water has been abundant on Mars. The northern hemisphere was probably a region of high heat flow, reflecting vigorous convection in the Martian interior, but after about 500 million years, the interior of Mars cooled so much that its magnetic dynamo ceased, and the global magnetic field disappeared.

Rock that melted and then solidified after this time, such as the rock of the northern lowlands, or the floor of the impact basin Hellas, is not magnetized.

By this time, Mars had probably lost much of its early atmosphere, and the great northern ocean (if it existed) froze. There are three proposed methods for the loss of the Martian atmosphere. First, following the formation of the planets came a period called the late heavy bombardment during which the planets were pummeled with all manner of space debris. With its low gravity, Mars would have been particularly susceptible to having great volumes of its atmosphere ejected into space by this bombardment. Second, surface water could have absorbed large quantities of carbon dioxide from the atmosphere and provided the environment where the carbon dioxide was converted into carbonate rock by chemical reactions. Third, after losing the protection of its global magnetic field, the upper Martian atmosphere could have had its gas stripped away by the solar wind.

Because it has had more time to collect them, older terrain has more craters per unit of area than younger terrain. Crater counts show that the northern lowlands are younger than the southern highlands and that the Tharsis Rise and Olympus Mons are younger than much of the northern terrain. Major volcanic outbreaks may have temporarily thickened the atmosphere, producing a warmer and wetter Mars, and it is quite possible that Mars has experienced several such episodes. Arsia Mons is one of three gigantic volcanoes on the Tharsis Rise. High-resolution images by MGS of lava flows within the Arsia Mons caldera show so few craters that the flows may be no more than 40 to 100 million years old, and some lava flows on Olympus Mons may be only 10 million years old. It is exciting that in geologic terms, these volcanoes may still be active.

The question of life on Mars is possibly the most intriguing and enduring question about Mars. The 1997 announcement of possible microfossils found in a meteorite from Mars added to the interest, but further investigation has cast doubt on this finding. Was there ever enough surface water to provide an environment in which Martian life could have evolved? Evidence from MGS data supports a tentative yes.

—Charles W. Rogers

See also: Jet Propulsion Laboratory; Magellan: Venus; Mariner 3 and 4; Mars Climate Orbiter and Mars Polar Lander; Mars Exploration Rovers; Mars Observer; Mars Odyssey; Mars Pathfinder; Mars Reconnaissance Orbiter; New Millennium Program; Planetary Exploration; Viking 1 and 2.

Further Reading

Beatty, J. Kelly. "In Search of Martian Seas." *Sky and Telescope* 4 (November, 1999): 38. An excellent summary of evidence for and against a possible northern ocean. The ocean may have frozen over, and the increasing weight of ice pushing southward may have forced underground water to the surface and thereby caused the observed catastrophic flooding.

Hartmann, William K. *Moons and Planets.* 5th ed. Belmont, Calif.: Thomson Brooks/Cole Publishing, 2005. Provides detailed information about all objects in the solar system. Suitable on three separate levels: high school student, general reader, and the college undergraduate studying planetary geology.

---. "Red Planet Rendezvous." *Astronomy* 4 (March, 1998): 50. An expert in planetary science looks at early MGS data and discusses how scientists hope to use future MGS results to answer questions left by Pathfinder.

Ladbury, Raymond. "Rediscovering Mars." *Physics Today* 3 (October, 1999): 33. A summary of ideas based upon MGS data. The Martian magnetic dynamo switched off after 500 million years. The differences between the northern and southern hemispheres are most likely due to internal processes, and there may have been a great northern ocean.

Morrison, David. "Mars Global Surveyor Photographs 'Face on Mars.'" *Skeptical Inquirer* 2 (July/August, 1998): 23. A discussion of the tabloid claims about the "Face on Mars." A comparison of the Viking 1 Orbiter photograph with an MGS photograph that clearly shows the feature is a natural hill.

Morrison, David, and Tobias Owen. *The Planetary System*. 3d ed. San Francisco: Addison-Wesley, 2003. Organized by planetary object, this work provides contemporary data on all planetary bodies visited by spacecraft since the early days of the Space Age. Suitable for high school and college students and the general reader.

Morton, Oliver. "Mystery of the Missing Atmosphere." *New Scientist* 4 (November, 1999): 35. If Mars ever had standing surface water, it must have had a thicker atmosphere. Evidence is given that it lost much of its early atmosphere during bombardment by asteroids and comets, and that the solar wind drove away some of the Martian atmosphere. Carbon dioxide from the atmosphere may also have been converted to carbonate rocks.

Parker, Samantha. "The Triumphant Turnaround of Mars Global Surveyor." *Sky and Telescope* 5 (August, 1998): 42. A collection of stunning, high-resolution images from MGS along with brief explanations of their significance. Includes images of Valles Marineris, Ophir Chasma, the splash-like pattern around a crater, and sand dunes in Hebes Chasma.

Winters, Jeffrey. "A Survey of Ancient Mars." *Discover* 6 (July, 1998): 112. Discusses evidence found in MGS images for water on Mars. Includes episodic floods, weathered craters, and the river channel of Nanedi Vallis.

Mars InSight

Type of Program: Planetary exploration
Date: May 5, 2018 to November 24, 2020 (projected)

Mars InSight is a National Aeronautics and Space Administration (NASA) Discovery Program mission that placed a single robotic lander on Mars to study the geophysics of the Martian subsurface. The InSight mission consists of a stationary Phoenix-class lander outfitted with a seismic experiment provided by the French space agency (CNES), and a heat flow and physical properties (HP³) experiment provided by the German space agency (DLR). An additional experiment led by the Jet Propulsion Laboratory (JPL) makes precise measurements of Mars' rotation.

Key Figures:

Thomas Zurbuchen, Associate Administrator, NASA Headquarters Science Mission Directorate

Richard Davis, Assistant Director, NASA Science Mission Directorate

W. Bruce Banerdt, InSight Principle Investigator, JPL

Suzanne Smrekar, Deputy Principle Investigator, JPL

Thomas Hoffman, Project Manager, JPL

Henry Stone, Deputy Project Manager, JPL

Chuck Scott, Deputy Project Manager, JPL

Philippe Lognonne, HP³ instrument Principle Investigator, DLR Institute of Planetary Research

William Folkner, RISE instrument Principal Investigator, JPL

Summary of the Mission

InSight is an acronym for Interior Exploration using Seismic Investigations, Geodesy and Heat Transport. The Mars InSight mission was designed to provide the first focused exploration of the Red Planet's interior using three primary instruments to map the Martian subsurface in unprecedented detail. Data will help determine the size, composition, and state of the planet's core. InSight seeks to analyze the thickness and structure of the Martian crust, determine the structure of the planet's mantle, investigate the thermal state of the Martian interior, document the rate of Mars' internal seismic activity, study the external Martian environment, and measure rotational variations exhibited by the planet.

Mars InSight is the twelfth of NASA's Discovery Program designated for investigation of the solar system with competitively selected, cost-capped missions. InSight's cruise stage, aeroshell, and lander were built by Lockheed Martin Space Systems. The InSight lander was based on the proven design of the successful Mars Phoenix lander from 2007, but incorporates advanced avionics and scientific instrumentation.

InSight was launched in the predawn hours of May 5, 2018 aboard an Atlas V-401 launch vehicle from Vandenberg Air Force Base, California, making this the first interplanetary launch from the West Coast of the United States. Also on the rocket was the Mars Cube One (MarCo) mission flown separately to Mars to test a new data relay system. InSight telecommunications data during the approach and landing phase were relayed to Earth through two MarCo miniaturized spacecraft, but the success of InSight's touchdown was not dependent on MarCo functioning properly as those CubeSats would only fly past Mars and ultimately get out of range for further data relay. Since the landing, InSight data are primarily relayed to Earth by the Mars Reconnaissance Orbiter and the Mars Odyssey orbiter.

InSight was specifically designed with a heat shield to withstand high-speed entry into Mars' atmosphere at 19,680 kilometers per hour, and to endure temperatures during atmospheric deceleration reaching 1811 kelvins. The instrument package also had to endure surface temperatures on Mars that ranged from 265 kelvins during the day to 178 kelvins overnight. The heat shield was further designed to survive "sandblasting" by suspended dust if InSight had to make its landing during a Martian dust storm. As with the Mars Phoenix lander, InSight did not use an air bag or "sky crane" landing scheme that NASA had successfully used to place large rovers on the surface. Use of a parachute and retrorockets made InSight a lighter lander, and thus helped give InSight a higher experiment payload to total launch mass ratio than the hefty Mars Exploration Rovers and Mars Curiosity rover. Upon entering the Martian atmosphere, InSight was initially slowed by deploying a parachute and then engaged descent engines to slow the lander to a gentle touchdown speed of 8.8 kilometers per hour. Suspended legs absorbed shock during touchdown. At touchdown, InSight weighed in at 607.81 kilograms. Because InSight's instruments were carried on a stationary lander and could record data no matter where they were positioned on Mars, InSight could touch down anywhere on the Red Planet with flat and stable terrain.

InSight successfully landed on Mars in the *Elysium Planitia* region (4.5°N, 135.6°E) at 19:52:59 UTC on November 26, 2018. Mission planners referred to Elysium Planitia as the "biggest parking lot on Mars" because of its relatively smooth, boulder-free, and impact crater-free surface.

With its solar panels deployed, InSight is 5.9 meters long and 1.525 meters wide. InSight's robotic instrument deployment arm can extend to a length of 1.725 meters. The arm has four motors and three joints that function as a shoulder, elbow, and wrist. There is a grapple fixture with five mechanical fingers at the end of the arm, and a camera mounted between the elbow and wrist joints. The grapple picked up InSight's experiment packages which operate optimally when in direct contact with the Martian surface: the Seismic Experiment for Interior Structure (SEIS), the Heat Flow and Physical Properties Package (HP³), and the seismometer's Wind and Thermal Shield. InSight was the first mission ever to use a mechanical arm to lift instruments off a spacecraft and gently place them on the Martian surface. The camera on the robot arm provides three-dimensional color views of the landing site, instrument placement, and experiment activities. Lander-mounted sensors measure weather and magnetic field variations. An Instrument Context Camera is attached below the lander deck to give a 120° "fisheye" view of the workspace.

InSight's surface operations began one minute after touchdown, and were programmed to be performed autonomously without the need for the lander to receive communication from the InSight science team. The lander began taking and transmitting stereo images back to Earth several minutes after touchdown. This provided three-dimensional information to aid in selecting the best locations to place the seismometer package and heat flow probe onto the Martian ground.

Science data were retrieved beginning the first week after the landing, but InSight's main focus initially was preparing to place InSight's instruments directly on the surface. It took ten weeks to place the instrument packages and set them up. It was anticipated that it could take up to seven additional weeks to position the heat flow probe or "mole." Alas during the initial test run, the self-hammering "mole" hit a snag before reaching its intended depth of 5 meters. Mission team members quickly tried to diagnose the problem and devise a solution. As of September 2019, that effort to get the "mole" sunk deep enough for meaningful data acquisition continued without resolution.

InSight has a planned mission duration of 709 Martian days (or Sols) which is equivalent to 728 Earth days. InSight is not an inexpensive mission. NASA spent $605.4 million on mission planning and lander hardware, and an additional $163.4 million for Atlas V launch services. CNES and DLR experiments required a $180 million investment, increasing the mission's total price tag to $993.8 million.

Contributions

Having a seismometer on the surface of Mars, and attempting to take heat flow measurements make Mars InSight singular. While the Viking landers did in fact attempt seismic research, those instruments unfortunately were not very effective because they were incorporated into the stationary landers and suffered from spacecraft vibrations that overpowered any seismic signal they might have picked up. Returning to seismic studies and starting investigations of the subsurface characteristics of Mars has been a long time coming.

The seismometers may aid in detecting subsurface water and volcanic plumes. A suite of magnetic field, pressure, wind, and temperature sensors calibrate the seismometers, and differentiate between geologic seismicity and vibrations caused by atmospheric phenomena. InSight is equipped with the Rotation and Interior Structure Experiment (RISE) to accurately track how much Mars' North Pole wanders during solar orbit. These observations provide details on the size of Mars' core, and whether the core is liquid or solid, and if elements other than iron make up the core's composition. The Heat Flow and Physical Properties Package (HP^3), includes a burrowing heat probe dubbed "the mole," which was supposed to bury itself at least 5 meters underground, deeper than any other previous probe, scoop, or drill on previous missions. The instrument was to measure heat flow leaving Mars' interior and illuminate the heat source in order to provide clues as to whether Mars formed and evolved geologically similar to the Earth and Moon. Alas as of 2019, "the mole" had been unable to penetrate very far into the Martian subsurface. However, InSight engineers continued to work on developing a means of surmounting the problem which could either be a large rock blocking the way or some issue involving cohesion with the soil.

It is hoped that the major scientific contribution of InSight will be to provide insight into the interior of a terrestrial planet other than Earth. The InSight team believes that by studying the deep interior of Mars, science can learn how other terrestrial planets, including Earth and the Moon, formed in the early solar system. Earth and Mars accreted from the same primordial materials over 4.5 billion years ago, yet are unique planets. So, why didn't they share the same developmental history? To date, we have only studied one terrestrial world in detail: our own planet Earth. To a minor extent the Moon also. The goal is to compare InSight data from Mars to the accepted model for Earth's interior scientists can develop an understanding of our solar system's evolution, and learn what characteristics to look for as we search for exoplanets that might support life.

Context

Mars is the fourth planet from the Sun, orbiting between Earth and the asteroid belt. Along with Mercury, Venus, and Earth, Mars is a rocky terrestrial planet. All four terrestrial planets, as well as Earth's Moon, share similar structural characteristics, having chemically differentiated and developed distinct crusts, mantles, and metallic cores. While these planets share bulk compositions somewhat similar to asteroids and meteorites, each body's physical structure is unique and none of the rocks associated with them are exactly like asteroid or meteorites. During the early formation of the terrestrial planets, their molten upper layers cooled and underwent fractional crystallization, differentiating into various magmatic minerals. While all terrestrial planets have current structures that resulted from fractional crystallization and differentiation, these complex geologic processes are poorly understood. When a young planet's molten outer layers cool, crystallize, and differentiate, the resulting minerals are dependent on temperature, pressure, and chemical composition of the magma. All these variables vary over time. Less dense minerals rise toward the planet's surface to form the crust, while heavier minerals sink to form the mantle. Even heavier iron and nickel components sink to the planet's center to form the core. These processes require hundreds of millions of years early in the planet's history. How these processes individually played out for each terrestrial world established their basic characteristics of rock composition, the presence and extent of volcanic or tectonic activity, the presence and chemical composition of an atmosphere, and the presence or lack of a magnetic field protecting that atmosphere. Planetary scientists begin to better understand the early evolution of terrestrial planets by studying the structural components of a planet's crustal thickness and stratification, mantle density and stratification, core composition and density, and the rate at which heat escapes from the planet's interior.

Mars currently has no global magnetic field. There are regions of its crust that are up to ten times more strongly magnetized than anything measured on Earth. This suggests those regions are remnants of an ancient global magnetic field. The center of Mars likely has a solid core composed of iron, nickel, and sulfur. The Martian core is not dynamic. Therefore Mars lacks a planet-wide magnetic field. Instead, it has sporadic magnetic field lines. Without a global magnetic field, radiation bombards the planet making it relatively inhospitable for humans.

The axis of Mars, like that of Earth, is tilted with relation to the Sun. This means that Mars is similar to Earth in that the amount of sunlight falling on certain parts varies widely during the year, giving Mars seasons. However, the tilt of Mars' axis shifts wildly over time because it is not stabilized by a large Moon.

The mantle of Mars is probably similar to Earth's, and is composed mostly of silicon-rich peridotite, oxygen, iron, and magnesium. Mars' crust is thought to be one piece. Unlike Earth, Mars has no crustal tectonic plates riding on a fluid mantle to reshape surface terrain. There is little to no movement in the crust. Molten rock at one time flowed to the surface at the same location for successive eruptions, building the huge volcanoes dotting the Martian surface. Evidence suggests that there have been no volcanic eruptions on Mars for millions of years, suggesting the mantle beneath the crust is largely dormant. The Martian crust is largely made of basalt, a volcanic rock common in crusts of the Earth and the Moon, although some crustal rocks in Mars' northern hemisphere may be andesite, a volcanic rock containing more silica than basalt. Mars is uniquely positioned in our solar system, large enough to have undergone fractional crystallization and differentiation shaping all the terrestrial plants but small enough in stature and free of atmospheric constraints to have retained the record of these early process, something Earth has not.

—Randall L. Milstein

See also: Jet Propulsion Laboratory; Mars Climate Orbiter and Mars Polar Lander; Mars Exploration Rovers; Mars Global Surveyor; Mars Observer; Mars Phoenix; Mars Odyssey; Mars Reconnaissance Orbiter; Planetary Exploration; Viking Program

Further Reading

Chapman, Mary., ed. *The Geology of Mars: Evidence from Earth-based Analogs*. Cambridge, United Kingdom: Cambridge University Press, 2011. Presents direct analogs between the geology and geologic processes and phenomena of Earth and Mars based on data sets from Mars landers, orbiters, and rovers.

Coles, Kenneth S., Kenneth L. Tanaka and Philip R. Christensen. *The Atlas of Mars: Mapping its Geography and Geology.* Cambridge, United Kingdom: Cambridge University Press, 2019. This book is an essential all-purpose guide describing the prominent features of Mars, and also describes the global characteristics, and regional geology and geography of the planet.

McCleese, Daniel J., ed. *Mars Exploration Strategy: 2009-2020.* Pittsburgh: Progressive Management, 2012. A summary of NASA plans for unmanned missions to explore Mars through 2020.

O'Neill, Ian. *"NASA's InSight Mission Triumphantly Touches Down on Mars."* Scientific American (November, 2018): A summary of the mission goals as well as description of the descent and successful landing of InSight on the Martian surface.

Soare, Richard J., Susan J. Conway and Stephen M. Clifford. *Dynamic Mars: Recent and Current Landscape Evolution of the Red Planet.* First Edition. Cambridge, Massachusetts: Elsevier Inc., 2018. Richly illustrated book, providing contemporary interpretations, observations, and explanations of geological processes and changes on the Martian surface and near subsurface.

Mars Observer

Date: September 22, 1992, to August 21, 1993
Type of program: Planetary exploration

Mars Observer was intended to have photographed the Martian surface using the most sophisticated camera yet carried on a civilian spacecraft. It was also designed to conduct various scientific experiments concerning the Martian atmosphere. However, the probe's propulsion system suffered a catastrophic failure while preparing for a major burn to enter Martian orbit.

Key Figures

Glenn E. Cunningham (b. 1943), Jet Propulsion
   Laboratory (JPL) project manager for Mars
   Observer
Suzanne Dodd, Mars Observer Mission Planning
   team chief
Arden L. Albee, Mars Observer project scientist
Sam Dallas, Mars Observer mission manager at
   JPL

Summary of the Mission

Mars Observer lifted off from Cape Canaveral, Florida, attached atop a Titan III rocket on September 25, 1992. After separation from the Titan, an onboard rocket burn of 150 seconds duration sent the spacecraft toward a conjunction with Mars to be completed after a deep-space journey lasting just less than one year.

Scientists modeled Mars Observer on Earth-orbiting weather and communications satellites. The rectangular body of the spacecraft (the "bus") carried seven scientific instruments wrapped in thermal blankets to maintain their operating temperatures in the hostile environment of space. Its instruments included a gamma-ray spectrometer, a thermal emission spectrometer, a laser altimeter, a pressure modulator infrared radiometer, a magnetometer/electron reflectometer, the Mars Observer camera, radio-communications equipment, and computer equipment to control the remote actions of the satellite

once it achieved Mars orbit. Mars Observer also carried radio equipment provided by French and Russian scientists.

The gamma-ray spectrometer was to detect and analyze gamma rays emitted by the Martian surface. Such analysis would provide an understanding of the mineral composition of Martian rocks and soil. The thermal emissions spectrometer, by measuring the heat produced by different areas of the Martian surface, was to provide information about weathering and mineral composition. The laser altimeter was to measure the topography of Martian surface features. The pressure modulator infrared radiometer was to measure the temperature, water content, and pressure of the Martian atmosphere throughout an entire Martian year. The magnetometer/electron reflectometer was to send back to Earth information concerning the Martian magnetic and gravity fields. Radio equipment aboard the spacecraft was to assist in the study of Martian magnetism, as well as relay information from all the instruments back to Earth. The Mars Observer camera represented the most sophisticated camera ever carried on a civilian spacecraft to that time. It was to have photographed much of the Martian surface at very high resolution. The Franco-Russian equipment was to retrieve and store data supplied by a Martian lander scheduled by scientists in France and Russia to touch down on the Martian

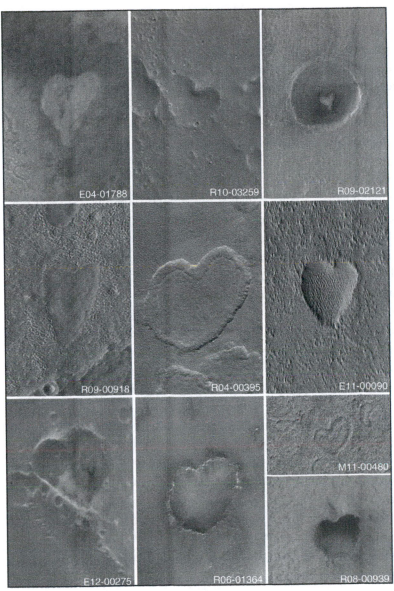

Heart-shaped features on Mars. (NASA)

In June, 1993, American space scientists had to delay the launch of the National Oceanic and Atmospheric Administration spacecraft NOAA-I when its Redundant Crystal Oscillator (RXO, a clock required for the operation of the spacecraft's central computers) failed. Mars Observer utilized the same type of RXO as did the NOAA-I spacecraft, making its reliability suspect. At the same time, the principal investigator of Mars Observer's photographic mission was coming under increasingly bitter criticism for his decisions concerning which areas of Mars's surface should have priority for photographic investigation.

In January, 1993, NASA scientists successfully tested the focus of the Observer's camera. Less than a month later other scientists successfully calibrated the thermal emission spectrometer. In April, those scientists responsible for the magnetometer part of the Observer's mission calibrated their instruments. In March and April, Mars Observer carried out the only successful experiment during its mission. In conjunction with two other spacecraft (Galileo and Ulysses), the instruments aboard Mars Observer attempted to gather data concerning low-frequency gravitational waves. Scientists hoped the data might offer confirmation for Albert Einstein's general theory of relativity.

During the flight, project scientists decided to alter the original orbital insertion plan. Taking advantage of larger-than-expected fuel reserves on the spacecraft, scientists moved ahead the planned date of insertion by three weeks. An earlier entry of the spacecraft into orbit would have allowed photography of Mars's surface to commence before the

surface in 1994. Unfortunately, that Russian lander was never built.

The mission objectives of Mars Observer, had they been realized, would have furnished American space scientists with much more detailed information about the planet Mars than had previously been available. Mars Observer accomplished none of its objectives. Almost from liftoff, foreshadowing of failure and controversy accompanied the spacecraft on its long path toward Mars.

dust-storm season began. The maneuver required shutting down all communications between NASA and the spacecraft for seventy-two hours prior to orbital insertion. The shutdown came on August 21, three days before orbital insertion. After the systems shut down, scientists were unable to reestablish communication with Mars Observer.

During the following months, project scientists made many attempts to salvage the mission. The last likely chance for reestablishing communications with the satellite failed in late September when scientists could not detect the radio beacon aboard the craft. When nothing proved successful, NASA scientists decided to terminate the failed mission. A news release from the Jet Propulsion Laboratory in California dated November 24, 1993, quoted Mars Observer Project Manager Glenn E. Cunningham as saying that the majority of the mission team had been reassigned to other projects. Cunningham said that although a few scientists would continue ground-tracking the Mars Observer, little hope of salvaging the mission remained.

Cunningham's announcement brought to a sad conclusion a much-heralded and triumphant "return to the Red Planet." If accomplished, the mission's objectives would have provided significant advances in human knowledge of the Martian surface and atmosphere. NASA would have benefited greatly from the favorable publicity generated by a successful reexamination of Mars, always a favorite with the public. Ending as it did in failure and controversy, the Mars Observer mission became a major setback for American efforts to explore the solar system in general and Mars in particular.

Contributions

Aside from data related to searching for low-frequency gravitational waves in interplanetary space, the Mars Observer mission did little to increase our knowledge about Mars. Two official inquiries into the failure do provide some negative knowledge: Scientists may have gained a better understanding of what not to do on future space missions.

Two committees that investigated the Mars Observer mission identified several possible causes for its ultimate failure. Although speculation of mission scientists immediately after losing contact with the spacecraft centered on the possible failure of the RXO, the investigatory committees concluded that other malfunctions were just as likely to have caused the failure. The Independent Mission Failure Review Board appointed by NASA Administrator Daniel S. Goldin agreed, and Jet Propulsion Laboratory's own Review Board identified several possible causes for loss of contact with Mars Observer. Potential malfunctions included electrical power loss due to a massive short in the power subsystems, loss of function that prevented both the spacecraft's main and backup computers from controlling the spacecraft, loss of both the main and backup transmitters due to the failure of an electronic part, and a breach of the spacecraft's propulsion system.

The investigatory committees identified three possible causes of potential malfunction:

(1) liquid oxidizer (nitrogen tetroxide) of the rockets may have seeped past a check valve in the pressurization lines, causing the lines to burst

(2) the pressure regulator of the fuel tanks may have failed, causing the tanks to explode

(3) a small pyrotechnic device called a squib, which was fired to open a valve in one of the pressure tanks, could have burst the tank.

These three possibilities all resulted from the in-flight decision to attempt to insert the spacecraft into Mars orbit three weeks ahead of the original schedule. Members of both investigative committees concluded that the exact cause of the mission failure would probably never be exactly identified.

Context

Mars Observer was not the first failed attempt to investigate the Red Planet. Some space scientists even speak of a "Mars jinx," which has dogged both American and Russian missions to the planet since the early 1960's. Soviet space scientists lost contact with Mars 1, launched on November 1, 1962, at some 106 million kilometers (65.9 million miles) from Earth. NASA's first attempt to investigate Mars also ended in disappointment in 1964 when Mariner 3's shroud failed shortly after the spacecraft had been successfully launched on November 5, 1964. Mariner 3's sister ship Mariner 4, launched on November 28 the same year, completed a successful flyby of Mars and sent back photographs on July 14, 1965. Several unannounced Soviet missions to Mars reportedly failed in the late 1960's.

In 1969, two NASA flyby missions to Mars experienced success. Mariner 6 (launched February 24) and Mariner 7 (launched March 27) both returned photographs of the Red Planet as they passed in its vicinity on July 31 and August 5, 1969, respectively. Mariner 8 fared less well, as its launch vehicle failed shortly after liftoff on May 8, 1971. Soviet scientists sent two missions to Mars in 1971, both designed to orbit and photograph the planet, and to soft-land instruments packages on Mars's surface. Mars 2, launched on May 19, arrived in Mars orbit on November 27, but sent back no useful data due to systems failures. Mars 3, launched on May 28, was more successful. It managed to send back a few photographs and some data.

The first major success in retrieving useful information from Mars through an uncrewed space probe came with NASA's Mariner 9 mission. After liftoff from Earth on May 30, 1971, Mariner 9 arrived in Mars orbit on November 13. Mariner 9 orbited the planet and photographed the Martian surface for almost a year, until October 27, 1972. The quality of the scientific data and photographs relayed to Earth far surpassed anything from previous missions.

Soviet Mars missions continued to disappoint the scientists who designed them. In 1973 Russian scientists launched Mars 4, Mars 5, Mars 6, and Mars 7 on July 21, 25, August 5, and 9, respectively. Mars 4 and 5 were orbiters designed to relay signals from the landers carried by Mars 6 and 7. Mars 4 failed to achieve orbit. Mars 5 arrived in orbit on February 12, 1974, but transmitted data for only a few days. Mars 6 and 7 arrived in orbit on March 9 and 12, 1974, respectively, but their landers lost contact with the orbiters before actually touching down on the Martian surface.

American space scientists followed up their Mariner 9 success with the spectacular Viking missions of 1975-1982. Viking 1 and Viking 2 left Earth, bound for Mars, on August 20 and September 7, 1975, respectively. Both carried landing craft and onboard relay equipment to send signals and data from the landers to NASA scientists and a world television audience. Viking 1 achieved Mars orbit on June 19, 1976, and successfully deployed its lander on July 20. Viking 2 achieved Mars orbit on August 7, 1976, and successfully deployed its lander on September 3. The photographs from the landers—the first from the surface of another planet—captivated people around the world as they were broadcast on television.

Russian space scientists were slow to attempt any new missions to Mars since the disappointing Soviet attempts in the early 1970's. Several United States Mars missions since the Viking triumphs, up to and including the Mars Observer, Mars Climate Orbiter, and Mars Polar Lander missions, have all ended in failure. Russia's Phobos 1 and Phobos 2, launched on July 7 and 12, 1988, respectively. One experienced signal malfunction before achieving Mars orbit, the other as it was nearing Phobos. Both carried landers and equipment packages more sophisticated than those of the Viking missions.

Despite these setbacks, NASA scientists announced new Mars missions almost simultaneously with finally admitting that the Mars Observer mission had failed. Three of these, Mars Global Surveyor, Mars Pathfinder, and Mars Odyssey, were successful, returning stunning images of the Martian surface that captivated the public. Though followed by the failed paired missions of the Climate Orbiter and Polar Lander, these successes ensured that the fascination of Mars would continue to attract the attention of space scientists despite any "Mars jinx." That jinx was again overcome by the tremendously successful Mars Exploration Rovers

Spirit and Opportunity, whose popularity fueled public fascination with Mars just as President George W. Bush proposed expanded human exploration of space, including a program to send people to investigate the Red Planet. Spirit and Opportunity lasted many years longer than their anticipated three-month life times. They were supplanted by the Mars Reconnaissance Orbiter and the Mars Curiosity rover. A Mars 2020 mission was nearing readiness for launch as of 2019.

—*Paul Madden, revised by David G. Fisher*

See also: Compton Gamma Ray Observatory; Cooperation in Space: U.S. and Russian; Jet Propulsion Laboratory; Mars Global Surveyor; Mars Odyssey; Mars Reconnaissance Orbiter; Planetary Exploration; Viking 1 and 2.

Further Reading

Burrows, William E. *This New Ocean: The Story of the First Space Age.* New York: Random House, 1998. This is a comprehensive history of the human conquest of space, covering everything from the earliest attempts at spaceflight through the voyages near the end of the twentieth century. Burrows is an experienced journalist who has reported for *The New York Times*, *The Washington Post*, and *The Wall Street Journal*. Many photographs and an extensive source list. Interviewees include Isaac Asimov, Alexei Leonov, Sally K. Ride, and James A. Van Allen.

French, Bevan M. *Return to the Red Planet: The Mars Observer Mission.* Washington, D.C.: United States Government Printing Office, 1993. A comprehensive description of the equipment and mission of the Mars Observer, prepared by one of the mission scientists. Relates the history of the mission from its inception until shortly before NASA scientists lost contact with the spacecraft. Includes photographs of the Mars Observer and many of its predecessors.

Hartmann, William K. *Moons and Planets.* 5th ed. Belmont, Calif.: Thomson Brooks/Cole Publishing, 2005. Provides detailed information about all objects in the solar system. Suitable on three separate levels: high school student, general reader, and the college undergraduate studying planetary geology.

Heppenheimer, T. A. *Countdown: A History of Space Flight.* New York: John Wiley, 1997. A detailed historical narrative of the human conquest of space. Heppenheimer traces the development of piloted flight through the military rocketry programs of the era preceding World War II. Covers both the American and the Soviet attempts to place vehicles, spacecraft, and humans into the hostile environment of space. More than a dozen pages are devoted to bibliographic references.

Lee, Wayne. *To Rise from Earth: An Easy to Understand Guide to Spaceflight.* New York: Checkmark Books, 1996. This is a good introduction to the science of spaceflight. Although written by an engineer with the NASA Jet Propulsion Laboratory, it is presented in easy-to-understand language. In addition to the theory of spaceflight, it gives some of the history of the human endeavor to explore space.

Mari, Christopher, ed. *Space Exploration.* New York: H. W. Wilson, 1999. Twenty-five articles (reprinted from magazines), covering the state of the space program at the time of publication, are divided into five sections: John H. Glenn, Jr.'s return to space, the exploration of Mars, the International Space Station, recent mining efforts by commercial industries, and new types of space vehicles and propulsion systems.

Mishkin, Andrew. *Sojourner: An Insider's View of the Mars Pathfinder Mission.* New York: Berkley Books, 2003. A thorough exploration of the Mars Pathfinder mission that also provides a detailed historical perspective on the exploration of the surface of Mars (begun by Viking).

Morrison, David, and Tobias Owen. *The Planetary System*. 3d ed. San Francisco: Addison-Wesley, 2003. Organized by planetary object, this work provides contemporary data on all planetary bodies visited by spacecraft since the early days of the Space Age. Suitable for high school and college students and the general reader.

National Aeronautics and Space Administration. *International Exploration of Mars: A Special Bibliography*. Washington, D.C.: Author, 1991. Comprehensive list of publications relating to Mars exploration space missions derived from STI database. Most complete reference available.

---. *Mars Observer Mission Failure Report: A Report to the Administrator, National Aeronautics and Space Administration on the Investigation of the August, 1993 Mission Failure of the Mars Observer Spacecraft*. Washington, D.C.: Author, 1993. An internal NASA report detailing the possible causes of the loss of contact with the Mars Observer. Concludes that while there exist many possible causes for the mission's failure, the exact cause cannot be ascertained.

National Aeronautics and Space Administration, Jet Propulsion Laboratory. *Mapping the Red Planet: The Mars Observer Global Mapping Mission*. Pasadena, Calif.: Author, 1992. A detailed explanation of the precise global mapping mission of the Mars Observer. Contains specifications and capabilities of the photographic equipment carried by the Observer.

---. *Mars Observer Loss of Signal: Special Review Board Final Report*. Pasadena, Calif.: Author, 1993. Report of independent investigative committee retained by JPL to ascertain the causes of the Mars Observer mission failure. Concludes that many factors could have caused the mission failure and that the true cause will probably never be known.

Sheehan, William. *Worlds in the Sky: Planetary Discovery from Earliest Times Through Voyager and Magellan*. Tucson: University of Arizona Press, 1992. Provides a brief account of the various space missions to Mars from 1962 to the Mars Observer mission. Puts Mars exploration into the broader perspective of the efforts of Earth nations in space exploration.

United States General Accounting Office. *Space Exploration: Cost, Schedule, and Performance of NASA's Mars Observer Mission*. Washington, D.C.: Author, 1988. Exhaustive analysis of the cost estimates for the proposed Mars Observer mission, NASA's ability to administer the project, and the performance estimates of the craft and its equipment.

Mars Odyssey

Date: April 7, 2001, to September, 2025 (projected)
Type of program: Planetary exploration

Mars Odyssey was a robotic spacecraft sent to enter Mars orbit as part of a series of missions over several years to study the Red Planet. Following a series of Mars mission failures, Mars Odyssey was a successful mission to Mars and resulted in a much-needed public relations boost for NASA. The spacecraft, 2001 Mars Odyssey, discovered evidence suggesting that Mars may have had water in the distant past.

Key Figures

Orlando Figueroa (b. 1955), Mars program
   director
Mark Dahl, Mars Odyssey program executive
Firouz Naderi (b. 1946), Mars program manager
Matthew Landano, Mars Odyssey project manager
Philip Varghese, Mars Odyssey project manager
Daniel McCleese, Mars program scientist
Michael Meyer, Mars program scientist
Robert Berry, Lockheed Martin Astronomics
   Odyssey program manager

Summary of the Mission

Originally intended to be a combination orbiter and lander, the mission to Mars designated for 2001 was redesigned as a single orbiter following the loss of the previous two missions, Mars Climate Orbiter and Mars Polar Lander. The new mission was re-named Mars Odyssey, and the spacecraft was dubbed *2001 Mars Odyssey* after the movie based on Arthur C. Clarke's novel *2001: A Space Odyssey* (1968).

2001 Mars Odyssey was launched April 7, 2001, at 16:02 Coordinated Universal Time (UTC) from Pad 17A at the Cape Canaveral Air Force Station, adjacent to the Kennedy Space Center, in Florida. The booster used was a Delta II 7925 rocket, one that included nine strap-on solid rocket boosters around the base of the rocket. The trip to Mars took the spacecraft two hundred days. On the way, *2001*

Mars Odyssey took photographs of the Earth and Moon. Given that the trip to Mars occurred near a period of solar maximum activity, radiation sensors on the spacecraft were used to study solar radiation during solar storms on the way to Mars.

On October 24, 2001, at approximately 02:18 UTC, the rocket motor on board 2001 Mars Odyssey fired to put the spacecraft into orbit around Mars. The initial Mars orbit was very elliptical, but in order to accomplish all goals of its mission, the spacecraft's orbit needed to be nearly circular. Rather than carrying more fuel for its rocket motor, the *2001 Mars Odyssey* was designed to use a technique called aerobraking to adjust its orbit. Aerobraking consists of using the planet's atmosphere rather than a rocket motor to slow the spacecraft. During the first two weeks, thrusters on board *2001 Mars Odyssey* began to decrease as the orbit around Mars approached 100 kilometers above the surface. A pass this low actually puts the spacecraft into the upper part of the tenuous Martian atmosphere. Atmospheric drag slows the spacecraft, which lowers the orbit's apapsis, or farthest distance from the planet. Such a maneuver must be done very carefully, because if the spacecraft dips too low into the Martian atmosphere, it will burn up. Eventually, after 332 aerobraking passes, the orbit was adjusted to be nearly circular at an altitude of 400 kilometers. Furthermore, during the aerobraking maneuvers, the spacecraft's orbit was slowly adjusted so that it was inclined nearly 93° with respect to the Martian equator. This orbit took the spacecraft nearly over the poles of the planet, allowing detailed studies of the Martian ice caps. The final circular orbit had a period of just under two hours. Furthermore, the orbit was designed to allow *2001 Mars Odyssey* to pass overhead each part of Mars at about the same time every Martian day. On May 22, 2004, *2001 Mars Odyssey* completed its ten thousandth orbit around Mars, and in August its mission was extended until at least September, 2006.

In addition to science missions, *2001 Mars Odyssey* was designed to act as a relay for future landers that arrived in early 2004. In 2003, the National Aeronautics and Space Administration (NASA) sent two Mars Exploration Rovers named Spirit and Opportunity, which landed in January and February, 2004, respectively. The European Space Agency (ESA) also planned to use *2001 Mars Odyssey* for the ESA lander *Beagle 2*, which arrived in December, 2003. Unfortunately, no contact was made with the *Beagle 2* after it entered the Martian atmosphere. Spirit and Opportunity operated successfully, and *2001 Mars Odyssey* was responsible for relaying larger portions of rover data back to Earth than the rovers themselves. More than 85 percent of the rover data in 2004 were relayed through *2001 Mars Odyssey*. The spacecraft coordinated with the Mars Reconnaissance Orbiter and Mars Curiosity rover missions. It also remained operational while the MAVEN spacecraft conducted its orbital mission, and is expected to play a role in the Mars 2020 rover program. In 2010 JPL revised the estimated life time of this long-lived Mars spacecraft. *2001 Mars Odyssey* was expected then to continue through 2016. Since that time, spacecraft operations in Martian orbit were projected to last through 2025.

The *2001 Mars Odyssey* spacecraft was one of the most asymmetrically shaped spacecraft that NASA had ever created. The main portion of the spacecraft looked basically like a big box. Sticking far out of the top of the box was a 6.2-meter-long boom, at the end of which was a gamma-ray spectrometer. Attached to one side of the box was a large solar panel for power. The high-gain antenna was a circular object at the end of a short boom sticking out of a bottom corner of the box, opposite the solar panels.

An imaging system was a major component of the spacecraft. The *2001 Mars Odyssey* Thermal Emission Imaging System (THEMIS) was able to image the surface of Mars with both visual and infrared light. THEMIS used five spectral bands in visual light and nine spectral bands in infrared light. The use of so many spectral bands permitted the identification of regions on the surface containing appreciable concentrations of certain minerals.

Another onboard science experiment was the Martian Radiation Environment Experiment (MARIE). MARIE was designed to study the radiation environment at Mars. It was also used to monitor solar and cosmic radiation on the way to Mars. The instrument had a 68° field of view, and it measured not only the direction of radiation particles but also their energy. MARIE continued operations until a series of massive solar storms in October, 2003, damaged the instrument.

The third science payload was the Gamma Ray Spectrometer (GRS), which was able to measure the energies of gamma rays emitted by certain atoms in the Martian soil after they are struck by cosmic rays. Measuring these gamma rays allowed scientists to determine the abundances of elements in various regions on Mars. The gamma-ray sensor head was on the end of a long boom extending from the body of the spacecraft. In addition to an instrument to measure gamma rays, GRS included two neutron detectors mounted on the main body of the spacecraft. The neutron detectors were sensitive to large concentrations of hydrogen located within the top meter of the Martian soil. Cosmic rays striking the protons in hydrogen atoms can create neutrons. The assumption is that a large concentration of hydrogen signals the presence of water. Water is essential for life, and if life were ever to have developed on Mars, then the planet must have had liquid water. Scientists are very interested in determining whether Mars ever had life.

Contributions

One of the major goals of the Mars Odyssey program was to determine whether Mars now has or once had abundant water. The neutron detectors on board *2001 Mars Odyssey* have revealed much evidence showing that hydrogen exists on Mars in abundance. Scientists believe that this hydrogen is in the form of water, which is composed of two atoms of hydrogen and one of oxygen. This water is believed to be in ice form, rather than liquid. Furthermore, most of the lowland surfaces in the northern hemisphere of Mars are so ice-rich that the soil in these areas is composed of more than 50 percent ice rather than dirt. So much ice has been found that current theories of Martian climate need to be changed.

In addition to finding surface ice at high latitudes, *2001 Mars Odyssey* found too much ice near the equator. In some places nearly 10 percent of the soil was composed of ice. So much ice was found that it cannot be in equilibrium with the atmosphere. This suggests that the Martian climate is evolving and that Mars may be emerging from an ice age.

THEMIS found several important minerals. One mineral, olivine, is easily destroyed in water, and it was found in abundance in basalt rocks in several locations on Mars. This suggests that Mars has been dry, without any liquid water, for a very long time. However, in other places THEMIS data show the presence of hematite, a form of which develops only in liquid water. This suggests that these areas of Mars may have been rich in liquid water at one time in the distant past. The data were used to select landing sites for the Mars Exploration Rovers. Both of those rovers have located hematite.

In addition to the geological findings, the *2001 Mars Odyssey* detected levels of radiation in Mars orbit in excess of 2.5 times the radiation level experienced in low-Earth orbit (the orbital plane occupied by craft such as the International Space Station). This high radiation level is believed to result from the lack of a significant magnetic field at Mars that would shield the planet from charged particles as Earth's magnetic field does. These levels of radiation, furthermore, suggest that astronauts on a future manned mission to Mars might receive their entire lifetime allotment of radiation in just the one trip.

Context

The Mars Observer mission was part of a series of NASA missions to Mars begun in the 1990's after a nearly twenty-year hiatus in Mars exploration. Furthermore, *2001 Mars Odyssey* was designed to relay signals from future missions to Mars. *2001 Mars Odyssey* also was to relay signals from the ESA's *Beagle 2* lander, in a rare instance of multinational cooperation between different space missions.

Due to the way that Mars and Earth orbit the Sun, the two planets are in position for a spacecraft to travel from one planet to the other for only about a month every two years. This period when a mission is possible is called a launch window. The Mars exploration program planned to send pairs of spacecraft to Mars each time a launch window opened. However, both of the 1999 missions were lost because of what later investigation found to be preventable mistakes.

The Mars Odyssey program and the *2001 Mars Odyssey* spacecraft were fashioned based on lessons learned from the previous mission losses. Mars missions are very difficult, and of all the missions sent to Mars by multiple nations around the world, nearly 60 percent have been failures. However, NASA was already under public scrutiny for a string of spacecraft failures, some of which were also caused by preventable mistakes that had seriously affected the missions and even caused the loss of some other spacecraft. Another failure would have been a major public relations disaster for NASA. *2001 Mars Odyssey* proved successful, and it returned far more information and made far bigger discoveries than had been expected.

—*Raymond D. Benge, Jr.*

See also: Mariner 3 and 4; Mars Curiosity; Mars Exploration Rovers; Mars Observer; Mars Reconnaissance Orbiter; MAVEN.

Further Reading

Godwin, Robert, ed. *Mars: The NASA Mission Reports*. Vol. 1. Burlington, Ont.: Apogee Books, 2000. A thorough presentation of NASA documents relating to the Mars programs from Mariner 4 through Mars Global Surveyor. Includes press kits and a CD-ROM filled with special programs and interviews.

---. *Mars: The NASA Mission Reports*. Vol. 2. Burlington, Ont.: Apogee, 2004. A collection of NASA documents pertaining to Mars exploration, including reports of the *2001 Mars Odyssey*.

Goldsmith, Donald. *The Hunt for Life on Mars*. New York: Penguin, 1998. Written before *2001 Mars Odyssey*, this book explains in layperson's terms the search to determine whether Mars ever had life, one of the main goals of the Mars program.

Hartmann, William K. *Moons and Planets*. 5th ed. Belmont, Calif.: Thomson Brooks/Cole, 2005. Provides detailed information about all objects in the solar system. Suitable for high school students, general readers, and undergraduates studying planetary geology.

---. *A Traveler's Guide to Mars: The Mysterious Landscapes of the Red Planet*. New York: Workman, 2003. Written in the unique style of a tour guide, this book offers a plethora of information on Martian geology and geological history.

Mishkin, Andrew. *Sojourner: An Insider's View of the Mars Pathfinder Mission*. New York: Berkley Books, 2003. A thorough exploration of the Mars Pathfinder mission that provides a detailed historical perspective on the exploration of the surface of Mars begun by Viking.

Russell, Christopher T., ed. *2001 Mars Odyssey*. Boston: Kluwer, 2004. Aimed at the professional, this highly technical work give extensive information about the *2001 Mars Odyssey* spacecraft.

Mars Pathfinder

Date: July 4 to September 27, 1997
Type of program: Planetary exploration

Mars Pathfinder was a spectacularly successful mission to Mars that sent back tens of thousands of close-up pictures of the Martian surface. It consisted of a lander and a small rover, which analyzed the surface rocks and the soil and provided extensive data on the thin Martian atmosphere and weather patterns.

Key Figures

Wesley T. Huntress, Jr., associate administrator, NASA Headquarters Office of Space Science

Joseph Boyce, Mars program scientist for Mars Pathfinder

Kenneth Ledbetter, director of the Mission and Payload Development division

Norman Ray Haynes (b. 1936), director for the Mars Exploration Directorate at the Jet Propulsion Laboratory (JPL)

Donna Shirley, JPL manager of the Mars Exploration program

Anthony Spear, JPL Mars Pathfinder project manager

Brian Muirhead, JPL deputy project manager and Flight Systems manager

Richard Cook, JPL Mars Pathfinder mission manager

Matthew Golombek, JPL Mars Pathfinder project scientist

Summary of the Mission

Mars is the fourth planet from the Sun, the next one beyond Earth. Both revolve around the Sun, with Earth taking 365 days, and Mars 687 days to complete one revolution. Periodically, when they are near each other on the same side of the Sun, they are said to be in conjunction. December 4, 1996, was one of these events: The Mars Pathfinder mission was launched on that day from Cape Canaveral, Florida, by the National Aeronautics and Space Administration (NASA). Pathfinder was a *Discovery*-class mission, one of NASA's "faster, better, cheaper" spacecraft, which cost only about $280 million. Two Viking missions to Mars, each with an orbiter and lander, cost about twenty times more when they were carried out during the 1970's. Hence, a primary objective of the Pathfinder mission was to demonstrate the feasibility of a low-cost method of placing a science instruments package on the Red Planet using a unique direct-entry descent and landing without first orbiting the planet. Pathfinder included three important science instruments: the Imager for Mars Pathfinder (IMP), an Atmospheric Structure Instrument and Meteorology Package (ASI/MET), both located on the lander, and the Alpha Proton X-Ray Spectrometer (APXS), located on the rover. In addition, the rover itself was used as a science instrument to conduct ten scientific experiments.

Mars Pathfinder was launched from Cape Canaveral on December 4, 1996, atop a Delta II launch vehicle. The Pathfinder underwent four Trajectory Correction Maneuvers (TCMs) to refine its flight path during its seven-month, 497-million-kilometer journey to Mars. A final TCM, six hours before entry into the Martian atmosphere, made sure that the spacecraft landed inside the 100-by-200-kilometer target ellipse. According to Project Scientist Matthew Golombek, "The hardest part of Pathfinder's mission was the five minutes during which the

IMP image of landing site in 1997. (NASA)

spacecraft went from the relative security of interplanetary cruising to the stress of atmospheric entry, descent, and landing." The Martian atmosphere, composed mostly of carbon dioxide, is about one hundred times thinner than Earth's atmosphere. The Pathfinder spacecraft entered the Martian atmosphere at a speed of 26,460 kilometers per hour, and it had to be slowed down to a speed of 50 kilometers per hour before it hit the ground to avoid serious damage to the scientific instruments on board.

To achieve safe landing, more than fifty critical events had to be triggered at exactly the right moments over a period of about thirty minutes. When launched from the Earth, Mars Pathfinder weighed about 895 kilograms, including its cruise stage, heatshield or aeroshell, solar panels, propulsion stage, medium- and high-gain antennae, and 94 kilograms of cruise propellant. The lander was tetrahedron—shaped like a small pyramid standing about 1 meter tall with three triangular-shaped sides and a base. The rover, named Sojourner after the African American crusader Sojourner Truth, weighed about 16 kilograms, and could be folded and stowed in a small space only about 18 centimeters high. When expanded it measured 65 by 48 by 30 centimeters in length, width, and height and moved on six wheels. The sides of the lander folded like petals, and the whole package was cocooned by large protective air bags.

Exactly thirty-four minutes before landing, at a distance of 8,500 kilometers from the Martian surface, the cruise stage separated from the rest of the lander. Four minutes before landing, at a height of 125 kilometers above the surface, the spacecraft entered the Martian atmosphere behind the protective aeroshell. A parachute unfurled two minutes before landing and the aeroshell was jettisoned.

About eighty seconds before landing, the lander was lowered beneath its back cover on a 20- meter-long bridle or tether. The air bags were inflated at a height of about 300 meters when there were just eight seconds to go. At a height of about 70 meters, the Pathfinder's radar altimeter triggered three retrorockets to slow the speed of landing further. The bridle was then cut, and the air-bag-enshrouded lander hit the Martian surface at a speed of about 50 kilometers per hour, on July 4, 1997. It then bounded more than 1 kilometer across the target area, rolling and bouncing at least fifteen times without losing air bag pressure. By a stroke of luck, the lander came to rest on its base, eliminating the need for a planned maneuver to stand the spacecraft right-side up. With that, one of the major objectives of the Mars Pathfinder mission was achieved. The excitement on the Earth, however, was just beginning. People were anxiously waiting for a close-up view of the mysterious Martian world through the Pathfinder's cameras. For the next three months,

Pathfinder sent more than sixteen thousand breath-taking pictures of the Martian landscape, which were flashed on magazines, newspapers, television screens, and the Internet all over the world.

Contributions

Mars Pathfinder landed on the mouth of an ancient floodplain called Ares Vallis, about 20 percent of which was covered by a variety of rocks. This interesting site was chosen with the help of the photographs taken by the Viking orbiters. On Earth a comparable site would be the Channeled Scabland in eastern Washington State. After the deflated air bags were retracted, the rover Sojourner rolled down its rear ramp and became the first moving vehicle to land on Mars. It had been specially designed to move over rough terrain, and in the ensuing days ground controllers from Earth were able to send the rover all around the lander to examine the soil and the rich variety of rocks. The rover traveled altogether 105 meters and explored more than 200 square meters of the Martian terrain around the lander during nearly three months of operation. Project scientists gave interesting nicknames—Barnacle Bill, Yogi, and Scooby Doo—to the rocks and carefully guided the rover to go and examine them. Sojourner's first analysis of a rock began with the study of Barnacle Bill, a nearby rock named for its rough surface.

The APXS on the rover was used to determine the elements that make up the rocks and the soil on Mars. A full study using APXS took about ten hours. It could identify and measure all elements except hydrogen. The APXS contained pellets of radioactive curium, which bombarded the target with alpha particles (helium nuclei made of two protons and two neutrons). The interaction of the alpha particles with the rock surface produced backscattered alpha particles, protons, and x-rays, which helped to determine the chemistry of the outermost rock layer.

Apart from the chemical analysis by the APXS located on the rover, mineralogical observations were made through the IMP stereo camera located on the lander. The IMP had twelve filters so that the Pathfinder scenes were imaged at different wavelengths ranging from 440 to 1,000 nanometers in the visible and infrared regions of the electromagnetic spectrum. Fantastic color images of the Martian landscape were obtained by combining the images at red, green, and blue wavelengths. To study the mineral content of the rocks, sunlight reflected by rock surfaces was viewed through different filters. Atoms of certain minerals absorb specific wavelengths of the reflected sunlight, so the absorption bands seen in the spectrum helped identify the minerals within the rocks. By combining the APXS's chemical analysis and IMP's mineralogical observations, planetary geologists were able to gather considerable knowledge on the nature and evolution of the rocks found in Ares Vallis.

The first rock examined by Sojourner, Barnacle Bill, proved to be rich in silica (silicon dioxide), similar to andesite rocks on Earth. The big rock Yogi, named after the famous cartoon character, proved to be a different type of rock even though it was situated very close to Barnacle Bill. Yogi had a weathered, comparatively smooth surface. It had much less silica and appeared more like the common basalts found on Earth. A third type of rock, like Scooby Doo, was bright pink in color and had a flat, tabular form. Sojourner was also used to carry out soil mechanics experiments in which varying amounts of pressure were applied by the studded wheels to determine the physical properties of the soil. During its trip to Yogi, the rover stirred the soil and exposed material from several centimeters in depth. Exposed material had the same bright pink color as Scooby Doo. Pathfinder also studied dust in the Martian atmosphere by collecting it on tiny magnets mounted on both the lander and the rover. Dust was found to be highly magnetic, possibly due to the presence of a mineral known as maghemite.

The ASI/MET package on Pathfinder was an engineering subsystem that acquired atmospheric information during the lander's descent, and during the entire mission. It had temperature, pressure, and

Sojourner rover on Mars on sol 22. (NASA)

wind sensors that indicated an atmospheric profile generally in agreement with the Viking data. At the landing site the temperature varied from 197 to 263 kelvins. Morning temperatures fluctuated with time and height. The sensors, located at heights of 25, 50, and 100 centimeters above the lander, showed different temperatures. This caused Golombek to make an interesting comment: "If you are standing on Mars, your nose would be at least 20° Celsius colder than your feet!" However, afternoon temperatures did not vary with height. The Martian atmospheric pressure reached its minimum of 6.7 millibars on the twentieth Martian day. The atmospheric pressure on the Earth is about 1,000 millibars.

Context

For a long time, people believed that water ran through channels on Mars, which gave rise to the folklore about little green Martians. However, after Mariner 9 was put in orbit around Mars in 1971 and after the Viking landings five years later, it was clearly established that there was absolutely no water on Mars in liquid form. It was difficult to reconcile this finding with the abundant visible evidence that water once freely flowed on Mars. Viking orbiter photographs clearly showed channels, presumably carved by running water. The Pathfinder mission provided very strong evidence that Ares Vallis is a floodplain where perhaps hundreds of cubic kilometers of water was catastrophically released, creating the channel in a few weeks and depositing many types of rocks in that region. Some jagged rocks are inclined toward the northeast, possibly an indication of the direction of water flow. The density of impact craters in that region indicated that this flooding happened probably two to three billion years ago. As there is not much evidence of subsequent erosion, it is clear that the liquid water disappeared later. Pathfinder has confirmed that Mars has a very thin atmosphere, which would make liquid water simply evaporate and escape from the planet.

Pathfinder data have provided valuable information on the evolution of Mars which is very useful in understanding the evolution of our own planet. Harry Y. McSween and Scott L. Murchie, two members of Pathfinder's Science Team, have developed a three-stage history for the landing site. The flood stage is inferred from the presence of maroon rinds around large, round boulders like Yogi. This was followed by significant meteoric bombardment, and the small gray rocks could be impact ejecta from nearby craters. A crater rim could be seen about 2 kilometers south of the landing site. The third stage, which continues to this day, is evident in the erosion of the maroon rinds from the windward side of the rocks. Pathfinder also provided the first evidence—wind abrasion of rocks and dune-shaped deposits—for the presence of sand on Mars. Until then, researchers knew only about the enormous amount of dust on Mars. The presence of sand supports the claim that Mars had plenty of running water long ago. The presence of andesitic rocks in the landing site came as a surprise to NASA geologists. If andesites are common in Martian highlands, they indicate that the ancient Martian crust is similar in composition to the continental crust on Earth.

Mars Pathfinder fell silent on September 27, 1997, after having nearly tripled its designed life span of thirty days. The NASA press release on October 8, 1997, said that "Mars is appearing more and more like a planet that was Earth-like in its infancy, with weathering processes and flowing water that created a variety of rock types and a warmer atmosphere that generated clouds, winds and seasonal cycles." Under those conditions, it is reasonable to surmise that life could have appeared on Mars around the same time it became a reality on Earth. The Mars Pathfinder lander is a trailblazer for delivering a set of science instruments and a rover to the surface of Mars, using a unique air-bag cushioned landing. Future landers and rovers would share the heritage of spacecraft designs and technologies first tested by the Pathfinder.

The Pathfinder mission received excellent media coverage, and NASA cleverly built very good political capital out of it. They certainly needed that, because even though the next mission to Mars, the Mars Global Surveyor, succeeded, the following two missions, Mars Climate Orbiter and Mars Polar Lander, ended in disaster. Some people began to question the "faster, better, cheaper" approach. NASA, however, did not give up on its Mars exploration program. If in the future human beings walk on Mars, the Pathfinder mission certainly will have laid the foundation for such a phenomenal achievement.

Mars Pathfinder laid the groundwork for the even more impressive Mars Exploration Rovers (MERs) that followed. Two rovers were independently launched in summer, 2004, on Delta II boosters and landed at Gusev Crater and the Meridiani Planum in January, 2005, in a fashion very similar to the manner in which Mars Pathfinder was delivered to the Martian surface. The Spirit and Opportunity MERs each were designed to last for a ninety-day primary mission and were the size of golf carts. Outfitted with a larger suite of sophisticated scientific instrumentation and onboard computer systems, the MERs quickly collected a treasure-trove of scientific data greater than that amassed by Mars Pathfinder, even producing definitive data that water had previously played a major role in the geological evolution of the Martian surface. Spirit lasted until March 22, 2010, and Opportunity until June 10, 2018. Between those dates Mars Curiosity arrived on the Red Planet to rove through Gale crater. The Mars 2020 rover was nearing preparation for launch as of 2019.

—Rajkumar Ambrose

See also: Dawn Mission; Funding Procedures of Space Programs; Hubble Space Telescope: Science; Jet Propulsion Laboratory; Mariner 3 and 4; Mars Climate Orbiter and Mars Polar Lander; Mars Curiosity; Mars Exploration Rovers; Mars Global Surveyor; Mars Observer; Mars Odyssey; Mars Reconnaissance Orbiter; Planetary Exploration; Viking Program; Viking 1 and 2.

Further Reading

Golombek, Matthew P. "The Mars Pathfinder Mission." *Scientific American* 279 (July, 1998): 40-48. The author was the project scientist for the mission. He has intimate knowledge of the Pathfinder data and knows how to interpret them. This article is strong in science content but is not too technical for a general audience. It has many useful diagrams, photographs, and just one table.

Hartmann, William K. *Moons and Planets*. 5th ed. Belmont, Calif.: Thomson Brooks/Cole Publishing, 2005. Provides detailed information about all objects in the solar system. Suitable on three separate levels: high school student, general reader, and the college undergraduate studying planetary geology.

Hawkes, Nigel. *The New Book on Mars*. London: Aladdin/Watts, 1998. This little book is primarily for a younger audience. It explores the features of the Red Planet and presents the Pathfinder mission in simple language with some good pictures.

McSween, Harry Y., Jr., and Scott L. Murchie. "Rocks at the Mars Pathfinder Landing Site." *American Scientist* 87 (January/February, 1999): 36-45. The authors have university backgrounds and are members of the Mars Pathfinder Science Team. The article gives a detailed account of the Pathfinder data from geological and chemical perspectives. Some background in these fields is needed to fully grasp the authors' interpretations and conclusions. Has many charts and photographs, and no mathematics.

Mishkin, Andrew. *Sojourner: An Insider's View of the Mars Pathfinder Mission*. New York: Berkley Books, 2003. A thorough exploration of the Mars Pathfinder mission that also provides a detailed historical perspective on the exploration of the surface of Mars (begun by Viking).

Naeye, Robert. "Blazing a Trail to the Red Planet." *Astronomy* 25 (October, 1997): 48-53. This is an excellent account of the Pathfinder mission in elegant language with many wonderful photographs. The author justifies NASA's "faster, better, cheaper" exploration strategy. Very enjoyable account for a general audience.

Petersen, Carolyn C. "Welcome to Mars!" *Sky and Telescope* 94 (October, 1997): 34-37. This article from the popular astronomy magazine has in pullout form some spectacular color photographs sent by the Pathfinder. It gives a succinct account of the mission and its achievement in the first few weeks. For a general audience.

Shirley, Donna. *Managing Martians*. New York: Broadway Books, 1998. The author heads the Mars exploration program and led a team of thirty engineers and technicians who spent four years designing and building the rover. The book has valuable inside information and describes the Pathfinder mission from its inception in great detail for a nontechnical audience. Reads like a fascinating story.

Mars Phoenix

Date: August 4, 2007 to November 2, 2008
Type of program: Planetary exploration

Mars Phoenix was a National Aeronautics and Space Administration (NASA) Scout mission placing a stationary lander on the surface of the Martian artic to study soil samples for the presence of water and collect data on the interaction between the Martian ground surface and atmosphere. The Phoenix payload consisted of a robotic arm for digging soil samples; a meteorological station; a microscopy, electrochemistry, and conductivity analyzer; a descent imager; a stereo imager; and a thermal and evolved-gas analyzer. Phoenix successfully completed its mission and provided ground-breaking discoveries about Mars' environmental and atmospheric conditions.

Key Figures

Michael D. Griffin, Administrator, NASA Headquarters

S. Alan Stern, Associate Administrator, NASA Science Mission Directorate

Peter Smith, Principle Investigator, University of Arizona, Lunar and Planetary Laboratory

Barry Goldstein, Project Manager, Jet Propulsion Laboratory (JPL)

Edward Sedlvy, Flight Systems Manager, Lockheed Martin Space Systems (LMSS)

Leslie Tamppsti, Project Scientist, Jet Propulsion Laboratory (JPL)

Deborah Bass, Deputy Project Scientist, Jet Propulsion Laboratory (JPL)

William Boynton, Lead Scientist, Thermal and Evolved-Gas Analyzer, University of Arizona

Mark Lemmon, Lead Scientist, Surface Stereo Imager Camera, Texas A&M University

Summary of the Mission

The Mars Phoenix lander was designed as a collaborative space exploration mission combining a partnership between academia, industry, and government agencies - specifically NASA; the Canadian Space Agency; the University of Neuchatel, Switzerland; the University of Copenhagen, Denmark; Aarhus University, Denmark; the Max Planck Institute, Germany; and the Finnish Meteorological Institute. Mars Phoenix was the first NASA Mars Scout class mission. Its goal was to provide information to answer whether there is a history of liquid water at the landing site, investigate if the arctic region of Mars can support life, assess the biological potential at the Martian soil-ice boundary, and determine how Martian climate and atmospheric conditions are affected by polar dynamics. A NASA Scout class mission is designed to be an innovative and low-cost complement to major Mars missions planned for NASA's Mars Exploration Program. Mars Phoenix came in at a cost of $386 million. The Phoenix mission's most desired result was to be the first probe to make contact with Martian water.

Mars Phoenix was launched by a Boeing Delta II 7925 launch vehicle from Cape Canaveral Air Force Station, Florida on August 4, 2007. The spacecraft took approximately 10 months to reach Mars. Phoenix's cruise assembly, consisting of solar panels and communication antennas, necessary for the long journey to Mars, were jettisoned five minutes prior to entering the Martian atmosphere. About 128 kilometers above the surface, Phoenix entered the Martian atmosphere using aerodynamic friction to decelerate as it descended. A heat shield protected the lander from extremely hightemperatures generated by hyper-velocity entryat speed at 20,800 kilometers per hour. When the lander had decelerated to Mach 1.7, a parachute deployed, the heat shield was jettisoned, the landing radar engaged, and the spacecraft's landing legs extended. Slowing more, the lander dropped to a kilometer above the Martian surface, and separated from its parachute while throttling up its landing thrusters for its final phase of deceleration prior to touchdown. At about 12 meters above the surface and traveling at a constant speed of close to 2.4 meters per second, the landing engines turned off and the lander descended to the surface.

Mars Phoenix successfully landed on May 25, 2008 to begin a planned three-month mission to study the ice, soil, and atmosphere of Mars. All surface operations of Phoenix were designed to operate based on a Martian day, called a Sol, equivalent to 24 hours and 40 minutes on Earth. Upon touchdown Phoenix deployed its solar array and Surface Stereo Imager (SSI). A short time after entry, descent, and landing data and images from the Mars Descent Imager (MARDI) began being sent back to Earth. At the beginning of Sol 2 the Thermal and Evolved-Gas Analyzer (TEGA) began using its mass spectrometer taking measurements of the Martian atmosphere. The Microscopy, Electrochemistry, and Conductivity Analyzer (MECA) and Robotic Arm Camera (RAC) were deployed, and the SSI began imaging the landing site to aid in selecting sampling sites for the robotic arm to dig. The Robotic Arm was just under 2.4 meters,, encased in a protective bio-barrier and had been sterilized prior to launch to prevent microbial contamination of Mars. Also, at the beginning of Sol 2 the Meteorological Station (MET) began sampling the weather and atmospheric conditions at the landing site to better understand the interaction between the Martian ground surface and atmosphere. Phoenix began digging on Sol 10, and would dig for 2.5 hours per sol. Phoenix was scheduled to continue digging and sample until

Sol 90, delivering samples to TEGA with every 15.24 centuneters of depth or if sediment layer was identified. Phoenix completed its initial three-month mission studying Martian "soil" with a chemistry lab, the Thermal and Evolved-Gas Analyzer, a microscope, a conductivity probe, and camera. It continued to operate an additional two months before diminished sunlight reaching its solar panels caused it to cease functioning. Phoenix was a solar-powered robotic mission and was not designed to work throughout the dark days, icing, and extremely cold conditions of a Martian arctic winter.

Context

Water is a common molecule on Earth. Earth is the only planet in the solar system known to harbor life. The medium to process life on Earth is water. On Earth when searching for life we "follow the water." Though life could conceivably evolve without water, the basic chemical and environmental conditions supporting life on Earth exist in a narrow range of parameters giving science a narrow paradigm with which to determine if recognizable life exists elsewhere. Locating water on celestial bodies such as Mars might lead to finding evidence for life. Liquid water alters soil chemistry and mineralogy in particular ways suggesting specific environmental conditions. Deciphering Mars' hydrogeologic history may suggest the possibility of environments hinting at either past or present life. Previous Mars landers and rovers were designed to search for water, rather than life, with the goal of finding environments where life could once have thrived. Currently, no liquid water has been observed to exist on the Martian surface. Imaging from numerous Mars mission have sent back extensive evidence of erosional and depositional geomorphic features indicating liquid water existed in the past on Mars, and could once have supported microbial life. Images have been taken of now dry riverbeds, waterfall drops, depositional fans, dendritic drainage, flood plains, gullies, canyons, flow channels, mudflows, hydro-depositional stratification patterns. Most of these observed water features date back to about 2 billion years, others suggest water may have still flowed on the Martian surface within the last 20 million years, while in the Martian arctic liquid water may have existed as recently as 100,000 years ago.

In addition to geomorphic features, certain mineral deposits can also suggest the past presence of liquid water. Many locations on Mars have high concentrations of hematite. On Earth, the mineral hematite can be found in association with liquid water in hydrothermal locations. Martian "soils" have been found in certain locations containing from 10 to 20 percent salt. Salt deposits are evaporitic in nature, and usually associated with previous liquid water. Analysis of Martian sedimentary materials suggests a past history of water deposition. Sedimentary structures, grain size, roundness, coarseness, surface markings, sorting, and depositional patterns all provide insight into the hydrologic history of Mars. Flowing rivers, lakes, and oceans may have been prominent features in Mars' past. During this time Mars would have had an atmosphere, weather, and been warm. All conditions that could have supported some form of life. Over time Mars' small size, lower gravity, and outgassing volcanoes releasing internal heat caused the planet to become a nearly solid mass, reducing its magnetic field to a point where it could no longer protect it from the solar wind. Mars' smaller mass and lower gravitational field makes it more difficult to hold and maintain larger molecules in an unprotected atmosphere. Once unprotected from the solar wind, evaporation and photodissociation accelerated the loss of water from Mars' surface. As temperatures and surface pressure lowered, water could no longer sublime to a liquid state. Remaining water on Mars froze or could only remain in a liquid state deep in the subsurface under increased pressures. There is some indication saline liquid water flows occasionally from deep Martian canyons and impact crater walls in the mid-latitudes during warm summer months. Currently, large deposits of water appear to be trapped within ice caps at the Martian poles. Warm summer temperatures shrink the polar ice caps, and the ice sublimes straight from solid ice to gaseous vapor. In winter, cold temperatures reverse the process. Mars' polar ice caps are an average of 3.2 kilometers thick and, if completely melted, could cover the Martian surface with about 6 meters of water. Radar data suggests a large lake of liquid salt water about 20.8 kilometers across lies under the Martian south pole nearly 1.6 kilometers beneath the ice. High resolution imaging of layered impact crater and canyon walls and indicates frozen water lies in the Martian subsurface. Permafrost patterns suggest Martian "soil" freezes and thaws over time. Ice ice sheets in the bottom of craters suggest liquid water occasionally pool under certain atmospheric conditions. Human missions to Mars will require access to water resources, Phoenix data may suggest how water may be acquired and exploited by human explorers.

Contributions

The Phoenix Lander design was based on a repurposed 2001 Mars Surveyor lander, a mission which was canceled. Phoenix's instruments were improved versions of those designed and flown on the ill-fated Mars Polar Lander which crashed on final descent to the Martian surface. MarsPhoenix safely touched down in the *Vastitas Borealis* region of the Martian arctic. It achieved a landing at the most northerly location of any spacecraft that had yet touched down on Mars. Phoenix was an exploration lander not an exploration rover. Phoenix never moved from its landing site. On July 31, 2008 NASA's Phoenix lander was the first scientific mission to identify water in a Martian soil sample. The Phoenix robotic arm retrieved a sample from 5 centimeters below the surface and delivered it to the lander's Thermal and Evolved-Gas Analyzer (TEGA) where the sample was heated and water vapors identified. The robotic arm camera collected over 25,000 images. Numerous images were also taken with Phoenix's atomic-force microscope, the first such microscope ever used off Earth. During the first five months of the Phoenix mission, water ice was identified at the landing site. Data analysis suggested the climate at the location was warmer and wetter in the past few million years. Additional analysis suggests the presence of potential nutrients in combination with water that meet criteria for habitability at the site. Phoenix collected samples indicating the presence of calcium carbonate. Others indicated evidence of perchlorate, a compound that attracts water and can pull humidity from the air, provide soil moisture, and be a potential energy/food source for microbial life. Phoenix was unable to identify any carbon-based organic compounds. It is possible the perchlorate could have destroyed any such compounds during heating the soil samples for testing aboard Phoenix. Phoenix was the first mission to identified Martian polar ice

clouds and the first to identify cloud-based precipitation (snow) of any kind on Mars; the clouds were 2.5 miles above the lander.

In 2007, NASA's Mars Phoenix team received the Arizona Governor's Innovation Award for academic contributions. In October, 2008 the Phoenix Team was presented with the National Space Club's Astronautics Engineer Award for significant contributions in rocketry and astronautics, as well as the 2008 Popular Mechanics Breakthrough Award for innovation. In November, 2008 the Phoenix team earned the 2008 Civil Space Award presented by the California Space Authority.

—*Randall L. Milstein*

See also: Jet Propulsion Laboratory; Mars Climate Orbiter and Mars Polar Lander; Mars Exploration Rovers; Mars Global Surveyor; Mars InSight; Mars Observer; Mars Odyssey; Mars Reconnaissance Orbiter; Planetary Exploration, Viking Program.

Further Reading

Boynton, W. V. et al., "Evidence for Calcium Carbonate at the Mars Phoenix Landing Site."*Science* (July 3, 2009): 61-64. Evidence suggests calcium carbonate identified at the Phoenix landing site may result from the presence of previous liquid water.

Harland, David M. *Water and the Search for Life on Mars*. Berlin, Germany, Springer-Praxis,2005. This book provides an account of the Spirit and Opportunity Mars Exploration Rover Missions and provides a historical summary of observations and theories about large bodies of water previously existing on Mars.

Hecht, M.H. et al., "Detection of Perchlorate and the Soluble Chemistry of Martian Soil at the Phoenix Landing Site." *Science* (July 3, 2009): 64-67. Chlorine detected at the Phoenix landing site appears as the highly water-soluble salt perchlorate.

Kessler, Andrew. *Martian Summer: My 90 Days with Interplanetary Pioneers, Temperamental Robots, and NASA's Phoenix Mars Mission*. New York, N.Y., Pegasus Books, 2011. A first-hand account of Andrew Kessler's three months of working with the Phoenix mission team exploring the Martian arctic and dealing with NASA internal politics.

Smith, P. H. et al., "H_2O at the Phoenix Landing Site." *Science* (July 3, 2009): 52-58. The paperreports the identification of a water ice layer between 5 and 15 centimeters at the Phoenix landing site at Mars' north pole.

Tokano, Tetsuya (ed.) *Water on Mars and Life*. Köln, Germany, Springer 2005. One of the bestoverviews on the possibilities of liquid water on Mars. The volume contains thirteen chapters with numerous maps, illustrations and diagrams; and despite being over a decade old, the information holds up.

Whiteway, J. A. et al., "Mars Water-Ice Clouds and Precipitation." *Science* (July 3, 2009): 68-70. Laser remote sensing from Mars surface shows water-ice clouds form during daytime and precipitate at night.

Mars Reconnaissance Orbiter

Date: Beginning August 12, 2005
Type of program: Planetary exploration

With its sophisticated scientific instruments, the Mars Reconnaissance Orbiter (MRO) was designed to return much more data on the atmosphere, surface, and subsurface of Mars than any previous mission. These data would provide significant support for future landers, rovers, and sample-return ventures.

Key Figures

James E. Graf, MRO project manager at JPL

B. Gentry Lee, chief engineer of the Planetary Projects directorate at JPL

Richard Zurek, project scientist at JPL

Kevin McNeill, Lockheed Martin's program manager for MRO

Dan Johnston, mission design manager

Ben Jai, mission operations manager

Howard Eisen, flight system manager

Thomas Fouser, project software manager

Summary of the Mission

The Mars Reconnaissance Orbiter (MRO) is in the tradition of such previous orbiters as the Mars Global Surveyor (1997) and Mars Odyssey (2001), but MRO was designed with the potential to surpass these previous projects in the number, power, and sophistication of its scientific instruments. At 2,100 kilograms (4,806 pounds), the latest Mars spacecraft weighed twice as much as Mars Global Surveyor and three times as much as Mars Odyssey, both of which were still orbiting Mars when the MRO joined their coordinated investigations of the Red Planet. MRO's cost, including its booster (an Atlas V rocket) and the spacecraft (along with mission operations for ten years), will be approximately $700 million.

The MRO mission has been and will continue to be managed for the National Aeronautics and Space Administration (NASA) Science Mission Directorate by the Jet Propulsion Laboratory (JPL) in Pasadena, California. The project's prime contractor is Lockheed Martin Space Systems in Denver. MRO's scientific equipment was designed and built in several states, including Arizona, California, and Maryland, and in one foreign country, Italy. In 2004, MRO personnel consisted of about 175 people at Lockheed Martin and 110 at JPL. In the spring of 2005 some of these scientists and technicians integrated MRO's systems and subsystems with the Atlas V launch vehicle.

MRO's mission, like previous flyby probes, orbiters, landers, and rovers, is to gather information on the atmosphere, climate, minerals, geologic history, water, and possible life (past and present) on Mars, but MRO, which will be by far the largest object ever put into orbit around Mars, will gather data that in quantity and quality should surpass data collected in all previous missions. These data will be quickly and efficiently communicated to Earth by Electra, a relay telecommunications system that was integrated into the spacecraft and tested in July of 2004.

The scientific instruments aboard MRO include JPL's Mars Climate Sounder (MCS), for measuring changes in temperature, water vapor, and dust in the Martian atmosphere. The Johns Hopkins Applied Physics Laboratory in Laurel, Maryland, was responsible for the Compact Reconnaissance Imaging Spectrometer for Mars (CRISM), designed to scan the Martian surface for water-related minerals.

Tectonic fractures within the Candor Chasma region of Valles Marineris, Mars, retain ridge-like shapes as the surrounding bedrock erodes away. This points to past episodes of fluid alteration along the fractures and reveals clues into past fluid flow and geochemical conditions below the surface. (NASA)

Camera (CTX), whose detailed pictures in wide swaths of the planet will enhance scientists' understanding of various Martian milieus. The Mars Color Imager (MARCI), with its fisheye lens, has the specific task of tracking Martian weather.

Throughout the long history of astronomical studies of Mars, the interrelated issues of life and liquid water on its surface have been fascinating and controversial. The long, linear *canali* crisscrossing the Martian surface that the Italian astronomer Giovanni Schiaparelli drew in 1888 on maps based upon his telescopic observations were later fancifully interpreted by the wealthy American astronomer Percival Lowell as artificial canals by which resourceful Martians brought water from the poles to their arid equatorial settlements. Using advanced scientific instruments astronomers, by the middle of the twentieth century, showed that these canals were a myth. Because of Mars's very low atmospheric pressure, liquid water was unable to exist on its surface. However, as NASA flyby probes, orbiters, and landers began exploring Mars, evidence accumulated that, at least in the past, liquid water very likely existed on the Red Planet. Schiaparelli's scientific descendants in the Italian Space Agency have designed MRO's Shallow Radar (SHARAD), whose ground-penetrating radio waves will probe for underground layers of rock and ice to see if liquid water exists there. MRO's SHARAD data would greatly expand upon radar data sets collected by the European Space Agency's Mars Express orbiter in 2004 and 2005.

Images from Mars appeal to both scientists and the public, and on board MRO are some of the most advanced cameras ever devised by NASA scientists. For example, a powerful telescopic camera, built by Ball Aerospace of Boulder, Colorado, for the University of Arizona in Tucson, is designed to reveal surface features as small as dishes on a kitchen table. Other examples are the Context

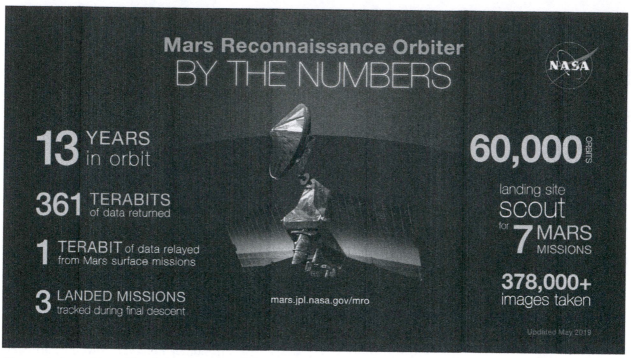

Since entering orbit on March 10, 2006, the spacecraft has been collecting daily science about the planet's surface and atmosphere, including detailed views with its High Resolution Imaging Science Experiment camera (HiRISE). HiRISE is powerful enough to see surface features the size of a dining room table from 186 miles (300 kilometers) above the surface. (Data as of May 2019) (NASA / JPL)

The launch window for MRO opened on August 10, 2005, but two delays resulted in liftoff on August 12 at 11:43 Universal Coordinated Time (UTC). The spacecraft was properly set along a trans-Mars trajectory and would take about seven months to reach the Red Planet. The Atlas-5 booster had done its job; this marked the first time an Atlas vehicle had been used to launch an interplanetary probe in twenty-two years. After spacecraft separation, MRO deployed its large high-gain antenna (to provide communications power) and set of solar panels (to provide electrical power). During the interplanetary cruise phase, all spacecraft instruments were powered and tested to configure MRO for orbital operations. The first in a series of planned trajectory maneuvers was executed successfully on August 27; six thrusters on the spacecraft fired for fifteen seconds to refine the approach to Mars. In order to achieve orbital insertion, MRO's rocket engines would use more than half of its fuel during a

26-minute burn. In the highly elliptical orbit that resulted from this insertion, MRO flew backwards, but the rear sections of the spacecraft, solar array, and antenna had been designed to withstand the high temperatures of aerobraking.

For about six months MRO dipped in and out of the thin Martian atmosphere while it transmitted to Earth large amounts of data at an unprecedented speed (three times faster than a high-speed residential telephone line). During the five to ten years that MRO was to be in orbit around Mars, JPL experimented with a high-frequency radio band that, scientists hope, wouldl provide more efficient interplanetary communications than previous systems. This experiment was successful, iand marked the start of an "interplanetary internet" that would allow future orbiters, landers, and rovers to have improved control, command, and communication between Earth and other planets.

During the period of its operation, MRO

travelled closer to the surface than any previous orbiter, and surveyed the entire planet with its high-resolution cameras, some of which have the ability to zoom in on interesting features. Detailed data enabled NASA scientists to select propitious sites for future missions as the Mars Phoenix lander (2007) and the Mars Science Laboratory Curiosity rover(2009). Because of the important questions the mission is seeking to answer, it was essential that the spacecraft and all its scientific instruments function properly for at least five years. Problems occurred while operating such systems as SHARAD on Earth. Since missions to Mars (for example, the American Mars Observer in 1992) have failed in the past, the possibility of malfunctions at launch, during orbital insertion, or in the data transmission from instruments while MRO is in orbit around Mars must be considered, despite statements by some members of the MRO team that "failure is not an option." Because the economic costs of this venture are so high and future missions will depend so heavily on data gathered by MRO, it is easy to understand why a total or partial failure of MRO was something few wish to contemplate. Fortunately, MRO outperformed even the most optimistic wishes of the planetary science community. MRO remained operational in 2019 supporting the Curiosity rover and also standing ready to support the anticipated Mars 2020 rover mission.

Contributions

Through MRO, space scientists hoped to acquire the most comprehensive knowledge of any solar system object, other than Earth, in the history of planetary science. This knowledge would be primarily concerned with the atmosphere, surface, and subsurface of Mars. Prolonged global weather observations would dramatically extend scientists' knowledge of the Martian atmosphere. With MRO's versatile and powerful cameras, the most detailed maps yet of Mars's surface features could be created. When interesting future landing sites get discovered, ultra-close-up images are taken to make sure that no obstacles, such as large boulders or deep crevasses, exist that might destroy an incoming lander or interfere with a future rover. These highly detailed maps created the knowledge base for NASA's distant goals, such as landing humans on the planet's surface. These pioneer crews will need to know the best places on which to land and survive and from which to return to Earth.

Because water is essential for all life, human and nonhuman, knowledge about Martian water deposits is indispensable both to settle the controversial question about possible past and present life on Mars and to provide the basis for future human life on the planet. After earlier discoveries of apparently water-carved channels, later surveys of Mars's surface composition provided less evidence of water-related minerals than some scientists anticipated

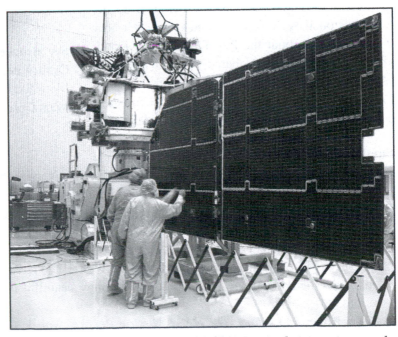

In the Payload Hazardous Servicing Facility, technicians inspect the solar panels for the Mars Reconnaissance Orbiter (MRO) during an electromagnetic interference verification test. (NASA)

and wished. MRO's imaging spectrometer (CRISM) was designed to identify various water-related minerals. According to JPL's Richard Zurek, these deposits most likely were small, more like the deposits of minerals at a hot spring in Yellowstone National Park than the immense Bonneville Salt Flats in Utah. With its penetrating radio waves, MRO's SHARAD instrument could determine whether the frozen water that Mars Odyssey detected in the upper 2 meters of some Martian soil extends deeper, perhaps to reservoirs of melted water. With its analysis of water vapor at different altitudes, the Climate Sounder (MCS) could discover where water vapor was entering the atmosphere from underground vents, providing other evidence that liquid water exists below the Martian surface.

Context

Previous flyby probes and orbiters began the quest for an ever more detailed portrait of Mars. For example, the Mariner 4 (1965), Mariner 6 (1969), and Mariner 7 (1969) flyby probes, with their revelations of a cratered, Moon-like world, proved that the Martian surface was vastly different from the one envisioned by Schiaparelli and Lowell. Mariner 9 entered orbit about the Red Planet in 1971 and, after a global dust storm abated, revealed Olympus Mons, an extinct volcano much larger than any on Earth, and Valles Marineris, the longest and broadest canyon system ever discovered. Mariner 9 images

revived the suggestion that Mars at one time had vast supplies of water; evidence of erosion and tremendous flooding appeared in the spacecraft's catalog of surface features.

In the 1970's and 1980's, two Viking orbiters and landers completed the picture of a present-day arid Mars with an atmospheric pressure so low that liquid water was impossible. However, two later orbiters, Mars Global Surveyor (1997) and Mars Odyssey (2001), uncovered an even more complex Mars than had the earlier missions, with an unexpected distribution of basaltic rocks and water-related minerals.

The Mars Reconnaisance Orbiter is part of this continuing series of robotic Mars missions, and it will try to answer such questions as how past conditions caused the present Martian surface, whether water that carved Martian channels is hidden in subsurface deposits, and whether fossils of extinct Martian life exist. If MRO is anything like previous missions, more questions will be raised than answered. However, that is scientific research at its finest.

—Robert J. Paradowski

See also: Jet Propulsion Laboratory; Mars Climate Orbiter and Mars Polar Lander; Mars Curiosity; Mars Exploration Rovers; Mars Global Surveyor; Mars Observer; Mars Odyssey; Mars Pathfinder.

Further Reading

Carr, Michael H. *Water on Mars*. New York: Oxford University Press, 1996. Using information from the Viking missions, Carr summarizes theories of the Martian atmosphere and geology. He espouses an ancient Mars that was warm and wet, but he also discusses other theories. Bibliography and index.

Crosswell, Ken. *Magnificent Mars*. New York: Free Press, 2003. Crosswell cleverly organizes his book by using the four ancient elements: in "Earth," he analyzes Martian geology; in "Air," the Martian atmosphere; in "Fire," Martian volcanoes; and in "Water," the rivers, lakes, and even oceans that Mars may once have had. The book is illustrated with many beautiful full-color pictures, some never published before.

Godwin, Robert, ed. *Mars: The NASA Mission Reports*. Vol. 1. Burlington, Ont.: Apogee Books, 2000. A thorough presentation of NASA documents relating to the Mars programs from Mariner 4 through Mars Global Surveyor. Includes press kits and a CD-ROM filled with special programs and interviews.

---. *Mars: The NASA Mission Reports*. Vol. 2. Burlington, Ont.: Apogee Books, 2004. A thorough presentation of NASA documents relating to the Mars programs from Mars Odyssey through the Mars Exploration Rovers. Includes a DVD of NASA data, bonus interviews, and NASA animation.

Hartmann, William K. *Moons and Planets*. 5th ed. Belmont, Calif.: Thomson Brooks/Cole, 2005. Provides detailed information about all objects in the solar system. Suitable for high school students, general readers, and undergraduates studying planetary geology.

---. *A Traveler's Guide to Mars: The Mysterious Landscapes of the Red Planet*. New York: Workman, 2003. Hartman, the first recipient of the American Astronomical Society's Carl Sagan Medal, has written a book that has been praised as "a masterpiece of scientific writing for the general reader." Because he was a participating scientist in the Mars Global Surveyor Mission, this book is particularly useful for those interested in orbital projects. Beautifully and extensively illustrated, with a glossary and an index.

Mishkin, Andrew. *Sojourner: An Insider's View of the Mars Pathfinder Mission*. New York: Berkley Books, 2003. A thorough exploration of the Mars Pathfinder mission that provides detailed historical perspective on the exploration of the surface of Mars begun by Viking.

National Aeronautics and Space Administration, Jet Propulsion Laboratory. "Mars Reconnaissance Orbiter." http://marsprogram.jpl.nasa.gov/mro. This MRO home page has features on how MRO will "follow the water" on Mars. It also contains updates on mission status.

Spitzer, Carl R., ed. *Viking Orbiter Views of Mars*. Washington, D.C.: National Aeronautics and Space Administration, 1980. This volume, the result of efforts by the Viking Orbiter Imaging Team, presents a judicious selection of fascinating images provided by "one of the longest-running successes in the history of space exploration." Includes a glossary and a list of sources.

Zubrin, Robert, with Richard Wagner. *The Case for Mars: The Plan to Settle the Red Planet and Why We Must*. New York: Free Press, 1996. The author, who was a senior engineer at Lockheed Martin, proposes a plan, based on data from Martian orbiters and landers, in which present technology can be developed to allow humans to explore Mars and live off its land. Includes a list of references and an index.

Marshall Space Flight Center

Date: Beginning July 1, 1960
Type of facility: Space research center

Marshall Space Flight Center (MSFC) is the National Aeronautics and Space Administration's (NASA's) principal center for development of large launch vehicles and propulsion systems. It is also one of four leading centers for space station research and development, providing expertise in the physical space sciences and space technologies.

Key Figures

Wernher von Braun (1912-1977), Director, 1960-1970

Eberhard F. M. Rees, Director, 1970-1973

Rocco A. Petrone (b. 1926), Director, 1973-1974

William R. Lucas, Director, 1974-1986

James R. Thompson, Director, 1986-1989

Thomas J. Lee, Director, 1989-1994

G. P. Bridwell, Director, 1994-1996

J. Wayne Littles, Director, 1996-1998

Arthur G. Stephenson, Director, 1998-2003

David A. King, Director 2003-2009

Robert M. Lightfoot, Jr., Director 2009-2012

Patrick Scheuermann, Director 2012-2015

Todd May, Director 2016-2018

Jody Singer, Director 2018-present

Summary of the Facility

Marshall Space Flight Center serves the NASA as the leading center for development of large space launch systems, about a third of the International Space Station, and a number of major space systems and payloads. The center's history dates to 1940, when a chemical munitions plant was located in Huntsville, Alabama. After World War II, the plant would have been shut down and sold as surplus, but the U.S. Army relocated a team of Army rocket engineers and scientists from Fort Bliss, Texas, to Huntsville, in 1950. The team included a core of 118 German engineers and scientists who had designed and launched V-2 rockets for Nazi Germany before surrendering to the U.S. Army in 1945. Popularly known as the von Braun rocket team, the group was led by the youthful Wernher von Braun, a charismatic engineer and scientist who would do much toward popularizing space travel in the United States. After early tests and development work at the White Sands Missile Range in New Mexico, the team sought larger facilities for production of a nuclear-tipped tactical ballistic missile later known as Redstone.

For the first eight years in Huntsville, the team, which evolved into the Army Ballistic Missile Agency (ABMA), developed the Redstone and larger Jupiter missiles and started design work on the super-sized Juno 5 missile for space exploration. Some effort was directed to development of a modified Redstone as a satellite launcher for the International Geophysical Year of 1957-1958, an eighteen-month period dedicated to space exploration. After failure of the primary launcher, the U.S. Navy's Vanguard, the Army team was told to prepare its Jupiter-C (later called Juno 1) for launch.

On January 31, 1958, the Army fired Explorer 1, the United States' first satellite, into orbit. The following October, NASA was formed around the old National Advisory Committee for Aeronautics. Non-military space activities were transferred from the Department of Defense. The Army resisted, but

Aerial view of the Marshall Space Flight Center. (NASA)

in 1959 it was ordered to transfer the von Braun team, made up of 4,670 federal employees, to NASA. The transfer took place in October, 1959. On July 1, 1960, ground was broken for a new headquarters building. The center was named in honor of George Catlett Marshall, the wartime chief of staff and postwar secretary of state, in the spirit of furthering the peaceful exploration of space.

The center's attention was initially focused on the development of large space launchers to overcome the apparent Soviet lead in this area. In the 1950's, the two superpowers had taken different paths in the nuclear arms race. The Soviets developed boosters that could launch the massive nuclear weapons common at that time, while the United States concentrated on making bombs smaller to fit mid-sized missiles believed to be easier to build. The first of these large boosters was called the C-1, later known as Saturn I.

In addition to the Saturn I, the new center inherited the U.S. Air Force's huge F-1 engine, which generated 6.67 million newtons of thrust alone, and was working on designs for large boosters that could place almost 200,000 kilograms of mass into orbit. President John F. Kennedy's proposal, declared in 1961, to send a man to the Moon brought this expertise and planning to the fore, and soon turned the C-5 program into the Saturn V booster for the Apollo Program. In 1963, Marshall was given the authority to proceed with the Saturn V rocket as the Moon launcher.

The magnitude of the Apollo Program required construction of many complex facilities to support development and testing of new technologies that would be used in the Saturn rockets. The style of the German team was to carry this work through production of the first few flight units, then to turn the work over to a contractor that would build production models. In this manner, the initial stages of the Saturn I and Saturn V vehicles were built in Huntsville by the Marshall team, then turned over to the Chrysler Corporation and Boeing Aircraft Company for production outside New Orleans, at a government-owned plant that built tanks and patrol boats during World War II. Subsequent stages of the Saturns, however, were built at contractor plants in California.

Important facilities built at Marshall include the F-1 test stand (completed in 1963), the vibration test stand for the complete Saturn V vehicle (completed in 1964), several smaller propulsion test facilities, a J-2 test stand (completed in 1965), and major machine shops.

As the Apollo Program progressed, Marshall spawned two new NASA centers. The first, soon known as Kennedy Space Center, was built to launch the Saturn V Moon rocket. The other facility was the Stennis Space Center, built inland of the Gulf Coast near Bay St. Louis, Mississippi, to remove Saturn testing from the Redstone Arsenal, for it had been causing broken windows and crockery in downtown Huntsville. In May, 1988, it was renamed the John C. Stennis Space Center in honor of U.S. Senator John C. Stennis for his steadfast leadership and staunch support of the nation's space program.

As it was building the rockets that would send Americans to the Moon, MSFC figured at the center of several controversies regarding management of the national space effort. With a personnel reduction in force effected in 1967, a federal judge ruled that mission support contracts were illegal. An eleven-year battle with the American Federation of Government Employees pushed the case to the Supreme Court, which ruled that the contracts were legal. The court ruled that NASA's charter and, by extension, the charter of any federal agency could be interpreted broadly.

Another MSFC project led to a revision of procurement practices. In 1969, the Senate Aeronautics and Space Science Committee learned that Marshall had built a Neutral Buoyancy Simulator (NBS) using more than $1 million of research funding after having been denied a construction of facilities request. The NBS is a water tank 22.9 meters wide and 10 meters deep in which spacewalks can be simulated. By using special space suits and flotation devices on heavy equipment, astronauts neither sink nor float and can move as if they were in space. The NBS has proved highly valuable in testing spacecraft designs and spacewalk procedures before flight.

The question whether MSFC would stay open was raised during the 1960's and well into the 1970's. "The Marshall problem" became a term that described the dilemma of any center that had facilities and personnel heavily vested in a single mission or line of work. One NASA official in the 1960's viewed Marshall as "that source for manpower needed elsewhere, and the place where surplus humanpower would occur as the Apollo Program phased down."

Indeed, the first of many humanpower reductions occurred in 1966; these cutbacks continued into the 1970's. Marshall's employment fell from a peak of 7,272 in July, 1967, to 5,851 by mid-1970. Its strength would be whittled even further in the 1970's, leveling off at 4,000 in the 1980's. More serious than the raw numbers and their implications

for the local economy was the loss of skilled management through layoffs, early retirement, or relegation to lesser positions. Many space veterans and one published history viewed a major portion of the layoffs as an effort "to get" the Germans. All but four or five of the original German rocket scientists were gone by the late 1970's because they did not have the rights held by most civil servants. A lawsuit was filed by two Germans alleging racial discrimination. In fact, there was resentment by many officials within NASA (and within MSFC) against the Germans and what was viewed as their autocratic, clannish management style.

Management styles changed radically at Marshall during the 1970's. At the urging of NASA officials, von Braun left MSFC for a post at NASA Headquarters, where he was to lead advanced planning for the United States' future in space. His patron, Administrator Thomas O. Paine, left NASA soon after, and interest of the Nixon White House in the space program declined. Von Braun left NASA for private industry in 1975. At Marshall, he was succeeded by another member of the German team, Eberhard F. M. Rees. Rees, too, retired and was replaced by Rocco A. Petrone, an American who had been with the Army missile program at Kennedy Space Center. Petrone stayed only a year before being transferred to NASA Headquarters.

Petrone was succeeded by William R. Lucas, a long-time civil servant who headed the program development branch from its inception. Lucas would have the longest tenure of any of Marshall's directors— twelve years—and his name would figure at the center of the post-accident investigation of the *Challenger* space shuttle accident in 1986. Lucas resigned in 1986 and was replaced by James R. Thompson, the former manager of the main engine program, who was heading a fusion project at Princeton University.

Diversification and the space shuttle program kept the gates open at MSFC during the 1970's and returned it to a central role as one of NASA's most vital centers in the 1980's. Earlier, in the

Ceremony of transfer from Army control to NASA control July 1, 1960. (U.S. Army)

mid-1960's, NASA officials had started the Apollo Applications Program, which would use Apollo and Saturn vehicles in missions outside the scope of a simple crewed lunar landing. It was an ambitious effort that was soon limited to the single Skylab launched in 1973 and crewed through 1974. Yet this project gave MSFC experience in developing a space station and a major science payload, the Apollo Telescope Mount (ATM), which carried a cluster of eight ultraviolet and x-ray telescopes to study the Sun.

Although a crewed space station seemed markedly different from large rockets, both involved integration and simultaneous operation of many complex systems. In this area, Marshall had excelled with the Saturn rockets. The center had also started developing a science capability in support of the engineering work on the rocket vehicles. This scientific expertise, in turn, expanded into experiments for these and other spacecraft.

Marshall's capability and innovation were clearly displayed in two projects in the early 1970's. The first was the Lunar Roving Vehicle, an electric "Moon buggy" that allowed astronauts to drive

several kilometers from their Lunar Module. Marshall and the Boeing Aircraft Company developed the rover in a short period of time and saw it operate successfully on the last three Apollo missions.

When Skylab launched in 1973, it was headed for a possible failure. During ascent, a combined sunshade and micrometeoroid shield tore loose, eliminating one solar power wing and jamming the other shut. MSFC was able to save the mission in less than a month. Marshall engineers modified a full-scale Skylab mock-up in the neutral buoyancy simulator to duplicate the damage and allow astronauts to practice repair procedures a few days before launch. Marshall's final involvement in Skylab came in 1978-1979 as the station started its spiral to reentry. MSFC engineers initially tried to develop a small, shuttle-launched robot stage to reboost the station. Yet Skylab would be on the ground again before the shuttle was launched, and by late 1978 the effort was abandoned. By the time Skylab reentered, much new experience had been gained in attitude control by momentum wheels (on Skylab's ATM), and the work with the robot stage had led to potential development of an orbital maneuvering vehicle that would act as a short-range space tug returning satellites to the shuttle in orbit.

Marshall's work on Skylab led to the High-Energy Astronomical Observatories (HEAO) program, which culminated in launches of three highly successful x-ray and cosmic-ray astronomy satellites from 1977 to 1979. The HEAO program substantially expanded the number of known x-ray sources, and revealed the universe to be more violent (that is, energetic) than previously thought. Skylab work also resulted in Marshall having lead responsibility for the docking module used on the joint Apollo- Soyuz Test Project (1975) with the Soviet Union.

Concerns about how to restart rockets and how to weld structures in space led to experiments in the fundamental behavior of fluids in a weightless environment. Experiments to test such behavior were carried aboard the Apollo spacecraft in 1971, and a larger suite of experiments was launched during Skylab and the Apollo-Soyuz Test Project. To span the gap between Skylab and Spacelab, a series of ten space processing applications rockets was flown from 1975 to 1980 to conduct basic research in the field. That, in turn, led to experiments aboard Spacelab 3 and the formation of a space commercialization office at MSFC.

In the late 1960's, Marshall and the Manned Spacecraft Center (later Johnson Space Center) were involved in research and development for a space shuttle. After several study cycles, which progressively reduced the size of the vehicle, NASA was authorized to proceed in 1972. MSFC was assigned to develop the high-performance main engines, their external fuel tank, and the twin solid-fueled rocket boosters. Johnson Space Center would manage the winged orbiter and the overall program. Several facilities at Marshall were modified to support shuttle testing. The Saturn vibration test stand was widened so that the complete shuttle "stack" could be assembled to simulate launch vibrations. The test stand built by the Army to fire the Saturn I first stage was modified to accommodate structural and pressure testing of a three-quarter-length solid-fueled rocket booster. All main engine testing was conducted at the Stennis Space Center under Marshall supervision. The need for advanced engine development, however, had led NASA officials to renovate one of the old Saturn test stands.

Marshall soon acquired oversight responsibility for the European Space Agency's Spacelab program, which would be a major shuttle payload. MSFC was designated lead agency for the first three Spacelab missions. This work broadened the center's systems capabilities and increased its

reputation as a science center rather than solely a builder of large rockets. Marshall was also charged with developing the Inertial Upper Stage, which boosts shuttle payloads to geostationary orbit, and advanced studies on reusable space tugs that would provide greater capability in the future. This work on Spacelab and the center's record with Skylab finally led to the assignment of more than 30 percent of NASA's space station program to MSFC in 1984. In the interim, between Apollo and the shuttle, Marshall's future again was in doubt, and rumors often circulated about its closing.

Marshall became the world leader in space propulsion and transportation systems. It was also making significant contributions to the International Space Station: As NASA's Lead Center for Microgravity Research, Marshall was at the forefront of that effort. Marshall also led the way in developing the Chandra X-Ray Observatory. Finally, its Space Optics Center was developing advanced optics manufacturing technologies designed to enhance future space observatories.

Marshall played a large role in preparing American modules for the International Space Station (ISS). Preliminary work was done at MSFC before those modules were transported to Kennedy Space Center for launch in the late 1990's and through 2011. After the Bush Administration's declaration that the space shuttle fleet would be retired after completion of ISS construction, Marshall began to play key roles in development of the Constellation Program's Ares I and Ares V rockets. With cancellation of Constellation by President Obama, those rockets morphed into the Space Launch System which, like the Ares family, incorporated upgraded space shuttle propulsion technologies. Marshall would play a large role in returning astronauts to the Moon in the 2020's, and perhaps sending them on to Mars in the 2030's.

Context

Marshall Space Flight Center is a strong, diverse facility. The center's staff is organized into four major groups. The programs and projects group covers the space shuttle, International Space Station, Hubble Space Telescope, Chandra X-Ray Observatory, and smaller payload projects. Program development includes preliminary design and analysis of advanced programs. Science and engineering provides research and technology, analytical, scientific, and other support to all project offices. Institutional and program support is the source of managerial and facilities support to all offices.

This organizational structure gives MSFC flexibility in supporting a wide range of projects. For example, work done by the program development office on an autonomous cargo version of the shuttle was supported by the Space Shuttle Projects office and various laboratories in the science and engineering office. One element of the Structures and Dynamics Laboratory has supported research on atmospheric science and on shuttle engine hot gas flow, because both involve modeling complex fluid flows. Marshall's Space Science Laboratory achieved international recognition for work in solar-terrestrial physics, x-ray astronomy, and materials sciences and has developed several payloads for the shuttle and other spacecraft.

Chief among the payloads were the core module, which will be used as laboratory and living quarters for the crew, and the resource nodes, which joined the modules. Marshall supplied the life-support systems, outfitted the Destiny Laboratory Module, and managed science operations aboard the crewed International Space Station. By overseeing the space laboratory, Marshall will continue to play a large role in materials and life science experiments to be conducted aboard the Space Station which is expected to remain operational through at least 2024 and perhaps as late as 2028.

Its experience with large projects also led to MSFC's being designated the lead center for development of the Hubble Space Telescope and the Chandra X-Ray Observatory. The Hubble project contains a 2.4-meter-aperture reflector telescope, which, though smaller than many ground-based telescopes, performs at least ten times more effectively because it is designed to function above Earth's atmosphere. Although the Space Telescope Science Institute in Baltimore operated the Hubble Space Telescope, Marshall retains responsibility for any necessary maintenance work in orbit. Chandra is an x-ray complement to the Hubble observatory and a high-resolution continuation of the HEAO program. MSFC also helped develop the Tethered Satellite System to explore the upper atmosphere and remained the lead center for several Spacelab missions.

In 2000, NASA partnered with industry to reduce the cost of space transportation to $2,000 per kilogram by 2010. Marshall managed a series of unpiloted, experimental, reusable launch vehicle demonstrators called X vehicles that are aimed at testing new technologies in flight. The lightweight, wedge-shaped X-33 was designed to take off vertically like a rocket and land horizontally like an airplane, traveling at more than thirteen times the speed of sound 100 kilometers above the Earth. The X-34 was designed to be air-launched from an L-1011 carrier aircraft and fly up to eight times the speed of sound and as high as 100 kilometers; it was expected to be a workhorse for testing high-reliability, low-cost technologies and operations needed to develop and operate the next generation of space vehicles. Unfortunately, budgetary concerns and technological issues led to the cancellation of both the X-33 and X-34. The X-37 was designed to be the first of NASA's fleet of reusable launch vehicle experimental demonstrators to operate in both the orbital and reentry phases of flight.

Beyond the X-planes, Marshall's Advanced Space Transportation Program is pushing technologies to reduce the cost of space transportation to only hundreds of dollars per kilogram by 2025. The key to continued advancement of the space program is development of new, cutting-edge technologies. One such emerging technology, intelligent vehicle health management systems, could allow the launch vehicle to determine its own health without human inspection.

Marshall's history of excellence in designing space propulsion systems has led to a long list of advancements. In addition to improving the shuttle main engine and fixing the solid-fueled rocket boosters, Marshall sponsors and conducts research in advanced propulsion areas such as the Space Transportation System booster and main engines, the joint NASA/Air Force advanced launch system, and an advanced solid-fueled rocket motor. Marshall is experimenting with a wide variety of propulsion technologies to dramatically reduce the cost of getting to space. Future launch vehicles could get a running start on a magnetic levitation tract that uses magnets and electricity to accelerate a vehicle at speeds up to 1,000 kilometers per hour before it leaves the ground. Another radical technology being developed at Marshall is a rocket engine that breathes oxygen from the air during the climb to orbit.

—Dave Dooling

See also: Ames Research Center; Cape Canaveral and the Kennedy Space Center; Goddard Space Flight Center; Jet Propulsion Laboratory; Johnson Space Center; Langley Research Center; Launch Vehicles; Lewis Field and Glenn Research Center; Saturn Launch Vehicles; Space Centers, Spaceports, and Launch Sites; Space Shuttle.

Further Reading

Allday, Jonathan. *Apollo in Perspective: Spaceflight Then and Now*. Philadelphia: Institute of Physics, 2000. This book takes a retrospective look at the Apollo space program, and the technology that was used to land humans on the Moon. The author explains the basic physics and technology of spaceflight, and conveys the huge technological strides that were made and the dedication of the people working on the program. All major aspects of the Apollo Program are covered, including crews, vehicles, and space suits.

Baker, David. *The Rocket: The History and Development of Rocket and Missile Technology*. New York: Crown, 1978. A highly detailed and comprehensive technical survey of the development of major and minor launch vehicles. Written for the technically oriented reader.

Belew, Leland F., ed. *Skylab: Our First Space Station*. NASA SP-400. Washington, D.C.: Government Printing Office, 1977. First in a series of books reporting Skylab results and experience. An introductory text written for the lay reader, with many details about MSFC. Well illustrated.

Bilstein, Roger E. *Stages to Saturn: A Technological History of the Apollo/Saturn Launch Vehicles*. Gainesville: University Press of Florida, 2003. Starting with the earliest rockets, Bilstein traces the development of the family of massive Saturn launch vehicles that carried the Apollo astronauts to the Moon and boosted Skylab into orbit. *Stages to Saturn* not only tells the important story of the research and development of the Saturn rockets and the people who designed them, but also recounts the stirring exploits of their operations, from orbital missions around Earth testing Apollo equipment to their journeys to the Moon and back.

Braun, Wernher von, and Frederick I. Ordway III. *Space Travel: A History*. Rev. ed. New York: Harper & Row, 1985. A revision of *The History of Rocketry and Space Travel*, which appeared during the 1960's. This book covers the entire space program for people unfamiliar with space travel. Includes surveys of the German rocket team and the Apollo-Saturn Program.

Compton, W. David, and Charles D. Benson. *Living and Working in Space: A History of Skylab*. NASA SP-4208. Washington, D.C.: Government Printing Office, 1983. An official NASA history of the Skylab program. Covers development work and management at Marshall as well as at other centers and contractor facilities. Includes discussion of the repair required after the sunshade was lost.

Davies, John K. *Astronomy from Space: The Design and Operation of Orbiting Observatories*. New York: John Wiley, 1997. This is a comprehensive reference on the satellites that have revolutionized twentieth century astrophysics. It contains in-depth coverage of all space astronomy missions. It includes tables of launch data and orbits for quick reference as well as photographs of many of the lesser-known satellites. The main body of book is subdivided according to type of astronomy carried out by each satellite (x-ray, gamma-ray, ultraviolet, infrared, millimeter, and radio). It discusses the future of satellite astronomy as well.

Dunar, Andrew J., and Stephen P. Waring. *Power to Explore: A History of Marshall Space Flight Center, 1960-1990*. NASA SP-4313. Washington, D.C.: Government Printing Office, 1999. A part of the National Aeronautics and Space Administration History Series, this is a highly detailed, official account of the Marshall Space Flight Center and its contributions to aeronautical and astronautical research. It covers the life of the center from its inception through its current activities. There are numerous illustrations and references, as well as numerous charts and tables.

Fifty Years of Rockets and Spacecraft in the Rocket City: NASA-Marshall Space Flight Center. Atlanta: Turner Publishing Company, 2003. This concise history of rocketry and the development of space travel over the past half-century centers on the contributions made to that effort by the Marshall Space Flight Center. Thoroughly laced with photographs, many of which are not typically included in other such works.

Launius, Roger D. *NASA: A History of the U.S. Civil Space Program*. Malabar, Fla.: Krieger Publishing Company, 1994. This is an in-depth look at America's civilian space program and the establishment of the National Aeronautics and Space Administration. It chronicles the agency from its predecessor, the National Advisory Committee for Aeronautics, through the present day.

Levine, Arnold S. *Managing NASA in the Apollo Era*. NASA SP-4102. Washington, D.C.: Government Printing Office, 1982. A highly detailed history of the difficulty of and lessons learned from managing a large, growing agency as it developed a complex program to place Americans on the Moon. Activities and problems at MSFC are discussed in the context of the agency as a whole.

McConnell, Malcolm. *Challenger: A Major Malfunction*. Garden City, N.Y.: Doubleday, 1987. An incisive account of how the *Challenger* accident came about and the roles played by people at Marshall and other centers. Written for a general audience.

National Aeronautics and Space Administration. *Marshall Space Flight Center, 1960-1985: Twenty-Fifth Anniversary Report*. Washington, D.C.: Government Printing Office, 1985. Celebratory booklet on Marshall's history. Includes many photographs of MSFC employees at work, contrasting early work with more recent activities. Included is a threepage time line showing activities on major projects, the management, and the supportive Huntsville community.

Ordway, Frederick I., III, and Mitchell Sharpe. *The Rocket Team*. Burlington, Ont.: Apogee Books, 2003. A revised edition of the acclaimed thorough history of rocketry fromearly amateurs to present-day rocket technology. Includes a disc containing videos and images of rocket programs.

Report of the Presidential Commission on the Space Shuttle Challenger Accident. Washington, D.C.: Government Printing Office, 1986. The summary of the activities of the commission organized to determine the cause of the *Challenger* accident. This thorough report provides technical and managerial details about Marshall and NASA and speculates about failures to monitor the booster and other problems on the shuttle. Recommends changes in procedure.

Materials Processing in Space

Date: Beginning January 31, 1971
Type of program: Scientific platforms

Materials processing on Earth has resulted in improved tools and devices and sophisticated composites that have contributed to higher standards of living worldwide. Materials processing in space, where gravitational effects are eliminated, promises even more dramatic technological gains.

Summary of the Technology

Materials processing in space was first attempted in January of 1971, by the astronauts on Apollo 14. The term "materials processing" means changing the characteristics of materials. For example, by freezing water it is changed from liquid to a solid. The process of changing from a liquid to a solid is called solidification, and the characteristics of the material are altered.

Materials are usually processed to obtain a desired product. Metal alloying, for example, is the process of mixing different metals together while they are in a liquid state, usually at a very high temperature, and then solidifying the mixture by cooling to obtain a metal alloy. Iron is a strong and useful metal; yet, it will oxidize (rust) easily. When iron is alloyed with chromium, manganese, and carbon, a new metal alloy called stainless steel, which does not rust easily, is produced. Therefore, the process of alloying these materials produces a new, improved end product.

There are many processes in which materials are combined to obtain different end products. On Earth, these processes can be adversely influenced by the force of gravity. Gravity can play a counterproductive role in processing. Sedimentation, buoyancy, and convection are the main gravity-driven effects that produce undesirable results in certain kinds of processing on Earth.

Sedimentation and buoyancy are really the same observable phenomenon described from different reference points. On Earth, if a material placed in a fluid, which is designated as the reference fluid, is more dense than the fluid, it will settle to the bottom. This process is called sedimentation. If the material is lighter than the fluid, it will float to the top and is said to be buoyant. Both sedimentation and buoyancy result in the separation of materials. On Earth, water is accepted as a common reference material, and the terms sedimentation and buoyancy are used to describe what happens when other materials are placed in water. Generalization of these terms, however, allows other reference materials to be designated.

Convection is a stirring action within a fluid. Usually the term "convection" is used to describe stirring that is induced by temperature differences within a fluid. Placing a heating source at the bottom of a container expands the molecules closest to the heat source and makes them buoyant with respect to the rest of the molecules in the gravitational field. The buoyant molecules move to the top of the container, inducing a stirring action. Placing a cooling source at the top of a container in a gravitational field will result in a similar stirring action. The stirring action, called convection, is usually caused by a temperature-induced movement of molecules in a fluid.

In space, these gravity-driven effects can be minimized. Theoretically, these effects can be eliminated, because they depend on the density (weight per unit volume) of one material versus that of

930

another. Weight is a measure of the gravitational force on a material or object. In the weightlessness of space, there is no gravity-induced sedimentation/buoyancy or convection.

Materials processing in space covers a wide range of activities across the processing spectrum. At one extreme the objective is to produce completely homogeneous products. At the other extreme the objective is to separate and isolate specific materials from others in a mixture. Materials processing in space is particularly applicable at these two extremes because in space the effects of sedimentation/buoyancy and convection will not adversely influence the processing.

Sedimentation/buoyancy can be counterproductive when obtaining homogeneous mixtures is the primary goal. In order to obtain homogeneous mixtures, the materials must be mixed in such a way that one unit volume of the mixture is the same as any other unit volume within the mixture. Any sedimentation/buoyancy effect would counteract this desired goal. This is especially true when the mixture needs to be solidified as a homogeneous solid, because most solidification processes require relatively long quiescent periods.

The absence of sedimentation/buoyancy in the microgravity environment of space allows attainment of higher levels of homogeneity in metal alloys and other solids. Lightweight, strong metals could be formed by mixing air with a metal that is in a liquid state, allowing bubbles to form in the metal, and then solidifying the end product. On Earth, this cannot be done easily or uniformly because of the difference in densities between air and metal. In space, metal and air can be mixed and solidified because sedimentation/buoyancy is absent and therefore does not contribute to separation. New products formed in this way are called foamed metals, and are strong yet lightweight.

In contrast to the process of mixing to obtain homogeneity, the process of separation on Earth is aided by sedimentation/buoyancy. When biological substances have weight, however, small differences in density and electrical charge create small-scale convection, which counteracts their separation. When measures are taken to minimize convective effects on Earth, the devices and mechanisms used create other problems. In the microgravity environment of space, where convection can be minimized, separation of biological substances that would be difficult on Earth can be achieved. Methods used to separate biological substances include electrophoresis, isoelectric focusing, chromatography, and filtering.

Electrophoresis is the process of separation using the differences in electrical charge between molecules. In this process, an electric potential is created across the material. With a positive charge on one side of the material and a negative charge on the other, molecules with a positive charge will migrate toward the negative side and molecules with a negative charge will migrate toward the positive side. This process requires that the materials being separated have the necessary charge differences to separate.

Isoelectric focusing also uses an electric potential across the material but incorporates the use of a solution with a pH (hydrogen-ion concentration) gradient. First, a pH gradient is established by "stacking" a series of carrier molecules (ampholytes) in the solution. Each ampholyte has the same molecular weight but a different stationary position (isoelectric point) within the fluid column in a specific electric field. Under the electric potential field, these ampholytes will form layers according to their isoelectric points. The result is a column with a natural pH gradient. Molecules introduced to this column will migrate to a corresponding stationary position. Sharp, concentrated, stable zones of like molecules are formed. This process of separation is useful for separating materials with isoelectric points as little as 0.01 pH apart.

Chromatographic methods such as ion exchange, molecular sieve, and affinity all use the principle of attraction. The molecules to be separated are attracted to a material that they will cling to called a "getter" material. The associative forces common to biological systems such as coulomb forces, van der Waals forces, and hydrophobic attractions are utilized to hold the molecules of interest while other, undesirable molecules are allowed to pass. Then the molecules of interest are removed from the "getter" and collected. Filtration methods involve forcing a mixture of molecules through a membrane of filtering material with a rigorously defined pore size; the molecules are separated according to molecular size.

Separating and sorting biological substances allows scientists to obtain ultrapure materials for study. For example, using ultrapure materials, they can grow very pure crystals and extract information about the molecular structures of substances. Crystal growth is the most common approach for obtaining structural information about biological substances.

Understanding the molecular structure of a substance allows scientists to manipulate it or vary its application. The more knowledge there is about the molecular structure of a substance, the less expensive and time-consuming it is to obtain the desired end product. Drug development, treatment of disease, and a host of other expensive, time-consuming problems can be minimized by a good understanding of the molecular structures involved.

Crystal growth is one of the best ways to obtain an understanding of molecular structures. The process involves several steps. First, an ultrapure sample of the material is needed. Such a sample is made through the separation and sorting techniques discussed earlier. Second, the substance is subjected to one of several methods of crystallization. After a crystalline form of the substance is obtained, the third step is to analyze the structure. Currently, the most common method of analyzing the structure is x-ray diffraction.

Crystallization is one process in which the systematic arrangement of identical molecules is accomplished. This orderly arrangement results in sufficient material for pattern recognition, which makes structural definition possible. To achieve the orderly arrangement of identical molecules on a microscopic level, it is necessary to allow enough time for the natural and appropriate orientation of each molecule as it takes its place in the structure. Consider this analogy. If 100,000 football fans had only five minutes to find their seats, there would be mass confusion. In many cases fans would occupy seats not legitimately belonging to them, and after they were in place it would be difficult, if not impossible, to extract them. Given more time, the process of achieving the proper seating arrangement would be accomplished more smoothly and acceptable positioning would result. Similarly, most macromolecules, especially mammal proteins, are made of 50,000 to 100,000 basic units of inheritance, or genes. Allowing enough time, without convection, for the natural and proper orientation of each molecule to take its proper place in the crystalline structure is vital.

There are several methods used to grow crystals, but the time consideration is common to all of them. There are other parameters that are important to the formation of crystals—such as the thermal environment, solution concentration, and externally imposed forces. Each of the crystallization methods provides advantages in controlling one or more of these parameters and therefore has its benefits. The most popular growing method for biological crystals is vapor diffusion. This method is used by more crystal growers in the biological field than any other.

There are many methods associated with crystal growth. Bulk crystallization occurs when a large quantity of solution is prepared and then given sufficient time for crystals to form. Batch crystallization occurs when a batch, or small quantity, of solution is prepared and given time to form crystals. Dialysis involves a semipermeable membrane used to separate the solution to be crystallized from the solution of the precipitating agent; dialysis of solute through the membrane is used to bring about nucleation conditions (conditions under which crystals will begin to form). Liquid/liquid diffusion occurs when two previously separated liquids are brought in contact with each other in a closed container and allowed through the process of liquid-through-liquid diffusion to reach nucleation conditions. Vapor diffusion, yet another process, occurs when a droplet of the solution to be crystallized is allowed to reach the nucleation condition by vapor diffusing through an air space between the droplet and a reservoir of diluted precipitating agent.

After a crystal has been grown, the next step is to analyze its pattern and derive the molecular structure. The method most commonly used is x-ray diffraction. In this approach, the crystal is placed in a beam of x-rays that are scattered in all directions by the electron complement of each atom in the crystal structure. The degree of scatter is proportional to the size and spacing of the atoms. When the lattice of the crystal is symmetrical, the distribution of the scattered x-rays will form a pattern that can be analyzed to deduce the arrangement of the atoms.

Processing in space clearly offers unique advantages. On Earth, materials that are processed at high temperatures may become contaminated by the very containers in which they are processed. The weightless environment of space affords the possibility of high-temperature processing without a container. In addition, ultrahigh processing, a method which would be useful for purifying materials, is possible in space. Because a constant stream of ions (an ion is an atom or group of atoms that carries an electric charge) is created by the orbital velocity in space, this process would probably require the use of a shield, or wake, to protect the materials being processed from the contamination of ions.

With the International Space Station operational, materials processing research has begun again in earnest. Conducting materials science research in microgravity gives scientists a unique opportunity to isolate and control gravity-related phenomena as well as investigate phenomena and processes normally masked by gravity's effects. One goal is to better understand how buoyancy-driven convection and sedimentation affect the processing of materials. Containerless processing may also be conducted on larger samples in microgravity than on Earth because the acoustic or electromagnetic forces used to manipulate them are not overwhelmed by gravity. Ultimately this research may result in improvements to production methods and materials on Earth. Better electronic devices, improved optical fibers for telecommunication, optoelectronic and photonic devices, and even bioceramic artificial bones are possible outcomes.

Only after extended periods of investigation in the microgravity environment of the International Space Station will scientists and entrepreneurs be able to determine if materials processing can result in viable commodities.

Contributions

Materials processing in space is a very young space technology. It has been shown, however, that processes with homogeneity or separation as their goal are greatly facilitated when compared to similar processing on Earth. In addition to metals and biological substances, insulators (such as glass and ceramics) and semiconductors have also been processed successfully in space.

The knowledge about materials processing in space comes from a smattering of sources. While there are no quantified analyses on the subject, the results obtained clearly show improvements in achieving materials homogeneity, materials separation, and crystal growth.

Context

It is doubtful that manufacturing facilities will be built in space to process large amounts of materials. It would not be economical to build manufacturing facilities in space simply to gain a minimal improvement in materials unless the materials were unique and valuable. It is more likely that the experiments involving materials processing in space will provide knowledge that will enable the processes on Earth to be improved.

—*David W. Jex*

See also: Get-Away Special Experiments; International Space Station: Design and Uses; International Space Station: Modules and Nodes; Skylab Space Station; Space Shuttle; Space Shuttle: Life Science Laboratories; Space Shuttle: Microgravity Laboratories and Payloads; Space Shuttle: Radar Imaging Laboratories; SPACEHAB; Spacelab Program.

Further Reading

Bugg, Charles E., et al. "Preliminary Investigations of Protein Crystal Growth Using the Space Shuttle." *Journal of Crystal Growth* 76 (1986): 681-693. A summary of the results of four different shuttle flights of a vapor-diffusion experiment to obtain protein crystals. It describes the advantages, techniques, strategy, and hardware design used for these four flights. Also describes the results of the experiments.

Chassay, Roger P., and Bill Carswell. *Processing Materials in Space: The History and the Future.* AIAA-87-0392. New York: American Institute of Aeronautics and Astronautics, 1987. An AIAA paper presented at the twenty-fifth Aerospace Sciences Meeting held in Reno, Nevada, in January, 1987. It gives a historical overview of materials processing in space and a description of the experiments performed. Describes the work being done at NASA centers and speculates on the future facilities available for materials processing in space and the technologies needed.

Doremus, Robert H., and Paul C. Nordine, eds. *Materials Processing in the Reduced Gravity Environment of Space.* Pittsburgh: Materials Research Society, 1987. Materials Research Society symposia proceedings were held in December, 1986, in Boston, Massachusetts. This is a compilation of the papers presented, which describe the highlights of ground-based experiments and plans for future experiments.

Feuerbacher, Berndt, Hans Hamacher, and Robert J. Naumann, eds. *Materials Sciences in Space: A Contribution to the Scientific Basis of Space Processing.* Berlin: Springer-Verlag, 1986. This book has three objectives: to stimulate new scientific experiments in space in order to expand the knowledge gained from microgravity research, to provide industry with the information obtained from space experiments, and to contribute to the scientific background for commercial space utilization.

Haskell, G., and Michael Rycroft. *International Space Station: The Next Space Marketplace.* Boston: Kluwer Academic, 2000. Covers uses of the ISS: commercial, scientific, technological, and educational.

Hazelrigg, George M., ed. *Progress in Astronautics and Aeronautics.* Vol. 108 in *Opportunities for Academic Research in a Low-Gravity Environment.* New York: American Institute of Aeronautics and Astronautics, 1986. A series of formal presentations on eight topics followed by a panel discussion on the policy implications of the identified research opportunities. The eight topics covered are infrastructures for low-gravity research, critical phenomena, gravitation, crystal growth, metals and alloys, containerless processing, combustion, and fluid dynamics.

McPherson, Alexander. *Preparation and Analysis of Protein Crystals.* New York: John Wiley, 1982. Basically a textbook describing the techniques and procedures used in the preparation and analysis of biological substances such as proteins, this book provides a working knowledge for the non-specialist who is familiar with protein crystallization.

National Aeronautics and Space Administration. *Space Station Science: Space Product Development.* http://spaceflight.nasa.gov/station/science/spaceproducts/index.html NASA Web site to encourage and discuss the commercial development of space utilizing the International Space Station. Accessed April, 2005.

National Research Council. *Future Materials Science Research on the International Space Station*. Washington, D.C.: National Academy Press, 1997. This composite work describes the International Space Station and materials science research in the following areas: microgravity research and the Space Station Furnace Facility Core, NASA's microgravity research solicitation and selection process, and the ability of the Space Station Furnace Facility Core to support materials science experiments that require a microgravity environment. Contains a table of references, a list of acronyms, and biographical sketches of committee members.

Naumann, Robert J., and Harvey W. Herring. *Materials Processing in Space: Early Experiments*. NASA SP-443. Washington, D.C.: Government Printing Office, 1980. A photographic presentation of the theories, applications, evolution, processes, results, and probable future of materials processing in space. Emphasis is on the theories and how they are supported, suggested by, and developed from the experiments conducted on the ground and in space up to and including the Apollo-Soyuz mission. It summarizes the state of the art at the time of publication and speculates on future facilities available for supporting materials processing in space.

Yates, Iva C., Jr. *Apollo 14 Composite Casting Demonstration Final Report*. NASA TM X-64641. Washington, D.C.: Government Printing Office, October, 1971. A description of the casting furnace experiment on Apollo 14. This experiment was one of three materials processing experiments performed on the mission. The other two were experiments investigating separation using electrophoretic techniques and fluid flow in selected configurations.

Mercury Project

Date: October 7, 1958, to June 12, 1963
Type of program: Piloted spaceflight

Project Mercury was the United States' first piloted orbital space program. In all, six piloted missions were flown, two suborbital and four orbital, yielding important data on human adaptability to space travel.

Key Figures

Robert R. Gilruth (1913-2000), manager, Project Mercury

Maxime A. Faget (1921-2004), flight director, Flight Systems Division, Space Task Group

Alan B. Shepard, Jr. (1923-1998), the first American in space (on the Mercury-Redstone 3 mission)

Virgil I. "Gus" Grissom (1926-1967), commander of the Mercury-Redstone 4 mission

John H. Glenn, Jr. (1921-2016), the first American to fly in Earth orbit, on the Mercury-Atlas 6 mission

M. Scott Carpenter (1925-2013), the second American in orbit, on the Mercury-Atlas 7 mission

Walter M. Schirra, Jr. (1923-2007), commander of the Mercury-Atlas 8 mission

L. Gordon Cooper, Jr. (1927- 2004), commander of the Mercury-Atlas 9 mission

Donald K. "Deke" Slayton (1924-1993), one of the original seven U.S. astronauts, replaced as commander of Mercury- Atlas 7 because of a heart murmur

Summary of the Program

Project Mercury officially began on October 7, 1958. Its stated goals were threefold: to place a piloted spacecraft in Earth orbit, to investigate human performance in space, and to recover the pilot and spacecraft safely. Beginning fifteen months after the first orbital satellite (Sputnik 1) was launched, Mercury would last nearly five years, send six humans into space, cost an estimated $400 million, and employ approximately thirty-three hundred engineers and scientists.

The prime spacecraft contractor, McDonnell Aircraft Corporation, was chosen in January of 1959. The first full-scale mockups were ready for inspection a mere two months later. The final vehicle was the classic cone-shaped "space capsule," which would become the traditional symbol of the United States' progress in space exploration. Mercury was a stubby black cone only 2.9 meters long and 1.89 meters in diameter at its base. The spacecraft tipped the scales at 1,355 kilograms and was small enough to impose a height limitation on the astronauts of 1.82 meters (5 feet, 11 inches).

Two booster rockets were selected. The smaller one was Redstone, a direct descendant of the German V-2 designed by Wernher von Braun. Also designed by von Braun. Redstone stood 21.5 meters tall, was 2 meters in diameter, and produced a sustained thrust of slightly more than 34,000 kilograms. It would be used for high-altitude structural tests and the first suborbital piloted flights. The second and larger booster was Atlas. With development beginning in 1951, Atlas would be the longest-lived of all American rockets, still launching satellites up through 2019. This "workhorse" of the American space program measured 23 meters long and carried a thrust of more than 250,000 kilograms.

The "Mercury Seven" astronauts pose with an Atlas model on July 12, 1962. Front row, left to right: Gus Grissom, Scott Carpenter, Deke Slayton and Gordon Cooper. Back row: Alan Shepard, Wally Schirra and John Glenn. (NASA)

With the official go-ahead, it was now necessary to concentrate on the third important element in this project: the astronauts. It was decided early in the project that military test pilots would be the perfect candidates. The original list consisted of 110 people: 5 Marine, 47 Navy, and 58 Air Force. By early March, 1959, the list had been whittled down to 32. The 32 became 18, and the 18 became the "Seven." In mid-April, the "Original Seven" were introduced to the public, becoming instant idols to millions of young boys and girls, subjects for harassment by the press, unofficial ambassadors of the United States, and "the best pilots in the world."

The original, and rather optimistic, flight schedule proposed in January, 1959, would have had the first piloted mission take place by January, 1960. Afterward, astronauts would fly every three to four weeks, completing the project by September of that year. It was planned that six suborbital and six orbital missions were to fly with astronauts aboard. Primarily because of the high failure rate of the Atlas rocket, however, Project Mercury got off to a slow start. Tests of both the Redstone and Atlas rockets were at first discouraging. Mercury-Atlas 1

and Mercury-Redstone 1 both failed in 1960. The first Mercury-Redstone test was finally successful just before the end of the year. In January, 1961, Ham the chimpanzee flew a suborbital arc on MR-2, experiencing six minutes of weightlessness. Despite problems with electronics aboard the Mercury spacecraft and much joking from their test-pilot friends about astronauts flying after monkeys, the Seven were heartened by Ham's success. Mercury-Atlas tests 2, 3, and 4, all robotic, were completed by September, 1961.

Meanwhile, the first piloted U.S. spaceflight was made on May 5, 1961, at 14:34 Coordinated Universal Time (UTC, or 9:34 a.m. eastern standard time). At that moment, the name of Alan B. Shepard joined those of Charles Lindbergh and the Wright brothers, as he became the United States' first human in space. Riding his spacecraft, *Freedom 7*, for a modest 15 minutes and 22 seconds, Shepard flew twenty-two days after Yuri A. Gagarin's stunning single-orbit mission. The secrecy surrounding the Soviets' Vostok flight, however, had made Shepard a hero to most of the world. The small Redstone rocket made orbital flight impossible; still, *Freedom 7* reached an altitude of 187.5 kilometers and a maximum velocity of more than 8,000 kilometers per hour.

Virgil I. "Gus" Grissom became the next hero, taking *Liberty Bell 7* on a repeat of Shepard's flight, lifting off at 12:20 UTC (7:20 a.m.) on July 21, 1961. Flying 9 seconds longer and 3 kilometers higher, Grissom's flight went as planned, until the landing. One major modification in Grissom's spacecraft was the use of explosive bolts on the hatch to make emergency escape much easier. Shortly after landing, while Grissom was waiting for recovery, the hatch blew open. *Liberty Bell 7* quickly filled with water, weighing 400 kilograms more than what the recovery helicopter could handle. The spacecraft was dropped and swiftly sank from sight into 4,600 meters of water. Meanwhile, Grissom struggled to stay afloat while his space suit filled with water as a result of an open valve. After an "eternity"—about five minutes—he found himself safely on board the helicopter returning to the carrier.

On February 20, 1962, an estimated 100 million people watched the televised broadcast of the first American to go into orbit. After a month-long series of frustrating launch delays, John H. Glenn, Jr., soared aloft in *Friendship 7*. For the next four and one-half hours, Glenn would take hundreds of photographs, observe African dust storms, describe mysterious "fireflies," and test dozens of intricate spacecraft systems. A potentially serious problem, however, came at the start of the second orbit. An indicator on the ground said that the heatshield had come loose and was being held in place only by the retropackage straps. Glenn was not told of the problem until the very end, however, and reported that everything was fine. He was finally instructed to leave the retropackage on during reentry to hold the heatshield in place. Nearing the end of the third orbit, Glenn fired the retrorockets to begin his slow glide toward Earth, and 4 hours and 55 minutes after launch, *Friendship 7* settled into the waters of the Atlantic Ocean.

With the success of *Friendship 7*, the next mission was to concentrate on science. M. Scott Carpenter was the pilot in the spacecraft dubbed *Aurora 7*. Carpenter's mission would take three orbits, lifting off on May 24, 1962. His many tasks included zero-gravity observations of liquid, weather photography, and the release of a 76-centimeter-diameter balloon to study air drag. As a result of his heavily loaded schedule of experiments, fuel consumption was unusually high, such that nearly 50 percent was used in the first orbit. Because of this and a malfunction in the spacecraft control systems, Carpenter had to effect a manual retrofire. Being distracted from his busy final preparations, he ignited the rockets three seconds too late with the

spacecraft in the wrong attitude. As a result, *Aurora 7* landed several hundred kilometers away from the intended splashdown site and required more than four hours to be rescued.

October 3, 1962, was the day on which Walter M. Schirra, Jr., lifted off at 12:15 UTC (7:15 a.m.) in *Sigma 7* for his six-orbit mission. One remarkable thing about Schirra's flight was just how unremarkable it was. Some called it perfect. Schirra agreed, calling it a textbook flight. Unlike Carpenter, Schirra managed to conserve fuel well, using in six orbits what Carpenter had used in the first half orbit. Schirra performed more photographic and systems experiments than were done on previous missions. He also tried extended periods of free drift, allowing the spacecraft to drift unguided. Reentry and landing were likewise uneventful, with Schirra hitting the ocean a scant 7.5 kilometers from the planned site. Unlike Glenn and Carpenter, he elected to ride *Sigma 7*, dangling from a helicopter's tether, all the way to the rescue carrier's deck. About forty-five minutes after splashdown, and 9 hours, 59 minutes after launch, Wally Schirra blew open the hatch to the jubilant shouts of the ship's crew.

On May 15, 1963, at 13:04 UTC (8:04 a.m.), the last Mercury spacecraft lumbered upward toward the sky. L. Gordon Cooper, Jr., in *Faith 7*, was on his way toward a twenty-two-orbit, thirty-four-hour mission. The primary goal was to test man's endurance in zero gravity. With a full day in space, Cooper was given eleven experiments to occupy his time, and like the earlier astronauts, he saw the "fireflies." One experiment had him launch a small beacon to test visual perception; other tasks were medical in nature. Cooper performed tests in transferring liquids from one container to another. He took radiation measurements and searched for Earth details, claiming that he could see roads, villages, and individual houses. Near the end of the flight, Cooper made observations of "airglow" and the "zodiacal light," mysterious dim glows seen in the night sky.

Photographs were taken to help in navigation studies for the Apollo Program.

A slow-scan television camera transmitted still cockpit pictures back to the ground every few seconds. On-board television had very little utility for the weight it took up and would not be used again until the first Apollo mission. (It is interesting to note that the Soviets used television from their very first flight.) A cranky pressure suit coolant system that alternated between extremes of heat and cold. More serious was an electrical short circuit that disabled Cooper's automatic control system. The latter problem required a manual reentry similar to Carpenter's. Unlike Carpenter, however, Cooper landed only 6.6 kilometers from the aircraft carrier *Kearsarge*. Like Schirra, Cooper elected to stay with his spacecraft as it was hoisted up to the deck. Forty minutes after landing, he blew the explosive bolts on his hatch.

Astronauts in simulated weightless flight in C-131 aircraft flying "zero-g" trajectory at Wright Air Development Center. Weightless flights were a new form of training for the Mercury astronauts and parabolic flights that briefly go beyond the Earth's tug of gravity continue to be used for spaceflight training purposes. These flights are nicknamed the "vomit comet" because of the nausea that is often induced. (NASA)

On June 12, 1963, NASA Administrator James Webb announced before the Senate Space Committee that there would not be another Mercury flight. Project Mercury had come to a close.

Contributions

Project Mercury proved that highly trained people could be sent into space, perform useful duties, and be recovered safely. These events alone fulfilled the primary objectives and provided a test bed for spaceflight management, communications, planning, training, and basic spacecraft engineering. In-flight experiments were divided into several areas: visual perception, photography, radiation, tethered balloon, aeromedical, and miscellaneous zero-gravity studies.

During several missions, flares were launched from the ground or intense beacons activated for the astronaut to sight. Poor weather hampered all attempts except on the last flight, when Cooper reported seeing one of the lights. The light was first visible from 530 kilometers away and appeared as a "star" of average brightness. Also on this same flight, a small beacon was launched from the retro-pack. This light flashed brightly about once a second and tested the utility of beacons for identifying space targets in later programs. Cooper sighted it on two orbits—once when it was about 21 kilometers away, and again when it was more than 28 kilometers in the distance. While the beacon was rather dim, Cooper stated that its flashing made it easily distinguishable from the stars.

In other simple visual studies, the astronauts were able to see ships' wakes, airplane contrails, railroad tracks (one actually saw a train), and small villages. All agreed that ground details were amazingly clear. Photography experiments revealed that Earth is best viewed in near-infrared light. This information would be of value for weather satellite design. Hundreds of ground photographs were taken, supplying useful geological and topographical data.

Radiation experiments showed that there were very low levels of radiation inside the spacecraft. Readings were taken on both Schirra's and Cooper's flights of radiation remnants from a July, 1962, atomic explosion. Results showed that radiation decayed by several orders of magnitude over the seven-month period between the missions. A balloon experiment failed on both missions.

As a result of the medical experiments on Cooper, it was shown that he withstood the stresses of flight with no evidence of degradation in performance. He did, however, suffer some dehydration. His pulse and blood pressure returned to normal between nine and nineteen hours after splashdown. Sleep in flight appeared to be relatively normal. There was no evidence of psychological disturbances during the thirty-four hour flight. All evidence pointed to the ability of humans to handle flights of a much longer duration, both physically and psychologically. This was welcome information, because Apollo Moon missions would last up to ten days.

On Schirra's mission, a number of panels made of differing ablative materials were attached to the outside of the spacecraft. These were to test the behavior of various materials to the reentry heat. None of the panels was clearly superior to the others. In-flight television transmissions were attempted from Cooper's mission, but the poor quality of the system rendered it of little value.

Context

As the United States' first piloted space program, Project Mercury served to pioneer the fundamentals of spaceflight. It answered the questions, "Could people be sent into orbit and recovered successfully, and while in space, could they perform useful work?" These missions laid the groundwork for the management, control, and training techniques required in later and more complex programs. Mercury provided training for both astronauts and

ground-control personnel. Three of the original seven astronauts were to go on to fly the two-person Gemini spacecraft: Virgil I. "Gus" Grissom in the first Gemini mission, Gemini 3, Schirra in Gemini 6, and Cooper in Gemini 5. Three would join Apollo crews: Schirra on Apollo 7, the first piloted Apollo flight; Shepard, who became the fifth person to walk on the Moon on Apollo 14; and Donald K. "Deke" Slayton, who never flew in Mercury as a result of a minor heart problem but was finally given his chance during the Apollo-Soyuz Test Project in 1975.

More specific flight elements required for lunar missions were not explored until Gemini. These included spacewalks, rendezvous and docking, navigational techniques, and missions of extended duration. Mercury flights also helped to galvanize the American public and government into accepting President John F. Kennedy's goal of a piloted lunar landing by the end of the decade. This declaration was made only fifteen days after Shepard's flight, when the National Aeronautics and Space Administration (NASA) had a mere total of 15 minutes and 28 seconds of piloted spaceflight time.

When compared to the Soviet's first piloted program, Vostok, Mercury seems rather primitive. Vostok landed on land, the Mercury Capsule in water. Vostok flew six orbital missions, the longest being five days, compared to Mercury's four orbital missions, with 34 hours being the longest flight duration time. Vostok cosmonauts accumulated a total of 16.46 days in space, compared to the minuscule 2.2 for The Seven. The Soviet spacecraft weighed a frightful 5,000 kilograms compared to the Mercury's featherweight 1,400 kilograms. What Mercury lacked in size and weight, however, it made up for in technology. While the Soviets were the undisputed leaders in the Space Race during this time, much of their success was a result of the brute-force nature of their technology. Their rockets were larger than those of the United States. This was out of necessity as they lagged behind in the important technology of miniaturization, and therefore manufactured heavier spacecraft. Furthermore, the early Soviet program was propelled with the need to "show off," giving science a back seat. For example, no repeat missions were allowed; each had to accomplish a clear-cut first for the history books. Mercury, by contrast, was a more methodical flight test program. This model presented by Mercury served the Gemini and Apollo Programs well, leading them to take a more cautious step-by-step approach.

—Michael Smithwick

See also: Apollo Program; Astronauts and the U.S. Astronaut Program; Atlas Launch Vehicles; Extravehicular Activity; Gemini Program; Launch Vehicles; Mercury Project Development; Mercury Spacecraft; Mercury-Redstone 3; Mercury-Redstone 4; Mercury-Atlas 6; Mercury-Atlas 7; Mercury-Atlas 8; Mercury-Atlas 9.

Further Reading

Ackmann, Martha. *The Mercury 13: The Untold Story of Thirteen American Women and the Dream of Space Flight*. New York: Random House, 2003. The story of thirteen remarkable women who underwent secret testing in the hopes of becoming America's first female astronauts.

Catchpole, John. *Project Mercury: NASA's First Manned Space Programme*. London: Springer- Verlag London Limited, 2001. A developmental resume of Project Mercury from associated infrastructure to launch vehicles.

Glenn, John, with Nick Taylor. *John Glenn: A Memoir*. New York: Bantam Books, 1999. Glenn tells his life story in this well-written and very interesting autobiography. The book covers his career from his days as a Marine pilot, through his Mercury-Atlas 6 orbital mission, and onward to his flight aboard STS-95 in 1998. In between, he was a husband, a father, and a senator from Ohio.

Godwin, Robert, ed. *Friendship 7: The NASA Mission Reports*. Burlington, Ont.: Apogee Books, 1999. This collection contains reprints of the Mercury-Atlas 6 preflight press release (in the days before press kits) and the results of the first United States manned orbital space flight. It also includes a CD-ROM featuring "*Friendship 7*," the official NASA film of the mission.

Gunston, Bill. *The Illustrated Encyclopedia of theWorld's Rockets and Missiles*. London: Salamander Books, 1979. A remarkable reference book, its sections are divided among the various kinds of missiles, including surface-to-air and air-to-air, and is then subdivided into countries. An attempt was made to provide photographs, drawings, and text for every known missile. Nearly all illustrations are in color. Highly recommended to those interested in model building.

Kraft, Christopher C., Jr. *Flight: My Life in Mission Control*. East Rutherford, N.J.: Penguin Putnam, 2002. The first NASA flight director gives an account of his life in Mission Control.

Montgomery, Scott, and Timothy R. Gaffney. *Back in Orbit: John Glenn's Return to Space*. Atlanta: Longstreet Press, 1998. This book, written prior to Glenn's return to space aboard the space shuttle *Discovery* in 1998, covers Glenn's life from his Project Mercury days. The authors are seasoned professionals: Montgomery is theWashington correspondent for the *Dayton Daily News*; Gaffney is the newspaper's military affairs/aerospace writer. There are a few technical errors in the book (they repeatedly misspell S. Christa McAuliffe's name), but overall it is a well-written book.

National Aeronautics and Space Administration. *Mercury Project Summary Including Results of Fourth Manned Orbital Flight, May 15-16, 1963*. NASA SP-45. Washington, D.C.: Government Printing Office, 1963. This work is the official NASA summary of the project. It contains twenty sections detailing Project

Mercury's medical experiments and booster and spacecraft performance. It is fairly technical in nature but should be suitable for general audiences. This volume also contains the official flight report for the last mission, *Faith 7*, along with transcripts of air-to-ground communications.

Newport, Curt. *Lost Spacecraft: The Search for Liberty Bell 7*. Burlington, Ont.: Apogee Books, 2002. Juxtaposes two stories: that of Gus Grissom and his Mercury flight in *Liberty Bell 7*, and Curt Newport's fourteen-year quest to raise the sunken space capsule from the depths of the Atlantic Ocean.

Schefter, James L. *The Race: The Uncensored Story of How America Beat Russia to the Moon*. New York: Doubleday Books, 1999. Journalist Schefter was given complete access to the biggest players at NASA during the Space Race, but here he reveals the full, unexpurgated story.

Shepard, Alan B., Jr., and Donald K. "Deke" Slayton, with Jay Barbree and Howard Benedict. *Moon Shot: The Inside Story of America's Race to the Moon*. Atlanta: Turner, 1994. This is, indeed, the inside story of the Apollo Program as told by two men who actively participated in it. Some of their tales appear here for the first time. Shepard and Slayton discuss Shepard's Mercury-Redstone 3 suborbital flight and tell some little known secrets of the Mercury astronauts. The book was adapted for a four-hour documentary in 1995.

Siddiqi, Asif A. *The Soviet Space Race with Apollo*. Gainesville: University Press of Florida, 2003. ---. *Sputnik and the Soviet Space Challenge*. Gainesville: University Press of Florida, 2003. These two volumes offer the first comprehensive history of the Soviet piloted space programs, covering a period of thirty years.

Slayton, Donald K., with Michael Cassutt. *Deke! U.S. Manned Space: From Mercury to the Shuttle*. New York: Forge, 1995. This is the autobiography of the last of the Mercury astronauts to fly in space. After being grounded from flying in Project Mercury for what turned out to be a minor heart murmur, Slayton was appointed head of the Astronaut Office. Slayton talks of his frustration at being grounded and how he worked to regain flight status. He also discusses the flights of his fellow Mercury astronauts.

Swenson, Loyd S., Jr., James M. Grimwood, and Charles C. Alexander. *This New Ocean: A History of Project Mercury*. NASASP-4201. Washington, D.C.: Government Printing Office, 1966. This publication is part of the NASA historical series and one of the "Special Publications" made available to the public. The history of Project Mercury is traced up through Cooper's flight. Includes material on both the technical and management sides of the program. Many rare photographs and diagrams are included. Suitable for ages twelve and above.

Wendt, Guenter, and Russell Still. *The Unbroken Chain*. Burlington, Ont.: Apogee Books, 2001. Wendt is the only person who worked with every astronaut who left the Cape bound for space.

Mercury Project Development

Date: January, 1958, to September 9, 1959
Type of program: Piloted spaceflight

The technical development of the Mercury spacecraft culminated in the Big Joe launch of September, 1959. The feasibility of the ablative heatshield and the survivability of a spacecraft during reentry and splashdown were demonstrated, and the use of an Atlas booster to launch Mercury spacecraft was proved effective.

Key Figures

Maxime A. Faget (1921-2004), flight director, Flight Systems Division, Space Task Group

Robert R. Gilruth (1913-2000), manager, Project Mercury

James A. Chamberlin (1915-1981), program manager, Project Mercury

Charles W. Mathews (1921-2002), operations manager, Project Mercury

John F. Yardley (1925-2001), the manager of Project Mercury at McDonnell Douglas

Andre J. Meyer, Jr., a developer of heat-shielding mechanisms for Project Mercury

Walter C. Williams (1919-1995), associate director, Project Mercury

Charles J. Donlan, associate director, Project Mercury

Alec Bond (b. c. 1922), Big Joe project engineer

Summary of the Program

The launching of the "boilerplate" Mercury capsule, named Big Joe, on September 9, 1959, capped almost two years of technical developments that ultimately resulted in the piloted spacecraft of Project Mercury. Big Joe's successful 20-minute flight proved that a capsule shaped like a frustum (or "Coke bottle" in the designers' vernacular) with an ablative heatshield would align itself properly, with its blunt end forward, during reentry and would land safely. The Big Joe flight also showed that efforts to make the Mercury compatible with existing rockets, such as the Atlas, had been successful.

The "father" of the Mercury capsule—and, to some extent, the later Gemini and Apollo craft—was Maxime A. Faget. In the early spring of 1958, he and his coworkers at Langley Memorial Aeronautical Laboratory in Virginia were already designing features for piloted spacecraft that were to become the mainstays of the U.S. space program for the next decade and beyond.

Faget's group first worked for the National Advisory Committee for Aeronautics (NACA). In July of 1958, NACA was merged into the new National Aeronautics and Space Administration (NASA). In September, 1958, plans for the program that was to be known as Project Mercury began to take shape and the scope of the technological challenge became clear. Mission objectives and the vehicle configuration were drawn up by a panel of experts from NACA and the Advanced Research Projects Agency (ARPA). A document was developed that outlined the retrograde firing rocket systems and the life-support, attitude control, recovery, and emergency escape systems. This panel, called the Space Task Group, also developed plans for tracking stations around Earth, craft-to-ground communication methods, and ground support and test program technology.

The objectives of the project were to "achieve at the earliest practicable date orbital flight and successful recovery of a piloted satellite, and to investigate the capabilities of man in this environment." The simplest and most reliable approach was always to be used, there was to be a minimum of new technical developments, and there was to be a steady progression of tests.

Debates had raged for years within NACA and ARPA and among aerodynamic theorists as to how it might be possible to retrieve a capsule safely, whether piloted or robotic, from Earth orbit. Because a spacecraft orbits Earth at speeds of about 30,000 kilometers per hour and must slow to a relatively safe post-entry speed of less than 100 kilometers per hour, there is a tremendous loss in kinetic energy. Most of this energy is released as heat. Theorists had predicted that reentry vehicles would experience temperatures ranging from 1,000° Celsius to as high as 3,000° Celsius and that these temperatures, because they are well above the thermal limits for most metal structures, would destroy the capsule. Three solutions had been proposed by various aerodynamicists in the United States, and each had advocates. They were an ablative heatshield, a beryllium heatsink, and a slow glider reentry.

The slow glider mechanism was rejected rather early in the NACA studies, although parts of the idea survived in the Rogallo wing, which was proposed for the final landing of the craft. It was believed that the first shock of the craft's hitting the air stream at the beginning of reentry would make deployment of glider wings a very unsound procedure.

Andre J. Meyer, Jr., kept tabs on development of both the beryllium heatsink and the ablative heatshield. In the late 1950's, fiberglass, ceramics, and other thermally resistant materials were in the earliest stages of development. It was not clear whether a heatsink made of beryllium would be able to carry heat away from the critical areas quickly enough. Beryllium, like titanium and vanadium, is a refractory metal. It maintains its structural integrity at relatively high temperatures. It was theorized that beryllium would get hot during reentry but would be able to spread the heat over its entire volume quickly. Thus, no part of the structure would get too hot to cause mechanical damage.

The ablative heatshield, in contrast, would consist of a very poor heat conductor, or insulator. The theory, as developed by investigators at the Langley and Ames Research Centers, was that most of the heat would be dissipated by shock waves. The shield would not conduct residual heat to the titanium shell of the spacecraft or to occupants within.

There was no accurate way to evaluate shielding devices of the size necessary to protect a piloted spacecraft. Wind tunnels could not produce air speeds high enough, and earlier rockets had relied on rather small nose cones for reentry. Beryllium, moreover, is a difficult metal to machine, and in the late 1950's no beryllium structures comparable to the required device had been built. There were beryllium coatings on engines and mirrors but nothing similar to a rather thick, well-formed, pure metal heatsink. Meyer soon formed the opinion that successful development of the mechanism would require a breakthrough in beryllium technology. With the flight of Big Joe and the success of the ablative heatshield, the beryllium heatsink idea was dropped from all subsequent piloted space programs. An Atlas 10D modified intercontinental ballistic missile (ICBM) launched Big Joe successfully. Even though the outboard engines had failed to detach correctly and the additional weight had caused Big Joe to fail to reach the desired speed, it did reach a speed of almost 25,000 kilometers per hour, which was acceptable for the heat studies.

The ablative heatshield worked effectively; only one-third of the heatshield melted during reentry. Fringe areas, where the heatshield was connected to the capsule, were hotter than expected and thicker beryllium shingles were placed there in subsequent Mercury flights.

Big Joe demonstrated that Mercury had the proper aerodynamic configuration and that upon reentry it would turn its blunt end forward. Had the retrorockets not fired to initiate reentry, it was calculated, the heatshield would have kept the capsule intact for a natural orbital decay. The launch also proved that fabrication techniques used on the titanium outer shell worked, that the Atlas could be used as a launcher, that the capsule could be landed safely on the ocean with the help of a parachute, and that recovery procedures could be effective 500 kilometers from the anticipated landing site. Big Joe's success made NASA personnel confident that Project Mercury could be piloted. A second test flight was deemed unnecessary.

Contributions

The Mercury project's development was an organizational and technological triumph. Titanium welding came of age at the McDonnell Douglas plant in St. Louis, where the titanium shell of the Mercury spacecraft was welded in an inert gas atmosphere. The layers were only 25 millimeters thick.

The success of Big Joe demonstrated that the heatshield approach would work even better than had been expected. Heating experienced by Big Joe was more intense than predicted, but it did not last as long as predicted. Paint on the titanium shell identifying it as a U.S. spacecraft sustained no damage during the flight. A piece of tape left on the outside surface returned undamaged. It was necessary to increase the thickness of the beryllium heat shingles at the interface of the craft with the heatshield. Only slight damage occurred at this interface. Some studies had suggested that a gradually decaying orbit might seriously damage the heatshield, but such reentries would be highly unlikely in future piloted flights. It was the flight of Mercury-Atlas 7 several years later that proved how efficacious the heatshield design really was; this capsule had a sustained-heating reentry trajectory.

The Atlas 10D, because it did not "stage" (detach from the spacecraft) properly, was classified a failure by the Air Force. To NASA officials,

however, the failure was almost irrelevant, because the spacecraft landed in such good shape.

After Big Joe, a series of launches using "Little Joe" rockets were conducted to test launch staging, escape and abort mechanisms, and other specialized features of what was to be the piloted Mercury craft. A rhesus monkey named Sam rode Little Joe 2 for four minutes and survived reentry and the shock of impact. Another monkey, dubbed Miss Sam, survived a gravitational force of 10 and was able to perform several functions during her ride.

Context

During early technical development stages of Mercury, the U.S. space program underwent several reorganizations. NACA and ARPA were competing agencies of sorts in early 1958, and there was considerable tension as to the role the Air Force Mercury Project Development 897 might play in directing future space efforts. Early Mercury-Redstone tests were partially under control of the Army. Various organizations were looking out for their own interests.

The successful Soviet launchings of Sputniks 1 and 2 in October and November of 1957 caused consternation within the space and aeronautical communities. Ames and Langley Research Centers, however, were succeeding in their technological investigations. Even though Atlas was designed to launch thermonuclear warheads, it could be modified for use as a launch vehicle for piloted spacecraft. Titanium airframes were being built by the aircraft industry, miniaturization of electronics was also beginning, and most of all, the country was developing a desire to get into space in response to what it saw as the Soviet challenge.

Basically, the Mercury capsule was a hull that could surround a pilot. The feasibility of using the Atlas booster with the Mercury capsule was demonstrated by Big Joe, as was the recoverability of a returning spacecraft after a splash landing. The Mercury techniques and design were carried over to the Gemini and Apollo Programs; the spacecraft that put the first humans on the Moon a decade later had the same basic features as Big Joe.

Within the space community, particularly at McDonnell Douglas and NASA, the idea of staged program management and meticulous testing of each feature systematically gained acceptance. The management teams that developed the early Mercury craft were talented, and their organizational abilities, high motivation, and clear decision making saw the U.S. space program off to an excellent start.

—John Kenny

See also: Apollo Program; Astronauts and the U.S. Astronaut Program; Atlas Launch Vehicles; Gemini Program; Launch Vehicles; Mercury Project; Mercury Spacecraft; Mercury-Redstone 3; Mercury-Redstone 4; Mercury-Atlas 6; Mercury-Atlas 7; Mercury-Atlas 8; Mercury-Atlas 9.

Further Reading

Catchpole, John. *Project Mercury: NASA's First Manned Space Programme.* London: Springer- Verlag London Limited, 2001. Project Mercury's development from infrastructure through launch vehicles.

Glenn, John, with Nick Taylor. *John Glenn: A Memoir.* New York: Bantam Books, 1999. Glenn covers his career from his days as a Marine pilot through his Mercury-Atlas 6 orbital mission to his flight aboard STS-95 in 1998. In between, he was a husband, a father, and a senator from Ohio.

Godwin, Robert, ed. *Friendship 7: The NASA Mission Reports.* Burlington, Ont.: Apogee Books, 1999. This collection contains reprints of the Mercury-Atlas 6 preflight press release (in the days before press kits) and the results of the first United States manned orbital space flight. It also includes a CD-ROM featuring "*Friendship 7,*" the official NASA film of the mission.

Kraft, Christopher C., Jr. *Flight: My Life in Mission Control.* East Rutherford, N.J.: Penguin Putnam, 2002. The first NASA flight director gives an account of his life in Mission Control.

Montgomery, Scott, and Timothy R. Gaffney. *Back in Orbit: John Glenn's Return to Space.* Atlanta: Longstreet Press, 1998. This book, written prior to Glenn's return to space aboard the space shuttle *Discovery* in 1998, covers Glenn's life from his Project Mercury days. The authors are seasoned professionals: Montgomery is the Washington correspondent for the *Dayton Daily News*; Gaffney is the newspaper's military affairs/aerospace writer. There are a few technical errors in the book (they repeatedly misspell S. Christa McAuliffe's name), but it is overall a well-written book.

Ordway, Frederick I., III, and Mitchell Sharpe. *The Rocket Team.* Burlington, Ont.: Apogee Books, 2003. Discloses much previously classified information, particularly involving the British intelligence effort to learn about Hitler's heralded V-1 and V-2 "vengeance weapons."

Rosholt, Robert L. *An Administrative History of NASA, 1958-1963.* NASA SP-4101. Washington, D.C.: Government Printing Office, 1966. This book focuses mainly on the administrative tangles in the aeronautics and space community at the time Mercury's technical developments were under way. The conflicts between the Air Force and the civilian space community are discussed, and the rationale for the national organization that was to emerge is well presented.

Shepard, Alan B., Jr., and Donald K. "Deke" Slayton, with Jay Barbree and Howard Benedict. *Moon Shot: The Inside Story of America's Race to the Moon.* Atlanta: Turner, 1994. This is, indeed, the inside story of the Apollo Program as told by two men who actively participated in it. Some of their tales appear here for the first time. Shepard and Slayton discuss the early days of Project Mercury, as well as the vehicles and spacecraft used. The book was adapted for a four-hour documentary in 1995.

Slayton, Donald K., with Michael Cassutt. *Deke! U.S. Manned Space: From Mercury to the Shuttle.* New York: Forge, 1995. This is the autobiography of the last of the Mercury astronauts to fly in space. After being grounded from flying in Project Mercury for what turned out to be a minor heart murmur, Slayton was appointed head of the Astronaut Office. Slayton talks about the early testing of the Mercury spacecraft and launch vehicle and the development of the astronaut training program.

Sobel, Lester A., ed. *Space: From Sputnik to Gemini.* New York: Facts on File, 1965. This small book contains a remarkably detailed account of all launches of the U.S. and Soviet space programs from 1957 to 1966. It includes brief statements about each Mercury flight, including technical development efforts, and gives a good account of the early days of the program. It is ordered chronologically.

Swenson, Loyd S., Jr., James M. Grimwood, and Charles C. Alexander. *This New Ocean: A History of Project Mercury.* NASASP-4201. Washington, D.C.: Government Printing Office, 1966. This book is part of the NASA History series. It is a complete and well-written account of all aspects of the space program until 1962 as they influenced the development of Mercury. It is a bit weak in outlining rivalries among the military and the civilian authorities, but it gives a good account of Big Joe and the early technical problems, such as those with the heatshield.

Thomas, Shirley. *Men of Space: Profiles of the Leaders in Space Research, Development, and Exploration.* 5 vols. Philadelphia: Chilton, 1960. This book contains the biographies of several of the key personnel associated with the early days of Mercury, such as Robert R. Gilruth and other members of the Space Task Group.

Mercury Spacecraft

Date: October 7, 1958, to June 12, 1963
Type of spacecraft: Piloted spacecraft

America's first spacecraft, the Mercury capsule tested technical and conceptual approaches, gave astronauts practical experience in outer space, and boosted the nation's sagging prestige early in the Space Race—all of which deeply influenced subsequent piloted space programs.

Key Figures

T. Keith Glennan (1905-1995), first NASA administrator, 1958-1961

Abe Silverstein (1908-2001), director of Space Flight Development

George M. Low (1926-1984), chief of the Office of Manned Space Flight

Robert R. Gilruth (1913-2000), project manager of the Space Task Group

Maxime A. Faget (1921-2004), conceptual designer of the Mercury spacecraft

Logan T. MacMillan, McDonnell Aircraft Corporation's Mercury project manager

Summary of the Program

In the early 1950's, aeronautical scientists and visionaries believed that the United States was ready to undertake piloted spaceflight. The idea stirred little public interest until the Soviet Union successfully orbited a satellite, Sputnik 1, on October 4, 1957. Sputnik spurred the U.S. government into supporting several potential spaceflight programs, including proposals for a space plane and a lifting body, but it was the "manned ballistic satellite" that produced the nation's first operational spacecraft.

The concept of a piloted ballistic satellite came from a panel of engineers and administrators called the Space Task Group (STG). After the National Air and Space Administration (NASA) was established in 1958, its first administrator, T. Keith Glennan, and two key subordinates—Director of Space Flight

Development Abe Silverstein and Head of the Office of Manned Space Flight George Low—threw their support behind STG and its leader, Robert R. Gilruth. Accordingly, STG formulated objectives and guidelines for the project, later named Mercury after the Roman messenger god, and its spacecraft. The overall mission objectives were to place a single person into Earth orbit for as long as twenty-four hours, study how humans perform in space, and safely recover the astronaut and spacecraft afterward.

For the spacecraft, STG recommended a launch escape system, a zero-lift body using drag braking and a retrorocket system for atmospheric reentry, and a water-landing system. The guidelines encouraged speed and economy in development. Developers were to employ existing technology as much as possible, design the simplest and most reliable systems with built-in redundancy (backup systems), and use existing launch vehicles.

Glennan accepted STG's proposal on October 7, 1958. The lead designer was NASA's Maxime A. Faget. McDonnell Aircraft Corporation won the primary contract to produce twelve capsules for $18.3 million; however, twenty vehicles were eventually delivered. Logan T. MacMillan, McDonnell's project manager, oversaw ten working groups and coordinated development with John F. Yardley at NASA and its seventeen working groups. The seven Mercury astronauts also exerted influence on the

President John F. Kennedy inspects Mercury capsule with astronaut John Glenn. (Cecil Stoughton, White House)

craft's development—insisting, for example, that a window be installed over the couch and that a manual control system be included.

Boilerplate versions of three cone shapes (known internally as types A, B, C) for the spacecraft's hull were tested but found to tumble during decent in the atmosphere. Eventually, NASA researchers produced a stable shape, type D, which had a conical crew compartment whose sides sloped at 25°. At the apex of the cabin was a cylindrical recovery section, and atop that was a second, smaller, truncated cylinder known as the antenna canister. At the base of the crew compartment was a heatshield, shaped like a shallow bowl. From heatshield to antenna canister, the spacecraft was 2.9 meters tall and 1.9 meters wide at the base. The retrograde package was strapped to the heatshield, adding another 38 centimeters. Attached at the top was the launch escape system: a three-nozzle rocket motor at the end

of a metal frame. This brought the total length of the vehicle to 7.9 meters. For suborbital flights the spacecraft was launched atop a Mercury-Redstone rocket; for orbital flights a modified Atlas-D intercontinental ballistic missile (ICBM) was used.

The core of the spacecraft was a pressure vessel with a volume of 1.7 cubic meters. A titanium outer shell capable of withstanding the temperatures encountered during reentry, approximately 2,000° Celsius, surrounded it. Suborbital Mercury spacecraft endured lower reentry temperatures and used beryllium heatsink heatshields. Orbital missions encountered much higher atmospheric friction and temperatures during reentry. They used ablative shields; that is, they were designed to absorb heat, to char, and then to break away in pieces during reentry to dissipate the heat. The heatshield was made of honeycombed aluminum stabilized by layers of glass fiber.

In space, control of the vehicle came from eighteen small hydrogen peroxide thrusters divided into two systems for redundancy: System A (two automated systems) had twelve thrusters, and system B (two manually controlled systems) had six. They controlled pitch (up and down motion), yaw (left and right motion), and roll (rotation on the vehicle's long axis). The retrograde package contained two sets of three solid-fueled rockets. Posigrade rockets had a thrust of 1,800 newtons and separated the spacecraft from the launch vehicle. The second set, the retrorockets, had a thrust of 4,500 newtons and slowed the spacecraft enough to drop out of orbit. Each retro fired for 10 seconds. One was sufficient to return the spacecraft to Earth if the other two failed. Between the heatshield and the cabin was an inflatable curtain that deployed just before the capsule to lessen the imipact at splashdown.

The recovery section held primary and reserve parachutes, a sound fixing and ranging (SOFAR) bomb to be dropped into the water to alert recovery ships, fluorescent green dye to stain the water around the vehicle, a communications antenna, and a flashing beacon and ultrahigh-frequency homing signal. The antenna canister contained high-frequency and ultrahigh-frequency antennae for communications from orbit, two horizon sensors, and a drogue parachute with two barostats (atmospheric pressure sensors) to trigger release. There was a small metal flap at the nose of the spacecraft called the "spoiler." If the spacecraft started to reenter nose-first (another stable reentry attitude for the capsule), airflow over the "spoiler" would flip the spacecraft around to the proper, heatshield-first reentry attitude.

The crew compartment was packed with equipment to keep the astronaut alive, functioning as the pilot, and able to communicate. Ceramic fiber insulation separated its titanium inner skin from its Rene-41 nickel alloy outer skin. The entrance was a rectangular hatch over the head and to the right of the single prone couch. The astronaut wore a pressure suit during flight, but the compartment also maintained breathable air and pressure with its Environmental Control System. The system cooled the suit and the compartment with water, supplied oxygen from two high-pressure tanks (each with enough for twenty-eight hours of operation), controlled air pressure and temperature, circulated air, and removed carbon dioxide by means of a canister of activated charcoal and lithium hydroxide.

The astronaut faced an instrument panel that gave him control over the capsule's environmental, communications, and guidance systems. The couch supported two hand controls. The left-hand control activated the abort sequence upon takeoff if the automatic system failed. The right-hand control maneuvered the capsule in outer space. The astronaut had drinking water available, and a hygienic urine collection system. Three pairs of 3,000-watt and 1,500-watt silver-zinc batteries provided electrical power. Specially designed sensors monitored the astronaut's vital signs, while one motion-picture camera recorded his face and another his actions on the instrument panel. A parabolic mirror on his chest permitted the viewing of the panel on the film. High-frequency and ultrahigh-frequency radios maintained communications with ground controllers and relayed telemetry while two radars provided navigational data.

Weight of the capsules varied somewhat with different Mercury missions; *Friendship 7*, the capsule in which astronaut John Glenn, Jr., orbited Earth three times, serves as an example. At launch with its escape tower attached, it weighed 1,932 kilograms, decreasing to about 1,360 kilograms in orbit, and just under 1,133 kilograms after landing. Following one failed launch attempt, there were five Mercury-Redstone missions (two robotic, one with a chimpanzee, and two piloted, all suborbital) and nine Mercury-Atlas missions (four robotic, one with a chimpanzee, and four piloted, the last six orbital). The final splashdown occurred on May 16, 1963. For an orbital mission, the Atlas booster lifted the spacecraft for about 2.5 minutes when it jettisoned its two outer booster engines. The spacecraft jettisoned its escape tower. After 5 minutes of flight, the Atlas's sustainer engine would shut down and the capsule separated from the booster. At mission's end, the astronaut pointed the capsule's heatshield in the direction of motion, fired the retrorockets, and jettisoned the retrograde package. Gravity pulled the craft down into the atmosphere, which slowed it. At an altitude of 10 kilometers, the drogue parachute deployed, followed by the main parachute at 3 kilometers. Just before hitting the ocean, the heatshield was released and the landing bag was extended for safe impact.

Contributions

The Mercury spacecraft began NASA's crusade to land Americans on the Moon. Not only was it a marked technological success for a first attempt at a spacecraft, but it gave astronauts nearly fifty-four hours of flight experience. That total pales next to the 13.5 days of flight experience accrued by Soviet cosmonauts aboard Russia's first spacecraft, Vostok, but Mercury permitted Americans to test much that the Russians could not.

First, cosmonauts were primarily passengers aboard Vostok, but American astronauts had actual control of their craft and could practice attitude control. This proved crucial, because during all six missions astronauts had to overcome malfunctions in the automated control system, and three of them had to position their spacecraft manually for reentry.

Second, the heavier Vostok came down for an Earth landing, requiring cosmonauts to eject beforehand and descend the last few thousand feet under separate parachute. Mercury proved the feasibility of a water landing to avoid risky ejections. While in orbit, astronauts performed more than two dozen scientific tasks involving Earth observations, photography, and radiation, proving that humans can work in microgravity. Furthermore, they established that humans can ingest nutrition, eliminate waste, and sleep while in orbit. The Mercury spacecraft showed that humans could live in space for short periods. A fact taken for granted today but was, at least for the general public, a serious concern at the time.

The capsule also proved the worth of ablative heatshields to protect the crew during reentry. The high-drag, low-lift conical hull design turned out to be reliable and stable in all environments. These flights gave engineers the opportunity to improve new technology, such as that of the medical sensors, and to develop the ground support system of flight controllers and the World-Wide Tracking Network.

Some design flaws, however, escaped notice. Most significant, Mercury astronauts breathed pure oxygen because it was simpler to supply than mixed gases. Pure oxygen is highly flammable, and its use on January 27, 1967, during the Apollo 1 mission contributed to the rapid spread of the fire in an accident that resulted in the deaths of all three astronauts on board.

Context

The United States was well behind in the Space Race when *Freedom 7* carried Alan Shepard, the first American in space, on a 15-minute suborbital flight on May 5, 1961. Cosmonaut Yuri Gagarin rode aboard *Vostok 1* on a one-orbit mission only three weeks earlier. The earlier launch of Sputnik 1 on October 4, 1957, and Gagarin's flight less than four years later had occurred during the height of the Cold War between the world's two superpowers: the United States, a democratic republic, and the Soviet Union, a totalitarian communist regime. Not long before, Americans had won the fight against totalitarian regimes during World War II by using the atomic bomb—only to see the rise of communism in the Soviet Union and the promise of its worldwide spread among developing nations.

Fear of communism and of Soviet military capability, especially in the post-atomic age, was as great or greater than fears of terrorism today. Soviet "firsts" in space—the first artificial satellite, Sputnik, and the first human in orbit around Earth, Gagarin—represented a Cold War victory and posed a true threat in the minds of American politicians and public alike. The sturdy little Mercury capsule gave Americans a much-need boost in prestige and morale. During dangerous Cold War tensions between the United States and Soviet Union, it showed that American technological ingenuity was equal to the challenge of space.

The success of the Mercury capsule also settled a political question within the American space community. Some engineers and scientists derided the Mercury program as "a man in a can"—an awkward, non-reusable ballistic projectile with limited maneuverability. Its chief competitor was the X-20 Dyna-Soar program, which sought to produce a reusable "space plane," something like a one-person space shuttle. Unlike the Mercury capsule, which was designed primarily with off-the-shelf components, the X-20 required development of many new technologies. That was expensive in both time and money. Secretary of Defense Robert McNamara decided that the country did not need parallel spacecraft development programs and in December of 1963 canceled the X-20 in favor of the proven capsule design.

Mercury therefore provided the basic configuration for the two-person Gemini spacecraft and the three-person Apollo craft that took Americans to the Moon. Its success also marked a turning point in favor of the United States during the Cold War Space Race.

—Roger Smith

See also: Apollo Program; Astronauts and the U.S. Astronaut Program; Atlas Launch Vehicles; Gemini Program; Gemini Spacecraft; Launch Vehicles; Mercury Project; Mercury Project Development; Mercury-Redstone 3; Mercury-Redstone 4; Mercury-Atlas 6; Mercury-Atlas 7; Mercury-Atlas 8; Mercury-Atlas 9; Space Shuttle: Ancestors.

Further Reading

Catchpole, John. *Project Mercury: NASA's First Manned Space Programme*. Chichester, England: Springer-Praxis, 2001. A thorough history of the Mercury program with several chapters, complemented by technical diagrams, concerning the capsule and its systems. The book also compares Mercury to the Russian Vostok and discusses subsequent American spacecraft designs.

Godwin, Robert, ed. *Friendship 7: The First Flight of John Glenn*. Burlington, Ont.: Apogee, 1999. A compendium of articles, graphics, photographs, and a CD-ROM with recordings of the television coverage of Glenn's mission. Two technically detailed chapters describe the Mercury capsule and its systems.

Swenson, Loyd S., Jr., James M. Grimwood, and Charles C. Alexander. *The New Ocean: A History of Project Mercury*. Washington, D.C.: National Aeronautics and Space Administration, 1998. A history of the Mercury program that focuses on the organizational structure and reviews individual missions. Of the book's three sections, one describes the development of the spacecraft. Also available online at the Project Mercury Web site, http://www.hq.nasa.gov/office/pao/History/SP-4201/toc.htm.

Mercury-Redstone 3

Date: May 5, 1961
Type of mission: Piloted spaceflight

Alan Shepard became the first American to reach space on Mercury-Redstone 3 in a 15- minute suborbital mission. In his Freedom 7 spacecraft, Shepard experienced five minutes of weightlessness. Although the United States was not the first country to put a human in space, Mercury-Redstone 3 gave President John F. Kennedy confidence to commit NASA to a lunar landing by the end of the decade.

Key Figures

Alan B. Shepard, Jr. (1923-1998), Mercury-Redstone 3 pilot

John H. Glenn, Jr. (1921-2016), Mercury- Redstone 3 backup pilot

Christopher C. Kraft, Jr. (b. 1924), assistant flight director, Flight Operations Division, NASA

James E. Webb (1906-1992), NASA administrator

Hugh L. Dryden (1898-1965), NASA deputy administrator

Robert R. Gilruth (1913-2000), director of the Space Task Group and Project Mercury manager

Maxime A. Faget (1921-2004), the spacecraft's designer

William K. Douglas, flight surgeon

Virgil I. "Gus" Grissom (1926-1967), astronaut

Donald K. "Deke" Slayton (1924-1993), astronaut

Summary of the Mission

On February 22, 1961, the Space Task Group revealed that three Mercury astronauts had been selected to begin concentrated training for piloted Mercury-Redstone (MR) suborbital flights. These three astronauts were Virgil I. "Gus" Grissom, Alan B. Shepard, Jr., and John H. Glenn, Jr. Although the identity of the prime pilot for MR-3 was kept secret, the astronauts themselves already knew who had won the competition to be first.

While the National Aeronautics and Space Administration (NASA) pressed forward to send one of these three humans into space, the Soviet Union orbited Yuri A. Gagarin in Vostok 1 on April 12, 1961. Losing the race into space to the Soviets was a bitter defeat for Project Mercury, but efforts were redoubled to proceed. NASA would not fly MR-3 until it was reasonably certain that both the booster and the spacecraft were ready to support a piloted mission safely.

Redstone number 7 was selected to support MR-3. The Mercury spacecraft to be used for this flight would not, however, incorporate all the changes the astronauts had requested. Spacecraft number 7 would have only a small porthole and periscope through which the astronaut would be able to view. The hatch was sealed by seventy bolts once the astronaut entered. Redstone number 7 arrived at Cape Canaveral in March, 1961; the spacecraft had been there since December 9, 1960.

The United States stood poised to enter space on May 2, 1961. Unlike the Soviets, the Americans planned to carry out their launch attempt before the eyes of the world. Newsprint, radio, and television reporters converged on the Cape to cover MR-3. The question asked most often concerned which astronaut would be making the flight. The announcement had been withheld in the event of a last-minute change. The weather was poor, and a hold was called at T minus 290 minutes when a storm broke out. Shepard and Glenn were awakened at 07:00

Coordinated Universal Time (UTC, or 2:00 a.m.) to eat breakfast, have a medical examination, and prepare for the flight. The press learned that Shepard had been selected as pilot and that Glenn was to be his backup. Shepard awaited a decision on weather for more than three hours while fully suited.

Shepard was born November 18, 1923, in East Derry, New Hampshire. He received his bachelor of science degree from the United States Naval Academy in 1944. As a naval aviator, Shepard ultimately achieved the rank of rear admiral in the Navy, and NASA selected him as one of the original seven Mercury astronauts in 1959. Following his MR-3 suborbital flight, Shepard served as backup pilot for Mercury-Atlas 9. He was then grounded from flight status because of an inner ear ailment. While grounded, until May 7, 1969, Shepard served as chief of the Astronaut Office. A successful ear operation restored Shepard to flight status, and he was assigned as commander of Apollo 14, becoming the only Mercury astronaut to walk on the Moon. From June, 1971, to August 1, 1974, Shepard resumed his post as chief astronaut. He retired from both NASA and the Navy. Shepard died July 22, 1998 after a long battle with leukemia. He was 74.

The May 2 launch attempt was scrubbed after a report of rain near the recovery area was made after 12:00 UTC (7:00 a.m.) A forty-eight-hour recycle was announced, but poor weather foiled a May 4 launch attempt. Countdown for the next attempt began at 01:30 UTC on May 5 (8:30 p.m. eastern daylight time on May 4). Shepard was awakened at 06:10 UTC (1:10 a.m.) on May 5. He showered and shaved before sharing a breakfast of orange juice, filet mignon, bacon, and scrambled eggs with Glenn

Astronaut Alan B. Shepard, Jr. sits in his Freedom 7 Mercury capsule, ready for launch. Just 23 days earlier, Soviet cosmonaut Yuri Gagarin had become the first man in space. (NASA)

and physician William K. Douglas. After a medical examination, biomedical sensors were attached to Shepard, and he donned his pressure suit. A transfer van transported Shepard, carrying a portable air conditioner, to the launch pad. At 10:15 UTC (5:15 a.m.), Shepard exited the van, briefly looked up at the Redstone booster, and entered the elevator to rise to the level of the spacecraft.

Shepard entered the spacecraft, which he had named *Freedom 7* (making allusions to the number of the booster, spacecraft, and Mercury astronauts), the hatch was bolted shut, and he began breathing pure oxygen. Weather conditions 15 minutes before scheduled launch were inadequate for proper photographic coverage, and a hold was called to await clearer skies. Meanwhile, a 115-volt, 400-hertz inverter was replaced on the Redstone. This hold ended after 52 minutes, and the countdown picked up at the T-minus-35-minute mark. At T-minus 15 minutes, a hold was again called, this time because of computer deficiencies at the Goddard Space Flight Center. This hold lasted 154 minutes. When the countdown resumed, it continued down to T-minus zero. Shepard had been inside *Freedom 7* for 4 hours and 14 minutes awaiting liftoff.

Astronauts L. Gordon Cooper, Jr., and Donald Slayton communicated with Shepard from the pad blockhouse and Mercury Control Center, respectively. Walter M. Schirra, Jr., flew overhead in an F-106 chase plane, ready to follow after MR-3. Glenn had helped prepare the spacecraft controls for Shepard, and Grissom served as the reserve pilot. Thus, although Shepard would fly the United States' first piloted spaceflight, MR-3 was an astronaut team effort.

As the firing command was given, Shepard's heart rate rose from 80 to 126 beats per minute. *Freedom 7* rose from the launch pad at 14:34 UTC (9:34 a.m.), and for the first 45 seconds of powered flight the ride was smooth. As *Freedom 7* passed into the transonic zone, aerodynamic buffeting vibrated the vehicle. Maximum dynamic pressure (3.8 pounds per square inch) was encountered 88 seconds after liftoff at an altitude of 10.6 kilometers. Shepard was shaken so violently that he was unable to read his instruments. After becoming supersonic, the vibration levels quickly diminished.

Shepard experienced 6 gravitational loads (6 Gs) two minutes after liftoff. T plus 142 seconds and at an altitude of 59 kilometers, the Redstone engine shut down. Ten seconds later, the spacecraft/booster clamp ring was released. A trio of solid-fueled posigrade rockets (rockets that increase the speed of a spacecraft, thus placing it in a higher orbit) at the back of *Freedom 7* (each packing 160 kilograms of thrust) pushed it free of the booster. The launch escape tower's jettison motor fired, pulling the tower safely away from *Freedom 7*. Shepard attempted in vain to watch the separation through the spacecraft porthole.

The Redstone booster accelerated *Freedom 7* to a speed of 8,214 kilometers per hour. Outside the spacecraft, the temperature was 104° Celsius; inside it was 32.8°, and Shepard's suit temperature was a comfortable 24°. Cabin pressure stabilized at 5.5 pounds per square inch. Shepard extended the periscope while the Automatic Stabilization Control System (ASCS) turned *Freedom 7* around so that it was flying heatshield first; oscillations were damped by ASCS thruster firings. Shepard performed pitch, yaw, and roll movements of the hand control stick, while *Freedom 7* was still under automatic control, to familiarize himself with the handling characteristics. He then switched to manual control and performed these movements one axis at a time, at no time moving more than 20° on a single axis.

Shepard had become weightless at booster burnout, but he experienced no debilitating symptoms, and he could read instruments and make limited movements allowed by his restrictive space suit. Shepard's vision was unimpaired; he was able to view Earth through his periscope. Unfortunately, Shepard had forgotten to remove a gray filter (used prior to liftoff to minimize glare) from the periscope, although he was able to distinguish clearly between cloud cover and landmasses, seeing first the west coast of Florida and the Gulf of Mexico and later Lake Okeechobee and the Bahamas.

Shortly after *Freedom 7* had achieved a maximum altitude of 186.4 kilometers, the retrofire sequence was initiated. (Since the spacecraft followed a ballistic trajectory, retrofire was unnecessary. However, this was a good test of the system under piloted flight conditions.) Shepard had pitched the spacecraft up to the 34° retroattitude, and a trio of retrorockets fired in turn for 10 seconds apiece, each burn overlapping the previous one by 5 seconds, to reduce spacecraft speed by 560 kilometers per hour. The retropack was held in place by a trio of steel straps equipped with explosive bolts so that the pack could be jettisoned. When retro-pack jettison was executed, Shepard heard a thud but saw no pack jettison light indication on the instrument panel. Astronaut Slayton informed Shepard that telemetry indicated retro-pack jettison. Shepard could see pieces of the pack and straps passing by his porthole, and switching to manual override, he got a green retro-pack jettison light.

The periscope was retracted when *Freedom 7* was restored to automatic control for the reentry phase. Shepard performed a dexterity test and vainly attempted to see stars through the porthole. At T plus 490 seconds, Shepard set up a two-revolution-per-minute roll to minimize landing dispersions. Deceleration was rapid and loads quickly reached 11.6 G. Shepard strained to make his voice communications readable but withstood the crushing force of reentry.

The drogue parachute mortar fired at an altitude of 6.4 kilometers at T plus 570 seconds. Four seconds later, the ambient air snorkel opened, and through his periscope Shepard could see the drogue parachute. Passing 3 kilometers altitude at T plus 600 seconds, the main parachute deployed. When fully blossomed, the parachute lowered *Freedom 7* to the water at a gentle 10 meters per second. *Freedom 7* splashed down 128 kilometers east-northeast of Grand Bahama Island, only 11.2 kilometers off target, at 14:49 UTC (9:49 a.m.) Within five minutes a Marine helicopter recovered *Freedom 7* from the water and transported Shepard and the spacecraft to the deck of the USS *Lake Champlain*.

Contributions

Gathering biomedical data on human response to spaceflight stresses and engineering data on the

Mercury-Redstone 3 (MR-3) spaceflight Earth observations of a cloudy Earth surface. (NASA)

Mercury-Redstone spacecraft-booster combination was the primary goal of MR-3. The ability of Astronaut Shepard to perform specific tasks during the flight and his usefulness as a pilot were carefully monitored and assessed after the flight. On June 6, 1961, a conference was held in the U.S. Department of State Auditorium by NASA in cooperation with the National Institutes of Health and the National Academy of Sciences to report the results of MR-3 investigations. This scientific meeting was open to both U.S. and foreign scientists.

Bioinstrumentation for real-time monitoring of pilot physiological responses during test flights had to be specially developed for Project Mercury. Biosensors to measure and record body temperature, respiratory activity, and heart rate were perfected for use on MR-3. (Blood pressure measurements were taken on later Mercury flights.) These sensors, attached directly to Shepard's body, did not interfere with his responsibilities as a pilot.

Shepard's vital signs were determined eight hours before flight. His body weight was 76.9 kilograms, rectal temperature was 37.2° Celsius, respiration rate was 16 breaths per minute, heart rate was 68 beats per minute, and blood pressure was 120 over 78 while he was seated. Shepard was given another physical examination on the USS *Lake Champlain* immediately following recovery, at which time his body weight was 76 kilograms, rectal temperature was 37.9° Celsius, pulse was 100 beats per minute, and blood pressure was 130 over 84 while seated. Three hours after the mission had ended, Shepard's status was measured on Grand Bahama Island. At this time Shepard's body weight was 75.6 kilograms, oral temperature was 36.7° Celsius, respiration rate was 20 breaths per minute, heart rate was 76 beats per minute, and blood pressure was 102 over 74 while standing and 100 over 76 while supine. Shepard performed programmed activities during the flight without major difficulty. He suffered no apparent physiological or psychological abnormalities as a result of his exposure to launch and reentry stresses and a brief spell of weightlessness (4 minutes and 45 seconds). There were no medical indications from MR-3 that would preclude American piloted orbital missions. Shepard's only medical complaint was that biomedical sensors caused minor skin irritations. Different adhesives were used on subsequent flights.

Spacecraft environmental control systems maintained comfortable space suit and cabin conditions. Shepard's suit temperature varied between 23.6 and 27.8° Celsius; the cabin temperature, between 33.3 and 37.8°. Only a portion of the available oxygen supply had been used, and there was an adequate cooling supply.

Shepard exercised all three methods of spacecraft control: automatic, manual, and fly-by-wire (a combination of manual and automatic). Manual control was very responsive, behaving similarly to procedures during training simulations except for a tendency toward a slight roll clockwise, which was caused by a tiny thrust expelled from leaky hydrogen peroxide thrusters. The ASCS consumed more fuel than desired when Shepard apparently forgot to turn off a manually controlled fuel-flow valve after he had switched to the automatic control mode. Attitude control and stabilization were maintained as desired with interactions between spacecraft, Mission Control, and the astronaut pilot.

Context

On May 5, 1986, five of the original seven Mercury astronauts and the wife of the late Virgil I. "Gus" Grissom were reunited in Los Angeles, California, for a celebration of the twenty-fifth anniversary of *Freedom 7*. The celebration overshadowed the difficulties faced by NASA in the wake of the accident of the space shuttle *Challenger*. Shepard, then fifty-two and a successful Houston businessman, was especially honored as the first American astronaut into space. Looking at the flight of MR-3 retrospectively after more than a quarter-century of piloted spaceflight, which has included such impressive space achievements as Apollo Moonlandings, Skylab and Salyut long-duration flights, and space shuttle missions, Shepard's 15-minute suborbital arc down the Atlantic Missile Range at first glance seems more like a spectacular stunt than an important milestone in space travel. Such an appraisal, however, clearly fails to recognize the proper place that *Freedom 7* deserves in the history of both the United States and piloted spaceflight.

The *Freedom 7* mission occurred on the heels of several politically embarrassing incidents for the fledgling Kennedy administration, including the Bay of Pigs fiasco. While the United States was still suffering fear and humiliation over the Soviet launching of Sputnik forty-two months earlier, the Soviets put the first human into space, Yuri A. Gagarin. The *Freedom 7* mission had several profound effects within the United States. First, it provided a renewed sense of national pride. Second, it served to crystallize support for NASA's plans for goals beyond Project Mercury. Third, it was used to illustrate the difference between the open society of the United States and the secrecy surrounding the Soviet space program. Fourth, it demonstrated to the nation and the rest of the world that the American program was not discouraged by its late entry into the Space Age and was capable of competing with the Soviets in the area of spaceflight.

Shepard was honored in Washington, D.C., on May 8, 1961, with a parade along Pennsylvania Avenue and a ceremony in the White House Rose Garden, where he received NASA's Distinguished Service Medal from President Kennedy. *Freedom 7* and Shepard drew headlines all over the world, much to the surprise and chagrin of Soviet premier Nikita Khrushchev, considering that the American suborbital mission occurred weeks after Gagarin had actually orbited Earth. *Freedom 7* gave the Kennedy administration confidence to propose a bold new initiative in an attempt to elevate the United States into a position of leadership in spaceflight, as well as a strong indication that both the American people and Congress would support and finance the effort. President Kennedy spoke before Congress on May 25, 1961, and publicly committed NASA to a piloted lunar landing before the end of the decade—effectively challenging the Soviets to a race to the Moon. This bold step was made before an American had even orbited the Earth.

By the fiftieth anniversary of *Freedom 7* (2011) only two of the original Mercury astronauts were still alive. Shepard was not one of them as he had passed away in 1998 from complications from a valiant struggle with leukemia. NASA used the historic importance of the first American in space to draw attention to space exploration. However, with the rise of commercial launch services which were intended to retrieve and reuse rockets in an attempt to lower the cost of putting payloads into space, the Shepard legacy was honored in a different manner. Jeff Bezos, CEO of Amazon.com, founded Blue Origin, a company dedicated to commercial space opportunities. One of its first major developments was the New Shepard rocket designed to provide reusable suborbital launch services for both payloads and paying tourists. The rocket was fully reusable and landed on legs, the capsule at the top of the rocket would be recovered on land by a parachute system. The first New Shepard rocket launched on April 29, 2015. A first crewed flight is anticipated as early as late 2019.

—David G. Fisher

See also: Mercury Project; Mercury Spacecraft; Mercury-Redstone 4; Space Shuttle Flights, January- June, 1985.

Further Reading

Carpenter, M. Scott, L. Gordon Cooper, et al. *We Seven, by the Astronauts Themselves.* New York: Simon & Schuster, 1962. Written by the astronauts in conjunction with the staff of *Life* magazine, this book portrays the original Mercury astronauts the way they were, and still are, revered. Fascinating reading. Includes photographs.

Glenn, John, with Nick Taylor. *John Glenn: A Memoir.* New York: Bantam Books, 1999. Glenn covers his career from his days as a Marine pilot through his Mercury-Atlas 6 orbital mission to his flight aboard STS-95 in 1998.

Godwin, Robert, ed. *Freedom 7: The NASA Mission Reports.* Burlington, Ont.: Apogee Books, 2001. Some of the rare official documentation of the voyage of *Freedom 7* is collected and made available for the first time. Included are the Mercury-Redstone 3 press kit, the complete text of "Results of the First United States Manned Suborbital Space Flight," and the "Invitation to Apply for Position of Research Astronaut-Candidate," NASA's presentation of the qualifications for the position of Mercury astronaut.

Grimwood, James M. *Project Mercury: A Chronology*. NASA SP-4001. Washington, D.C.: Government Printing Office, 1963. This book chronologically traces the general developments of piloted spaceflight capability, research and development of Project Mercury, and the operational phase of Project Mercury. Includes numerous diagrams, photographs, charts, and eight appendices that are key to a complete understanding of Mercury's achievements.

Kraft, Christopher C., Jr. *Flight: My Life in Mission Control*. East Rutherford, N.J.: Penguin Putnam, 2002. The first NASA flight director gives an account of his life in Mission Control.

McDonnell Astronautics Company. *Project Mercury Familiarization Manual*. SEDR 104. St. Louis: Author, 1961. Once classified, this contractor document provides the most detailed description available of the Mercury spacecraft and its systems. Contains structural diagrams, block diagrams, wiring diagrams, and photographs. For the serious researcher.

National Aeronautics and Space Administration. *The Mercury-Redstone Project*. TMX-53107. Huntsville, Ala.: Marshall Space Flight Center, 1964. Reports in a single volume a complete history of Redstone's development for robotic, chimpanzee, and piloted Mercury suborbital spaceflights. Highly technical, providing flight data in chart, graph, and tabular forms.

National Aeronautics and Space Administration, with the National Institutes of Health and the National Academy of Sciences. *Proceedings of the Conference on the Results of the First U.S. Manned Suborbital Spaceflight*. Washington, D.C.: Government Printing Office, 1961. Proceedings of a conference held on June 6, 1961. Provides a summary of Project Mercury, *Freedom 7*'s biomedical data, pilot training and evaluation of pilot in-flight performance, and Shepard's flight report. Includes charts, diagrams, tables, and photographs.

Olney, Ross R. *Americans in Space: A History of Manned Space Travel*. Rev. ed. Nashville, Tenn.: Thomas Nelson, 1973. This volume includes general summaries of American spaceflights from *Freedom 7* through Apollo 13. Perfect for younger readers and novices. Contains photographs, appendices, and a glossary, as well as numerous quotations from mission air-to-ground conversations.

Shepard, Alan B., Jr., and Donald K. "Deke" Slayton, with Jay Barbree and Howard Benedict. *Moon Shot: The Inside Story of America's Race to the Moon*. Atlanta: Turner, 1994. This is, indeed, the inside story of the Apollo Program as told by two men who actively participated in it. Some of their tales appear here for the first time. Shepard and Slayton discuss Shepard's Mercury-Redstone 3 suborbital flight and tell some little-known secrets of the Mercury astronauts. The book was adapted for a four-hour documentary in 1995.

Silverberg, Robert. *First American into Space*. Derby, Conn.: Monarch Books, 1961. Published shortly after Mercury-Redstone 3, this paperback book demonstrates the American people's reaction to Shepard's historic flight, one of relief and pride. Details the flight of *Freedom 7* and provides personal biographies of astronauts Shepard, Grissom, and Glenn.

Slayton, Donald K., with Michael Cassutt. *Deke! U.S. Manned Space: From Mercury to the Shuttle*. New York: Forge, 1995. This is the autobiography of the last of the Mercury astronauts to fly in space. After being grounded from flying in Project Mercury for what turned out to be a minor heart murmur, Slayton was appointed head of the Astronaut Office. Slayton talks of his frustration at being grounded and how he worked to regain flight status. He also discusses the flights of his fellow Mercury astronauts.

Swenson, Loyd S., Jr., James M. Grimwood, and Charles C. Alexander. *This New Ocean: A History of Project Mercury*. NASASP-4201. Washington, D.C.: Government Printing Office, 1966. An excellent NASA History series text, providing a fascinating report of research and development, management, and flight operations of Project Mercury. Extensive photographs, appendices, and references are included. An important reference for serious spaceflight researchers.

Thompson, Neal. *Light This Candle: The Life and Times of Alan Shepard—America's First Spaceman*. New York: Crown Publishing Group, 2004. This account of Shepard's life is based on Thompson's exclusive access to private papers and interviews with Shepard's family and closest friends—including John H. Glenn, Jr., Walter M. Schirra, Jr., and L. Gordon Cooper, Jr.

Wendt, Guenter, and Russell Still. *The Unbroken Chain*. Burlington, Ont.: Apogee Books, 2001. Wendt is the only person who worked with every astronaut bound for space.

Mercury-Redstone 4

Date: July 21, 1961
Type of mission: Piloted spaceflight

The flight of Liberty Bell 7, Mercury-Redstone 4, ended Project Mercury's suborbital test program. Astronaut Gus Grissom duplicated the successful suborbital profile flown by Alan Shepard in Freedom 7. Although Liberty Bell 7 sank after the spacecraft hatch blew off prematurely, Grissom was safely recovered.

Key Figures

Virgil I. "Gus" Grissom (1926-1967), Mercury-Redstone 4 pilot

John H. Glenn, Jr. (1921-2016), Mercury-Redstone 4 backup pilot

Christopher C. Kraft, Jr. (b. 1924), assistant flight director, Flight Operations Division

James E. Webb (1906-1992), NASA administrator

Hugh L. Dryden (1898-1965), NASA deputy administrator

Robert R. Gilruth (1913-2000), director of the Space Task Group and Project Mercury manager

Maxime A. Faget (1921-2004), spacecraft designer

William K. Douglas, astronaut and flight surgeon

Alan B. Shepard, Jr. (1923-1998), astronaut

Donald K. "Deke" Slayton (1924-1993), astronaut

Summary of the Mission

The National Aeronautics and Space Administration (NASA) announced in early July, 1961, that Air Force Captain Virgil I. "Gus" Grissom had been selected as the primary pilot for Mercury-Redstone 4 (MR-4), the United States' second suborbital flight. Marine Lieutenant Colonel John H. Glenn, Jr., would serve as backup pilot for Grissom, as he had for Shepard's Mercury-Redstone 3 flight in May, 1961. Launch of MR-4 was originally scheduled for July 18, 1961.

Grissom was born April 3, 1926, in Mitchell, Indiana. He earned a bachelor of science degree in mechanical engineering from Purdue University in 1950. As a military pilot, Grissom ultimately achieved the rank of lieutenant colonel in the Air Force. NASA selected Grissom as one of the original seven Mercury astronauts in 1959. Grissom, in addition to his *Liberty Bell 7* suborbital flight, later flew as command pilot of Gemini 3 and served as backup command pilot for Gemini VI. Assigned as commander of the first piloted Apollo flight, Grissom perished in the Apollo 204 flash fire on Pad 34 at Cape Kennedy on January 27, 1967.

Meteorological forecasts for July 18 predicted cloud coverage that would have severely hindered optical coverage of the launch vehicle during ascent. A one-day delay in launch was ordered. On July 19, however, clouds and precipitation postponed the launch once more. MR-4 was rescheduled for July 21. The two-day delay was ordered because the Redstone booster's liquid oxygen supply had to be removed and its cryogenic tanks purged and dried before the next launch attempt.

Grissom was awakened at 06:10 Coordinated Universal Time (UTC, or 1:10 a.m. eastern standard time) on the morning of the launch. Within an hour, he had eaten breakfast and had been given a physical examination. After suiting up, Grissom was driven to the launch pad. He climbed into Mercury spacecraft number 11, which he had named *Liberty Bell 7*, at 08:58 UTC (3:58 a.m.) Grissom would wait nearly three and a half hours inside the spacecraft before lifting off.

Mercury spacecraft number 11 incorporated a number of new innovations, encouraged by the astronauts themselves, which Shepard's spacecraft did not have. The two most important changes were the inclusion of a new trapezoidal window, which greatly increased the pilot's viewing ability, and an explosive hatch, which greatly reduced the problem of exiting the spacecraft after splashdown. Originally, egress from the Mercury spacecraft was through the antenna compartment, a procedure requiring removal of a pressure bulkhead. This maneuver proved difficult for the astronauts and would be disadvantageous in the event the astronaut was injured or disabled, for the only alternative route to the pilot required external removal of seventy bolts around the hatch.

Weather was favorable during the early morning hours of July 21. The countdown proceeded without delay from T minus 180 minutes to T minus 45 minutes. Proper installation of a misaligned hatch bolt forced a 30-minute hold, and at T minus 30 minutes, the countdown held for 9 minutes while pad searchlights, which interfered with Redstone telemetry during launch, were turned off. The final hold, 41 minutes in duration, was called at T-minus 15 minutes as Mission Control waited for better cloud cover conditions to prevail. The countdown resumed, and MR-4 lifted off the pad at 12:20 UTC (7:20 a.m.).

Proper flight path angle was maintained by the Redstone control system during ascent. As the vehicle entered the transonic region at an altitude of 11 kilometers, Grissom experienced less noise and vibration than Shepard reported at the similar point in his flight. (Damping material and alternate

Astronaut Virgil I. Grissom climbs into "Liberty Bell 7" spacecraft the morning of July 21, 1961. (NASA)

aerodynamic bearings had been added to *Liberty Bell 7* to reduce these vibrations.) Grissom was able to read his instruments clearly and communicate with Mission Control. Pausing briefly to peer out the window, he saw nothing but blue sky above him. The vehicle had just passed through a thin layer of clouds. Grissom later reported that the sky had turned from a beautiful blue to pitch black in a matter of seconds; shortly after, he was able to see a star.

The Redstone engine cut off at T plus 2 minutes, 23 seconds. At the same time, the escape tower clamp ring was released and both the escape and tower jettison rockets fired. The gravitational force

(g) of six times Earth's gravity was suddenly replaced by weightlessness. Grissom saw two streams of smoke pass by his window and the launch escape tower off to the right of the spacecraft. Ten seconds after booster burnout, the spacecraft's booster adapter clamp ring separated, and posigrade rockets fired to separate *Liberty Bell 7* from the spent Redstone. The spacecraft automatic stabilization and control system provided five seconds of rate damping and turned the spacecraft around to its flight attitude of −34° with respect to the horizon.

Grissom then assumed manual control of *Liberty Bell 7*'s attitude at T plus 3 minutes, 5 seconds. He performed pitch and yaw movements to check out the manual proportional control system, dividing his attention between looking out the window and controlling the spacecraft. Grissom yawed to the left to view the coast of Florida. Alan Shepard, serving as capsule communicator, reminded Grissom to return to retroattitude. Retrofire sequence was initiated by a timer, and thirty seconds later, *Liberty Bell 7* reached its maximum altitude, 188.8 kilometers.

When the retrorocket firing sequence began, Grissom keenly perceived their effect. Until retrofire he had had the distinct feeling that he was flying backward. (The heatshield pointed near the direction of the spacecraft velocity vector.) After retrofire he experienced a sensation as though he had changed direction and was now flying forward. Actually, what Grissom felt was a reduction in his retrograde motion. He controlled spacecraft attitude within proper limits during retrofire, and after T plus 5 minutes, 43 seconds, he manipulated the spacecraft attitude by using the manual rate command system. *Liberty Bell 7*'s retropack was jettisoned at T plus 6 minutes, 7 seconds.

Grissom switched from ultrahigh-frequency to high-frequency radio systems. He attempted to inform Mission Control about the tremendous view he saw but was unable to establish radio contact. Failing on the high-frequency wavelength, Grissom returned to the ultrahigh-frequency wavelength;

glancing down into the periscope, he was able to see the retropack floating away from the spacecraft. The spacecraft was pitched to the 14° reentry attitude. Loads on *Liberty Bell 7* increased as it plunged through the upper atmosphere. Eventually Grissom experienced 10.2g, slightly less than what Shepard had been subjected to aboard *Freedom 7*.

At an altitude of 20 kilometers, Grissom reported being able to see white, wispy contrails. The drogue parachute deployed to stabilize the spacecraft. The main parachute was deployed 33 seconds later at an altitude of 3,300 meters. Grissom watched the main parachute blossom into its full shape, noting a small triangular rip and a quarter-sized hole as its only imperfections. Through his periscope, Grissom could see the Atlantic Ocean's surface rapidly approaching and prepared for impact. Splashdown came at T plus 15 minutes, 37 seconds. Grissom had traveled 785 kilometers (488 miles) down the Atlantic Missile Range from liftoff to splashdown. He had been weightless for 5 minutes and 18 seconds, 37 seconds longer than Shepard.

Splashdown imposed no excessive loads on the spacecraft, and *Liberty Bell 7* tipped over on its left side. The parachute compartment, heavily laden with Grissom's reserve parachute, dropped below the water level. Grissom waited until the reserve chute package popped above the water and then ejected it. Thirty seconds later, the spacecraft turned itself to an upright position. Waves were gentle, and Grissom was in good shape and in contact with recovery helicopters. Meanwhile, Grissom disconnected his suit attachments, except for an inlet hose that provided cooling, disconnected his helmet, and rolled up the suit's neck dam. He then began reading the items on his post-splashdown switch checklist. As a recovery helicopter closed in on *Liberty Bell 7*, Grissom removed the cover on the detonator for the explosive bolts on the hatch and pulled out the safety pin. (To activate the explosive hatch, a plunger off the astronaut's right shoulder had to be pulled.) Grissom sat back and awaited instructions from the recovery helicopter.

Unexpectedly, the spacecraft hatch blew off. Grissom, seeing water pouring in through the open hatch sill, instinctively removed his helmet, grabbed the instrument panel, and thrust himself into the water. With his suit neck dam up, Grissom would have been able to float easily. Unfortunately, he failed to close one suit port, through which water entered. The helicopter crew grappled the loop on top of the spacecraft, but *Liberty Bell 7* filled with water. The recovery helicopter, unable to keep *Liberty Bell 7* afloat, cut its attachment line loose, allowing the spacecraft to sink in deep ocean water. Recovery forces turned their attention now to Grissom, who was struggling to stay afloat because of excess water in his suit. A horse collar was then dropped to Grissom, and he was extracted from the ocean and flown to the recovery vessel USS *Randolph*.

When *Liberty Bell 7* was retrieved from the ocean floor in 1999, it was hoped that the question of how the hatch blew would be answered. The hatch was not recovered. It should be noted that all of the pilots after Grissom bruised their hands blowing their hatch of the spacecraft. There were no bruises on Grissom's hands.

Contributions

Because of the brevity of the mission, there were no purely scientific investigations included in the flight plan; all knowledge gained on MR-4 was biomedical or engineering in nature. Grissom was assigned fewer spacecraft tasks to perform than Shepard so that he could use more time for observations through his trapezoidal window.

Apart from feeling somewhat tired and having a mild sore throat, Grissom was in excellent shape after his flight. His first post-flight examination was conducted on the USS *Randolph*, 15 minutes after splashdown. Grissom appeared tired and breathed heavily, which could have been attributed to his ordeal in the water following splashdown. After a brief nap and a breakfast meal, Grissom was flown to Grand Bahama Island for more tests. Three hours

after splashdown, his appearance and vital signs were much improved, and he was subjected to more medical, psychological, and neurological examinations over the next forty-eight hours. As a result of the medical evaluations, a number of conclusions were reached. Grissom was in good health both before and after MR-4, and his immediate post-flight examination results were consistent with exertion and exposure to salt water. No specific functional abnormality was found to be attributable to spaceflight stresses, and there were no biochemical alterations.

The flight profiles of MR-3 and MR-4 were quite similar, but Redstone performance differed slightly. Grissom's Redstone engine burned 0.3 second in excess of prediction, which pushed the craft 4.8 kilometers higher and 14.4 kilometers farther downrange than scheduled. Shepard's Redstone engine burned a half second short of schedule.

The loss of the spacecraft forced a review of Mercury recovery plans. Navy and Marine recovery forces expressed a need for checklists with specific detailed recovery functions and responsibilities. Use of larger, more powerful helicopters, availability of flotation gear for helicopters, and use of flotation collars to be attached by frogmen to the spacecraft were given consideration for future Mercury flights as a result of the MR-4 experience. *Liberty Bell 7* need not have been lost. The recovery helicopter crew cast the spacecraft loose when a warning light indicated overheating of the helicopter's engines. Later examination revealed no problem with the engines; the warning light was faulty.

Although there was no official NASA or military recovery effort for the lost $2 million spacecraft, in 1999 a salvage expedition sponsored by cable television's Discovery Channel successfully retrieved *Liberty Bell 7* from the ocean floor. The spacecraft, which was moved to the Kansas Cosmosphere and Space Center in Hutchinson, Kansas, has been restored for public display.

Context

NASA's Project Mercury was a measured response to the perceived and very real potential of the Soviet Union to place the first human in space. This suspicion was largely based on the heavier lift capability of existing Soviet boosters, as proved by some of the early Sputnik launches. The Atlas intercontinental ballistic missile (ICBM), already in development, was selected to place Mercury astronauts into orbit. Recognizing that the Mercury-Atlas (MA) rocket would not be safe and reliable until mid-to-late 1961, NASA pursued a parallel program to gain piloted spaceflight operational status as early as possible, in order to beat Soviet cosmonauts into space. This parallel program, Mercury-Redstone (MR), used a modified Redstone intermediate range ballistic missile (IRBM) as a booster to propel the Mercury spacecraft at suborbital speeds on ballistic arcs originating at Cape Canaveral and terminating with a splashdown in the Atlantic Ocean. MR-4 was the last mission of the MR program. In mid-August, 1961, NASA announced that additional planned piloted suborbital flights would be canceled. Spacecraft number 15 and 16, originally manufactured for two extra MR flights, were diverted to the Mercury-Atlas program. NASA said all MR program test objectives had been achieved with the conclusion of MR-4, *Liberty Bell 7*.

MR-1 was a miserably disappointing failure. When ignition was commanded on November 21, 1960, a cloud of smoke surrounded the launch pad and a piece of hardware accelerated rapidly through that cloud. Only the Mercury capsule's launch escape tower had lifted off. The parachute canister popped off and the parachutes were ejected, yet both the booster and the spacecraft remained fixed to the pad. The capsule was repaired and given a new booster, parachute compartment, and launch escape tower. MR-1A was successfully launched on December 19, 1960. Although experiencing slight over-acceleration, the spacecraft demonstrated the entire suborbital flight profile.

MR-2 was launched on January 21, 1961, with a chimpanzee named Ham as its passenger. Ham was a biomedical test specimen to collect data on the effects of weightlessness and launch and reentry stresses. He was subjected to as much as 18g when the launch vehicle followed a steeper flight path than desired, resulting in abort conditions. Ham reached an apogee of 251 kilometers and landed down range 77 kilometers farther than planned; he was not injured during this severe Mercury spacecraft test.

These two MR flights experienced Redstone booster over-accelerations. At the suggestion of Wernher von Braun, another robotic MR flight test using a boilerplate Mercury spacecraft was inserted into the program schedule before attempting a piloted MR flight. Designated MR-BD, this test took place on March 24, 1961. The design changes to correct the over-acceleration problem also corrected booster performance, clearing the way for piloted Mercury suborbital flights.

Before Project Mercury could launch astronauts, the Soviet Union sent a man, Yuri A. Gagarin, into Earth orbit. Nevertheless, Project Mercury proceeded with a pair of piloted suborbital flights, MR-3 and MR-4. Despite these successes, the disparity between Mercury and Vostok was underscored when Cosmonaut Gherman Titov spent a full day in space later in 1961.

—*David G. Fisher*

See also: Gemini 3; Mercury Project; Mercury-Redstone 3. Mercury-Redstone 4 919

Further Reading

Carpenter, M. Scott, L. Gordon Cooper, Jr., et al. *We Seven, by the Astronauts Themselves*. New York: Simon and Schuster, 1962. Written by the astronauts in conjunction with the staff of *Life* magazine, this book portrays the original Mercury astronauts the way they were and continue to be revered. Includes photographs.

Glenn, John, with Nick Taylor. *John Glenn: A Memoir*. New York: Bantam Books, 1999. Glenn tells his life story in this well-written and very interesting autobiography. The book covers his career from his days as a Marine pilot, through his Mercury-Atlas 6 orbital mission, and onward to his flight aboard STS-95 in 1998. In between, he was a husband, a father, and a senator from Ohio. He talks about the flight of *Liberty Bell 7* and his participation as backup pilot.

Grimwood, James M. *Project Mercury: A Chronology*. NASA SP-4001. Washington, D.C.: Government Printing Office, 1963. Chronologically traces general developments of piloted spaceflight capability, the research and development of Project Mercury, and the operational phase of Project Mercury. Numerous diagrams, photographs, and charts. Includes eight appendices essential to a total understanding of Mercury's achievement.

Kraft, Christopher C., Jr. *Flight: My Life in Mission Control*. East Rutherford, N.J.: Penguin Putnam, 2002. The first NASA flight director gives an account of his life in Mission Control.

National Aeronautics and Space Administration, Manned Spacecraft Center. *Results of the Second U.S. Manned Suborbital Space Flight, July 21, 1961*. Washington, D.C.: Government Printing Office, 1961. Provides a summary of Project Mercury, *Liberty Bell 7* biomedical data, pilot training and evaluation of pilot in-flight performance, and Grissom's flight report. Charts, diagrams, tables, and photographs.

Newport, Curt. *Lost Spacecraft: The Search for Liberty Bell 7*. Burlington, Ont.: Apogee Books, 2002. Focuses on two periods, one beginning in 1959, the other in 1985, interweaving the stories of Grissom and his Mercury flight with Curt Newport's fourteen-year quest to raise *Liberty Bell 7* from the depths of the Atlantic Ocean.

Shepard, Alan B., Jr., and Donald K. "Deke" Slayton, with Jay Barbree and Howard Benedict. *Moon Shot: The Inside Story of America's Race to the Moon*. Atlanta: Turner, 1994. This is, indeed, the inside story of the Apollo Program as told by two men who actively participated in it. Some of their tales appear here for the first time. Shepard and Slayton discuss Shepard's Mercury-Redstone 3 suborbital flight and tell some little-known secrets of the Mercury astronauts. The book was adapted for a four-hour documentary in 1995.

Silverberg, Robert. *First American into Space*. Derby, Conn.: Monarch Books, 1961. Published shortly after Mercury-Redstone 3, this paperback book demonstrates the American people's response to the United States' first steps in space: one of relief and pride. Although it details the flight of *Freedom 7*, the book provides personal biographies of astronauts Shepard, Grissom, and Glenn.

Slayton, Donald K., with Michael Cassutt. *Deke! U.S. Manned Space: From Mercury to the Shuttle*. New York: Forge, 1995. This is the autobiography of the last of the Mercury astronauts to fly in space. After being grounded from flying in Project Mercury for what turned out to be a minor heart murmur, Slayton was appointed head of the Astronaut Office. Slayton talks of his frustration at being grounded and how he worked to regain flight status. He also discusses the flights of his fellow Mercury astronauts.

Swenson, Loyd S., Jr., James M. Grimwood, and Charles C. Alexander. *This New Ocean: A History of Project Mercury*. NASASP-4201. Washington, D.C.: Government Printing Office, 1966. Excellent NASA History series text. Fascinating report of research and development, management, and flight operations of Project Mercury. Extensive photographs, appendices, and references. An essential reference for serious spaceflight researchers.

Wendt, Guenter, and Russell Still. *The Unbroken Chain*. Burlington, Ont.: Apogee Books, 2001. Wendt is the only person who worked with every astronaut bound for space.

Mercury-Atlas 6

Date: February 20, 1962
Type of mission: Piloted spaceflight

The Mercury-Atlas 6 (MA-6) mission, better known as the flight of Friendship 7, was the United States' first piloted Earth-orbiting flight. John H. Glenn, Jr., the astronaut on board, proved that humans could work in a microgravity environment and that the Mercury spacecraft design was sound.

Key Figures

John H. Glenn, Jr. (b. 1921-2016), Mercury-Atlas 6 pilot, the first American to fly in Earth orbit

M. Scott Carpenter (1925-2013), Mercury-Atlas 6 backup pilot

Robert R. Gilruth (1913-2000), manager, Project Mercury

Christopher C. Kraft, Jr. (b. 1924), flight director

Walter C. Williams (1919-1995), mission director

William M. Bland, Jr., the chief designer of the capsule

Summary of the Mission

Until 1962, the United States had been second to the Soviet Union in the international Space Race. The Soviets, after orbiting the world's first satellite and sending the first probe to the Moon, captured the imagination of millions with the first piloted orbital mission. Yuri A. Gagarin became instantly famous after his one-orbit mission, which was soon upstaged by Gherman Titov's seventeen-orbit flight. By the end of 1961, the Soviets had accumulated more than twenty-seven hours of flight time, the Americans a scant thirty-one minutes. (Actually, the chimpanzee Enos flew a two-orbit Mercury mission in November, 1961. This event prompted one cartoonist to depict Enos walking away from the spacecraft, helmet in hand, saying, "We're a little behind the Russians and a little ahead of the Americans.") Clearly, 1962 was the year for Americans to come from behind, the year in which the United States could at last demonstrate its prowess in space.

Forty-one-year-old John H. Glenn, Jr., would join the likes of Charles A. Lindbergh and the Wright brothers as one of the world's most popular adventurers. Serving as backup astronaut to both Alan B. Shepard and Virgil I. "Gus" Grissom in their brief suborbital flights, Glenn was the natural choice to make the first orbital mission. M. Scott Carpenter would be his backup pilot.

Mercury spacecraft number thirteen was not much different from that flown by Grissom in July, 1961. A classic cone-shaped capsule, the black spacecraft measured 2.9 meters high and 1.89 meters across the base. On its nose perched the launch escape system, a fiery red solid-fueled rocket balanced atop a ladder-like tower. This mechanism was designed to propel the spacecraft away from the launch vehicle in case of an emergency. The spacecraft weighed 1,935 kilograms at liftoff. Once in orbit, its weight would drop down to 1,355 kilograms. It would weigh 1,099 kilograms upon landing. (In comparison, the Soviet's Vostok spacecraft weighed 5,000 kilograms.)

Glenn's launch vehicle would be the venerable Atlas. First developed in 1951, the Atlas would prove to be the longest lived of all American missiles, still launching satellites up through the late 1980's. This "workhorse" of the American space program was 23 meters long and had a thrust of more than 2.45 million newtons at liftoff. The Atlas is unique in that it is virtually an aluminum "balloon." To keep the booster lightweight, its metal skin was made so thin that it could not even support its own weight. Therefore, the rocket was pressurized at all times, inflated like a balloon, to keep it rigid.

The original—and overly optimistic—schedule for Project Mercury had the first orbital flight slated for April, 1960. This flight was rescheduled to December, 1961, a month after the successful mission of Enos the chimpanzee. Soon other problems caused the flight's postponement to January 16, 1962, and later to January 23. Weather problems continued to delay the flight. On January 27, all looked well, and Glenn suited up and climbed into the capsule. Five hours later he was instructed to climb back out. Questionable weather caused another delay. More weather problems resulted in further postponements. Finally, almost one month later, on February 19, the countdown began.

Glenn's three-orbit flight would help verify and evaluate the integrity of the Mercury spacecraft's design. Glenn would also make astronomical observations while on the dark side of Earth. Data would give researchers an idea of how the stars might be used for navigational purposes. While in daylight, he was to observe weather patterns and take photographs. Also, many questions regarding human capabilities in the weightless environment remained unanswered. Would it affect his judgment, his eyesight, his sense of balance?

Glenn was awakened at 7:05 Coordinated Universal Time (UTC, or 2:05 a.m. eastern standard time) on February 20, 1962. After donning his space suit, he slid into the couch of the spacecraft at 11:03 UTC (6:03 a.m.). At 12:00 UTC (7:00 a.m.), weather forecasters at Cape Canaveral gave a favorable report for the flight. Fifty-five minutes before

View of Mercury Control at Cape Canaveral Air Force Station, in Florida (USA) during the Mercury-Atlas 6 mission, in February 1962. (U.S. Navy)

launch time the tower was rolled back, exposing the gleaming rocket.

At 14:47:39 UTC (9:37 a.m. eastern standard time), the Atlas engines came to life, propelling John H. Glenn, Jr., into space. "The clock is operating, we're under way," Glenn called. Two minutes and 10 seconds into flight the two outer engines shut down and dropped away while the center, so-called sustainer, engine continued firing for another few minutes. Glenn was pressed back into his seat with a force of nearly eight times Earth's gravity. After only five minutes Glenn was in a 158-by-256-kilometer orbit, circling Earth.

Once in orbit, Glenn immediately began status checks and measurements. The astronaut tested the maneuverability of the spacecraft. As he quickly moved from one tracking station to another, he commented on the beauty of the sunset, the blackness of the sky, and the brilliance of the stars. Over the Indian Ocean he reported again on the stars, the constellations he could recognize, and a high-altitude band of light in the atmosphere. He watched the Moon rise above the darkened horizon, its soft white light illuminating the ground below him. During all this time, Glenn's heartbeat stayed a calm eighty to eighty-five beats per minute.

Starting a tradition that would continue for years, the residents of Perth, Australia, turned on all of their lights for the orbiting pilot. At fifty-five minutes into the mission, Glenn reported to Capsule Communicator L. Gordon Cooper, Jr., "Just to my right I can see a big pattern of lights."

It was during his first sunrise that Glenn reported one of the most intriguing observations of his flight, mysterious "fireflies" that surrounded his spacecraft. These were later found to be particles of ice that had broken away from the spacecraft and shimmered brightly in sunlight.

Beginning with the second orbit, Glenn reported a slow sideways drift at about 1 degree per second. This drift was the result of a failed thruster, a thruster that was to be used for fine motions. When Glenn reached a certain attitude, more powerful thrusters would automatically fire. Thus, he switched over to manual control, a method that consumed fuel much more quickly but that allowed for more precise navigation.

At about this time, telemetry code indicated a potential problem with the landing system. Because of the forces of splashdown, the spacecraft engineers designed an air bag to be used to cushion the impact. Tucked under the heatshield, this air bag would normally be deployed well after reentry. Yet telemetry suggested that the landing bag had already deployed, meaning the heatshield was loose. A loose heatshield could have subjected Glenn to temperatures of up to 1,600° Celsius.

The decision was made not to inform Glenn of this malfunction until later so as to avoid distracting him. Still, the test pilot's opinion was needed to diagnose the problem. He was asked whether he heard strange sounds (indicating the loose heatshield), whether the landing bag indicator light was on (it was not), and whether certain switches were in the right positions.

Christopher C. Kraft, Jr., flight director, immediately devised a plan to leave the rear-mounted retrorockets on during reentry. Normally, the package of three rockets, strapped to the heatshield, is jettisoned directly after firing. In this case, Mission Control hoped that these retrorockets would hold

the heatshield in place. Of primary concern were the aerodynamics of the spacecraft as it hit the atmosphere. This configuration had never been tested.

Meanwhile, Glenn continued watching "fireflies," taking photographs of sunrises and sunsets, and reporting data to ground controllers. It was not until his last pass over Hawaii that Glenn was finally informed of the potentially life-threatening problem. He was given new landing instructions. Glenn would need to use manual control for the reentry sequence.

The retrorockets fired at 4 hours and 32 minutes after liftoff. Soon Glenn was hitting the upper atmosphere. He heard the roar of the air as it began to tear at the titanium shingles of the spacecraft, the noises that sounded like "small things brushing against the capsule." One of the straps from the retropackage broke loose, swinging around and slapping the spacecraft's window. Large chunks of the package flew by the window, and an orange glow crept up the side. Glenn noticed that the interior of the spacecraft was becoming hotter, and for a moment he thought that he might not make it. Ionized air prevented any communications with the outside. Glenn was completely alone in his white-hot spacecraft.

With two minutes left before the drogue parachute was to be deployed, the fuel was exhausted. At an altitude of 8.5 kilometers, the drogue was finally released, stabilizing *Friendship 7* for the main parachute, which was released soon afterward.

John H. Glenn, Jr., landed 11 kilometers from the recovery ship, the destroyer *U.S.S. Noa*. Within seventeen minutes, *Noa* had pulled alongside the small bobbing capsule and the recovery crew quickly winched the spacecraft aboard. Glenn opened the hatch and stepped into the cool Atlantic air.

Contributions

John H. Glenn, Jr.'s mission again demonstrated that people could go into space, perform useful duties, and return with no ill effects. The spacecraft design was tested in real-life flight situations. One of the most important aspects of any mission is the astronaut's ability to control his spacecraft. Glenn's flight showed that, by using external references, the pilot could yaw (move left and right) the vehicle more easily than he could pitch or roll it. Furthermore, it was easier to yaw in the daylight than in the dark.

The utility of having a pilot on board was clearly demonstrated when the thruster problem arose. Had the flight been robotic, it would have been terminated early because of excessive fuel use. Furthermore, Glenn's on-site observations of the heatshield problem provided useful data that could not be gathered from the ground.

Glenn took six spectrograms of the Orion region of the sky. They were used to determine the kind of light that could pass through the window. This information would help compensate for spectral distortion in the future. Overall, Glenn took only two rolls of film and produced rather poor photographs. His photographs did reveal cloud patterns, ground details, sunrises and sunsets, and the so-called fireflies (later called the Glenn effect).

Glenn reported that clouds of all types were easily seen with the naked eye. Cities were clearly visible on both the dayside and nightside. Colors appeared much as they would from a high-altitude aircraft. On the dark side of Earth, Glenn could observe clouds, weather fronts, and landmasses in the moonlight. Without the Moon, looking at Earth was like "looking into the black hole at Calcutta." Lightning was seen in storms over the Indian Ocean.

From the in-flight problems of the thrusters and heatshield, much was learned about coordinating ground control with the pilot's observations. The decision to withhold information about the possible landing bag problem was later deemed imprudent. It was determined that for future missions, the pilot would be informed of problems as quickly as possible.

The medical team concluded that spaceflight had no ill effect on physically fit humans, or that whatever physical effects the flight might have had on Glenn were so short-lived that they disappeared before the postflight medical examination.

Context

The flight of *Friendship 7* was the first of four piloted Earth-orbiting Mercury flights. It proved that people had a place in space, and it disproved the theory that space travel is only safe for robots. Glenn's flight also demonstrated that the basic design of the spacecraft was sound and could be used to make future designs.

Because of the unusual environment, Glenn felt rushed to perform all of his duties. Subsequent flight plans would be reworked to allow the astronaut more time to perform his tasks. It was decided that the first orbit should be used both for systems checkout and to allow the pilot to get accustomed to the space environment. Air-to-ground communications were simplified based on Glenn's having to report all switch positions and gauge readings twice during each orbit. The mission flight plan would be finalized earlier so the pilot could become more familiar with the schedule.

The next flight, MA-7, would be a virtual repeat of Glenn's, used to gain additional experience for piloted spaceflight operations and to test spacecraft modifications. MA-8 would orbit Earth six times instead of three and perform more of the same experiments. MA-9, the last mission, was 34 hours long and designed to test a human's endurance in space. It lasted 22 orbits.

In 1961, the McDonnell Douglas Corporation, Mercury's manufacturer, was asked to begin development of the next generation of piloted spacecraft. This two-person Mercury, later known as Gemini, would be built using the experience gained with the original Mercury.

John H. Glenn, Jr., retired from the National Aeronautics and Space Administration (NASA) in 1964. The oldest of the Seven (the name by which the seven original Mercury astronauts were best known collectively), Glenn had little prospect for any new flight assignments. Gemini astronauts would be training for Apollo flights, and by that time he would be nearing fifty years old. Ten years after his retirement from NASA, Glenn, was elected senator from his home state of Ohio. In 1984, he ran an unsuccessful campaign for president on the Democratic ticket.

On October 29, 1998, John H. Glenn, Jr., became the oldest human to go into space when he flew aboard space shuttle *Discovery* on the STS- 95 mission. During the flight, he conducted experiments to determine the effects of spaceflight on his seventy-seven-year-old body. His journey marked the end of the cold-war-in-space era. Shortly thereafter, cooperation between the two space superpowers would be required to construct and maintain the International Space Statiton.

John Glenn passed away in 2016 having reached the age of 95. Special services were held in Columbus, Ohio and in Washington, D.C. to honor Glenn's service to the United States as a Marine pilot, an astronaut, and a Senator from the state of Ohio. Glenn was buried with full military honors in Arlington National Cemetary.

—Michael Smithwick

See also: Astronauts and the U.S. Astronaut Program; Lewis Field and Glenn Research Center; Mercury Project; Mercury Project Development; Mercury-Redstone 3; Mercury-Redstone 4; Mercury- Atlas 7; Mercury-Atlas 8; Mercury-Atlas 9; Space Shuttle Flights, 1998.

Further Reading

Baker, David. *The History of Manned Space Flight*. New York: Crown, 1982. This comprehensive book, more than 530 pages long, details all piloted spaceflight programs up to 1982. Contains hundreds of photographs. Recommended for anyone with even a passing interest in space history.

Glenn, John, with Nick Taylor. *John Glenn: A Memoir*. New York: Bantam Books, 1999. Glenn tells his life story in this well-written and very interesting autobiography. The book covers his career from his days as a Marine pilot, through his Mercury-Atlas 6 orbital mission, and onward to his flight aboard STS-95 in 1998. In between, he was a husband, a father, and a senator from Ohio.

Godwin, Robert, ed. *Friendship 7: The NASA Mission Reports*. Burlington, Ont.: Apogee Books, 1999. This collection contains reprints of the Mercury-Atlas 6 preflight press release (in the days before press kits) and the results of the first United States manned orbital space flight. It also includes a CD-ROM featuring "*Friendship 7*," the official NASA film of the mission.

Kraft, Christopher C., Jr. *Flight: My Life in Mission Control*. East Rutherford, N.J.: Penguin Putnam, 2002. The first NASA flight director gives an account of his life in Mission Control.

Montgomery, Scott, and Timothy R. Gaffney. *Back in Orbit: John Glenn's Return to Space*. Atlanta: Longstreet Press, 1998. This book, written prior to Glenn's return to space aboard the space shuttle *Discovery* in 1998, covers Glenn's life from his Project Mercury days. The authors are seasoned professionals: Montgomery is the Washington correspondent for the *Dayton Daily News*; Gaffney is the newspaper's military affairs/aerospace writer. There are a few technical errors in the book (they repeatedly misspell S. Christa McAuliffe's name), but it is overall a well-written book.

Shepard, Alan B., Jr., and Donald K. "Deke" Slayton, with Jay Barbree and Howard Benedict. *Moon Shot: The Inside Story of America's Race to the Moon*. Atlanta: Turner, 1994. This is, indeed, the inside story of the Apollo Program as told by two men who actively participated in it. Some of their tales appear here for the first time. Shepard and Slayton discuss Glenn's Mercury-Atlas 6 orbital flight and tell some little-known secrets of the Mercury astronauts. The book was adapted for a four-hour documentary in 1995.

Slayton, Donald K., with Michael Cassutt. *Deke! U.S. Manned Space: From Mercury to the Shuttle*. New York: Forge, 1995. This is the autobiography of the last of the Mercury astronauts to fly in space. After being grounded from flying in Project Mercury for what turned out to be a minor heart murmur, Slayton was appointed head of the Astronaut Office. Slayton talks of his frustration at being grounded and how he worked to regain flight status. He also discusses the flights of his fellow Mercury astronauts.

Swenson, Loyd S., Jr., James M. Grimwood, and Charles C. Alexander. *This New Ocean: A History of Project Mercury*. NASASP-4201. Washington, D.C.: Government Printing Office, 1966. This NASA publication traces the history of Project Mercury through Gordon Cooper's flight in *Faith 7*. Both the technical and managerial sides of the program are discussed. Many rare photographs and some diagrams are included.

Thomas, Shirley. *Men of Space: Profiles of the Leaders in Space Research, Development, and Exploration*. 5 vols. Philadelphia: Chilton, 1960. Covers the people who managed the early development of Project Mercury. Includes biographical material on Robert R. Gilruth and other members of the Space Task Group.

Wendt, Guenter, and Russell Still. *The Unbroken Chain*. Burlington, Ont.: Apogee Books, 2001. Wendt is the only person who worked with every astronaut bound for space.

Mercury-Atlas 7

Date: May 24, 1962
Type of mission: Piloted spaceflight

Mercury-Atlas 7 was the first U.S. space mission devoted to piloted scientific research in space. This second orbital mission for the United States, flown by M. Scott Carpenter, investigated the capability of a human in space to perform various experiments, ranging from photographic trials to investigations of the characteristics of Earth's atmosphere at the edge of space for navigational purposes.

Key Figures

M. Scott Carpenter (1925-2013), Mercury-Atlas 7 pilot

Walter M. Schirra, Jr. (1923-2007), Mercury-Atlas 7 backup pilot

James E. Webb (1906-1992), NASA administrator

D. Brainerd Holmes (b. 1921), NASA's director of Manned Spaceflight

Kurt H. Debus (1908-1983), director of NASA's Cape Canaveral launch facilities

Donald K. Slayton (1914-1993), the original Mercury-Atlas 7 pilot and later Chief of Flight Operations

Summary of the Mission

American piloted spaceflights that preceded the Mercury-Atlas 7 (MA-7) flight were conducted primarily to determine fundamental questions, such as vehicle performance and human ability to survive in space. Following the examples of Alan B. Shepard, Jr., Virgil I. "Gus" Grissom, and John H. Glenn, Jr., M. Scott Carpenter in MA-7 was to inquire into a whole new set of questions about piloted spaceflight. For the first time, the agenda had been cleared for basic scientific research in an American piloted spacecraft. Carpenter was to be allowed three orbits, requiring an in-orbit flight time of approximately four and one-half hours. He was assigned an assortment of scientific experiments in addition to piloting and attending to the

spacecraft. He would deploy an inflated, tethered balloon from the capsule to study the tenuous atmosphere at his orbital altitude as well as the reflectivity of sunlight on the balloon's surface. Carpenter would also be making weather observations from orbit with a camera equipped with special filters and film types. His scientific itinerary also included the study of liquids in a gravitational force of zero (the apparent "weightless" environment of orbital free fall), an investigation of the luminous band of light around Earth's horizon as seen from space (which would be used for future navigational references), looking for flares set off on the ground, testing the human ability to use star sights for space navigation, and investigating a phenomenon discovered on Glenn's flight, "space fireflies." Carpenter's schedule was literally packed with tasks that needed attention every minute, a fact that would cause eventual problems during the flight

The first launch date of MA-7 had been set for May 15, 1962. Problems with the Atlas booster rocket delayed the flight, however, and then the Mercury capsule (named *Aurora 7* by Carpenter both because it represented the "dawn of a new age" and in honor of Project Mercury, which he described as "a light in the sky") developed problems with its attitude control system. The difficulties were corrected, and at the same time a modification was developed and installed in the parachute deployment

Launch of Mercury-Atlas 7. (NASA)

system. Finally, May 24, 1962, was established as the launch date.

Carpenter lifted off from Launch Pad 14 at Cape Canaveral, Florida, at 12:45:16 Coordinated Universal Time (UTC, or 7:45 a.m.) on May 24, 1962, for the United States' second orbital flight. Five minutes after leaving the Florida launch tower, the Atlas missile completed its task of placing MA-7 into orbit and separated, falling away from the capsule. The Mercury capsule had attained orbital velocity, flying at a speed of 28,000 kilometers per hour.

Carpenter immediately began to follow his flight plan, turning the spacecraft around. Then he felt compelled to maneuver his capsule in space, discovering that there was absolutely no sensation of speed or even disorientation as he inverted *Aurora 7* to look down at the world passing beneath him. Yet Carpenter had much work to accomplish, and with only three orbits in which to do so, he set about his assigned tasks.

He maneuvered his capsule about, attempting to see the flares over darkened Australia, but the country was obscured by clouds. He was forced by requirements of his many photographic assignments to place the capsule in a variety of positions— so many, in fact, that on several occasions he used excessive fuel in trying to maneuver the capsule into position as rapidly as possible. He also made mistakes on several occasions, activating the manual and automatic thruster modes simultaneously and thereby wasting even more fuel. In these terms, the first orbit was to be costly.

Carpenter got his first look at the firefly phenomenon on his first encounter with night. He described them as resembling snowflakes and hypothesized that they were "frost from a thruster"—a speculation that would prove surprisingly accurate.

A regulator inside his suit had not been able to keep up with its rising temperature. Although the heat in his suit never rose above 36° Celsius (96.8° Fahrenheit), the system designed to remove the humidity did not function properly. In addition, Carpenter's biological temperature monitor was malfunctioning, indicating to worried ground controllers a body temperature of 38.8° Celsius (nearly 102° Fahrenheit). A persistent problem throughout his flight, the heat would account for his losing 7 pounds of body weight to perspiration.

Carpenter released the balloon at 1 hour and 38 minutes into the flight. He would later describe it as "a mess." It did not inflate properly, did not deploy behind the spacecraft as predicted, and in the end refused to release when commanded. Carpenter trailed the balloon until retrofire, "like a tin can attached to the bumper of a car." Although he confidently attempted some analysis of its deployment, it was impossible to obtain any meaningful drag data from it. Because of its partially inflated state, reflection data were for all practical purposes useless. Nevertheless, the unexpected results themselves would yield valuable scientific data.

By the final orbit, Carpenter was genuinely low on fuel. He set the spacecraft on an automatic control system to place it in position for firing of the braking rockets (retrorockets). In doing so, he found that the automatic system was malfunctioning, wasting even more of his dangerously depleted fuel. He switched back to the manual mode. With the two systems operating at once, fuel requirements were doubled. Carpenter would need what little fuel he had remaining to orient the capsule for reentry into Earth's atmosphere. If he ran out before this procedure was completed, he would enter at the wrong angle and could burn up. Worse, he might not be able to orient the capsule to fire the retrorockets and become stranded in space as a result.

To complicate matters further, just as Carpenter was orienting the spacecraft for return, he bumped the side of *Aurora 7* with his hand, and a series of the mysterious fireflies flew past the window. Then he bumped the walls again, releasing even more of them, which he identified conclusively as frost particles.

Nevertheless, the moment of reentry was nearly at hand. Carpenter, dwelling on the fireflies, completed the orientation of his capsule and fought the automatic control problem as the short countdown on the retrofire began. The firing was supposed to be automatic, but it never came. Waiting three seconds, Carpenter finally hit the manual fire switch

and the rockets fired later than planned. Because of problems with his automatic control system, the spacecraft was oriented 25° off center and the rockets delivered less thrust than planned. These seemingly small factors magnified themselves at 28,000 kilometers per hour and acted to bring the spacecraft in 463 kilometers off target.

Though Carpenter had fired his retrorockets and his craft had begun the long fall to Earth, he was not home yet. He still needed fuel to orient the capsule for the interface with the atmosphere so that the capsule would descend in a controlled manner. He used fuel from his automatic tanks to assist efforts at maintaining control just before he reentered the atmosphere.

Reentry itself was affected by the sparse use of available fuel. *Aurora 7* began to oscillate excessively. As the spacecraft buffeted from side to side, Carpenter heard the craft "bang and whump." He finally used every last drop of fuel in an attempt to restrain these motions. *Aurora 7* then began wide oscillations in an arc of about 270°, and Carpenter began to fear that the capsule would invert and go completely out of control. Thus, at 7,900 meters, he deployed his drogue chute to control the motions of the spacecraft. Carpenter splashed down northeast of the Virgin Islands five hours after liftoff. Because he had overshot his targeted landing zone, Carpenter would have a long wait in the water. He exited his spacecraft and waited in a life raft, then in the company of two Navy recovery divers before he was recovered and transported safely to the deck of the USS *Intrepid* some four hours later.

Contributions

No previous space pilot had maneuvered his vehicle as extensively as Carpenter. Not only was *Aurora 7* loaded with experiments to perform, but Carpenter's automatic control system malfunctioned as well, requiring even more maneuvering. He literally pushed the tiny space capsule to its maximum abilities, providing practical knowledge on the limits and performance of the Mercury spacecraft system.

Carpenter and MA-7 represented the first piloted space mission dedicated primarily to science. In past space voyages, tolerance of the space environment had been a fundamental area of inquiry with regard to both human and machine. MA-7 was the first mission, however, to place a person in space with the express aim of scientifically investigating the effects of the largely unknown environment. MA-7 proved that humans could achieve Earth orbit, survive there, and maneuver a space vehicle to obtain useful scientific data.

Carpenter discovered that cloud cover obscured any attempt to communicate with him using flares from the ground. While seemingly a commonsensical discovery, it did prove that high altitudes of orbit affected visual observation in much the same way as lower ones. Until Carpenter's mission, that idea was only conjecture.

The mission of MA-7 also proved that the density of the atmosphere was so insignificant that when traveling at 28,000 kilometers per hour at an altitude of 268 kilometers there was not enough drag to stretch out the balloon. This was a surprise to the experiment's designers, who had wanted Carpenter to report on the effect of drag. MA-7's finding would influence nearly all space missions to follow and would ultimately affect the design of future space stations.

Carpenter provided some of the first meteorological photographs of Earth taken from space. These images were taken with several filters that would allow later comparison of weather formations and be instrumental in determining the design of satellite requirements ranging from weather satellites to the Earth resources satellites. The human ability to change photographic filters and aim at specific features was at that time not possible using robotic vehicles. MA-7 provided badly needed yet otherwise unobtainable data.

Carpenter solved a substantial space mystery. On his earlier flight, Glenn had described what appeared to be luminous fireflies dancing outside the window of his spacecraft. One of Carpenter's assignments was to find out more about these mystifying objects. He discovered these to be flakes of frost that had accumulated on the sides of the space vehicle. Again, the ability of a human in space to make these on-the-scene evaluations was well beyond the capability of any robotic probe.

Finally, Carpenter was assigned two vital navigation tasks. He was to see if he could spot specific stars from the window of his spacecraft and investigate the band of light at Earth's visible horizon. He was able to distinguish Earth's horizon clearly, and spot target stars distinctly, proving that people would someday be able to use these guideposts to navigate in space.

Context

MA-7 was the sixth piloted space mission flown in history, the fourth by the United States. It was the NASA's second orbital mission, and the first mission devoted substantially to scientific research in space. The second piloted mission to fly into space atop an Atlas booster rocket, MA-7 still holds the record for missing its intended landing zone, by some 463 kilometers. Nevertheless, Carpenter's flight proved conclusively not only that people could achieve orbit and survive but also that they could work there and collect data.

By early 1962, there had been few spaceflights at all. The question of simple survival had been answered conclusively, first by the Soviet Union some thirteen months earlier with the flight of Vostok 1. Because the Soviets were not sharing their information, however, American scientists could rely only on their own data. The Cold War between the United States and the Soviet Union had been heating up, and the high ground of space was being eyed for military use. The U.S. Air Force had already initiated Dyna-Soar, a planned space laboratory in which it would conduct military exercises on a nearly continuous basis. Dyna-Soar was replaced by the Manned Orbiting Laboratory, which itself would be canceled some seven years later.

In 1962, when Carpenter flew on MA-7, the United States and the Soviet Union had just entered the so-called Space Race, initiated one year earlier by President John F. Kennedy's challenge to land a man the Moon by the end of the decade. This proclamation gave the nation something for which to strive, a goal. Namely, to reach the Moon and return safely. Although this was the focus of the space program in the early 1960's, other vital space applications were being developed as well. The first meteorological, Earth resources, military, and navigation satellites were also being developed and launched.

Thus, the mission of MA-7 came at a time of energetic space science development, of which there were two primary focal points: piloted spaceflight leading to a landing on the Moon, and robotic investigations of many varieties, ranging from Earth resources to military surveillance. Carpenter's mission benefited both goals substantially by providing key pieces of information.

NASA marked the fiftieth anniversary of all the historic early flights of the Space Age. Fifty years after *Aurora 7* only two of the original Mercury astronauts were still alive, Scott Carpenter being one of the two. Carpenter passed away one year later (2013) having never gotten a second chance to fly in space but having been given more recognition as the second astronaut to orbit Earth than he had received in the aftermath of *Aurora 7* having splashed down so far off target.

—*Dennis Chamberland*

See also: Mercury Project; Mercury Project Development; Mercury-Atlas 6; Mercury-Atlas 8.

Further Reading

Carpenter, M. Scott, and Kris Stoever. *For Spacious Skies: The Uncommon Journey of a Mercury Astronaut.* New York: Harcourt, 2003. Carpenter tells the story of the science, training, and biomedicine of early spaceflight as well as his own famous spaceflight aboard *Aurora 7.*

Glenn, John, with Nick Taylor. *John Glenn: A Memoir.* New York: Bantam Books, 1999. Glenn covers his career from his days as a Marine pilot through his Mercury-Atlas 6 orbital mission to his flight aboard STS-95 in 1998.

Kraft, Christopher C., Jr. *Flight: My Life in Mission Control.* East Rutherford, N.J.: Penguin Putnam, 2002. The first NASA flight director gives an account of his life in Mission Control.

Shepard, Alan B., Jr., and Donald K. "Deke" Slayton, with Jay Barbree and Howard Benedict. *Moon Shot: The Inside Story of America's Race to the Moon.* Atlanta: Turner, 1994. This is, indeed, the inside story of the Apollo Program as told by two men who actively participated in it. Some of their tales appear here for the first time. Shepard and Slayton discuss Glenn's Mercury-Atlas 6 orbital flight and tell some little-known secrets of the Mercury astronauts. The book was adapted for a four-hour documentary in 1995.

Slayton, Donald K., with Michael Cassutt. *Deke! U.S. Manned Space: From Mercury to the Shuttle.* New York: Forge, 1995. This is the autobiography of the last of the Mercury astronauts to fly in space. After being grounded from flying in Project Mercury for what turned out to be a minor heart murmur, Slayton was appointed head of the Astronaut Office. Slayton talks of his frustration at being grounded and how he worked to regain flight status. He also discusses the flights of his fellow Mercury astronauts.

Wendt, Guenter, and Russell Still. *The Unbroken Chain.* Burlington, Ont.: Apogee Books, 2001. Wendt is the only person who worked with every astronaut bound for space.

Mercury-Atlas 8

Date: October 3, 1962
Type of mission: Piloted spaceflight

Sigma 7, the Mercury-Atlas 8 mission, was the United States' third piloted Earth-orbiting spaceflight. Astronaut Walter M. Schirra, Jr., demonstrated that astronauts could work in a microgravity environment for an extended time.

Key Figures

Walter M. Schirra, Jr. (1923-2007), Mercury-Atlas 8 pilot

L. Gordon Cooper, Jr. (1927-2004), Mercury-Atlas 8 backup pilot

Robert R. Gilruth (1913-2000), manager, Project Mercury

Christopher C. Kraft, Jr. (b. 1924), flight director

Walter C. Williams (1919-1995), mission director

Summary of the Mission

With the success of two three-orbit flights by mid-1962, the United States decided that its space program was ready for longer Mercury missions. Because the Mercury spacecraft was designed for only a three-orbit, five-hour-long flight, several modifications on its design would be required. There would no longer be space for extra supplies. The atmospheric leak rate of the vehicle had to be cut from 1,000 to 600 cubic centimeters per minute. A new fuel-saving plan was implemented to minimize the use of attitude fuel. Excessive fuel use had been a problem that had plagued the flights of both John H. Glenn, Jr., and M. Scott Carpenter. Finally, a new plan was developed to conserve electrical power; the pilot would turn off systems when not actually in use.

Thirty-nine-year-old Walter M. Schirra, Jr., was the pilot selected for the third Mercury orbital mission. L. Gordon Cooper, Jr., was his backup pilot. This mission was essentially an engineering flight

to test the new conservation measures, paving the way for still longer missions. Schirra was given very few scientific experiments. Instead, he was to concentrate on observing the behavior of the spacecraft and its systems. Schirra named his spacecraft *Sigma 7.* "Sigma" is an engineering term for "summation," and this flight was to be a summation of all previous ones.

While preparing for the flight of *Sigma 7*, officials at the National Aeronautics and Space Administration (NASA) were apprehensive about the next steps the Soviet Union might take. The Soviets' last mission had lasted a full day in orbit. Americans believed that, with some luck, it might be possible to launch a daylong Mercury mission before any more Soviet spectaculars were reported, effectively overtaking them. This pressure gave added importance to the long-duration *Sigma 7* flight. On August 11, 1962, however, the Soviets launched Vostok 3, with cosmonaut Andriyan Nikolayev at the helm. A day later, Radio Moscow announced that Vostok 4 had lifted off, piloted by cosmonaut Pavel Popovich. For three days, the two Soviets sent live television images back to Earth, chatted with each other, and stole the world's headlines. The United States was clearly trailing in the Space Race. (The two cosmonauts landed within minutes of each other, after four and three days in space, respectively.)

Because of the length of the mission, *Sigma 7* would fly over portions of Earth without the benefit

Astronaut Walter M. Schirra Jr, (right), Mercury-Atlas 8 (MA-8) pilot, discusses the MA-8 flight plan with Flight Director Christopher C. Kraft Jr., Chief of the Flight Operations Division at the Manned Spacecraft Center, Houston, during MA-8 preflight preparations at Cape Canaveral, Florida. They are seated at a console in the Mercury Control Center. (NASA)

of tracking stations. As Schirra's spacecraft traveled around Earth, the planet itself would rotate under him 27° each orbit—causing his flight path to shift west. This shift would gradually take him away from the normal set of ground stations, leaving him with communications lapses of up to thirty minutes. Until Schirra's flight, ten minutes without ground communications had been the accepted maximum. Therefore, for this mission, three tracking ships were added to the network. The *Huntsville*, *Watertown*, and *American Mariner* were stationed close to Midway Island, near Hawaii. Another land-based station was added at Quito, Ecuador, to aid communications on the final orbit.

Sigma 7 would land in the Pacific Ocean, while all the previous missions had landed in the Atlantic. The Department of Defense assigned more than seventeen thousand personnel, eighty-three airplanes and helicopters, and twenty six ships to recovery operations. The aircraft carrier USS *Kearsarge* was designated the primary recovery ship.

On the morning of October 3, 1962, Schirra climbed aboard *Sigma 7*. An automobile ignition key that had been hung inside the cabin by a good-natured technician added a playful spirit to the day's activities. Schirra made a quick inventory of gear in the cabin: star charts, flight plan, camera equipment, and the like. Checking in the "glove compartment," where personal items were stowed, Schirra discovered a second gift from the ground crew: a steak sandwich.

Launch was scheduled for 12:00 Coordinated Universal Time (UTC, or 7:00 a.m. eastern standard time), but a radar malfunction at the Canary Island tracking station delayed the countdown by fifteen minutes. At precisely 12:15:11 UTC (7:15 a.m.), the Atlas rocket was ignited. After only ten seconds, however, the mission was nearly aborted. The Atlas had made an unexpected clockwise roll because of a misalignment of the booster engines. Vernier rockets (small attitude control motors) stopped the roll before it could trigger an abort condition. The remainder of the launch was uneventful, much less dramatic than Schirra had expected. The sustainer engine fired ten seconds longer than planned, putting *Sigma 7* in a slightly higher orbit than intended: some 167 by 283 kilometers, the highest orbit of all four Mercury orbital flights.

Schirra first cartwheeled the spacecraft around to watch the Atlas rocket drift into space. He then performed manual attitude tests and began to monitor spacecraft systems. While flying over Zanzibar, Schirra could feel his space suit become warmer. The suit's delicate environmental control system had sent its temperature soaring from 23.3 to 32.2° Celsius. On the ground, Christopher C. Kraft, Jr., the flight director, suggested that the mission be terminated after one orbit. Schirra carefully adjusted the suit's control knob and managed to stabilize the temperature. Kraft gave permission for a second orbit. By the time Schirra was passing over Australia for the second time, the temperature had dropped to a comfortable 22.2° Celsius.

Over Australia, Schirra was supposed to watch for flares that would be fired from the ground. As it had been on past missions, the launching area was covered with clouds. Nothing could be seen of the ground.

Another test was scheduled to verify the utility of a periscope mounted under the main instrument panel. Carpenter had claimed that it was useless, taking up much-needed space and weight, but Schirra believed that it could be used for more accurate attitude alignment. At the post-flight press conference, however, it was revealed that Schirra had not been able to use the periscope effectively.

Over Muchea, Australia, on the second orbit, Schirra performed the night yaw experiment, designed to determine whether the spacecraft could be properly aligned by using the stars as a guide. The small window and incorrect star charts made it difficult to identify constellations. Nevertheless, ground telemetry showed Schirra's error to be no more than 4°.

Approaching California for the second time, Schirra radioed to Capsule Communicator John H. Glenn, Jr., that he saw the "fireflies," bright particles that Glenn had observed on his *Friendship 7* mission. Schirra also noticed that he could generate more "fireflies" by knocking the side of the spacecraft. He reported seeing the Salton Sea, Mount Whitney, and several roads in the Mojave Desert. Unlike most astronauts, Schirra was rather unimpressed with the view. Although he was ten times higher than he had ever flown before, the details and landscape looked to him like those viewed from high-altitude aircraft. "Same old deal, nothing new," he stated at the debriefing.

On the third orbit, Schirra performed an experiment suggested a year before by his training officer. He closed his eyes and attempted to touch certain target points on the control panel. In nine trials, he made only three errors. Schirra concluded that weightlessness created no significant disorientation.

By the end of the third orbit, Schirra began photographing various regions from California to Cuba. He then measured radiation levels in the cabin, but the levels were so low that they were virtually unreadable. Kraft urged Schirra to look for the large silver Echo balloon satellite when he passed over Zanzibar. He was unable to find it.

On Schirra's fourth orbit, he took more photographs, performed communications checks with the ships *Watertown* and *Huntsville*, and observed thunderstorms over Australia. Nearing California once again, at 6 hours and 8 minutes after liftoff, Schirra was given two minutes of live network radio time to report on his status to the entire world.

Flying over South America for the last time, Schirra bid the Quito, Ecuador, communications crew farewell as he prepared for reentry. Fuel conservation procedures had succeeded. *Sigma 7* still had 78 percent of its fuel left in its tanks. Less fuel had been used in six orbits than in the three revolutions on each of the previous two missions. Orienting for reentry consumed more fuel, and the supply dropped to 52 percent. With the blunt heatshield forward, the rockets fired one at a time at five-second intervals. The retropackage dropped away, and Schirra began his fiery fall toward the Pacific Ocean.

The friction of reentry heated the small capsule to more than 1,600° Celsius. Schirra reported seeing a brilliant green glow outside the window. A retropackage strap still attached to the heatshield slapped against his window much as it had for John H. Glenn, Jr., a few months before. The small drogue parachute opened at an altitude of 13 kilometers, stabilizing the spacecraft. The single main chute opened at 5 kilometers altitude. Some nine hours after liftoff, *Sigma 7* settled into the Pacific Ocean a mere 7.5 kilometers from the aircraft carrier USS *Kearsarge*. As had Glenn, Schirra elected to stay in the capsule until it was placed on the deck. The reporters shouted to him, "How do you feel, Wally?" He replied "Fine" and headed down to the ship's sick bay.

Contributions

The *Sigma 7* mission was intended to test different flight procedures so as to correct problems encountered during the previous two missions. Crowded flight plans during Mercury-Atlas missions 6 and 7 had rushed the astronauts too much, causing them to waste both fuel and energy. Schirra did not have to tend many scientific experiments, so he had more time for each flight test. New procedures on Mercury-Atlas 8 dealt with factors critical to long-duration space missions, specifically, the conservation of fuel and electrical power. Attitude changes were kept at a minimum, and those that were affected took more time than on previous flights. As a result, Schirra's first attitude change at 4° per second (turning around to observe the detached booster) consumed only 0.14 kilogram of propellant, compared to 2.45 kilograms for the same maneuver on John Glenn, Jr.'s flight.

The bulky periscope was tested to see if it could aid in the adjustment of the spacecraft's attitude. When the periscope was used at high power, Schirra reported that it was only a bit faster, but not any more accurate, than other methods. It was recommended that the periscope be dropped from future missions.

Various ablative panels were attached to the outside of the spacecraft. These were used to test the reactions of different materials to the reentry heat. None of the panels was clearly superior to the others.

Previous mission flight rules regarding a ten-minute maximum communications gap were changed, because the longer mission would carry Schirra farther from the prime tracking stations. The decrease in pilot communications time did not appear to hinder the mission in any way.

Psychomotor tests proved that an astronaut's spatial perception did not change significantly in weightlessness. In fact, only one significant observation concerning Schirra's physical condition was made. After the mission, Schirra's change in blood pressure and heart rate when standing and lying down was somewhat greater than it had been before flight. This remained constant until one day after splashdown. In-flight exercise was recommended to counteract any such changes in heart rate caused by future long-duration missions.

Context

The *Sigma 7* flight was called an "engineering evaluation" by Schirra. Drawing from the experience gained from the first two missions, NASA officials used *Sigma 7* to verify new approaches required for long-duration flights. Many of these new approaches were tested further by L. Gordon Cooper, Jr., in the final Mercury flight, the thirty-four hour-long *Faith 7* mission. The *Sigma 7* experience would also affect the way flight plans were organized and pilots were trained. Furthermore, as a result of Schirra's mission, the pilot was given a more autonomous role, and the need for continuous communications became less urgent.

Compared with the Soviets, the Americans were still a distant second in the Space Race, with only a total of nineteen hours in space compared to the Soviets' eight days.

Walter M. Schirra, Jr., would go on to command the fourth piloted Gemini mission—Gemini VI with Thomas P. Stafford in December, 1965. The pair would perform the world's first rendezvous between two piloted spacecraft. Three years later, Schirra would command the first piloted Apollo flight, Apollo 7. Donn F. Eisele and Walter Cunningham accompanied him for the 163-orbit flight. With his participation in the Apollo Program, Schirra became the only astronaut to fly in all three piloted programs during the 1960's.

Walter Schirra had remained an acclaimed and popular astronaut after his final spaceflight, *Apollo 7* in October 1968, having had a career as an analyst for CBS News helping Walter Cronkite cover early spaceflights from Apollo Moon missions through Skylab expeditions and the early space shuttle missions. Schirra passed away in mid-2007 at the age of 84 while being treated for abdominal cancer. As such he nearly witnessed the first fifty years of the Space Age (relative to the launch of Sputnik 1) but missed NASA's celebration of the fiftieth anniversary of any of his three historic space missions, each of which (*Sigma 7, Gemini 6A*, and *Apollo 7*) were given special recognition as the space agency sought to honor the special golden anniversaries of all early flights that led up to the first lunar landing.

—Michael Smithwick

See also: Apollo 7; Gemini V; Gemini 7/6A; Mercury Project; Mercury-Atlas 7; Mercury-Atlas 9.

Further Reading

Baker, David. *The History of Manned Space Flight.* New York: Crown, 1982. A detailed reference work, more than 530 pages long and filled with photographs. Unlike many well illustrated books, this source has a generous amount of text.

Glenn, John, with Nick Taylor. *John Glenn: A Memoir.* New York: Bantam Books, 1999. Glenn covers his career from his days as a Marine pilot through his Mercury-Atlas 6 orbital mission to his flight aboard STS-95 in 1998.

Godwin, Robert, and Steve Whitfield, eds. *Sigma 7: The Six Orbits of Walter M. Schirra: The NASA Mission Reports.* Burlington, Ont.: Apogee Books, 2003. Includes the overall details of the Mercury-Atlas 8 mission, the surface to air transcripts, and an interview with the pilot, Wally Schirra. Documents include the MA-8 press kit and the complete *Results of the Third U.S. Manned Orbital Space Flight.*

Kraft, Christopher C., Jr. *Flight: My Life in Mission Control.* East Rutherford, N.J.: Penguin Putnam, 2002. The first NASA flight director gives an account of his life in Mission Control.

National Aeronautics and Space Administration. *Mercury Project Summary Including Results of Fourth Manned Orbital Flight, May 15-16, 1963.* NASA SP-45. Washington, D.C.: Government Printing Office, 1963. The official summary of Project Mercury, this book contains material on medical experiments and the performance of the booster and spacecraft. Technical in nature but suitable for a general readership.

Shepard, Alan B., Jr., and Donald K. "Deke" Slayton, with Jay Barbree and Howard Benedict. *Moon Shot: The Inside Story of America's Race to the Moon.* Atlanta: Turner, 1994. This is, indeed, the inside story of the Apollo Program as told by two men who actively participated in it. Some of their tales appear here for the first time. Shepard and Slayton discuss the Mercury-Atlas 7 orbital flight and tell some little-known secrets of the Mercury astronauts. The book was adapted for a four-hour documentary in 1995.

Slayton, Donald K., with Michael Cassutt. *Deke! U.S. Manned Space: From Mercury to the Shuttle.* New York: Forge, 1995. This is the autobiography of the last of the Mercury astronauts to fly in space. After being grounded from flying in Project Mercury for what turned out to be a minor heart murmur, Slayton was appointed head of the Astronaut Office. Slayton talks of his frustration at being grounded and how he worked to regain flight status. He also discusses the flights of his fellow Mercury astronauts.

Swenson, Loyd S., Jr., James M. Grimwood, and Charles C. Alexander. *This New Ocean: A History of Project Mercury.* NASA SP-4201. Washington, D.C.: Government Printing Office, 1966. Part of the NASA History series. A complete and well-written account of all aspects of Project Mercury. Gives a good description of early technical problems, such as those with the capsule's heatshield.

Wendt, Guenter, and Russell Still. *The Unbroken Chain.* Burlington, Ont.: Apogee Books, 2001. Wendt is the only person who worked with every astronaut bound for space.

Mercury-Atlas 9

Date: May 15 to May 16, 1963
Type of mission: Piloted spaceflight

The Mercury-Atlas 9 (MA-9) mission was the United States' fourth piloted orbital flight. Astronaut L. Gordon Cooper, Jr., aboard his Faith 7 spacecraft demonstrated that humans could work in a microgravity environment for more than one day.

Key Figures

L. Gordon Cooper, Jr. (1927-2004), Mercury-Atlas 9 pilot

Alan B. Shepard, Jr. (1923-1998), Mercury-Atlas 9 backup pilot

Robert R. Gilruth (1913-2000), manager, Project Mercury

Christopher C. Kraft, Jr. (b. 1924), flight director

Walter C. Williams (1919-1995), mission director

Summary of the Mission

On May 15, 1963, L. Gordon Cooper, Jr., was situated atop an Atlas booster in his Mercury spacecraft *Faith 7*. Cooper would shortly be launched on the most complicated Mercury flight ever. It would also be the last mission of Project Mercury.

MA-9 got its start following the successful flight of MA-8 (*Sigma 7*), piloted by Astronaut Walter M. Schirra, Jr. The Mercury spacecraft was originally built for a simple three-orbit, five-hour-long mission. With the success of the Soviet Union in long-duration flights lasting several days, not to mention delays with the United States' two-man Gemini spacecraft, it became apparent that a lengthy Mercury flight was in order. First, both spacecraft and flight procedures had to be modified to support longer stays in space. These modifications were successfully tested by Schirra in his six-orbit mission of October, 1962. Still, a new set of problems had to be solved for Cooper's flight, as it was to last for more than one day.

Engineers dissected the Mercury capsule, looking for every gram of excess weight that could be replaced with extra fuel, oxygen, and experiments. Based on Schirra's recommendations, the bulky periscope was the first item to be removed, saving 34 kilograms. Two backup radio transmitters and an extra automatic control system were also taken out of the spacecraft. These changes made room for more batteries, more cooling water, nearly double the amount of drinking water, and more oxygen. A total of 183 changes were made to the Mercury spacecraft. In the end, it weighed 1,963 kilograms—only 1.8 kilograms more than Schirra's *Sigma 7*.

Cooper's flight was a controversial one. Many wanted Mercury to end on the high note of Schirra's textbook-perfect mission. In fact, this feeling was so strong and the changes in Cooper's spacecraft so extensive that for a while MA-9 was considered a separate program. In a quarterly report on Project Mercury dated November, 1962, it was stated, "This report will be the final in the series of Project Mercury, as such, because the MA-8 flight was the last mission of Project Mercury." MA-9 was now called the Manned One-Day Mission, or MODM, project.

Another controversy arose when Cooper announced the name of his spacecraft. *Faith 7* was selected, symbolizing for Cooper his trust in God, his country, and his teammates.

Faith 7 would be a scientific mission. Previous Mercury flights had been much too short for serious scientific research. Cooper called *Faith 7* a "flying camera," because it contained a 70-millimeter Hasselblad (the same camera used on the lunar missions), a 35-millimeter still camera, a 16-millimeter general-purpose motion-picture camera, and a television system, the first on an American piloted flight. Experiments included releasing a flashing beacon from the rear of the spacecraft to test the pilot's visual ability to track other objects in space. There would be a tethered balloon to study air drag. Studies of the behavior of liquids in weightlessness would be made, and photographs were to be taken to aid in weather satellite design, celestial navigation, and studies of the upper atmosphere.

Cooper would experience long gaps in communications with ground controllers, much as Schirra had on his flight, because *Faith 7* would be moving

An image of Tibet-Kashmir, looking northwest, as photographed from the Mercury-Atlas 9 capsule by Astronaut L. Gordon Cooper Jr. Lake Ch'in-Tzu-Hu is visible in the upper right, Lake Yen-K'o-Ling-Ts in the lower left centre, and The Korakaram Range in the upper centre portion of the image. (NASA / L. Gordon Cooper)

away from the established tracking network. Two new ships were added to fill in some of the gaps in communications: *Twin Falls Victory* and *Range Tracker*.

At 13:04:13 Coordinated Universal Time (UTC, or 8:04 a.m. eastern standard time) on May 15, the nearly $18 million Mercury-Atlas 9 spacecraft was launched. Five minutes later, *Faith 7* was in an orbit of 267 by 161 kilometers. Cooper immediately began a slow turn to observe the Atlas booster tumbling behind his spacecraft. Using fuel-saving procedures that Schirra had pioneered, Cooper maneuvered his spacecraft. *Faith 7* consumed only 0.09 kilogram of fuel for that maneuver, compared to 0.14 kilogram on Schirra's flight and 2.45 kilograms on Glenn's flight.

Cooper was the most relaxed Mercury astronaut. He had been caught dozing in his spacecraft during countdown and was awakened several times from catnaps throughout the entire flight. On his first pass over Australia, he saw the lights of Perth and observed the so-called Glenn effect, the mysterious "fireflies" first reported by John H. Glenn, Jr. He released the beacon on the third orbit but was unable to see it until the next orbit.

On the sixth orbit Cooper tried releasing the balloon, a sphere 75 centimeters in diameter attached to a 30-meter line. A strain gauge was to measure the differences in air drag between the highest and lowest points of the orbit, but the device failed for unknown reasons, just as it had when M. Scott Carpenter had tried to use it one year earlier.

Cooper performed liquid experiments on the seventh orbit, transferring urine samples and water from tank to tank. Syringes he used were unwieldy and leaked. He observed that in microgravity liquid "tends to stand in pipes, and you have to actually force it through." Next, he took measurements of residual radiation from a July, 1962, atomic blast. These measurements would be compared with similar measurements taken by Walter M. Schirra, Jr., seven months earlier.

Cooper spent much time performing vision tests. Early astronauts had reported the amazing clarity with which they could see objects on Earth. Schirra claimed to have seen individual roads and railroad tracks. Cooper caught sight of a 44,000-watt xenon light located at Bloemfontein, South Africa. Astronauts on previous missions had attempted similar tests, but clouds had always obscured their views. Other visual observations made by Cooper would stir much controversy. On the ninth orbit, while passing over the Himalayas and later over the southwestern United States, Cooper claimed that he could see individual houses with smoke emanating from their chimneys. He reported seeing fields and roads, and believed he actually saw a vehicle on one of the roads. Over northern India, Cooper watched a steam locomotive, and detected the wake of a boat in a Burmese river. These observations were made without any visual aids whatsoever. Even after long post-flight debriefings, many would maintain that the astronaut must have had some sort of visual suggestion. At this time Cooper also took some of the best photographs ever taken during Project Mercury.

At 13 hours and 35 minutes into the mission, Cooper said good night to John H. Glenn, Jr., who was Capsule Communicator (CapCom) on board the ship *Coastal Sentry Quebec*. For the next eight hours Cooper dozed, waking periodically to record status reports into the onboard tape recorder. Later, Cooper recorded the first prayer from orbit. In his casual Oklahoman drawl, he gave thanks for both the success of the mission and the privilege of being on the flight. He prayed for help in future space endeavors. On the fifteenth orbit, Cooper received greetings from the Salvadoran president. Later, as he soared above Zanzibar, Cooper sent greetings to African leaders meeting in Addis Ababa, Ethiopia.

The spacecraft had performed nearly flawlessly until the seventeenth orbit, when the level of carbon dioxide began to climb. A higher level could slow Cooper's reactions and dull his senses (although he could activate his emergency oxygen supply if necessary). On the nineteenth orbit, Cooper had a more serious problem. The light signifying the beginning of reentry switched on, indicating that the spacecraft was experiencing deceleration. This malfunction had the effect of triggering the automatic recovery sequence. Cooper quickly deactivated the system, but the power supply to the automatic stabilization control system short-circuited. He switched to the backup system, but it, too, failed. Because all attitude readings were lost, Cooper would have to perform a manual reentry, a procedure attempted on M. Scott Carpenter's 1962 Mercury mission. As if this problem were not worrisome enough, Cooper noticed that the carbon dioxide levels in his suit and cabin were increasing again.

During this emergency, Cooper calmly photographed cloud formations and the Moon setting behind Earth. He also took time-exposure photographs of "dim light" phenomena, which included high-altitude "airglow" (a glow caused by solar radiation ionizing the thin gases in the upper atmosphere) and the "zodiacal light" (a dim glow from the Sun's atmosphere stretching millions of miles from the Sun).

On the twenty-second orbit, Cooper reported that he was in retrograde attitude, with all tasks on the checklist completed. CapCom Glenn gave a ten-second countdown, and Cooper, keeping his pitch at 34°, fired his retrorockets. With the spacecraft traveling nearly 12 kilometers per second, the slightest error could throw him off course. His timing was perfect, and manual control during reentry flawless. L. Gordon Cooper, Jr., landed nearest the recovery point of any Mercury astronaut, only 1.8 kilometers away from the target. He had flown 34 hours and 21 minutes.

Like Glenn and Schirra, Cooper elected to ride his spacecraft all the way to the carrier. Forty minutes later, he opened the hatch. Project Mercury concluded, and the celebrations began. President John F. Kennedy awarded all the astronauts medals, and a ticker-tape parade in New York City followed. Radio Moscow recognized Cooper's flight and the entire Project Mercury, expressing hope for future Soviet-U.S. cooperation in exploring the universe.

Contributions

Perhaps the most controversial aspect of the *Faith 7* flight had to do with Cooper's visual reports. He claimed to have seen individual houses, a locomotive on its tracks, roads, and even a vehicle on a road. Well after the mission, there was still much debate over whether he had truly seen these things.

On the third orbit, Cooper released a flashing beacon. For two or three orbits' time, he was able to see the beacon, one time when it was estimated to be 28 kilometers away. Even though the beacon was rather dim, Cooper said that its flashing made it easily distinguishable from the stars. This information would aid spacecraft planners when they began designing rendezvous devices for the two spacecraft Apollo missions.

Photography experiments performed aboard MA-9 revealed that Earth is best viewed in near infrared light, an important piece of data for weather satellite designers. The value of space-based photographs was debated until Cooper returned with the hundreds that he took. These images showed that much could be learned from high-quality photographs. Photography from space would become an integral part of future missions.

Radiation experiments showed that there were very low levels of radiation inside the spacecraft. Readings taken on board *Faith 7* were compared to those taken on board *Sigma 7*, seven months earlier. Residual radiation from an atomic test of July, 1962, was seen to decrease by several orders of magnitude.

Medical experiments showed that Cooper "withstood the stresses of the flight situation with no evidence of degradation" of his performance. He did, however, suffer from mild dehydration. His pulse and blood pressure returned to normal between nine and nineteen hours after splashdown. There was no evidence of psychological disturbances during the thirty-four hours in orbit. All evidence pointed to the ability of man to handle, both physically and psychologically, missions of a much longer duration. This news was welcome, because Apollo Moon flights would last up to ten days.

The liquid flow experiment gave only limited results; it essentially confirmed previous data gathered in ground-based laboratories. The experiment would, however, provide information needed to design weightless fuel systems required for transferring fuel during future missions.

Zodiacal light photographs were underexposed and yielded little data as to the light's possible origins. Airglow photographs were overexposed but still useful. Scientists determined that the airglow appeared at an altitude of about 88 kilometers and that it was about 24 kilometers thick.

Context

Gordon Cooper's spaceflight was a milestone: It was the first scientific piloted space mission for the United States. It was a fitting end to Project Mercury. Mercury had started some five years earlier, had cost more than $400 million, and had involved 3,345 scientists and engineers. The flight of *Faith 7* combined everything that had been learned up to that time into a single, highly successful mission. Space was now actually being used, not simply explored. The mission proved that the long-duration procedures rehearsed by Walter M. Schirra, Jr., during the previous flight were valid and that long-term weightlessness had no ill effect on humans. This final determination was especially important, considering how long Apollo missions would last.

Cooper's success with the manual reentry justified the expense of sending man along with machine into space. Had *Faith 7* been robotic, it would likely have been stranded in orbit.

An onboard television camera was the first in the American piloted program, although the Soviets had used television beginning with their first piloted Vostok flight. The poor quality of Cooper's camera rendered it nearly useless, and television was not to be used again until the first Apollo flight, some six years later.

Interesting sightings made by Cooper of roads, houses, and the like prompted NASA to send him into space again, only two years later, to follow up on his reports. In 1965, he flew the longest flight up to that time, with Charles "Pete" Conrad, Jr., on Gemini V. It lasted more than eight days. Cooper later served as commander of the Apollo 10 backup crew, but he never flew again.

Up until the MA-9 mission, there was serious talk of having yet another Mercury flight, MA-10. That idea was rejected because of the tremendous success of *Faith 7*, although there were still several unused Mercury spacecraft (three of which were modified for long-duration flight). This proposed mission would have lasted three days or longer and would have been flown by Alan B. Shepard, Jr., the United States' first man in space. In anticipation of this, a Mercury Capsule even had *Freedom 7-II* painted on its side, after Shepard's first spacecraft, *Freedom 7*.

Cooper passed away from heart failure in 2007 at age 77 on the anniversary of the *Sputnik 1* launch which dawned the Space Age. Three years later some of Cooper's ashes were sent aloft from New Mexico aboard a commercial suborbital rocket. The capsule containing those ashes was eventually recovered from a mountainous region and returned to family members Some of Cooper's ashes again returned to space, this time in orbit, onboard SpaceX's Dragon capsule's Demo Flight 2 on May 22, 2012 just a year in advance of the fiftieth anniversary of *Faith 7*. On that anniversary, NASA paid special tribute to the last American astronaut to fly in space alone.

—Michael Smithwick

See also: Ethnic and Gender Diversity in the Space Program; Gemini V; Mercury Project; Mercury-Redstone 3; Mercury-Atlas 8.

Further Reading

Baker, David. *The History of Manned Space Flight*. New York: Crown, 1982. This book details the evolution of space programs throughout the world. Well illustrated with both color and black-and-white photographs. Recommended for the general reader with an interest in space history.

Cooper, L. Gordon, with Bruce Henderson. *Leap of Faith: An Astronaut's Journey into the Unknown*. New York: Harper Torch, 2000. Cooper recalls his adventures in planes and spacecraft and looks toward the next millennium of space travel.

Glenn, John, with Nick Taylor. *John Glenn: A Memoir*. New York: Bantam Books, 1999. Glenn covers his career from his days as a Marine pilot through his Mercury-Atlas 6 orbital mission to his flight aboard STS-95 in 1998.

Kraft, Christopher C., Jr. *Flight: My Life in Mission Control*. East Rutherford, N.J.: Penguin Putnam, 2002. The first NASA flight director gives an account of his life in Mission Control.

National Aeronautics and Space Administration. *Mercury Project Summary Including Results of Fourth Manned Orbital Flight, May 15-16, 1963*. NASA SP-45. Washington, D.C.: Government Printing Office, 1963. The official summary of Project Mercury, this book focuses on the *Faith 7* flight. Contains a discussion of scientific experiments and details the design of the capsule. The official flight report of this last mission is also included, along with transcripts of the ground-to-air communications.

Shepard, Alan B., Jr., and Donald K. "Deke" Slayton, with Jay Barbree and Howard Benedict. *Moon Shot: The Inside Story of America's Race to the Moon*. Atlanta: Turner, 1994. This is, indeed, the inside story of the Apollo Program as told by two men who actively participated in it. Some of their tales appear here for the first time. Shepard and Slayton discuss the Mercury-Atlas 8 orbital flight and tell some little-known secrets of the Mercury astronauts. The book was adapted for a four-hour documentary in 1995.

Slayton, Donald K., with Michael Cassutt. *Deke! U.S. Manned Space: From Mercury to the Shuttle*. New York: Forge, 1995. This is the autobiography of the last of the Mercury astronauts to fly in space. After being grounded from flying in Project Mercury for what turned out to be a minor heart murmur, Slayton was appointed head of the Astronaut Office. Slayton talks of his frustration at being grounded and how he worked to regain flight status. He also discusses the flights of his fellow Mercury astronauts.

Sobel, Lester A., ed. *Space: From Sputnik to Gemini*. New York: Facts on File, 1965. This small book provides a complete account of the pertinent data concerning launches from 1957 to 1966 in both the Soviet Union and the United States. Ordered chronologically, it contains details about each Mercury flight.

Swenson, Lloyd S., Jr., James M. Grimwood, and Charles C. Alexander. *This New Ocean: A History of Project Mercury*. NASA SP-4201. Washington, D.C.: Government Printing Office, 1966. One of the special publications made available to the general public as part of the NASA History series, this text traces Project Mercury through Cooper's flight. Includes material on both the technical and managerial aspects of the program. With photographs and diagrams.

Wendt, Guenter, and Russell Still. *The Unbroken Chain*. Burlington, Ont.: Apogee Books, 2001. Wendt is the only person who worked with every astronaut bound for space.

MESSENGER

Date: August 3, 2004, to 2012 (projected)
Type of spacecraft: Planetary exploration

Mercury, the innermost planet in the solar system, is both Earth-like and Moon-like: Earth-like in that it is a terrestrial planet with a magnetic field, and Moon-like in that it is heavily cratered. Prior to the MESSENGER (Mercury Surface, Space Environment, Geochemistry, and Ranging) program, only the Mariner 10 spacecraft, in 1974 and 1975, had imaged this planet's surface from close proximity during three brief flyby encounters.

Key Figures

Orlando Figueroa (b. 1955), director of NASA's Office of Solar System Exploration

Max R. Peterson, MESSENGER project manager at The Johns Hopkins University's Applied Physics Laboratory

Sean C. Solomon, MESSENGER principal investigator from the Carnegie Institution of Washington, D.C.

Edward Weiler, NASA associate administrator for space science

Summary of the Mission

In late March, 2002, the National Aeronautics and Space Administration (NASA) received budget authorization to design and build the first spacecraft to orbit the innermost planet in the solar system. Named MESSENGER, which stands for Mercury Surface, Space Environment, Geochemistry, and Ranging, the program was selected in July, 1999, as the seventh mission in NASA's relatively young Discovery Program, aimed at rapid development of highly focused, lower-cost space science investigations. The project had been approved for a total cost of $286 million and was to be managed by the Applied Physics Laboratory at The Johns Hopkins University.

Originally planners envisioned a five-year journey to Mercury following launch in 2004, permitting a thorough multidisciplinary one-year orbital investigation of Mercury. This plan would have taken MESSENGER on a trajectory that would include three Venus flybys, one each in November of 2004, August of 2005, and October of 2006, and two Mercury flybys, one each in October of 2007 and July of 2008. Orbital insertion around Mercury would have occurred in July, 2009.

MESSENGER was equipped with seven separate scientific instruments, some of which could be operated cooperatively. MESSENGER's two cameras would produce high-resolution images of nearly the entire surface of Mercury. Detailed surface topography data would be generated by a laser altimeter. The spacecraft also carried four spectrometers and a magnetometer. The suite of spectrometers specifically included a gamma-ray and neutron spectrometer, a Mercury atmospheric and surface composition spectrometer, an x-ray spectrometer, and an energetic particle and plasma spectrometer.

To protect some of those instruments and the basic spacecraft structures and systems from the intense heat encountered in the neighborhood of Mercury, MESSENGER was outfitted with a large, curved sunshield. The magnetometer stuck out far from the main bus to keep it free of electromagnetic interference generated by onboard electronics. In

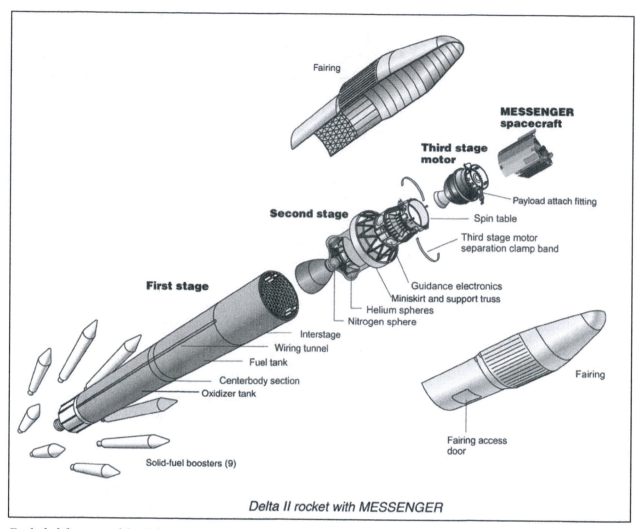

Fairing

MESSENGER
spacecraft

Third stage
motor

Payload attach fitting

Spin table

Second stage

Third stage motor
separation clamp band

First stage

Guidance electronics
Miniskirt and support truss
Helium spheres
Nitrogen sphere

Interstage
Wiring tunnel
Fuel tank
Centerbody section
Oxidizer tank

Fairing

Fairing access
door

Solid-fuel boosters (9)

Delta II rocket with MESSENGER

Exploded diagram of the Delta II launch vehicle for the MESSENGER spacecraft. (NASA / JHU / APL)

addition, the spacecraft used composite materials and carbon fiber in its construction in order to withstand the heat while also lightening spacecraft weight.

After four years of design, assembly, and testing, and with only six months to go before scheduled launch, MESSENGER in late December, 2003, was shipped from The Johns Hopkins University to NASA's Goddard Space Flight Center for structural testing of the spacecraft prior to its delivery to the launch site. There, MESSENGER was subjected to extreme thermal, vibrational, and acceleration loads. After passing those tests, MESSENGER was secured within a special air-conditioned payload

transportation van and then delivered to Kennedy Space Center/Cape Canaveral Air Force Station, arriving there on March 10, 2004. At this point, launch remained scheduled for May 11, 2004. While in a high bay clean room, the spacecraft's solar arrays were attached to the main bus.

In late March, NASA decided to delay MESSENGER's launch in order to permit additional testing of the spacecraft's fault-protection system software. This delay forced an alteration of the spacecraft's trajectory and changed the timing of MESSENGER's arrival at Mercury. Launch was reset for no earlier than July 30, with a fifteen-day launch window that would delay insertion into orbit around Mercury to 2011. The new trajectory would incorporate an Earth flyby one year after launch for a gravity assist; a pair of Venus flybys in October, 2006, and June, 2006; and three Mercury flybys in January and October, 2008, and September, 2009, prior to Mercury orbital insertion.

MESSENGER was taken to Launch Complex 17, Pad B in mid-July and installed atop the heavy-lift model of the Delta II launch vehicle, one equipped with nine strap-on solid rocket boosters, a liquid-fueled first and second stage, and a solid-fueled third stage. After several delays and one scrubbed launch, MESSENGER stood poised to depart Earth. MESSENGER had a twelve-second-long launch window on August 3, and the launch team was able to dispatch the Delta II booster on time at 06:15:56 Coordinated Universal Time (UTC). For the spacecraft, this began a 7.8-billion-kilometer trip to reach Mercury.

MESSENGER weighed 1,100 kilograms at launch, with 600 kilograms being consumed as hydrazine propellant and nitrogen tetroxide as oxidizer. Six of the booster's nine solid rocket strapons ignited at liftoff. The other three ignited in the air. All had burned out and separated by the 160- second mark in the ascent. First-stage shutdown occurred 4 minutes and 38 seconds after liftoff. Shortly thereafter, while the second-stage engine burned, MESSENGER's payload shroud was safely jettisoned. The second-stage shutdown occurred just seconds before the 9-minute point of ascent. Its engine restarted at the T-plus-46-minute mark and burned for another three minutes. This increased the spacecraft's apogee to 6,400 kilometers. The third stage ignited at 50 minutes and 20 seconds after liftoff, and the spacecraft achieved escape velocity from Earth's gravitational hold. Five minutes after burnout, MESSENGER separated from its spent third stage. Spacecraft solar panels unfurled properly and were secured for the lengthy cruise phase to Mercury.

During the first week after launch, the operations team checked MESSENGER's communications system—including its high-, medium-, and low-gain antennae—and started testing the guidance and control system. An initial trajectory correction burn was performed on August 24, 2004, at 09:03:55 UTC using four medium-sized and eight small thrusters firing in concert. The burn lasted only 3.6 minutes and slowed the spacecraft's speed by 18 meters per second. By this time, testing of scientific instruments had commenced, and no problems were discovered. Thrusters on MESSENGER were fired for 23 seconds on July 21, 2005; this was only the fifth trajectory correction since launch. This firing altered the spacecraft's speed by a mere one-sixth of a meter per second, setting it up for the first Earth flyby encounter. MESSENGER flew within 2,347 kilometers of Mongolia at 19:13 UTC on August 2, 2005. The narrow-angle camera snapped high-resolution photographs of the Earth as a test of the spacecraft's imaging systems. If all proceeded as

At Astrotech in Titusville, Fla., technicians with The Johns Hopkins University Applied Physics Laboratory (APL) prepare the MESSENGER spacecraft for a move to a hazardous processing facility in preparation for loading the spacecraft's complement of hypergolic propellants. (NASA)

planned, MESSENGER would enter orbit about Mercury in 2011.

Contributions

Mercury was known to the ancients, appearing periodically in the evening and morning skies briefly just before sunset and sunrise, respectively. The Romans named it for the messenger of the Gods in part to indicate the speed of its periodic motion across the heavens. Until Mariner 10 imaged a portion of Mercury's surface during three flybys in 1975, in modern times little more was known about the planet closest to the Sun apart from its solar illumination, its rates of rotation and revolution, its tremendous temperature variation from lit to dark sides, the fact that its surface was heavily cratered, and the fact that its density suggested a large amount of iron in its core. Being so close to the Sun, Mercury receives eleven times more sunlight than Earth, and the surface temperature of the illuminated side can reach 700 kelvins or more at maximum, with the difference between lit and dark sides being several hundred kelvins.

Mercury ranges in its orbit from between 46 and 69 million kilometers from the Sun. It revolves about the Sun every 88 Earth days, while rotating about its axis at the slow rate of once every fifty-nine days. This means that at a given location, the time between successive sunrises, the Mercurian day, is the equivalent of 176 days on Earth. The planet's mass is only 5.5 percent that of Earth, its density is 5,430 kilograms per cubic meter, its diameter is 4,850 kilometers, and the strength of its magnetic field at its equator is slightly less than 1 percent of Earth's.

Mariner 10 saw only a little less than half the planet, so it was anticipated that MESSENGER investigations would raise plenty of questions that only future spacecraft might be able to address. However, MESSENGER was designed to investigate a number of basic science questions: Why would Mercury be the only terrestrial planet apart from Earth to have a global magnetic field? Does Mercury's magnetic field, like Earth's, originate from a dynamo effect from a molten iron core, or is the core solid and the magnetic field frozen in place? What elements are in the crust, and in what concentration are they present? Why does Mercury have such a large concentration of iron, thus making it the densest planet in the solar system? How does Mercury fit into the present-day understanding of the formation of the solar system? Did Mercury, like Earth, once have a crust that may have been boiled away by the Sun? Considering the high temperatures Mercury endures, how might the innermost planet have ice in its polar regions?

Context

The nine known planets of the solar system could be divided into two categories, the gas giants and the terrestrial planets. Mercury, Venus, Earth, and Mars represent the terrestrial planets. Jupiter, Saturn, Uranus, and Neptune represent the gas giants. Outermost Pluto does not fit into either category, and some astronomers are prone to dismiss Pluto as a planet in its own right.

Through studying each planet within these two categories and contrasting it against the others in the same category—the discipline of comparative planetology—much more can be learned about a planet than if one examined it exclusively. Much has been learned about the nature of the Earth by contrasting it with what is observed on Mars and Venus, and to a lesser extent by comparing it to Mercury. However, only one spacecraft—Mariner 10, launched on November 3, 1973—has ever visited Mercury, and it was able to take images and make readings of the planet's physical conditions during only three brief flybys in 1974 and 1975. (No Soviet or Russian spacecraft was sent to investigate Mercury during the twentieth century.) Because Mercury is so close to the Sun, it has been difficult for a spacecraft to reach Mercury and survive the thermal environment. It is therefore no surprise that so few spacecraft were directed to Mercury during the first fifty years of the Space Age.

More than three decades would transpire before NASA would again be granted authorization for a return voyage to Mercury. Whereas Mariner 10 could only rapidly fly by the innermost planet in the solar system, the MESSENGER spacecraft is designed to perform at least a yearlong sequence of imaging and taking measurements of physical characteristics of Mercury from an orbital position. If even part of its mission is successful, MESSENGER will greatly increase our understanding of this elusive planet.

—David G. Fisher

See also: Dawn Mission; Mariner 10; Mercury Spacecraft; Planetary Exploration.

Further Reading

Beatty, Kelly J., and Andrew Chaikin, eds. *The New Solar System*. Cambridge, Mass.: Cambridge University Press, 1990. A thorough description of the solar system based largely upon spacecraft data. Designed as an introductory-level textbook for the undergraduate student, but readily available to the interested reader.

Murray, Bruce G. *Earthlike Planets: Surfaces of Mercury, Venus, Earth, Moon, and Mars*. New York: W. H. Freeman, 1981. Provides a comparative-planetology perspective on the understanding of the inner solar system. Although dated for all planets except Mercury, an excellent read for anyone interested in planetary science.

Strom, Robert G. *Mercury: The Elusive Planet*. Washington, D.C.: Smithsonian Institution Press, 1987. Provides a historical perspective for exploration of the innermost planet in the solar system from ancient times through the Mariner 10 flyby.

Strom, Robert G., and Ann L. Sprague. *Exploring Mercury: The Iron Planet*. London: Springer-Verlag, 2003. Provides a CD-ROM of Mariner 10 and telescope images of Mercury along with a wealth of information about the planet closest to the Sun.

Meteorological Satellites

Date: Beginning April 1, 1960
Type of spacecraft: Meteorological satellites

Since 1960, meteorological satellites have helped predict the weather, save lives in storms, protect crops during droughts, and improve life on Earth. These satellites have revolutionized meteorological science, and became an indispensable part of modern living.

Summary of the Satellites

The first successful meteorological experiment was flown in 1959 on the United States' Explorer 7 satellite, which measured reflected sunlight, infrared radiation emitted from Earth, and energy radiated from the Sun. These components of Earth's radiation are fundamental to deriving atmospheric and oceanic conditions that give rise to daily changes in weather patterns.

In 1960, the Television Infrared Observations Satellite (TIROS) program began. With a special television camera called a vidicon, TIROS 1 was able to provide the first cloud images from space and thus become the first dependable, long-term weather satellite. The TIROS series demonstrated that satellites could be used to survey global weather conditions and study other surface features from space. TIROS 1 transmitted to Earth more than twenty thousand high-quality cloud cover photographs from a 122.5-kilogram spacecraft.

TIROS 2 proved the accuracy and reliability of experimental television and infrared equipment for global meteorological information data gathering. The TIROS series proved the cornerstone of the effort to develop twenty-four-hour weather-monitoring of Earth. The Improved TIROS Operational System (ITOS) and the Environmental Science Services Administration (ESSA) and National Oceanic and Atmospheric Administration (NOAA) systems that have followed simply improved on the basic design.

RCA was the prime contractor for the TIROS series, and the project was managed by the National Aeronautics and Space Administration (NASA) with data handled by the United States Weather Bureau (later renamed ESSA, still later titled NOAA). Ten TIROS satellites were successfully launched. Only TIROS 5 experienced an infrared imaging system failure.

The satellites of the ESSA were designed to follow up on the successful TIROS series. In this series, dependability increased to the point that, for the first time, weather forecasters could use satellite data routinely in preparing daily weather forecasts, storm and marine advisories, gale and hurricane warnings, cloud analyses, and navigational assistance. Again, RCA was the prime contractor. Nine ESSA satellites were extensions of and improvements on the original TIROS design.

ESSA spacecraft carried either the automatic picture transmission systems or the advanced vidicon camera system. These systems included two eight-hundred-line cameras with nearly twice the resolution of a normal television camera. They could photograph in real time a 3,000-kilometerwide area with 3-kilometer resolution. Two television cameras were mounted 180° apart on the sides, with a 40-centimeter receiving antenna on top, solar cells covering the sides and top, and four whip antennae extending from the baseplates. Generally, it was some 50 centimeters high and nearly 100 centimeters wide, shaped like an eighteen-sided cylindrical

A GOES-12 visible image of Hurricane Katrina shortly after landfall on August 29, 2005. (NASA Goddard Space Flight Center)

polygon. Two tape recorders could store up to 48 pictures for later transmission.

ESSA satellites provided global weather data to the United States Department of Commerce's command and data acquisition stations in Wallops Island, Virginia, and Fairbanks, Alaska, and then relayed those data to the National Environmental Satellite Service at Suitland, Maryland, for processing and forwarding to the major forecasting centers in the United States and around the world. ESSA provided the world's first true meteorological satellites as well as the world's first operational applications satellite.

In 1969, an image from ESSA 7 made history by revealing that snow cover in parts of the Midwest was three times thicker than normal. Measurements showed that there was equivalent of 15 to 25 centimeters of water covering thousands of square kilometers. A disaster was declared, and before the floods came the area was prepared. By the time ESSA 9 was in orbit there were some 400 receiving stations in operation around the world, as well as 26 universities, up to 30 American television stations, and an unknown number of private citizens receiving the photographs.

In 1970, a second generation, called the Improved TIROS Operational System (ITOS), was introduced. The National Oceanic and Atmospheric Administration had taken over the duties of the ESSA. Thus, the second ITOS was also known as NOAA-1 when launched in December, 1970, from Vandenberg Air Force Base. Gradually ITOS and the NOAA satellites began to fulfill the functions of the remaining ESSA satellites. These spacecraft were manufactured by RCA. ITOS-B failed to achieve orbit as a result of launch vehicle failure, and ITOS-C was never used as a designation. The NOAA series formally began with NOAA-6. Like the ITOS spacecraft, the NOAA satellites were developed by RCA.

TIROS-type satellites proved that an operational weather satellite system had considerable value, but the series still had limited capabilities. Modern weather forecasting is done numerically, with the aid of computers. Some of the most important data are the vertical temperature structure of the atmosphere, the motion of the winds (both speed and direction), and the atmosphere's moisture content. The ESSA system could provide no direct data about these factors. The United States was well aware of these limitations and eventually turned to the Nimbus system, which had remote sensors that could measure atmospheric temperatures and moisture levels.

The Nimbus series (*nimbus* is Latin for rain cloud) was originally conceived of as only a weather forecasting program, without experimental capabilities. The later satellites, Nimbus 5 through Nimbus 7, were upgraded to provide data for a larger range of scientific programs such as agriculture, cartography, geography, geology, and oceanography. The Nimbus program was especially important for gathering weather data over the poles. The Nimbus series was developed by the General Electric Company and launched from Vandenberg Air Force Base to reach polar orbits. NASA's

Goddard Space Flight Center managed the satellite series, using seven Nimbus satellites to test and improve measuring instruments. Noteworthy experiments were performed. For example, the cloud imaging vidicon camera on Nimbus 2 was equipped to transmit images of weather to local receiving stations by a very high frequency (VHF) signal. Thus, many low-cost receiving stations, which were often located in developing countries, could receive and use data from weather satellites for the first time. In 1969, instruments that were able to probe the atmosphere's temperature and moisture layers by means of a selected spectral apparatus placed on Nimbus 3.

Of special significance in the late 1960's were the launchings of NASA's Applications Technology Satellites (ATS's) 1 and 3. These geosynchronous satellites were actually early communications satellites that orbited over one specific spot on Earth. They carried sensors that, from a stationary position high above the equator, provided a constant view of changing weather patterns. For the first time meteorologists could track with precision the movement and growth of weather systems from space. ATS satellites were thus the first series of meteorological functioning satellites in a geosynchronous orbit, and were positioned to view 45 percent of Earth's surface. This program was managed by NASA, with Hughes Aircraft Company the primary spacecraft contractor. The second, fourth, and fifth ATS's failed to gain the proper orbit, and were thus excluded from meaningful experiments. ATS 3 not only performed meteorological experiments but also performed experiments involving communications, navigation, and Earth reconnaissance. Later it was moved to a more favorable orbit to better monitor any storms developing over the United States.

The Synchronous Meteorological Satellite (SMS) series was the first series actually designed to be geosynchronous. The satellites were designed by Ford Aerospace and Communications Corporation and managed by NASA for NOAA. Parked over a part of the globe, they enabled meteorologists to make twenty-four-hour forecasts. So successful was this program that it was succeeded by NOAA's Geostationary Operational Environmental Satellite (GOES) program. SMS 1 (sometimes known as SMS-A) and SMS 2 (or SMS-B) were developmental satellites leading up to the GOES program, and GOES-A also carried the designation SMS-C.

The first GOES spacecraft were produced by Ford, and after they were launched by NASA they were turned over to NOAA, which used them to provide worldwide meteorological data and observations of ocean currents and river water levels. The GOES spacecraft provided pictures of approximately one-fourth of the globe at thirty-minute intervals day and night with an infrared image maker. The GOES-D was the first U.S. spacecraft capable of near-continuous measurements of atmospheric water vapor and temperature. The spacecraft enabled scientists to provide more accurate weather predictions.

GOES-A was launched on October 16, 1975. Early GOES satellites were spin-stabilized and viewed the Earth only about 10 percent of the time. These satellites were in operation from 1975 until 1994. From April 13, 1994, to the present, a new generation of three-axis stabilized spacecraft (GOES I-M) has been in operation. GOES-8, the first of the new generation, was launched April 13, 1994. Since then, GOES-9 and GOES-10 have been launched. This generation of satellites views the Earth 100 percent of the time, taking continuous images and soundings. GOES satellites provide data for severe storm evaluation and information on cloud cover, winds, ocean currents, fog distribution, storm circulation, and snow melt, using visual and infrared imagery. The satellites also receive transmissions from free-floating balloons, buoys, and remote automatic data collection stations around the world.

GOES satellites are a mainstay of weather forecasting in the United States. They are the backbone of short-term forecasting. Real-time weather data gathered by GOES satellites, combined with data from Doppler radars and automated surface observing systems, greatly aid weather forecasters in providing warnings of thunderstorms, winter storms, flash floods, hurricanes, and other severe weather. These warnings help save lives and preserve property.

The United States operates two meteorological satellites in geostationary orbit, one over the East Coast and one over the West Coast, with overlapping coverage over the United States. Currently, GOES-8 and GOES-10 are in operation. The GOES satellites are a critical component of the ongoing National Weather Service modernization program, aiding forecasters in providing more precise and timely forecasts. GOES-L was carried in space aboard a Lockheed Martin Atlas-2A rocket on May 3, 2000. Twenty-seven minutes later, the spacecraft separated from the Centaur stage. GOES-M supported NOAA's dual-satellite geostationary observing system. Five more GOES satellites were launched, so that by 2019 the most-recently commissioned one was GOES-S (there was no GOES-Q). By 2019, GOES-M was decommissioned. In 2019 three GOES satellites were operational, and one was placed in orbital storage (GOES-14).

On March 28, 1983, the first of the Advanced TIROS-N (ATN) satellites, designated NOAA-8, was launched. These satellites are physically larger and have more power than their predecessors, to accommodate more equipment. NOAA continues to operate the ATN series of satellites with improved instruments. The current configuration is NOAA-14, launched December 12, 1994, and NOAA- 15, launched May 13, 1998. NOAA-15 (NOAA-K) is the first in a series of five satellites with improved imaging and sounding capabilities and is expected to operate until about 2010. NOAA-16 (NOAA-L) was launched from Vandenberg Air Force Base on a Titan II on September 21, 2000. NOAA-17 (NOAA-M) launched from Vandenberg Air Force Base on June 24, 2002. NOAA-N launched on May 20, 2005, from Vandenberg Air Force Base on a Delta II booster. Upon reaching orbital position, the spacecraft was renamed NOAA-18. NOAA-N prime's launch was planned for 2008; this spacecraft had been severely damaged in a processing accident in which it fell from a transportation platform and had to be repaired.

In the 1980's, NOAA needed to balance the high cost of space systems and the growing need to provide a complete and accurate description of the atmosphere at regular intervals as inputs to numerical weather prediction and climate-monitoring support systems. This led NOAA to enter into discussions and agreements at the international level with the European Organisation for the Exploitation of Meteorological Satellites (EUMETSAT). The goal of this cooperation is to provide continuity of measurements from polar orbits, cost sharing, and improved forecast and monitoring capabilities through the introduction of new technologies.

Building upon the Polar Operational Environmental Satellites (POES) program, an agreement is in place between NOAA and EUMETSAT on the Initial Joint Polar-orbiting Operational Satellite System (IJPS). This program will include two series of independent but fully coordinated NOAA and EUMETSAT satellites, exchange of instruments and global data, cooperation in algorithm development, and plans for real-time direct broadcast. Under terms of the IJPS agreement, NOAA will provide NOAA-N and NOAA-N prime satellites for flight in the afternoon orbit while EUMETSAT makes available METOP-1 and METOP-2 satellites for flight in the mid-morning orbit. The first METOP satellite was originally planned to launch in mid-2003. However, the program experienced difficulties, and the METOP-1 launch was pushed back to October 19, 2006. METOP-2 launched on September 17, 2012, and METOP-3 on November 7, 2018. Once in orbit these three became known as METOP-A, B, and C.

On May 5, 1994, President Bill Clinton made the landmark decision to merge the nation's military and civil operational meteorological satellite systems into a single, national system capable of satisfying both civil and national security requirements for space-based remotely sensed environmental data. Convergence of these programs is the most significant change in U.S. operational remote sensing since the launch of the first weather satellite in April, 1960. For the first time, the U.S. government is taking an integrated approach to identifying and meeting the operational satellite needs of both the civil and national security communities. The joint program formed at President Clinton's direction is the National Polar-orbiting Operational Environmental Satellite System (NPOESS). It is expected to provide more than $1.8 billion savings in acquisition and operational costs through the System Life Cycle of the program, compared to the cost of continuing the planned separate satellite systems within the Departments of Defense and Commerce.

The U.S. government has traditionally maintained two operational weather satellite systems, each with a thirty-plus-year heritage of successful service: NOAA's Polar Operational Environmental Satellite (POES) and the Department of Defense's Defense Meteorological Satellite Program (DMSP). Changes in geopolitis and declining agency budgets prompted a reexamination of combining the two systems. These eight satellites, the first of which was launched in October, 1971, included a precision sensor on top. Designed and built by RCA, the DMSP spacecraft served as the primary military meteorological reconnaissance satellites. Similar to TIROS, DMSP satellites transmit weather data to the United States Air Force Global Weather Control at Strategic Air Command headquarters at Offutt Air Force Base in Nebraska and to other military installations around the world. Satellite sensors included an electron measurement instrument to evaluate atmospheric conditions that might affect military communication, an instrument to measure temperature, and a cloud cover imager.

On October 3, 1994, NOAA, the Department of Defense (DoD), and NASA created an Integrated Program Office (IPO) to develop, manage, acquire, and operate the NPOESS system. The IPO concept provides each of the participating agencies with lead responsibility for one of three primary functional areas. NOAA has overall responsibility for the converged system and is also responsible for satellite operations. NOAA is also the primary interface with the international and civil user communities. DoD is responsible for supporting the IPO for major systems acquisitions, including launch support. NASA has a primary responsibility for facilitating the development and incorporation of new cost-effective technologies into the converged system. Although each agency provides certain key personnel in their lead role, each functional division is staffed by tri-agency work teams to maintain the integrated approach.

On December 13, 1999, a new DoD meteorological satellite was launched by the U.S. Air Force and is being operated by NOAA. The satellite is the next in a series of the Defense Meteorological Satellite Program and is the first DMSP whose post-launch checkout was conducted from NOAA's Satellite Operations Control Center in Suitland, Maryland.

The first converged NPOESS satellite was expected to be available for launch in the latter half of the first decade of the twenty-first century, approximately 2008, depending on when the remaining Polar Operational Environmental Satellite (POES) and DMSP program satellite assets were exhausted. NPOESS would have provided significantly improved operational capabilities and benefits to satisfy the nation's critical civil and national security requirements for space-based, remotely sensed environmental data. NPOESS would have delivered higher resolution and more accurate atmospheric and oceanographic data to support improved accuracy in short-term weather forecasts and severe storm warnings, as well as to serve the data-continuity requirements of the climate community for improved climate prediction and assessment. NPOESS would also have provided improved measurements and information about the space environment necessary to ensure reliable operations of space-based and ground-based systems, as well as continue to provide surface data collection and search-and-rescue capabilities. However, on February 1, 2010 the Obama White House announced that the NPOESS partnership would be dissolved in favor of pursuing other avenues of space-based meteorological systems.

Contributions

Basically, meteorological satellites are platforms for "topside observation," or electromagnetic scanning of the atmosphere of Earth from above. Their scanning is passive in the sense that satellites merely make use of existing radiation emitted or reflected from the atmosphere, without adding to it as radar does. Many experiments, especially those conducted with the Nimbus satellite series, improve and perfect weather forecasting.

Some satellites also do special experiments. For example, there have been many important experiments measuring both direct and reflected energy from the Sun. Orbiting satellites provide an ideal platform for such measurements. The first successful meteorological satellite experiment, on Explorer 7, directly measured the Sun's energy for the first time. Additional radiation experiments have been conducted on TIROS, Nimbus, and NOAA satellites.

In general, meteorological satellites perform five major functions. They are able to take images of clouds and cloud patterns and relay them back to Earth; they can observe the movement of clouds and weather systems (this work was previously accomplished through the use of tracer balloons); they can measure the atmosphere's moisture content and temperature; they can help forecast storms, especially severe thunderstorms, through cloud patterns and upper-air movements; and they can help track tropical storms by observing cloud patterns.

A meteorological satellite utilizes three classes of instruments with which to gather data, forecast weather, and perform scientific experiments.

Radiometers measure Earth's infrared and reflected solar radiance and use small, selected wavelengths (ultraviolet to microwave) to measure temperature, ozone, and water vapor in the atmosphere. Radiometers are sensitive to one or more wavelength bands in the visible and invisible ranges. If visible wavelengths are used, the satellite can detect cloud vistas from reflected sunlight, resulting in a slightly blurred version of those images photographed directly by astronauts. Using invisible emissions, satellites can capture terrestrial radiation, producing images from Earth's radiant energy.

Such radiometers, combined with sensitive optical devices, can measure clouds as small as 1 kilometer. As the satellite spins, the radiometer scans parts of Earth. These radiometric data are then transmitted to each ground processing station or recorded for later replay. The ground processing station then produces a computer-generated image with landmark features, coastlines, and sometimes even artificial political boundaries.

Sounding sensors are more complex than radiometers. These sonar-like devices probe the atmosphere, and aid in understanding temperature and moisture, among other things. For example, Nimbus 3 measured the global distribution of ozone in the atmosphere. Tracking and data-relay systems are special transponders that receive signals from Earth stations and relay back other data. These systems help identify wind patterns and ocean currents.

Context

TIROS satellites first proved the feasibility of gathering meteorological data from space, and in 1962 and 1963 helped save lives during a period of severe hurricanes. Meteorological satellites continually examine cloud formations, estimate atmospheric water vapor, and measure air and water temperatures. These data are then used routinely to forecast storms and provide basic information for modeling weather conditions. Aircraft and ship travel would be far more difficult without the use of meteorological satellites. Nearly all Americans are familiar with the work of these satellites from the weather forecasts on local television news programs.

The huge panoramic views of the atmosphere afforded by meteorological satellites confirmed the structures of large cloudy weather systems that had previously emerged only after painstaking assembly and analysis of synoptic data. Few can even appreciate the work that was required in the 1950's to produce a cloud map half as accurate as one poor satellite photograph. Satellite images were remarkably clear and precise, and with the continual improvement of equipment they became better and better. The relatively high resolution of the images (a few kilometers compared with tens of thousands of kilometers of the earlier, coarser maps) revealed a bewildering range of subsynoptic scale structures in cloud systems, many of which are still not well understood. For the first time there was uniform weather information. Meteorological satellites provide a consistent flow of images, covering oceans and landmasses heretofore impossible to observe.

The development of meteorological satellites has been particularly advanced by international cooperation. For example, several different nations contributed the instruments that the United States used in its Nimbus and TIROS programs. The Bahamas, Brazil, and other countries in Latin America use the United States' GOES and NOAA satellites in daily forecasting and research.

In the longer run, the availability of decades of daily coverage of Earth for rain, temperature, cloud behavior, and other meteorological data have enabled researchers to develop climatologies—that is, baselines of what is normal; thus, deviations can be compared. These baselines are especially important for detecting drought, temperature change, and snow caps. Previously, scientists had small descriptions but lacked data for the entire planet. With the complement of instruments covering the entire planet, scientists are able to attain a better understanding of what is normal weather for Earth. In addition, NOAA's Advanced Very High-Resolution Radiometer (AVHRR) was developed in such a way that infrared signals could be analyzed to determine the state of vegetation on Earth. Used over a number of years, this instrument can monitor slow but significant changes in large-scale vegetation cover brought about by droughts and floods.

—Douglas Gomery

See also: Environmental Science Services Administration Satellites; Heat Capacity Mapping Mission; Interplanetary Monitoring Platform Satellites; ITOS and NOAA Meteorological Satellites; Landsat 1, 2, and 3; Landsat 4 and 5; Meteorological Satellites: Military; Nimbus Meteorological Satellites; Seasat; SMS and GOES Meteorological Satellites; TIROS Meteorological Satellites; Upper Atmosphere Research Satellite.

Further Reading

Ahrens, C. Donald. *Essentials of Meteorology: An Invitation to the Atmosphere.* 4th ed. Pacific Grove, Calif.: Thomson Brooks/Cole, 2005. This is a text suitable for an introductory course in meteorology. Comes complete with a CD-ROM to help explain concepts and demonstrate the atmosphere's dynamic nature.

American Meteorological Association. *The Conception, Growth, Accomplishments, and Future of Meteorological Satellites.* NASA SP-2257. Springfield, Va.: National Technical Information Service, 1982. An important collection of articles about the history and practice of the United States meteorological program. Clearly written.

Anthes, Richard A. *Meterology.* 7th ed. Upper Saddle River, N.J.: Prentice Hall, 1997. Includes color illustrations and maps, bibliographical references, and an index.

Bader, M. J., G. S. Forbes, and J. R. Grant, eds. *Images in Weather Forecasting: A Practical Guide for Interpreting Satellite and Radar Imagery*. New York: Cambridge University Press, 1997. The aim of this work is to present the meteorology student and operational forecaster with the current techniques for interpreting satellite and radar images of weather systems in mid-latitudes. The focus of the book is the large number of illustrations.

Barrett, E. C. *Climatology from Satellites*. New York: Harper and Row, 1974. A systematic look at the applications and uses of satellites in all phases of meteorology. Written for the advanced student, although the second chapter lays out in clear detail the extent of the program in the early 1970's.

Eagleman, Joe R. *Meteorology: The Atmosphere in Action*. New York: Van Nostrand Reinhold, 1980. This basic textbook provides a context for the importance of the meteorological satellites as tools of the modern-day scientist. Written in clear and understandable language.

Henderson-Sellers, Ann, ed. *Satellite Sensing of a Cloudy Atmosphere*. London: Taylor and Francis, 1982. A collection of articles about the various technologies and uses of meteorological satellites. Written in conjunction with the Global Atmospheric Research Program.

Moran, Joseph M., Michael D. Morgan, and Patricia M. Pauley. *Meteorology: The Atmosphere and the Science of Weather*. 5th ed. Upper Saddle River, N.J.: Prentice Hall, 1997. Comprehensive treatment of the science of weather. Includes color illustrations and maps, bibliographical references, and an index.

National Aeronautics and Space Administration. *Meteorological Satellites: Past, Present, and Future*. NASA SP-2227. Springfield, Va.: National Technical Information Service, 1982. An important collection of articles about how the United States' meteorological satellite program began. It covers the programs until the beginning of the 1980's. Accessible to the beginner.

Scorer, Richard S. *Cloud Investigation by Satellite*. New York: Halsted Press, 1986. A wonderful overview, filled with photographs illustrating the uses of meteorological satellites. The images provide a clear sense of the importance of the various advancements in the satellite meteorological program.

Smith, W. L., et al. "The Meteorological Satellite: Overview of Twenty-Five Years of Operation." *Science* 231 (January 31, 1986): 455-462. This is an important review of the contributions of the meteorological satellite programs. Written for the layperson.

United States Congress. House Committee on Science and Technology. *Space Activities of the United States, Soviet Union, and Other Launching Countries/Organizations: 1957-1984*. Report prepared by Congressional Research Service, the Library of Congress, 99th Congress, 1st session. Washington, D.C.: Government Printing Office, 1985. This is a clear analysis of the various activities in space. Includes an interesting section on meteorological satellites.

Zimmerman, Robert. *The Chronological Encyclopedia of Discoveries in Space*. Westport, Conn.: Oryx Press, 2000. Provides a complete chronological history of all piloted and robotic spacecraft and explains flight events and scientific results. Suitable for all levels of research.

Meteorological Satellites: Military

Date: Beginning April 1, 1960
Type of spacecraft: Meteorological satellites

Military meteorological satellites provide cloud-cover photographs and other weather data from orbit. These data are used for the scheduling of reconnaissance satellite launches to the planning of military operations. Much of this important information could not be obtained from ground instruments.

Summary of the Satellites

Weather is a determining factor in all human activities—including military activities. History is filled with examples of weather's impact on battles, and military strategists know that commanders must be able to predict the next day's weather. For example, General Dwight D. Eisenhower's decision to launch the invasion of Europe on June 6, 1944, was based on a forecast of marginally acceptable weather.

When the first studies of satellites were made in the late 1940's, it was quickly realized that these spacecraft could provide weather data on a worldwide basis. In the late 1950's, the U.S. Army considered the possibility of using a satellite equipped with a television camera for battlefield reconnaissance. By the fall of 1958, this project became a meteorological satellite and was transferred to the National Aeronautics and Space Administration (NASA) as a joint civil-military project. It was called the Television Infrared Observations Satellite (TIROS). TIROS 1 was launched on April 1, 1960, into a 740-by-692-kilometer orbit. Within days it was clear that the science of meteorology had been fundamentally altered.

It was during this time that Discoverer reconnaissance satellites began returning the first satellite photographs of the Soviet Union. To support these satellites, reliable weather forecasts were needed of specific sites inside the Soviet Union, China, and Eastern Europe. Film supplies of satellites were limited; none would be wasted on photographs of clouds. Even partly cloudy conditions result in poor photographs, because of large shadows cast by the clouds. (U-2 overflights of the Soviet Union and, later, Cuba often had to be delayed because of weather.) During the early years of United States reconnaissance satellite operations, weather support was provided by the civilian TIROS and Nimbus satellites. By early 1963, however, it was becoming clear that military and civilian requirements were too different. Whereas civilian weather forecasters needed widespread coverage, the military required information on specific areas. Accordingly, a separate military meteorological satellite program was approved.

The first of these satellites was launched on January 19, 1965, from Vandenberg Air Force Base in California. The Thor booster put it into an 822-by-471-kilometer orbit, inclined 98.8°. The satellite passed over a given spot on Earth at the same local time each day. A total of six Thor launches were made until March, 1966. (One launch failed.)

On September 16, 1966, the satellite program became known as the Defense Meteorological Satellite Program (DMSP). The satellites were built by the Radio Corporation of America. Called the DMSP Block 4A satellites, they weighed 82 kilograms and were spin-stabilized. In 1968, the Block 4B was introduced, and the Block 5A followed in 1970.

While the first DMSP satellites were being launched, the United States was becoming

This image of Earth's city lights was created with data from the Defense Meteorological Satellite Program (DMSP) Operational Linescan System (OLS). Originally designed to view clouds by moonlight, the OLS is also used to map the locations of permanent lights on the Earth's surface. (NASA Goddard Space Flight Center)

increasingly involved in the Vietnam War. Knowledge of weather conditions was critical, particularly for air strikes. Air Force and Navy fighter pilots had to spot their targets visually from 3,660 meters. Tanker aircraft, which refueled the strike aircraft, needed to operate in areas that were free of clouds and turbulence. In South Vietnam, Laos, and Cambodia, close air support missions required good weather at low altitudes. It was difficult to provide the necessary forecasts for these activities: There were few weather stations in Southeast Asia, the North Vietnamese regularly falsified or coded their data, and the seasonal monsoon weather caused additional problems.

Many different types of satellites were used to forecast the weather in Southeast Asia during this time. Civilian weather satellites, equipped with a feature called automatic picture transmission (APT), transmitted images to ground stations constantly so they could be detected by any receiver within range. (The Chinese and the North Vietnamese may have also made use of this technology.) The civilian satellites made their passes from 7:00 a.m. to 9:00 a.m. or 12:00 to 14:00 Coordinated Universal Time (UTC) and from 11:00 a.m. to 1:00 p.m. The DMSP satellites provided photographs in the visible and infrared spectra at 7:00 a.m. (12:00 UTC), 12:00 p.m. (05:00 UTC), 7:00 p.m. (00:00 UTC), and 12:00 a.m. (05:00 UTC). Unlike the civilian photographs, those from the DMSP were encoded. The Air Force ground stations were located at an air base in South Vietnam, outside Saigon, and at a Thai air base. The South Vietnamese facility had a mobile van with an APT antenna, a large DMSP dish antenna, and two sandbagged DMSP trailers. Photographs were transmitted via microwaves to a U.S. Air Force headquarters facility. (Unfortunately, the Navy lagged behind the Air Force in readout equipment during the early years of the war. That was corrected by 1970. The USS *Constellation* was the first aircraft carrier to use shipboard readout equipment.)

The DMSP Block 5D-1 version made its debut in 1976 in the United States. The 473-kilogram satellite was a gold-foil-wrapped box with a solar panel on a long boom. It was 5.2 meters long and 1.8 meters wide. Television and infrared devices had two resolutions: 0.56 kilometer and 2.78 kilometers. Atmospheric temperature and water vapor could also be measured. The first DMSP Block 5D-1 was launched on September 11, 1976, into an 834-by-806-kilometer, Sun-synchronous orbit. After launch, a high-pressure nitrogen leak caused the satellite to tumble. Because the solar panel was no longer directed toward the Sun, the satellite lost power and ceased to function. On October 5, the solar panel began to be illuminated by the Sun and generate power. Ground controllers were able to raise the altitude of the satellite and slow its spin. This effort was made more difficult when a gyroscope problem occurred in February, 1977. Finally, on March 24, the satellite was fully stabilized. Four more satellites from this series were launched.

The first improved DMSP Block 5D-2 satellite was launched on December 21, 1982. The booster was an Atlas E, an intercontinental ballistic missile converted for satellite launching. The Block 5D-2 carried a larger sensor payload and had a longer life span (thirty-six months versus eighteen months for the earlier Block 5D-1 series). A second Block 5D-2 was launched on November 18, 1983, and a third on June 20, 1987. The operating network consists of two satellites: the "early morning bird," which makes a south to north crossing of the equator at 6:30 a.m. local time, and one that makes its crossing at noon.

On October 3, 1994, the National Oceanic and Atmospheric Administration (NOAA), the Department of Defense (DoD), and NASA created an Integrated Program Office (IPO) to develop, manage, acquire, and operate the National Polar-orbiting Operational Environmental Satellite System (NPOESS) system. The IPO concept provides each of the participating agencies with lead responsibility for one of three primary functional areas. NOAA has overall responsibility for the converged system and is also responsible for satellite operations. NOAA is also the primary interface with the international and civil user communities. DoD is responsible to support the IPO for major systems acquisitions, including launch support. NASA has a primary responsibility for facilitating the development and incorporation of new cost-effective technologies into the converged system. Although each agency provides certain key personnel in its lead role, each functional division is staffed by tri-agency work teams to maintain the integrated approach.

On December 13, 1999, a new Department of Defense meteorological satellite was launched by the U.S. Air Force and is being operated by NOAA. The satellite is the next in a series of the Defense Meteorological Satellite Program and the first DMSP whose post-launch checkout was conducted from NOAA's Satellite Operations Control Center in Suitland, Maryland.

The DMSP system was intended to be replaced by the Defense Weather Satellite System, but the Obama White House cancelled the program in 2012. Then in 2017 a Weather System Follow-on Microwave (WSF-M) satellite was contracted by the Air Force to be a next-generation defense meteorological satellite.

Contributions

DMSP satellites have provided weather data for the planning of reconnaissance satellite coverage, thus preventing the waste of valuable film. In Vietnam, these satellites proved critical. Air Force officials have said that the DMSP was among the most significant innovations during the war. For three years the Navy had made repeated attacks on the Thanh Hoa Bridge, which was one of the two main rail lines to the south. One of the problems was weather over the target. Only eighteen kilometers inland, it was covered with low clouds, fog, smoke from burning fields, and haze during much of the year. Sometimes there would be only two to four days of clear weather per month. The DMSP photographs indicated when the weather was about to change. In the late 1960's, improved sensors increased effectiveness. The infrared scanner revealed the burning rice paddies, and warnings could be given to the pilots.

During the November, 1970, raid on the SonTay prisoner-of-war camp in North Vietnam, DMSP satellites gave a highly accurate three- to five-day forecast. In May, 1975, Cambodians captured the freighter *Mayaguez* on the high seas. During the military action that followed, the DMSP provided most of the weather information. Air refueling areas were moved on May 14 based on DMSP data, and decisions were made to land several damaged helicopters in Thailand rather than abandon them.

Context

Military meteorological satellites provide a support function. They can make military operations more effective but they cannot undertake such activities as reconnaissance surveys or air strikes. Because of their limited role, they face budgetary problems that do not affect other military satellite programs. In the DMSP, these problems gave rise to a number of innovative solutions. During the early 1970's, the program was run by forty military and civilian personnel. Many Air Force officers were of junior rank but held doctorates or had specific technical qualifications. This meant that personnel with ranks as low as captain held senior positions. Their tours were also longer than normal, giving a cohesiveness to the program, while saving funds.

In addition, the Block 4 and early Block 5 satellites had no built-in redundancy, making the program even more cost-efficient. Spacecraft with built-in redundancy are equipped with duplicate systems to prevent failure of the mission in the case of one component's malfunction. Thus, Block 5A and Block 5B spacecraft had a variety of life spans; they would function from three months to twenty-three months. Even with the increased priority in the early 1970's, the DMSP Block 5D had only "selective redundancy," that is, backup systems for certain critical areas. This modification was intended to ensure a longer lifetime. By using the satellite's stellar inertial platform as the guidance system for the rocket booster, designers were also able to reduce the weight of the DMSP satellites—making them less expensive to launch.

The design and contracting process was also innovative. The concept for the infrared scanner, used in all the Block 5 satellites, was proved by three Air Force and two Aerospace Corporation engineers. Hardware development was then undertaken by Westinghouse.

Despite its military origins, the DMSP has its civilian importance. The Photographic data have been available to civilian weather forecasters since 1974. Meteorologists have been able to take advantage of the satellite's improved resolution. Moreover, the DMSP Block 5D has served as the basis of the civilian TIROS-N weather satellite.

—Curtis Peebles

See also: Electronic Intelligence Satellites; Interplanetary Monitoring Platform Satellites; ITOS and NOAA Meteorological Satellites; Landsat 1, 2, and 3; Meteorological Satellites; Nuclear Detection Satellites; Nuclear Energy in Space; Telecommunications Satellites: Military; TIROS Meteorological Satellites; United States Space Command.

Further Reading

Ahrens, C. Donald. *Essentials of Meteorology: An Invitation to the Atmosphere.* 4th ed. Pacific Grove, Calif.: Thomson Brooks/Cole, 2005. This is a text suitable for an introductory course in meteorology. Comes complete with a CD-ROM to help explain concepts and demonstrate the atmosphere's dynamic nature.

Asrar, Ghassem, and Jeff Dozier. *EOS: Science Strategy for the Earth Observing System.* New York: Springer-Verlag, 1994. This illustrated book takes a look at the history of the Earth Observing System. It also discusses the scientific equipment used in the program. There is a list of acronyms and a bibliography.

Bader,M. J., G. S. Forbes, and J. R. Grant, eds. *Images inWeather Forecasting: A Practical Guide for Interpreting Satellite and Radar Imagery.* New York: Cambridge University Press, 1997. The aim of this work is to present the meteorology student and operational forecaster with the current techniques for interpreting satellite and radar images of weather systems in mid-latitudes. The focus of the book is the large number of illustrations.

Hall, Cargill R. *A History of the Military Polar-Orbiting Meteorological Satellite Program*. Chantilly, Va.: Office of the Historian, National Reconnaissance Office, 2001. This report details the development of meteorological satellite sensing for the Department of Defense.

Klass, Philip J. *Secret Sentries in Space*. New York: Random House, 1971. The first book on military satellites. It covers the historical background and development of reconnaissance satellites and briefly discusses U.S. military weather satellites.

Parkinson, Claire L. *Earth from Above: Using Color-Coded Satellite Images to Examine the Global Environment*. Sausalito, Calif.: University Science Books, 1997. A book for non-specialists on reading and interpreting satellite images. Explains how satellite data provide information about the atmosphere, the Antarctic ozone hole, and atmospheric temperature effects. The book includes maps, photographs, and fifty color satellite images.

Peebles, Curtis. *Guardians: Strategic Reconnaissance Satellites*. Novato, Calif.: Presidio Press, 1987. Covers the history and technology of reconnaissance satellites and the profound impact they have had on international relations. The book has a brief mention of U.S. military weather satellites. Suitable for high school and college readers.

Richelson, Jeffrey T. *America's Space Sentinels: DSP Satellites and National Security*. Lawrence: University Press of Kansas, 1999. This is the story of America's Defense Support Program satellites and their effect on world affairs. Richelson has written a definitive history of the spy satellites and their use throughout the Cold War. He explains how DSP's infrared sensors are used to detect meteorites, monitor forest fires, and even gather industrial intelligence by "seeing" the lights of steel mills.

Seinfeld, John H., and Spyros Pandis. *Atmospheric Chemistry and Physics: Air Pollution to Climate*. New York: John Wiley, 1997. This is an extensive reference on atmospheric chemistry, aerosols, and atmospheric models. While the book may be too complex for the average reader, it is extremely useful as a research tool on the science of atmospheric phenomena.

Turnill, Reginald. *The Observer's Book of Unmanned Spaceflight*. New York: Frederick Warne, 1974. A brief overview of uncrewed satellites. It includes a section on the Meteor satellites. Suitable for general audiences.

United States Congress. Senate Committee on Aeronautical and Space Sciences. *Soviet Space Programs: 1971-1975*. Vol. 1. Report prepared by Congressional Research Service, the Library of Congress. 94th Congress, 2d session, 1976. Committee Print. This volume is an earlier version of the source listed below. It includes material on the Meteor weather satellite. Recommended for high school and college readers.

United States Congress. Senate Committee on Commerce, Science, and Transportation. *Soviet Space Programs: 1976-1980. Part 3, Unmanned Space Activities*. Report prepared by Congressional Research Service, the Library of Congress. 99th Congress, 1st session, 1985. Committee Print. This book includes a section on the Meteor weather satellites, a table of launches, and illustrations of the satellites. Recommended for high school and college readers.

Wilding-White, T. M. *Jane's Pocket Book of Space Exploration*. New York: Collier Books, 1977. This source focuses on the achievements of space exploration. It provides a capsule summary of the history and statistics of satellite programs and includes discussion of both the Meteor and DMSP Block 5D satellites.

Mission to Planet Earth

Date: Beginning 1990
Type of program: Earth observation satellites

The Mission to Planet Earth (MTPE) is a long-term program to study how the global environment is changing. It uses the unique perspective available from space to observe, monitor, and assess large-scale environmental processes, with an emphasis on climate change. Satellite data are complemented with data collected by aircraft and ground stations.

Key Figures

Charles F. Kennel, NASA associate administrator for the Office of Mission to Planet Earth

Ghassem R. Asrar (b. 1951), Earth Observing System program scientist

Michael King, Earth Observing System senior project scientist

Summary of the Program

Earth has always experienced changes in its environment and climate. Until very recently, however, such changes were viewed as gradual and of interest only to scientists. Today, evidence of ozone depletion, global warming, deforestation, desertification, acid rain, rising sea levels, extreme weather conditions, and reduction in biodiversity has heralded rapid, large-scale changes in the global environment. There is a growing amount of evidence that the normal rate of global environmental change is being accelerated by human activities. Exhaust fumes from automobiles, factories, and power plants increase the level of greenhouse gases in the atmosphere. Certain chemicals used in manufacturing deplete the ozone layer that protects us from ultraviolet light. Stripping and burning of forests changes the overall balance of life on the planet. Within only a few decades, we have made significant changes in the world about us without understanding the long-term effects on the ability of the environment to sustain life.

In order to understand the global implications of our activities, we must observe and monitor the Earth as a whole. Scientific communities within the United States are working with international scientific communities to examine these issues on a sound scientific basis. These research efforts are being coordinated under the U.S. Global Change Research Program (USGCRP), the International Geosphere-Biosphere Program (IGBP), and the World Climate Research Program (WCRP). NASA's contribution to this effort is Mission to Planet Earth (MTPE), which uses the unique perspective of space to understand how the Earth's environment is changing and humanity's role in that change.

MTPE is a long-term program to study the Earth using data from spacecraft, supplemented with data from aircraft and ground stations, and making those data available to scientists around the world. A research program supports scientific analysis of the data, and the results of these scientific investigations will be used by decision makers to help them make economic and environmental policy. Interdisciplinary research, education, and international coordination are all major elements of MTPE. In order to accomplish its mission, MTPE will use a constellation of satellites organized in two groups: Earth Probes and the Earth Observing System (EOS).

Most of the Earth Probes were deployed during the Phase I Program from 1990 to 1998 and consist of satellites and instruments addressing specific Earth science investigations. There are currently over thirty such probes planned or operational. The motivation behind these probes is to provide focused missions in a faster, better, and cheaper manner. They are all small to moderate in size with highly focused objectives. Some examples of Earth Probes are the Upper Atmosphere Research Satellite (UARS), the Ocean Topography Experiment (TOPEX/Poseidon), and the Total Ozone Mapping Spectrometer (TOMS/Earth Probe). In addition to Earth Probes already approved, small Earth Probes will be launched as the national and international science community requests particular observations or as data gaps develop.

While the Earth Probes are very important and will provide scientists with valuable data, the heart of MTPE is the fifteen-year-long Earth Observing System (EOS) program. EOS satellites began launching during the Phase II Program in 1998 and continued to 2014. These were a series of polar-orbiting and low-inclination satellites for long-term global observations of the land surface, biosphere, solid Earth, atmosphere, and oceans. EOS satellites will carry instruments supplied by NASA as well as instruments from researchers selected through a competitive process.

Planning for the EOS mission began in the early 1980's and was included in the 1990 presidential initiative for Mission to Planet Earth. Originally, there were three groups of instruments: EOS-A spacecraft, EOS-B spacecraft, and instruments to be attached as payloads on then planned Space Station Freedom. In 1991, however, Congress directed the plans for EOS to be restructured to focus the science objectives of EOS on global climate change, increase the flexibility and survivability of the program by flying the instruments on multiple smaller platforms instead of a few large satellites, and reduce the cost of EOS from $17 billion to $11 billion through fiscal year 2000. In 1992, Congress further reduced the budget for EOS through fiscal year 2000 to $8 billion, and to $7.25 billion in 1994. Budget cuts required elimination of some satellite missions, consolidation of others, and a greater reliance on foreign contributors. This left EOS with three main satellite programs, in addition to several smaller ones, for a planned total of seventeen satellites. The main programs are EOS-AM, EOS-PM, and EOS-CHEM, with three satellites in each of these programs.

EOS-AM is studying the land and ocean surfaces, clouds, aerosols in the air, and the radiative balance (the amount of heat coming into and leaving Earth). EOS-PM is studying clouds, precipitation, the radiative balance, terrestrial snow, sea ice, sea-surface temperature, and atmospheric temperature. EOS-CHEM is studying atmospheric chemicals and their transformations and oceanic surface stress.

All satellites in these programs are in Sun-synchronous polar orbits, meaning that they orbit over both of the Earth's Poles and they always cross the equator with the same angle relative to the Sun. EOS-AM-1, renamed Terra, was successfully launched on December 18, 1999, atop an Atlas-2AS. On February 24, 2000, Terra began collecting what will ultimately become a new, fifteen-year global data set on which to base scientific investigations about our complex home planet. NOAA-N launched on May 20, 2005, from Vandenberg Air Force Base on a Delta II booster. Upon reaching orbital position, the spacecraft was renamed NOAA-18. NOAA-N prime's launch was planned for 2008; this spacecraft had been severely damaged in a processing accident in which it fell from a transportation platform, and required repairs before launch.

Terra has an instrument mass of 1,155 kilograms, provides an average power of 2.5 kilowatts, and provides an average data rate of 18 million bits per second (Mb/s). All other spacecraft will support an instrument mass of 1,100 kilograms, provide an average power of 1.2 kilowatts, and provide an average data rate of 7.7 mb/s.

All satellites in the three series will be placed into orbits with altitudes of 705 kilometers and an inclination of 98.2°. Because Terra studies mainly surface features, it observes the Earth in the morning when cloud cover is at a minimum. It crosses the equator going from north to south at 10:30 a.m. local Sun time. Likewise, Aqua provides complementary observations of the Earth in the afternoon and crosses the equator from south to north at 1:30 p.m. local Sun time. Aura crosses the equator from south to north at 1:45 p.m. local Sun time. These orbits allow the satellite to view the same region on the surface of the Earth every 233 orbits, or about every sixteen days. The sequence of satellites from Aqua to Terra was often called the A-Train, and these satellites were easily visible to the naked eye reflecting in sunlight under proper conditions.

Space-based observations are not sufficient to accomplish all mission objectives, and extensive ground- and airborne-based observations will be necessary to provide a complete picture. These campaigns are important components of MTPE. More than any other factor, the key to success for MTPE is the commitment to make Earth science data easily available to researchers everywhere. This will be accomplished with the EOS Data and Information System (EOSDIS). EOSDIS is a comprehensive data and information system designed to perform a wide variety of functions to support scientists everywhere. Some of the services provided by EOSDIS are for the casual user, while some are restricted and designed for select scientists chosen by NASA. Many other services will fall between.

NASA designed EOSDIS as a distributed, open system. This permits distribution of EOSDIS components to various locations to take best advantage of different institutional capabilities and science expertise. An EOSDIS Core System (ECS) provides centralized control and site-unique extensions. Although physically distributed, the components are integrated together and will appear as a single entity to users.

Most interaction with EOSDIS occurs through nine EOSDIS Distributed Active Archive Centers (DAACs). Most of this interaction occurs through human-computer interface over the Internet, but each DAAC also has a User Support Services to assist users in data acquisition, search, access, and usage. EOSDIS charges users no more than the cost of fulfilling an order. This cost may include charges for machine use to execute searches, electronic-copy or hard-copy delivery, and costs incurred in performing any unique processing of the data. EOSDIS may also charge for packaging and media used for data delivery but will not charge for the institutional costs of a DAAC. To promote the use of EOSDIS, first-time users receive a credit balance. The user will be charged only after this credit has been used.

Ultimately, the product of MTPE is to educate decision makers and the public concerning the effects of human activities on global climate change. One of the four goals of the program, as cited in the Mission to Planet Earth Strategic Plan, is to "foster the development of an informed and environmentally aware public." In support of the NASA education initiative, the Office of MTPE is working with NASA's Education Division to establish a focused education strategy. This strategy has the objectives of training the next generation of scientists; educating and training educators, raising awareness of decision makers and the public regarding global climate change, improving science and math literacy, improving the interface between educators and scientists, increasing resources availability, increasing the knowledge base, and encouraging the development of external resources capable of translating scientific research into usable forms for a variety of customers.

Contributions

With most of MTPE's missions flying in the twenty-first century, results will be collected for several decades to come. Already, MTPE has had an impact on our understanding of global climate change. The results of just one satellite mission under MTPE, TOPEX/Poseidon, provide a hint of what scientists expect to learn from MPTE. In 1995, TOPEX/Poseidon, a joint mission between NASA and the French space agency Centre National d'Études Spatiales (CNES), successfully completed its three-year primary mission to help scientists study how the Earth's oceans affect our climate. By improving our understanding of how oceans circulate, information gathered by the Ocean Topography Experiment (TOPEX/Poseidon) is enabling oceanographers to study the way the oceans transport heat and nutrients and how oceans interact with weather patterns. These data allow scientists to produce global maps of ocean circulation. Information has also provided oceanographers with unprecedented global sea level measurements with an accuracy to less than 5 centimeters. Data have shown a global rise in sea level of 0.3 centimeter per year during the mission time frame. TOPEX/Poseidon also detected data concerning El Niño in the equatorial Pacific Ocean that have been linked to global weather patterns.

Context

Research findings since the 1970's reveal that the Earth's climate is not static but is actually continuously changing. Increasing evidence that humankind's activities contribute to this change has provided the incentive to launch a major, large-scale study of the global environment. Mission to Planet Earth is NASA's contribution to this worldwide effort. MTPE will study the global climate from space in an effort to increase understanding of many environmental issues facing humankind today. Support for MTPE ebbed and flowed with the changing political environment in Washington, D.C.

One of these issues is global warming. Scientists know that the Earth's average global temperature has been increasing since the beginning of the Industrial Revolution. What is currently unknown is exactly what is causing this rise. It could be a natural, cyclical event, or it could be due to gases emitted by machines that trap heat in the atmosphere. Some of these gases are carbon dioxide and methane and are called greenhouse gases. Measurements of global levels of greenhouse gases show that these levels have steadily increased, and in 1990 were more than 14 percent higher than in 1960. Increases in temperature could alter precipitation patterns, change growing seasons, melt polar ice and thus result in coastal flooding, and create new deserts where none currently exists. Many MPTE investigations will be to study factors that contribute to global warming, to predict further trends, to determine humanity's role in this change, and to discover what effect changes in human activities will have.

Another case of human activities affecting the environment is ozone depletion. Ozone is a molecule consisting of three oxygen atoms and exists high in the atmosphere in small amounts. These amounts are great enough to absorb much of the Sun's deadly ultraviolet light and protect those who occupy Earth's surface. Ozone is destroyed when it reacts with chlorine, bromides, and other compounds in the presence of light. The main source of chlorine in the atmosphere is chlorofluorocarbons (CFCs), human-made chemicals used in air conditioning, refrigeration, industrial solvents, and firefighting agents. Once released into the atmosphere, they gradually drift upward until they reach the ozone layer. Under the proper conditions these CFCs destroy ozone. Space studies have long documented the depletion of ozone, and these data have been supplemented with airborne measurements. As a result, most countries, including the United States, signed the Montreal Protocol in 1989 calling for phasing out production and use of CFCs by the year 2000. The United States no longer manufactures CFCs. There is still much to learn, and MTPE will continue to study ozone depletion.

Another issue that will be studied by MTPE is deforestation. As our cities grow, we have cleared land to make room for structures and have harvested forests for timber or for agriculture. Deforestation has three major impacts on the environment: It reduces the planet's ability to absorb carbon dioxide, a major greenhouse gas; it influences local weather, especially precipitation and water storage; and it reduces biodiversity. Plants store carbon dioxide in their structure. Through burning of vast areas of timber, carbon dioxide is released into the air. At the same time, the number of plants removing carbon dioxide from the air has been reduced. MTPE will study global vegetation and other land processes so we can better understand their role in the global environment.

These are just a sampling of the issues confronting society today that MTPE will be dedicated to research. Mission to Planet Earth should extend our understanding greatly and let us know, once and for all, just how much our activities affect the environment in which we live.

In June, 2004, NASA began the transformation of its Earth and space science programs by combining them into an integrated Science Mission Directorate. One specific goal of the Vision for Space Exploration is the scientific investigation of the Earth, Moon, Mars, and beyond, with emphasis on understanding the history of the solar system, searching for evidence of habitats for life on Mars, and preparing for future human exploration. Another goal is the search for Earth-like planets and habitable environments around other stars. A third goal is to explore the solar system for scientific purposes and to support human exploration in order to establish a sustained "presence" throughout the solar system.

Observations from space have also demonstrated that Earth's land surfaces are becoming greener because of longer growing seasons. NASA has documented dramatic changes in land use and cover at global scales. The El Niño/La Niña cycles were revealed and based on that understanding, which has allowed scientists to begin modeling Earth's climate system in a meaningful way. Earth's Arctic region has seen a dramatic decrease in sea ice cover, a change that could be seen only using new technologies from space. Decreasing ice cover will affect ocean circulation and exchange of energy and water vapor between the ocean and atmosphere, which can result in worldwide changes in climate and agriculture. NASA has partnered with operational agencies such as the U.S. Department of Agriculture, National Oceanic and Atmospheric Administration, and Environmental Protection Agency to incorporate space-based observations into prediction and warning systems for wildfires, global famine, air quality, and global weather and climate.

—Christopher Keating,
updated by Russell R. Tobias

See also: Atmospheric Laboratory for Applications and Science; Dynamics Explorers; Earth Observing System Satellites; Explorers: Atmosphere; Geodetic Satellites; Global Atmospheric Research Program; Heat Capacity Mapping Mission; Landsat 1, 2, and 3; Landsat 4 and 5; Landsat 7; Seasat; SMS and GOES Meteorological Satellites; Upper Atmosphere Research Satellite.

Further Reading

Asrar, Ghassem, and Jeff Dozier. *EOS: Science Strategy for the Earth Observing System.* New York: Springer-Verlag, 1994. This illustrated book takes a look at the history of the Earth Observing System. It also discusses the scientific equipment used in the program. There is a list of acronyms and a bibliography.

The Earth Observer. The bimonthly newsletter of the EOS Project Office provides current reports on the status of various elements of the EOS Program. Issues dating back to November/ December, 1992, are available on the Internet at http://eospso.gsfc.nasa.gov. Suitable for high school and college-level audiences.

Federal Coordinating Council for Science, Engineering, and Technology. Committee on Earth and Environmental Sciences. *Our Changing Planet: The FY [Year] U.S. Global Change Research Program.* Collingdale, Pa.: DIANE Publishing Company. This publication, which appeared annually in the 1990's, outlines all of the U.S. federal government activities in the area of global climate change. Ground, airborne, and space-based programs are all covered, as well as economic research. Budgets are presented by agency and by scientific element. This report is expected to be published annually. In the title, replace the word "Year" with the year desired. Suitable for high school and college-level audiences.

Science@NASA: The Science Mission Directorate Web Site. http://science.hq.nasa.gov. This site details the combined missions of the Science@NASA Program.

Mobile Satellite System

Date: Beginning 1987
Type of spacecraft: Communications satellites

After the conception in 1987 of the Iridium system, satellite communications experienced rapid and dramatic advances. In direct competition with Iridium and other Big low-Earth-orbiting (Big LEO) satellites, communication systems such as ICO, Globalstar, and Teledesic (the so-called Little LEOs) and LEO One emerged as low-cost alternatives for two-way communications with small data packets. The global market for these LEOs increased steadily after the 1990's.

Key Figures

Barry Bertiger, Motorola engineer and Iridium
system proposer
Ray Leopold, Motorola engineer and Iridium
system proposer
Ken Peterson, Motorola engineer and Iridium
system proposer
Edward F. Staiano, flight director executive officer
of Iridium

Summary of the Satellites

With the installation of optical fiber cables throughout the world in the 1990's, it was envisioned that fixed satellite services would be severely challenged. Fiber cables carry digital data at very high data rates (HDR), equal to or greater than 155 megabits (million bits) per second (Mb/s), and deliver signal quality and error performance as good as or better than satellites (with much less time delay). It became clear that in order to survive in a cable environment, satellite services would have to demonstrate their advantages for HDR transmission and networking in the same manner as they do for more modest data rates such as 1.5 mb/s. Although the availability of fiber optics would undoubtedly move much HDR traffic, it became necessary that they also open new opportunities for HDR satellites in services such as high-definition television (HDTV) distribution and in the emerging field of distributed high performance computing (DHPC).

In 1987, Motorola engineers Ray Leopold, Ken Peterson, and Barry Bertiger proposed the Iridium system, consisting of a constellation of low-orbiting satellites interfacing with existing terrestrial telephone systems around the world through a number of ground station gateways. In 1990, the Iridium system was announced at simultaneous press conferences in Beijing, London, Melbourne, and New York City. At these conferences, Iridium unveiled its revolutionary concept for global personal communications: to link existing terrestrial telephone networks, using the Iridium satellite constellation as a base.

A major boost for Iridium occurred in 1991, when Motorola incorporated Iridium as a separate company to develop and deploy the network. The same year, the United States government reserved radio frequencies for the Iridium low-orbit satellites. Another favorable development for Iridium at this time was the granting of an experimental license by the U.S. government's Federal Communications Commission (FCC). Iridium subsequently signed a $3.37 billion contract with Motorola for system development, construction, and delivery. In 1992, Iridium proposed "multimode" phones that would access existing cellular systems, as well as the Iridium satellite constellation.

An operational license for the Iridium system was granted by the U.S. FCC in 1995. The date for the commercial activation of the Iridium system was set for 1998. A generic design was created for the ground station gateways, and eleven gateway contracts were signed with investor organizations. In October, 1995, the first Iridium satellite flight bus subsystem was delivered by Lockheed Martin to Motorola Satellite Communications facilities in Chandler, Arizona.

The first complete Iridium satellite was delivered by Motorola in 1996. The same year, the first ground station gateway was inaugurated in Japan, and construction was completed on the Iridium Satellite Network Operations Center, located in Leesburg, Virginia. Meanwhile, Iridium agreed with other mobile satellite service providers to a frequency-use plan, allowing them to cooperate in efforts to secure global authorizations for radiofrequency spectrum use. Dr. Edward F. Staiano was appointed vice chairperson and chief executive officer of Iridium in 1996.

In 1997, Iridium successfully placed forty-seven satellites into orbit. Its board members received the first Iridium pager message delivered by orbiting satellites. That year, Iridium selected Allied Signal as its aeronautical strategic partner to develop global wireless telecommunications for aircraft passengers and crew. By 1998, Iridium had completed the constellation of sixty-six LEO satellites with 100 percent launch success, and following extensive testing, the Iridium system entered commercial service.

At approximately the same time, several other mobile satellite communication systems emerged. Principal among these were the Odyssey (which has since been canceled), ICO, Globalstar, and Teledesic systems. With the exception of Teledesic, these systems are commonly known as Big or Voice LEOs; they are targeted at providing real-time voice services through handheld mobile terminals. Of these, the ICO system (ICO96, HAR95, INM95) is a time-division multiple-access (TDMA),

medium-Earth-orbiting (MEO) system, with ten satellites and two spares in two inclined circular orbits. Its MEO altitude of 10,390 kilometers provides for slow-moving satellites as seen from the Earth, leading to fewer and simpler handover arrangements than in a LEO system.

The Globalstar system (GLO96, GAF94, MAZ93, ROU93) has forty-eight low-Earth-orbiting satellites in eight planes. The constellation is designed for 100 percent single satellite coverage between 70° north and 70° south latitude, and 100 percent dual or higher satellite coverage between 25° and 50° north latitudes. Globalstar chose Qualcomm's terrestrial code division multiple access (CDMA) technology for the mobile link, and for the feeder link frequency division multiplexed (FDM) uplink and frequency division multiple access (FDMA) downlink. CDMA was chosen to increase capacity on the mobile link through frequency reuse and voice activity detection, for its ability for spectrum sharing, and for improved multipath performance.

The Teledesic satellite system (SHA95, GRI95, STU95, TUC94) is by far the most ambitious of the proposed systems. At a cost of $9 billion, it consists of 840 active satellites (924 satellites, including in-orbit spares) in twenty-one planes in a Sun-synchronous, inclined circular low-Earth orbit. Teledesic aims to provide high data rate (broadband) fixed and mobile services, continuous global coverage, fiber-like delay, and bit error rates less than one in ten billion. Thus, rather than targeting voice and supporting low bit rate data for fax and messaging as the Big LEOs do, Teledesic focuses on providing wireless broadband services with a fiber-like quality, focusing on data and supporting voice. The term Broadband LEO is therefore more suitable for describing Teledesic than is Big LEO.

The Little LEO and LEO One systems, proposed in 1990 and 1993, respectively, have some significant advantages over the MEOs and Big LEOs. Satellites in geosynchronous orbit, because of their orbit altitude, require significantly more power to complete transmissions than do satellites in lower orbits. The power requirement and frequencies used result in more expensive satellites and terminal equipment. MEOs and Big LEOs also require more powerful transmitters and sophisticated antenna technology, thus increasing the terminal cost compared with that used by Little LEOs and LEO One. In addition, the network infrastructure of the LEO One system is based on a frame relay terrestrial backbone and avoids the more expensive inter-satellite links deployed by some Big LEOs and MEOs. The LEO One system is specifically designed to serve the small packet messaging marketplace. The system operates in a store-and-forward environment, thus greatly increasing the reliability of message delivery. Any error in transmission simply results in a retransmission of the packet. Finally, the ultrahigh-frequency (UHF) and very high frequency (VHF) frequencies allocated to Little LEO systems have been used for many years for terrestrial radio applications—thus components for terminal equipment are readily available at low cost.

Technological developments quite revolutionary in nature arise almost every year or two in the twentieth-first century making many of these original mobile satellite service system quite outdated. As of 2019 SpaceX founder and chief executive officer Elon Musk had begun setting up a string of Starlink satellites to ultimately provide worldwide broadband Internet services. The system is intended to consist of perhaps thousands of small satellites to achieve that goal.

Contributions

As mentioned, the Little LEOs have several competitive advantages over other satellite systems. There are also many significant operational differences between the systems. Low-Earth-orbiting satellites (LEOs) orbit the Earth at altitudes of 800 to 1,600 kilometers. Geosynchronous satellites (GEOs) must orbit the Earth at an exact altitude (approximately 35,200 kilometers) in order to maintain a stationary view of the Earth. Medium-Earth-orbiting satellites (MEOs) have an orbit altitude between that of LEOs and GEOs (around 9,600 kilometers).

The size of the communications footprint of a satellite on the Earth is a direct result of its orbit altitude. Because LEOs have very small footprints, it takes many more satellites to provide communications to the entire Earth in real time. By comparison, a GEO satellite can cover about one-third of the Earth with its footprint, while MEOs can cover the Earth with six to ten satellites, depending upon the orbit.

Satellite systems may also be characterized by the types of services they provide. Geosynchronous satellites, because of their orbit altitude and frequencies used, generally provide broadcast services (DBS television) or high-speed data and voice services. MEO satellite systems are designed to offer high-speed data, teleconferencing, videoconferencing, and, in some cases, mobile voice services. Big LEOs such as Iridium, Globalstar, and ICO, which use multiple satellites in low-Earth orbit, have been designed primarily for voice communications. The only systems with a satellite and network architecture designed specifically for two-way communications for small data packets are the Little LEOs.

Among the Big LEOs, Teledesic redesigned its constellation from 840 to 288 active satellites, thereby raising its altitude from one similar to Iridium's to one similar to Globalstar's. Therefore, Teledesic now has twelve planes with twenty-four active satellites per plane at an altitude of 1,296 kilometers, and uses laser inter-satellite links. Iridium, on the other hand, has sixty-six satellites forming a cross-linked grid in space, making it the first low-Earth-orbiting system for wireless telephone service. Only 776 kilometers above the Earth, these satellites work differently from those at a much higher orbit (35,200 kilometers) in two major ways. First, they are close enough to receive the signals of a handheld device; and second, they act like cellular towers in the sky. Thus, wireless signals do not need to move through ground-based cells and may be transmitted and received among the satellites themselves.

Each LEO One satellite weighs approximately 192 newtons on orbit and has a design life of five years with fuel on board for seven years. The orbit altitude of each plane is 944 kilometers. Each of the eight orbital planes contains six equally positioned satellites, with each plane equally spaced around the equator at an inclination of 50°. Each satellite provides a circular coverage footprint of approximately 3,639 kilometers in diameter. The orbital period of the satellites is approximately 104 minutes, and the typical period of visibility of a satellite to a user on the Earth is about 7 to 10 minutes. A single operating frequency band of 148.00-150.05 megahertz has been allocated to LEO One's subscriber and gateway uplink. On the other hand, two separate frequency bands, in the ranges 137.00- 138.00 megahertz and 400.15-401.00 megahertz, have been allocated to LEO One's subscriber and gateway downlink. Corresponding data rates are 24,000 bits per second (bps) and 50,000 bps for the subscriber and gateway downlinks, respectively; 2,400-9,600 bps for the subscriber uplink; and 50,000 bps for the gateway uplink. LEO One's design is to connect with the Internet, private networks, and all public switched telephone and data networks. Those rates are slow by twenty-first century standards.

LEO One arrived in the wake of the Little LEO service concept initiated around 1990. The project was initially led by LEO One's founder and chairperson, David A. Bayer, and its president and CEO, Tom Rudd. In 1990, Orbcomm and other satellite companies filed applications with the FCC for frequency allocations to provide Little LEO services for monitoring and text messaging. In 1992, the World Radio Conference allocated spectra in the VHF and UHF bands for Little LEO services. In response to the FCC's request and growing interest in Little LEO systems, the World Radio Conference allocated additional uplink spectrum(but no additional downlink spectrum) for LEO One and its

competitors. Finally, after several applicants withdrew their applications in 1997, the FCC issued a Report and Order incorporating an agreement signed by all remaining applicants, dividing the spectrum among them. In 1998, LEO One received its Little LEO license from the FCC and was allotted the full amount of spectrum requested. In April, 1999, LEO One announced the completion of a prototype for an evolutionary integrated communications facility. Complete deployment and commissioning of the facility was expected within a few years. Although there were nine launches after late 2001, the FCC canceled the license for this commercial outfit in March, 2004.

As of 2019, Iridium Satellite LCC remained the only satellite voice and data provider capable of global coverage. It maintains 66 low-Earth-orbiting, cross-linked satellites; twelve in-orbit spares were are available. Despite tremendous customer volumes for satellite communications, the actual business opportunities did not meet earlier expectations for commercial expansion into this area. SpaceX founder Elon Musk seeks to provide global Internet coverage inexpensively.

Context

On a more cautious note, it must be mentioned that both Iridium and ICO Global Communications, two of the major companies involved in the satellite mobile phone communications business, filed for bankruptcy in August, 1999. Several reports, however, expressed the possibility of the companies being restructured and rescued. Needless to say, however, the field of mobile satellite communications will impact technology and society for decades to come. As was predicted in the late 1980's, the global communications satellite market has expanded very rapidly into personal communications services and new mobile satellite services (PCS and MSS, respectively), low-Earth-orbiting (LEO) satellite systems, Global Positioning System (GPS) navigation, and new direct broadcast satellite services. LEO satellite services (Big and Little) have become operational; their growth is dependent on competitive factors for which it is still premature to make predictions. It is expected that conventional fixed satellite services (FSS) and maritime mobile satellite services (MMSS) should continue to grow steadily, but not as rapidly as before.

The world of satellite communications is changing quickly. New opportunities for mobile, broadcast, and personal services may appear to threaten traditional fixed services. The United States, long an agent of change in these areas, may no longer take its role for granted in the future. The dominant role played by U.S. industry and technology in the first twenty-five years of satellite service is now under a serious challenge from other countries.

During the first twenty-five years of the growth and development of geosynchronous satellites, the emergence of international and long-distance fixed satellite services (FSS) helped create the global electronic village. Beginning with the global viewing of the first lunar landing in July, 1969, communications satellites have indeed become the greatest force for the "super-tribalization" of the human species. Their impact and potential are still far from being fully realized.

—Monish R. Chatterjee

See also: Intelsat Communications Satellites; Private Industry and Space Exploration; Telecommunications Satellites: Maritime; Telecommunications Satellites: Military; Telecommunications Satellites: Passive Relay; Telecommunications Satellites: Private and Commercial; Tracking and Data-Relay Communications Satellites.

Further Reading

Ahrens, C. Donald. *Essentials of Meteorology: An Invitation to the Atmosphere*. 4th ed. Pacific Grove, Calif.: Thomson Brooks/Cole, 2005. This is a text suitable for an introductory course in meteorology. Comes complete with a CD-ROM to help explain concepts and demonstrate the atmosphere's dynamic nature.

Andrade, Alessandra A. L. *The Global Navigation Satellite System: Navigating into the New Millennium*. Montreal: Ashgate, 2001. Provides an international view of issues of availability, cooperation, and reliability of air navigation services. Attention is specifically paid to the American GPS and Russian GLONASS systems, although the development of the Galileo civilian system in Europe is also presented.

Baker, David, ed. *Jane's Space Directory, 2005-2006*. Alexandria, Va.: Jane's Information Group, 2005. Extensive bibliographic presentation of all space programs, broken down into programmatic categories.

Benson, Charles D., and William B. Faherty. *Gateway to the Moon*. Gainesville: University Press of Florida, 2001. This text was originally part of a NASA history series. It provides a detailed management and engineering history of the construction of the Kennedy Space Center in support of the Apollo Program.

Comparetto, Gary, and Rafols Ramirez. "Trends in Mobile Satellite Technology." *Computer* 30 (February, 1997): 44-52. Discusses the demand for sophisticated personal communication services and the design of low-orbit, more computer resource-consuming communications satellites.

Ingley, Carol. "Little LEOs: Riding the Wave of Market Forces." *Satellite Communications* 23, no. 12 (December, 1999): 28. Provides a description of the niche market positions available to little low-Earth-orbiting (LEO) satellite systems, projected to 2003.

Leverington, David. *New Cosmic Horizons: Space Astronomy from the V2 to the Hubble Space Telescope.* New York: Cambridge University Press, 2001. Examines space-based astronomical observations from the end of World War II to the Hubble Space Telescope and other major NASA space-based observatories.

Martin, Donald H. *Communication Satellites.* 4th ed. New York: American Institute of Aeronautics and Astronautics, 2000. Covers the development of communications satellites and worldwide networks from Project Score to modern satellite communication systems.

Mowry, Clayton. "The Year of the Mobile Satellite." *Satellite Communications* 22 (January, 1998): 62. The writer predicted here that 1998 would be the year of the mobile satellite, with Iridium, Globalstar, and Orbcomm leading the way in low-Earth-orbiting (LEO) systems.

Pratt, Timothy, Charles W. Bostian, and Jeremy E. Allnut. *Satellite Communications.* New York: Wiley, 2002. This can serve as a textbook for college-level satellite communications but also provides a wealth of information that can be used by both experienced professionals and the novice with a strong background in basic science and computer skills.

Smith, Bruce A. "Without Fast Cash, Iridium May Deorbit." *AviationWeek and Space Technology* 152, no. 11 (March, 2000): 37. Discusses the bankruptcy woes of Iridium, the pacesetter in Big LEO communications satellite constellations.

Swanson, Glen E. *Before This Decade Is Out: Personal Reflections on the Apollo Program.* Gainesville: University Press of Florida, 2002. This history of the Apollo Program provides insights into the thoughts of the people who accepted President Kennedy's lunar challenge, sent astronauts to walk upon the Moon, and returned them safely to Earth.

Tassoul, Jean-Louis, and Monique Tassoul. *A Concise History of Solar and Stellar Physics.* Princeton, N.J.: Princeton University Press, 2004. A comprehensive study of the historical development of humanity's understanding of the Sun and the cosmos, written in easy-to-understand language by a pair of theoretical astrophysicists. The perspective of the astronomer and physicist are presented.

Yenne, Bill. *Secret Weapons of the Cold War: From the H-Bomb to SDI.* New York: Berkley Books, 2005. A contemporary examination of Cold War superweapons and their influence on American-Soviet geopolitics.

Zimmerman, Robert. *The Chronological Encyclopedia of Discoveries in Space.* Westport, Conn.: Oryx Press, 2000. Provides a complete chronological history of all piloted and robotic spacecraft and explains flight events and scientific results. Suitable for all levels of research.

National Aeronautics and Space Administration

Date: Beginning October 1, 1958
Type of organization: Aerospace agency

The National Aeronautics and Space Administration (NASA) was formed in 1958. Its purpose is to unite under one administration all U.S. space exploration activities. Although it is a civilian organization, it sometimes undertakes special military projects.

Key Figures

T. Keith Glennan (1905-1995), NASA Administrator, 1958-1961

James E. Webb (1906-1992), NASA Administrator, 1961-1968

Thomas O. Paine (1921-1992), NASA Administrator, 1969-1970

James C. Fletcher (1919-1991), NASA Administrator, 1971-1977

Robert A. Frosch (b. 1928), NASA Administrator, 1977-1981

James M. Beggs (b. 1926), NASA Administrator, 1981-1985

James C. Fletcher (1919-1991), NASA Administrator, 1986-1989

Richard H. Truly (b. 1937), NASA Administrator, 1989-1992

Daniel S. Goldin (b. 1940), NASA Administrator, 1992-2001

Sean C. O'Keefe (b. 1956), NASA Administrator, 2001-2004

Frederick D. Gregory (b. 1941), acting NASA Administrator, 2005

Michael D. Griffin (b. 1949), NASA Administrator, 2006-2009

Charles F. Bolden, Jr., (b. 1946), NASA Administrator, 2009-2017

James F. Bridenstine (b. 1975), NASA Administrator, 2018-present

Summary of the Organization

The National Aeronautics and Space Administration (NASA) came into being October 1, 1958, when President Dwight D. Eisenhower signed into law the National Aeronautics and Space Act of 1958.

On October 4, 1957, the Soviets launched the world's first artificial satellite, Sputnik 1. At that time, the United States had several space efforts spread across a large number of government agencies. Sputnik's launch convinced U.S. officials that in order to compete with the Soviet Union in space, the United States needed to establish one comprehensive space agency. To that end, NASA was founded. NASA absorbed the existing National Advisory Committee for Aeronautics (NACA) and acquired personnel and projects from other government programs, including Project Vanguard from the Naval Research Laboratory, lunar probe programs from the Army, and lunar probe and rocket engine programs from the Air Force.

Initially, NASA's resources included eight thousand employees, three laboratories, two flight stations, and an annual budget of $100 million. Later, the Jet Propulsion Laboratory, in Pasadena, California, and the Army Ballistic Missile Agency (ABMA), in Huntsville, Alabama, were added to the facilities. NASA has centers throughout the nation, including NASA Headquarters in Washington,

D.C.; Ames Research Center, Mountain View, California; Armstrong Flight Research Center, Edwards, California (previously known as Dryden Flight Research Center); Goddard Space Flight Center, Greenbelt, Maryland; the Jet Propulsion Laboratory, Pasadena, California; Johnson Space Center, Houston, Texas; Kennedy Space Center, Cape Canaveral, Florida; Langley Research Center, Hampton, Virginia; the John H. Glenn Research Center at Lewis Field, Cleveland, Ohio; Marshall Space Flight Center, Huntsville, Alabama; John C. Stennis Space Center, Bay St. Louis, Mississippi; and Wallops Flight Facility, Wallops Island, Virginia. In addition, Marshall Space Flight Center operates two more centers: the Michoud Assembly Facility, in New Orleans, and Computer Science Corporation (formerly Slidell Computer Complex), in Slidell, Louisiana. The White Sands Test Facility, in New Mexico, is operated by Johnson Space Center. Kennedy Space Center is responsible for the operation of the Space Transportation System Resident Office at Vandenberg Air Force Base, California. Plum Brook Station, which provides large-scale, specialized research installations, is operated by NASA Glenn.

NASA Headquarters manages the spaceflight centers, research centers, and other NASA installations. Headquarters officials direct the planning and management of NASA research and development programs, determine what projects and programs will be undertaken, and review and analyze all phases of the activities.

Ames Research Center performs research and development in aeronautics, space science, life science, and spacecraft technology. Ames had responsibility for the Pioneer series of spacecraft, and Ames scientists study the origins of life and provide medical support for crewed missions. Ames contributes to the space shuttle program by researching heat protection systems and conducting wind-tunnel experiments.

Dryden Flight Research Center is administered by Ames Research Center. Its primary research goal is the study of high-speed aircraft, but its personnel also work on vertical takeoff and landing, low-speed flight, supersonic flight, hypersonic flight, and flight vehicle reentry.

Goddard Space Flight Center (GSFC) conducts automated spacecraft and sounding rocket experiments to provide data about Earth's environment, Sun-Earth relationships, and the universe. Goddard is the home of the National Space Science Data Center, the repository of data collected from spaceflight experiments. The center is responsible for the Delta launch vehicle and has the lead role in the management of the international Search and Rescue Satellite-Aided Tracking (SARSAT) program.

NASA's Jet Propulsion Laboratory (JPL) is a government-owned facility that is staffed and managed by the California Institute of Technology. The Laboratory is active in deep-space missions and data acquisition and analysis for those missions. JPL scientists also study solid- and liquid-propellant spacecraft engines and spacecraft guidance and control systems. The Laboratory operates the Deep Space Communications Complex, which is one station of the Deep Space Network. JPL has tracked and controlled probes to Mercury, Venus, Mars, Jupiter, Saturn, Uranus, and Neptune, including Cassini, Deep Space 1, Deep Space 2, Galileo, Magellan, Mariners 2 through 10, Mars Climate Orbiter, Mars Exploration Rovers, Mars Global Surveyor, Mars Observer, Mars Pathfinder, Mars Polar Lander, Pioneers 10 and 11, Ranger, Stardust, Surveyor, Ulysses, Vikings 1 and 2, and the Voyager interstellar missions.

Johnson Space Center (JSC) was established in September, 1961. It is NASA's primary center for the design, development, and manufacture of piloted spacecraft; selection and training of spaceflight crews; and ground control of piloted flights. JSC is the lead NASA center for management of the space shuttle. The Mission Control Center is one of NASA's best-known facilities, because it is from there that piloted flights, from Gemini IV to the space shuttle and space station missions, have been monitored. Television broadcasts of spaceflights have featured the activity at Mission Control. JSC also operates the White Sands Test Facility, which is responsible for the space shuttle propulsion system and power system and for materials testing.

Kennedy Space Center (KSC) serves as the main facility for the testing and launch of space vehicles, piloted and robotic. It also oversees launches at the Air Force's Western Space and Missile Center at Vandenberg Air Force Base in California. KSC concentrates on the assembly, testing, and launch of space shuttle vehicles and their payloads. KSC operates the Space Transportation System Resident Office at Vandenberg Air Force Base in California. The office supports the Air Force in the design, construction, and operation of the space shuttle launch and landing site.

Langley Research Center's primary mission is to research and develop new aircraft and spacecraft. The center's scientists study ways to increase the performance and efficiency of air and space vehicles. Langley has a variety of wind tunnels to aid this research. The National Transonic Facility, a cryogenic, high-pressure wind tunnel, is also located at Langley.

The John H. Glenn Research Center at Lewis Field is NASA's main center for research and development in aircraft propulsion, spacecraft propulsion, space power, and satellite communications. Power system research includes studies on the conversion of chemical and solar energy into electricity. NASA Glenn manages the Centaur launch vehicle, a second-stage rocket used with the Atlas first stage. Glenn Research Center also operates Plum Brook Station, which provides specialized research installations.

Marshall Space Flight Center (MSFC) was established in 1960 by a team of former Army rocket experts headed by Wernher von Braun. MSFC is responsible for the development of the space shuttle's main engines, solid-fueled rocket boosters, and external propellant tank. MSFC is also responsible for developing the Hubble Space Telescope and

Chandra X-Ray Observatory, the Spacelab research facility, and many other programs.

The Michoud Assembly Facility and Computer Science Corporation in Slidell, Louisiana, are operated by MSFC. Michoud's primary function is the design, engineering, manufacture, assembly, and testing of the space shuttle's External Tank. The computer complex is responsible for NASA's computational requirements. It also provides computational services for the John C. Stennis Space Center.

The John C. Stennis Space Center became a separate field installation in 1974; it was previously called the Mississippi Test Facility and, later, the National Space Technology Laboratories (NSTL). Since 1975, NSTL's function had been to support the development of the space shuttle's main engine. Between 1965 and 1970, NSTL oversaw the static test firing of the first and second stages of the Saturn V, the launch vehicle used in the Apollo piloted lunar-landing missions and the Skylab program. In May, 1988, it was renamed the John C. Stennis Space Center in honor of U.S. senator John C. Stennis for his steadfast leadership and staunch support of the nation's space program.

Wallops Flight Facility is part of Goddard Space Flight Center. Wallops's main responsibility is to manage NASA's suborbital sounding rocket projects, and its responsibility is complete; it covers this program from mission planning to landing and recovery. Wallops personnel design and develop payloads, control launches, track rockets, and acquire data. They also monitor, schedule, and control all NASA balloon activities, and to this end, they operate the National Scientific Balloon Facility at Palestine, Texas.

Located in Fairmont, West Virginia, the NASA Independent Verification and Validation (IV&V) Facility was established in 1993 as part of an agency-wide strategy to provide the highest achievable levels of safety and cost-effectiveness for mission critical software. The IV&V Facility was founded under the NASA Office of Safety and

Mission Assurance as a direct result of recommendations made by the National Research Council (NRC) and the Report of the Presidential Commission on the space shuttle *Challenger* Accident (the Rogers Commission's report). Since then, the IV&V Facility has experienced continual growth in personnel, projects, capabilities, and accomplishments. The IV&V Facility's efforts have contributed to the improved safety record of NASA since its inception. Today, the IV&V Facility is governed by the Goddard Space Flight Center, houses more than 150 fulltime employees, and leverages the expertise of more than twenty in-house partners and contractors.

When Moffett Field Naval Air Station in Mountain View, California, was closed by the government in 1994, NASA acquired the 200-acre field adjacent to the Ames Research Center. NASA is turning it into a research and development campus to include the California Air and Space Center (CASC) and the Computer Museum History Center (CMHC).

The CASC will be a unique facility in Silicon Valley to enhance training for elementary and secondary teachers and their students in the disciplines of math, science, and technology. In December, 1998, the cities of Mountain View and Sunnyvale approved a landmark agreement to join in partnership with NASA Ames Research Center to spearhead this project. Each will appoint board members to the California Air and Space Center Educational Foundation, who will, in turn, establish the independent, nonprofit entity known as the CASC. Subsequently, NASA Ames Research Center will make historic Hangar One available to the foundation for the purpose of developing a Teacher Institute, an Educator Resource Center, a public facility with interactive exhibits and displays for all ages, and much more.

Established in 1996, the Computer Museum History Center is a nonprofit entity dedicated to the preservation and celebration of computing history. It is home to one of the largest collections of computing artifacts in the world, a collection comprising more than three thousand artifacts, two thousand films and videotapes, five thousand photographs, two thousand linear feet of cataloged documentation, and many gigabytes of software. The collection is housed in a visible storage building at Moffett Field.

NASA has made a number of international agreements, results of the mandate given it by the 1958 National Aeronautics and Space Act, which required NASA to cooperate with other nations in peaceful aeronautical and space activities. Cooperation with other nations contributes to broad national goals by stimulating scientific and technical contributions from abroad, providing access to foreign areas for tracking stations and possible emergency landing sites, enhancing satellite experiments with foreign scientific data, increasing the possibility for the development of space technology, extending ties to foreign scientific and engineering communities, and supporting U.S. foreign policy.

One of the best-known agreements involved the Apollo-Soyuz Test Project. In July of 1975, three American astronauts in an Apollo spacecraft and two Soviet cosmonauts in a Soyuz spacecraft met in space by means of a docking module. The two spacecraft remained docked for forty-four hours while the astronauts and cosmonauts exchanged visits. It was hoped at the time that increased cooperation between the two countries would result from this joint mission.

Other international projects have included cooperative spaceflights involving American and foreign astronauts, cooperative satellite experiments in which all or part of a satellite has been built by foreign governments, foreign space missions that carried U.S. experiments, and solar energy projects. More such projects are under way, including the International Space Station, and at least seventy-two countries have participated in scientific and technical information exchanges with the United States.

NASA's budget is substantial. In 1965, it was $5.092 billion. It had dropped to $3.269 billion by

1975, but it rose to $7.251 billion over the next ten years. The NASA budget request for Fiscal Year 2001 was reflected in four appropriations: Human Space Flight ($5.5 billion); Science, Aeronautics, and Technology ($5.9 billion); Mission Support ($2.6 billion); and Inspector General ($22,000). In the aftermath of the *Columbia* accident, President George W. Bush proposed a return to the Moon by 2020 and human exploration of Mars and beyond. In order to jump-start that expansion of NASA's mission, in its Fiscal Year 2006 budget NASA became one of the few federal agencies to receive a significant funding boost. The $16.5 billion budget request represented a 2.4 percent increase over the previous year. The budget process for NASA in the Bush and Obama White House years went through "roller coaster-like" changes in priorities. In 2019 the Trump Administration's NASA budget amounted to $21.5 billion, and included rather well-defined program priorities which surprisingly enjoyed bipartisan support in Congress, at least with regard to human space exploration beyond low-Earth orbit. However, the political winds of change in Washington, D.C. could easily mess with plans to return astronauts to the Moon's surface by 2024.

Context

A nation receives a good return on the money it spends on a space program. One of the benefits of a space program is the information it can provide about the solar system and the universe. For example, the Voyager flybys of Jupiter and Saturn allowed U.S. scientists to study those planets' atmospheres in detail. Information obtained from such studies may appear to have no application, but, in fact, it sheds light on the structure of Earth's atmosphere.

Another space program benefit is improved military technology. In most space studies, rockets or missiles must be used to lift the payload or experiment, and the rockets' engineering must be reliable. Although NASA is a civilian agency, it contracts with the military for various projects. Also, any rocket that can put a satellite in orbit for peaceful purposes can put one in orbit for military purposes.

Perhaps most important are the space program "spin-offs." A spin-off is the application of space-age technology to other uses. For example, when the question of humans entering space was first raised, NASA scientists quickly determined that medical data would have to be transmitted from the spacecraft back to Earth. Medical technology had to be developed that would transmit data on astronauts' heart activity, respiration rate, and temperature. When the devices to perform these functions were developed, they were quickly adapted for use in hospitals. Many patients may owe their lives to the fact that an electrocardiogram could be read at some distance from a hospital bed and thereby alert medical personnel to an impending heart attack. Other spin-offs include image processing, advanced aircraft, drag reduction techniques for racing yachts, eyeglass filters, solar water heaters, water filters, relaxation systems, speech aids, and a "cool suit." The same image processing techniques that remove interference from data returned by deep-space probes, such as Voyager, can be used to make ordinary x-ray radiographs clearer. The cool suit is based on technology developed at Ames Research Center; a liquid-cooled helmet liner for military pilots was invented after heat exhaustion appeared to be the cause of some accidents. A national space program also has intangible benefits. Humans seem to need the kinds of challenges offered by space exploration.

—T. Parker Bishop

See also: Astronauts and the U.S. Astronaut Program; Cooperation in Space: U.S. and Russian; Ethnic and Gender Diversity in the Space Program; Private Industry and Space Exploration; Rocketry: Modern History; Space Centers, Spaceports, and Launch Sites; Space Shuttle; Space Stations: Origins and Development; Space Suit Development; United Space Alliance; United States Space Command.

Further Reading

Couper, Heather, and Nigel Henbest. *Space Frontiers*. New York: Viking Press, 1978. This book contains more than one hundred color illustrations. It begins with the early astronomy of the Egyptians and Greeks and continues through modern astronomy, including radio astronomy. NASA's role in space exploration is discussed in the chapter "Man Conquers Space." The possibility of space colonization is evaluated. Suitable for general audiences.

Dethloff, Henry. *Suddenly Tomorrow Came: A History of Johnson Space Center*. Washington, D.C.: Government Printing Office, 1994. NASA's official history of the Manned Spacecraft Center and, as it was later known, the Johnson Space Center. It gives a great deal of detail about the Center, as well as the personnel who operated it. Along the way, the history of the American space program is told.

DeWaard, E. John, and Nancy DeWaard. *History of NASA: America's Voyage to the Stars*. New York: Exeter Books, 1984. Illustrated with many color and black-and-white photographs, this book begins with a discussion of humankind's early attempts to fly and proceeds through descriptions of NASA's programs. It also speculates about future space exploration. For general audiences.

Dunar, Andrew J., and Stephen P. Waring. *Power to Explore: A History of Marshall Space Flight Center, 1960-1990*. NASA SP-4313. Washington, D.C.: Government Printing Office, 1999. A part of the National Aeronautics and Space Administration History Series, this is a highly detailed, official account of the Marshall Space Flight Center and its contributions to aeronautical and astronautical research. It covers the life of the center from its inception through its current activities. There are numerous illustrations and references, as well as numerous charts and tables.

Glennan, T. Keith. *The Birth of NASA: The Diary of T. Keith Glennan*. Edited by J. D. Hunley. NASA SP-4105. Washington, D.C.: Government Printing Office, 1993. This is the semiautobiographical history of NASA's early days and of its first director. It details the difficulties, as well as the triumphs, that the space agency experienced during the transitional period of the late 1950's and early 1960's.

Glover, Daniel R. *History of the Lewis Research Center*. Washington, D.C.: National Aeronautics and Space Administration, 1995. This is the story of the Lewis Research Center and the aeronautical and astronautical research conducted there. It also provides biographical information on George W. Lewis and about the National Advisory Committee for Aeronautics.

Haggerty, James J. *Spinoff*. Washington, D.C.: Government Printing Office, 1985. *Spinoff* is one of NASA's annual reports. This issue contains approximately 130 pages and is illustrated throughout with color photographs. The publication covers the many technological developments for which NASA is responsible and that have applications in fields other than space science. For general audiences.

Hallion, Richard. *On the Frontier: Flight Research at Dryden, 1946-1981*. Washington, D.C.: Government Printing Office, 1984. This is one of the titles in the NASA History series, which provides an official look at the space agency, its programs, and its facilities. The information is presented in chronological order, and it covers such noted aerospace craft as the X-1, X-15, HL-10, X-24A, X-24B, and space shuttle. Also detailed is the research that assisted the development of the Gemini and Apollo spacecraft. There are many black-and-white photographs and line drawings, an index, and an impressive bibliography. Appendices include program flight chronologies on the X-1, D-558, X-2, X-3, X-4, X-5, XF-92A, X-15, lifting bodies, XB-70A, and space shuttle approach and landing test program.

Hansen, James R. *Spaceflight Revolution: NASA Langley Research Center from Sputnik to Apollo*. NASA SP-4308. Washington, D.C.: Government Printing Office, 1995. A part of the NASA History series, this book looks at the contributions Langley researchers have made to the exploration of the atmosphere and space.

Herring, Mack R. *Way Station to Space: A History of the John C. Stennis Space Center*. Washington, D.C.: National Aeronautics and Space Administration, 1997. This is a look into the John C. Stennis Space Center and its contributions to the Saturn launch vehicles and the space shuttle. It describes facilities and the history of this Mississippi research center. There are numerous illustrations and a bibliography.

Klerkx, Greg. *Lost in Space: The Fall of NASA and the Dream of a New Space Age*. New York: Pantheon Books, 2004. The premise of this work is that NASA has been stuck in Earth's orbit since the Apollo era, and that space exploration has suffered as a result.

Koppes, Clayton R. *JPL and the American Space Program: A History of the Jet Propulsion Laboratory*. New Haven, Conn.: Yale University Press, 1982. This volume discusses research activities at JPL during World War II and the years that followed. Describes JPL's internal organization and the relationship between JPL and NASA. Most of the text is devoted to JPL space projects.

Lambright, W. Henry, ed. *Space Policy in the Twenty-First Century*. Baltimore: Johns Hopkins University Press, 2003. This book addresses a number of important questions: What will replace the space shuttle? Can the International Space Station justify its cost? Will Earth be threatened by asteroid impact? When and how will humans explore Mars?

Launius, Roger D. *NASA: A History of the U.S. Civil Space Program*. Malabar, Fla.: Krieger Publishing Company, 1994. This is an in-depth look at America's civilian space program and the establishment of the National Aeronautics and Space Administration. It chronicles the agency from its predecessor, the National Advisory Committee for Aeronautics, through the present day.

Levine, Arnold S. *Managing NASA in the Apollo Era*. NASA SP-4102. Washington, D.C.: Government Printing Office, 1982. A highly detailed history of the difficulties encountered and lessons learned in managing NASA, a growing agency, as it developed a complex program to place humans on the Moon.

Logsdon, John M., moderator. "Legislative Origins of the National Aeronautics and Space Act of 1958: Proceedings of an Oral History Workshop." Monograph in *Aerospace History* 8. Washington, D.C.: Government Printing Office, 1998. The transcript of a round-table discussion with Paul Dembling, Eilene Galloway, George E. Reedy, Gerald W. Siegel, Willis H. Shapley, H. Guyford Stever, and Glen P. Wilson.

National Aeronautics and Space Administration. *Marshall Space Flight Center 1960-1985: Twenty-Fifth Anniversary Report*. Washington, D.C.: Government Printing Office, 1985. A celebratory booklet on Marshall's history and its role in the U.S. space program. Includes many photographs of Marshall personnel at work, contrasting early and later activities. Contains a time line showing the dates for major projects.

---. *NASA: The First Twenty-Five Years, 1958-1983*. NASA EP-182. Washington, D.C.: Government Printing Office, 1983. Designed to be a teacher's resource, this illustrated volume covers the history of NASA and its many programs. Includes sections on the pre-NASA U.S. space program, crewed spaceflight, and the uses of space technology. An appendix lists all major NASA launches through 1983. Suitable for high school and college students.

Phillips, W. Hewitt. *Journey in Aeronautical Research: A Career at NASA Langley Research Center*. Washington, D.C.: Government Printing Office, 1998. This is a personal account of a researcher who spent his years at Langley. It is an intriguing behind-the-scenes look at aeronautical research and the way NASA conducts it.

Time-Life Books. *Life in Space*. Boston: Little, Brown, 1984. A volume in a Time-Life series, this work contains many photographs and illustrations. It covers the Mercury, Gemini, Apollo, Skylab, and space shuttle programs. Suitable for the nonspecialist.

Tompkins, Phillip K., and Emily V. Tompkins. *Apollo, Challenger, and Columbia: The Decline of the Space Program*. New York: Roxbury Publishing Company, 2004. Subheaded "A Study in Organizational Communications," this work examines changes in NASA's internal communications since its inception through the space shuttle accidents. Focuses more on sociology than engineering.

Wolf, Marvin J. *Space Pioneers: The Illustrated History of the Jet Propulsion Laboratory and the Race to Space*. Santa Monica, Calif.: General Publishing Group, 1999. This is an in-depth look at the Jet Propulsion Laboratory and the space missions—both piloted and robotic—to explore the depths of space. The book covers JPL from its inception through its current endeavors in aeronautics and astronautics. There are numerous photographs and tables.

National AeroSpace Plane

Date: 1986 to 1994
Type of spacecraft: Piloted spacecraft

The National AeroSpace Plane (NASP) was a program to design and build a single-stage-to-orbit (SSTO) vehicle that would have landed and taken off on conventional runways. The plane, traveling at hypersonic speeds, would have required the development of new materials and technologies to become a reality.

Key Figures

Robert Heaps, U.S. Air Force colonel and program director for NASP

Robert Barthelemy, former program director for NASP

Phillip Aitken-Cade, U.S. Air Force colonel and deputy program director for NASP

George Baird, chief program engineer for NASP

Frank Berkopec, chief of Space Vehicle Propulsion, NASA Lewis Research Center

Stephan Wolanczyk, Subsystem Technology Development manager for NASP

Margaret Whalen, co-leader of Slush Technology program at NASA's Lewis Research Center

Summary of the Technology

President Ronald W. Reagan in his February, 1986, State of the Union address asked for congressional support of a National AeroSpace Plane that he referred to as the Orient Express. Reagan's vision became the X-30 National AeroSpace Plane (NASP), a technological device capable of reaching Mach 25 (twenty-five times the speed of sound or 28,000 kilometers per hour) and delivering payloads into low-Earth orbit. The NASP program was to have led to a new concept of aerospace vehicles including a commercial transport, a space plane replacing the shuttle, and a series of military Transatmospheric Vehicles (TAVs).

The NASP program was started secretly in the early 1980's by the Defense Department's Advanced Research Projects Agency (ARPA). The engineering and scientific research tasks were allocated to various government and industrial labs across the country, with the main program office located at Wright Patterson Air Force Base in Dayton, Ohio. The military importance of TAVs was reflected in the NASP funding. The U.S. Air Force, U.S. Navy, ARPA, and the Strategic Defense Initiative Organization (SDIO, now called the Ballistic Missile Defense Organization) all contributed 80 percent to the costs, while NASA's share was only 20 percent. The total cost to build and fly the X-30 was estimated to exceed $5 billion.

The decision to build the NASP was based upon the view that less costly access to space travel would benefit both commerce and the military. The launch of a space shuttle payload costs thousands of dollars per kilogram, with the time between launches often measured in months. In contrast, there are significant savings to launch, land, and service an SSTO type craft. The reduction estimates vary from only one-tenth to only one one-hundredth of the shuttle's cost per kilogram of payload placed in a low-Earth orbit.

A radically new design concept like the NASP emerged from earlier research aircraft that were given an X classification. The North American X-15 was able to achieve Mach 6.7 (more than 8,000 kilometers per hour) and reach near-space altitudes in excess of 100 kilometers. The X-15 flights yielded valuable information on frictional heating from the atmosphere. A metal alloy known as Inconel-X was used in the metallic skin of the aircraft, which could withstand temperatures to 700° Celsius. Other areas of the plane heated to 1,100° Celsius but were coated with an ablative heatshield.

The X-24's were a series of lifting-body aircraft with the purpose of demonstrating that high-speed craft with low lift and high drag coefficients could land on conventional runways. The X-24 lifting bodies attained Mach 1.8 (2,200 kilometers per hour) yet made unpowered, accurate, and precise landings. This wingless craft generated lift in the atmosphere through a streamlined but stubby shape. The shape and construction of both of these unusual aircraft influenced the design of the X-30.

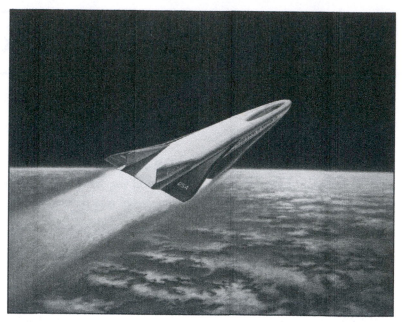

Artist's concept of the X-30 aerospace plane flying through Earth's atmosphere on its way to low-Earth orbit. (NASA / James Schultz)

The X-30, like the X-15, the X-24, and the shuttle, would have used rocket propulsion, but not for the entire flight. Unlike the shuttle, the X-30 would not have discarded its booster rockets but would have retained them for reentry. This concept is contrary to conventional practice, which uses a series of rocket stages to decrease the vehicle's weight in order to increase thrust. An SSTO craft would have required the engine efficiency be as high as 95 percent to extract as much thermal energy as possible from each kilogram of fuel. Researchers also believe that the vehicle's empty weight must be less than 25 percent of its takeoff weight to achieve orbit.

The thrust required to deliver the X-30 into orbit would have been produced from a propulsion system based on the ramjet and scramjet, as a single air-consuming engine type will not operate over the required range of altitudes and speeds. Ramjet engines have been in operation since the 1940's on missiles. A ramjet employs a cone-shaped structure in the front of the engine to reduce the speed of the incoming air from supersonic to subsonic range. The air becomes compressed and heated, passing over fuel injectors that ignite the mixture. Resulting hot gases expand out of the tube-shaped engine at a higher velocity than the incoming air, providing thrust.

Ramjet engines operate best from Mach 1 (the speed of sound) to Mach 6; at greater speeds they become overheated and ineffective due to the drag induced by the compressed air. To exceed Mach 6, the ramjet must be able to effectively mix fuel with air moving through the engine at supersonic speeds. Engineers compare this task to that of igniting a match in hurricane force winds. The principle of producing combustion in a supersonic airflow is termed a supersonic-combustion ramjet or scramjet.

With air moving with such high velocities inside the scramjet, combustion must be successfully achieved within only one or two milliseconds. Hydrogen becomes the desired fuel due to the rapid burn-rate, low weight, and high thermal energy, but there are problems. The low density means that sufficient fuel to propel the SSTO craft will occupy a large volume. Hydrogen is an extremely inflammable gas, as aviation history reveals, and requires special facilities for storage and refueling.

An engine under serious consideration for the NASP was a long and rectangular hybrid of the ramjet and scramjet. This engine would have been able to shift from the ramjet to scramjet mode at higher speeds without substantially changing the internal airflow path. Engineers indicated that a single engine combining both modes of operation was preferable to building and attaching the two separate engines because of the savings in overall weight. To allow the engine to run under such a range of conditions, fuel injection must be varied in response to the combustion region, which moves upstream with an increase in flight speed. Groups of fuel injectors would have been installed at critical points inside the combustion chamber walls.

Ramjet and scramjet engines both require air to sustain combustion. The scramjet would have been functional at very high altitudes, but just how high is unknown. At these high altitudes and speeds the engine's thrust would have decreased at the expense of drag. When drag forces overcome the thrust, the aircraft must turn off the scramjet engines and rely on rocket propulsion to reach orbit. The X-30 would have used the same rocket engines to gain reentry from orbit and enter a gliding trajectory back to Earth. The X-30, unlike the shuttle, would have been able to restart its engines once it reentered the atmosphere, allowing a greater margin of safety for landings.

Five contractors working with NASP's Joint Program Office in Dayton, Ohio, designed a composite configuration. The configuration that emerged was a two-seat aircraft about the size of a Douglas DC-10 airliner. The craft, a massive structure of engines and cryogenic fuel tank, measured between 45 and 60 meters long and had a mass of between 100,000 and 140,000 kilograms. The fuselage of the craft was very broad, to provide lift and accommodate multiple scramjets underneath. The wings were very stubby, providing flight control but little lift.

The wider fuselage permitted a more efficient airflow path, allowing air collection and compression prior to the engine inlets. The wide body design also accommodated a larger fuel tank without significantly increasing drag forces. The X-30 was designed so that at high speeds the thrust, drag, and lift forces all would pass through the center of gravity. To achieve this, the wings were to be movable and placed in the neutral position upon reaching hypersonic speeds. At lower speeds, the wings provided lift that acts as a control surface to stabilize the craft. At hypersonic speeds, control surfaces are not necessary since the forces are stabilized through the center of gravity.

Actual testing of the X-30 design was limited to wind tunnels that could not attain the required air speeds that the full-scale prototype would reach. Engineers overcame some of these drawbacks by modeling airframes on supercomputers. Airflow down to as little as six one-hundredths of a square millimeter across the airframe can be modeled. Supercomputer time alone over the first five years of the project amounted to close to 50 percent of the national total. Flight materials and systems were also tested when attached to conventional rocket launch vehicles.

A major consideration surrounding the X-30 design required the development and testing of entirely new materials. Sections of this aircraft had to be able to withstand temperatures as high as 2,800° Celsius while resisting tremendous pressures generated by hypersonic flight in the atmosphere and from orbital reentry. These materials had to maintain high strength yet be very light in weight. Titanium aluminum boron alloys sustain strength to 750° Celsius and carbon-carbon composites can resist temperatures to 3,000° Celsius.

These materials alone would not have been sufficient to absorb all of the heat generated by this vehicle. Active cooling systems utilizing the fuel as a coolant have been used on the SR-Blackbird reconnaissance plane. The hottest sections of the airframe— the nose, engines, and leading edges—can be actively cooled with cold circulating fuel. The X-30's fuel tanks would have held liquid hydrogen as a slush cooled to minus 242° Celsius. The semisolid hydrogen slush that could be contained in a smaller volume than liquid hydrogen alone would have been pumped through the hottest portions of the aircraft, absorbing heat.

The NASP program never built any test devices to demonstrate the capabilities of the various technologies. Large funding requests delayed obtaining the required budget from Congress. The NASP study was terminated in 1994, when it was concluded that the high-temperature materials and air-breathing propulsion technology required for such prolonged high speeds within Earth's atmosphere would take many more years to mature than had originally been estimated.

An X-30 model in a wind tunnel. (NASA)

Contributions

Research and development stemming from the NASP program have resulted in new devices, materials, and technologies. NASP contractors have produced a titanium alloy that would be used in the medical field and in chemical processing. The light weight and strength make the alloy suitable for hips and other human joints. The alloy's resistance to corrosion would find use in pipes and valves that transport corrosive gases.

Composites developed for aircraft engine components could be used in other types of power-generating turbine machinery that are exposed to high temperatures. Carbon-carbon composites have been developed that are able to resist temperatures as high as 1,700° Celsius, which were expected to be encountered on the leading edges of the flight surfaces of the NASP. If given an antioxidant coating of these carbon materials, power plant combustion chambers should become more efficient, with less pollution.

Texas Instruments' Metallurgical Materials Division, under contract to the NASP program, succeeded in developing a titanium-aluminum alloy that could be rolled to foil thickness. Direct outcomes of the process were a higher yield and a cost savings: from $6,600 per kilogram to only $1,500 to $2,000 per kilogram. The foils could be applied to metal matrix composites for gas turbine power plants as well as to combustor and exhaust components. The foil would find other commercial applications in heart-valve assemblies and pacemakers due to its high strength, low weight, and compatibility with human tissue.

Titanium foils are being manufactured into honeycomb materials and heat exchangers. Honeycomb materials of titanium are light in weight, are strong, and resist high temperatures, and they find use in the aircraft industry. In the construction of heat exchangers for NASP, Texas Instruments bonds separate layers of titanium, copper, and nickel foil to a stainless steel sheet. Heating of the stainless steel sheets allows the foils to alloy into a brazing material. The titanium-copper-nickel brazing material forms joints of higher yield and better quality at a lower cost.

In order to model high-speed airflow, NASP researchers have modified fluid dynamics software to study structural and thermal analysis of airframes and engines. The huge volume of computational data needed to model these physical systems has produced new computer algorithms that can run at high speeds. This field, known as computational fluid dynamics, is expected to be applied to the study of commercial engine combustion and brake systems, as well as to wind and ocean current circulation patterns.

NASP's supercryogenic fuel requirements have led to the development of special fuel tanks constructed of graphite epoxy that provides high strength and low weight. Advanced turbomachinery pumps developed for the cooling systems will allow engineers to reduce the overall weight by as much as twelve times. The fuel under development for the NASP will be a slush, a mixture of both solid and liquid hydrogen, as more hydrogen can be carried in a fuel tank this way. Tests conducted by NASA have already demonstrated the feasibility of producing large amounts of slush hydrogen.

Context

Progress in the areas of propulsion, high-temperature materials, and supercomputer modeling distinguished the NASP program from earlier aerospace planes and vehicles. Kerosene, used for most conventional jet aircraft, is not a suitable fuel for hypersonic transports designed to travel two or more times faster than the speed of sound. Air-consuming propulsion systems, like the scramjet, by using atmospheric instead of onboard oxygen, will be able to carry much larger payloads. A scramjet engine alone, however, will not be capable of reaching orbital altitudes that are well above the atmosphere.

The NASP would have had rocket engines to operate in space and for reentry but, unlike the shuttle, would not have discarded them. A vehicle able to take off and land from a runway and attain an orbit

without resorting to rocket staging offers many advantages, including more frequent return flights and cost effectiveness. An SSTO craft like the NASP had to burn a low-density fuel such as hydrogen to save weight.

To carry enough hydrogen for the flight required very large fuel tanks, which contributed to a large, bulging fuselage. The fuselage had to be designed to produce both lift and directed airflow. One solution to the problem of large fuel tanks was resolved with the realization that a larger quantity of hydrogen could be carried in these tanks if at least part of it was in a solid state. The solution was to develop a slush hydrogen technology that could produce large quantities of this liquid-solid mixture.

A major challenge to production of the NASP was the development of materials that could maintain strength under the extreme conditions of high temperatures and pressures encountered during hypersonic flight. A major breakthrough was preventing carbon-carbon composites, which are very light and strong, from burning in the presence of oxygen. Silicon-carbide ceramic coatings, for example, would seal out oxygen but were subject to cracking due to differences in the thermal expansion rates of these two materials. The answer was to layer the material with a silicon sealer and to add an oxygen inhibitor to the carbon matrix.

The ability to investigate fluid dynamics on supercomputers has enabled researchers to model characteristics of high-speed flight that would not otherwise be available experimentally. The basic design of the NASP airframe, as well as the ramjet and scramjet engine performances modeled by computer, have provided data that have been validated in supersonic wind-tunnel testing. Computational modeling, when appropriate, can lead to results that are reasonably predictive and cost-effective.

When viewed only as applied research, the NASP, like other major government-industry joint ventures, involved considerable risks with no guarantees for successes or applications. The potential technology spin-offs from basic research, on the other hand, have prompted other countries to develop their own hypersonic vehicles. If the United States should drop the NASP program, then countries like Japan, Germany, and England would catapult to leadership roles in aerospace technology.

Late in 2002, NASA announced plans to proceed with an Orbital Space Plane capable of both crew transport and crew return missions from the International Space Station (ISS). The Orbital Space Plane is one of three parts making up NASA's Integrated Space Transportation Plan (ISTP). The ISTP consists of three major programs: Space Shuttle, Orbital Space Plane, and Next Generation Launch Technology. The plan makes investments to extend the shuttle's operational life for continued safe operations.

The Orbital Space Plane will provide a crew transfer capability, as early as possible, to ensure access to and from the ISS. The OSP is a crucial component of the new ISTP as it focuses on the development of a crew transport vehicle. The concept of an Orbital Space Plane reflects NASA's need to ferry Space Station crew members and to ensure that a capability exists to get the crew home if there is an emergency.

By 2012, the Orbital Space Plane system is to have the capability to ferry crew and light cargo to and from the Space Station. In time, the system could become the foundation for a crew transfer vehicle routinely flown to space on a new launch vehicle.

—*Michael L. Broyles*

See also: Ames Research Center; Launch Vehicles: Reusable; Lewis Field and Glenn Research Center; National Aeronautics and Space Administration; Space Shuttle: Ancestors; Space Shuttle Flights, 1998.

Further Reading

Brown, Stuart F. "X-30: Out of the World in a Scramjet." *Popular Science* 239 (November, 1991): 70. A feature article covering the historical development of the National Aero- Space Plane. A good discussion of aerodynamics and propulsion systems including ramjets, scramjets, and rockets. Gives the general reader a feeling for the economics and global interest in the program.

Burrows, William E. *This New Ocean: The Story of the First Space Age*. New York: Random House, 1998. This is a comprehensive history of the human conquest of space, covering everything from the earliest attempts at spaceflight through the voyages near the end of the twentieth century. Burrows is an experienced journalist who has reported for *The New York Times*, *The Washington Post*, and *The Wall Street Journal*. There are many photographs and an extensive source list. Interviewees in the book include Isaac Asimov, Alexei Leonov, Sally K. Ride, and James A. Van Allen.

Hallion, Richard. *On the Frontier: Flight Research at Dryden, 1946-1981*. Washington, D.C.: Government Printing Office, 1984. This is one of the titles in the NASA History series, which provides an official look at the space agency, its programs, and facilities. The information is presented in chronological order, and it covers such noted aerospace craft as the X-1, X-15, HL-10, X-24A, X-24B, and space shuttle. Also detailed is the research that assisted the development of the Gemini and Apollo spacecraft. There are many black-and-white photographs and line drawings, an index, and an impressive bibliography. Appendices include program flight chronologies on the X-1, D-558, X-2, X-3, X-4, X-5, XF-92A, X-15, lifting bodies, XB-70A, and space shuttle approach and landing test program.

Harland, David M. *The Space Shuttle: Roles, Missions, and Accomplishments*. Hoboken, N.J.: John Wiley, 1998. *The Space Shuttle* is written thematically, rather than purely chronologically. Topics include shuttle operations and payloads, weightlessness, materials processing, exploration, Spacelabs and free-flyers, and the shuttle's role in the International Space Station.

Heppenheimer, T. A. *Countdown: A History of Space Flight*. New York: John Wiley, 1997. A detailed historical narrative of the human conquest of space. Heppenheimer traces the development of piloted flight through the military rocketry programs of the era preceding World War II. Covers both the American and the Soviet attempts to place vehicles, spacecraft, and humans into the hostile environment of space. More than a dozen pages are devoted to bibliographic references.

Kandebo, Stanley. "TI Finding Commercial Uses for NASP Materials." *Aviation Week and Space Technology* 137 (September, 1992): 56-58. The author has kept the aviation reader well informed on the progress of the NASP program in recent years. Discusses advancements in commercialized materials and processes developed in connection with the NASP program by Texas Instruments as a prime contractor. Applications for the thin metal alloy foils are listed.

Murray, Charles J. "NASP: A Leap into the Unknown." *Design News* 47 (August, 1991): 70-74. An excellent review covering the complete history of the aerospace plane. Nontechnical and easy to understand for the lay reader. Problems and possible solutions encountered in the design and testing of this revolutionary craft. Materials, fuel systems, and industrial spin-offs are discussed. The author excerpts interviews from prominent individuals who are familiar with the program.

Reed, R. Dale, and Darlene Lister. *Wingless Flight: The Lifting Body Story*. NASA SP-4220. Washington, D.C.: National Aeronautics and Space Administration, 1997. *Wingless Flight* is a story about the development of the lifting body research aircraft at Edwards Air Force Base. A small group of individuals pooled their talents and aspirations to accomplish one of the most amazing feats in aeronautical history by flying eight different wingless aircraft-spacecraft designs.

Reithmaier, Larry. *Mach 1 and Beyond: The Illustrated Guide to High Speed Flight*. New York: TAB Books, 1995. A short but informative chapter is provided on the NASP program. Both objectives and values of the overall project are listed. The reader is given information on the technical problems that must be overcome for the NASP to become a reality. Profile diagrams of the proposed design along with an artistic rendition of the completed craft highlight the chapter.

Taylor, Michael J. H., ed. *Jane's Aviation Review*. London: Jane's Publishing, 1987. A complete chapter written by Graham Warwick is devoted to trans-atmospheric vehicles (TAVs) along with a brief history of the NASP program. Includes five conceptual illustrations of proposed aerospace planes. Discussion of problems of obtaining high Mach numbers with ramjets and scramjets and efforts to overcome airframe temperatures caused by high-speed flight. The British version of the aerospace plane is also presented.

National Commission on Space

Date: July 16, 1984, to August, 1986
Type of organization: Aerospace agency

Created by Congress in 1984, the National Commission on Space (NCOS) was assigned to "define the long-range needs of the Nation that may be fulfilled through the peaceful uses of outer space" and "articulate goals and develop options for the future direction of the Nation's civilian space program." In response, NCOS prepared Pioneering the Space Frontier (1986), a thorough look at long-term space goals that includes a "Declaration for Space," which many consider to be as important to space-age civilization as the Declaration of Independence is to the United States.

Key Figures

Ronald W. Reagan (1911-2004), fortieth president of the United States, 1981-1989

Thomas O. Paine (1921-1992), NCOS chairperson and former NASA administrator

Laurel Wilkening, NCOS vice chair

Luis Alvarez (1911-1988), Nobel Prize-winning physicist at Lawrence Berkeley Laboratory

Neil A. Armstrong (1930-2012), Apollo 11 commander, first man to walk on the Moon

Gerard K. O'Neill (1927-1992), president of the Space Studies Institute and flight director executive officer at Geostar Corporation

Kathryn D. Sullivan (b. 1951), the first American woman to walk in space

Marcia Smith, NCOS executive director specialist on aerospace policy at the Library of Congress

Theodore Simpson, NCOS director of Planning

Leonard David, NCOS director of Research and editor of *Space World*

John H. Glenn, Jr. (1921-2016), Mercury and space shuttle astronaut, U.S. senator, and nonvoting NCOS member

Slade Gorton (b. 1928), U.S. senator and non-voting NCOS member

Summary of the Organization

In 1984, the space shuttle and space station programs were billed by NASA as the next logical steps in space exploration. Some members of the U.S. Congress, however, believed that the U.S. space program had had no real objective or focus since the Apollo Program ended in the mid-1970's. The Senate Committee on Commerce, Science, and Transportation and the House Committee on Science and Technology created a private citizens' commission to determine the goals and the pacing of the American space effort, both piloted and robotic.

These committees held hearings. Testifiers included Thomas O. Paine, former National Aeronautics and Space Administration (NASA) administrator, and James M. Beggs, the NASA administrator at that time. Paine testified that, if a study were performed, it should be done by NASA, which would have to implement the recommendations. Beggs testified that NASA had file cabinets filled with earlier studies. Congress, however, decided that the earlier reports were unsatisfactory and stressed the need for a study by people outside government but familiar with the space effort, a study that would balance all scientific and political interests.

The result, Title II of Public Law 98-361, the National Aeronautics and Space Act of 1984, was approved July 16, 1984. It created the National Commission on Space (NCOS) and included requirements that the NCOS should plan for the next twenty years, "define the long-range needs of the Nation that may be fulfilled through the peaceful uses of outer space" and "articulate goals and develop options for the future direction of the Nation's civilian space program." It stated that the NCOS should consider a permanently crewed space station a necessity. The act included a so-called sunset provision, requiring the commission to disband within sixty days of submitting its report to Congress and the president of the United States.

The act also required President Ronald W. Reagan to appoint fifteen people (of whom no more than three could be federal employees) to the commission within ninety days. The members would review classified documents; therefore, Federal Bureau of Investigation (FBI) clearance would be required. The time needed to process these clearances delayed the naming of the members. On March 29, 1985, Reagan appeared at the National Space Club in Washington, D.C., where he announced the names of fourteen of the fifteen members. He later named the fifteenth member, after an FBI clearance was received.

Nonvoting NCOS members included Senator Slade Gorton and Senator John H. Glenn, Jr., two members of the House of Representatives, and nine *ex officio* members (from the National Science Foundation, the Office of Science and Technology Policy, and the U.S. Departments of Agriculture, Commerce, Transportation, and State). Marcia Smith, executive director; Leonard David, director of Research; and Theodore Simpson, director of Planning, headed the staff of nine.

The commission began work quickly. It personally invited more than three hundred space experts, including many from NASA, to speak at eight hearings to convene between May and December, 1985, in various cities. (The five people on the commission staff loaned from NASA performed only administrative work. In line with Paine's 1984 congressional testimony, the commission invited NASA policy experts to the hearings because the NCOS believed that NASA would more readily implement directives that it had helped establish.)

Even before the first hearings, the commissioners recognized that planning for the next twenty years only, as Congress had requested, would be insufficient, because many programs have lead times of more than ten years. They decided to look at what the United States wanted to be doing in fifty years, and what would be needed in the next twenty years to lay the groundwork for the fifty-year goals.

Even with the quick start, the NCOS did not have a full year before the deadline because of the administrative and clearance delays in naming the commission members. Chairperson Paine and Vice Chairperson Laurel Wilkening returned to Congress, requesting a six-month extension of the deadline. They also asked for funding for a thirty-minute video. Congress agreed to both requests. The total appropriation came to $1.4 million.

Continuing its diligent approach, the National Commission on Space held fifteen public hearings to receive comments from as wide a cross section of the public as possible. These hearings—intentionally held around the country, from Honolulu, Hawaii, to Iowa City, Iowa, and Boston, Massachusetts— occurred between September, 1985, and January, 1986. More than six hundred people, of all ages and from all walks of life, presented their views. Besides these public hearings, the NCOS arranged to have a "Life in the Twenty-First Century Workshop" on October 18, 1985. It also asked the American Institute of Aeronautics and Astronautics to sponsor a "Workshop on the Commercialization of Space," which took place on October 31, 1985. In addition to organizing these many hearings and workshops, NCOS commissioners spoke individually to numerous groups, invariably requesting the members of the audience to contribute their ideas by sending either letters or electronic mail.

More ideas came from an unexpected direction. Astronomer Carl Sagan wrote an article for *Parade* magazine (a national Sunday newspaper supplement) in early February, 1986, asking American readers to write the NCOS outlining what they believed their nation's space goals should be. His request specifically pointed to a joint U.S.-Soviet crewed Mars mission. By the end of February, when the NCOS was completing its report, it had received more than one thousand letters sparked by Sagan's article. Frank White, another concerned planner, worked closely with Commissioner George Field on the "Declaration for Space." NCOS member Gerard K. O'Neill commented that White's work "contributed freely to the National Commission on Space at a critical point in its deliberations, [and] became the organizing theme about which its report was written."

This reaching out for ideas on space goals went beyond the borders of the United States. The commission realized that the United States could not be a leader in space if it did not know what other nations were doing. Chairman Thomas Paine and Executive Director Marcia Smith visited Moscow to obtain Soviet input. Paine also went to Paris to determine what the European Space Agency (ESA) had planned.

Many suggestions received through the letters, electronic mail, workshops, hearings, and consultations helped the commissioners formulate their report. Very early in their planning, the commissioners recalled an illustrated report on the United States' future in space that had appeared in a national magazine in 1951. They realized that the illustrations that had accompanied that piece were still distinctly in their memory. Yet the text, which had been written by Wernher von Braun, was not as memorable. The commissioners decided that their report should be well illustrated. They clearly wanted the publication to be as accessible to the public as possible.

On May 23, 1986, a commercial publisher released the commission's 218-page report, *Pioneering the Space Frontier: The Report of the National Commission on Space*. The report recommended that NASA review the report's findings, and, by December 31, 1986, suggest a long-range implementation plan, including a specific agenda for the next five years.

The prologue to the report, entitled "Declaration for Space," states the pioneering mission for twenty-first century America:

> To lead the exploration and development of the space frontier, advancing science, technology, and enterprise, and building institutions and systems that make accessible vast new resources and support human settlements beyond Earth orbit, from the highlands of the Moon to the plains of Mars.

The report provides a rationale for exploring and settling the solar system. It states that the solar system is humanity's extended home; the human species is "destined to expand to other worlds." It adds that American freedoms must be carried into space, and individual initiative and free enterprise in space must be stimulated. Comparing the American frontier to the space frontier, the report advocates combining space's vast resources with solar energy to create new wealth. This must be done, it asserts, logically and wisely, sustaining investment at a small but steady fraction of the gross national product (GNP).

The report advises that the United States work with other nations in exploring the universe. It states that, with the United States' economic strength, technological ability, and frontier background, it will lead in the space effort and challenge and inspire individuals and nations to contribute their best efforts. It calls for common sense in settling space, in a sustained effort combining technology, scientific research, exploration, and development of space resources. Government's role, it states, is to support exploration, science, and critical technologies and provide the transportation systems and access to this new territory. The NCOS report affirms that Americans must not lose their values, such as peaceful intent, equal opportunity, planetary ecological considerations, and respect for alien life-forms.

Part 1, "Civilian Space Goals for Twenty-First Century America," discusses the proposed long-range three-pronged interlocking program: stimulating space enterprise; increasing understanding of Earth, the solar system, and the universe; and exploring and settling the solar system. To accomplish these three goals, NCOS recommends in part 2, "Low-Cost Access to the Solar System," that the United States commit to providing low-cost access to space and advancing technology across a broad spectrum.

Part 3 proposes twenty-year civilian space programs, with budget planning five years in advance. It assumes that NASA's budget will grow at the rate the GNP grows, remaining below 0.5 percent of GNP (one-half the peak percentage during Apollo). The projected fifty-year total is $700 billion. Among the twenty-year goals stated are cargo vehicles with operating costs of under $200 per 0.45 kilogram orbited by the year 2000, low-cost aerospace (ground to orbit) planes, orbital maneuvering vehicles, Space Station operation by 1994 (the International Space Station was launched in 1998), permanent human lunar outposts by 2005 (the target date is now between 2015 and 2020), and uncrewed Mars sample return mission by 2005 (launch is now planned between 2011 and 2014), a variable-gravity research facility, and fellowships in space science and engineering. Among the fifty-year goals listed in part 4 are a permanent human Mars outpost by 2015, full Moon manufacturing by 2017, full Mars manufacturing by 2027, and space-based factories. The benefits, *Pioneering the Space Frontier* avers, include achieving advances in science and technology, providing direct economic returns from new space-based enterprises, and opening new worlds, with resources that can free humanity's aspirations.

The NCOS also produced a thirty-minute videotape, for which it had been funded by Congress. It has been shown worldwide. The commission also provided copies to all the Teacher-in-Space candidates and made it available to all science teachers.

Because of problems with government schedules (caused, in part, by an international crisis concerning Libya), the NCOS could not officially deliver its report to either Congress or the President until July 22, 1986. On that day, both the House Committee on Science and Technology and the Senate Committee on Commerce, Science, and Transportation held hearings on the report. The committees agreed that the National Commission on Space had properly discharged its responsibilities. They complimented the Commission on its inspiring report but voiced concern at the proposed costs and benefits. Chairman Thomas Paine and Vice Chairperson Laurel Wilkening presented the report to President Reagan later that day.

In August, 1986, as decreed by the sunset provision, the National Commission on Space disbanded. The many letters, videotapes, and reports resulting from the hearings and public forums are stored in the National Archives.

Context

The NCOS report, the most thorough study of the United States' space goals, was the first such report made by private citizens. It legitimized the ideas long studied by the space community and provided, in its "Declaration for Space," what may be the equivalent of the Declaration of Independence to future civilization.

Earlier efforts to establish long-term goals for the U.S. space program began in 1969, when Vice President Spiro Agnew chaired the Space Task Group. (Thomas O. Paine had been a member of this group.) After reviewing the findings of the group, President Richard M. Nixon had decided on what seemed at first the least expensive option— proceeding with the building of a space shuttle only.

Later, in 1975, President Gerald Ford and the Congress ignored NASA's report "Outlook for Space," which suggested broad goals except for a space station and a Mars return. Just before the publication of *Pioneering the Space Frontier*, the National Research Council's Space Science Board advocated the return to a fleet of both piloted and robotic launch vehicles, rather than sole reliance on shuttles. It saw no scientific need for a space station during the next two decades.

The January, 1986, *Challenger* accident—in which the crewed space shuttle exploded shortly after liftoff—overshadowed the NCOS. Preoccupied, NASA did not immediately respond to the NCOS report's call to suggest, by December 31, 1986, long-range implementation plans.

Former Astronaut Michael Collins chaired the NASA Advisory Council Task Force on Space Program Goals, reporting in March, 1987. The task force's objective was to assess NASA's response to the NCOS report and advise on any plans, emphasizing certain shorter-term goals and broad policy issues. It recommended crewed Mars missions, preceded by extensive research.

NASA also responded with the August, 1987, *Leadership and America's Future in Space: A Report to the Administrator* by astronaut Sally K. Ride, which coordinated various study findings. This report acknowledged the NCOS and *Challenger* reports. It listed initiatives around which to focus a spacegoals discussion: the exploration of the solar system, an outpost on the Moon, and a crewed mission to Mars. Ride was then the head of the Office of Exploration, formed in June, 1987, to develop technical options needed to realize space goals. Also in 1987, Congress approved NASA's Civil Space Technology Initiative to revitalize technology, enhance orbit access, and advance in-orbit science missions.

The Iran-Contra affair and other crises preoccupied President Reagan, and Science Adviser William R. Graham, Jr., stymied NASA's attempts to gain Reagan's support. Finally, on February 11, 1988, President Reagan unveiled his National Space Policy. It incorporated an interagency review of *Pioneering the Space Frontier*, an assessment of the implications of the 1986 *Challenger* accident, and a review of previous presidential decisions. It supported the goals of a strong commercial space program, international cooperation, obtaining benefits through space-related activities, and expanding humanity throughout the solar system.

It must be noted that few of the NCOS recommendations were implemented according to the time schedule projected in its final report.

—*Patricia Jackson*

See also: Ames Research Center; Asteroid and Comet Exploration; Deep Impact; Hubble Space Telescope: Science; International Space Station: 2004; Jet Propulsion Laboratory; Planetary Exploration; Ranger Program; Space Shuttle Mission STS-1; Stardust Project; Telescopes: Air and Space.

Further Reading

Bova, Ben. *The High Road*. Boston: Houghton Mifflin, 1981. Bova, president of the National Space Society and former *Omni* magazine editor, discusses solving energy, environment, and nuclear-war problems with space resources. He shows how little extra energy is required to travel to the Moon and to asteroids to mine raw materials once a vehicle is in low-Earth orbit.

Burrows, William E. *This New Ocean: The Story of the First Space Age*. New York: Random House, 1998. This is a comprehensive history of the human conquest of space, covering everything from the earliest attempts at spaceflight through the voyages near the end of the twentieth century. Burrows is an experienced journalist who has reported for *The New York Times*, *The Washington Post*, and *The Wall Street Journal*. Many photographs and an extensive source list. Interviewees include Isaac Asimov, Alexei Leonov, Sally K. Ride, and James A. Van Allen.

David, Leonard. "America in Space: Where Next?" *Sky and Telescope* 74 (July, 1987): 23-29. David, the NCOS Director of Research, looks at the state of space in the United States and what the next goal should be. He compares space science obtained by astronauts versus robots and reviews the NCOS report.

Klerkx, Greg. *Lost in Space: The Fall of NASA and the Dream of a New Space Age*. New York: Pantheon Books, 2004. The premise of this work is that NASA has been stuck in Earth orbit since the Apollo era, and that space exploration has suffered as a result.

Lambright, W. Henry, ed. *Space Policy in the Twenty-First Century*. Baltimore: Johns Hopkins University Press, 2003. This book addresses a number of important questions: What will replace the space shuttle? Can the International Space Station justify its cost? Will Earth be threatened by asteroid impact? When and how will humans explore Mars?

McDonald, Frank B. "Space Research: At a Crossroads." *Science* 235 (February 13, 1987): 751-754. Assesses the current and future U.S. space science program in view of the *Challenger* accident, NCOS, and the Gramm-Rudman-Hollings Budget Reduction Act.

McDougall, Walter A. *The Heavens and the Earth: A Political History of the Space Age*. 2d ed. Baltimore: Johns Hopkins University Press, 1997. This scholarly book traces the origins of the Space Age. McDougall considers whether the seemingly unending technocracy race against foreign competition will erode the basic values of Western civilization.

Mendell, Wendell W., ed. *Lunar Bases and Space Activities of the Twenty-First Century*. Houston: Lunar and Planetary Institute, 1985. Papers presented at the first (1984) Lunar Bases symposium. The authors suggested that improved transportation technology would lead to routine payloads to and from the Moon by the year 2000. These papers consider lunar base concepts; transportation issues; lunar science, construction, materials, and processes; astronomy from the Moon; lunar oxygen production; life-support and health maintenance; and societal issues. Several papers deal with Mars issues. Some illustrations.

---. "Solar System Bonanza: The Burden of Proof." *Space World* W-6-270 (June, 1986): 18-19. The NCOS held a public meeting in November, 1985, in San Francisco. This is a transcript of Commissioner Gerard K. O'Neill and Carl Sagan discussing the commercialization of the solar system.

Michaud, Michael A. G. *Reaching for the High Frontier: The American Pro-Space Movement, 1972-1984*. New York: Praeger, 1986. The pro-space movement (including more than fifty advocacy groups and more than 200,000 Americans) has developed since the end of the Moon landing program. Michaud traces key groups that have subtly influenced space policy and identifies their origins and goals.

National Commission on Space. *Pioneering the Space Frontier: The Report of the National Commission on Space*. New York: Bantam Books, 1986. This highly readable text resulted from the commission's thorough research. It sets forth goals and scenarios for space exploration into the twenty-first century. Illustrated.

O'Neill, Gerard K. *The High Frontier: Human Colonies in Space*. Garden City, N.Y.: Anchor Books, 1982. An interesting look at concepts for space colonies, farms, and factories. O'Neill, an NCOS member, shows how they can be built from materials sent by "mass drivers" from lunar mines.

---. *2081: A Hopeful View of the Human Future*. New York: Simon & Schuster, 1981. Discusses predicting the future, shows the drivers of change—computers, increased automation, and space colonies—and provides scenarios of how life, including routine space travel, will be in the year 2081.

Reichhardt, Tony. "Predicting the Space Frontier: A Conversation with Laurel Wilkening." *Space World* W-10-274 (October, 1986): 8-13. An interview with Wilkening, the NCOS vice chairperson, about the NCOS report and reactions to it.

Reichhardt, Tony, and I. Gilman. "Destination Mars: A Conversation with Michael Collins." *SpaceWorld* X-7-283 (July, 1987): 16-20. Former astronaut Collins chaired the Task Force on Space Programs Goals for the NASA Advisory Council. This article is an interview with him concerning the report.

White, Frank. *The Overview Effect: Space Exploration and Human Evolution.* Boston: Houghton Mifflin, 1987. White, who greatly influenced the Commission's "Declaration for Space," interviewed astronauts and cosmonauts for this book. He reports on the Copernican perspective, which views Earth as part of the solar system, and the "universal insight," which focuses on comprehending Earth's place in the universe. The space travelers share their unique visions.

Navigation Satellites

Date: Beginning April 15, 1960
Type of spacecraft: Navigational satellites

The United States and the former Soviet Union each began launching a series of intrinsically different types of navigation satellites in 1960. These satellites are military spacecraft to which civilian interests have been allowed access. They have enabled ships, aircraft, and even land-based vehicles to pinpoint their positions on Earth, saving billions of dollars in fuel and lost time and helping to ensure safe travel for millions of people.

Summary of the Satellites

Edward Everett Hale made the first mention of a satellite in modern literature in *The Atlantic Monthly* in 1869. Hale's idea, set in his story "The Brick Moon," was to orbit a brick moon nearly 65 meters in diameter. The purpose of the brick moon was to provide navigators with a visual object by which to determine their positions. Thus, Hale must be credited with originating the notion of using artificial satellites for navigation.

Nearly a century later, the Soviet Union launched the first human-made satellite, Sputnik 1, an 83.3-kilogram object whose primary purpose was to beam repetitive signals to the Earth. The fact that a growing military power with an adversarial relationship to the United States could accomplish such a feat stirred much concern in the West. The immediate fear was that the Soviet Union could orbit nuclear weapons and drop them on any target in the United States at will. This fear gave rise to the need to track foreign satellites precisely so that their activities could be carefully monitored.

It quickly became clear that visual tracking alone did not provide experts with enough information. Two physicists at The Johns Hopkins University in Baltimore, Maryland, decided that a radio tracking system could provide them with the answer. Such a locating device had already been tested by scientists in West Germany. Eventually, William Guier and George Weiffenbach developed a system that measured the frequency shift of a satellite as it approached and again as it departed to determine its exact orbital characteristics—that is, making use of what is known as the Doppler effect.

A third physicist, Frank McGuire, had joined Guier and Weiffenbach. McGuire decided that if the satellite's exact position in orbit at any given time were known, the process could be reversed to determine the observer's position on Earth. The United States Navy seized upon the idea, and its scientists quickly worked to develop and launch the world's first navigation satellite, Transit 1B, on April 15, 1960. This satellite effectively reversed the science of determining spacecraft position using the Doppler principle.

This first satellite was to be one of a series of test satellites. As soon as the Navy had gathered data on them, it would build permanent ground stations and receivers that would be placed on U.S. naval vessels. The system developed after completion of all the tests would become known as the Operational System. The Navy's primary purpose was to provide precise navigation for its submarines that carried nuclear-tipped ballistic missile warheads. In the event that a missile was launched at sea, any error of known position at launch would be magnified in proportion to the distance to the target. Before the Navy launched the first navigation satellite, it had had to rely on Earth-based radio navigation systems and sometimes celestial navigation. The Navy had also devised an onboard navigation system known as the Shipboard Inertial Navigation System (SINS, or INS, the latter including Inertial Navigation Systems employed on aircraft and land-based vehicles), which tracked the submarine's position based on recorded movements of the ship and worked with electronic navigation inputs. These systems were not precise enough for accurate targeting of sea-launched ballistic missiles.

The Transit satellites were launched into orbits that were called polar because they traveled over the Earth's Poles at 1,000 kilometers in altitude. In this orbit, as the Earth rotated under them, every square kilometer of the Earth's surface would ultimately pass beneath them. As soon as the first Transit satellites were in orbit, scientists discovered several conditions that necessitated alterations to the satellite design. The original purpose of the Transit test series was to test the system designers' expectations regarding the satellites' behavior. It was discovered that orbital vehicles were subject to unexpected fluctuations, so that a more complex system design became necessary. The position of the Earth-based unit could not be determined with accuracy unless the precise position of the orbiting navigation satellite was known. Thus, these test orbits helped determine how the Earth-based system had to work so that the satellite's exact position could be continually monitored.

The experimental Transit system underwent almost four years of development, during which time the space-based navigation system and its Earth-based links were designed and built. During this entire period, the Transit system remained a carefully guarded military secret, a system tailored to the needs of the U.S. Department of Defense.

The Transit system became operational in late 1964, at first as a secret military program. It was not long, however, before private companies became aware of the Navy's new navigation system, and pressure began to be applied on the U.S. Congress to open the system for commercial use. Finally, in July of 1967, President Lyndon B. Johnson agreed to allow the Transit system to be used by civilian interests. Though businesses were given permission to build receivers to pick up and decipher the satellite's signals, the Transit system remained very much a military program. The Transit system and its nascent successor, the Global Positioning System (GPS), were both designed, financed, and maintained by the U.S. Department of Defense, even though civilians were allowed to use them. In this sense, then, all navigation satellites are military satellites.

The U.S. Transit program has had many names over its lifetime. In 1968, for example, the acronym Navsat was the name of a series of naval navigation satellites. The designations Timation (from time navigation), Triad, Navigation Technology Satellite (NTS), Transit Improvement Program (TIP), and Nova were all used at one time or another to describe Transit-type satellites. Users of the system have often applied the term "Satnav" to the system as a whole.

The Transit-type satellites allowed Earth-based observers to determine their position, receiving within two minutes the data transmitted from a single spacecraft. The ground-based observer need not transmit to the satellite. The ability to obtain a position (called a "fix") is determined by whether a satellite is within the observer's "receiving horizon," or a given distance above the receiver's actual horizon. Because of the altitude of the Transit satellite, a given satellite would be in a position to give an observer four fixes in a single day. Because normally there were five operating Transit satellites in orbit, an observer could count on twenty fixes per day, coming just over an hour apart, with an accuracy range of about 1.8 kilometers.

While the American Transit and the Soviet K-192-type systems are still being utilized and replenished by both nations, new satellite navigation systems have been developed by both the United States and Russia. The U.S. version is called the GPS, and the Russian system, the Global Navigation Satellite System (GLONASS). The systems operate on very similar principles.

The GPS satellite is named Navstar. Orbits of these spacecraft are twenty times higher than those of Transit (20,000 kilometers), are not polar, have an orbital period of twelve hours, and are made up of a constellation of at least eighteen satellites. The first GPS satellite was launched on February 22, 1978. The first ten Navstars were designated Block I and were used to test and validate the system. The results of that test were spectacular. The GPS system, according to one published report, made it possible for a ground-based receiver to pinpoint positions to a reported accuracy of 2 meters. (The system's advertised accuracy is 10 meters.)

The GPS system uses between one and four satellites to "fix" a position. Using four satellites to formulate the fix enables multidimensional positioning, especially valuable to aviation users. The GPS system can fix position in latitude, longitude, altitude, velocity, and time. Hence, GPS has application to all forms of transportation from ships to aircraft to land-based vehicles.

Like Transit, the GPS system is designed to be used by both military and civilian users. The precision made available to civilian users, however, is less accurate. Civilian receivers' transmissions make use of a code termed the standard positioning system, which ensures an accuracy of 100 meters. The military uses a highly classified code, the precise positioning system, which permits the highest accuracy. GPS became fully operational in March, 1994, when the last of the Navstar II satellites was placed in orbit.

The Russian GLONASS system was made available to the world in May, 1988, through details released to the International Civil Aviation Organization in Montreal. Signals similar to those of the U.S. standard and precise positioning systems show that the Russian system is nearly identical in scope, design, and purpose to the U.S. system. GLONASS satellites were placed in orbit and work in coordination with the GPS. However, many of the satellites were no longer functional. For example, in 2004, only eleven satellites were functional; a fully operational system required eighteen. Russia signed an agreement with India to expand on the diminished GLONASS system. The GPS network is continually upgraded with new satellites of increasing capabilities.

Contributions

The Transit test series confirmed that Earth's gravitational attraction was not uniform over the planet, so that the spacecraft's altitude fluctuated slightly. Tests also confirmed that the density of the atmosphere was not uniform at the level of the satellites' orbits; this variation also affected their altitudes. This finding was important to the designers because in any given orbit the altitude of a spacecraft determines such things as its speed and exact position. Of more fundamental importance, however, was the simple fact that new and valuable knowledge of Earth's gravitational fluctuations and the behavior of the upper atmosphere had been gained.

Satellite navigation was enabled by making a reverse application of the knowledge and techniques gained from the first consistent measurements of spacecraft in orbit. Yet a method for determining an orbital body's precise orbit had to come first, even in an operational satellite navigation system. Once satellite navigation systems had been developed, the Earth-based leg of the system itself worked to refine the method of determining a spacecraft's precise orbital position, providing data for the very science responsible for its inception. This system also contributed to the knowledge needed to develop exact rules for Doppler positioning of other kinds of satellites.

These discoveries would be vitally important to the total body of astronautics. Precise determination of the positions of spacecraft by ground-based observers would become an integral component of crewed spaceflights that require exact calculations of orbits for rendezvous. Such rendezvous would be vital for the crewed lunar missions and later for linking with space stations such as Skylab.

Precise positioning was also essential in determining exact positions when igniting booster rockets of interplanetary spacecraft in parking orbits prior to departure for the Moon or distant planets. Though space-based navigation was designed to determine the position of Earth-based observers, the science itself, in all of its reversible, interchangeable dimensions, would be used for both Earth and space navigation.

Direct knowledge was gained regarding the design and use of space-based navigation systems, so that the accuracy of the GPS improved on that of Transit by more than a hundredfold. The ability to schedule, build, and launch a system to allow for uninterrupted use over decades has been refined and is reflected in modern systems that place satellite spares in orbit, lying dormant until called upon. This practice ensures service free of disruptions.

Microelectronics made possible the development of satellite navigation receivers whose cost was such that even recreational boaters could afford access to satellite signals. Systems now allow private and commercial access to the extremely accurate GPS. At least one company designed a system that will use both the American GPS and the Soviet GLONASS, selectable with the flip of a switch. Another uses a hybrid INS/GPS for ultra-precise positioning. These products have become available to anyone with a receiver, from commercial to military to recreational users.

Context

Transit 1B was the world's first navigation satellite. Until the inception of the Transit series of satellites, the art and science of navigation had relied on techniques that could not ensure accurate positioning of ships and aircraft. Most vessels could not be sure of their position to within about 2 kilometers at sea, regardless of the navigation technique employed.

With the Transit program and ultimately GPS, it became possible to fix one's position constantly, anywhere on Earth—on sea, land, or air—with an accuracy of 2 meters, a time standard accurate to 0.1 microsecond, and a velocity of plus or minus 0.1 meter per second.

The process of designing the system enabled Earth-based observers to track spacecraft in orbit precisely. It also provided a database on the conditions of the upper atmosphere and their effect on orbiting spacecraft. The program and its antecedents also made the first fundamental discoveries of the fluctuations of Earth's gravitational field and their effect on orbital vehicles.

The science of space-based navigation originated as a result of reversing the knowledge gained in one of the first space sciences: precise tracking of orbital space vehicles. During the ensuing process of developing the space-based navigation network, it became necessary to track the navigation satellites meticulously, so that the system itself refined the progenitor science of space vehicle tracking.

Though navigation spacecraft were developed as military vehicles, they quickly became important to commercial users after the military allowed them access to the signals broadcast from the spacecraft. Their use has made possible the saving of billions of dollars in fuel and time since their inception by allowing precise tracking of ships and aircraft along their routes. This precise knowledge of position has also allowed for a greater margin of safety for ships and aircraft.

The Soviet Union pursued the same investigations as the United States, almost a decade behind in the early years of navigation, but nearly catching up with the inception of the GLONASS system. The GLONASS system was released by the Soviets in 1988, marking the first time one of its space systems was freely opened for world use. This change in Soviet policy came about the time Soviet General Secretary Mikhail Sergeyevich Gorbachev instituted his policies of *perestroika* (social and economic restructuring) and *glasnost* (openness).

Use of the GPS and GLONASS systems has revolutionized navigation worldwide with the use of low-cost receivers on civilian ships, recreational boats, aircraft, land vehicles such as trucks and automobiles, and even hikers and campers. In the twenty-first century GPS technologies pervades all facets of modern life.

—*Dennis Chamberland*

See also: Air Traffic Control Satellites; Amateur Radio Satellites; Global Positioning System; Nuclear Detection Satellites; Ocean Surveillance Satellites; Private Industry and Space Exploration; Search and Rescue Satellites; Spy Satellites; Telecommunications Satellites: Maritime; Telecommunications Satellites: Military; Telecommunications Satellites: Passive Relay; Telecommunications Satellites: Private and Commercial.

Further Reading

Andrade, Alessandra A. L. *The Global Navigation Satellite System: Navigating into the New Millennium*. Montreal: Ashgate, 2001. Provides an international view of issues of availability, cooperation, and reliability of air navigation services. Attention is specifically paid to the American GPS and Russian GLONASS systems, although the development of the Galileo civilian system in Europe is also presented.

Chamberland, Dennis. "Space Based Navigation." In *Proceedings of the United States Naval Institute*. Annapolis, Md.: Naval Institute Press, 1988. An article examining the unclassified military (primarily naval) use of the navigation satellite systems of the United States and the Soviet Union. This nontechnical article compares the latest system developments and naval applications. Includes photographs and historical charts.

Dahl, Bonnie. *The User's Guide to GPS: The Global Positioning System*. Evanston, Ill.: Richardsons' Marine Publishing, 1993. An explanation of GPS aimed at recreational boaters. Includes maps and illustrations.

Farrell, Jay A. *The Global Positioning System*. New York: McGraw-Hill, 1998. A concisely written, technical reference on the Global Positioning System for the engineer. It makes for fascinating reading for the rest of us.

Hassard, Roger. "A Layman's Guide to the Global Positioning System." *Navigator*, July/ August, 1985, 22-25. This excellent article provides a concise and easy-to-understand description of the Global Positioning System (GPS). It makes comparisons with Transit type satellites, examines the military versus civil uses, and briefly discusses civil receivers under development at the time of its publication.

Huang, Jerry. *All About GPS: Sherlock Holmes' Guide to the Global Positioning System*. San Jose, Calif.: Acme Services, 1999. This book is intended to bring the reader's interest toward fundamental sciences and modern technologies. The aspects of concepts, philosophy, methodology, and history are also emphasized.

Kaplan, Elliott D. *Understanding GPS: Principles and Applications*. Boston: Artech House, 1996. An overview of the Global Positioning System, accessible to the general reader.

Logsdon, Tom. *The Navstar Global Positioning System*. New York: Van Nostrand Reinhold, 1992. Overview of the Navstar system. Includes illustrations.

---. *Understanding the Navstar: GPS, GIS and IVHS*. New York: Van Nostrand Reinhold, 1995. Comprehensive explanation of the entire Navstar system and its multiple functions.

Maloney, Elbert S. *Dutton's Navigation and Piloting*. 14th ed. Annapolis, Md.: U.S. Naval Institute Press, 1985. This text is considered one of the definitive works on navigation. A rather technical, stiff presentation of the science of navigation of all kinds. Nevertheless, it is a valuable reference for one interested in satellite navigation in that it presents several superb pages of narrative dealing with satellite navigation systems and detailing exactly how they are used. Enlightening for the more serious student of satellite navigation.

Paul, Günter. *The Satellite Spin-Off: The Achievements of Space Flight*. Translated by Alan Lacy and Barbara Lacy. Washington, D.C.: Robert B. Luce, 1975. This book describes the beneficial spin-offs of all kinds of satellite systems. The work lists in chapter-by-chapter fashion different kinds of satellites, from meteorological to navigation; gives a historical synopsis; and reviews the broader use scenario. Includes numerous drawings. Suitable for all readers interested in a general review of satellite systems up to the mid-1970's. An eminently readable translation from the German.

The Soviet Year in Space: 1987. Colorado Springs, Colo.: Teledyne Brown Engineering, 1988. This report in book format is the seventh annual report on Soviet space activities published by Teledyne Brown Engineering. It constitutes an intriguing look in surprising detail at what is otherwise considered one of the world's best-kept secrets. Contains an entire section discussing navigation satellites, covering both the K-192-type system and GLONASS. It is oriented to all readers in an easy-to-understand format with many photographs and drawings.

Yenne, Bill. *The Encyclopedia of U.S. Spacecraft*. New York: Exeter Books, 1985. This work is a pictorial reference, listing all unclassified satellites alphabetically, with photographs of many. It is a useful review of the Transit series, though the reader must keep in mind that the Transit-type spacecraft had many names over its operational lifetime. It is suitable for all readers.

Zimmerman, Robert. *The Chronological Encyclopedia of Discoveries in Space*. Westport, Conn.: Oryx Press, 2000. Provides a complete chronological history of all crewed and robotic spacecraft and explains flight events and scientific results. Suitable for all levels of research.

New Horizons Pluto-Kuiper Belt Mission

Date: January, 2006, to 2026 (projected)
Type of program: Planetary exploration

The New Horizons spacecraft was the first human-made probe to explore Pluto, its moon Charon, and the distant Kuiper Belt Object 2014 MU69 (also known as Ultima Thule). The mission provided insights into the origin and evolution of the outer solar system, including the geology and geochemistry of Pluto, its atmosphere, Charon, and the Kuiper Belt in general. This first reconnaissance of the Kuiper Belt by the New Horizons spacecraft has led to an increased understanding of how stars, planets, and solar systems form and evolve.

Key Figures

S. Alan Stern, principal investigator

Thomas B. Coughlin, and Helene Winters, project managers

Mark Holdrige, deputy project director

Bill Gibson, payload manager

Andrew Francis, Hal Weaver, project scientist

Summary of the Mission

Shortly after the discovery of the first Kuiper Belt object in 1992, the Pluto Fast Flyby mission was outlined by the National Aeronautics and Space Administration (NASA). Subsequently named the Pluto-Kuiper Express mission, its goal was to send a robotic spacecraft to study Pluto and its moon, Charon, in 2012 and 2013 (after a December, 2004, launch), then move outward to investigate the Kuiper Belt. One of the primary objectives was to characterize the geology, surface composition, and atmosphere of Pluto. Initially, the mission was to be a joint effort of the United States and Russia. Zond probes, which would separate from the flyby spacecraft and relay data prior to their impact with Pluto, were to be included in the mission. However, in

September, 2000, budgetary considerations forced NASA to cancel the Pluto-Kuiper Express mission.

In early 2001, NASA proposed another mission to go to Pluto and beyond. After competitive bidding, Lockheed Martin's New Horizons proposal was chosen on November 29, 2001, as the one that would provide the design of the spacecraft, scientific instruments, and ground systems for the mission. On February 26, 2003, the New Horizons Pluto-Kuiper Belt Mission was approved as part of NASA's budget. Total mission cost was estimated at approximately $550 million. The Johns Hopkins University's Applied Physics Laboratory in Laurel, Maryland, was chosen to manage the mission, with Thomas B. Coughlin serving as the project manager. Dr. S. Alan Stern of the Southwest Research Institute in Boulder, Colorado, was selected as the principal investigator for the project.

Scheduled to be launched in January 2006 on a Lockheed Martin Atlas V551 booster, the New Horizons Pluto- Kuiper Belt spacecraft was planned to reach Jupiter in March 2007. For a time in 2005, concerns over the availability of nuclear fuel for the probe's power generation plants threatened to delay launch another year, which would alter the probe's trajectory to the Pluto-Charon system. Fortunately, that delay did not materialize. Spacecraft assembly was completed during April 2005. During that time a comprehensive performance test verified functionality of major spacecraft systems and New Horizons' scientific instruments. High-fidelity flight simulations began on April 30. Engineers ran another comprehensive performance test during the first half of May. Intensive environmental testing and analysis followed that test. In late May through early June 2005, NASA Headquarters managers conducted a mission readiness review. The spacecraft's preparation remained on schedule and was launched on January 19, 2006.

During the spacecraft's passage through the Jupiter system, the spacecraft carried out four months of investigations that included imaging Jupiter and some of its moons. The New Horizons spacecraft had a trajectory that took it outward through Jupiter's magnetic field "tail" which allowed the first such study of a planetary magnetosphere. Passage close to Jupiter allowed the spacecraft to perform a gravity-assisted slingshot maneuver that greatly increased its velocity and gave it a trajectory toward the Pluto-Charon system for a close approach to Pluto on July 15, 2015 at a distance of 9,600 kilometers.

Beginning about three months prior to its closest encounter with Pluto, New Horizons cameras acquired images of Pluto and its moons and its compliment of instruments began an intensive campaign of observing Pluto's environment. The New Horizons spacecraft, with hydrazine fuel included, had an initial mass of 465 kilograms upon launch. Upon its arrival near Pluto, approximately 228 watts of power was available to the spacecraft from its radioisotope thermoelectric generator (RTG). A 2.5-meter dish antenna on top of the triangular-shaped spacecraft provided the necessary Radio Science communications with the Earth. Five scientific instruments were aboard the spacecraft. The Long Range Reconnaissance Imager (LORRI) was a high-resolution charge-coupled device (CCD) that

produced images in visible light. The Pluto Exploration Remote Sensing Investigation (PERSI) instrument consisted of a visible CCD imager, as well as near-infrared and ultraviolet imaging spectrometers, which were used to determine the atomic and molecular species that make up Pluto's atmosphere. The main component of the third instrument, the Radio Science Experiment (REX), is an ultrastable oscillator that was used to investigate surface composition and temperatures. The spectrometer for analyzing plasmas and high-energy particles (PAM) was composed of the Solar Wind Around Pluto (SWAP) detector and a time-of-flight ion and electron sensor. The fifth separate scientific instrument, a student-built dust counter (SDC) constructed at the University of Colorado, made dust measurements in the outer regions of the solar system.

The first major goal of the Pluto-Kuiper Belt Mission was to characterize the geology, geomorphology, surface composition, temperatures, atmospheres, and internal structure of Pluto and Charon from data gathered using the visible wavelength cameras, infrared spectral mapping, radio waves, ultraviolet spectroscopy, and in situ plasma sensors. High-resolution images of Pluto and Charon, far superior to those taken by the Hubble Space Telescope, were collected for a period of over seventy-five days. Global maps of Pluto's surface were generated with a 40- kilometer resolution, and hemispheric maps were made with a 1-kilometer resolution. These maps allowed scientists to characterize the diverse geologic processes occurring on Pluto and Charon. Localized visible color maps with up to a 3-kilometer resolution and infrared spectral maps with a 7-kilometer resolution allowed characterization of the composition and physical state of surface frost, composed of methane, carbon monoxide, water and nitrogen ices, on Pluto and Charon. The Radio Science Experiment mapped surface temperatures with a 50-kilometer resolution. Particle detectors sampled escaping material from Pluto's atmosphere.

After gathering data for approximately 150 days in the Pluto-Charon system, the spacecraft traveled outward through the Kuiper Belt. On January 1, 2019, the spacecraft performed a flyby of the Kuiper Belt Object (KBO) 2014 MU69. The surface of 2014 MU69 was imaged and mapped at infrared and visible wavelengths in order to analyze its composition. Due to the primordial nature of KBOs, insights into their origin and evolution provide constraints on the origin and evolution of our solar system.

Contributions

The Pluto-Charon system and the Kuiper Belt had never been explored by spacecraft before New Horizons, and thus a great deal of new knowledge was gained from the mission. Using the experience, observations, and analogies derived from missions to other bodies in our solar system, as well as information gathered from ground-based, airborne, and Earth-orbiting telescopes, scientists crafted the New Horizons mission to optimize the knowledge gained from the Pluto flyby. From the data returned from the New Horizons mission, fundamental questions about Pluto's atmosphere, surface properties, geology, and interior makeup of Pluto, Charon, and KBOs were answered, and many new more specific questions were formulated. Additionally, spacecraft observations provided basic information on what happens to the solar wind as it interacts with bodies in the outer regions of the solar system. The images and data gathered while New Horizons was near Jupiter provided new knowledge about the moons and Jupiter' giant magnetosphere.

While approaching Pluto, the New Horizons spacecraft searched unsuccessfully for rings that might exist around Pluto as well as for other satellites of Pluto. During the time of the spacecraft's closest approach to Pluto, a sequence of high-resolution images were taken that allowed scientists to search for time-variable phenomena associated with Pluto, including meteorology, clouds, atmospheric waves, and active volatile transport over its surface and through its atmosphere.

Instrumentation on the spacecraft provided a deeper understanding of Pluto's atmospheric composition, its weather, winds, and atmospheric escape into space from the top of the atmosphere. The complex geology determined from the features imaged by New Horizons showed that Pluto has one of the most diverse surfaces among planetary bodies in the solar system.

The known frost on the surface of Pluto is composed of nitrogen, methane, carbon monoxide, and water, and the frost on Charon is composed primarily of water and ammonia. These frosts were analyzed from high-resolution images and spectral analysis data gathered by the spacecraft. These observations and subsequent studies have provided insights into the possibilities of simple microbial life associated with the liquid water possibly beneath the surface of Pluto. Many of the known properties of Pluto, particularly its red color, resemble those of Neptune's moon Triton. The New Horizons mission was able to reveal other similarities and differences between these two bodies that reflected their separate origins and independent evolution.

By mapping the surfaces of Pluto, its five moons Charon, Styx, Nix, Kerberos, Hydra, and the distant KBO Ultima Thule, the New Horizons mission has helped answer questions about their contrasting diversity. From the New Horizons measurements of cosmic dust, insights were gained into the source of water in the Kuiper Belt. Planetologists believe that KBOs represent primordial remnants from the formation of the outer planets around 4.5 billion years ago. This makes KBO among the oldest known objects in the solar system, and thus they contain clues as to the nature of the primordial nebula from which the Sun and planets formed. The New Horizons' data on KBOs has provided the best information to date on these primordial planetary building blocks.

Context

By providing the first close reconnaissance of Pluto and its moons as well as Ultima Thule, New Horizons mission has led to a dramatic increase in our understanding of the outer solar system and its history. Since the center of mass of the Pluto-Charon system lies between Pluto and Charon, the Pluto-Kuiper Belt Mission has given us the first close-up inspection of a true double-planet system. Because processes similar to what are believed to be occurring in the Kuiper Belt have been observed in apparent "Kuiper Belts" surrounding other stars in the Milky Way galaxy—particularly Vega and Beta Pictoris—the New Horizons mission is helping scientists better understand the development and evolution of other solar systems. Since the KBOs have probably not changed since the beginning of the solar system, their properties provide important constraints for theoretical models of the formation of stars and planets in general and of their evolution. The New Horizons mission has also provided valuable knowledge about spacecraft and instrumentation that are best suited for possible future missions into the outer realms of the solar system, as well as providing technology transfer to other branches of science.

There is still controversy as to whether or not Pluto merits planetary designation, rather than a designation as a Kuiper Belt Object or as a dwarf planet. From what has been learned from the New Horizons mission, Pluto is a complex and diverse world with a rich and equally complex history. Given the discovery of amazingly diverse planetary type bodies elsewhere in the galaxy, the study of Pluto and its categorization among these bodies is an important part of understanding the full range of planetary possibilities.

—Alvin K. Benson
Michael E. Summers

See also: Funding Procedures of Space Programs; National Aeronautics and Space Administration; National AeroSpace Plane; Space Task Group; United Space Alliance; United States Space Command.

Further Reading

Davies, John Keith. *Beyond Pluto: Exploring the Outer Limits of the Solar System*. New York: Cambridge University Press, 2001. Davies details the story of the various astronomers who have observed and theorized about Kuiper Belt objects, beginning with Kenneth Edgeworth in 1943 until the time of the proposed Pluto-Kuiper Express mission. The associated scientific methods and theories are documented.

Hartmann, William K. *Moons and Planets*. 5th ed. Belmont, Calif.: Thomson Brooks/Cole, 2005. Provides detailed information about all objects in the solar system. Suitable for high school students, general readers, and undergraduates studying planetary geology.

McBride, Neil, and Iain Gilmour, eds. *An Introduction to the Solar System*. New York: Cambridge University Press, 2004. Compiled by a group of astronomy experts, this book provides an excellent overview of the solar system and the known pertinent information about Pluto, Charon, the Kuiper Belt, and projected missions to the outer parts of the solar system.

Moche, Dinah L. *Astronomy: A Self-Teaching Guide*. 6th ed. New York: John Wiley & Sons, 2004. This edition features amazing new astronomical discoveries and the latest developments in astronomy, from the Neptune flyby to the Hubble Space Telescope to the Pluto-Kuiper Belt Mission. It contains up-to-date graphics and photos.

Petersen, Carolyn Collins, and John C. Brandt. *Visions of the Cosmos*. New York: Cambridge University Press, 2003. Using worldwide observatory and spacecraft mission data and images, this well-illustrated, comprehensive exploration of astronomy includes discussions of what is known about Pluto, Charon, and Kuiper Belt objects, as well as future planned missions to Pluto and the Kuiper Belt.

Stern, S. Alan. *Pluto and Charon: Ice Worlds on the Ragged Edge of the Solar System*. New York: John Wiley & Sons, 1998. Stern presents an excellent account of the discovery and investigation of Pluto and what has been learned about this planet from space missions and Hubble Space Telescope images.

---, ed. *Worlds Beyond: The Thrill of Planetary Exploration as Told by Leading Experts*. New York: Cambridge University Press, 2003. This work documents the exploration of worlds beyond Earth, from Mercury to Pluto, through the use of telescopes and robotic missions. It is complemented by many color photos and comprehensive bibliographies.

Stern, S., and David Grinspook, *Chasing New Horizons: Inside the First Epic Mission to Pluto*, Picador, 2018. This book give the inside story of how New Horizons became the first spacecraft to explore the most distant realm of our solar system. It relates the many discoveries made by the New Horizons spacecraft as it passed close to Jupiter, Pluto and its moon Charon, and finally the distant Kuiper Belt Object known as Ultima Thule.

Cruikshank, Dale P., and William Sheehan, *Discovering Pluto: Exploration at the Edge of the Solar System*. The University of Arizona Press, 2018. This book tells the story of Pluto's discovery and how our understanding of this planet from the "third zone" of the solar system has changed since its discovery to the first reconnaissance by made by the New Horizons spacecraft.

New Millennium Program

Date: From 1995 to 2015
Type of program: Planetary exploration

Developed in 1995, the first missions in NASA's New Millennium Program were launched in October, 1998, with Deep Space 1 and in January, 1999, with Deep Space 2. The program employed research laboratories and space missions to develop and test new, space-applicable technologies intended to revolutionize future space exploration at reduced cost and risk.

Key Figures

Fuk Li, manager of the New Millennium Program, Jet Propulsion Laboratory (JPL)

David Crisp, program scientist for the New Millennium Program, JPL

David Lehman, JPL project manager for Deep Space 1

Marc D. Rayman (b. 1956), JPL chief mission engineer for Deep Space 1

Robert Nelson, JPL project scientist for Deep Space 1

Sarah Gavit, JPL project manager for Deep Space 2

Kari Lewis, JPL chief mission engineer for Deep Space 2

Suzanne Smrekar, JPL project scientist for Deep Space 2

Summary of the Program

In 1995, NASA's Office of Space Science and Office of Earth Science created the New Millennium Program (NMP) with a view to cutting down on the risk of future space missions and attempting to demonstrate whether new cutting-edge technologies could reduce cost, achieve Earth orbit, and reach deep space in the new millennium. In this effort, revolutionary technologies such as ion propulsion and artificial intelligence (AI) software would be tested through relatively low-cost missions in order to ascertain their reliability in more expensive and complex missions.

NMP was unique among space programs in several ways. It brought together technologists from government, industry, and academia to develop reliable and innovative new technologies. If proven successful, these technologies would revolutionize future space exploration. NMP had two main goals, which were (1) to test new, space-applicable technologies in space and determine if they are viable; and (2) to reduce the risk and cost to future missions by first conducting such dedicated-technology-testing missions at low cost.

Each of NMP's experimental missions was designed by a team of technologists, engineers, and scientists. A key element of the design was to ensure that an innovative technology was thoroughly tested in flight, to ensure that it has the capability of performing its tasks successfully in future missions. The projects included within NMP were also required to operate under the constraints of a tighter budget and schedule.

Of the five main missions under NMP, DS1 was launched from Cape Canaveral, Florida, on October 24, 1998, using a Delta 7326-9.5 med-Lite rocket (first use of this model), while DS2 was launched from the same site on January 3, 1999, using a Delta II (7425) rocket. Of the two, DS1 has proven to be considerably more successful in fulfilling its objective of testing twelve new technologies.

On July 28, 1999, DS1 flew to within 25.6 kilometers of asteroid 9969 Braille. This was by far the closest flyby of an asteroid. Its infrared sensor indicated that Braille is similar to Vesta, one of the largest members of the asteroid belt between Mars and Jupiter. Physically, Braille is considerably smaller than Vesta, its longest dimension being 2.1 kilometers compared with Vesta's 496-kilometer diameter. Both asteroids possess a high visual reflectivity, leading to speculation about whether they are siblings or may have once belonged to a larger whole. The Braille flyby used a new space autopilot system called AutoNav, and its successful piloting of DS1 further validated the technologies on board the spacecraft. During much of 1999, DS1 successfully completed its primary technology-validation mission. Subsequently, its mission was extended to include new tasks, such as pointing its main antenna toward the Earth, sending data from Mars observations taken in November, 1999, and transmitting data at a high rate for extended periods without the aid of its star-tracker sensor, which failed in November, 1999. As of early 2000, DS1 was about 256 million kilometers from the Earth, a distance approaching 2 astronomical units (one AU is the mean distance from Earth to Sun).

In contrast with the notable success of NMP's DS1 mission, the DS2 mission, which included the Mars Polar Lander (MPL) spacecraft, accompanied by two advanced microprobes, is now generally acknowledged as having been a failed mission. The MPL carried the two lightweight probes (2.4 kilograms each) with the intention of releasing them upon arrival just above the south polar region of Mars around December 3, 1999. In reality, however, mission controllers for DS2 made several unsuccessful attempts to get the lander to talk to Earth via NASA's Mars Global Surveyor (already in orbit around Mars), and by other means for at least two weeks beyond the lander's scheduled arrival at the designated site on the Martian surface between December 3 and 4, 1999. On December 7, 1999, the

Lander's project manager, Richard Cook, declared, "The Mars Polar Lander flight team played its last ace." In addition, there was no communication from the microprobes accompanying the Polar Lander. DS2 Project Manager Sarah Gavit observed within days of the expected landing that since the probes' batteries could not hold charge beyond four days, the hopes of making contact with the probes had just about evaporated thereafter. A major investigation by review boards at NASA and the Jet Propulsion Laboratory (JPL) in Pasadena was launched in order to ascertain the cause of the apparent loss and measures to prevent any recurrence.

Apart from DS1 and DS2, NMP also includes three additional projects with launch dates originally extending to late 2003. These projects are, in chronological order, Earth Observing 1 (EO-1), Space Technology 3 (ST3), and Space Technology 5 (ST5). It must be noted that an earlier project, named Space Technology 4 or the Champollion mission, was eventually canceled on July 1, 1999, due to budgetary constraints.

The EO-1 mission has been designated to fly three advanced land (terrestrial) imaging instruments and seven "crosscutting" spacecraft technologies. The advanced imaging instruments are intended to be lighter, higher-performance, and lower-cost versions of Landsat-type imaging instruments (the latter being a satellite-based terrestrial imaging system). The new crosscutting space technologies would enable space-based Earth observations with unique spatial, spectral, and temporal characteristics.

ST3, the New Millennium Interferometer, would fly test technologies intended to benefit NASA's Origins Program, which seeks to study distant stars and their planets in order to find answers to questions about the origins of our own Milky Way galaxy, our solar system, and the universe in general. The New Millennium Interferometer would pave the way for more ambitious spacecraft such as the Space Interferometry Mission, the Terrestrial

Planet Finder, and the Planet Imager—all designed to pave the way for the detection and imaging of extrasolar planets.

ST5, also known as the Nanosat Constellation Trailblazer mission, flew three miniature spacecraft high above the Earth after launching in 2006. The spacecraft, each weighing around 22.7 kilograms, were used to test methods of operating a constellation of spacecraft together as a system. Space Technology 6 consisted of two separate demonstrations, the Autonomous Sciencecraft Experiment that flew aboard Earth Observing 1 Satellite and the Inertial Stellar Compass which was flown aboard the TacSat-2, both in 2006. Space Technology 7 was a technology demonstration for gravity wave observations as part of the European Space Agency's LISA Pathfinder launched late in 2015.

ST7 was actually flown after program cancellation. The New Millennium Program was not included in NASA's Fiscal Year 2009 budget authorization, thereby concluding this novel opportunity to test new space technologies.

Contributions

Led by Project Manager David Lehman, the DS1 mission has successfully tested technologies (including Xenon ion propulsion) for future space and Earth-observing missions. These technologies will make future spacecraft lighter, smaller, less expensive, and more capable of independent decision making than those that currently rely on tracking and intervention by ground controllers.

Deep Space 1, the first mission of NASA's New Millennium Program, has tested risky technologies designed to make future missions smaller, faster, and cheaper—a policy strongly espoused by NASA Administrator Daniel S. Goldin. The mission utilized onboard software that, for the first time, assumed total control of the spacecraft. Despite the handicap imposed by the malfunctioning star tracker on board DS1 (which ceased operating in

November, 1999), the operations team devised and successfully implemented a new method of controlling the spacecraft so that its main antenna could still be pointed to the Earth. The technique, based on monitoring the strength of DS1's radio signal, has been used to communicate with the spacecraft. A still more novel pointing method, built around the autonomous navigation system's ability to analyze pictures taken by the onboard camera and driven by new software, has also been tested. This technology allows a spacecraft to operate without frequent assistance from Earth.

As mentioned, DS1 successfully flew within 26 kilometers above asteroid 9969 Braille on July 28, 1999. This was by far the closest flyby of any asteroid. About ten minutes after the flyby, signals from the spacecraft reached the Earth and indicated via a marked Doppler shift (a shift in signal frequency due to movement past an object) that the spacecraft was turning back to face the asteroid. More significant, several hours prior to the flyby, the spacecraft experienced a critical "safing" event, which involved the detection of a software glitch and subsequent triggering of a protective program that caused the spacecraft to halt noncritical activity, turn its solar panels to the Sun, point light- and heat-sensitive instruments away from the Sun, and revert to its low-gain antenna for commands. The safing event was deemed an additional measure of success.

Around the time of its scheduled descent on the Martian surface, a potentially critical flaw was discovered in the MPL, launched in January, 1999, on board the DS2 mission. A NASA propulsion expert discovered that the craft's engine fuel lines were in danger of freezing and inhibiting the operation of the engine. Although this problem was likely fixed by turning the vehicle's heaters on earlier than scheduled, events far more detrimental occurred soon thereafter. It turned out that the Polar Lander failed to beam back a message signaling its arrival near Mars's south pole. Significant among initial findings was the determination that a probable cause for the device's failure was a mix-up of metric and nonmetric units used in the design of critical components of the lander and its microprobes (which also failed to communicate) by Lockheed Martin, a contractor for JPL. Two additional causes have since been proposed: that the craft suffered a technical problem just after radio communication with Earth broke off, as expected, before landing or that it entered the Martian atmosphere intact but landed on such a steep slope that it fell over. A complex series of mechanical operations was due to take place after the communications break, but with no word from the lander, engineers were unable to determine how these progressed. After several weeks of futile efforts to contact the lander, it was eventually declared a complete loss.

The loss of MPL represented the third failure in the United States' last five attempts to send a mission to Mars. While some experts wonder whether to redesign future probes to yield more information if they fail, others want NASA to change its "faster, better, cheaper" policy for space exploration.

Context

DS1's mission was to test important, high-risk technologies in order to reduce the cost and risk of future scientific missions in space. In February, 2000, a symposium was conducted in which detailed engineering information on all aspects of the new technologies was disseminated. According to Marc D. Rayman, the new capabilities are like tools in the toolboxes of designers, making previously unaffordable or impossible missions feasible in the future. Included among these new technologies are ion propulsion, autonomous systems, advanced microelectronics, and telecommunications systems. In summary, NASA's willingness to test these technologies in DS1 represents a step forward for future planetary and deep-space missions.

EO-1 launched on a Delta II booster from Vandenberg Air Force Base on November 21, 2000, and following deployment from the second stage, entered a 705-kilometer circular, Sun-synchronous orbit with a 98.7° inclination with respect to the equator. This orbit was within a minute of Landsat 7's orbit, so comparisons of identical images could be made during ground-based analysis. The EO-1 spacecraft carried three instruments that incorporated revolutionary land-imaging technologies, which enabled future Landsat and Earth Observing missions to classify and map global land utilization more accurately. In addition, seven unique technologies reduced the cost, mass, and complexity of future Earth Observing spacecraft, thereby increasing scientific payload potential.

Unlike any spacecraft launched by NASA in the past, ST3 would consist of two separate spacecraft that would be used to test the techniques of interferometry and formation flying in space. ST3 would become the first space-borne stellar interferometer. The knowledge gained from this mission could be used in follow-up interferometer missions as part of NASA's Origins Program, which will seek answers to the origins of the universe by imaging and studying distant planets and stars.

In addition to testing the operation of a constellation of spacecraft, the ST5 mission tested eight new technologies in the harsh space environment near the boundary of the Earth's protective magnetic field known as the magnetosphere.

Admittedly, the failure of the DS2 mission was a setback for NASA. Questions have been raised by both technical experts and politicians regarding the wisdom of sending low-cost, high-risk missions off to space in a hurry. Clearly, when such a mission is successful, the general perception is that the risk and expenditure are justified. A failure often casts long shadows of doubt and uncertainty. However, judging by NASA's accomplishments, failures are relatively rare, and those that do occur every once in a long while (including those involving loss of human life, such as the 1986 *Challenger* and 2003 *Columbia* accidents) help scientists and engineers learn critical lessons from them, using them to make future missions and projects safer and less risky. Humanity cannot, and must not, be deterred by occasional failures during the course of carrying out missions in space, a frontier to which its destiny is inexorably tied.

—*Monish R. Chatterjee*

See also: Cooperation in Space: U.S. and Russian; Mars Climate Orbiter and Mars Polar Lander; New Horizons Pluto-Kuiper Belt Mission.

Further Reading

Hecht, Jeff. "Calling Mars." *New Scientist* 165, no. 2224 (February, 2000): 11. An account of the Mars Polar Lander and the failure of space probes.

Kerr, Richard A. "Deep Space 1 Traces Braille Back to Vesta." *Science* 285, no. 5430 (August, 1999): 993-994. Provides an informative account of space probes and asteroid encounters.

---. "Yet Another Loss to the Martian Gremlin." *Science* 286, no. 5447 (December, 1999): 2051. An account of the Mars Polar Lander, the Mars Climate Orbiter, and the failure of space probes.

Lambright, W. Henry, ed. *Space Policy in the Twenty-First Century*. Baltimore: Johns Hopkins University Press, 2003. This book addresses a number of important questions: What will replace the space shuttle? Can the International Space Station justify its cost? Will Earth be threatened by asteroid impact? When and how will humans explore Mars?

Normile, Dennis. "NASA Craft to Take the Controls in Flight." *Science* 282, no. 5389 (October, 1998): 604-605. Discusses asteroid encounters and flybys, as well as the control of artificial satellites.

Seife, Charles. "The Nick of Time." *New Scientist* 164, no. 2213 (November, 1999): 15. An account of the Mars Polar Lander, the Mars Climate Orbiter, and the failure of space probes.

---. "The Nightmare Continues." *New Scientist* 164, no. 2216 (December, 1999): 4. An account of the Mars Polar Lander and the failure of space probes.

Zimmerman, Robert. *The Chronological Encyclopedia of Discoveries in Space*. Westport, Conn.: Oryx Press, 2000. Provides a complete chronological history of all piloted and robotic spacecraft and explains flight events and scientific results. Suitable for all levels of research.

Nimbus Meteorological Satellites

Date: August 28, 1964, to mid-1986
Type of spacecraft: Meteorological satellites

Nimbus satellites were used to develop new techniques for observing Earth, especially its atmosphere and oceans, by remote sensing from orbit. A number of methods that are now used routinely to gather data for weather forecasting, for example, were first tried on an experimental basis on one of the Nimbus satellites.

Key Figures

Ronald K. Browning, Nimbus project manager at the Goddard Space Flight Center (GSFC)

Charles McKenzie, Nimbus project manager at GSFC

William R. Bandeen, Nimbus project scientist at GSFC

Morris Tepper (b. 1916), Nimbus project scientist at GSFC

Albert J. Fleig, Nimbus project scientist at GSFC

William Forney Hovis, Jr., Nimbus 7 principal investigator

Summary of the Satellites

The Nimbus Earth observatory program consisted of seven satellite launches, separated by roughly two-year intervals, ranging from Nimbus 1 on August 28, 1964, to Nimbus 7 on October 24, 1978. In each case, the spacecraft's appearance and orbit were similar to the others'; the payloads, however, progressively increased in mass and sophistication as new experiments were developed and tested. Nimbus 1 weighed less than 400 kilograms; Nimbus 7, nearly 1,000 kilograms. All Nimbus satellites were built by the General Electric Company of Valley Forge, Pennsylvania. The dozens of experiments came from a wide range of institutions in the United States and England.

Nimbus has been described as a butterfly-shaped spacecraft. It was a cone 3 meters high and nearly 2 meters across near the base, with two large panels carrying solar cells to convert the Sun's energy into electricity, extending like wings at either side. The scientific instruments were inside, or hanging below, a doughnut-shaped "sensory ring" attached at the base of the cone. The satellite was stabilized by gyroscopes, so the base of the sensory ring faced toward Earth at all times as the satellite orbits the planet.

All the Nimbuses except the first were placed in nearly circular orbits about 1,000 kilometers above Earth's surface, and all were in orbits that passed close to the North and South Poles of the planet, so that views of the whole of Earth's surface were possible. In addition, the orbits were Sun-synchronous, which means that a person at a particular place on the surface would see Nimbus go overhead at exactly the same times twice each day. A special type of Sun-synchronous orbit was used so that the Sun would be at noon when the satellite passed above an observer during the day. The second crossing would take place at local midnight. It has been estimated that, during their useful lives, Nimbus spacecraft traveled about 7 billion kilometers in all.

Nimbus 1 was launched by a Thor-Agena B rocket from Vandenberg Air Force Base in California, the launch site that was to be used for the whole series. The launch was imperfect and resulted in an orbit that was too low and fairly eccentric. Furthermore, the spacecraft malfunctioned after twenty-four days, when the tracking system that

Artist's conception of the NIMBUS satellite. (NASA Goddard Space Flight Center)

kept the solar panels pointing at the Sun jammed, causing a serious loss of power. Nevertheless, many useful data and experience were gained. The first attempt to launch Nimbus 3, in 1968, was a complete failure because of launch vehicle problems. A duplicate spacecraft was assembled and successfully launched in the following year. All other launches in the series went well. By the time the relatively advanced and heavy Nimbus 7 was launched, the Thor first stage included nine Thiokol solid-fueled boosters to increase the thrust, and a Delta second stage was being used. Project management and mission operations were provided by the National Aeronautics and Space Administration (NASA) Goddard Space Flight Center in Greenbelt, Maryland.

The scientific payload of Nimbus 1 consisted of three sensors. The advanced vidicon camera system (AVCS) was a television camera that observed Earth with a resolution of about 1 kilometer. The automatic picture transmission system was an early version of the now-commonplace technique of transmitting pictures taken by a camera on a satellite directly to any user equipped with a low-cost

receiving station. It was intended mainly for meteorologists, who need pictures of cloud formations as soon as they occur. Finally, the high-resolution infrared radiometer was an imaging system that could operate at night by making pictures from scanned maps of thermal infrared, or heat, emissions from the surface and clouds. Although Nimbus 1 was both in the wrong orbit and short-lived, all the experiments functioned successfully before the mission was terminated.

Nimbus 2, launched May 15, 1966, repeated the Nimbus 1 experiments. All of them functioned well for thirty-three months, during which time more than 100,000 pictures were transmitted to Earth. In addition, this satellite carried the medium resolution infrared radiometer to study Earth's heat balance, or the difference between the amount of heat absorbed from the Sun and the amount radiated from Earth as infrared waves. These two components must be the same for the whole planet, but they are quite different in different isolated regions, and these differences drive weather systems. One of the first really sophisticated weather satellites, Nimbus 2 provided data for, and stimulated the development of, computer models of the atmosphere that are the basis of accurate forecasting.

Nimbus 3 had a similarly long life, beginning on April 14, 1969, and it carried both high- and medium-resolution infrared sensors. It had an improved camera, called the image dissector camera system, which transmitted to ground-based stations. Most significantly, it had two particularly novel infrared sounders, the Infrared Interferometer Spectrometer (IRIS) and the Satellite Infrared Sounder (SIRS). The former was a fairly high-resolution spectrometer that scanned nearly all the infrared wavelengths at which Earth emits radiation, thereby sensing individual gases such as water vapor and ozone and allowing inferences about atmospheric composition and behavior to be made. SIRS used selected spectral channels specifically to measure the vertical profile of atmospheric temperature by monitoring atmospheric carbon dioxide emissions.

In addition to its meteorological experiments, Nimbus 3 carried three technology experiments: the IRLS (Interrogation, Recording, and Location Subsystem), the RMP (Rate Measuring Package), and the System for Nuclear Auxiliary Power 19 (SNAP-19). IRLS was used to collect data from surface stations, RMP was a test of a gas-bearing gyroscope, and SNAP was an early test of a nuclear isotope-driven power source for satellites. The plutonium in SNAP was valuable enough to be worth retrieving from 100 meters below the sea after the failed attempt to launch the first Nimbus 3 in 1968.

Nimbus 4 was launched April 8, 1970, on board a Thor-Agena D. In addition to improved versions of the image dissector camera, IRIS, SIRS, and IRLS from Nimbus 3, four new experiments were carried to test still more ways of monitoring the atmosphere by remote sensing. Three of these were infrared spectrometers similar in principle and objectives to, although quite different in detail from, IRIS and SIRS. The most innovative sensor was the backscatter ultraviolet spectrometer, which allowed the amounts of ozone in the upper atmosphere to be inferred from maps of the solar ultraviolet radiation reflected back from the ozone layer. In addition, the first of four British experiments on successive Nimbus satellites used a special technique to measure temperature at greater altitudes than previous Nimbuses had (around 50 rather than 30 kilometers) and so was optimal for the study of the structure and dynamics of the stratosphere.

There were fewer but larger instruments on Nimbus 5, which was launched December 11, 1972. They included the first microwave sounders: the Nimbus E microwave sounder, or NEMS (Nimbus satellites were known by letter designations, A through G, before launch and were numbered after achieving orbit), and the Electrically Scanning

Microwave Radiometer (ESMR). These instruments succeeded in their goal of proving microwave sounders' ability to penetrate clouds and measure the temperature of the surface beneath. The infrared temperature profile radiometer demonstrated how to eliminate cloud interference by making infrared observations with high spatial resolution and using ratios of adjacent soundings to eliminate images of rapidly varying features, on the usually reasonable assumption that these are clouds. Nimbus 5 also had an improved SCR and a surface composition mapping radiometer. At about the time of Nimbus 5, a series of satellites using the same basic configuration and called ERTS, for Earth Resources Technology Satellite, was instigated. They were to do for Earth's surface what Nimbus did for the atmosphere, and they carried some of the same instruments. The first ERTS was later named Landsat 1.

Nimbus 6, launched June 12, 1975, and Nimbus 7, launched October 24, 1978, completed the series. Nimbus 6 had an improved ESMR; a new Scanning Microwave Sounder, called SCAMS; a pressure modulator radiometer; and an improved Earth radiation budget experiment. The newest instruments were TWERLE, for Tropical Wind Energy and Reference Level Experiment, and the Limb Radiance Inversion Radiometer (LRIR). TWERLE was designed to obtain meteorological data by tracking balloons below. The LRIR was the first infrared limb-scanning instrument, which is to say it measured emissions while looking sideways at the atmosphere at the edge of Earth's disk, rather than downward. Most infrared sensors now use this technique, and Nimbus 7 had two such sensors: LIMS, for Limb Infrared Monitor of the Stratosphere, an improved LRIR; and SAMS, for Stratospheric and Mesospheric Sounder, a limb-viewing version of the pressure modulator radiometer. Both of these devices measured temperature and a range of minor gas abundances in the stratosphere. Nimbus 7 also had an ocean monitoring device, the coastal zone color scanner, which could detect variations in plankton and other marine life, as well as an Earth radiation budget experiment.

Contributions

A large part of the new knowledge gained from the Nimbus program was the ability to apply new sensor technology, which, having been tested, went on to be widely used on operational weather, oceanographic, and Earth resources satellites. As a result, the oceans, the surface, and especially the atmosphere were observed in unprecedented detail, and many significant scientific projects were conducted.

From as early as 1964, with the short-lived Nimbus 1, hurricanes Cleo and Gladys were observed from space in advanced vidicon camera pictures and high-resolution infrared radiometer maps. The television images showed the character and evolution of these systems along with the rest of Earth's weather. Infrared maps added nighttime coverage and the vertical dimension, because cloud heights could be inferred from radiometric temperature readings. Nimbus images of the surface were also revolutionary; for example, a mountain in Antarctica was shown to be 75 kilometers from its presumed location, and a range shown on existing maps as double was clearly seen to be single.

The automatic picture transmission system on the early Nimbus satellites brought the lofty perspective of the Earth spacecraft to the ordinary user for any of a hundred applications, provided the user had a basic receiving station. One of these applications was the mapping of sea ice and the identification of channels in ice sheets, which previously had required a patrol using aircraft. The resolution from Nimbus 2's vidicon camera was good enough to permit tracking of individual floes, allowing currents to be studied. Later versions could observe volcanic plumes, brush fires, and even dust storms. Nimbus 2 also produced temperature maps of the ocean and spearheaded the development of computerized data processing techniques for "cloud clearing," so that an extended region could be

mapped without obscuration. These maps helped scientists to develop a first tentative understanding of the relation between ocean surface temperature and climatic behavior, including hurricane development.

The Nimbus series pioneered the study of Earth's ozone layer from space, including the monitoring of the flux of energetic ultraviolet radiation from the Sun, which produces ozone from oxygen. The brightness of the Sun varies significantly at the wavelengths of importance for ozone formation, and the gas itself is easily destroyed by a number of reactions. Starting with Nimbus 3, the satellites began an ongoing process of monitoring and studying the ozone layer. A correlation between stratospheric ozone and the pressure nearer the surface was discovered. Seasonal changes were also identified, including strong variability over the Poles. On Nimbus 6 and 7, not only was ozone monitored with accuracy and higher vertical resolution through the use of the limb scanning technique, but measurements also were made of the global distribution of other minor constituents that affect ozone chemically. Among these are the oxides of nitrogen, produced in large part by human activities, which are thought to be making important changes in global ozone. Earth's atmospheric water budget has also been studied on a planet-wide scale for the first time.

Predominant among the techniques pioneered by Nimbus is the measurement of atmospheric temperature structure, first in the lower atmosphere and then, through instruments such as the pressure modulator radiometer and SAMS, in the stratosphere and mesosphere. Many features of global temperature fields were discovered or first characterized fully by Nimbus instruments. Among these features are the various planetary wave modes that affect the general circulation, unexpected seasonal effects such as the warm winter mesopause, and dramatic phenomena such as the stratospheric sudden warmings, in which the air temperature can increase by 100 kelvins in a few days.

Context

The Nimbus satellites provided new information about Earth's atmosphere, oceans, and surface on a scale never before contemplated. Even more important, however, Nimbus scientists pioneered, developed, and proved techniques and instrumentation that now form the backbone of the science of remote sensing. Sensors and subsystems developed from technologies first flown on Nimbus satellites now play major roles in data gathering for computerized weather forecasting, hurricane detection, climate research, agriculture, and even prospecting.

Earlier weather satellites—of which the most important were those known as TIROS, for Television Infrared Operations Satellite—were much less capable of providing the observations that meteorologists require. These pioneering satellites were stabilized by their own spinning instead of by gyroscopes, were in orbits which did not view Earth continuously, did not cross the polar regions, and were too small, at about 300 kilograms, to carry instruments of the sophistication that Nimbus made possible. The eight original TIROS satellites, launched from 1960 to 1963, made important achievements; Nimbus, however, was the first significant platform in space for Earth observations.

Research into the various phenomena that make up the weather and routine operations such as forecasting require global data. Before satellites, these data came mainly from a network of stations that launched balloons carrying radio transmitters, which provided only fragmentary coverage. When the stabilized, polar-orbiting platform became available in the form of Nimbus 1, it rapidly stimulated the invention of new sensors that could map Earth in four dimensions—latitude, longitude, altitude, and time—with good coverage in all four. The availability of these data led in turn to the growth of

Graphic showing difference of coverage of inclined orbit satellite versus polar orbit satellite. (NOAA)

computer processing methods that could make use of them, this advance being aided enormously by the rapid improvements in computer technology that were being made at the same time. From these processing methods has come the numerical weather forecast, in which the state of the atmosphere one day or a few days into the future is predicted by solving the physical equations that represent the fluid motions. To do this with sufficient accuracy and resolution requires large, fast computers and the rapid availability of extensive data about the "initial state," or today's weather. Therefore, although numerical forecasting was understood in principle as long ago as the 1930's, it was not feasible until the era of Nimbus. In the years to come, refinements of this technique may lead to reliable forecasts that extend, although with less detail, years or even decades ahead.

The overall state of Earth's atmosphere is subject to change, and the changes have profound effects on the suitability of the surface for the survival of lifeforms, including humans. The great ice ages were examples of such changes, and even today there are smaller extremes of climate that lead to localized disasters: Missing rainy seasons lead to drought, and excessive monsoons lead to catastrophic flooding. There is currently much concern that Earth's climate is drifting permanently toward a more extreme, less comfortable state, possibly pushed by human activities such as the burning of fossil fuels or the release of chemicals harmful to the ozone layer. Satellite observations, most significantly those from Nimbus 7, have made it possible to commence an in-depth scientific study of some aspects of the ozone problem in particular and of large-scale, long-term atmospheric behavior in general. These studies have helped to emphasize the seriousness of the global habitability situation, and, in time, they may suggest solutions.

Spacecraft derived from Nimbus will continue to gather meteorological data. The Nimbus design became obsolete for advanced scientific work at the end of the 1970's, however, and it has been replaced by the Upper Atmosphere Research Satellite (UARS), also managed by Goddard Space Flight Center and built by General Electric. This satellite is more than five times as large as Nimbus 7 and outperforms the Nimbus satellites in factors such as stability, which controls a satellite's ability to obtain very high-resolution pictures or soundings, and data rate, which determines the number of observations that can be made in a given time. In 1991, NASA launched a more comprehensive program to study the Earth as an environmental system, now called the Earth Science Enterprise. The Earth Science Enterprise has three main components: a series of Earth-observing satellites, an advanced data system, and teams of scientists who will study the data. Phase I of the Earth Science Enterprise was made up of focused, free-flying satellites, space shuttle missions, and various airborne and ground-based studies. Phase II began in 1999 with the launch of the first Earth Observing System (EOS) satellite, Terra (formerly AM-1), Landsat 7, Aqua, and other robotic spacecraft.

—F. W. Taylor

See also: Environmental Science Services Administration Satellites; Global Atmospheric Research Program; ITOS and NOAA Meteorological Satellites; Meteorological Satellites; Meteorological Satellites: Military; Seasat; SMS and GOES Meteorological Satellites; TIROS Meteorological Satellites; Upper Atmosphere Research Satellite.

Further Reading

Ahrens, C. Donald. *Essentials of Meteorology: An Invitation to the Atmosphere*. 4th ed. Pacific Grove, Calif.: Thomson Brooks/Cole, 2005. This is a text suitable for an introductory course in meteorology. Comes complete with a CD-ROM to help explain concepts and demonstrate the atmosphere's dynamic nature.

Asrar, Ghassem, and Jeff Dozier. *EOS: Science Strategy for the Earth Observing System*. New York: Springer-Verlag, 1994. This illustrated book takes a look at the history of the Earth Observing System. It also discusses the scientific equipment used in the program. There is a list of acronyms and a bibliography.

Bader, M. J., G. S. Forbes, and J. R. Grant, eds. *Images in Weather Forecasting: A Practical Guide for Interpreting Satellite and Radar Imagery*. New York: Cambridge University Press, 1997. The aim of this work is to present the meteorology student and operational forecaster with the current techniques for interpreting satellite and radar images of weather systems in mid-latitudes. The focus of the book is the large number of illustrations.

Barrett, E. C. *Climatology from Satellites*. New York: Harper and Row, 1974. Includes a general discussion of meteorological satellite systems, including Nimbus. Contains particularly good discussions of the applications of satellite data to climatic aspects of interest to geography and agriculture students. Also casts light on physics and mathematics. For college-level readers.

Chen, H. S. *Space Remote Sensing System: An Introduction*. New York: Academic Press, 1985. This book describes satellite sensors from an engineer's point of view, but it is kept at a very basic level and so is suitable for the technically minded general reader. It is well illustrated and includes references.

Houghton, J. T., F. W. Taylor, and C. D. Rodgers. *Remote Sounding of Atmospheres*. New York: Cambridge University Press, 1984. Describes the various types of satellites, including Nimbus, that have been used to make atmospheric measurements. Gives details on the instruments and techniques used and the methods of analyzing the data. Intended for advanced college students, but early chapters are suitable for general readers. Contains many references to books and technical articles dealing with satellite observations of the atmosphere.

Hubert, Lester F., and Paul E. Lehr. *Weather Satellites*. Waltham, Mass.: Blaisdell, 1967. A good introduction for the non-specialist audience to the goals, methods, and achievements of weather satellites. Explains in general terms how satellite data are used for forecasting and research. Includes descriptions, with many illustrations of TIROS and early Nimbus satellites and their measurements.

Parkinson, Claire L. *Earth from Above: Using Color-Coded Satellite Images to Examine the Global Environment*. Sausalito, Calif.: University Science Books, 1997. A book for non-specialists on reading and interpreting satellite images. Explains how satellite data provide information about the atmosphere, the Antarctic ozone hole, and atmospheric temperature effects. The book includes maps, photographs, and fifty color satellite images.

Philosophical Transactions of the Royal Society. *Studies of the Middle Atmosphere*. London: Author, 1987. An up-to-date account of scientific work on the higher regions of the atmosphere, including the ozone layer, this work consists of individual review papers by specialists. Suitable mainly for those with a college-level background in atmospheric science.

United States Committee for the Global Atmospheric Research Program. *Understanding Climatic Change: A Program for Action*. Detroit: Grand River Books, 1980. This is a reprint of the 1975 work published by National Academy of Sciences. It gives a variety of information about the atmospheric research projects, including the Global Atmospheric Research Program. It is fairly detailed and, at times, quite technical.

United States Congress. House Committee on Science. *U.S. Global Change Research Programs*. Washington, D.C.: Government Printing Office, 1996. This congressional report details data collection and scientific priorities used in several terrestrial and space-based studies of Earth's global climate changes. It includes sections on the Global Atmospheric Research Program. There is a bibliographical listing included.

Zimmerman, Robert. *The Chronological Encyclopedia of Discoveries in Space*. Westport, Conn.: Oryx Press, 2000. Provides a complete chronological history of all crewed and robotic spacecraft and explains flight events and scientific results. Suitable for all levels of research.

Nuclear Detection Satellites

Date: Beginning October 17, 1963
Type of spacecraft: Military satellites

Nuclear detection is the spotting of secret nuclear explosions in space and within Earth's atmosphere in an effort to enforce the nuclear test ban treaties. Nuclear detection was the first example of an arms-control treaty verified through satellites.

Summary of the Satellites

Nuclear detection satellites had their origins in talks during the late 1950's and early 1960's to ban nuclear tests in the atmosphere, under water, under ground, and in space. Policing a ban on nuclear tests in space posed difficulties. The verification system would have to detect explosions in the upper atmosphere, in near-Earth space, behind the Moon, and in deep space. Making this task more difficult was the natural background of solar radiation, cosmic rays, and the Van Allen radiation belts. One early proposal in 1958 involved placing five or six large nuclear detection satellites in 29,000-kilometer-high orbits. Additionally, 170 ground stations would be spread across the globe. Yet even this extensive network might not detect a weapon encased in radiation shielding.

To solve this verification problem, the Atomic Energy Commission and the U.S. Department of Defense jointly began Project Vela in the fall of 1959. (Vela is Spanish for "watchman.") One part of the project was called Vela Hotel. This part of the project envisioned the development of nuclear detection satellites able to spot an explosion as small as 10 kilotons and as far away as 160 million kilometers from Earth. Satellites would carry sensors to detect the x rays, neutrons, and gamma rays emitted by the fireball. Sensors were designed using data from satellites on the normal background radiation of space and five high-altitude nuclear tests. These measurements were made by the Explorer 4 satellite during the 1958 U.S. nuclear test series.

Vela sensors were designed by the Lawrence Radiation Laboratory and built by the Los Alamos National Laboratory and the Sandia Corporation. The prime contractor for the satellite was TRW. The work went well, and on June 22, 1961, the Advanced Research Projects Agency gave approval for a five-launch program. Each launch was to carry a pair of Vela satellites. The first pair were to be launched in April, 1963, with the rest to follow at three-month intervals.

Over the next two years, as the Vela sensors were being developed, both the Soviet Union and the United States conducted high-altitude nuclear tests. Radiation from these tests was trapped by Earth's magnetic field and damaged several satellites, including the Telstar communications satellite. In addition to American and Soviet satellite measurements of these trapped radiation fields, Vela experiments were flown aboard the Discoverer 29 and 31 reconnaissance satellites.

It was not until August, 1963, that the United States, the Soviet Union, and Great Britain were finally able to reach an agreement on limiting nuclear tests. The treaty banned nuclear tests in the atmosphere, under water, and in space. Underground tests were permitted as long as no radiation escaped. The Nuclear Test Ban Treaty went into effect on October 10, 1963.

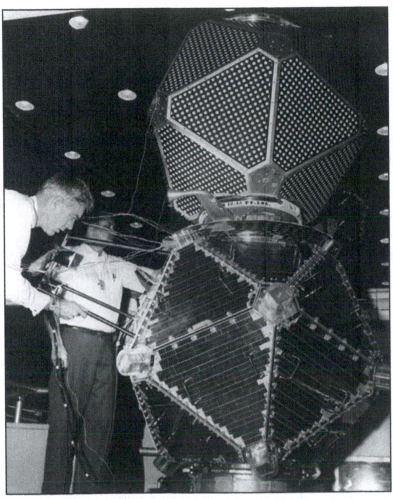

Stress and strains are being measured on the lower space craft after being loaded with a duplicate vehicle and the spin-up interstage between the two units. (U.S. Department of Energy)

On October 17, 1963, the first pair of Vela satellites was launched by an Atlas-Agena D from Cape Canaveral. The Agena placed the two Velas into 103,600-by-208-kilometer initial orbit. Eighteen hours after launch, a radio signal fired the first Vela's onboard engine, placing it into a 110,868-by-101,851-kilometer orbit. This was the highest orbit achieved by any military satellite and was equivalent to one-quarter of the distance to the Moon.

On October 19, the second Vela's engine was fired, placing it into a similar orbit. The satellites were placed 180° apart, so that their sensors could look into space in opposite directions. The detection package weighed 36 kilograms and was composed of twelve x-ray detectors and two diagnostic detectors on the outside of the satellite and four gamma-ray and neutron detectors inside. The Vela itself was a sphere made up of twenty triangular faces. Placement of the x-ray detectors at the points where the triangles met gave each detector a field of view greater than a full hemisphere. Once in its final orbit, the Vela satellite weighed about 136 kilograms and was spin-stabilized at two revolutions per second.

The second pair of Velas was launched on July 17, 1964. A successful launch was marred when the Agena's engine continued to fire briefly after the two Velas had separated. The Agena bumped one of the satellites, damaging a few of the detectors and changing the spin axis slightly. The third pair went into orbit after a night launch on July 20, 1965. These two Velas carried improved instrument packages, which included an optical flash detector. These early Velas had a planned lifetime of only six months, yet they were still working after five years. Accordingly, the fourth and fifth pairs were not launched.

By this time, Vela's role had started to expand. In October, 1964, the People's Republic of China (PRC) exploded its first atomic bomb. As the PRC had not signed the test-ban treaty, the explosion was in the atmosphere. A Vela could, with optical flash detectors and other instruments, detect atmospheric nuclear tests and measure such things as the weapons yield. This, along with data from other sources, would indicate the status of the Chinese nuclear weapons program.

Accordingly, in March, 1965, TRW was awarded a contract to develop an advanced Vela. It would carry a larger instrument package—63 kilograms. This package included a pair of optical flash detectors. Called Bhangmeters, they could indicate the size of a nuclear test by measuring the brightness of its flash. Two were used to cover a wide range of explosive yield: One Bhangmeter was more sensitive than the other. Because the Bhangmeters had to face Earth, the advanced Vela was stabilized by gas jets and gyros rather than by spinning. The sensors that made up the rest of the instrument package included eight x-ray detectors, an x-ray analyzer, four gamma-ray detectors, a neutron detector, two heavy-particle detectors, an extreme ultraviolet detector, two Geiger counters, an electron-proton spectrometer, a solid-state spectrometer, and electromagnetic pulse detectors. The latter picked up the extremely strong burst of energy emitted by a nuclear fireball, which can damage electronic components such as transistors by generating very high currents and burning them out. The advanced Vela weighed about 227 kilograms and was a twenty-six-sided sphere.

The first pair of advanced Velas was launched by a Titan III-C on April 28, 1967, from Cape Kennedy. They were placed into orbits measuring 112,585 by 109,089 and 114,587 by 107,489 kilometers. A second pair followed on May 23, 1969, and the third was launched on April 8, 1970. The third pair carried an enlarged sensor payload weighing 74 kilograms. This was also the last Vela launch. Later, nuclear detection sensors would be carried piggyback on early-warning satellites. The advanced Velas performed as well as did the earlier ones—designed to operate for eighteen months, three of the six were still working ten years later.

It appears that this piggyback approach was used by the Soviets, because there were no Soviet satellites that can clearly be identified as dedicated to nuclear detection. The lone exceptions were Elektrons 1, 2, 3, and 4, which were launched in pairs on January 30 and July 10, 1964, from the Baikonur Cosmodrome. One satellite went into a low orbit, while the other of the pair went into a highly elliptical orbit. It was thought at the time that they might have a nuclear detection role in addition to serving as orbiting geophysical observatories. Nevertheless, no subsequent launches were made using a similar profile. It must be assumed that any Soviet nuclear detection sensors were flown piggyback on other satellites rather than on specially designed satellites.

The shift by the United States to piggyback nuclear detection instruments began on June 12, 1973, with the launch from Cape Canaveral of a Program 647/Defense Support Program early-warning satellite. It used a Titan III-C booster and went into a 35,786-by-35,777-kilometer orbit. This satellite had proton counters and x-ray detectors on two of its solar panels. Optical flash detectors were fitted on the telescope housing.

Studies also began in early 1975 on fitting Bhangmeters and electromagnetic pulse sensors to Navstar navigation satellites. The advantage was increased coverage. Although the Navstars orbited at a lower altitude than did either the Velas or the early-warning satellites, their higher inclination (63° versus 33° for the Velas and less than 10° for the early-warning satellites) would give increased coverage of the polar areas. Also, because a network of as many as eighteen satellites would be used, the probability was that several Navstars would observe any suspected nuclear tests. Ford Aerospace and Communications Corporation was selected to build the instruments in October, 1975. The first Navstar to carry the nuclear detection instruments was launched on April 26, 1980, by an Atlas F booster from Vandenberg Air Force Base. The instrument package weighed 27 kilograms. The Navstar was placed into a 20,288-by-170-kilometer orbit.

Scientists at the Los Alamos National Laboratory in New Mexico have begun to study lightning from space. Flashes and thunder are but a fraction of the energy blasts from lightning: The bolts are fountains of radio waves as well—so powerful, in fact, that they are the closest thing on the radio dial to a nuclear explosion. The mini-satellite called FORTE (Fast On-orbit Recording of Transient Events) is capturing millions of flashes and radio blasts from lightning all over the tropics. What FORTE is hearing by radio challenges a long-held notion that lightning occurs up to ten times more often over continents than over oceans. That is why Los Alamos scientists launched FORTE in August, 1997. Early nuclear-detection satellites were so overwhelmed by radio noise from Earth that their radio detectors got a bad reputation.

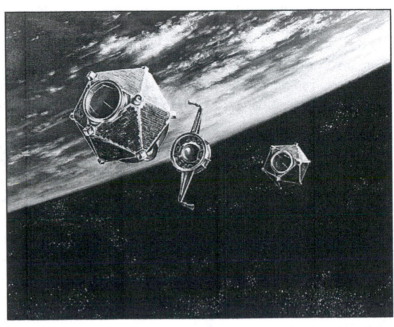

Artist's conception of the post-launch speration of Vela 5A and 5B. (NASA)

FORTE is the first all-composite spacecraft, its framework made entirely of graphite-reinforced epoxy. The 2-meter-tall satellite, weighing 210 kilograms fully loaded, carries three decks with aluminum honeycomb cores and composite facing to support the onboard instruments. The FORTE payload consists of three instruments: an RF (radio frequency) system, an optical system, and an event classifier. The RF system incorporates three broad bandwidth RF receivers covering the frequency range 30-300 megahertz, a polarization-selective antenna, and high-speed waveform digitizers. The optical system consists of a coarse imager that is based on a NASA/MSFC design and has a 10-by-10-kilometer ground resolution for lightning flash location (five hundred frames per second) and a fast photodetector (fifty thousand samples per second) for recording individual light curves. The event classifier, based on digital signal-processing technology, will provide on-orbit characterization of impulsive RF events that have satisfied trigger criteria.

In addition to their primary role of detecting nuclear explosions on the Earth's surface, nuclear detection spacecraft have also been used to detect and observe galactic events, such as supernovae.

Contributions

Beyond the role they play as watchmen of the Nuclear Test Ban Treaty, the nuclear detection satellites have also provided important scientific data. Vela 10 (one of the pair launched on May 23, 1969) provided measurements of the x-ray star Cygnus X-1 from May, 1969, until its x-ray detectors failed on June 19, 1979. From these data it was determined that Cygnus X-1 is a black hole orbiting a blue giant. The black hole is only about 8 kilometers across but has a mass between ten and fifteen times that of the Sun. This small size and high density mean that not even light can escape from it. As the black hole orbits the blue giant, it pulls hydrogen gas from the star's surface; the gas forms a ring around the black hole. As the hydrogen spirals into the black hole, it is heated to tens of millions of degrees and emits x rays, which can vary wildly in intensity over a period of a day.

Other objects of study are x-ray and gamma-ray bursters. The first is a normal star with a neutron star; the latter is the crushed core of a star after a supernova explosion. The neutron star pulls hydrogen gas from the normal star. This gas coats the neutron star's surface until pressure and temperatures become so high that a thermonuclear explosion takes place—a natural hydrogen bomb. The cycle repeats every few hours or days. The source of the gamma-ray burst is not yet clear. Two possibilities are a "star quake" on a neutron star and the impact of an asteroid on a neutron star. In any case, they are much more powerful than an x-ray burst and do not repeat. The bursts were first discovered in 1967 by Ian B. Strong from Vela data. Thus, the Vela can be considered the start of orbital x-ray astronomy. Before their launch, the only data available were from brief sounding-rocket flights.

Context

The success of nuclear detection satellites is the result of a number of factors. One is the directness of the test-ban treaty—it has none of the confusion or loopholes of other arms-control agreements. Another is data from earlier atmospheric nuclear tests. The American 1962 nuclear tests were planned with the belief that this could be the last opportunity for atmospheric explosions, and detailed information was recorded. A major reason, however, is the

verification system in place; with not only Vela and the other satellites but also seismic networks and atmospheric fallout-sampling aircraft, the chance of making successful secret tests is too small for the data that could be gained.

Nuclear detection satellites provide the means to spot secret tests by would-be nuclear powers. Despite their capabilities, however, nuclear detection satellites are subject to false alarms. One such false alarm occurred on September 22, 1979, when a Vela satellite spotted what was thought to be the flash from a 2- or 4-kiloton explosion in an area of the South Atlantic. A year of analysis finally determined that it was a false alarm caused by a small bit of debris knocked off the Vela by a dust-sized meteoroid. The debris drifted in front of the Bhangmeters and was seen as a flash that mimicked one caused by a small nuclear explosion. Given both the variety of nature and the ingenuity of humans, a small level of uncertainty is inevitable.

—Curtis Peebles

See also: Attack Satellites; Early-Warning Satellites; Electronic Intelligence Satellites; Meteorological Satellites: Military; Nimbus Meteorological Satellites; Ocean Surveillance Satellites; Spy Satellites; Strategic Defense Initiative; Telecommunications Satellites: Military.

Further Reading

Butrica, Andrew J. *Beyond the Ionosphere: Fifty Years of Satellite Communications*. NASA SP-4217. Washington, D.C.: Government Printing Office, 1997. Part of the NASA History series, this book looks into the realm of satellite communications. It also delves into the technology that enabled the growth of satellite communications. The book includes many tables, charts, photographs, and illustrations; a detailed bibliography; and reference notes.

Cox, Christopher. *The Cox Report: U.S. National Security and Military/Commercial Concerns with the People's Republic of China*. Washington, D.C.: Regnery Publishing, 1999. Investigates U.S.-Chinese security interaction and reports that China successfully engaged in harmful espionage and obtained sensitive military technology from the United States. Some of the technology obtained includes information on American reconnaissance and attack satellites.

Gavaghan, Helen. *Something New Under the Sun: Satellites and the Beginning of the Space Age*. New York: Copernicus Books, 1998. This book focuses on the history and development of artificial satellites. It centers on three major areas of development—navigational satellites, communications satellites, and weather observation and forecasting satellites.

Hansen, Chuck. *U.S. Nuclear Weapons*. New York: Orion Books, 1988. Covers the physics of nuclear weapons, the history of American weapons programs, and the development of individual weapons themselves. Illustrated. Suitable for college readers (some knowledge of nuclear physics may be helpful).

Klass, Philip J. *Secret Sentries in Space*. New York: Random House, 1971. The first book to deal with military satellites. Covers the historical background and development of reconnaissance satellites. Includes a section on Vela.

Peebles, Curtis. *Guardians: Strategic Reconnaissance Satellites*. Novato, Calif.: Presidio Press, 1987. Covers the history and technology of reconnaissance satellites and their profound impact on international relations. Includes a full chapter on nuclear detection. Suitable for high school and college readers.

Richelson, Jeffrey. *American Espionage and the Soviet Target*. New York: William Morrow, 1987. An overview of U.S. efforts to obtain information on Soviet military activities. Includes several mentions of fallout sampling and monitoring of nuclear testing.

Seaborg, Glenn T. *Kennedy, Khrushchev, and the Test Ban*. Berkeley: University of California Press, 1981. Written by the man who was chairperson of the Atomic Energy Commission at the time the test-ban treaty was negotiated. The book covers events leading up to the treaty. Includes a chapter on the 1962 high-altitude nuclear tests.

Sullivan, Walter. *Assault on the Unknown*. New York: McGraw-Hill, 1961. A history of the International Geophysical Year by a science writer with *The New York Times*. Includes a chapter on the high-altitude nuclear tests of 1958.

Turnill, Reginald. *The Observer's Book of Unmanned Spaceflight*. New York: Frederick Warne, 1974. A brief overview of uncrewed satellites. Includes a section on military satellites with a mention of nuclear detection.

Yenne, Bill. *Secret Weapons of the Cold War: From the H-Bomb to SDI*. New York: Berkley Books, 2005. A contemporary examination of Cold War superweapons and their influence on American-Soviet geopolitics.

Zimmerman, Robert. *The Chronological Encyclopedia of Discoveries in Space*. Westport, Conn.: Oryx Press, 2000. Provides a complete chronological history of all crewed and robotic spacecraft and explains flight events and scientific results. Suitable for all levels of research.

Nuclear Energy in Space

Date: Beginning 1954
Type of technology*:* Spacecraft propulsion and power

Space travel requires a large quantity of stored energy confined to a small space. Nuclear power can meet this need, supplying energy to a spacecraft for decades, without the need for refueling. Missions to explore deep space and the surfaces of certain planets would not be possible without nuclear energy sources.

Summary of the Technology

Research on nuclear energy systems for prospective space applications, particularly onboard electrical power and propulsion, began in the mid-1950's. Amid the realization of space travel and exploration, the National Aeronautics and Space Administration (NASA) funded and conducted numerous studies involving the effective use of nuclear energy as a power source. On January 16, 1959, President Dwight D. Eisenhower and a group of U.S. Atomic Energy Commission (AEC) officials met at the White House to discuss the world's first atomic battery, termed a radioisotope thermoelectric generator (RTG), a nuclear energy source specifically developed by the AEC to produce electric power during space missions. A radioisotope of an element is an isotope (same number of protons, but differing number of neutrons, in the nucleus) that undergoes radioactive decay, while "thermoelectric" refers to producing current in an electrical wire from temperature differences in the circuit. Many of NASA's scientific space missions are also equipped with radioisotope heater units (RHUs) that generate heat energy from radioactive decay. RHUs keep instruments warm during cold Moon and Mars nights, as well as during deep-space missions.

Propulsion, heat, and electrical energy for space missions are provided by RTGs, RHUs, and nuclear reactors. RTGs and nuclear reactors generate heat energy that can be transformed into useful electrical energy. Preliminary RTGs and space nuclear reactors were classified under the general title Systems for Nuclear Auxiliary Power (SNAPs). On June 29, 1961, the first RTG used on a space mission (SNAP-3B8) was launched aboard a Navy transit navigation satellite, and the RTG reportedly performed for about fifteen years after the launch. Since that time, the United States has developed and sent dozens more RTGs into space to provide energy for more than twenty-five space missions, including Voyager, Pioneer, Viking, Apollo, Galileo, Ulysses, Cassini, New Horizons, and the Curiosity rover. RHUs were used for Apollo missions 11 through 17, the Galileo mission, and the Cassini mission. Spurred by the research efforts of Stanislaw Ulam, Theodore Taylor, and Freeman Dyson, engineers designed and tested several nuclear reactor rocket engines in the 1960's, but there was only one U.S. nuclear reactor mission. On the other hand, the former Soviet Union has sent many nuclear reactors into space, but only a few RTGs.

The U.S. space mission of April 21, 1964, was aborted because of launch vehicle failure, and the RTG burned up on reentry, dispersing some plutonium 238 (Pu 238) into the atmosphere over the Southern Hemisphere. Such accidents are of great concern when using nuclear energy devices on space missions. On April 3, 1965, the United States launched its only space nuclear reactor with the SNAPSHOT mission. During the late 1960's and

Down-Sun picture of the RTG of Apollo 14's ASLEP with the Central Station in the background. The fins on the RTG provide radiative cooling. The smaller object in the far background is the LRRR. The mortar pack is at the right edge. (NASA / Alan Shepard)

early 1970's, astronauts on five different Apollo missions left RTG units on the lunar surface to power the Apollo Lunar Surface Experiments Packages (ALSEPs). In April, 1970, when the Apollo 13 Lunar Module *Aquarius* burned up in the atmosphere over the Pacific Ocean, a cask containing plutonium meant to power a lunar surface ALSEP dropped into the deep water. No radiation could be detected from the wayward RTG radioactive core. In 1972, funding to build or test space nuclear reactor systems was stopped until the late 1980's.

On October 18, 1989, Galileo carried 22.3 kilograms of Pu 238 and became the first RTG-powered mission to be launched by a space shuttle, *Atlantis*. In October, 1990, the Ulysses mission, a joint enterprise of the European Space Agency (ESA) and NASA, was launched. For this mission, a single RTG provided all the power for instruments and other equipment, and would do so for several years, as the Sun and interstellar space were explored. The Mars-96 mission was launched on November 16, 1996, but the spacecraft went out of control and reentered the Earth's atmosphere one day later. The United States Space Command reported that the craft fell intact into the ocean off of the coast of Chile, and the 9 kilograms of Pu 238 contained in the RTG were recovered. The Cassini mission to Saturn, carrying three RTGs with a total of nearly 33 kilograms of Pu 238, was launched in 1997, as another joint venture between the ESA and NASA.

In 2005, nearly two dozen RTGs were in interplanetary space; of those, eleven orbited the Earth, six were on the Moon, and five were on Mars, while one nuclear reactor orbited the Earth. All but two of the RTGs have used Pu 238 as the primary source for energy production because of its extensive half-life (87.7 years, which is the time it takes half of the parent atoms to radioactively decay) and because of its comparatively low level of radiation emission (the emitted radioactive particles are easily absorbed by light shielding in the heat source). Pu 238 is not weapons-grade material and is not usable as an explosive in nuclear weapons. Uranium 235 was the fuel used in the sole U.S. flight of a nuclear space reactor.

Then in 2012 the large Mars Curiosity rover landed on Mars exclusively powered by an RTG system. The Mars 2020 rover likewise was going to be so powered. However, the Juno spacecraft orbiting Jupiter had been designed during a period between 2005 and 2012 when RTG systems were viewed less favorably due to problems with procurement of Pu 238 for non-military uses. As a result, despite the fact that Juno had to go to the outer solar system where solar illumination was quite diminished relative to that at Earth by the simple inverse square law, Juno was designed to incorporate extremely large solar arrays rather than be powered by RTG-based technologies. In 2019 availability of nuclear fuel for RTGs was getting better, much to the relief of designers of future spacecraft that would travel far from the inner solar system.

Contributions

Nuclear power technologies have been developed by NASA designers to propel spacecraft and pilot space systems into orbit. Because nuclear fuel is very compact, larger payloads can be delivered at a greatly reduced cost compared to that of conventional combustion fuels. In addition to payload transportation, nuclear power can provide propulsion to enhance mobility once the craft is in orbit. Two options have been pursued, Nuclear Electric Propulsion (NEP) and Nuclear Thermal Propulsion (NTP). NEP systems consist of electric ion thrusters powered by a nuclear reactor, while NTP systems feature a nuclear reactor that heats a propellant (a working fluid of hydrogen), which drives the spacecraft forward. Advantages of NEP and NTP systems over conventional chemical propulsion methods include reduced travel times as well as reduced masses for science and human space missions.

In addition to propelling spacecraft into orbit, nuclear energy has proven very useful for producing heat and electrical energy for spacecraft instruments and experiments. Radioisotope energy sources are the enabling technology for space and terrestrial applications requiring proven, reliable, and maintenance-free power supplies capable of producing up to several kilowatts of power, and operating under severe environmental conditions for many years. By providing energy through the natural radioactive decay of plutonium, RTGs enable spacecraft to operate at significant distances from the Sun. Heat source technology developed by the Department of Energy (DOE) has resulted in several models of an RTG energy system, evolving from the SNAP-RTG, to the multi-hundred-watt-RTG, to the General Purpose Heat Source (GPHS)-RTG used on Galileo, Ulysses, and Cassini spacecraft. More than thirty years have been invested in the engineering, safety analysis, and testing of RTGs. Incorporated safety features have demonstrated that RTGs can withstand physical conditions more severe than those expected in most accidents.

Much learning has emerged regarding the necessary characteristics that nuclear fuel must possess to mitigate potential health effects that could occur if fuel were to be released. The culmination of more than twenty-five years of design evolution has led to the production of RTG fuels that are heat-resistant, ceramic forms of plutonium dioxide, which greatly reduce the chance of vaporization in case of a fire or upon reentry into the Earth's atmosphere. The fuel is also highly insoluble, has a low chemical reactivity, and primarily fractures into large particles and chunks that will not invade the respiratory system. In addition, the fuel is divided among numerous small, independent modular units, each with its own heatshield and impact shell, thereby reducing the chances of fuel release in a mishap because the modules would not receive equal impact in an accident. Furthermore, multiple layers of protective materials, including high-strength graphite blocks, are used to protect the fuel and prevent any accidental release. Prior to each launch, a three-step, multi-agency review process must be completed to ensure the safety of the spacecraft, particularly nuclear energy devices.

Although RTGs are excellent proven devices for low-power applications, nuclear reactors are necessary for space applications needing more power, such as a lunar base station or large mechanized rovers. After the end of the Cold War, U.S. nuclear laboratories purchased some Russian Topaz II nuclear reactors, like those used in Soviet space missions, and tested them thoroughly. Further developments have led to a reactor that is very reliable, a source of high power, with a long lifetime (more than three years), small overall dimensions, and complete radiation safety. The United States has developed a fast neutron space reactor (SP-100) that has an operating life of ten years. The fuel is a uranium nitride ceramic designed to be shock-resistant and durable at very high temperatures. Along with reactors that use conventional fission (splitting heavy nuclei into fragments to release energy), reactors that use controlled fusion (combining light nuclei to form a heavier nucleus and release energy) reactors are being developed for use in interstellar flight. In addition, ongoing research involves the design and testing of new breeds of space nuclear reactors based on advanced principles of efficient direct energy conversion.

NASA is working with the DOE to identify power requirements of future spacecraft, and to design smaller and more efficient nuclear energy systems. The Advanced Radioisotope Power Source Program of NASA and DOE is intended to replace RTGs with an advanced nuclear energy generator that will convert heat into electricity with efficiencies of up to 20 to 30 percent, as compared to 5 to 10 percent for conventional RTGs. These new power systems are being designed to carry only about 9 to 15.5 kilograms of nuclear material for energy generation versus the 11 kilograms necessary for a traditional RTG.

Context

Radioisotope power systems have been used in space and terrestrial applications for more than forty years. These systems are reliable, maintenance free, generally safe, and capable of producing either heat or electricity for many years under the conditions required for deep-space and robotic Earth missions. Unique characteristics of these systems make them especially suited to applications where large arrays of solar cells or batteries are not practical, particularly at large distances from the Sun where there is little sunlight, or in harsh environments near the Sun.

Space travel made possible through the use of nuclear energy devices—including RTGs, RHUs, and space nuclear reactors—has enhanced our understanding of the Earth and has helped scientists, doctors, and engineers solve many important problems, with benefits to humankind. The development of computers by engineers to regulate spacecraft and nuclear energy sources has spurred the proliferation of computer technology worldwide. Physicians have learned more about our bodies and have made advancements in medicine as the result of space travel made possible with nuclear energy devices. Scientists know more about the Earth's weather and can give us much more accurate warning of impending storms and other conditions with the help of nuclear-powered satellites. From space, scientists can see where oil and valuable minerals might be found inside the Earth. In addition, changes in the way that plants grow can be viewed from space. All this information leads to applications that allow humankind to take better care of the Earth. Furthermore, nuclear-powered spy satellites and orbiting weaponry are used to track and counter airborne enemy missiles.

Robotic, nuclear-powered space probes sent to other planets have provided information about many previously unanswered questions about our solar system. Astronauts have landed on the Moon and left instruments powered by nuclear energy that relay information back to Earth about conditions there. Mercury, Venus, Mars, Jupiter, Saturn, Uranus, Neptune, Pluto, and a Kuiper Belt Object have been explored by spacecraft powered by nuclear energy devices, providing a better understanding of the origin and development of our solar system and the possibility of placing space stations between the Earth and other planets in the future. These stations might provide homes for groups of people living and working in space. Without nuclear energy systems, critical national security satellite activities and NASA missions to explore deep space and the surfaces of neighboring planets would not occur. Development of advanced nuclear propulsion was proposed by the Bush administration in 2004 under the name Project Prometheus. The flagship mission of the project involved the Jupiter Icy Moons Observer (JIMO), a vehicle that would steer through the Jovian system with a minimum of chemical propulsion. Unfortunately the high cost associated with Project Prometheus led to its rather quick demise. Overall, nuclear power has a vast potential to expand the ability to explore space. It is currently the best and essentially the only option that can provide vast quantities of power in a small, lightweight, and reliable package.

—Alvin K. Benson

See also: Nuclear Detection Satellites.

Further Reading

Angliss, Sarah. *Cosmic Journeys: A Beginner's Guide to Space and Time Travel.* New York: Copper Beech Books, 1998. A nontechnical look at the future of space travel, including nuclear fission-powered spacecraft and time travel. Contains many excellent pictures and illustrations.

Booth, Nicholas. *Exploring the Solar System.* New York: Cambridge University Press, 1996. Chronicles more than three decades of planetary exploration, including robotic explorers on missions into deep space, scientific techniques, and image processing. Describes and explains important advancements in space exploration, and shows diagrams of some of the nuclear energy devices. Over 300 full-color photographs from NASA missions show remarkably realistic views of planetary surfaces.

El-Genk, Mohamed S., ed. *A Critical Review of Space Nuclear Power and Propulsion.* New York: Springer-Verlag, 1994. A collection of papers for more advanced readers that details past, present, and possible future developments for using nuclear energy in space. Reviews advancements made in the development and usage of RTGs and space nuclear reactors.

Grossman, Karl. *The Wrong Stuff: The Space Program's Nuclear Threat to Our Planet.* New York: Common Courage Press, 1997. Clear discussion of the use of nuclear energy in space missions and some of the associated nuclear accidents. Because, on average, there has been one accident for each seven nuclear-powered space missions, Grossman expresses his concerns for possible future accidents and dispersal of plutonium around the world.

Herbst, Judith. *Star Crossing: How to Get Around in the Universe.* New York: Maxwell Macmillan International, 1992. Written for a general audience, it discusses the scientific developments and concerns that have led to current achievements in space exploration and that will be necessary for future space travel. Contains historical development of nuclear-powered spacecraft.

Kerrod, Robin. *The Journeys of Voyager.* New York: Mallard Press, 1990. Explains the use of RTGs in the Voyager missions, including diagrams showing RTG implementation. Loaded with beautiful colored pictures of Jupiter, Saturn, Uranus, Neptune, and some of their moons that were obtained during the missions.

Lambright, W. Henry, ed. *Space Policy in the Twenty-First Century.* Baltimore: Johns Hopkins University Press, 2003. This book addresses a number of important questions: What will replace the space shuttle? Can the International Space Station justify its cost? Will Earth be threatened by asteroid impact? When and how will humans explore Mars? Nuclear Energy in Space 1029

Mason, John W. *Spacecraft Technology.* New York: Bookwright Press, 1990. An introduction to space technology, discussing principles of rockets, various types of satellites, travel in the solar system, and space stations.

Murray, Bruce C. *Journey into Space: The First Three Decades of Space Exploration*. New York: W. W. Norton, 1990. Tells the story of America's robotic space program, including nuclear energy applications.

Yenne, Bill. *Secret Weapons of the Cold War: From the H-Bomb to SDI*. New York: Berkley Books, 2005. A contemporary examination of Cold War superweapons and their influence on American-Soviet geopolitics.

Ocean Surveillance Satellites

Date: Beginning September 18, 1967
Type of spacecraft: Military satellites

Ocean surveillance involves locating ships, identifying them, and determining their speed and course. As satellites pass over all Earth's oceans, they have a unique vantage point for this activity.

Summary of the Satellites

During the mid-1960's, designers in the United States Navy explored the feasibility of ocean surveillance satellites. In 1969, development began on the Program 749 satellite, which would use active radar. Technical problems were too great, however, and the program was canceled in 1973.

To replace it, the Navy selected a three-step approach. The first was to borrow United States Air Force satellites to gain experience in orbital ocean surveillance. There has been speculation that this involved use of high-resolution photo reconnaissance satellites, launched by a Titan III-B rocket and equipped with an infrared scanner. This scanner could pick up the hot gases from a ship's smokestack and the warm water discharged from a nuclear submarine's reactor. (ELINT, or electronic intelligence, satellites may also have been used.)

The next step was an advanced ELINT satellite, code-named White Cloud. The first was launched on April 30, 1975, by an Atlas F from Vandenberg Air Force Base. The payload went into a 1,128-by-1,092-kilometer orbit; then the three White Cloud satellites separated and went into parallel orbits, with the satellites a few kilometers apart. Each satellite was 2.4 meters long, 0.9 meter wide, and 0.3meter thick. The upper side was covered with solar cells, while the underside carried the antennae to pick up transmissions from foreign ships.

The third step in the United States Navy's ocean surveillance plan was development of a radar-equipped satellite, code-named Clipper Bow. During 1978 and 1979, doubts arose regarding its cost, usefulness, and possible duplication of data from other orbital radar reconnaissance projects. By mid-1980, Clipper Bow had been canceled.

To locate ships, White Cloud used a technique known as interferometry. Radar and radio signals from a ship arrived at each satellite at a slightly different time. This difference was used to determine the ship's location. A similar procedure was suggested as the basis for a satellite navigation system, which developed into the Global Positioning System. It was first tested on a December 14, 1971, launch. A long-tank, thrust-augmented Thor-Agena D (LTTAT-Agena D) placed three satellites into an orbit similar to that used later by White Cloud. From a 1,126-kilometer orbit, a White Cloud cluster could pick up transmissions from ships as far away as 3,218 kilometers. This wide-area coverage, and the fact that the cluster passed over the same spot on Earth twice each day, meant multiple position reports. To increase coverage further, a three-cluster network was used; each cluster of three satellites was positioned 120° apart. The full network was not completed until March 2, 1980, when the third White Cloud was orbited.

The White Cloud Naval Ocean Surveillance System (NOSS) performed wide-area ocean surveillance, primarily for the Navy. White Cloud was used to determine the location of radio and radar transmissions, using triangulation. The identity of naval units could be deduced by analysis of the operating frequencies and transmission patterns of the emitters. Each NOSS launch placed a cluster of one primary satellite and three smaller subsatellites (that trail along at distances of several hundred kilometers) into low polar orbit. This satellite array could determine the location of radio and radar transmitters, using triangulation, and the identity of naval units, by analysis of the operating frequencies and transmission patterns.

NOSS used the ELINT technique called "time difference of arrival" (TDOA) rather than true interferometry. Conceptually, TDOA and interferometry are very similar, though distinct, techniques. They may also use the frequency-domain version of TDOA, FDOA, which exploits Doppler shifts somewhat in the way the COSPAS/SARSATs do. Although there did not appear to be a definitely fixed constellation size for White Cloud, at the beginning of 1990 the constellation apparently consisted of two clusters of primary and secondary satellites, launched on February 9, 1986, and May 15, 1987. No launches under this program were conducted after 1987.

A Space Based Wide Area Surveillance System (SB-WASS) replaced White Cloud. This program, which was initiated in the early 1980's, was used to track ships and aircraft on a global basis. Originally, SB-WASS was supposed to be a joint Air Force-Navy program, but the cost as well as disagreement over the type of sensors resulted in postponement of full-scale development. In the interim, the Navy developed a White Cloud successor, referred to as the SB-WASS (Navy) for convenience, but its real designation is not known. Originally it was to have been launched by the shuttle, but after the *Challenger* accident in 1986 it was decided to use the Titan IV booster instead.

The satellites are larger and heavier than their predecessors. The White Cloud system massed about 1.5 metric tons in orbit, with the main satellite about 600 kilograms and each subsatellite about 200 kilograms. In the new system, the whole lot amounted to 8 metric tons in orbit. This extra mass is consistent with the presence of an advanced scanning infrared sensor on the subsatellites. The apparent size of the primary (3 or more metric tons) suggests that it may have a secondary SigInt (signal intelligence) mission; this idea is reinforced because the primary in each launch (USA-59, USA-72, and USA-119) has disappeared. It appears that the program was to have consisted of four clusters, one in each orbital plane. However, the third launch attempt, in 1993, went spectacularly wrong when the Titan IV booster blew up shortly after launch. At the time this was described as the most expensive U.S. space failure since *Challenger*. Operation of SB-WASS is similar to White Cloud. Orbits of 1,000 by 1,100 kilometers at about 63° are employed, but the subsatellites are much closer together (30 to 110 kilometers). It is possible that the subsatellites communicate with one another by laser, rather than microwave link as White Cloud did. A laser used for this purpose would be virtually impossible to intercept or jam. It would also have a much higher bandwidth, which could be needed to handle the data generated by the infrared sensors. Martin Marietta and Lockheed were the prime contractors for this program.

Refurbished Titan II boosters launched three satellites in 1988, 1989, and 1992. These seem to have been the Air Force version of SB-WASS. They were launched into 780-by-800-kilometer, 85° orbits and exhibited regular flashing reflection patterns, as would be expected from the rotating reflector radar antenna planned for the Air Force SB-WASS. The project appears to have been terminated. TRW was the prime contractor.

There appears to be the intention within the United States defense establishment to proceed with development of a single SB-WASS system to be used by the Air Force and Navy. The apparent intention is to consolidate operations at one site in an attempt to save money. Martin Marietta (now Lockheed Martin) was awarded the development contract in 1994. The SB-WASS spacecraft may be a 7.5-tonne platform that could be launched into a nominal 180-kilometer orbit at 63°, from either Vandenberg or Cape Canaveral.

The U.S. Air Force, the Defense Department's Advanced Research Projects Agency (ARPA), and the National Reconnaissance Office (NRO) jointly selected three contractor teams on February 22, 1999, for Phase One of the Discoverer II space-based radar technology demonstrator program. Lockheed Martin Astronautics, Spectrum Astro, and TRW Defense Systems Division lead these teams. The goal of the demonstration program was to develop, build, and launch two research and development satellites capable of detecting and tracking moving targets on the Earth's surface, producing high-resolution imagery and collecting high-resolution digital terrain-mapping data in the early twenty-first century

Contributions

For both the United States and the former Soviet Union, control of the seas during the Cold War was critical. In the event of a war in Europe, the strategy of the North Atlantic Treaty Organization (NATO) envisioned large convoys to resupply equipment and troops. If the Soviets were to stop these convoys, their ships and submarines had to know their positions. The stakes were high. In World Wars I and II, German U-boats were almost successful in starving England into submission. A battle in the Atlantic could easily decide the fate of Europe. If the United States Navy and other NATO navies were to ensure security, they had to know the location of attacking Soviet ships and submarines.

North Atlantic convoy routes are not the West's only points of vulnerability. Most of the oil that fuels the West's economies comes through the Persian Gulf. Any interruption, such as a blockade, could spark inflation, unemployment, and social disruption.

Despite the critical role ocean surveillance satellites played for the United States, it was relatively slow to deploy these types of satellites. The first White Cloud was not orbited until nearly a decade after the first Soviet ocean surveillance satellites. Two different radar satellites were canceled by the United States before they were flown.

With the dawn of the twenty-first century, the Air Force and the Navy, in conjunction with the National Reconnaissance Organization, have established a well-coordinated space-based spying system. Using a combination of visible light, infrared, and radar observation satellites, the United States has kept track of all oceangoing traffic above and below the waves. In addition, these satellites have turned their lenses to peaceful, scientific research, studying the oceans and landmasses.

Context

Questions have been raised about the safety of the orbital graveyard where former satellites reside. Altitudes above 900 kilometers have the greatest amount of "space junk," and the expended boosters cross them; thus, collisions are possible. A reactor in one of these satellites hit in a collision could be sent into an elliptical orbit and might reenter far sooner than expected. The reactor could also be fragmented. Fragments could hit other reactors, producing more debris, until there were clouds of shrapnel.

For the most part, however, the need for ocean surveillance satellites both in the spy business and in scientific research far outweighs the danger of an impact. Both the Navy and Air Force have been working on anti-satellite programs aimed at these sentinels in the sky. Should the need arise, an errant satellite or other large orbiting object could be destroyed at an altitude that would diminish the impact of such an explosion. The object could be destroyed or deflected into a safe orbit.

—Curtis Peebles, updated by Russell R. Tobias

See also: Attack Satellites; Early-Warning Satellites; Electronic Intelligence Satellites; Manned Orbiting Laboratory; Meteorological Satellites: Military; Nuclear Detection Satellites; Nuclear Energy in Space; Spy Satellites; Strategic Defense Initiative; Telecommunications Satellites: Military.

Further Reading

Baker, David, ed. *Jane's Space Directory, 2005-2006*. Alexandria, Va.: Jane's Information Group, 2005. Extensive bibliographic presentation of all space programs, broken down into programmatic categories.

Butrica, Andrew J. *Beyond the Ionosphere: Fifty Years of Satellite Communications*. NASA SP-4217. Washington, D.C.: Government Printing Office, 1997. Part of the NASA History series, this book looks into the realm of satellite communications. It also delves into the technology that enabled the growth of satellite communications. The book includes many tables, charts, photographs, and illustrations; a detailed bibliography; and reference notes.

Cox, Christopher. *The Cox Report: U.S. National Security and Military/Commercial Concerns with the People's Republic of China*. Washington, D.C.: Regnery Publishing, 1999. Investigates U.S.-Chinese security interaction and reports that China successfully engaged in harmful espionage and obtained sensitive military technology from the United States. Some of the technology obtained includes information on American reconnaissance and attack satellites.

Gavaghan, Helen. *Something New Under the Sun: Satellites and the Beginning of the Space Age*. New York: Copernicus Books, 1998. This book focuses on the history and development of artificial satellites. It centers on three major areas of development—navigational satellites, communications satellites, and weather observation and forecasting satellites.

Hofmann-Wellenhof, Bernhard, and Helmut Moritz. *Physical Geodesy*. London: Springer- Praxis, 2005. This is an update to a text considered by some to be the introductory book of choice for the field of geodesy. Includes terrestrial methods and discusses contributions made through the Global Positioning System (GPS).

Kennedy, William V. *Intelligence Warfare*. New York: Crescent Books, 1983. A survey of the various forms military intelligence can take, this volume includes a chapter on ocean surveillance. Suitable for high school and college audiences.

Peebles, Curtis. *Guardians: Strategic Reconnaissance Satellites*. Novato, Calif.: Presidio Press, 1987. The book covers the history, technology, and impact on international relations of reconnaissance satellites. It includes chapters on United States ocean surveillance programs.

Richelson, Jeffrey. *American Espionage and the Soviet Target*. New York: William Morrow, 1987. This book is a detailed survey of United States intelligence activities. Some material on ocean surveillance is included.

Yenne, Bill. *Secret Weapons of the Cold War: From the H-Bomb to SDI*. New York: Berkley Books, 2005. A contemporary examination of Cold War superweapons and their influence on American-Soviet geopolitics.

Zimmerman, Robert. *The Chronological Encyclopedia of Discoveries in Space*. Westport, Conn.: Oryx Press, 2000. Provides a complete chronological history of all crewed and robotic spacecraft and explains flight events and scientific results. Suitable for all levels of research.

Orbiting Astronomical Observatories

Date: April 8, 1966, to August 21, 1972
Type of spacecraft: Space telescope

The Orbiting Astronomical Observatories (OAOs) provided astronomers with an opportunity to conduct observations at specific wavelengths above Earth's atmosphere. Their data significantly contributed to an understanding of certain astronomical objects and phenomena. Development of these observatories presented new challenges, the solutions to which made the satellites some of the most complex of their time.

Key Figures

Lyman Spitzer, Jr. (1914-1997), principal investigator, OAO 32-inch ultraviolet telescope

John E. Rogerson, Jr., executive director, OAO 3 32-inch ultraviolet telescope

Albert Boggess, Jr., principal investigator, OAO B

Summary of the Satellites

Astronomers have always been plagued by problems over which they have little or no control, including poor weather at observing sites and the atmosphere's absorption of certain wavelengths of light. These conditions often result in limited observations, which in turn can diminish the quality and quantity of collected data.

With the advent of the Space Age and satellite technology, it became possible to place observatory satellites in Earth orbit. Such a satellite project, called the Orbiting Astronomical Observatory (OAO), enabled astronomers to overcome the problem of atmospheric interference.

The National Aeronautics and Space Administration (NASA) chose Grumman Aerospace to be the major contractor for the OAOs, satellites that would allow the study of astronomical objects in the ultraviolet, x-ray, and gamma-ray ranges of the spectrum. The first OAO was scheduled to be launched in 1964, but several problems postponed the launch until 1966. These difficulties involved the OAO control and guidance system, and the development and completion of one of the first OAO experiments, a project of the Smithsonian Astrophysical Observatory, designated "Celescope." Budget overruns and a lack of agreement on how such a program should proceed were also problems. Many scientists and engineers believed that the technology for such an advanced satellite program would have to evolve slowly, for it did not exist at the time, and that several smaller, less complex, and less expensive OAOs should first be constructed and launched.

The cost of the OAOs, as estimated by the NASA comptroller's office, was about $55,000 per satellite kilogram. When compared with the cost of other programs, however, that amount was not excessive. The Orbiting Geophysical Observatory program had cost about $70,000 per satellite kilogram, the Surveyor satellites had demanded $85,000 to $90,000 per kilogram, and the Lunar Orbiters had cost about $95,000 per kilogram. Moreover, crewed missions cost hundreds of thousands of dollars per spacecraft kilogram.

The OAO's basic design included large paddle-like panels covered with solar cells that would furnish power. Specially designed star trackers were used to orient the satellite. The trackers operated by selecting several stars and locking onto their positions, thereby establishing a frame of reference for the OAO and allowing it to orient itself toward any desired object. The observatory's scientific equipment, along with the necessary satellite equipment, was installed in a framework that was the same for all OAO missions. Scientific equipment and experiments could be varied on each mission, depending on the equipment's availability and the mission's objectives.

A special network of ground-based control stations was built for the OAO program. It included stations at Quito, Ecuador; Rosman, North Carolina; and Santiago, Chile. These stations were linked via radio to Goddard Space Flight Center, in Greenbelt, Maryland.

The first OAO was launched by an Atlas-Agena D booster rocket; later OAOs were launched by the Atlas-Centaur. OAO 1 was launched from the Eastern Test Range in Florida on April 8, 1966, at 2:36 p.m. eastern standard time or 19:36 Coordinated Universal Time (UTC). The observatory satellite's experiments included a University of Wisconsin package, a Massachusetts Institute of Technology (MIT) experiment, and a Lockheed experiment.

The University of Wisconsin equipment, supplied by the Washburn Observatory, included four telescopes with 20.3-centimeter-diameter mirrors, one telescope with a 40.6-centimeter-diameter mirror, two scanning spectrometers, and some photoelectric detectors. Equipment was controlled by five hundred high-reliability, low-power, digital logic elements. At the focusing point of the 40.6-centimeter telescope, which weighed 33.6 kilograms, was a photoelectric photometer, a device that measures an object's brightness. The four 20.3-centimeter telescopes, each weighing 12.7 kilograms, were brought to focus at a diaphragm,

OAO-1 in assembly. (NASA / GRC)

which can limit the size of the field of view, and a special filter wheel with optical filters. The University of Wisconsin experiment was designed to measure the radiation of stars and nebulae (interstellar clouds of gas and dust).

The MIT experiment's purpose was to detect high-energy gamma rays using a device similar to that flown on the Explorer 11 spacecraft. On Explorer 11, the experiment had not worked well because of the spacecraft's proximity to the Van Allen radiation belts.

The Lockheed experiment was designed to measure soft x rays, which had recently been detected by high-altitude sounding rockets, using a special counter. This instrument, similar to a Geiger counter, was many times more sensitive than those flown on the sounding rockets.

After a successful launch and orbital insertion in a 790-by-800-kilometer orbit, all appeared well. On the second day, however, a primary battery failed. The malfunction appeared to spread to the other battery systems, and the OAO 1 ceased to operate. Lessons learned from this failure were applied to future missions; equipment was redesigned, and procedures for activating satellite power were changed.

OAO 2 was successfully launched from the Eastern Test Range on December 7, 1968, at 3:40 a.m. eastern standard time (08:40 UTC). The observatory assumed an orbit that was 761 kilometers at its perigee (the closest approach to Earth) and 770 kilometers at its apogee (the farthest point from Earth). The satellite had eleven telescopes on board, representing experimental packages of the University of Wisconsin and the Smithsonian Astrophysical Observatory.

The Smithsonian Astrophysical Observatory's Celescope was built around a telescope with a 30.5-centimeter-diameter mirror. At the telescope's point of focus there were four television-type tubes, or uvicons, each of which operated at a different wavelength. A special calibration system, using an ultraviolet lamp source coupled with pinholes of various sizes, was used to align and calibrate the telescope and its associated equipment. Digital techniques were used to send images to the ground stations without delays. (The University of Wisconsin experiment stored data and later relayed it to a ground station.) The Celescope's main purpose was to record data for the construction of a star map in ultraviolet light.

OAO B was to orbit a single reflecting telescope with a 91.4-centimeter-diameter mirror, a project of the Laboratory for Optical Astronomy at NASA's Goddard Space Flight Center. The telescope, coupled with a spectrometer, was to have measured phenomena in the ultraviolet-to-blue regions of the spectrum. The objects to be observed included variable stars, emission and reflection nebulae, star clusters, stellar objects in the nearby Magellanic Clouds, and member galaxies of the Local Group, a cluster of twenty-eight known galaxies of which the Milky Way is a member. Unfortunately, the launch of OAO B failed, and the satellite never reached its planned 746-kilometer-high orbit.

The final planned mission of the Orbiting Astronomical Observatory series, designated OAOC before launch and OAO 3 upon placement in Earth orbit, was named Copernicus, after the great astronomer who promoted a heliocentric model of the solar system. OAO 3 was successfully launched on August 21, 1972, at 6:28 a.m. eastern standard time (11:28 UTC). Its orbit had a perigee of 739 kilometers, an apogee of 751 kilometers, and a period of 99.7 minutes.

Overall, Copernicus was similar to OAO 2. Several changes had been made, however, including improvements to the star tracking system and the Sun baffles. There was also a new computer system. Two experiments were aboard: a Princeton University project and an experiment designed by the University College in London and included as a result of NASA's international cooperation policy.

The Princeton University project was based on an 81.3-centimeter-diameter reflecting telescope designed to observe objects in the ultraviolet region of the spectrum. The telescope's mirror was specially constructed by the Corning Glass Works. Most telescope mirrors of this size are solid cast, but the Copernicus mirror was made of thin plates of silica fused into an egg crate pattern. The egg crate structure was then sandwiched between thin front and rear disks of glass. This method of construction reduces a mirror's weight by a factor of three; the Copernicus mirror weighed about 44 kilograms. The mirror was also designed to perform in the varying temperatures of space. It had an aluminized surface coated with protective lithium fluoride.

The Copernicus telescope's tracking instrumentation was capable of unprecedented accuracy. One

NASA official stated that the telescope could locate an object the size of a basketball at a distance of 640 kilometers. Three small x-ray telescopes were the basis of the project, designed by the University College in London. The telescopes were designed to observe already identified x-ray sources.

Copernicus was the final mission in the OAO series. Two of the four satellites were highly successful. The OAO technology also served as a foundation for new generations of space observatories, including the High-Energy Astronomical Observatory and the Hubble Space Telescope. The OAO project produced the most massive and complex uncrewed satellites ever launched at that time.

The OAOs' contributions to astronomy were significant, even though simpler satellites could have been built for less money and orbited sooner. Moreover, important technological knowledge was gained from designing and constructing the OAOs.

Contributions

The opportunity to observe objects without the interference of Earth's atmosphere began a new era in astronomical research. The two OAOs that completed their missions, OAO 2 and OAO 3, made significant contributions, especially to ultraviolet radiation observational astronomy.

OAO 2 had several observational goals, including the observation of young, hot stars. Such stars expend a large amount of energy in the ultraviolet region of the spectrum, and, because of atmospheric absorption of ultraviolet light, they cannot be studied from ground-based observatories.

OAO 2 completed the first survey of space in ultraviolet light as part of the Smithsonian Astrophysical Observatory's program, using the SAO's experimental package. OAO 2 was the first satellite to detect ultraviolet radiation originating from the center of M31, the Andromeda galaxy. The Andromeda galaxy is a spiral galaxy much like the Milky Way and is part of the Local Group.

OAO 2 also made the first space-based measurements of a comet. It detected a large hydrogen cloud surrounding the Comet Tago-Sato-Kosaka, discovered in 1969. This finding was significant because free hydrogen had never been seen associated with a comet. Additional cometary data indicated the presence of hydroxyl molecules. Other OAO 2 results included information on stellar xray, gamma ray, and infrared emissions.

Some of the observations conducted by OAO 3, Copernicus, were continuations of OAO 2 experiments. Some unique and useful investigations, however, were also carried out. OAO 3 collected data on Cygnus X-1, an object that many astronomers believe is a black hole. (A black hole is formed by the gravitational collapse of a star with a mass three times that of the Sun; no matter or energy of any form may leave a black hole beyond a certain point in its collapse called the Schwarzschild radius.) Data returned by Copernicus suggested that Cygnus X-1, an x-ray emission source, is indeed a black hole.

Copernicus also collected data on some supernovae remnants, stars that, near the end of their lives, throw off the outer layers of their atmospheres in cataclysmic explosions caused by the rapid conversion of elements and the resulting extreme rises in temperature and pressure. These studies of the remnants, or planetary nebulae, had results that varied from object to object. Copernicus provided evidence that some planetary nebulae produce x rays as a result of the supernova explosion and that some, such as the Crab nebula in the constellation of Taurus, produce radiation many times stronger than others and have a more discrete radiation source.

Copernicus measured the amounts of deuterium, a hydrogen isotope that is twice the mass of ordinary hydrogen, present in the universe. Scientists use this type of information when constructing models of the universe's size. Other investigations included observations of the flow of particle radiation from stars ("stellar wind") and additional hydrogen, x-ray, and gamma-ray studies.

Context

The two Orbiting Astronomical Observatories successfully launched by NASA, OAO 2 and Copernicus, began a new era, both in astronomical observations and in spacecraft design and engineering. The OAOs required entirely new instrumentation and designs for spacecraft operation and experimentation packages. The necessity of developing sophisticated new technology delayed the original launch target two years, from 1964 to 1966, and the spacecraft proved to be more expensive than was originally intended. Nevertheless, engineering problems and delays were overcome, and one of the most successful and extensive astronomical studies of the time was conducted. Many of the special instrumentation packages and spacecraft designs would be adapted for use in future missions.

Observations conducted via the OAOs allowed astronomers to perform studies on radiation at the extreme ends of the spectrum: x rays, gamma rays, infrared rays, and ultraviolet rays. Ultraviolet radiation studies were especially useful and were the primary observations performed by OAO 2 and Copernicus.

Studies of such phenomena allow astronomers to do more than collect information in specific wavelengths of the spectrum; they allow astronomers to act as historians. Many sources of radiation are so far away that their light may take billions of years to reach Earth. (Light travels at 300,000 kilometers per second; the light from the closest star to Earth besides the Sun, Proxima Centauri, takes more than four years to reach Earth.) Data collected from the two OAO missions allowed astronomers to construct particular theories regarding cosmology, or the beginnings and development, of the universe. The life of a star may last millions or billions of years, depending on several factors, the most important being mass. Instrumentation carried by the OAOs allowed astronomers to measure the ages of many types of objects.

The OAOs collected data for several years. Some scientists—comparing the OAOs' life spans with the life spans of sounding rockets, which had performed similar experiments—said that one month of OAO data was worth fifteen years of research with sounding rockets.

Finally, the OAOs gave astronomers and engineers an opportunity to study the potential of, and problems with, Earth-orbiting astronomical observatories. The development of future observatory platforms would rely on the experience gained through the pioneering Orbiting Astronomical Observatories.

—*Mike D. Reynolds*

See also: Chandra X-Ray Observatory; Compton Gamma Ray Observatory; Gamma-ray Large Area Space Telescope; Hubble Space Telescope; Hubble Space Telescope: Science; Infrared Astronomical Satellite; Orbiting Geophysical Observatories; Orbiting Solar Observatories; Spitzer Space Telescope; Telescopes: Air and Space.

Further Reading

Davies, John K. *Astronomy from Space: The Design and Operation of Orbiting Observatories*. New York: John Wiley, 1997. This is a comprehensive reference on the satellites that revolutionized twentieth century astrophysics. It contains in-depth coverage of all space astronomy missions. It includes tables of launch data and orbits for quick reference as well as photographs of many of the lesser-known satellites. The main body of the book is subdivided according to type of astronomy carried out by each satellite (x-ray, gamma-ray, ultraviolet, infrared, and radio). It discusses the future of satellite astronomy as well.

Golub, Leon, and Jay M. Pasachoff. *Nearest Star: The Surprising Science of Our Sun*. Boston: Harvard University Press, 2002. Although written by two of the most active research astrophysicists, this book is accessible to a general audience. It describes most contemporary advances in solar physics.

Heppenheimer, T. A. *Countdown: A History of Space Flight.* New York: John Wiley, 1997. A detailed historical narrative of the human conquest of space. Heppenheimer traces the development of piloted flight through the military rocketry programs of the era preceding World War II. Covers both the American and the Soviet attempts to place vehicles, spacecraft, and humans into the hostile environment of space. More than a dozen pages are devoted to bibliographic references.

Lee, Wayne. *To Rise from Earth: An Easy to Understand Guide to Spaceflight.* New York: Checkmark Books, 1996. This is a good introduction to the science of spaceflight. Although written by an engineer with the NASA Jet Propulsion Laboratory, it is presented in easy-to-understand language. In addition to the theory of spaceflight, it gives some of the history of the human endeavor to explore space.

Mari, Christopher, ed. *Space Exploration.* New York: H. W. Wilson, 1999. Twenty-five articles (reprinted from magazines), covering the state of the space program at the time of publication, are divided into five sections: John H. Glenn, Jr.'s return to space, the exploration of Mars, the International Space Station, recent mining efforts by commercial industries, and new types of space vehicles and propulsion systems.

Newell, Homer E. *Beyond the Atmosphere: Early Years of Space Science.* NASA SP-4211. Washington, D.C.: Government Printing Office, 1980. An excellent overview of program and spacecraft development within NASA, this source offers a candid look at a variety of projects and programs, details some problems and experiences, and summarizes program results. A historical approach is taken. Suitable for readers with some background in space science.

"Observing a Comet from Space." *Sky and Telescope* 39 (March, 1970): 143. Discusses the OAO 2 observations of the Comet Tago-Sato-Kosaka. A number of excellent articles outlining the OAO program, its development, and its results have been published in this popular astronomy and space sciences magazine.

"The Orbiting Astronomical Observatory." *Sky and Telescope* 24 (December, 1962): 339-340. Details the original concept of and plans for the Orbiting Astronomical Observatory program.

Watts, Raymond N., Jr. "Another Orbiting Astronomical Observatory." *Sky and Telescope* 40 (December, 1970): 349-350. This article details OAO B's planned experiments and equipment; it was published prior to the satellite's launch failure.

---. "An Astronomy Satellite Named Copernicus." *Sky and Telescope* 44 (October, 1972): 231-232, 235. Discusses the final OAO of the series. Information on the satellite's launch, experiments, and equipment is presented.

---. "The Celescope Experiment: Ultraviolet Telescopes on Orbiting Astronomical Observatory." *Sky and Telescope* 36 (October, 1968): 228-230. Outlines the Smithsonian Astrophysical Observatory experiment and equipment that was flown on OAO 2.

---. "More About the OAO." *Sky and Telescope* 28 (August, 1964): 78-79. An article about the University of Wisconsin experiment and equipment that was flown on OAOs 1 and 2.

---. "Orbiting Astronomical Observatory." *Sky and Telescope* 31 (May, 1966): 275-276. Details the launch, in-orbit problems, and ultimate failure of OAO 1.

Zimmerman, Robert. *The Chronological Encyclopedia of Discoveries in Space.* Westport, Conn.: Oryx Press, 2000. Provides a complete chronological history of all crewed and robotic spacecraft and explains flight events and scientific results. Suitable for all levels of research.

Orbiting Geophysical Observatories

Date: September 5, 1964, to July 14, 1972
Type of spacecraft: Space telescope

The six Orbiting Geophysical Observatories (OGOs) returned significant data on various geophysical phenomena, including the solar wind, Earth's atmosphere and magnetic field, the radiation belts surrounding Earth, and numerous properties of the Earth-Moon space environment.

Key Figures

Wilfred E. Scull, project manager for all six OGOs
G. H. Ludwig, project scientist for OGOs 1 and 3
C. D. Ashworth, program manager for OGOs 1 through 4
T. L. Fischetti, program manager for OGOs 5 and 6

Summary of the Satellites

The Orbiting Geophysical Observatory (OGO) program consisted of six missions, based upon a generation of spacecraft that were capable of operating a number of scientific instruments and experiments simultaneously and returning large amounts of data to Earth at rates considerably greater than had been possible with previous satellites. Although earlier spacecraft were responsible for the more spectacular discoveries in the near-Earth environment—such as the Van Allen radiation belts (the bands of highly energetic, charged particles trapped in Earth's magnetic field), the solar wind (a flow of charged particles from the Sun), and the magnetosphere (the region around Earth where its magnetic field interacts with the solar wind)—the OGO missions provided more detailed data on the complexities of these (and other) phenomena and their interactions.

In the late 1950's and early 1960's, researchers at the Goddard Space Flight Center of the National Aeronautics and Space Administration (NASA) developed the concept of the OGO spacecraft, and on January 6, 1961, the TRW Systems Group of Redondo Beach, California, was selected as prime contractor for the program. Wilfred E. Scull, at Goddard Space Flight Center, was named project manager for all six OGO missions; for OGO 1, G. H. Ludwig was project scientist, C. D. Ashworth program manager, and A. W. Schardt program scientist.

Beginning on September 5, 1964, with the launch of OGO 1, the six satellites were eventually placed (at the rate of one launch per year) alternately in two different types of orbits about Earth. The Eccentric Geophysical Observatory (EGO) satellites, OGOs 1, 3, and 5, used eccentric orbits with apogee (highest distance from Earth's surface) altitudes of approximately 150,000 kilometers and perigee (closest distance to Earth's surface) altitudes of approximately 300 kilometers, giving each spacecraft an orbital period (time for one trip around Earth) of approximately sixty-four hours. These orbits carried the satellites through the radiation belts and far enough from Earth to allow data collection in near interplanetary space. Closer to Earth, the three Polar Orbit Geophysical Observatory (POGO) satellites (OGOs 2, 4, and 6) had apogees of approximately 1,000 kilometers and perigees of approximately 400 kilometers, resulting in orbital periods of approximately one hundred minutes. These orbits were oriented to carry the satellites close to Earth's polar regions, allowing studies of ionospheric and atmospheric phenomena involving the higher

Drawing of the OGO's deployment sequence. (NASA)

equipment on the satellite itself were mounted on one of several booms extending from the vehicle; these included two 6.7-meter booms and four 1.8-meter booms. Electrical power was generated by solar arrays that could provide up to 550 watts; these charged two 28-volt nickel-cadmium storage batteries, which were used for peak demands in power requirements by the experiments or during eclipses (shadowing of the spacecraft by Earth during part of each orbit). Attitude (orientation) control, important for solar power generation as well as for accurate pointing of the scientific instruments, was achieved through the use of horizon sensors (which determine the vehicle's orientation relative to Earth's visible edge), gas jets, and reaction wheels (electrically driven wheels that use the action-reaction principle to change the satellite's orientation). The OGO spacecraft were the first scientific satellites to be three-axis stabilized, with all three axes held relatively stable in space. For thermal control of each satellite's components, both active (requiring onboard power) and passive means were employed. Active control was limited to individual sites on the spacecraft's periphery. Louvers, radiating surfaces whose positions determine the rate of cooling of the vehicle, provided a means of ejecting excess heat from the main body of the satellite. Alternatively, they could be adjusted to minimize heat radiation during times when the vehicle was eclipsed and in danger of cooling too much. Two 100-milliwatt transmitters and one 10-watt transmitter were used to aid in tracking each OGO satellite. Commands to the vehicle from the ground control station were received by two redundant receivers. Up to 86 million bits of data collected by the instruments could be stored on

intensities of the magnetic field at those locations. All the eccentric orbit missions used Atlas-Agena launch vehicles and were launched from the Eastern Test Range (Cape Canaveral, Florida), while the polar missions employed thrust-augmented Thor-Agena vehicles and were launched from the Western Test Range (Vandenberg Air Force Base, California). Scheduling of the missions was such that, at times, as many as three satellites were returning data concurrently; while this imposed an additional burden on ground support, it afforded unprecedented opportunities for simultaneous measurements (for example, of variations in Earth's magnetic field intensity) at different points in space.

A nearly identical design was used for all six OGO spacecraft, following the program philosophy of demonstrating the feasibility of a standard observatory satellite that could house a relatively large payload (many scientific experiments and instruments). The main body of each OGO satellite was rectangular in shape, measuring 0.9 by 0.9 by 1.8 meters. One of the sides was kept pointing toward Earth; experiments could be mounted both on this side and on the opposite face. Instruments sensitive to magnetic fields generated by electrical tape recorders for later transmission to Earth via the two redundant telemetry transmitters.

OGO 1 housed twenty experiments, including studies of solar cosmic rays, interplanetary dust, plasmas (gases consisting of charged particles), positrons (positively charged particles with mass equivalent to that of electrons), gamma rays (highly energetic photons), radio astronomical sources, radio propagation, the geomagnetic field, and ion composition. Following a failure to deploy two of its booms (thereby prohibiting operations of the three-axis stabilization system), OGO 1 was placed in a backup attitude control mode, in which it was spin stabilized (made to spin at a constant rate about a symmetry axis, relying on gyroscopic effects to keep that axis relatively fixed in space). Such spinning limited the data-gathering capabilities of the sensors, because their pointing directions were then constantly changing. This mission was generally considered quite successful, and it was decided to use the basic design of OGO 1 for the subsequent five missions. Operational support of OGO 1 was terminated on November 1, 1971.

OGO 2, carrying twenty experiments, was launched into a polar orbit on October 14, 1965. After exhausting all of its attitude control propellant ten days after launch, it went into the backup spin-stabilized mode, but the spin axis wobbled so much that the performance of the major subsystems degraded rapidly, requiring ground controllers to shut down the spacecraft approximately two years later; it was revived intermittently during the following four years. Operational support for OGO 2 was terminated on November 1, 1971.

OGO 3, carrying twenty-one experiments, was launched into an eccentric orbit on June 7, 1965. After forty-six days in orbit, its attitude control system failed, resulting in activation of the backup spin-stabilized mode. Operational support for this satellite was terminated on February 9, 1972.

OGO 4 carried twenty experiments into a polar orbit on July 28, 1967. It maintained nominal attitude control for eighteen months, until a failure in

the data recorder system required that the attitude control system be shut down, resulting in activation of the spin-stabilized mode. The spinning motion was such that seven of the experiments no longer generated useful data, and the spacecraft was placed in standby mode, with only intermittent operations during the following two years. Operational support for OGO 4 was terminated on September 27, 1971.

OGO 5 carried twenty-five experiments into an eccentric orbit on March 4, 1968. After forty-one months its attitude control system failed, and the backup spinning mode was activated. Ground control revived the spacecraft from standby for a one-month period just prior to terminating operational support on July 14, 1972.

OGO 6, with twenty-six experiments, was launched into a polar orbit on June 5, 1969. After seventeen days of successful data collecting, solar panel failures led to reduced data storage capability and degraded operation of the experiments. After two years, the spacecraft was placed in the spin-stabilized mode, but it was returned to three-axis stabilized mode for two months just prior to the termination of operational support on July 14, 1972.

Contributions

Because of the long span of operations (September, 1964, to July, 1972), the OGO satellites provided data on geophysical phenomena influenced by the Sun during one of the peak activity periods for sunspots (regions of intense magnetic disturbances on the solar surface), which occur approximately every eleven years. A large part of the data collected pertains to specialized areas in space physics; only those findings of a general interest are mentioned here.

OGO 1 conducted a thorough study of the outer magnetosphere and identified the existence of the plasmasphere (the definite outer boundary of Earth's ionosphere). OGO 2 helped map the geomagnetic field for the World Magnetic Survey (an international cooperative effort involving satellites from the United States and the Soviet Union). These measurements improved scientists' geomagnetic model immeasurably. OGO 2 also mapped the ion composition as a function of latitude, providing some of the first substantial data on this variation. OGO 4 performed the first global measurement of nitric oxide concentrations in the atmosphere.

Context

The OGO satellites served important roles, from both scientific and technological perspectives. Many of their scientific results, particularly the magnetic field studies, have been employed in scientific research, with the consequence that these data have appeared in numerous articles and textbooks. Many of the data were collected simultaneously with similar measurements from other spacecraft (such as the Interplanetary Monitoring Platforms, the Applications Technology Satellites, the Injun satellites, and the International Satellites for Ionospheric Studies). By correlating the data from these spacecraft with those from the OGOs, scientists were able to separate the temporal and spatial characteristics of such phenomena as cosmic rays, solar particles, charged particles trapped in Earth's magnetic field, and variations in the magnetic fields surrounding Earth and in interplanetary space.

Technologically, the OGOs served to demonstrate the feasibility of standard, general-purpose satellites into which experimental packages could be placed and operated successfully without the experiments' having to be integrated into the design of the overall vehicle. In addition, the OGOs demonstrated the feasibility of maintaining three-axis stabilization for this modular design, and thereby provided the necessary conditions for experiments with precise pointing requirements. The successful use of backup modes (resulting in extended spacecraft operational lifetimes) was demonstrated repeatedly with the spin-stabilized standby mode of attitude control.

—Robert G. Melton

See also: Explorers: Air Density; Explorers: Atmosphere; Explorers: Ionosphere; Hubble Space Telescope: Servicing Missions; International Ultraviolet Explorer; Interplanetary Monitoring Platform Satellites; Launch Vehicles; Nuclear Detection Satellites; Ocean Surveillance Satellites; Orbiting Astronomical Observatories; Orbiting Solar Observatories.

Further Reading

Baker, David, ed. *Jane's Space Directory, 2005-2006*. Alexandria, Va.: Jane's Information Group, 2005. This informative volume is a good reference for novices and space buffs alike. Written in clear language, it provides concise descriptions of the missions, programs, and spacecraft of the world. Illustrated. Contains an index.

Corliss, William R. *Scientific Satellites*. NASA SP-133. Washington, D.C.: Government Printing Office, 1967. Gives a history of scientific satellite missions from 1958 to 1967. Describes major subsystems common to all satellites, devoting significant coverage to scientific instrumentation for spacecraft use. Includes an appendix of all U.S. scientific missions (with descriptions of the satellites and their experiments) flown during the period covered. A rather technical work.

Davies, John K. *Astronomy from Space: The Design and Operation of Orbiting Observatories*. New York: JohnWiley and Sons, 1997. This is a comprehensive reference on the satellites that have revolutionized twentieth century astrophysics. It contains in-depth coverage of all space astronomy missions. It includes tables of launch data and orbits for quick reference as well as photographs of many of the lesser-known satellites. The main body of the book is subdivided according to type of astronomy carried out by each satellite (x-ray, gamma-ray, ultraviolet, infrared, and radio). Discusses the future of satellite astronomy as well.

Gavaghan, Helen. *Something New Under the Sun: Satellites and the Beginning of the Space Age.* New York: Copernicus, 1998. Subjects written about include the history of artificial satellites, astronautics, and civil aviation. Bibliographical references and an index are also included.

Jackson, John E., and James I. Vette. *The Observatory Generation of Satellites.* NASA SP-30. Washington, D.C.: Government Printing Office, 1963. A collection of six papers: Two pertain to OGO; the others describe similar observatory-type spacecraft. Written before the first OGO launch, these are useful overviews of the program and the engineering design of the spacecraft. For general audiences, although moderately technical.

---. *OGO Program Summary: The Orbiting Geophysical Observatories.* Springfield, Va.: National Technical Information Service, 1975. Provides an overview of the six OGO missions. Describes each satellite, including engineering systems and all scientific experiments on board (along with names of the associated principal investigators). Describes scientific findings from each experiment. For technical audiences.

Parks, George K. *Physics of Space Plasmas: An Introduction.* 2d ed. Boulder, Colo.: Westview Press, 2004. Provides a scientific examination of the data returned during what might be called the "golden age" of space physics (1990-2002), when over two dozen satellites were dispatched to investigate space plasma phenomena. Written at the undergraduate level for an introductory course in space plasma, there is also detailed presentation of NASA and ESA spacecraft missions.

Zimmerman, Robert. *The Chronological Encyclopedia of Discoveries in Space.* Westport, Conn.: Oryx Press, 2000. Provides a complete chronological history of all crewed and robotic spacecraft and explains flight events and scientific results. Suitable for all levels of research.

Orbiting Solar Observatories

Date: March 7, 1962, to September 26, 1978
Type of spacecraft: Space telescope

Orbiting Solar Observatories (OSOs) were designed to study the structure of the Sun and its outward flow of high-energy particles. They were used to study the influence of the Sun on Earth, and to provide a basis for the study of more distant stars.

Key Figures

L. T. Hogarth, program manager
John C. Lindsay, project manager
John M. Thole, project manager
William E. Behring, project scientist
Stephen P. Maran, project scientist
Roger J. Thomas, project scientist
G. K. Oertel, flight director of Solar Physics, NASA

Summary of the Satellites

The Orbiting Solar Observatory (OSO) program was the first series of satellites to operate as orbiting observatories. The program was conceived to monitor the Sun continuously for long periods of time, particularly during one complete eleven-year solar sunspot cycle. (Sunspots are relatively cool regions on the Sun that appear dark in contrast with the hotter surrounding material.) The occurrence of sunspots follows a semi-regular cycle of twenty-two years as the Sun's magnetic field reverses from the north to south pole, and returns. This drives sunspot activity and a maximum is observed twice during each solar cycle (roughly once every eleven years).

The study of the Sun from space began in the late 1940's, when V-2 rockets were launched to obtain ultraviolet solar spectrograms. (A spectrogram is a picture of the light from a radiant body separated into its component parts.) The major limitation of this type of research was that the rockets could stay above the atmosphere of Earth for only a few minutes. Observation above the atmosphere is essential to solar research, because the atmosphere filters out much of the lethal, but informative, radiation that comes to Earth from the Sun.

The OSOs were designed to carry solar experiments in a low orbit around Earth. Orbiting once every ninety minutes, they could view the Sun continuously for up to one hour before passing into the night side of the orbit. The observatories were designed to last from six months to a year, and a series of satellites was planned to cover an entire solar cycle.

All satellites in the OSO series were of the same basic design. Each consisted of a nine-sided spinning base about 38 centimeters high, with a diameter of about 112 centimeters. Attached to it by a rod was a stationary sail-shaped platform about 58 centimeters high. The base rotated at a speed of about thirty to forty rotations per minute, allowing experiments housed there to scan the Sun every two seconds. The base also held the power, command, and communications systems. The sail section held experiments that could be continuously pointed at the Sun and the solar cell panels, which provided power to the spacecraft and experiments. As the wheel rotated, different sensors in the wheel pointed first at the sky and then at the Sun to compare radiation coming from different directions. Nitrogen gas jets were used on both the wheel and sail sections in order to keep the experiments aligned correctly and to adjust the spin rate of the base.

The spacecraft contained sensors to measure x rays, gamma rays, and ultraviolet radiation. These ranges of radiation are of wavelengths shorter than those of visible light and are highly energetic. Experiments were also carried to study radio emissions, which are of wavelengths longer than those of visible light. The same basic satellite design could accommodate a variety of experiments as the program progressed. In many cases, observations from the OSO satellites were coordinated with those of ground-based observatories to maximize the scientific usefulness of the data.

As data were collected, they were recorded and stored on a continuous-loop magnetic tape. Upon command from the ground, the tape would deliver ninety minutes of observations in the five minutes it was within range of a receiving station. Tracking, data acquisition, and command generation were

Dr. Nancy Roman, one of the nation's top scientists in the space program, is shown with a model of the Orbiting Solar Observatory (OSO). She retired from NASA in 1979, but continued working as a contractor at the Goddard Space Flight Center. Throughout her career, Dr. Roman was a spokesperson and advocate of women in the sciences. (NASA)

handled by NASA's Space Tracking and Data Acquisition Network (STADAN), later the Spaceflight Tracking and Data Network (STDN), with tracking stations located around the world. As data were received at each of these stations, they were transmitted to the OSO control center at Goddard Space Flight Center and then to the various experimental laboratory locations. Among these were the Naval Research Laboratory, the University of California at San Diego, and the University of New Hampshire.

Life expectancies of the satellites ranged from six months to one year. Several of the satellites performed for a period well over their expected lifetimes, providing useful information for up to three years.

OSO 1 was launched March 7, 1962, from Cape Canaveral. It was given the nickname Streetcar because of its boxlike design and interchangeability of instrumentation. Although it was expected to perform for six months, a solar power generation system malfunction on May 22 caused the satellite to fail. During its short lifetime, the satellite was able to transmit more than one thousand hours' worth of useful data and record measurements on some 140 solar flares. Solar flares are large, sudden outbursts of energy from the Sun. They are phenomena normally associated with sunspot groups.

OSO 2 was launched February 3, 1965. It was originally scheduled to be launched in April of 1964 but was delayed because of a preflight accident in which the launch rocket ignited prematurely and exploded. Three technicians were killed, thirteen others were injured, and the spacecraft was severely damaged. OSO 2 incorporated many improvements over the first OSO, including the ability to scan across the entire solar disk rather than be confined to a single point on the Sun.

The third satellite in the series, OSO-C, was launched August 25, 1965, but its launch vehicle failed to reach orbit. OSO 3 was designed as a replacement, but it was not launched until March of 1967. OSO 4 followed in October of the same year. This satellite focused on the structure and energy balance of the solar chromosphere, the layer of the Sun's atmosphere directly above the visible surface. It carried a device that could observe the Sun in the extreme ultraviolet portion of the light spectrum.

OSO 5 and OSO 6 were both launched in 1969. Among their other experiments, these two spacecraft concentrated on solar flares. The eventual goal in this study was to provide solar eruption predictions that could serve as an early warning to astronauts on crewed spaceflights and extravehicular activity missions. With OSO 6 came an improvement in pointing accuracy and scanning capability. While previous satellites were able to point only at the center of the Sun or scan the entire disk, OSO 6 could aim at any desired place on the disk or in the corona and scan a select area. Space programs of Great Britain and Italy furnished two of the experiments flown aboard OSO 6.

A problem occurred in the launch of OSO 7 on September 29, 1971. A failure in the launch vehicle sent the satellite into an unplanned orbit. The spacecraft was spinning out of control and was unable to orient itself toward the Sun. Ground controllers were finally able to stabilize the satellite and position it properly, and all experiments began functioning normally. The primary target of OSO 7 was the solar corona, the outermost layer of the Sun's atmosphere. This part of the Sun is normally seen only during a solar eclipse, when the shadow of the Moon blocks the bright light from the disk of the Sun. A circular occulting disk on the spacecraft produced an artificial eclipse to allow the onboard cameras to observe the corona. OSO 7 was also used in conjunction with experiments aboard the orbiting crewed space laboratory Skylab.

OSO 7 continued earlier experiments conducted by OSOs 5 and 6 to study solar flare prediction techniques for use during crewed missions. It also studied the effect of solar flares on weather and communications on Earth.

The last satellite in the series, OSO 8, was launched June 21, 1975. While improvements had been made to each successive satellite in the series, OSO 8 was by far the most sophisticated. Its instrument package was larger, had more resolution, could be directed more accurately, and was able to cover a wider range of wavelengths than that of any OSO satellite before it. It observed fine details in the photosphere and explored the various ways energy is transported in the chromosphere and the corona.

OSO 8 also pointed its instruments away from the Sun in order to investigate other celestial x-ray sources. Of special interest was the x-ray background emission that comes from all directions in space, an emission that is now believed to be a remnant from the beginning of the universe. The French space program contributed to the experiment package on OSO 8, with an instrument designed to study the fine structure of the Sun's chromosphere. (The chromosphere is the layer of the Sun's atmosphere directly above the visible surface of the Sun.)

Contributions

The largest body of knowledge scientists gained about the Sun in the early days of the Space Age came from experiments flown aboard the OSOs. The first OSO alone gathered more than four thousand times the information previously known about the Sun. For the first time, scientists were able to study comprehensive data from the entire disk of the Sun in wavelengths and with resolution impossible from the surface of Earth.

Solar flares were one of the most exciting areas of discovery. Spectra taken showed some flares being heated to an excess of 30 million kelvins. Fast periodic pulses of x rays were found to be emitted by flares, and gamma-ray emissions were also detected. The first images of the birth, buildup, and death of a flare were recorded. Flares seem to occur in two stages, showing two distinctly different bursts of x rays.

A new model of prominences emerged from OSO data. Prominences are bright, flamelike masses of gas that can be seen on the edge of the Sun. They appear to consist of a relatively cool material concentrated in threads and surrounded by a hot sheath that rises to the same temperature as the corona as it rises over a distance of a few thousand kilometers.

While the light and heat output of the Sun remains fairly constant, large fluctuations were found in other wavelengths of energy. During active periods of the Sun (times with more sunspot and flare activity), it was found that ultraviolet and x-ray emissions can be four times as intense as usual. An important result of one OSO experiment was the ability to generate a daily x-ray map of the Sun, along with a map of solar radio emissions and sunspots. This mapping allowed for a systematic approach to the study of the evolution of active regions on the Sun.

Many discoveries were made regarding the solar corona, usually visible only during a total solar eclipse. Evidence of gamma-ray emission was found. This indicates there are nuclear reactions occurring in solar flares themselves, rather than solely deep within the Sun, as was previously thought. OSO discovered "coronal holes," areas of reduced emission of radiation at high-energy wavelengths. In a coronal hole, the temperature is about 600,000 kelvins cooler than in the surrounding corona, and the pressure of the gases in the area is about one-third lower. The solar wind, the flow of particles away from the Sun, seems to be increased in the area of a coronal hole.

Using an experiment designed by a team of French physicists, researchers found that there are huge periodic oscillations of the Sun occurring every fourteen minutes. The entire atmosphere pulses to a distance of about 1,300 kilometers. It is believed that sound waves are responsible for the pulsations.

Toward the end of the OSO program, resolution on the satellites had improved in such a way that equipment could record fine details of the solar surface, structures resembling granules. These granulations are constantly in motion and have a lifetime of only a few minutes. They contain clues about how energy is transferred in the Sun's atmosphere.

OSO discoveries were not restricted to the Sun. The satellites also studied Earth's atmosphere, and the zodiacal light, a band of faint light extending along the path of the Sun in the sky. This light is visible in the dark sky just after sunset and before sunrise. It was found that this light is not evenly distributed; it is much less apparent near the poles. Other atmospheric studies showed that lightning strikes more often over land than water and that certain land areas seem to experience more lightning than others. In other areas of the sky, OSO satellites searched for and mapped out other sources of x rays, discovering many new sources and verifying the positions of other known sources.

Context

The Sun, while the most vital and central member of the solar system, is perhaps the least understood. With the advent of orbiting observatories such as the OSO series, the knowledge of the Sun and its effects on Earth could be increased.

Visible and infrared radiations, which are the emissions from the Sun that scientists can most readily measure from the surface of Earth, are nearly constant. Yet the Sun's energy varies considerably in other wavelengths, such as in the ultraviolet and radio regions. At apparently random intervals, the Sun will unleash a burst of energetic particles. Until researchers had the means to measure these emissions and variations, the data went unnoticed. With the invention of radio, however, these bursts were discovered, because they interfered with radio waves in the upper atmosphere and created a disturbance in radio transmission.

In comparison with instruments launched since the end of the OSO series, these satellites seem rather out-of-date. In the context of the times, however, these were the most sophisticated satellites that had been launched, the first of a new class of orbiting observatories. It was the first time an artificial satellite had been applied to astrophysical problems in a comprehensive way. Information that was obtained from these satellites was therefore revolutionary to the study of the Sun.

Because little was known of the Sun at that time, scientists were uncertain as to what might be learned from OSO data. One hope was that the study of the Sun might lead to its use as an unlimited and pollution-free power source for Earth. In fact, the understanding of solar physics is considered to be essential to the understanding of the physics of Earth and of the other planets. The study of the Sun is closely related to geology and biology, because the record of rocks and fossils on Earth confirms what scientists are discovering about the Sun. It is theorized that variations in the Sun's output of energy may have been responsible for the ice ages that have occurred at intervals throughout the history of Earth.

Besides its importance to Earth, the Sun provides astronomers with their only opportunity to study a star at close range. The next nearest star is 48 trillion kilometers farther away than the Sun.

With each OSO came improvements in the accuracy and capability of the spacecraft and in experiment capability. The OSO series can also be seen, then, as a test for the more sophisticated satellites that were to come later: the Orbiting Astronomical Observatories (OAOs), the International Ultraviolet Explorer (IUE), the Solar Maximum Mission (SMM), and the crewed space station Skylab. In fact, OSO 7 was in orbit at the same time as Skylab and was used in conjunction with the space station.

The OSO program was also a testbed for spaceflight in general. Besides performing experiments that were directed at astronomical phenomena, satellites such as OSO 2 performed experiments to test the effects of solar radiation on different surface preparations and paint used on spacecraft. One of OSO's major missions was to find a method to predict solar flares, which would affect future missions, particularly the crewed Apollo flights. The OSO program can, therefore, be seen as an essential stepping-stone in the space program, in terms of both scientific research and spaceflight. Later came the Solar Max satellite and the Solar Dynamics Observatory to name but a few subsequent space-based solar investigations, all of which built upon the legacy of early OSO research.

—Divonna Ogier

See also:; Compton Gamma Ray Observatory; Explorers: Solar; International Ultraviolet Explorer; Launch Vehicles; Orbiting Astronomical Observatories; Orbiting Geophysical Observatories; Solar Maximum Mission; Space Shuttle; Telescopes: Air and Space.

Further Reading

Cornell, James, and Paul Gorenstein, eds. *Astronomy from Space: Sputnik to Space Telescope*. Cambridge, Mass.: MIT Press, 1985. An overview of twenty-five years of astronomical research from space. Summarizes what has been learned in different areas of astronomy in the form of short articles written by experts in each field. Suitable for those with some science background.

Davies, John K. *Astronomy from Space: The Design and Operation of Orbiting Observatories*. New York: John Wiley, 1997. This is a comprehensive reference on the satellites that have revolutionized twentieth century astrophysics. It contains in-depth coverage of all space astronomy missions. It includes tables of launch data and orbits for quick reference as well as photographs of many of the lesser-known satellites. The main body of the book is subdivided according to type of astronomy carried out by each satellite (x-ray, gamma-ray, ultraviolet, infrared, and radio). It discusses the future of satellite astronomy as well.

Eddy, John A. *A New Sun: The Solar Results from Skylab*. NASA SP-402. Washington, D.C.: Government Printing Office, 1979. Describes the Skylab mission in detail and discusses what is known about the Sun, including the findings from Skylab. Written for the layperson with an interest in astronomy, although some background is helpful. Illustrated with color photographs, many taken aboard Skylab.

Fire of Life: The Smithsonian Book of the Sun. Washington, D.C.: Smithsonian Exposition Books, 1981. A collection of articles written by experts in the field, geared toward general audiences. Includes a history of beliefs about the Sun. Contains beautiful photography. Poetic as well as informative.

Gibson, Edward G. *The Quiet Sun*. NASA SP-303. Washington, D.C.: Government Printing Office, 1973. A fairly technical manual on current solar theory. Includes information obtained from the OSO program. Describes solar structure and processes in detail and includes those questions that remain unanswered.

Golub, Leon, and Jay M. Pasachoff. *Nearest Star: The Surprising Science of Our Sun*. Boston: Harvard University Press, 2002. Although written by two of the most active research astrophysicists, this book is accessible to a general audience. It describes most contemporary advances in solar physics.

Henbest, Nigel, and Michael Marten. *The New Astronomy*. New York: Cambridge University Press, 1986. Compares optical, infrared, ultraviolet, radio, and x-ray observations of well-known astronomical objects. Written specifically for general audiences. Illustrated.

Maran, S. P., and R. J. Thomas. "Last OSO Satellite: Orbiting Solar Observatory." *Sky and Telescope* 49 (June, 1975): 355-358. Describes the last OSO satellite and reports on the program's status and results of observations. Geared toward amateur astronomers with some background in astronomical and space-flight principles. Illustrated.

Mari, Christopher, ed. *Space Exploration*. New York: H. W. Wilson, 1999. Twenty-five articles (reprinted from magazines), covering the state of the space program at the time of publication, are divided into five sections: John H. Glenn, Jr.'s return to space, the exploration of Mars, the International Space Station, recent mining efforts by commercial industries, and new types of space vehicles and propulsion systems.

"OSO-8 Program Keyed to Skylab Data: Orbiting Solar Observatory." *Aviation Week and Space Technology* 102 (June 30, 1975): 45. Describes the satellite and its discoveries. Reports on plans for satellites not yet launched. Written for professionals in the field of avionics; thus, the language is technical. Illustrated.

Tassoul, Jean-Louis, and Monique Tassoul. *A Concise History of Solar and Stellar Physics*. Princeton, N.J.: Princeton University Press, 2004. A comprehensive study of the historical development of humanity's understanding of the Sun and the cosmos, written in easy-to-understand language by a pair of theoretical astrophysicists. The perspective of the astronomer and physicist are presented.

Zimmerman, Robert. *The Chronological Encyclopedia of Discoveries in Space*. Westport, Conn.: Oryx Press, 2000. Provides a complete chronological history of all crewed and robotic spacecraft and explains flight events and scientific results. Suitable for all levels of research.

OSIRIS-REx

Date: Launched September 8, 2016
Type of Mission: Uncrewed spacecraft

The Origins, Spectral Interpretation, Resource Identification, Security, Regolith Explorer (OSIRIS-REx) spacecraft was launched in 2016 and began orbiting the carbon-rich asteroid Bennu in 2018. The OSIRIS-REx spacecraft will characterize the asteroid, collect a sample from its surface, and deliver the sample for study in laboratories on Earth in 2023.

Key Figures

Michael J. Drake (1946-2011), planetary scientist and original OSIRIS-Rex Principal Investigator

Dante Lauretta (b.1970), Planetary scientist at the University of Arizona and OSIRIS-Rex Principal Investigator

Heather Enos, OSIRIS-REx Deputy Principal Investigator

Rich Kuhns, Lockheed Martin Space Systems OSIRIS-REx Project Manager

Jason Dworkin, OSIRIS-REx Project Scientist

Victoria Hamilton, OSIRIS-REx Lead Spectral Scientist

Summary of the Mission

The Origins, Spectral Interpretation, Resource Identification, Security, Regolith Explorer (OSIRIS-REx) was selected as the third mission in NASA's New Frontiers program in May 2011. The OSIRIS-REx mission concept was developed by planetary scientists at the University of Arizona in collaboration with Lockheed Martin Space Systems and NASA's Goddard Spaceflight Center. OSIRIS was originally proposed as a sample return mission to the lower-cost NASA Discovery program by a team led by Michael Drake, a professor at the University of Arizona. But NASA did not select the OSIRIS mission, so the science team enlarged the scope of the mission, adding instruments to more completely characterize the target asteroid, and proposed the new mission to NASA's New Horizons program. Drake's death, shortly after the mission was selected, left Dante Lauretta, originally the Deputy Principal Investigator, leading the mission.

After more than five years of development the OSIRIS-REx spacecraft was launched from Cape Canaveral Air Force Station, Florida on an Atlas V rocket at 7:05 p.m. EDT on September 8, 2016. A deep space maneuver on 28 December 2016 placed OSIRIS-REx in a one-year orbit around the Sun. This put OSIRIS-REx in position for an Earth gravity assist on 22 September 2017, which moved the spacecraft's orbit out of the ecliptic plane and into the orbital plane of asteroid 101955 Bennu. Bennu is a 0.3 mile diameter asteroid that orbits the Sun every 436 days and makes a very close approach to Earth every six years. By August 2018 OSIRIS-REx was close enough to detect the asteroid, allowing more precise navigation to the target. OSIRIS-REx entered orbit around Bennu on 31 December 2018, beginning its two-year study of the asteroid.

The 4,650 pound OSIRIS-REx spacecraft carries five instruments designed to explore Bennu: a Camera Suite (OCAMS), consisting of three cameras, a Laser Altimiter (OLA), a Thermal Emission Spectrometer (TES), a Visible and InfraRed Spectrometer (OVIRS) and a Regolith X-ray Imaging Specrometer (REXIS). These scientific instruments were selected to measure the physical, geological, and chemical properties of Bennu and to allow selection of a safe and scientifically interesting sampling site.

During the summer of 2020 OSIRIS-REx will slowly descend towards the surface of Bennu, deploying a Touch-And-Go Sample Acquisition System (TAGSAM) designed to collect at least two ounces of regolith from Bennu's surface. The sampler will only touch Bennu's surface for about five seconds, injecting a burst of pure nitrogen gas that will push loose material into the sample chamber. Should the first collection attempt fail, OSIRIS-REx carries enough nitrogen for two additional attempts at sample collection. Once the sample is collected it will be transferred to the sample return capsule, a slightly modified version of the reentry capsule used on NASA's Stardust mission, which successfully delivered samples from Comet Wild 2 to the Earth in 2006. The sample is expected to be delivered to Earth for laboratory study in September 2023. After arrival, the OSIRIS-REx science team will have two years to characterize a representative sample of the material before NASA makes the samples available to the rest of the worldwide science community for more intensive scientific research.

Of the 192 near-Earth asteroids that were determined to be accessible within the limitations of a New Frontiers mission, asteroid Bennu was selected as the target because telescopic observations indicated it was a carbon-rich asteroid with a reflection spectrum similar to that of some hydrous, carbon-rich meteorites. These meteorites have been the subject of intensive study because they contain clues to the origin of the rocky bodies of the system and contain organic matter that could have provided raw material for the origin of life. However, the meteorites may have been altered by the shock and heat experienced by ejection from their parent bodies and they can be contaminated during deceleration in the Earth's atmosphere and by terrestrial microorganisms or water after they reach the Earth's surface. Thus, laboratory analysis of the Bennu samples is expected to provide an unprecedented look at the formation and evolution of the minerals and organic matter in primitive, carbon-rich asteroids.

Contributions

Because of its frequent close approaches to the Earth and its classification as a Potentially Hazardous Asteroid, since it has the possibility of hitting the Earth in the 22nd century, Bennu had been studied extensively by high-powered radar and astronomical telescopes. Aside from the main mission objective to collect and deliver to Earth a sample of a primitive, carbon-rich asteroid, OSIRIS-REx was designed to assess Bennu's resource potential, better constrain its impact probability with Earth, and provide "ground-truth" for the extensive astronomical data set collected by ground-based and space based instruments. The latter objective was particularly important since many asteroids have been studied remotely, but only a few have been examined close-up in order to validate the interpretation of the remote sensing data.

During the year between launch and the Earth gravity assist, OSIRIS-REx approached the *Sun-Earth Lagrangian point,* a region of space where some planetary scientists had speculated there might be an undetected population of "Earth-Trojans," asteroids or comets trapped in the gravitationally stable region, called a Lagrangian Point, that co-orbits the Sun following ahead or behind the Earth. A population of Jupiter-Trojans has been observed from ground-based telescopes in the gravitationally stable region co-orbiting with Jupiter. However, none were found by OSIRIS-REx at the Earth's Lagrangian points.

Prior to arriving at Bennu instruments on OSIRIS-REx were used to search for a dusty environment surrounding the asteroid, a natural satellite, or any unexpected asteroid characteristics that could adversely impact the mission's safety or the planned observation strategy. Observations in

September 2018 placed an upper limit on the average dust production from Bennu's surface to an only a few ounces every second, well below the production rate that would constitute a safety hazard. Satellites larger than a few meters in size would have been detectable, but none were identified.

Astronomical observations had classified Bennu as rare B-type asteroid, a type that is primitive and carbon-rich. In the visible and near-infrared the OVIRS spectra are featureless with a blue slope, with a very low reflectivity for visible light, consistent with the ground-based observations. The near-infrared and thermal-infrared spectral features observed on Bennu are most similar to spectra of the aqueously altered carbonaceous chondrite meteorites, also consistent with the remote sensing observations. But water in the Earth's atmosphere prevents detection of the spectral features of water using ground-based telescopes. The observation of a globally distributed a near-infrared absorption, near 2.7 micrometers, indicates the presence of abundant water distributed widely across the surface of Bennu, likely present as clay minerals. From this, they suggested that Bennu is a "rubble pile," an aggregate of smaller fragments held together only weakly by gravity.

Remote sensing allowed researchers to determine the size and and shape of Bennu from radar observations. But the best resolution possible from Earth was inadequate to reveal details of its surface. The OCAMS images revealed that Bennu looks like a spinning top with an equatorial bulge, consistent with the images obtained by Earth-based radio telescopes. By combining shape measurements, which provide a volume of Bennu, with the asteroid's mass determined from OSIRIS-REx's orbital period and radio science measurements, the science team determined that the bulk density of Bennu is only slightly greater than that of water and much less than the minerals that make up the bulk of the asteroid. From this they concluded that Bennu has a

very high porosity, larger than any of the carbon-rich meteorites.

Based on measurements of Bennu taken by the Spitzer Space Telescope, the OSIRIS-REx science team expected the surface to be covered by small, sand-sized particles with large, flat areas suitable for sample collection. But the early high-resolution images from OSIRIS-REx showed that Bennu's surface is globally rough, covered by boulders some tens of feet across. The number of large boulders indicates that a precision landing will be needed to sample a safe touchdown zone. Bennu's thermal emissivity is lower than expected for a surface covered by large boulders, which is interpreted to indicate the boulders are covered by a layer of more insulating dust below the resolution limit of the cameras.

Comparison of the rotation rate of Bennu measured over several years by ground-based instruments with measurements as the spacecraft approached Bennu showed that the spin rate of Bennu is increasing over time. The time to complete a full rotation is getting shorter by about 1 second per century. The OSIRIS-REx science team attributes this increase in the rotation rate to the "YORP effect," which results from sunlight illuminating one side of the asteroid, heating the sunlit surface, which reradiates the energy into space as the heated region rotates into darkness. This exerts a windmill-like force on the asteroid's surface, causing it to spin faster or slower depending on the direction of the force. Although the rate at which the rotation is increasing may seem small, if it continues Bennu could eventually spin fast enough to tear itself apart since rubble pile objects have little cohesive strength and material on the surface of a rapidly rotating body is thrown into space when the rotation rate becomes excessive.

The density of craters found on Bennu indicates its surface is between 100 million and 1 billion years old. This is much longer than dynamical modeling indicates an asteroid can remain in a near-Earth orbit, so the OSIRIS-REx science team concluded that many of the craters on Bennu's surface record events from Bennu's time in the main asteroid belt, in the region between Mars and Jupiter. The observation of fractures in many of the boulders suggests impact or thermal processes affected the surface of Bennu in the time period since the boulders were exposed at the surface.

Context

When OSIRIS-REx entered orbit around Bennu it set two Guinness World Records. Bennu became the smallest celestial body ever orbited by a spacecraft, and OSIRIS-REx entered the closest orbit ever achieved around another celestial body. These achievements demonstrated technology needed for future efforts, being pursued by several private companies, to mine asteroids for use of their mineral and water resources.

The similarity of Bennu's reflection spectrum to that of hydrous carbon-rich meteorites validated the astronomical observations, and demonstrated that Bennu is a representative member of a class of asteroids that are suspected of having brought water and organic compounds to the early Earth. Studies of the organics and water in these carbon-rich meteorites are frequently hampered by terrestrial contamination. This delivery of uncontaminated samples from the surface of Bennu will make possible, for the first time, the detailed characterization of the organic matter in an uncontaminated sample of one of these carbon-rich bodies. The widespread detection of the spectral absorption feature indicative of the presence of hydrated silicates supports the idea that water was delivered to the early Earth by primitive asteroids.

The greatest scientific return from OSIRIS-REx is expected to come from the laboratory analysis of the Bennu samples, since measurements with these large, heavy, power consuming laboratory instruments are generally much more sensitive, accurate, and precise than the instruments that can be carried on spacecraft. Although the two-ounce minimum sample size may seem small compared to the more than 800 pounds of lunar samples collected by the Apollo astronauts, NASA's Stardust spacecraft collected and delivered to Earth only a few hundred very small particles of comet dust, much less than the minimum two ounces of the Bennu sample. Nonetheless, laboratory analysis of the dust collected by Stardust reshaped ideas about the composition of comets and the formation and transport of dust in the early Solar System. The similarity of Bennu to the very primitive, carbon-rich meteorites indicates that the dirt and gravel collected from Bennu's surface will preserve the record of early solar system processes, a record that is overprinted in Earth rocks billions of years of geological activity. The Bennu samples are expected to help scientists better understand the processes of mineral formation, grain aggregation, and planet formation during the early days of the solar system.

The OSIRIS-REx observation of numerous large boulders on the surface of Bennu is inconsistent with the interpretation of remote sensing data, which indicated Bennu was relatively flat and covered by material of much smaller sizes. This calls into question the selection of landing sites for future missions based entirely on remote sensing data or images with inadequate resolution to compellingly identify safe landing sites.

—*George J. Flynn*

See also: Asteroid Redirect Mission; Near Earth Asteroid Rendezvous

Further Reading

Balram-Knutson, S. S., et al. "OSIRIS-REx: Sample Return from Asteroid (101955) Bennu." *Space Science Reviews*, vol. 212, no. 1-2, Oct. 2017, pp. 925–984., doi:10.1007/s11214-017-0405-1. Although intended for space scientists, this comprehensive, very well-illustrated article describes the OSIRIS-REx mission, the science objectives, and the instruments in a manner accessible for general audiences.

Hamilton, Vicky. "Flying By Home: Testing OSIRIS-REx's Tools on the Way to Asteroid Encounter." *The Planetary Report*, vol. 38, no. 4, Dec. 2018, pp. 6–11. A well-illustrated, first-hand account by the head of OSIRIS-REx's Spectral Analysis Working Group, of the OSIRIS-REx Earth flyby, the instruments, and the plans for exploration at Bennu.

Lauretta, D. S., et al. "The OSIRIS-REx Target Asteroid (101955) Bennu: Constraints on Its Physical, Geological, and Dynamical Nature from Astronomical Observations." *Meteoritics & Planetary Science*, vol. 50, no. 4, 2014, pp. 834–849., doi:10.1111/maps.12353. This investigation provides information on the orbit, shape, mass, rotation state, radar response, photometric, spectroscopic, thermal, regolith, and environmental properties of Bennu.

Lauretta, Dante S. "The Seven-Year Mission to Fetch 60 Grams of Asteroid." *Scientific American*, vol. 315, no. 2, Aug. 2016, pp. 62–69., doi:10.1038/scientificamerican0816-62. A well-illustrated account, intended for general audiences, by the OSIRIS-REx principal investigator describing how this mission to explore the asteroid Bennu, collect a sample, and deliver it to Earth will answer questions about the past history of our Solar System and possibly the origin of life on Earth.

Powell, Corey. "First Person: Dante Lauretta." *American Scientist*, vol. 102, no. 4, 2014, p. 247., doi:10.1511/2014.109.247. An interview with OSIRIS-REx principal investigator Dante Lauretta, who describes the mission and the expected science results.

Parker Solar Probe

Date: Launched August 12, 2018
Type of Mission: Orbiter

The Parker Solar Probe will help scientists learn more about the Sun and other stars. The spacecraft was named for physicist Eugene Parker who coined the term Solar wind. The main goal of the mission is to study how solar particles accelerate and are ejected by the Sun. They also hope to determine why the corona is hotter than the Sun's surface. The spacecraft made its first perihelion on November 6, 2018 and sent back its first images the following December.

Key Figures

APL John Hopkins University's Applied Physics Laboratory, designed and built spacecraft

Eugene Parker (b. 1927), Astrophysicist that coined the term "solar wind"

Andrew Driesman (b. 1963-) Mission project manager at APL

Summary of the Mission

The design and objectives of the Parker Solar Probe originated from the cancelled Solar Orbiter program in the 1990s. The project was originally named Solar Probe and was designed to answer why the Sun's corona is hotter than its photosphere, how energy and heat move throughout the corona, and determine what accelerates solar wind. In the early 2010s, the program was replaced with a simpler, lower cost version named Solar Probe Plus. To save money, the probe would now use multiple Venus gravity assists to take a more direct trajectory to the Sun and would be powered with solar panels. The Solar Probe Plus also would have a higher perihelion than its predecessor, which meant that it could operate with a simpler thermal protection system. This system was designed to keep the spacecraft and its instruments safe from the intense heat and radiation of the Sun.

In 2017, the mission was renamed the Parker Solar Probe, in honor of physicist Eugene Parker. It is the first spacecraft named after a living person. Parker, professor emeritus at the University of Chicago, theorized the existence of supersonic solar wind in the 1950s. He also predicted the shape of the sun's magnetic field in the outer solar system, which also now bears his name. In 1987, he hypothesized that the corona has higher temperatures than

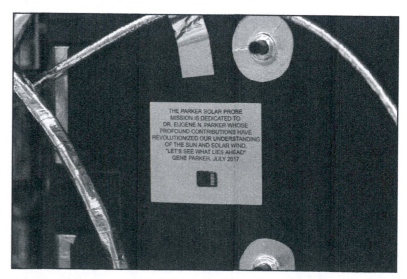

1.1 million names submitted by the public were loaded into a memory card and mounted on a plaque bearing a dedication to the mission's namesake, heliophysicist Dr. Eugene Parker. (NASA)

the Sun's photosphere because it is heated by a large quantity of "nano-flares", similar to solar flares.

The spacecraft is the first to fly into the Sun's outer atmosphere, the corona. The Parker Solar Probe was launched August 12, 2018. On October 29, 2018, it broke the record for a man-made object being nearest the Sun. The previous record holder was Helios 2 that passed within 42.5 million kilometers (26.55 million mile) of the Sun in April 1976. By comparison, the Parker Solar Probe was only 24 million kilometers (15 million miles) above the Sun's surface. The spacecraft is following a highly elliptical orbit around the Sun that allows it to use Venus to help decrease its orbit. The probe will pass Venus seven times and will make twenty-four close passes of the Sun. Each perihelion with bring the spacecraft closer to the Sun. The final planned perihelion, in 2025, will put the spacecraft within 6 million kilometers (3.8 million miles) of the Sun's surface. The Parker Solar Probe will also travel faster than any other man-made object during its perihelions, another record previously held by Helios 2. During its closest approach, the Parker Solar Probe will be traveling 688,000 kilometers per hour (430,000 miles per hour).

When designing the spacecraft, scientists at the Applied Physics Laboratory had to find a way to protect it from the Sun's intense heat and radiation. The solar radiation at perihelion is 475 times that at Earth's orbit. The probe is equipped with a hexagon shaped heat shield that is 2.25 meters (7.5 feet in) diameter, 11.4 centimeters (4.5 inches) thick, and coated with a white ceramic layer to help reduce absorption. The heat shield is designed to withstand temperatures up to 1644 kelvins (2.500 degrees Fahrenheit). Without this protection, the spacecraft would be damaged and non-functional in tens of seconds. The spacecraft has four light sensors to

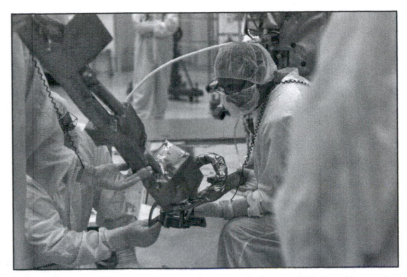

Technicians and engineers deploy the magnetometer boom on the probe. (NASA)

detect the first hint of direct sunlight and then will reposition itself in the shadow of the heat shield.

It takes approximately eight minutes for a signal from the probe to reach Earth. While the Parker Solar Probe is within 0.25 astronomical units (AU), it is in the science phase of the mission. This is because radiation from the Sun will interfere with communications and sometimes the shield will be blocking the antenna. The rest of the orbit will be the communication phase, when the spacecraft can safely transmit data back to Earth.

The Parker Solar Probe mission has four main scientific objectives. The primary goal is to answer a question that scientists have been investigating for over sixty years: determining how energy flows through the corona and accelerates the solar wind. The spacecraft will also study the structure and dynamics of the Sun's magnetic field at the origins of the solar wind. Scientists will further attempt to determine how the particles of solar wind are transporting and accelerating. Lastly, the mission is hoping to explain why the Sun's outer atmosphere has a higher temperature than the surface. Data will be collected by four instrument suites that are designed to investigate each of these scientific goals. The first image captured by Parker Solar Probe was released by NASA December 12, 2018.

Contributions

Parker Solar Probe is equipped with four scientific instrument suites to collect data to reach the mission's science goals. The Electromagnetic Fields Investigation (FIELDS) is comprised of two flux-gate magnetometers, a search-coil magnetometer, and five plasma voltage sensors. FIELDS measures the scale and shape of the Sun's magnetic and electric fields within its atmosphere. It observes turbulence within the heliosphere to help understand the process that causes the magnetic field lines to re-align. FIELDS was built and is operated by scientists at the University of California's Berkeley Space Science Laboratory.

The spacecraft's imaging system is known as WISPR, Wide-Field Imager for Parker Solar Probe. WISPR takes photographs of coronal mass ejections and other ejections from the Sun. It also images the corona and solar wind before the spacecraft travels through it. WISPR will help link activity within the Sun's atmosphere overall with the measurements the probe makes when traveling through the corona and solar wind. WISPR was developed by the Naval Research Laboratory's Solar and Heliosphysics Physics Branch in Washington, D.C.

The Solar Wind Electrons Alphas and Protons Investigation (SWEAP) is made up of two complimentary instrument systems; Solar Probe Cup (SPC) and Solar Probe Analyzers (SPAN). They will count the number of electrons, protons, and helium ions within the solar wind. The instruments will also measure the velocity, density, and temperature of the particles. This will help scientists better understand solar wind and coronal plasma. SWEAP is a joint project between the Space Science Laboratory and the Smithsonian Astrophysical Observatory in Cambridge, Massachusetts.

The fourth experiment is the Integrated Science Investigation of the Sun, abbreviated ISOIS, (pronounced ee-sis). The acronym also incorporates the symbol for the Sun. Its two instruments, Energetic Particle Instruments (EPI), measure particles over a vast range of energies. It will investigate the life cycles of electrons, ions, and protons, where they originate from, what caused their acceleration, and how they travel through the solar system. ISOIS was a collaboration between the Applied Physics Laboratory at John Hopkins University, CalTech, NASA's Goddard Space Flight Center, and the Southwest Research Institute in San Antonio. The project is operated by the University of New Hampshire in Durham.

NASA released the first photographs taken by Parker Solar Probe on December 12, 2018. Those images are the first ever taken from within the Sun's outer atmosphere. They show bright streams which are coronal streamers, emanating from the sun. Mercury appears in the images as a bright spot.

Context

Helios 1 and 2 were a joint mission between NASA and West Germany. Helios 1 was launched from Cape Canaveral December 10, 1974, followed by Helios 2 in January of 1976. The orbiters were built in Germany and were the first constructed outside

Encapsulated in its payload fairing, the Parker Solar Probe is transported out of the Astrotech processing facility to Cape Canaveral. (NASA)

the U.S. or Russia to leave Earth. Helios 1 reached first perihelion in late February 1975, becoming the closest object to reach the Sun. On its second perihelion, temperatures of the spacecraft reached 405 kelvins (270 degrees Fahrenheit) causing some of the instruments to not function properly. Thermal insulation was increased on Helios 2, along with other small changes learned from the first spacecraft. Because of this, Helios 2 was able to travel even closer to the Sun. It reached its closest perihelion in April 1976, a distance of 0.29 AU (about 43.4 million kilometers or 27 million miles) and set the record for fastest man-made object traveling at 257,500 kilometers per hour (160,000 miles per hour). Helios 2 held both records until the Parker Solar Probe reached its first perihelion in October 2018. The Helios orbiters studied solar wind, the Sun's magnetic field, cosmic rays, and dust and ion tails of three comets. Helios 2 had a problem with a

radio transponder and was deactivated December 23, 1979. Helios 1 remained operational for over ten years, before being shut down February 18, 1985.

Several other spacecraft have been launched following the Helios mission, but remain in Earth's orbit, follow Earth's orbit, or orbit near L1 Lagrange point. The earliest, Global Geospace Geoscience (GGS) WIND was launched in 1994. GGS WIND studies solar wind, plasma and particles emitted from the Sun and is creating a baseline for comparison with data collected by the Parker Solar Probe. Other probes study the Sun's magnetic field cycles, solar flares, coronal mass ejections, and how these affect the Earth's magnetic field, climate, and life.

—*Jennifer L. Campbell*

See Also: MESSENGER; Solar and Heliospheric Observatory

Further Reading

Anderson, Paul Scott. "1st Image from inside Sun's Atmosphere." *EarthSky*, 18 Dec. 2018, earthsky.org/space/parker-solar-probe-1st-image-from-inside-suns-atmosphere. Article summarizing the Parker Solar Probe's first close flyby of the Sun, including the first image the probe sent back to Earth.

Driesman, Andrew, et al. "Journey to the Center of the Solar System: How the Parker Solar Probe Survives Close Encounters with the Sun." *IEEE Spectrum*, vol. 56, no. 5, May 2019, pp. 32–53., doi:10.1109/mspec.2019.8701197. Article written by mission scientists about how the spacecraft will survive its close flybys of the sun and traveling through the corona.

"Parker Solar Probe." *Johns Hopkins University Applied Physics Laboratory*, National Aeronautics and Space Administration, www.parkersolarprobe.jhuapl.edu/. Website and blog for the Parker Solar Probe mission produced by the Applied Physics Laboratory.

"Parker Solar Probe." *National Aeronautics and Space Administration*, www.nasa.gov/parkersolarprobe. NASA's official website with news and information about the Parker Solar Probe mission and findings.

"Parker Solar Probe: A Mission to Touch the Sun." *Parker Solar Probe - Media Resources*, National Aeronautics and Space Administration, Aug. 2018, www.nasa.gov/content/parker-solar-probe-media-resources. The informational packet NASA provided to the media ahead of the spacecraft's launch. Includes fast face sheets as well as detailed explanations of the science goals, instruments onboard, and spacecraft particulars.

University of Michigan. "Solving the Sun's Super-Heating Mystery with Parker Solar Probe." *ScienceDaily*, 4 June 2019, www.sciencedaily.com/releases/2019/06/190604162532.htm. Article from the University of Michigan scientists that have a theory as to why the Sun's corona is hotter than the surface, and hope that the Parker Solar Probe will help prove their theory.

Pegasus Launch Vehicles

Date: Beginning April 5, 1990
Type of technology: Reusable launch vehicles

Pegasus is a satellite launch vehicle, developed by the Orbital Sciences Corporation, that uses a novel air-launching system. Pegasus is dropped from an aircraft, flying at about 12,000 meters (40,000 feet), that serves as a low-cost, recoverable first stage, reducing the cost of satellite launching compared to conventional ground-launched rockets.

Summary of the Technology

The Orbital Sciences Corporation, located in Dulles, Virginia, developed a novel satellite launch vehicle, the Pegasus, that can place small satellites into orbit around the Earth at a cost of about half that of the traditional expendable launch vehicles, like the Scout, that were available at the time Pegasus first flew. Pegasus obtains its cost advantage over traditional satellite launch vehicles by using the air-launching technique. Pegasus is a winged satellite launch vehicle that is carried aloft and dropped from below a high-flying aircraft, with this reusable aircraft functioning as the boost vehicle for Pegasus. The first Pegasus rocket was launched on April 5, 1990, and it successfully placed Pegsat, a satellite that released chemicals used to study the Earth's upper atmosphere, into a 409-by-507-kilometer near-circular orbit.

The original Pegasus launch vehicle was a four-stage rocket, weighing about 19,000 kilograms, with a length of 15.5 meters and a body diameter of 1.3 meters. The first three stages used solid propellant, but the fourth stage, called the Hydrazine Auxiliary Propulsion System, burned liquid hydrazine. Pegasus could place a payload of 375 kilograms in a 200-kilometer orbit. The last of the original Pegasus rockets was launched on October 22, 1998, after Orbital Sciences Corporation had developed an upgraded version of the Pegasus. Nine original Pegasus launch vehicles were flown. Of these, seven successfully placed satellites into orbit, a success rate of 77 percent. The upgraded Pegasus, the Pegasus XL, was first launched in 1994. The Pegasus XL is a three-stage, solid-propellant rocket. The Pegasus XL measures 17.6 meters long, has a body diameter of 1.3 meters, and weighs about 24,000 kilograms. The Pegasus XL can place a 460-kilogram payload in a 200-kilometer circular orbit, or a 200-kilogram payload into a 1,000-kilometer circular orbit. The first two Pegasus XL flights were failures. The first Pegasus XL was destroyed on launching, on June 27, 1994. The second Pegasus XL suffered a failure of its second-stage rocket and was destroyed by the range safety officer on June 22, 1995. In its first nineteen flights, through December 4, 1999, the Pegasus XL successfully placed satellites in orbit sixteen times, a success rate of 84 percent. Orbital Sciences Corporation has developed a fourth stage for the Pegasus XL. Using this fourth stage, the Pegasus XL can send payloads of about 100 kilograms on Earth-escape trajectories.

During development of the Pegasus launch vehicle, a B-52 aircraft, which had been used by NASA to air-launch other rocket vehicles, was used to carry the Pegasus aloft for launching. The final launching of a Pegasus from a B-52 occurred in December, 1994, and placed the Advanced

A Pegasus launch vehicle before being mated to a B-52. (NASA)

Photovoltaic and Electronic Experiments (APEX) satellite into orbit. Once the success of the Pegasus rocket had been demonstrated, Orbital Sciences Corporation purchased a Lockheed L-1011 aircraft, which it called *Stargazer*, to carry the Pegasus aloft.

A typical Pegasus XL launching begins with the L-1011 aircraft carrying the Pegasus to an altitude of about 12,000 meters (40,000 feet) and traveling at a speed of about 235 meters (770 feet) per second. The Pegasus, which is held in a horizontal position below the aircraft, is released, and it free falls for about five seconds before its first-stage engine ignites. The first-stage rocket motor burns for about seventy-three seconds. During this time period the delta-winged Pegasus climbs to an altitude of about 63,000 meters (207,000 feet) and reaches a speed of about 2,500 meters (8,300 feet) per second. At this point the first stage, which includes the delta wing, drops away, and the second-stage rocket motor begins its seventy-three-second burn. The second stage carries the payload to about 216,100 meters (709,000 feet) and reaches a speed of 5,400 meters (17,800 feet) per second. During the second-stage burn, the payload fairing, which covers the third-stage rocket and the satellite, drops away. After the second-stage rocket burns out, the second and third stages remain attached, coasting for about six and a half minutes before the small third-stage motor ignites, about ten minutes after launching. The third stage burns for sixty-five seconds, carrying the payload to orbital altitude, several hundred miles above the Earth's surface, at a speed of about 7,500 meters (24,700 feet) per second. The entire launch sequence takes about eleven minutes.

Because the Pegasus is air-launched, launchings can be conducted from any site where the appropriate support and tracking facilities are available. Pegasus launchings have been conducted from the Air Force Western Test Range, at Vandenberg Air Force Base in California; the Air Force Eastern Test Range, at Cape Canaveral in Florida; the National Aeronautics and Space Administration (NASA) Wallops Flight Facility, in Virginia; and the Canary Islands, off the coast of Africa.

The Pegasus XL payload fairing was designed to accommodate the third-stage rocket motor as well as several satellites. By launching multiple satellites, Orbital Sciences Corporation further minimizes the cost of placing each satellite in orbit.

Pegasus suffered one failure with long-term implications. During the May, 1994, launching the Hydrazine Auxiliary Propulsion System (HAPS) failed to burn to completion, thrusting for only 275 seconds rather than 300 seconds. As a result of the premature engine shutdown, the STEP-2 satellite, a military satellite designed to test space technology, was placed in a lower orbit than had been planned. This premature cutoff left unburned fuel in the rocket's tanks. On June 3, 1996, the HAPS stage exploded, producing 150 fragments large enough to be tracked in orbit, along with more numerous fragments of space debris too small to be tracked by ground-based radar. The Air Force tracks more than six thousand pieces of space debris, much of it from explosions of the upper stages of satellite launch vehicles. This space debris poses a collision hazard to other Earth-orbiting satellites, particularly large objects like the International Space Station.

Orbital Sciences Corporation has also developed a ground-launched version of the Pegasus. This rocket combines the first and second stages of the Air Force Minuteman II intercontinental ballistic missile with two stages from the Pegasus XL. Since the Minuteman II missiles were deactivated in compliance with the Strategic Arms Reduction Treaty in 1991, these surplus missiles provide another low-cost satellite launch vehicle. The first of these new vehicles was launched successfully from Vandenberg Air Force Base on January 26, 2000. As of early 2005, the Pegasus booster had been launched thirty-eight times with only six failures. Notable spacecraft it had placed into orbit were the Fast Auroral Snapshot Explorer (FAST), the Galaxy Evolution Explorer (GALEX), the Handheld Earth-oriented, Real-time, Cooperative, User-friendly, Location-targeting and Environmental System (HERCULES), High Energy Transient Explorer (HETE), the Transition Region and Coronal Explorer (TRACE), and the X-43A scramjet demonstration vehicles.

Contributions

Air-launching of rockets was a relatively well-developed technology prior to Pegasus. The Air Force and NASA had launched a series of rocket-powered research aircraft, from the Bell X-1, which broke the sound barrier in 1947, to the X-15, which flew to the edge of space in the 1960's from B-29 and B-52 bombers. The Air Force also developed a Satellite Interceptor, which was air-launched from a fighter aircraft. However, the development of the Pegasus launch vehicle demonstrated the feasibility of a lofted

satellite launch vehicle. Because the aircraft, which serves as the first stage of the Pegasus, is recovered and reused, perfection of the air-launching technique for satellites lowered the cost per pound for payloads delivered to Earth orbit.

The comparatively low cost of launching a satellite using the Pegasus launch vehicle has opened new opportunities for commercialization of space. ORBCOMM, which is a partnership between Orbital Sciences Corporation and Teleglobe Incorporated, has become the first commercial provider of global data and message communications through a series of satellites in low-Earth orbit. ORBCOMM satellites relay the radio signals, which are used by corporations to track rail cars, fishing vessels, trailers, and other valuable assets, as well as monitor utility meters, contents of storage tanks, and performance of wells and pipelines. Pegasus has also been used to launch two communications relay satellites for Brazil: the Data Collection Satellite-1, launched in 1993, and the Data Collection Satellite-2, launched in 1998. These satellites relayed data collected by remote meteorological stations in the Amazon River Basin of South America to scientists who have used the data to better understand the

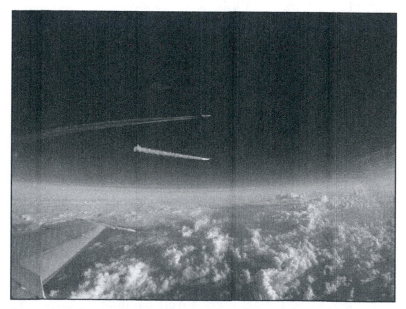

Pegasus rocket igniting seconds after dropping from Orbital ATK's L-1011 Stargazer aircraft. (NASA)

environmental changes taking place in the rain forest.

By combining multiple payloads in a single launch, Orbital Sciences Corporation has minimized the cost of orbiting small payloads. On April 21, 1997, Pegasus XL launched a 209-kilogram Minisat-1, carrying an extreme ultraviolet spectrograph to study interstellar gases and a gamma-ray burst detector. The Minisat-1 was launched for the Instituto Nacional de Tecnica Aeroespacial (INTA) in Spain. However, the Minisat-1 satellite did not use all the available Pegasus XL payload mass. This provided an opportunity to launch a small commercial satellite, Celestis, at a minimal cost. Celestis, Inc., which developed the Celestis satellite, provides "space funerals," launching the cremated remains of individuals into orbit. The first Celestis satellite carried the remains of twenty-five individuals, including Star Trek creator Gene Roddenberry, space physicist Gerard O'Neill, rocket engineer Krafft Ehricke, and the founder of the International Space University, Todd Hawley, at a cost of $4,800 per person.

The Pegasus has become the launch vehicle of choice for NASA's Small Explorer Satellite (SMEX) program, launching all but the first satellite in that program. Small Explorer satellites launched by the Pegasus include the Fast Auroral Snapshot Explorer, launched in 1996 to collect real-time measurements of the plasma density, electron temperature, and magnetic field properties while it was passing through the northern auroral zone; the Transition Region and Coronal Explorer, launched in 1998, which carried a telescope to image the Sun, exploring the connection between the fine-scale magnetic fields and the behavior of the plasma in the outer regions of the Sun; the Submillimeter Wave Astronomy Satellite (SWAS), launched in 1998, which carried a submillimeter wave telescope to investigate the chemical and isotopic composition of dense interstellar clouds; and the Wide-Field Infrared Explorer, launched in 1999, which studied high-frequency changes in output that provide information on the structure of the deep interior of the stars, showing that Alpha Ursa Major, the brightest star in the Big Dipper, is expanding rapidly, on its way to becoming a giant star.

Pegasus is also used as the launch vehicle for satellites in the Student Explorer Demonstration Initiative (STEDI), a NASA program to provide university students with the opportunity to participate in the design and development of small research satellites. The first STEDI satellite, the Student Nitric Oxide Explorer (SNOE), was launched in 1998. SNOE was built at the University of Colorado to study the effects of the Sun's x-ray emissions on the density of nitric oxide as a function of height in the atmosphere.

Pegasus launch vehicles have orbited a variety of scientific research satellites, including the Total Ozone Mapping Spectrometer, in 1996, to study variations in the Earth's ozone layer; the High Energy Transient Explorer, in 1996, to study an unusual astronomical phenomenon called gamma-ray bursts; and the Fast On-Orbit Recording of Transient Events satellite, in 1997, to develop technology to monitor compliance with nuclear test ban treaties. Pegasus has also launched a series of commercial satellites including Seastar, in 1997, a commercial Earth-surveillance satellite for the Orbital Imaging Corporation, and a series of ORBCOMM communications satellites, providing communications for private industry.

Context

When NASA developed the space shuttle, NASA planned to abandon all expendable launch vehicles and launch all commercial, military, and scientific satellites into orbit using the shuttle. After the *Challenger* failure in 1986, and the two-year suspension of shuttle operations, NASA began to reconsider its decision to shift all satellite launchings to the shuttle. In August, 1986, President Ronald W. Reagan announced that, when the space shuttle returned to service, it would carry no commercial satellites. In May, 1987, NASA announced that it would also purchase expendable rockets to launch its small satellites, reserving the space shuttle for missions that required a human presence in space.

These decisions created a new demand for expendable launch vehicles. Orbital Sciences Corporation, which had been founded to develop an "orbital transfer rocket," a rocket that would be used to boost satellites carried into orbit by the space shuttle into higher orbits, saw this new demand as an opportunity. The company focused on the smallest satellites and examined ways to use a small air-launched rocket to carry satellites into orbit at minimal cost.

Use of an aircraft to carry the Pegasus rocket to 12,000 meters (40,000 feet) significantly lowered the cost of placing small satellites in Earth orbit compared to expendable launch vehicles such as the Scout. By providing lower-cost access to space, Pegasus made it possible to launch more scientific research satellites within the same research budget than if conventional launch vehicles had been employed. At the same time Pegasus was being developed, NASA began to shift its focus from launching a few large, expensive research satellites to the "faster, better, cheaper" concept in which highly focused, small research satellites were funded. The Pegasus has served as the launch vehicle for all but the first satellite in NASA's Small Explorer program and in the Student Explorer Demonstration Initiative Program.

Because of the comparatively low cost of launching satellites using the Pegasus, new opportunities have opened up for commercial development of space. By providing low-cost launch access to space for a variety of private enterprises, Pegasus has spawned the development of a variety of space enterprises. Orbital Sciences Corporation itself is a partner in two of these enterprises, ORBCOMM and ORBVIEW.

Pegasus launched two ORBVIEW satellites, which obtained color images of the Earth for commercial and scientific use. The ORBVIEW satellites are the first privately owned satellites to provide color images of the Earth's land and oceans. The ORBVIEW satellites collect color images that assist commercial fishing fleets in finding schools of fish, forestry and agriculture specialists in monitoring tree and crop health and distribution, and NASA in monitoring the Earth's carbon cycle and its effects on global warming.

—George J. Flynn

See also: Launch Vehicles; Launch Vehicles: Reusable; Private Industry and Space Exploration; Saturn Launch Vehicles; Small Explorer Program; Space Centers, Spaceports, and Launch Sites; Telecommunications Satellites: Private and Commercial.

Further Reading

Butrica, Andrew J. *Single Stage to Orbit: Politics, Space Technology, and the Quest for Reusable Rocketry.* Baltimore: Johns Hopkins University Press, 2003. NASA-piloted launch vehicles have traditionally used a multistage approach to reach orbit. This work tells the story of the attempts by research groups and industrial teams to develop a single-stage-to-orbit technology that promises more routine access to space and a lessening of the cost per kilogram for placing payloads into orbit.

Dorsey, Gary. *Silicon Sky: How One Small Start-Up Went Over the Top to Beat the Big Boys into Satellite Heaven.* Reading, Mass.: Perseus Books, 1999. A history of Orbital Sciences Corporation, covering the time period from about 1992 through 1995, focusing on its attempts to design, develop, and launch the ORBCOMM series of satellites. This book won the 1999 Distinguished Literary Contribution award from the Institute of Electrical and Electronics Engineers for its behind-the-scenes account of the engineering and management team discussions, decision making, and problem-solving strategies that resulted in the successful launching of ORBCOMM.

Isakowitz, Steven J., Joseph P. Hopkins, Jr., and Joshua B. Hopkins. *International Reference Guide to Space Launch Systems*. 3d ed. Reston, Va.: American Institute of Aeronautics and Astronautics, 1999. A reference guide that contains an up-to-date guide to launch vehicles around the world, including performance figures describing each launch system in detail, including cost, performance graphs, flight history and failure descriptions, vehicle design, payload capabilities, and vehicle history. Well illustrated throughout.

Zimmerman, Robert. *The Chronological Encyclopedia of Discoveries in Space*. Westport, Conn.: Oryx Press, 2000. Provides a complete chronological history of all crewed and robotic spacecraft and explains flight events and scientific results. Suitable for all levels of research.

Pioneer Missions 1-5

Date: October 11, 1958, to June 26, 1960
Type of spacecraft: Planetary exploration

The Pioneer probes began the exploration of the solar system. Although Pioneer 5 was the only unqualified success, achieving its aim of a heliocentric orbit between the paths of Earth and Venus, all five early Pioneers made important discoveries about the radiation belts around Earth.

Key Figures

Louis Dunn, president of Space Technology
  Laboratories (STL)
Ruben F. Mettler, executive vice president of STL
Abe Silverstein (1908-2001), director of Space-
  flight Development, NASA
William H. Pickering (1910-2004), director of the
  Jet Propulsion Laboratory
James A. Van Allen (1914-2006), participating
  scientist

Summary of the Missions

The first Pioneer project, whose goal was to launch uncrewed spacecraft toward the Moon for the International Geophysical Year (IGY), began in 1957 when the Advanced Research Projects Agency (ARPA) authorized the program. In March, 1958, Secretary of Defense Neil H. McElroy announced that the U.S. Air Force would launch three probes in an attempt to place a scientific payload in the vicinity of the Moon. When the National Aeronautics and Space Administration (NASA) was created in 1958, it assumed responsibility for the nation's space programs, including the Pioneer project. One of the purposes in forming NASA was to unify the diverse and competing space programs of the Navy, Army, and Air Force. At that time, NASA's intention was to compete with the Soviet Union in the conquest of space. Abe Silverstein, director of Spaceflight Development, made it clear that he hoped that the United States would leap ahead of the Soviet Union in lunar and planetary exploration with the Pioneer program.

Because the majority of the early Pioneers were failures, they never won much public respect, but they were interesting spacecraft that lived up to their name—they pioneered uncrewed interplanetary travel. These probes were modest vehicles, weighing around 45 kilograms, designed to investigate the medium between the planets. The series started inauspiciously on August 17, 1958. An explosion in the first-stage engine ripped open the vehicle after it had traveled about 16 kilometers above Earth. Although "Pioneer" was a name applied by NASA only to successfully launched deep-space vehicles, this initial launch was sometimes unofficially referred to as Pioneer 0.

On October 11, 1958, another attempt was made to "shoot the Moon." The Pioneer 1 probe was perched atop a three-stage experimental rocket configuration: The first or bottom stage was a Thor intermediate range ballistic missile, the second stage was a modified Vanguard, and the third stage was an advanced version of the Vanguard. The overall objective of the mission was to circle the Moon and relay to Earth infrared images of its far side. Other objectives were to measure radiation, micrometeoritic density, magnetic fields, and temperatures in interplanetary space. A secondary but essential goal was to get all three main stages to fire in proper sequence.

Pioneer 1 was launched at 4:42 a.m. eastern daylight time or 08:42 Coordinated Universal Time (UTC), and all three stages fired properly. After second stage burnout, eight small rockets mounted sideways imparted a spin of 120 revolutions per minute to the third and fourth stages to stabilize them in altitude. Unfortunately, an error in the Thor guidance system resulted in a speed slightly less than escape velocity (the speed necessary to break loose from Earth's gravitational pull) and a 3.5° inaccuracy in the angle at which the first stage was lofted into space. Later analysis revealed that the launch would still have been a success were it not for the third stage swerving sharply to one side as the rocket ignited. Pioneer 1 did reach a record distance from Earth of 115,000 kilometers, nearly a third of the distance to the Moon, before falling back and reentering Earth's atmosphere over the South Pacific forty-eight hours later.

According to Louis Dunn, technical director of the entire project, Pioneer 1 was a success, despite its failure to reach the Moon, because this was the first time that complexmechanisms involving rockets, explosive bolts, and precise timers had worked in perfect sequence. Pioneer 1 had broken all altitude records, and it had sent back the first measurements of radiation above 4,000 kilometers. According to Dunn, the launch demonstrated the soundness of the vehicle design, which was capable of performing a wide variety of space missions.

Pioneer 2 had the same objectives as Pioneer 1, though some modifications had been made in the payload. For example, an image-scanning television system created by the Space Technology Laboratories (STL) had replaced the infrared device on

Pioneer 1. Changes had also been made in the rockets to ensure cleaner separation of the stages, such as improved retrorocket batteries better able to withstand cold temperatures. Despite these improvements, Pioneer 2 proved to be a disaster. After a successful launch at 2:30 a.m. (07:30 UTC) on November 8, 1958, and a successful separation of the first and second stages, the third stage failed to ignite. Pioneer 2 climbed to an altitude of only 1,600 kilometers before falling back to Earth. The instrument package burned up as the probe plunged into the atmosphere above east-central Africa. The flight had lasted less than 45 minutes.

Thor-Able I with the Pioneer I spacecraft atop, prior to launch at Eastern Test Range at what is now Kennedy Space Center. (NASA)

Problems that plagued the first three Pioneers continued to plague Pioneer 3. This time, Pioneer's target would not be the Moon. Instead, it was to orbit the Sun. The objectives of the mission were to measure radiation at extremely high altitudes and to test a moonlight-activated trigger mechanism for a photographic experiment. Overall vehicular engineering for Pioneer 3 was done jointly by the Army Ballistic Missile Agency (ABMA), under the technical direction of Werner von Braun, and by the Jet Propulsion Laboratory (JPL), a NASA facility. The first stage was a modified Jupiter intermediate range ballistic missile. The second, third, and fourth stages were solid-fueled JPL rockets. The Army called its combination of rockets the Juno 2.

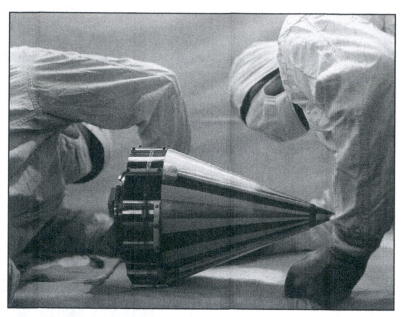

These technicians, wearing "cleanroom" attire, inspect the Pioneer III probe before shipping it to Cape Canaveral. (NASA)

At 12:45 a.m. (05:45 UTC) on December 6, 1958, the Juno 2 began to lift the 5.9 kilograms of delicate instruments from the launch pad at Cape Canaveral. Shortly after launch, T. Keith Glennan disclosed that the course angle was 3° too low and the rocket's speed was 1,600 kilometers an hour slower than the desired escape velocity. Von Braun blamed the first-stage Jupiter, which had stopped burning 3.7 seconds short of the planned burning time of 3 minutes. The shortened firing time was probably caused by improper adjustment of a valve designed to keep the rocket fuel under constant pressure. Initially, Jack Froehlich held out hope that the other stages could make up the deficit, but William H. Pickering later told a news conference that the payload would not reach the vicinity of the Moon. Pioneer 3 soared to an altitude of 107,313 kilometers before Earth's gravity pulled it back to a flaming end in the atmosphere over French West Africa at 5:15 p.m. eastern standard time on December 8, 1958 (00:15 UTC, December 9, 1958). In one way, Pioneer 3 was a fruitful failure, because,

as it fell back to Earth, it transmitted data on the newly discovered zone of radiation around the planet.

After four failures, further disappointment was in store for U.S. space program planners. On January 2, 1959, the Soviet Union sent a much heavier payload (361 kilograms) past the Moon and into orbit around the Sun—a feat the United States had been trying to accomplish with its Pioneer program. Thus, it was anticlimactic when Pioneer 4 was shot into orbit around the Sun a few months later. Pioneer 4 had the same program objectives as Pioneer 3, although an enhanced Geiger tube encased in additional lead shielding was added to improve the measuring of radiation.

An Army team from the Redstone Arsenal in Huntsville, Alabama, headed by Kurt H. Debus, was in charge of this launch. The Juno 2 with its Pioneer 4 probe left the launch pad at Cape Canaveral at 12:10:30 a.m. (05:10:30 UTC) on March 3, 1959. Hugh L. Dryden soon announced that the 6-kilogram, gold-plated payload would pass about 56,350 kilometers from the Moon. Unfortunately, this would not be close enough to trigger the probe's photoelectric sensor, sample the Moon's radiation, or measure its magnetic field.

Although Pioneer 4 became an artificial satellite around the Sun, it was a silent one since its tiny batteries allowed intermittent transmissions for only a few months. Pioneer 5 became the first probe to test radio communications at interplanetary distances. This probe was mounted in the nose cone of a three-stage Thor-Able 4 rocket that launched from Cape Canaveral at 8:02 a.m. (13:02 UTC) on March 12, 1960. Pioneer 5 was successfully placed in an 848.5-million-kilometer heliocentric orbit. Its radio was powered by solar energy through 4,800 photovoltaic cells covering the satellite's four extended vanes. The spacecraft radioed back information on magnetic fields, cosmic radiation, solar particles, micrometeorite collisions, and interplanetary temperatures. It continued to telemeter data to Earth from a distance of more than 36 million kilometers, a record for long-distance communication that went unchallenged for more than two and a half years.

Pioneer 5 was a case of *finis coronat opus* (the end crowns the work). It had been five months since the last successful American space project, and NASA anxiously desired a success. Abe Silverstein saw Pioneer 5 as an important stepping-stone in the ten-year program of space exploration that he had helped to develop. Pioneer 5 had proven that a spacecraft could endure the rigors of interplanetary space and radio useful information back to Earth. The way was now open for uncrewed exploration of Mars and Venus.

Contributions

The greatest scientific contribution of the early Pioneer probes was to clarify the ways in which various solar emissions interact with Earth's magnetic field. Explorer 1 had begun the discovery of Earth's radiation zones, called the Van Allen radiation belts after James A. Van Allen, who had been in charge of the satellite and space-probe experiments that led to their discovery. The early Pioneers provided a more detailed understanding of the two doughnut-shaped radiation zones ringing the planet. Pioneer 1, for example, determined the radial extent of the radiation belt and first observed that it actually is a band. Pioneer 2 discovered that Earth's equatorial region has a higher energy radiation than previously thought.

Helped by these early findings, Pioneer 3 made the program's greatest discoveries in its two passes through these radiation zones. It found that there are two widely separated radiation belts around Earth: an inner band between 2,250 and 5,500 kilometers from the planet and an outer band extending from 13,000 to 19,000 kilometers. Geiger counters aboard Pioneer 3 showed that radiation grew more intense near the center of the Van Allen belts, whereas 1,000 kilometers away the radiation dwindled to a low level.

The most striking result of Pioneer 4 was its discovery that an immensely greater quantity of trapped radiation existed in the outer zone on March 3, 1959 (Pioneer 4), than on December 6, 1958 (Pioneer 3). Pioneer 4 reported the same radiation intensity in the inner belt, but in the outer belt it found conditions radically different from those reported by Pioneer 3. During the time between these probes, radiation had increased considerably and the belt had expanded in cross section. Van Allen suggested that these changes were the result of a solar magnetic storm, leading to five consecutive nights of strong auroral activity in the days immediately preceding Pioneer 4's launch. The period preceding Pioneer 3's flight had been geomagnetically quiet.

Besides its great accomplishment of long-range radio transmission, Pioneer 5 also investigated the space between the planets. It observed cosmic rays in space, completely free of any Earthly effects, showing the rays were truly galactic, not solar, phenomena. It detected particles accelerated by solar flares and found that energetic electrons in Earth's outer radiation zone arose from an acceleration mechanism within its geomagnetic field rather than direct injection of energetic electrons from the Sun. Pioneer 5 also found that Earth's magnetic field

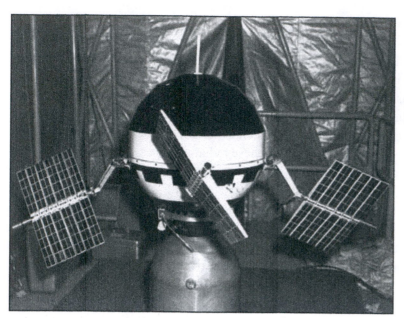

Pioneer 5 mounted to its Thor Able launcher. (NASA)

ended about fourteen Earth radii from its daylight side, a much greater distance than predicted earlier.

Context

The Pioneer program was begun prior to the creation of NASA and was a phenomenon of the earliest days of American space development. Despite the inevitable failures of a new program, sufficient successes occurred to convince several important scientists that similar interplanetary spacecraft were a necessity for future explorations of space. Indeed, the early Pioneers pointed to the need for further exploration, because they had raised more questions than they answered—questions about micrometeorites and magnetic fields, about the radiation milieu in outer space, and about the transient effects of solar flares.

The first group of Pioneer probes also encouraged progress in other areas. For example, to communicate with these flights, tracking hardware had to be developed. JPL was in the forefront of this development, and to support the Pioneer flights JPL built what ultimately became the Deep Space Network. Managed by JPL for NASA, this communications network began by tracking the Pioneer probes

toward the Moon and into deep space. By late 1958, as the first Pioneers were launched, JPL had established tracking stations at Cape Canaveral, Puerto Rico, and Goldstone Lake, California. The basic functions performed by these stations were to track spacecraft positions with high precision, to issue commands to the spacecraft, and to acquire and process scientific data from the spacecraft. Because of JPL's experience with the early Pioneers, NASA assigned more responsibilities to the laboratory in its Ranger, Surveyor, and Mariner programs.

Besides illustrating the institutional context of the early U.S. space program, the history of the Pioneer 1 through 5 missions also reveals something of its political context. Although NASA was created to eliminate certain rivalries in the space program, the Air Force's failures with the first three Pioneers and the eventual Army successes with the later Pioneers show that this rivalry continued even after NASA's creation. More important than this rivalry, however, was the competition between the United States and the Soviet Union. NASA wanted to surpass the Soviet Union by launching the first deep-space probe, but because of the failure of Pioneer 3, Luna 1 (later renamed Mechta, or "Dream") became the first artificial satellite orbiting the Sun. The Soviet Union had again bested its American rivals. These Soviet successes encouraged NASA officials to press for a more vigorous space program.

This political rivalry played a role in the creation of later Pioneers. The early Pioneers showed what could be done by modifying existing technologies, but they also revealed the need for new approaches. The later Pioneer spacecraft were therefore considerably more complex, with average weights of three and a half times the early Pioneers. While the new instruments still included a preponderance of particle and field sensors, more sophisticated imaging devices were used. Because JPL was already so heavily involved in lunar and planetary programs, the new Pioneers became a major responsibility of the Ames Research Center, with the Goddard Space Flight Center also contributing. Unlike the first group of Pioneers, which, except for Pioneer 5, were plagued by unreliable equipment, the second group, Pioneers 6 through 9, were extremely reliable. Although the early Pioneers failed in their ambitious overall objectives, they achieved many other goals and opened the path to the planets for later spacecraft.

—*Robert J. Paradowski*

See also: Explorers: Solar; Jet Propulsion Laboratory; Launch Vehicles; Lunar Exploration; Magellan: Venus; Pioneer Missions 6-E; Pioneer 10; Pioneer 11; Planetary Exploration; Ulysses: Solar Polar Mission; Voyager Program; Voyager 1: Jupiter; Voyager 1: Saturn; Voyager 2: Saturn.

Further Reading

Corliss, William R. *Summary*. Vol. 1 in *The Interplanetary Pioneers*. NASA SP-278. Washington, D.C.: Government Printing Office, 1972. The first of three volumes on the Pioneer program and the most accessible for the general reader. Although he emphasizes the second group of Pioneer missions (Pioneers 6 through 9), Corliss, in his well-illustrated and extensively documented account, makes some interesting comparisons between the first and second groups of probes.

Heppenheimer, T. A. *Countdown: A History of Space Flight*. New York: John Wiley, 1997. A detailed historical narrative of the human conquest of space. Heppenheimer traces the development of piloted flight through the military rocketry programs of the era preceding World War II. Covers both the American and the Soviet attempts to place vehicles, spacecraft, and humans into the hostile environment of space. More than a dozen pages are devoted to bibliographic references.

Hirsch, Richard, and Joseph John Trento. *The National Aeronautics and Space Administration*. New York: Praeger, 1973. Hirsch was aerospace assistant to the National Aeronautics and Space Council. He died before completing this popular history of NASA. Using Hirsch's notes and files, Trento finished the book as he thought Hirsch himself would have done. Though the book does not avoid controversial issues, its emphasis is on NASA's remarkable accomplishments, including some of the flights of the early Pioneer spacecraft.

Kivelson, Margaret G., and Christopher T. Russell. *Introduction to Space Physics*. New York: Cambridge University Press, 1995. A thorough exploration of space physics. Some aspects are suitable for the general reader. Suitable for an introductory college course on space physics.

Koppes, Clayton R. *JPL and the American Space Program: A History of the Jet Propulsion Laboratory*. New Haven, Conn.: Yale University Press, 1982. JPL played an important part in some of the early Pioneer missions, and Koppes analyzes these in the context of the laboratory's evolution. This widely praised book relates the scientific and technical history of the American space program.

Lee, Wayne. *To Rise from Earth: An Easy to Understand Guide to Spaceflight*. New York: Checkmark Books, 1996. This is a good introduction to the science of spaceflight. Although written by an engineer with the NASA Jet Propulsion Laboratory, it is presented in easy-to-understand language. In addition to the theory of spaceflight, it gives some of the history of the human endeavor to explore space.

McDougall, Walter A. *The Heavens and the Earth: A Political History of the Space Age*. 2d ed. Baltimore: Johns Hopkins University Press, 1997. McDougall is a professor of history at the University of California in Berkeley, and his book focuses on the race between the United States and the Soviet Union for technological supremacy in space. His book, which won the 1986 Pulitzer Prize in History, demonstrates the ways in which technology can bring about social and political change, and how politics can influence technology.

Mari, Christopher, ed. *Space Exploration*. New York: H. W. Wilson, 1999. Twenty-five articles (reprinted from magazines), covering the state of the space program at the time of publication, are divided into five sections: John H. Glenn, Jr.'s return to space, the exploration of Mars, the International Space Station, recent mining efforts by commercial industries, and new types of space vehicles and propulsion systems.

Newell, Homer E. *Beyond the Atmosphere: Early Years of Space Science*. NASA SP-4211. Washington, D.C.: Government Printing Office, 1980. This book, part of the NASA History series, vividly captures the early years of space science. Newell tells a multifaceted tale, ranging from the technical to the political, the personal to the institutional, the national to the international. He presents space science as a continuation of traditional science.

Nicks, Oran W. *Far Travelers: The Exploring Machines*. NASA SP-480. Washington, D.C.: Scientific and Technical Information Branch, 1985. A popularly written account of the first twenty-five years of space exploration. The author's approach is thematic rather than chronological, and the Pioneer missions are not discussed until the end of the book, in an interesting chapter entitled "Spinners Last Forever." As a senior NASA official during most of the period about which he writes, Nicks played a major role in shaping and directing NASA's lunar and planetary programs, and his narrative makes excellent use of his personal experiences.

Parks, George K. *Physics of Space Plasmas: An Introduction*. 2d ed. Boulder, Colo.: Westview Press, 2004. Provides a scientific examination of the data returned during what might be called the "golden age" of space physics (1990-2002), when over two dozen satellites were dispatched to investigate space plasma phenomena. Written at the undergraduate level for an introductory course in space plasma, there is also detailed presentation of NASA and ESA spacecraft missions.

Zimmerman, Robert. *The Chronological Encyclopedia of Discoveries in Space*. Westport, Conn.: Oryx Press, 2000. Provides a complete chronological history of all crewed and robotic spacecraft and explains flight events and scientific results. Suitable for all levels of research.

Pioneer Missions 6-E

Date: Beginning December 16, 1965
Type of spacecraft: Planetary exploration

Pioneers 6 through E were the first spacecraft specifically prepared to obtain synoptic information on the effects in interplanetary space of solar activity that varies with the solar cycle, such as the incidence of solar flares.

Key Figures

Glenn A. Reiff (b. 1923), program manager, 1963-1970

Charles F. Hall (1920-1999), project manager until 1980

Richard O. Fimmel (b. 1946), project manager from 1980

Ralph W. Holtzclaw, Spacecraft Systems manager, Ames Research Center

Summary of the Missions

In 1962, in response to a request from Edgar M. Cortright, deputy director of the Office of Space Science for the National Aeronautics and Space Administration (NASA), Space Technology Laboratories (STL) performed a two-and-a-half-month feasibility study for the Pioneer 6 through E spacecraft for the Ames Research Center. This Pioneer project was approved by NASA Associate Administrator Robert C. Seamans, Jr., on November 9, 1962. Following competitive bidding procedures, STL was selected to provide the five spacecraft; the definitive contract was approved by NASA Headquarters on July 30, 1964.

In order to maximize scientific returns, the spacecraft were equipped with spin stabilization such that the spin axis could be oriented perpendicular to the ecliptic plane (the plane of Earth's orbit) and a high-gain transmitting antenna directed at Earth. This choice for the direction of the spin axis meant that the scientific experiments could scan all azimuthal directions in the ecliptic plane. Also, solar cells that provided electrical power to operate the spacecraft could all be oriented parallel to the spacecraft's spin axis, thereby minimizing their weight. Finally, a relatively simple transmitting antenna, called a modified Franklin array, provided a disk-shaped transmission pattern centered on the ecliptic plane, thus maximizing the distance from Earth at which data could still be returned. The 8-watt transmitters were relatively high powered for such small spacecraft. The orbits of the five spacecraft were to be essentially in the ecliptic plane. Long spacecraft lifetimes, at least six months, were another scientific requirement. Masses of the five spacecraft, including 16 to 19 kilograms of experiments, ranged from 62 kilograms for Pioneer 6 to 67 kilograms for Pioneer 9. The main body of these spacecraft was a right cylinder (a cylinder whose side is perpendicular to its base) 0.89 meter high and 0.95 meter in diameter.

The experiments for the five spacecraft were solicited from the scientific community and had to measure interplanetary plasma and the magnetic field or study cosmic-ray gradients and radio propagation. Eighteen proposals were evaluated for experiments for Pioneers 6 and 7 and fifteen for Pioneers 8 and 9; seven experiments were selected for Pioneers 6 and 7 and eight for Pioneers 8 and 9. Because Pioneer E used spare parts from the earlier four spacecraft, it was decided that the Pioneer 8

The design for Pioneer 6, 7, 8, 9, and E. (NASA)

Pioneers 7 and 8 took trajectories farther from the Sun with aphelia (the points in their orbits farthest from the Sun) of 1.1 AU. The two trajectories that passed beyond Earth's orbit also passed through Earth's geomagnetic wake, which is similar to a shadow in the plasma flowing from the Sun. Consequently, experiments on those two spacecraft could collect data on this phenomenon.

Pioneer E was to have a special inward-outward trajectory that would keep it relatively near Earth for more than half a year. The hydraulic pressure in the first stage of the launcher became too low while this stage was firing, however, and was lost altogether about seven seconds before that engine was to complete its firing. This caused the upper stages to move too far from their proper course, and their destruction was commanded about eight minutes after launch.

and 9 experiments should be used. In addition to having the basic plasma, magnetic field, and cosmic-ray experiments carried by Pioneers 6 and 7, Pioneers 8, 9, and E included additional cosmic dust and electric field wave experiments, at the expense of eliminating a second solar plasma experiment.

The five spacecraft, Pioneers 6 to 9 and Pioneer E, were launched from December 16, 1965, to August 27, 1969. The basic launch vehicle was the McDonnell Douglas Thrust-Augmented Improved Delta.

The trajectories of these spacecraft were heliocentric (centered on the Sun) to study phenomena such as cosmic-ray gradients over a range of distances from the Sun. Pioneers 6 and 9 took trajectories closer to the Sun, with perihelia (the points in their orbits closest to the Sun) of 0.81 astronomical unit (one astronomical unit, or AU, is the mean distance of the Earth from the Sun in its orbit) for Pioneer 6 and 0.75 astronomical unit for Pioneer 9.

After each Delta third stage burned out and was separated from the spacecraft, three spacecraft booms unfolded. These booms housed an orientation system nozzle, the magnetometer experiment sensor, and a wobble damper. Then, each spacecraft was automatically oriented, using the timed release of pulses of compressed nitrogen to move its spin axis so that it was perpendicular to the spacecraft-Sun direction. Finally, each spacecraft was moved in a similar way, but under ground control, so that it was perpendicular to the spacecraft-Earth direction as well. Experiments were activated, and high data rates were possible through use of a high-gain antenna.

Plasma and magnetic field data collected as Pioneer 6 departed from Earth showed the magnetopause, or boundary of Earth's magnetic field in space, at an altitude of 11.8 Earth radii. Subsequently, the bow shock, which is "upstream" from

Earth in the solar wind, was encountered at an altitude of 19.5 Earth radii. The Pioneer plasma experiments were improved over those used previously and thus were more detailed in their measurements of the properties of shocked plasma and interplanetary plasma, and of the properties of the bow shock itself.

The Pioneer 6 experiments, soon after launch, were able to fulfill the plan to measure the effects of solar flares in interplanetary space. A flare on December 30, 1965, produced energetic solar protons, measured by cosmic-ray experiments. In this case, effects were strong enough that the measurements were fairly detailed. After study of solar proton data from a number of events, combined with measurements of the interplanetary magnetic field, it was found that energetic solar protons usually began to arrive first from the direction of the magnetic field. Also, for some events, fast solar plasma associated with the solar flares was observed. In addition, the relation between the speed of propagation and the time histories of the energetic solar proton fluxes, along with the longitudes of the solar flare sources, was examined.

Another contribution was an improved description of the discontinuous structure of the interplanetary plasma, using data from various experiments aboard Pioneers 6 and 7. Also, a four-sector structure of the interplanetary magnetic field was found using magnetometer data from the first month after the launch of Pioneer 6. As the Sun rotates in space, the interplanetary magnetic field is first directed toward it and then away from it, forming the sector pattern. It is known that four such sectors are not always present; sometimes there are only two sectors. Such changes reflect the long-term variations of the solar magnetic field itself.

The Stanford University radio propagation experiment collected data on many solar plasma events while interplanetary electron density was measured. Using a different technique, transient phenomena near the Sun were also detected using the spacecraft transmitter—at times when one of these Pioneer spacecraft passed behind the Sun, as seen from Earth.

In early August, 1972, a series of four large solar flares produced intense fluxes of energetic solar particles and large increases in the speed of the solar wind. Pioneer 9 was in a favorable position then in its orbit around the Sun to measure these effects. Increased solar plasma fluxes can produce important effects on Earth, such as geomagnetic storms, and these Pioneer 9 data, in combination with those from other spacecraft and from the ground, provided important information on the propagation speeds of solar plasma disturbances and of solar particles. As a result, understanding of many geophysical effects was increased.

During Apollo piloted lunar explorations from 1969 through 1972, data from Pioneers 6 through 9 were used to give indications of solar particles to which the astronauts might be exposed. Pioneer data were sent to a solar disturbance forecast center in Boulder, Colorado, for this purpose.

The Pioneer 7 and 8 spacecraft provided opportunities to explore the geomagnetic wake farther downstream from Earth. As concluded from the study of the plasma and magnetic field data, the geomagnetic wake is not ordered and regular inside the Moon's orbit as it is nearer Earth; instead, it is mixed with the solar wind, possibly in a turbulent or filamentary manner. Pioneer 7 initially traversed this wake region at a distance of about 1,000 Earth radii downstream from Earth, while Pioneer 8 initially did so at about 500 Earth radii. Following its heliocentric orbit, Pioneer 7 again passed through this wake region in 1977, at about 3,100 Earth radii, and plasma data were again collected showing the presence of the wake region. Again in 1987, Pioneer 7 passed through this region at a distance of about 3,000 Earth radii, but by then the decrease in power from the spacecraft's solar cells meant that only the University of Chicago cosmic-ray experiment could be operated; thus, the wake region was not detected in the data. Similarly, Pioneer 8 in 1985 again passed through this region, at about 1,650 Earth radii downstream. The power available from this spacecraft was also limited and only the electric field wave experiment could be operated, but the wake region apparently was detected in the data. The structure of this wake has now been determined in more detail, out to a distance of about 220 Earth radii, by measurements made in 1983 by the International Sun-Earth Explorer-3 spacecraft.

The Pioneer 9 spacecraft was last tracked on May 18, 1983. Subsequent attempts to locate its transmissions were unsuccessful. The last of these attempts was in November, 1986, and it is not known exactly why the transmitted signal could no longer be located.

During 1986, while passing near the Sun, Halley's comet also passed fairly close to Pioneer 7 (within 12 million kilometers of it, or only 8 percent of the distance from the Sun to Earth). Plasma and cosmic-ray experiments were operated during several days of tracking, and there was an indication in the plasma data nearest the comet of solar wind helium being altered by the presence of cometary gas. The European Giotto spacecraft detected similar altered solar wind helium much closer to Halley's comet. Plasma data collected from Pioneer 7 had to be interpreted with a technique developed once the spacecraft's Sun sensor stopped operating in February of 1969.

Contributions

As the first spacecraft in the series, Pioneer 6 left Earth in December, 1965, and obtained new, more detailed data from plasma and magnetic field experiments concerning Earth's interaction with the solar wind. New features of Earth's bow shock and of the shocked plasma behind it were also measured, because the experiments carried were more sophisticated than earlier ones.

As time passed, data on the effects in interplanetary space of many solar flares were obtained from Pioneers 6 through 9. The evolution over time of energetic solar proton fluxes associated with flares was often found to progress from alignment close to the direction of the interplanetary magnetic field toward an isotropic distribution. The gradient of the solar protons was sometimes observed to have more intense fluctuations closer to the Sun. The effect of a flare's solar longitude relative to the Pioneer spacecraft was examined for some events, and it was concluded that a magnetic field line connection between the source and the spacecraft favored prompt, relatively intense effects. Fast solar plasma, accelerated in association with the flare, was observed for some events.

In August, 1972, particularly large solar flare events occurred, and solar wind plasma, magnetic field, and energetic particle data from Pioneer 9 proved valuable in combination with data from other spacecraft in determining the speeds and the longitudinal and radial extents of the associated accelerated interplanetary plasma and energetic solar particles.

The structure of the interplanetary medium was found to be characterized by discontinuous changes in the magnetic field and the solar wind plasma parameters by experiments on these Pioneer spacecraft. Also, experience was gained from the radio propagation experiments in the detection of solar plasma events and in the measurement of interplanetary electron densities.

For the first time, Earth's magnetic wake in the solar wind was observed at fairly large distances downstream by the Pioneer 7 and 8 spacecraft. Data from about 500 and 1,000 Earth radii downstream indicated that Earth's magnetic field, carried away by the solar wind, had generally lost its ordered near-Earth characteristics. At the greater distances, this wake may have become turbulent. In March of 1986, it was possible to collect interesting data from Pioneer 7 on the interaction of Halley's comet with the solar wind.

Context

Before traversal by Pioneer 6 in 1965 of the magnetopause and bow shock boundaries of Earth's magnetic field, the general locations of these boundaries were known because of experiments aboard other spacecraft. Plasma data collected by Pioneer 6, however, provided actual measurements of the plasma flow vector, which previously had not been fully defined. Measurements of electrons in the solar wind provided by Pioneer 6 considerably improved upon those previously available.

Solar wind plasma, magnetic field, and energetic particle data collected by Pioneer 6, and by the later Pioneer spacecraft of this series, permitted scientists to prove the discontinuous nature of the solar wind near Earth's orbit. Hints of this characteristic had been present in earlier, less complete data.

Scientists had already understood that solar flares can generate energetic particles and had studied transmission of these particles and the accelerated solar wind associated with them by the time that Pioneer 6 was launched. Serious research on these topics had been possible through measurements of geomagnetic activity and of effects associated with the energetic particles that could be measured from Earth, such as changes of the ionosphere, neutrons generated in the upper atmosphere, and the incidence of ionizing radiation measured with balloon-borne experiments. The Pioneer spacecraft, however, provided more complete, accurate, and sensitive data, unmodified by Earth's close proximity. New data permitted important advances in the understanding of the physical effects in the interplanetary medium, and on Earth, of these solar phenomena.

Prior to the passage of Pioneer 7 in 1966 through Earth's magnetic wake, nothing was known about this phenomenon at those distances. Pioneer 7 data indicated that this distant wake had a disordered nature, a characteristic that was confirmed with data from Pioneer 8 a little more than a year later. Pioneer 7 data were used to detect Earth's wake in the solar wind near 3,100 Earth radii downstream in 1977.

Pioneer 7 solar wind plasma data obtained in the vicinity of Halley's comet during March, 1986, augmented the results obtained by other spacecraft by performing a relatively unsophisticated but fairly sensitive experiment at an extreme distance.

—J. D. Mihalov

See also: Explorers: Solar; International Sun- Earth Explorers; Jet Propulsion Laboratory; Pioneer Missions 1-5; Pioneer Venus 2; Ulysses: Solar Polar Mission; Voyager Program; Voyager 1: Jupiter.

Further Reading

Burrows, William E. *This New Ocean: The Story of the First Space Age*. New York: Random House, 1998. This is a comprehensive history of the human conquest of space, covering everything from the earliest attempts at spaceflight through the voyages near the end of the twentieth century. Burrows is an experienced journalist who has reported for *The New York Times*, *The Washington Post*, and *The Wall Street Journal*. There are many photographs and an extensive source list. Interviewees in the book include Isaac Asimov, Alexei Leonov, Sally K. Ride, and James A. Van Allen.

Corliss, William R. *The Interplanetary Pioneers*. 3 vols. NASA SP-278, 279, and 280. Washington, D.C.: Government Printing Office, 1972. An official history of these Pioneer spacecraft. Contains numerous photographs, diagrams, and illustrations.

---. *Scientific Satellites*. NASA SP-133. Washington, D.C.: Government Printing Office, 1967. An ambitious work that presents the rationales and engineering and experimental details for scientific spacecraft of the period. Includes a useful diagram of the electrostatic deflection arrangement for the Pioneer 6 and 7 Ames Research Center plasma experiments. Contains some college-level material. Provides numerous diagrams and photographs.

Gibson, Edward G. *The Quiet Sun.* NASA SP-303. Washington, D.C.: Government Printing Office, 1973. This volume was prepared by a Skylab scientist-astronaut to organize the available knowledge about the Sun, particularly in its undisturbed state. Contains considerable general information. Despite the title, a reasonable discussion of the solar flare phenomenon is included. Contains numerous photographs and illustrations.

Kennel, Charles F., et al., eds. *Solar System Plasma Physics.* 3 vols. Amsterdam: North-Holland Publishing, 1979. Volume 1 contains a discussion of solar flares that generally is at the graduate level, although some introductory material is also included. Volume 3 provides a discussion of some detrimental effects on Earth of solar activity. These three volumes contain photographs and diagrams.

Kivelson, Margaret G., and Christopher T. Russell. *Introduction to Space Physics.* New York: Cambridge University Press, 1995. A thorough exploration of space physics. Some aspects are suitable for the general reader. Suitable for an introductory college course on space physics.

Lee, Wayne. *To Rise from Earth: An Easy to Understand Guide to Spaceflight.* New York: Checkmark Books, 1996. This is a good introduction to the science of spaceflight. Although written by an engineer with the NASA Jet Propulsion Laboratory, it is presented in easy-to-understand language. In addition to the theory of spaceflight, it gives some of the history of the human endeavor to explore space.

Mari, Christopher, ed. *Space Exploration.* New York: H. W. Wilson, 1999. Twenty-five articles (reprinted from magazines), covering the state of the space program at the time of publication, are divided into five sections: John H. Glenn, Jr.'s return to space, the exploration of Mars, the International Space Station, recent mining efforts by commercial industries, and new types of space vehicles and propulsion systems.

Nicks, Oran W. *Far Travelers: The Exploring Machines.* NASA SP-480. Washington, D.C.: Scientific and Technical Information Branch, 1985. Discusses all major NASA planetary spacecraft during NASA's first quarter-century. Written by a senior NASA official involved with lunar and planetary programs during that era.

Parks, George K. *Physics of Space Plasmas: An Introduction.* 2d ed. Boulder, Colo.: Westview Press, 2004. Provides a scientific examination of the data returned during what might be called the "golden age" of space physics (1990-2002), when over two dozen satellites were dispatched to investigate space plasma phenomena. Written at the undergraduate level for an introductory course in space plasma, there is also detailed presentation of NASA and ESA spacecraft missions.

Zimmerman, Robert. *The Chronological Encyclopedia of Discoveries in Space.* Westport, Conn.: Oryx Press, 2000. Provides a complete chronological history of all crewed and robotic spacecraft and explains flight events and scientific results. Suitable for all levels of research.

Pioneer 10

Date: March 2, 1972, to January 22, 2003
Type of spacecraft: Planetary exploration

Pioneer 10 was the first spacecraft to conduct a close-up reconnaissance of Jupiter, the largest planet in the solar system, and to sample directly its magnetic and particle environment. It was also the first spacecraft to cross the asteroid belt between Mars and Jupiter, and the first to achieve escape velocity from the solar system. Silently Pioneer 10 like its sister ship Pioneer 11 is on its way to another star system.

Key Figures

Charles F. Hall (1920-1999), Pioneer project
  manager
John H. Wolfe, project scientist
Robert R. Nunamaker, Flight Operations manager
Norman J. Martin, Flight Operations manager
Richard O. Fimmel (b. 1946), Science manager
Gilbert Schroeder, Spacecraft manager
Joseph Lepetich, Experiments manager
Ralph W. Holtzclaw, Spacecraft Systems manager
Robert Hofstetter, Launch Vehicle and Trajectory
  Analysis coordinator
Alfred Siegmeth, Pioneer Tracking and Data
  Systems manager
J. W. Johnson, Cape Kennedy Launch Operations
  Representative for the Pioneer Jupiter project
Bernard O'Brien, project manager at the TRW
  Systems Group

Summary of the Mission

The Pioneer 10 mission performed the first close flyby of the planet Jupiter. In 1967, as a part of the activities of the National Aeronautics and Space Administration's (NASA) Lunar and Planetary Missions Board, an outer planet panel chaired by Dr. James A. Van Allen of the University of Iowa (discoverer of Earth's radiation belts) recommended low-cost missions to the outer planets. In June of 1968, the Space Science Board of the National Academy of Sciences stated that Jupiter was

probably the most interesting planet from a physical point of view, and that it was technically feasible to send probes to that planet. The board recommended that "Jupiter missions be given high priority, and that two exploratory probes in the Pioneer class be launched in 1972 or 1973."

A mission to Jupiter was officially approved by NASA Headquarters in February of 1969, and the program was assigned to the Program Office, Office of Space Science and Applications. The Pioneer Project Office at the NASA Ames Research Center was selected to manage the project, and TRW Systems Group, in Redondo Beach, California, was awarded a contract to design and fabricate two identical Pioneer spacecraft for the mission. The first feasible launch opportunity ran from late February through early March of 1972, and the first spacecraft, "Pioneer F," was scheduled to make this launch window. After launch, the spacecraft was renamed Pioneer 10.

At the Ames Research Center, Charles F. Hall became Pioneer progject manager. Experiments on the spacecraft were the responsibility of Joseph Lepetich.s Spacecraft systems were the responsibility of Ralph W. Holtzclaw. The Flight Operations manager was Robert R. Nunamaker and later Norman J. Martin. Robert Hofstetter was launch vehicle and trajectory analysis coordinator, Richard O. Fimmel was science chief, and Gilbert

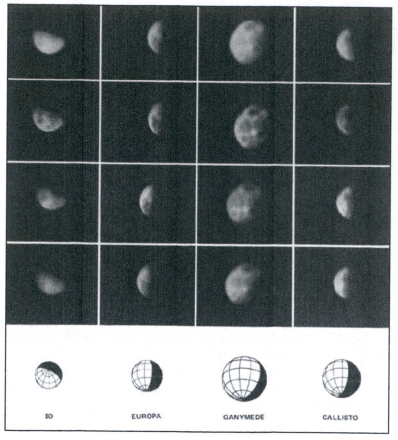

Best images of the four largest moons of Jupiter taken by the Pioneer 10 and Pioneer 11 spacecraft in 1973 and 1974. (NASA)

Schroeder was spacecraft chief. The California Institute of Technology's Jet Propulsion Laboratory (JPL), in Pasadena, California, provided tracking and data systems support with Alfred Siegmeth as the Pioneer tracking and data systems manager, and NASA's Goddard Space Flight Center in Greenbelt, Maryland, provided worldwide communications to the various stations of the Deep Space Network. NASA's Lewis Research Center (now NASA Glenn Research Center at Lewis Field) in Cleveland, Ohio, was responsible for the launch vehicle system. J. W. Johnson represented the Pioneer Jupiter project for launch operations at NASA's Kennedy Space Center, and Bernard O'Brien was project manager at TRW Systems Group.

The Pioneer 10 spacecraft was spin-stabilized so that it continually rotated, always pointing in the same direction, with the center of its dish-shaped communications antenna pointed toward Earth. The spacecraft was 2.9 meters long, from the end of its conical medium-gain antenna to the adapter ring that fastened it to the third stage of the launch vehicle. Its structure was centered around a 36-centimeter-deep flat equipment compartment. The top and bottom of this compartment consisted of regular hexagons with sides 71 centimeters long. Attached to one side of this compartment was a smaller compartment that contained most of the instruments for the scientific experiments. The main communications antenna, 2.74 meters in diameter and 46 centimeters deep, was attached to the front of the equipment compartment. Radioisotope thermoelectric generators were held about 3 meters from the spacecraft center. These provided power for the long flight time to Jupiter by converting heat from the radioactive decay of plutonium 238 into electricity. Solar cells would not be of much use in this mission, because, at the planet Jupiter, sunlight has only 3.7 percent of its intensity on Earth. A third single-rod boom, 120° from the two trusses, projected from the experiment compartment to position a magnetometer sensor about 6.6 meters from the center of the spacecraft. Both trusses and the boom were stowed before launch and extended from the spacecraft after launch in order for everything to fit within the 3-meter shroud of the Atlas- Centaur launch vehicle.

Besides the Magnetometer Experiment (for which Edward J. Smith of JPL served as principal investigator), the other scientific experiments (listed with principal investigators in parentheses) included a Plasma Analyzer Experiment (John H. Wolfe, Ames Research Center), Charged Particle

Composition Experiment (John A. Simpson, University of Chicago), Cosmic-Ray Energy Spectra Experiment (Frank B. McDonald, Goddard Space Flight Center), Jovian Charged Particle Experiment (James A. Van Allen, University of Iowa), Jovian-Trapped Radiation Experiment (R. Walker Filius, University of California, San Diego), Asteroid- Meteoroid Astronomy Experiment (Robert K. Soberman, General Electric Company and Drexel University), Meteoroid Detection Experiment (William H. Kinard, Langley Research Center), Ultraviolet Photometry Experiment (Darrell L. Judge, University of Southern California), Imaging Photopolarimetry Experiment (Tom Gehrels, University of Arizona), and Jovian-Infrared Thermal Structure Experiment (Guido Munch, California Institute of Technology). In addition, two experiments used information obtained from the radio communications link, the Celestial Mechanics Experiment (John D. Anderson of JPL) and the Occultation Experiment (Arvydas J. Kliore, also of JPL).

Radiation is further explored over an even broader range of energies by a trapped radiation detector, equipped on both Pioneer 10 and 11. (NASA)

Pioneer 10 could be launched between February 25 and March 20, 1972, arriving at Jupiter sometime between October, 1973, and July, 1974. Arrival had to be timed so that Jupiter and Pioneer 10 would not be too close to the Sun's direction in the sky. Initial electrical problems and high-wind conditions delayed the launch for several days. On March 2, 1972, at 8:49 p.m. eastern standard time or 01:49 Coordinated Universal Time (UTC) on March 3, Pioneer 10 was launched from Cape Canaveral by an Atlas-Centaur equipped with an additional boost stage. After seventeen minutes of flight, Pioneer 10 was traveling 51,682 kilometers per hour, faster than any previous human-made object. After only eleven hours of flight, Pioneer 10 was beyond the orbit of the Moon. On March 7, a small

correction was made to the spacecraft velocity to ensure an arrival time at Jupiter that optimized the results of the scientific experiments. After only ten days, all scientific experiments had been turned on so that the health of each of the instruments could be monitored during the long flight time to Jupiter. Although there had been a few unexpected readings from the spacecraft, there were no serious problems. All the experiments had survived the launch in operating condition. On July 15, Pioneer 10 became the first spacecraft to enter the asteroid belt between the orbits of Mars and Jupiter. Also in July, a trajectory correction was made so that Pioneer 10 would be occulted by Jupiter's innermost main satellite, Io, near its closest approach to the planet.

During the portion of its trajectory between Earth and Jupiter, Pioneer 10 was active in collecting scientific measurements of the characteristics of charged particles, interplanetary plasma, and the zodiacal light—a faint glow in the plane of the zodiac that is visible in dark Earth skies after sunset and before sunrise. Pioneer also had the chance to observe the influence on the solar wind—the stream of plasma that moves outward from the Sun—of several unprecedented storms on the visible surface of the Sun. These measurements were compared with similar ones taken from spacecraft still in orbit around the Sun in different parts of the sky, i.e. Pioneers 6, 7, 8, and 9.

Although scientists estimated that Pioneer 10 had a 90 percent chance of passing through the asteroid belt undamaged, there was still some concern. Encounter with any object as big as half a millimeter in diameter at speeds that could be as great as fifteen times the speed of a high-powered rifle bullet would do serious damage to the spacecraft. Pioneer 10 emerged from the asteroid belt in February of 1973, completing the seven-month asteroid belt passage without harm.

In early November of 1973, controllers readied Pioneer 10 for the most active phase of its mission— the encounter with Jupiter. Its trajectory was nearly equatorial with respect to Jupiter, and it would come within 140,000 kilometers of the Jovian cloud tops. By November 16, Pioneer 10 had crossed the bow shock where Jupiter's magnetic field affects the solar wind. This bow shock was farther from the planet than had been expected. On November 27, Pioneer crossed the magnetopause, the boundary between the shocked solar wind and the magnetic field of Jupiter itself. Pictures of Jupiter began coming in from the imaging photopolarimeter's narrow-angle telescope. Images were returned in two colors, red and blue, and a detailed color image of the planet was reconstructed later by mixing green with the image in proportions as seen from Earth-based observations.

Because it had no onboard computer, commands had to be transmitted to the spacecraft daily, increasing to four thousand commands per day as Pioneer 10 moved toward its closest approach to Jupiter. A series of contingency commands was periodically sent so that the spacecraft could be corrected in case of spurious signals generated by Jupiter's powerful radiation field. Some spacecraft systems showed effects from the powerful radiation environment, with several particles and fields experiments reaching measurement saturation points.

Although there was concern that some instruments might be destroyed in the deluge of radiation received from Jupiter at closest approach, the spacecraft continued to function well when it emerged from behind Jupiter just after periapsis—closest approach—on December 3.

Transmitting a series of crescent-shaped images of Jupiter, Pioneer 10 left the Jovian environment on a trajectory that followed the heliotail—that part of the solar wind swept by the interstellar wind—gathering data about the solar wind at extreme distances from the Sun, crossed the orbit of Neptune, and was used to seek a possible tenth planet. Pioneer 10 sent its last signal to Earth on January 22, 2003. Pioneer 11, a virtual twin, would reach Jupiter about a year after Pioneer 10 and gather more information about the planet, particularly its polar regions, eventually encountering the planet Saturn being directed out of the solar system in a different direction than Pioneer 10.

Contributions

Between Earth and Jupiter, Pioneer 10 found that the solar wind temperature behaved differently from theory and had many non-uniformities from irregularities in the solar corona. In its mission past Jupiter, Pioneer 10 discovered that the heliopause (the boundary of the heliosphere, or expanding solar wind) was beyond the orbit of Neptune. Pioneer 10 experimenters found that the stream of uncharged hydrogen atoms that make up the gas between stars—the interstellar wind—enters the solar system along the path of Earth's orbit, but at a direction $60°$ away from the direction the solar system is traveling through interstellar space. On the way to Jupiter, the concentration of small particles was not found to be particularly greater in the asteroid belt than anyplace else in the solar system.

Near Jupiter, Pioneer 10 mapped the intensity, direction, and structure of the planet's magnetic field. The outer portion of the magnetic field was similar in structure to that of Earth but turned in the opposite direction. It was also tilted $11°$ away from the rotational axis and offset from the planet's center. Closer to the planet, between the cloud tops and a distance of three Jovian radii, the field was extremely complicated and extremely strong—at its cloud top level more than ten times the strength of Earth's magnetic field at its own surface. The outer part of the field expanded and contracted under the influence of the solar wind and was blunted in the solar wind direction. Between 20 and 60 Jovian radii, the field was found to be extremely distorted by trapped plasma; there, ionized particles formed a sheet of electric current around Jupiter that produced its own magnetic field. Peak intensities of electrons in Jupiter's radiation belts were ten thousand times greater than the maximum in Earth's belts; protons were several thousand times more intense.

Imaging and infrared measurements of Jupiter's atmosphere of Jupiter showed that dark regions were warmer than light regions. The Great Red Spot, a long-observed oval in the southern hemisphere, was cool and had clouds higher than anywhere else

Pioneer 10 in the final stage of construction in at the TRW plant in Southern California. (NASA)

on the planet. The temperature of the atmosphere reached a minimum of about 110 kelvins, near a pressure of one-tenth that at Earth's surface, and warmed up to about 173 kelvins at a pressure equal to that at Earth's surface. At lower pressures in Jupiter's stratosphere, the temperature warmed up again. Jupiter was found to emit about 1.7 times as much heat energy as it absorbed from solar radiation.. Jupiter's ionosphere was found to rise some 4,000 kilometers above the visible cloud tops. It has at least five distinct layers, similar to Earth's ionospheric layers.

Low-resolution images were made of Jupiter's second and third innermost large moons, Europa and Ganymede, respectively. Analysis of changes in the radio signal from the spacecraft as it went behind Io showed that the satellite had an ionosphere that extended 700 kilometers above its day side. Masses and sizes of the large satellites were observed with sufficient precision to determine that their densities decreased uniformly outward from Jupiter, suggesting predominantly rocky compositions for the innermost moons and predominantly icy compositions for the outermost satellites.

Context

Prior to the Pioneer 10 mission, the only knowledge about Jupiter came from Earth-based observations and theoretical considerations. Scientific interest in Jupiter is centered on the facts that it is the largest planet in the solar system and that its bulk density, like those of the other outer planets—Saturn, Uranus, and Neptune—indicates that it is primarily composed of hydrogen and helium gas, unlike the inner planets—Mercury, Venus, Earth, and Mars. Theory suggests that a large region of the interior of Jupiter is composed of metallic hydrogen. The measured behavior of the magnetic field conformed to this expectation by showing the generation of an immense magnetic field by a dynamo at the center of the planet with a complicated structure and gravitational measurements of the planet that confirmed that it is almost entirely fluid. Measurements of the radiation belts and electrical flow revealed details of an electromagnetic environment that has, for many years, made Jupiter known as the "brightest" source of radio emissions in the sky apart from the Sun due to its proximity to Earth.

Jupiter's atmosphere is mostly molecular hydrogen, but it also contains helium. The flow of heat from the interior, in excess of the energy received from the Sun, is consistent with the slow cooling of such a large body from the time of its formation. Preliminary infrared measurements of Jupiter by aircraft had indicated that even more heat was emitted by the planet. Because of the flow of heat from the interior and the planet's rapid rotation (it has a ten-hour period), weather patterns appear quite different from those on Earth. Familiar pressure systems with clockwise and counterclockwise flow are stretched over many degrees of longitude; major features are stretched all the way around the planet. Visible and infrared results are consistent with a picture in which bright and cool bands are regions of upwelling atmosphere and dark and warm areas are regions of subsidence. Rapid convection of the atmosphere causes incrementally higher temperatures toward the interior; the warm

stratosphere is consistent with absorption of sunlight by methane and other hydrocarbon gases present in the atmosphere and by haze particles.

Pioneer 10 was the first spacecraft to visit Jupiter, and its scientific results are best viewed together with its "twin," Pioneer 11, which differed by the addition of another magnetometer experiment and a trajectory that took it closer to the planet to allow imaging and infrared instruments to view the polar regions. Pioneer results are often overlooked in the wealth of high-resolution imaging and detailed remote-sensing spectral data obtained just six years later by Voyagers 1 and 2. For a relatively inexpensive mission, Pioneer 10 provided a treasure of information, some of which was not duplicated or improved by Voyager, such as the cloud photometry and polarimetry of the imaging system.

Besides being the first spacecraft to reach Jupiter, Pioneer 10 was the first spacecraft to penetrate the asteroid belt. It traversed and communicated from greater distances than ever before. It was also the first planetary spacecraft to use all nuclear electrical power. It demonstrated the viability of spin-scan imaging, and its probing of the asteroid belt and the radiation environment of Jupiter paved the way for the later sophistication of the Voyager spacecraft. It also showed that a probe could survive penetration into the Jovian atmosphere and an orbiter could survive many months in the neighborhood of the planet.

Pioneer 10's final transmitted signal was received through the Deep Space Network on January 22, 2003. At this point, signals from the spacecraft, 12.23 billion kilometers (7.6 billion miles) distant from Earth, took eleven hours and twenty minutes to arrive. It had continued to send data concerning the nature of the far reaches of the outer solar system until its radioisotope thermal generator's performance diminished. The spacecraft would continue to head out of the solar system as a silent ambassador of humanity.

—*Glenn S. Orton*

See also: Ames Research Center; Cassini: Saturn; Galileo: Jupiter; Huygens Lander; Pioneer 11; Planetary Exploration; Ulysses: Solar Polar Mission; Voyager Program; Voyager 1: Jupiter; Voyager 1: Saturn; Voyager 2: Saturn.

Further Reading

Beatty, J. Kelly, Carolyn Collins Petersen, and Andrew Chaikin, eds. *The New Solar System*. 4th ed. New York: Sky Publishing, 1999. A general description of solar-system bodies that contains detailed articles pertinent to Jupiter and Pioneer discoveries. The book is readable at high school or college levels. In particular, chapters by James A. Van Allen, Edward J. Smith, Andrew P. Ingersoll, and J. W. Johnson discuss magnetospheres and the interplanetary medium, the Voyager mission (and pre-Voyager information, including a brief description of Pioneer results), the atmosphere of Jupiter, and the Galilean satellites (the four largest moons of Jupiter).

Belton, Michael J. S., Gary Hunt, and Robert West, eds. *Time-Dependent Phenomena in the Jovian System*. Washington, D.C.: Government Printing Office, 1988. This book is a collection of articles that reviews time-dependent phenomena that are known or suspected in the Jovian magnetospheric environment in Jupiter's atmosphere, and on Jupiter's satellites (particularly Io's volcanic activity). The college- and postgraduate-level material is intended to review what is known from existing data and from theoretical expectations.

Fimmel, Richard O., William Swindel, and Eric Burgess. *Pioneer Odyssey*. NASA SP-396. Washington, D.C.: Government Printing Office, 1977. An authorized history of the Pioneer 10 and 11 missions to Jupiter. This work is a revision of the original NASA Special Publication with more Pioneer 11 results added, including several images of the Galilean satellites. It is suitable for high school and college levels. Appendices include a list of all images taken of Jupiter by Pioneers 10 and 11.

---. *Pioneer Odyssey: Encounter with a Giant*. NASA SP-349. Washington, D.C.: Government Printing Office, 1974. An authorized history of the Pioneer 10 mission to Jupiter with some early Pioneer 11 results included. It is suitable for high school and college levels and describes the mission from the earliest planning stages to its accomplishments by 1973. It contains many illustrations of the spacecraft, its instrumentation, the scientists involved with the experiments, and many of the images obtained of Jupiter by the imaging photopolarimeter. Appendices offer complete information on the details of image acquisition and the personnel involved with the mission. 1078 Pioneer 10

Fimmel, Richard O., James A. Van Allen, and Eric Burgess. *Pioneer: First to Jupiter, Saturn, and Beyond*. NASA SP-446. Washington, D.C.: Government Printing Office, 1980. An authorized history of the Pioneer 10 and 11 missions to Jupiter and Saturn and their extended missions. This book is the most recent edition of the NASA series on the Pioneer 10 and 11 missions, and it includes all the information on the Pioneer 11 encounter with Saturn. It is suitable for readers with high school or college science backgrounds. Additions to the appendices include a list of Saturn images made by Pioneer 11.

Fischer, Daniel. *Mission Jupiter: The Spectacular Journey of the Galileo Spacecraft*. New York: Copernicus Books, 2001. Provides a summary of Galileo's extensive findings in the Jovian system as well as the discoveries of the Pioneer and Voyager spacecraft that preceded it.

Gehrels, Tom, ed. *Jupiter*. Tucson: University of Arizona Press, 1976. A collection of articles written shortly after the Pioneer 10 and 11 encounters with Jupiter. The authors are primarily from the United States, and final results of the Pioneer missions at Jupiter, as well as observations from Earth-based telescopes at the time, are described. This work is a primary professional reference, and it contains information suitable to readers with college or postgraduate science backgrounds.

Harland, David M. *Jupiter Odyssey: The Story of NASA's Galileo Mission*. London: Springer- Praxis, 2000. A detailed scientific and engineering history of the Galileo program, but also includes extensive discussion of Voyager program events and results.

Hartmann, William K. *Moons and Planets*. 5th ed. Belmont, Calif.: Thomson Brooks/Cole Publishing, 2005. Provides detailed information about all objects in the solar system. Suitable on three separate levels: high school student, general reader, and the college undergraduate studying planetary geology.

Irwin, Patrick G. J. *Giant Planets of Our Solar System: Atmospheres, Composition, and Structure*. London: Springer-Praxis, 2003. Provides an in-depth comparison of Jupiter, Saturn, Uranus, and Neptune, incorporating data obtained from astronomical observations and planetary spacecraft encounters.

Lee, Wayne. *To Rise from Earth: An Easy to Understand Guide to Spaceflight*. New York: Checkmark Books, 1996. This is a good introduction to the science of spaceflight. Although written by an engineer with the NASA Jet Propulsion Laboratory, it is presented in easy-to-understand language. In addition to the theory of spaceflight, it gives some of the history of the human endeavor to explore space.

Mari, Christopher, ed. *Space Exploration*. New York: H. W. Wilson, 1999. Twenty-five articles (reprinted from magazines), covering the state of the space program at the time of publication, are divided into five sections: John H. Glenn, Jr.'s return to space, the exploration of Mars, the International Space Station, recent mining efforts by commercial industries, and new types of space vehicles and propulsion systems.

National Aeronautics and Space Administration. *Voyager to Jupiter and Saturn*. NASA SP-420. Springfield, Va.: National Technical Information Service, 1977. Summary of the Voyager mission to explore planets of the outer solar system. The spacecraft, its trajectories, and its scientific instruments are described, along with relevant investigations. Color graphics, pictures of the spacecraft and its instruments, and the well-known Voyager images are included.

Pioneer 11

Date: April 5, 1973, to November, 1995
Type of spacecraft: Planetary exploration

Pioneer 11 collected critical data on the outer solar system, obtained images of Jupiter and Saturn, and continues to collect important data from the interplanetary space beyond Saturn.

Key Figures

Charles F. Hall (1920-1999), project manager until 1979
Richard O. Fimmel (b. 1946), project manager
John H. Wolfe, project scientist
Palmer Dyal, project scientist
Edward J. Smith, principal investigator
Tom Gehrels, principal investigator
Andrew P. Ingersoll, principal investigator

Summary of the Mission

The Pioneer 11 spacecraft mission was approved by the National Aeronautics and Space Administration (NASA) as a backup to the Pioneer 10 mission to Jupiter. Both spacecraft were managed by the Pioneer Project Office of NASA's Ames Research Center. Pioneer 11 was initially targeted to follow the path of Pioneer 10 through the asteroid belt and past Jupiter. If the asteroid belt or the radiation environment of Jupiter had proved hazardous to Pioneer 10, Pioneer 11 would have been retargeted to avoid the hazards.

Pioneer 11, like other spacecraft designed to travel to the outer solar system, had to be very lightweight and extremely reliable. It also needed power sources other than solar cells, because the Sun's power is too faint at large distances. Finally, Pioneer 11 needed communications systems designed to operate over billions of miles.

Pioneer 11 was designed and built by TRW in Redondo Beach, California. The designers chose a spin-stabilized spacecraft with a large dish antenna for communications and four radioisotope thermo-electric generators (RTGs), mounted on external booms, for power.

The communications dish antenna is 2.7 meters in diameter and 46 centimeters deep, and it is mounted on the main equipment compartment, which surrounds a hydrazine fuel tank that feeds the propulsion units. Ten propulsion rockets are located at the rim of the antenna and are used to control the spin rate, attitude, and velocity of the spacecraft. All electronic spacecraft components are housed in the main equipment compartment. A smaller hexagonal compartment attached to the side of the main compartment houses most of the twelve scientific instruments. A thermal insulation blanket surrounds both compartments to maintain the electronics at a comfortable temperature. On the bottom of the main equipment compartment are a number of thermally activated louvers, which open and close to expel excessive heat generated by the electronic equipment. Extending from the equipment compartment are two 3-meter booms holding the RTGs and one 6.6-meter boom holding the helium vector magnetometer instrument. The total weight of the spacecraft at launch was only 270 kilograms, including 30 kilograms of scientific instruments.

The scientific instruments were designed to obtain data on interplanetary space, Jupiter, and Saturn. The twelve instruments comprise two magnetometers, an infrared radiometer, a cosmic-ray

This image from Pioneer 11 shows Saturn and its moon Titan. The irregularities in ring silhouette and shadow are due to technical anomalies in the preliminary data later corrected. At the time this image was taken, Pioneer was 2,846,000 km (1,768,422 miles) from Saturn. (NASA Ames)

detector, a charged particle instrument, a trapped radiation detector, an ultraviolet photometer, a Geiger tube telescope, an imaging photopolarimeter, a plasma analyzer, meteoroid detector panels, and an asteroid/meteoroid detector.

Pioneer 11 was launched at 9:11 p.m. eastern standard time, April 5, 1973, or 02:11 Coordinated Universal Time (UTC) on April 6, from Cape Canaveral aboard an Atlas-Centaur three-stage launch vehicle. The launch vehicle propelled Pioneer 11 to a speed of more than 51,000 kilometers per hour, fast enough to pass the orbit of the Moon in just eleven hours. At the time of Pioneer 11's launch, the sister spacecraft Pioneer 10 had been in flight for thirteen months and was still eight months from its Jupiter encounter.

After the successful encounter of Pioneer 10 with Jupiter on December 3, 1973, at a closest approach of 132,252 kilometers above the cloud tops, the final decision was made to retarget Pioneer 11. On April 19, 1974, a pair of rockets on Pioneer 11 fired to add an additional 63.7 meters per second to the spacecraft's velocity and to make it aim for an altitude of 43,000 kilometers above Jupiter's cloud tops. This very close approach caused the spacecraft to be accelerated by Jupiter's tremendous gravity to a velocity fifty-five times that of the muzzle velocity of a high-speed rifle bullet, or 173,000 kilometers per second, so that the spacecraft would intercept Saturn five years after passing Jupiter.

The Jupiter encounter trajectory was such that the spacecraft would approach Jupiter on the left side, as viewed from Earth, and hurtle almost straight up, thus obtaining the first polar view of Jupiter. This path had the added benefit of quickly crossing the planet's magnetic equator, where the most intense radiation belts are concentrated, thus minimizing the spacecraft's total radiation exposure.

On November 2, 1974, the initial Pioneer 11 images of Jupiter were taken and transmitted back to Earth.. Those images were obtained by the imaging photopolarimeter instrument designed by scientists at the University of Arizona. The instruments used the spacecraft's rotation (4.8 revolutions per minute) to scan across Jupiter with a small telescope. On one rotation of the spacecraft, a red filter was placed in front of the telescope and a digital image of a thin strip of the planet was transmitted to Earth. On the next rotation, a blue filter was used to obtain a digital image of the same strip of the planet. On the third rotation, the telescope was moved a tiny amount to a new viewing angle, and a red filter was again used. This sequence of filter changes and angle adjustments was repeated until the whole planet had been scanned. After ground equipment had converted the digital signals to a video signal, green was added to the combined red and blue signals to produce full-color pictures. As the image was created strip by strip the television screen in the Pioneer Mission Operations Center displayed a rather oddly shaped planet. Instead of having the familiar spherical shape, Jupiter appeared quite elongated, like a beach ball with an air leak. This curious shape was the result of forward motion of the spacecraft, which had moved a considerable distance between transmissions of successive strips of the picture. Later, ground computers corrected for spacecraft motion by placing the strips in the geometrically correct position.

Between November 2, 1974, and December 2, 1974, approximately twenty-five images per day were obtained, each one progressively filling more of the field of view as the spacecraft moved closer to Jupiter. At 8:21 a.m. Pacific standard time (16:21 UTC) on December 2, 1974, the last full-disk picture was taken. Subsequent pictures would show only portions of the planet. At 4:00 p.m. (24:00 UTC) that day, a two-hour scan produced a detailed image of the famous Red Spot, a puzzle to astronomers for centuries.

On December 2, 1974, at 9:02 p.m. Pacific standard time (05:02 UTC on December 3), twenty-two minutes before closest approach, Pioneer 11 passed behind Jupiter. Its onboard memory was busy recording data to be transmitted to Earth later, assuming the spacecraft's electronic equipment survived the fierce radiation. At 9:44 p.m. (05:44 UTC on December 3), the spacecraft came out from behind Jupiter, but controllers on Earth had to wait an additional forty minutes to hear anything because of the time it took the signal to travel the 720 million kilometers from Jupiter to Earth. Eleven seconds after 10:24 p.m. Pacific standard time (06:24 UTC on December 3), the tracking station at Canberra, Australia, picked up the first faint signal from the spacecraft and sent it on to the Pioneer Mission Operations Center at Ames Research Center. Pioneer 11 had survived the ordeal. The massive dose of radiation had caused minor irregularities in the functioning of the plasma analyzer, the infrared radiometer, the meteoroid detector, and the imaging system. Engineers quickly sent a string of 108 commands to the spacecraft to reconfigure the instruments so they could continue to provide data as the spacecraft departed Jupiter.

During the spring of 1978, engineers and scientists decided that the spacecraft should pass just outside Saturn's bright rings. Hydrazine rockets were used to adjust the spacecraft's velocity so that Pioneer 11 would swing under the ring plane at a distance of 35,400 kilometers and come within 21,400 kilometers of the cloud tops. Later, this trajectory would carry Pioneer 11 within 355,600 kilometers of Titan, the largest of Saturn's moons.

By August 2, 1979, Pioneer 11 had accelerated to a speed of 30,600 kilometers per hour under the influence of Saturn's enormous gravity. With increasing speed, the spacecraft continued its plunge toward Saturn. At 7:36 a.m. Pacific daylight time (14:36 UTC) on September 1, 1987, it crossed the plane of the rings. By this time its speed had increased to 112,000 kilometers per hour. Because of the large distance of Saturn from Earth (1.547 billion kilometers), project engineers had to wait eighty-six minutes for signals to reach their computer screen at the Pioneer Mission Operations Center. Data confirmed that the spacecraft had not sustained any damage by particles in the ring plane, as had been feared. Images continued to arrive, showing beautiful close-ups of the rings around Saturn.

At 9:31 a.m. Pacific daylight time (16:31 UTC), Pioneer 11 hurtled through its closest approach to Saturn, only 20,930 kilometers above the cloud tops, at 114,150 kilometers per hour. At 11:04 a.m. Pacific daylight time (18:04 UTC) on September 2, 1979, Pioneer 11 made its closest approach to Titan, Saturn's largest satellite. By September 3, 1979, the spacecraft was moving away from the ringed planet at 36,210 kilometers per hour.

Pioneer 11 and its sister ship, Pioneer 10, were the first human-made objects to travel through the asteroid belt and obtain images of Jupiter and Saturn. They continued to provide exciting scientific data as they traveled toward the edge of the solar system. Pioneer 11's signal ceased in

November, 1995, when its power source ran out; however, Pioneer 10 continued transmitting until January 22, 2003.

Contributions

Pioneer 11's flyby of Jupiter revealed high-energy electron intensity in the radiation belts to be as predicted, but that the proton flux was about one-tenth of what was anticipated based on extrapolation from Pioneer 10 data. Particle and field experiments verified that Jupiter's intense radiation belts are dangerous only at lower latitudes, and pose relatively few hazards to spacecraft flying through them at high altitudes.

Images of the cloud tops at Jupiter's poles showed that they are significantly lower than at the equator and that they are covered by a thick, transparent atmosphere. Blue sky, caused by multiple molecular scattering of light by the gases in the atmosphere, was clearly visible at the poles. The Jupiter encounter also provided new details about circulation and convection patterns in the clouds around the Great Red Spot.

After the Jupiter encounter, Pioneer 11 looped high across the ecliptic plane and across the solar system, providing new information about the Sun's magnetic field. Magnetic field detectors on board the spacecraft showed that solar rotation produces a warped "current sheet" (a disk-shaped region separating the north and south magnetic fields around the Sun). The sheet wobbles up and down, as seen from Earth and the other planets, and this explains fluctuations of the solar magnetic field that had puzzled scientists for years.

During the Saturn encounter, Pioneer 11 produced spectacular pictures of the ring plane from underneath, with the Sun shining through the gaps of the rings from above. The rings, which from

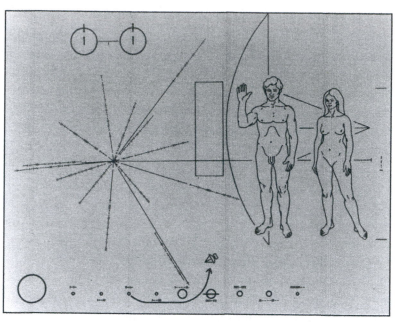

Both Pioneer 10 and 11 included a gold-anodized aluminum plaque featuring a pictorial message in case either probe was intercepted by intelligent extraterrestrial life. The plaques show the nude figures of a human male and female along with several symbols that are designed to provide information about the origin of the spacecraft. The plaque was designed by astrophysicist Carls Sagan and Frank Drake. (NASA)

Earth appear bright, were now seen as dark. The Sun's light, scattering off particles in the spaces between the rings, produced bright regions, which from Earth appear dark. A new ring, the F-ring, was discovered just outside the A-ring, which had been thought to be the outermost.

The close encounter also produced evidence—based on absorptions of charged particles—of additional Saturnian satellites. This was the first time that previously unknown satellites had been inferred from charged particles and magnetic field measurements.

Data from the infrared radiometer instrument showed that Saturn is still hot inside and that it emits more heat than it absorbs from the Sun. The magnetic field was shown to be almost exactly aligned with the axis of rotation, unlike the fields of Earth and Jupiter.

Images and data obtained during the Titan encounter showed Titan as a fuzzy ball with a slight orange tint and a suggestion of blue around the edge caused by its thick atmosphere. Radiometric data proved that Titan is in equilibrium with the solar radiation and has no internal heat source.

As Pioneer 11 sped out of the solar system, it continued to provide particle and field measurements from regions where no other spacecraft had traveled. In addition, engineers gained valuable information about the reliability of spacecraft components on extended missions. Techniques developed to control and maneuver spacecraft at large distances from Earth have contributed to a valuable information base for future exploration of the universe.

Context

Pioneer 11 was the second spacecraft to traverse the asteroid belt and proceed to Jupiter to take close-up pictures. Pioneer 10, launched in the spring of 1972, traveled through the asteroid belt in the summer of 1972 and made a flyby of Jupiter in December, 1973. The best Earth-based observations of Jupiter had previously established that the giant planet is a beautifully colored globe with bands of swirling clouds parallel to its equator. The Giant Red Spot, just south of the equator, had intrigued astronomers for centuries.

The Pioneer 10 flyby of Jupiter in 1973 answered many questions about the intensity of the radiation belts and provided exquisite pictures of the cloud bands. Because it followed an almost equatorial trajectory, however, no information was obtained about the latitudinal distribution of the radiation belts, and no pictures of the polar regions were obtained. Pioneer 11 was the first spacecraft to fly by Jupiter on a near-polar trajectory and thus was able to complement Pioneer 10's data by providing measurements in the third dimension. Unexpectedly, Pioneer 11 discovered that the cloud tops are substantially lower near the poles than at the equator. Scientists were astounded to see a blue atmosphere at the poles.

Before Pioneer 11 visited Saturn, the only information about this mysterious planet had come from Earth-based observations. As far back as 1675, the astronomer Jean-Dominique Cassini had studied the rings and identified a large gap, the Cassini Division, between the outer two rings. Before the Pioneer 11 flyby, astronomers had speculated that the rings consisted of ice or ice-coated rocks from several centimeters to several meters in size. Pioneer's perspective, not possible to achieve from Earth, allowed it to observe the rings illuminated from behind. Gaps between the rings were found to contain small particles that scattered the light, but a small amount of sunlight passed through. This allowed scientists to assess much more accurately the thickness of the ring material. From temperature and heat balance measurements of the rings and the ring shadow on the planet, scientists determined that the rings cannot be more than 4 kilometers thick. Sensitive measurements of the motion of the spacecraft as it was influenced by Saturn's gravity allowed scientists to estimate the mass of the rings to be less than one three-millionth of the mass of Saturn itself.

The infrared photopolarimeter and the ultraviolet spectrometer provided new information about the size and atmosphere of Saturn's moon Titan. The diameter was estimated to be approximately 5,600 to 5,800 kilometers. Analysis of the polarized light suggested a haze of methane particles high into the atmosphere. The discovery of a cloud of hydrogen atoms, extending at least 300,000 kilometers along the orbit, suggested that methane in Titan's atmosphere is being broken down into hydrogen and carbon by solar radiation.

Pioneer 11 is historically significant because it was the first spacecraft to observe Saturn. The information it provided had a direct influence on the planning and design of the Voyager missions to Jupiter, Saturn, and beyond.

The last communication from Pioneer 11 was received in November, 1995, shortly before the Earth's motion carried it out of range of the spacecraft's antenna. The spacecraft is headed toward the constellation of Aquila (The Eagle), northwest of the constellation of Sagittarius. Pioneer 11 may pass near one of the stars in the constellation in about four million years.

—Manfred N. Wirth

See also: Ames Research Center; Cassini: Saturn; Galileo: Jupiter; Huygens Lander; Pioneer 10; Planetary Exploration; Ulysses: Solar Polar Mission; Voyager Program; Voyager 1: Jupiter; Voyager 1: Saturn; Voyager 2: Saturn.

Further Reading

Elliot, James, and Richard Kerr. *Rings: Discoveries from Galileo to Voyager*. Cambridge, Mass.: MIT Press, 1984. This book describes planetary ring systems discovered by ground-based, airborne, and spacecraft telescopes. Suitable for high school and college students, the volume provides good insight into the characteristics and composition of planetary rings. The text is supported by numerous illustrations and diagrams.

Encrenas, Therese, R. Kallenbach, T. Owen, and C. Sotin. *The Outer Planets: A Comparative Study Before the Exploration of Saturn by Cassini-Huygens*. New York: Springer, 2005. A comparative study of the formation and evolution of the outer planets, the atmospheres of the outer planets and Titan, and moons and ring systems. Includes early Cassini data.

Fimmel, Richard O., James A. Van Allen, and Eric Burgess. *Pioneer: First to Jupiter, Saturn, and Beyond*. NASA SP-446. Washington, D.C.: Government Printing Office, 1980. Contains a good description of the Pioneer 10 and Pioneer 11 missions to Jupiter and Saturn. Suitable for high school and college students, the publication describes in detail the probes' launches, journeys through the asteroid belt, and first encounters with Jupiter and Saturn. Contains pictures transmitted from Jupiter and Saturn and illustrations and photographs of the spacecraft and their scientific instruments.

Fischer, Daniel. *Mission Jupiter: The Spectacular Journey of the Galileo Spacecraft*. New York: Copernicus Books, 2001. Provides a summary of Galileo's extensive findings in the Jovian system as well as the discoveries of the Pioneer and Voyager spacecraft that preceded it.

Gehrels, Tom, ed. *Jupiter*. Tucson: University of Arizona Press, 1976. A collection of scientific essays, this book is the authoritative reference on Jupiter. Its 212 contributors from around the world present scientific analyses of all aspects of Jupiter; many of the data are derived from the Pioneer missions. Suitable for college students, this book lists thousands of references to scientific papers in professional journals.

Hanlon, Michael, and Arthur C. Clarke. *The Worlds of Galileo: The Inside Story of NASA's Mission to Jupiter*. New York: St. Martin's Press, 2001. This text presents the Galileo spacecraft's exploration of asteroids and the Jupiter system while instilling the reader with the excitement of the voyage. The book also discusses the potential for a planetary ocean on the moon Europa.

Irwin, Patrick G. J. *Giant Planets of Our Solar System: Atmospheres, Composition, and Structures*. New York: Springer-Verlag, 2003. Reviews the current understanding of Jupiter, Saturn, Uranus, and Neptune. For the more advanced reader.

Morrison, David, and Tobias Owen. *The Planetary System*. 3d ed. San Francisco: Addison-Wesley, 2003. Organized by planetary object, this work provides contemporary data on all planetary bodies visited by spacecraft since the early days of the Space Age. Suitable for high school and college students and for the general reader.

Nicks, Oran W. *Far Travelers: The Exploring Machines*. NASASP-480. Washington, D.C.: Scientific and Technical Information Branch, 1985. Discusses all major NASA planetary spacecraft during NASA's first quarter-century. Written by a senior NASA official involved with lunar and planetary programs during that era.

Washburn, Mark. *Distant Encounter: The Exploration of Jupiter and Saturn*. San Diego: Harcourt Brace Jovanovich, 1983. Describes the images obtained by the Pioneer and Voyager missions to Jupiter, Saturn, and their satellites. Provides a good account of the activities and events occurring in the Pioneer Mission Operations Center at the time of the Pioneer 11 Saturn encounter. Suitable for high school and college students, this book contains numerous illustrations and photographs, many in exquisite color.

Wolverton, Mark. *The Depths of Space: Story of the Pioneer Planetary Probes*. New York: Joseph Henry Press, 2004. Written by a journalist who covered the Pioneer 10, 11, and Venus missions, the text presents these spacecraft as the "little probes that could."

Pioneer Venus 1

Date: May 20, 1978, to October 8, 1992
Type of spacecraft: Planetary exploration

Pioneer Venus 1 obtained important information on Venus's topography and atmosphere. Previous American missions to Venus were quick flybys, but the Pioneer Venus orbiter, over many months, mapped most of the planet's surface and investigated in detail its atmosphere and ionosphere.

Key Figures

Charles F. Hall (1920-1999), project manager
Richard O. Fimmel (b. 1946), project manager for extended mission
Ralph W. Holtzclaw, Spacecraft Systems manager
Bruce C. Murray (1932-2013), director of the Jet Propulsion Laboratory
Gordon H. Pettengill, leader, Orbiter Radar Mapping team

Summary of the Mission

In 1967, shortly after the American Mariner 5 spacecraft flew by Venus and the Soviet Venera 4 spacecraft probed its atmosphere, the Pioneer Venus project began. Three scientists, Richard Goody of Harvard University, D. M. Hunten of Kitt Peak National Observatory, and N. W. Spencer of the Goddard Space Flight Center, formed a team to study the possibility of sending a probe to investigate Venus's atmosphere. Meeting at the Goddard Space Flight Center in Greenbelt, Maryland, these scientists considered several approaches for the Venus mission, including orbiters, atmospheric probes, and balloon probes. By 1969, the National Aeronautics and Space Administration (NASA) merged some of these ideas into what became known as the universal bus, a probe-orbiter combination that could be used to orbit the planet and send probes into its atmosphere. In 1970, twenty-one scientists of the Space Science Board and the Lunar and Planetary Missions Board of NASA analyzed possible missions to Venus and issued a report, *Venus: Strategy for Exploration*, informally referred to as the "Purple Book" because of its cover's color. This report recommended that exploration of Venus be an important item on NASA's agenda for the 1970's and 1980's.

Congress was reluctant to fund new space programs in the early 1970's, and as a result NASA's Venus program fell behind its Soviet counterpart, whose Venera spacecraft were piling up successes. After the American program was transferred to the Ames Research Center in California, a study team was organized. This team worked closely with a science steering group, formed of interested scientists, to define payloads for the mission. In 1972, this group published a report, informally referred to as the "Orange Book," that became the American guide to Venus exploration by spacecraft. This Pioneer Venus report recommended that three missions to Venus be supported: a multiple probe in 1976, an orbiter in 1978, and a probe in 1980. Because of financial restrictions, NASA decided in August, 1972, to limit the project to a multi-probe in 1977 and an orbiter in 1978. During this same period, the European Space Research Organization expressed an interest in the orbiter mission and, after a period of study, a group of European and American scientists recommended that the spacecraft's mission should cover a period of one rotation of Venus, that is, 243 Earth days.

In 1974, NASA approved the Pioneer Venus missions and selected the scientific instruments to be developed for the orbiter and multi-probe. After competitive studies, NASA chose Hughes Aircraft Company's Space and Communications Group to build the spacecraft. Unfortunately, Congress continued to withhold funding for the Venus program, and, after much political maneuvering, NASA decided to delay the multi-probe until 1978, so that both the multi-probe and orbiter could use the same launch opportunity, thereby reducing operational costs. Nevertheless, political problems were not at an end; in 1975, the House cut $48 million intended for the Pioneer missions, causing many organizations to lobby intensely for restoration of Pioneer Venus's funding. Eventually, funding was restored.

Meanwhile, scientists had been building and testing various scientific instruments for the mission. For example, they found ways to compress more than a thousand microcircuits and many intricate mechanical devices into a radar mapper that weighed only 11 kilograms. By February, 1978, all scientific instruments for the orbiter had been shipped to Hughes Aircraft Company in El

Segundo, California, where, after further testing, they were installed on the spacecraft. The orbiter was then shipped to the launch site at Cape Canaveral in Florida, where it was mated to an Atlas-Centaur rocket, its launch vehicle.

The Pioneer Venus Orbiter began its 480-million kilometer voyage to Venus at 9:13 a.m. eastern daylight time (13:13 Coordinated Universal Time or UTC) on May 20, 1978. Pioneer Venus 1 traveled outside Earth's orbit for three months and then moved inside it for the next four months. NASA scientists chose this long, indirect route to minimize the accelerating influence of solar gravity and reduce the amount of fuel needed to go into orbit around Venus. Because cosmic rays had caused errors in the spacecraft's memory circuits, controllers were uneasy about the orbital insertion maneuver that would take place while the orbiter was hidden behind Venus. On December 3, technicians loaded the orbiter's memory circuits with the sequence of commands needed to fire orbital insertion rockets the following day. At 7:51 a.m. eastern standard time (12:51 UTC) on December 4, the orbiter passed behind Venus and communications with Earth ceased. When the orbiter finally emerged, it sent a signal that took three minutes to travel 56 million kilometers to Earth. When that signal was received, controllers responded with shouts of joy.

The orbiter had been inserted into a highly eccentric, nearly polar Venusian orbit that would take it as close to Venus as 150 kilometers (perigee) and as far away from Venus as 66,900 kilometers (apogee). On December 5, the orbiter was maneuvered so that its antenna pointed to Earth, and several of its instruments were activated. By December 6, it beamed the first black-and-white images of Venus to Earth. During this early period of the mission, the radar mapper performed

Pioneer Venus 1 is presented to the press during the launch preparations. (NASA / KSC)

erratically and was deactivated for a month. Then, with redesigned operating procedures, it worked perfectly for the rest of the mission. Such was not the case with the infrared radiometer, which failed on the seventieth orbit. It was the only permanent instrument failure of the mission.

As the orbiter began its scientific tasks, not much was known about the upper atmosphere of Venus. As more and more data were transmitted to Earth, it became practical, through trial and error, to make orbital corrections. During the first phase of the orbiter's mission, the surface of Venus was mapped by radar. Radar mapping took 243 Earth days to accomplish (the time for Venus to rotate once on its axis). The radar mapper continued to function through 243 more orbits—a second Venus day—and with the completion of orbit 600 on July 27, 1980, NASA officials announced that phase 1 of the Pioneer Venus mission had been completed, though the radar mapper continued to return data through orbit 834, nearly eight months later. Other instruments were still active, however, and the orbiter continued to investigate the interaction of solar radiation with Venus's ionosphere over an entire solar cycle (from sunspot minimum to maximum to minimum).

After orbiting Venus for more than fourteen years, the Pioneer Venus Orbiter spacecraft ceased operating on October 8, 1992. The spacecraft passed through the lowest part of its orbit and out of radio contact. A radio signal should have been received by ground stations when it emerged from behind the planet.

Contributions

Venus is perpetually shrouded by layers of pale yellow clouds, and most of the twelve scientific instruments aboard the cylindrical orbiter were developed to observe the planet's atmosphere and global weather patterns. Venus's surface had been totally hidden until Earth-based radar began to penetrate its veil of clouds. Earthbound efforts were crude, however, and it was not until the Pioneer Venus

mission that the surface could be mapped. The orbiter's radar was able to map about 93 percent of the Venusian surface by sending radar pulses downward and measuring the time lag until the echo returned. In this way, the radar altimeter could detect features as small as 30 kilometers across and about 200 meters high.

The topographic map derived from the orbiter's radar data revealed that Venus is generally smoother than the other terrestrial planets (Mercury, Earth, and Mars), but that it is also a world of great mountains, expansive plateaus, enormous rift valleys, and shallow basins. The Venusian surface can be divided into three regions: rolling plains, lowlands, and highlands. Plains, which cover about 65 percent of the mapped surface, are pockmarked with circular features that may be the remains of impact craters. Lowlands, which comprise about 27 percent of the imaged surface area, are much less abundant than on Earth, where ocean basins cover about two-thirds of the globe. Venus's highlands, which comprise only 8 percent of the imaged surface area, are like Earth's continents. Venus has two major highland areas: Ishtar Terra and Aphrodite Terra. Venus's highest point, a mountain massif higher than Mount Everest on Earth, is known as Maxwell Montes. This huge area of uplifted terrain occupies the entire east end of Ishtar Terra, 11,800 meters above the average level and 9,000 meters above the adjoining Lakshmi Planum.

Besides the radar mapper, the orbiter carried other instruments for studying Venusian phenomena, including a telescope to observe the clouds in ultraviolet light, an infrared radiometer to measure heat radiated from the atmosphere, an ultraviolet spectrometer to track dark streaks in the clouds, and a variety of other sensors to examine the physical and chemical properties of the upper atmosphere. The orbiter found that the clouds that enshroud Venus horizontally also have an enormous vertical extent, about 50 kilometers. The orbiter's data also provide a more detailed picture of the temperature structure of Venus's atmosphere. Scientists have divided the atmosphere into two regions. In the lower region (called the troposphere), which extends from the surface to an altitude of 100 kilometers, the temperature decreases with height. Above the troposphere lies a thinner region (called the thermosphere), which is heated by ultraviolet solar radiation; thus, its temperature increases with height. One of the orbiter's most exciting discoveries was the enormous change in temperature between day and night in the upper atmosphere. Scientists have coined the term "cryosphere" (cold sphere) to describe the cold region of the upper atmosphere on the nightside of Venus. On Earth, the thermosphere is present day and night, whereas on Venus, the thermosphere disappears on the nightside.

Using such instruments as the photopolarimeter and ultraviolet spectrometer, the orbiter transmitted data to Earth about Venus's clouds that led to a detailed understanding of their morphology, composition, and motions. For example, ultraviolet photographs made on consecutive days showed that the dominant wind pattern on Venus drives cloud markings around the equatorial region in only four Earth days. The orbiter's instruments were also able to penetrate beneath the clouds to measure the high amount (96 percent) of carbon dioxide in Venus's atmosphere. Because Venus's dense carbon dioxide atmosphere inhibits absorbed sunlight from being reradiated into space as heat (the greenhouse effect), Venus has a higher surface temperature than any other planet.

Finally, the orbiter gathered considerable information about Venus's ionosphere, the region of its upper atmosphere characterized by a high density of electrically charged particles. Orbiter instruments also gathered data on how the ionosphere

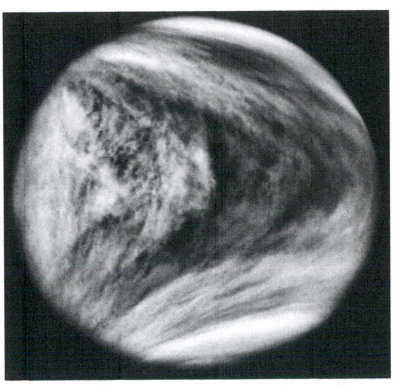

This image, acquired by Pioneer Venus 1, shows a thick layer of clouds that completely obscure the surface of Venus, which lies beneath them. (NASA)

interacts with the solar wind, the outward flow of atomic particles from the Sun. Venus has no appreciable magnetic field, but the interaction of its ionosphere with corpuscular radiations from the Sun produces a well-developed bow shock. Because the solar wind travels faster than any atmospheric pressure wave that could divert its flow around Venus, a shock wave, or bow shock, forms in the solar wind in front of Venus analogous to the shock wave in front of a supersonic aircraft. The Venusian bow shock is in many ways similar to that of Earth, but there are differences. At Venus the ionosphere deflects the solar wind; at Earth the strong terrestrial magnetic field deflects it.

Context

Until the Pioneer Venus missions, Earth-based observations had contributed little detailed knowledge about the cloud-covered planet. NASA's flyby missions, Mariners 2, 5, and 10, along with the Soviet

Union's Venera spacecraft, had shown that Venus's atmosphere is composed largely of carbon dioxide and that the surface is hot enough to melt such metals as lead, tin, and zinc. These previous missions offered only fleeting glimpses of the planet, however, whereas the Pioneer Venus orbiter permitted repeated sensing of Venus's surface, lower and upper atmosphere, ionosphere, and solar wind interaction. The Pioneer Venus missions clearly marked a milestone in the American exploration of Venus.

Pioneer Venus 1 was the latest in a series of uncrewed probes that had begun in the late 1950's. This series of probes sent back important information on magnetic fields and radiation in interplanetary space. Pioneers 10 and 11, which crossed the asteroid belt and studied Jupiter's atmosphere, conducted investigations of the interplanetary medium beyond Mars. Ames Research Center, which had taken over the Pioneer missions in 1962, viewed Pioneer Venus as a logical development within the tradition of small, relatively inexpensive Pioneer spacecraft.

From orbital insertion on December 4, 1978, through the following decade, Pioneer Venus Orbiter produced a wealth of scientific data on all aspects of the Venusian environment. Many of the instruments continued to be fully functional throughout this period. Even though the resolution of the orbiter's radar map of Venus is crude in comparison with that available for planets such as Mercury and Mars, this map does reveal enough about Venus to fuel speculations concerning its geology and evolution. Certain features—for example, the vertical uplift of the Lakshmi Planum— suggest tectonic activity. Some scientists think that ridges on Ishtar Terra may be the result of plate motion, though there is little evidence for integrated plate movements similar to continental drift on Earth.

In textbooks written before the Pioneer Venus missions, Venus was often depicted as Earth's twin because of their similar sizes and stable atmospheres. Data from the Pioneer orbiter has revealed that Venus is no twin of life-nurturing Earth. This is not to say that there are no similarities between the planets. Like Earth, Venus appears to have experienced volcanism, impact cratering, and a complex geologic history, and some models used to understand the circulation of the atmosphere on Earth can be used to understand Venus's weather patterns. Nevertheless, the differences on Venus are even more striking: the poisonous atmosphere, the sulfuric acid rain, and the furnace like surface temperatures.

The Pioneer Venus Orbiter's mission has also raised a host of intriguing questions for future exploration. What caused the greenhouse effect on Venus? Was there ever a large amount of water on Venus, and if so, what happened to it? Is Venus now quiet geologically, or is it active? Are the Venusian highlands like Earth's continents, or are they gigantic volcanic piles? Are the rolling plains extremely old or relatively recent in origin? These questions, in addition to the Pioneer Venus mission's many scientific accomplishments, are the lasting legacy of the orbiter mission. Knowledge of Venus was extended by the subsequent Magellan spacecraft, which orbited the planet, mapping the by means of radar, and determined the variations in Venus's gravitational field.

—*Robert J. Paradowski*

See also: Ames Research Center; Compton Gamma Ray Observatory; Magellan: Venus; Mariner 1 and 2; Mariner 8 and 9; Pioneer 11; Pioneer Venus 2; Planetary Exploration.

Further Reading

Briggs, Geoffrey, and Frederick Taylor. *The Cambridge Photographic Atlas of the Planets*. New York: Cambridge University Press, 1982. This atlas of the solar system contains the official maps of the planets and their satellites as well as more than two hundred photographs. The chapter on Venus makes excellent use of the data and photographs from the Pioneer Venus missions. The approach is descriptive and nontechnical.

Burgess, Eric. *Venus: An Errant Twin*. New York: Columbia University Press, 1985. An informative, well-illustrated volume by a skilled science writer. He perceptively recounts the history of the major discoveries about Venus, including those of Soviet and American exploration. He is willing to speak his mind, and his discussions of both the well-established findings and the controversial areas are entertaining as well as enlightening.

Cattermole, Peter, and Patrick Moore. *Atlas of Venus*. New York: Cambridge University Press, 1997. Filled with photography from telescopes and the Mariner, Pioneer Venus, and Magellan spacecraft, this work provides a complete atlas of Venus and a gazetteer of Venusian place-names.

Fimmel, Richard O., Lawrence Colin, and Eric Burgess. *Pioneer Venus*. NASA SP-461. Washington, D.C.: Government Printing Office, 1983. All three authors have been deeply involved in the Pioneer Venus missions, Fimmel as project manager, Colin as project scientist, and Burgess as a science journalist. Their attractively illustrated book is both authoritative and clearly written. Though they do not shirk analyses of technical matters, they avoid advanced mathematical and physical concepts, and their approach is accessible to the layperson.

Grinspoon, David Harry. *Venus Revealed: A New Look Below the Clouds of Our Mysterious Twin Planet*. New York: Perseus Book Group, 1998. This work provides both romantic and scientific explanations of the planet closest to Earth, incorporating the latest data from the Magellan spacecraft.

Hartmann, William K. *Moons and Planets*. 5th ed. Belmont, Calif.: Thomson Brooks/Cole Publishing, 2005. Provides detailed information about all objects in the solar system. Suitable on three separate levels: high school student, general reader, and the college undergraduate studying planetary geology.

Hunten, D. M., et al., eds. *Venus*. Tucson: University of Arizona Press, 1983. A scientific celebration of the exploration of Venus by spacecraft from Mariner 2 in 1962 to the Pioneer Venus and Venera missions of the late 1970's and early 1980's. Though the articles are technical, some of the more general ones are accessible to the layperson, especially if use is made of the helpful glossary at the end of the book. Most of the articles, however, are intended for readers with a knowledge of physics, chemistry, and advanced mathematics.

Jones, Barrie William. *The Solar System*. Elmsford, N.Y.: Pergamon Press, 1984. A presentation of the contemporary picture of the solar system. Written at an introductory level, the book assumes no previous knowledge of planetary astronomy. Jones's chapter on Venus discusses its interior, surface, and atmosphere in the light of data from the Pioneer Venus 1 Orbiter and the Pioneer Venus 2 Multiprobe.

Lee, Wayne. *To Rise from Earth: An Easy to Understand Guide to Spaceflight*. New York: Checkmark Books, 1996. This is a good introduction to the science of spaceflight. Although written by an engineer with the NASA Jet Propulsion Laboratory, it is presented in easy-to-understand language. In addition to the theory of spaceflight, it gives some of the history of the human endeavor to explore space.

McBride, Neil, and Iain Gilmour. *An Introduction to the Solar System*. New York: Cambridge University Press, 2004. This work provides a comprehensive tour of the solar system best suited to a high school or college course on planetary astronomy.

Morrison, David, and Tobias Owen. *The Planetary System*. 3d ed. San Francisco: Addison-Wesley, 2003. Organized by planetary object, this work provides contemporary data on all planetary bodies visited by spacecraft since the early days of the Space Age. Suitable for high school and college students and for the general reader.

Muenger, Elizabeth A. *Searching the Horizon: A History of Ames Research Center, 1940-1976*. NASA SP-4304. Washington, D.C.: Government Printing Office, 1985. Muenger wrote this book for NASA's internal history program. Ames has made many important contributions to NASA space missions, especially the Pioneer projects. Although Muenger does not deal directly with the Pioneer Venus program (it lies outside her chronological limits), her account of Ames's technological achievements in the context of its managerial evolution sheds light on the early history of the Pioneer program and makes the later successes of the Pioneer Venus project more understandable.

Pioneer Venus 2

Date: August 8 to December 9, 1978
Type of spacecraft: Planetary exploration

Pioneer Venus 2, often called the multiprobe, was a cluster of five spacecraft designed to penetrate Venus's cloud cover and gather information about all levels of its atmosphere at widely separated locations.

Key Figures

Charles F. Hall (1920-1999), project manager
Richard O. Fimmel (b. 1946), project manager
Lawrence Colin, project scientist
Gordon H. Pettengill, leader, multiprobe's radio
    science experiment

Summary of the Mission

During the 1960's, the Soviet Union and the United States used two different methods to explore Venus. The Soviets, with greater booster rockets, flew probe and lander missions as well as flybys, whereas the United States used flybys only. Conflicting information was sometimes obtained. For example, the Venera 4 lander recorded a surface temperature of 265° Celsius, while in the same year the Mariner 5 flyby recorded a surface temperature of 526° Celsius. Because of the many unanswered questions about Venus, a new approach was needed—a multi-faceted mission to orbit Venus and probe its dense atmosphere. The impetus for this new approach came mainly from scientists.

By 1968, the Space Science Board of the National Academy of Sciences had completed a study, *Planetary Exploration, 1968-1975*, which concluded that planetary explorations should be undertaken as an integrated plan involving a wide range of scientific disciplines. A specific recommendation was for the National Aeronautics and Space Administration (NASA) to initiate a program to put Pioneer spinning spacecraft into orbit around Mars and Venus. In 1969, the Goddard Space Flight Center published a report, *A Venus Multiple-Entry-Probe, Direct-Impact Mission*, which advised development of a program to send seven entry probes to Venus to measure its atmospheric temperature, pressure, and wind speeds. In 1970, twenty-one scientists of the Space Science Board and the Lunar and Planetary Missions Board of NASA studied the scientific potential of a mission to Venus and produced a report, *Venus: Strategy for Exploration*, which recommended two multiprobe missions for 1975 and two orbiter missions for 1976. Because of congressional unwillingness to provide funding, these missions never materialized.

NASA established a Pioneer Venus science steering group in 1972 to involve the scientific community in the Pioneer Venus missions. This group published a report known as the "Orange Book" that became a widely used guide to Venus exploration. Because of restricted budgets, NASA decided to limit the Pioneer Venus program to two flights, a multiprobe in 1977 and an orbiter in 1978. NASA then invited scientists to suggest experiments for the missions. A small number of instruments were made for these experiments, usually by the principal investigator. The instruments had to be miniaturized for inclusion in small, sealed shells. Unfortunately, Congress balked at the program, refusing to authorize mission starts, resulting in cancellations and a decision by NASA to launch both the multiprobe and the orbiter in 1978 to save costs. The biggest setback came in 1975, when the House

Charlie Hall inspects the Pioneer Venus 2 multiprobe at Hughes Aircraft Co. in Dec. 1976. (NASA)

of Representatives cut $48 million from NASA's appropriation for the Venus missions. By this time, however, many scientists had become ardent supporters of the program, and they successfully lobbied Congress to restore the funds.

Meanwhile, Hughes Aircraft Company, the primary contractor for the spacecraft, began assembling and testing the instruments at its plant in El Segundo, California. All instruments were ready in time for the mission. During April, 1978, the multiprobe completed its preshipment review at Hughes. Then the large probe was shipped to Cape Canaveral and placed on the bus, the spacecraft whose main function was to carry the probes to Venus and

target their entries into the atmosphere. Explosive bolts were also installed at KSC. The multiprobe was then transferred to the launch pad and mated with the launch vehicle, an Atlas SLV-3D booster and a Centaur D-1A second stage. The scheduled launch was August 6, 1978, but this was missed when a problem occurred in loading liquid helium into the Centaur.

Pioneer Venus 2 began its 350-million-kilometer voyage to Venus at 3:33 a.m. eastern daylight time (07:33 Coordinated Universal Time or UTC) on August 8, 1978. During its trip, the multiprobe had to undergo several critical maneuvers. For example, on August 17, mission controllers, through a series of carefully timed rocket thrusts, effected a course change that put the spacecraft on target for encounter with Venus on December 9. Then on November 9, when the multiprobe was about 13 million kilometers from Venus, controllers oriented the bus so that the large probe would separate in the proper direction. Unfortunately, tracking stations on Earth encountered problems concerning the precise orientation of the bus. Some scientists thought that there might be a propellant leak; others believed that the problem arose from difficulties in observing a spacecraft racing away from a rotating Earth, which itself was traveling in orbit around the Sun and wobbling in concert with the Moon. Because of these unresolved problems, the project manager decided to delay the scheduled release of the large probe from the bus. After an all-night session, NASA scientists agreed on a compromise timer setting, and on November 16 the large probe was successfully released toward its planned entry point on Venus.

The next critical maneuver involved pointing the bus toward Venus so that the three small, identical probes could be correctly released. The spin rate of the bus had to be precise, 49.60 revolutions per minute, to ensure that the probes would separate along paths that would take them to their individual targets on Venus. On November 20, when the bus was twenty days away from the planet, the small probes were successfully released. Upon separation, the probes became silent, because they lacked the power to replenish their batteries, but their internal timers had been set to reactivate their instruments three hours before descent into the Venusian atmosphere.

On December 9, radio contact with the four probes resumed. The first radio signal came from the large probe; then, one by one and within minutes of one another, the three small probes were detected. All instruments on all probes were operating satisfactorily. Now the exciting entry phase of the mission began. The large probe, which was the first to enter, rapidly decelerated as it penetrated the ever-thickening atmosphere. Its speed was further slowed by deployment of a Dacron parachute. At 45 kilometers above the surface, the parachute was jettisoned. The large probe hit the surface at 32 kilometers per hour, landing near the equator, some 55 minutes after first encountering the Venusian atmosphere. Its radio signals ceased immediately upon impact.

The three small probes, entering the atmosphere within three minutes of one another, were all slowed rapidly, dense gases retarding their fall without the use of parachutes. During their descents, windows opened on the probes and sensors began encountering the atmosphere and telemetering data to Earth. Like the large probe, the small probes took about 55 minutes to reach the surface. One of the probes, called the north probe, landed in darkness near the north polar region. Another probe, called the day probe, landed in the southern hemisphere on the day side. The third, the night probe, landed in the southern hemisphere on the night side. Although radio signals from the north and night probes ended at impact, transmissions from the day probe

continued for another 68 minutes before it became silent.

Meanwhile, the bus hurtled toward Venus close behind the probes. Its entry into the atmosphere occurred about 88 minutes after the last probe's entry. The bus plunged into the atmosphere on the day side. Unlike the small probes, the bus had no heatshield, and it burned up within two minutes. During this time, however, radio transmissions poured back to Earth, carrying scientific data on the composition of the very high atmosphere of Venus. The entire entry phase, involving all five spacecraft, took only 98 minutes, but in that time the probes and bus generated data that would cause scientists to take a new look at the complex atmosphere of Earth's sister planet.

Contributions

Scientific instruments on the probes measured temperature, pressure, and density from the upper atmosphere through the clouds to the surface. These instruments located sources and sinks of solar and infrared radiation in the lower atmosphere. Because of the various locations of the probes' descents, they were able to explore the atmosphere under daytime, nighttime, low-latitude, and high-latitude conditions. Enough data were acquired from these probes that a general meteorological model of Venus could be developed and compared with the meteorologies of other planets.

One of the important questions the probes were designed to answer is why Venus's surface has such a high temperature. Ubiquitous cloud cover on Venus is so reflective that the planet actually absorbs less solar radiation than Earth does. Furthermore, the probes showed that only a small fraction of this absorbed radiation actually penetrates the clouds and the dense lower atmosphere to reach the surface. Nevertheless, Venus remains extremely hot because, like a gigantic greenhouse, its atmosphere allows passage of incoming solar radiation but greatly restricts the radiation of heat back into space. The probes also found water vapor in the

A parachute system, designed to carry an instrument-laden probe down through the dense atmosphere of torrid, cloud-shrouded Venus, is tested in KSC's Vehicle Assembly Building. (NASA / KSC)

below the clouds, there is very little thermal contrast between day and night or between the equatorial and polar regions.

The probes also detected several distinct layers in Venus's atmosphere. The dense cloud layer that enshrouds the planet begins at an altitude of about 70 kilometers and then disappears at about 50 kilometers. A lower haze layer extends down to 30 kilometers, and below that the atmosphere is remarkably clear. Data from a spectrometer aboard the large probe revealed that the Venusian clouds contain nearly pure sulfuric acid. Another probe discovered a large quantity of atmospheric sulfur dioxide that declined after a time. Some scientists interpret this as indicating that sulfur dioxide had been ejected by a volcano and then settled to lower levels.

The Pioneer probes also measured wind speeds. The winds of Venus are dominated by a global east-to-west circulation that reaches a maximum of about 150 meters per second at the altitude of the cloud tops. For the most part, wind speeds on Venus decline with decreasing altitude, and at the surface are only about 1 meter per second. Venus itself turns from east to west, but it takes 243 Earth days to complete a single rotation. When this slow rotation is compared with the rapid speed of Venus's high-altitude winds, it becomes clear why many scientists say that the atmosphere of Venus superrotates, for at the cloud tops the atmosphere moves more than sixty times as fast as the planet does. In contrast, Earth turns west to east, and its atmosphere rotates nearly synchronously with the solid planet below it. Less dramatic than this global circulation is the movement of atmospheric matter from the equator to the pole and back again. This

lower atmosphere in sufficient amounts to trap infrared radiation even further.

Another discovery made by the probes is the enormous temperature difference between Venus's dayside and nightside upper atmospheres. Even with twice the incoming solar radiation, Venus somehow manages to keep a cooler upper atmospheric temperature than Earth's, but the real surprise is the low temperature of the upper atmosphere on Venus's nightside. The basic difference between the atmosphere of Venus and that of Earth is that the atmosphere of Venus is hot at the bottom and cold at the top, whereas on Earth the reverse is true. In the lower Venusian atmosphere, the probes found that, gigantic circulation—in which heated air rises at the equator and cooled air descends at the poles, traveling more or less horizontally in between, poleward above the clouds and equatorward below—is called a Hadley cell. On Venus these cells exist in a much simpler state than they do on Earth.

Finally, a surprising discovery resulted from the large probe's neutral mass spectrometer. Its data indicated that two isotopes of argon, argon 36 and argon 40, are present in Venus's atmosphere in equal amounts, whereas on Earth argon 40 is four hundred times more abundant than argon 36 is. This unexpected presence on Venus of argon 36— relatively rare on Earth and Mars—might lead to a total revision of theories about planetary formation.

Context

The Pioneer Venus multiprobe was an important part of the massive exploration of Venus by American and Soviet spacecraft in December, 1978. The multiprobe's success was particularly important for the United States, which had never before attempted to penetrate the clouds of Venus. Three Mariner spacecraft had reconnoitered the planet on flyby missions in 1962, 1967, and 1974, but it had been the Soviet Union that was the most significant explorer of Venus's atmosphere and surface. Following the missions of Pioneer Venus and of Veneras 11 and 12, Soviet and American scientists formally exchanged data and held several meetings at which results and interpretations were discussed. The Joint U.S./U.S.S.R. Working Group on Near-Earth Space, the Moon, and Planets fostered these cooperative efforts. These meetings ushered in a period of scientific détente between the two space superpowers, at least with regard to the exploration of Venus.

Soviet and American scientists agreed that the multiprobe mission resulted in a major increase in knowledge about Venus's gaseous environment. Unfortunately, space missions return ambiguous, even erroneous, data along with the unambiguous

data and results. Thus, in addition to key scientific questions about Venus that are now answered, there remain several that are not. For example, the composition of many of the particles in Venusian clouds remains to be determined. More information about lightning on Venus is necessary before scientists can speak with certainty about its origin. Why a westward super rotation is the dominant circulation of the Venusian atmosphere remains a great mystery. Another intriguing question left unresolved by the multiprobe mission is the reason for the lack of water in Venus's atmosphere. Some scientists think that the high deuterium-to-hydrogen ratio in the water of Venus's atmosphere is an important clue toward solving this puzzle; other scientists are more skeptical.

The multiprobe mission was like much scientific research in that answering one question often raises many others. New mysteries of Venus were created by the multiprobe mission, and new space missions will be needed to resolve them. Some of this further exploration has occurred. For example, Veneras 13, 14, 15, and 16 built on the foundation established by Pioneer Venus 1 and 2. The multiprobe's success demonstrated the practicality of focused interplanetary missions, and it contributed to the success of such missions as the Voyager explorations of Saturn and Jupiter. Pioneer Venus became a model for exploring the surfaces and atmospheres of the other planets of the solar system. The Magellan orbiter used a far more sophisticated radar system to map nearly the entire Venusian surface at far greater resolution than Pioneer Venus could, and produced a detailed gravity field map before it was purposely plunged into the upper atmosphere of Venus.

—*Robert J. Paradowski*

See also: Ames Research Center; Compton Gamma Ray Observatory; Magellan: Venus; Mariner 1 and 2; Pioneer Venus 1; Planetary Exploration. 1098 Pioneer Venus 2

Further Reading

Burgess, Eric. *Venus: An Errant Twin*. New York: Columbia University Press, 1985. Burgess, a research scientist and journalist, presents a survey of modern knowledge about Venus for the nonscientist. His book emphasizes the modern explorations of Venus by spacecraft, but he also discusses previous attempts to understand the veiled planet by telescope and radar. He presents a knowledgeable discussion of the Pioneer multiprobe in his chapter on Pioneer Venus. His well-illustrated book also contains an adept examination of various theories about Venus's origin and evolution.

Cattermole, Peter, and Patrick Moore. *Atlas of Venus*. New York: Cambridge University Press, 1997. Filled with photography from telescopes and the Mariner, Pioneer Venus, and Magellan spacecrafts, this work provides a complete atlas of Venus and a gazetteer of Venusian place-names.

Fimmel, Richard O., Lawrence Colin, and Eric Burgess. *Pioneer Venus*. NASA SP-461. Washington, D.C.: Government Printing Office, 1983. This handsomely illustrated book was prepared at the Ames Research Center with the help of many of the scientists who were directly involved in the mission, as were Fimmel and Colin. The authors place the Pioneer Venus missions in context with previous explorations of the planet. There are also excellent chapters on the history of Pioneer Venus, the development of the orbiter and the multiprobe, the actual mission to the planet, and an analysis of the scientific results.

Grinspoon, David Harry. *Venus Revealed: A New Look Below the Clouds of Our Mysterious Twin Planet*. New York: Perseus Book Group, 1998. This work provides both romantic and scientific explanations of the planet closest to Earth, incorporating the latest data from the Magellan spacecraft.

Hartmann, William K. *Moons and Planets*. 5th ed. Belmont, Calif.: Thomson Brooks/Cole Publishing, 2005. Provides detailed information about all objects in the solar system. Suitable on three separate levels: high school student, general reader, and the college undergraduate studying planetary geology.

Hunten, D. M., et al., eds. *Venus*. Tucson: University of Arizona Press, 1983. Sixty-five authors have collaborated with the editors in analyzing the new data presented to scientists by the many spacecraft explorations of Venus. Topics discussed include the interior, surface, and atmosphere of Venus. Most of the authors are drawn from the Pioneer Venus and Venera scientific communities. The thirty chapters are almost evenly divided between major surveys and detailed technical discussions. The papers are all in English (Russian papers have been translated), but they require a knowledge of advanced mathematics, physics, and chemistry for a complete understanding.

Jones, Barrie William. *The Solar System*. Elmsford, N.Y.: Pergamon Press, 1984. A survey of contemporary knowledge about the solar system. The author presupposes no previous knowledge of planetary astronomy on the part of the reader. The chapter on Venus uses the Pioneer Venus data to discuss the interior, surface, and atmosphere of Venus. There is also a good discussion of why so little water exists in the Venusian atmosphere.

McBride, Neil, and Iain Gilmour. *An Introduction to the Solar System*. New York: Cambridge University Press, 2004. This work provides a comprehensive tour of the solar system best suited to a high school or college course on planetary astronomy.

Morrison, David, and Tobias Owen. *The Planetary System*. 3d ed. San Francisco: Addison- Wesley, 2003. Organized by planetary object, this work provides contemporary data on all planetary bodies visited by spacecraft since the early days of the Space Age. Suitable for high school and college students and for the general reader.

Muenger, Elizabeth A. *Searching the Horizon: A History of Ames Research Center, 1940-1976.* NASA SP-4304. Washington, D.C.: Government Printing Office, 1985. Muenger wrote this book for NASA's internal history program. Ames Research Center (ARC) has made many important contributions to several space missions for NASA and was intimately involved with the Pioneer program from Pioneer 6 onward. Although she briefly mentions the Pioneer Venus missions, her focus is on ARC's technological achievements in the context of its managerial development. This emphasis helps the reader to grasp the early history of the Pioneer program, which in turn makes the Pioneer Venus mission more comprehensible in terms of NASA's institutional evolution.

Nicks, Oran W. *Far Travelers: The Exploring Machines.* NASA SP-480. Washington, D.C.: Scientific and Technical Information Branch, 1985. Discusses all major NASA planetary spacecraft during NASA's first quarter-century. Written by a senior NASA official involved with lunar and planetary programs during that era.

Pater, Imke de, and Jack J. Lissauer. *Planetary Science.* New York: Cambridge University Press, 2001. This is an advanced text about the physical, chemical, and geological processes at work in the solar system.

Planetary Exploration

Date: Beginning 1962
Type of program: Planetary exploration

American, European, and Soviet robotic planetary space probes from 1962 to the present have explored all the known planets in the solar system. The greatest beneficiary of knowledge gained from those investigations has been the field of planetary geology. By comparing our planet to others, a greater understanding of Earth has been acquired. This has also added to the understanding of planetary formation, and is of great interest to those searching for planets beyond our solar system.

Summary of the Missions

Nearly six decades of planetary exploration by spacecraft dispatched from Earth cannot be completely recounted in an article of this length. What follows is a synopsis of many of the highlights of robotic investigations throughout the solar system. Some of the story is presented sorted by solar system object, and part is chronological in nature. For more detailed descriptions see other articles devoted to individual missions. Successful robotic exploration began in 1962 when the American Mariner 2 probe reached Venus. The first robotic mission to draw major public attention was the Mariner 4 flyby of Mars in 1965. That spacecraft returned a small number of close-range photographs of the Martian surface showing heavy cratering, but also some evidence of flowing water in past geologic ages.

During the mid-1960's, the United States gained valuable experience in interplanetary exploration with the Ranger and Surveyor Programs, designed to prepare the way for the Apollo piloted lunar program. Ranger vehicles returned thousands of pictures before impacting the surface; the Surveyor series soft-landed to collect and analyze samples of the lunar surface. Extensive mapping was down by five Lunar Orbiters which helped scientists pick the Apollo landing sites.

The Soviet probe Venera 3 became the first human-made object to impact a planet, in 1966. Venera 4 and the American Mariner 5 both arrived at Venus in 1967 within hours of each other. Venera 4 released an instrument package that was designed to land on the planet, but stopped transmitting some 30 kilometers above the surface. Mariner 5 passed radio signals through the atmosphere to determine its composition.

In 1969, Mariners 6 and 7 returned much larger numbers of photographs of Mars of far higher quality than those produced by Mariner 4, revealing Mars to a be a planet of very complex geology. Mariner 9, which reached Mars in 1971, became the first probe to orbit the planet rather than just make a flyby, providing scientists with much time to use its instruments to gather data. In the same year, a Soviet probe attached to Mars 3—part of a sequence of mostly unsuccessful missions by the Soviet Union in the early 1970's—reached the surface of Mars but transmitted for only about ninety seconds. (Following these failures, the Soviet Union turned its attention for the next fifteen years to Venus with a series of more successful Venera orbiters and landers.)

Pioneers 10 and 11 were the first missions to the outer planets. Pioneer 10 passed Jupiter in late 1973 and headed on a trajectory that would take it beyond

This view of Jupiter's clouds was imaged by Voyager 1. The Great Red Spot is seen at top right as a brown oval. Below the Great Red Spot are various bands of bluer wavy clouds at smaller scales with smaller light blue spots. (NASA / JPL-Caltech)

the bounds of the solar system; it transmitted until late 1997. Pioneer 11 visited both Jupiter (1974) and Saturn (1979) and continued transmitting through 1995. Mariner 10 made three flybys of Mercury in 1974-1975, photographing about half of the planet's surface. En route, it passed Venus and photographed the planet's cloud cover. The spacecraft was the first to use the gravitational field of one planet to assist in propelling it to the vicinity of another.

Two Viking missions to Mars in 1976 became the first successful landers on the planet. Viking 1 enthralled the public with the first photographs from the Martian surface and a dramatic set of experiments designed to detect evidence of possible Martian microbial life. The Viking landers continued to transmit meteorological reports for several years. The orbiters that delivered the Viking landers to Mars remained in orbit, adding to the depth and detail of our knowledge of surface features. Several of the Mariner and Viking missions also returned

photographs of the two tiny Martian satellites Deimos and Phobos.

Perhaps the highlights of robotic planetary exploration in the twentieth century were the epic missions of Voyagers 1 and 2 to the outer solar system's gas giant planets and beyond. Launched in 1977, Voyager 1 reached Jupiter early in 1979 and Saturn in late 1980. In order to bring it into position to examine Saturn's satellite Titan, scientists bent Voyager 1's trajectory out of the plane containing the orbits of the major planets. Voyager 2 arrived at Jupiter in 1979 and reached Saturn in 1981. Timed for launch when planetary alignments made possible an almost incredible "Grand Tour" of the outer solar system, the mission continued on to Uranus in 1986, and Neptune in 1989. Before exiting the system, it returned some of the most spectacular photographs in history.

A pair of Pioneer Venus spacecraft reached their objective in 1978, the first of which entered orbit and transmitted information until 1992. The second carried probes that impacted on the planet's surface. Following a hiatus of more than a decade in robotic planetary exploration, activity resumed in 1989 with the launch of Magellan, which orbited Venus. Magellan used radar to map most of the surface of Venus, which is almost totally obscured by clouds.

Also in 1989, the complex Galileo expedition to Jupiter got under way. Originally intended to be launched out of Earth orbit by the *Atlantis* shuttle, Galileo had to be redesigned for surface launch following the *Challenger* accident. This required a complex series of gravitational boosts from Venus and Earth to acquire the necessary velocity and greatly lengthened the mission. Galileo did not reach Jupiter until the end of 1995. It released a probe into the Jovian upper atmosphere that survived nearly an hour. Galileo then went into orbit around Jupiter to study the planet and its major satellites, especially volcanic Io and enticing Europa. Some scientists believe Europa harbors an ocean beneath its frozen surface. After a greatly extended mission, Galileo was purposely plunged into Jupiter's atmosphere to prevent it from colliding with and contaminating Europa or any other Jovian moon. Galileo was followed by the Juno spacecraft which launched on August 5, 2011, and reached Jovian orbit on July 5, 2016. The seven-year mission was intended to include 37 orbits about Jupiter with its science mission to concentrate on magnetic and gravity fields, particle detections, plasma wave observations, and investigations using an ultraviolet imaging spectrometer. Also Juno's imaging system was far superior than Galileo's, and did not suffer from a low transmission rate for data. As of 2019 Juno remains operational, providing surprises about Jupiter so intriguing that its mission was extended until at least 2021.

Robotic exploration of Mars resumed in 1988 with a number of extremely ambitious missions. Spectacular failures punctuated attempts to return to the planet. In August, 1993, ground stations lost contact with the American Mars Observer shortly before its scheduled arrival, the victim of an explosion in its propulsion system plumbing; in 1988-1989, two complex Soviet missions, Phobos 1 and 2— loaded with international experiments and assisted by the American Deep Space Tracking Network— reached Mars orbit but failed in novel attempts to place landers on the Martian satellites; in 1996 a Russian probe called Mars '96 failed to reach escape velocity from the Earth.

A huge success finally came in July, 1997, when Mars Pathfinder used a radical method of landing on Mars, encasing the entire vehicle in a cluster of large air bags to cushion the impact. After settling on the surface, Pathfinder deployed a small robot vehicle called Sojourner, which could receive commands from Earth. Sojourner spent nearly three months exploring the immediate vicinity of the landing site. In September, 1997, the Mars Global Surveyor arrived to begin making highly detailed physiographic maps of the Martian surface. Surveyor was the first vehicle to establish an orbit around another planet using atmospheric braking, which gradually transformed a highly elliptical orbit into a nearly circular one.

Catastrophe returned to haunt the American Mars exploration program in September, 1999, with the loss of the Mars Climate Orbiter, which evidently burned up in the Martian atmosphere as the result of confusion by ground controllers between U.S. and metric units of measurement in

They might look like trees on Mars, but they're not. Groups of dark brown streaks were photographed by the Mars Reconnaissance Orbiter in 2008 near the North Pole of Mars. At that time, dark sand on the interior of Martian sand dunes became more and more visible as the spring Sun melted the lighter carbon dioxide ice. When occurring near the top of a dune, dark sand may cascade down the dune leaving dark surface streaks -- streaks that might appear at first to be trees standing in front of the lighter regions, but cast no shadows. (NASA) plotting the course. Perhaps even more of a setback was the loss, just three months later, of the Mars Polar Lander, a much-anticipated mission to explore the southern polar regions of the planet and search for water ice. Ground controllers lost contact with the lander—which also carried two micro-probes designed to search for water or ice beneath the surface—shortly after it entered the Martian atmosphere. These much-publicized misfortunes prompted full-scale review of the Mars exploration program and missions scheduled for future launch. Tremendous success followed when a pair of Mars Exploration Rovers called Spirit and Opportunity landed independently at vastly separated sites in January, 2004. Both rovers were much larger and more capable than Mars Pathfinder, traversing distances on the surface measured in kilometers rather than meters. Each continued to produce important results well after its first year on Mars. Among the most exciting of these was the definitive identification of rocks and minerals that required the presence of water on Mars in the past. Results hinted at the potential for past life on Mars, but no direct evidence was found. Mars studies enjoyed a great deal of success during the early portion of the twenty-first century. NASA sent the Mars Odyssey and Mars Reconnaissance Orbiter to act as scientific platforms, imaging systems, and relays to surface robots. Spirit continued to operate until it became stuck in soft sand and was lost in 2010. Opportunity lasted even longer roving across the Martian surface. It encountered a nearly complete planetary dust storm which left it without the ability to recharge its solar battery, and its mission was declared over in 2019. For a time there were three rovers operating on the Red Planet. The Mars Science Laboratory or Curiosity rover was delivered to the Red Planet in 2012. It landed in Gale crater and moved toward the centrally located Mount Sharp to seek evidence of sedimentary layers. As of 2019 Curiosity was the only rover working on the Martian surface, but plans are on track to launch the Mars 2020 rover during the coming summer. But surface

operations on Mars early in the twenty-first century also involved stationary landers. On May 25, 2008 the Mars Phoenix spacecraft landed at a high latitude in the Martian Northern Hemisphere. Its robotic arm was able to reveal evidence of subsurface water ice. Then on November 26, 2018 the InSight lander touched down in Elysium Planitia to perform heat flow and seismology research on Mars. As of 2019 the seismometer had detected Marsquakes, but the heat flow experiment was having trouble digging itself deep enough to deploy its temperature sensors.

Cassini, intended to be the first orbital mission of the Saturn system, left Earth in October, 1997, carrying the Huygens probe, designed to land on Titan, the planet's largest satellite. A joint effort of NASA and the European Space Agency (ESA), the spacecraft entered Saturn's orbit in July, 2004, and began its studies of the planet, its system of moons, and the ring plane. Late in 2004, the Huygens probe was detached from the main spacecraft, and on January 14, 2005, it descended through the atmosphere of Titan and touched down safely on that large moon's surface. Cassini remained in orbit about Saturn for over twelve years. The orbiter flew past Titan a great many times at close range, discovered that the small moon Enceladus sported water geysers near its south pole and thereby developed an interest in this world for both planetary scientists and astrobiologists, studied the ring system of the planet in great detail, and basically rewrote the textbooks on the solar system's most beautiful planet. To avoid potential plutonium contamination of any world in the Saturn system, when the mission was drawing to a close, Cassini was maneuvered to fly through the ring plane, and on September 15, 2017, be destroyed in the planet's atmosphere.

Clementine, a joint venture of NASA and the United States Department of Defense, signified renewed interest in lunar exploration and spent two months of 1994 producing highly detailed maps of the surface. Lunar Prospector, launched in 1998, spent eighteen months in orbit studying lunar geology. Controllers caused it to impact near the lunar south pole in July, 1999, in an unsuccessful attempt to reveal the presence of water ice.

The planet Mercury had not been revisited since the initial expedition, Mariner 10, in 1975. A Mercury orbiter called MESSENGER (Mercury Surface, Space Environment, Geochemistry, and Ranging) was launched on August 3, 2004. After a series of gravity assists, the spacecraft entered Mercury orbit in 2011, and remained operational until April 30, 2015 when it was crashed purposely into the planet's surface.

Expeditions to smaller objects in the solar system contribute significantly to our knowledge of planetary evolution. An international flotilla of probes encountered Comet Halley in 1986. The Near Earth Asteroid Rendezvous (NEAR) mission, launched by the United States in 1996, entered orbit around the asteroid Eros in 2000. Stardust, launched in 1999, rendezvoused with Comet Wild 2 on January 2, 2004, and captured cometary dust samples; the spacecraft returned those samples to Earth in 2006. The Genesis spacecraft had demonstrated the method of sample return to be used by Stardust when it came back to Earth over the salt flats of Utah on September 8, 2004, carrying solar wind particles trapped in aerogel-based collectors. Unfortunately, the spacecraft crashed into the ground and cracked open rather than having its parachute snagged safely by a recovery helicopter. Fortunately for the Genesis program, samples survived the crash, but the incident created consternation as to whether or not Stardust would suffer a similar fate upon return to Earth. The Dawn mission launched on September 27, 2007, and flew to the asteroid belt. It first entered orbit about Vesta, and remained there studying

that large asteroid for nearly 14 months. Dawn then broke out of orbit and headed for the dwarf planet Ceres. During a period of over 3.5 years Dawn discovered a number of unexpected features on Ceres, not the least of which was a large crater with two very bright spots inside. Dawn was the only spacecraft to enter orbit about one solar system body only to go and orbit yet another outside the Earth-Moon system.

Throughout the last half of the twentieth century, vastly improved Earth-based and orbital telescopes, radar imaging, and radio astronomy supplemented the findings of robotic probes. For example, as early as 1956, radio astronomers confirmed the high temperatures of the surface and atmosphere of Venus. Telescopes detected rings around Uranus and a previously unknown satellite for Pluto in 1978. In 1992, radar mapping of Mercury suggested possible

Long ago, there were large crescent-shaped (barchan) dunes that moved across this area, and at some point, there was an eruption. The lava flowed out over the plain and around the dunes, but not over them. The lava solidified, but these dunes still stuck up like islands. However, they were still just dunes, and the wind continued to blow. Eventually, the sand piles that were the dunes migrated away, leaving these "footprints" in the lava plain. These are also called "dune casts" and record the presence of dunes that were surrounded by lava. This dune cast is notable for its resemblance to the Starfleet insignia from popular television series Star Trek. (NASA / JPL / University of Arizona)

water ice deposits near the poles. Observation of the impacts of fragments of Comet Shoemaker-Levy on Jupiter in 1994 illustrated the potentially disastrous consequences of impacts even by small bodies, and in 1998-1999 radar signals returned conflicting data for a possible hydrocarbon ocean on Titan. Growing evidence of a vast number of planetesimals in orbit far beyond Pluto greatly complicated our image of the solar system. In the 1990's, astronomers began to detect evidence of planets, Jupiter-sized or much larger, orbiting other stars. As these discoveries continue, and improved technology begins to reveal smaller planets as well, there will be an invaluable comparative basis upon which to better understand our own solar system. Those studies continued in the early twenty-first century, and were joined by investigations performed by space-based telescopes such as the Hubble Space Telescope and Spitzer Space Telescope.

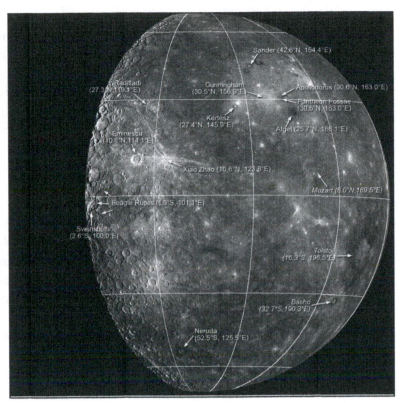

The International Astronomical Union (IAU) recently approved new names for features on Mercury that were all seen for the first time in images taken by MESSENGER during the spacecraft's first flyby of the planet. (NASA)

Contributions

Robotic planetary exploration generated far more knowledge about the solar system in the last third of the twentieth century and the first two decades of the twenty-first century than had been accumulated in all previous periods of history combined. Photographic returns alone represented such a stunning advance over fuzzy images from Earth-bound telescopes that textbooks about the solar system had to be completely rewritten. Other planets and their satellites turned out to be far more varied and individually peculiar than could have been imagined. Major accomplishments include a nearly complete topographic map of Venus and working theories of how that planet, so similar to Earth in size, could have developed a runaway greenhouse effect leading to

its thick atmosphere and extremely high temperatures and pressures. During the first billion or so years of its existence, Venus may have evolved along lines similar to Earth, perhaps even with oceans, but later developed a hellish environment resulting from this runaway greenhouse effect.

Mars also shows many signs of early evolution along terrestrial lines. Although heavily cratered and far colder today than even Antarctica, and lacking all but the thinnest atmosphere of carbon dioxide, the topography of Mars is rich with hints of huge amounts of flowing water during its first billion years. The comparative flatness of the planet's northern hemisphere suggests the existence of a primordial ocean, and for liquid water to have been present on the surface, the atmosphere must have been much denser and ambient temperatures much higher than at present. Despite such signs, both

Venus and Mars are significantly different from Earth; both, for example, nearly lack magnetic fields, required to deflect dangerous radiation.

The outer planets—Jupiter, Saturn, Uranus, and Neptune, once thought to be more or less alike—revealed many differences. The atmospheric composition of Jupiter, for example, as analyzed by the Galileo probe, is not consonant with formation of the planet at its current distance from the Sun. Jupiter's major satellites have vastly different conditions. Europa appears covered with water ice, but the fractures in the ice indicate a liquid ocean beneath, perhaps kept above freezing by volcanism and tidal stresses as the satellite resonates with Jupiter and other moons. Ganymede and Callisto also may be covered with water ice and may have subsurface salty oceans. Io, caught in powerful gravitational fields within the system, is the most geologically active body in the solar system, completely resurfacing itself with lava flows about every hundred million years. Saturn revealed the immense complexity of its rings (though all the gas giants turned out to have thin ring systems); Voyager photographs discovered a multitude of previously unknown satellites. The number of satellites of Uranus increased to eighteen, and those of Neptune to eight; again the larger satellites showed great individuality. Geologic activity appears to be present on Neptune's largest satellite, Triton. Post-mission analysis of Voyager data, coupled with telescopic observations, found many more moons around the gas giants.

Context

Although planetary probes have accounted for a tiny percentage of robotic missions, they generate disproportionate public interest through both their spectacular successes and their much-publicized failures. Earlier missions were relatively expensive, and the odds against success continue to be daunting. Many links exist between public attitudes toward piloted missions and these presumed robotic precursors. The captivating nature of deep-space photography, robotic systems, and other instrumentation—when they succeed—serve the argument that piloted missions are dangerous and unnecessary; the failures often do the same. Others argue that a human presence could deal with malfunctions and that planning and development time—especially added to flight time to the outer planets—is so long that when a mission arrives at its destination, its technology is two decades old.

Inevitably, much public attention has been invested in findings that might suggest life, or at least the conditions for life, elsewhere in the solar system. Witness the suspenseful coverage of test programs of Martian soil samples on Vikings 1 and 2. Increasingly, robotic missions explore for water or water ice (now known to be relatively abundant), in the hope that some form of life might also be present or that they might supply constituents for rocket propellants and sustain eventual human colonization. Something else that spacecraft search for at Mars is methane. The Curiosity rover in 2019 detected a change in methane emission at the surface. Previous orbiting spacecraft had noted significant methane

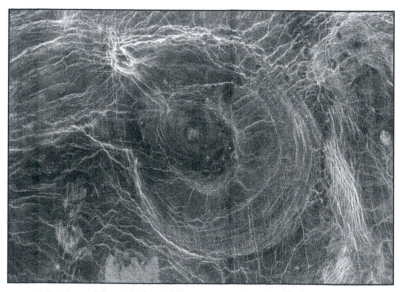

Arachnoid Trotula Corona on Venus radar image by Magellan. (NASA)

on Mars. The open question remains whether that methane originated geologically or by biological means.

The real beneficiaries of this kind of exploration thus far have been the planetary sciences. Our knowledge of volcanism, plate tectonics, and planetary evolution has expanded enormously with the data returned from other planets as a comparative base. Other models of atmospheric circulation add to our understanding of atmospheric physics and climatology. The complex gravitational resonances in the satellite systems of the outer planets show that the overall gravitational structure of the solar system is far more complex than previously believed. Compared to Mars, whose angle of axial inclination appears to have varied greatly over geologic time, with consequent upheavals in climate, scientists now value the presence of a large satellite such as the Moon in lending stability to a planetary system. Growing concerns about the number of small asteroids discovered in the vicinity of Earth orbit—punctuated by a consensus that major asteroid impacts may have led to the near-extinction of life on Earth on several occasions—have completely changed how scientists and the informed public view the significance of space exploration.

Many other planetary science missions were conducted since the dawn of the space age than the ones listed in this summary article. What constitutes a planet remained somewhat controversial even in 2019. At a meeting of the International Astronomical Union in Prague in 2006, four special criteria had been established for what determining what constitutes a planet. That classification scheme resulted in our solar system having terrestrial planets (Mercury, Venus, Earth, and Mars), gas giants (Jupiter and Saturn), ice giants (Uranus and Neptune), and dwarf planets. Pluto had been demoted from planetary status and was referred to in 2019 as a dwarf planet like Ceres. Pluto was encountered by the New Horizons spacecraft, and the interested reader is directed to a separate article concerning that historic mission.

—*Ronald W. Davis, updated by David G. Fisher*

See also: Asteroid and Comet Exploration; Cassini: Saturn; Clementine Mission to the Moon; Dawn Mission; Galileo: Jupiter; Juno; Magellan: Venus; Mariner 1 and 2; Mars 2020; Mars Curiosity; Mars Exploration Rovers; Mars InSight; Mars Pathfinder; Mars Phoenix; Mars Reconnaissance Orbiter; MESSENGER; New Horizons Pluto-Kuiper Belt Mission; Search for Extraterrestrial Life; Stardust Project; Viking Program; Voyager Program.

Further Reading

Adamson, Thomas K. *The Secrets of Jupiter (Planets)*. Washington, D.C.: National Geographic, 2015. For the young adult. Filled with pictures of Jupiter and explanations of the science in easy to understand descriptions for the interested student.

Adamson, Thomas K. *The Secrets of Neptune (Planets)*. Washington, D.C.: National Geographic, 2015. One of several books for children in the NatGeo "planets" series, this work describes Neptune's atmosphere, rings, and moons as seen by Voyager 2 and the Hubble Space Telescope. Written to excite a young mind.

Adamson, Thomas K. *The Secrets of Uranus (Planets)*. Washington, D.C.: National Geographic, 2015. One of several books for children in the NatGeo "planets" series, this work describes the atmosphere, rings, and moons of the seventh planet. Written to excite a young mind.

Baines, Kevin H., F. Michael Flasar, Norbert Krupp, and Tom Stallard. *Saturn in the Twenty First Century*. Cambridge, England: Cambridge University Press, 2019. For the serious reader. Fully describes the state of knowledge about Saturn after the Cassini missions and several centuries of astronomical interest and investigation.

Beatty, J. Kelly, Carolyn Collins Petersen, and Andrew Chaikin, eds. *The New Solar System*. 4th ed. New York: Sky Publishing, 1999. One of the best summaries of discoveries about other planets in the 1980's and 1990's, as well as how these discoveries have been synthesized into a new and more complex understanding of the solar system. Raises new questions requiring further research.

Brandt, John C., and Robert D. Chapman. *Introduction to Comets*. New York: Cambridge University Press, 2004. Provides a detailed exposé about virtually every cometary phenomenon.

Carlson-Berne, Emma. *The Secrets of Venus (Planets)*. Washington, D.C.: National Geographic, 2015. Part of a series about the planets intended for the younger mind curious about the solar system and space flight. Contrasts Earth and Venus and puts the second planet into context with all the solar system planets.

David, Leonard. *Mars: Our Future on the Red Planet*. Washington, D.C.: National Geographic, 2016. A companion book for a National Geographic Channel dramatization of what live on Mars would be like a quarter century after the publication date. Well written, and fascinating reading. Plenty of pictures but far more than a typical "coffee table" book.

David, Leonard. *Moon Rush: The New Space Race*. Washington, D.C.: National Geographic, 2019. Describes a new effort to reach the Moon, and set up for long-term exploration of Earth's nearest neighbor in space and for the exploitation of its natural resources. Places lunar science in the context of Apollo and prior scientific investigations of the Moon.

Grinspoon, David Harry. *Venus Revealed: A New Look Below the Clouds of Our Mysterious Twin Planet*. New York: Perseus Book Group, 1998. This work provides both romantic and scientific explanations of the planet closest to Earth, incorporating the latest data from the Magellan spacecraft.

Harland, David M. *Jupiter Odyssey: The Story of NASA's Galileo Mission*. London: Springer- Praxis, 2000. A detailed scientific and engineering history of the Galileo program, but also includes extensive discussion of Voyager program events and results.

---. *Mission to Saturn: Cassini and the Huygens Probe*. London: Springer-Praxis, 2002. An in-depth history of the Cassini program that also includes lengthy discussion of the Voyager program.

Irwin, Patrick G. J. *Giant Planets of Our Solar System: Atmospheres, Composition, and Structure*. London: Springer-Praxis, 2003. Provides an in-depth comparison of Jupiter, Saturn, Uranus, and Neptune, incorporating data obtained from astronomical observations and planetary spacecraft encounters.

Kaufman, Marc. *Mars Up Close: Inside the Curiosity Mission*. Washington, D.C.: National Geographic, 2014. Recommended by Buzz Aldrin. Shows Mars as a world that is perplexing and intriguing. Explains the findings of the Curiosity rover in Gale Crater.

Miner, Ellis D., and Randii R. Wessen. *Neptune: The Planet, Rings, and Satellites*. London: Springer-Praxis, 2002. Miner, the assistant project scientist for the Voyager 2 Neptune encounter composed this thorough review of our contemporary understanding of the Neptune system.

Mishkin, Andrew. *Sojourner: An Insider's View of the Mars Pathfinder Mission*. New York: Berkley Books, 2003. A thorough exploration of the Mars Pathfinder mission that also provides a detailed historical perspective on the exploration of the surface of Mars (begun by Viking).

Morrison, David, and Tobias Owen. *The Planetary System*. 3d ed. San Francisco: Addison- Wesley, 2003. Organized by planetary object, this work provides contemporary data on all planetary bodies visited by spacecraft since the early days of the Space Age. Suitable for high school and college students and for the general reader.

Radomski, Kassandra Kathleen. *The Secrets of Saturn (Planets)*. Washington, D.C.: National Geographic, 2015. One of several books in the NatGeo series about the planets, this work describes the ringed planet Saturn and its multitude of moons. Intended to excite a young mind about the solar system and space travel.

Sparrow, Giles. *Mars*. New York: Quercus, 2015. Heavily illustrated with images taken by spacecraft in orbit about and on the surface of Mars. Explains the findings of the Mars Curiosity rover as well as describing the findings of previous investigations of the Red Planet.

Strom, Robert G., and Ann L. Sprague. *Exploring Mercury: The Iron Planet*. New York: Springer-Praxis, 2003. A detailed history of our changing understanding of the planet closet to the Sun. Includes Mariner 10 data and describes the goals of the MESSENGER mission.

Private Industry and Space Exploration

Date: Beginning January 1, 1955
Type of issue: Socioeconomic

Since the mid-1950's, utilization of launch vehicles, artificial satellites, and space shuttles by private companies that produce or consume space-related technologies and services has grown to multibillion-dollar proportions, creating new challenges as well as opportunities.

Summary of the Issue

After the mid-1950's, with the development of increasingly sophisticated rocketry, missiles, space shuttles, and space laboratories—and their support technologies—it became clear that space afforded economic opportunities for individual and corporate private enterprises.

Commercial and industrial interest in space exploitation has been affected by shifts in the national policy-making climate. Ever since the eighteen-month International Geophysical Year (July, 1957, through December, 1958), heavy emphasis has been placed on peaceful, cooperative use of space, and every American president since Dwight D. Eisenhower has reaffirmed those principles; nevertheless, by the 1960's space had become one more arena for U.S.-Soviet competition.

For astute business interests, however, there were positive signs. Created in 1958, the National Aeronautics and Space Administration (NASA) was charged with maintaining U.S. superiority in space science and technology, and with contributing to the peaceful exploitation of space. By 1962, with its communications satellite program under way, NASA asked private enterprises to enter with it into joint public/private ventures. For private interests this meant a sharing of investment, a relative abundance of money, and a reduction of risk. There was general recognition, too, that the United States enjoyed the technological edge in space, despite the Soviet Union's launching of Sputnik, the first

satellite, in 1957. It had more experience; its launch vehicles lifted the heaviest payloads. Not only did it possess the world's largest and richest scientific establishment, but it also was then the leader in computerization and communications. Until the mid-1980's, the aerospace defense corporations—Litton, EG&G, and Rohr Industries, among others—enjoyed close working relationships with NASA and the Department of Defense (DoD), and also were comfortably placed in the most profitable sector of the U.S. economy.

Added incentives arose from the entrepreneurial sense of adventure, the desire to serve the national interest, the prospect of making hundreds of millions or even billions of dollars, and the awareness that competition elsewhere was building rapidly. By the early 1970's, Western European nations, realizing aspirations that they had harbored for twenty years, had launched the European Space Agency (ESA). Japan, China, India, and Brazil were advancing claims to the limited resources of inner space. The Soviet challenge, whose strength could not be accurately gauged, continued.

NASA's public/private ventures were effective in encouraging private enterprise in space. By the early 1980's, Ford Aerospace, McDonnell Douglas, American Telephone and Telegraph (AT&T), Martin Marietta, Boeing Aircraft Company, and forty other major corporations—some well known, such as General Electric and General Dynamics, and some not, such as Loral, Rockwell

International, Morton Thiokol, and United Technologies—had moved partially under NASA's umbrella. NASA, with annual budgets exceeding $5 billion and with more than twenty thousand employees, had created an economic and scientific imperium of its own. By 1983, it included thirteen flight, space, and research centers (the Goddard Space Flight Center, the Kennedy Space Center, the Johnson Space Center, and the Ames Research Center, for example); the Jet Propulsion Laboratory in Pasadena, California, run for NASA by the California Institute of Technology; the Slidell Computer Complex; and the Landsat (land satellite) and Seasat (sea satellite) programs.

SpaceShipTwo (central fuselage) carried under its twin fuselage mother ship, White Knight Two. SpaceShipTwo is an air-launched suborbital spaceplane type designed for space tourism. It is manufactured by The Spaceship Company, a California-based company owned by Virgin Galactic. (Virgin Galactic / Mark Greenberg)

Changes in this NASA conglomerate began in 1983. First, James A. Abrahamson, Jr., NASA's director, decided to begin using space shuttles to launch payloads instead of Titan, Atlas-Centaur,, and Delta missiles, known generically as expendable launch vehicles (ELVs). Giants of aerospace such as Martin Marietta, McDonnell Douglas, and General Dynamics, which produced these missiles, were outraged, and they pointed to the missiles' excellent performance records. Their protests, however, were to no avail. This initial step toward opening the space transportation business to competition was followed in May, 1983, by President Ronald W. Reagan's executive decision to sell NASA's spare rocket parts and lease its launch pads to private enterprises. The field of space transportation, even in 1983 a billion-dollar market, thus was rendered more competitive.

Almost immediately, more than twenty transportation enterprises began to produce ELVs, minishuttles, or shuttles, among them Starstruck, Pacific American Launch Services (PALS), Space Services Incorporated of America (SSIA), and Earth Space Transportation System. Many, like Robert C.

Truax's Truax Engineering, had been trying since the 1960's to develop space products—in Truax's case, a Volksrocket ("people's rocket"). Gary Hudson, one of the pioneers of space launchers and a founder of PALS, had been looking for opportunities since the early 1970's. SSIA, a Houston firm, swiftly raised $6 million from sixty investors, bought equipment from NASA, and soon succeeded in launching its Conestoga successfully and joining with Space America in exploring the economic potential of the remote sensors that have been part of many satellite missions. Investors William and Klaus Heiss, heads of Space Transportation Company, were able to offer NASA a one billion-dollar bid to buy a space orbiter from NASA and lease it back to the agency if NASA would allow STC to market the shuttle fleet to private firms. A doubling of this bid by a company seeking to buy a fifth shuttle from NASA was indicative of the competition to tap the ostensibly lucrative space transportation market.

Space-based communications were placed on a business footing somewhat earlier than space transportation. A Christmas message from President Dwight D. Eisenhower was broadcast in 1958 from a U.S. military satellite, and two years later NASA's Echo 1 balloon relayed signals over intercontinental distances. AT&T soon persuaded NASA to launch its Telstar 1 satellite, the first active satellite with a transmitter, so that it might be tested and so that the United States could be assured of superiority in space applications. Telstar carried the first live transatlantic television broadcast, underscoring its immense commercial potential. Because the Telstars were limited by being line-of-sight transmitters, Hughes Aircraft developed its Syncoms (Synchronous Communication Satellites), which provided immediate and inclusive communications. The development of more powerful rocketry by 1964 allowed the placing of communications satellites in high orbit 35,680 kilometers above the equator, where they could orbit with the rotational speed of Earth (in a geostationary position) and provide continuous worldwide transmissions. Meanwhile, the Communications Satellite Act of 1963 made Communications Satellite Corporation (COMSAT) the first private enterprise in space, with NASA providing launch services and funds for research and development but obedient to a largely private board of directors that sold stock publicly. Under American auspices, the internationalization of space communications, directly and indirectly involving more than one hundred American firms alone, produced an economic phenomenon: By 1988, 7.2 percent of the world's communications assets were space-based—$13 billion of a $165 billion market.

Domestically, the Federal Communications Commission (FCC) authorized use of the first communications satellites, thereby creating business opportunities independent of federal funding. Satellites were used to provide long-distance phone service and, later, live and cable television. By 1988, more than eighty satellites were in service and the FCC had been licensing as many as twenty new satellite systems annually. Hughes Aircraft, Ford Aerospace, RCA, TRW, and General Electric were major contractors in the production of communications satellites. Moreover, the complexity of the satellites necessitated subcontracting to hundreds of firms, not counting subcontracts for launch services, ground control facilities, production of transponders, and production of other specialized equipment for data transmission.

Technology underlying the profitable deployment of space communications satellites was essentially the same as technology for the development of remote-sensing satellites. These are satellites that monitor Earth from remote points in space, either by photographing objects or by using infrared, radar, radio-wave, or multispectral scanners. Since 1960, the United States' Television Infrared Observations Satellite (TIROS) spacecraft have been photographing Earth. NASA's Landsat and Seasat series of satellites have provided immense quantities of data concerning crop yields, the state of forests, fish populations, weather prediction, the availability of water, ocean currents, air pollution, water quality, topography, and the locations of mineral resources. Although some of these data are in the public domain, others have come close to commercial viability. In 1984, the U.S. government turned over the tasks of Landsat operation and data distribution to a commercial entity, Earth Observation Satellite Company (EOSAT). This for-profit company, a joint venture between Hughes and RCA, operated the Landsat 4 and 5 spacecraft and sold the satellites' data. EOSAT was also responsible for the development of Landsat 6 and 7, although government funding paid for the spacecraft. Overall Landsat program management is the responsibility of NASA, NOAA (National Oceanic and Atmospheric Administration), and the U.S. Geological Survey.

Because NASA could manage cargoes on its space shuttle ranging in size from 90 to 27,000 kilograms, its Materials Processing Space Division had been selling cargo space since 1978. To stimulate sales, it started the Get-Away Special Experiments, which in only a few years brought more than three hundred users into the program, among them Coors

Brewing Company, Dow Chemical, Dupont, Columbia Pictures, Corning Ware, and Ford Motor Company.

To market space-manufactured biological products, including pharmaceuticals—which alone were expected to constitute a twenty-billion-dollar market—NASA entered into an agreement with Johnson and Johnson and McDonnell Douglas for exclusive use of its continuous flow electrophoresis (CFE) process. The unique gravity-free environment of space permits CFE, and variations of the process, to produce purer products. The Johnson and Johnson CFE experiments in the 1980's, moreover, yielded quantities five hundred times greater than would have been possible on Earth.

Such private industrial demands and visions prompted President Ronald W. Reagan in 1984 to direct NASA to have a space station orbiting within a decade and to press plans for a U.S. space laboratory. In the 1980's and 1990's, the United States orbited more than one hundred satellites, nearly all of them engaged in commerce-related missions. By the year 2005, the predominantly private aerospace industries and related companies represented one of the nation's leading growth industries. That only grew dramatically in the subsequent 15 years to the point where space-related commerce was a normal part of the business world and no longer thought of as something novel and apart from ordinary Earthly business operations.

In addition to the commercialization of the space shuttle and the International Space Station, private industry continues to build, launch, operate, and service communications satellites, navigational satellites, weather satellites, digital television and Internet satellites, and Earth observation satellites. Commercial enterprises also construct and fly their own launch vehicles, launch spacecraft for the government, operate several launch complexes, and plan for the future of piloted and robotic spaceflight.

In 1991, International MicroSpace, Inc., of Herndon, Virginia, contracted with Canadian-based Bristol Aerospace, Ltd. to develop a small launch vehicle called the Orbital Express. The vehicle was to have been capable of delivering a payload of up to 180 kilograms to low-Earth orbit. MicroSpace managed to land a deal to fire off up to ten payloads as part of the Pentagon's Strategic Defense Initiative, but the contract died when the Clinton administration took office and dismantled the Star Wars program.

In 1996, Peter H. Diamandis, the former owner of MicroSpace, established the X Prize Foundation, an organization with a clear mission: to spur space travel for the general populace. The X Prize itself was a $10 million award, to go to the first group to build a vessel capable of taking three adults (6-foot, 2-inch, 198-pound adults maximum) to an altitude of 100 kilometers twice in fourteen days. The prize was Diamandis's idea, but it was jump-started by St. Louis businesses, which donated the first $2 million. Zegrahm Space Voyages, one of two U.S. companies taking reservations for suborbital flights that hoped to have launched as early as 2002, fielded inquiries from ten thousand people in seventy-seven countries and by 2000 had received seventy-five deposits on the 2.5-hour trip's $98,000 fare. By 2005, none of those inquiries had led to flight experiences. Meanwhile, seventeen teams vied for Diamandis's X Prize, and many others built their own space-tourism dreams, from moonwalker Buzz Aldrin's plan for developing big, reusable rocket planes that will evolve into commercial space liners, to Las Vegas real estate tycoon Robert Bigelow's promise to spend half a billion dollars developing a lunar orbiting cruiser. The X Prize was won by the SpaceShipOne team on October 4, 2004, when two piloted flights of the same vehicle were flown within five days of each other.

The Space Transportation Association (STA) represents the interests of organizations and people who are engaged in developing, building, operating, and using space transportation vehicles, systems, and services to provide reliable, economical, safe, and routine access to space for private users and government, civil, and military users. STA's founder, General Daniel O. Graham, saw the urgency in seeking and developing the potential and promise of true commercial space transportation. To respond to this need, he created STA and began the timely effort that resulted in today's government/ space industry support of reusable launch vehicle development. Reusable space transportation technology and airline-like operations are coming into being in an attempt to address these objectives in other potentially even more effective ways. A reduction in per-flight costs and daily scheduling capabilities heralds the early 2000's as a major turning point for space activities. This led to the SpaceX reusable Falcon 9 and Falcon

New Shepard is a vertical-takeoff, vertical-landing (VTVL), suborbital crewed rocket that is being developed by Blue Origin as a commercial system for suborbital space tourism. Blue Origin is owned and led by Amazon.com founder and businessman Jeff Bezos and aerospace engineer Rob Meyerson. (NASA)

Heavy launch vehicles, and the Dragon cargo freighter and Crew Dragon spacecraft as well as the Orbital ATK (which later became Northrup Grumman) Cygnus freighter and the Boeing CST-100 piloted Starliner spacecraft.

On July 30, 1998, the U.S. Senate approved legislation that would open new opportunities for commercial launch firms in the United States. The Commercial Space Act, House Resolution 1702, allows the Federal Aviation Administration (FAA) to license the launch and landing of reusable launch vehicles. The bill also mandates the use of commercial launch services for most government payloads, the purchase of space science data from private companies, a study on the commercialization of the International Space Station, and improved licensing regulations for remote-sensing satellites. The ability to issue launch and reentry licenses was seen by many analysts as the key section of the bill. With new reusable launch vehicles being developed by private industry, such regulation is critical to permit them to be launched from the United States.

In August, 1998, the Mars Society ratified a declaration to further the goal of the exploration and settlement of the Red Planet. According to the declaration, this would be done by broad public outreach to instill the vision of pioneering Mars, to support aggressive government-funded Mars exploration programs around the world, and to encourage Mars exploration on a private basis. Starting small, with hitchhiker payloads on government-funded missions, the Mars Society intends to use the credibility that such activity will engender to mobilize larger resources that will enable standalone private robotic missions and ultimately human exploration.

After the *Challenger* accident in January, 1986, NASA scrubbed plans to launch the shuttle from Vandenberg Air Force Base, and Space Launch Complex 6 (SLC-6) was placed in mothballs. In 1995, the Air Force awarded a twenty-five-year lease of SLC-6 to Spaceport Systems International (SSI), including the payload processing facility and more than 100 acres of land for commercial launch facility construction. In 2000, SSI launched two satellites from the facility. The Joint Air Force Academy-Weber State University Satellite (JAWSAT) was launched aboard the Orbital Suborbital Program Space Launch Vehicle (dubbed Minotaur), a combination of rocket motors from the Minuteman II and Pegasus XL launch vehicles, on January 26. The MightySat II satellite was successfully launched on July 19 atop the Minotaur.

The Rotary Rocket Company of San Bruno, California, completed the manufacture of structural components for the Roton ATV (atmospheric test vehicle) in November, 1998. These composite structural parts were later assembled to form the test vehicle, which stood 19 meters high by 6.7 meters in diameter. The components were constructed by Scaled Composites in its Mojave, California facility. The test vehicle was designed to demonstrate the ability of the Roton ATV to fly at varying speeds under full control in a forward direction— exactly the same mode of flying that would be needed by a returning space vehicle maneuvering to land at an airport.

On July 23, 1999, a two-person crew piloted the vehicle for the first flight. The crew comprised the pilot, Marti Sarigul-Klijn, a retired U.S. Navy commander and Roton's chief engineer, with Brian Binnie, retired U.S. Navy commander and Roton's flight test director, as copilot. Both crew members were highly qualified and experienced flight test pilots. During the test, the Roton ATV performed three takeoff and landing maneuvers. These maneuvers demonstrated the crew members' ability to control the vehicle in the critical touchdown phase of the landing approach. They also verified the accuracy of the ATV's integrated flight simulator, which the crew had used prior to the test for flight rehearsals. The scheduled nominal test duration was five minutes. The actual test duration was 280 seconds. During the test, the ATV flew at a height of approximately 2.5 meters, which centered the ATV within the 1.5- to 3-meter nominal hover height planned. Hydrogen peroxide rotor tip rockets were used to fly the ATV up to its operating altitude.

The ATV approach and landing demonstrator made its first translational (forward) flight in the envelope expansion flight program, flying 1.3 kilometers along a Mojave airport runway on October 12, 1999. The same two-person crew from the first flight piloted the ATV. The test was to investigate the longitudinal stability and control characteristics of the Roton ATV in forward flight. During the test, the ATV reached a maximum altitude of 23 meters above the Mojave runway and a maximum ground speed of approximately 85 kilometers per hour.

As of 2019 SpaceX was beginning testing of a Starhopper vehicle similar in nature to the ATV as part of its plans to develop its Mars rocket. Many other companies in the early twenty-first century such as Blue Origin and Virgin Galactic, to name but two, are working toward novel transportation systems for both cargo and humans in suborbital and orbital space alike. The field of commercial participants in space activities would likely only expand in the coming years and decades.

Contributions

The private, or semiprivate, commercialization of space was largely a dream in the 1950's. In the next decade, under the auspices of NASA, communications satellites were being orbited and the inner space frontier was being exploited, the technological lead firmly in American hands. The late 1980's found a broadened aerospace market for an increasingly wide range of ventures, products, facilities, and services. For private business, the period from the 1950's to the 1980's involved much trial and error, ingenious negotiations between private companies and government, and the continuous accumulation of an immense body of hard-earned experience—technological, financial, political, and legal. Few directly applicable precedents existed in any of these areas to which private enterprises could turn for guidance. Astrobusiness was new and risky. A failed launch vehicle, an unsatisfactory orbit, or malfunctioning transponders or solar energy cells spelled disaster: years of planning, and often tens of millions of dollars, lost.

Because American private enterprises were going to space for profit, they first learned important lessons about the financial characteristics of their novel undertakings. Commonly requiring between thirty and sixty million dollars for development, and sometimes several hundred million dollars, space ventures are capital-intensive. Pioneering firms may enjoy some protection from competition, but those that develop later face lesser financial rewards. Moreover, space investments are long-term propositions, and they are perceived by both institutional and individual investors as entailing very high risks. Investors cannot be certain that the sophisticated, often experimental technology will work and that market conditions will be favorable, and they cannot know how they may be affected by domestic and international political changes. The almost exclusive dependence on high technology has increased the risks, and many potential investors or entrepreneurs have chosen to remain outside aerospace ventures until more years of experience have been acquired. Those who have ventured, however, have been able to draw on an outstanding pool of talent, and management quality is now viewed as critical to success.

NASA is a repository of immense quantities of data, information, experience, and expertise essential to novel enterprises. As it was intended to do, NASA has directly and indirectly shared expenditures, the better to curtail risks and encourage space ventures. Similarly, risks have been shared by groups of private corporations and by private companies and the federal government. COMSAT, a company formed in 1963 under the Communications Satellite Act, represents this type of hybridization; that is, it was created by the federal government, but it functions as a private, profit-making company. Indeed, when the Federal Communications Commission sought in 1980 to regulate COMSAT's soaring profits, COMSAT, though formed with a monopoly on U.S. satellite communications

with other countries, promptly joined with RCA, AT&T, IBM, and Xerox, among others, to enter the domestic communications satellite business.

Other means to reduce risks have been discovered. In the early days of space ventures, only one major American insurance company, Associated Aviation Underwriters, would insure spacecraft. By 1972, however, RCA was able to purchase insurance for its Satcom satellite, and the way was paved for a sharing of losses in the $200 million range. A recognition of the benefits of risk sharing, which occurred early with communications satellites under Intelsat (International Telecommunications Satellite Consortium), dawned on other U.S. enterprises, so that many private firms began sharing financing, design, construction, allocation of payloads, and losses and profits with foreign companies and governments, as was the case with Skylab, use of the space shuttles, and the launch vehicles of the ESA.

Context

With the federal government's use of NASA as a handmaiden to U.S. astrobusiness, two overriding precepts have established a basic framework for American enterprise in space. The first precept holds that the United States must maintain world leadership in the peaceful and military use of space. The second precept is that inner and outer space be opened as widely as possible to U.S. private enterprise. Many Space Age presidencies, fluctuating domestic economic conditions, a changing international scene, and startling technological advances have affected the application of these precepts to the United States' private space efforts.

The word "private" invites qualification. Without U.S. military experience with rocket launch vehicles during the decade after World War II and, later, the military's classified communications, navigation, weather, and spy satellites, it is doubtful that much private investment in space activities would have been forthcoming. Public monies originally paved and paid the way for the costly experimentation essential to opening private prospects in space. Just as had been the case with Columbus's voyages, with the founding of many of the American colonies, and with the construction of the nation's great railway system in the nineteenth century, stimulus, seed money, and security came from government. In return, space enterprises have added enormously to the economy at large. Initial investments from the public sector have been more than repaid by the generation of tax revenues, ideas, and technology, and most of the original publicly borne risks were perceived to have been undertaken in the national interest.

Although every national administration has been eager to broaden private participation in space programs, the Reagan administration in particular vigorously sought to transfer an increasing measure of responsibility for them to the private sector. It continued leasing ELVs, launch sites, and NASA equipment to private firms. It encouraged private companies to undertake the construction of launch vehicles and space shuttles. It took the position that any well-conceived space project can be privately financed without government subsidies, guaranteed loans, or any other kinds of direct or indirect investment. Nevertheless, the aerospace industry still considered certain governmental support desirable, even essential, for fledgling projects. Consequently, many aerospace companies called for government to help underwrite demonstration projects, to provide cheap payload integration services, and to provide free, or very low-cost, shuttle flights. They wanted speedier access to government information on new technologies, the removal of what they believed to be discriminatory taxation, and eligibility for tax credits for investment and research. They also wanted government to assist them with legislation or regulations making it easy for them—as it was for the aircraft industry—to compete or, as occasion demands, cooperate with foreign interests in the development of space stations.

Although the federal government has consistently espoused privatization, the stronger push in this direction has come from the aerospace industries. Generally, they have supported legislative efforts to deregulate space telecommunications, and to place licensing and regulation of private launchings in the hands of the Department of Commerce or the Department of Transportation. Such views imply that NASA should function principally as a research and development resource that would ensure the United States' primacy in space. Some have advocated that NASA concentrate on long-term space projects, such as development of permanent space research, mining, and manufacturing stations; placement of large space structures such as space lasers and antennae-farm satellites in orbit; and establishment of a lunar colony that would mine lunar ores and serve as a scientific outpost along the way to Mars.

One interesting outgrowth of privatization of space enterprises is the implication for local government: Florida's governor and legislature created the Spaceport Florida Authority (SFA) as a state government space agency in 1989. SFA's mission is to retain, expand, and diversify the state's space-related industry. SFA has governmental powers similar to other types of transportation authorities (such as those for airports and seaports) to support and regulate the state's space transportation industry. With regard to spaceport development and operations, SFA is broadly empowered to own, operate, construct, finance, acquire, extend, equip, and improve launch pads, landing areas, ranges, spaceflight hardware, payloads, payload assembly buildings, payload processing facilities, laboratories, and space business incubators. In addition to these specific types of infrastructure, SFA is empowered to support facilities and equipment for the construction of payloads, spaceflight hardware, rockets, and other launch vehicles, and for other spaceport facilities and related systems (utility infrastructure, fire and police services, mosquito control, and so forth). A seven-member governor-appointed board of supervisors administers SFA. The U.S. Navy's Trident land-based Launch Complex 46 at Cape Canaveral

Air Station was reconfigured by the SFA during 1996 to allow the assembly, integration, and launch of medium expendable launch vehicles such as the Lockheed Martin LMLV 1 and LMLV 2 and the Orbital Sciences Corporation Taurus. The complex was reworked specifically to accommodate commercial launch vehicles such as those designed around the CASTOR 120 motor, built by Thiokol's Defense and Launch Vehicles Division, Brigham City, Utah. In 1998, the Lunar Prospector probe was launched from Complex 46 aboard a three-stage Lockheed Martin Athena II rocket. Kennedy Space Center (KSC) in the aftermath of the shuttle fleet's retirement (in 2011) became a multi-user space port. Launch Complex 39-A was heavily used by SpaceX for *Falcon 9* launches. *Falcon 9* rockets were also launched from facilities at Cape Canaveral and Vandenberg Air Force Base. KSC drew space businesses into using space shuttle Orbiter Processing Facility bays, and even part of the Vehicle Assembly Building for the vertical integration of Northrup Grumman's new OmegA rocket. Opportunities abounded as the 2020's approach.

—Clifton K. Yearley and Kerrie L. MacPherson

See also: Funding Procedures of Space Programs; Global Positioning System; Langley Research Center; Marshall Space Flight Center; Pegasus Launch Vehicles; Planetary Exploration; Space Centers, Spaceports, and Launch Sites; Space Shuttle; SPACEHAB; SpaceShipOne.

Further Reading

Aviation Week and Space Technology 120 (June 25, 1984). This entire volume is devoted to prospects for the commercialization of space. The articles are readily understandable by the layperson. A few footnotes are included with the articles, but there are no appendices and no index. Despite the lack of these aids, the articles are germane and worth reading.

Bainum, Peter M., and Friedrich von Bun, eds. *Europe/United States Space Activities with a Space Propulsion Supplement: 23d Goddard Memorial Symposium, 19th European Space Symposium.* San Diego: American Astronautical Society, 1985. These Goddard symposia draw upon experts in many space-related fields. Their papers are intended for intelligent but not necessarily specialist audiences. Twelve of the twenty papers presented relate to this topic. Profusely illustrated with drawings, charts, graphs, and photographs. Reference endnotes are appended to papers, but there is no overall bibliography. Author index only.

Berinstein, Paula. *Making Space Happen: Private Space Ventures and the Visionaries Behind Them.* Medford, N.J.: Plexus Publishing, 2002. This work provides insights into the private organizations and entrepreneurs who seek to develop commercial space transportation systems and open up the solar system to economic development.

Butrica, Andrew J. *Single Stage to Orbit: Politics, Space Technology, and the Quest for Reusable Rocketry.* Baltimore: Johns Hopkins University Press, 2003. NASA-piloted launch vehicles have traditionally used a multistage approach to reach orbit. This work tells the story of the attempts by research groups and industrial teams to develop a single-stage-to-orbit technology that promises more routine access to space and a lessening of the cost per kilogram for placing payloads into orbit.

Finch, Edward Riley, Jr., and Amanda Lee Moore. *Astrobusiness: A Guide to the Commerce and Law of Outer Space.* New York: Praeger, 1984. A concise and readable review of the development and future of American space commerce. Only twenty pages deal with national and international space law; attention is focused on a condensed overview of space commerce. The text is augmented by many pictures and schematics. There is no overall bibliography, but there are four very informative appendices and a useful, if minimal, index.

Goldman, Nathan C. *Space Commerce: Free Enterprise on the High Frontier*. Cambridge, Mass.: Ballinger, 1985. Written in authoritative style for non-specialist readers, this is a very useful review of American commercial space enterprises. It is both synthetic and specific. Charts, tables, and a few photographs augment the text. End-of-chapter notes partially compensate for lack of a bibliography. The six appendices are informative, and the index is sufficient.

Gump, David, ed. *Space Processing, Products, and Profits, 1983-1990*. Arlington, Va.: Pasha, 1983. Contains specific descriptions and analyses of the commercial potentials offered by space's low-gravity, high-vacuum environment and the opportunities for electrophoretic biological separation, container-less liquid processing, and crystal manufacture for semiconductors and solar cells. Aimed at a narrow business audience, this is still an interesting, readable study. There are adequate notes, a bibliography, and an index.

Haskell, G., and Michael Rycroft. *International Space Station: The Next Space Marketplace*. Boston: Kluwer Academic, 2000. Addresses issues of ISS utilization and operations from all perspectives, especially the commercial viewpoint, as well as scientific research, technological development, and education in the widest sense of the word. Of interest to those working in industry, academia, government, and particularly public-private partnerships.

McCurdy, Howard E. *The Space Station Decision: Incremental Politics and Technical Choice*. Baltimore: Johns Hopkins University Press, 1990. The author is a professor of public affairs at American University in Washington, D.C. The events that led up to the decision (1984) to build a permanently occupied space station in low-Earth orbit provide his primary subject matter in the present monograph, but the author's deeper interest has to do with the politics of Big Science. The story is arrestingly told in this nicely produced volume, which provides thirteen pages of plates plus detailed notes and references.

McLucas, Charles, and Charles Sheffield, eds. *Commercial Operations in Space, 1980-2000: 18th Goddard Memorial Symposium*. San Diego: American Astronautical Society, 1981. The editors are representative of the oldest profitable private American enterprise in space: communications satellites. Each of the eighteen papers, or addresses, is authoritative and relevant; the papers cover topics such as manufacturing in space, space power systems and technology, Earth resources location, commercial launch operations, and international commercial opportunities. Papers include numerous charts, graphs, and photographs. There is no bibliography and only an inadequate index.

National Research Council. *Future Materials Science Research on the International Space Station*. Washington, D.C.: National Academy Press, 1997. This composite work describes the International Space Station and materials science research in the following areas: microgravity research and the Space Station Furnace Facility Core, NASA's microgravity research solicitation and selection process, and the ability of the Space Station Furnace Facility Core to support materials science experiments that require a microgravity environment. Included are a table of references, a list of acronyms, and biographical sketches of committee members.

O'Neill, Gerard K. *The High Frontier: Human Colonies in Space*. Garden City, N.Y.: Anchor Books, 1982. The bright, imaginative, and eminently readable author was head of Geostar and a member of the Space Studies Institute at Princeton University. He was especially interested in lunar and asteroid mining. The book is delightful and is intended for a general readership, despite O'Neill's scholarly credentials. There is an adequate bibliography and index.

Schwarz, Michiel, and Paul Stares, eds. *The Exploitation of Space: Policy Trends in the Military and Commercial Uses of Outer Space*. London: Butterworth, 1986. Taken from a special issue of *Futures* that was devoted to space, these are eminently readable and highly informed articles by business or scholarly specialists, intended for nonspecialist readers. Tables, charts, and graphs abound throughout. Notes and references conclude each article. There is no index or overall bibliography, nor are there appendices. Nevertheless, it is an excellent series.

Ranger Program

Date: February 23, 1961, to March 24, 1965
Type of program: Lunar exploration

The Ranger program, the first part of NASA's three-stage plan leading to piloted exploration of the Moon, provided some of the earliest detailed information about the lunar surface. Images sent back by Rangers 7, 8, and 9 helped scientists to identify feasible landing sites for the Apollo missions.

Key Figures

T. Keith Glennan (1905-1995), NASA administrator
James E. Webb (1906-1992), NASA administrator
Abe Silverstein (1908-2001), director of Spaceflight Programs
Homer E. Newell (1915-1983), assistant director of Spaceflight Programs
William H. Pickering (1910-2004), director of the Jet Propulsion Laboratory
James D. Burke, project manager
Harris M. Schurmeier, project manager
Gerard P. Kuiper (1905-1973), principal investigator

Summary of the Program

The National Aeronautics and Space Administration (NASA) first considered the Ranger program as early as 1959; authorities had thought that the early lunar missions could act as an appropriate answer in part to the successful Earth-orbiting missions launched by the Soviet Union. Because the best Earth-based telescopes could achieve only a limited resolution, it became obvious that a reconnaissance of the lunar surface at much higher resolution was needed for the benefit of later lunar landing missions. It was important, for example, to know whether the flat parts of the lunar surface, the so-called maria (plural of Latin *mare*, or sea), were littered with rocks and other debris. Also, scientists needed to know the number of smaller craters, which were invisible to the telescope, and how extensively they covered the floors of the seas. Finally, there was the possibility that the lunar surface was covered with a dust layer, perhaps several meters deep. If such a dust layer were determined to be present, it would pose considerable dangers for a landing spacecraft.

The Ranger program was expected to help supply answers to these questions. The spacecraft, directed toward selected points of the lunar hemisphere, were not supposed to land softly on the Moon; before crashing, however, they would carry out various studies of the surface and transmit the results back to Earth. A particularly important part of the program involved taking television pictures of the surface with increasing resolution as the spacecraft approached the Moon. Such a reconnaissance mission gained particular favor after May, 1961, when President John F. Kennedy called for the country to put a man on the Moon and bring him back safely before the end of 1969; the Ranger program was a necessary preliminary for this more ambitious project, which was later known as the Apollo Program.

As originally conceived, the Ranger program was to carry out some other types of observations in addition to the visual imaging experiment. After some reverses in the early attempts, however, designers agreed in mid-1961 that only a restricted version of the program, called the Block 3 project, would be carried out. This project—realized later by Rangers 6 through 9—was limited to imaging experiments using television cameras. There was, nevertheless, some doubt remaining whether a mere picture-taking experiment would provide all the information needed for planning the Apollo missions. An even more technically demanding soft-landing project (the Surveyor Program) was initiated, as was a project for high-resolution mapping of the whole lunar surface (the Lunar Orbiter program).

Block 3 spacecraft were launched by Atlas-Agena rockets from Cape Canaveral, Florida. Each craft weighed about 370 kilograms and was equipped with solar energy panels, a high-gain directional antenna for telecommunications, and an instrument system consisting of a battery of television cameras. The contractor for the imaging system was RCA. The cameras' focal lengths were 25 millimeters or 76 millimeters; cameras A and B had wide fields while cameras P1 through P4 had restricted fields. The last complete pictures in the successful missions were taken with the A and B cameras between two and five seconds before impact, with the P cameras less than one second before impact. The resulting maximum resolution was about 1 meter with Rangers 7 and 8; somewhat better, about 0.5 meter, with Ranger 9.

The picture-scanning rate was generally slower than in commercial systems; this made possible the use of a narrow electrical bandwidth, greatly simplifying the telecommunications process. The signals from the spacecraft were received with two 26-meter antennae near Goldstone, California. Commands from the mission center at the Jet Propulsion Laboratory (JPL) were also sent through the Goldstone antennae.

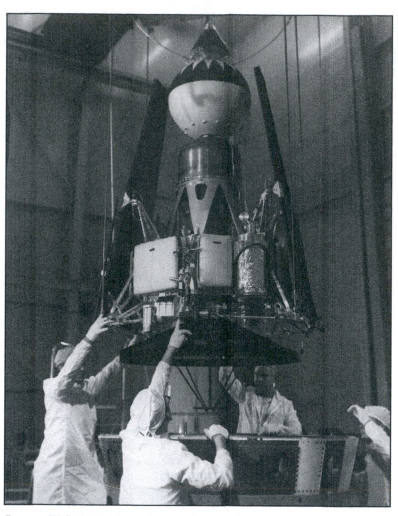

Ranger IV. (NASA / Glenn Research Center)

Ranger 6, the first mission of the restricted program (which was to provide images only), was launched on January 30, 1964. It proved unsuccessful: After its flawless flight, the craft's camera systems failed, and no pictures were transmitted before the probe's impact on the Moon. The remaining missions, Rangers 7, 8, and 9, however, were spectacularly successful. Ranger 7, launched on July 28, 1964, crashed as planned in the Sea of Clouds, one of the lunar seas, or maria. These maria were apparently flat, roughly circular areas with diameters ranging from a few hundred to a thousand kilometers. The first close-up images of the floor of the Sea of Clouds, showing a wealth of detail, were greeted with worldwide enthusiasm; the region around the impact site was renamed the Sea of Knowledge. These first photographs of the lunar surface clearly suggested that the mare basins would not prove as dangerous as expected to landing missions.

After Ranger 7 tested the Sea of Clouds, Ranger 8, launched on February 17, 1965, was sent to another lunar sea, because NASA wished to discover whether the maria were similar to one another. The target chosen for Ranger 8, the Sea of Tranquility, indeed revealed similarities to the Sea of Clouds. Later, Apollo 11's Lunar Module, carrying the first humans to set foot on the Moon, would also land in the Sea of Tranquility.

Because its predecessors had already gathered important practical information about the nature of the lunar lowlands, Ranger 9 was sent on a purely scientific mission. Alphonsus, a large crater in the central highland of the Moon, showed patches of unusual coloration and a central peak where reports suggested possible volcanic activity, was to be investigated. Ranger 9 made impact only a few miles from its assigned target point, close to the central peak of the crater, and also achieved a somewhat higher resolution by taking its last pictures even closer to the surface prior to impact.

Contributions

In total, the Ranger 7, 8, and 9 missions sent back more than seventeen thousand pictures, showing the lunar surface with resolutions more than one thousand times greater than that available to Earth-based telescopes. Images taken by Rangers 7 and 8 showed the floors of the seas to be flat, slightly undulating lowlands, mostly free of large debris. Craters of various sizes, down to about 1 meter and probably smaller in diameter, were numerous, but the sizable ones, those which could offset an attempted landing, occupied no more than 1 to 2 percent of the surface. The depth of a possible dust layer proved more difficult to judge, but

experiments tentatively decided that this layer was probably less than one millimeter thick.

Floors of the two maria studied by Rangers 7 and 8 proved to be basically similar in nature; all lunar lowlands probably share the same features. Ranger 9's target was a different type of object: the large crater Alphonsus. No confirmation of any recent or ongoing volcanism was found, but the study of a different type of lunar feature proved highly rewarding. The crater floor itself resembled the mare basins studied in the earlier missions.

In addition, two previously unknown features emerged from the study of the Ranger images. Along the conspicuous "rays," long straight streaks of brighter surface material emanating from several of the large craters (known for centuries from telescopic studies), the pictures show an occasional dense clustering of smaller craters, ranging in size from 100 to 200 meters. These small craters are obviously of secondary origin; that is, they were formed by swarms of rocks or other debris hurled out when the large primary crater was formed. The second discovery was a new and unexpected type of lunar crater, the dimple crater: These are shallow depressions without sharp edges and are located on the mare and crater floors. In size, they range from a few meters up to about 100 meters. Scientists have not been able to agree on the nature of these craters. If they are collapse features (caused by surface matter slumping into a cavity beneath), they might indicate the lunar surface's inability to bear heavy weights.

Context

Hitting the Moon with the Ranger spacecraft and returning pictures in the final moments before destructive impact proved more difficult than imagined. The program experienced frustrating setbacks, but with the high priority it enjoyed because of the lunar-landing goal set by President Kennedy, it continued   receiving   adequate   funding   until achievement of the long-sought data. Ranger 1 launched on August 23, 1961, but failed to leave Earth's orbit. The same fate befell Ranger 2 on November 18, 1961. Ranger 3 left Earth's orbit on June 26, 1962, but contact with the spacecraft was lost and it missed the Moon by approximately 37,000 kilometers. Ranger 4, launched on April 26, 1962, scored an impact on the Moon, but the mission was still a failure; Ranger 4's sequencer failed and the spacecraft returned no data. Ranger 5 launched on

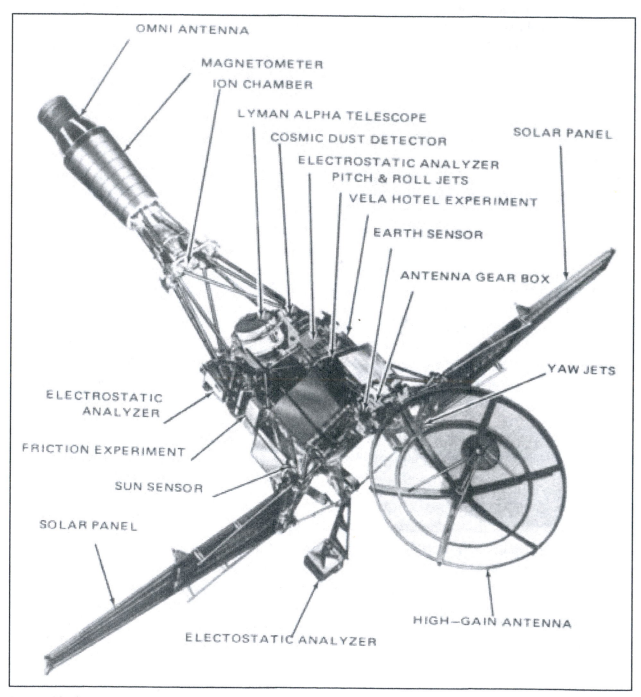

Ranger block I spacecraft diagram. (NASA)

October 18, 1962, lost contact with Earth, and flew past the Moon at a distance of 725 kilometers. Everything appeared to be ripe for program success with Ranger 6 as it followed the proper trajectory to its selected target and its instruments responded to command. However, when the spacecraft was ready to begin sending images during final approach to impact, on February 2, 1964, its television cameras unexpectedly failed. All program goals were accomplished with highly successful Rangers 7, 8, and 9 missions.

The Ranger missions were intended to prepare the way for the crewed lunar missions of the Apollo Program by gathering knowledge of the small-scale structure of the lunar surface. The most important result of the program was the discovery that the lunar lowlands presented no serious surface hazards to landing spacecraft. The presence of a deep dust layer could not be disproved with absolute certainty, but the Ranger missions did render it rather improbable. Nevertheless, the bearing strength of the surface, even without a significant dust layer, remained problematic; discovery of dimple craters emphasized this problem. This question was the only one not resolved by the otherwise successful Ranger program. As a spokesman for the program reported in May, 1966, "the bearing strength of the lunar surface cannot be determined by photographs, even at this high resolution."

Fortunately, the subsequent soft-lander missions of the Surveyor project, as well as their Soviet counterparts, the Luna missions, clearly demonstrated the lunar surface's ability to bear up under massive structures such as the Apollo Lunar Module. The first soft landings on the Moon (Luna 9 and Surveyor 1) followed within fifteen months of the flight of Ranger 9. With the results of the lunar-landing studies of the soil, even the spectacular Ranger pictures were quickly replaced by new knowledge; they became mere documentation of the progress toward the first Apollo landing in July, 1969.

—*T. J. Herczeg*

See also: Apollo Program; Apollo Program: Geological Results; Apollo Program: Orbital and Lunar Surface Experiments; Atlas Launch Vehicles; Cape Canaveral and the Kennedy Space Center; Clementine Mission to the Moon; Explorers 1-7; Launch Vehicles; Lunar Exploration; Pioneer Missions 1-5; Surveyor Program.

Further Reading

Burrows, William E. *This New Ocean: The Story of the First Space Age*. New York: Random House, 1998. This is a comprehensive history of the human conquest of space, covering everything from the earliest attempts at spaceflight through the voyages near the end of the twentieth century. Burrows is an experienced journalist who has reported for *The New York Times*, *The Washington Post*, and *The Wall Street Journal*. There are many photographs and an extensive source list. Interviewees in the book include Isaac Asimov, Alexei Leonov, Sally K. Ride, and James A. Van Allen.

French, Bevan M. *The Moon Book*. New York: Penguin Books, 1977. This nontechnical overview focuses on the information gained during the 1960's and portrays the excitement as well as the facts of the search. Includes descriptions of the various lunar spacecraft and their experiments. Very well illustrated.

Hall, R. Cargill. *Lunar Impact: A History of Project Ranger*. NASA SP-4210. Washington, D.C.: Government Printing Office, 1977. A detailed history of the Ranger program, this highly readable volume is well documented and brings out the human story behind the technical developments.

Koppes, Clayton R. *JPL and the American Space Program: A History of the Jet Propulsion Laboratory.* New Haven, Conn.: Yale University Press, 1982. This text provides virtually the entire history of the Jet Propulsion Laboratory; it also contains considerable information on the pre-Apollo lunar probes, including the various Rangers.

Kuiper, Gerard P. "Lunar Results from Rangers 7 to 9." *Sky and Telescope* 29 (May, 1965): 293- 308. This article summarizes the results achieved by the program. Written for the reader with only a minimal background in science.

Lee, Wayne. *To Rise from Earth: An Easy to Understand Guide to Spaceflight.* New York: Checkmark Books, 1996. This is a good introduction to the science of spaceflight. Although written by an engineer with the NASA Jet Propulsion Laboratory, it is presented in easy-to-understand language. In addition to the theory of spaceflight, it gives some of the history of the human endeavor to explore space.

Mari, Christopher, ed. *Space Exploration.* New York: H. W. Wilson, 1999. Twenty-five articles (reprinted from magazines), covering the state of the space program at the time of publication, are divided into five sections: John H. Glenn, Jr.'s return to space, the exploration of Mars, the International Space Station, recent mining efforts by commercial industries, and new types of space vehicles and propulsion systems.

Shoemaker, Eugene M. "The Moon Close Up." *National Geographic* 126 (November, 1964): 690-707. This well-written summary provides a general overview of the results of the Ranger program. Includes a large selection of photographs.

Smith, Gerald M., et al. *Ranger VII, Photographs of the Moon: Part I, Camera A Series.* NASA SP- 61. Washington, D.C.: Government Printing Office, 1964.

---. *Ranger VII, Photographs of the Moon: Part II, Camera B Series.* NASA SP-62. Washington, D.C.: Government Printing Office, 1965.

---. *Ranger VII, Photographs of the Moon: Part III, Camera P Series.* NASA SP-63. Washington, D.C.: Government Printing Office, 1965.

---. *Ranger VIII, Photographs of the Moon: Cameras A, B, and P.* NASA SP-111. Washington, D.C.: Government Printing Office, 1966.

---. *Ranger IX, Photographs of the Moon: Cameras A, B, and P.* NASA SP-112. Washington, D.C.: Government Printing Office, 1966. These volumes, filled with spectacular images taken by the various successful Ranger missions, are enjoyable for anyone interested in astronomy. Each book contains a short technical description of the spacecraft and instrumentation.

Swanson, Glen E. *Before This Decade Is Out: Personal Reflections on the Apollo Program.* Gainesville: University Press of Florida, 2002. This oral history of the Apollo program provides insights into the thoughts of the people who accepted President Kennedy's lunar challenge, sent astronauts to walk upon the Moon, and returned them safely to Earth.

Zimmerman, Robert. *The Chronological Encyclopedia of Discoveries in Space.* Westport, Conn.: Oryx Press, 2000. Provides a complete chronological history of all crewed and robotic spacecraft and explains flight events and scientific results. Suitable for all levels of research.

Rocketry: Early History

Date: c. 400 b.c.e. to c. 1880 c.e.
Type of program: Rocket research and development

Developments in black powder and simple missiles for more than two millennia established the theoretical and practical basis for rocket science to develop in the twentieth century. Early rockets were developed in Asia, spreading west into Europe by the fifteenth century and thence into the Americas. Although the tangible results of rockets as weapons were negligible, their potential continued to attract experimenters.

Key Figures

Archytas of Tarentum (fl. 406-365 b.c.e.), ancient Greek inventor

Hero of Alexandria (fl. third century c.e.), ancient Greek inventor

Sir Isaac Newton (1642-1727), English physicist

Christopher Friedrich von Geissler, German artillery expert

Sir William Congreve (1772-1828), British artillery expert

William Hale, British inventor

Summary of Events

Since prehistoric times, projectiles have been used for hunting and fighting. For thousands of years warriors depended primarily on handheld weapons, such as swords and spears, and missiles powered by kinetic energy, such as arrows fired from bows and bolts fired from crossbows. Roman armies employed artillery in the form of large catapults, known as onagers, that hurled boulders at enemy fortifications. These early missiles also used kinetic energy, transferred to the projectile by a launcher rather than thrust from the missile itself.

According to the Roman Aulus Gellius, a Greek named Archytas of Tarentum, in southern Italy, used steam to provide thrust to propel a wooden pigeon traveling on wires around in a circle in 360 b.c.e. Another Greek, Hero of Alexandria, created an engine around 300 c.e. that used steam to provide

thrust, which rotated a centrally mounted sphere. Hero seems to have used his engine for amusement rather than for practical applications.

There is clear evidence that true rockets, in the form of tubes using chemical reactions to provide thrust and thus lift, originated in China, although the date for their first appearance is controversial. The rocket became possible with the Chinese invention of black powder, later known as gunpowder. Early black powder was a mixture of charcoal dust, sulfur, and saltpeter. In general, the first use of black powder to create rockets is believed to have occurred accidentally. Bamboo tubes filled with black powder were tossed into ceremonial fires, providing a form of firecracker. Imperfectly sealed bamboo tubes would shoot out of fires, with the pressure from the quick-burning black powder providing thrust from one end of the tube rather than building up and exploding. Opinions differ as to when the Chinese began to fill bamboo with black powder. References to exploding bamboo in fires during the Han Dynasty (206 b.c.e.-220 c.e.) could refer to bamboo tubes filled with black powder or might simply refer to the tendency of air chambers inside bamboo to pop when burned. Chroniclers during the Han Dynasty mentioned the existence of "fire arrows"; however, again the context is unclear regarding whether the flight of these arrows was powered either in part or wholly by the burning of black powder or if the "fire" referred instead to an attached incendiary device.

Fireworks were popular in China during the Tang Dynasty (618-907 c.e.). The writings of a Chinese government official in 1045 c.e. showed that the Chinese were well acquainted with black powder. Possibly by 969 c.e. they were using rockets in war. By 1180, their use of rockets as weapons is definite. Bamboo tubes to which spearheads were attached were filled with black powder and launched against the enemy. During the twelfth century, in prolonged warfare between China's Song Dynasty (960-1279 c.e.) and their Mongol neighbors, the Chinese used the earliest known cannons and mortars. In the early thirteenth century, rocket-propelled fire arrows were in widespread use. Chinese records show the use of very large fire arrows in 1232 at the Battle of Kai-fung-fu against the Mongols. These large rockets possibly carried a warhead in the form of black powder encased in iron, which became shrapnel after the powder exploded, and well as incendiary materials. By one account, the surrounding area was destroyed for a radius of 2 kilometers (1.6 miles) from the point of impact.

Depiction of a fire arrow rocket launcher, or shen huo chien phai, from the Ming Dynasty book Huo Long Jing, circa 14th century. (Jio Yu and Liu Ji)

Unfortunately for the Chinese and others, the Mongols quickly assimilated the technology, introducing rockets to Europe in the Battle of Sejo, against the Magyars, in 1241, near what is now Budapest. Europeans showed little initial interest in rockets. Instead, Europeans adopted the hand-carried gun and cannon to their warfare, and neglected rockets. The Arabs were on the receiving end of Mongol rocket barrages during the capture of Baghdad (1258), and soon incorporated rockets for their own use. Arabs employed them against French

Crusaders in 1268. It is most likely that Europeans adopted the rocket as a weapon from the Arabs rather than directly from the Mongols.

Rocket use spread north from the Mediterranean coast of Europe by the early fifteenth century. A French army used rockets in the Siege of Orleans against the English in 1429. Rockets appeared in Germany in the early sixteenth century and spread to England from there. A 1647 treatise on artillery published in London contained a section on the use of rockets. Dutch and German experiments with rockets increased their size and payloads, if not their effectiveness. A German artillery officer, Colonel Christopher Friedrich von Geissler, built military rockets ranging between 25 and 54 kilograms (55 to 120 pounds) in the 1730's, although these failed to make any impact on warfare of the day.

More theoretical, yet of more lasting import, was the work of the English physicist Sir Isaac Newton, whose three laws of motion would later provide much of the scientific underpinning for the ability of rockets to operate in the near vacuum of space. Despite Newton's theories to contrary, the erroneous notion that the rocket moved by thrust "pushing" against the air remained common.

Although rockets were more of a curiosity in Europe, Asian armies continued to employ them. Through contact with China, various indigenous armies of independent Indian states had long used rockets in warfare. The British Indian Army found itself on the receiving end of terrifying rocket barrages in 1792 and 1799. Although the British noted that the main uses of these rockets were psychological or as a means of signaling distant units, they recognized their effectiveness at these tasks. The British colonel William Congreve, an expert in artillery, designed the rocket system that would bear his name. The Congreve rocket was essentially a tube of black powder with a 4.1-kilogram (9-pound) ball at one end. The tube was mounted on a long stick, which in theory would provide stability in flight. The entire package weighed 13.6 kilograms (30 pounds). It was placed in a V-shaped launcher, pointed in the general direction of its target, and lit. Congreve rockets allowed the delivery of a ball over a distance that would have taken a massive cannon to duplicate. Later versions would range in size up to 136 kilograms (300 pounds).

Congreve rockets first saw action in 1806 in the attack on the French city of Boulogne. The two thousand rockets so terrified the city's defenders that they surrendered without returning a shot. The British used Congreve rockets both as a ship-to-shore weapon and as a land-based weapon. The rockets came either as an incendiary or loaded with case-shot, which would explode into shrapnel. However impressive the sight of a rocket barrage might have been, the rockets' main effect was more psychological than physical. Congreve rockets were wildly inaccurate and depended on employment in massive numbers to bring firepower onto an intended target. Even direct hits produced minimal damage to fortifications, as each rocket carried little kinetic or chemical energy. Congreve rockets became memorialized in the United States when British ships, firing them at Fort McHenry during the War of 1812, inspired Francis Scott Key to include "the rockets' red glare" in his poem "The Star-Spangled Banner," which later became the words for the U.S. national anthem.

In 1843, another Englishman, William Hale, experimented with spin stabilization to provide better accuracy. By attaching small plates to the bottoms of rockets to direct the thrust slightly to the side, he induced a spin that allowed greatly increased accu-

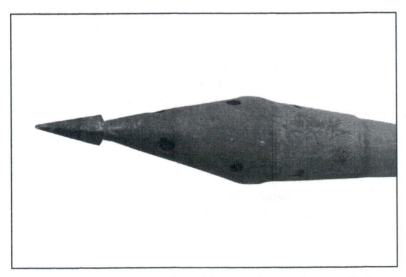

Tip of an early Congreve rocket of the Napoleonic Wars, on display at Paris Naval Museum. (via wikimedia Commons)

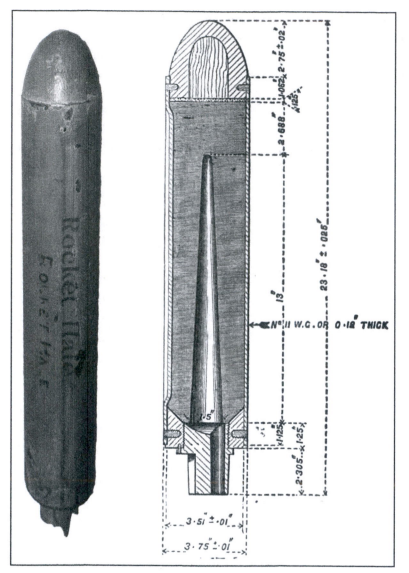

William Hale's rotary rocket. (Smithsonian Institute)

Mexico City. The unit was disbanded after the war. The American military would again employ rockets during the Civil War (1861-1865). Although both Union and Confederate forces employed rockets sporadically, neither side found them an especially effective weapon.

By the middle of the nineteenth century, rockets fell out of favor as a weapon because of improvements in the range, power, and accuracy of artillery, which made rockets obsolete. The Prussian army made this point clear during the Austro-Prussian War of 1866. New Prussian breech-loading rifled artillery, which fired exploding projectiles, proved far superior to the Austrians' rockets. Rockets as a weapon of war had reached their nadir.

Although rockets had fallen from favor as a weapon, a handful of researchers continued to experiment with rockets throughout the nineteenth century. Charles Golightly received a British patent for a steam-propelled flying machine, although he apparently built no prototype. In 1855, Lieutenant-Colonel E. M. Boxer of the Royal Laboratory in Britain developed a two-stage rocket, which greatly improved the distance over which lifelines could be sent to rescue people from sinking ships. In the whaling industry, rocket-propelled harpoons became common about the time of the American Civil War. Thus as the rocket was discounted as a weapon, its continued used in fireworks, lifesaving, and whaling ensured its survival as an applied technology.

racy. His version of the Congreve rocket would become known as the Hale rocket.

Americans were slow to adopt the rocket as a weapon. The first "rocketeer" company did not develop until the Mexican War (1846-1848). Accompanying Major General Winfield Scott's expedition against Mexico City, the first such military unit saw action on March 24, 1847, during the Siege of Veracruz, Mexico. It was equipped with fifty 1.02-kilogram (2.25-pound), 15-centimeter (6-inch) Hale rockets. The unit later fought at Telegraph Hill and

Contributions

Most early developments in rockets were aimed at their use in warfare or as fireworks. In discovering the practical problems of using rockets this way and in devising solutions and improvements, early developers of rockets laid the foundations for the modern science of propulsion. For example, early experimenters eventually found that a drag stick could provide stability, which in turn gave way to the use of fins. Induced spin further increased stability of the rocket in flight. Multistage rockets, originally used for fireworks and later lifelines, allowed increased altitudes to be reached.

Although the employment of rockets on the battlefield ultimately failed to have a major impact on warfare, fascination with the technology of chemical propulsion and the potential for non-military uses for rockets ensured continued interest in the face of minimal practical results. The use of rockets for entertainment, primarily in fireworks, continued, with the Chinese and much later the Italians developing complex aerial displays while gaining an understanding of the chemical and aeronautical aspects of rockets. Such early uses eventually led to additional experiments in thrust, propellants, and design of the projectiles or rockets themselves, providing a basis for later scientific advances in rocketry in the late nineteenth and twentieth centuries. Hence, although rockets before the twentieth century were far too limited in size and power to contemplate their use in space exploration in the immediate future, their long-term potential continued to attract adherents.

Context

Despite early Greek experiments with steam thrust, true rockets seem to have been invented once, in China, and spread around the world from there. Although most practical applications involved the rocket as a weapon, their use in fireworks, whaling, and delivering rescue lines at sea should not be discounted—for these non-military applications forced inventors and manufactures to address real problems in accuracy and distance when the military ultimately abandoned its interest in rockets.

Before the twentieth century, science-fiction writers were more likely to propose springs, cannons, sails, balloons, or birds to send humans into outer space, but rockets continued to have their supporters as a likely mode for future space travel. The ability of rockets to capture the human imagination would ultimately lead to their fictional and then real use as a method for lofting objects, including humans, into space.

—Barry M. Stentiford

See also: Rocketry: Modern History.

Further Reading

Berinstein, Paula. *Making Space Happen: Private Space Ventures and the Visionaries Behind Them*. Medford, N.J.: Plexus Press, 2002. This work provides insight into the private organizations and entrepreneurs who seek to develop commercial space transportation systems and open up the solar system to economic development.

Butrica, Andrew J. *Single Stage to Orbit: Politics, Space Technology, and the Quest for Reusable Rocketry*. Baltimore: Johns Hopkins University Press, 2003. NASA launch vehicles used in piloted missions have traditionally used a multistage approach to reach orbit. This work tells the story of the attempts by research groups and industrial teams to develop a single-stage-to-orbit technology that promises more routine access to space and less cost per kilogram for placing payloads into orbit.

Gruntman, Mike. *Blazing the Trail: The Early History of Spacecraft and Rocketry*. Reston, Va.: American Institute of Aeronautics and astronautics, 2004. Written for the educated lay reader, this work focuses on Congreve and early American rocket pioneers.

Macinnis, Peter. *Rockets: Sulfur, Sputnik, and Scramjets*. East Melbourne, New South Wales, Australia.: Allen and Unwin, 2003. Entertaining history of rocketry from the Chinese through European pioneers and into the future of space travel. Macinnis explores many forgotten consequences of gunpowder and rocketry..

Ordway, Frederick I., III, and Mitchell Sharpe. *The Rocket Team*. Burlington, Ont.: Apogee books, 2003. A revised edition of the acclaimed, thorough history of rocketry, from early amateurs to present-day rocket technology. Includes a disc containing videos and images from rocket programs.

Winter, Frank. *The First Golden Age of Rocketry: Congreve and Hale Rockets of the Nineteenth Century*. Washington, D.C.: Smithsonian Institution Press, 1990. This history focuses mainly on the use of rockets by the military. Demonstrates that, although rockets showed promise and had their ardent supporters, eventually developments in artillery led to the abandonment of rockets by the military in the late nineteenth century.

Rocketry: Modern History

Date: Beginning c. 1880
Type of program: Rocket research and development

From the late nineteenth through the twenty-first century, the rocket developed from a largely unreliable device with few practical applications to a highly sophisticated marvel of modern technology capable of such varied feats as launching multiple independently targeted nuclear missiles or helping people land on the Moon.

Key Figures

Robert H. Goddard (1882-1945), American physicist who developed the first liquid-fueled rocket

Wernher von Braun (1912-1977), German American rocket scientist whose greatest achievements were the V-2 and Saturn rockets

Hermann J. Oberth (1894-1989), Hungarian German engineer who was one of the founders of modern rocket science

Konstantin Tsiolkovsky (1857-1935), Russian physicist who was a visionary pioneer of spaceflight

Sergei Pavlovich Korolev (1907-1966), Soviet designer of guided missiles, powerful rockets, and spacecraft

Summary of Events

According to many scholars, modern rocketry had three fathers: Konstantin Tsiolkovsky, Hermann Oberth, and Robert Goddard. These three pioneers not only foresaw much of the future development of rocketry and astronautics but also took the first significant steps toward making rocket-assisted space exploration a reality. Although space exploration was the primary motivation of these pioneers, their work resulted in modern rockets that were useful for achieving military as well as scientific goals.

Some have called Tsiolkovsky the "father of astronautics," because he showed in detail how rockets could be built that were capable of traveling to outer space. In his *Exploration of Cosmic Space by Means of Reaction Devices* (1903), he explained how liquid oxygen, when combined with either kerosene or liquid hydrogen in a combustion chamber, could provide the propulsive force needed—especially when "rocket trains" (multistage rockets) were used—to attain velocities necessary to escape from the Earth's gravity. He understood that gyroscopes would be needed to stabilize rockets in flight. However, despite his insightful speculations, he never actually constructed a rocket.

The person who, more than any other, solved many practical problems involved in building a modern liquid-fueled rocket was Robert Goddard. He obtained his doctorate in physics, and his first rocket patents in 1914. His monograph *A Method of Reaching Extreme Altitudes* (1919) anticipated many later rocket technologies, and in 1926 he became the first person to launch a liquid-propellant rocket. Powered by the combustion of liquid oxygen and kerosene, it reached only modest heights and speeds, but in retrospect it was a turning point in rocket history. During the 1930's, with institutional funding for his largely independent research, he was able to develop the first gyro-stabilized rockets and other innovations that helped make transform the rocket into a complex device capable of achieving great heights and speeds in controlled flights.

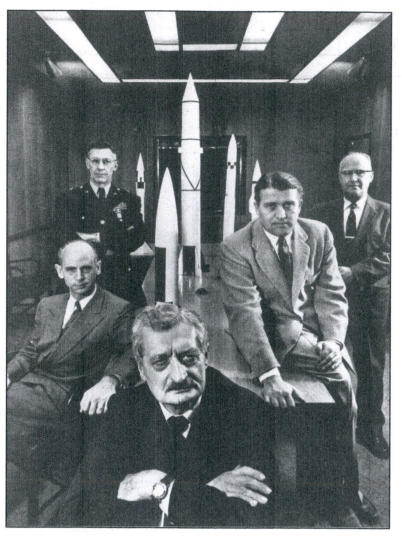

Hermann Oberth (forefront) with officials of the Army Ballistic Missile Agency at Huntsville, Alabama in 1956. Left to right around Oberth: 1) Dr. Ernst Stuhlinger (seated). 2) Major General H.N. Toftoy, Commanding Officer and person responsible for "Project Paperclip," which took scientists and engineers out of Germany after World War II to design rockets for American military use. Many of the scientists later helped to design the Saturn V rocket that took the Apollo 11 astronauts to the Moon. 3) Dr. Wernher von Braun, Director, Development Operations Division (sitting on table). 4) Dr. Robert Lusser, a Project Paperclip engineer who returned to Germany in 1959. (U.S. Army)

The lure of space travel also stimulated Hermann Oberth's interest in rocketry. Unable to get his dissertation on rocket design accepted, he published such books as *Die Rakete zu den Planetenräumen* (1923; *The Rocket into Planetary Space*), which contained new ideas about rocket design: for example, the advantages of alcohol and hydrogen as propellants. His books inspired others to work on rockets, and the first European liftoff of a liquid-propellant rocket (fueled by a mixture of methane and oxygen) occurred in Germany on March 14, 1931. During the 1920's Oberth had developed a "cone-jet nozzle" for introducing liquid propellants into the combustion chamber. During the 1930's he worked with a young rocket enthusiast, Wernher von Braun, who had been the first member of a German rocket society to be employed by the German army's rocket program. When this program moved from Kunersdorf to Peenemünde, Oberth joined the staff that, in World War II (1939-1945), constructed the gigantic A-4 rocket (later named the V-2), which some scholars have designated a technological achievement second only to the American development of the atomic bomb.

While Germans were engaged in the research, development, and manufacture of the V-2, Americans were concentrating on such short-range rocket launchers as the bazooka and on the Jet-Assisted Take-Off (JATO) project, which has been called the start of practical rocketry in the United States. JATO rockets reduced by a third the distance and time needed for bombers to take off. Eschewing long-range missiles, the Allies had to use conventional airplanes in bombing Nazi Germany. Meanwhile in Germany, von Braun, his associates, and many slave laborers produced about five thousand V-2s during the war, and more than a thousand of them hit targets in England, but with such inaccurate trajectories that they failed to halt the Allies' reconquest of Europe.

Near the end of the war, in Operation Paperclip, Americans captured as many German rocket scientists and technicians as they could, including von Braun. These experts had a great impact on American rocketry in the postwar period. U.S. forces also captured V-2's, and in Project Hermes they studied and test-launched some of these rockets, mainly at White Sands Proving Grounds in New Mexico. Soviet forces also captured German rocket technicians and their equipment, transporting them to Russia, where these technicians became the nucleus of the Soviet development of rockets for guided missiles and space exploration.

In the United States—first at Fort Bliss, Texas, and later at Huntsville, Alabama—von Braun and his team developed the Redstone rocket, the nation's first intermediate range ballistic missile (IRBM). Based on the V-2 and other rockets, the Redstone, which used kerosene and liquid oxygen (LOX) as propellants, produced a thrust of 667 kilonewtons. During the period between 1953 and 1958, several versions of the Redstone were tested at Cape Canaveral in Florida, establishing its range of 320 kilometers and its usefulness as a support for army ground forces.

While this research on military missiles was proceeding, other research was under way in connection with U.S. participation in the International Geophysical Year (IGY), a cooperative project for the comprehensive study of the Earth in 1957 and 1958. In connection with IGY both the United States and the Soviet Union intended to use rockets to launch satellites to study the Earth's outerspace environment. A powerful R-7 rocket developed by Sergei Korolev for Soviet intercontinental ballistic missiles (ICBMs) was used to place in orbit Sputnik 1, the world's first artificial satellite, on October 4, 1957. During the twelve years following the end of World War II, Korolev had designed a series of increasingly powerful rockets, including the world's first IRBM (tested in 1956) and its first ICBM

(tested in 1957), well before Americans tested their IRBMs (Jupiter and Thor) and ICBMs (Atlas and Titan). In 1961 the Soviets used a version of the R-7 outfitted with a spacecraft named Vostok (meaning "East") to place the first man in orbit around Earth.

In the United States, which had tried to keep its military and civilian rocket programs separate, a three-stage Vanguard rocket was to have been the launch vehicle for the first American satellite. However, after the shock of the early Soviet successes and the dismal failures of the first Vanguard rocket, President Dwight D. Eisenhower gave von Braun's team permission to use a modified Redstone rocket, known as the Jupiter-C, to put Explorer I into orbit. Public pressure also played a role in the creation of the National Aeronautics and Space Administration (NASA) in 1958. The four-stage Scout, the first rocket developed by NASA itself, became the launch vehicle for light payloads. The Delta, the first rocket built specifically for NASA (by Douglas Aircraft), was a modified Air Force Thor IRBM.

During the late 1950's and early 1960's, Soviet rockets were more powerful than those being developed in the United States. Americans began to close the gap, however, with the Atlas missile. One of its innovations was its arrangement of two dispensable Rocketdyne boosters and one inboard Rocketdyne sustainer, which eliminated the need for complex staging. After a series of tests, the Atlas, in combination with either an Agena or a Centaur rocket, became NASA's workhorse launch vehicle, successfully delivering many satellites into orbit and other payloads into outer space, where they helped scientists explore the planets and their moons. (The Atlas design was modified several times after its original creation. Only the Atlas 5 design remained available for launch service through 2019.)

The second ICBM to be converted into a space launcher was the Titan. With a different configuration of rockets from that of the Atlas, the two-stage Titan generated significantly more thrust. Later, more powerful Titans were developed to lift heavy payloads into orbit. For example, the Titan II successfully launched all ten piloted Gemini spacecraft in the mid-1960's. The Titan III, which had two solid-fueled strap-on boosters, was capable of lifting very heavy payloads into space, such as the Viking landers, which went on to search for life on Mars. After a quarter century of military and NASA use, the Titan became commercial when the *Challenger* accident made it necessary to use launch vehicles other than the space shuttle. The final Titan IV launch from Cape Canaveral occurred on April 29, 2005. The last Titan IV launch from Vandenberg Air Force Base would mark the end of the long-lived Titan program, leaving heavy-lift capability to the space shuttle (until 2011), Atlas-5, Delta IV heavy boosters, or Falcon Heavy commercial rockets.

American space programs were finally able to surpass the Soviets in large rocket development with the Saturn series. The massive Saturn V, with its five clustered F-1 rocket engines, generated 33.3 meganewtons (7.5 million pounds) of thrust. The design of the various Saturn rockets (Saturn I, Saturn IB, and Saturn V) owed much to von Braun, and the Saturn family of rockets operated practically flawlessly in the Apollo, Skylab, and Apollo-Soyuz missions.

With the launch of the space shuttle *Columbia* in 1981, the United States entered a new era, since the solid-propellant rocket boosters and the shuttle orbiter were recoverable. However, questions were raised—even before the tragic explosion of *Challenger* shortly after liftoff in 1986—about the economics and safety of reusable rockets. Consequently at the end of the twentieth and in the early years of the twenty-first century, scientists have

Robert Goddard, bundled against the cold weather of March 16, 1926, holds the launching frame of his most notable invention — the first liquid-fueled rocket. (Esther Goddard)

reverted to expendable launch rockets, though they continue to do research on new families of rockets.

In late 2019 piloted space flight technology is nearly ready to take yet another evolutionary step, that being the launching of astronauts by commercial entities. SpaceX had developed the Crew Dragon, and Boeing the CST-100 Starliner. Both spacecraft are believed to be very close to resuming sending astronauts into space from American soil after the space shuttle's retirement in 2011.

Contributions

In the late nineteenth century, rockets powered by black powder (a mixture of saltpeter, sulfur, and charcoal) had some military uses, but these rockets often behaved erratically. In the early decades of the twentieth century, Robert Goddard developed reliable liquid-fueled rockets that could be controlled by valve manipulations. He also used sounding rockets that carried instruments to collect meteorological information at high altitudes. Wernher von Braun claimed that, because of war restrictions, he gained no knowledge from Goddard's patents, but Goddard, who lived to inspect a captured V-2, believed that the Germans had copied many of his ideas. Other American rocket scientists came to recognize that the V-2 embodied systems of propellant injection, guidance, and control that were far in advance of any rockets that they had developed during World War II.

During the postwar period, rocket developments were accelerated by military necessity and the Space Race between the United States and the Soviet Union. Because IRBMs and ICBMs needed to be instantly operational, sophisticated solid-propellant rocket motors were developed. Some solid fuels consisted of synthetic rubber with an oxidizer kneaded in. The use of such liquid fuels as hydrogen and oxygen required cryogenic conditions and an electric spark to start the chemical reaction. On the other hand, hypergolic systems, such as nitrogen tetroxide and monomethylhydrazine, ignite on contact.

Both American and Soviet rocket scientists gained valuable knowledge from interactions between their military and space-research projects. New ideas such as internally pressurized fuel tanks and strong, lightweight stainless-steel construction helped scientists and technicians fashion powerful and reliable rockets. Tests often revealed inefficiencies. For example, all three rocket engines of the Atlas ignited before liftoff, whereas in the Titan only its first-stage engines fired at liftoff, while its upper stage ignited only after first-stage burnout. The three-stage Saturn V was the culmination of years of highly complex developments. Its five gigantic F-1 rocket engines required new

manufacturing and testing procedures. Its regeneratively cooled combustion chamber had hundreds of tubes intricately interconnected, and as fuel flowed through these tubes, the chamber was cooled prior to fuel injection.

Through the development of these families of rocket boosters—Atlas, Titan, and Saturn—the knowledge gained in research on solid- and liquid-fueled rockets was used in constructing the space shuttle. The shuttle has sixty-seven rockets to lift it into orbit, maneuver it through space, and control its reentry into Earth's atmosphere. Forty-nine of these rockets are liquid-fueled; the other eighteen are solid-fueled. Rocket scientists in the twenty-first century can choose from a variety of propellants, such as kerosene, hydrazine, or hydrogen, and a variety of oxidizers, such as nitric acid and LOX. Designers of modern rocket systems can choose from a variety of engines, and they may combine these in different ways, depending on the results required. in their knowledge of propellants, structural materials, and guidance and control systems in constructing rockets that perform efficiently and safely.

Rocketry in the twentieth century was pushed by military and geopolitical concerns. Those influences remained in the early twenty-first century, but the biggest driver became commercialization of launch services with the need for reusability in order to drive down the cost per kilogram of sending payloads or humans into space.

Context

Although rockets had military uses in the late nineteenth and early twentieth centuries, these applications were limited. For example, combatants used rockets to illuminate battlefields in World War I. Rockets were much more extensively used in World War II. Americans utilized bazookas and barrage rockets, and Germans fired V-2 rockets into London and other cities.

After the war, the increasing power of rockets and the sophistication of their guidance systems made possible the ICBM, which in turn fostered an arms race between the United States and the Soviet Union. These military rockets, when suitably modified, allowed scientists to launch into space military and civilian satellites, astronauts, space stations, and planetary probes. These rockets also allowed humans to orbit and land upon the Moon (1969) as well as unmanned orbiters and landers to explore other planets in the solar system.

Rockets have also been involved in the commercialization of space. Corporations as well as countries now launch communications and weather satellites, which have generated substantial revenues. Although the transport of payloads and humans into space is by no means inexpensive or perfectly reliable, Goddard would have been pleasantly surprised by the achievements that grew out of his crude liquid-fueled rockets in the half century after his death.

—Robert J. Paradowski

See also: Astronauts and the U.S. Astronaut Program; Cooperation in Space: U.S. and Russian; Ethnic and Gender Diversity in the Space Program; International Space Station: Development; Private Industry and Space Exploration; Rocketry: Early History; Russia's Mir Space Station; Space Shuttle.

Further Reading

Baker, David. *The Rocket: The History and Development of Rocket and Missile Technology*. New York: Crown, 1978. This illustrated history emphasizes rocketry's political and military contexts. Bibliography and index.

Berinstein, Paula. *Making Space Happen: Private Space Ventures and the Visionaries Behind Them*. Medford, N.J.: Plexus Press, 2002. This work provides insight into the private organizations and entrepeneurs who seek to develop commercial space transportation systems and open up the solar system to economic development.

Braun, Wernher von, and Frederick I. Ordway III. *History of Rocketry and Space Travel*. New York: Thomas Y. Crowell, 1975. This profusely illustrated third edition of a highly praised book stresses the development of many specific rockets and missiles. Bibliography and index.

Butrica, Andrew J. *Single Stage to Orbit: Politics, Space Technology, and the Quest for Reusable Rocketry*. Baltimore: Johns Hopkins University Press, 2003. NASA piloted launch vehicles have traditionally used a multistage approach to reach orbit. This work tells the story of the attempts by research groups and industrial teams to develop a single-stage-to-orbit technology having the promise of more routine access to space and a lessening of the cost per kilogram for placing payloads into orbit.

Hall, Rex D., and David J. Shaylor. *Rocket Men: Vostok and Voskhod, the First Soviet Manned Spaceflights*. Chichester, England: Springer-Praxis, 2001. Because the authors have had access to recently released archival information, their account of the development of Russian rockets is much richer than previous accounts. Index.

Launius, Roger D., and Dennis R. Jenkins, eds. *To Reach the High Frontier: A History of U.S. Launch Vehicles*. Lexington: University Press of Kentucky, 2002. In this book experts analyze the history of the most important American launch vehicles. Notes on contributors and an index.

Ley, Willy. *Rockets, Missiles, and Men in Space*. New York: Viking, 1968. Ley was an excellent popularizer of rocketry, and this revised and expanded edition of his classic work, the last before his death, provides a vivid account of the conquest of space.

Ordway, Frederick I., III, and Mitchell Sharpe. *The Rocket Team*. Burlington, Ont.: Apogee books, 2003. A revised edition of the acclaimed, thorough history of rocketry, from early amateurs to present-day rocket technology. Includes a disc containing videos and images of rocket programs.

Siddiqi, Asif A. *Sputnik and the Soviet Space Challenge*. Gainesville: University Press of Florida, 2003. This two-volume set provides a comprehensive history of Soviet space efforts at the dawn of the Space Age.

Van Riper, A. Bowdoin. *Rockets and Missiles: The Life Story of a Technology*. Westport, Conn.: Greenwood Press, 2004. After a survey of early developments, the author focuses on rocketry in twentieth century Europe and America. Glossary, Further Reading, and an index.

Winter, Frank H. *Rockets into Space*. Cambridge, Mass.: Harvard University Press, 1990. This popular guide to military and civilian rockets emphasizes their growing sophistication. Source notes and index.

Russia's Mir Space Station

Date: February 20, 1986, to 2001
Type of spacecraft: Space station, piloted spacecraft

Mir, a third-generation Soviet/Russian orbital station, was home to numerous cosmonauts and international visitors between 1986 and 2000. It also provided experience for NASA astronauts before the International Space Station (ISS) was placed in orbit.

Key Figures

Sergei Pavlovich Korolev (1907-1966), widely regarded as a founder of the Soviet space program

Vladimir Pavlovich Barmin (1909-1993), pioneer of the rocket program in the USSR who led the development of launch infrastructure for Russian rocketry

Vladimir Nikolaevich Chelomei (1914-1984), Soviet rocket scientist and flight director designer who led the development of the Almaz space station

Leonid Kizim (1941-2010), Salyut 7 Expedition Five, Mir Expedition One commander

Anatoly Yakovlevich Solovyev (b. 1948), Salyut 7 Expedition Five, Mir Expedition One flight engineer

Yuri Romanenko, Mir Expedition Two commander

Alexander Laveikin, Mir Expedition Two flight engineer

Summary of the Mission

Mir's core module was launched on February 20, 1986. Mir was launched largely without any research equipment. It required outfitting during early expeditions. Mir's first crew briefly flew Soyuz T-15 to Salyut 7 to retrieve equipment for use aboard Mir. On July 16, cosmonauts Leonid Kizim and Anatoly Solovyev departed from Mir, leaving it unoccupied for the rest of 1986.

The second crew achieved Mir's first long-duration occupation. Yuri Romanenko and Alexander Laveikin were launched aboard Soyuz TM-2 on February 6, 1987. They reactivated Mir's systems, unloaded supplies inside a previously launched Progress freighter, and established residence for eleven months, initiating research involving materials science and Earth resources imaging. Orbital construction began when the Kvant astrophysics module was launched on March 31, 1987. Difficulty with automatic rendezvous equipment developed shortly before Kvant attempted docking at Mir's aft port. Ten days later Kvant achieved a soft docking but not a secured physical mating. Cosmonauts Romanenko and Laveikin undertook an extravehicular activity (EVA), or spacewalk, to remove a foreign object obstructing the docking mechanism. Mission Control Moscow then retracted Kvant's docking mechanism and achieved a hard mating. Over subsequent months, the cosmonauts received additional Progress freighters bearing fresh consumables, performed spacewalks installing new solar arrays that expanded Mir's available electrical power, activated Kvant's x-ray telescopes, and briefly hosted other cosmonauts and a Syrian guest who arrived on Soyuz TM-3. Laveikin developed minor cardiovascular irregularities, and was

The view of Mir from Space Shuttle Discovery in 1998 as it left the station during STS-91. (NASA)

replaced as a resident crew member by TM-3 Cosmonaut Alexander Alexandrov. Laveikin, TM-3 cosmonaut Alexander Viktorenko, and the Syrian guest returned home in the older Soyuz TM-2, leaving the fresh Soyuz spacecraft behind.

Soyuz TM-4's crew, Vladimir Georgievich Titov and Musa Manarov, relieved Romanenko and Alexandrov four days before Christmas. Romanenko and Alexandrov returned home in Soyuz TM-3 four days after Christmas, and Titov and Manarov started a year-long residence. These two hosted three brief visits by cosmonauts and researchers. They were joined in late summer by Yuri Polyakov, a physician, who over two separate lengthy visits would accumulate station time equivalent to a round trip to Mars He evaluated human physiological response when subjected to long-term weightlessness. Titov and Manarov returned home on December 21, 1988, aboard Soyuz TM-6, precisely one year after launch. Crew rotation was clearly established, with returning crews using older available Soyuz TM transports for reentry while a fresh one brought up briefly visiting crews or resident replacements. It was time to resume Mir's expansion.

Original plans predicted that Mir's orbital construction would be completed within three years, but economic and political difficulties in the faltering Soviet Union delayed the four remaining specialized research modules. While waiting for them, a new-generation Progress vehicle entered service. Progress M freighters would be equipped with separable spacecraft that would survive reentry, returning data and samples, while the freighter would undergo atmospheric destruction. Throughout 1989, crew and Soyuz rotations continued.

The Kvant 2 module was launched on November 26, 1989. Completing rendezvous, the new module approached Mir automatically, and like the first expansion module, it underwent docking delays. Unsecured solar arrays prevented the module from maintaining adequate attitude control. After that problem was solved, Kvant 2 attached itself to Mir's forward port. Later, cosmonauts used a manipulator arm to transfer it to one of four radial ports available at the core module's forward end. Kvant 2 added research facilities and incorporated a spacious airlock and large exterior hatch from which cosmonauts could begin and terminate spacewalks more easily. It also housed additional gyrodynes that increased the efficiency of Mir's attitude control system.

Kristall, the third expansion module, arrived June 10 after another aborted docking attempt several days earlier. Like Kvant 2, it initially docked at Mir's forward port, and then the cosmonauts moved Kristall to the radial port opposite Kvant 2. Several days later, Cosmonauts Solovyev and Alexander

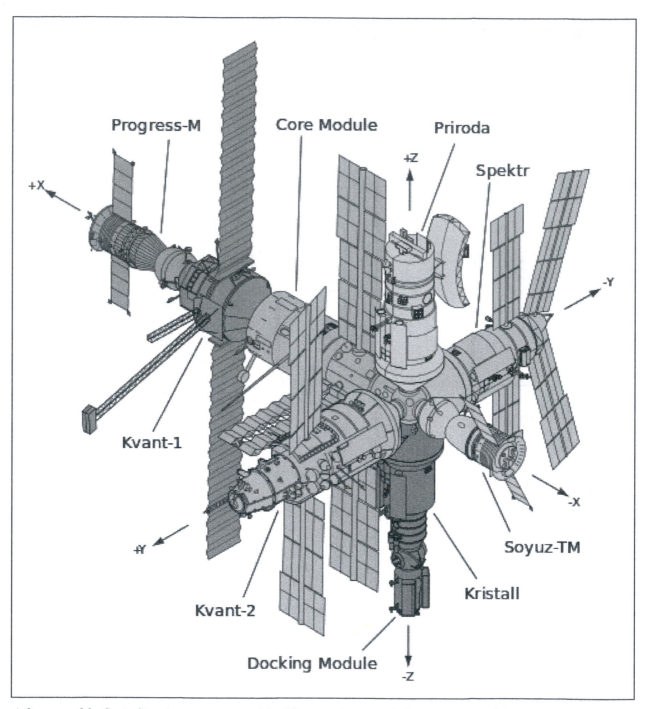

A diagram of the Soviet/Russian space station Mir following the arrival of the Priroda module and the deployment of new solar arrays on Kvant-1 at the end of May 1996, shown with a docked Progress spacecraft and Soyuz spacecraft. (via Wikimedia Commons)

Balandin performed a contingency spacewalk securing thermal blankets that had debonded from Soyuz TM-9's descent module's hull. When that spacewalk ended, Kvant 2's outer airlock hatch would not close. Fortunately, that airlock was double-chambered. The cosmonauts sealed the inner one while leaving the outer one exposed to a vacuum.

In 1991, despite the Soviet Union's dissolution, regular crew rotations continued. Numerous EVAs were performed by several cosmonauts, some including beam construction. Crews conducted varied research, hosted international guests, and received numerous Progress freighters. As 1991 ended, however, rumors surfaced that Russia might sell Mir. Severe funding problems beset the Russian Space Agency (RSA) as economic conditions in the country worsened.

Mir operations in 1992 and 1993 experienced financial shortfalls and program uncertainties following the Soviet Union's dissolution. Late hardware deliveries resulted in mission delays, but financial help arrived when the Bush Administration initiated studies of Soyuz spacecraft and Mir's compatibility in connection with National Aeronautics and Space Administration's (NASA's) Space Station Freedom. This planted the seed of the Phase I program for the ISS—the station design the Clinton Administration backed—a program that set up joint flight opportunities for cosmonauts and astronauts. Meanwhile, cosmonauts continued research and hosted international guests, which provided additional financial help and permitted continuous occupation.

Phase I operations began when STS-63 was launched on February 3, 1994, carrying cosmonaut Vladimir Georgievich Titov among its crew. *Discovery* flew the first shuttle rendezvous to Mir, coming within 10 meters (33 feet) of Mir and blazing the path for subsequent dockings. Early that year Polyakov began an attempted endurance record. At year's end RSA announced major delays in launching Spektr, a new research module that

NASA's first astronaut to live aboard Mir, Norman E. Thagard, had expected to use extensively.

Thagard was launched aboard Soyuz TM-21 on March 14, 1995, and became the first American to ride a Russian rocket. Thagard was hosted by cosmonauts Vladimir Nikolaevich Dezhurov and Gennady Mikhailovich Strekalov but briefly overlapped with Viktorenko, Elena V. Kondakova, and Polyakov's residence early in his stay. The latter three left Mir aboard Soyuz TM-20 on March 22, ending Polyakov's record-setting endurance visit at 438 consecutive days, a milestone likely to stand for quite some time.

Spektr was launched on May 20 and, after Kristall's relocation, docked at Mir's forward port on June 1, making it the first expansion module to achieve docking on its initial attempt. The next day Spektr was moved to a remaining radial port. Mir was now in proper configuration for STS-71, the first shuttle-Mir docking mission. *Atlantis* lifted off on June 27 with cosmonauts Solovyev and Nikolai Budarin slated for residence on Mir. It docked to Kristall two days later. When the astronauts entered Mir, the total population aboard reached ten, which set a record. Thagard reunited with his training backup Bonnie J. Dunbar. After logistical transfers and official ceremonies, *Atlantis* departed on July 4 with Thagard aboard. When *Atlantis* touched down at Kennedy Space Center (KSC) three days later, Thagard had established a new NASA space endurance record.

Next, NASA sent Shannon W. Lucid to Mir on STS-76, which was launched on March 22, 1996. This time *Atlantis* docked to a new docking module attached to Kristall's end, a Russian structure that STS- 74 had delivered on November 15, 1995, on the second shuttle-Mir docking mission. Lucid began an even longer stay than Thagard's. The final expansion module, Priroda, which had been planned to support much of Lucid's scientific research, was launched on April 23. Three days later it docked to Mir's forward port and was subsequently positioned at the only free radial port, thereby completing

Mir's orbital construction eight years after core module launch.

Lucid's stay lasted longer than expected after delays in getting *Atlantis* ready for its next docking mission. STS-79 retrieved Lucid in September. When Lucid finished her stay she had completed 188 days in space, a new NASA record. Lucid's replacement, John E. Blaha, traded places with her on the STS-79 shuttle-Mir docking mission. Blaha spent 128 days in space, was retrieved by STS-81, and was replaced by Jerry M. Linenger in January, 1997.

A lengthy series of crises occurred in 1997. During Linenger's stay, an international mission overlapped with a long-duration residence. With six people aboard, Mir's Elektron oxygen generation unit required supplementation by burning lithium perchlorate canisters. When Alexander Lazutkin changed out a canister inside Kvant, leaking chemicals ignited. Although the intense flame was attacked with fire extinguishers, it ended only when the canister's chemical supply ran out. The fire caused no significant structural damage, but thick smoke pervaded Mir. If it had not dissipated or if oxygen masks had not been available, the cosmonauts might have had to abandon Mir.

C. Michael Foale replaced Linenger. *Atlantis* was launched on May 15, 1997, carrying Foale and cosmonaut Elena V. Kondakova among the crew. It landed at KSC on May 24 and returned Linenger after 132 days in space.

Foale encountered 1997's worst station crisis. During a manual docking test on June 25, Commander Vasili Tsibliyev did not receive necessary telemetry, nor did he have adequate control over Progress M-34 as it impacted Mir and therefore damaged radiators and solar arrays. The cosmonauts scrambled into action upon hearing pressure-loss alarms. Lazutkin and Foale sealed off Spektr's hatch, and powered up their Soyuz in the event they needed to abandon Mir. Meanwhile, Mir lost attitude and power dropped precipitously.

Power-hungry systems were deactivated, and it took several days to reconfigure Mir's essential systems.

Over the next several weeks, Mir's computer periodically malfunctioned, forcing cosmonauts repeatedly into a lengthy sequence of restoring power, attitude control, and life-support. Additionally, carbon dioxide scrubbers and Elektron oxygen generation units required frequent maintenance. When Spektr was abandoned, many of Foale's personal property and much of his access to research equipment were lost.

Soyuz TM-26 was launched on August 5. It brought new tools and replacement parts, and cosmonauts Solovyev and Pavel Vinogradov to replace Tsibliyev and Lazutkin. While spacewalking inside Spektr, Vinogradov inserted electrical lines through the hatch and connected Spektr's functional solar arrays, which provided additional power. Attempts to isolate Spektr's hull breach all proved unsuccessful.

Mir's continued diminished condition caused serious Phase I review. Some believed that Mir was unfit for further flights. Despite external criticism, NASA decided to dispatch David A. Wolf to replace Foale. Three more shuttle-Mir dockings were achieved. Wolf began his stay on September 27. His visit was without the crises Linenger and Foale had survived, but frequent nuisance malfunctions continued. Wolf was replaced by Andrew S. W. Thomas on January 24, 1998. He, in turn, was picked up by STS-91, ending the Phase I program on June 8.

Cosmonauts kept Mir's habitation going until the twenty-seventh expedition departed in summer, 1999. Mir's future remained uncertain, but attempts to continue it beyond Phase I added to the ISS delays as Russia fell behind on its commitments to the new station. Finally, on November 17, 2000, news agencies announced that Russian Space Agency head Yuri Koptev had reported the agency's decision to dump the aging space station into the Pacific Ocean early in 2001 because Mir had reached the point "where it would be normal for any system to fail."

Contributions

Russia's Mir Space Station was launched when NASA's shuttle program appeared impotent in the wake of the *Challenger* accident. Meant as an evolutionary step in Russian space station development, Mir was designed to include considerable orbital construction of separately launched modules, in-flight repairs, and equipment changeouts performed by space-walking cosmonauts.

A view of the interior of the core module's docking node, showing the crowded nature of the station. (NASA)

Approaching the end of its life late in 2000, Mir had accumulated an impressive scientific record despite its rather significant and media celebrated problems in later years. More than 22,000 individual scientific experiments had been run using more than 240 major pieces of apparatus. Many were launched inside expansion modules, and the rest were delivered aboard Soyuz, Progress, or space shuttles. Among Mir's final clutter was fourteen tons of science hardware. Although many research projects were short-term, twenty were long-term, and some ran during virtually Mir's entire lifetime.

Including all missions up to the twenty-seventh expedition, a total of seventy-seven spacewalks had been conducted in support of station expansion, maintenance, repairs, technology demonstrations, and scientific research. Crews encountered and responded effectively to approximately 1,500 malfunctions and accidents. For the vast majority of the fourteen years that Mir had been piloted there were only several periods during which it had been mothballed and unoccupied.

During Mir's lifetime an impressive number of cosmonauts each accumulated well over a year total time spent in space spread over several separate missions. The longest single habitation ran 438 days, accomplished by Polyakov, who also held the total time record at 681 days. He was surpassed by Sergei Avdeyev on the piloted mission of 1999. Avdeev's new record-holding stay lasted 748 days. Both of these cosmonauts had spent more than enough time in space to equal a round trip to Mars, and suffered no long-term physiological or psychological maladies.

Context

Russian space station operations began in 1971 with Salyut 1. Three cosmonauts spent a record time aboard that station before returning to Earth. Although an accident resulted in their deaths during atmospheric entry, this mission marked an important step toward development of permanent space station operations. Skylab was NASA's response: a station launched virtually fully equipped, ultimately to be occupied by three separate teams staying for increasing durations in 1973 and 1974. Ten years later, NASA attained presidential authorization to build a new station called Freedom. Unfortunately, that project suffered considerable congressional interference and numerous redesigns spanning nearly a decade. Ultimately, it was reorganized into the ISS and incorporated the Russians as major partners along with the European Space Agency, the Canadian Space Agency, and the Japanese Space Agency.

Between Skylab and the ISS the Russians accumulated an impressive history of space station operations with Salyuts 3, 4, and 5, which primarily bore resemblance to the initial Salyut 1. The second-generation Salyut 6 and 7 stations provided routine resupply missions using robotic Progress freighters by incorporating multiple docking ports. During the Salyut era, a large number of cosmonauts accumulated impressive amounts of time in space, sometimes as long as six months or considerably more on a single visit.

Mir represented a third-generation Russian space station. It provided additional specific research modules to the core module. Originally, Mir was designed to be completely assembled within five years, with the addition of five add-on modules, four attached radially and one axially behind the core module. Later, it would be incorporated into or superseded by Mir 2, an even larger station that might house upward of a dozen cosmonauts and be regularly visited by Russian shuttles. With the Soviet Union's dissolution, Mir suffered economic shortfalls, and both the Russian shuttle and Mir 2 programs were canceled. Mir became the only focus of Russian piloted spaceflight, and its mission was extended. Including the Russians into the ISS provided a groundbreaking preparatory stage wherein NASA astronauts could gain long-duration station experience during the Phase I Russia's Mir Space Station 1139 program. Seven astronauts spent periods of time ranging from three to six months aboard Mir with cosmonauts. Other international visitors stayed aboard for shorter durations. Lessons learned proved to be extremely valuable for future ISS operations. Continuing Mir's operations beyond Phase I delayed fulfillment of Russian commitments to the ISS program, forcing serious delays in the early ISS orbital construction. Such considerations played a role in the final decision to deorbit Mir.

—*David G. Fisher*

See also: Cooperation in Space: U.S. and Russian; Extravehicular Activity; International Space Station: Living and Working Accommodations; International Space Station: 1999; International Space Station: 2000; International Space Station: 2001; Soyuz and Progress Spacecraft; Soyuz Launch Vehicle; Space Shuttle-Mir: Joint Missions.

Further Reading

Burrough, Bryan. *Dragonfly: NASA and the Crises Aboard Mir*. New York: Harper Collins, 1998. A nonchronological account of Mir operations during NASA's Phase I involvement with the Russian space program, largely zeroing in on behind-the-scenes interactions of principal managers, astronauts, and cosmonauts. Spends considerable time discussing Mir's lengthy list of major problems encountered in 1997.

Godwin, Robert, ed. *Rocket and Space Corporation Energia*. Burlington, Ont.: Apogee Books, 2001. The story of the R-7 rocket and its many offspring, including the current Soyuz booster, is one which still remains a mystery in the West. The book contains a pictorial record encompassing the entire history of the Russian space program, from its inception at the end of World War II to the present day. Included are details of the Mir Station and its development.

Hall, Rex, and David J. Shayler. *Soyuz: A Universal Spacecraft*. Chichester, England: Springer- Praxis, 2003. The authors review the development and operations of the reliable Soyuz family of spacecraft, including lesser-known military and unmanned versions. Using authentic Soviet and Russian sources this book is the first known work in the West dedicated to revealing the full story of the Soyuz series, including a complete listing of vehicle production numbers.

Harland, David M. *The Story of Space Station Mir*. Chichester, England: Springer-Praxis, 2005. The book tells how the Soviet Union's experience with a succession of Salyut space stations led to the development of Mir, which became an international research laboratory whose technology went on to form the "core modules" of the International Space Station. The book runs through to Mir's deorbiting in March, 2001, providing the definitive account of the Mir Space Station. The book reviews the origins of the Soviet space station program, in particular the highly successful Salyuts 6 and 7, describes Mir's structure, environment, power supply and maneuvering systems, and provides a comprehensive account of how it was assembled and how it operated in orbit.

Johnson, Nicholas L. *The Soviet Year in Space, 1987*. Colorado Springs, Colo.: Teledyne Brown Engineering, 1988. Excellent, thorough review of Soviet space program activities in 1987, both piloted and, robotic, by an acknowledged expert in Soviet spaceflight history and present-day operations. A similar volume was published by this author for each of the years 1988, 1989, and 1990.

Linenger, Jerry M. *Off the Planet*. New York: McGraw-Hill, 2000. This is a personal account of Linenger's Phase I stay aboard Mir. It must be noted that his account paints a more serious situation with regard to the fire than either the official Russian or NASA account. Provides insight into interpersonal relationships between cosmonauts and astronauts, particularly those with whom Linenger served.

Newkirk, Dennis. *Almanac of Soviet Manned Space Flight*. Houston: Gulf Publishing Company, 1990. A thorough encapsulation of Soviet spaceflight activities until the end of 1990. Mir activities during its first four years are particularly well documented. Readers will find it interesting to read future projections and compare those with what actually transpired.

Saturn Launch Vehicles

Date: April, 1957, to July, 1975
Type of technology: Expendable launch vehicles

The Saturn launch vehicle, which evolved through three phases, made possible the placement in orbit of very large payloads. These payloads would later include the technology to allow the launching of three astronauts and their subsequent safe return to Earth. The Saturn family of rockets were necessary to send Apollo astronauts to the Moon.

Key Figures

Wernher von Braun (1912-1977), director of Marshall Space Flight Center

Edmund F. O'Connor, director of Industrial Operations, Marshall Space Flight Center

Kurt H. Debus (1908-1983), director of Kennedy Space Center who developed the Saturn launch facilities

Rocco A. Petrone (1926-2006), director of Launch Operations, Kennedy Space Center

Summary of the Technology

In April of 1957, a scientific group headed by Wernher von Braun began study of a vehicle with a booster that could launch payloads of between 9,074 and 18,149 kilograms in orbital missions, or between 2,722 and 5,445 kilograms for "escape" (that is, missions designed to place a spacecraft outside Earth's gravitational field). In December, 1957, the von Braun group, together with the Army Ballistic Missile Agency (ABMA), presented a proposal to the U.S. Department of Defense (DoD) for the creation of a vehicle capable of 337,079 newtons of thrust. In August, 1958, the Advanced Research Projects Agency (ARPA) initiated the Saturn program, which provided for the clustering of rocket engines already in existence. Various configurations were explored, including the use of the Atlas-Titan and Centaur for second and third stages. The S-3D engine used on both the Thor and Jupiter missiles could be modified to 42,247 newtons of thrust (becoming the H-1), and the Redstone and Jupiter tools and fixtures could be used with little modification. Redstone and Jupiter liquid oxygen and fuel tanks could also be adapted to become tanks in the proposed new booster. The idea behind these adaptations and modifications was to save time and resources in the creation of what was at first called Juno 5. In January, 1959, a contract was awarded to the Rocketdyne Division of North American Aviation to develop and test a single engine capable of 337,079 newtons of thrust, using liquid oxygen and RP-1, a kerosene-type fuel. The program name was formally changed to Saturn on February 3, 1959.

Three distinct Saturn vehicles were developed during the course of the program, with different types of engines and boosters used. The testing procedures were complicated and extremely thorough; the first stage of Saturn IB was tested more than five thousand times as a single engine, then checked seventy-two more times in vehicle tests. Various elements were built as far away as the Douglas Aircraft facilities in California, then taken for testing to the Mississippi Test Facility (MTF) or to Kennedy Space Center (KSC), then returned for adaptation or repair. Launchings took place either at Cape Canaveral (also called Cape Kennedy) or at KSC. The logistics of moving the giant boosters were solved with a huge, adapted aircraft, called the "Pregnant

Guppy," and with barges constructed especially for this purpose. A canal was even dredged for easier access to the MTF.

The first Saturn vehicle series was designated Saturn I. Ten successive flights were labeled SA-1 through SA-10, and launched from Cape Canaveral. The Saturn I (Block I) variant used only a live first stage. This first stage, S-I, was powered by eight H-1 engines and fueled with liquid oxygen and RP-1. The Saturn I (Block II) carried a second stage, S-IV, propelled by six RL-10 engines that used liquid oxygen and liquid hydrogen.

SA-1 was launched on October 27, 1961. It stood 49.4 meters high and weighed 417,422.9 kilograms at liftoff. It flight-tested the cluster of H-1 (adapted Thor-Jupiter) engines, the S-I (the first stage) clustered propellant tank structure, the S-I control system, and other structural functions. The second stage had no engines installed, carried only water for ballast, and was topped with a Jupiter nose cone.

Von Braun with the F-1 engines of the Saturn V first stage at the U.S. Space and Rocket Center. (NASA)

SA-2, Project Highwater, was launched April 25, 1962. It carried almost 86,208 kilograms of water, which it delivered at an altitude of 106.6 kilometers. Scientists were able to observe conditions as the ionosphere regained equilibrium following the water dump.

SA-3, launched on November 16, 1962, was also a research and development flight and, like SA-2, delivered a payload of water. Flight SA-4, launched on March 28, 1963, had much the same characteristics and goals as SA-3. In addition, a planned early cutoff of one of the eight engines proved that a mission cou ld continue in spite of an engine failure. On November 27, 1963, the first extended-duration firing of the J-2 engine occurred. This engine

powered the upper stages of both the Saturn IB and V vehicles.

Another significant engine test took place in December, 1963—the F-1 initial firing at Marshall Space Flight Center (MSFC). The F-1 was later used in the first stage (SIC) of the Saturn V vehicle.

The next flight, SA-5, was launched on January 29, 1964. It was the first in a series of more sophisticated trials, using the Block II vehicle with a live second stage and instrumentation for onboard guidance. The first and second stages were separated in flight, and eight cameras were carried, seven of which were recovered.

Flight SA-6, launched on May 28, 1964, contained an active guidance system that was able to correct a deviation from the planned trajectory, caused by a premature shutdown of one engine. A boilerplate (simulation) was placed in orbit, where it stayed for 3.3 days, for a total of fifty orbits. Twelve thousand performance measurements were telemetered to ground stations, until battery power was depleted during the fourth orbital pass.

SA-7 was significant in that the Saturn I launch vehicle was declared operational following the flight, a full three missions earlier than planned. The orbit attained by the spent second stage and the payload was similar to that of a three-person lunar mission. The payload closely resembled that of a lunar mission as well, containing boilerplate Apollo spacecraft CSMs and instrumentation.

The last three Saturn I flights carried Pegasus meteoroid detection satellites designed by Fairchild Hiller Corporation. Once released from its protective Apollo boilerplate, Pegasus spread its wings to more than 29 meters. It carried solar panels to supply its power to collect data, sort information, and transmit. This satellite helped determine how thick the walls of spacecraft needed to be to provide protection from meteoroids during spaceflight.

The second series of vehicles flown was the Saturn IB. Eight H-1 engines, fueled by liquid oxygen and RP-1, powered the first stage, S-IB. The second stage, S-IVB, used one J-2 engine, which burned liquid oxygen and liquid hydrogen. It was 43 meters long, its weight at liftoff was 588,475 kilograms, and its Earth-orbit payload was 18,149 kilograms. There were nine Saturn IB vehicles launched. One of the prime objectives of Apollo-Saturn (AS) 201, the first flight, was to test the Apollo Command Module's ablative heatshield during reentry. It was launched on February 26, 1966, from KSC.

One of the primary objectives of AS-203, launched July 5, 1966, was to perform an engineering study of the behavior of liquid hydrogen during orbit. The robotic satellite placed in orbit was the heaviest to date. The flight of AS-202, on August 25, 1966, provided valuable inputs into the behavior of the S-IVB-stage fuel dynamics. This stage would be used as the third stage of the Saturn V on lunar missions.

Tragedy struck during a piloted launch pad test on what was initially called AS-204. The Apollo 1 mission was to have been the first piloted Earth orbital flight. On January 27, 1967, a flash fire in the Command Module (CM) killed the three astronauts: Virgil I. "Gus" Grissom, Edward H. White II, and Roger B. Chaffee. The fourth successful Saturn IB launch came nearly a year later. Using the AS-204 vehicle, it was launched on January 22, 1968, as Apollo 5. It was the first flight of a Lunar Module (LM). It carried instrumentation, an adapter, the LM, and a nose cone. Its objective was to check the Ascent and Descent Propulsion Systems and the abort staging function for future piloted flights. The first piloted Saturn IB flight was also the first piloted mission in the Apollo Program, Apollo 7, an Earth-orbital mission. It was launched on October 11, 1968.

Thirteen flights were made in the third series of Saturn launch vehicles, the Saturn V. It had three stages, with a total vehicle length of almost 922 meters. The first stage, S-IC, was powered by five F-1 engines, for a total thrust of 1,710,112 newtons, and burned liquid oxygen and RP-1. Stage two, S-II, was propelled by five J-2's, with a total thrust of 258,427 newtons; it was fueled by liquid oxygen and liquid hydrogen. The third stage, the S-IVB, used only one J-2 engine, propelled by liquid oxygen and liquid hydrogen. The Saturn V weight at liftoff was 2,903,211 kilograms. Its translunar payload capability was 45,372 kilograms; the Earth-orbit capability was 129,310 kilograms.

Few major changes were made from flight to flight. The only alterations made were performed to reduce weight, to improve safety or reliability, or to increase the possibilities of a larger payload.

On May 14, 1973, Skylab 1 was put into orbit. The primitive space station was built inside an S-IVB stage. The first two stages of the Saturn V were used to launch the workshop. Three flights of

Launch of AS-202 with a Saturn IB vehicle. (NASA)

the Saturn IB launched the crews for their extended visits. The last flight of a Saturn IB vehicle carried Thomas P. Stafford, Vance DeVoe Brand, and Donald K. "Deke" Slayton to their rendezvous with their former rivals during the 1975 Apollo-Soyuz mission.

Although the remaining vehicles have been retired to museums and space centers, Saturn has proved to be not only effective but also reliable. The Saturn program was an engineering and managerial marvel.

Contributions

The most significant knowledge acquired from the Saturn program was the technological knowhow needed to produce a rocket booster capable of launching large payloads of more than 5,000 kilograms to destinations as far away as the Moon. Development of engines of enormous thrust, combined with the development of a range of boosters, was a tremendous breakthrough in the space program.

Testing facilities and procedures were also greatly advanced to meet the demands of the huge boosters. New types of static and gimbal test facilities were used, and the transporter with crawler treads was developed to facilitate the Saturn program. Transportation problems were resolved with adaptations to aircraft and watercraft, and test areas were further developed to accommodate these craft.

In the entire Saturn program, only two launch vehicles failed to fly precisely according to flight plan. On one robotic Saturn V flight, Apollo 6, two of the second stage engines shut down early, and the third stage failed to fire during a restart test. What is more significant is that no vehicle failure prevented the accomplishment of a mission. The Saturn launch vehicle was remarkably successful and extremely reliable. On the Apollo 13 Saturn V launch, the center engine on the second stage shut down early but other engines made up for the difference, and the S-IVB with Apollo 13 spacecraft made Earth orbit safely.

The Saturn vehicle made possible the retrieval of a tremendous amount of data from the many varied missions for which it has been used, beginning with Project Highwater in April of 1962.

Context

The American space program started on the heels of the Soviet program. Cosmonaut Yuri A. Gagarin was successfully launched into space only three weeks ahead of U.S. astronaut Alan Shepard. The Soviet Union also launched the first multiple crew into space, as well as the first woman. The Saturn launch vehicle thrust the United States into the lead for the "race for the Moon," placing the American public firmly behind the future of the space program. The Soviet Union was working on the N-1 lunar vehicle booster at the same time. A Soviet cosmonaut never walked on the Moon. The development of the Saturn launch vehicle, capable of delivering immense payloads, made it possible for the United States to achieve such goals. Each of four N-1 test flights failed, and the Soviet Moon program was cancelled in the mid-seventies.

The Saturn launch vehicle invigorated the American public's support of the development of space technology. Following the Apollo 1 tragedy involving the CM, eighteen months elapsed before another piloted flight was attempted. The course of space exploration was considerably slowed as a result.

By the end of the Saturn launchings, however, the American public had begun to lose interest in space exploration. The final three Moon missions were canceled. The Saturn program had been extraordinarily expensive, and the launch vehicles were not reusable (hence the name "expendable launch vehicle"). The public seemed to wonder whether the returns were worth the billions of dollars spent. The American space program began to move in the direction of a spacecraft that could be reused, in the belief that costs could thereby be cut. In addition, space technology seemed to be directed toward the development of a space station, the ultimate goal being to reach other terrestrial planets via an inhabitable way station. Many payloads would be required to launch and outfit such a facility, and it was thought that a space shuttle would serve that end. The research and development spent on the Saturn program helped prepare the way for this next stage of the space program.

—Ellen F. Mitchum

See also: Apollo Program; Atlas Launch Vehicles; Delta Launch Vehicles; Launch Vehicles; Russia's Mir Space Station; Skylab Program; Skylab 2; Skylab 4; Soyuz Launch Vehicle; Titan Launch Vehicles; Viking Program.

Further Reading

Allday, Jonathan. *Apollo in Perspective: Spaceflight Then and Now*. Philadelphia: Institute of Physics, 2000. This book takes a retrospective look at the Apollo space program and the technology that was used to land humans on the Moon.

Baker, David. *The Rocket: The History and Development of Rocket and Missile Technology*. New York: Crown, 1978. A highly detailed, well-illustrated volume telling the story of rocketry from the invention of gunpowder to the landing of the first human on the Moon. Suitable for a general audience.

Bilstein, Roger E. *Stages to Saturn: A Technological History of the Apollo/Saturn Launch Vehicles*. Gainesville: University Press of Florida, 2003. Starting with the earliest rockets, Bilstein traces the development of the family of massive Saturn launch vehicles, from the people who designed them to their missions.

Cernan, Eugene A., and Don Davis. *The Last Man on the Moon: Astronaut Eugene Cernan and America's Race in Space*. New York: St. Martin's Press, 1999. The story of the last two men to walk on the Moon is told by Cernan, commander of Apollo 17, and Don Davis, an experienced journalist. This autobiography tells the story behind the story of Gemini and Apollo. Cernan, whose spaceflight career spanned both programs, fittingly narrates it. He was the first person to spacewalk in orbit around the Earth and the last person to leave footprints on the lunar surface.

Ley, Willy. *Rockets, Missiles, and Men in Space*. New York: Viking Press, 1967. A complete overview of rocketry through 1967. Begins with humankind's earliest dreams of flight and continues through the Saturn program. Technical appendices provide more technical data. Illustrated. College level.

Marshall Space Flight Center. *Saturn Illustrated Chronology*. Huntsville, Ala.: Author, 1968. A detailed presentation of all stages of development of the Saturn program. Many unretouched photographs give a realistic account of the launch sites and hardware. College-level material.

National Aeronautics and Space Administration. *Apollo Program Summary Report*. Houston: Johnson Space Center, 1975. This clear, succinct narrative of the Apollo Program includes a treatment of the role of the Saturn launch vehicle in that program. College level.

---. *Countdown! NASA Launch Vehicles and Facilities*. Washington, D.C.: Government Printing Office, 1978. A collection of short articles giving data on various NASA launch vehicles, both active and inactive, and a description of NASA facilities. Suitable for general audiences.

Shepard, Alan B., Jr., and Donald K. "Deke" Slayton, with Jay Barbree and Howard Benedict. *Moon Shot: The Inside Story of America's Race to the Moon*. Atlanta: Turner, 1994. This is, indeed, the inside story of the Apollo Program as told by two men who actively participated in it. Some of their tales appear here for the first time. The book was adapted into a four-hour documentary in 1995.

Slayton, Donald K., with Michael Cassutt. *Deke! U.S. Manned Space: From Mercury to the Shuttle*. New York: Forge, 1995. This is the autobiography of the last of the Mercury astronauts to fly in space. After being grounded from flying in Project Mercury for what turned out to be a minor heart murmur, Slayton was appointed head of the Astronaut Office. During his reign he assigned each of the Apollo crew members to their flights. Later, he commanded the Apollo-Soyuz flight in 1975. This is a behind-the-scenes look at America's attempt to land humans on the Moon.

World Spaceflight News. *Saturn V: America's Apollo Moon Rocket*. Mount Laurel, N.J.: Author, 2000. This report features more than two hundred images, illustrations, drawings, schematics, tables and charts. Although the layout leaves a lot to be desired, the information makes a decent Saturn V reference.

World Spaceflight News. *Saturn V Flight Manual: Astronaut's Guide to the Apollo Moon Rocket*. Mount Laurel, N.J.: Author, 2001. This flight manual (produced for the Apollo 8 mission) was designed for the astronauts and there is special emphasis on flight systems, events, and crew interactions. Every page is packed with details about the launch vehicle, clearly reproduced from an original NASA document.

Search and Rescue Satellites

Date: Beginning September 1, 1982
Type of spacecraft: Search and rescue satellites

Search and Rescue Satellites detect emergency beacons of downed aircraft, capsized boats, and individuals involved in exploration. In its first few years, the COSPAS/SARSAT program helped to save more than thirteen hundred lives.

Summary of the Satellites

COSPAS/SARSAT is an international program using satellites to aid in search-and-rescue operations. SARSAT stands for Search and Rescue Satellite-Aided Tracking. COSPAS is a Russian acronym for Space System for Search of Vessels in Distress.

The idea for a satellite-aided search-and-rescue program arose at almost the same time that artificial satellites were first placed in Earth orbit. It was not until the 1970's, however, that the National Aeronautics and Space Administration (NASA) began to experiment with the Doppler effect using the Nimbus satellites. The Doppler effect is the apparent change in frequency (the number of wave crests passing a point per unit of time) of an electromagnetic wave when an object moves toward or away from the source of the wave. A satellite in low-Earth orbit would observe an emergency beacon to have a higher frequency as it approached the beacon and a lower frequency as it receded from the beacon. This frequency shift allows the satellite to calculate the location of the beacon's source. The Nimbus satellites succeeded in locating weather buoys, drifting balloons, and other remote sensors, and a search-and-rescue system was proved to be feasible.

The first operational Doppler data collection system was the French ARGOS carried on the U.S. National Oceanic and Atmospheric Administration's TIROS (Television Infrared Observations Satellite). Later systems evolved from ARGOS.

In 1976, the COSPAS/SARSAT program became an international effort when the United States, France, and Canada signed agreements to test a satellite-aided search-and-rescue system. The United States would contribute its Advanced TIROS-N (ATN) weather satellites, Canada would supply electronic repeaters (devices that receive a radio signal, amplify it, and relay it to a ground station), and France would supply electronic processors for collection of identification data transmitted by the system's users. In 1980, the Soviet Union joined the program by agreeing to place the same type of electronic equipment in its Kosmos satellites. The system became operational on September 1, 1982.

Other countries began participating in the system, although their participation was limited to ground operation of a local user terminal and/or a Mission Control Center. Local user terminals receive distress signals relayed from the repeaters in the satellites. Mission Control Centers collect information and send it to the appropriate rescue control center. In 1981, Norway and Sweden began operating local user terminals. The United Kingdom joined in 1983; Finland, in 1984. Norway and the United Kingdom also operate Mission Control Centers. Additional nations joined the program with the passage of time.

A number of other countries (Chile, Denmark, India, Italy, Japan, Pakistan, Sweden, Switzerland, and Venezuela) either use the system, operate a user terminal, or are discussing possible operation of user terminals or control centers

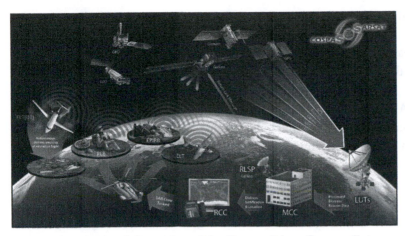

The Components and Operation of the Cospas-Sarsat System. (International Cospas-Sarsat Programme)

COSPAS/SARSAT works in the following manner. An emergency transmitter—either an emergency locator-transmitter (ELT) or an emergency pointing/indicating radio beacon (EPIRB)—is activated when an emergency occurs. ELTs are carried on general aviation aircraft, and EPIRBs are carried on marine vessels that venture into open ocean. The signal from an ELT or EPIRB has a frequency of 121.5 or 243 megahertz. The signal is received by a COSPAS/SARSAT satellite and relayed to a local user terminal at a frequency of 1544.5 megahertz. Some more advanced ELTs can transmit a 406 megahertz signal that provides data on the sender's identification and nationality as well as the transmission's time and location. If necessary, the information can be stored until the satellite is in range of a ground station. After the information is processed by the local user terminal, it is relayed to the appropriate Mission Control Center, which may be in another country. The Mission Control Center then passes the information on to a rescue control center, which is then responsible for the rescue.

The type of rescue effort varies with geography, national boundaries, and available resources. In the United States, the Air Force, sometimes with help from the Civil Air Patrol, coordinates inland airplane rescue attempts. The Coast Guard is called on for rescue attempts in the ocean to a distance of 320 kilometers from the U.S. coastline; farther out, the Air Force is responsible for searches. COSPAS/SARSAT's pinpointing of the signal sender's location helps reduce the amount of money spent on the search and, more important, time spent finding downed aircraft or ships in distress. Studies show that the survival rate for airplane crash victims is 50 percent if they are rescued within eight hours. If the rescue takes place more than two days after the disaster, however, the chance of survival drops to 10 percent.

Contributions

In the 1970's, using satellites in search and rescue was proven feasible. In the early 1980's, enough satellites were placed in orbit and enough ground stations were set up to allow the system to operate.

The first COSPAS/SARSAT rescue took place in September, 1982. A young couple's plane went down in British Columbia in July, 1982, and the Canadian government launched an extensive search that ultimately cost nearly two million dollars. The couple was not found, and the search was stopped. The young man's father, along with a pilot and a friend, decided to embark on their own search-and-rescue mission, which continued into September, 1982.

During this search, however, their plane crashed in a mountainous, tree-covered area. They were injured, but alive. An ELT had been activated by the crash, and as Soviet COSPAS 1 passed over, it relayed the information to the Trenton, Ontario, Air Rescue Station. A rescue control center was contacted, and the three victims became the first persons to be rescued with the aid of a satellite.

The two disasters serve as contrasting examples of search-and-rescue operations. The location of the first crash was not known, and consequently, much time and money were expended in searching. The second crash location was known to within 22.5 kilometers, so only a relatively small area had to be searched; costs were much lower, and the victims were found while they were still alive.

In July, 1985, the COSPAS/SARSAT steering committee, which includes experts from Canada, France, the Soviet Union, and the United States, adopted the 406 megahertz frequency for signals broadcast by ELTs. Because the 406 megahertz signal allows for more precise location calculations than does the 121 megahertz signal, it makes faster rescues possible. Moreover, such a signal can carry identification data.

A problem that plagues the COSPAS/SARSAT system is the large number of false alarms. In 1988, the false alarm rate was 98 percent for ELTs and more than 50 percent for EPIRBs. False alarms are caused by unintentional activation of an ELT or EPIRB beacon resulting from improper handling, equipment failure, or improper shipment or testing. Because each distress signal must be tracked down, much time and effort are wasted. False alarms probably can be reduced by better enforcement of laws governing the use of emergency frequencies, redesign of equipment so that it is harder to trigger a false alarm, and better education for ELT and EPIRB users.

Context

Before the COSPAS/SARSAT program, search-and-rescue operations were conducted on a hit-or-miss basis. During the 1970's, NASA showed that it was possible to locate radio signal sources on Earth by making use of the Doppler effect, and this technology spurred the development of COSPAS/SARSAT. New knowledge has been gained in the area of locating points on Earth's surface, and as a result, rescue teams can locate disaster victims much more quickly.

COSPAS/SARSAT saves money as well as lives. When the area to be searched is a few square

kilometers instead of hundreds or thousands of square kilometers, fewer searches are needed. More efficient searches also mean that rescue planes or ships can be used for shorter times. COSPAS/SARSAT has effected savings of $20 million per year, according to estimations by Owen Heeter, commander of the Air Force's Aerospace Rescue and Recovery Service.

COSPAS/SARSAT is important for one other reason: international cooperation. The United States and the Soviet Union were partners in this program almost from its beginning. For nearly six years, it functioned only on a memorandum of understanding, but on July 1, 1988, an international agreement requiring nations to cooperate in COSPAS/SARSAT was signed by the United States, Canada, France, and the Soviet Union. William E. Evans, undersecretary of commerce for Ocean and Atmosphere, signed for the United States. This agreement is binding for the first ten years, with automatic renewal every five years thereafter. Countries and organizations such as the United Nations International Maritime Organization can require that ships and/or aircraft have the emergency 406 megahertz beacon on board. In the late 1980's, NASA was trying to develop low-cost 406 megahertz ELTs.

As of 2005, there were seven COSPAS/SARSAT satellites in low-altitude Earth orbit and three satellites in geostationary orbit, eighteen ground segment providers, and eight user states. One SARSAT satellite had suffered malfunctions, resulting in intermittent loss of service, that could affect an entire or just partial satellite pass. More than 800,000 distress beacons were estimated to be deployed. By 2003 more than seventeen thousand people had been rescued in more than 4,800 responding incidents. NASA and others continue to seek new methods to cut costs and time in search-and-rescue operations while saving even more lives.

—T. Parker Bishop

See also: Amateur Radio Satellites; Cooperation in Space: U.S. and Russian; National Aeronautics and Space Administration; Saturn Launch Vehicles; SMS and GOES Meteorological Satellites; Telecommunications Satellites: Maritime; TIROS Meteorological Satellites.

Further Reading

Andrade, Alessandra A. L. *The Global Navigation Satellite System: Navigating into the New Millennium*. Montreal: Ashgate, 2001. Provides an international view of issues of availability, cooperation, and reliability of air navigation services. Attention is specifically paid to the American GPS (Global Positioning System) and Russian GLONASS systems, although the development of the Galileo civilian system in Europe is also presented.

Bailey, James T. "Satellites Answer SOS." *Mariner's Weather Log* 32 (Spring, 1988): 8-11. A nontechnical description of search-and-rescue satellites, this article requires minimal technical knowledge. Contains several photographs and one illustration showing how the COSPAS/SARSAT system works and features stories about searches that demonstrate the usefulness and cost-effectiveness of the COSPAS/SARSAT system. Emphasizes international cooperation.

Gavaghan, Helen. *Something New Under the Sun: Satellites and the Beginning of the Space Age*. New York: Copernicus Books, 1998. This book focuses on the history and development of artificial satellites. It centers on three major areas of development—navigational satellites, communications satellites, and weather observation and forecasting satellites.

Haggerty, James J. *Spinoff 1984*. NASA TM-85596. Washington, D.C.: Government Printing Office, 1984. This multicolor pamphlet contains a summary of NASA's major accomplishments in space and the ways in which those accomplishments have benefited humankind. One page is devoted to a brief description of how the COSPAS/SARSAT system operates. Illustrated. For general audiences.

Kachmar, Michael. "SARSAT/COSPAS: Saving Lives Through Cooperation In Space." *Microwaves and RF* 23 (October, 1984): 33-35. This journal contains a news section in which uses of microwaves and radio frequency waves are described. Includes photographs. Technical language is used mostly without explanation, but some terms are defined in the text.

McElroy, John H., and James T. Bailey. "Saving Lives at Sea . . . Via Satellite." *Sea Technology* 26 (August, 1985): 30-34. A nontechnical description of the COSPAS/SARSAT international satellite network. Includes illustrations of a rescue at sea and a discussion of searches and their costs. Suitable for general audiences.

National Aeronautics and Space Administration. *COSPAS/SARSAT*. Greenbelt, Md.: Author, 1986. Describes the COSPAS/SARSAT system and gives a brief history of how the system was developed. Outlines the operation's successes and the ways in which it will expand in the future. Contains color diagrams. Suitable for general audiences.

---. *Space Network Users' Guide (SNUG)*. Washington, D.C.: Government Printing Office, 2002. This users' guide emphasizes the interface between the user ground facilities and the Space Network, providing the radio frequency interface between user spacecraft and NASA's Tracking and Data-Relay Satellite System, and the procedures for working with Goddard Space Flight Center's Space Communication program.

National Research Council Staff. *The Global Positioning System: A Shared National Asset: Recommendations for Technical Improvements and Enhancements*. Washington, D.C.: National Academy Press, 1995. This book provides insights into the global positioning satellites and recommends some improvements to enhance military, civilian, and commercial use of the system.

Ola, Per, and Emily D'Aulaire. "The Starduster's Last Flight." *Reader's Digest* 131 (July, 1987): 75-80. This is a nontechnical account of a successful search-and-rescue operation. It is part of the Drama in Real Life series of articles that appears in *Reader's Digest*. Written as a historical account of an air disaster, with a description of the efforts of the Air Force Rescue Coordinator Center to help in the search. Suitable for general audiences.

United States Coast Guard. *National Search and Rescue Manual*. Washington, D.C.: Author, 1986. This two-volume work gives detailed information on the procedures for performing search-and-rescue operations. These manuals could be used in training exercises. Satellite-aided search-and-rescue operations are discussed. For general audiences.

United States Department of Commerce. *NESDIS Programs, NOAA Satellite Operations*. Washington, D.C.: Author, 1985. This publication provides a very brief description of the COSPAS/SARSAT system and a diagram of how the system operates. Most of this publication covers other topics, such as the weather satellites of the NESDIS program. For general audiences.

United States Department of Transportation. *1986 SAR Statistics*. Washington, D.C.: Author, 1986. This publication offers tables, photographs, and diagrams detailing search and rescue statistics for 1986. Does not distinguish between satellite-aided and nonsatellite-aided rescues. For general audiences.

Search for Extraterrestrial Life

Date: Beginning 1976
Type of program: Planetary exploration

The notion of extraterrestrial life has fascinated humanity for centuries. Since the mid-twentieth century, however, technological advances in radio astronomy have allowed scientists to search for evidence of intelligent life beyond Earth. Spacecraft dispatched throughout the solar system have produced tantalizing suggestions for the possibility of microbial life in our own celestial neighborhood.

Key Figures

Frank Drake (b. 1930), director of Project Ozma, the initial radio search

Carl Sagan (1934-1996), astronomer who popularized the notion of contact with extraterrestrial intelligences

H. Paul Shuch (b. 1946), founding director of the SETI Institute

Summary of the Program

One of the most captivating and controversial aspects of space exploration is the search for extraterrestrial life. Speculation about life on other worlds has been a part of scientific and popular cosmology since the Renaissance, but only in the second half of the twentieth century was it possible to begin searching systematically for evidence. Two main lines of investigation have been followed: experiments carried aboard robotic planetary probes to test for indirect evidence of life or conditions conducive to life, and radio astronomy programs designed to detect possible signals from intelligent life on planets orbiting other stars. (A third approach—detection of atmospheric or other evidence of life on planets in other solar systems—began in the 1990's but requires further technological development to generate significant results.)

The prototypes of experiments to detect signs of life were aboard the Viking 1 and 2 landers, deployed in 1976 on Mars, the planet that historically has been the object of the lion's share of speculation about possible life in the solar system. By the time of the Viking missions, prevailing views about possible Martian life had long since matured from popular fantasies about intelligent aliens to a consensus that if such life existed, it must be microscopic in size. Experiments aboard the Viking landers focused on a key assumption for detection of possible extraterrestrial life: Anything living must reproduce, and it must metabolize or in some other manner consume energy; consequently it will leave chemical or atmospheric by-products as "fingerprints." Three different experiments on the landers sampled nearby Martian soil, seeking to detect photosynthesis or some other process that might use carbon dioxide containing radioactive carbon 14, or bathing the samples in nutrients containing carbon 14 and attempting to detect radioactive gases given off by any metabolic process.

Certain conditions are widely believed to be indispensable for the existence and evolution of life—above all large quantities of water in a liquid state over geologic periods of time. Robotic missions to explore for water, although also having more practical purposes—notably to judge the feasibility of eventual long-term piloted occupation of other planets—also implicitly relate to the search for life. Evidence continues to accumulate that Mars had significant bodies of surface water early in its

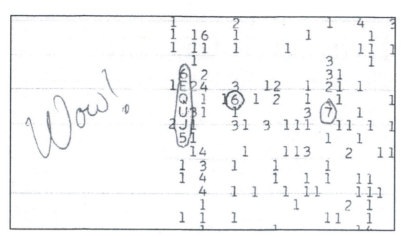

The Wow! signal was a strong narrowband radio signal received on August 15, 1977, by Ohio State University's Big Ear radio telescope in the United States, then used to support the search for extraterrestrial intelligence. The signal appeared to come from the direction of the constellation Sagittarius and bore the expected hallmarks of extraterrestrial origin. (Big Ear Radio Observatory)

geologic history and that large quantities still exist frozen beneath the surface. The search for water or water ice was a high priority for the unsuccessful Mars Polar Lander mission in 1999. The Mars Phoenix lander provided in 2007-2008 direct evidence of subsurface water ice in the high northern latitudes of the Red Planet. Robotic missions and orbital and ground-based telescopes have focused a great deal of scientific and public attention on Europa, one of the major satellites of Jupiter, because there is strong evidence of a liquid water ocean beneath its frozen surface.

The search for intelligent life elsewhere in the universe relies primarily on radio astronomy. The earliest systematic attempt to detect intelligent signals was Project Ozma in 1958, directed by Harvard astronomer Frank Drake, using a radio telescope at Green Bank in West Virginia. In 1984 scientists formed the Search for Extraterrestrial Intelligence Institute (SETII) to coordinate research and educational programs. The Institute obtained more than $100 million in funding from the National Aeronautics and Space Administration (NASA), philanthropists, and other sources to conduct a decade of research utilizing some of the largest radio telescopes

and arrays in the world, as well as ever-increasing computer technology and speed to search millions of potential frequencies. In 1994 the United States Congress canceled funding for the NASA SETII Project, of which the Institute was a major grantee. Project Phoenix, a privately funded effort, carried on the search. Also, in the aftermath of Congress forcing NASA to withdraw its support for SETI research, an industrialist founded the nonprofit, membership-driven SETI League for which microwave engineer and SETI enthusiast Dr. H. Paul Shuch served as initial executive director and principal investigator for the League's Project Argus, an all sky survey of radio emissions. The public became engaged in SETI data analysis through SETI@home in which interested volunteers provided screen-saver computing time for data analysis; for many the thought that they might be the one to identify a signal from an intelligence beyond Earth was thrilling.

Radio astronomers organize the search on a number of fairly speculative assumptions. They reason that radio and television broadcasts must be fingerprints of any advanced civilization, and that some may be deliberately propagated to announce the presence of alien civilizations. Given that the universe is awash in all sorts of electromagnetic radiation, including radio signals from natural sources, SETII searches generally have concentrated on the microwave region of the spectrum, from 1,000 to 100,000 megahertz. Here the universe is relatively "quiet," with only a faint signature left over from the Big Bang from which the universe evolved Microwave transmitters can propagate strong signals with only modest power. Searchers calculate that other advanced civilizations also will have realized the advantages of the microwave bands and thus search and broadcast in these frequencies. Project Phoenix has directed increased attention to relatively nearby, Sun-like stars.

Discoveries since the 1990's of planets around other stars holds great promise for expanding the search for extraterrestrial life. By the mid-twenty-first century telescopes and deep-space interferometers identified planets as small as Earth. These instruments are capable of analyzing the atmospheres around Earth-like planets. The presence of free oxygen in the atmosphere of a planet, for example, because there are few natural processes to account for it, would be a strong fingerprint of life processes. Carl Sagan, to whom the public owes more perhaps than to anyone else for the popularization of the extraterrestrial life debate, once suggested that atmospheric methane, which most likely would be generated by the digestive processes of ungulate-like animals—basically flatulent cows—would be another clue worth searching for.

Contributions

As of 2019 not one shred of irrefutable evidence existed for the presence of any form of life, microscopic or otherwise, other than on Earth. However, the continuing search for extraterrestrial life should not be disregarded. It has seldom been conducted to the exclusion of other forms of space research. For example, the biology experiments aboard the Viking landers, while they did not return positive results, nevertheless revealed much about what seems to be the highly reactive composition of Martian soils. The search for water on other planets and satellites, closely bound in many ways to the search for extraterrestrial life, has fundamentally revised our views of the solar system, wherein we now suspect water to be abundant. Inasmuch as water is potentially a source of free hydrogen and oxygen, it can be a resource for expanding human exploration and eventual settlement in the system. Several discoveries of what radio astronomers initially thought could be signals not of natural origin turned out to reveal previously unknown types of bodies in deep

space, the study of which has added to our theories of cosmology.

Actual discovery of unequivocal evidence of extraterrestrial life would be one of the most profound events in human history. The media and the public got a taste of what might be in store when NASA announced in 1996 that it believed scientists had detected fossilized microbes in the meteorite ALH84001, which was found in Antarctica and probably originated on Mars. Even heads of state called news conferences to comment on the find, later to become highly controversial as other teams of scientists produced plausible nonbiological explanations for the features.

Context

Perhaps the most significant and revealing element of the search for extraterrestrial life is the debate itself and how its evolution reflects the growing sophistication of knowledge about our solar system and beyond. Much of that debate, for example, turns on probability projections. Frank Drake devised a widely debated equation relating variables involved in determining the probability of extraterrestrial life, but hard data to refine some of those variables still eludes scientists. Carl Sagan's writings reflect a broad scientific consensus that, given the billions upon billions of stars in the Milky Way, and the billions upon billions of other galaxies in the universe, conditions favorable to life on other planets almost certainly exist, and that contact with one or more alien civilizations is only a matter of time.

Over the course of the last half century views about the tenacity of life also have changed. Microbial life has been discovered deep within the rocks of Antarctica under the most severe conditions. Hydrothermal vents on the ocean floor are now known to support a wide variety of microbial and even more complex life in total darkness under enormous pressures. Once thought to be fragile, the processes of life now appear to be capable of flourishing almost anywhere on Earth, and, implicitly, on other worlds. Many scientists now believe that eventually we shall find evidence of microscopic life-forms, and perhaps the life-forms themselves, in a number of places in the solar system, especially where liquid water is available. Evidence continues to mount that Mars was a warmer, much wetter world with a less tenuous atmosphere during the first billion or so years of its existence, and a similar scenario may apply to Venus. Perhaps simple life forms got a start on Mars but no longer survive the harsh environment; perhaps they do survive deep underground, protected from the lethal ultraviolet radiation striking the planet now almost barren of atmosphere.

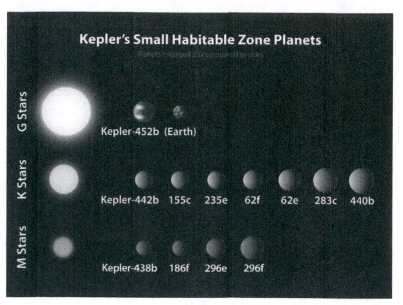

Of the 1,030 confirmed planets from Kepler, a dozen are less than twice the size of Earth and reside in the habitable zone of their host stars. In this diagram, the sizes of the exoplanets are represented by the size of each sphere. (NASA / Ames / JPL-Caltech)

As scientists learn more about the universe, new reasons also have appeared to be less than optimistic about the possibility of extraterrestrial life. Most important, researchers still do not know enough about processes leading to the origin of life on Earth to say with any confidence what might be the probability of similar processes operating elsewhere. In general, our notions about the origins of life are tending toward ever greater complexity. Research in terrestrial geology and paleontology in the last two decades of the twentieth century revealed an unsettling pattern of near-extinction of life on Earth and radical redirection of evolution—the most spectacular being extinction of the dinosaurs some sixty-five million years ago—caused by asteroid or cometary impacts, perhaps generated in turn by as yet unknown long-term cycles of periodic disturbance of the solar system neighborhood. The presence of a single large Moon orbiting the Earth—a highly unusual circumstance as far as scientists know—is believed to have prevented wild swings in the Earth's axial inclination which could have altered climate sufficiently to extinguish primitive life-forms. Plate tectonics, a force not known to exist in robust form elsewhere in the solar system,

have been crucial in renewing the Earth's surface and in stimulating evolution. Plant evolution created an atmosphere with large amounts of free oxygen, a feature unknown thus far on other worlds. In sum, the evolution of life on Earth, particularly complex life, appears more and more to be the product of a conjunction of unusual circumstances of almost astronomical improbability of being replicated elsewhere.

Discoveries of planets orbiting other stars, which began in the 1990's, confirm that planets seem to be abundant in the universe, but that Earth-like planets in stable orbits may not be so numerous A large proportion of extrasolar planets discovered thus far are close to the mass of Jupiter or many times as massive, and most have highly elliptical orbits that may eliminate the possibility of emergence of life in any case. Most disturbing is that many of these extrasolar planets are extremely close to their stars, suggesting that huge, gas-giant planets may evolve in the outer reaches of star systems and then spiral inward over billions of years, destroying any smaller, Earth-like planets more likely to harbor life-forms.

These discoveries have led to a new appreciation of Jupiter in determining the success of life on Earth. Jupiter may be responsible for sweeping up most of the otherwise deadly asteroids and comets on a collision course with Earth, thus creating a more placid inner solar system in which life could take hold on Earth and perhaps elsewhere.

Accumulating knowledge about the universe has led exobiologists increasingly to theorize in two different directions about the probability of extraterrestrial life. Simple, microbial life—or other forms of organisms that replicate and metabolize—might turn out to be relatively abundant, or at least to have started to evolve on planets such as Mars. On the whole, the probability of such life seems substantially higher than was the case based on our knowledge of the universe in, say, 1960, when robotic planetary exploration first got under way. In contrast, the probability of complex life, much less intelligent life, at least in the near vicinity of the solar system, has greatly diminished. Moreover, if intelligent life exists elsewhere, scientists may not detect it within hundreds or even thousands of light-years from Earth. The speed and power of equipment searching for radio signals have increased by hundreds of millions of times since the first attempt in 1958, with no result and perhaps none to be expected for centuries or millennia. However, the state of understanding of exoplanets changes rapidly. The Kepler Space Telescope and Transiting Exoplanet Survey Satellite data sets contain a wide range of planetary systems to study.

The ultimate context in which to understand the search for extraterrestrial life is cosmological and religious. The question of whether humanity is alone in the universe, as an intelligent life-form with a culture capable of even asking such a question, must be resolved. The very nature of that question guarantees the search will go on.

—Ronald W. Davis

See also: Ames Research Center; Mariner 8 and 9; Mission to Planet Earth; Search and Rescue Satellites; Viking 1 and 2.

Further Reading

Aczel, Amir D. *Probability 1: Why There Must Be Intelligent Life in the Universe*. New York: Harcourt Brace, 1998. Argues that the probability of intelligent life somewhere else in the universe is overwhelming.

Cooper, Henry S. F., Jr. *The Search for Life on Mars: Evolution of an Idea*. New York: Holt, Rinehart and Winston, 1980. A summary of the debate about life on Mars through the period of the Viking experiments in the mid-1970's. Also provides excellent insights on the nature of the scientific process of designing the Viking experiments.

Davies, Paul. *The Fifth Miracle: The Search for the Origin and Meaning of Life*. New York: Simon and Schuster, 1999. Discusses the search for extraterrestrial life within the context of our rapidly changing knowledge about the nature and tenacity of life in general. Excellent summation of the search for life on Mars and the debate over meteorite ALH84001.

Dick, Steven J. *Life on Other Worlds: The Twentieth Century Extraterrestrial Life Debate*. New York: Cambridge University Press, 1998. Places the debate about extraterrestrial life in historical perspective, suggesting that based on discoveries in the 1990's the universe appears more supportive of life than earlier cosmological arguments permitted.

Jakosky, Bruce. *The Search for Life on Other Planets*. New York: Cambridge University Press, 1998. A fairly dispassionate account of the search and assessment of the arguments for and against various forms of life in the universe.

McConnell, Brian S. *Beyond Contact: A Guide to SETI and Communicating with Alien Civilizations*. New York: O'Reilly, 2001. Covers the history of the search for extraterrestrial intelligence, including the latest efforts to include the general public in the SETI project. Investigates how communication might be attempted in the event that a signal from ETs is detected.

Sagan, Carl. *The Cosmic Connection: An Extraterrestrial Perspective*. Garden City, N.Y.:

Doubleday, 1973. The classic statement about the question of extraterrestrial life and how it fits into our broader views of ourselves and our universe, by perhaps the most renowned science writer of the latter twentieth century.

Shapiro, Robert. *Planetary Dreams: The Quest to Discover Life Beyond Earth*. New York: Wiley, 1999. Highly readable synopsis of the search for extraterrestrial life by a biochemist and firm believer in its existence.

Sullivan, Walter. *We Are Not Alone: The Continuing Search for Extraterrestrial Intelligence*. Rev. ed. New York: Plume, 1994. This work is a revision of a 1964 publication. Examining the two together is one of the best means to appreciate the enormous technological leaps in radio astronomy as well as the evolution of discourse about extraterrestrial life.

Ward, Peter Douglas. *Rare Earth: Why Complex Life Is Uncommon in the Universe*. New York: Copernicus, 2000. Predicts that microbial life will be found to be fairly common in the universe, but that unusual combinations of factors connected with the emergence of higher forms of life on Earth seem to make its replication unlikely. An excellent summation of the state of thinking in astrobiology at the end of the twentieth century.

Seasat

Date: June 26 to October 6, 1978
Type of spacecraft: Earth observation satellites

Seasat was a satellite designed to perform a variety of experiments, including photographic and remote-sensing procedures, above the world's oceans. Though short-lived, it provided invaluable data about ocean currents, wave action, water temperature, wind direction, ice floes, and other marine phenomena.

Summary of the Satellite

In the post-Sputnik era, the use of satellites for communication, reconnaissance, and remote sensing of Earth's surface became commonplace. Early experiments with ground-controlled orbital spacecraft demonstrated the usefulness of such technology for cartography, natural resource identification, and the monitoring of agricultural production. It was only a matter of time before scientists would begin to explore the uses of satellite technology for the study of the world's oceans.

On January 9, 1975, the National Aeronautics and Space Administration (NASA) announced a satellite program to monitor the world's oceans and provide continuous data on sea conditions and ocean weather. The satellite, dubbed Seasat-A, was scheduled for launch in 1978. Its purpose was to provide evidence that an artificial scientific satellite could function in this role. Thus, it was not an operational system, although indications were that such a system might be launched if Seasat accomplished its mission successfully. Instrumentation aboard the satellite would measure wave height, current direction, surface wind direction, and the temperature of the surface of the ocean for a period of one year.

It was hoped that the information gathered by Seasat could be used to predict the weather, help ships avoid storms and icebergs, provide coastal disaster warnings, and locate currents that could be used to advantage by ships. The satellite was also designed to provide data on ocean circulation, interaction between the atmosphere and the sea, and the movement of heat and nutrients by ocean currents.

At the time of the announcement, the cost of Seasat was projected to be $58.2 million. In November of 1975, a $20 million contract for the design and construction of Seasat was awarded to Lockheed Missiles and Space Company of Sunnyvale, California, by the Jet Propulsion Laboratory (JPL).

As the launch date approached, NASA began to seek potential users of the data that it expected would be forthcoming from Seasat. Early in 1977, representatives of a group of European nations—including Denmark, Finland, France, West Germany, Great Britain, and Spain—came forward to express an interest in the project. These potential data users suggested two common goals: that Seasat be useful in forecasting floods in the North Sea region, and that the information it provided be useful in designing ships and offshore installations such as oil-drilling platforms and in-harbor structures.

Among U.S. organizations interested in Seasat were the National Oceanic and Atmospheric Administration (NOAA), the National Science Foundation, the Office of Naval Operations of the U.S. Coast Guard, and the U.S. Geological Survey. Early studies done by NASA suggested that an operational oceanographic satellite data-gathering system

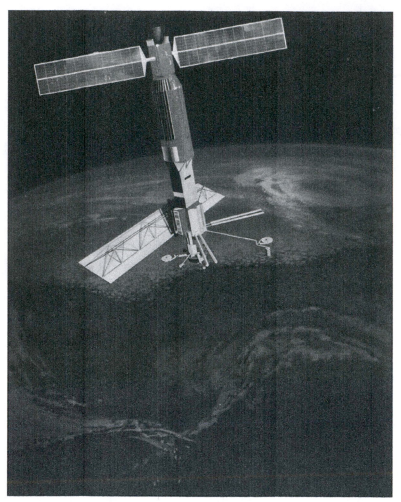

Artist's conception of Seasat. (NASA / JPL)

minutes to complete, and during each thirty-six-hour period, 95 percent of Earth's surface was covered. After an initial adjustment, the orbit was to be stabilized and devoid of variation for three months at a time, in an effort to create the best operating environment for one of the onboard instruments.

Seasat was fitted with five remote-sensing instruments, designed and programmed by various NASA agencies. These devices included a radar scatterometer, a synthetic aperture radar (SAR) system, a scanning multispectral microwave radiometer, a radar altimeter, and a visual and infrared radiometer.

The microwave wind scatterometer, built under the direction of the Langley Research Center, measured surface wind speeds over the oceans in a range of between 4 and 28 meters per second.

The SAR system measured the direction and size of ocean waves, day and night. It was able to detect ice, oil spills, and ocean current configurations, even through fog and moderate precipitation. It was designed by JPL.

could produce returns valued at up to $2 billion by the end of the twentieth century. The semi-commercial nature of the venture was important in overall strategic planning at a time when NASA was being encouraged by the U.S. government to find markets for its programs.

Seasat was launched successfully on June 26, 1978, from Vandenberg Air Force Base in California. The satellite itself, an Agena rocket stage with sensor module attached, was the second stage of the launch vehicle. The first stage was an Atlas-F rocket. Seasat's overall length was 12 meters, and it weighed 2,273 kilograms. It was placed in an orbit 800 kilometers above Earth and made 14.33 orbits of Earth each day. Each orbit took one hundred

The five-channel multispectral scatterometer, also designed by JPL, was able to detect the surface temperature of the ocean to within 2 kelvins. It also detected wind speed to 50 meters per second and mapped ice fields. It measured atmospheric moisture content as a housekeeping chore, allowing controllers to correct altimeter and scatterometer readings. It also measured radiation on five wavelengths.

The radar altimeter measured the distance between the ocean surface and the satellite, with an accuracy of plus or minus 10 centimeters, and could detect currents, tides, and weather-related storm surges, of importance to shipping and coastal population areas. It was designed by the Applied Physics Laboratory at The Johns Hopkins University for NASA's Wallops Flight Center.

The scanning visible and infrared radiometer observed surface features during clear weather only. It was designed to help in the identification and location of phenomena such as intense currents, storm systems, and ice floes.

Soon after Seasat was launched, users began to extol the high quality of the heavy volume of data being generated by its sensors and transmitted to ground stations around the world. The mission was widely proclaimed a success, despite equipment malfunctions that cut it short after only four months of operation. Each day of its life, Seasat generated more data than had accumulated over decades using land-based techniques and aircraft, with their relatively narrow fields of vision. Seasat had met the expectations of NASA and led to the development and eventual deployment of advanced sensing instrumentation for Earth resources satellites. Soon, NASA and other space agencies began to plan construction and deployment of similar satellites, as the space era moved into the 1980's.

Contributions

Before the advent of satellites, oceanographers had been able to obtain information about the seas, but the efficiency of operation and quantity of data were limited by the relatively narrow field of vision of traditional sensing technology and the expense of deployment and operation. For example, ocean vessels and aircraft were able to contribute to the body of knowledge about the weather, currents, ice fields, and the like by relaying visual-sighting information to federal agencies responsible for monitoring such activity. Sensing equipment had also been mounted on automatic transmission buoys on the surfaces of oceans around the world. Using radio signals, these buoys could detect and transmit information about ocean surface temperatures, wave action, wind direction, and salinity.

When satellites did appear on the scene, these buoys were able to receive data for relay to control sites around the world. Seasat, on the other hand, was able to acquire and transmit a much higher volume of significantly more sophisticated data in real time, twenty-four hours a day.

Until Seasat most satellite systems contained only passive sensors. Among their functions were the measurement of radiation emission, infrared and microwave, and reflected solar radiation. Such passive systems are useful in nighttime detection of icebergs and ice floes. Sea ice emits a different rate of microwave radiation than seawater, a fact that is key to the process of oceanographic sensing of the delineation between them. Furthermore, old sea ice emits radiation at a different rate than new sea ice, giving scientists another dimension to the picture: the relative age of the ice field and of its individual components.

In addition to monitoring radiation, passive systems could collect visual images of clouds, ice fields, and ocean surfaces during daylight. They could also determine the amount of water vapor in the atmosphere and thus constituted a useful tool in the creation of global precipitation maps. Yet passive systems had certain limitations.

Seasat carried three different types of radar, two of which were active, including a new and relatively untried sensor, a scatterometer. The scatterometer measured back-scattered radiation from the ocean surface at a specific wavelength. The theory behind its design was that the intensity of such radiation and its direction related to the amount of wind at the surface and the direction of that wind. Empirical analysis of the data received from the scatterometer aboard Seasat suggested that it was extremely accurate in its findings.

The other active system aboard Seasat was the SAR system, which provided radar images of the ocean surface. Scientists were surprised to discover that it also detected waves below the surface and bottom topography, even in relatively deep water.

For the first time, scientists were able to witness the effect the ocean floor has on the ocean surface under varying weather and wave conditions.

Seasat was also able to detect time variations of intermediate-sized eddies in the Atlantic Ocean to the east of the North and South American continents, a development that has led researchers to conclude that weather forecasters will soon be able to include eddy maps in their portfolios of atmospheric maps, also generated from satellite data.

The one major limitation of active sensing radar is the fact that seawater is opaque to infrared and microwave radiation, so that this kind of sensing is useful only in monitoring the surface. Once the radio waves slip beneath the surface, they are reflected by objects such as the ocean floor and do not show transitory characteristics of ocean movements. Thus, their usefulness in other than relatively shallow waters is quite limited.

Seasat set the standard for the application of satellite technology to oceanography. This experimental program delivered on its promise of advancements in the study of the world's oceans. Its function was twofold: to prove that Seasat satellite technology would work, and to provide evidence that commercial applications exist for such technology. In both cases the evidence was overwhelming that an operational satellite system would be extremely useful to oceanographers.

Context

The Seasat program was developed largely at the request of a number of academic, scientific, and governmental entities. Satellite technology in the mid-1970's had come to represent a viable, dependable, economical alternative to existing techniques for the gathering and analysis of oceanographic data. In addition, international cooperation in the development of space technology was at an all-time high.

Satellites already had become important to the maritime industry for a number of reasons. The fishing industry, for example, had used satellite photography to track such periodic sea phenomena as red tides and abnormal currents, which have a significant effect on commercial fishing. In some fishing grounds, commercially important species of sea life tend to gather near the outer edges of major currents and, under certain weather conditions, along coastal areas, where large concentrations of nutrients congregate. Satellite imagery was useful to commercial fishing boats because it provided detailed, up-to-the-minute information on the location of these fish, allowing significant savings on the cost of fuel and the amount of time necessary to obtain such data. During 1975, the year in which the Seasat program was announced, Exxon, the giant U.S. oil company, saved more than $350,000 in fuel for fifteen oil tankers by using satellite imagery to track the Gulf Stream and the Gulf Loop current. The tankers rode the currents when going in the same direction and avoided them on the return trip.

Seasat overlapped other remote-sensing satellite programs in many ways. Among these other programs was Landsat, the U.S. Earth resources satellite series that aided in the location and identification of natural resources, such as mineral and oil deposits. These satellites were also used to monitor urban growth, track crop yields, monitor snowmelt, and map shallow lakes and oceans. In fact, Landsat sensors were able to penetrate clear water up to a depth of 20 meters, allowing them to chart underwater features in most lakes and along coastal areas, including much of the shallow Caribbean basin. Other satellites of a similar configuration were the ITOS, TIROS, and other meteorological satellites that monitored weather conditions and developing storm centers.

Seasat was the first satellite with remote-sensing capabilities devoted exclusively to the study of oceans. The success of its instrumentation resulted in modifications to existing Landsat equipment, making it more reliable and sophisticated. Many other satellites have been designed to engage in multitask service, monitoring the earth and sea, yet simultaneously providing communications and navigation capabilities to a variety of users. In addition, other nations and international consortia began to develop satellite programs similar to Seasat.

Oceanographers continue to propose and develop Earth-based systems to support and, in many cases, refine findings derived from data acquired by Seasat and other scientific satellites. Among these are buoys equipped with sensing instrumentation and telemetry for relaying data to satellites, ships, aircraft, or radio receiving stations. Others include specially equipped aircraft that can be sent to the area of a developing storm, tidal surge, or ice field for direct observation.

Satellites can also be used to police the oceans.

Seasat went beyond its mission by focusing attention on human-made as well as natural phenomena. It detected oil spills and air pollution and was capable of detecting ocean dumping from ships at sea. It was a multidimensional satellite that set the agenda for oceanographic research for many years after its launch.

—Michael S. Ameigh

See also: Geodetic Satellites; Heat Capacity Mapping Mission; Jet Propulsion Laboratory; Landsat 1, 2, and 3; Private Industry and Space Exploration; Search for Extraterrestrial Life; Vandenberg Air Force Base.

Further Reading

Braun, Wernher von, and Frederick I. Ordway III. *Space Travel: A History.* Rev. ed. New York: Harper & Row, 1985. An excellent account of the evolution of rocketry and satellite technology, beginning with the very early days, long before the Sputnik era. This book contains a thorough account of the accomplishments of the U.S. space program during the 1970's and includes an assessment of the most successful of the U.S. applications satellites that were deployed just prior to the launch of Seasat, which was a proof-of-concept mission rather than an operational system. Includes photographs and an index.

Brun, Nancy L., and Eleanor H. Ritchie. *Astronautics and Aeronautics, 1975.* Washington, D.C.: National Aeronautics and Space Administration, 1979. This annual represents a collection of press accounts and NASA publicity releases documenting national and international events related to space exploration during 1975. Includes accounts of various aspects of the planning stages of the Seasat program. Contains an index.

Burrows, William E. *This New Ocean: The Story of the First Space Age.* New York: Random House, 1998. This is a comprehensive history of the human conquest of space, covering everything from the earliest attempts at spaceflight through the voyages near the end of the twentieth century. Burrows is an experienced journalist who has reported for *The New York Times*, *The Washington Post*, and *The Wall Street Journal*. There are many photographs and an extensive source list. Interviewees in the book include Isaac Asimov, Alexei Leonov, Sally K. Ride, and James A. Van Allen.

Corliss, William R. *Scientific Satellites.* NASA SP-133. Washington, D.C.: Government Printing Office, 1967. Most of the scientific satellites launched during the first decade of the Space Age by various countries are described in highly technical accounts. Also included is a chronology of international satellite launches. Contains a chapter describing geophysical instruments and experiments, preceded by an excellent overview of space science. Includes photographs and illustrations. Indexed.

Gatland, Kenneth. *The Illustrated Encyclopedia of Space Technology: A Comprehensive History of Space Exploration.* New York: Salamander, 1989. Contains numerous chronologies of Soviet, American, and international space programs. Earth observation systems are discussed in detail. Specific examples of successful applications of space technology in this area are cited, and a very good description of the Seasat program is given, with technical parameters of the satellite and its instrumentation. Well illustrated. Indexed.

Kivelson, Margaret G., and Christopher T. Russell. *Introduction to Space Physics*. New York: Cambridge University Press, 1995. A thorough exploration of space physics. Some aspects are suitable for the general reader. Suitable for an introductory college course on space physics.

Lee, Wayne. *To Rise from Earth: An Easy to Understand Guide to Spaceflight*. New York: Checkmark Books, 1996. This is a good introduction to the science of spaceflight. Although written by an engineer with the NASA Jet Propulsion Laboratory, it is presented in easy-to-understand language. In addition to the theory of spaceflight, it gives some of the history of the human endeavor to explore space.

Mari, Christopher, ed. *Space Exploration*. New York: H. W. Wilson, 1999. Twenty-five articles (reprinted from magazines), covering the state of the space program at the time of publication, are divided into five sections: John H. Glenn, Jr.'s return to space, the exploration of Mars, the International Space Station, recent mining efforts by commercial industries, and new types of space vehicles and propulsion systems.

National Research Council of the National Academies, Committee on Microgravity Research. *Assessment of Directions in Microgravity and Physical Sciences Research at NASA*. Washington, D.C.: National Academies Press, 2003. Provides detailed reports on microgravity research conducted on robotic missions, the space shuttle, and the International Space Station.

Parkinson, Claire L. *Earth from Above: Using Color-Coded Satellite Images to Examine the Global Environment*. Sausalito, Calif.: University Science Books, 1997. A book for nonspecialists on reading and interpreting satellite images. Explains how satellite data provide information about the atmosphere, the Antarctic ozone hole, and atmospheric temperature effects. The book includes maps, photographs, and fifty color satellite images.

Ritchie, Eleanor H. *Astronautics and Aeronautics, 1976: A Chronology*. NASA SP-4021. Washington, D.C.: National Aeronautics and Space Administration, 1984. Abstracts of press accounts of space activity during 1976 are compiled here in chronological order. These accounts were gleaned from popular publications and space agency memoranda made available to the general public. Early activity in the Seasat program is documented in trade publications and NASA releases. Indexed.

Wells, Neil. *The Atmosphere and Ocean: A Physical Introduction*. London: Taylor and Francis, 1986. A primer on the relationship between the oceans and the physical elements of the atmosphere, this book contains an excellent account of the accomplishments of the Seasat project in terms of its oceanographic research techniques, the instrumentation aboard the satellite, and the significance of the data acquired from that instrumentation. Highly technical. Indexed.

Zimmerman, Robert. *The Chronological Encyclopedia of Discoveries in Space*. Westport, Conn.: Oryx Press, 2000. Provides a complete chronological history of all crewed and robotic spacecraft and explains flight events and scientific results. Suitable for all levels of research.

Shuttle Amateur Radio Experiment

Date: Beginning November, 1983 to 2011
Type of program: Scientific platform

Amateur radio operators (hams) have communicated with space shuttle astronauts orbiting the Earth since 1983. NASA's intention in making astronauts available for the Shuttle Amateur Radio Experiment (SAREX) is educational in nature, involving a large number of people in technology and the space program.

Summary of the Program

The SAREX project is a continuing program of an educational nature that combines the missions of the space shuttle with amateur radio. It is sponsored by NASA, Radio Amateur Satellite Corporation (AMSAT), and the American Radio Relay League (ARRL), with the approval of the Federal Communications Commission (FCC). During a SAREX mission, the astronauts typically make several types of amateur radio contacts, including scheduled radio contacts with schools, random contacts with the ham community, and personal contacts with the astronauts' families. The contacts are made during breaks in the astronauts' work schedule. The costs of this ongoing mission are borne by radio amateurs who donate their time and equipment on the shuttle and on the ground.

In 1983, the first SAREX mission was carried out when Owen K. Garriott, a mission specialist aboard the shuttle *Columbia*, was the first to carry his amateur radio equipment into orbit during STS-9. Before any communications could take place, however, there were many complex problems that had to be overcome by ground stations.

The problems of communicating between an Earth station and a satellite (in this case, the shuttle in orbit) present the amateur radio operator with a new set of challenges. Ordinary communication between fixed Earth stations is dependent on frequency, time of day, and season of the year and is related to the cycle of sunspots recurring over a course of eleven years. While these factors are well understood, and they allow a long or short communications link depending on the station the amateur wishes to contact, the resulting communication (or QSO, in amateur parlance) will be of a quality that varies greatly: Interference, both human- induced and natural, as well as fading, will affect the signal's readability.

Communicating with an orbiting satellite, however, is both simpler in terms of frequency choices involved and more complex in that it requires that the amateur know considerably more about the station with which he or she is communicating. When successful, the signals exchanged will be eminently readable. For example, two Earth stations wishing a communications link find that signals are subject to the whims of the ionosphere, the chief cause, along with overcrowding, of variability in the communications in the most common ham bands (1.8 megahertz to 30 megahertz or the short-wave frequencies). For satellite work, however, the frequencies chosen are more limited: Direct, line of sight communications make sense when the distance involved is about 250-300 kilometers (150-200 miles) away, as in the case of the shuttle, as opposed to thousands of miles distant, as in normal Earth communications. As a result, the frequencies of choice for SAREX missions and other satellite communications are what are known as VHF, or very high

Astronaut Michel Tognini, mission specialist, uses the SAREX-II on Columbia's flight deck. (NASA)

frequency. VHF frequencies have the virtue of traveling short distances but doing so in a straight (line of sight) path. This is normally a relative disadvantage on Earth, but in space communications it is eminently predictable. However, where does one point the antenna for a line of sight communication with an orbiting body? Not only does the antenna on Earth need to be oriented in azimuth (a north-south-east-west manner), but the elevation above the horizon must be set, too.

Fortunately, computers aid in determining precisely where the satellite (in this case, the shuttle) is at any given time. To do that job, two things are necessary: a computer with appropriate software and Keplerian elements. Keplerian data are orbital or tracking elements used to pinpoint the location of a satellite. They provide the computer and its software with a "snapshot" of the orbital track the shuttle is following, and they allow users to determine where in space the shuttle is located at any given moment. This enables the observer to know precisely when the shuttle will appear above his or her horizon (the window of time that the shuttle's signal can be heard may last only eight minutes). These data are updated frequently and available via amateur radio and on the Internet (using techniques such as FTP, File Transfer Protocol).

Armed with the data yielded by a computer program and the Keplerian elements, the amateur next readies the station. Typically, a SAREX Earth station consists of a 2-meter FM transmitter and receiver (one that operates on the VHF frequency band of 144-148 megahertz) capable of an average output power of 50 to 100 watts, plus an antenna. The antenna is crucial to successful communications with the shuttle because the shuttle protocol allows the amateur operators on board primarily handheld equipment with antennae that are limited in scope and, therefore, gain. Indeed, the amateur operators on board the shuttle can place an antenna only directly facing the windows on the flight deck. On Earth, the ham station will use a circularly polarized (not directional) antenna of the crossed-Yagi type. Successful communications have been established with sufficient power from the transmitter using only vertical (straight up and down) antennae, but more modest stations will need antennae that are capable of being adjusted in two ways. First, the azimuth must be altered as the need arises. Second, the elevation or degrees above the horizon must be equally variable.

Finally, there is one additional issue the operator may wish to consider: the Doppler effect. As the shuttle moved through space at about 27,350 kilometers (17,000 miles) per hour, its position was constantly changing with reference to a ground station. For part of the time, the shuttle would approach that station. As a result, the signal it transmits would appear to be slightly higher in frequency than its nominal signal. Conversely, as it flew away from the station, its signal appeared to be somewhat lower. A station on Earth, then, may choose to set its local transmitter frequency approximately several kilohertz above the frequency set as nominal and its local receiver frequency correspondingly lower. This situation was reversed when the shuttle moved out of range. While not critical in achieving basic voice communications for the average station, the effects of Doppler shift on packet communications may be greater.

While Garriott's communications equipment aboard STS-9 consisted of little more than a handheld 2-meter (144-megahertz) transceiver and an antenna mounted in the window on the shuttle's flight deck, the shuttle's amateur station grew somewhat over the years. In more recent shuttle operations, it has consisted of approximately 60 pounds of equipment, a not inconsiderable weight when one must account for every spare pound due to orbital constraints. Typically, this equipment was a handheld transceiver or one similar in nature, operating on the 2-meter amateur radio band; a module to permit a means of interconnecting SAREX equipment with the standard crew headset and microphone; an equipment assembly cabinet, which held a converter for SSTV, or Slow-Scan Television (the converter takes normal television from a camera or the shuttle television distribution system and makes still television pictures from it so that they may be transmitted on a voice frequency without taking up too much bandwidth), packet radio terminal node controller (to allow digital reception and transmission using an amateur-written protocol), and power supplies, displays, and connectors; a television camera to televise via slow-scan technology scenes within the orbiter and external scenes viewable from the windows; a television monitor for viewing the output of the SSTV converter; an antenna; and a payload general support computer, which acted as a data terminal for the packet radio portion of the experiment.

There were a number of different configurations of SAREX equipment, and the choice of configuration for a specific flight depends on the number of amateur operators among the astronauts (some crews, notably of STS-37, STS-56, and STS-74, consisted entirely of hams) and the amount of space available for that particular operation. The configurations, designated by a letter of the alphabet starting with A and running through E (with a separate configuration for approaches to the Space Station Mir designated Configuration M), vary from the simple station brought aboard by Garriott, to a Configuration D, which included fast-scan television. Configuration A included the modes of transmission mentioned but only permits slow-scan television. Configuration C did not include facilities for television but did include the handheld transceiver and the digital packet radio.

The shuttle has been equipped with an experimental antenna mounted on the outside of the orbiter in addition to the usual window antenna on the flight deck. Amateur radio operators were helpful in testing this antenna when it was used on STS-63.

Contributions

Consistent with its stated goal of introducing a large number of people to the technology of the space program, SAREX was employed to bring space to locations such as the classroom. For each mission, a school completed a SAREX application and wrote an educational proposal. These proposals were collected by the ARRL and forwarded to the SAREX Working Group for final selection in collaboration with the astronauts involved. The educational proposal is an important element of an application, because it described how the SAREX activity will be incorporated into the school's curriculum. For example, a school might sponsor an essay or poster contest or encourage letter writing to secure more information about an experiment planned for a given shuttle flight. The proposal also specified the capabilities of the school organizer to set up the necessary equipment, usually with the aid of experienced hams, who may or may not be associated with the school. Even schools whose applications were not chosen could participate in the SAREX activity, as can all stations with at least a receiver and an antenna.

It should be emphasized that communications between a student and a given amateur radio operator aboard the shuttle were not at all rehearsed. Questions about geography, about if a bird can fly in space, about how astronauts sleep in space or move about the shuttle, or about what it feels like to return to Earth are generally easy to answer, but they provide the young student with the unmatched realism that comes from someone on the spot.

Of course, the astronaut-hams had not forgotten the typical, random, contact that amateurs make. Garriott's method of contacting earthbound amateur operators were relatively simple. When operating, he transmitted on even minutes and listened on odd minutes; a station wishing to contact him would send his or her call sign a few times during odd minutes (time was synchronized via WWV, the National Bureau of Standards atomic clock in Colorado) and then listen. This was about the extent of his QSOs (two-way communications) then, but much changed over the years. Nevertheless, many stations established communications using that mode. On subsequent flights, slow-scan television and packet radio via a robot station have been added. In addition, FSTV, or Fast Scan Television, has been added to the mix so that amateurs can receive live broadcasts from the shuttle on amateur radio.

Context

The SAREX goal was educational in nature, and as such, it was a never-ending quest during the shuttle era. The questions it answered were not crucial to the flight in question but could awaken a certain interest in a young student. It was likely that shuttle amateur radio would be used for the foreseeable future, and contacts on voice, packet radio, or television (depending on which configuration the shuttle takes into orbit) will continue.

Indeed, contacting human beings in space is international in flavor. With information made available weekly in a newsletter, amateur operators the world over can contact more than the orbiting space shuttle. The Space Station Mir, a Russian project, accommodated amateur radio, too, making it possible to talk to space on a regular basis. Using approximately the same frequencies as SAREX missions did, the Mir Space Station passed within reach of most North American locations at least six to eight times each day for up to ten minutes each pass. The equipment used by the shuttle to establish contact with Mir before docking was the same equipment the shuttle astronauts use for SAREX missions.

SAREX is invaluable for a number of reasons. First, it serves the purposes that created it: Namely, it awakens interest in technology among the youngest as they talk to an astronaut about real matters. Second, it encourages those students interested to become amateur radio operators themselves. Third, it provides countless other amateurs and short-wave radio listeners with an insight into the astronauts' daily living conditions in space. Finally, it serves to make all this public. It is indeed a successful experiment.

With the advent of the International Space Station, SAREX has matured to become ARISS, Amateur Radio on the International Space Station. ARISS is sponsored by the American Radio Relay League (ARRL), the Radio Amateur Satellite Corporation (AMSAT), and NASA. The space shuttle *Atlantis* carried the initial ARISS equipment on mission STS-106 in September, 2000. Two new call signs were issued for U.S. Amateur Radio operations— NN1SS and NA1SS—to the International Space Station Amateur Radio Club on October 11, 2000. A technical team, called ISS Ham, has been officially established to serve as the interface to support hardware development, crew training and on-orbit operations.

ARISS provides students with the unique opportunity to talk by amateur radio with crew members on the International Space Station (ISS) while they orbit Earth. With the help of amateur radio operators on the ground, students can contact the crew members by voice and packet (computer) radio, and in the future, they will be able to communicate by amateur television. Crew members make ham radio contacts with students around the world, sparking their interest in space, science, and technology. The crew members also contact their family and friends, as well as individual ham radio operators.

—*Joseph T. Malloy*

See also: Seasat; Space Shuttle Flights, 1997.

Further Reading

Amateur Radio on the International Space Station Web site. http://www.rac.ca/ariss/ oindex.htm. This is the official site of ARISS and contains information about the equipment and program. Written for high school students, it explains how one can make contact with the ISS crew during missions. Accessed March, 2005.

Butrica, Andrew J. *Beyond the Ionosphere: Fifty Years of Satellite Communications*. NASA SP-4217. Washington, D.C.: Government Printing Office, 1997. Part of the NASA History series, this book looks into the realm of satellite communications. It also delves into the technology that enabled the growth of satellite communications. The book includes many tables, charts, photographs, and illustrations, a detailed bibliography, and reference notes.

Davidoff, Martin. *The Satellite Experimenter's Handbook*. 2d ed. Newington, Conn.: American Radio Relay League, 1990. Basic information on communications via the large number of satellites of interest to amateur radio operators. Contains advice for those who would like to receive weather, amateur radio, or TV broadcasts from spacecraft. Does not cover SAREX expressly, but the information may be applied toward receiving SAREX transmissions.

---, et al. *ARRL Satellite Anthology*. 3d ed. Newington, Conn.: American Radio Relay League, 1994. Contains recent QST satellite articles on all amateur spacecraft from OSCAR (Orbital Satellite Carrying Amateur Radio) 10 through OSCAR 27. Includes how to work long distances via OSCAR's 10 and 13, and how to get on the "Pacsats" and the Russian "Easysats." Gives information regarding the future of advanced amateur satellites.

Gavaghan, Helen. *Something New Under the Sun: Satellites and the Beginning of the Space Age*. New York: Copernicus Books, 1998. This book focuses on the history and development of artificial satellites. It centers on three major areas of development—navigational satellites, communications satellites, and weather observation and forecasting satellites.

National Aeronautics and Space Administration. *International Space Station Reference: Ham Radio*. http:// spaceflight.nasa.gov/station/reference/radio. This is NASA's official Web guide to the Amateur Radio on the International Space Station program. Information about the equipment is available, as well as how to communicate with the ISS crews. Accessed March, 2005.

---. *The Shuttle Amateur Radio Experiment*. Washington, D.C.: Author, 1994. A collage of five pictures of astronauts in the shuttle making communications with schoolchildren on the ground during flights STS-37 and STS-47.

---. "STS-9 and Amateur Radio." *NASA Educational Briefs*. EB-83-9. Washington, D.C.: Author, 1983. Gives a cursory overview of SAREX and Owen K. Garriott's mission; details how one can get a QSL card (a card confirming reception or a two-way communication) with SAREX.

Skylab 2

Date: May 25 to June 22, 1973
Type of mission: Space station, piloted spaceflight

The crew of Skylab 2 installed a makeshift sunshade to protect the Orbital Workshop from overheating, released the panel of solar power cells that had been jammed as a result of the Skylab 1 launch accident, and conducted a twenty-eight-day program of medical, astronomical, and Earth resources experiments, establishing a new record for the longest piloted Earth-orbiting flight.

Key Figures

Charles "Pete" Conrad, Jr. (1930-1999), Skylab 2 mission commander
Paul J. Weitz (1932-2017), Skylab 2 pilot
Joseph P. Kerwin (b. 1932), Skylab 2 science pilot

Summary of the Mission

The crew of Skylab 2 launched on a Saturn IB rocket from Launch Complex 39B at Kennedy Space Center (KSC) at 13:00:00 Coordinated Universal Time (UTC, or 9 a.m. eastern daylight time) on May 25, 1973, following eleven days of hectic activity. The launch had been postponed while engineers at the Manned Spacecraft Center (MSC) and Marshall Space Flight Center (MSFC) sought ways to repair the overheated and underpowered Orbital Workshop (OWS). The crew carried with them three improvised sunshields: a "parasol" that could be extended through an airlock located in the center of the area exposed to the Sun, a fabric "sail" that astronauts might attach to the Workshop while remaining in the Command Module (CM), and a "twin-pole sail" to be stretched over two long poles by crew members working from inside the Workshop. They also carried several metal-cutting tools and other devices that engineers hoped would enable the astronauts to free the jammed solar panels.

Arriving seven and one-half hours after launch, Charles "Pete" Conrad, Jr. and his crew described the damaged Skylab OWS and sent back television pictures to Mission Control. They confirmed that one array of solar panels was missing and that a metal strap, apparently debris from the lost meteoroid shield, held the other down. No other damage was obvious, and the area to be covered was clear of debris. Conrad then soft-docked the CM to the Workshop, using three of the twelve docking latches. After discussing strategy with flight controllers, the astronauts began an attempt to free the solar array.

After the astronauts had put on their pressure suits, Conrad maneuvered the CM nearer the workshop while Paul J. Weitz stood up in the open hatch and grappled for the solar array with a long "shepherd's crook." In the absence of gravity, Weitz could not exert enough force to break the restraining strap, and after nearly an hour of frustrating labor Conrad abandoned the attempt and returned the CM to the docking port for the night. Three attempts at docking failed. The crew members were finally forced to don their suits, depressurize the CM, and disassemble the docking probe to wire around an apparent electrical fault. It was nearly midnight (eastern daylight time) when they successfully docked, ending a twenty-two-hour working day.

Shortly after noon the next day the crew entered the Workshop, finding a dry, desert-like heat approaching 47° Celsius, but tolerable for short periods. Over the next four hours they performed several tasks to start up Workshop systems. Late in the afternoon they attached the canister containing the parasol to the solar air lock and pushed the parasol out some 6 meters, using extension rods. The parasol opened, and its four supporting arms were extended, spreading the aluminum-coated nylon-and-Mylar fabric shield to cover an area 6.7 by 7.3 meters. The external temperature of the workshop immediately began dropping; internal temperature followed more slowly, falling below 35° Celsius within twenty-four hours and eventually stabilizing at 24° Celsius.

Meanwhile, ground-based technicians were constructing a mock-up of the Workshop solar array, using descriptions and television pictures provided by the crew, to work out procedures for freeing it. After experimenting in the large water tank at the MSFC, where the buoyancy of water provided an approximation of weightlessness, technicians concluded that the job could be done without danger to the astronauts. Tests continued, for the power shortage in the workshop was not yet critical.

In the cooling Workshop, Conrad, Weitz, and Joseph P. Kerwin began their program of experiments on May 28, taking blood samples and performing some initial medical evaluations and checking out the solar instruments in the Apollo Telescope Mount (ATM). At midday they conferred with Mission Control, reporting that they were in good physical shape and were adapting easily to weightlessness. Physicians in Houston welcomed this news, for they had feared that freedom of motion in the cavernous Workshop might trigger nausea and vomiting while the astronauts' inner ears adjusted to weightlessness. One out of every three Apollo crew persons had suffered from this malaise, and it was not at all understood.

Skylab 2 crew - Joseph Kerwin, Charles Conrad and Paul Weitz. (NASA)

On May 29, the Skylab 2 crew began operations, even though power was limited. Kerwin made four series of solar observations, and his crew mates prepared Earth-observing instruments for use the following day. Conrad reported difficulty in running one of the major medical experiments, a bicycle ergometer that measured his metabolism while he performed physical work. In the absence of gravity, it proved difficult to ride the bicycle. The harness designed to hold the subject in position did not work as expected, and in the heat the prescribed exercises could not be completed at the expected levels of exertion. A week would elapse before the crew could use the ergometer as it was intended.

The first use of Earth-sensing instruments on May 30 made clear the importance of freeing the solar panel. The Workshop's batteries were only at half capacity, whereupon they were cut out of the circuit—a feature designed into the system to protect the batteries from damage by excessive discharge. One battery failed to reconnect to the system after recharging, leaving Skylab with only 4,200 watts of power. Of this supply, 3,600 watts were required for operation of the workshop's essential systems, leaving only 600 watts for experiments and seriously curtailing the science program. On June 7, engineers on the ground held a long conference with the crew, discussing procedures they had worked out for releasing the solar panels. Conrad was only cautiously optimistic about success, because they had not trained for this exercise, and estimated their chances at about 50 percent.

The next day, Conrad and Kerwin suited up and went outside to attempt the repair. After considerable difficulty caused by the lack of adequate body restraints, Kerwin used a cutting tool (a pair of tree-trimming shears attached to an 8.3-meter pole) to snip the 1-centimeter metal strap holding the array. With the aid of a hook attached to a long nylon rope, Conrad and Kerwin were able to break a frozen hydraulic cylinder, allowing the array to come free. In a few hours, the solar panels extended fully, adding 3,000 watts to the power supply and clearing the way for the planned science program. The astronauts completed their three-and-one-half-hour excursion by changing a film magazine on one of the solar telescopes and freeing a jammed door on another.

After the two major repairs, Skylab 2 could proceed more or less as planned. Investigators were eager to make up for lost time, however, and the crew occasionally complained that flight controllers were rushing them through the experiments and not allowing time for the difficulties of working in weightless conditions. Soon, however, they settled into a routine of experiments, housekeeping chores, and occasional recreation that seemed humdrum after the excitement of the first two weeks.

On June 19, Conrad and Weitz made their last excursion outside the Workshop to retrieve exposed film from the solar telescopes. Before going back inside, Conrad, following instructions from Houston, sharply rapped one of the malfunctioning battery modules with a hammer; technicians on the ground had decided that the problem was a stuck relay that could be released by mechanical shock. Their diagnosis proved correct. The battery immediately began recharging and soon became fully operational.

Three days later, on their twenty-ninth day in space, the crew of Skylab 2 left the Workshop. In spite of their difficulties they had completed nearly all the planned medical experiments and 80 percent of the scheduled solar observations. Completed Earth observations, however, came to only 60 percent of what had been expected, largely because most of them had been scheduled during the first half of the mission, when the power shortage was most acute.

The Skylab 2 CM landed in the Pacific Ocean 1,340 kilometers southwest of San Diego, California, at 13:49:49 UTC on June 22, 1973. Half an hour later, crew and spacecraft were taken aboard the USS *Ticonderoga*, having set a new world endurance record for piloted flight in Earth orbit (twenty-eight days, 49 minutes, and 49 seconds).

Contributions

Skylab 2 investigations made major contributions in space physiology and solar physics. The astronauts were the subjects of three major medical studies of the human body's adjustment to weightlessness: effects on the muscular and skeletal systems, effects on the cardiovascular system, and effects on the vestibular system (the inner ear, which controls balance). Earlier spaceflights had indicated that there was a possibility of serious physiological harm from long-duration missions. Skylab's medical program was designed to study physiological changes during weightlessness over progressively longer periods to see whether such changes continued.

Skylab 2 showed that a loss of bone and muscle tissue continued throughout the mission, an effect attributed to the absence of compressive forces on weight-bearing bones (similar results are seen in patients confined to bed for long periods). Absolute losses were not large enough to constitute a problem, but the fact that losses continued for twenty-eight

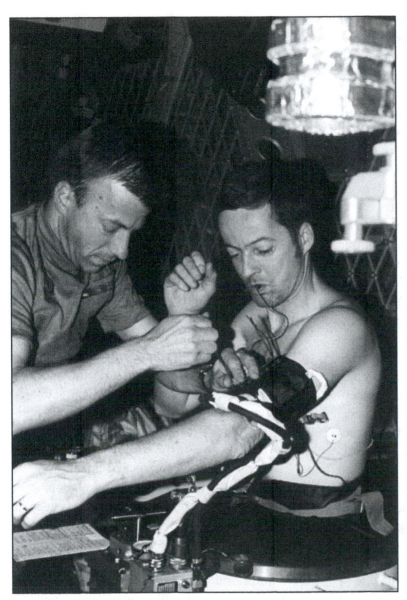

Astronaut Weitz assists Astronaut Kerwin with blood pressure cuff. (NASA)

the heart was measured by changes in blood pressure and pulse rate. On Skylab 2, the crew had difficulty completing this exercise, developing near-fainting symptoms. At one point, Kerwin strongly urged discontinuing the experiment, but investigators persisted in order to determine whether adaptation would occur. For the first Skylab crew it did not, and they did not regain their normal preflight responses for nearly three weeks after returning to Earth.

The bicycle ergometer and metabolic analyzer showed that the body's tolerance for exercise did not diminish during the mission. When they returned to normal gravity, however, the crew members could no longer perform this exercise regimen at preflight levels of efficiency, which indicated that some adaptation to weightlessness had occurred. Again, readjustment to Earth's gravity after the mission required almost three weeks.

Response of the human vestibular system to zero gravity was tested during flight by seating the crew members in a rotating chair and having them make rapid up-and-down head motions. The Skylab 2 crew showed no tendency to become ill under the most severe conditions tested, whereas on the ground all the crew members could be brought to the verge of nausea. Nor did they succumb to motion sickness on entering orbit, as many Apollo astronauts had.

The ATM produced the largest return of scientific data from Skylab 2. The astronauts spent 117 hours at the control console and took more than twenty-eight thousand photographs. Skylab's solar telescopes had been designed to allow simultaneous observation of different layers of the Sun: its thin,

days implied some risk for missions lasting several months.

The cardiovascular system was markedly affected by nearly a month of weightlessness. In the absence of gravity, the heart and major blood vessels function at a slower rate. This deconditioning was measured in flight by applying a partial vacuum to the lower body, simulating the effect of gravity by pulling blood into the legs; the resulting stress on hot corona (outer atmosphere), visible on Earth only during solar eclipses; the chromosphere (outermost surface layer), which radiates most of the Sun's visible light; and the underlying photosphere. The instruments took advantage of Skylab's orbital altitude to study those wavelengths that do not penetrate Earth's atmosphere—ultraviolet and x-rays. A white-light coronagraph, which blocks off the Sun's disk so that the faint corona can be seen, produced more data than had been obtained in all Earth-based studies preceding the mission.

Although thorough analysis of the data would require years, astronomers immediately recognized the immense value of the Skylab data, which will ultimately contribute to an understanding of the processes taking place in the Sun and their effects on Earth's atmosphere. The coronagraph, for example, along with the x-ray telescopes, confirmed the existence of "coronal holes," huge voids in the corona through which subatomic particles flow outward; coronal mass ejections through these "holes" cause magnetic storms and atmospheric disturbances on Earth. Skylab revealed a much more active Sun than scientists had anticipated and facilitated the investigation of phenomena for which little information had previously existed.

The Earth-observing instruments, added late in development of the Skylab science program, were in large part designed to assess the value of orbiting sensors for the study of Earth. Among the methods evaluated were those used for the determination of changing land utilization, the search for undetected mineral resources, geodesy (measurement of the detailed shape of Earth), detection of water pollution, and crop surveys.

Besides major experimental projects, Skylab 2 conducted some research relating to manufacturing in space. Using a specially designed furnace, the crew melted and resolidified samples of metals and semiconductors, investigated welding and brazing metals, and attempted to cast spherical specimens of metals in zero gravity. Such evaluations provided basic data on the possible use of a zero-gravity facility (for example, a space station) to carry out processes not easily effected on Earth.

Context

Skylab 2 was the National Aeronautics and Space Administration's first step in a program that, piloted spaceflight enthusiasts believed, would establish the value of humans in scientific research in space. To that end, the mission made its intended contribution, but its more immediately important contribution was the demonstration of human adaptability to unexpected situations. The repair in orbit of the severely damaged Orbital Workshop saved the entire Skylab program. Although a backup OWS had been built and was available for launch, the estimated $250 million it would cost might have been an insurmountable barrier to continuing the program. In a time of shrinking space budgets, declining public interest in space, and growing public antipathy toward large technological projects, the resourcefulness of the Skylab team revived something of the spirit of earlier times in the space program.

Because it was only the first of three missions, Skylab 2 can hardly be considered in isolation. Still, on the first long-term piloted flight, the easy adaptation of the crew to the weightless environment and their general good health and spirits throughout the mission boded well for subsequent missions and for future Earth-orbital projects. After an initial period of adjustment, crew and flight planners worked out a system for scheduling their daily activities that was improved further on the later missions.

—W. David Compton

See also: Apollo 9; Extravehicular Activity; Gemini V; Skylab Program; Skylab 3; Skylab Space Station; Skylab 4; Space Shuttle Mission STS-6; Space Shuttle-Mir: Joint Missions.

Further Reading

Belew, Leland F., ed. *Skylab: Our First Space Station*. NASASP-400. Washington, D.C.: Government Printing Office, 1977. Description of the entire program (evolution, plans, spacecraft, and missions); for high school and college students.

Bilstein, Roger E. *Stages to Saturn: A Technological History of the Apollo/Saturn Launch Vehicles*. Gainesville: University Press of Florida, 2003. Traces the development of the Saturn launch vehicles, which boosted Skylab into orbit.

Compton, W. David, and Charles D. Benson. *Living and Working in Space: A History of Skylab*. Washington, D.C.: Government Printing Office, 1983. The officially sponsored history of the Skylab project, this volume exhaustively details the development of Skylab from earliest concepts to the missions and their results. Two chapters discuss the launch accident and the first piloted mission. The book is intended for serious students of the space program but is not beyond the general reader. Numerous illustrations include several spectacular photographs from the Apollo Telescope Mount (ATM)instruments and the Earth resources cameras.

Cooper, Henry S. F., Jr. *A House in Space*. New York: Holt, Rinehart and Winston, 1976. This slim volume is a collection of the author's articles first published in *The New Yorker* magazine— a chatty journalistic account of all three Skylab flights, based on transcripts of the air-to-ground communications and interviews with participants.

Cromie, William J. *Skylab*. New York: David McKay, 1976. Written mainly for high school students, this book describes the spacecraft, missions, and experiments on all three Skylab missions.

Ertel, Ivan D., and Roland W. Newkirk. *Skylab: A Chronology*. Washington, D.C.: Government Printing Office, 1977. A chronological tabulation of important events in the development of Skylab (and some other early space station concepts) from1960 to 1975. Appendices contain summaries of flight data and other factual information.

Ise, Rein, ed. *A New Sun: The Solar Results from Skylab*. NASA SP-402. Washington, D.C.: Government Printing Office, 1979. A discussion of the Apollo Telescope Mount solar telescopes, the data they yielded, and their importance to solar physics. Profusely illustrated.

Johnston, Richard S., Lawrence F. Dietlein, and Charles A. Berry, eds. *Biomedical Results from Skylab*. NASA SP-377. Washington, D.C.: Government Printing Office, 1977. This volume is directed toward the biomedical professional and summarizes the medical findings from all three Skylab missions.

Lundquist, Charles A., ed. *Skylab's Astronomy and Space Sciences*. NASA SP-404. Washington, D.C.: Government Printing Office, 1979. A discussion of the corollary experiments on Skylab: stellar and galactic studies and studies of Earth's atmosphere. For high school and college students.

National Aeronautics and Space Administration. *Skylab Explores the Earth*. NASA SP-380. Washington, D.C.: Government Printing Office, 1977. A technical summary of Skylab's Earth-resources experiments and their results, for a technically literate audience. Includes many photographs illustrating the scope of the Earth-sensing instruments and the crew's observations of surface phenomena.

---. *Skylab Mission Press Kits*. http://www-lib.ksc.nasa.gov/lib/skylabpresskits .html. Provides detailed preflight information about each of the Skylab missions.

Shayler, David J. *Skylab: America's Space Station*. Chichester, England: Springer-Praxis, 2001. Shayler tells the Skylab story well, but without footnotes. From the perspective of more than a quarter century after the missions, Shayler uses official NASA documentation and interviews with the astronauts and key personnel to present the story of Skylab. Also presents an assessment of lessons learned in the context of current programs.

Skylab 3

Date: July 28 to September 25, 1973
Type of mission: Space station, piloted spaceflight

Skylab 3 continued the occupation and operation of the Skylab Orbital Workshop for fifty-nine days. After an initial period of motion sickness, the crew adapted well to weightlessness and exceeded the objectives of most of their experiments. Skylab 3 was the first mission that truly proved the capability of a space station to produce results that would be useful on Earth, therefore paving the way for the International Space Station.

Key Figures

Alan L. Bean (1932-2018), Skylab 3 mission
    commander
Jack R. Lousma (b. 1936), Skylab 3 pilot
Owen K. Garriott (1930-2019), Skylab 3 science
    pilot

Summary of the Mission

Skylab 3 began with the launch of the crew from Launch Complex 39B, Kennedy Space Center (KSC), at 11:10:51 Coordinated Universal Time (UTC, or 7:10 a.m. eastern daylight time) on July 28, 1973. Their Command Module (CM) docked with the Skylab Orbital Workshop (OWS) eight and one-half hours later, and the crew began activating the laboratory's systems shortly thereafter. All three crew people experienced motion sickness on entry into orbit, the first time an entire crew had been thus affected on any piloted mission. For the first three days, Alan L. Bean, Jack R. Lousma, and Owen K. Garriott were partially incapacitated by nausea. Flight controllers adjusted the astronauts' work load to allow for prolonged rest periods during each day. Only on the sixth day in orbit were they able to handle a normal work schedule.

A serious anomaly appeared on launch day when one of the CM's attitude control thrusters began to leak; four such units were used to orient the spacecraft and served as the backup system to bring it out of orbit in case the main propulsion system failed.

After some analysis, engineers concluded that the mission could be completed with only three thrusters operating, but on the sixth mission day a second unit developed an apparently similar leak. Fearing that the entire attitude control system might fail, in which case the crew could not return to Earth, mission officials ordered a rescue mission to be made ready. Launch teams at KSC began round-the-clock preparation of the launch vehicle and spacecraft that had been scheduled to be used on the last Skylab mission. The CM was be modified to carry five people, so that a crew of two could fly to the OWS and bring back the three Skylab astronauts. Preparations continued until engineers satisfied themselves that no generic problem existed and that the Skylab 3 CM could return safely using modified procedures. The problem was later traced to loose fittings in the lines carrying oxidizer to the thrusters.

Once they had recovered from nausea, the Skylab 3 crew set out to make up for lost time. On August 1, program officials extended their stay from the planned fifty-six days to fifty-nine. Experience on Skylab 2 indicated that recovery closer to a seaport was desirable, to minimize the time spent aboard ship after recovery. The new mission duration did allow recovery closer to a port. On August 3 the astronauts made the first of thirty-nine Earth-observing passes; four days later Garriott activated the

Skylab 3 crew - Owen Garriott, Jack Lousma and Alan Bean. (NASA)

Apollo Telescope Mount (ATM) for solar observations. Medical experiments occupied a part of every mission day. This crew never found their days to be "humdrum," as Joseph P. Kerwin had described the last two weeks of Skylab 2. They felt no daily need for more than six hours of sleep, and during the second week Commander Bean told Mission Control that they were not working as hard as they had in preflight training. Flight planners then increased their workday from eight hours to twelve. This made Skylab 3 highly productive, but it set a pace that would create problems for the next crew.

Eleven days into the mission, Garriott and Lousma went outside the OWS to rig the "twin-pole sail," or sunshade. Assembling two 16.8-meter poles from sections of tubing, Garriott secured them to the ATM and extended the mover the parasol deployed by the first crew. He and Lousma then hoisted the 3.6-by-7.3-meter sunshade by ropes until it covered the exposed area. The difficulty of working in zero gravity stretched the job from an anticipated two hours to four. Lousma then retrieved and replaced film cartridges in four ATM instruments, removed a balky door latch from another, and set out three new experiments.

Mechanical problems arose in mid-August. A dehumidifier in the environmental control system sprang a leak. An electrical short circuit destroyed one of two video display tubes on the ATM control console, and the cooling system for the workshop electronics appeared to be leaking. A continuing annoyance to Mission Control was erratic behavior of the rate gyroscopes, which sensed rotation of the workshop and provided input to the attitude control system computer. These had gone awry after the launch accident, and the Skylab 3 crew had brought replacements. On their second trip outside the OWS, the crew connected the new gyroscopes into the system, giving ground controllers better ability to regulate the Workshop's maneuvers. Finally, the mechanism that drove a scanning antenna on one of the Earth-resources experiments failed. This and the other defects would be left for repair by the last crew.

While major experiment programs occupied most of their time, the Skylab 3 crew found opportunities to conduct several small experiments and demonstrations. Owen K. Garriott brought some live minnows with him, along with fertilized minnow eggs and two common spiders, to see how other living organisms might behave in weightlessness. He observed that the full-grown minnows seemed unable to orient themselves; they swam in tight circles, perhaps searching for the gravity force that would determine a downward direction. Hatchlings from the minnow eggs, however, seemed to have no difficulty, and the spiders, after an initial period of apparent confusion, soon learned to spin normal webs.

Among experiments important to future spaceflight was a series of tests of astronaut maneuvering aids, which the Skylab 3 crew operated in the large upper compartment of the Workshop. The most complex device, a gyroscope-stabilized, thruster-propelled manned maneuvering unit, proved extremely useful and easy to operate in spite of being large and cumbersome (it resembled a large chair into which the astronaut strapped himself). Its ease of operation enabled Garriott to learn to use it in a short period of on-the-job training. A handheld gas pistol much like the one used on early Gemini flights was less precise and controllable, and a foot-controlled unit (called "jet shoes") was less useful still. The large unit was later to be developed for use on space shuttle flights.

Weekly meetings of program officials evaluated the crew's performance during Skylab 3 and assessed the state of OWS systems. Had any serious anomaly developed, the flight could have been terminated early. Yet no problems arose to justify ending the flight prematurely, and the crew continued to collect scientific data for the full fifty-nine days. In early September, Bean asked for a mission extension, but his request was turned down because medical investigators wanted to evaluate the fifty-nine-day data. On September 25, the Skylab 3 astronauts deactivated the workshop, powered up their CM, and returned to Earth. They were picked up by the recovery ship USS *New Orleans* late that

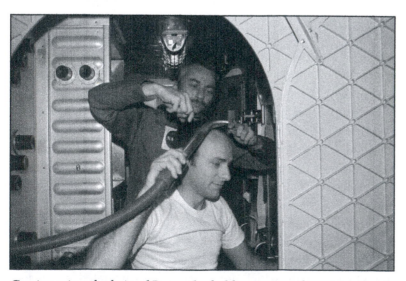

Garriott trims the hair of Bean who holds a vacuum hose to gather in loose hair. (NASA)

afternoon, about 400 kilometers southwest of San Diego.

Contributions

Skylab 3 added substantially to the store of information about the Sun and Earth. The crew returned nearly twenty-five thousand photographs of the Sun, almost seventeen thousand photographs of Earth, and more than 25,000 meters of magnetic tape containing data on Earth resources. In all experiment categories the crew had exceeded preflight plans, in several cases by more than 50 percent. They had observed several rare occurrences on the Sun, among them coronal transients (outbursts of energy and matter from the Sun that distort the corona as they pass through it).

Of more importance to piloted spaceflight, Skylab 3 showed that over long periods of time the human body slowly acclimates to weightlessness. Skylab 2 astronauts had experienced deterioration of their cardiovascular systems throughout their flight; the Skylab 3 crew returned in better condition. Physicians concluded that adaptation began between thirty and forty days into the mission. After their disabling nausea at the outset, the Skylab 3 astronauts experienced no further trouble with motion sickness. Nevertheless, the episode worried officials who were planning missions for the space shuttle; they were contemplating flights lasting no more than seven days, and the prospect of illness among the crew for half that time was not encouraging.

Context

Skylab 3, lacking the urgency and drama of the first piloted mission, was more indicative of what humans might accomplish on long-term Earth-orbital missions. This, indeed, was the theme that the National Aeronautics and Space Administration (NASA) had emphasized in justifying the first post-Apollo project: the use of Apollo-developed capability to produce results that would be useful on Earth. Both the Skylab 3 crew and their flight planners strove to maximize the time spent on experiments, and in the context of a normal mission they developed considerable facility in using the available time to best effect.

A major science projects on Skylab meshed well with national concerns in 1973. A growing shortage of energy (to be exacerbated by an oil embargo imposed by Arab states later in the year), concern for environmental pollution, and a growing fear of depletion of natural resources all heightened concern for problems that Skylab's Earth resources experiments might help to solve. Although contributions of these experiments were actually minimal, NASA officials and influential newspapers continually stressed the practical aspects of the piloted space program.

—W. David Compton

See also: Skylab Program; Skylab Space Station; Skylab 2; Skylab 4.

Further Reading

Belew, Leland F., ed. *Skylab: Our First Space Station*. NASASP-400. Washington, D.C.: Government Printing Office, 1977. This publication describes the Skylab program in detail (its evolution, plans, spacecraft, and missions). Appropriate for high school and college students.

Compton, W. David, and Charles D. Benson. *Living and Working in Space: A History of Skylab*. Washington, D.C.: Government Printing Office, 1983. The official history of Skylab, this volume details the development of Skylab from earliest concepts to the missions and their results. Includes discussion of the launch accident and the first piloted mission. Intended for serious students of the space program but is not beyond the general reader. Numerous illustrations include several spectacular photographs from the Apollo Telescope Mount instruments and the Earth-resources cameras.

Cooper, Henry S. F., Jr. *A House in Space*. New York: Holt, Rinehart and Winston, 1976. This slim volume, a collection of the author's articles first published in *The New Yorker* magazine, provides an informal, journalistic account of all three Skylab flights. Based on transcripts of the air-to-ground communications and interviews with participants.

Cromie, William J. *Skylab*. New York: David McKay, 1976. Written mainly for high school students, this book describes the spacecraft, missions, and experiments on all three Skylab missions.

Ertel, Ivan D., and Roland W. Newkirk. *Skylab: A Chronology*. Washington, D.C.: Government Printing Office, 1977. A chronological tabulation of important events in the development of Skylab (and some other early space station concepts) from 1960 to 1975. Includes appendices with summaries of flight data.

Ise, Rein, ed. *A New Sun: The Solar Results from Skylab*. NASA SP-402. Washington, D.C.: Government Printing Office, 1979. Included in this volume is a discussion of the Apollo Telescope Mount solar telescopes, the data they yielded, and their importance to solar physics. Profusely illustrated.

Johnston, Richard S., Lawrence F. Dietlein, and Charles A. Berry, eds. *Biomedical Results from Skylab*. NASASP-377. Washington, D.C.: Government Printing Office, 1977. Written for the biomedical professional, this volume summarizes the medical findings from all three Skylab missions.

Lundquist, Charles A., ed. *Skylab's Astronomy and Space Sciences*. NASA SP-404. Washington, D.C.: Government Printing Office, 1979. Includes a discussion of the corollary experiments on Skylab: stellar and galactic studies and studies of Earth's atmosphere. For high school and college students.

National Aeronautics and Space Administration. *Skylab Explores the Earth*. NASA SP-380. Washington, D.C.: Government Printing Office, 1977. This technical summary of Skylab's Earth-resources experiments and their results is written for a technically literate audience. Includes many photographs illustrating the scope of the Earth-sensing instruments and the crew's observations of surface phenomena.

---. *Skylab Mission Press Kits*. http://www-lib.ksc.nasa.gov/lib/skylabpresskits .html. Provides detailed preflight information about each of the Skylab missions.

Shayler, David J. *Skylab: America's Space Station*. Chichester, England: Springer-Praxis, 2001. Shayler tells the Skylab story well, but without footnotes. From the perspective of more than a quarter century after the missions, Shayler uses official NASA documentation and interviews with the astronauts and key personnel to present the story of Skylab. Also presents an assessment of lessons learned in the context of current programs.

Skylab 4

Date: November 16, 1973, to February 8, 1974
Type of mission: Space station, piloted spaceflight

Skylab 4 was the last flight to the United States' first space station. The three astronauts on Skylab 4 spent a total of eighty-four days in Earth orbit, making this mission the longest piloted U.S. spaceflight up to that time.

Key Figures

Gerald P. Carr (b. 1932), Skylab 4 mission commander
Edward G. Gibson (b. 1936), Skylab 4 pilot
William R. Pogue (1930-2014), Skylab 4 science pilot

Summary of the Mission

The Skylab 4 mission was launched from the Kennedy Space Center (KSC) on November 16, 1973, at 14:01:23 Coordinated Universal Time (UTC, or 9:01 a.m. eastern standard time). Gerald P. Carr, Edward G. Gibson, and William R. Pogue were ferried to the Skylab space station via an Apollo spacecraft, which was boosted into orbit by a Saturn IB launcher. Each of these astronauts was embarking on his first flight into space.

Two other crews had used the Skylab space station prior to the Skylab 4 flight. Skylab 2 astronauts Charles "Pete" Conrad, Jr., Joseph P. Kerwin, and Paul J. Weitz spent a total of twenty-eight days aboard Skylab. Skylab 3 astronauts Alan L. Bean, Owen K. Garriott, and Jack R. Lousma more than doubled their predecessors' stay by remaining aboard Skylab for fifty-nine days.

Skylab 4's launch did not occur as originally scheduled. Hairline cracks in stabilizing fins at the base of the Saturn IB launch vehicle were discovered. Launch was delayed nine days in order for engineers to replace the fins. Once orbit was reached, it took three attempts for the crew to complete a successful docking with Skylab. The three astronauts orbited at an altitude of approximately 435 kilometers.

Many significant scientific experiments were planned for the Skylab 4 mission. This flight would be longer than the flights of the previous two missions. Thus, the experiments aboard Skylab 4 could be increased in number and sophistication. The crew of Skylab 2 had spent a major portion of its twenty-eight days in space repairing faulty equipment, and space officials hoped that the Skylab 4 mission would not be similarly compromised.

Yet the Skylab 4 crew also had problems with equipment. Three control-moment gyroscopes, mounted on three sides of the Apollo Telescope Mount (ATM), were used to control the position of the spacecraft. (The ATM was used for observations of the Sun, utilizing a variety of ultraviolet and x-ray instrumentation.) Shortly after the crew's arrival, one of the three gyroscopes failed, and the performance of a second gyroscope began to deteriorate. This malfunction required the use of the station's attitude control system, normally reserved for large attitude changes. Aside from the gyroscope failures, a few smaller repair tasks also demanded the crew's attention.

The National Aeronautics and Space Administration (NASA) had proposed four major objectives for Skylab. Skylab crews were to make Earth-resources observations, aid scientists in their study of

Skylab 4 crew - Gerald Carr, Edward Gibson and William Pogue. (NASA)

materials processing in weightlessness, advance astronomical knowledge about objects in the universe, and contribute to a better understanding of piloted spaceflight capabilities and basic biological processes. All four broad goals were met during the Skylab 4 mission.

To prepare for Earth-resources observations, Carr, Gibson, and Pogue had spent twenty hours in lectures given by nineteen scientists in that field. This background provided the crew with an insight into the significance of particular phenomena and features on Earth, the type of data desired, and procedures for conducting the observations. Some 165 features and phenomena were identified prior to the mission as those with which scientists were principally concerned.

Photographic equipment used by the Skylab 4 crew included binoculars and two handheld cameras, a 70-millimeter Hasselblad and a 35-millimeter Nikon. A variety of camera lenses were used to provide narrow to wide fields of view. Color Ektachrome slide film was used for most of the photography, but some images were taken with Ektachrome infrared film. The crew took thousands of photographs. In addition, more than 850 verbal descriptions were made.

A variety of geologic features were observed during the mission. These included desert regions, global tectonic features, meteoritic impact craters, and volcanic regions. Studies of crops and their relationship to the environment were performed. Crew members also observed land-sea interaction and certain oceanic events. In addition, meteorological observations were made as time and conditions allowed.

Carr, Gibson, and Pogue observed major dust storms while passing over Africa. In addition, extensive foliage burning was observed. Observations of other Earth features provided data important for understanding desert formation. Studies of the southwestern United States and the adjacent areas of Mexico contributed information about major fault zones in Baja California, southeastern California, and Sonora, Mexico. Other tectonic studies focused on the Alpine fault in New Zealand, the African rift zone, the Zagros and Asian Caucasus Mountains, Guatemalan fault zones, and the Atacama fault in Chile.

The Manicouagan impact area in Quebec, Canada, one of many meteoritic impact areas on Earth, was observed from Skylab 4. Carr, Gibson, and Pogue also had a rare opportunity to observe and photograph an erupting volcano, that of Sakurajima in Japan. The Skylab 4 crew took photographs of this feature, which included a set of stereophotographs, the first such images produced in space. Glacial development in the Gulf of Saint Lawrence, eddies in ocean currents, upwelling areas, and many other oceanic phenomena were observed and photographed. Meteorological experiments included height determinations of multilayered clouds; analyses of cloud structure, cloud movement, and cloud patterns; and tropical storm studies.

Materials processing experiments conducted during Skylab 4 were continued from previous Skylab studies. In Earth orbit, the extremely low gravity level—or microgravity—allows for the production of certain materials that cannot be processed on Earth. Skylab 4 experimentation with materials processing confirmed that space factories do indeed have a place in the future of space exploration.

The approach of Comet Kohoutek presented an unusual opportunity to add to the scientific knowledge of astronomical phenomena. The proximity of the comet, discovered earlier in the year, made it possible for the crew to study it without interference from Earth's blanket of air. Observations of Kohoutek included those made by Carr and Pogue during both a seven-hour spacewalk on Christmas Day, 1973, and another spacewalk four days later. Observations of the comet were also made from within the space station itself.

One of the primary interests of scientists involved with Skylab was a study of the Sun. The Skylab 4 crew was able to observe the birth, development, and death of a medium-sized solar flare. It was the first time such an event was observed from space. Much information about the Sun was collected. More than seventy-three thousand photographs of the Sun were taken during the eighty-four-day mission. Other solar observations included a study of the corona in white light and a study of the corona in extreme-ultraviolet light.

Most solar observations were made from the ATM. This instrument, controlled from the multiple docking adapter, weighed about 10,000 kilograms on Earth. Results from the observations were in either photographic or spectrographic format. (Spectrographic data reveal the components of light emitted by the Sun.)

This dummy was left behind in the Skylab space station by the Skylab 3 crew to be found by the Skylab 4 crew. The dummy is dressed in a flight suit and propped upon the bicycle ergometer. The name tag indicated that it represents William Pogue, Skylab 4 pilot. The dummy for Gerald Carr, Skylab 4 commander, was placed in the Lower Body Negative Pressure Device. The dummy representing Edward Gibson was left in the waste compartment. (NASA)

Many biological experiments were performed on this final Skylab mission. The most obvious gain in this area would be determining the reaction of the human body to long-term weightlessness. The Skylab 4 crew recovered from the effects of microgravity more quickly than had any previous long-endurance flight crew. During the mission Carr, Gibson, and Pogue actually grew taller by at least a few centimeters as a result of the stretching of the spinal column and the shift in body fluids from the lower to upper body extremities. Yet the astronauts returned to their preflight height after their return. The crew spent much time on the station's bicycle ergometer and portable treadmill. A strict exercise regimen in space probably contributed to the astronauts' excellent condition upon their return to Earth. Additional biological and medical experimentation included studies of body fluids, red blood cells, bones, human vestibular function, metabolic activity, and mineral balance.

Student projects were also a part of Skylab 4. The projects, selected by NASA and the National Science Teachers' Association, utilized the space environment to study the effects of weightlessness in a variety of ways.

The flight came to an end on February 8, 1974, with the crew's Apollo CM landing in the Pacific Ocean southwest of San Diego, California. Skylab 4 was the longest piloted flight up to that time. The mission lasted 2,017 hours and 16 minutes. It included four spacewalks totaling 22 hours and 21 minutes. The final mission of Skylab had provided scientists with important information about Earth, the Sun, materials processing in space, and the human body and its reaction to weightlessness.

Contributions

When the Skylab program was first proposed, space planners had specific objectives in mind. The flights of the three piloted Skylab missions, however, went beyond the anticipated goals of the project.

The potential of studying Earth from orbit was realized early in the space program. Yet most spaceflights were not long enough to provide a sustained overview. The longest U.S. spaceflight before Skylab was the fourteen-day Gemini VII mission in 1965. The Skylab missions provided an opportunity for sustained scientific study of Earth from space, and the flight of Skylab 4 was a prime example of this capability.

A better understanding of Earth's geologic features resulted from studies made by the Skylab 4 crew. Data collected provided geologists with information on desert conditions and formations, volcanic formation and eruptions, meteoritic crater formation, faults, and mountains. The study of the eruption of the Sakurajima volcano provided scientists with spectacular stereoscopic imagery. Data collected by the Skylab 4 crew contributed important information about the height of the eruption plume.

Crops were studied from orbit. Changes in vegetation patterns and the effects of weather on crops were observed. Meteorological events were also discernible from Skylab. The crew could determine where snow had fallen and what its general depth was.

Materials processing experiments made clear to scientists the advantages of microgravity. The weightless environment allows for a faster rate of materials processing and results in a purer product; it also allows for production of materials that simply cannot be made on Earth. Many believe that space factories, of which Skylab was a forerunner, will be an important aspect of space exploitation in the future.

Earth's atmosphere, while essential for sustaining life on the planet, prevents astronomers from making accurate observations. Space-based telescopes and observatories such as those on Skylab provide astronomers with more accurate data on astronomical phenomena. The data collected by the Skylab 4 crew led to a better understanding of the Sun and comets. An improved understanding of solar activities leads to an improved understanding of stars in general.

Photograph taken from the hatch into the airlock module looking the length of the Skylab Orbital Workshop. Gibson and Astronaut Carr look up the passageway with trash bags around them. (NASA)

In the past, people thought that the space environment would be too harsh for human beings. It was known that humans could be protected from the extremes of heat and cold, excessive radiation, and the vacuum of space. Yet many believed that the weightless environment might be the one factor that would prevent humans from becoming space travelers. The Skylab 4 mission demonstrated that humans could survive a long time in space. Additional experiments provided more information on the effects of the weightless environment on other living things.

Context

If humans are to work in space on a full-time basis, then several questions must first be answered. These questions concern the importance of such a plan, the types of equipment and spacecraft necessary, and the reaction of the human body to the space environment.

Since the early days of the space program, some have questioned the benefit of space exploration. Early satellites and piloted spacecraft have since provided information and services that have proved their usefulness. Yet others argued that the problems of long-duration piloted spaceflight might outweigh the benefits. Skylab 4 proved that the gains are worth the risks. The crew returned important information about Earth as a planet. This information contributed to a better understanding of the geological, meteorological, agricultural, and hydrological sciences.

Production and processing of certain materials in space would prove advantageous to future space stations. The crew of Skylab 4, along with the crews of two previous Skylab missions, demonstrated that materials processing can be performed successfully and that there are important benefits from processing materials in space.

Astronomical observations made from Skylab provided important data about the Sun. Data would help astronomers and solar physicists better predict sunspot activity and solar flare eruptions. Such solar events directly affect life on Earth in various ways, from determining general weather cycles to interfering with radio transmissions.

Comets are thought to be very old objects. An understanding of these bodies, may lead to a better understanding of the history of the solar system. The Skylab 4 astronauts' opportunity to study the Comet Kohoutek provided astronomers with new observations.

Even though NASA officials experienced significant problems with Skylab, they proved that a space station could be constructed and that such a station could be used for worthwhile experimentation during long-duration flights. Possibly more important, NASA proved that human beings could repair satellites and spacecraft in orbit. While the first Skylab crew, that of Skylab 2, did the major repair work on the space station, the Skylab 4 crew effected several repairs also.

If humans are to inhabit space, then the effects of the weightless environment must be understood.

The Skylab 4 mission proved that with proper in-orbit exercise and diet, the effects of space are not detrimental. The future of long-term flights depended on this one important observation.

Even though many Russian flights in the Mir Space Station would surpass the U.S. record set by Skylab 4, the mission of Skylab 4 will be remembered as a milestone. It proved that humans could adapt to the space environment and that this environment had much to offer those who could make use of it. It also paved the way for later efforts, especially the International Space Station at the dawn of the twenty-first century.

—Mike D. Reynolds

See also: International Space Station; Skylab 3; Space Shuttle-Mir: Joint Missions.

Further Reading

Baker, David. *Conquest: A History of Space Achievements from Science Fiction to the Shuttle*. Topsfield, Mass.: Salem House, 1985. A general overview of space exploration. The text summarizes significant advances and programs with appropriate illustrations. Suitable for general audiences.

Belew, Leland F., and Ernst Stuhlinger. *Skylab: A Guidebook*. NASA EP-107. Washington, D.C.: Government Printing Office, 1974. This text provides the reader with details of the Skylab project. It outlines the history, missions, operation and design, and experimental proposals of the Skylab program.

Bilstein, Roger E. *Stages to Saturn: A Technological History of the Apollo/Saturn Launch Vehicles*. Gainesville: University Press of Florida, 2003. A thorough treatment of the Saturn program, including the personnel and managerial aspects as well as the technology. A good resource for in-depth understanding. For technical audiences, but of value to the general reader as well.

Braun, Wernher von, and Frederick I. Ordway III. *Space Travel: A History*. Rev. ed. New York: Harper & Row, 1985. A complete and detailed history of space exploration. Covers the development of the rocket and the evolution of the Soviet and U.S. space programs. Well illustrated.

Gatland, Kenneth. *The Illustrated Encyclopedia of Space Technology: A Comprehensive History of Space Exploration*. New York: Crown, 1981. This encyclopedia is a collection of chapters written by well-known experts in the space sciences. Each of the twenty-one chapters presents a different stage in the history of space exploration. Excellent references at the end of each chapter.

---. *Manned Spacecraft*. Rev. ed. New York: Macmillan, 1976. An excellent reference for both Soviet and American piloted space exploration. Text provides complete details on spacecraft design and lists mission highlights. Fully one-quarter of the book is illustrations, including illustrations of Soviet spacecraft. A useful text for anyone desiring additional detailed information.

National Aeronautics and Space Administration. *Skylab Explores the Earth*. NASA SP-380. Washington, D.C.: Government Printing Office, 1977. The text is a detailed log of the many geological, meteorological, and hydrological observations made from Skylab 4. The chapters are actually papers given by prominent scientists. Illustrated with photographs returned from the Skylab 4 mission.

---. *Skylab Mission Press Kits*. http://www-lib.ksc.nasa.gov/lib/skylabpresskits .html. Provides detailed preflight information about each of the Skylab missions.

Shayler, David J. *Skylab: America's Space Station*. Chichester, England: Springer-Praxis, 2001. Shayler tells the Skylab story well, but without footnotes. From the perspective of more than a quarter century after the missions, Shayler uses official NASA documentation and interviews with the astronauts and key personnel to present the story of Skylab. Also presents an assessment of lessons learned in the context of current programs.

Skylab Program

Date: August 6, 1965, to February 8, 1974
Type of program: Space station, piloted spaceflight

Skylab, the first American space station, saw three crews spend a total of 171 days in space. The astronauts accumulated volumes of scientific data, establishing the value of humans as space-based researchers.

Key Figures

James E. Webb (1906-1992), NASA administrator, 1961-1968

Thomas O. Paine (1921-1992), NASA administrator, 1969-1970

George E. Mueller (1918-2001), associate administrator for Manned Spaceflight, 1963-1969

Dale DeHaven Myers (b. 1922), associate administrator for Manned Spaceflight, 1970-1974

William C. Schneider (1923-1999), Skylab program director

Leland F. Belew, Skylab project manager, Marshall Space Flight Center

Robert F. Thompson (b. 1925), Skylab project manager, Manned Spacecraft Center, 1967- 1970

Kenneth S. Kleinknecht (1919-2007), Skylab project manager, Manned Spacecraft Center, 1970- 1974

Summary of the Program

The project that evolved into Skylab originated in the summer of 1965, when researchers at the National Aeronautics and Space Administration (NASA) were developing programs to follow the piloted lunar landing. Engineers at Marshall Space Flight Center (MSFC) proposed a "spent-stage experiment," in which astronauts would enter the empty upper stage (the S-IVB stage) of a Saturn IB launch vehicle and performexperiments in weightlessness. Almost nothing was known about how easily human beings could work in zero gravity:

The hydrogen tank of the S-IVB, 6.5 meters in diameter and nearly 9 meters in length, could provide a protected environment to test mobility aids and restraint devices and experiment with various tools and techniques.

The spent-stage experiment, also called the Orbital Workshop (or the "wet workshop," because the fuel tank was to be filled with fuel at launch), was assigned to the Apollo Applications Program (AAP), a program established in August, 1965, in the Office of Manned Space Flight (OMSF). AAP developed ambitious plans to use Apollo spacecraft and launch vehicles for frequent flights in low-Earth orbit, synchronous orbit, and lunar orbit, as well as long-duration lunar surface missions (up to fourteen days). Its major objectives were to use the Apollo hardware to produce useful data and to keep the Apollo team together while a major post-Apollo goal was defined and developed.

As defined in early 1967, the Orbital Workshop (OWS) was a semi-permanent space station adaptable to many types of research. Besides the Workshop itself, the station comprised an airlock, through which astronauts could leave the OWS for extravehicular activity, and a Multiple Docking Adapter (MDA) carrying extra docking ports to permit additional spacecraft, experiment modules, and supply vehicles to be attached. In 1966, AAP acquired a major scientific project, the Apollo Telescope Mount (ATM), which consisted of six high-resolution telescopes designed for systematic study of the

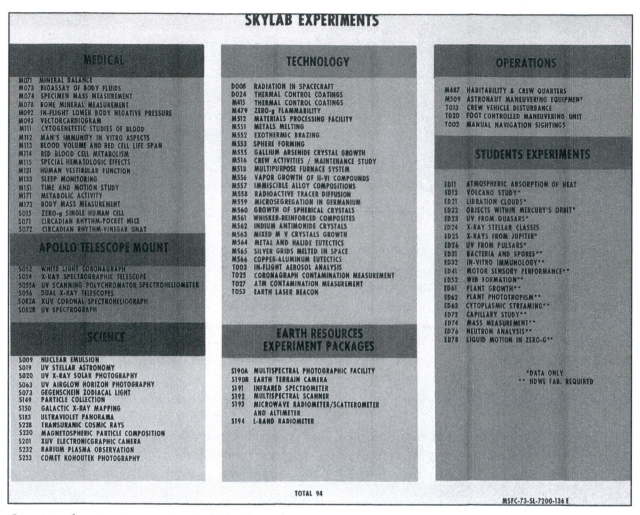

SKYLAB EXPERIMENTS

MEDICAL

M071	MINERAL BALANCE
M073	BIOASSAY OF BODY FLUIDS
M074	SPECIMEN MASS MEASUREMENT
M078	BONE MINERAL MEASUREMENT
M092	IN-FLIGHT LOWER BODY NEGATIVE PRESSURE
M093	VECTORCARDIOGRAM
M111	CYTOGENETIC STUDIES OF BLOOD
M112	MAN'S IMMUNITY IN VITRO ASPECTS
M113	BLOOD VOLUME AND RED CELL LIFE SPAN
M114	RED BLOOD CELL METABOLISM
M115	SPECIAL HEMATOLOGIC EFFECTS
M131	HUMAN VESTIBULAR FUNCTION
M133	SLEEP MONITORING
M151	TIME AND MOTION STUDY
M171	METABOLIC ACTIVITY
M172	BODY MASS MEASUREMENT
S015	ZERO-g SINGLE HUMAN CELL
S071	CIRCADIAN RHYTHM-POCKET MICE
S072	CIRCADIAN RHYTHM-VINEGAR GNAT

APOLLO TELESCOPE MOUNT

S052	WHITE LIGHT CORONAGRAPH
S054	X-RAY SPECTROGRAPHIC TELESCOPE
S055A	UV SCANNING POLYCHROMATOR SPECTROHELIOMETER
S056	DUAL X-RAY TELESCOPES
S082A	XUV CORONAL SPECTROHELIOGRAPH
S082B	UV SPECTROGRAPH

SCIENCE

S009	NUCLEAR EMULSION
S019	UV STELLAR ASTRONOMY
S020	UV X-RAY SOLAR PHOTOGRAPHY
S063	UV AIRGLOW HORIZON PHOTOGRAPHY
S073	GEGENSCHEIN ZODIACAL LIGHT
S149	PARTICLE COLLECTION
S150	GALACTIC X-RAY MAPPING
S183	ULTRAVIOLET PANORAMA
S228	TRANSURANIC COSMIC RAYS
S230	MAGNETOSPHERIC PARTICLE COMPOSITION
S201	XUV ELECTRONICGRAPHIC CAMERA
S232	BARIUM PLASMA OBSERVATION
S233	COMET KOHOUTEK PHOTOGRAPHY

TECHNOLOGY

D008	RADIATION IN SPACECRAFT
D024	THERMAL CONTROL COATINGS
M415	THERMAL CONTROL COATINGS
M479	ZERO-g FLAMMABILITY
M512	MATERIALS PROCESSING FACILITY
M551	METALS MELTING
M552	EXOTHERMIC BRAZING
M553	SPHERE FORMING
M555	GALLIUM ARSENIDE CRYSTAL GROWTH
M516	CREW ACTIVITIES / MAINTENANCE STUDY
M518	MULTIPURPOSE FURNACE SYSTEM
M556	VAPOR GROWTH OF II-VI COMPOUNDS
M557	IMMISCIBLE ALLOY COMPOSITIONS
M558	RADIOACTIVE TRACER DIFFUSION
M559	MICROSEGREGATION IN GERMANIUM
M560	GROWTH OF SPHERICAL CRYSTALS
M561	WHISKER-REINFORCED COMPOSITES
M562	INDIUM ANTIMONIDE CRYSTALS
M563	MIXED M V CRYSTALS GROWTH
M564	METAL AND HALIDE EUTECTICS
M565	SILVER GRIDS MELTED IN SPACE
M566	COPPER-ALUMINUM EUTECTICS
T003	IN-FLIGHT AEROSOL ANALYSIS
T025	CORONAGRAPH CONTAMINATION MEASUREMENT
T027	ATM CONTAMINATION MEASUREMENT
T053	EARTH LASER BEACON

EARTH RESOURCES EXPERIMENT PACKAGES

S190A	MULTISPECTRAL PHOTOGRAPHIC FACILITY
S190B	EARTH TERRAIN CAMERA
S191	INFRARED SPECTROMETER
S192	MULTISPECTRAL SCANNER
S193	MICROWAVE RADIOMETER/SCATTEROMETER AND ALTIMETER
S194	L-BAND RADIOMETER

OPERATIONS

M487	HABITABILITY & CREW QUARTERS
M509	ASTRONAUT MANEUVERING EQUIPMENT
T013	CREW VEHICLE DISTURBANCE
T020	FOOT CONTROLLED MANEUVERING UNIT
T002	MANUAL NAVIGATION SIGHTINGS

STUDENTS EXPERIMENTS

ED11	ATMOSPHERIC ABSORPTION OF HEAT
ED12	VOLCANO STUDY*
ED21	LIBRATION CLOUDS*
ED22	OBJECTS WITHIN MERCURY'S ORBIT*
ED23	UV FROM QUASARS*
ED24	X-RAY STELLAR CLASSES
ED25	X-RAYS FROM JUPITER*
ED26	UV FROM PULSARS*
ED31	BACTERIA AND SPORES**
ED32	IN-VITRO IMMUNOLOGY**
ED41	MOTOR SENSORY PERFORMANCE**
ED52	WEB FORMATION**
ED61	PLANT GROWTH**
ED62	PLANT PHOTOTROPISM**
ED63	CYTOPLASMIC STREAMING**
ED72	CAPILLARY STUDY**
ED74	MASS MEASUREMENT**
ED76	NEUTRON ANALYSIS**
ED78	LIQUID MOTION IN ZERO-G**

*DATA ONLY
** HDWE FAB. REQUIRED

TOTAL 94

MSFC-73-SL-7200-136 E

Overview of most major experiments. (NASA)

Sun. Missions of twenty-eight and fifty-six days were planned, and longer stays were projected.

Technical problems multiplied as the OWS missions were planned in detail, and following the fatal fire in Apollo 1 (January 27, 1967), the OWS project was seriously underfunded. Until the Apollo Program was successfully completed, AAP garnered little support. Between 1966 and 1969 most of the projected AAP missions had to be canceled; only the OWS remained. An alternative plan, long considered as an advanced project to follow the wet workshop, was to equip the S-IVB stage as a laboratory before flight (a "dry workshop"). Such a laboratory, however, could be launched only on the much larger Saturn V, and no Saturn V could be made available until the success of the lunar landing was assured. By early 1969, however, the dry workshop appeared to be the only solution to the many problems of the OWS missions. On July 22, 1969, the change to a dry workshop was implemented, and the development of Skylab began.

The redefined OWS (given its new name, Skylab, in February, 1970) comprised four modules. The workshop itself was an S-IVB stage outfitted on two levels as a laboratory and living space. On the lower level, separate compartments were provided for scientific work, dining, sleeping, and personal hygiene. The upper level was mostly open; storage lockers for film, food, clothing, and scientific equipment lined the walls, and two small airlocks permitted extension of scientific instruments into space. Atop the workshop at launch sat the air-lock module, basically a tunnel capable of being sealed at each end and equipped with a hatch opening to space. On its outer structure the airlock carried tanks of oxygen and nitrogen for the OWS atmosphere and the electrical power system for the cluster (batteries, chargers, and regulators connected to two large arrays of solar cells, one on the ATM and one on the OWS). The upper end of the airlock opened into the MDA, where the control console for the ATM was located. Topping off the launch stack was the ATM itself, mounted on a truss structure hinged to permit deployment of the telescope canister at right angles to the long axis of the cluster. The air lock, MDA, and ATM were enclosed at launch in a shroud that was jettisoned in orbit. The entire cluster measured about 30 meters in length and weighed nearly 100,000 kilograms at launch.

Major experiment programs planned for three piloted missions involved medical investigations to determine the effects of long-term weightlessness and solar physics investigations. In 1970, a third set of experiments was added—a group of Earth-pointed sensors designed to explore the utility of human-tended instruments in studying Earth. Adding this package required changing the planned orbital inclination from 30° to 50° so the OWS could fly over the entire United States as well as most of the populated area of the world.

Skylab progressed through 1970 toward a launch date in July, 1972. By 1971, however, delays in development pushed that launch date to April, 1973. While the cluster modules were built and flight operations plans developed, launch facilities at Kennedy Space Center (KSC) were modified for the project. Launch Complex 39 was built for the Saturn V, and a 39-meter pedestal was built on top of one of the mobile launch platforms to raise the smaller Saturn IB (to be used for crew launches), where it could mate properly with ground-support equipment. Skylab cluster modules began arriving at

KSC in July, 1972, for the most extensive preflight test program ever conducted for a piloted mission. Testing soon required one more launch postponement. It was rescheduled for May 14, 1973. By late April, both launch pads at Launch Complex 39 were occupied simultaneously for the first time ever: the Workshop on its Saturn V at Pad 39A and the first crew's Apollo Command and Service Module (CSM) on its Saturn IB at Pad 39B.

Skylab 1 was launched from KSC at 17:30:00 Coordinated Universal Time (UTC, or 1:30 p.m. eastern daylight time), May 14, 1973, on the last Saturn V ever to fly. The orbital cluster went into its 435-kilometer orbit as planned, but before the first revolution was completed the mission was in serious trouble. Temperature readings on the skin of the OWS were off the high end of the scale (above 82° Celsius), and neither of the two solar panel arrays on the Workshop was producing power. Flight controllers soon deduced that the Workshop had lost its micrometeoroid shield during launch. This shield, a thin metal girdle surrounding the OWS (designed to prevent micrometeoroids from striking the OWS), had been tightly secured to the Workshop at launch, but in orbit became detached, standing 13 centimeters off the outer surface of the OWS. (Thermal engineers later incorporated a passive thermal control system into the shield, using coatings on either side to regulate the flow of heat from the shield to the Workshop.) When the shield was ripped away in orbit, the Workshop surface absorbed much of the solar heat to which it was exposed. In the week after launch, the temperature inside OWS approached 50° Celsius, far above tolerable limits, and engineers worked frantically to design a temporary shield that could be taken up and installed by the first crew. A backup Workshop had been built, but to abandon the first one and postpone the mission until the backup could be prepared for launch would require some $250 million, which the project could not afford.

In the eleven days following the launch of Skylab 1, two designs for a temporary shield were produced and tested: a parasol that could be extended through one of the air locks in the OWS and a "twin-pole sail," which could be stretched over two long poles by astronauts working outside the OWS. The first crew (Skylab 2, launched May 25, 1973) carried the parasol and successfully installed it; the temperature inside the OWS soon dropped to a tolerable level. The Skylab 2 crew discovered that one of the Workshop's two solar arrays had been torn off and that the second was held down by a fragment of the micrometeoroid shield. After freeing it, they were able to complete their twenty-eight day mission without incident.

A post-mission investigation concluded that a design flaw, which had gone undetected throughout development, had allowed air pressure to lift the micrometeoroid shield away from the OWS. At maximum dynamic pressure, 63 seconds after liftoff, the shield had become detached. Pieces of the shield had ripped the latches that held down the solar arrays; one had been torn by the blast from the retrorocket that separated the second stage from the OWS, and a strap of metal from the shield had wrapped around the second array, holding it against the OWS.

Crew members of Skylab 3 installed the twin-pole sail, further protecting the OWS against solar heating; their fifty-nine-day flight and the eighty-four-day mission of the third crew were completely successful. After the third mission ended on February 8, 1974, the OWS was shut down and left in a 435-kilometer orbit, where it was expected to stay for nine years. Tentative plans were made to visit the derelict workshop on an early flight of the space shuttle orbiter so that a propulsion unit could be attached to boost the OWS into a much higher orbit. Too big to burn up when it reentered the atmosphere, the Skylab workshop was a potential hazard.

Yet events overtook plans; space shuttle development was delayed, and atmospheric resistance pulled the OWS down much faster than had been predicted. In mid-1978, a team of engineers reestablished contact with the Workshop and took control of its attitude in orbit. This way it was possible to control its descent to some extent, because atmospheric drag was lower in certain attitudes. For ten months, flight controllers maneuvered the OWS by telemetry, trying to make sure that its final dive into the atmosphere would take place over an unpopulated area. On July 11, 1979, they successfully guided it to reentry over the southeastern Indian Ocean. Some pieces fell on the sparsely populated ranch country of southwestern Australia, but no injury or damage was reported. The Skylab OWS had spent 2,248 days in space and completed 34,981 revolutions of Earth.

Contributions

As intended, Skylab missions accumulated a vast amount of scientific data, principally on the effects of long-term weightlessness on the human body and on the processes that take place on the Sun. Data from the three piloted missions showed that no permanent ill effects resulted from nearly three months of weightlessness and that astronauts readapted rapidly to Earth's environment. Solar scientists were rewarded with more data than

The floor grating of Skylab under construction. (NASA)

they could readily interpret. Eventually, the ATM data would lead to a better understanding of how energy is produced on the Sun and how solar radiation is transmitted into space and eventually interacts with Earth's atmosphere. Earth observations showed that instruments and astronauts could gather information useful in oceanography, pollution control, and exploration for mineral resources. Finally, experiments in zero-gravity manufacturing suggested that the environment in orbit might enable advances in the production of semiconductor crystals and the casting of alloys that could not be made on Earth.

Context

Skylab had been conceived at a critical time for piloted spaceflight. In 1965, the first lunar landing was at least four years in the future, and little effort could be spared for post-Apollo planning; at the same time, failure to get started on a new venture could lead to a serious hiatus in piloted spaceflight operations after Apollo. Support for expensive space projects was waning, and the nation faced internal and external problems that demanded attention. Like other federal programs, piloted spaceflight felt the political pressure to reduce expenditures in the face of an expanding war in Vietnam and the Johnson administration's costly social programs. In these circumstances, and lacking any mandate for a program comparable to Apollo, OMSF director George E. Mueller proposed to use the tremendous capacity developed for Apollo to produce useful results. His proposal

attracted little support, even within NASA. Administrator James E. Webb was fully committed to the lunar landing but reluctant to propose any large subsequent project until he could feel sure of support from the White House and Congress. This support came only grudgingly, with the result that the AAP muddled along with an inadequate budget until Apollo succeeded and NASA settled on the space shuttle as its next major piloted project. Only then did the OWS appear to bridge a gap between Saturn/Apollo and the shuttle, providing information that would be essential in further planning.

When Skylab became the only piloted project available for several years, managers, eager to exploit this opportunity, tended to overload the missions with experiments. The result was increased difficulty in flight operations planning and crew training. Workdays were crowded and poorly organized until ground-based personnel realized the difficulties of working in orbit, especially on the last mission. Despite all of its problems Skylab temporarily was the most productive piloted project ever flown in terms of its advancement of scientific knowledge and its proof of the utility of human beings in orbital operations.

—W. David Compton

See also: Explorers: Solar; Extravehicular Activity; Funding Procedures of Space Programs; Gemini Spacecraft; Get-Away Special Experiments; Manned Orbiting Laboratory; Saturn Launch Vehicles; Skylab Space Station; Skylab 2; Skylab 3; Skylab 4; Space Suit Development.

Further Reading

Bilstein, Roger E. *Stages to Saturn: A Technological History of the Apollo/Saturn Launch Vehicles*. Gainesville: University Press of Florida, 2003. Starting with the earliest rockets, Bilstein traces the development of the Saturn launch vehicles, which carried the Apollo astronauts to the Moon and boosted Skylab into orbit.

Compton, W. David, and Charles D. Benson. *Living and Working in Space: A History of Skylab*. Washington, D.C.: Government Printing Office, 1983. An official overview of the Skylab program and all of its results, this volume details the origin of the program and all four of the piloted missions. The launch accident and the repairs performed on subsequent missions are covered. Copiously illustrated, including several excellent shots of the ATM instrumentation and the Earth-resources cameras.

Cooper, Henry S. F., Jr. *A House in Space*. New York: Holt, Rinehart and Winston, 1976. Containing essays originally published in *The New Yorker*, this slim volume offers a readable account of the Skylab flights. Its journalistic tone is a refreshing change from other texts concerning spaceflight.

Cromie, William J. *Skylab*. New York: David McKay, 1976. A full description of the Skylab spacecraft, mission aims, and data collected on all the Skylab flights, this book is written for the beginning student of space exploration.

Ertel, Ivan D., and Roland W. Newkirk. *Skylab:A Chronology*. Washington, D.C.: Government Printing Office, 1977. The development of Skylab is traced from its conception to the uses of the data it brought back. Includes appendices on flight information and summaries of the missions.

National Aeronautics and Space Administration. *Skylab Mission Press Kits*. http://wwwlib. ksc.nasa.gov/lib/skylabpresskits.html. Provides detailed preflight information about each of the Skylab missions.

Shayler, David J. *Skylab: America's Space Station*. Chichester, England: Springer-Praxis, 2001. Shayler tells the Skylab story well, but without footnotes. From the perspective of more than a quarter century after the missions, Shayler uses official NASA documentation and interviews with the astronauts and key personnel to present the story of Skylab. Also presents an assessment of lessons learned in the context of current programs.

Skylab Space Station

Date: August 6, 1965, to July 11, 1979
Type of spacecraft: Space station, piloted spacecraft

Skylab, America's first space station, was a "monolithic" station, intended to be constructed and launched in one piece and then occupied by a crew later. The International Space Station, by contrast, is a "modular" station, consisting of a core structure with modules added over the course of time to increase its volume and capabilities. Skylab contained all of its essential supplies and experimental equipment when it was launched and was then abandoned when they were exhausted. The 91-metric-ton Skylab was in Earth orbit from 1973 to 1979, and was occupied by crews three times in 1973 and 1974.

Key Figures

Davy Jones, first Skylab program director
James C. Fletcher (1919-1991), NASA
   administrator
William C. Schneider (b. 1923), Skylab program
   director, 1968-1974
Leland F. Belew, Skylab program director, Marshall Space Flight Center

Summary of the Spacecraft

America's first space station began as most ambitious undertakings begin, slowly and carefully planned. Many learned individuals set about to fulfill the dreams of science-fiction writers. Skylab, as it would come to be known, evolved during the most prolific decade of human space travel. While American astronauts walked on the Moon (1969) and their Soviet counterparts trained for long-duration missions, engineers at the Marshall Space Flight Center (MSFC) began work on a variety of space station concepts.

The Apollo Applications Program (AAP), which in 1970 became the Skylab program, developed ambitious plans to use Apollo spacecraft and launch vehicles for frequent flights in low-Earth orbit, as well as long-duration missions. Their Orbital Workshop (OWS) was to be a semi-permanent orbital station on which a crew of three would conduct a variety of astronomical and terrestrial studies and experiments in the microgravity environment.

The goals of the Apollo Applications Program were well defined. Astronaut-scientists would enrich scientific knowledge of Earth, the Sun, the stars, and cosmic space; study the effects of microgravity (weightlessness) on living organisms, including the astronauts; develop new and valuable processing and manufacturing techniques in microgravity; and devise and test new methods of gathering information about the Earth's surface.

Severe damage sustained during launch on May 14, 1973 of the last Saturn V (Saturn-Apollo 513), included the loss of the station's micrometeoroid shield/sunshade and one of its main solar panels. Debris from the lost micrometeoroid shield complicated matters by pinning the remaining solar panel to the side of the station, preventing its deployment, and thus leaving the station with a huge power deficit.

The complete Skylab space station assembly, comparable in volume to a modest three-bedroom home, was 36.1 meters long and 8.2 meters in diameter at the widest point, weighing 91 metric tons. Skylab carried at launch 953 kilograms of food; 2,722 kilograms of water; and nitrogen, oxygen, and other life-sustaining essentials. A payload shroud provided cover for the telescope mount, airlock, and docking adapter during launch.

The Orbital Workshop contained 295 cubic meters of space and weighed 35,380 kilograms. Except for attitude control thrusters, there was no propulsion system. Within the OWS, aluminum open-grid floors and ceilings were installed to divide the two-story space cabin. Crew quarters in the aft end were divided by solid partitions into sleep, waste management, and experiments compartments. The thermal control and ventilation system was designed to maintain temperatures ranging from 16 to 32° Celsius, while the nitrogen-oxygen atmosphere was constant at 3.45 newtons per square centimeter. Outside the workshop shell was a meteoroid shield to provide thermal control and decrease the possibility of hazardous punctures. Once in orbit, the shield was to be deployed and held 12.2 centimeters from the workshop shell.

An overhead view of the Skylab Orbital Workshop in Earth orbit as photographed from the Skylab 4 Command and Service Modules (CSM) during the final fly-around by the CSM before returning home. (NASA)

The OWS was a converted Saturn IB second stage (from the AS-212 vehicle), a leftover from the Apollo Program originally intended for one of the canceled Apollo Earth-orbital missions. This stage was modified internally to work as a large orbiting space habitat rather than a propulsive stage. Crew members spent most of their time in the OWS, conducting experiments, observing, eating, sleeping, and attending to their personal needs.

Mounted on opposing sides of the OWS were the "wings" of the solar array panels, which provided electrical power. At the aft end, cold gas storage bottles and a refrigeration radiator replaced the S-IVB engine. The crew quarters section, in the aft end of the former hydrogen tank, was divided into a wardroom with about 9.3 square meters of floor space, a waste management compartment of 2.8 square meters, a sleep compartment of about 6.5 square meters, and an experiment area of about 16.7 square meters. The forward compartment was separated from the crew quarters by a 20-centimeter beam structure with a grid on each side, serving as both floor and ceiling. In the forward compartment were lockers for storing food, clothing, film, and other items, and tanks holding enough water for the entire mission. On the water tank mounting ring were 25 lockers holding supplies such as bundles of urine bags, portable lights, electrical cables, hoses, umbilicals, pressure suits, tape recorders, charcoal filters, fans, lamps, and intercom boxes. Major items on the floor and around the wall included the food lockers and freezers, experiment equipment, astronaut maneuvering equipment, suits for extravehicular activities (EVAs, or spacewalks), and various scientific instruments.

The thermal control and ventilation system provided the astronauts with a habitable environment with temperatures ranging from 15.6 to 32.2° Celsius and an oxygen-nitrogen atmosphere with internal pressure of 3.45 newtons per square centimeter. Two elements attached to the OWS were the Airlock Module (AM) and the Multiple Docking

Adapter (MDA). The AM, between the MDA and the OWS, was 5.3 meters long, weighed 22,226 kilograms, and had 17.4 cubic meters of habitable volume. The Structural Transition Section (STS) connected the tunnel assembly to the MDA. The tunnel had an airlock and hatch to permit astronauts to perform extravehicular activities without depressurizing the entire spacecraft. The STS contained the AM control panels, lights, ducts, stowage containers, and cabin heat exchanger. Although relatively small, the AM tunnel contained dozens of items of equipment, including lights, a tape recorder module, portable timers, spare batteries, light bulbs, and a teleprinter.

Separated from the OWS and the MDA by doors, the AM could be evacuated for egress or ingress of a space-suited astronaut through a side hatch. Oxygen and nitrogen storage tanks needed for Skylab's life-support system were mounted on the external truss work of the AM. Major components in the AM included Skylab's electric power control and distribution station, environmental control system, communications system, and data-handling and data-recording systems.

The MDA was a cylindrical structure, 5.2 meters long and 3 meters in diameter. It weighed 6,260 kilograms and contained about 32 cubic meters of space. It had an axial docking port at the forward end, to which the Apollo Command and Service Module (CSM) docked, and a radial port used as a backup if necessary. The MDA served as the docking interface for the Command Module and permitted the transfer of personnel, equipment, power, and electrical signals between the docked CSM and the Airlock Module and OWS. In orbit, the MDA was a major experiment control center for solar observations, metals and materials processing, and Earth resources experiments.

The Apollo Telescope Mount was the first piloted astronomical observatory for performing solar research from Earth orbit. It weighed 11,181 kilograms, and was 4.4 meters long and 31 meters wide with solar arrays extended. The ATM had five major

hardware elements: an experiment canister, an attitude and pointing control system, solar array wings, a control and display console (in the MDA), and the rack assembly. Mounted on the ATM were major elements of Skylab's Attitude and Pointing Control System, which provided three-axis stabilization and maneuvering capability for the vehicle.

Contributions

Successful in all respects despite early mechanical difficulties, three three-person crews occupied the Skylab Orbital Workshop for a total of 171 days and 13 hours. The OWS was the site of nearly three hundred scientific and technical experiments: medical experiments on humans' adaptability to microgravity, solar observations, and detailed Earth resources experiments.

Skylab included eight separate solar experiments on its Apollo Telescope Mount: two x-ray telescopes, an x-ray and extreme ultraviolet camera, an ultraviolet spectroheliometer, an extreme ultraviolet spectroheliograph and an ultraviolet spectroheliograph, a white light coronagraph, and two hydrogen-alpha telescopes.

The effectiveness of Skylab crews exceeded expectations, especially in their ability to perform complex repair tasks. They demonstrated excellent mobility, both inside and outside the space station, showing that the human presence was an asset in conducting research from space. By selecting and photographing targets of opportunity on the Sun and by evaluating weather conditions on Earth and recommending Earth-resources opportunities, crew members were instrumental in attaining extremely high-quality solar and Earth-oriented data. The astronauts recorded more than 177,000 frames of the Sun and more than 46,000 frames of Earth. The missions also accumulated more than forty hours of spacewalks.

Experimental results on motion sickness seemed to indicate that space malaise was a highly individualized problem, unpredictable in any particular case. The drugs used during the program reduced

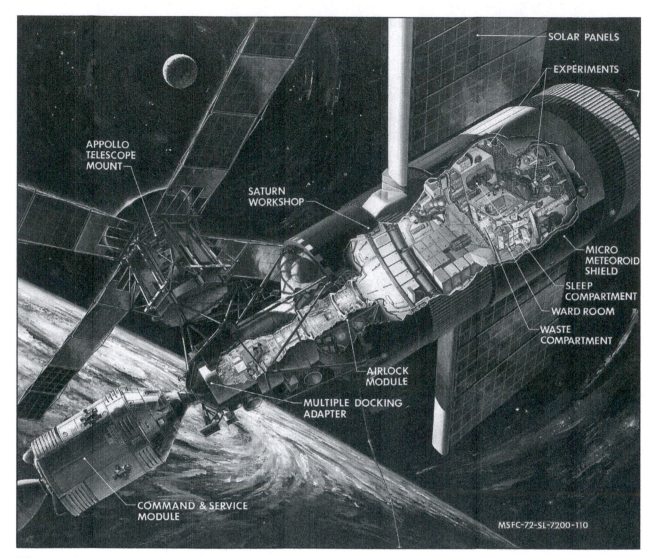

This artist's concept is a cutaway illustration of the Skylab with the Command/Service Module being docked to the Multiple Docking Adapter. (NASA / MFSC)

the severity of symptoms but did not prevent them. All the crew members, however, adapted within the first week, and illness did not recur for the rest of the mission. Motion sickness was obviously complicated, and Skylab did not provide enough information to understand it thoroughly. However, many of the medical investigations conducted on Skylab contributed to a fuller picture of what happens to the human body during weightlessness.

Skylab's Earth-resources experiments differed in several ways from the medical and solar experiments. Given the wider variety of instruments, the

larger number of investigators, and the diversity of objectives, no clear assessment of the value of the Earth-sensing experiments could emerge quickly. Early reports by investigators focused narrowly on individual projects. In the independent but related visual observations program, however—an exercise conducted largely by the third crew—it was possible to assess the value of humans as observers of Earth's surface features.

By all standards, Skylab was an impressive success. Its cost remained relatively low because most of the major components were taken from previous projects. Skylab clearly showed that it was feasible to live for extended periods in orbit without becoming disoriented or encountering major problems with the lack of a gravity field. Microgravity proved to be simply another work environment, one to which all the crew members adjusted in their own time. Some tasks were actually easier in microgravity; moving massive objects, for example, was not hard at all, provided there were adequate handholds to control them. Small objects were more troublesome; hand tools, screws, and other small parts would not stay put. Crews quickly learned, however, that there was little danger of losing something of this kind, because air currents in the workshop would sooner or later carry small objects to the screen covering the intake of the ventilation system.

Context

All told, Skylab orbited Earth 2,476 times during the three piloted Skylab missions. Astronauts performed ten spacewalks totaling 42 hours and 16 minutes. Skylab logged about two thousand hours of scientific and medical experiments, including eight solar experiments. Many of the experiments concerned the astronauts' adaptation to extended periods of microgravity, and each Skylab mission set a record for the duration of time astronauts spent in space.

Skylab was not the first space station, having been preceded by one successful Soviet Salyut (Russian for "salute") space station. Salyut 1, launched April 19, 1971, was so named as a salute to the first space traveler, Yuri A. Gagarin, who had orbited the Earth ten years earlier on April 12, 1961. Jinxed from the beginning, its first crew (arriving

on Soyuz 10) was unable to board Salyut 1 because of a failure in the docking mechanism; its second crew (Soyuz 11) died during reentry when a pressure-equalization valve in the descent module opened prematurely.

Five other Salyut space stations and Mir, the first modular space station, followed Skylab. Overall, Skylab had a greater mass (91 metric tons) than any Salyut and three times the habitable volume (295 cubic meters). Salyut led to the development of the Mir complex. Together, these nine stations are the ancestors of the International Space Station (ISS). By comparison, when completely assembled, the ISS will have a habitable volume of 1,200 cubic meters and a mass of 419 metric tons.

Following the third and final piloted visit to the station, Skylab was put in a parking orbit that was expected to last at least eight years. However, increased solar activity heated the outer layers of Earth's atmosphere and thereby increased drag on Skylab. This, in turn, led to an early reentry on July 11, 1979, when Skylab disintegrated over western Australia and the Indian Ocean. The only casualty was an unfortunate Australian cow.

—Russell R. Tobias

See also: Funding Procedures of Space Programs; Get-Away Special Experiments; International Space Station: Development; International Space Station: Modules and Nodes; Manned Orbiting Laboratory; Marshall Space Flight Center; Russia's Mir Space Station; Saturn Launch Vehicles; Skylab Program; Skylab 2; Skylab 3; Skylab 4; Space Shuttle-Mir: Joint Missions; Space Suit Development.

Further Reading

Belew, Leland F., ed. *Skylab: Our First Space Station.* NASA SP-400. Washington, D.C.: Government Printing Office, 1977. A detailed history of the Skylab program that includes many color photographs taken during the flights. Available online at http://history.nasa.gov/ SP-400/sp400.htm.

Belew, Leland F., and Ernst Stuhlinger. *Skylab: A Guidebook.* NASA EP-107. Washington, D.C.: Government Printing Office, 1974. Completed prior to the launch of the Skylab station, this document gave a detailed preview of the station and its goals. Available online at http://history.nasa.gov/EP-107/contents.htm.

Compton, W. David, and Charles D. Benson. *Living and Working in Space: A History of Skylab*. SP-4208. Washington, D.C.: Government Printing Office, 1983. The definitive history of the Skylab program, filled with facts, photos, and diagrams relating to all aspects of the vehicles, crews, and support personnel. Available online at http://history.nasa.gov/SP- 4208/sp4208.htm.

Lundquist, Charles A., ed. *Skylab's Astronomy and Space Sciences*. Washington, D.C.: Government Printing Office, 1979. This book discusses the astronomy and space science experiments conducted by the astronauts during their stay aboard Skylab. It is filled with details and photographs. Available online at http:// history.nasa.gov/SP-404/sp404.htm. Accessed May, 2005.

National Aeronautics and Space Administration. *Skylab Mission Press Kits*. http://wwwlib. ksc.nasa.gov/ lib/SKYLABPRESSKITS.html. Provides detailed preflight information about each of the Skylab missions.

Newkirk, Roland W., and Ivan D. Ertel, with Courtney G. Brooks, eds. *Skylab: A Chronology*. Vol. 4. Washington, D.C.: Scientific and Technical Information Division, Office of Technology Utilization, National Aeronautics and Space Administration, 1978. A record of the day-by-day events that occurred during the Skylab program including its inception, development, and completion. Available online at http://history. nasa.gov/SP-4011/ cover.htm.

Shayler, David J. *Skylab: America's Space Station*. Chichester, England: Springer-Praxis, 2001. From the perspective of more than a quarter century after the missions, Shayler uses official NASA documentation and interviews with the astronauts and key personnel to present the story of Skylab.

Small Explorer Program

Date: Beginning April 4, 1989
Type of program: Scientific platform

The Small Explorer Satellite (SMEX) program is an effort sponsored by NASA that provides frequent opportunities to fly highly focused and relatively inexpensive scientific research satellites. The Small Explorer spacecraft, which weigh less than 250 kilograms and consume less than 200 watts of electric power, have studied particle emission by the Sun, the Earth's aurora, the corona of the Sun, and the composition of interstellar clouds.

Key Figures

Glenn M. Mason, Science Team leader, Solar Anomalous and Magnetospheric Particle Explorer

Charles Carlson, Science Team leader, Fast Auroral Snapshot Explorer

Alan Title, Science Team leader, Transition Region and Coronal Explorer

Gary J. Melnick, Science Team leader, Submillimeter Wave Astronomy Satellite

Perry B. Hacking, Science Team leader, Wide-Field Infrared Explorer

Reuven Ramaty (1937-2001), solar physics and gamma-ray astronomer

Summary of the Satellites

The National Aeronautics and Space Administration (NASA) introduced its Small Explorer (SMEX) satellite program to provide opportunities for scientists to develop relatively inexpensive scientific satellites to perform highly focused experiments. SMEX spacecraft are expected to weigh less than 250 kilograms and use no more than 200 watts of electric power. Projects selected for the SMEX program are expected to cost about $35 million for the design, development, and orbital operations. The weight, power, and cost limitations on SMEX projects required the development of innovative instrumentation to perform high-quality science. On April 4, 1989, NASA officially announced the SMEX program. A total of fifty-one proposals to employ satellites to study important questions in space physics, astrophysics, and upper atmosphere science were submitted to NASA, and three were selected to begin the SMEX program.

The first satellite in the SMEX program was launched on July 3, 1992, only three years after the program was announced. The Solar Anomalous and Magnetospheric Particle Explorer (SAMPEX) was placed into orbit by a Scout rocket fired from Vandenberg Air Force Base in California. Glenn M. Mason, of the University of Maryland, led a team that included ten other scientists from institutions in the United States and Germany that developed SAMPEX. The SAMPEX spacecraft weighs 157 kilograms, carrying 40 kilograms of instruments that consume an average of 22 watts of electric power. The SAMPEX satellite carried four instruments that monitored the charged particles emitted by the Sun in order to investigate the isotopic composition of these particles. SAMPEX used a novel momentum reaction system to keep its instruments pointed at the Sun.

The second satellite in the SMEX program was the Fast Auroral Snapshot Explorer (FAST), launched on August 21, 1996, by a Pegasus XL rocket over the Air Force Western Test Range. The

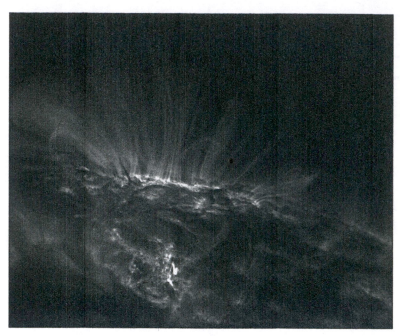

Image of a sunspot taken by TRACE. (NASA)

Pegasus is an air-launched rocket; it minimizes launching costs because it is dropped from the Orbital Sciences Corporation Lockheed L1011 aircraft, which serves as the first stage of the launch vehicle. Charles Carlson, from the University of California at Berkeley, led a team of scientists from the Lockheed Martin Palo Alto Research Laboratory, California, and the University of California campuses at Berkeley and Los Angeles who developed FAST. The FAST spacecraft weighs 191 kilograms and carries 51 kilograms of instruments that consume an average of 19 watts of electric power. To allow FAST to collect real-time measurements while it was passing through the northern auroral zone, a Transportable Orbital Tracking Station was deployed in Alaska.

The third SMEX satellite, the Transition Region and Coronal Explorer (TRACE), was launched by a Pegasus XL on April 2, 1998, over the Air Force Western Test Range. Alan Title of Stanford's Lockheed Martin Palo Alto Research Laboratory, California, led a team that included thirteen other scientists from the United States, Sweden, the United Kingdom, and the Netherlands who developed

TRACE. The TRACE satellite, which weighs 250 kilograms, consumes an average of 35 watts of electric power. TRACE carried a telescope, with a 30-centimeter aperture and 8.6-meter focal length, to image the Sun. The objective of the TRACE mission is to better understand the forces at work on the Sun by exploring the connection between the fine-scale magnetic fields and the behavior of the plasma in the outer regions of the Sun.

The fourth SMEX satellite, the Submillimeter Wave Astronomy Satellite (SWAS), was launched by a Pegasus XL on December 5, 1998, over the Air Force Western Test Range. Gary J. Melnick, of the Harvard-Smithsonian Center for Astrophysics, Cambridge, Massachusetts, headed a team of twelve scientists from institutions across the United States and Cologne, Germany, who developed the SWAS satellite. SWAS, which weighs 285 kilograms, carries a single research instrument, a Submillimeter Wave Telescope. This telescope, built by the Ball Aerospace Systems Group, was used to investigate the chemical and isotopic composition of dense interstellar clouds. SWAS can observe two or three astronomical objects during its 97-minute orbit. However, to obtain high-quality measurements, SWAS can observe the same object on successive orbits, improving the measurements by adding all of the data together. Using this technique, SWAS has observed the same object for periods as long as seventy hours, providing far better measurements than previously available.

The fifth SMEX satellite, the Wide-Field Infrared Explorer (WIRE), was launched by a Pegasus XL on March 4, 1999, over the Air Force Western Test Range. Perry B. Hacking of NASA's Jet Propulsion Laboratory, Pasadena, California, led the team that developed WIRE. The WIRE spacecraft, which weighs 250 kilograms, carries a 30-centimeter

Cassegrain imaging telescope to detect faint astronomical sources in two infrared wavelength bands. WIRE was designed to study the evolution of unusual galaxies, called starburst galaxies, and to search for distant ultra-luminous galaxies. The WIRE spacecraft was placed in its planned orbit, and all the instruments functioned properly. WIRE failed, however, in its primary scientific mission when an error in the computer programming resulted in the instrument cover being ejected earlier than planned, causing the satellite to spin uncontrollably. This allowed radiation from the Sun to enter the telescope, causing the temperature to rise. By the time ground controllers regained control of WIRE, a week later, all of the cryogenic hydrogen, required to cool the infrared detectors, had boiled away.

NASA has selected the next two SMEX missions. The High Energy Solar Spectroscopic Imager (HESSI) was launched by a Pegasus XL rocket on February 5, 2002, off the coast of Florida from the Cape Canaveral area. Designed to observe the Sun, HESSI studies how particles are accelerated and how energy is released in solar flares. The Galaxy Evolution Explorer (GALEX) was launched by a Pegasus XL rocket on April 28, 2003, also off the Florida coast from Cape Canaveral. GALEX carried an ultraviolet telescope to explore the origin and early evolution of galaxies and stars.

Next among the funded SMEX satellites was the Aeronomy of Ice in the Mesosphere (AIM) mission, slated for a launch in September, 2006. This mission would investigate Earth's highest-level clouds as part of a study of climate change. On January 26, 2005, NASA announced that several new Small Explorer missions had been selected from more than two dozen proposals. The Interstellar Boundary Explorer (IBEX) was intended to study galactic cosmic rays and indirectly detect the edge of the solar system. IBEX launch was tentatively scheduled for 2008. The Nuclear Spectroscopic Telescope Array (NuSTAR) was intended to become the first x-ray telescope specifically designed to detect black holes. NuSTAR was funded as a feasibility study; a decision would be made in early 2006 about whether to develop NuSTAR and proceed to flight development. As of 2019, AIM, IBEX, NuSTAR, and IRIS were operational SMEX satellites. Plans were in the works for three more SMEX satellites to be launched in 2021 and 2022.

An extension of the SMEX is SMEX-Lite. The SMEX-Lite program is intended to provide ultralow- cost small spacecraft with performance that exceeds that accomplished with the initial five SMEX missions. This initiative capitalizes on NASA's past experiences, initiates technology development programs, and shrinks the institutional infrastructure in a manner that promises to cut the cost of SMEX class spacecraft in half while improving system reliability.

Contributions

NASA's first SMEX satellite, SAMPEX, monitored the energetic particles from the Sun and the local interstellar medium, as well as electrons within the Earth's magnetosphere, the region of space influenced by the Earth's magnetic field. The deflection of these energetic particles caused by the Earth's magnetic field was measured by the SAMPEX instruments, allowing the origin, type, and energy of each particle to be determined. SAMPEX measurements determined the precise location of trapped anomalous cosmic rays in the magnetosphere, measured the elemental composition of the carbon, nitrogen, oxygen, and neon in anomalous cosmic rays trapped in the Earth's magnetic field, and discovered that trapped anomalous cosmic rays are the dominant component of high-energy ions heavier than helium in the magnetosphere. The satellite detected the "early" return of the anomalous cosmic-ray component in the 1992 solar minimum. SAMPEX also determined the "normal" solar system isotopic abundances for neon and magnesium in the large solar particle events of October and November, 1993.

The TRACE satellite obtained images, at high spatial resolution and short time resolution, of the transitional region between the solar photosphere, the outermost region of the atmosphere of the Sun, and the solar corona, a hotter region below the photosphere. The corona has a temperature of millions of kelvins, while the photosphere is at a temperature of 6,000 kelvins. This large difference in temperature results in many interesting physical processes in the transitional zone between the photosphere and the corona. The TRACE satellite took more than one million images of this region, allowing the fine structure to be monitored. TRACE measurements indicate that solar flares, the rapid emissions of charged particles from the Sun, can increase by a factor of one hundred in intensity in only thirty seconds.

Before the TRACE measurements became available, scientists had difficulty modeling the physical processes in the Sun's atmosphere because they lacked detailed knowledge of the behavior of the plasma in the transitional region. TRACE filled in some of these gaps, allowing more realistic models of the solar atmosphere to be developed.

The FAST spacecraft carried four scientific instruments to monitor auroras. The electric field experiment uses three sensors to determine the plasma density and electron temperature. The magnetic field experiment uses two magnetometers to determine the strength, direction, and time variation of the magnetic field. The Time-of-Flight Energy Angle Mass Spectrograph (TEAMS) measures the three-dimensional distribution of the major ions in the plasma. There were sixteen electrostatic analyzers placed around the perimeter of the spacecraft to measure the energies of the electrons and ions in the plasma. FAST measurements were part of a worldwide auroral campaign that took place from January 1 through March 15, 1997, as part of the International Auroral Study. FAST measurements provided a better understanding of how natural radio emissions are generated throughout the solar system. Electric currents, detected by the FAST satellite, turn the

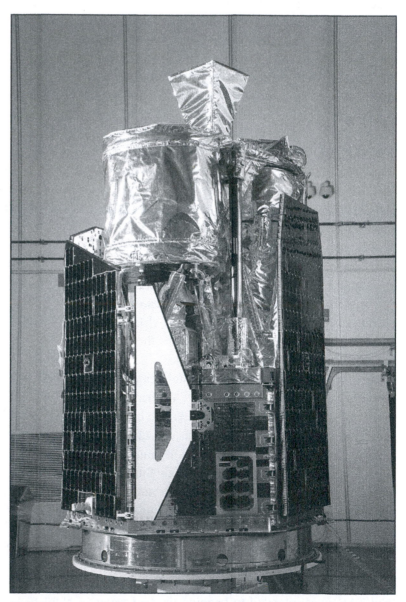

NuSTAR in the clean room at Orbital Sciences Corporation in Dulles, Virginia. (NASA / JPL-Caltech / Orbital)

Earth into a giant radio transmitter capable of broadcasting billions of watts of high-frequency radio waves into space. This powerful radio emission, called the auroral kilometric radiation, is not detected on the ground because it is blocked by the Earth's upper atmosphere. Measurements by the FAST satellite also resulted in the discovery of an invisible aurora, which exists as a companion to the familiar visible aurorae, or northern and southern lights. Researchers detected the invisible aurora by consistently detecting upward flows of electrons interspersed with the downward flowing electrons that produce the visible aurora.

The SWAS spacecraft studied the chemical composition of interstellar galactic clouds to help determine the process of star formation. SWAS instruments looked at molecules of water and oxygen as well as atomic carbon and the individual isotopes of carbon by detecting their submillimeter wave radiation. During its first year of operation, SWAS observed more than thirty star-forming regions in the galaxy in an effort to determine the detailed mechanism by which star formation takes place. SWAS also measured the compositions of molecular clouds in an effort to determine the cooling mechanisms that result in the collapse of these clouds and the condensation of dust.

The WIRE spacecraft failed in its primary mission when all the hydrogen used to cool its infrared detectors was lost before the infrared sensors could be activated. However, Derek Buzasi, an astronomer at the Berkeley campus of the University of California, realized that the small guiding telescope on the WIRE could be used for an entirely different purpose, to monitor rapid changes in the light from the brightest stars. Engineers at NASA's Goddard Space Flight Center developed techniques to point the spacecraft's 5-centimeter diameter telescope at these bright stars, making ten observations of the light emission every second. These rapid measurements allowed scientists to study the high-frequency changes in output, which provided information on the structure of the deep interior of the star.

Buzasi used the telescope to observe stars in the Big Dipper and in Centaurus. He found that Alpha Ursa Major, the brightest star in the Big Dipper, is expanding rapidly, on its way to becoming a giant star.

HESSI began studying hard x-ray emissions in solar flares. After being commissioned, it was renamed RHESSI, after Reuven Ramaty, a pioneer NASA scientist who worked in the areas of solar physics and gamma-ray astronomy until his death in 2001. GALEX began providing surprising clues about the nature of early galaxy formation. Indeed, its most startling finding was that galaxies formed far sooner after the Big Bang than had previously been thought.

Overall, the SMEX program has demonstrated that NASA can develop, test, and launch a successful, low-cost scientific research satellite with a development time of three years or less. The quick recovery from the loss of the planned WIRE mission, permitting the satellite to be used for another purpose, demonstrated flexibility in redirecting mission objectives, allowing an otherwise nonfunctional satellite to perform useful scientific research.

Context

When NASA began development of the space shuttle in the 1970's, it was decided to shift all satellite launching from expendable satellite launch vehicles, such as the Scout and the Delta, to the space shuttle. The large launching capability of the space shuttle, tens of tons, compared to the hundreds to thousands of pounds that a Scout or a Delta could place into orbit, resulted in a change in design philosophy from small spacecraft focused on a single experiment to large spacecraft designed to perform multiple tasks linked by a common theme. As a consequence of this requirement to integrate multiple payloads, the lead time between the proposal of an experiment and its flight lengthened significantly, with some projects requiring five to ten years between proposal and flight. After the loss of the shuttle *Challenger* in 1986, NASA began to shift from launching a few large satellites, such as the

Hubble Space Telescope, to more frequent projects to launch smaller and less expensive satellites.

One objective was to shorten the design and development time for scientific research satellites from five to ten years to two to three years. One of the new projects that emerged from this rethinking of NASA's approach to space research was the SMEX. The SMEX program was initiated by NASA to provide frequent flight opportunities for highly focused and relatively inexpensive space science missions. The first five SMEX satellites demonstrated that small spacecraft, developed and operated on limited budgets, can perform high-quality scientific research.

—George J. Flynn, updated by David G. Fisher

See also: Galaxy Evolution Explorer; Pegasus Launch Vehicles; Skylab 4.

Further Reading

Baker, D. N., G. M. Mason, O. Figueroa, G. Colon, J. G. Watzin, and R. M. Aleman. "An Overview of the Solar, Anomalous, and Magnetospheric Particle Explorer (SAMPEX) Mission." *Institute of Electrical and Electronics Engineers (IEEE) Transactions on Geoscience and Remote Sensing* 31 (1993): 531-541. A description of the SAMPEX satellite, its instrumentation, and the early results of the mission. Intended as an introduction to a series of articles reporting the specific results of the SAMPEX mission.

Carlson, C. W., R. F. Pfaff, and J. G. Watzin. "The Fast Auroral Snapshot Mission." *Geophysical Research Letters* 25 (1998): 2031-2016. A description of the FAST satellite, its instrumentation, and the early results of the mission. Intended as an introduction to a series of articles reporting the specific results of the FAST mission.

Lemaire, J. F., D. Heynderickx, and D. N. Baker. *Radiation Belts: Models and Standards*. Washington, D.C.: American Geophysical Union, 1996. Presents the new results from the SAMPEX satellite, describing the physical sources of the energetic particles that are trapped in the Van Allen radiation belts.

Lin, Robert P., Brian R. Dennis, and A. O. Benz. *The Reuven Ramaty High Energy Solar Spectroscopic Imager (RHESSI)—Mission Description and Early Results*. New York: Springer, 2003. As the title states, this book presents early science returns from RHESSI. For the more scientifically inclined reader.

Suess, Steven T., and Bruce T. Tsurutani. *From the Sun: Auroras, Magnetic Storms, Solar Flares, Cosmic Rays*. Washington, D.C.: American Geophysical Union, 1998. A comprehensive account, intended for the general reader, of the latest research on auroras, solar flares, and cosmic rays, including the results of the SAMPEX and FAST satellites. The book consists of a series of separate articles, each describing a different area of research. The article on anomalous cosmic rays provides a good description of the understanding of this phenomenon as a result of SAMPEX observations.

Zimmerman, Robert. *The Chronological Encyclopedia of Discoveries in Space*. Westport, Conn.: Oryx Press, 2000. Provides a complete chronological history of all crewed and robotic spacecraft and explains flight events and scientific results. Suitable for all levels of research.

SMS and GOES Meteorological Satellites

Date: Beginning May 17, 1974
Type of spacecraft: Meteorological satellites

Synchronous Meteorological Satellites (SMS) were prototypes placed in orbits over the equator at parameters that made them appear stationary in relation to Earth's surface. They provided continuous coverage of weather conditions such as temperature, wind speed and direction, and cloud cover. Geostationary Operational Environmental Satellites (GOES) eventually replaced the SMS, engaging in the same type of reconnaissance as part of an operational system under the direction of NASA.

Summary of the Satellites

During the 1960's, launch capabilities in the United States increased to the point where craft could be placed in orbits high enough to allow them to become synchronous with the turning of Earth on its axis. In order to accomplish this synchronicity, they had to reach altitudes of around 35,880 kilometers directly above the equator and move with the turning of Earth at a speed that made them appear to stand still when viewed from Earth's surface. This concept is precisely what makes possible satellite communication with permanently positioned satellite receiving antennae such as backyard dishes. Such geosynchronous, or geostationary, orbits are useful for continuous, uninterrupted photo reconnaissance of a specific region of Earth's surface.

In the mid-1960's, the National Aeronautics and Space Administration (NASA) began to apply geosynchronous technology with a series of Applications Technology Satellites (ATS's) that carried high-resolution cameras for monitoring the atmosphere. This series was experimental but did achieve success, leading NASA to launch two Synchronous Meteorological Satellites as precursors to an operational system, under the aegis of the Global Atmospheric Research Program (GARP) of the United States Department of Commerce.

SMS 1 was the first of the two satellites designed for the Goddard Space Flight Center, under the direction of NASA's Office of Applications. It was launched from Cape Canaveral aboard a Thor-Delta launch vehicle on May 17, 1974, and placed at 45° west longitude. After being placed in orbit and tested, it was turned over to the National Oceanic and Atmospheric Administration (NOAA).

SMS 1 was a spin-stabilized cylinder 190.5 centimeters in diameter and 254 centimeters long. It was covered with solar cells and weighed 628 kilograms. The satellite carried a visible infrared radiometer, a meteorological data collection system, and a space environment monitoring system.

SMS 1 was equipped to provide day and night imagery of cloud cover, take radiance temperatures of Earth's atmosphere, and measure proton, electron, and solar x-ray fluxes and magnetic fields. It could also transmit processed information from NOAA control facilities to regional stations and pick up and transmit data from thousands of piloted and robotic weather-monitoring sites. High-resolution photographs of the Western Hemisphere were transmitted every thirty minutes. The primary instrument aboard SMS 1 was a visible infrared spin-scan radiometer.

SMS 2 was launched from the Eastern Test Range on February 6, 1975, and placed at 115° west longitude.

The Geostationary Operational Environmental Satellite (GOES) program followed SMS. NASA

GOES-N being encapsulated in a Delta IV launch vehicle. (NASA)

centimeters long and 190 centimeters in diameter; it weighed 243 kilograms. Like the SMS series, it contained a radiometer and data collection and transmission instrumentation. It also contained a telescope. It worked in concert with SMS 2 to provide twenty-four-hour-a-day coverage of the Western Hemisphere.

GOES-2 was launched on June 16, 1977, GOES-3 in June, 1978, and GOES-4, GOES-5, and GOES-6 during the 1980's. The latter three satellites were equipped with advanced sensing technology, including a visible infrared spin-scan radiometer and atmospheric sounder that provides improved imagery. This sophisticated technology allows scientists to determine the three-dimensional configuration of Earth's atmosphere at any given time.

The SMS/GOES series was also used to relay meteorological data that had a bearing on navigation. During 1976, a program was established by the U.S. Coast Guard to use a channel of GOES-1 to relay radar imagery of ice fields from aircraft to control centers, which then distributed the analyzed data to ships for navigation purposes. This program, called Project Icewarn, was conducted over the Great Lakes during the winter and spring seasons in an effort to keep shipping lanes open longer. The SMS's were also used to monitor forest conditions in remote regions as part of an early-warning system against forest fires.

These satellites were also equipped with maneuvering rockets, which allowed them to be moved from one location to another by ground controllers. As more GOES spacecraft were deployed, the older SMS and early GOES craft were moved into

had contracted with the Department of Commerce to build and operate SMS 1 and SMS 2 as well as the first of the GOES series, SMS-C, which became GOES-1 after it was launched and tested. Five additional GOES satellites were developed to give the program full global coverage and backup. The entire program was eventually taken over by NOAA.

GOES-1 was launched from the Eastern Test Range aboard a Thor-Delta rocket on October 16, 1975. It was a spin-stabilized cylinder, 344 positions that would permit them to serve as backups for newer, more sophisticated equipment. Working together, they provided early warning of hurricanes, typhoons, and tropical storms. This information was of major importance to coastal areas and island locations in which weather information had not been readily available by other means.

The instrumentation aboard all these satellites also gave controllers the opportunity to monitor phenomena in space such as solar flares, which might not have a direct impact on the weather but which appear to play a role in the formation of magnetic storms.

The SMS/GOES project was incorporated into an international program known as the Global Atmospheric Research Program, a model of international cooperation. After the launch of GOES-3, GOES-1 was positioned over the Indian Ocean to collect and transmit data to a ground station in Spain operated by the European Space Agency (ESA), where it was analyzed and from which it was distributed. Control functions were turned over to the Darmstadt site in West Germany.

Contributions

While the ATS series proved the concept that weather satellites could function in geostationary orbit, SMS 1 and SMS 2 proved the reliability of satellite technology for providing continuous, real-time coverage of developing weather conditions from the same orbital location above the equator. The sophisticated equipment aboard these satellites was the first to provide continuous high-quality color reconnaissance of Earth's surface. The photographs from these satellites were processed and looped together to create a visual progression of weather fronts from which meteorologists were able to track and predict the progress of a weather system. This imagery also gave scientists the opportunity to study the formations in an effort to understand more fully what caused them and what conditions caused them to develop in one way or another.

SMS/GOES also acted as part of an early-warning system operated by the U.S. government's National Environmental Satellite Service. By 1976, several hundred sensors for forecasting natural disasters—loods, tidal waves, earthquakes, and forest fires—had been installed in various remote regions of the country. It was projected that eventually several thousand such instruments would be deployed. In the winter of 1976, two such sensors placed in a watershed in the state of Washington warned of impending flood conditions upstream from Deming, Washington. At the time, GOES-1 was stationed over the West Coast of the United States, while SMS 2 was stationed over the East Coast. Both satellites picked up signals from the sensors and relayed them to NOAA facilities in Maryland, where the information was analyzed and an advisory was transmitted to Deming area authorities. The same technology has been employed to keep track of ocean vessels, aircraft, and highway traffic.

During that same month, SMS 2 was also employed to transmit data from twenty-three ground stations in an area of one thousand square miles in northern California. Famous for its fragile redwood forests, the area was susceptible to forest fires. Sensors in each of these ground stations kept track of air temperature, humidity, wind speed and direction, solar radiation, rainfall, air pollution, and the moisture content of the forest floor, which was blanketed by dry pine needles and grasses. Data from each of these sensors were sent to the satellite for relay to ground stations.

The principal advancement achieved with the SMS/GOES series was the full-time, day and night coverage of the Western Hemisphere in real time. Earlier programs had established the dependability of satellites as data gatherers, but the non-synchronous orbits of earlier systems had meant relatively long delays between sweeps of the same area.

The earliest meteorological satellites—Television Infrared Observations Satellites (TIROS), Environmental Science Services Administration satellites (ESSA), and Improved TIROS Operational

System Satellites (ITOS)—were placed in polar Sun-synchronous orbits. From that configuration, the more advanced ITOS satellites were designed to cover 95 percent of Earth's surface in thirty-six hours, which was not fast enough to track a developing tropical storm that might turn into a hurricane, threatening island and coastal regions. Nor were many of these early satellites able to provide nighttime imagery. The infrared sensors aboard SMS/GOES, developed to complement or replace less sophisticated technology aboard the earlier satellites, allowed meteorologists to update information on developing weather systems much more frequently.

Another major advancement was the establishment of a satellite system that could be maneuvered at will to serve a multitude of purposes, as described above. Semiretired ATS's were moved into position to relay television coverage of the 1968 Summer Olympics in Mexico City after an international communications satellite failed at launch, thus providing a dependable backup that later served in similar capacities. Since their launches, both SMS's and several of the GOES's have been maneuvered from one location to another along the equatorial plane to accomplish a variety of tasks.

The geostationary equatorial position of the SMS/GOES system is ideal for the United States and much of Europe and Asia. Russia and nations of the former Soviet Union, on the other hand, use a combination of geostationary and polar orbital configurations, because a large portion of the Eurasian landmass is in extreme northern latitudes that cannot be seen adequately from a position above the equator.

Context

As the space era entered the 1980's, the space shuttle program demonstrated its ability to transport satellites into space and even to repair them while in orbit. Thus the era of the serviceable, reusable satellite was at hand, offering operators the opportunity to upgrade onboard systems and make repairs rather than replace entire spacecraft.

In the 1960's, when the ATS program was launched, scientists had begun to look for ways to make satellites capable of performing various tasks over long periods of time. Early satellites had been in orbit for short periods, often only a few days or weeks. The need had been established for long-term, dependable, multifunction satellites.

A major problem in those early days had been that rocket technology had not attained the capability of boosting satellites or other spacecraft into the orbits required for geosynchronization. By the time the ATS series was ready for launch, however, more powerful rockets and second- and third-stage jump motor technology were available to accomplish the task.

The SMS and GOES series, along with telecommunications satellites, were among the first to take advantage of the geosynchronous capability. From their stationary vantage points, they were able to provide high-quality imagery of Earth's surface and simultaneously to monitor extraterrestrial phenomena such as solar flares and interplanetary radiation. They were also equipped with communications circuits that served dependably when unexpected demand outstripped supply of space channels for international communications traffic, including transoceanic broadcasts. They also served as relay platforms for a variety of Earth-based sensing instruments that provided critical monitoring of remote areas and natural-disaster prone regions of the Western Hemisphere and its oceans.

As the GOES series continued to provide reliable data for a multitude of users, international cooperation continued to grow, allowing the program to be tied in with those of other nations to assure complete coverage of the globe in real time. The three-dimensional character of the imagery available from the advanced GOES-4, GOES-5, and GOES-6 has also enhanced the capabilities of other programs, including Landsat, which monitors Earth resources such as oil, minerals, and water. Scientists are still looking for ways to use the deluge of data from these satellites to enhance such endeavors as urban planning and environmental protection, perhaps putting the variable of climatology into the mix with infrastructure and available water resources.

A major concern in the scientific community over the decades following the launch of SMS 1 was the reported depletion of the ozone layer of Earth's atmosphere. SMS/GOES spacecraft were among the first to relay reliable information regarding the state of worldwide atmospheric ozone.

GOES-7 was launched on April 28, 1983. The satellite was designed to sense meteorological conditions from a fixed location above the Earth, and to provide this data to operational forecasters and private interests on the ground. It was designed to replace GOES-5 and provide continuous vertical profiles of atmospheric temperature and moisture. After GOES-I was deployed on April 13, 1994, as GOES-8 (GOES-EAST), GOES-7 remained in geostationary orbit and is still used for satellite communications.

GOES-8 also provides a continuous relay of Weather Facsimile (WEFAX) and other data to users, independent of all other functions. A "fringe benefit" of GOES-8 is its ability to relay distress signals from people, aircraft, or marine vessels to the search-and-rescue ground stations of the Search and Rescue Satellite-Aided Tracking (SARSAT) system. The GOES-8 spacecraft is operational as GOES-EAST at 75°W and is still providing clear imagery.

GOES-9 was launched on May 23, 1995, and made operational as GOES-WEST. It was deactivated in August, 1998, because of failing bearings in the momentum wheels. GOES-10 was launched on April 25, 1997, to perform the same basic functions as GOES-8 and GOES-9. It was positioned at 105° west longitude. GOES-11 was launched on May 3, 2000. NASA turned it over to NOAA as an orbital backup to either GOES-8 or GEOS-10. By 2019 the GOES satellite had evolved into its fourth design. The GOES-17 spacecraft had been launched on March 1, 2018, by an Atlas V from Cape Canaveral's Space Launch Complex 41. GOES-T and GOES-U are planned to be launched in 2020 and 2024, respectively.

—*Michael S. Ameigh*

See also: Environmental Science Services Administration Satellites; Global Atmospheric Research Program; ITOS and NOAA Meteorological Satellites; Landsat 7; Meteorological Satellites; Nimbus Meteorological Satellites; Seasat; Small Explorer Program; TIROS Meteorological Satellites; Upper Atmosphere Research Satellite.

Further Reading

Ahrens, C. Donald. *Essentials of Meteorology: An Invitation to the Atmosphere*. 4th ed. Pacific Grove, Calif.: Thomson Brooks/Cole, 2005. This is a text suitable for an introductory course in meteorology. Comes complete with a CD-ROM to help explain concepts and demonstrate the atmosphere's dynamic nature.

Asrar, Ghassem, and Jeff Dozier. *EOS: Science Strategy for the Earth Observing System*. New York: Springer-Verlag, 1994. This illustrated book takes a look at the history of the Earth Observing System. It also discusses the scientific equipment used in the program. There is a list of acronyms and a bibliography.

Bader, M. J., G. S. Forbes, and J. R. Grant, eds. *Images in Weather Forecasting: A Practical Guide for Interpreting Satellite and Radar Imagery*. New York: Cambridge University Press, 1997. The aim of this work is to present the meteorology student and operational forecaster with the current techniques for interpreting satellite and radar images of weather systems in mid-latitudes. The focus of the book is the large number of illustrations.

Brun, Nancy L., and Eleanor H. Ritchie. *Astronautics and Aeronautics, 1975.* Washington, D.C.: National Aeronautics and Space Administration, 1979. A chronologically arranged compilation of press releases and accounts from popular publications regarding key events in the space program during 1975. The reports cover not only NASA activities but also the projects and discoveries of other nations' programs. Includes material regarding SMS and GOES spacecraft. Indexed.

Gatland, Kenneth. *The Illustrated Encyclopedia of Space Technology: A Comprehensive History of Space Exploration.* New York: Salamander, 1989. Gatland has assembled a number of chronologies of American, Soviet, and international space programs. This well-illustrated volume includes a chapter that discusses in detail weather observation by satellites and specifically summarizes the SMS/GOES program and its accomplishments. Specific examples of successful applications of space technology in this area are cited. Indexed.

Gavaghan, Helen. *Something New Under the Sun: Satellites and the Beginning of the Space Age.* New York: Copernicus Books, 1998. This book focuses on the history and development of artificial satellites. It centers on three major areas of development—navigational satellites, communications satellites, and weather observation and forecasting satellites.

Hirsch, Richard, and Joseph John Trento. *The National Aeronautics and Space Administration.* New York: Praeger, 1973. A well-executed chronology of the accomplishments of NASA during the first decade of space exploration. Discusses early plans for NASA's weather observation satellite program, which eventually led to SMS, GOES, and the NOAA operational systems. Photographs supplement the text. Includes an index.

Parkinson, Claire L. *Earth from Above: Using Color-Coded Satellite Images to Examine the Global Environment.* Sausalito, Calif.: University Science Books, 1997. A book for non-specialists on reading and interpreting satellite images. Explains how satellite data provide information about the atmosphere, the Antarctic ozone hole, and atmospheric temperature effects. The book includes maps, photographs, and fifty color satellite images.

Radzanowski, David P. *U.S. Civil Earth-Observation Programs: Landsat, Mission to Planet Earth, and the Weather Satellites.* Washington, D.C.: Congress Research Service, Library of Congress, 1992. A comprehensive review of weather satellites and the interpretation of their data.

Ritchie, Eleanor H. *Astronautics and Aeronautics, 1976: A Chronology.* NASA SP-4021. Washington, D.C.: National Aeronautics and Space Administration, 1984. In chronological order, offers abstracts of press accounts of space activity during the extremely active year of 1976. These accounts include the names of hundreds of individuals associated with scores of international space programs. Perhaps most useful are summaries of updates on programs such as SMS/GOES, which were ongoing at that time.

Seinfeld, John H., and Spyros Pandis. *Atmospheric Chemistry and Physics: Air Pollution to Climate.* New York: John Wiley, 1997. This is an extensive reference on atmospheric chemistry, aerosols, and atmospheric models. While the book may be too complex for the average reader, it is extremely useful as a research tool on the science of atmospheric phenomena.

Zimmerman, Robert. *The Chronological Encyclopedia of Discoveries in Space.* Westport, Conn.: Oryx Press, 2000. Provides a complete chronological history of all piloted and robotic spacecraft and explains flight events and scientific results. Suitable for all levels of research.

Solar and Heliospheric Observatory

Date: Beginning December 2, 1995
Type of program: Scientific platform

Armed with twelve instruments to study the entire Sun in detail, the Solar and Heliospheric Observatory (SOHO) traveled to an orbit 1.5 million kilometers from Earth. This stable vantage point allows SOHO to study the Sun continuously without the regular interruptions plaguing Earth-orbiting satellites as they pass through Earth's shadow.

Key Figures

Joseph Gurman, project scientist, Goddard Space Flight Center

Bernhard Fleck, European Space Agency (ESA)

Roger Bonnet, ESA director of Science

Vincente Domingo, ESA project scientist for Definition, Development, and Early Flight phases

Arthur Poland, NASA project scientist for Definition, Development, and Early Flight phases

Ken Sizemore, NASA project manager

Summary of the Satellite

Launched on December 2, 1995, the Solar and Heliospheric Observatory (SOHO) is a joint mission of the European Space Agency (ESA) and the National Aeronautics and Space Administration (NASA). SOHO's mission is to answer longstanding mysteries about the Sun's behavior by returning continuous solar observations of unprecedented accuracy and detail.

Early missions designed to study the Sun did so from an Earth orbit. As they orbited Earth, they were periodically in Earth's shadow and therefore unable to observe the Sun for roughly half of each orbit. To achieve a stable vantage point allowing continuous observations of the Sun, SOHO traveled to a point 1.5 million kilometers directly toward the Sun from the Earth. This point, L1, is one of the five Lagrangian points where the gravitational forces from the Sun and Earth are balanced. More important, L1 is the closest to Earth and Sun of these Lagrangian points. This Lagrangian point is normally unstable, meaning that if SOHO is perturbed a small amount from its orbit, it will continue to drift rather than return to its proper location. However, a proper orbit around this Lagrangian point can be stable; hence, SOHO orbits the Lagrangian point. After SOHO reached this point on February 14, 1996, its instruments were able to begin continuously observing the Sun.

SOHO is armed with twelve instruments designed to study the full range of solar phenomena. GOLF, SOI/MDI, and VIRGO are three of these instruments and are designed to study the solar interior. An additional four instruments, named CELIAS, COSTEP, ERNE, and SWAN, study the stream of particles flying out from the Sun's outer atmosphere, called the solar wind. The remaining five instruments, named SUMER, CDS, EIT, UVCS, and LASCO, study the Sun's outer atmospheric layers.

Just as researchers cannot directly probe Earth's interior, they cannot directly probe the interior of the Sun. There are, however, indirect techniques to study both. In a branch of geology known as seismology, scientists use vibrations on Earth's surface generated by earthquakes to probe Earth's interior indirectly. Similarly, a branch of solar physics known as helioseismology allows scientists to probe the Sun's interior from surface oscillations. GOLF (Global Oscillations at Low Frequencies) and SOI/MDI (Solar Oscillations Investigations/Michelson Doppler Imager) measure the speeds of the Sun's low- and high-frequency surface oscillations. VIRGO (Variability of Solar Irradiance and Gravity Oscillations) measures the Sun's energy output very precisely to track the very small changes associated both with these oscillations and with the eleven-year sunspot cycle.

The visible surface of the Sun is called the photosphere. Above the photosphere is a warmer layer called the chromosphere. The outermost and hottest layer of the Sun's atmosphere is the corona. Particles streaming out from the outermost part of the corona form the solar wind. Unlike the photosphere, the corona emits much of its energy in the ultraviolet range. SUMER (Solar Ultraviolet Measurements of Emitted Radiation), CDS (Coronal Diagnostic Spectrometer), EIT (Extreme-Ultraviolet Imaging Telescope), and UVCS (Ultraviolet Coronagraph Spectrometer) are designed to study the chromospheric and coronal ultraviolet emissions in order to probe temperatures, densities, and velocities in these regions, as well as the origin of the solar wind. LASCO (Large Angle Spectroscopic Coronagraph) blocks the Sun's visible photosphere in order to study the visible light from the corona and its transition to the solar wind.

SWAN (Solar Wind Anisotropies) uses the interactions between hydrogen atoms sweeping through the solar system and the Sun's outer atmosphere to study the shape of the solar wind. Three additional instruments study the solar wind particles as they reach SOHO. CELIAS (Charge, Element and Isotope Analysis System), COSTEP (Comprehensive Suprathermal and Energetic Particles), and ERNE (Energetic and Relativistic Nuclei and Electron Experiment) study the mass, composition, charge, and energy distribution of the solar wind particles.

SOHO reached its operational destination in early 1996, but on three separate occasions the observatory was nearly lost. In 1998, after a software change was effected, the observatory went into a flat spin. With its solar panels producing insufficient electrical power, SOHO almost went dead. Three months of heroic and painstaking efforts on the part of the control team restored SOHO to nominal operation; fortunately there was only minimal damage to the instruments, and they were all fully recommissioned by November 5, 1998. Also in 1998, SOHO's last navigational gyroscope failed. By early 1999, the control team had devised a means of maintaining attitude without gyroscopes. SOHO thus became the first three-axis stabilized spacecraft to be controlled without gyroscopes. Then, in June, 2003, the observatory suffered a stuck motor drive that threatened to stop the flow of data through the primary antenna. A maneuver that involved flipping SOHO upside down for portions of its orbit allowed the continued use of the main antenna to transmit data. With continued ingenuity, SOHO was capable of continuing to send high-priority solar data for years to come.

Contributions

Helioseismology instruments have revealed secrets of the Sun's interior. The outer layer of the Sun's interior is called the convective zone because convection currents transfer the Sun's energy to the surface. This convective layer extends 28.7 percent of the distance, approximately 200,000 kilometers, from the photosphere to the center. Below the convective zone to the Sun's core, energy is transferred by radiation in the radiative zone. The rate at which the Sun's surface rotates depends on the latitude, with the equator rotating faster. SOHO reveals that these differential rotation rates persist into the interior of the Sun through the convection zone. However, the radiative zone rotates more uniformly. The shearing that occurs in the transition between these two zones may cause the Sun's magnetic field.

SOHO has also found unexpectedly complex wind-like motions within the convective zone. Solar jet streams blowing 130 kilometers per hour relative to nearby gas circle the Sun 40,000 kilometers below the top of the convective zone at 75° solar latitude. The convective zone also has slower equatorial belts (16 kilometers per hour relative to nearby gas), reminiscent of those seen on Jupiter and Saturn. They extend to nearly half the depth of the high-latitude streams. In addition to the rotation, the top 25,000 kilometers of the convective zone is also moving toward increasing latitudes north and south from the equator at 90 kilometers per hour.

In addition to the regular long-lived interior motions, SOHO's helioseismology instruments made the first discovery of a sunquake in 1996. The sunquake consisted of transient but more powerful oscillations associated with a burst of x-ray emission.

In a further analogy to terrestrial disasters, SOHO discovered giant "tornadoes" in the Sun's atmosphere near the polar regions. They are not tornados in a strict technical sense because they have a different physical nature and cause from those of terrestrial tornadoes. However, they spiral up from the base of the solar atmosphere in a shape that resembles terrestrial tornadoes. As wide as Africa, they have steady wind speeds of 50,000 kilometers per hour, with maximum gusts ten times as fast.

The Sun's photosphere, the Sun's visible surface, is the coolest layer on the Sun at a temperature of 5,800 kelvins. The chromosphere, the next higher layer, is warmer. The very tenuous outer layer, the corona, is much hotter, with temperatures exceeding 1 million kelvins. SOHO has helped scientists understand this temperature increase. SOHO observed a magnetic carpet on the Sun's surface that may heat the corona. Each day, roughly four thousand magnetic field lines on the Sun's surface loop up from the interior then back down like the loops in a carpet. The Sun's turbulence soon snaps these loops, releasing bursts of energy that heat the corona.

SOHO observations coupled with those of the SPARTAN 201 probe have also helped solve another long-standing solar mystery, the origin of the solar wind. The wind particles surf waves in the solar magnetic field lines. The solar wind has fast and slow components. The fast component, with speeds of up to 800 kilometers per second, had been thought to originate near the Sun's poles and was twice as fast as theory predicted it should be. The SOHO observations, however, suggest that the fast magnetic field lines in the solar corona also vibrate with a variety of frequencies. Field lines vibrating at the right frequency for a particular type of particle can accelerate the particle. The particle then rides the magnetic wave outward from the Sun into the solar wind just as a surfer rides an ocean wave. In addition to the mass ejected in the solar wind, SOHO observes mass ejected from the Sun in clumps of billions of tons called coronal mass ejections (CMEs).

MDI has been able to explore the subsurface structure of sunspots, leading to a better understanding of how sunspots are formed. A comparison of EIT data between solar minima and solar maxima have provided a better understanding of how solar activity varies over solar cycles. It had been assumed that there are more coronal mass ejections as a solar maximum approached, but SOHO provided data to prove the validity of this assumption. SOHO has also produced a better understanding of the effects of solar storms, showing that a solar storm ejects radiation from the Sun immediately, that high-energy particles are ejected for a period of anywhere from fifteen minutes to several days, and that low-energy particles can be ejected for upwards of four days following the appearance of a storm.

A side benefit of SOHO imaging is that it allows for the detection of comets in the near solar space. LASCO's wide field and disk blocks the Sun's bright photosphere, allowing SOHO to observe comets much closer to the Sun than would ordinarily be possible. A large number of these comets are kamikaze comets, diving destructively into the Sun. By January, 2005, SOHO had discovered its nine hundredth comet. One of these comets, Kudo-Fujikawa, was shown live on the Internet as it passed through SOHO's field of view. Another comet, seen in 2003 and named NEAT, was observed by SOHO as it was hit by a severe solar storm. That was the first recording of such an event.

SOHO images of the Sun have proved exciting for public consumption, and SOHO comet images have had public relations and educational value as well. A contest was established to predict the timing of SOHO's discovery of its one thousandth comet. The winner would receive a Solar Max DVD, a SOHO T-shirt, and solar viewing glasses, among other educational incentives.

In addition to discovering many new comets, SOHO observed comets discovered from Earth as they passed near the Sun, including the widely observed bright Comets Hyakutake and Hale-Bopp. SWAN observed large, tenuous hydrogen clouds around these comets, produced by their outflow of water vapor. At its peak, Hale-Bopp evaporated nearly 50 million metric tons of water per day. SWAN also observed a 150-million-kilometer-long shadow of this comet on the other side of the Sun. SWAN's ability to see the other side of the Sun also allows it to see solar storms beyond the limb of the Sun and give researchers advance warning when such a storm heads toward Earth.

Context

Mariner 2 discovered the mysteriously high speed of the fast component of the solar wind in the year John H. Glenn, Jr., first orbited the Earth, 1962. The SPARTAN 201 probe, which, along with SOHO, helped solve the mystery, was flown on the space shuttle mission STS-95, when Glenn took his long-awaited second spaceflight.

Prior to SOHO, helioseismology relied on the Earth-bound observatories, such as the Global Oscillations Network Group (GONG). GONG is a series of solar observatories that must span the globe to observe the solar oscillations continuously. SOHO did not shut down GONG, but it did provide a more detailed view and is not limited by atmospheric obscurations. Several more years of continued uninterrupted observations of the Sun's

oscillations will help scientists probe deeper into the Sun's interior. Eventually they may obtain information about the Sun's core.

With its strong magnetic field, the Sun has a considerable amount of magnetic activity. This activity includes sunspots, which are dark spots on the Sun's surface; flares, which are bright bursts of energy; prominences, or material that shoots up from the Sun's surface into the corona and then loops back down along magnetic field lines; and coronal mass ejections. The Sun has long been known to have a twenty-two-year cycle in the amount of its magnetic activity in that the field reverses direction roughly every eleven years and then returns to the original direction during the next eleven years. Sunspot activity peaks during each half of the overall solar cycle. There may also be longer cycles in the amount of sunspot activity at the maximum period. The cause of these cycles is poorly understood, but they are thought to originate in the swirling and turbulence SOHO observes in the Sun's interior. The turbulence twists and knots the solar magnetic field lines, giving rise somehow to solar magnetic activity. SOHO's unprecedented views of the solar interior and its swirling circulation patterns, if continued over at least one complete solar magnetic activity cycle, should provide clues to the origin of both magnetic activity and magnetic activity cycles.

It has been suggested, but not proven, that the Sun's overall energy output varies with solar activity cycles and that the energy output changes over the longer cycles contribute to long-term climate cycles on Earth. It has not been possible to measure the Sun's energy output from Earth with sufficient accuracy to test this hypothesis. Previous satellite observations of the Sun's energy output show that it does vary a small amount with the twenty-two year solar activity cycle. SOHO can continue this work and thereby help us understand possible long-term climate cycles on Earth.

SOHO had been planned as a two-year mission. In 2019 SOHO was still providing useful solar physics data 23.5 years after its launch, clearly one of the great scientific satellite success stories. The Solar Dynamics Observer (SDO) had surpassed SOHO as the premier solar physics platform, and in 2019, science from the Parker Solar Probe reached observing distances far closer to the Sun that SOHO or even SDO could attain. However, the need to keep SOHO alive remains.

—Paul A. Heckert and Christina M. Nestlerode

See also: SMS and GOES Meteorological Satellites.

Further Reading

Day, Charles. "SOHO Observations Implicate 'Magnetic Carpet' as Source of Coronal Heating in Quiet Sun." *Physics Today* 51, no. 3 (March, 1998): 19-21. This article describes the discovery by SOHO of the source of the coronal heating in the Sun, which is one of the longstanding mysteries about the Sun that SOHO helped solve.

Gianopoulos, Andrea. "Sun Shines on SOHO and SPARTAN." *Astronomy* 27, no. 2 (February, 1999): 32-34. This is a brief news article describing the recovery of contact with the SOHO spacecraft.

Glanz, James. "Two Spacecraft Track the Solar Wind to Its Source." *Science* 278, no. 5337 (October, 1997): 387-388. This news article reports on SOHO's observations on the origin of the solar wind. The accompanying inset article describes the explanation of the solar coronal heating from SOHO observations.

Golub, Leon, and Jay M. Pasachoff. *Nearest Star: The Surprising Science of Our Sun.* Boston: Harvard University Press, 2002. Although written by two of the most active research astrophysicists, this book is accessible to a general audience. It describes most contemporary advances in solar physics.

Lang, Kenneth R. "SOHO Reveals the Secrets of the Sun." *Scientific American* 276, no. 3 (March, 1997): 40-48. A typically detailed and well-illustrated *Scientific American* essay.

McBride, Neil, and Iain Gilmour. *An Introduction to the Solar System.* New York: Cambridge University Press, 2004. This work provides a comprehensive tour of the solar system. Suitable for a high school or college course on planetary astronomy.

---. "SOHO Reveals the Secrets of the Sun." *Scientific American Special Edition* 9, no. 1 (Spring, 1998): 50-56. These two articles, although they have the same title, are similar, but not exactly the same. They summarize the knowledge scientists have gained from SOHO.

---. *Sun, Earth, and Sky.* New York: Springer-Verlag, 1995. A good source of general information about the Sun and solar phenomena as scientists understood them prior to SOHO's launch.

---. "Unsolved Mysteries of the Sun." Parts 1 and 2. *Sky and Telescope* 92 (August- September, 1996): 38-42, 24-28. An informative series of two popular articles on aspects of the Sun that scientists do not yet understand. The second article in the series concentrates on the mysteries that SOHO will help solve.

Nesme-Ribes, Elizabeth, Sallie L. Baliunas, and Dmitry Sokoloff. "The Stellar Dynamo." *Scientific American* 275, no. 2 (August, 1996): 46-52. A popular article on the Sun's magnetic activity cycle. This article also notes the connection between the amount of the Sun's magnetic activity and its total energy output.

Zimmerman, Robert. *The Chronological Encyclopedia of Discoveries in Space.* Westport, Conn.: Oryx Press, 2000. Provides a complete chronological history of all crewed and robotic spacecraft and explains flight events and scientific results. Suitable for all levels of research.

Solar Maximum Mission

Date: February 14, 1980
Type of program: Scientific platform

The Solar Maximum Mission (SMM) was designed to study the Sun during the 1980 peak of the eleven-year solar cycle. In addition, the satellite was the world's first to be retrieved, repaired, and redeployed in space.

Key Figures

Robert L. Crippen, Jr. (b. 1937), STS 41-C commander
Francis R. "Dick" Scobee (1939-1986), STS 41-C pilot
Terry J. Hart (b. 1946), STS 41-C mission specialist
James D. A. "Ox" Van Hoften (b. 1944), STS 41-C mission specialist
George D. "Pinky" Nelson (b. 1950), STS 41-C mission specialist
Frank J. Cepollina, Multimission Modular Spacecraft and Flight Support System project manager, Goddard Space Flight Center

Summary of the Mission

The Solar Maximum Mission (SMM), also known as Solar Max, was initiated to continue the investigation of the Sun begun by Skylab's Apollo Telescope Mount and by the Orbiting Solar Observatory satellites. Solar Max's mission was to study activity on the Sun during the 1980 peak of solar activity, simultaneously recording information in a broad spectrum of wavelengths. (The spectrum refers to the electromagnetic spectrum, the entire range of wavelengths of electromagnetic energy, from gamma rays to radio waves and including visible light.) A primary focus of the mission was to study the mechanism behind flare activity. (A solar flare is a tremendous eruption on a small area of the Sun's surface that generates highly energetic charged particles and light.) The original estimated lifetime of the Solar Maxsatellite was one to two years.

Solar Max was not a solitary venture but was a key component in the International Solar Maximum Year's program to study the Sun. More than fifty observatories around the world participated in the International Solar Maximum Year, coordinating their observations of the Sun during the time of its maximum activity. Observations from orbiting instruments such as Solar Max and the International Sun-Earth Explorers were supported by simultaneous observations from ground based observatories. From a control room at Goddard Space Flight Center, current images of the Sun could be obtained from several observatories. All the active regions of the Sun were monitored and predictions made as to likely targets for Solar Max. Amateur observers were also involved, photographing and sketching those flare events that were intense in visible light.

The Solar Max spacecraft was the first satellite to use a new system designed specifically to take advantage of the capabilities of the space shuttle. This multi-mission modular spacecraft (MMS) was a standardized base used for a variety of satellites. Multiple missions could be achieved using a system of modules designed to be replaced in space by shuttle crews. Such replacements would require the removal of only two bolts and could be accomplished with a special tool designed for use in zero gravity. Previously, expensive satellites could be completely disabled by problems as trivial as a

The crew of STS-41C practices retrieval maneuvers in the Neutral Buoyancy Simulator. This voyage initiated a series of firsts for NASA; the first satellite retrieval, the first service use of a new space system called the Marned Maneuvering Unit (MMU), the first in-orbit repair, the first use of the Remote Manipulator System (RMS), and the Space Shuttle Challenger's first space flight. After the repairs were completed, Solar Max was redeposited in orbit with the assistance of the RMS. (NASA)

blown fuse. With the space shuttle and this new modular design, satellites could be repaired in space and restored to usefulness for a fraction of the cost of replacing them. Originally, the National Aeronautics and Space Administration (NASA) had planned to retrieve Solar Max with the space shuttle in 1984 and return it to Earth before the spacecraft reentered Earth's atmosphere.

The instruments aboard Solar Max were the most diverse and sophisticated yet orbited to study solar activity. There were six major experiments to record information in wavelengths ranging from visible light to gamma rays. A group of Dutch scientists built the first orbiting instrument with the ability to photograph the Sun in "hard," or penetrating, x-rays. Another instrument was designed to record gamma-ray emissions in solar flares, and other instruments included hard and soft x-ray detectors, a device to record the ultraviolet spectrum of the Sun, and one to produce images of the Sun's corona and follow the effects of flares into interplanetary space. (The corona is the part of the Sun's

atmosphere above the visible surface and is observable only during a total solar eclipse.)

A seventh experiment, called the Active Cavity Radiometer Irradiance Monitor (ACRIM), was intended to observe variations in the solar constant in wavelengths from the far ultraviolet to the far infrared. (The solar constant is the amount of solar energy falling on a unit area of Earth every second.) ACRIM produces one solar constant measurement every two minutes. All the instruments were designed to look at the same area of the Sun at the same time.

Solar Max was launched on February 14, 1980, into a circular orbit 570 kilometers above Earth. Instruments aboard began recording flares almost immediately. The spacecraft was to operate virtually automatically, monitoring preselected regions on the disk of the Sun for signs of impending activity. The areas were to be chosen from daily activity forecasts prepared by a solar observatory at NASA's Marshall Space Flight Center in Alabama. Solar data gathered there would reveal areas where solar activity was most likely to occur.

As an area brightened rapidly, the x-ray detector aboard the satellite would electronically alert the other instruments, which then would focus on the region and conduct a series of preplanned observations. In this way, activity on the Sun could be studied from the "preflare" phase through the first major release of energy and then through the entire process.

Solar Max functioned perfectly for about ten months, returning useful information on flare and sunspot activity. Then in November, 1980, the spacecraft suffered a malfunction. The fuses began to blow in its primary attitude control system (the system that controls the satellite's orientation toward its targeted areas of study). In the vacuum of space, the small fuses had degraded to the point at which they could no longer carry their load of current. By mid-December, three of four attitude controls had been lost, and the spacecraft was disabled. Although the mission ended before its estimated lifetime was over, the wealth of information returned by the satellite made the mission a successful one.

In the spring of 1981, a team of engineers from NASA's Johnson Space Center in Houston began studying the possibility of an in-orbit repair of the satellite. Such a repair would require extravehicular activity (EVA) by a shuttle astronaut, who would first stop the satellite's motion by using a special grappling device. The shuttle's Remote Manipulator System would then take over, moving the satellite into the shuttle's payload bay, where the failed modules would be replaced. Brought back to full function, the satellite was expected to be useful for two years or more.

Besides restoring an expensive and useful satellite, the repair project was seen as an opportunity to demonstrate the capability of a space shuttle crew to retrieve and repair satellites in orbit. This demonstration would be important to civil and military space planners and would be a crucial factor in planning upcoming space missions. In early 1982, however, it appeared that the repair mission would be canceled because of funding priorities, but the mission was considered important enough to transfer funding from other projects. After two years of planning and rehearsal, the mission was scheduled for April of 1984; *Challenger*'s STS 41-C crew would make the attempt.

Although Solar Max was approached, a first attempt to retrieve the spacecraft with the Manned Maneuvering Unit failed. Because there was a danger that the depleted batteries would destroy sensitive instruments, a second attempt was made two days later. On April 10, 1984, Solar Max was successfully secured in *Challenger's* cargo bay. Repairs were completed, and the satellite returned to its own independent orbit on April 12. Within a

month, all the spacecraft's systems were again operational.

In the interval between its failure and repair, improvements were made to the Solar Maximum Mission. NASA's Tracking and Data-Relay Satellite (TDRS) was launched in 1983, and it provided a much more efficient way to communicate with Solar Max. Astronomers could receive images from Solar Max immediately and formulate new observing sequences based on the solar activity in progress. The more than three years that Solar Max was dysfunctional provided scientists with the opportunity to analyze the data they had already received. Perhaps even more important, the time allowed scientists to alter some of the experiments aboard the satellite.

Because the solar cycle was approaching a minimum after the repair, Solar Max studied the different types of activity that appeared during a decline in solar activity. The satellite was also expected to last until the 1991 solar maximum. Solar Max also studied other objects in the sky. Beginning in late 1986, investigators attempted to measure x- and gamma-ray spectra from Cygnus X-1, an unusual object that is suspected to harbor a black hole. Solar Max observed Comet Halley in 1986 when the comet was too close to the Sun for ground-based observation, and the satellite was used to study the supernova that appeared in January, 1987, in the Large Magellanic Cloud. The gamma-ray instrument aboard Solar Max is the only orbiting instrument sensitive enough to detect emissions coming from a supernova.

As the mission stretched toward the beginning of a new solar maximum, it continued to provide solar data not only at its maximum activity but also during the entire solar cycle. Solar Max also extended the reach of its sophisticated instruments beyond the Sun to study the processes in other stars. From a spectacular beginning and a disappointing end to an unexpected revival, Solar Max challenged the astrophysical community with information that began to create a new understanding of the Sun.

Solar Max recorded its final data on November 24, 1989, and reentered on December 2, 1989.

Contributions

A "new" Sun is emerging from the results obtained from Solar Max, along with studies from previous orbiting solar satellites. Together, these solar satellites have contributed a major percentage of scientists' knowledge of solar processes. The primary area of interest has been the study of solar flares. The 1980 solar maximum was especially active, and Solar Max recorded information on thousands of flares. Solar flares are usually associated with sunspots, regions on the Sun's surface that appear dark and are associated with intense magnetic fields. Solar Max provided the first direct evidence that the interaction of solar magnetic fields can give rise to a flare.

At the onset of a flare, there are bursts of high-energy X and ultraviolet radiation. The timing of the bursts gives information about where they take place. It was found that the bursts occur simultaneously, and that they occur at the locations where magnetic fields are anchored in the lower solar atmosphere. Surprisingly, the largest flares do not necessarily produce the largest amount of radiation. Some flares have been known to produce ten times the gamma rays that are produced by flares more than twice their size.

Researchers have found that flare mechanisms can produce higher temperatures than were thought to exist on the Sun. Curiously, the solar material does not expand when heated but increases in density, indicating that something is pressurizing it. This is an important finding, because thermonuclear fusion researchers are trying to accomplish the same effect on Earth.

It was previously believed that the chemical composition of the Sun was uniform and constant.

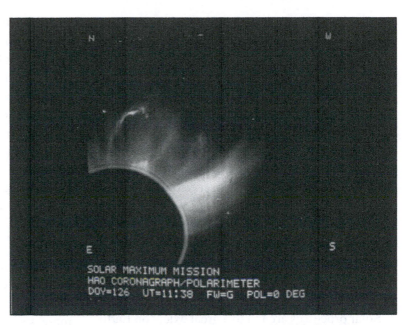

A coronal transient as seen by the SMM on May 5, 1980. (NASA)

Solar Max observations, however, have shown evidence of variations in the abundance of calcium from flare to flare and in the proportions of other chemicals in different levels of the Sun's atmosphere.

Solar Max has also made important observations on the nature of coronal transients. These are huge bubbles of plasma (superheated gases) often containing 9 billion kilograms of matter, which are thrown away from the corona at speeds up to 1.6 million kilometers per hour. It seems from the data that these transients may precede the flare itself and not be caused by it, as was previously theorized. Thus, flares may not cause the many phenomena associated with them but may be merely one step in the entire process.

It has been observed that as a group of sunspots crosses the face of the Sun there is a slight drop in the Sun's total output of energy. It is not yet known whether this is a true drop in energy or whether the energy is being redirected in some way. In fact, the variability of the solar constant is one of the most notable discoveries made by Solar Max. ACRIM data show a downward energy trend of 0.019 percent per year between 1980 and 1985. As new data are obtained throughout the next solar cycle, researchers will be looking for this trend to reverse, possibly indicating a variation linked with the solar activity cycle.

Context

The Solar Maximum Mission came at a time when solar physicists had had several years to study data returned by previous solar studies, particularly from the series of Orbiting Solar Observatories and from the Apollo Telescope Mount aboard Skylab. As much as those studies advanced knowledge of solar processes, they raised a new set of questions requiring a new, more sophisticated generation of instrumentation. Solar Max was designed in direct response to these needs.

Solar processes are felt to a great extent on Earth. During a large flare, ejected particles, x-rays, and gamma rays disrupt Earth's atmosphere, in turn disturbing radio communications and electrical power. Familiar manifestations of this influence are auroral displays seen in polar regions. Radiation during the largest flares could also be lethal to astronauts who are above the protective layer of Earth's atmosphere.

Weather patterns and climate are ultimately determined by the interaction between Earth and radiation from the Sun. Theoretically, a change in the Sun's output by as little as 0.5 percent per century could produce profound changes in Earth's climate. A decrease of 6 percent in the Sun's radiation would cover the planet with ice. It is only by monitoring the solar constant and its effects that scientists will be able to determine this effect and predict future changes in climate.

Scientists now have data showing that the solar constant does indeed vary. By monitoring this variability over time, it may be possible to predict long-term climatic cycles and changes. With Solar Max able to record the Sun's activity for more than a complete solar cycle, an important record is being made to establish a baseline on the Sun's activity.

The Sun is the most important factor influencing life on Earth. Its study, therefore, is of utmost importance. Besides being of vital concern to life, the Sun is also a conveniently nearby star and thus provides an excellent laboratory for the study of stars. Moreover, because the Sun provides the energy needs of Earth, there may come a time when the Sun's power can be harnessed to power human technology. Perhaps with further study of the Sun, more secrets of its generation of power will be revealed.

In addition to the vast harvest of scientific data, however, Solar Max was an important milestone in space science. The reusable design of the satellite and its in-orbit repair can be seen as a first step toward humanity's increased ability to live and work in space.

—Divonna Ogier

See also: Compton Gamma Ray Observatory; Explorers: Solar; Launch Vehicles; Manned Maneuvering Unit; Orbiting Solar Observatories; Parker Solar Probe; Solar and Heliospheric Observatory; Solar Dynamics Observer; Space Shuttle Mission STS-6; Space Shuttle Flights, 1984; Space Shuttle Mission STS 41-B; Space Shuttle Mission STS 41-C; Space Shuttle Flights, July-December, 1985.

Further Reading

Chaikin, Andrew. "Solar Max: Back from the Edge." *Sky and Telescope* 67 (June, 1984): 494- 497. This article, one of several published by *Sky and Telescope* about the Solar Maximum Mission, discusses the status and results of the mission. Describes the satellite and includes illustrations of the spacecraft and images taken by its instruments. For the amateur astronomer.

Cornell, James, and Paul Gorenstein, eds. *Astronomy from Space: Sputnik to Space Telescope.* Cambridge, Mass.: MIT Press, 1985. An overview of the previous twenty-five years of astronomical research from space. Written by experts in the fields covered, these pieces are intended for those with some scientific background.

Eddy, John A. *A New Sun: The Solar Results from Skylab*. NASA SP-402. Washington, D.C.: Government Printing Office, 1979. Describes the Skylab mission in detail and discusses what Solar Maximum Mission 1223 is known about the Sun. Written for the layperson with an interest in astronomy.

Fire of Life: The Smithsonian Book of the Sun. Washington, D.C.: Smithsonian Exposition Books, 1981. A collection of articles geared for general audiences. Includes cultural history as well as projections of how the Sun might be used once a better understanding of its secrets is gained. Beautifully illustrated.

Gregory, William H. "Aftermath of a Rescue." *Aviation Week and Space Technology* 120 (April 23, 1985): 13. This article is part of a series of articles on the space shuttle mission to repair Solar Max. Written for professionals in the field of avionics, but readable for advanced college students. Illustrated.

Shayler, David J. *Walking in Space: Development of Space Walking Techniques*. Chichester, England: Springer-Praxis, 2003. Shayler provides a comprehensive overview and analysis of EVA techniques, drawing on original documentation, personal interviews with astronauts with experience in EVAs, and accounts by those involved in suit design and EVA planning and operations.

Strong, Keith T., Bernhard M. Haisch, J. T. Schmelz, and Julia L. R. Saba, eds. *The Many Faces of the Sun: A Summary of the Results from NASA's Solar Maximum Mission*. New York: Springer-Verlag, 1999. NASA's Solar Maximum Mission satellite's observations of the Sun have led to many discoveries in solar physics and atomic physics. This book collects the results in a single volume to provide a snapshot of the current state of knowledge of solar physics. An expert in solar physics has written each chapter.

Soyuz and Progress Spacecraft

Date: Beginning November 28, 1966
Type of spacecraft: Piloted spacecraft

Originally designed as part of Soviet programs for piloted orbital flight and a later-abandoned piloted landing on the Moon, the Soyuz spacecraft program pioneered docking in space, spacewalking between spacecraft, and robotic missions. After the United States' victory in the "race to the Moon" (1969), the Soyuz spacecraft made the first space stations possible, becoming the workhorse vehicle in supplying and ferrying cosmonauts to the Soviet/Russian space stations Salyut and Mir. For some time after the U.S. shuttle accidents in which first Challenger (1986) and then Columbia (2003) were lost, Soyuz and its robotic version, Progress, have been the major vehicles to transport astronauts, cosmonauts, and supplies to the International Space Station.

Key Figures

Sergei Pavlovich Korolev (1907-1966), Soyuz chief designer
Vasili Mishin (1917-2001), Progress chief designer
Alexei Isayev (1908-1971), rocket designer

Summary of the Mission

Created as a multipurpose spacecraft for operations in Earth orbit and for use as a cargo ferry, the Soyuz was designed in the mid-1960's by the legendary Soviet rocket scientist Sergei Korolev. It basically consists of three sections: an orbital module used as a working area; a descent module, which contains controls and housing for the crew and which carries cosmonauts into space and back to Earth; and a service module, which houses communications, power, and KDTU-35 propulsion units (main and backup) designed by the rocket design bureau of Alexei Isayev. Depending on circumstances, it has carried either two or three cosmonauts. While U.S. astronauts in pre-shuttle spacecraft returned for landings in the water, Soviet cosmonauts returned on land. The Soyuz descent module features a drag parachute, a large main parachute, and retrorockets to slow the module as it approaches the ground.

Soyuz (meaning "union") was in some ways a Soviet answer to the U.S. Gemini spacecraft, which carried two astronauts. At 3,500 kilograms, Gemini was smaller than Soyuz, which weighs more than 6,000 kilograms. Gemini was an spacecraft intermediate between the smaller, single-astronaut Mercury spacecraft, weighing only about a one-fourth as much, and the larger Apollo Command Module (CM), which carried three suited astronauts and was used as part of the lunar landing program. While weighing twice as much as Soyuz, the Apollo CM provided for only 6 cubic meters of living space, compared to the 9 cubic meters available in the Soyuz orbital module. The U.S. shuttle, able to carry a crew of nine, dwarfs them all.

Soyuz has been the most heavily utilized of all Soviet spacecraft, but two other versions were also planned: a lunar flyby model named Zond, which omitted the orbital module, and a larger version (weighing more than 10,000 kilograms) intended to be part of the eventually abandoned Soviet Moon-landing program. Zond ("probe" in Russian) flew around the Moon on missions 4, 5, 6, 7, and 8.

The first launch of Soyuz without cosmonauts aboard occurred on November 28, 1966, as Kosmos 133. The first piloted flight, Soyuz 1, occurred on

April 23, 1967. Early Soyuz missions used the 7K-OK module, which was designed for a piloted lunar mission and could support three crew members without pressurized suits. It had a docking port that allowed two Soyuz spacecraft to join. The Soyuz launch vehicle, a three-stage rocket designated the Soyuz 11A511, was itself a modification of the Vostok 8K72K rocket used in the Vostok piloted missions and the Voskhod 11A57 rocket used for the Voskhod two-person missions.

Hardware and docking difficulties plagued the early flights of Soyuz. Soyuz 1, launched on April 23, 1967, at 00:35 Coordinated Universal Time (UTC), carried a single cosmonaut, Vladimir Komarov (1927-1967). The mission was presented as a test of space conditions and a project to conduct scientific and medical experiments. It was supposed to rendezvous with Soyuz 2, to be launched the next day carrying three cosmonauts. Problems with Soyuz 1's orientation detectors complicated maneuvering the craft. The Soyuz 2 launch was canceled and Soyuz 1 was deorbited as soon as it passed over the Soviet Union. The main parachute did not unfurl because of problems with a pressure sensor, and the manually deployed reserve chute tangled, making the spacecraft fall to Earth nearly unbraked. Komarov was killed by the impact.

It would be eighteen months before the next Soyuz flight, the joint mission between the robotic Soyuz 2 and the piloted Soyuz 3. The two craft rendezvoused successfully, but cosmonaut Georgi Beregovoi could get within only a meter of Soyuz 2. Docking would wait until the next joint mission.

Because there was no passageway or entrance through the docking ports of early Soyuz spacecraft, a crew transfer would require a spacewalk

Control panel within a Soyuz. (via Wikimedia Commons)

from one vehicle to another. This was achieved during the Soyuz 4 and 5 flights on January 16, 1969. Cosmonauts Yevgeny Khrunov, Soyuz 5 research engineer, and Aleksei Yeliseyev, Soyuz 5 flight engineer, conducted the world's first spacewalk, or EVA, between spacecraft. They transferred from Soyuz 5 to the Soyuz 4 orbital module (which also served as an airlock) and returned to Earth with the commander of Soyuz 4, Vladimir Shatalov. At the time, this mission was intended as a prelude to a Soviet lunar landing mission, which would require a cosmonaut to spacewalk to an orbiting spacecraft.

A second version of Soyuz, the 7K-11, removed the orbital module in order to create extra space for the cosmonauts and for a reserve parachute. It was designed to circle the Moon, but the design was abandoned after failures of the reentry system. Also trouble-prone was the Soyuz model 7K-OKS, the first to feature a docking tunnel that allowed direct transfer from one orbital module to the other. The spacecraft was pressurized, but there was not enough space for the cosmonauts to wear pressurized suits. This model was abandoned after tragedy befell the crew of Soyuz 11, which was launched on June 6, 1971. After docking with the first space station, Salyut 1, all three crew members died on reentry when a pressurization valve on Soyuz failed.

In order to create space for cosmonauts to wear protective pressurized suits, the next model, the 7KT, was designed for only two cosmonauts. In November, 1980, this model was used in the Soyuz T-3 mission, which included an improved navigation system that could fly the spacecraft automatically. Other versions of the Soyuz spacecraft have included the Soyuz TM, introduced in 1986, which featured an improved system for rendezvous and docking with the Mir Space Station, as well as improved communications and landing systems. There is also a version of Soyuz designated 7K-T/ A9, which was designed for flying to the Almaz military space stations. Details of its structure are largely classified.

In the Apollo-Soyuz Test Project (ASTP) of July, 1975, a Soyuz 7K-M and Apollo spacecraft successfully docked, and Soviet cosmonaut Alexei Leonov became the first non-American to enter an American spacecraft. Because of American concerns about compatibility, including the different cabin pressures on the two vehicles, modifications were made to Soyuz. U.S. astronauts were reportedly surprised that Soviet cosmonauts on Soyuz calculated burn times with a stop watch and used paper tape, instead of a computer, for many flight calculations.

The Soyuz spacecraft has undergone four major changes since the first model appeared in 1967. The Soyuz T (Transport), introduced in 1979, featured larger solar panels for longer

independent flights to the Salyut space stations and carried a crew of two. Soyuz TM (Transport Modification) began service in 1986. It featured multiple improvements in the design, including the introduction of a weight-saving computerized flight-control system and improved emergency escape system. These upgrades allowed for three crew members, while they could be still protected with pressure suits. Soyuz TMA (Transport Modification Anthropometric) contains redesigned seats and suspension to accommodate American astronauts, who on average are taller than cosmonauts, and a new set of computer displays. It made its first crewed flight, Soyuz TMA-1, on October 30, 2002, and carried the fifth International Space Station visiting crew. The first next-generation vehicle, Soyuz MS-1 launched on July 7, 2016, and carried cosmonaut Ivanishin, Japanese astronaut Onishi, and NASA astronaut Rubins to the International Space Station. As of 2019 the Soyuz MS-13 spacecraft was docked to the International Space Station in service to the Expedition Sixty and Sixty One station residents. Soyuz is ultimately intended to be replaced by a new spacecraft called Federation.

On January 20, 1978, supplies and other cargo were ferried to the Salyut 6 space station by the first

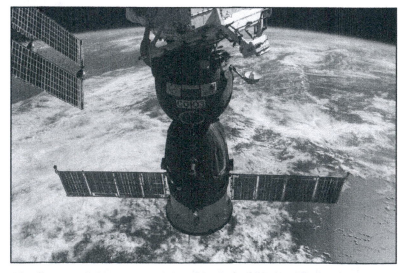

The Soyuz MS-01 spacecraft is seen docked to the International Space Station. (NASA)

Progress robot cargo ship that could carry 2,300 kilograms of cargo to a space station. At some 8 meters in length, it is slightly longer than the piloted Soyuz craft. It was calculated that the average cosmonaut would consume up to 30 kilograms of materials per day. Because the storage space in Soyuz was too small to furnish such materials on a constant basis, Vasili Mishin's Central Design Bureau of Experimental Machine Building (TsKBEM), now S. P. Korolev Rocket and Space Corporation Energia, worked to maximize cargo space by eliminating life-support systems. In place of a reentry module, Progress features a forward pressurized module for clothes, food, correspondence, and other equipment. A second compartment carries fuel, with much of the ducting being located on the outside of the spacecraft, so that poisonous gases will not enter the space station. The Progress retains the Soyuz's third, or rear, propellant module, with engines to orient the spacecraft for automatic docking. Progress always docks to the aft port of the station it was resupplying. After delivering supplies, Progress is generally loaded with waste material and sent to burn up in the atmosphere.

The Progress M was essentially the same spacecraft as the original Progress, but it featured improvements from the Soyuz T and Soyuz TM. It could spend up to thirty days in autonomous flight and was able to carry 100 kilograms more to Mir. In addition, for the first time it could return items to Earth. This was accomplished by using the Raduga (Russian for "rainbow") capsule, which could carry up to 150 kilograms of cargo. The supplies were brought to Mir in the Progress M cargo craft's dry cargo compartment. For return, the capsule would be substituted for the Progress's docking probe before it left the space station. After the Progress M performed its deorbit burn, the capsule was ejected at an altitude of 120 kilometers to reenter the atmosphere independently. It would then parachute to a landing area in Russia.

It was 1.5 meters long and 60 centimeters in diameter and had a "dry weight" of 350 kilograms. For the first time, Progress could dock to the forward port of the station and still transfer fuel. It also used the same rendezvous system as the Soyuz and featured solar panels for the first time.

Progress M freighters included a redesigned refueling section to allow more fuel to be delivered to space stations. Progress M-1 launched in 1989. Progress M-67 ended the series with its launch in 2008. Progress M freighters flew to both Mir and the International Space Station. This model was replaced by the MS version. Progress MS-1 launched on December 21, 2015, and docked to the International Space Station two days later. It undocked on July 2, 2106. As of 2019 the Progress MS-12 freighter had been launched. There was no estimate at that time as to whether or not the MS version would be upgraded further.

A Progress resupply spacecraft is seen docked to the International Space Station. (NASA)

Contributions

Although much of the scientific work in the Soviet Union's (later Russia's) space program was carried out on the nation's space stations, significant knowledge was also gained through experiments and observations made on various Soyuz missions themselves. Soyuz 6 included experiments with welding in a microgravity vacuum and photographing Earth in different spectral bands. Weather and geological observations were made on Soyuz 9, during which the Siberian snow cover was studied and a storm warning was sent to a Siberian town well in advance of weather forecasters. Earth's surface was studied with an eye to economic benefits. Fluorescent lights were used to grow plants on Soyuz 11. The stars were studied with the large astrophysical camera, Orion 2, on Soyuz 13. The behavior of turtles and plants in weightlessness was investigated during Soyuz 20. A specially built Carl Zeiss camera on Soyuz 22 allowed six photographs to be taken of the same section of Earth simultaneously with exposures in different parts of the visible and electromagnetic spectrum.

Russian cosmonaut Dmitry Kondratyev, Expedition 27 commander, photographs the departure of the unpiloted Progress 41 supply vehicle from a window in the Zvezda Service Module of the International Space Station. (NASA)

Since Soyuz missions involved placing cosmonauts in space for extended lengths of time, particularly valuable knowledge was gained about human behavior over long periods lived in conditions of microgravity. Soyuz 9 proved the importance of having cosmonauts exercise in space and the dangers of the resulting fatigue that exceeded the expected "space sickness"—so much so that when the crew returned to Earth, the ground crew reported they were slow to respond and lost concentration easily. Even on the tragic Soyuz 11 mission, the cosmonauts were required to exercise for two hours a day on a bicycle, treadmill, and chest exerciser. As a result, the crew did not report fatigue until the third week and were able to complete more than 340 orbits.

Context

The Soyuz project was very much affected by the desire of the Soviet government to outdistance the United States in space. Although it was originally designed as part of the plans of Korolev to land Soviet cosmonauts on the Moon, the project was delayed by political considerations. Soviet premier Nikita Khrushchev wanted impressive Soviet achievements to match those of the U.S. Gemini Program and insisted that the Soyuz project, planned to begin in 1964, be delayed in favor of Soviet space "spectaculars" through the Voskhod program, which achieved the first flights of multiperson spacecraft and the first walk in space. By the time the Soyuz program was implemented in 1966, the United States was well on its way to Moon landings. As a result, the goals of the Soyuz project focused on long-term orbital flights and Soyuz became primarily a support vehicle for the Salyut and Mir space stations.

Korolev's death in 1966 and Khrushchev's ouster in 1964 deprived the nation's space program of its most important designer and most important sponsor, and the end of the Cold War in the late 1980's created additional problems. The space program's budget was severely slashed. With the dissolution of the Soviet Union in 1991, the space program was required to pay more than $100 million to the newly independent republic of Kazakhstan just to use the major launch facilities at Baikonur. Yet the success of the robotic Progress ferry and its promise as a commercial vehicle have given new impetus Russia's almost continuous presence in space.

In June, 1997, the Mir Space Station almost had to be abandoned when the Progress M-34 spacecraft crashed into the station and caused a loss of hull pressure. After the loss of the shuttle *Columbia*, Soyuz and Progress were the only means to supply the International Space Station. Malfunctions and other problems continue to trouble the program. In May, 2003, when International Space Station Expedition Six returned to Earth, the craft landed so far off target that rescuers could not find it for two hours.

Nevertheless, Soyuz and Progress continue to be the most frequently used space vehicles for global space programs, with the Progress spacecraft compiling a record of more than ten thousand days of robotic missions in space. Soyuz has accumulated more than thirteen thousand days in space and has transported more than 150 individuals.. Some of the seats have been offered commercially.

The European Space Agency (ESA) and Japanese Aerospace Exploration Agency (JAXA) both developed their own supply freighters. The European freighter was called the Automated Transfer Vehicle. Five of the ATVs flew before the vehicle was cancelled. The Japanese freighter was called the H-II Transfer Vehicle (HTV). As of 2019 JAXA was preparing to launch HTV-8 during the fall season. Both of these freighters were capable of carrying much more than a Progress vehicle. Commercial resupply vehicles were developed by SpaceX and Orbital ATK (eventually Northrup

Grumman). The SpaceX vehicle was called Dragon, the Orbital vehicle called Cygnus. As of 2019 SpaceX was in the process of sending the CRS-18 Dragon to the space station, and Northrup Grumman the NS-12 Cygnus. Both of those commercial vehicles easily surpassed the resupply capabilities of Progress vehicles, but could not hold as much as either ATV or HTV.

In 2011 NASA retired the space shuttle fleet. As a result, the only way to send humans to the International Space Station was aboard the Soyuz transport. Soyuz was to have been replaced as a primary vehicle for astronaut crew rotations shortly after the shuttle fleet retirement, but Commercial Crew Program development proved to be more difficult and costly than originally planned. Although the first SpaceX Crew Dragon and Boeing Corporation CST-100 Starliner piloted missions were expected before the end of 2019, by the time of the fiftieth anniversary of Apollo 11, astronauts were still launching along with their cosmonaut counterparts from the Tyuratam Cosmodrome (Baikonur) aboard Soyuz transports. In fact, on the very day of the fiftieth anniversary of the Apollo 11 Moon landing (July 20, 2019), the Soyuz MS-13 spacecraft launched from Kazakhstan with NASA astronauts Morgan, ESA astronaut Parmitano, and RSA cosmonaut Skvortsov aboard. After six orbits they docked to the International Space Station.

As of 2019 the need for Soyuz and Progress vehicles remains strong.

—Niles R. Holt, Russell R. Tobias,
and David G. Fisher

See also: Apollo-Soyuz Test Project; Escape from Piloted Spacecraft; International Space Station: Crew Return Vehicles; International Space Station: 2001; International Space Station: 2002; Russia's Mir Space Station; Soyuz Launch Vehicle; Space Shuttle; Space Shuttle-Mir: Joint Missions; Space Shuttle Mission STS-71/Mir Primary Expedition Eighteen. Soyuz and Progress Spacecraft 1229

Further Reading

Bova, Ben. *Workshops in Space*. New York: Dutton, 1974. A portion of this book describes the scientific work done during the Apollo-Soyuz joint mission. It features many photos of rockets, modules, and models and includes illustrations of the method by which the Apollo and Soyuz craft carried out rendezvous and docking operations. Appropriate for elementary and middle school students.

Briggs, Carole S. *Women in Space*. Minneapolis: Lerner, 1999. Two Soviet women cosmonauts are among the figures profiled who have had major roles in space exploration. The book also contains photographs of women prominent in the space programs of both the United States and the Soviet Union/Russia. Appropriate for elementary and middle school students

Hall, Rex, and David Shayler. *Soyuz: A Universal Spacecraft*. Chichester, England: Springer- Praxis, 2003. The first comprehensive work in English specifically devoted to the Soyuz program, this book traces the history of the Soyuz spacecraft since 1967 and the Progress robotic spacecraft since 1978. The book details many of the design modifications made to the T and TM series of Soyuz spacecraft, and it includes a table listing the spacecraft's many variations, developmental dates, and the dates of first launches for each version. It uses Soviet sources and provides many pictures and drawings. Dedicated to Komarov and the three cosmonauts who died in the Soyuz 11 mission. Appropriate for college students and general readers.

Hardy, David A., and Patrick Moore. *Future: Fifty Years in Space—The Challenge of the Stars*. New York: HarperCollins, 2004. A beautifully illustrated book that examines how rockets have changed our view not only of the solar system but also of the universe. Hardy and Moore speculate regarding where future space missions might travel and what they might study. Appropriate for high school students, college students, and general readers.

Harford, James. *Korolev: How One Man Masterminded the Soviet Drive to Beat America to the Moon*. New York: John Wiley & Sons, 1997. A detailed biography of the life and achievements of Korolev, the designer of many of the early Soviet spacecraft, particularly the Soyuz. Emphasis is placed on Korolev's struggles to convince the Soviet government to approve his vision of the country's space program. The book explores one of Korolev's greatest disappointments: that the Soviet government wished him to remain anonymous and allowed him to be identified only as "the chief designer." Includes a detailed chronology. Appropriate for college students and general readers.

Harvey, Brian. *Race into Space: The Soviet Space Programme*. Chichester, England: Ellis Horwood Publishers, 1988. A comprehensive review of the Soviet space program through the 1980's—from Sputnik to the Soviet space stations—this volume contains a chronology of major events in the Soviet program and a list of Soviet piloted missions. It also includes photographs of various figures in the Soviet program, especially cosmonauts. Appropriate for college students and general readers.

Soyuz Launch Vehicle

Date: Beginning 1957
Type of technology: Expendable launch vehicles

The Soyuz launch vehicle's reliability not only made possible the Salyut and Mir space station projects but also allowed the Soviet Union to set records for the amount of time cosmonauts remained in space and to conduct the first spacewalk between spacecraft. In the aftermath of the space shuttle Columbia accident, Soyuz has been the sole launch vehicle available to supply and ferry astronauts to and from the International Space Station.

Key Figures

Sergei Pavlovich Korolev (1907-1966), Soyuz project director
Valentin Petrovitch Glushko (1908-1989), rocket design pioneer
Alexei Isayev (1908-1971), rocket designer

Summary of the Vehicle

Soyuz launch vehicles were derived from the first Soviet intercontinental ballistic missile, designed during the 1950's by the OKB-1 design bureau of legendary Soviet rocket visionary Sergei Pavlovich Korolev. Korolev had been a designer for the Soviet Union's first liquid-fueled rocket, the "09" rocket, developed in the 1930's. Although he was imprisoned for a time by Soviet dictator Joseph Stalin, Korolev eventually became the director of the Soviet space program. Valentin Glushko. who also survived Stalin's purges, became the chief engine designer for Soviet rockets. When Russian troops captured the German rocket research and construction center of Peenemünde in 1945, both Korolev and Glushko were sent to Germany to examine the program. In the late 1940's, they designed the Pobeda ("victory") missile.

During the early and mid-1950's, Soviet scientists began discussing the use of the country's new intercontinental ballistic missile, the Raketa 7 (R-7), then in development, to launch Earth satellites.

The "secret" designation for large ballistic missiles and space launchers consisted of the letter R followed by a sequential number, followed by letters indicating a modification to the basic design (R-1, R-2, R-3, R-5; R-5M for modernized or maritime version; R-14U for universal version; and so on). Korolev made sure the rockets he designed had the "lucky" odd numbers (R-3, R-5, R-7, R-9, R-11, but not R-13). NATO used so-called Reporting Names and referred to Soviet surface-to-surface missiles as "SS." To NATO the R-7 was known as the SS-6 or Sapwood.

A two-stage missile, the R-7 (*semyorka*, or "number seven") stood 34 meters tall, was 3 meters in diameter, and weighed 280 metric tons. It was a two-stage vehicle, powered by rocket motors using liquid oxygen (LOX) and kerosene and was capable of delivering its payload around 8,800 kilometers, with an accuracy of around 5,000 meters. It featured a central core with a single four-nozzle RD-108 engine and four strap-on boosters, each with one four-nozzle RD-107 engine. The "public" designation, 8K71PS, may be considered the "real" designation of the rocket. The "8" was for the army missile forces in the 1950's. The "K" was used for missiles until 1966. The "71" was a two-digit sequential number, allocated within a single product group. The "PS" was an alphabetical suffix used to differentiate submodels.

The Soyuz MS-04 spacecraft arrives at the launch pad after being rolled there by train on Monday, April 17, 2017 at the Baikonur Cosmodrome in Kazakhstan. (NASA / Aubrey Gemignani)

First launched in 1957, the R-7 was larger than United States' 25-meter-tall Redstone rocket but smaller than the 47-meter-tall Atlas rocket, both of which boosted the U.S. Mercury capsules. The R-7 became the workhorse launcher for early Soviet space projects during the 1950's, placing in orbit the world's first artificial Earth satellite, Sputnik 1 ("satellite" or "fellow traveler"). A third stage was added (the vehicle was now the 8K72) for launching Luna probes to the Moon beginning in 1959. Luna 3 orbited the Moon and took pictures of its far side.

In 1962, Korolev made plans for a program named Soyuz (meaning "union"), in which two or more spaceships would be launched into Earth orbit and then carry a crew of three cosmonauts into lunar orbit. If these plans succeeded, possibly by 1965, Korolev planned to construct a descent module that would make possible the first human landing on the Moon as early as 1966. By 1962, however, the United States' space program had advanced to the point of launching two astronauts into orbit in the Gemini Program, using a modification of the two-stage Titan intercontinental ballistic missile, the Titan II Gemini Launch Vehicle (GLV). Soviet premier Nikita Khrushchev, concerned that the Soyuz missions would not be ready for two years, pressed

Korolev to focus instead on the Voskhod program, which achieved the first spacewalk and the first launching of a multi-cosmonaut capsule.

The Soyuz program was revived after several setbacks. Korolev died in 1966, and the giant Moon rocket he had envisioned, the 110-meter-tall N-1 (SL-15) rocket, proved accident-prone. In contrast to the United States' success with the Saturn V Moon rocket, the N-1 blew up on the launch pad in 1969, the same year the United States landed astronauts on the Moon. In fact, on the same day of the American Moon landing, the Russian Luna 15 probe was in lunar orbit, surveying the surface for possible landing sites. Controllers attempted to land it on the Moon, but communications were lost at an altitude of 3 meters above the lunar surface and it crashed in the Sea of Crises.

While the Soyuz launch vehicle Soyuz 11A511 (the first "11" stands for Space Forces launch vehicles, the "A," meaning sealed unit) is based on the R-7 rocket, there were two intervening rocket designs. Vostok (translated as "East") 8K72K (SL-3), was a three-stage rocket design that launched the world's first piloted Earth-orbital flight by Soviet cosmonaut Yuri A. Gagarin in April, 1961, beating the orbital flight of American astronaut John Glenn by a full ten months. It utilized the same first and second stages as the R-7, both designed by Glushko's Gas Dynamics Laboratory. The first stage was nearly 20 meters long and weighed 3.5 metric tons. The second stage, 29 meters in length, weighed some 6.5 metric tons. A second design, the Voskhod (translated as "sunrise") 11A57 (SL-4), was used for two piloted missions. It kept the first two stages, but featured a new third stage, which measured 3 meters in length and weighed 1.5 tons and had been originally designed to launch interplanetary probes.

All stages used liquid oxygen and kerosene as propellants.

Although the Soyuz launch vehicle retained all three stages of the Voskhod rocket, the 11A57-2 third stage was redesigned to create greater lift capability (nearly 7 metric tons versus some 5.5 metric tons with the Voskhod). One result was to make a true rocket escape system possible, replacing the ejector seat that allowed Voskhod cosmonauts to escape from launch aborts.

The Soviet Union pioneered the concept of "clustering" engines, and the clustered engines of the central core and boosters, with their high degree of reliability, proved an excellent platform for a variety of upper stages. New upper stages with newer fuels, new fuel-injection techniques, higher energy designs, and multichamber engines contributed to the longevity of the Soyuz series of launchers.

The Soyuz series of launch vehicles began with the 11A511, which could carry an additional 550 kilograms of payload. Subsequent variants include the 115A11U, also known as the Soyuz U, which used chilled fuel to create a higher density in the central core and, thus, more power. It is used to launch the robotic Progress space station supply ship, as well as the piloted Soyuz missions. The 11A511U2, which could carry an increased payload, used synthetic kerosene and was utilized in missions to Mir until 1996, when the production of the synthetic kerosene was halted. The Soyuz FG, which includes improvements to the central core, strap-on boosters, and fuel injection, has been used to launch the Soyuz TMA spacecraft to the ISS since 2003. The Soyuz-2 (industrial designation 14A14, also known as Soyuz-2K and Soyuz-M) has an RD-0124 (14D23) closed-cycle engine on its third stage and an all-digital flight control system with a terminal guidance system. The first and second stages are equipped with 14D21 and 14D22 engines with an improved injection system. All the upgrades combined increase the payload of the vehicle by 1,200 kilograms in comparison with the base launcher.

The Soyuz launch vehicle, some 49 meters high and with more than 3,900 kilonewtons of thrust, is larger and more powerful than early U.S. launchers for piloted space missions. The Mercury-Atlas launcher, a modified Atlas D used for the orbital Mercury missions, was some 29 meters in height and featured a central core engine and two side boosters. Using RP-1 as fuel and liquid oxygen as oxidizer, it developed slightly under 1,590 kilonewtons of thrust. A smoother ride was provided for American astronauts by the Gemini launch vehicle, the Titan II GLV, a modification of the Titan II intercontinental ballistic missile. A two-stage booster, it developed close to 1,900 kilonewtons of thrust using unsymmetrical dimethylhydrazine and nitrogen tetroxide as propellants. The giant Saturn V launch vehicle, which launched the Apollo Moon orbiting and landing missions, was a three-stage booster that used RP-1 and liquid oxygen for its first stage and liquid hydrogen and liquid hydrogen for the two upper stages. At 111 meters tall, it developed more than 33.4 meganewtons of thrust. The most distinctive American launch vehicle, the space shuttle, was designed partly as transport to space stations. On the shuttle, two solid rocket boosters were attached to a returnable shuttle vehicle that functions as a glider upon its return to Earth. Also attached is an expendable liquid hydrogen and liquid oxygen tank, some 50 meters in height, which provides fuel for some 1.8 meganewtons of thrust from each of the three main engines.

The escape system of the Soyuz launch vehicle worked successfully during an aborted Soyuz launch in September, 1983. During the launch of Soyuz 18-1 in April, 1975, the Soyuz third stage failed to separate from the core rocket and the entire assembly appeared to be out of control. The Soyuz spacecraft's own propellant system was used to pull the capsule away from the rocket. The cosmonauts, subjected to more than 14g acceleration, landed more than 1,500 kilometers from their launch pad. Overall, the Soyuz booster has compiled a remarkable record for reliability, although a Soyuz launch

The Soyuz MS-13 rocket is launched with Expedition 60 Soyuz Commander Alexander Skvortsov of Roscosmos, flight engineer Drew Morgan of NASA, and flight engineer Luca Parmitano of the European Space Agency. (NASA / Joel Kowsky)

vehicle exploded only seconds after liftoff on October 15, 2002, killing one person and leading to the loss of the Photon-M satellite it carried.

Most Soyuz launches have been from the Baikonur Cosmodrome, also called Tyuratam, the world's oldest and largest working space launch facility. It is situated about 200 kilometers to the east of the Aral Sea, on the north bank of the Syr Darya, near the town of Tyuratam, in the south-central part of the country. The name Baikonur was chosen to mislead the West as to the actual location of the site

by suggesting that the site was near Baikonur, a mining town about 320 kilometers northeast of the space center. A northern cosmodrome, Plesetsk, is located about 800 kilometers north of Moscow and south of Arkhangelsk. It was originally developed by the Soviet Union as a launch site for intercontinental ballistic missiles. During the 1990's, when Baikonur became part of the new republic of Kazakhstan, an additional Russian cosmodrome was opened at Svobodny, the former strategic missile base located 120 kilometers north of Blagoveshensk and closed down after an agreement on the Strategic Arms Limitations Treaty START-2. In the twenty-first century at the insistence of Vladimir Putin a new eastern cosmodrome was built at Vostochni. The first Soyuz booster launch from the new cosmodrome occurred on April 28, 2016. As of 2019 four of five attempted Soyuz launches from Vostochni were successful.

Whichever site is used, the launch procedures have been similar. Before moving the rockets and payload to the launch stand, the equipment is carefully checked in the Launch Vehicle Assembly and Testing Facility. Typically, two days before launch, the rocket and payload are attached to a vertical erector on a rail car and transported by a train engine that moves at about 3 kilometers per hour to a launch pad that consists of a concrete platform surrounded by a water reservoir. The spacecraft and booster are lifted from the transport car and positioned on the pad for launch. After the vehicle is placed in the vertical position and its railroad erector is removed, two service trusses rise from both sides, enveloping the rocket into an array of access bridges. The booster is fueled, starting about five to six hours before launch. The service towers are removed twenty-five minutes before launch. Combustion chambers of side and central engine pods are purged with nitrogen about three minutes prior to launch at T minus 3:15. Fuel and oxidizer hoses are removed at T minus 2:15; electrical lines come off about T minus 1:00, leaving the rocket to function off its own batteries. At T minus 0:20, the launch command is given and the central and booster engines are ignited. At T minus 0:05, the first-stage engines reach maximum thrust, and at T minus 0:00, the fueling separates from the vehicle and liftoff is achieved.

Unlike American launches, in which rockets are held on the launch pad until sufficient thrust is created, the Soyuz launch vehicle leaves its pad when the rockets overcome the force of gravity. The strap-on boosters fire for about 120 seconds (until T plus 1:58) and are jettisoned. The escape tower and launch shroud surrounding the Soyuz capsule separate. The core section (second stage) continues to fire for another 120 seconds before it separates at an altitude of 170 kilometers. The third stage ignites immediately and thrusts for another four minutes to lift the Soyuz or Progress spacecraft into orbit. At T plus 9:00 (nine minutes after launch), the third stage cuts off and the spacecraft separates from the booster.

The role of the Soyuz launch vehicle in the Soviet and Russian space program is similar to the role played by the shuttle and other launch vehicles in the U.S. space program. During the 1980's and 1990's, a Russian space shuttle was developed. The Buran ("snowstorm") shuttle vehicle resembled the American shuttle, since this was the shape necessary to fly a similar mission: vertical launch and airplane-like landing. Buran was designed to be capable of both piloted and robotic flight and had automated landing capability. Although the robotic version flew once, on November 15, 1988, the piloted version never did. After the flight, the project was suspended for lack of funds and the political situation in the Soviet Union. Buran would have been mated to a more powerful and expendable Energia rocket and would not have its own engines, relying instead on Energia to reach orbit.

The Soyuz booster has emerged as the most often used launch vehicle in the world, becoming an indispensable booster for global piloted space programs. The Soyuz booster has also been marketed commercially by a Russian-French commercial venture, Starsem. Starsem has also used the Soyuz Fregat, which employs a Fregat upper stage designed by the Soviet/Russian Organization for Scientific Production or Research (NPO) Lavochkin design bureau. The Soyuz Fregat can boost a payload of up to 1,350 kilograms into a geostationary transfer orbit. It has launched the European Space

The Soyuz MS-01 spacecraft launches from the Baikonur Cosmodrome with Expedition 48-49 crewmembers Kate Rubins of NASA, Anatoly Ivanishin of Roscosmos and Takuya Onishi of the Japan Aerospace Exploration Agency. (NASA / Bill Ingalls)

Agency's Cluster satellites, which have studied plasma, or ionized particles, trapped in Earth's magnetic field. Future ventures with the European Space Agency are also planned. Soyuz—in its new version as Soyuz/ST—is planned to be brought into service by the European Space Agency in 2007 under a Russo-European joint venture. A launch pad in French Guiana was used to launch this variant, the first one lifting off on October 21, 2011 marking the first time that a Soyuz had been launched outside Russia.

Contributions

Unlike the U.S. Moon-landing program, the early Soviet space program failed to master the use of liquid hydrogen as a rocket fuel. Liquid hydrogen is a powerful propellant that is difficult and hazardous to utilize. However, Soviet engineers learned that a liquid-oxygen-and-kerosene core rocket with strap-on boosters was not only highly reliable but also sufficient for the task of making frequent launches of orbital flights. By mating more advanced second and third stages to the central core and strap-on boosters of the R-7, Soviet and Russian engineers have created a modular launch vehicle that has taken advantage of more advanced fuels, fuel-injection techniques, and designs that allow longer burn times. These improvements paved the way for the 11A511U, 11A511U2, Soyuz FG, and Soyuz-2 designs.

The improvements have made possible not only heavier Soyuz payloads but also the Progress spacecraft itself, with its heavier payload of fuel and supplies. Some innovations in the Soyuz launch vehicle have also proved applicable to other Soviet launchers, as when synthetic kerosene (Sintin), used in the Soyuz 11A511U2, was also utilized in the upper stages of the Proton rocket. The modular approach has also proved workable with the payload shrouds, which have been redesigned as necessary to accommodate a variety of Soyuz and

Progress spacecraft. Because of what one Soviet cosmonaut has called the "adaptability" of the Soyuz launch vehicle, it was not necessary to design a new launch vehicle for the Progress spacecraft. A new payload shroud was sufficient. At the same time, the continually evolving Soyuz launch vehicles have made it possible to launch larger and heavier Progress spacecraft; compared to the lift capability of the Soyuz FG, the Soyuz-2 is able to launch a Progress spacecraft weighing nearly 1,000 kilograms more.

Context

Rockets became a major part of the Soviet Union's drive to superpower status, but rocket science in Russia has a long history, dating to the "father" of Russian rocketry, Konstantin Tsiolkovsky (1857-1935), who calculated the "escape velocity" that space ships would have to achieve to leave Earth's gravity and who experimented with weightlessness. Interest in Tsiolkovsky's work revived among Soviet scientists in the 1920's, when Fredrick Tsander (1887-1933) and Yuri Kondratyuk (1897-1942) worked on the concept of multistage rockets and designed hybrid vehicles that would combine rocket and aircraft power. Although captured German rocket scientists were transported to the Soviet Union after World War II, Soviet rocket achievements during the 1950's were largely homegrown. (The master of Nazi Germany's rocket program, Wernher von Braun, took pains to surrender to U.S. forces during World War II and directed the successful American Saturn V Moon landing rocket program.)

Like some of the early rockets of the U.S. space program, the space launchers of the Soviet Union were based on intercontinental ballistic missiles. Because Soviet atomic weapons were not miniaturized to the extent that U.S. nuclear weapons were, much larger boosters were required for the first Soviet ICBMs. This gave the Soviets a weight advantage in early Earth-orbiting missions. In turn, the reliability of the Soyuz booster and the achievements of the Soyuz program provided a stimulus for the U.S. space program.

The Russian space program has experienced difficult times since the collapse of the Soviet Union, and budgetary restraints have caused Soyuz launch vehicles to be offered for commercial use. Nevertheless, for nearly fifty years the R-7 and its offspring have successfully launched Soviet and Russian spacecraft. The reliability of the Soyuz booster has not been matched.

—Niles R. Holt and Russell R. Tobias

See also: Apollo-Soyuz Test Project; Atlas Launch Vehicles; Delta Launch Vehicles; Escape from Piloted Spacecraft; Launch Vehicles; Saturn Launch Vehicles; Soyuz and Progress Spacecraft; Titan Launch Vehicles.

Further Reading

Bond, Peter. *Heroes in Space: From Gagarin to Challenger*. New York: Blackwell, 1987. This book describes Soviet and U.S. space missions until the *Challenger* accident of 1986. It offers drawings of all of the major spacecraft of the period, including Soyuz and *Challenger*. Appropriate for college students and general readers.

Chaikin, Andrew. *Space: A History of Space Exploration in Photographs*. Buffalo: Firefly Books, 2004. Incorporating impressive photographs of U.S. and Russian space missions, this book includes sections on the Soyuz program and on the use of the Soyuz rocket and capsules to supply space stations, particularly the International Space Station. Appropriate for high school students, college students, and general readers.

Clark, Phillip. *The Soviet Piloted Space Program: An Illustrated History of the Men, the Missions, and the Spacecraft*. New York: Orion Books, 1988. The focus of this book is on the "hardware"—the launching rockets and spacecraft in the Soviet program. It includes detailed tables of specifications for various Soviet rockets and spacecraft and is lavishly illustrated with photos and drawings of rockets, cosmonauts, and specific missions and procedures. Appropriate for high school students, college students, and general readers.

Godwin, Robert, ed. *Rocket and Space Corporation Energia: The Legacy of S. P. Korolev*. Burlington, Ont.: Apogee Books, 2001. Appearing in English for the first time, the book traces the role of one of the main bureaus in the Soviet space program from the time of the creation of Sputnik to the formation of plans for a Russian space shuttle. It contains a wealth of photographs and diagrams. Appropriate for college students and general readers.

Hall, Rex, and David J. Shayler. *Rocket Men: Vostok and Voskhod, the First Soviet Manned Spaceflights*. London: Springer-Verlag, 2001. Beginning with the work of Tsiolkovsky, this book traces the history and the reasons for the successes of the early Soviet space program, emphasizing the importance of Korolev and the R-7 launch vehicle. Previously unavailable photographs and archival materials are included. Appropriate for college students and general readers.

Harvey, Brian. *Russia in Space: The Failed Frontier*. Chichester, England: Springer-Praxis, 2001. Much of this book is concerned with the Russian space program after the end of the Cold War and the dissolution of the Soviet Union. It also details new Russian space projects, including the opening of a new cosmodrome. Numerous tables detail launches, launch rates and failures, Russian design bureaus, and the key features of the Soyuz capsules. Appropriate for college students and general readers.

Heppenheimer, T. A. *Countdown: A History of Space Flight*. New York: John Wiley and Sons, 1997. This book explains the history of twentieth century rocketry, beginning with the programs of Nazi Germany and Stalinist Russia. It is particularly detailed on the topic of the superpower rivalry between the Soviet and U.S. rocket programs into the 1990's. Other topics covered are the faltering of the Russian program in the late 1980's and the planned commercial uses of Russian spacecraft. Appropriate for high school students, college students, and general readers.

Space Centers, Spaceports, and Launch Sites

Date: Beginning 1945
Type of facility: Space research center

With the advent of the German V-2 rocket in World War II, areas separated from population centers for testing this new weapon became a necessity. As the rockets' size grew and as their purpose changed from carrying warheads to launching satellites, more and larger testing facilities were needed.

Summary of the Facilities

The primary launch sites for space vehicles in the United States are the John F. Kennedy Space Center (KSC) on Merritt Island and the Cape Canaveral Air Force Station, both in Florida, and the Vandenberg Air Force Base located just outside Lompoc, California. Each facility lies on the coastline of an ocean, permitting relatively safe launches over large, unpopulated areas. Two other key launch sites are the U.S. Army's White Sands Missile Range, between Las Cruces and Alamogordo, New Mexico, and Wallops Flight Facility, of the National Aeronautics and Space Administration's Goddard Space Flight Center, in Virginia on the Chesapeake Bay's Eastern Shore. White Sands and Wallops are used primarily for sounding rockets, small rockets— usually from surplus military inventories— that carry scientific experiments on brief, suborbital flights. Wallops also manages the National Scientific Balloon Facility (NSBF) in Palestine, Texas, where many experiments are launched on huge balloons. Wallops supports sounding rocket and balloon campaigns worldwide, as well, using mobile facilities in locations from Andoya, Norway, to Alice Springs, Australia.

The Apollo lunar-landing program led to an expansion of operations from Cape Canaveral to the adjacent Merritt Island in 1962 to accommodate the giant Saturn V launch vehicle. In July, 1962, the site was named the Launch Operations Center. It was renamed the John F. Kennedy Space Center in November, 1963, after the recently assassinated President Kennedy. The surrounding Cape Canaveral was also renamed Cape Kennedy, but this change was unpopular with the local people and the name reverted in 1973.

KSC is 240 kilometers south of Jacksonville and 80 kilometers east of Orlando. KSC and the Cape Canaveral Air Force Station form a complex that stretches for 55 kilometers and varies in width from 8 to 16 kilometers. The center has a workforce of approximately two thousand National Aeronautics and Space Administration (NASA) civil servant employees and between twelve and thirteen thousand personnel who work for private companies under contract to NASA.

Two launch complexes are situated on the Atlantic coast portion of KSC. Launch Complexes 39A and 39B were accustomed to sending the mighty Saturn V into space and onward toward the Moon. Two identical complexes were built to permit launch preparations to proceed on two vehicles concurrently—the only way NASA could achieve the 1969 deadline for an Apollo piloted lunar-landing mission. The first Saturn V test launch, Apollo 4 (Apollo-Saturn 501), was launched on November 9, 1967. The first piloted launch from KSC was Apollo 8 in December, 1968.

1982 Space Shuttle Columbia landing at Northrop Strip at the White Sands Missile Range. (NASA)

After completion of the Apollo lunar landing mission, KSC concentrated on supporting the space shuttle. The first space shuttle (known as STS-1, for Space Transportation System 1) was launched from Launch Complex 39A on April 12, 1981. Many other launches from the Florida site take place at Cape Canaveral Air Force Station, which is adjacent to KSC. All the launches using the Delta rocket, for example, are from the Air Force station. KSC also operates a Vandenberg launch site resident office, which supports NASA activities at Vandenberg Air Force Base.

Vandenberg was formed when an operational site was needed to train Air Force crews to launch intercontinental and intermediate range ballistic missiles. The Department of Defense decided to use an old Army facility, known as Camp Cooke, which occupied a strip of land on the Pacific Coast of California halfway between Los Angeles and San Francisco. The site was named Cooke Air Force Base in June, 1957, and the name was changed to Vandenberg Air Force Base in October, 1958, in honor of the late Hoyt S. Vandenberg, the second Air Force chief of staff.

It was desirable to have spy satellites launched into a polar orbit—one that circles the globe over the poles rather than around the equator. This would provide for constant surveillance of desired targets. The launch site, jutting out into the Pacific, offered the perfect place for these satellite launches.

The first missile was launched from Vandenberg in December, 1958—a Thor intermediate range ballistic missile (IRBM). The mission was a success. In February, 1959, Discoverer 1, the first satellite placed in a polar orbit, was launched from the base. Discoverer was a precursor to the first successful U.S. reconnaissance satellite, Discoverer 13, which was launched from Vandenberg in August, 1960. Known as America's western spaceport, Vandenberg is the only U.S. military installation to launch both land-based intercontinental ballistic missiles and space boosters. Vandenberg is also used for the launch of nonmilitary satellites in polar orbits. Clementine, a probe that tested sensors and spacecraft components under extended exposure to the space environment, was launched from Vandenberg on January 25, 1994. Clementine made scientific observations of the Moon and the near-Earth asteroid 1620 Geographos.

Covering more than 396 square kilometers, Vandenberg is the third-largest U.S. Air Force installation. The facilities are linked by 837 kilometers of roads, 27 kilometers of railroad tracks, 129 kilometers of gas lines, 476 kilometers of water mains, and 727 kilometers of electrical power lines. Much of the base is rugged, mountainous, and undeveloped; predominant groundcover includes chaparral, with coastal sage scrub and oak woodland.

Delta Space Launch Complex (SLC-2, "slick two"), used to launch the Delta launch vehicle, comprises two independent launch facilities designated SLC-2E and SLC-2W. Atlas Space Launch Complex (SLC-3) is used to launch the Atlas vehicle and has two different pads, designated SLC-3E and SLC-3W. Titan Space Launch Complex

(SLC-4) used to launch the Titan vehicle has two launch pads. One is designated SLC-4E and the other is SLC-4W. Scout Space Launch Complex (SLC-5) is used to launch the Scout vehicle; it has only one launch pad, designated SLC-5.

The Advanced Keyhole (KH-12) spy satellite was a driving force behind the decision to build Space Launch Complex 6 (SLC-6) at Vandenberg. The satellite needed a polar orbit for coverage, and Vandenberg could provide near-polar and retrograde azimuth launches. These launches could not be satisfactorily achieved from Cape Canaveral, and the importance of accommodating the new reconnaissance satellites was the reason that the Defense Department maintained the need for a West coast launch site. However, SLC-6 was plagued by problems, including faulty construction, unanticipated operational hazards (such as the weather), and the need for the space shuttle in order to boost the heavy KH-12. These problems delayed the initial operation of SLC-6 as well as the KH-12's debut, which, prior to the cancellation of West coast shuttle operations, was scheduled for the second Vandenberg shuttle flight. The expensive and problem-ridden SLC-6 complex itself came under increasing fire as critics urged rapid development of new expendable launch vehicles capable of boosting heavy payloads into polar orbit.

After Vandenberg was chosen as an STS launch site, the Air Force argued that conversion of SLC-6's partially complete Titan III facilities—the remains of the canceled Manned Orbiting Laboratory (MOL) program—would save more than $100 million by precluding "bare ground" construction of shuttle facilities. Nonetheless, modification of existing MOL facilities was extensive.

The original plans called for shuttle operations to be conducted both at North Vandenberg and at South Vandenberg. The runway, orbiter maintenance and checkout facility, orbiter lifting facility, thermal protection facility, supply warehouses, and most of the support personnel are at North Vandenberg. SLC-6, which included the launch control center, payload preparation room, payload changeout room, shuttle assembly building, access tower, launch mount, mobile service tower, and three exhaust ducts, is at South Vandenberg.

After the *Challenger* accident in January, 1986, NASA scrubbed plans to launch the shuttle from Vandenberg and SLC was placed in mothballs. In 1995, the Air Force awarded a twenty-five-year lease of SLC-6 to Spaceport Systems International (SSI), including the payload processing facility and more than 100 acres of land for commercial launch facility construction. In 2000, SSI launched two satellites from the facility. The Joint Air Force Academy- Weber State University Satellite (JAWSAT) was launched aboard the Orbital Suborbital Program Space Launch Vehicle (dubbed Minotaur), a combination of rocket motors from the Minuteman II and Pegasus XL launch vehicles, on January 26. The Mighty Sat II Satellite was successfully launched on July 19 atop the Minotaur. Since 2003, the Boeing Aircraft Company has used the site to launch its commercial Delta IV Evolved Expendable Launch Vehicle.

The 30th Space Wing at Vandenberg Air Force Base, California, is the Air Force Space Command organization responsible for all Department of Defense space and missile launch activities on the West Coast. The wing supports West Coast launch activities for the Air Force, Department of Defense, NASA, and various private industry contractors. The wing launches a variety of expendable vehicles, including Atlas- 5, Delta IV, Titan IV, Delta II, Pegasus, Minotaur, Taurus, and Falcon. The wing also supports Force Development and Evaluation of all intercontinental ballistic missiles.

The Army's White Sands Missile Range (WSMR), in the Tularosa Basin of southern New Mexico, is 160 kilometers long by 65 kilometers wide—larger than the states of Delaware and Rhode Island and the District of Columbia combined. The range stretches more than half the distance from El Paso, Texas, to Albuquerque, New Mexico. In area, it is the largest military reservation in the United States.

WSMR was established on July 9, 1945, as the White Sands Proving Ground; the name was changed in 1958. The first missile fired at the range was a Tiny Tim sounding rocket, fired in September, 1945. The facility supports missile development and test programs for the Army, Navy, and Air Force, and for NASA and other government agencies.

An overhead view of the space shuttle Enterprise moving toward the shuttle assembly building at Vandenberg Air Force Base Space Launch Complex 6. (U.S. Air Force / William W. Thompson)

Since 1960, WSMR has had part-time use of a 4,225-square-kilometer area adjoining the range's northern boundary. Two other areas, adjacent to the western boundary, also have been used to extend the range. Used many times a year, these areas— which total approximately 5,150 square kilometers— permit testing of longer-range missiles. When firings are scheduled in these areas, residents leave their homes, usually for a maximum of twelve hours. The ranch families are paid for the use of their land and for the hours they must spend away from home during these evacuations.

WSMR has served as an impact area for Army Sergeant and Pershing missiles launched from sites in Utah as far as 643 kilometers away. In 1982, the range added a launch complex near Mountain Home, Idaho, thereby acquiring the capability of firing the Pershing 2 missile and other test missiles with ranges of more than 1,200 kilometers.

On the northern portion of the range, on July 16, 1945, the world's first atomic device was detonated. The spot, known as Trinity Site, is in a missile impact area and is open to the public only once a year.

WSMR is part of the Developmental Test Command (DTC), which reports to the United States Army Test and Evaluation Command (ATEC) and is designated as an activity within the Defense Department's Major Range and Test Facility Base (MRTFB). The range possesses extensive capabilities and infrastructure used by the Army, Navy, Air Force, NASA, and other government agencies, as well as universities, private industry, and foreign militaries.

The Wallops Flight Facility is managed by Goddard Space Flight Center. Wallops is 64 kilometers southeast of Salisbury, Maryland, and approximately 241 kilometers southeast of Goddard, which is in Greenbelt, Maryland. Composed of a main base, the Wallops Island launch site, and the Wallops mainland, the site covers more than 25 square kilometers and has eighty-four major facilities valued at about $105 million. Approximately 380 civil service workers and 560 contractor employees staff the installation, which has an annual payroll of more than $30 million.

Development of Wallops was started in 1945 when the National Advisory Committee for Aeronautics (NACA) authorized the Langley Research Center to establish a site for research on rocket-propelled vehicles. Since then, Wallops has been used as a launching site for scientific missions as well as a facility for aeronautical research. The first rocket launch on Wallops Island took place on July 4, 1945, making it one of the oldest in the world.

The Navy decided in 1958 to close its Chincoteague Naval Air Station, about 11 kilometers northwest of Wallops Island. A year later, Wallops took over those facilities, which included buildings, utilities, hangars, and an excellent airport. Wallops is at the center of NASA's suborbital programs. Sounding rockets, balloons, and aircraft are used in NASA programs concerned with space science, applications, advanced technology, and aeronautical research.

Sounding rockets carry scientific payloads to altitudes ranging from 48 to 965 kilometers. Experiment time above the atmosphere is usually about fifteen minutes. Scientific data are collected and returned to Earth by telemetry links, and the payloads are parachuted to Earth for refurbishment and reuse. Scientific balloons carry payloads to altitudes of up to 48 kilometers and normally remain aloft for from one to sixty hours. The balloon program supports approximately forty-five launches each year. Between 1975 and 1986, 493 balloons were launched, with an overall success rate of 85 percent. In addition, more than twenty satellites have been launched from Wallops since 1961, including Explorer 9, the first satellite to be launched by an all-solid-fueled rocket.

Along with its headquarters in Washington, D.C., NASA operates nine major space centers in the United States. Ames Research Center, Mountain View, California, was founded in 1940 and is located on 1.7 square kilometers of land adjacent to the U.S. Naval Air Station at Moffett Field.

Goddard Space Flight Center, in Greenbelt, Maryland, was established in 1959. Goddard is 16 kilometers northeast of Washington, D.C. It has 4.45 square kilometers of land and employs approximately twelve thousand civil service and contractor employees at Greenbelt and at its subsidiary, Wallops Flight Facility.

The Jet Propulsion Laboratory, in Pasadena, California, is a government-owned facility operated by the California Institute of Technology under a NASA contract. It is 32 kilometers northeast of Los Angeles.

The Lyndon B. Johnson Space Center is about 32 kilometers southeast of Houston. The center was established in 1961 as NASA's primary center for piloted spaceflight. Most of the one hundred buildings on the 6.6-square-kilometer site house offices and laboratories, some of which are dedicated to astronaut training and mission operations. Kennedy Space Center (KSC) is responsible for the assembly, testing, and launch of space shuttles and their payloads, for shuttle landing operations, and for the servicing of space shuttle orbiters between missions.

Langley Research Center is in the Tidewater area of Virginia between Norfolk and Williamsburg. The center occupies 3 square kilometers, one of which is used under permit from the U.S. Air Force. An additional 13.3 square kilometers of marshland near Langley are used as a model-drop zone.

The John H. Glenn Research Center (GRC) at Lewis Field is adjacent to the Cleveland Hopkins International Airport, approximately 32 kilometers southwest of Cleveland. Established in 1941, it is staffed by twenty-seven hundred civil service employees and thirteen hundred contractor personnel. It was renamed the John H. Glenn Research Center (GRC) at Lewis Field on March 1, 1999, in honor of the Ohio-born astronaut and former U.S. senator.

Marshall Space Flight Center, Huntsville, Alabama, is situated on 7.3 square kilometers inside the Army's Redstone Arsenal. The center has thirty-five hundred civil service employees, of whom 58 percent are scientists and engineers. Formed in July, 1960, Marshall has been most often identified as NASA's launch vehicle development center. Marshall

Vandenberg Air Force Base Space Launch Complex 6 under construction in July 1982. (U.S. Air Force / SRA Eric C. Baker)

manages two other sites: the Michoud Assembly Facility, in New Orleans, where space shuttle External Tanks are made, and Computer Science Corporation, in Slidell, Louisiana, which provides computer service support to Michoud.

Stennis Space Center, Bay St. Louis, Mississippi, is located on the East Pearl River, which provides deep-water access to oversize cargo. Stennis occupies an area of 562 square kilometers, 54.6 of which are covered by the operational base. The center conducts static test firings of space shuttles' main engines.

In January, 1998, the Alaska Aerospace Development Corporation (AADC) began building a commercial spaceport at Narrow Cape on Kodiak Island, about 400 kilometers south of Anchorage and 40 kilometers southwest of the city of Kodiak. The location, combined with low-cost operations, was promoted for launching telecommunications, remote sensing, and space science payloads of up to 3,500 kilograms into low-Earth polar orbits. Through an agreement with the State Division of Land, AADC was granted a thirty-year lease of 1,200 hectares at Narrow Cape with an option for a second thirty-year term. On November 5, 1998, the

USAF conducted the launch of the AIT (atmospheric interceptor technology) suborbital rocket, marking the first launch from the Kodiak Launch Complex (KLC). The first orbital launch of an Athena-1 came on September 30, 2001.

The Mojave Spaceport, also known as the Mojave Airport and Civilian Flight Test Center, is the first facility in the United States licensed for horizontal launches of reusable spacecraft. Certified as a spaceport by the Federal Aviation Administration on June 17, 2004, it is also the first inland spaceport in the United States. The spaceport has been a test site for several teams in the Ansari X Prize. Most notably, it is the test launch site for SpaceShipOne, developed by Scaled Composites, which conducted the first privately funded human spaceflight on June 21, 2004. Other groups based at the Mojave Spaceport include XCOR Aerospace, Orbital Sciences Corporation, and Interorbital Systems.

In December, 2004, the U.S. Congress passed the Commercial Space Launch Amendments Act of 2004. That legislation gave the Federal Aviation Administration (FAA), among other duties, the goahead to start shaping rules on medical requirements for a spaceship passenger—termed a "space-flight participant"—an individual (who is not crew) carried within a launch vehicle or reentry vehicle. Along with Scaled Composites and Virgin Galactic, XCOR, Rocketplane, SpaceX, Armadillo Aerospace, and others are working to complete reusable launch vehicles in the hopes of carrying passengers in the near future.

The Oklahoma Space Industry Development Authority (OSIDA) was founded in 1999, with the signing of the Space Industry Tax Incentive Act by the Oklahoma State Legislature. That legislation also directed that the OSIDA be given municipal authority to develop a 435-square-kilometer (168-square-mile) Spaceport Territory. The old Clinton-Sherman Air Force Base at Burns Flat is the site for the Oklahoma Spaceport, due to begin flight operations in 2006 or 2007.

New Mexico is establishing the Southwest Regional Spaceport at Upham, an undeveloped location in Southern New Mexico approximately 72 kilometers north of Las Cruces and 48 kilometers east of Truth or Consequences. The proposed site is approximately 70 square kilometers of open, generally level rangeland with an average elevation of 1,500 meters. The complete lack of conflicting operations, facilities, and environmental constraints provides a unique opportunity to design and develop a purpose-built launch complex that meets the needs of spaceport customers. The spaceport will include a launch complex, a 400-meter runway and aviation complex, a payload assembly complex, a support facilities complex, a system development complex, and site infrastructure.

As of 2019 commercial space flight was still a developing technology. Kennedy Space Center was deep in preparation to use modified shuttle-era facilities for the launch of the new Space Launch System rocket/Orion spacecraft to resume piloted flights to the Moon. Commercial companies

such as SpaceX and Boeing were using facilities at Kennedy Space Center and Cape Canaveral for commercial launch services intended to lower the cost per pound of putting payloads into orbit, but also were heavily involved with the development of spacecraft that could begin launching American astronauts to space from the United States once again after space shuttle fleet retirement in 2011. As of 2019, both companies were on the verge of launching their spacecraft called Crew Dragon (SpaceX) and Starliner (Boeing) on their maiden piloted voyages to the International Space Station. Other commercial companies such as Virgin Galactic and Blue Origin were developing launch services for commercial uses as well as space tourism for the 2020's.

Context

At the end of World War II, the United States was operating five small missile sites: one in West Virginia, three in California, and one in Texas. The maximum range of the missiles being tested at those facilities was less than 15 kilometers. To meet the greater distance requirements of the postwar era, three facilities were created in 1945. The first of these was Wallops Flight Facility, which was established by the National Advisory Committee for

The Wallops Flight Facility flight control room during a launch attempt for the Antares A-ONE mission. (NASA / Keith Kohler)

Aeronautics (NACA) with an 80-kilometer range. The second was the 161-kilometer-wide White Sands Missile Range, set up adjacent to the already established Hueco Range at Fort Bliss. The third was the Naval Air Facility, established at Point Mugu, California, with a 100-kilometer range.

Hardly were these installations established, however, before officials recognized that they were not large enough. With the development of intermediate and intercontinental ballistic missiles already under way, the need for sites with ranges of thousands of kilometers became obvious. Moreover, further expansion of the existing ranges would be extremely difficult. As a result, in 1947, a War Department research committee was established to find a suitable range for testing medium and long-range weapons.

The committee selected three possible sites. In order of preference, they were El Centro Naval Station, in California; Cape Canaveral, in Florida; and a third site, in Washington. The selections were made based on favorable weather and the location of island chains downrange on which tracking stations could be established. El Centro was found unsuitable when Mexico refused rights to some of its islands, and the weather in the Aleutians proved a setback for the Washington site. Great Britain was more cooperative with its Bahamas, and Cape Canaveral was chosen.

In October, 1949, President Harry S. Truman established the Joint Long Range Proving Ground (later known as the Air Force Eastern Test Range), a huge over-water range extending 8,000 kilometers across the Atlantic from Cape Canaveral to Ascension Island. The first launch from the Cape was conducted by a military-civilian team on July 24, 1950. The rocket was a modified German V-2 with an upper stage, and it attained an altitude of 16 kilometers. In the early 1950's, the focus turned from missile tests to satellite launches. On January 31, 1958, the United States' first satellite, Explorer 1, was launched from the Cape by a military-civilian team led by Kurt H. Debus, a key member of the famed Wernher von Braun rocket team. Thereafter, Cape Canaveral became the launch site for Project Mercury, in the 1960's for the Gemini and Apollo Programs, and ultimately the main launch site for the Space Transportation System (shuttle) and ensuing projects such as the U.S. contributions to the International Space Station.

—*James C. Elliott and Russell R. Tobias*

See also: Ames Research Center; Cape Canaveral and the Kennedy Space Center; Goddard Space Flight Center; Jet Propulsion Laboratory; Johnson Space Center; Langley Research Center; Lewis Field and Glenn Research Center; Marshall Space Flight Center.

Further Reading

Hartman, Edwin P. *Adventures in Research: A History of Ames Research Center, 1940-1965*. NASA SP-4302. Washington, D.C.: Government Printing Office, 1970. Published in celebration of Ames Research Center's twenty-fifth anniversary, this work captures the excitement of the people who staffed the center in its early years. Includes appendices and references.

Koppes, Clayton R. *JPL and the American Space Program: A History of the Jet Propulsion Laboratory*. New Haven, Conn.: Yale University Press, 1982. Discusses research at JPL during World War II and the years that followed. Describes the relationship between the California Institute of Technology and JPL and between JPL and NASA. More than half the volume is devoted to JPL's space projects.

National Aeronautics and Space Administration, John F. Kennedy Space Center. *America's Spaceport*. Washington, D.C.: National Aeronautics and Space Administration, 1987. Published in celebration of the center's twenty-fifth anniversary, this comprehensive overview of the history and facilities of Kennedy Space Center is illustrated with works from the NASA art program.

Ordway, Frederick I., III, and Mitchell Sharpe. *The Rocket Team*. Burlington, Ont.: Apogee Books, 2003. This book looks at the individuals who developed the rockets and missiles in the early days of spaceflight. The principal launch sites are discussed to some extent.

Rosenthal, Alfred. *The Early Years, Goddard Space Flight Center: Historical Origins and Activities Through December, 1962*. Washington, D.C.: Government Printing Office, 1964. This commemorative manual provides a comprehensive look at the founding of Goddard Space Flight Center.

Sloan, Aubrey B. "Vandenberg Planning for the Space Transportation System." *Astronautics and Aeronautics* 19 (November, 1981): 44-50. A detailed description of the original plan for the Vandenberg shuttle complex. Provides a good history of the decision-making process involved in bringing the shuttle complex to Vandenberg. Includes illustrations, diagrams, and a useful bibliography for further study. Full of technical information but still readable.

Wallops Flight Facility, Office of Public Affairs. *Wallops: A Guide to the Facility*. Greenbelt, Md.: Goddard Space Flight Center, 1988. This guide, prepared by the Office of Public Affairs, provides a thorough explanation of the facilities and programs at Wallops.

Weil, Elizabeth. *They All Laughed at Christopher Columbus: An Incurable Dreamer Builds the First Civilian Spaceship*. New York: Bantam Books, 2003. The story of Rotary Rocket, founded by Gary Hudson.

Space Shuttle

Date: January 5, 1972 to August 31, 2011
Type of program: Piloted spaceflight

The Space Transportation System (STS), popularly known as the space shuttle, was designed and built to be a reusable system that could transport humans, satellites, and equipment to and from Earth orbit on a regular basis. It would also provide support for a wide range of other activities until its retirement in 2011.

Key Figures

James M. Beggs (b. 1926), NASA Administrator
James C. Fletcher (1919-1991), NASA Administrator
Charles F. Bolden, Jr. (b. 1946), NASA Administrator
Sean C. O'Keefe (b. 1956), NASA Administrator
Michael D. Griffin (b. 1949), NASA Administrator
Robert A. Schmitz, program manager, NASA Headquarters
John S. Theon, program scientist, NASA Headquarters
Donald K. "Deke" Slayton (1924-1993), manager, Orbital Flight Test Program
Maxime A. Faget (1921-2004), director of Engineering and Development, Johnson Space Center
Robert F. Thompson (b. 1925), program manager of the Space Shuttle Office, Johnson Space Center
James W. Bilodeau, the chief of Crew Procedures for shuttle missions*Richard M. Nixon* (1913-1994), President of the United States who authorized the shuttle
George W. Bush (b. 1946), President of the United States who retired the shuttle

Summary of the Program

The concept of a reusable launch vehicle and spacecraft that could return to Earth was developed early in the American rocket program. The National Advisory Committee for Aeronautics (NACA), the predecessor of the National Aeronautics and Space Administration (NASA), and NASA itself cooperated with the U.S. Air Force on early studies in the X-15 rocket research program and the Dyna-Soar hypersonic vehicle program in the late 1950's and 1960's.

In 1963, NASA and the Air Force began to work on a design for a piloted vehicle that would be launched into orbit and then return to Earth. The craft was called an aerospace plane and could take off and land horizontally in the manner of a conventional aircraft. In addition, joint tests of wingless lifting bodies, such as the M2 series, HL-10, and eventually the X-24, laid the foundations for a future craft that could safely reenter the atmosphere.

At about the same time, NASA scientists began to talk about a spacecraft that would serve as a cargo transport to other vehicles or space stations in Earth orbit or on the Moon. Experts at NASA's Marshall Space Flight Center engaged in research on the recovery and reuse of the Saturn V launch vehicle. The Department of Defense and private industry also became involved in the development of a reusable transport spacecraft during the late 1960's. In its 1967 budget briefing, NASA referred to an advanced studies program for a "ferry and logistics vehicle." The President's Science Advisory Committee agreed that developing a reusable, economic space transportation system was necessary.

Between 1969 and 1971, NASA awarded contracts to major aerospace industries to study and define such a system. After considering these findings, NASA decided in 1972 to develop the Space Transportation System (STS). Eventually, this program would be known simply as the space shuttle. On January 5, 1972, President Richard M. Nixon officially authorized the space shuttle program. NASA's ambitious schedule called for atmospheric flight tests by 1977 and the first orbital tests by 1979. The shuttle was scheduled to begin regular launchings by 1980.

NASA's goal was to establish a national space transportation system capable of substantially reducing the cost of space operations by providing

President Nixon (right) with NASA Administrator Fletcher in January 1972, three months before Congress approved funding for the Shuttle program. (NASA)

support for a wide range of scientific, military, and commercial applications. Space officials hoped that the space shuttle would operate at a fraction of the cost of the expendable rockets that were in use at the time.

Designed to be a true aerospace vehicle, the space shuttle would take off like a rocket, maneuver in space and attain an Earth orbit, and return to Earth and land like an airplane under a pilot's control. The four-part vehicle would include the reusable orbiter (it would be able to make one hundred launches) mounted atop the expendable External Tank (ET) and two solid-fueled rocket boosters. The boosters, too, would be recoverable and reusable.

The reusable space shuttle would make spaceflight and cargo transport relatively routine and cost-effective, thereby encouraging and enhancing the commercial use of space. The system could be used as a base from which to deploy payloads, repair and service satellites, and launch or retrieve satellites. It could also serve as a platform for

scientific research and the manufacture of certain materials requiring a zero-gravity environment.

Additional advantages would be the shuttle's ability to carry large payloads, such as the Hubble Space Telescope, into orbit and to provide a vantage point from which to observe astronomical events, weather disturbances, and environmental changes on Earth. Very important, the shuttle could carry the component parts of a space station into orbit and then act as the transportation system between the station and Earth.

About the same length and weight as a commercial DC-9, the wedged-shaped, delta-winged orbiter could carry a crew of three to seven persons. The crew would consist of a commander, a pilot, and several mission specialists, all astronauts. There would also be room for one or two payload specialists, non-career astronauts responsible for conducting specific experiments and nominated for flight by the payload sponsor. Certified by NASA for flight, they could be chosen from the civilian population. The fact that "ordinary" people might travel on the shuttle added to the program's appeal.

A typical mission would last between a week to sixteen days; the longest mission was 17.5 days (STS-80) The crew would live and work in a shirt-sleeve environment, without cumbersome space suits or breathing apparatuses. Maneuvering in the microgravity environment would prove the biggest challenge to crew members.

In January, 1977, tests of the shuttle's approach and landing capabilities began, with and without crews on board, at Dryden Flight Research Center, Edwards Air Force Base, California. An orbiter prototype, *Enterprise*, was the first shuttle-type vehicle tested, and it flew successfully.

On April 12, 1981, two years behind schedule, the first of four piloted orbital test flights was launched from Kennedy Space Center (KSC) at Cape Canaveral, Florida. The flight was designated STS-1, and the orbiter was named *Columbia*. The two-day mission demonstrated the spacecraft's ability to reach orbit and return safely. The mission provided data on temperatures and pressures at various points on the orbiter. There were also tests of the cargo bay doors, attitude control systems, and orbital maneuvering system. STS-1 landed safely at Edwards Air Force Base.

STS-2 was launched in November of 1981. The orbiter *Columbia* was used again. For the first time, the Remote Manipulator System (RMS) was tested. STS-2 also marked the first time that a spacecraft had ever flown twice.

STS-3, launched in March, 1982, was the longest of the initial test flights. The spacecraft stayed in space eight days, and activities included a special test of the RMS and experiments in materials processing. This mission was the first to use the secondary landing site at White Sands Missile Range in New Mexico. The final test flight of this series, conducted in the summer of 1982, featured another test of the RMS, further materials processing experiments, and the launch of the first Department of Defense payload. Once these tests were completed, the space shuttle was declared operational.

From 1981 to 1983, NASA launched a total of nine STS missions. All were launched from KSC. The space shuttles *Columbia* and *Challenger* were used for these missions, and they carried a variety of payloads and experiments. Highlights included the launching of commercial and government communications satellites (the first Tracking and Data-Relay Satellite, or TDRS), the first retrieval of an object from orbit, the first shuttle-based extravehicular activity, and the launching of the first Spacelab—a portable science laboratory carried in a shuttle's cargo bay.

Beginning with the first shuttle launch of 1984, NASA began to use a new numbering system to identify missions. A first number would refer to the year, a second number would refer to the launch site (1 for KSC, 2 for Vandenberg Air Force Base), and a letter would refer to the order of assignment in that year. The first 1984 mission, known as STS 41-B, used the orbiter *Challenger* and marked the first landing on a concrete runway specifically designed for shuttle landings at KSC. The shuttle's tenth flight featured the introduction of the Manned Maneuvering Unit (MMU), a backpack propulsion unit that allowed astronauts to maneuver in space independent of the orbiter. The next mission, 41-C, was important because it demonstrated the ability of the orbiter and crew to retrieve, repair, and redeploy a malfunctioning satellite.

Throughout 1984 and 1985, the shuttle program evolved. With each mission, payloads became more sophisticated, and the orbiters continued to meet NASA's expectations. Spacelab was flown two more times, and several missions were devoted to Department of Defense programs. Two new orbiters, *Discovery* and *Atlantis*, were added to the shuttle fleet.

Shuttle flights were considered so safe and routine that civilian scientists and even a U.S. senator traveled on the spacecraft. In 1984, at the suggestion of President Ronald W. Reagan, a national search for a candidate to be the first schoolteacher

Members of the Rogers Commission arrive at Kennedy Space Center. (NASA)

in space was started. S. Christa McAuliffe, a New Hampshire high-school teacher, was chosen; she was scheduled to fly on STS 51-L. The prospect of a civilian schoolteacher riding aboard a shuttle captured the imagination of the nation. The attention of the world, especially the schoolchildren, was focused on the launch pad at KSC on the cold morning of January 28, 1986. Seventy-three seconds after liftoff, the space shuttle *Challenger* was destroyed, killing all seven crew members, including McAuliffe. Millions watching television had viewed the accident. Once the initial shock and grief passed, another kind of anguish replaced it.

President Reagan immediately appointed an independent board of inquiry headed by former Secretary of State William P. Rogers. Shuttle astronaut Sally K. Ride and former astronaut Neil A. Armstrong also served on the commission. NASA conducted its own inquiry, and the U.S. Congress oversaw NASA's investigation. As the committees began to probe, it became obvious that NASA was in a difficult position. It was revealed that warnings about faulty equipment had been ignored because of scheduling pressures and that there was a general lack of communication between NASA, its contractors, and the government. NASA's Administrator, James M. Beggs, resigned and was replaced by a former NASA Administrator, James C. Fletcher. The old controversy over a piloted program versus a robotic program reemerged. The space shuttle was put on hold, and it appeared that it might never recover from the devastating blow. In addition to the serious social and moral ramifications, the scientific and economic costs were high. A one billion dollar orbiter, one-fourth of the space shuttle fleet, had been destroyed, and the deployment of several expensive and important scientific projects would have to be delayed indefinitely.

In June of 1986, the official findings of the Rogers Commission were released. Failure of the O-rings, critical connecting seals in the Solid Rocket Boosters (SRBs), was identified as the primary cause of the accident. The report also revealed that there had been warnings that the rings might fail in the abnormal cold of January 28, 1986, warnings that had been ignored so that the shuttle could fly on schedule. In the wake of the report, harsh criticism fell on NASA management.

NASA began to reorganize the space shuttle program from its very foundations. Every aspect of the system was scrutinized, from the SRBs to the orbiter. More than forty major changes were made to the SRBs, at a cost of $450 million. Thirty-nine changes were made to the liquid-fueled main engines, and sixty-eight modifications were made to the shuttle itself. Perhaps the most significant changes, however, concerned the way NASA conducted business, especially with respect to safety. In July, 1986, a new safety program was instituted. NASA officials believed that their new system would safeguard against any poor or uninformed decision that could endanger the lives of shuttle crew members.

On September 29, 1988, approximately two and one-half years after the *Challenger* accident, the space shuttle *Discovery* (STS-26) was successfully launched from KSC. On October 3, after sixty-four orbits and 2.7 million kilometers of successful spaceflight, it safely touched down on the runway at Edwards Air Force Base. The improved SRBs and modified main engines performed perfectly. NASA's goal had been reached: The space shuttle program had been reborn.

During 1989, five shuttle missions were flown, including two Department of Defense flights, STS-28 and STS-33. Communications and interplanetary exploration were the prime payloads for the other missions. STS-29 deployed the Tracking and Data-Relay Satellite-D (TDRS-D) in March during the four-day mission aboard *Discovery*. With the deployment, the Tracking and Data-Relay Satellite System was complete and operational. The Magellan probe to Venus was launched from the payload bay of *Atlantis* on May 4 during the four-day STS-30 flight. The Galileo orbiter and probe were launched atop an Inertial Upper Stage on October 18, from *Atlantis*.

Two more Department of Defense missions, STS-36 and STS-38, flew in 1990. The Defense Department's Synchronous Communication Satellite IV-F5 (Syncom IV-F5) was deployed from *Columbia* in January, during STS-32. During the ten-day flight the Long Duration Exposure Facility (LDEF) was, at long last, retrieved. It had been deployed in 1984. In April, the crew of *Discovery* placed the Hubble Space Telescope in orbit during the STS-31 flight. Seven months later, the Ulysses Solar Polar mission was launched from *Discovery* on STS-41. The year's activities were concluded with the December flight of *Columbia*. The primary objectives of STS-35 were round-the-clock observations of the celestial sphere in ultraviolet and x-ray astronomy with the ASTRO-1 observatory, consisting of four telescopes. The flight

crew-operated ultraviolet telescopes were mounted on Spacelab elements in the cargo bay.

Six shuttle flights were conducted in 1991. In April, the Compton Gamma Ray Observatory became the second of NASA's Great Observatories to begin studying the cosmos when it was deployed during STS-37. The September deployment of the Upper Atmosphere Research Satellite from the space shuttle initiated NASA's Mission to Planet Earth, a two-decade-long coordinated research program to study Earth as a complete environmental system. In June, NASA's Life Sciences and Flight Systems Divisions oversaw the flight of Spacelab Life Sciences 1 (SLS-1) aboard the space shuttle *Columbia*, in which seven astronauts conducted nine days of experiments to study the effects of weightlessness on the human body.

STS-39 in April was one of the most complicated missions ever flown. *Discovery* performed dozens of maneuvers, deploying canisters from the cargo bay, releasing and retrieving a payload with the RMS, all of which allowed the Department of Defense to gather important plume observation data and information for the Strategic Defense Initiative Organization (now called the Ballistic Missile Defense Organization). STS-43 in August set a record as the heaviest mission flown to date with a liftoff weight of *Atlantis* at 115,000 kilograms. The Tracking and Data-Relay Satellite-E was deployed, keeping the network that supports shuttle missions and other spacecraft, such as the Hubble Space Telescope, at full operational capability. NASA's fleet of reusable space planes returned to full strength in 1991, when the space shuttle program took delivery of *Endeavour* on April 25 in a ceremony at Rockwell's facility in Palmdale, California.

In January, 1992, the shuttle manifest showed eight flights scheduled, and at year's end, all eight had been flown. Seven of the eight missions launched on the day set at the flight readiness review and the eighth was one day late. The shuttle system flew so trouble-free that two missions were extended for additional science gathering. The year also saw the longest mission ever flown to date, STS-50, which lasted fourteen days.

Highlighting the missions conducted was *Endeavour*'s maiden voyage in May on the STS-49 mission. The crew rescued a wayward satellite and in the process set three new records for spaceflight: four spacewalks on a single mission, the longest spacewalk ever conducted (8 hours, 29 minutes), and the first three-person spacewalk ever performed. Three Spacelab missions were flown in 1992 to explore the effects of space on protein crystals, electronic materials, fluids, glasses, ceramics, metals, and alloys. Missions flown aboard the space shuttle included the International Microgravity Laboratory flown in January, United States Microgravity Laboratory-1 in June, and United States Microgravity Payload-1 in October. The September flight of Spacelab-J, the Japanese Spacelab, also included NASA-sponsored microgravity experiments.

The STS-46 mission in July demonstrated new technology in space with the Tethered Satellite System payload. *Columbia* and the STS-52 crew in October showed the orbiter's ability to fly a combination mission as they deployed the LAGEOS satellite and then conducted microgravity research with the United States Microgravity Payload. The last dedicated Department of Defense mission flown by the shuttle was during the STS-53 flight in early December.

The space shuttle once again showed its versatility in 1993. During that year, the shuttle deployed and retrieved various payloads, served as laboratory for scientists and researchers, and at the end of the year became an orbiting service station as NASA astronauts removed and replaced various elements of the Hubble Space Telescope.

The STS-54 mission in January saw the deployment of the sixth in the series of NASA's Tracking and Data-Relay Satellites. During shuttle mission STS-51 in September, a new Advanced Communications Technology Satellite (ACTS) was delivered to geostationary orbit. During shuttle mission STS-57 in June, NASA astronauts retrieved the EURECA (European Retrievable Carrier) satellite, which had spent almost a year in orbit. After being stowed in the cargo bay, it was brought back to Earth and the experiments aboard were delivered to the European Space Agency (ESA). Two shuttle missions in 1993 carried the ESA-developed pressurized Spacelab module, allowing the shuttle to become an orbiting laboratory.

The STS-55/Spacelab-D2 mission, launched April 26, saw the second flight of a mission devoted primarily to Germany for conducting a wide range of experiments in the microgravity environment of space. The STS-58/Spacelab Life Sciences 2 mission, launched October 18, involved NASA astronauts continuing the agency's efforts to gain more knowledge of how the human body adapts in a weightless condition and provide insight into medical problems experienced by people on Earth.

A new era in the commercial development of space began in June during shuttle mission STS-57, when the privately developed middeck augmentation module known as SPACEHAB was carried in the shuttle's cargo bay. The module provided additional access to crew-tended, middeck lockers and experiments. The shuttle became an orbiting astronomical observatory on several missions during 1993. The Diffuse X-ray Spectrometer (DXS) payload carried on STS-54 in January, the Atmospheric Laboratory for Applications and Science-2 (ATLAS-2) payload carried on STS-56 in April, and the Orbiting and Retrievable Far and Extreme Ultraviolet Spectrometer-Shuttle Pallet Satellite (ORFEUS-SPAS) payload deployed and retrieved on STS-51 in September investigated such issues as the origin and nature of the matter that fills the space between stars, the relationship between the Sun's energy output and studies of Earth's atmosphere, and the life-cycle of stars.

During three shuttle missions in 1993, NASA astronauts conducted a series of extravehicular activities (EVAs), or spacewalks. The EVAs, conducted during STS-54 in January, STS-57 in June, and STS- 51 in September were designed to refine training methods for spacewalkers by helping them to understand differences between true microgravity and ground simulations used during training, preparing them for the extensive series of EVAs associated with the STS-61 Hubble Space Telescope servicing mission, and expanding the EVA experience levels of the astronauts' flight controllers and instructors in preparation for construction of the International Space Station. NASA's final shuttle mission of 1993, STS-61, was the much anticipated first servicing mission to the Hubble Space Telescope (HST). On five consecutive nights, audiences around the world watched as astronauts aboard shuttle *Endeavour* removed and replaced various components on HST. The five EVAs performed on the STS-61 mission set a new record for most spacewalks on a single shuttle flight, and STS-61

The Space Radio Laboratory-2 in Endeavour's payload bay on STS-68. (NASA)

Astronaut Thomas D. "Tom" Akers became the American with the most EVA time in space with a total time to date of 29 hours, 40 minutes.

In 1994, NASA launched seven highly successful science and technology missions that acquired a total flight time of more than eighty-one days in orbit. The shuttle fleet deployed 832 tons of cargo into space, carried an additional 105 tons of cargo to orbit and back, and lofted forty-two astronauts into space, including crew members from Russia, Japan, and the European Space Agency. The space shuttle *Discovery* launched STS-60 on time at 7:10 a.m. eastern standard time, February 3, in a historic mission that featured the first flight of a Russian cosmonaut aboard a U.S. spacecraft. The presence of veteran cosmonaut Sergei Konstantinovich Krikalev signaled the beginning of a three-phase cooperative effort between the United States and Russia. A preview of the microgravity research work that would be conducted on the International Space Station was available during the STS-62 mission from March 4 to 18. It was the second flight of the United States Microgravity Payload (USMP). The highly successful mission included experiments that could lead to better semiconductors and stronger metals and alloys.

The space shuttle *Endeavour* carried the international Space Radar Laboratory (SRL) into orbit for the first of two flights, STS-59, in 1994. Comprising two radars and an atmospheric instrument, SRL made unprecedented measurements of the Earth's surface and continued observations of the atmosphere that began with STS-3 in 1982. SRL's radars used multiple frequencies and polarizations of radar waves to create images of the Earth's land, water, snow, and ice surfaces. Data obtained are being used in studies of the Earth's water cycle, vegetation, volcanoes, and oceans. During the first flight in April, scientists were able to see the progression of the "thaw line" as ice in northern sites began to melt. A ground team of more than two thousand scientists was deployed at sites around the globe to support the mission.

Columbia launched July 8 on a fourteen-day microgravity research mission. STS-65, the second International Microgravity Laboratory flight, was a worldwide research effort into the behavior of materials and life in the microgravity environment of space. The seven-member crew of STS-65 conducted eighty-two experiments developed by more than two hundred scientists from thirteen different countries. A new technique for remote sensing flew aboard *Discovery* during the STS-64 mission. By firing a powerful laser down through the Earth's atmosphere and measuring the portion of laser energy reflected back to the shuttle, scientists were able to observe clouds invisible to conventional weather satellites and to study the structure of a powerful typhoon. Laser ranging equipment acquired more than forty hours of high-quality data.

The shuttle *Endeavour* on STS-68 launched the second Space Radar Laboratory mission September 30 for a highly successful flight that repeated many of the April SRL investigations. The October flight, which covered the same sites and investigations as the April flight, allowed the scientists to observe the changes of seasons in different ecological settings. Using a technique called interferometry, the team also obtained very precise elevation data on some sites. Both SRL missions carried an instrument to study levels of carbon monoxide in the Earth's atmosphere. Scientists use measurements of carbon monoxide, which is produced in large amounts by fossil-fuel consumption and the burning of forests and other vegetation, to estimate the atmosphere's ability to cleanse itself of greenhouse gases.

NASA's Office of Mission to Planet Earth completed a series of space shuttle flights dedicated to studying the Earth's atmosphere and its relation to the Sun. Designated the Atmospheric Laboratory for Applications and Science (ATLAS) series, these flights in 1992, 1993, and 1994 provided scientists with three snapshots of the Sun and the chemistry of the Earth's atmosphere, focusing on ozone depletion. During the ATLAS-3 flight from November 3 to November 14, scientists were able to peer inside the ebbing Antarctic ozone hole and "see" the lower concentrations of ozone and higher levels of ozone-depleting chemicals. Data also clearly differentiated between human-induced ozone depletion and that caused by atmospheric dynamics.

Seven shuttle flights flew in 1995, including three to the Russian Mir Space Station. STS-63, the first shuttle flight of 1995, included several history making achievements. It was the first flight of a female shuttle pilot (Eileen M. Collins). Part of Phase I of the International Space Station program, it was also the second flight of a Russian cosmonaut on the shuttle, and the first approach and fly-around by shuttle of the Mir Space Station. During STS-67 in March, *Endeavour* logged 11 million kilometers, completing the longest shuttle flight to date, allowing sustained examination of the "hidden universe" of ultraviolet light. The primary payload, the Astro Observatory, had flown once before—on STS-35 in December, 1990—but the second flight had almost twice the duration. Planned Astro-2 observations built on discoveries made by Astro-1, as well as seeking answers to other questions. Astro-2 marked the second flight of the three ultraviolet telescopes flown on Astro-1.

STS-71 marked a number of historic firsts in human spaceflight history: the one hundredth U.S. human space launch, the first U.S. shuttle-Mir docking and joint on-orbit operation, the largest spacecraft ever in orbit, and the first on-orbit changeout of a shuttle crew. Docking occurred at 9:00 a.m. eastern daylight time, June 29, using the R-bar or Earth radius vector approach, with *Atlantis* closing in on Mir from directly below. The R-bar approach allows natural forces to brake the orbiter's approach more than would occur along a standard approach directly in front of the Space Station; also,

The Microgravity Science Laboratory (MSL) was a collection of microgravity experiments housed inside a European Spacelab Long Module (LM). (NASA)

the R-bar approach minimizes the number of orbiter jet firings needed for approach. The primary objective of the STS-70 mission in July was accomplished when the Tracking and Data-Relay Satellite-G was deployed from the orbiter payload bay about six hours after liftoff. Approximately one hour after deployment, the Inertial Upper Stage (IUS) booster attached to TDRS-G completed the first of two scheduled burns to place TDRS-G in geosynchronous orbit. Once it completed on-orbit checkout, TDRS-G became an operational spare, completing the existing TDRS network of advanced tracking and communications satellites.

The September flight of STS-69 marked the first time two different payloads were retrieved and deployed during the same mission. It also featured an extravehicular activity to practice for space station activities and to evaluate space-suit design modifications. The first of two primary payloads, SPARTAN 201-03, was deployed on flight day two. This was the third SPARTAN 201 mission in a planned series of four. The primary objective was to study the Sun's outer atmosphere and its transition into the solar wind, which constantly flows past Earth. The second primary payload, the Wake

Shield Facility-2 (WSF-2) was deployed on flight day five and became the first spacecraft to maneuver itself away from the orbiter, rather than the other way around, by firing a small cold gas nitrogen thruster to maneuver away from *Endeavour*. WSF-2 was a 3.66-meter-diameter stainless steel disk designed to generate an ultra-high vacuum environment in space within which to grow thin films for next-generation advanced electronics.

In October, STS-73 marked the second flight of the United States Microgravity Laboratory (USML) and built on the foundation of its predecessor, which had flown on *Columbia* during mission STS-50 in 1992. Research during USML-2 concentrated within the same overall areas of USML-1, with many experiments flying for the second time. The crew was divided into two teams to work around the clock in a 7-meter-long Spacelab module located in *Columbia*'s payload bay. Research was conducted in five areas: fluid physics, materials science, biotechnology, combustion science, and commercial space processing. USML-2 activities were directed by NASA's Spacelab Mission Operations Control facility at Marshall Space Flight Center. The final flight of 1995, STS-74, marked the second docking of the U.S. space shuttle to the Russian space station Mir, continuing Phase I activities leading to the construction of the International Space Station.

The first NASA shuttle mission of 1996 saw space shuttle *Endeavour* and its six-person crew retrieve a Japanese satellite, deploy and retrieve a NASA science satellite, and conduct two spacewalks to demonstrate and evaluate techniques to be used in the assembly of the International Space Station. Launch of *Endeavour* on STS-72 occurred on January 11. Reflight of the U.S.-Italian Tethered Satellite System (TSS-1R) was marred by the loss of the satellite on flight day three, although valuable scientific data were still gathered. The other primary payload, the United States Microgravity Payload-3 (USMP-3), performed nominally. TSS had flown previously on mission STS-46 in June, 1992, but experiment operations had been curtailed because of a jammed tether. The TSS concept was designed to study electrodynamics of a tether system in the electrically charged portion of Earth's atmosphere called the ionosphere.

The transfer in March of veteran astronaut Shannon W. Lucid to Mir to become the first American woman to live on the station highlighted the third linkup between the space shuttle and the Russian space station Mir. Lucid would be succeeded by Astronaut John E. Blaha during STS-79 in August, giving her the distinction of membership in four different flight crews, two U.S. and two Russian. Her stay on Mir began a continuous U.S. presence in space for the next two years. The fourth shuttle flight of 1996, in May, was highlighted by four rendezvous activities with two different payloads. The primary payloads, all located in the cargo bay, were the SPACEHAB-4 pressurized research module; the Inflatable Antenna Experiment (IAE) mounted on the SPARTAN 207 free flyer; and a suite of four technology demonstration experiments known as Technology Experiments for Advancing Missions in Space (TEAMS).

Five space agencies (NASA, the European Space Agency, the French Space Agency, the Canadian Space Agency, and the Italian Space Agency) and research scientists from ten countries worked together on the primary payload of STS-78, Life and Microgravity Spacelab (LMS). More than forty experiments flown were grouped into two areas: life sciences, which included human physiology and space biology, and microgravity science, which included basic fluid physics investigations, advanced semiconductor and metal alloy materials processing, and medical research in protein crystal growth. In September, STS-79 was highlighted by the return to Earth of U.S. astronaut Lucid after 188 days in space, the first U.S. crew exchange aboard

the Russian space station Mir, and the fourth shuttle-Mir docking. Lucid's long-duration spaceflight set a new U.S. record as well as a world record for a woman. STS-79 also marked the second flight of the SPACEHAB module in support of shuttle-Mir activities and the first flight of the SPACEHAB double module configuration.

The final shuttle flight of 1996, STS-80, was highlighted by the successful deployment, operation, and retrieval of two free-flying research spacecraft. Two planned extravehicular activities (EVAs) were canceled. The Orbiting Retrievable Far and Extreme Ultraviolet Spectrometer-Shuttle Pallet Satellite II (ORFEUS-SPAS II) was deployed on flight day one to begin approximately two weeks of data gathering. Making its second flight aboard the shuttle, ORFEUS-SPAS II featured three primary scientific instruments: the ORFEUS-Telescope with the Far Ultraviolet (FUV) Spectrograph and Extreme Ultraviolet (EUV) Spectrograph. The ORFEUS-SPAS II mission was dedicated to astronomical observations at very short wavelengths to investigate the nature of hot stellar atmospheres, investigate cooling mechanisms of white dwarf stars, determine the nature of accretion disks around collapsed stars, investigate supernova remnants, and investigate the interstellar medium and potential star-forming regions. Wake Shield Facility-3 (WSF-3) was deployed on flight day 4. The third flight was highly successful, with a maximum seven thin film growths of semiconductor materials achieved and the satellite hardware performing almost flawlessly. WSF-3 was retrieved after three days of free-flight. Two planned six-hour EVAs were designed to evaluate equipment and procedures that would be used during construction and maintenance of the International Space Station. However, the crew could not open the outer airlock hatch, and when troubleshooting did not reveal the cause mission managers concluded it would not be prudent to attempt the two EVAs and risk unnecessary damage to hatch or seals. Post-landing assessment of the hatch indicated that a small screw had become loose from an internal assembly and had lodged in an actuator—a gearbox-type mechanism that operated the linkages that secure the hatch—preventing the crew from opening the hatch. The hatch opened easily when the replacement actuator was installed.

The first shuttle flight of 1997, STS-81, was highlighted by the return of astronaut John E. Blaha to Earth after a 118-day stay aboard the Russian space station Mir and the largest transfer to date of logistics between the two spacecraft. *Atlantis* also returned carrying the first plants to complete a life cycle in space—a crop of wheat grown from seed to seed. This fifth of nine planned dockings continued Phase IB of the NASA/Russian Space Agency cooperative effort. The same payload configuration flown on previous docking flights—featuring the SPACEHAB double module—was flown again. The February STS-82 mission demonstrated anew the capability of the space shuttle to service orbiting spacecraft. The six-member crew completed the servicing and upgrading of the Hubble Space Telescope during four planned extravehicular activities (EVAs) and then performed a fifth, unscheduled spacewalk to repair insulation on the telescope.

The first flight of the Microgravity Science Laboratory 1 (MSL-1) on STS-83 in April was cut short over concerns about one of three fuel cells, marking only the third time in the history of the shuttle program that a mission ended early. (STS-2 in 1981 and STS-44 in 1991 were the other two times.) Fuel cell No. 2 had shown some erratic readings during prelaunch startup but had been cleared to fly after an additional checkout and test. Shortly after on-orbit operations began, the fuel cell No. 2 substack No. 3 differential voltage began trending upward. There are three fuel cells on each orbiter, each containing three substacks made up of two banks of sixteen cells. In one substack of fuel cell No. 2, the difference in output voltage between the two banks of cells was increasing. Fuel cells use a reaction of liquid hydrogen and liquid oxygen to generate electricity and produce drinking water. Although one

fuel cell produced enough electricity to conduct on-orbit and landing operations, shuttle flight rules required all three to be functioning well to ensure crew safety and provide sufficient backup capability during reentry and landing.

The May flight of STS-84 was the sixth shuttle-Mir docking and was highlighted by the transfer of the fourth successive U.S. crew member to the Russian space station. Astronaut C. Michael Foale exchanged places with Jerry M. Linenger, who had arrived at Mir January 15 with the crew of shuttle mission STS-81. Linenger had spent 123 days on Mir and just over 132 days in space from launch to landing, placing him second behind astronaut Shannon W. Lucid for most time spent on orbit by an American. Another milestone reached during his stay was the one-year anniversary of a continuous U.S. presence in space that had begun with Lucid's arrival at Mir on March 22, 1996.

The July flight of STS-94 marked the first reflight of the same vehicle, crew, and payloads, following the shortened STS-83 mission in April due to indications of a fuel cell problem. The primary payload was the Microgravity Science Laboratory 1 (MSL-1). A quick turnaround in processing *Columbia* for the reflight was accomplished in part by the first reservicing of a primary payload, MSL-1, in the orbiter. In August, STS-85 carried a complement of payloads in the cargo bay that focused on Mission to Planet Earth objectives as well as preparations for International Space Station assembly: the Cryogenic Infrared Spectrometers and Telescopes for the Atmosphere-Shuttle Pallet Satellite-2 (CRISTASPAS-2), the Japanese Manipulator Flight Development (MFD), the Technology Applications and Science-01 (TAS-1) package, and the International Extreme Ultraviolet Hitchhiker-02 (IEH-02).

The seventh Mir docking mission, in September on STS-86, continued the presence of a U.S. astronaut on the Russian space station with the transfer of physician David A. Wolf to Mir. Wolf became the sixth U.S. astronaut in succession to live on Mir to continue Phase IB of the NASA/Russian Space

Agency cooperative effort. C. Michael Foale returned to Earth after spending 145 days in space, 134 of them aboard Mir. His estimated mileage logged was 93 million kilometers, making his the second longest U.S. spaceflight, behind Shannon W. Lucid's record of 188 days. His stay was marred by a collision on June 25 between a Progress resupply vehicle and the station's Spektr module, damaging a radiator and one of four solar arrays on Spektr.

The primary payload of STS-87, the last flight of 1997, was the United States Microgravity Payload-4. It performed well. Research using the other major payload, the SPARTAN-201-04 free-flyer, was not completed. USMP-4 research was deemed highly successful. This fourth flight of the United States Microgravity Payload focused on materials science, combustion science, and fundamental physics.

The first flight of 1998, STS-89, featured the docking of *Endeavour* to Mir on January 24. The transfer of Andrew S. W. Thomas to Mir and the return of David A. Wolf to the orbiter occurred at 6:35 p. m., January 25. Initially, Thomas thought his Sokol pressure suit did not fit, and the crew exchange was allowed to proceed only after Wolf's suit was adjusted to fit Thomas. Once on Mir, Thomas was able to make adequate adjustments to his own suit (which would be worn should the crew need to return to Earth in the Soyuz spacecraft), and this remained on Mir with him. Wolf spent a total of 119 days aboard Mir, and after landing his total on-orbit time was 128 days. Neurolab's 26 experiments aboard STS-90 targeted one of the most complex and least understood parts of the human body: the nervous system. Primary goals were to conduct basic research in neurosciences and expand the understanding of how the nervous system develops and functions in space. Test subjects were crew members and rats, mice, crickets, snails, and two kinds of fish. The mission was a cooperative effort of NASA, several domestic partners, and the space agencies of Canada (Canadian Space Agency, CSA), France (Centre National d'Études Spatiales, CNES), and Germany (DARA), as well as the European Space Agency (ESA) and the National Space Development Agency of Japan (NASDA). Most experiments were conducted in the pressurized Spacelab long module located in *Columbia*'s payload bay. This was the sixteenth and last scheduled flight of the Spacelab module, although Spacelab pallets would continue to be used on the International Space Station.

The docking of *Discovery* to Mir, the first for that orbiter, occurred at 12:58 p. m., June 4, during STS-91. At hatch opening, Andy Thomas officially became a member of *Discovery*'s crew, completing 130 days of living and working on Mir. The transfer wrapped up a total of 907 days spent by seven U.S. astronauts aboard the Russian space station as long-duration crew members. During the next four days,

With Unity in place, Astronaut Nancy Currie begins positioning Zarya for mating during STS-88. (NASA)

the Mir 25 and STS-91 crews transferred more than 500 kilograms of water, and almost 2,100 kilograms of cargo experiments and supplies were exchanged between the two spacecraft. During this time, long-term U.S. experiments aboard Mir were moved into *Discovery*'s middeck locker area and the SPACEHAB single module in the orbiter's payload bay, including the Space Acceleration Measurement System (SAMS) and the tissue engineering cocul-ture (COCULT) investigations, as well as two crystal growth experiments. The crews also con-ducted Risk Mitigation Experiments (RMEs) and Human Life Sciences (HLS) investigations. When the hatches closed for undocking at 9:07 a. m., June 8, and the spacecraft separated at 12:01 p.m. that day, the final shuttle-Mir docking mission was con-cluded and Phase I of the International Space Sta-tion (ISS) program came to an end.

The primary objectives of STS-95 in October in-cluded conducting a variety of science experiments in the pressurized SPACEHAB module, the deploy-ment and retrieval of the SPARTAN freeflyer pay-load, and operations with the Hubble Space Tele-scope Orbiting Systems Test (HOST) and the International Extreme Ultraviolet Hitchhiker pay-loads being carried in the payload bay. The scien-tific research mission also returned space pioneer John H. Glenn, Jr., to orbit—thirty-six years after he became the first American to orbit Earth.

The final mission of 1998 was the twelve-day mission to begin assembly of the International Space Station (ISS). All objectives of STS-88 were met. On December 5, the 12.8-ton Unity connecting module was first connected to *Endeavour*'s docking system; on December 6, using the 15-meter-long robot arm, the Zarya Control Module was captured from orbit and mated to Unity; and astronauts Jerry L. Ross and James H. Newman conducted three spacewalks to attach cables, connectors, and hand-rails. The two modules were powered up after the astronauts' entry. Other EVA objectives were met as Ross and Newman tested a Simplified Aid for Ex-travehicular Activity Rescue (SAFER) unit, a

self-rescue device should a spacewalker become separated from the spacecraft during an EVA; nudged two un-deployed antennae on Zarya into position; removed launch restraint pins on Unity's four hatchways for mating future additions of sta-tion modules and truss structures; installed a sun-shade over Unity's two data-relay boxes to protect them against harsh sunlight; stowed a tool bag on Unity and disconnected umbilicals used for the mating procedure with Zarya; installed a handrail on Zarya; and made a detailed photographic survey of the station. A new spacewalk record was estab-lished as Ross completed his seventh walk, totaling 44 hours, 9 minutes. Newman moved into third place with four walks totaling 28 hours, 27 minutes.

Only three shuttle missions were flown in 1999, the first of which was conducted at the International Space Station. All major objectives were accom-plished during the STS-96 mission. On May 29, *Discovery* made the first docking to the Interna-tional Space Station (ISS). Kent V. Rominger eased the shuttle to a textbook linkup with Unity's Pres-surized Mating Adapter 2 as the orbiter and the ISS flew over the Russian-Kazakh border. The forty-fifth spacewalk in shuttle history and the fourth of the ISS era lasted 7 hours and 55 minutes, making it the second-longest ever conducted. Tamara E. Jernigan and Daniel T. Barry transferred a U.S.-built crane, called the Orbital Transfer Device, and parts of the Russian crane Strela from the shuttle's payload bay and attached them to locations on the outside of the station. The astronauts also installed two new portable foot restraints that would fit both American and Russian space boots and attached three bags filled with tools and handrails that would be used during future assembly operations. The cranes and tools fastened to the outside of the sta-tion totaled 300 kilograms.

The July flight of STS-93 was the first mission in space shuttle history to be commanded by a woman, Commander Eileen M. Collins. Also, this was the shortest scheduled mission since 1990. On the first day of the scheduled five-day mission, the Chandra X-Ray Observatory was deployed from *Columbia*'s payload bay. Chandra's two-stage IUS propelled the observatory into a transfer orbit of 330 by 72,000 kilometers in altitude. It was later lifted to its observation orbit, which has the shape of an ellipse and takes the spacecraft more than a third of the way to the Moon before returning to its closest approach to Earth of 10,000 kilometers.

The final flight of 1999, STS-103, restored the Hubble Space Telescope to working order and upgraded some of its systems, allowing the decade-old observatory to get ready to begin its second scheduled decade of astronomical observations. During the first few days of the eight-day mission, the crew prepared for the rendezvous with and capture of the Hubble Space Telescope and the three maintenance spacewalks to follow. After a thirty-orbit chase, Commander Curtis L. Brown, Jr., and Pilot Scott J. Kelly maneuvered the orbiter to a point directly beneath Hubble and then moved upward toward it. Mission Specialist Jean-François Clervoy grappled Hubble using the orbiter's robotic arm and placed it on the Flight Support System in the rear of *Discovery*'s cargo bay. Three spacewalks were needed for the servicing, and then Hubble was released from *Discovery*'s cargo bay on Christmas Day. Mission STS-103 saw the third time in the U.S. space program that a crew has spent Christmas in space.

During the first flight of 2000, STS-99, the Shuttle Radar Topography Mission (SRTM) mast was deployed successfully to its full length, and the antenna was turned to its operation position. After a successful checkout of the radar systems, mapping began at 12:31 a. m., February 12, less than twelve hours after launch. Crew members, who had split into two shifts so they could work around the clock, began mapping an area from 60° north to 56° south. Data were sent to the Jet Propulsion Laboratory for analysis, and early indications showed the data to be of excellent quality. In May, the STS-101 crew completed a successful mission to service and

supply the International Space Station. After a flawless docking with the station and a five-day stay and undocking, Commander James D. Halsell, Jr., landed space shuttle *Atlantis* at Kennedy Space Center on May 29. During the mission, *Atlantis* had logged 6.6 million kilometers.

STS-106 was launched in September, 2000, as a logistics and resupply mission to the ISS. This would be the last supply mission prior to the beginning of a permanent presence on the station. STS-92 brought the Integrated Truss Structure (ITS) Z1 and Pressurized Mating Adapter 3 (PMA-3) to ISS. In October, Soyuz TM-31 brought the ISS Permanent Expedition One crew for a five-month stay. The Soyuz would be left as a lifeboat for the next crew. The Integrated Truss Structure P6 and the photovoltaic module were brought to the station by the STS-97 crew in November.

All six shuttle missions in 2001 were flown to the Space Station. The Destiny Laboratory was delivered aboard STS-98 in February. Destiny is the primary research laboratory for U.S. payloads, supporting a wide range of experiments and studies contributing to health, safety, and quality of life for people all over the world. In March, *Discovery* spent nine days docked to the Space Station. The crew attached the Leonardo Multi-Purpose Logistics Module (MPLM), transferred supplies and equipment to the station, and completed two spacewalks. They also carried the second permanent crew to the station and returned the first crew to Earth.

STS-100 (May, 2001) delivered and installed a new robotic arm and transferred equipment and supplies between the orbiter and the station. *Endeavour* and its crew spent eight days in joint operations with the station crew. In July, STS-104 delivered the Quest Airlock and installed it on the station's Unity Node. *Atlantis* spent thirteen days in orbit, eight of those days docked with the station. The airlock permits astronauts and cosmonauts aboard the station to leave the safety of the pressurized vessel and venture out into space on assembly and repair missions.

In August, 2001, the STS-105 crew attached the Leonardo MPLM, transferred supplies and equipment to the station, completed two spacewalks, and deployed a small spacecraft called Simplesat. *Discovery* also delivered the Expedition Three crew and returned the second crew to Earth. The final mission of 2001, STS-108, was the twelfth shuttle flight to visit the station and the first since the installation of the Russian airlock called Pirs on the station. *Endeavour* delivered the Expedition Four crew to the orbital outpost and returned the Expedition Three crew. While at the station, the crew conducted one spacewalk and attached the Raffaello MPLM to the station. About 2.7 metric tons of equipment and supplies were unloaded. The crew later returned Raffaello to *Endeavour*'s payload bay for the trip home.

The STS-109 crew began 2002 with the successful servicing of the Hubble Space Telescope. Upgrades and servicing by the crew left Hubble with a new power unit, a new camera, and new solar arrays. This was the fourth shuttle mission dedicated to servicing Hubble. STS-109 spent a total of 10 days, 22 hours, and 39 minutes in space. This was *Columbia*'s twenty-seventh flight and its first since undergoing modifications in 1999. It would also be *Columbia*'s last successful flight.

The four remaining missions of 2002 were to the ISS. *Atlantis* installed the 13-meter-long S0 Truss—the backbone for future station expansion. While in orbit, the STS-110 crew members performed four spacewalks and used the shuttle and station robotic arms to install and outfit the S0. They prepared the station for future spacewalks and spent a week in joint operations with the Expedition Four crew. They also prepared the Mobile Transporter for use along the truss as a conveyor of robotic systems and equipment.

STS-111 delivered the Expedition Five crew to the station and returned the Expedition Four crew to Earth. *Endeavour* also delivered the Mobile Base System, or MBS. Among the objectives completed were the permanent installation of the MBS onto the station and the replacement of a wrist roll joint on the station's robotic arm. The STS-111 crew also unloaded supplies and science experiments from the Leonardo MPLM, which made its third trip to the orbital outpost.

While at the International Space Station in October, 2002, the STS-112 crew conducted joint operations with the Expedition Five crew, installed and activated the S1 Truss, and performed three spacewalks. During a fourteen-day mission in November and December, 2002, *Endeavour* and the STS-113 crew extended the Space Station's backbone and exchanged the Expedition Five and Six crews. STS-113 was the sixteenth shuttle mission to the station. It continued the station's outward expansion with the delivery of the P1 Truss.

On February 1, 2003, seventeen years after the *Challenger* accident, NASA suffered the loss of another orbiter, *Columbia*, and its crew of seven upon reentry after nearly completing the mission. STS-107 marked the first flight of the SPACEHAB Research Double Module. The Fast Reaction Experiments Enabling Science, Technology, Applications and Research (FREESTAR) payload included six separate experiments mounted on a crossbay-support structure. This sixteen-day mission had been dedicated to research in physical, life, and space sciences, conducted in approximately 80 separate experiments, comprising hundreds of samples and test points. The seven astronauts worked twenty-four hours a day, in two alternating shifts before attempting to return home. *Columbia* broke up approximately 16 minutes before landing, during reentry over Texas, en route to the Kennedy Space Center. The STS-107 crew members—Commander Rick D. Husband; Pilot William C. McCool; Mission Specialists Michael P. Anderson, David M. Brown, Laurel B. Clark, and Kalpana Chawla; and Payload Specialist Ilan Ramon of Israel—were killed and the world's first reusable space vehicle was destroyed.

For more than two years, the shuttle fleet—*Atlantis*, *Discovery*, and *Endeavour*—was on hiatus, while NASA upgraded flight hardware and visual tracking and inspection equipment to ensure the STS-114 "Return to Flight" mission would be successful. *Discovery*, which played the same return-to-flight role after the 1986 *Challenger* accident, was successfully launched on July 26, 2005 under the command of Eileen Collins.

NASA engineers made dozens of changes to the External Tank design, including one to a key mechanism that joins it with the orbiter. Jutting from the upper third of the tank, the "bipod fitting" is susceptible to icing from the ultra-cold fuel that tank contains. Until the *Columbia* accident, the part was protected from ice buildup using thick sheets of foam. The improved bipod design instead relied on electric heaters to keep the area clear.

Another major safety improvement to the space shuttle fleet was the expanded use of enhanced imaging equipment to record the launch. At KSC, NASA upgraded the short-, medium-, and long-range tracking camera system around the Center's Launch Pads 39A and 39B, along with those lining the nearby Atlantic coastline. *Discovery* received new imaging equipment with the installation of a digital External Tank camera. Making the most of current consumer photography equipment, the orbiter's External Tank camera has been switched from film to a digital model. With the simplicity and increased speed of a digital system, the image files taken during the STS-114 launch were transmitted to Earth shortly after *Discovery* reached space.

Once in orbit, the orbiter's visual inspection continued with the help of a new piece of robotic technology. The RMS included a Canadian-built

Orbiter Boom Sensor System (OBSS). The OBSS boom extension housed a camera and laser-powered measuring device that astronauts used to scan the orbiter's exterior. The boom attached to the end of the existing robotic arm and doubled its length to 30 meters. The extra length allowed the arm to reach around the spacecraft for the best possible views. With the new boom, *Discovery*'s astronauts took a good look at features like the orbiter's leading wing edges and underbody tiles. During this inspection, and subsequent examination by the International Space Station crew before docking, relatively minor damage was found on critical areas of the orbiter. There was no damage to the wings' leading edges, and the only significant find on the underbody was the protrusion of two tile-gap fillers. Gap fillers were used in areas to restrict the flow of hot gas into the gaps between thermal protection system components. They

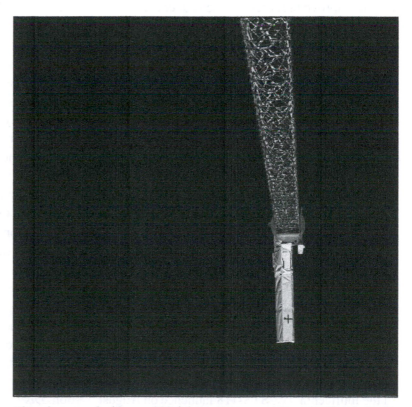

This photograph shows a 200-ft long mast supporting the Shuttle Radio Topographic Mission jutted into space from the Space Shuttle Endeavour on STS-99. (NASA)

consisted of a layer of coated Nextel fabric and were normally about 0.5 millimeter thick. Despite days of anticipation and intense planning, space-walking STS-114 astronaut Steve Robinson made it look easy as he gently pulled out the two gap fillers on the ninth day of the mission.

The orbiter's leading wing edges were outfitted with 22 temperature sensors to measure how heat was distributed across their spans. Each wing had 66 accelerometers to detect impacts and gauge their strength and location. The sensors were highly sensitive and took 20,000 readings per second. This new network of sensors running along the wings provided an electronic nervous system that gave engineers a valuable way to monitor the wings' condition. During the STS-114 flight, no unusual measurements were recorded. *Discovery* landed on August 9, 2005 restoring faith in the Space Transportation System, but also leaving more work to be done to improve the safety of the orbiter fleet.

There were only two shuttle missions in 2006. STS-121 had been delayed in order to make changes to the External Tank foam situation in the aftermath of shedding events experienced during STS-114's climb to orbit, i.e. the first Return To Flight mission. In a way, STS-121 was also part of the Return To Flight effort because the changes in ET foam had to be verified before more routine missions would follow. *Discovery* launched on July 4, 2006, and flew to the International Space Station with logistical supplies in the Leonardo MPLM. A crew rotation was also affected before *Discovery* landed at the end of nearly 13 days aloft. ISS assembly resumed with STS-116 which launched on December 9, 2006. *Discovery* delivered the P5 truss segment to the orbital complex, and affected a crew rotation during a 13-day flight.

The first shuttle flight of 2007 was *Atlantis'* STS-117 mission which installed the station's S3/S4 truss segment and its solar arrays. *Atlantis* landed on the fourteenth day. STS-118 launched on August 8, 2007. *Endeavour* delivered the S5 truss segment and new station supplies. This nearly 13-day shuttle

mission saw the flight of Barbara Morgan, Christa McAuliffe's backup teacher, in the role of an educator astronaut with mission specialist designation. *Discovery* launched on October 23, 2007 under the command of Pamela Melroy, only the second woman to command a shuttle mission. Her STS-120 flight delivered the Harmony module to the station, and attached it to the forward end of the Destiny laboratory. In addition the P6 module was relocated from atop Unity to the port end of the main truss. Its solar arrays required EVA-based repairs after grommets snagged while the solar arrays unfurled after P6 attachment to the truss. That EVA was a contingency spacewalk performed without ground-based training for the unexpected repair operation which was successfully accomplished by Scott Parazyncki.

Atlantis flew the first shuttle mission of 2008. STS-122 launched on February 7, 2008, and delivered the European Space Agency's *Columbus* laboratory which was attached to Harmony. STS-123 launched on March 11, 2008, and during a nearly 16-day mission *Endeavour* delivered a major part of the Japanese Aerospace Exploration Agency's (JAXA's) station components which was attached to Harmony. JAXA's Kibo (Hope) laboratory was delivered by *Discovery* to the ISS on STS-124 which launched on May 31, 2008. The Japanese laboratory was attached to Harmony, and given its other components that had been delivered during STS-123. On November 14, 2008, *Endeavour* launched on the STS-126 mission and flew to the ISS for a nearly 16-day mission that involved crew rotation and resupply with the Leonardo MPLM.

There were five shuttle missions flown in 2009. Time was growing short for the anticipated retirement of the fleet of orbiters, and there remained quite a bit of ISS construction to complete. Four of these flights were devoted to station, but one last one was flown to an orbit other than that of the station. *Discovery* launched on March 15, 2009 on the 12-day STS-119 mission to install the S6 truss segment and complete the truss' solar power generation system. On May 11, 2009 *Atlantis*, with *Endeavour* on the pad as a potential rescue vehicle, launched on the STS-125 final Hubble Space Telescope Servicing Mission. Over the course of five consecutive days spacewalking astronauts repaired essential systems on the observatory including two major instruments, and installed the Cosmic Origins Spectrograph. The crew left Hubble in such good shape that it remained operational in 2019 with no end in immediate sight. *Atlantis* returned to Earth safely, and *Endeavour* was freed to be prepared for the STS-127 mission which then launched on July 15, 2009 for a nearly 16-day flight to install Japan's Exposed Facility and other station structures outside the pressurized modules. *Discovery* launched on August 28, 2009 for 13 days and carried the Leonardo MPLM full of supplies to the station. This STS-128 mission ended with the final shuttle landing at Edwards Air Force Base. STS-129 launched on November 16, 2009. *Atlantis* took EXPRESS Logistics Carriers and plenty of supplies to the ISS.

It would not be possible to end shuttle operations in 2010 as had originally been planned in the aftermath of the *Columbia* accident; the fleet flew three missions during 2010. *Endeavour* launched on February 8, 2010 on the STS-130 mission, and delivered to the station the Tranquility Node which was installed to the Harmony Node. Also installed was the Cupola, a set of multiple high-quality windows, atop Tranquility. *Discovery's* STS-131 mission launched on April 5, 2010. This 15-day logistical flight delivered a great deal of supplies aboard the Leonardo MPLM. This flight featured the program's last night launch. *Atlantis* launched on May 14, 2010 and delivered the Russian mini-research module Rassvet to the ISS as well as logistical supplies. Rassvet was docked to the nadir part of the station's first element - Zarya.

Each of the remaining orbiters flew one last time in 2011, each mission devoted to station assembly and outfitting. *Discovery's* final flight, STS-133, launched on February 24, 2011, and carried the Leonardo MPLM which was left behind at the station as the Permanent Multipurpose Module to provide crews with extra stowage space. *Endeavour* launched on May 16, 2011 and carried logistical facilities for the station's exterior and installed the $2 billion Alpha Magnetic Spectrometer built to study antimatter and cosmic rays. This mission lasted nearly 16 days. *Atlantis* flew the program's final mission, STS-135, launching on July 8, 2011 with the Raffaello MPLM and as many supplies as the orbiter could carry. *Atlantis* landed at night at KSC after nearly 13 days in space.

Contributions

The space shuttle was unique in its design and function. Thus, the development of the spacecraft contributed much to the fields of aerodynamics and rocket research. Early test flights confirmed the capabilities and versatility of e vehicle that acted as rocket, spacecraft, and airplane in the course of a single mission. In addition, equipment and systems developed for the shuttle—such as the Remote Manipulator System, which allowed for the deployment and retrieval of payloads—raised the level of space technology and built a foundation for further advances. In fact, thousands of new products and techniques in such diverse fields as medicine and archaeology have been developed indirectly from advanced shuttle technology. The knowledge gained from the missions themselves also covered a broad spectrum of disciplines.

The shuttle's early flights demonstrated and tested the capabilities of the craft and its systems. In addition, STS-2 carried a payload for NASA's Office of Space and Terrestrial Applications; experiments concerning land resources, environmental quality, ocean conditions, and meteorological phenomena were performed. A precedent was set for scientific study.

STS-3 carried the first Get-Away Special payloads, small, self-contained, low-cost experiments that were packaged in canisters. These payloads were available to educational organizations, industries, and governments. STS-3 also carried the first student project, an experiment designed to collect data on the effects of flight motion on insects. The first materials processing experiment was also conducted on STS-3, with the Monodisperse Latex Reactor (MLR). The experiment produced micron-sized latex particles of uniform diameter for commercial use in laboratories. It marked the beginning of the shuttle program's commercial materials production capabilities.

As shuttle flights became routine, the number and sophistication of experiments conducted in or from the orbiter increased. In 1983, STS-9 carried

A grid on the floor is used to organize recovered debris of the STS-107 Columbia disaster. (NASA)

the first Spacelab. Spacelab 1 was an orbital laboratory and observation platform designed to remain inside the shuttle's cargo bay. When the bay doors were open, it was directly exposed to space. Spacelab 1 was funded by the European Space Agency as a major contribution to the STS program. It had the capability of performing numerous experiments in the areas of plasma physics, astronomy, solar physics, material sciences, life sciences, and Earth resources. Vast amounts of data collected in this and the subsequent Spacelab missions would take decades to analyze. The essential assumptions of the Spacelab program were proved: that non-NASA astronauts could perform as trained payload specialists working closely with a scientific command center on Earth,that the Tracking and Data-Relay Satellite System could return information to ground stations, and that Spacelab could support complex experiments in space.

Shuttle missions also included many experiments on the effects of spaceflight, and especially of zero gravity, on human beings. It was discovered that zero gravity affects every component of the motor control system. The heart and other large muscles decrease in size because of the absence of gravity's pull. Astronauts also experienced a decrease in bone tissue and red blood cells. Certain parts of the endocrine system may be affected, too. Finally, space sickness, a type of motion sickness, is not uncommon in microgravity.

Medical experiments and tests provided important data on zero gravity's effects and the ways in which those effects could be controlled. Medical experiments also raised questions about how humans would respond to long-term missions in space—missions undertaken on a space station, for example.

Over the course of the space shuttle program, hundreds of experiments and observations in almost every scientific discipline—from computers to agronomy—were conducted. As the program moved forward and technology improved, the database continued to grow.

Context

Human technology has often been spurred by human imagination. Nowhere has this been illustrated better than in the space shuttle program. The ability to launch piloted vehicles into space, maneuver them around the universe, and return them home safely was once the exclusive province of science-fiction characters such as Buck Rogers. The space shuttle changed all that.

Based on years of research in rocketry and aerodynamics, the flights of *Enterprise* and the later orbiters placed humankind on the threshold of a new era. The ability to conduct routine space missions had arrived. The space shuttle was the first vehicle to travel into space and return, to be used again. The ramifications of that capability have been far-reaching.

Satellites were deployed, repaired, and retrieved by shuttle astronauts. Thousands of scientific and medical experiments and hundreds of hours of solar, Earth, atmospheric, and cosmic observations were conducted aboard the shuttle. Critical communications satellites and Department of Defense payloads were launched from the shuttle, and the potential for the manufacture of commercial alloys, crystals, and other materials was enormous.

With construction of the International Space Station, the space shuttle fleet finally began the mission for which it was first proposed in 1972. Crews, some modules, and limited supplies could be launched to the station aboard robotic vehicles. However, massive experimental payloads and sufficient provisions for a permanent presence had to be transported on the shuttle. NASA's ambitious plan for an international space station in low-Earth orbit by the end of the twentieth century depended upon the shuttle's viability. The loss of *Columbia* in 2003 caused the cancellation of all non-ISS-related shuttle flights. Even so, with a fleet of only three orbiters, construction of the Space Station slowed.

The space shuttle program cost $196 billion in 2011 dollars, and ran, from authorization in 1972, to 2011. Six vehicles were built, five of which were launched into orbit. Two orbiters, *Columbia* and *Challenger*, and fourteen astronauts were lost. The orbiters spent a total of 1,322 days 19 hours 21 minutes and 23 seconds in space. As for overall statistics, the orbiters carried 1,597,108 kilograms of cargo to space and returned 104,151 kilograms of material to Earth, completed 20,830 orbits, flew 833 crew members to space and returned 789 people to Earth, carried 355 different people of whom 306 were men and 16 were women, launched 180 satellites and ISS components, returned 52 payloads to Earth, made 37 dockings to the ISS, made 9 dockings to Mir, completed 7 satellite repairs and re-deploys, and provided the vehicle for returning to Earth orbit of one original Mercury astronaut (John Glenn) as well as the vehicle for two women (Eileen Collins and Pamela Melroy) to command an American space flight.

The space shuttle orbiter fleet was decommissioned, and after considerable discussion the disposition of *Enterprise, Discovery, Atlantis,* and *Endeavour* was determined as follows. *Enterprise* was given to New York City for display on the U.S.S. Intrepid air and space museum. *Discovery* was given to the Smithsonian Institution for display within the Udvar-Hazy extension to the National Air and Space Museum located outside Washington, D.C. *Discovery* was put on display as if it had just landed. Atlantis was given to the Kennedy Space Center Visitor Center where a special building called *Atlantis* Experience was constructed to display *Atlantis* as if in orbit performing a rendezvous to capture the Hubble Space Telescope. *Endeavour* was given to the California Science Center for display in Los Angeles. In 2019 *Endeavour* was being prepared to be attached to a set of Solid Rocket Boosters and External Tank so that it would be displayed as if in launch configuration. The space shuttle orbiters are popular attractions at these museums a decade after they last flew in orbit.

—Lulynne Streeter, Russell R. Tobias,
and David G. Fisher

See also: Extravehicular Activity; Launch Vehicles; Space Centers, Spaceports, and Launch Sites; Space Shuttle: Ancestors; Space Shuttle: Approach and Landing Test Flights; Space Shuttle: Life Science Laboratories; Space Shuttle: Living Accommodations; Space Shuttle: Microgravity Laboratories and Payloads.

Further Reading

Baker, David, ed. *Jane's Space Directory, 2005-2006*. Alexandria, Va.: Jane's Information Group, 2005. Updated annually, this resource is invaluable for a quick overview of progress made in space exploration. Spacecraft summaries of piloted and robotic missions are provided, and the text is heavily illustrated with diagrams and black-and-white photographs. A helpful index is also included.

Bizony, Piers. *Island in the Sky: Building the International Space Station*. London: Aurum Press Limited, 1996. Bizony tells how the International Space Station will be assembled in orbit during an extended sequence of shuttle flights, dockings, and spacewalks over the next five years. With unrivaled access to NASA and the astronautic sources worldwide, his lively text contains a wealth of information. There are one hundred photographs, sixty in color.

Burrows, William E. *This New Ocean: The Story of the First Space Age*. New York: Random House, 1998. This is a comprehensive history of the human conquest of space, covering everything from the earliest attempts at spaceflight through the voyages near the end of the twentieth century. Burrows is an experienced journalist who has reported for *The New York Times*, *The Washington Post*, and *The Wall Street Journal*. There are many photographs and an extensive source list. Interviewees in the book include Isaac Asimov, Alexei Leonov, Sally K. Ride, and James A. Van Allen.

Godwin, Robert, ed. *Space Shuttle STS Flights 1-5: The NASA Mission Reports*. Burlington, Ont.: Apogee Books, 2001. This book covers the space shuttle through the test-flight stage and on to its first so-called operational flight. Included are the text from the five NASA press kits and post-flight mission operation reports. The accompanying CD-ROM includes film footage from each of the five flights.

Harland, David M. *The Space Shuttle: Roles, Missions, and Accomplishments*. Hoboken, N.J.: John Wiley, 1998. This book is written thematically, rather than purely chronologically. Topics include shuttle operations and payloads, weightlessness, materials processing, Space Shuttle 1263 exploration, Spacelabs and free-flyers, and the shuttle's role in the International Space Station.

Harrington, Philip S. *The Space Shuttle: A Photographic History*. San Francisco, Calif.: Brown Trout, 2003. With one hundred full-color photographs by Roger Ressmeyer and others and with text by popular astronomy writer Harrington, this book tells the story of the space shuttle program from 1972 to 2003. Its beautiful photographs allow the general reader to survey the history of the space shuttle program and be uplifted by the pioneering spirit of one of humanity's grandest enterprises.

Haskell, G., and Michael Rycroft. *International Space Station: The Next Space Marketplace*. Boston: Kluwer Academic, 2000. Addresses issues of ISS utilization and operations from all perspectives, especially the commercial viewpoint, as well as scientific research, technological development, and education in the widest sense of the word. Of interest to those working in industry, academia, government, and particularly public-private partnerships.

Heppenheimer, T. A. *Countdown: A History of Space Flight*. New York: John Wiley, 1997. A detailed historical narrative of the human conquest of space. Heppenheimer traces the development of piloted flight through the military rocketry programs of the era preceding World War II. Covers both the American and the Soviet attempts to place vehicles, spacecraft, and humans into the hostile environment of space. More than a dozen pages are devoted to bibliographic references.

Jenkins, Dennis R. *The History of the American Space Shuttle*. Forest Lake, Minnesota: Specialty Press, 2019. Covers the thirty year flight history of the space shuttle fleet. Covers triumphs and tragedies, and the evolution of the program.

Jenkins, Dennis R. *Space Shuttle: Developing an Icon 1972-2013.* Forest Lake, Minnesota: Specialty Press, 2017. The author worked for NASA for 33 years in engineering and management roles for the space shuttle program. Covers the entire space shuttle program from inception, through flight operations, to fleet retirement. Jenkins, Dennis R. *Space Shuttle: The History of the National Space Transportation System: The First 100 Missions.* Stillwater, Minn.: Voyageur Press, 2001. This is a concisely written technical reference account of the space shuttle and its ancestors, the aerodynamic lifting bodies. It details some of the advantages and inherent disadvantages of using a reusable space vehicle. Each of the vehicles is illustrated by line drawings with important features pointed out with lines and text. The book follows the space shuttle from its original concepts and briefly chronicles its first one hundred flights.

"Launch Vehicles." *Aviation Week and Space Technology*, January 17, 2000, 144-145. This table details the specifications for each of the 2000 launch vehicles and spacecraft, as well as the status.

Shayler, David J. *Disasters and Accidents in Manned Spaceflight.* Chichester, England: Springer-Praxis, 2000. The author examines the challenges that face all crews as they prepare and execute their missions. The book covers all aspects that make up spaceflight by a human crew—training, launch to space, survival in space, and return from space—followed by a series of case histories that tell of the major incidents in each of those categories over the past forty years. The sixth section looks at the International Space Station and its ability to prevent major incidents during the lifetime of the orbital complex.

Space Shuttle: Ancestors

Date: 1928 to 1971
Type of program: Piloted test flights

Ancestors of the space shuttle helped aerospace engineers learn how to build a reusable vehicle that could withstand both the rigors of outer space and reentry into Earth's atmosphere. Some experimental craft gave pilots vital experience in flying at supersonic and hypersonic speeds.

Key Figures

Wernher von Braun (1912-1977), German American rocket engineer and space exploration visionary

Eugen Sänger (1905-1964), German aerospace scientist

Fritz von Opel (1889-1971), German industrialist and early rocketeer

Walter Dornberger, rocket plane designer

Krafft Ehricke, rocket plane designer

Darrell C. Romick, rocket plane designer

Maxime A. Faget (1921-2004), space shuttle designer

Friedrich Stamer, early German rocket plane test pilot

Charles E. "Chuck" Yeager (b. 1923), American rocket plane test pilot

A. Scott Crossfield (1921-2006), American rocket plane test pilot

Joseph A. Walker (1921-1966), American rocket plane test pilot

Summary of the Missions

From the outset, space travel visionaries proposed reusable vehicles for carrying people into Earth orbit and beyond. Spacecraft designers themselves preferred reusable craft, because they would be much less expensive than the use-once rockets and spacecraft of the early American and Soviet piloted space programs. When in the late 1960's American aerospace engineers had an opportunity to build a reusable craft for the Space Transportation System, they had two decades of technological development on which to draw. Following World War II, the United States military and the National Advisory Committee for Aeronautics (NACA) cooperated in testing two types of craft: space or rocket airplanes and lifting bodies. These are the ancestors of the space shuttle.

A forebear of the shuttle in spirit, if not in direct line of development, the first rocket plane was a glider with solid rockets strapped to it. Sponsored by a German glider club, the rocket plane carried Pilot Friedrich Stamer more than 200 meters in 1928. The next year, German car manufacturer Fritz von Opel flew an improved design for about ten minutes and at nearly 120 kilometers per hour. Because these hybrids did not promise quick improvement on the internal combustion engine then used in airplanes, despite quasi-military support, experimentation continued only sporadically.

In 1935 German engineers, including Wernher von Braun, designed and tested rocket engines for military aircraft. Shortly before and during World War II, the Germans saw at least two models through the prototype test stage, but military interest turned to jet engines late in the war, and rocket planes saw little combat. The Japanese, however, used a rocket-propelled suicide bomber, the Baka, late in the war. The most notable contribution from the Axis powers to the history of rocket planes came from a secret

German study by Eugen Sänger. He proposed a winged rocket as a long-range bomber. Carrying 80 metric tons of bombs, this "antipodal bomber" (antipodes are two points on opposite sides of the Earth) would take off from a runway and boost to about 42 kilometers altitude, above the densest layers of atmosphere. It would save fuel on the way to its target by skipping repeatedly off the atmosphere much as a flat stone, thrown at a shallow angle, skips off the surface of still water. Finally, the bomber would land under its own power. The Sänger report, which was not widely distributed among Nazi scientists, did not prompt developmental efforts until long after the war. A similar proposal in 1949 by California Institute of Technology professor Hsue Shen Tsien envisioned a winged rocket for passenger service.

Chuck Yeager in front of the X-1 that he nicknamed the Glamorous Glennis. (U.S. Air Force)

Meanwhile, the American military had been interested in advanced propulsion systems since early in the war. In 1944, Congress approved a research program to explore both jet- and rocket-powered airplanes. NACA (later the National Aeronautics and Space Administration, NASA), the Navy, the Army, and the Air Force were to share in the design and testing. The program produced the X-1, America's first rocket plane.

Designed to climb to 24,000 meters and reach 2,800 kilometers per hour (kph), the X-1 was astonishingly successful for a first research craft. Cigar-shaped with straight wings and tail fins, the 10-meter-long craft was launched in air from a B-29 bomber. In 1947, Air Force Captain Charles E. "Chuck" Yeager accelerated it to 1,126 kph, becoming the first person to fly faster than Mach 1, the speed of sound. In 1953, NACA Test Pilot A. Scott Crossfield flew a Navy-sponsored rocket plane, the D-558-II, past Mach 2.

Despite several crashes, further designs of the X-2 proceeded, especially steadily increased speed and altitude records, until the X-plane research program culminated in the X-15. After launch from a B-52 bomber, the X-15 was intended to soar to the edge of outer space at speeds up to Mach 10. Engineers faced serious design problems to meet these goals: The airframe had to withstand temperatures of up to 650° Celsius, acceleration of seven orders of gravity (that is, the change in velocity would increase its weight seven times), and turbulence at hypersonic speeds (greater than Mach 5). Because it would climb out of the atmosphere into near vacuum, the pilot had to steer by firing small control rockets, a new technique. The final design, shaped something like a ballpoint pen with short triangular, or delta, wings and three tail fins, eventually climbed to more than 111 kilometers altitude (in 1963) and a speed of nearly Mach 6. The NASA test pilot who flew to the record altitude, Joseph A. Walker, became the first rocket plane pilot to achieve the status of astronaut, awarded to all who fly above 83 kilometers (50 miles). Among the other pilots in the X-15 program was Neil A. Armstrong, later an Apollo astronaut and the first man to walk on the Moon. Proponents of rocket planes wanted to mount the X-15 on a big booster and lift it to Earth orbit, but NASA officials worried the vehicle could not survive reentry. Besides, Project Mercury had already successfully put Alan B. Shepard, Jr., and John H. Glenn, Jr., into space. NASA administrators decided to devote American efforts to the spacecraft programs and eventually discontinued the X-15. On October 24, 1968, the 199th and final test of the X-15 was flown.

Even without the X-15, the idea of a reusable space plane had steady and powerful support. First of all, it held an important place in von Braun's grand vision for space exploration and colonization, and von Braun had long guided American space policy. Beginning in 1952, he articulated the vision in popular books and articles. He wanted a space station built in orbit that would serve as an outpost for travel to the planets, Mars first. The station would require regular ferry service from Earth. For that, his solution was a massive three-stage vehicle, two boosters and a winged spaceship that could rendezvous with the station and then land under its own power on a runway. Darrell C. Romick independently presented a proposal for a three-staged winged passenger vehicle, the Meteor, at the American Rocket Society annual convention in 1954. At the same time, engineers Walter Dornberger and Krafft Ehricke, drawing upon the ideas of Sänger, developed plans for a reusable, piloted booster to start a Bomber-Missile space plane (BOMI) on its way between continents; the booster would return to base on its own.

These proposals impressed the United States Air Force. Beginning in 1957, it started development of the X-20, or Dynamic Soaring program, which was unfortunately and prophetically nicknamed Dyna-Soar. NASA joined the project in 1958. The X-20 had triangular wings with a 6-meter span and was 10.6 meters long. A one-person glider with a rounded ceramic nose, it was to be boosted into space by a Titan III-C and an orbit-transfer stage. Retrorockets and gas jets would slow it for reentry and permit it to maneuver to a landing strip. Planners intended the program to identify and solve problems encountered in reentering the atmosphere and test new technology involved in the solutions.

Although piloted orbital flights were the goal, rising costs, delays, and uncertainty about the program's benefit to the Apollo Program caused cancellation of Dyna-Soar in 1963. However, by then scientists had conducted wind-tunnel tests on models, built full-scale mock-ups, started a pilot training program with simulators, and created and tested much new hardware. In 1963, just before Dyna-Soar was closed down, a related program, Spacecraft Technology and Advanced Reentry Test (START), launched a scaled-down version of the glider to measure acceleration, vibrations, temperature, and structural pressure as it dived back to Earth.

START thereafter began a new phase as the Precision Recovery Including Maneuvering Entry (PRIME) project. PRIME was to test lifting bodies, especially their maneuvering capabilities upon reentry from space and landing. A lifting body is a wedge-shaped vehicle whose entire fuselage acts as a wing to support it in the air. The project tested three robotic X-23A vehicles, launched on Atlas boosters, in 1966 and 1967. A piloted version, the M2-F1, had already been used to practice lowspeed landings. Dropped from B-52 bombers, piloted supersonic lifting bodies such as the M2-F2, M2-F3, HL-10, X24A, and X24B tested the aerodynamics and maneuvering properties of the basic design from 1966 to 1975.

Both the testing programs and the design ideas of space pioneers influenced the first space shuttle designs in the late 1960's. Several configurations called for a rocket plane or lifting body piggybacked on a piloted, winged booster that could itself land and be reused, similar to Romick's Meteor. Other designs bracketed a lifting body or X-15-like vehicle with boosters or required a single engine that could operate as a jet in the atmosphere and as a rocket in space, a versatility beyond the technology of the 1960's. Maxime A. Faget, principal designer for the shuttle, initially favored a rocket plane with straight wings, much like the X- 1 and X-2. However, because the Air Force demanded a large payload bay and cross-orbital maneuvering capabilities, Faget changed to a delta-wing configuration, which was adopted into the final design in 1971.

Contributions

Although most were far too grandiose for the technology of their times, early rocket plane proposals, such as those by von Braun and Sänger, furnished important ideas for the Space Transportation System and other programs. They introduced the delta-wing configuration that the space shuttle uses. They suggested lowering costs by launching spacecraft on a reusable booster, which the space shuttle program partially adopted in the form of two recoverable solid rocket boosters. Most significant, they implanted the idea that a spacecraft could be amphibious—an airplane in the atmosphere and a rocket in space.

More practically, rocket-plane and lifting-body experiments taught essential lessons in piloting and vehicle design. Many scientists believed that the speed of sound amounted to a "brick wall in the sky," as rocket pioneer Theodore von Kármán facetiously put it. The fears were not entirely unreasonable. They worried that supersonic speeds would compress air along the leading edges of aircraft and create turbulence. Aircraft might then turn unstable and uncontrollable. The X-1 was designed to settle the stability question, and it proved quickly and finally that no insurmountable sonic barrier exists. Moreover, the X-15 demonstrated that hypersonic speeds are also manageable. Pilots of these craft developed skills to handle the difficulties of extreme velocities in the atmosphere, especially attitude control, and to wrest back control if the craft began to spin. Data from the X-15 flights suggested piloted vehicles are superior to robotic craft because thoroughly trained pilots can react more quickly and effectively to problems than can ground controllers. The lifting bodies proved that a space plane can land on the glide and did not need power from an auxiliary source, such as jet engines, which increases a vehicle's weight and complexity.

The X-15, Dyna-Soar, and lifting bodies contributed fundamentally to technology and techniques for controlling the heating of a craft's skin upon reentry. The aerodynamics to reduce drag was studied, but it was learned that by positioning the body to reenter belly-first, the friction-induced heat could be spread over a larger area and that then only this area had to be provided with a heavy heatshield. Researchers also found that the delta-wing shape maintained lower average skin temperatures than a straight-wing configuration. Furthermore, the various metals in the skins of these experimental craft provided data on heat shedding and structural integrity at high temperatures and during vibration.

Finally, shuttle ancestors tested control and life-support systems. The small attitude control rockets, such as those used under the X-15's wings and nose, gave pilots invaluable experience in handling a craft in vacuum and let engineers find the best placement and power for thrusters. Guidance systems, sensors, onboard instruments, escape systems, fuel mixtures and pressurization, use of devices such as fences and slats on wings to increase stability, and many other features received crucial trials. At the same time, medical researchers studied how the human body behaves under high acceleration and how to design suits and seats to protect the body.

Context

Released in 1968, the feature film *2001: A Space Odyssey* depict a sleek space plane streaking up from Earth to rendezvous with a huge, wheel-shaped space station. Based on the novel of the same name by science-fiction writer Arthur C. Clarke, the film indicate how deeply ingrained the space plane and space station concepts had become among proponents for piloted spaceflight, thanks primarily to von Braun. It also impressed audiences so deeply that the scene has since been an icon of a bold technological future. Imaginative systems such as those portrayed in the film and the actual testing of rocket planes and lifting bodies thus figured centrally in both the professional and popular visions of space exploration and assumed a place in modern culture.

Space shuttle precursors also reveal much about the national and international politics behind large technological research programs. From the earliest German rocket planes through the testing of lifting bodies, involvement of military planners was typical and often crucial. In the United States, the Air Force initiated and conducted much of the research on the X-planes and lifting bodies. Even for the space shuttle, billed as a civilian program, the final design derived to a large extent from military requirements.

Although NACA, and later NASA, played key roles all along, these research programs needed the weight of the military for economic reasons.

Von Braun and William R. Lucas, the first and third Marshall Space Flight Center directors, viewing a Spacelab model in 1974. (NASA)

First, the extensive system of Air Force bases with generous resources and financing, Navy ships for recovery at sea, the many highly trained military pilots, and the numerous technical support personnel made programs cheaper to start up and run than if they had depended on building new facilities and assembling strictly civilian staffs. What is more important, the budget-conscious Congresses were much more likely to appropriate money for programs that had military participation and possible military applications. This militarism derived from competition with the Soviet Union, both military and civilian. That the Soviets might use space for piloted weapons systems argued powerfully for a U.S. military presence in space as well. National prestige was also at stake: The Soviet Union had launched the first spacefarer in a spacecraft, and so the U.S. did not want the Soviets to get ahead in other piloted ventures as well.

The shuttle precursors had more than a national effect, however. On the basis of rocket-plane and lifting-body research as well as that for the space shuttle, the Soviet Union, the European Space

Agency, and Japan set up their own shuttle programs.

Furthermore, more so than the American space shuttle, the X-planes are the direct antecedents of various proposals in the United States and Europe for a single-stage space plane. The Air Force sponsored X-30 program, for example, studied prototypes for a National AeroSpace Plane (NASP), designed as a single-stage-to-orbit (SSTO) vehicle that would have landed and taken off on conventional runways. The plane, traveling at hypersonic speeds, would have required the development of new materials and technologies to become a reality. The NASP study was terminated in 1994, when it was concluded that the high-temperature materials and air-breathing propulsion technology required for such prolonged high speeds within Earth's atmosphere would take many more years to mature than had originally been estimated.

The X-33, X-34, and X-38 CRV programs were designed to pave the way to full-scale, commercially developed reusable launch vehicles. In 2001, NASA announced that the problem-plagued X-33 space plane project, a venture that aimed to create a single-stage-to-orbit spaceliner, had been scrapped. In addition, the American space agency announced that the X-34 was axed. The X-33 was to have been the flagship technology demonstrator for technologies that would have dramatically lowered the cost of access to space. It was unpiloted, taking off vertically like a rocket, reaching an altitude of up to 100 kilometers and speeds between Mach 13 and 15 (13 to 15 times the speed of sound), and landing horizontally like an airplane. The X-34 was a reusable, suborbital, air-launched vehicle that would have flown at speeds approaching Mach 8 at altitudes up to 80 kilometers.

During the first years of the International Space Station's life on orbit, a Russian Soyuz robotic spacecraft was always present to provide crewmembers with the means to evacuate the station quickly. In the early 1990's, NASA began development of a new emergency Crew Return Vehicle (CRV) for the International Space Station. The Soyuz can stay on orbit for only six months, as opposed to three years estimated for the CRV. The X-38 was scheduled to be launched aboard the space shuttle released in the ISS orbit inclination (51.6°), and with Baja California as the primary landing site (secondary sites are Argentina and Australia).

On April 29, 2002, NASA announced cancellation of the X-38 program because of budget pressures associated with the International Space Station (ISS). The X-38 was two years short of completing its flight test phase. This cancellation was part of a larger plan that emerged late in 2002, which NASA would proceed with an Orbital Space Plane capable of both crew transport and crew return missions from the ISS, but that too was cancelled. Sierra Nevada Corporation kept alive the possibility of a commercial mini-space plane as first a crewed transport and later only as a logistical resupply vehicle to the ISS. As of 2019, it had not flown in space.

—Roger Smith, updated by Russell R. Tobias

See also: Rocketry: Early History; Rocketry: Modern History; Space Shuttle.

Further Reading

Godwin, Robert, ed. *X-15: The NASA Mission Reports*. Burlington, Ont.: Apogee Books, 2001. The book details the X-15 program, pilots, and vehicles. Included are biographies of each X-15 pilot, original proposals for the vehicle, and pilot reference manuals. The CD-ROM includes hundreds of images of the X-15 program. Hours of rare video, including footage of the "pink" X-15A-2; the dramatic explosion of the XLR-99 engine; comments from Joseph A. Walker and A. Scott Crossfield, Pete Knight's record-breaking high-speed flight; Neil A. Armstrong's final flight before joining the Astronaut Corps; and rare silent footage of the first six research pilots. The complete documentation of every X-15 flight including flight-plans, surface-to-air transcripts, and post flight reports in the pilots' own words are included.

Hallion, Richard. *On the Frontier: Flight Research at Dryden, 1946-1981*. Washington, D.C.: Government Printing Office, 1984. This is one of the titles in the NASA History series, which provides an official look at the space agency, its programs and facilities. The information is presented in chronological order and it covers such noted aerospace craft as the X-1, X-15, HL-10, X-24A, X-24B and the space shuttle. Also detailed is the research that assisted the development of the Gemini and Apollo spacecraft. There are many black-and-white photographs and line drawings, an index and an impressive bibliography. Appendices include program flight chronologies on the X-1, D-558, X-2, X-3, X-4, X-5, XF-92A, X-15, lifting bodies, XB-70A, and space shuttle approach and landing test program.

Harland, David M. *The Space Shuttle: Roles, Missions, and Accomplishments*. Hoboken, N.J.: John Wiley, 1998. This book is written thematically, rather than purely chronologically. Topics include shuttle operations and payloads, weightlessness, materials processing, exploration, Spacelabs and free-flyers, and the shuttle's role in the International Space Station.

Harrington, Philip S. *The Space Shuttle: A Photographic History*. San Francisco, Calif.: Brown Trout, 2003. With one hundred full-color photographs by Roger Ressmeyer and others and with text by popular astronomy writer Harrington, this book tells the story of the space shuttle program from 1972 to 2003. Its beautiful photographs allow the general reader to survey the history of the space shuttle program and be uplifted by the pioneering spirit of one of humanity's grandest enterprises.

Jenkins, Dennis R. *Hypersonic: The Story of the North American X-15*. North Branch, Minn.: Specialty Press, 2003. The book was written with the cooperation of surviving X-15 pilots as well as many other program principals and is based on six years of research in Air Force, NASA, and North American archives. It covers the tasks of converting and testing the B-52 carrier airplanes, building the first full-pressure suits to protect the pilot, building the first engineering mission simulators, acquiring the remote lake bed landing sites, and building the radar range. It also covers the flight program in detail, including the most authoritative flight log ever assembled; in many instances, information in this log was derived from the original flight data recordings.

---. *Space Shuttle: The History of the National Space Transportation System: The First 100 Missions*. Stillwater, Minn.: Voyageur Press, 2001. This is a concisely written technical reference account of the space shuttle and its ancestors, the aerodynamic lifting bodies. It details some of the advantages and inherent disadvantages of using a reusable space vehicle. Each of the vehicles is illustrated by line drawings with important features pointed out with lines and text. The book follows the space shuttle from its original concepts and briefly chronicles its first one hundred flights.

Landis, Tony R., and Dennis R. Jenkins. *X-15 Photo Scrapbook*. North Branch, Minn.: Specialty Press, 2003. An in-depth history of the X-15 program, this book is a collection of illustrations that provides an excellent visual look at the X-15 research program.

Miller, Jay. *X-Planes: X-1 to X-45*. 3d ed. Stillwater, Minn.: Voyageur Press, 2001. This well-illustrated book is the definitive study on the X-series experimental aircraft. It contains complete flight records and details each craft. Included in the photograph coverage are rare cockpit illustrations of every piloted X-Plane to progress beyond the drawing board stage. Each X-Plane is also illustrated by an accurate and detailed multiview drawing. These also provide color scheme information and scale data.

Reed, R. Dale, and Darlene Lister. *Wingless Flight: The Lifting Body Story*. Washington, D.C.: National Aeronautics and Space Administration, 1997. This is a story about the development of the lifting body research aircraft at Edwards Air Force Base. A small group of individuals pooled their talents and aspirations to accomplish one of the most amazing feats in aeronautical history by flying eight different wingless aircraft-spacecraft designs.

Rotundo, Louis C., and Charles E. "Chuck" Yeager. *Into the Unknown: The X-1 Story*. Washington, D.C.: Smithsonian Books, 2001. The story of the experimental X-1 program and the fifty glider and jet-powered flights in 1946-1947, each of which was a learning experience for the pilots and technicians.

Thompson, Milton O., and Curtis Peebles. *Flying Without Wings: NASA Lifting Bodies and the Birth of the Space Shuttle*. Washington, D.C.: Smithsonian Institution Press, 1999. A comprehensive look at the ancestors of the space shuttle. The authors detail the development of the shuttle's current configuration and future lifting bodies like the X-33, X-34, and X-38.

Winter, Frank H. *Rockets into Space*. Cambridge, Mass.: Harvard University Press, 1990. A pleasantly written, general history of the Space Age. The sixth chapter concerns the space shuttle, and Winter summarizes both the visionary and practical projects for a space plane. He pays particular attention to lifting bodies and alternative designs for the shuttle, although there is little technical detail. Illustrations of four early designs.

Space Shuttle: Approach and Landing Test Flights

Date: September 8, 1976, to October 26, 1977
Type of program: Piloted test flights

Enterprise, the first space shuttle orbiter, tested the approach and landing techniques of the United States' Space Transportation System (STS). Engineers also used it for ground handling, vibration, and landing brake net tests.

Key Figures

Fred W. Haise, Jr. (b. 1933), NASA astronaut
Charles Gordon Fullerton (1936-2013), NASA astronaut
Joseph H. Engle (b. 1932), NASA astronaut
Richard H. Truly (b. 1937), NASA astronaut
Fitzhugh L. Fulton, shuttle carrier aircraft pilot
Thomas C. McMurtry, shuttle carrier aircraft copilot

Summary of the Missions

In September, 1976, the National Aeronautics and Space Administration (NASA) unveiled the prototype for a new class of reusable piloted spacecraft. The delta-wing vehicle *Enterprise* was the first space shuttle orbiter, the piloted component of the space shuttle vehicle. The complete space shuttle was constituted by the orbiter and a large expendable fuel tank flanked by two solid-fueled rocket boosters (SRBs). The space shuttle would be launched from a rocket, orbit like a spacecraft, and then land like an airplane.

Before any of the reusable craft ventured into space, tests of the landing system had to be made; these tests were called approach and landing tests (ALTs). The first orbiter, which bore the airframe designation OV-101 (OV standing for orbiter vehicle), was designed to undergo such tests. Construction of OV-101 began on June 4, 1974. OV-101 was not intended for spaceflight, so it did not contain many of the systems needed for an orbital craft. For example, OV-101 did not have the three rocket engines necessary for boost to space, nor did it contain any of the orbital maneuvering engines. Such spaceflight components as the star trackers, unified S-band antennae, and rendezvous radar were also not part of the design. Because OV-101 would never venture beyond Earth's atmosphere, it was not covered with any of the thermal tiles (ceramic blocks of silicon material that can withstand extremely high temperatures and insulate the orbiter's aluminum structure from the heat of reentry) needed for protection during the fiery return from space. On OV-101, blocks of polyurethane foam simulated the thermal protection tiles. Glass fiber panels on the nose cap and wing leading edges simulated the reinforced carbon-carbon structures planned for later orbiters.

On September 8, 1976, NASA Administrator James C. Fletcher met with President Gerald Ford to discuss the name of OV-101. For several months prior to the meeting, fans of the beloved television series *Star Trek* had conducted a letter writing campaign suggesting the name of the vehicle be changed from *Constitution* to *Enterprise*, the name of the starship in the sci-fi series. After an estimated sixty thousand letters arrived at the White House and

The two crews for the Space Shuttle Approach and Landing Tests (ALT), from left to right: Astronauts C. Gordon Fullerton, pilot of the first crew; Fred W. Haise Jr., commander of the first crew; Joe H. Engle, commander of the second crew; and Richard H. Truly, pilot of the second crew. The DC-9 size airplane-like Orbiter 101 is in the background. (NASA)

NASA Headquarters, President Ford approved the name.

Slightly more than a week later, on September 17, 1976, Fletcher, U.S. senator Barry Goldwater, Rockwell International board Chairperson Willard Rockwell, and about five thousand others stood outside a hangar at Rockwell International's Palmdale, California, plant. As the band played the theme music from *Star Trek* for a cheering crowd, a red, white, and blue tractor towed the *Enterprise* from behind the hangar. *Enterprise* had a wingspan of 23.1 meters, a length of 37.1 meters, and weighed 65,000 kilograms.

On January 31, 1977, NASA and Rockwell engineers moved *Enterprise* out of Palmdale, 58 kilometers to the Dryden Flight Research Center at Edwards Air Force Base. *Enterprise* made the journey, which took nearly twelve hours, on a 90-wheel trailer. At Dryden, engineers had a modified commercial passenger jet waiting to be used with *Enterprise* for the landing tests. Because the space shuttle

orbiter returned from space unpowered, getting the shuttle airborne to test the landing system posed a unique challenge. The solution was to mount the orbiter piggyback on top of a large aircraft that could carry it aloft and then release it. In addition, the aircraft could ferry space shuttle orbiters for cross-country travel.

On June 17, 1974, NASA purchased a Boeing 747 from American Airlines for use as the Shuttle Carrier Aircraft (SCA) and subsequently modified it to carry a 68,000-kilogram load on its back. All passenger accommodations—seats, galleys, and the like—were removed. Bulkheads and reinforcements had to be added to the fuselage's main deck. The 747's standard engines were replaced with higher-thrust engines. Three supports for the orbiter were added to the SCA's top, and tip fins were added to the horizontal stabilizer. Other changes to the aircraft included modifications to its trim system, air conditioning system, and electrical wiring, and the addition of an escape system for the flight crew.

On February 7, 1977, *Enterprise* was mounted atop the SCA for the first time. Eight days later, engineers began a series of taxi tests. During these, the 747 taxied along the runway at speeds just less than what was needed to become airborne. These tests showed no unusual problems, so preparations were made for the first flight of the tandem aircraft. The first five flights of the approach and landing test program were so-called captive inert flights to verify the handling of the SCA/space shuttle orbiter combination. For these, *Enterprise* did not carry a crew. The program then progressed to "captive active" flights, for which *Enterprise* was "powered up" and occupied but remained attached to the SCA. Finally, there were the free flights, during which

Enterprise separated from the SCA and made an unpowered approach and landing.

For all but the last two free flights, which tried to duplicate the return from space of an orbiter as closely as possible, *Enterprise*'s aft end was covered with an aerodynamic fairing. This fairing, or tailcone, smoothed the airflow off the orbiter's base, reducing drag and buffeting on the SCA's tail. For cross-country flights with operational orbiters, the fairing also protected the three space shuttle main engines.

The first captive inert flight occurred on February 18. For 2 hours and 10 minutes, Fitzhugh L. Fulton and Thomas C. McMurtry flew the SCA/*Enterprise* combination over the California esert. This flight evaluated the airworthiness of the configuration and verified the preflight stability and control predictions. Four more captive inert flights followed during the next two weeks, each exploring a different portion of the flight envelope.

After the captive inert flights, the program moved into the captive active phase. The first captive active flight was on June 18, 1977. Fred W. Haise, Jr., and Charles Gordon Fullerton occupied the orbiter's flight deck. During a 56-minute flight, they tested various orbiter systems and gathered additional information about buffeting of *Enterprise*'s vertical tail. Ten days later, astronauts Joseph H. Engle and Richard H. Truly occupied *Enterprise* for the second captive active flight. Haise and Fullerton again occupied *Enterprise* for the final captive flight of the ALT program, a dress rehearsal for the free flights.

On August 12, 1977, *Enterprise* flew independently of the SCA for the first time. Haise and Fullerton piloted *Enterprise*, while Fulton and McMurtry flew the SCA. About 48 minutes after takeoff, the piggyback aircraft reached an altitude of 8,650 meters. Fullerton and McMurtry began a shallow dive, a maneuver called "pushover." At an altitude of 7,350 meters, Haise pushed the separation button in *Enterprise*, and seven explosive bolts fired; *Enterprise* was on its own. Fulton pitched the

SCA down and rolled left to clear the free-flying space shuttle. Haise and Fullerton pitched the orbiter's nose up and gently rolled *Enterprise* to the right to clear the SCA. They straightened the craft, then eased the orbiter's nose up, practicing a landing flare maneuver. After this maneuver, the crew of the *Enterprise* executed a 180° turn to the left, aligning *Enterprise* with the Dryden runway. *Enterprise* touched down 5 minutes and 22 seconds after separating from the SCA.

Some relatively minor problems were encountered during the first free flight. For example, one of the general purpose computers (GPCs) stopped working at separation; however, the other onboard computers sensed the fault and automatically took the malfunctioning GPC off-line. Because Haise and Fullerton remained flexible, all mission objectives were achieved, and the handling, stability, and flight performance characteristics were as predicted.

Engle and Truly piloted *Enterprise* for its second free flight on September 13, 1977. During this flight, the pilots executed a 1.8-g turn to the left as they lined *Enterprise* with the runway, duplicating the maneuvers of an orbiter returning from space. The abbreviation "g" refers to the acceleration of gravity. Sitting still on Earth, one experiences an acceleration of 1g, or a gravitational force of 1, the normal sensation of gravity. During periods of changing acceleration, such as a banking turn in an airplane, the so-called g-loading (gravitational loading) will change. As Engle and Truly banked the *Enterprise*, they felt as though they weighed twice as much as normal. The second flight lasted 5 minutes, 28 seconds.

Haise and Fullerton were again at *Enterprise*'s controls on September 23, 1977, for the third free flight of the ALT program. During this flight, the pilots tested the orbiter's automatic landing system. After the flight, ALT program managers decided to proceed with the tailcone-off flights, eliminating two planned missions. For these flights, the tailcone was removed, duplicating the aerodynamic characteristics of an orbiter returning from space.

The fourth free flight, also the first tailcone-off flight, occurred on October 12, 1977. Engle and Truly flew OV-101. While the SCA climbed to separation altitude, the 747's tail was visibly buffeted by the turbulence coming off the base of the orbiter. After separation, Engle and Truly flew *Enterprise* on a straight course to Dryden. Without the tailcone, drag on *Enterprise* was much higher, and the flight lasted 2 minutes, 35 seconds.

Haise and Fullerton again piloted *Enterprise* for the fifth and final free flight on October 26, 1977. This would be the first landing on a paved runway. (All previous landings had been on dry lakebed runways.) This free flight lasted 2 minutes, 5 seconds. During landing, after making a near touchdown, the orbiter's nose suddenly rose, then settled back down. The nose rose once more, made a second touchdown, skipped off the runway briefly, then finally settled down for a third, and final, touchdown. Despite the difficulties, no further free flights were deemed necessary, so the most visible part of the ALT program ended.

After the free flights, engineers evaluated one more aspect of the space shuttle's flight characteristics: how the SCA/orbiter combination handled on cross-country ferry flights. For the ferry flights, the orbiter's front support on the back of the 747 was lowered from 4° to 2° to reduce drag and improve the aircraft's cruise characteristics. Following a series of tests, the SCA/*Enterprise* took off from Dryden on March 10, 1978, bound for the Marshall Space Flight Center (MSFC) in Huntsville, Alabama.

At MSFC, engineers joined *Enterprise* with an external propellant tank and two SRBs in a test stand. They then applied vibrations of varying frequencies and intensities to the vehicle to see how the space shuttle reacted. These tests simulated the vibrations expected during launch.

By early 1979, the so-called mated ground vibration tests were over, and on April 10, the SCA ferried the *Enterprise* from MSFC to the Kennedy Space Center (KSC) in Cape Canaveral, Florida. At the Cape, *Enterprise* was assembled with the tank and boosters atop the mobile launch platform and taken to the launch pad. This was the first time a complete space shuttle was processed for launch, and technicians tested how well all the plumbing and electrical fittings at the launch pad interfaced with the vehicle. On May 1, 1979, a space shuttle vehicle stood on Launch Complex 39A for the first time.

Following launch pad assembly and fit checks, *Enterprise* was used for several public exhibitions. In May, 1983, NASA took the *Enterprise* to the Paris Air Show. After the French exposition, *Enterprise* was also viewed by millions of people in West Germany, Italy, England, and Canada. The following year, from May through November, *Enterprise* was exhibited at the Louisiana World Exposition in New Orleans. For this trip, the orbiter was transported on a barge part of the way.

On November 18, 1985, *Enterprise* made its last flight, as NASA delivered it to the Smithsonian Institution at Dulles International Airport in Virginia. At a ceremony on December 6, NASA formally turned the *Enterprise* over to the Smithsonian Institution. In June, 1987, however, NASA engineers found one more use for OV-101, as they tested an emergency net designed to keep returning orbiters from running off the runway.

Contributions

As the prototype space shuttle orbiter, *Enterprise* validated the design of a new family of spacecraft. Also, by testing the landing system, *Enterprise* proved the validity of using glide return for piloted spacecraft. In the course of the flight test program, NASA engineers learned how to land a 90,000- kilogram, delta-winged spacecraft. The flights verified both pilot-guided and automatic approach and landing systems and showed that the orbiter could land on a paved runway. This had been particularly worrisome, because the orbiter lands at relatively

Enterprise takes flight for the first time in August 1977 during the Approach and Landing Tests. (NASA / Dryden Flight Research Center)

high speeds (about 350 kilometers per hour) and tire wear is a problem. (In fact, subsequent landings by orbiters returning from space showed this to be a major problem.)

Ground vibration tests were a crucial step toward validating the entire space shuttle "stack" for launch. In the course of these tests, engineers at MSFC ballasted the External Tank with varying amounts of deionized water, simulating the consumption of propellants during flight. In addition, the SRBs were ballasted with inert propellant for the tests. Thus, the shuttle's designers had actual measurements of the vehicle's response to dynamic flight conditions. These data were used to validate researchers' analytical math models and predictions of the space shuttle's in-flight behavior.

By taking *Enterprise* to Kennedy Space Center for launch pad fit checks, engineers could verify that all the electrical, hydraulic, and fuel lines on the launch pad interfaced properly with the space shuttle. This was particularly important, because the shuttle used facilities originally built for the Apollo Program in the 1960's. The *Enterprise* also provided a dress rehearsal for launch pad crews to handle and assemble a complete space shuttle before the first actual flight vehicles arrived.

Context

The idea of winged, reusable spacecraft had long appealed to engineers as the most economical means for opening the space frontier. Throughout the 1960's, NASA and military engineers discussed the possibilities of an aircraft-type space vehicle and advanced numerous designs. One of the best known was the United States Air Force Dyna-Soar, a piloted glider planned for launch by a Titan III launch vehicle. Other designs, though never built, bore such exotic names as Triamese (a shuttle comprising three identical vehicles connected for launch, one of which would reach orbit), Meteor, and Astro Rocket. By the late 1960's, NASA planners were developing a program to succeed the Apollo piloted lunar missions. They finally decided on a reusable space shuttle. In April, 1972, the United States Congress approved NASA's request to proceed with the space shuttle. On August 9, 1972, NASA managers authorized North American Rockwell (later, Rockwell International) to build the space shuttle orbiter.

Engineers proposed numerous designs for the space shuttle before choosing what became the *Enterprise*. The orbiter contained a cargo bay capable of carrying payloads up to 4.5 meters in diameter, 18.3 meters in length, and 29,500 kilograms in weight. The space shuttle would lift off like a rocket, orbit like a spacecraft, and then glide back for an airplane-style landing.

Winged spacecraft had existed for nearly two decades, in the form of the North American X-15. Between 1959 and 1968, three of these remarkable aircraft made 199 flights. On several occasions, X-15 pilots flew above 80 kilometers, qualifying them as astronauts. Experiences with the rocket-powered X-15 aircraft, which made unpowered, high-speed landings, were directly applicable to the space shuttle program. Yet before the plans for the space shuttle could be put into practice, particularly the notion of landing a spacecraft like an airplane, a test vehicle was needed. The *Enterprise* served that function. Thus, *Enterprise* bridged the gap between X-15 research aircraft flights and the first space-flight of the OV-102 orbiter *Columbia* in 1981.

—*Gregory P. Kennedy*

See also: Apollo Program: Lunar Lander Training Vehicles; Launch Vehicles; National Aeronautics and Space Administration; National Aero- Space Plane; Space Shuttle: Ancestors; Space Shuttle Mission STS-1; Space Shuttle Flights, 1983; Space Shuttle Mission STS-6.

Further Reading

Grey, Jerry. *Enterprise*. New York: William Morrow, 1980. This popular book on the space shuttle program deals extensively with the politics of building the space shuttle and starting the program.

Hallion, Richard P. *On the Frontier: Flight Research at Dryden, 1946-1981*. NASA SP-4303. Washington, D.C.: Government Printing Office, 1984. This volume in the NASA History series describes flight-testing activities at the Dryden Flight Research Center from 1946 to 1981. Provides an excellent perspective on flight research activities at Dryden up to the first space shuttle mission. Also included are chapters on the X-15 and "lifting body" programs, which were precursors of the space shuttle.

Harland, David M. *The Space Shuttle: Roles, Missions, and Accomplishments*. New York: John Wiley, 1998. The book details the origins, missions, payloads, and passengers of the Space Transportation System (STS), covering the flights from STS-1 through STS-89. This large volume is divided into five sections: "Operations," "Weightlessness," "Exploration," "Outpost," and "Conclusions." "Operations" discusses the origins of the shuttle, test flights, and some of its missions and payloads. "Weightlessness" describes many of the experiments performed aboard the orbiter, including materials processing, electrophoresis, phase partitioning, and combustion. "Exploration" includes the Hubble Space Telescope, Spacelab, Galileo, Magellan, and Ulysses, as well as Earth observation projects. "Outpost" covers the shuttle's role in the joint Russian Mir program and the International Space Station. Contains numerous illustrations, an index, and bibliographical references.

Harrington, Philip S. *The Space Shuttle: A Photographic History*. San Francisco, Calif.: Brown Trout, 2003. With one hundred full-color photographs by Roger Ressmeyer and others and with text by popular astronomy writer Harrington, this book tells the story of the space shuttle program from 1972 to 2003. Its beautiful photographs allow the general reader to survey the history of the space shuttle program and be uplifted by the pioneering spirit of one of humanity's grandest enterprises.

Jenkins, Dennis R. *Rockwell International Space Shuttle*. Osceola, Wis.: Motorbooks International, 1989. Includes a brief yet concise history of the orbiter and its predecessors. Contains dozens of close-up color and black-and-white photographs, detailing the orbiter's exterior and interior features, including the major subsystems. Some of the text, especially the data tables, is printed in extremely small type.

---. *Space Shuttle: The History of the National Space Transportation System: The First 100 Missions*. Stillwater, Minn.: Voyageur Press, 2001. This is a concisely written technical reference account of the space shuttle and its ancestors, the aerodynamic lifting bodies. It details some of the advantages and inherent disadvantages of using a reusable space vehicle. Each of the vehicles is illustrated by line drawings with important features pointed out with lines and text. The book follows the space shuttle from its original concepts and briefly chronicles its first one hundred flights.

Stockton, William, and John Noble Wilford. *Spaceliner: The New York Times Report on the Columbia's Voyage.* New York: Times Books, 1981. An excellent narrative of the space shuttle program up to the first flight of *Columbia* in April, 1981. Included in the narrative are chapters devoted to the design, development, and testing of the space shuttle system, including *Enterprise.*

Space Shuttle: Life Science Laboratories

Date: June, 1991, to May, 1998
Type of program: Scientific platforms

Space Transportation System missions deployed life science and microgravity laboratories and payloads for biological experiments that investigated six of the human body's systems.

Key Figures

James M. Beggs (b. 1926), NASA administrator

James C. Fletcher (1919-1991), NASA administrator

Robert A. Schmitz, program manager, NASA Headquarters

John S. Theon, program scientist, NASA Headquarters

Donald K. "Deke" Slayton (1924-1993), manager, Orbital Flight Test Program

Maxime A. Faget (1921-2004), director of Engineering and Development, Johnson Space Center

Robert F. Thompson (b. 1925), program manager of the Space Shuttle Office, Johnson Space Center

James W. Bilodeau, the chief of Crew Procedures for shuttle missions

Summary of the Program

STS-40 was launched on June 5, 1991. It was the fifth dedicated Spacelab mission, carrying Spacelab Life Sciences 1 (SLS-1), and thus the first Spacelab mission dedicated solely to life sciences. The mission featured the most detailed and interrelated physiological measurements in space since the 1973-1974 Skylab missions. The subjects were humans, thirty rodents, and thousands of tiny jellyfish. The primary SLS-1 experiments studied six body systems. Of eighteen investigations, ten experiments involved humans, seven involved rodents, and one used jellyfish. The six body systems investigated were the cardiovascular/cardiopulmonary system (heart, lungs, and blood vessels), renal/endocrine system (kidneys, hormone-secreting organs, and glands), blood system (blood plasma), immune system (white blood cells), the musculoskeletal system (muscles and bones), and the neurovestibular system (brains, nerves, eyes, and inner ear).

STS-42 was launched on January 22, 1992. The primary payload was the International Microgravity Laboratory-1 (IML-1). The IML-1 was making its first flight and used the pressurized Spacelab module. The international crew divided into two teams for around-the-clock research on the human nervous system's adaptation to low gravity and the effects of microgravity on other life-forms, such as shrimp eggs, lentil seedlings, fruit fly eggs, and bacteria.

STS-58 went into orbit on October 18, 1993. This was the second dedicated Spacelab Life Sciences mission (SLS-2). Fourteen experiments were conducted in four areas: regulatory physiology, cardiovascular/cardiopulmonary, musculoskeletal, and neuroscience. Eight experiments focused on the crew. Six other experiments focused on forty-eight rodents. The crew collected more than 650 different samples from themselves and rodents, thus increasing the statistical base for life sciences research.

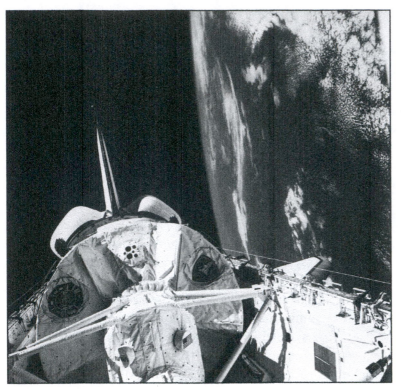

Space Life Science-1 (SLS-1), launched aboard Space Shuttle Orbiter Columbia (STS-40) on June 5, 1991, was the first Spacelab mission dedicated solely to life sciences research. The laboratory for the research took place in a module, shown here, carried in the cargo bay of the Columbia. (NASA / MSFC)

Cardiovascular investigations included in-flight study of cardiovascular deconditioning, cardiovascular adaptation to zero gravity, and pulmonary function during weightlessness.

Musculoskeletal investigations were composed of the following: protein metabolism during spaceflight, effects of zero gravity on the functional and biochemical properties of antigravity skeletal muscle, effects of microgravity on the electron microscopy, histochemistry and protease activities of rat hindlimb muscles, and pathophysiology of mineral loss during spaceflight (bone, calcium). Histochemistry is the study of the chemical components of cells and tissues. A protease is an enzyme that digests proteins.

Neuroscience investigations were to study the effects of space travel on mammalian gravity receptors and conduct vestibular experiments in Spacelab.

The anatomical and zoological meaning of vestibule is any cavity or space serving as an entrance or exit to another cavity or space, such as the vestibule of the inner ear, which leads into the cochlea.

Regulatory physiology investigations were as follows: fluid electrolyte regulation during spaceflight, regulation of blood volume during spaceflight, regulation of erythropoiesis in rats during spaceflight, and influence of spaceflight on erythrokinetics in humans. Erythropoiesis is the body process of making red blood cells, and erythrokinetics is red-blood-cell dynamics within the body.

For one of the neurovestibular experiments, the Rotating Dome Experiment, the crew worked with the first flight prototype of Astronaut Science Advisor (ASA). ASA is a laptop computer designed to assist astronauts conducting experiments. It is also called "principal investigator in a box" because it can increase the efficiency of experiment activities. Six rodents were sacrificed and dissected during the mission. This yielded the first tissue samples collected in space and not altered by reexposure to Earth's gravity.

STS-78 lifted off on June 20, 1996. Five space agencies—the National Aeronautics and Space Administration (NASA), the European Space Agency (ESA), the French Space Agency, the Canadian Space Agency, and the Italian Space Agency—and research scientists from ten countries worked together on the primary payload of STS-78, the Life and Microgravity Spacelab (LMS).

The LMS investigations were conducted via the most extensive telescience up to that time. Investigators were located at four remote European and four remote U.S. locations. This is similar to what was planned for the International Space Station.

The mission also made extensive use of video imaging to help crew members perform in-flight maintenance procedures on equipment hardware.

More than forty experiments flown were categorized into two areas: life sciences, which included human physiology and space biology, and microgravity science. One series of experiments measured muscle performance and function. These utilized the Torque Velocity Dynamometer, a device much like exercise equipment, which provides precise measurements of muscle use, including strength, the amount of force produced, and fatigue.

Blood, saliva, and other body samples were collected for metabolic experiments designed to understand the biochemical changes and effects of spaceflight on humans. These specimens were for measurement of calcium intake and loss from the body, protein metabolism, and caloric intake and use. The first of several tests of the Astronaut Lung Function Experiment was performed. This investigation examined spaceflight's effects on lung function and respiratory muscles during rest and heavy exercise. An alternative oxygen supply was connected to the lung experiment device. The alternative source of oxygen allowed performance of a pulmonary test to measure the diffusion capacity of the lung. This is the ability of gases to move from the air spaces into the blood and vice versa. The Torso Rotation Experiment was designed to determine how eye, head, and body coordination is changed by longer stays in space.

Some experiments focused primarily on the effects of weightlessness on human physiology. STS-78 marked the first time that researchers collected samples of muscle tissue both before and after flight. Crew members were also scheduled to undergo magnetic resonance imaging (MRI) scans almost immediately after landing.

On STS-78 there occurred the first comprehensive study of sleep cycles, twenty-four-hour circadian rhythms, and task performance in microgravity. While orbiting the Earth, the spacecraft passed through sixteen sunrises and sunsets in a single twenty-four-hour period. This could disrupt normal body rhythms. During two seventy-two-hour time blocks, crew members completed questionnaires and measured such functions as eye movement and muscle activity during sleep. In the Performance Assessment Work Station, crewmembers carried out a series of drills involving math problems and other mental tests to measure microgravity effects on cognitive or thinking skills.

The STS-90 (Neurolab) took off on April 17, 1998. The Neurolab's twenty-six experiments targeted one of the most complex and least understood parts of the human body: the nervous system. Primary goals were to conduct basic research in space neurosciences and expand our understanding of how the nervous system develops and functions in space. The test subjects were crew members, rats, mice, crickets, snails, and two kinds of fish. The work was a cooperative effort of NASA, several domestic partners, and the space agencies of Canada (Canadian Space Agency, CSA), France (Centre National d'Études Spatiales, CNES), and Germany (DARA) as well as the ESA and the National Space Development Agency of Japan (NASDA). Most experiments were conducted in the pressurized Spacelab long module located in *Columbia*'s payload bay, and many were the same as those carried out during the flights of STS-58 and STS-78.

Space neuroscience is a specialized discipline within the field of neuroscience. It studies the adaptation of the nervous system when exposed to the space environment and its readaptation upon return to Earth. A number of characteristics of the space environment affect the functioning of the nervous system including microgravity, radiation, loss of temporal cues, and the spacecraft environment. The most striking of these is exposure to microgravity.

A number of crew members received injections of radioactively labeled norepinephrine into their bloodstreams, and blood samples were later taken from them. Norepinephrine is a chemical messenger that allows investigators to measure how fast the substance is released into and removed from the blood's circulation and determines whether the blood-pressure control system is underutilized in the absence of gravity.

Another set of experiments focused on effects of microgravity on the vestibular system in the inner ear. In space, the vestibular system sometimes becomes confused as to which way is up and which down, leading to nausea and disorientation. Using specially designed headgear to monitor head movement and eye coordination, crew members performed tests to determine how the head and eyes track visual and motion targets in microgravity.

In this onboard photo of STS-78 mission specialists Richard Linnehan and Charles Brady, Linnehan is drawing blood from Brady as part of the mission's many experiments. (NASA)

Contributions

The combined data from the shuttle's life science experiments will help build a comprehensive picture of how humans and animals adapt to weightlessness. Findings from comparison of the tissue samples, along with various musculoskeletal tests conducted during the mission, could lead to effective countermeasures to reduce in-flight muscle atrophy. Some findings were that the decrease in bone density that occurs during spaceflight is due to increased bone breakdown that is not compensated for by a subsequent increase in bone formation.

One experiment that traced development of fish embryos seemed to indicate that the samples in orbit were developing at a slower rate than ground-controlled samples. One of the biggest mysteries in science is how a single cell develops different types of structures and tissues. This experiment indicates that gravity may be an important factor in this development.

Upon return to normal gravity, space travelers commonly are unable to stand without fainting. This condition, known as orthostatic intolerance, results from insufficient blood being pumped to the brain and reflects the adaptation of the cardiovascular system to microgravity. In space, the heart no longer has to pump against gravity to keep blood flowing to the brain. Some possible causes are a lower level of constriction in blood vessels and impairment of neural reflexes that control the balance between heart rate and blood pressure.

Experiments on STS-90 showed that there are residual effects of weightlessness. When subjects close their eyes, there is a tendency to point low at a previously viewed target. During spaceflight, subjects often misjudge the position of passively moved limbs, indicating that the receptors that sense limb position are altered in the absence of gravity. Upon return to Earth most astronauts experience some instability and difficulty in walking and standing. This seems to be due to an increased reliance upon visual cues and a possible change in the way the receptors in the joints sense the angle of the limbs against the force of gravity.

One component of the nervous system, the autonomic nervous system, governs diverse physiological functions including heart rate, blood pressure, hormone release, and respiration. Exposure to microgravity alters processes that can affect autonomic nervous system activity. These include neurovestibular changes (changes in sense of balance and orientation), removal of the force of gravity from muscles, and a microgravity-induced shift of body fluid toward the head.

Context

Some of the major changes experienced by space shuttle crews have been shifts in body fluids, muscle atrophy, and decalcification of bone tissue. These changes seem to be reversible after short-duration flights, but the effects of long-duration missions such as those on the Space Station are not known. Knowledge gained from the STS-78 (LMS) experiments aided in the development of countermeasures and contribute to the basic understanding of human physiology.

Results from the studies of muscle activity, performance, and sleep will help future mission planners organize crew schedules for greater efficiency and productivity. Similarly, results from the Torsion Rotation Experiment could help researchers identify causes of motion sickness during spaceflight, develop countermeasures, and lead to practical ways on Earth to avoid motion sickness in cars, boats, or aircraft.

The study of fish embryo development in a microgravity environment may have great impact upon the future of long-duration spaceflight, both how it is planned, and how it is carried out. Knowledge of the impact of microgravity on vertebrate development is needed if space exploration goes to the extent of including families with young children.

Some of the research will aid studies on osteoporosis and the affects steroids have on bones, and may also help doctors on Earth develop treatments for muscle diseases like muscular dystrophy. With the information gathered, better ways will probably be found to keep people in space healthier and help them fight off muscle and bone degeneration, which will benefit people on Earth.

On-orbit results from the musculoskeletal/ ergometer experiments will be compared with pre- and post-flight data to determine the effects of microgravity on muscle activity, ability to control muscles, and capacity to secrete growth hormones. The tests will provide investigators with qualitative measurements of the stress induced by exercise and may help develop measures to reduce in-flight muscle atrophy.

Results from the few animal studies conducted in space and ground-based experiments using models of microgravity suggest that exposure to microgravity does cause changes in the developing nervous system. Additional research is needed to understand these effects completely. Future research will take advantage of the capability of the Spacelab module and the Space Station to support experiments using animals, to conduct such studies. Examining nervous system development in microgravity will lead to a better understanding of the capacity of the growing nervous system to respond to environmental influences and how the nervous system normally develops on Earth.

—Dana P. McDermott

See also: Biosatellites; Space Shuttle: Microgravity Laboratories and Payloads; Space Shuttle Flights, 1991; Space Shuttle Flights, 1992; Space Shuttle Flights, 1993; Space Shuttle Flights, 1994; Space Shuttle Flights, 1998; Spacelab Program.

Further Reading

Buckey, Jay C., and Jerry L. Homick, eds. *The Neurolab Spacelab Mission: Neuroscience Research in Space: Results from the STS-90, Neurolab Spacelab Mission*. Washington, D.C.: U.S. Government Printing Office, 2003. The book reveals the results of Neurolab, a sixteen-day space shuttle mission dedicated to studying how weightlessness affects the brain and nervous system. This book shows the complex and sometimes surprising changes in the brain and nervous system that allow astronauts to adapt to weightlessness. The results suggest that the developing nervous system may need gravity to develop normally and that some concept of how gravity works may be "built in" to the brain.

Churchill, Susanne E., and Heinz Oser, eds. *Fundamentals of Space Life Sciences*. 2 vols. Melbourne, Fla.: Krieger Publishing Company, 1997. An international collection of papers considering the fundamental issues, existing data, and future research directions of space life sciences. Volume 1 presents information on the space environment and living systems' responses to it. Volume 2 explores psychosocial issues of spaceflight and lifesupport systems in space.

Harland, David M. *The Space Shuttle: Roles, Missions, and Accomplishments*. Hoboken, N.J.: John Wiley, 1998. This book is written thematically, rather than purely chronologically. Topics include shuttle operations and payloads, weightlessness, materials processing, exploration, Spacelabs and free-flyers, and the shuttle's role in the International Space Station.

Jenkins, Dennis R. *Space Shuttle: The History of the National Space Transportation System: The First 100 Missions*. Stillwater, Minn.: Voyageur Press, 2001. This is a concisely written technical reference account of the space shuttle and its ancestors, the aerodynamic lifting bodies. It details some of the advantages and inherent disadvantages of using a reusable space vehicle. Each of the vehicles is illustrated by line drawings with important features pointed out with lines and text. The book follows the space shuttle from its original concepts and briefly chronicles its first one hundred flights.

Konstantinova, I. V., and B. B. Fuchs. *Immune System in Space and Other Extreme Conditions*. Newark, N.J.: Gordon & Breach Publishing Group, 1991. Data drawn from twenty-five years of Soviet spaceflights and analyzed by scientists throughout the world form the basis of a review of the immune systems of both humans and animals under such conditions as prolonged hypokinesia, isolation, and extreme temperatures. Of special concern are disorders of bone-calcium metabolism provoked by long-term hypokinesia and weightlessness, and diseases accompanied by osteoporosis. Seven of the ten chapters discuss humans; one, animals; and one, experiments on isolated cells.

Moore, David, Peter Bie, and Heinz Oser, eds. *Biological and Medical Research in Space: An Overview of Life Sciences Research in Microgravity*. New York: Springer-Verlag, 1996. This book provides a critical review of the whole space life sciences research field. Chapters 1 to 7 are scientific reviews that have been prepared by recognized experts in cell biology, human physiology, radiation biology, and exobiology. Chapter 8 provides a statistical summary of life sciences research in space.

Rath, H. J. *Microgravity Sciences: Results and Analysis of Recent Spaceflights*. New York: Pergamon Press, 1995. Description and analyses of the research carried out in the microgravity laboratories on the space shuttle during the early 1990's.

Zigmond, Michael J., Floyd E. Bloom, Story C. Landis, and Larry R. Squire, eds. *Fundamental Neuroscience*. New York: Academic Press, 1998. This volume provides historical context and addresses the progress of neuroscience and physiology disciplines. It provides comprehensive coverage of molecular, cellular, developmental, organismal, behavioral, and cognitive neuroscience, as well as clinical research and applications.

Space Shuttle: Living Accommodations

Date: Beginning April 12, 1981
Type of spacecraft: Piloted spacecraft

Safe and comfortable living conditions in a microgravity environment must be provided for space shuttle astronauts in order to ensure the success of assigned scientific and military tasks.

Key Figures

Maxime A. Faget (1921-2004), director of Engineering and Development, Johnson Space Center (JSC)

Charles A. Berry (b. 1923), director of Medical Research and Operations, JSC

Robert E. Smiley, head of the Crow Systems division, JSC

Robert F. Thompson (b. 1925), program manager of the Space Shuttle Office, JSC

James W. Bilodeau, the chief of Crew Procedures for space shuttle missions

Alan B. Shepard, Jr. (1923-1998), head of the Astronaut Office, Manned Spacecraft Center

Summary of the Facility

Daily life aboard the U.S. space shuttle is much more luxurious than that on the earliest piloted space missions, although interior decorating is not a high priority. "The decor could be called modern metal file cabinet," according to Rick Gore of *National Geographic* magazine (March, 1981). The nose section of the shuttle orbiter contains the bi-level, pressurized crew cabin. Approximately 72 cubic meters of space are available for astronaut activities. Commander and pilot observe and operate shuttle functions from the upper-level flight deck, and a work area for other crew members is located behind the command center. The lower level of the cabin, known as middeck, serves as living quarters for the entire crew; experiments requiring oxygen are also housed here during some missions.

Fans force cabin air through an array of filters. Particulates, including dust, bacteria, dead skin cells, and hair, are filtered directly; lithium hydroxide canisters remove carbon dioxide, a waste product of respiration; and activated charcoal filters remove odors. Humidity is kept low to discourage bacterial growth. The astronauts' breathing mixture is 80 percent nitrogen and 20 percent oxygen. (Earth air is 78 percent nitrogen, 21 percent oxygen, and 1 percent other gases.) Internal cabin pressure is maintained at 14.7 pounds per square inch, the pressure of Earth's atmosphere at sea level. Water—a by-product of the fuel cells that generate electricity—is provided to the crew cabin at a rate of 3 kilograms per hour. Cabin temperature is maintained by water-pipe heat exchangers that transfer heat to Freon-fueled cargo bay radiators.

Early spacefarers survived on unpalatable food pastes squeezed out of devices resembling toothpaste tubes. Shuttle astronauts enjoy a wide variety of foods and even select their own menus. Each day's intake must provide 2,800 to 3,000 kilocalories and the recommended daily allowances of minerals and vitamins. Special attention is given to potassium, calcium, and nitrogen; in weightlessness, the human body loses these minerals first. Everything from scrambled Mexican eggs to candy-coated chocolates can be found among the ninety-two foods and thirty-seven beverages available.

The shuttle's galley, or kitchen, contains food lockers, which hold each day's meals in the order in which they will be consumed, a convection oven to

A smiling Robert L. Crippen, STS-1 pilot, is about to prepare a meal aboard the space shuttle Columbia in Earth orbit. (NASA)

heat precooked foods to 82° Celsius, and a hot and cold water dispenser, which injects fluid into rehydratable food packages with a needle to prevent spillage. Velcro strips on lockers and walls allow food items to be fixed in place while meals are prepared. Fresh foods, including fruit, vegetables, and baked goods, are loaded shortly before launch. The galley also has a washing station for cleaning hands and utensils.

For certain special missions in which space is at a premium, the entire galley is removed and the astronauts make do with a cold water dispenser that can rehydrate a reduced menu of foods. A small, portable warmer substitutes for the convection oven. Emergency food, for unexpectedly lengthened missions, and additional snacks are stored in the pantry, which contains enough extra food to provide 2,100 kilocalories per day per astronaut for two additional mission days.

There is no refrigerator on board the shuttle because of weight considerations, so foods are prepared and packed in several ways for storage at room temperature. Freeze-dried, rehydratable food and drink come in small, sealed plastic bowls or pouches. Thermostabilized foods are heat sterilized to discourage bacterial spoilage and packaged in metal cans or flexible pouches. Meats are sterilized by exposure to ionizing radiation and packaged in flexible foil. Intermediate-moisture foods, such as dried apricots, dried peaches, and beef jerky, are packed in transparent plastic. Items such as nuts and cookies, designated "natural form foods," are packed in plastic containers, and condiments are provided in dropper bottles. Even salt and pepper are fluidized in water or oil to make them dispensable.

Mealtime in the shuttle may find the astronauts rooted to a surface by suction cups, sitting in a seat with meal trays strapped to their laps, upside down with trays attached to the ceiling, sitting at the small shuttle table with feet in loops, or even floating freely through the cabin. Knives, forks, and spoons three-quarters of the size are used for shuttle meals; their smallness helps minimize food spillage and cleanup problems for the vehicle's air recycling systems.

Keeping clean and disposing of waste is no easy task in space, but it is vital for the health of the space shuttle crew. The confined space and effects of microgravity could allow disease-inducing bacteria to multiply out of control if sanitation were not carefully maintained. The microgravity environment of low-Earth orbit allows water droplets and crumbs of debris to float around the shuttle cabin, posing a threat to instrumentation and crew members.

Garbage from food preparation, used clothing, and waste from experimental activities is sealed in plastic containers for storage under the middeck floor until return to Earth. All areas of the spacecraft used by the crew are cleaned in flight with disposable wipes and disinfectant solution.

The space shuttle lavatory contains a small sink, a toilet, mirrors, and a light. Washing is performed with a minimum of water. Because fluid adheres to skin in a weightless environment, little soap or water is necessary. Crew members take short sponge baths rather than taking showers, as they did in Skylab. A fan sucks water into the basin drain, substituting for the ordinary effect of gravity on Earth. Hot water is dispensed from a gun set at temperatures from 18 to 35° Celsius. Male astronauts wishing to shave must use ordinary shaving cream and safety razors, wiping the razors with disposable towels to keep whiskers from escaping into the cabin environment. Towels and personal necessities are clipped to the wall for easy access. The zero-gravity toilet drains by means of a fan, which transports the waste materials to a storage area. Originally, wastes were shredded; now, they are disinfected, deodorized, and dried for storage until return to Earth. In microgravity, to remain in place on the toilet, astronauts use a seat belt and place their feet in toeholds while holding onto handles. The toilet's cycle time is approximately fifteen minutes, so it can be used about four times in an hour. Space-sick astronauts use Velcro-sealable pouches,

similar to airsickness bags, which are disposed of in the commode. The same bags can be used as an alternative method of fecal collection if the zero-gravity toilet malfunctions.

Shuttle astronauts wear ordinary trousers, shirts, and jackets covered with Velcro-fastened pockets. Ordinary clothes contribute to a sense of normality and comfort as the astronauts go about their many tasks. For extravehicular activities (spacewalks outside the vehicle or in the exposed cargo bay), protective space suits are required. Each suit is really a tiny spaceship that provides a breathable atmosphere, comfortable temperatures, and adequate internal pressure. Propulsion is provided by separate maneuvering units.

Shuttle suits, called extravehicular mobility units (EMUs), are much more sophisticated than those used on past space missions. In addition to offering greater flexibility and comfort, they can be put on relatively quickly without assistance. The modular suits have three primary and several secondary components, all of which come in several sizes so as to fit the exact dimensions of each astronaut. The main part of the suit consists of a hard covering for the upper torso and flexible pants, a detachable helmet with a visor, gloves, and a bag containing about twenty ounces of drinking water. The gloves are the only component that is fitted to each crew member. The torso is composed of many layers, each with an important job. A Teflon-coated outside layer resists tears and protects against damage from micrometeoroids, the next several layers of aluminized Mylar plastic reflect heat away from the suit, and the interior layers are made of insulating Dacron unwoven fabric. Inside the outer suit, a separate, water-cooled, liner garment is worn; it resembles long underwear. The small tubes sewn all over it conduct water to lower the astronaut's body temperature. Under the liner, there is a urine collection device that retains liquid waste for later transferal to the shuttle's waste management system. Physiological functions are controlled by the primary life-support system, which circulates and cools the water in the liner, absorbs carbon dioxide, supplies temperature-controlled oxygen for breathing, and maintains suit pressure. Filters remove unpleasant odors from the suit. All these complicated and vital functions are controlled by a tiny computer that displays information on the suit's chest section. Automatic checking programs test various suit functions, provide instructions for astronauts donning their suits, and sound an alarm if any suit functions begin to fail.

Sleeping accommodations vary with the demands of a particular mission. For uncrowded missions, one vertical and three horizontal bunks are available. Each sleeping pallet has storage areas, a light, pillows, a fan, a communications station, microgravity restraint sheets, and a noise-suppression blanket. For crowded missions, up to four sleeping bags attached to provision lockers are used, although some astronauts have preferred to catch naps while simply tethered to a cabin wall.

Communication among crew members in various parts of the shuttle is accomplished via simple headsets that connect to eight intercom terminals in the crew compartment. Books, tape recorders and tapes, playing cards, and other games are supplied, and a regular exercise regimen prevents physiological deconditioning.

Contributions

Keeping humans alive and well in space is a tremendously complicated task. Space shuttle designers must plan each subsystem and then integrate it with the entire human systems design scheme. Shuttle missions carry up to eight astronauts for periods of seven to fourteen days; shuttle designers

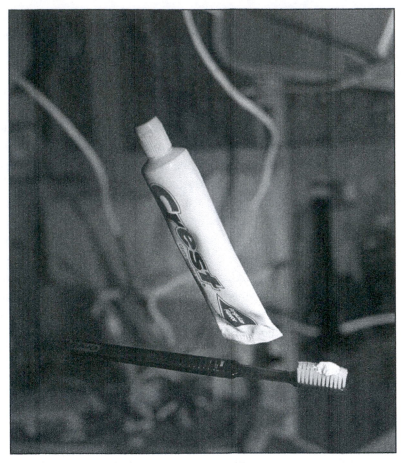

Toothpaste and toothbrush floating on the flight deck of Discovery, STS-70. (NASA)

therefore face challenges quite different from those presented by the three Skylab missions, with their smaller numbers of astronauts and longer duration missions.

As the Space Transportation System (STS) became operational, much was learned about problems with the various living arrangements. Solutions to these problems were gradually refined as more missions were flown. Strong odors are particularly disturbing to persons working in the confined area of a spacecraft. It was found that the odor of certain fresh fruits, such as bananas, was terribly annoying, and such items had to be stored separately or eliminated from the cargo.

Space sickness has been a problem for a number of astronauts on the shuttle, and scientists have made considerable efforts to understand and prevent the syndrome. Senator Jake Garn experienced significant space sickness during his 1985 voyage on *Atlantis*. He graciously offered to serve as a "guinea pig" for important studies on the symptomatology and physiology of the complaint.

The zero-gravity toilet was notoriously unreliable during many of the shuttle missions. Problems with the system were particularly demoralizing to the crew, presented a potential health hazard, and contributed to cabin odors. After the first few missions, the shredder/slinger was removed, because it did not function well in microgravity. The system was changed to allow wastes to be diverted to the side of the receiving vessel.

Debris in the cabin proved to be difficult to control, even with considerable prior planning. It is very important, for example, to have low-lint clothing and towels. During some experiments with small animals, most notably those on the April, 1985, *Challenger* mission, soiled bedding and unused food pellets escaped from the containment units and caused a major annoyance to the astronauts aboard. Such experiences have led to increasingly better designs for daily use items and experimental apparatus.

The maintenance of normal sleep cycles is very important to the crew's productivity and alertness. Schedules that keep astronauts on a regular twenty-four-hour cycle were found to be far superior to radically different schedules.

In the limited environment of a spacecraft, mealtimes become significant events. The space shuttle has the most sophisticated eating arrangements of any American spacecraft. It is possible that the preparation and consumption of food substitutes for the social and personal rituals that are lacking on board the shuttle.

Context

Just as astronauts' experiences on the three Skylab missions affected the design of the space shuttle living quarters, crew members' experiences aboard the shuttle have helped engineers to design the U.S. Space Station and the spacecraft that may go to Mars and the Moon. Human performance and well-being in space is the single largest factor determining the success of piloted space missions. It is also the area in which the United States has less cumulative experience than the former Soviet Union. Setbacks in the shuttle program have slowed U.S. progress in understanding human needs in space.

The Soviet Union's and, later, Russia's piloted missions have almost all been of long duration and have involved only a few astronauts at a time. The few times that psychological stress, depression, and conflict among cosmonauts emerged during a mission usually occurred after thirty days. It does not appear that any of these symptoms arise when astronauts spend equally long periods in space.

The demanding work of launching and repairing satellites or recovering damaged satellites for later repair on Earth requires that the crew be in topnotch physical condition. Such projects have served as

The STS-112 crew members sleep on the middeck of the space shuttle Atlantis. Pictured are mission specialists Sandra Magnus, David Wolf, Piers Sellers and Commander Jeffrey Ashby. (NASA)

models for future situations in which spacefarers will be faced with demanding tasks under stressful conditions. The International Space Station requires high performance standards in the demanding work of constructing large space structures in orbit. What scientists learned about human performance from the first hundred shuttle missions has been valuable in planning the activities of space station workers.

The lengthy consideration of human daily life—from sleeping, to eating, to exercising—in the alien environment of space has helped to advance the sciences of ergonomics, human performance, and stress psychology and the technologies of air and water recycling, food sterilization, and food packaging. Systems on the shuttle provide rigorous, immediate feedback on theories about human behavior and human engineering. If the designs are faulty, that is instantly apparent in the demanding shuttle environment.

Keeping human beings alive and comfortable in an environment as hostile as space shows that humankind's domain can be extended far into the solar system. Although unpiloted missions offer new perspectives on the outer planets and the universe, piloted missions are the key to moving human life into the realm of space.

When the orbiter has docked with the International Space Station, it is comparable to parking one's automobile in the garage. Free to roam the vast expanse of the station, astronauts no longer have to remain in close proximity to their crewmates. The orbiter's systems are monitored from the ground and crew can spend time working on the station. Eventually, the size of the station's shuttlecraft will be reduced to a fraction of its current size. Its only purpose will be that of a transport vehicle and, like any practical earthbound transport vehicle, it will be compact and get very good mileage.

—Penelope J. Boston

See also: Astronauts and the U.S. Astronaut Program; Cooperation in Space: U.S. and Russian; Ethnic and Gender Diversity in the Space Program; Extravehicular Activity; International Space Station: Living and Working Accommodations; Space Shuttle.

Further Reading

Bizony, Piers. *Island in the Sky: Building the International Space Station*. London: Aurum Press Limited, 1996. Bizony tells how the International Space Station will be assembled in orbit during an extended sequence of shuttle flights, dockings, and spacewalks over the next five years. With unrivaled access to NASA and the astronautic sources worldwide, his lively text contains a wealth of information. There are one hundred photographs, sixty in color.

Burrows, William E. *This New Ocean: The Story of the First Space Age*. New York: Random House, 1998. This is a comprehensive history of the human conquest of space, covering everything from the earliest attempts at spaceflight through the voyages near the end of the twentieth century. Burrows is an experienced journalist who has reported for *The New York Times*, *The Washington Post*, and *The Wall Street Journal*. There are many photographs and an extensive source list. Interviewees in the book include Isaac Asimov, Alexei Leonov, Sally K. Ride, and James A. Van Allen.

Connors, Mary M., et al. *Living Aloft: Human Requirements for Extended Spaceflight*. NASA SP-483. Washington, D.C.: Government Printing Office, 1985. Discusses the physical and social stresses of living in space and explores medical considerations and possible ways to deal with those stresses. Includes sections on exercise, leisure time, the need for privacy, astronaut work schedules and other aspects of human performance, the selection of crews, communications, and responses to crises. For college-level readers.

Harland, David M. *The Space Shuttle: Roles, Missions, and Accomplishments*. Hoboken, N.J.: John Wiley, 1998. This book is written thematically, rather than purely chronologically. Topics include shuttle operations and payloads, weightlessness, materials processing, exploration, Spacelabs and free-flyers, and the shuttle's role in the International Space Station.

Harrington, Philip S. *The Space Shuttle: A Photographic History*. San Francisco, Calif.: Brown Trout, 2003. With one hundred full-color photographs by Roger Ressmeyer and others and with text by popular astronomy writer Harrington, this book tells the story of the space shuttle program from 1972 to 2003. IBeautiful photographs allow the general reader to survey the history of the space shuttle program and be uplifted by the pioneering spirit of one of humanity's grandest enterprises.

Haynes, Robert. *Space Shuttle Food Systems*. NASA Facts NF-150/1-86. Washington, D.C.: National Aeronautics and Space Administration, 1986. This volume in the NASA Facts Series deals with the foods provided for the space shuttle astronauts. It is well illustrated with pictures of the various food packs, lockers, ovens, and hand-washing facilities aboard the shuttle. Includes a picture of an astronaut eating from a food tray in space. Sample menus and actual foods carried on the first four space shuttles are listed. Accessible to a general readership.

Heppenheimer, T. A. *Countdown: A History of Space Flight*. New York: John Wiley, 1997. A detailed historical narrative of the human conquest of space. Heppenheimer traces the development of piloted flight through the military rocketry programs of the era preceding World War II. Covers both the American and the Soviet attempts to place vehicles, spacecraft, and humans into the hostile environment of space. More than a dozen pages are devoted to bibliographic references.

Jenkins, Dennis R. *Space Shuttle: The History of the National Space Transportation System: The First 100 Missions*. Stillwater, Minn.: Voyageur Press, 2001. This is a concisely written technical reference account of the space shuttle and its ancestors, the aerodynamic lifting bodies. It details some of the advantages and inherent disadvantages of using a reusable space vehicle. Each of the vehicles is illustrated by line drawings with important features pointed out with lines and text. The book follows the space shuttle from its original concepts and briefly chronicles its first one hundred flights.

"Launch Vehicles." *Aviation Week and Space Technology*, January 17, 2000, 144-145. This table details the specifications for each of the 2000 launch vehicles and spacecraft, as well as the status.

Launius, Roger D. *NASA: A History of the U.S. Civil Space Program*. Malabar, Fla.: Krieger Publishing Company, 1994. This is an in-depth look at America's civilian space program and the establishment of the National Aeronautics and Space Administration. It chronicles the agency from its predecessor, the National Advisory Committee for Aeronautics, through the present day.

Logsdon, John M. *Together in Orbit: The Origins of International Participation in the Space Station*. Washington, D.C.: National Aeronautics and Space Administration, 1998. Describes the politics and science behind the effort to bring together many nations in the effort to build a space station.

McElroy, Robert D., Norman V. Martello, and David T. Smernoff. *Controlled Ecological Life Support Systems: CELSS 1985 Workshop*. NASA TM-88215. Springfield, Va.: National Technical Information Service, 1986. A compendium of ideas for life-support methods on the space shuttle, the Space Station, and future space missions. Discusses systems for recycling water, disposing of waste, reconstituting gases for use as breathable air, and producing food from algae, bacteria, and higher plants. College-level material.

Shayler, David J. *Disasters and Accidents in Manned Spaceflight*. Chichester, England: Springer- Praxis, 2000. The author examines the challenges that face all crews as they prepare and execute their missions. The book covers all aspects that make up spaceflight by a human crew—training, launch to space, survival in space, and return from space—followed by a series of case histories that tell of the major incidents in each of those categories over the past forty years. The sixth section looks at the International Space Station and its ability to prevent major incidents during the lifetime of the space station.

United States Air Force Academy. Department of Behavioral Sciences and Leadership. *Psychological, Sociological, and Habitability Issues of Long-Duration Space Missions*. NASA T-1082K. Houston: National Aeronautics and Space Administration, 1985. This book thoroughly assesses human engineering for current and future space missions. Topics covered include work-rest cycles; astronauts' sleep needs and performance levels; the design of astronauts' garments, food, and private accommodations; and the effects of all these factors on space personnel. Advanced college-level material.

Space Shuttle: Microgravity Laboratories and Payloads

Date: January, 1992, to December, 1997
Type of program: Scientific platforms

Various space shuttle missions have deployed microgravity laboratories and payloads for low-gravity experiments. Experiments have been conducted to help scientists develop better synthetic drugs, less expensive alloys and metal products, improved environmental methods, a better understanding of Earth's weather and climate, and a greater knowledge of how the human body functions in the space environment.

Summary of the Program

STS-42 was launched on January 22, 1992. The primary payload of STS-42 was the International Microgravity Laboratory-1 (IML-1), making its first flight and using the pressurized Spacelab module. The international crew divided into two teams for around-the-clock research on the human nervous system's adaptation to low gravity and the effects of microgravity on other life-forms such as shrimp eggs, lentil seedlings, fruit fly eggs, and bacteria. Materials-processing experiments were also conducted. These included crystal growth from a variety of substances such as enzymes, mercury iodide, and a virus.

STS-50 began its flight on June 25, 1992. The primary payload was the United States Microgravity Laboratory-1 (USML-1) which was making its first flight. The experiments conducted were Crystal Growth Furnace (CGF), Drop Physics Module (DPM), Surface Tension Driven Convection Experiments (STDCE), Zeolite Crystal Growth (ZCG), Protein Crystal Growth (PCG), Glovebox Facility (GBX), Space Acceleration Measurement System (SAMS), Generic Bioprocessing Apparatus (GBA), Astroculture-1 (ASC), Extended Duration Orbiter Medical Project (EDOMP), and Solid Surface Combustion Experiment (SSCE). SAMS was designed to provide information about the acceleration environment in which the other USML-1 experiments were being conducted.

STS-52 took off on October 22, 1992. One of the two primary objectives of STS- 52 was the operation of the United States Microgravity Payload-1 (USMP-1). USMP- 1, which was activated on flight day one, included three experiments mounted on two connected Multipurpose Experiment Support Structures (MPESS's) that were mounted in the cargo bay. The USMP-1 experiments were Lambda Point Experiment (LPE), the French-sponsored Matériel Pour l'Étude des Phénomènes Intéressant la Solidification sur Terre et en Orbite (MEPHISTO, Material for the Study of Interesting Solidification Phenomena on Earth and in Orbit), and SAMS. MEPHISTO was a cooperative program between the National Aeronautics and Space Administration (NASA) and the French space agency, Centre National d'Études Spatiales (CNES), which also built the payload.

STS-62 was the first Extended Duration Orbiter and launched on March 4, 1994. Two of the USMP-2 experiments focused on directional solidification, a well-known industrial process for making semi-conductors and metals. The goal of the Advanced Automated Directional Solidification Furnace (AADSF) was to exploit the gravity- free environment of space to gain understanding of the effects of

Commander Peggy Whitson is working on the OsteoOmics bone cell study that utilizes the Microgravity Science Glovebox inside the U.S. Destiny laboratory. (NASA)

gravitational forces on the material properties of semiconductors. The sample material, mercury cadmium telluride, is used in infrared detectors for applications such as remote sensing and astronomy. The other directional solidification experiment, MEPHISTO, flew on the first USMP as well.

The Isothermal Dendritic Growth Experiment (IDGE) also studied solidification of materials, but on a very different scale. Dendrites are tiny crystalline forms that develop as materials solidify under certain conditions. (Their Christmas-tree-like shape gave rise to their name, "dendrite," from the Greek word meaning tree.)

The Critical Fluid Light Scattering Experiment/ Zeno (CFLSE/Zeno) studied fluid behavior, specifically of a material in a state called the critical point, where portions of the substance are simultaneously a gas and a liquid. The inert gas xenon was the test material. The fifth USMP-2 payload was the SAMS, which had flown previously.

STS-73 launched on October 20, 1995. It was the second flight of theUSMLand built on the foundation of its predecessor, which flew on *Columbia* during mission STS-50 in 1992. Research of the USML- 2 was concentrated within the same overall areas of USML-1, with many experiments flying for the second time.

Research was conducted in five areas: fluid physics, materials science, biotechnology, combustion science, and commercial space processing. Experiments went smoothly. In some cases, results confirmed existing theories, while in other cases results were new and unique. Highlights included unprecedented results from the Surface Tension Driven Convection Experiment, which flew for the second time and studied in great detail basic fluid mechanics and heat transfer of thermocapillary flows. These are motions created within fluids by nonuniform heating of their free surfaces. Flying for the first time was the Fiber Supported Droplet Combustion experiment.

STS-75 set off on February 22, 1996. The USMP-3, flying on the shuttle for the third time, included U.S. and international experiments, all of which had flown at least once before. The experiments were the Advanced Automated Directional Solidification Furnace (AADSF), Critical Fluid Light Scattering Experiment (Zeno), Isothermal Dendritic Growth Experiment (IDGE), and MEPHISTO.

In the MEPHISTO experiment, changes in the microgravity environment caused by orbiter thruster firings were correlated with fluid flows in a crystal sample. In AADSF, three lead-tin-telluride crystals were grown while the orbiter flew at three different altitudes to determine effect on crystal growth. Data were also collected on the crystal's freezing point temperature.

STS-83 launched on April 4, 1997. The first flight of the Microgravity Science Laboratory 1 (MSL-1) was cut short because of concerns about one of three fuel cells, marking only the third time in the shuttle program's history that a mission ended early. STS-2 in 1981 and STS-44 in 1991 were the other two missions. The crew was able to conduct some science in the MSL-1 Spacelab module despite the early return. Work was performed in the German electromagnetic levitation furnace facility (TEMPUS) on an experiment called Thermophysical Properties of Undercooled Metallic Melts. This experiment studies the amount of undercooling that can be achieved before solidification occurs. Another experiment performed was the Liquid-Phase Sintering II Experiment in the large Isothermal Furnace. This investigation uses heat and pressure to test theories about how a liquefied substance bonds with the solid particles of a mixture without reaching the melting point of a new alloy combination being created.

Two fire-related experiments were also conducted. The Laminar Soot Processes Experiment allowed scientists to observe for the first time the concentration and structure of soot from a fire burning in microgravity. The Structure of Flame Balls at Low Lewis Number (SOFBALL) experiment completed two runs. This experiment is designed to determine under what conditions a stable flame ball can exist, and if heat loss is responsible in some way for the stabilization of the flame ball during burning.

STS-94 was launched on July 1, 1997, and marked the first reflight of the same vehicle, crew, and payloads due to the shortened STS-83 mission in April, 1997. The crew maintained twenty-four-hour, two-shift operations. Using the Spacelab module as a test bed, MSL-1R tested some of the hardware, facilities, and procedures that will be used on the International Space Station. The thirty-three investigations conducted also yielded new knowledge in the principal scientific fields of combustion, biotechnology, and materials processing.

The USMP-4 research was deemed to be highly successful. This fourth flight of the USMP focused on materials science, combustion science, and fundamental physics and was launched on November 19, 1997. With MEPHISTO, researchers were able to separate for the first time two separate processes of solidification. The Particle Engulfment and Pushing by a Solid/Liquid Interface (PEP) experiment, conducted with the Glovebox facility, examined the solidification of liquid metal alloys. For the first time, researchers observed large clusters of particles being pushed, forcing them to reassess theories on how alloys solidify.

Contributions

MEPHISTO, which flew on missions STS-52, 62, 75, and 87, focused on the direction in which a material becomes solid as it goes from a liquid to a solid state. When a sample of material is melted and then solidified from one end, there will be an interface or surface where solid meets liquid. What happens at this surface influences the final composition, structure, and properties of the solid. MEPHISTO studied the location and shape of the interface, building on data collected on the first flight.

During STS-73 (USML-2), there were unprecedented results from the STDCE, which studied in great detail basic fluid mechanics and heat transfer of thermocapillary flows. These are motions created within fluids by nonuniform heating of their free surfaces. During the Fiber Supported Droplet Combustion experiment, more than twenty-five droplets of a variety of fuels were ignited. The results confirmed theories about how fuels burn in microgravity. The results revealed a larger droplet extension diameter (size of drop as it burns out) than can be studied on Earth, with burning ten times longer.

Five small potatoes were grown in orbit from tubers in the Astroculture Plant Growth Facility. It seemed that starch accumulation in potatoes is greater under microgravity conditions than on Earth.

A record number of PCG samples, around fifteen hundred, were flown on USML-2. Initial results indicated many had produced crystals that were to be further studied after landing. In the CGF, which flew the first time on USML-1, a crystal was grown for the first time as a liquid bridge to minimize contact with its container wall, thus decreasing the number of defects in the crystal. Eight semiconductor crystals were grown, also a very thin crystal and two crystals, which could lead to products such as computer chips that are faster and use less power than traditional computer chips.

During STS-83 (MSL-1) and STS-94 (MSL-1R), SOFBALL made the biggest news with the tiniest fires, flame balls about the size of a pinhead and glowing with one-fiftieth of the energy of a birthday candle. The flame balls, generated by electric sparks, burned—motionless in their chamber— for five hundred seconds when the experiment was designed to blow them out. These are believed to be the weakest fires ever stoked. They should lead to clues on how to design engines that burn with leaner fuel-air mixtures and thus produce less pollution.

The Laminar Soot Process (LSP) Experiment produced flames twice as large as those formed on Earth and which appeared as steady as freeze frames on television. The laminar (smooth flow) flames formed soot, a pollutant, sooner then expected. Scientists also saw flames extinguished by energy radiating from soot, a new phenomenon that will alter studies for years.

Experiments processed in the TEMPUS during STS-83/MSL-1 yielded the first measurements of specific heat and thermal expansion of glass-forming metallic alloys. This basic research information is necessary for modeling industrial materials systems to manufacture new and better products.

Context

Much of the information gathered could be described as basic research. The phenomena and experiments were designed to gain basic information into how physical processes behave or perform under low-gravity conditions. Thus, studies were carried out that could not be performed on Earth. Essentially all of the information obtained was new. For example, under microgravity conditions, ethanol burns very well to total consumption of the fuel, whereas methanol puts out its own fire. Evidently methanol absorbs much of the water that is a key product of its own combustion. This water

absorption causes the methanol fire to go out. This phenomenon had never been observed on Earth and has great implications for those designing alcohol-burning engines. Methanol will not work as a fuel.

The work of the PCG project can provide a better understanding of the body's immune system and the function of individual genes, and can aid in the development of more effective drugs for the treatment of diseases such as cancer, diabetes, and acquired immunodeficiency syndrome (AIDS). Pure, well-ordered protein crystals of large size, which can be produced in microgravity, are much in demand by the pharmaceutical industry to facilitate drug discovery and drug delivery.

Many of the metal products on which we rely in our daily lives, such as automobiles and jet engine blades, are formed under conditions that yield dendrites. On STS-62/USMP-2, a single dendrite was grown and photographed under several different sets of experimental parameters, with the growth process repeated thirty-five to forty times.

The STDCE Experiment produced oscillations on USML-2 samples that had never been observed on Earth. Researchers controlling this experiment from the ground were able to pinpoint when fluid flows changed from stable to unstable. This research has direct applications on Earth, in that unwanted fluid flows during melting and resolidifying can create defects in high-tech crystals, metals, alloys, and ceramics.

Studying the critical point on Earth is difficult due to the effects of gravity. In the near weightlessness of space, the Zeno Experiment showed that the critical point zone is widened and researchers may have gained a one-hundred-times-more-accurate estimate of the behavior of the fluid near the temperature at which the critical point occurs.

The combustion investigations provided valuable information for improved fire safety on future spacecraft and for development of cleaner, more efficient internal combustion engines. These missions also produced progress in learning how to control and position liquid drops that could lead to improvements in chemical manufacturing, petroleum technology, and the cosmetics and food industries.

The International Space Station (ISS) provides an environment for constant microgravity experimentation. The space shuttle *Endeavour* transported the Microgravity Science Glovebox to the Space Station during STS-111, ISS Flight UF2, in June, 2002. The Microgravity Science Glovebox—a sealed container with built-in gloves—provides an enclosed workspace for investigations conducted in the unique microgravity environment created as the ISS orbits Earth. There are good reasons for using a glovebox to contain experiments with fluids, flames, particles, and fumes. In an Earth-based laboratory, liquids stay in beakers or test tubes. In the near-weightlessness of the Space Station, they float away. They might get into the cabin air and irritate a crew members' skin or eyes or even make them sick. They could damage the Space Station's sensitive computer and electrical systems or contaminate other experiments.

To make laboratory-type investigations inside the Space Station possible, engineers and scientists at NASA's Marshall Space Flight Center in Huntsville, Alabama, worked with the European Space Agency (ESA) to build the Microgravity Science Glovebox—a facility that will support Space Station investigations for up to ten years. In exchange for developing the Microgravity Science Glovebox, the ESA will have use of other facilities inside the Destiny Laboratory Module until its Space Station laboratory, the Columbus Orbital Facility, is attached to the Space Station. Launch is set for 2007 on STS-122.

The 10-metric ton, $1.4 billion lab—the ESA's major contribution to the ISS—will be delivered to a berthing site on Node 2, adjacent to the Destiny and directly across from the Japanese Experiment Module. The facility will accommodate ten racks, five of them for ESA use, the other five for NASA. It will be used primarily for research and experimentation in microgravity conditions.

—Dana P. McDermott,
updated by Russell R. Tobias

See also: Get-Away Special Experiments; International Space Station: Living and Working Accommodations; Materials Processing in Space; Private Industry and Space Exploration; Space Shuttle: Life Science Laboratories; Spacelab Program.

Further Reading

Barczy, P., ed. *Solidification and Microgravity*. Zurich, Switzerland: Trans Tech Publications, 1992. A fairly extensive collection of materials on various experimental areas of materials science under microgravity conditions. It has chapters on microgravity experiments and space devices, and solidification research. Very specific chapters on isothermal dendritic growth during a USMP-2 spaceflight experiment, experiment facilities for microgravity missions, and directional solidification of metal alloys.

Harland, David M. *The Space Shuttle: Roles, Missions, and Accomplishments*. Hoboken, N.J.: John Wiley, 1998. This book is written thematically, rather than purely chronologically. Topics include shuttle operations and payloads, weightlessness, materials processing, exploration, Spacelabs and free-flyers, and the shuttle's role in the International Space Station.

Holden, Alan, and Phylis S. Morrison. *Crystals and Crystal Growing*. Cambridge, Mass.: MIT Press, 1982. This work is a discussion of the ways in which solids form and a penetrating introduction to solid state physics. It discusses crystallography and crystal formation.

Jenkins, Dennis R. *Space Shuttle: The History of the National Space Transportation System: The First 100 Missions*. Stillwater, Minn.: Voyageur Press, 2001. This is a concisely written technical reference account of the space shuttle and its ancestors, the aerodynamic lifting bodies. It details some of the advantages and inherent disadvantages of using a reusable space vehicle. Each of the vehicles is illustrated by line drawings with important features pointed out with lines and text. The book follows the space shuttle from its original concepts and briefly chronicles its first one hundred flights.

Moore, David, Peter Bie, and Heinz Oser, eds. *Biological and Medical Research in Space: An Overview of Life Sciences Research in Microgravity*. New York: Springer-Verlag, 1996. This book provides a critical review of the whole field of space life sciences. Chapters 1 to 7 are scientific reviews that have been prepared by recognized experts in cell biology, human physiology, radiation biology, and exobiology. Chapter 8 provides a statistical summary of life sciences research in space.

National Research Council of the National Academies, Committee on Microgravity Research. *Assessment of Directions in Microgravity and Physical Sciences Research at NASA*. Washington, D.C.: National Academies Press, 2003. This in-depth report looks at NASA's microgravity research using robotic platforms, the space shuttle, and the International Space Station.

Rath, H. J. *Microgravity Sciences: Results and Analysis of Recent Spaceflights*. New York: Pergamon Press, 1995. Description and analyses of the research carried out in the microgravity laboratories on the space shuttle during the early 1990's.

Schiffman, Robert A., ed. *Experimental Methods for Microgravity Materials Science Research*. Warrendale, Pa.: Minerals, Metals & Materials Society, 1989. Proceeding of the Second International Symposium on Experimental Methods for Microgravity Materials held in February, 1988, in Phoenix, Arizona. The twenty-five papers included in this volume detail research techniques being used in Earth-based simulations, and also planned experimentation techniques to be used upon resumption of the space shuttle program.

Space Shuttle: Radar Imaging Laboratories

Date: 1994 to 2000
Type of program: Scientific platforms

Several Space Transportation System missions used a technology called imaging radar, which bounced a radar signal off the ground and then measured how long the signal took to come back and how strong it was. This technology facilitates very accurate pictures of the surface, regardless of whether it was day or night, cloudy or clear. A mission in February, 2000, used interferometry with imaging radar to create three-dimensional pictures of Earth's surface.

Summary of the Technology

An imaging radar works very much like a flash camera in that it provides its own light to illuminate an area on the ground and take a snapshot picture, but at radio wavelengths. A flash camera sends out a pulse of visible light (the flash) and records on film light reflected back at it through the camera lens. Instead of a camera lens and film, radar uses an antenna and digital computer tape to record its images. In a radar image, one can only see light reflected back toward the radar antenna.

Typical radar (radio detection and ranging) measures the strength and round-trip time of the microwave signals that are emitted by a radar antenna and reflected off a distant surface or object. The radar antenna alternately transmits and receives pulses at particular microwave lengths. The range of wavelengths is typically 1 centimeter to 1 meter, which corresponds to a frequency range of about 300 megahertz to 30 gigahertz.

Space Radar Laboratory-1 (SRL-1) was a payload launched aboard the space shuttle *Endeavour* (STS-59) on April 9, 1994. The SRL-1 comprised two elements: a suite of radar instruments called Spaceborne Imaging Radar-C/X-Band Synthetic Aperture Radar (SIR-C/X-SAR) and the Measurement of Air Pollution from Satellites (MAPS) instrument. The National Aeronautics and Space Administration (NASA) with two other space agencies, the DLR of Germany and ASI of Italy, jointly developed the SIR-C/X-SAR radar. The Jet Propulsion Laboratory (JPL) in Pasadena, California and the Ball Communication System built and managed the SIR-C portion of the mission for NASA's Office of Mission to Planet Earth, a program to study Earth's land, oceans, atmosphere, and life as a total integrated system. The instrument is a two-frequency radar including L-band, 23-centimeter wavelength, and C-band, 6-centimeter wavelength. The X-SAR instrument was built by the Dornier and Alenia Spazio companies for DARA and ASI, and is a single-frequency radar with X-band, 3-centimeter wavelength.

The objectives of the SIR-C/X-SAR were to provide information about Earth's land surfaces, including vegetation coverage, snow pack extent, wetlands, geologic features, volcanic processes, ocean wave heights, and wind speeds over the oceans. The most useful feature of imaging radar is its ability to make measurements over any region at any time regardless of weather or sunlight. The SIR-C/X-SAR is a synthetic aperture radar that transmits pulses of microwave energy from the shuttle toward Earth and measures the strength and time delay of the energy scattered back to the SIR-C/X-SAR antenna. The motion of the shuttle between the transmission of the beam and the reception of backscattered radiation was used to "synthesize" or create an antenna (aperture) much longer than the actual antenna, hence the name "synthetic aperture radar." This technique can result in finer-resolution images because the elongation allows the gathering of more data points per unit of the Earth's surface area.

A SAR radar image acquired by the SIR-C/X-SAR radar on board the Space Shuttle Endeavour shows the Teide volcano in the Canary Islands, Spain. (NASA)

The Space Radar Imaging Laboratory-2 (SRL-2) was a payload launched aboard space shuttle *Endeavour* (STS-68) on September 30, 1994. Flying SRL-2 during different seasons allowed comparison of changes between the first and second SRL flights. SRL-2 activated on flight day one. Astronauts split into two teams conducted around-the-clock observations. Besides repeating data taken over the same locations as on the first flight, unusual events were also imaged, including an erupting volcano in Russia, and the islands of Japan after an earthquake had taken place. The ability of SRL-2 imaging radars, Spaceborne Imaging Radar-C (SIR-C) and X-Band Synthetic Aperture Radar (X-SAR), to discern differences between human-induced phenomena such as an oil spill in the ocean and naturally occurring events was tested.

The mission also took advantage of opportunities to study fires set in British Columbia, Canada, for forest management purposes. Special readings were taken with another SRL element, Measurement of Air Pollution from Satellites (MAPS), to gain better understanding of carbon monoxide emissions from burning forests. Flying for the fourth time on the shuttle, MAPS was designed to measure global distribution of carbon monoxide.

On flight day six, the Mission Management Team extended the mission by one day. A different data-gathering method was tried. Called interferometry, the method required repeated, nearly coincidental imaging passes with SIR-C/X-SAR over target sites. In one instance, *Endeavour* piloted to within 9 meters of where it was flown on the first flight in April, 1997. This was a precursor to the SRTM on flight STS-99. Interferometric passes were completed over central North America, Amazon forests of central Brazil, and volcanoes on Russia's Kamchatka Peninsula.

The Shuttle Radar Topography Mission (SRTM) flew aboard space shuttle *Endeavour*, launched on February 11, 2000. The STS-99 mission was a partnership between NASA and the National Imagery and Mapping Agency (NIMA). In addition, the German and Italian space agencies contributed an experimental high-resolution imaging radar system. To acquire topographic (or elevation) data, the SRTM instrument was configured with two receiving antennae separated by a specific distance. This configuration set up the use of interferometry. An interferogram arises when two beams of electromagnetic radiation such as microwaves or radio waves interact or "interfere" with each other. The result of this interference is called the "Fourier transform" of the object. A single mountain will give a Fourier transform shaped much like a sine or cosine wave. An interferogram of the Himalayas would be a superposition or sum of many sine and cosine waves. There are computer programs that can "invert" the interferogram or Fourier transform back to the individual mountain peaks and thus give topographical and three-dimensional maps.

The SRTM payload consisted of three main sections: (1) radar electronics and antennae located in the payload bay; (2) a mast that deployed to 60 meters once in space; and (3) outboard antennae attached to the end of the mast. The mast that held the two radar antennae apart was the largest "unfolding" structure ever to fly in space. "Images" received by the two antennae were carefully combined to give

precise information about the height of the terrain below—a three-dimensional image. With the radar sweeping most of the land surfaces of the Earth, SRTM acquired enough data during eleven days of operation to obtain the most complete near-global high-resolution database of Earth's topography.

Contributions

The SIR-C/X-SAR scientific team identified more than four hundred sites where data were taken. Nineteen of the sites were designated "supersites," making them priority targets for scientific investigations. There were fifteen additional backup supersites. The supersites were chosen to represent different environments within each scientific discipline. The following were areas of investigation and supersites for the SRL missions:

(1) Ecology: Manaus, Brazil; Raco, Michigan; Duke Forest, North Carolina; Central Europe. Radar images were used to study land use, vegetation extent, effects of fires, floods, clear-cutting, soil moisture, and forest dynamics.

(2) Hydrology: Chickasha, Oklahoma; Otzal, Austria; Bebedouro, Brazil; Montespertoli, Italy. Radar images were used to study snow cover, wetlands, and soil moisture pattern.

(3) Oceanography: Gulf Stream, Northeast Atlantic Ocean; Southern Ocean. Radar images were used to study surface and internal waves, oceanic wind speed, and currents.

(4) Geology: Galápagos Islands; Sahara Desert; Death Valley, California; Andes Mountains, Chile; Mount Pinatubo.

Radar images were used to map geologic structures, areas of erosion and volcanic activity, paleoclimatic sites in arid regions, geologic evidence of past climate changes, and surface roughness.

Surface features of the Sahara Desert (Landsat)

buried river bed

Ancient features hidden beneath the surface (radar)

Two images of the Safsaf Oasis in The Sahara. The top image (taken by the Landat Thematic Mapper) is the surface. The bottom (taken by the Spaceborne Imaging Radar-C/X-band Synthetic Aperture Radar (SIR-C/X-SAR) on board the Space Shuttle Endeavour on April 16, 1994) is the rock layer underneath, revealing black channels cut by the meandering of an ancient river. (NASA / JPL)

Each SIR-C/X-SAR mission collected a total of about fifty hours of data. This corresponded to roughly 50 million square kilometers (19 million square miles) of ground cover. The two missions in 1994 discovered an ancient river channel buried under layers of sand in the Sahara Desert in Africa. It enabled scientists to examine the origin of the Great Bend of the Nile River. Probably sometime between ten thousand years and one million years ago, the Nile was forced to abandon its bed, and took up a new course to the south. The buried channel proved that this region of the Nile has been tectonically active and showed how that forced the river to change its course.

The eleven-day flight of the SRTM mapped about 122.8 million square kilometers (47.6 million square miles) of the planet covering 99.958 percent of the planned mapping area at least once and 94.594 percent of it twice. Almost all land surfaces between 60° north latitude and 60° south latitude were mapped by SRTM. Analysts used SRTM data to generate three-dimensional topographic maps of the Earth's surface called digital elevation models.

Context

The SRTM was the first to map a substantial portion of the Earth's terrain in three dimensions. The radar system represents a breakthrough in the science of remote sensing and created topographic maps thirty times as precise as those previously used. Traditionally, topographic maps have been generated from stereo pairs of photographs acquired from high-altitude aircraft and satellites. However, such optical systems cannot penetrate the cloud cover that blankets nearly 40 percent of the Earth's surface. In some tropical regions the cloud cover is virtually continuous and, as a result, significant portions of our planet's surface had never before been mapped in detail.

Although various countries have produced their own topographic maps, many are in different resolutions. Scientists lacked a common, unified map of all populated areas around the globe. The completed mosaic would be used to better understand how nature and people affect the land, and for studies of volcanoes and earthquakes, research into the movement of glaciers, urban and disaster planning, crop and forest management, and identifying the consequences of acid rain.

The military, which funded one-third of the SRTM, wanted highly accurate elevations to pinpoint targets from space and to plan flight patterns. Following a lengthy calibration and validation phase, 9 terabytes of raw data were processed continent by continent into digital topographic maps, and the last data set was delivered to the National Geospatial-Intelligence Agency (NGA) in January, 2003. NGA, through its contractors, edited and verified the SRTM data to bring them into conformance with National Map Accuracy Standards and to format them to their Digital Terrain Elevation Data (DTED) specifications. These "finished" data were returned to NASA for distribution to the public through the United States Geological Survey.

Scientists can use the digital elevation maps of the Earth's surface to study planetary geophysics and geology, aid in earthquake research, monitor volcanoes, model hydrologic drainage systems, and create more realistic flight simulators for military aircraft. Data will even be of value for commercial uses such as finding better locations for cellular phone towers and creating improved maps for backpackers. C-band data is available through the United States Geological Survey's EROS Data Center, while X-band data is obtained through the German Aerospace Center (Deutsches Zentrum für Luft- und Raumfahrt, or DLR).

—Dana P. McDermott

See also: Magellan: Venus; Planetary Exploration; Space Shuttle: Microgravity Laboratories and Payloads; Space Shuttle Flights, 1994; Space Shuttle Flights, 2000.

Further Reading

Ambroziak, Brian, and Jeffrey R. Ambroziak. *Infinite Perspectives: Two Thousand Years of Three-Dimensional Mapmaking*. Princeton, N.J.: Princeton Architectural Press, 1999. This is a cartographic anthology that examines verticality in mapping from ancient Iraq to the twentieth century. In the colorful pages, mountains and molehills bubble up in relief maps of Imperial Roman highways and Leonardo da Vinci's Tuscany. Meanwhile, the dramatic contours of the Grand Canyon are captured accurately in three dimensions, courtesy of the futuristic Ambroziak Infinite Perspective Projection.

Harland, David M. *The Space Shuttle: Roles, Missions, and Accomplishments*. New York: John Wiley, 1998. The book details the origins, missions, payloads, and passengers of the Space Transportation System (STS), covering the flights from STS-1 through STS-89 in great detail. This large volume is divided into five sections: "Operations," "Weightlessness," "Exploration," "Outpost," and "Conclusions." "Operations" discusses the origins of the shuttle, test flights, and some of its missions and payloads. "Weightlessness" describes many of the experiments performed aboard the orbiter, including materials processing, electrophoresis, phase partitioning, and combustion. "Exploration" includes the Hubble Space Telescope, Spacelab, Galileo, Magellan, and Ulysses, as well as Earth observation projects. "Outpost" covers the shuttle's role in the joint Russian Mir program and the International Space Station. Contains numerous illustrations, an index, and bibliographical references.

Henderson, Floyd M., and Anthony J. Lewis. *Manual of Remote Sensing: Principles and Applications of Imaging Radar*. 3d ed. New York: John Wiley, 1998. The manual offers a survey of theory, methods, and applications of imaging radar. It discusses basic principles of imaging radar, traces research activity across many sciences where radar remote sensing may be applied, and provides a snapshot of related technology such as radargrammetry, polarimetry, and interferometry. It also combines technical coverage of systems, data interpretations, and other fundamentals with a generous coverage of practical applications in fields such as forestry, oceanography, urban analysis, and archaeology.

Soumekh, Mehrdad. *Synthetic Aperture Radar Signal Processing with MATLAB Algorithms*. New York: John Wiley, 1999. Originally introduced for military radar systems, synthetic aperture radar boasts numerous commercial and military applications, ranging from topographic imaging as was done during STS-99/SRTM, to oil explorations to air traffic control and to medical imaging techniques. This volume clearly explains how, using signal processing, this intriguing technology allows a small antenna to achieve as powerful and accurate effects as a much larger one.

Stimson, George W. *Introduction to Airborne Radar*. 2d ed. Mendham, N.J.: SciTech Publishing, 1999. This is the first text that completely covers the wide range of techniques employed in modern airborne and space-based radar. It fulfills the need of those who want to learn about radar, regardless of their technical backgrounds. Lavishly produced in full-color, the book contains more than 1,100 graphics. Virtually every concept is illustrated with a simple diagram that appears adjacent to the text it depicts. Every illustration is accompanied by a concise caption, enabling it to stand on its own.

Sullivan, Roger J. *Microwave Radar: Imaging and Advanced Concepts*. Norwood, Mass.: Artech House, 2000. Beginning with a systematic introduction to the fundamental principles of microwave radar, this book delivers an extensive discussion of radar imaging, offering the most comprehensive general-purpose imaging radar book presently available. It provides the latest information on image superresolution, automatic target recognition, moving target indication, and space-time adaptive processing (STAP).

United States Geological Survey EROS Data Center. http://srtm.usgs.gov. Under agreement with NASA, the USGS EROS Data Center distributes and archives SRTM data in accordance with a joint-partnership memorandum of understanding between NASA and NGA.

World Spaceflight News. *21st Century Complete Guide to Radar Imaging from Space.* Mount Laurel, N.J.: Author, 2002. This electronic book, on CD-ROM, provides comprehensive coverage of NASA's radar imaging of Earth from space, including the Shuttle Radar Topography Mission (SRTM), SIR-C, and X-SAR. Over 350 image files in JPG and GIF format are provided for use in any computer graphics program, and fifteen flyover simulation movies in MOV and MPG format are included.